U L T I M A T E

SO-AEY-449

VISUAL
dictionary

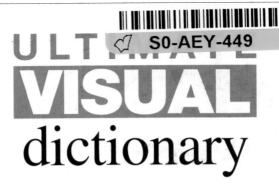

Glabella

Eye

Thoracic pleurae

Tail shield

Tail area

Date: 7/19/17

**423.17 ULT
Ultimate visual dictionary.**

**PALM BEACH COUNTY
LIBRARY SYSTEM**

3650 Summit Boulevard

West Palm Beach, FL 33406-4198

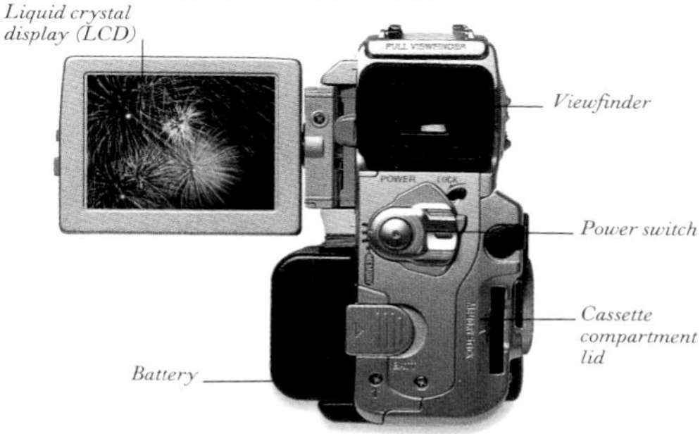

DIGITAL VIDEO CAMERA

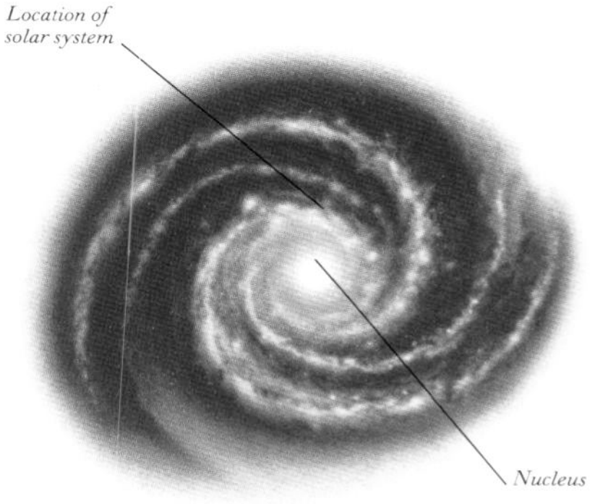

Liquid crystal display (LCD)

Viewfinder

Power switch

Cassette compartment lid

Battery

OVERHEAD VIEW OF OUR GALAXY

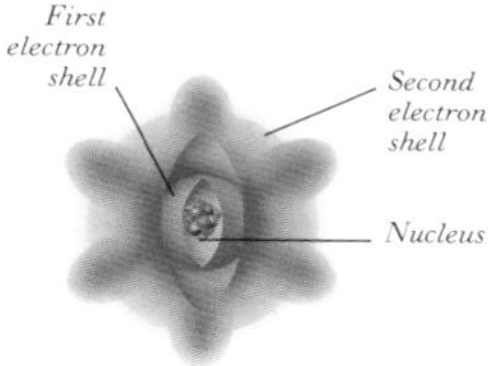

Location of solar system

Nucleus

First electron shell

Second electron shell

Nucleus

ANATOMY OF A FLUORINE-19 ATOM

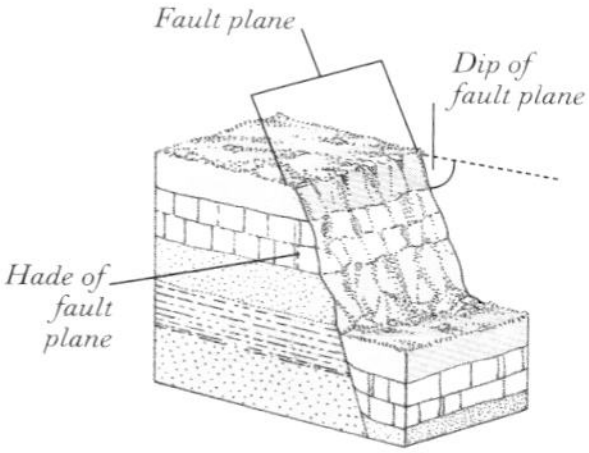

Fault plane

Dip of fault plane

Hade of fault plane

STRUCTURE OF A FAULT

Windshield

Steering wheel

Radiator

Headlight

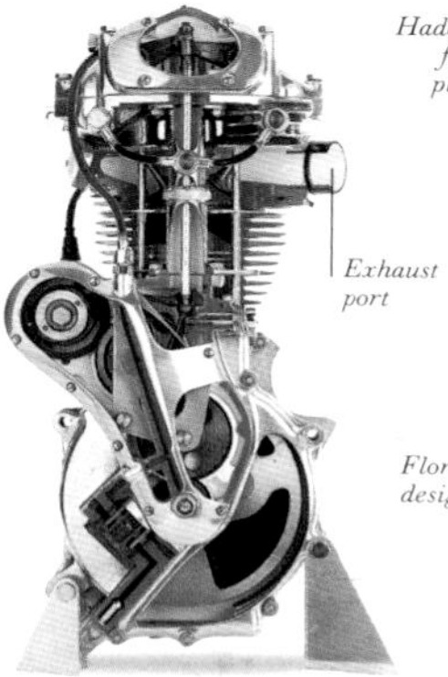

Exhaust port

VELOCETTE OHV ENGINE

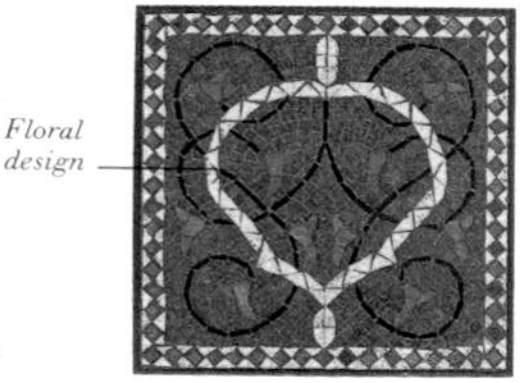

Floral design

MOSAIC DESIGN

MODEL T FORD

ULTIMATE VISUAL
dictionary

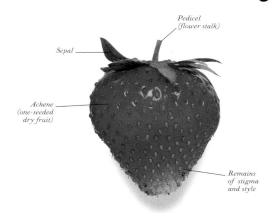

Pedicel
(flower stalk)

Sepal

Achene
(one-seeded
dry fruit)

Remains
of stigma
and style

STRAWBERRY

THIS EDITION

DK LONDON

Editorial Consultants Ian Graham, Darren Naish, Carole Stott
Picture Researcher Karen VanRoss
Jacket Designer Silke Spingies
Digital Conversion Coordinator Linda Zacharia
Production Editor Joanna Byrne
Production Controller Linda Dare
Managing Editor Julie Ferris
Managing Art Editor Owen Peyton Jones
Art Director Philip Ormerod
Associate Publishing Director Liz Wheeler
Publishing Director Jonathan Metcalf

DK DELHI

Managing Art Editor Arunesh Talapatra
Managing Editor Saloni Talwar
Deputy Managing Art Editor Priyabrata Roy Chowdhury
Senior Art Editor Rajnish Kashyap
Senior Editor Neha Gupta
Art Editors Arijit Ganguly, Pooja Pipil
Assistant Art Editor Pooja Pawwar
DTP Manager Balwant Singh
DTP Designer Jaypal Singh Chauhan
Managing Director Aparna Sharma

Anatomical And Botanical Models Supplied By Somso Modelle, Coburg, Germany

ORIGINAL EDITION (*Ultimate Visual Dictionary*)

Project Art Editors Heather McCarry, Johnny Pau, Chris Walker, Kevin Williams
Designer Simon Murrell
Project Editors Luisa Caruso, Peter Jones, Jane Mason, Geoffrey Stalker
Editor Jo Evans
DTP Designer Zirrinia Austin
Picture Researcher Charlotte Bush
Managing Art Editor Toni Kay
Senior Editor Roger Tritton
Managing Editor Sean Moore
Production Manager Hilary Stephens

FIRST AMERICAN EDITION PUBLISHED UNDER THE TITLE
ULTIMATE VISUAL DICTIONARY, 1994

THIS REVISED EDITION PUBLISHED IN 2017 BY
DK PUBLISHING
345 HUDSON STREET
NEW YORK, NEW YORK 10014

17 18 19 20 21 10 9 8 7 6 5 4 3 2 1
001—299759–JAN/17
REVISED EDITIONS IN 1996, 1997, 1998, 1999, 2000, 2002, 2006, 2011, 2016, 2017

COPYRIGHT © 1994, 1996, 1997, 1998, 1999, 2000, 2002, 2006, 2011, 2016, 2017 DORLING KINDERSLEY LIMITED

ALL RIGHTS RESERVED UNDER INTERNATIONAL AND PAN-AMERICAN COPYRIGHT CONVENTIONS.
NO PART OF THIS PUBLICATION MAY BE REPRODUCED, STORED IN A RETRIEVAL SYSTEM, OR
TRANSMITTED IN ANY FORM OR BY ANY MEANS, ELECTRONIC, MECHANICAL, PHOTOCOPYING,
RECORDING OR OTHERWISE, WITHOUT THE PRIOR WRITTEN PERMISSION OF THE COPYRIGHT OWNER.
PUBLISHED IN GREAT BRITAIN BY DORLING KINDERSLEY LIMITED.

A CATALOG RECORD FOR THIS BOOK IS AVAILABLE FROM THE LIBRARY OF CONGRESS.
ISBN 978-1-4654-5894-0

PRINTED AND BOUND IN CHINA

A WORLD OF IDEAS:
SEE ALL THERE IS TO KNOW
www.dk.com

*Prosoma
(cephalothorax)*   *Spinneret*

Leg

**EXTERNAL FEATURES
OF A SPIDER**

Canopy   *Fin*

*Main landing
gear*

SIDE VIEW OF ARV SUPER 2 AIRPLANE

Heat shield

*Third
stage
motor*

*Delta II
launch
vehicle
second
stage*

MARS PATHFINDER

CONTENTS

INTRODUCTION 6

THE UNIVERSE 8

PREHISTORIC EARTH 54

PLANTS 110

ANIMALS 164

THE HUMAN BODY 208

GEOLOGY, GEOGRAPHY,
AND METEOROLOGY 262

PHYSICS AND CHEMISTRY 304

RAIL AND ROAD 322

SEA AND AIR 370

THE VISUAL ARTS 428

ARCHITECTURE 456

MUSIC 500

SPORTS 522

THE MODERN WORLD 564

APPENDIX 616

INDEX 624

Barrel

*Permanent
black ink*

FOUNTAIN PEN AND INK

*Face light
emitting
diodes
(LEDs)*

*Movable
tail*

**SONY AIBO
ROBOT DOG**

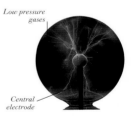

*Low pressure
gases*

*Central
electrode*

**BALL CONTAINING HIGH
TEMPERATURE GAS (PLASMA)**

*Parallel
bands*

ONYX

*Nonbreakable
plastic*

*Shock
absorber*

FOOTBALL HELMET

Introduction

THE VISUAL DICTIONARY is a completely new kind of reference book. It provides a link between pictures and words in a way that no ordinary dictionary ever has. Most dictionaries simply tell you what a word means, but the *Visual Dictionary* shows you—through a combination of detailed annotations, explicit photographs, and illustrations. In the *Visual Dictionary*, pictures define the annotations around them. You do not read definitions of the annotated words, you see them. The highly accessible format of the *Visual Dictionary*, the thoroughness of its annotations, and the range of its subject matter make it a unique and helpful reference tool.

How to use the VISUAL DICTIONARY

You will find the *Visual Dictionary* simple to use. Instead of being organized alphabetically, it is divided by subject into 14 sections—THE UNIVERSE, PREHISTORIC EARTH, PLANTS, ANIMALS, THE HUMAN BODY, etc. Each section begins with a table of contents listing the major entries within that section. For example, The Visual Arts section has entries on *Drawing, Tempera, Fresco, Oils, Watercolor, Pastels, Acrylics, Calligraphy, Printmaking, Mosaic,* and *Sculpture.* Every entry has a short introduction explaining the purpose of the photographs and illustrations, and the significance of the annotations.

If you know what something looks like, but don't know its name, find the term you need by turning to the annotations surrounding the pictures; if you know a word, but don't know what it refers to, use the comprehensive index to direct you to the appropriate page.

Suppose that you want to know what the bone at the end of your little finger is called. With a standard dictionary, you wouldn't know where to begin. But with the *Visual Dictionary* you simply turn to the entry called *Hands*—within THE HUMAN BODY section—where you will find four fully annotated, color photographs showing the skin, muscles, and bones of the human hand. In this entry you will quickly find that the bone you are searching for is called the distal phalanx, and for good measure you will discover that it is attached to the middle phalanx by the distal interphalangeal joint.

Perhaps you want to know what a catalytic converter looks like. If you look up "catalytic converter" in an ordinary dictionary, you will be told what it is and possibly what it does—but you will not be able to tell what shape it is or what it is made of. However, if you look up "catalytic converter" in the index of the *Visual Dictionary,* you will be directed to the *Modern engines* entry on page 344—where the introduction gives you basic information about what a catalytic converter is—and to page 350—where there is a spectacular exploded-view photograph of the mechanics of a Renault Clio. From these pages you will find out not only what a catalytic converter looks like, but also that it is attached at one end to an exhaust pipe and at the other to a muffler.

Whatever it is that you want to find a name for, or whatever name you want to find a picture for, you will find it quickly and easily in the *Visual Dictionary.* Perhaps you need to know where the vamp on a shoe is; or how to tell obovate and lanceolate leaves apart; or what a spiral galaxy looks like; or whether birds have nostrils. With the *Visual Dictionary* at hand, the answers to each of these questions, and thousands more, are readily available.

The *Visual Dictionary* does not just tell you what the names of the different parts of an object are. The photographs, illustrations, and annotations are all specially arranged to help you understand which parts relate to one another and how objects function.

With the *Visual Dictionary* you can find in seconds the words or pictures that you are looking for; or you can simply browse through the pages of the book for your own pleasure. The *Visual Dictionary* is not intended to replace a standard dictionary or conventional encyclopedia, but is instead a stimulating and valuable companion to ordinary reference volumes. Giving you instant access to the language that is used by astronomers and architects, musicians and mechanics, scientists and sportspeople, it is the ideal reference book for specialists and generalists of all ages.

Sections of the VISUAL DICTIONARY

The 14 sections of the *VISUAL DICTIONARY* contain a total of more than 30,000 terms, encompassing a wide range of topics:

•In the first section, THE UNIVERSE, spectacular photographs and illustrations are used to show the names of the stars and planets and to explain the structure of solar systems, galaxies, nebulae, comets, and black holes.

•PREHISTORIC EARTH tells the story in annotations of how our own planet has evolved since its formation. It includes examples of prehistoric flora and fauna, and fascinating dinosaur models—some with parts of the body stripped away to show anatomical sections.

•PLANTS covers a huge range of species— from the familiar to the exotic. In addition to the color photographs of plants included in this section, there is a series of micrographic photographs illustrating plant details—such as pollen grains, spores, and cross-sections of stems and roots—in close-up.

•In the ANIMALS section, skeletons, anatomical diagrams, and different parts of animals' bodies have been meticulously annotated. This section provides a comprehensive guide to the vocabulary of zoological classification and animal physiology.

•The structure of the human body, its parts, and its systems are presented in THE HUMAN BODY. The section includes lifelike, three-dimensional models and the latest false-color images. Clear and authoritative annotations indicate the correct anatomical terms.

•GEOLOGY, GEOGRAPHY, AND METEOROLOGY describes the structure of the Earth—from the inner core to the exosphere—and the physical phenomena—such as volcanoes, rivers, glaciers, and climate—that shape its surface.

•PHYSICS AND CHEMISTRY is a visual journey through the fundamental principles underlying the physical universe, and provides the essential vocabulary of these sciences.

•In RAIL AND ROAD, a wide range of trains, trams and buses, cars, bicycles, and motorcycles are described. Exploded-view photographs show mechanical details with striking clarity.

•SEA AND AIR gives the names for hundreds of parts of ships and airplanes. The section includes civil and fighting craft, both historical and modern.

•THE VISUAL ARTS shows the equipment and materials used by painters, sculptors, printers, and other artists. Well-known compositions have been chosen to illustrate specific artistic techniques and effects.

•ARCHITECTURE includes photographs of exemplary architectural models and illustrates dozens of additional features such as columns, domes, and arches.

•MUSIC provides a visual introduction to the special language of music and musical instruments. It includes clearly annotated photographs of each of the major groups of traditional instruments—brass, woodwind, strings, and percussion—together with modern electronic instruments.

•The SPORTS section is a guide to the playing areas, formations, equipment, and techniques needed for many of today's most popular sports.

•In THE MODERN WORLD, items that are a familiar part of our daily lives are taken apart to reveal their inner workings and give access to the language used by their manufacturers. It also includes systems and concepts, such as the internet, that increasingly influence our 21st century world.

THE UNIVERSE

ANATOMY OF THE UNIVERSE······················ 10
GALAXIES······················· 12
THE MILKY WAY······················· 14
NEBULAE AND STAR CLUSTERS······················· 16
STARS OF NORTHERN SKIES······················· 18
STARS OF SOUTHERN SKIES······················· 20
STARS······················· 22
SMALL STARS······················· 24
MASSIVE STARS······················· 26
NEUTRON STARS AND BLACK HOLES······················· 28
THE SOLAR SYSTEM······················· 30
THE SUN······················· 32
MERCURY······················· 34
VENUS······················· 36
THE EARTH······················· 38
THE MOON······················· 40
MARS······················· 42
JUPITER······················· 44
SATURN······················· 46
URANUS······················· 48
NEPTUNE AND PLUTO······················· 50
ASTEROIDS, COMETS, AND METEOROIDS······················· 52

Anatomy of the universe

Fireball of rapidly expanding, extremely hot gas lasting about one million years

THE UNIVERSE CONTAINS EVERYTHING that exists, from the tiniest subatomic particles to galactic superclusters (the largest structures known). No one knows how big the universe is, but astronomers estimate that it contains at least 125 billion galaxies, each comprising an average of 100 billion stars. The most widely accepted theory about the origin of the universe is the Big Bang theory, which states that the universe came into being in a huge explosion—the Big Bang—that took place between 10 and 20 billion years ago. The universe initially consisted of a very hot, dense fireball of expanding, cooling gas. After about one million years, the gas began to condense into localized clumps called protogalaxies. During the next five billion years, the protogalaxies continued condensing, forming galaxies in which stars were being born. Today, billions of years later, the universe as a whole is still expanding, although there are localized areas in which objects are held together by gravity; for example, many galaxies are found in clusters. The Big Bang theory is supported by the discovery of faint, cool background radiation coming evenly from all directions. This radiation is believed to be the remnant of the radiation produced by the Big Bang. Small "ripples" in the temperature of the cosmic background radiation are thought to be evidence of slight fluctuations in the density of the early universe, which resulted in the formation of galaxies. Astronomers do not yet know if the universe is "closed," which means it will eventually stop expanding and begin to contract, or if it is "open," which means it will continue expanding forever.

FALSE-COLOR MICROWAVE MAP OF COSMIC BACKGROUND RADIATION

Pink indicates "warm ripples" in background radiation

Pale blue indicates "cool ripples" in background radiation

Deep blue indicates background radiation corresponding to -454°F (-270°C); (remnant of the Big Bang)

Low-energy microwave radiation corresponding to -454°F (-270°C)

Red and pink band indicates radiation from our galaxy

High-energy gamma radiation corresponding to 5,400°F (3,000°C)

ORIGIN AND EXPANSION OF THE UNIVERSE

Quasar (probably the center of a galaxy containing a massive black hole)

Universe about five billion years after Big Bang

Protogalaxy (condensing gas cloud)

Galaxy spinning and flattening to become spiral shaped

Dark cloud (dust and gas condensing to form a protogalaxy)

Elliptical galaxy in which stars form rapidly

Universe today (13–17 billion years after Big Bang)

Cluster of galaxies held together by gravity

Elliptical galaxy containing old stars and little gas and dust

Irregular galaxy

Spiral galaxy containing gas, dust, and young stars

OBJECTS IN THE UNIVERSE

CLUSTER OF
GALAXIES IN VIRGO

FALSE-COLOR IMAGE
OF 3C273 (QUASAR)

NGC 4406
(ELLIPTICAL GALAXY)

NGC 5236
(BARRED SPIRAL GALAXY)

NGC 6822
(IRREGULAR GALAXY)

THE ROSETTE NEBULA
(EMISSION NEBULA)

THE JEWEL BOX
(STAR CLUSTER)

THE SUN
(MAIN SEQUENCE STAR)

EARTH

THE MOON

Galaxies

SOMBRERO,
A SPIRAL GALAXY

A GALAXY IS A HUGE MASS OF STARS, nebulae, and interstellar material. The smallest galaxies contain about 100,000 stars, while the largest contain up to 3 trillion stars. There are three main types of galaxy, classified according to their shape: elliptical, which are oval shaped; spiral, which have arms spiraling outward from a central bulge (those whose arms spiral from a bar-shaped bulge are called spirals); and irregular, which have no obvious shape. Sometimes, the shape of a galaxy is distorted by a collision with another galaxy. Quasars (quasi-stellar objects) are thought to be galactic nuclei but are so far away that their exact nature is still uncertain. They are compact, highly luminous objects in the outer reaches of the known universe: while the farthest known "ordinary" galaxies are about 12 billion light-years away, the farthest known quasar is about 13 billion light-years away. Active galaxies, such as Seyfert galaxies and radio galaxies, emit intense radiation. In a Seyfert galaxy, this radiation comes from the galactic nucleus; in a radio galaxy, it also comes from huge lobes on either side of the galaxy. The radiation from active galaxies and quasars is thought to be caused by material falling into central black holes (see pp. 28-29).

OPTICAL IMAGE OF NGC 4486 (ELLIPTICAL GALAXY)

Globular cluster containing very old red giants

Central region containing old red giants

Less densely populated region

Neighbouring galaxy

OPTICAL IMAGE OF LARGE MAGELLANIC CLOUD (IRREGULAR GALAXY)

Tarantula Nebula

Dust cloud obscuring light from stars

Emission nebula

Light from stars

OPTICAL IMAGE OF NGC 2997 (SPIRAL GALAXY)

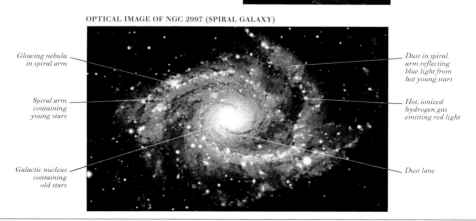

Glowing nebula in spiral arm

Spiral arm containing young stars

Galactic nucleus containing old stars

Dust in spiral arm reflecting blue light from hot young stars

Hot, ionized hydrogen gas emitting red light

Dust lane

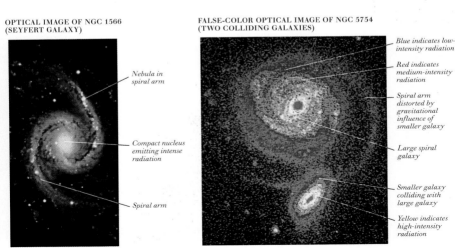

OPTICAL IMAGE OF CENTAURUS A (RADIO GALAXY)

Dust lane crossing elliptical galaxy

Galactic nucleus containing powerful source of radiation

Light from old stars

FALSE-COLOR RADIO IMAGE OF CENTAURUS A

Radio lobe

Red indicates high-intensity radio waves

Blue indicates low-intensity radio waves

Radiation from galactic nucleus

Outline of optical image of Centaurus A

Radio lobe

Yellow indicates medium-intensity radio waves

FALSE-COLOR RADIO IMAGE OF 3C 273 (QUASAR)

Radiation from jet of high-energy particles moving away from quasar

Quasar nucleus

White indicates high-intensity radio waves

Blue indicates low-intensity radio waves

OPTICAL IMAGE OF NGC 1566 (SEYFERT GALAXY)

Nebula in spiral arm

Compact nucleus emitting intense radiation

Spiral arm

FALSE-COLOR OPTICAL IMAGE OF NGC 5754 (TWO COLLIDING GALAXIES)

Blue indicates low-intensity radiation

Red indicates medium-intensity radiation

Spiral arm distorted by gravitational influence of smaller galaxy

Large spiral galaxy

Smaller galaxy colliding with large galaxy

Yellow indicates high-intensity radiation

The Milky Way

VIEW TOWARD GALACTIC CENTER

THE MILKY WAY IS THE NAME GIVEN TO THE FAINT BAND OF LIGHT that stretches across the night sky. This light comes from stars and nebulae in our galaxy, known as the Milky Way Galaxy or simply as "the Galaxy." The Galaxy is believed to be a barred spiral, with a dense central bar of stars encircled by four arms spiraling outward and surrounded by a less dense halo. We cannot see the spiral shape because the solar system is in one of the spiral arms, the Orion Arm (also called the Local Arm). From our position, the center of the Galaxy is completely obscured by dust clouds; as a result, optical maps give only a limited view of the Galaxy. However, a more complete picture can be obtained by studying radio, infrared, and other radiation. The central part of the Galaxy is relatively small and dense and contains mainly older red and yellow stars. The halo is a less dense region in which the oldest stars are situated; some of these stars are as old as the Galaxy itself (possibly 13 billion years). The spiral arms contain main sequence stars and hot, young, blue stars, as well as nebulae (clouds of dust and gas inside which stars are born). The Galaxy is vast, about 100,000 light-years across (a light-year is about 5,870 billion miles/9,460 billion km); in comparison, the solar system seems small, at about 12 light-hours across (about 8 billion miles/13 billion km). The entire Galaxy is rotating in space, although the inner stars travel faster than those farther out. The Sun, which is about two-thirds out from the center, completes one lap of the Galaxy about every 220 million years.

SIDE VIEW OF OUR GALAXY

Disk of spiral arms containing mainly young stars

Central bulge containing mainly older stars

Halo containing oldest stars

Nucleus

100,000 light-years

OVERHEAD VIEW OF OUR GALAXY

Central bulge

Nucleus

Perseus Arm

Crux-Centaurus Arm

Emission nebula

Sagittarius Arm

Dust in spiral arm reflecting blue light from hot young stars

Location of solar system

Orion Arm (Local Arm)

Patch of dust clouds

PANORAMIC OPTICAL MAP OF OUR GALAXY AND NEARBY GALAXIES

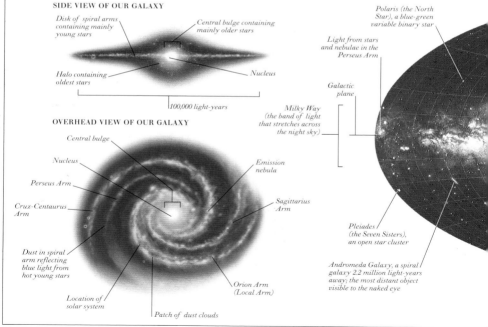

Polaris (the North Star), a blue-green variable binary star

Light from stars and nebulae in the Perseus Arm

Galactic plane

Milky Way (the band of light that stretches across the night sky)

Pleiades (the Seven Sisters), an open star cluster

Andromeda Galaxy, a spiral galaxy 2.2 million light-years away; the most distant object visible to the naked eye

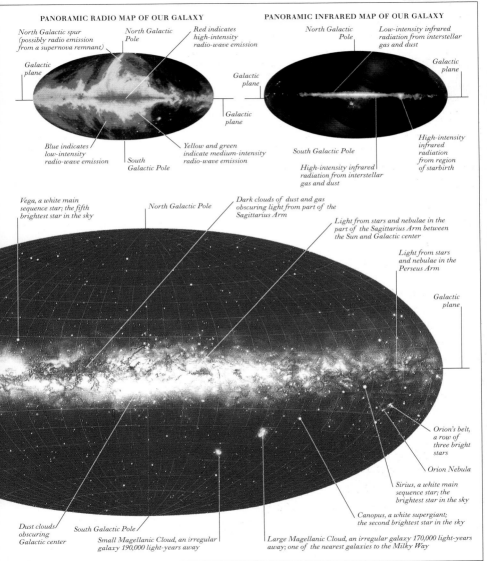

PANORAMIC RADIO MAP OF OUR GALAXY

North Galactic spur (possibly radio emission from a supernova remnant)

North Galactic Pole

Red indicates high-intensity radio-wave emission

Galactic plane

Galactic plane

Galactic plane

Blue indicates low-intensity radio-wave emission

South Galactic Pole

Yellow and green indicate medium-intensity radio-wave emission

PANORAMIC INFRARED MAP OF OUR GALAXY

North Galactic Pole

Low-intensity infrared radiation from interstellar gas and dust

Galactic plane

Galactic plane

High-intensity infrared radiation from region of starbirth

South Galactic Pole

High-intensity infrared radiation from interstellar gas and dust

Vega, a white main sequence star; the fifth brightest star in the sky

North Galactic Pole

Dark clouds of dust and gas obscuring light from part of the Sagittarius Arm

Light from stars and nebulae in the part of the Sagittarius Arm between the Sun and Galactic center

Light from stars and nebulae in the Perseus Arm

Galactic plane

Orion's belt, a row of three bright stars

Orion Nebula

Sirius, a white main sequence star; the brightest star in the sky

Canopus, a white supergiant; the second brightest star in the sky

Dust clouds obscuring Galactic center

South Galactic Pole

Small Magellanic Cloud, an irregular galaxy 190,000 light-years away

Large Magellanic Cloud, an irregular galaxy 170,000 light-years away; one of the nearest galaxies to the Milky Way

15

Nebulae and star clusters

**HODGE 11, A
GLOBULAR CLUSTER**

A NEBULA IS A CLOUD OF DUST AND GAS inside a galaxy. Nebulae become visible if the gas glows, or if the cloud reflects starlight or obscures light from more distant objects. Emission nebulae shine because their gas emits light when it is stimulated by radiation from hot young stars. Reflection nebulae shine because their dust reflects light from stars in or around the nebula. Dark nebulae appear as silhouettes because they block out light from shining nebulae or stars behind them. Two types of nebula are associated with dying stars: planetary nebulae and supernova remnants. Both consist of expanding shells of gas that were once the outer layers of a star. A planetary nebula is a gas shell drifting away from a dying stellar core. A supernova remnant is a gas shell moving away from a stellar core at great speed following a violent explosion called a supernova (see pp. 26-27). Stars are often found in groups known as clusters. Open clusters are loose groups of a few thousand young stars that were born from the same cloud and are drifting apart. Globular clusters are densely packed, roughly spherical groups of hundreds of thousands of older stars.

TRIFID NEBULA (EMISSION NEBULA)

Reflection nebula

Emission nebula

Dust lane

Starbirth region (area in which dust and gas clump together to form stars)

**PLEIADES (OPEN STAR CLUSTER)
WITH A REFLECTION NEBULA**

Wisps of dust and hydrogen gas. The cluster is passing through a region of interstellar material

Young star in an open cluster of more than 1,000 stars

Reflection nebula

HORSEHEAD NEBULA (DARK NEBULA)

Glowing filament of hot, ionized hydrogen gas

Alnitak (star in Orion's belt)

Dust lane

Emission nebula

Star near southern end of Orion's belt

Emission nebula

Horsehead Nebula

Reflection nebula

Dark nebula obscuring light from distant stars

ORION NEBULA (DIFFUSE EMISSION NEBULA)

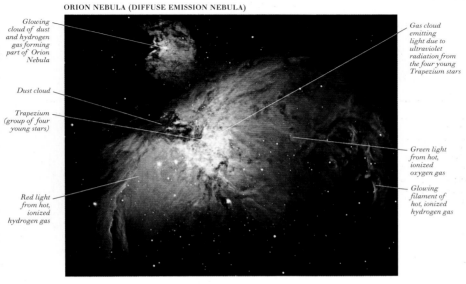

Glowing cloud of dust and hydrogen gas forming part of Orion Nebula

Dust cloud

Trapezium (group of four young stars)

Red light from hot, ionized hydrogen gas

Gas cloud emitting light due to ultraviolet radiation from the four young Trapezium stars

Green light from hot, ionized oxygen gas

Glowing filament of hot, ionized hydrogen gas

VELA SUPERNOVA REMNANT

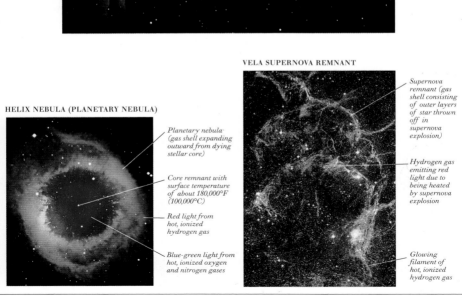

Supernova remnant (gas shell consisting of outer layers of star thrown off in supernova explosion)

Hydrogen gas emitting red light due to being heated by supernova explosion

Glowing filament of hot, ionized hydrogen gas

HELIX NEBULA (PLANETARY NEBULA)

Planetary nebula (gas shell expanding outward from dying stellar core)

Core remnant with surface temperature of about 180,000°F (100,000°C)

Red light from hot, ionized hydrogen gas

Blue-green light from hot, ionized oxygen and nitrogen gases

Stars of northern skies

WHEN YOU LOOK AT THE NORTHERN SKY, you look away from the densely populated Galactic center, so the northern sky generally appears less bright than the southern sky (see pp. 20-21). Among the best-known sights in the northern sky are the constellations Ursa Major (the Great Bear) and Orion. Some ancient civilizations believed that the stars were fixed to a celestial sphere surrounding the Earth, and modern maps of the sky are based on a similar idea. The North and South Poles of this imaginary celestial sphere are directly above the North and South Poles of the Earth, at the points where the Earth's axis of rotation intersects the sphere. The celestial North Pole is at the center of the map shown here, and Polaris (the North Star) lies very close to it. The celestial equator marks a projection of the Earth's equator on the sphere. The ecliptic marks the path of the Sun across the sky as the Earth orbits the Sun. The Moon and planets move against the background of the stars because the stars are much more distant; the nearest star outside the solar system (Proxima Centauri) is more than 50,000 times farther away than the planet Jupiter.

ORION

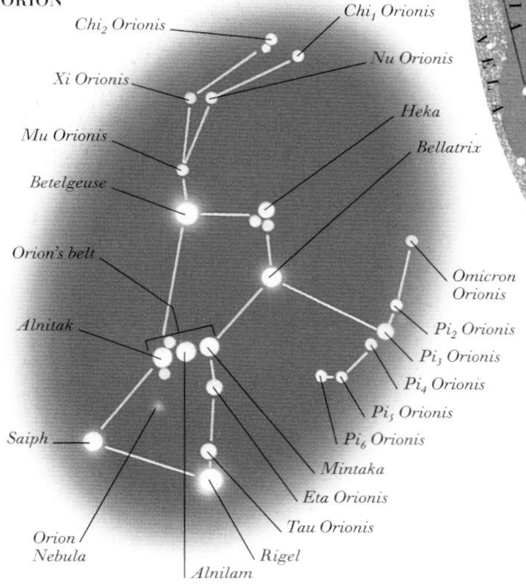

Chi₂ Orionis
Chi₁ Orionis
Xi Orionis
Nu Orionis
Heka
Mu Orionis
Bellatrix
Betelgeuse
Orion's belt
Omicron Orionis
Alnitak
Pi₂ Orionis
Pi₃ Orionis
Pi₄ Orionis
Pi₅ Orionis
Saiph
Pi₆ Orionis
Mintaka
Eta Orionis
Tau Orionis
Orion Nebula
Rigel
Alnilam

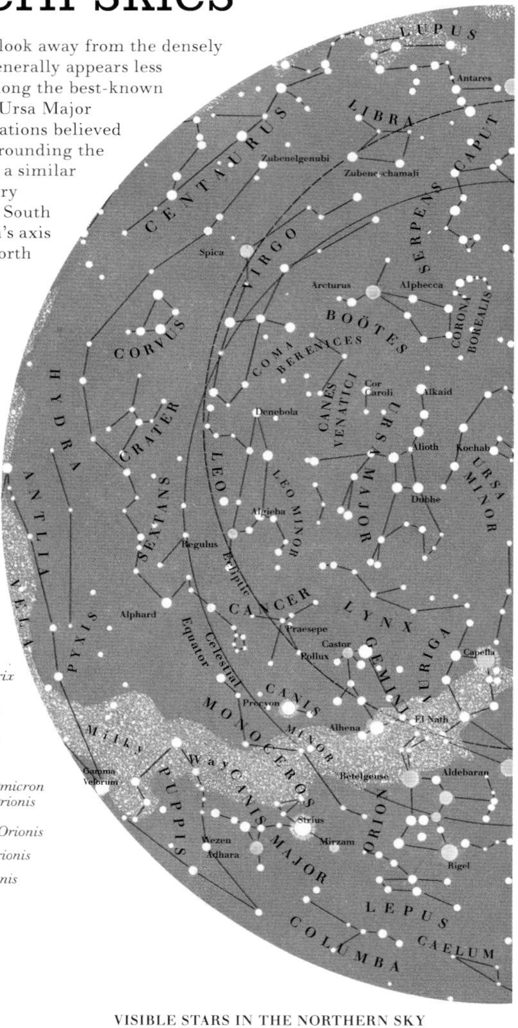

VISIBLE STARS IN THE NORTHERN SKY

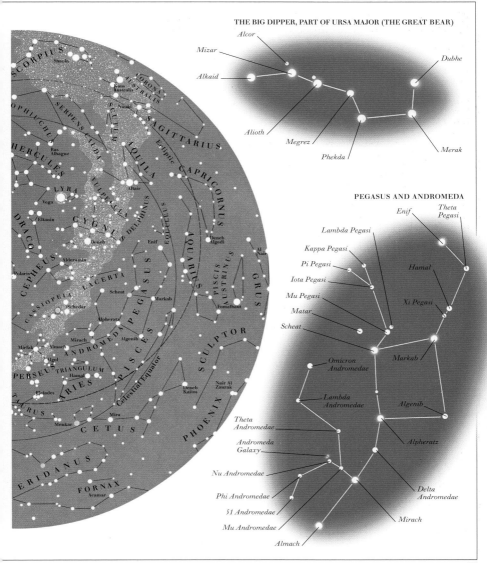

THE BIG DIPPER, PART OF URSA MAJOR (THE GREAT BEAR)

Alcor
Mizar
Alkaid
Dubhe
Alioth
Megrez
Phekda
Merak

PEGASUS AND ANDROMEDA

Enif
Theta Pegasi
Lambda Pegasi
Kappa Pegasi
Pi Pegasi
Hamal
Iota Pegasi
Mu Pegasi
Xi Pegasi
Matar
Scheat
Omicron Andromedae
Markab
Lambda Andromedae
Algenib
Theta Andromedae
Andromeda Galaxy
Alpheratz
Nu Andromedae
Delta Andromedae
Phi Andromedae
51 Andromedae
Mirach
Mu Andromedae
Almach

Left hemisphere map labels:

SCORPIUS
Shaula
CORONA AUSTRALIS
OPHIUCHUS
SERPENS CAUDA
Kaus Australis
Nunki
SAGITTARIUS
HERCULES
Ras Alhague
AQUILA
Ecliptic
CAPRICORNUS
LYRA
Vega
Altair
Eltanin
CYGNUS
VULPECULA
DELPHINUS
DRACO
Deneb
EQUULEUS
AQUARIUS
Deneb Algedi
Enif
PISCIS AUSTRINUS
Al Nair
CEPHEUS
Alderamin
LACERTA
PEGASUS
GRUS
Polaris
Scheat
Fomalhaut
CASSIOPEIA
Markab
Schedar
PISCES
Alpheratz
SCULPTOR
ANDROMEDA
Algenib
Mirach
Almach
Algol
Mirfak
TRIANGULUM
Celestial Equator
Nair Al Zaurak
PERSEUS
ARIES
Hamal
Deneb Kaitos
Pleiades
TAURUS
CETUS
Mira
PHOENIX
Menkar
ERIDANUS
FORNAX
Acamar

Stars of southern skies

WHEN YOU LOOK AT THE SOUTHERN SKY, you look toward the Galactic center, which has a huge population of stars. As a result, the Milky Way appears brighter in the southern sky than in the northern sky (see pp. 18-19). The southern sky is rich in nebulae and star clusters. It contains the Large and Small Magellanic Clouds, which are two of the nearest galaxies to our own. Stars make fixed patterns in the sky called constellations. However, the constellations are only apparent groupings of stars, since the distances to the stars in a constellation may vary enormously. The shapes of constellations may change over many thousands of years due to the relative motions of stars. The movement of the constellations across the sky is due to the Earth's motion in space. The daily rotation of the Earth causes the constellations to move across the sky from east to west, and the orbit of the Earth around the Sun causes different areas of sky to be visible in different seasons. The visibility of areas of sky also depends on the location of the observer. For instance, stars near the celestial equator may be seen from either hemisphere at some time during the year, whereas stars close to the celestial poles (the celestial South Pole is at the center of the map shown here) can never be seen from the opposite hemisphere.

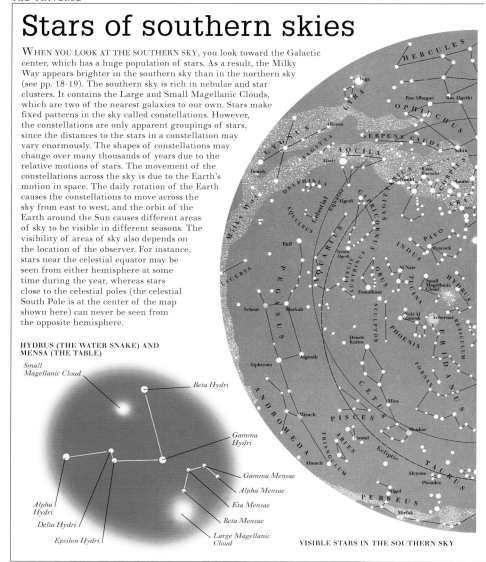

HYDRUS (THE WATER SNAKE) AND MENSA (THE TABLE)

Small Magellanic Cloud

Beta Hydri

Gamma Hydri

Gamma Mensae

Alpha Mensae

Eta Mensae

Beta Mensae

Alpha Hydri

Delta Hydri

Epsilon Hydri

Large Magellanic Cloud

VISIBLE STARS IN THE SOUTHERN SKY

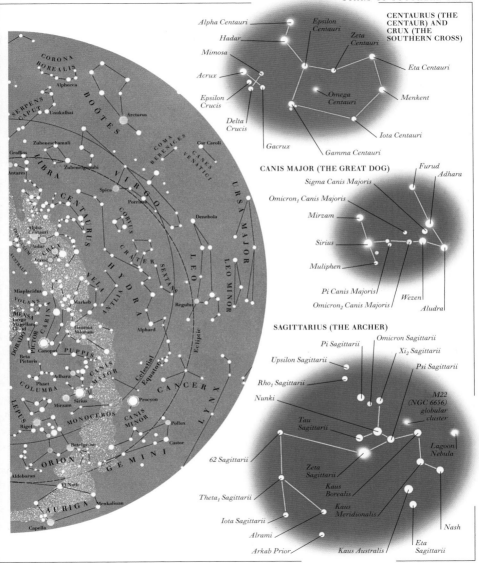

CENTAURUS (THE CENTAUR) AND CRUX (THE SOUTHERN CROSS)

Alpha Centauri
Epsilon Centauri
Zeta Centauri
Hadar
Mimosa
Eta Centauri
Acrux
Epsilon Crucis
Omega Centauri
Menkent
Delta Crucis
Iota Centauri
Gacrux
Gamma Centauri

CANIS MAJOR (THE GREAT DOG)

Furud
Adhara
Sigma Canis Majoris
Omicron₁ Canis Majoris
Mirzam
Sirius
Muliphen
Pi Canis Majoris
Wezen
Omicron₂ Canis Majoris
Aludra

SAGITTARIUS (THE ARCHER)

Pi Sagittarii
Omicron Sagittarii
Upsilon Sagittarii
Xi₂ Sagittarii
Psi Sagittarii
Rho₁ Sagittarii
Nunki
M22 (NGC 6656) globular cluster
Tau Sagittarii
62 Sagittarii
Lagoon Nebula
Zeta Sagittarii
Theta₁ Sagittarii
Kaus Borealis
Iota Sagittarii
Kaus Meridionalis
Alrami
Nash
Arkab Prior
Kaus Australis
Eta Sagittarii

Star map labels: CORONA BOREALIS, Alphecca, SERPENS CAPUT, BOÖTES, Unukalhai, Arcturus, Zubeneschamali, COMA BERENICES, Graffias, LIBRA, Zubenelgenubi, VIRGO, CANES VENATICI, Cor Caroli, Antares, Spica, CENTAURUS, Porrima, Denebola, URSA MAJOR, CORVUS, HYDRA, CRATER, SEXTANS, LEO, LEO MINOR, Alpha Centauri, CRUX, Hadar, Acrux, VELA, Markeb, ANTLIA, Regulus, Miaplacidus, VOLANS, MENSA, Large Magellanic Cloud, PICTOR, CARINA, Gamma Velorum, PUPPIS, Alphard, CANCER, Celestial Equator, LYNX, DORADO, Beta Pictoris, Canopus, COLUMBA, Phact, CANIS MAJOR, Adhara, Sirius, Mirzam, CANIS MINOR, Procyon, Pollux, Castor, LEPUS, Rigel, MONOCEROS, Betelgeuse, GEMINI, ORION, Aldebaran, El Nath, TAURUS, Menkalinan, AURIGA, Capella, Ecliptic

21

Stars

OPEN STAR CLUSTER AND DUST CLOUD

STARS ARE BODIES of hot, glowing gas that are born in nebulae (see pp. 24-27). They vary enormously in size, mass, and temperature: diameters range from about 450 times smaller to over 1,000 times bigger than that of the Sun; masses range from about a twentieth to over 50 solar masses; and surface temperatures range from about 5,500°F (3,000°C) to over 90,000°F (50,000°C). The color of a star is determined by its temperature: the hottest stars are blue and the coolest are red. The Sun, with a surface temperature of 10,000°F (5,500°C), is between these extremes and appears yellow. The energy emitted by a shining star is usually produced by nuclear fusion in the star's core. The brightness of a star is measured in magnitudes—the brighter the star, the lower its magnitude. There are two types of magnitude: apparent magnitude, which is the brightness seen from Earth, and absolute magnitude, which is the brightness that would be seen from a standard distance of 10 parsecs (32.6 light-years). The light emitted by a star may be split to form a spectrum containing a series of dark lines (absorption lines). The patterns of lines indicate the presence of particular chemical elements, enabling astronomers to deduce the composition of the star's atmosphere. The magnitude and spectral type (color) of stars may be plotted on a graph called a Hertzsprung-Russell diagram, which shows that stars tend to fall into several well-defined groups. The principal groups are main sequence stars (those which are fusing hydrogen to form helium), giants, supergiants, and white dwarfs.

STAR SIZES

Red giant from 10 to 100 million miles (15 to 150 million km) wide

The Sun (main sequence star; diameter 870,000 miles/1.4 million km)

White dwarf (diameter of 2,000 to 30,000 miles/3,000 to 50,000 km)

ENERGY EMISSION FROM THE SUN

Nuclear fusion in core produces gamma rays and neutrinos

Neutrinos travel to Earth directly from Sun's core in about 8 minutes

Lower-energy radiation travels to Earth in about 8 minutes

Earth

Sun

High-energy radiation (gamma rays) loses energy while traveling to surface over 2 million years

Lower-energy radiation (mainly ultraviolet, infrared, and light rays) leaves surface

STAR MAGNITUDES

APPARENT MAGNITUDE   **ABSOLUTE MAGNITUDE**

Brighter stars

-9

Sirius: apparent magnitude of -1.46

Rigel: apparent magnitude of +0.12

Rigel: absolute magnitude of -7.1

0

Sirius: absolute magnitude of +1.4

Objects of magnitude higher than about +6.0 cannot be seen by the naked eye

+9

Fainter stars

NUCLEAR FUSION IN MAIN SEQUENCE STARS LIKE THE SUN

Positron

Deuterium nucleus

Proton

Neutron

Proton (hydrogen nucleus)

Neutrino

Gamma rays

Helium-3 nucleus

Helium-4 nucleus

HERTZSPRUNG-RUSSELL DIAGRAM

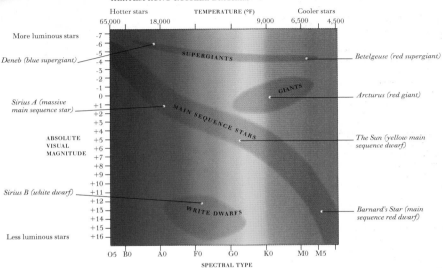

More luminous stars

Deneb (blue supergiant)

Betelgeuse (red supergiant)

Arcturus (red giant)

Sirius A (massive main sequence star)

The Sun (yellow main sequence dwarf)

ABSOLUTE VISUAL MAGNITUDE

Sirius B (white dwarf)

Barnard's Star (main sequence red dwarf)

Less luminous stars

Hotter stars   TEMPERATURE (°F)   Cooler stars

SUPERGIANTS

GIANTS

MAIN SEQUENCE STARS

WRITE DWARFS

SPECTRAL TYPE

STELLAR SPECTRAL ABSORPTION LINES

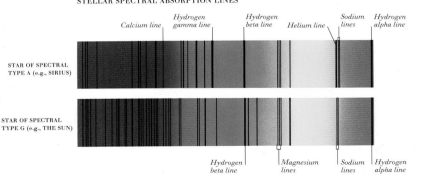

Calcium line

Hydrogen gamma line

Hydrogen beta line

Helium line

Sodium lines

Hydrogen alpha line

STAR OF SPECTRAL TYPE A (e.g., SIRIUS)

STAR OF SPECTRAL TYPE G (e.g., THE SUN)

Hydrogen beta line

Magnesium lines

Sodium lines

Hydrogen alpha line

Small stars

REGION OF STAR FORMATION IN ORION

SMALL STARS HAVE A MASS of up to about one and a half times that of the Sun. They begin to form when a region of higher density in a nebula condenses into a huge globule of gas and dust that contracts under its own gravity. Within a globule, regions of condensing matter heat up and begin to glow, forming protostars. If a protostar contains enough matter, the central temperature reaches about 27 million °F (8 million °C). At this temperature, nuclear reactions in which hydrogen fuses to form helium can start. This process releases energy, which prevents the star from contracting more and also causes it to shine; it is now a main sequence star. A star of about one solar mass remains on the main sequence for about 10 billion years, until much of the hydrogen in the star's core has been converted into helium. The helium core then contracts, and nuclear reactions continue in a shell around the core. The core becomes hot enough for helium to fuse to form carbon, while the outer layers of the star expand and cool. The expanding star is known as a red giant. When the helium in the core runs out, the outer layers of the star may be blown away as an expanding gas shell called a planetary nebula. The remaining core (about 80 percent of the original star) is now in its final stages. It becomes a white dwarf star that gradually cools and dims. When it finally stops shining altogether, the dead star will become a black dwarf.

STRUCTURE OF A MAIN SEQUENCE STAR

Core containing hydrogen fusing to form helium

Radiative zone

Convective zone

Surface temperature 10,000°F (5,500°C)

Core: 27 million °F (15 million °C)

STRUCTURE OF A NEBULA

Young main sequence star

Dense region of dust and gas (mainly hydrogen) condensing under gravity to form globules

Hot, ionized hydrogen gas emitting red light due to being stimulated by radiation from hot young stars

Dark globule of dust and gas (mainly hydrogen) contracting to form protostars

LIFE OF A SMALL STAR OF ABOUT ONE SOLAR MASS

Cool cloud of gas (mainly hydrogen) and dust

Dense globule condensing to form protostars

NEBULA

Glowing ball of gas (mainly hydrogen)

Natal cocoon (shell of dust blown away by radiation from protostar)

PROTOSTAR
Duration: 50 million years

About 1.4 million km

Star producing energy by nuclear fusion in core

MAIN SEQUENCE STAR
Duration: 10 billion years

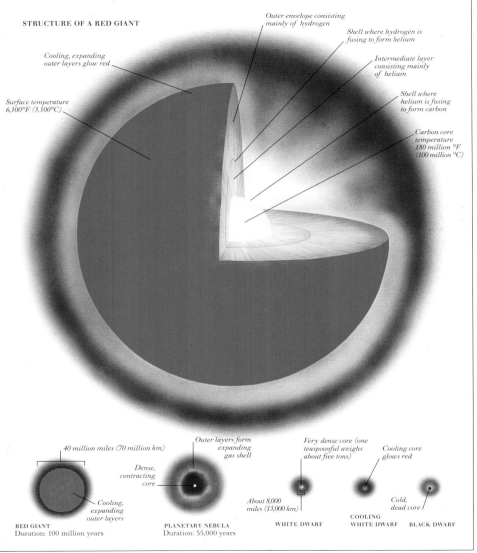

STRUCTURE OF A RED GIANT

Outer envelope consisting mainly of hydrogen

Shell where hydrogen is fusing to form helium

Cooling, expanding outer layers glow red

Intermediate layer consisting mainly of helium

Shell where helium is fusing to form carbon

Surface temperature 6,300°F (3,500°C)

Carbon core temperature 180 million °F (100 million °C)

40 million miles (70 million km)

Outer layers form expanding gas shell

Very dense core (one teaspoonful weighs about five tons)

Cooling core glows red

Dense, contracting core

Cooling, expanding outer layers

About 8,000 miles (13,000 km)

Cold, dead core

RED GIANT
Duration: 100 million years

PLANETARY NEBULA
Duration: 35,000 years

WHITE DWARF

COOLING WHITE DWARF

BLACK DWARF

Massive stars

MASSIVE STARS HAVE A MASS AT LEAST THREE TIMES that of the Sun, and some stars are as massive as about 50 Suns. A massive star evolves in a similar way to a small star until it reaches the main sequence stage (see pp. 24-25). During its life as a main sequence star, it shines steadily until the hydrogen in its core has fused to form helium. This process takes billions of years in a small star, but only millions of years in a massive star. A massive star then becomes a red supergiant, which initially consists of a helium core surrounded by outer layers of cooling, expanding gas. Over the next few million years, a series of nuclear reactions form different elements in shells around an iron core. The core eventually collapses in less than a second, causing a massive explosion called a supernova, in which a shock wave blows away the outer layers of the star. Supernovae shine brighter than an entire galaxy for a short time. Sometimes, the core survives the supernova explosion. If the surviving core is between about one and a half and three solar masses, it contracts to become a tiny, dense neutron star. If the core is greater than three solar masses, it contracts to become a black hole (see pp. 28-29).

SUPERNOVA

TARANTULA NEBULA BEFORE SUPERNOVA

STRUCTURE OF A RED SUPERGIANT

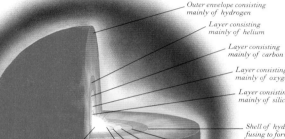

Outer envelope consisting mainly of hydrogen

Layer consisting mainly of helium

Layer consisting mainly of carbon

Layer consisting mainly of oxygen

Layer consisting mainly of silicon

Shell of hydrogen fusing to form helium

Shell of helium fusing to form carbon

Shell of carbon fusing to form oxygen

Shell of oxygen fusing to form silicon

Shell of silicon fusing to form iron core

Surface temperature 5,500°F (3,000°C)

Cooling, expanding outer layers glow red

Core of mainly iron at 5.4-9 billion °F (3-5 billion °C)

LIFE OF A MASSIVE STAR OF ABOUT 10 SOLAR MASSES

Dense globule condensing to form protostars

Cool cloud of gas (mainly hydrogen) and dust

NEBULA

Glowing ball of gas (mainly hydrogen)

Natal cocoon (shell of dust blown away by radiation from protostar)

PROTOSTAR
Duration: a few hundred thousand years

About 2 million miles (3 million km)

Star producing energy by nuclear fusion in core

MAIN SEQUENCE STAR
Duration: 10 million years

FEATURES OF A SUPERNOVA

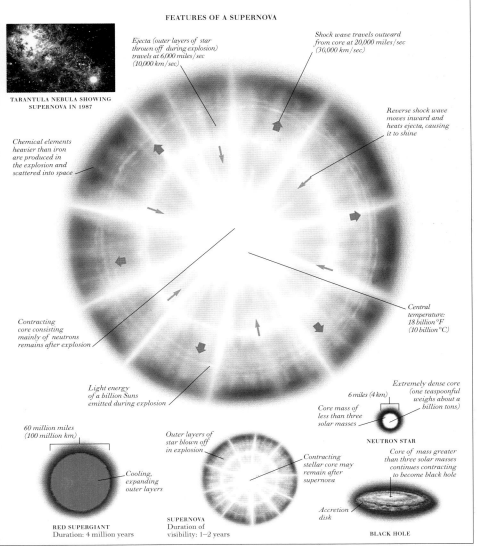

TARANTULA NEBULA SHOWING
SUPERNOVA IN 1987

Ejecta (outer layers of star
thrown off during explosion)
travels at 6,000 miles/sec
(10,000 km/sec)

Shock wave travels outward
from core at 20,000 miles/sec
(30,000 km/sec)

Reverse shock wave
moves inward and
heats ejecta, causing
it to shine

Chemical elements
heavier than iron
are produced in
the explosion and
scattered into space

Central
temperature:
18 billion °F
(10 billion °C)

Contracting
core consisting
mainly of neutrons
remains after explosion

Light energy
of a billion Suns
emitted during explosion

60 million miles
(100 million km)

Outer layers of
star blown off
in explosion

Contracting
stellar core may
remain after
supernova

6 miles (4 km)

Extremely dense core
(one teaspoonful
weighs about a
billion tons)

Core mass of
less than three
solar masses

NEUTRON STAR

Cooling,
expanding
outer layers

Core of mass greater
than three solar masses
continues contracting
to become black hole

Accretion
disk

RED SUPERGIANT
Duration: 4 million years

SUPERNOVA
Duration of
visibility: 1–2 years

BLACK HOLE

Neutron stars and black holes

Neutron stars and black holes form from the stellar cores that remain after stars have exploded as supernovae (see pp. 26-27). If the remaining core is between about one and a half and three solar masses, it contracts to form a neutron star. If the remaining core is greater than about three solar masses, it contracts to form a black hole. Neutron stars are typically only about 6 miles (10 km) in diameter and consist almost entirely of subatomic particles called neutrons. Such stars are so dense that a teaspoonful would weigh about a billion tons. Neutron stars are observed as pulsars, so-called because they rotate rapidly and emit two beams of radio waves, which sweep across the sky and are detected as short pulses. Black holes are characterized by their extremely strong gravity, which is so powerful that not even light can escape; as a result, black holes are invisible. However, they can be detected if they have a close companion star. The gravity of the black hole pulls gas from the other star, forming an accretion disk that spirals around the black hole at high speed, heating up and emitting radiation. Eventually, the matter spirals in to cross the event horizon (the boundary of the black hole), thereby disappearing from the visible universe.

Nebula of gas and dust surrounds pulsar

Rapidly rotating pulsar

Beam of radiation from pulsar

X-RAY IMAGE OF PULSAR AND CENTRAL REGION OF CRAB NEBULA (SUPERNOVA REMNANT)

PULSAR (ROTATING NEUTRON STAR)

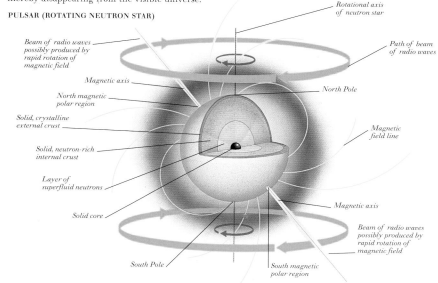

Rotational axis of neutron star

Beam of radio waves possibly produced by rapid rotation of magnetic field

Path of beam of radio waves

Magnetic axis

North Pole

North magnetic polar region

Solid, crystalline external crust

Magnetic field line

Solid, neutron-rich internal crust

Layer of superfluid neutrons

Solid core

Magnetic axis

Beam of radio waves possibly produced by rapid rotation of magnetic field

South Pole

South magnetic polar region

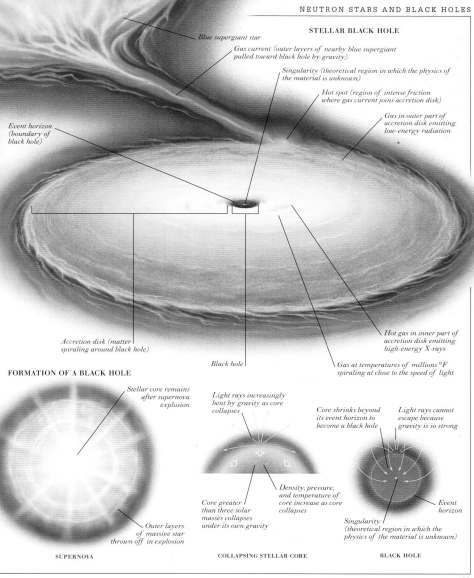

STELLAR BLACK HOLE

Blue supergiant star

Gas current (outer layers of nearby blue supergiant
pulled toward black hole by gravity)

Singularity (theoretical region in which the physics of
the material is unknown)

Hot spot (region of intense friction
where gas current joins accretion disk)

Gas in outer part of
accretion disk emitting
low-energy radiation

Event horizon
(boundary of
black hole)

Hot gas in inner part of
accretion disk emitting
high-energy X-rays

Accretion disk (matter
spiraling around black hole)

Black hole

Gas at temperatures of millions °F
spiraling at close to the speed of light

FORMATION OF A BLACK HOLE

Stellar core remains
after supernova
explosion

Light rays increasingly
bent by gravity as core
collapses

Core shrinks beyond
its event horizon to
become a black hole

Light rays cannot
escape because
gravity is so strong

Density, pressure,
and temperature of
core increase as core
collapses

Core greater
than three solar
masses collapses
under its own gravity

Event
horizon

Singularity
(theoretical region in which the
physics of the material is unknown)

Outer layers
of massive star
thrown off in explosion

SUPERNOVA

COLLAPSING STELLAR CORE

BLACK HOLE

29

The solar system

THE SOLAR SYSTEM consists of a central star (the Sun) and the bodies that orbit it. These bodies include eight planets and their more than 160 known moons; dwarf planets; Kuiper Belt objects; asteroids; comets; and meteoroids. The solar system also contains interplanetary gas and dust. The planets fall into two groups: four small rocky planets near the Sun (Mercury, Venus, Earth, and Mars); and four planets farther out, the giants (Jupiter, Saturn, Uranus, and Neptune). Between the rocky planets and giants is the asteroid belt, which contains thousands of chunks of rock orbiting the Sun. Beyond Neptune is the Kuiper Belt and, more distant, the Oort Cloud. Most of the bodies in the planetary part of the solar system move around the Sun in elliptical orbits located in a thin disk around the Sun's equator. All the planets orbit the Sun in the same direction (counterclockwise when viewed from above) and all but Venus and Uranus also spin about their axes in this direction. Moons also spin as they, in turn, orbit their planets. The entire solar system orbits the center of our galaxy, the Milky Way (see pp. 14-15).

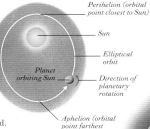

Perihelion (orbital point closest to Sun)

Sun

Elliptical orbit

Planet orbiting Sun

Direction of planetary rotation

Aphelion (orbital point farthest from Sun)

Aphelion of Neptune: 2.8 billion miles

ORBITS OF INNER PLANETS

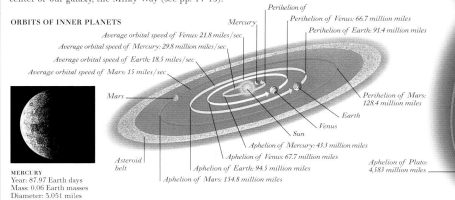

Perihelion of Mercury

Perihelion of Venus: 66.7 million miles

Perihelion of Earth: 91.4 million miles

Average orbital speed of Venus: 21.8 miles/sec

Average orbital speed of Mercury: 29.8 million miles/sec

Average orbital speed of Earth: 18.5 miles/sec

Average orbital speed of Mars: 15 miles/sec

Mars

Perihelion of Mars: 128.4 million miles

Earth

Venus

Sun

Aphelion of Mercury: 43.3 million miles

Aphelion of Venus: 67.7 million miles

Asteroid belt

Aphelion of Earth: 94.5 million miles

Aphelion of Mars: 154.8 million miles

Aphelion of Pluto: 4,583 million miles

MERCURY
Year: 87.97 Earth days
Mass: 0.06 Earth masses
Diameter: 3,051 miles

VENUS
Year: 224.7 Earth days
Mass: 0.81 Earth masses
Diameter: 7,521 miles

EARTH
Year: 365.26 days
Mass: 1 Earth mass
Diameter: 7,926 miles

MARS
Year: 1.88 Earth years
Mass: 0.11 Earth masses
Diameter: 4,217 miles

JUPITER
Year: 11.87 Earth years
Mass: 317.83 Earth masses
Diameter: 88,850 miles

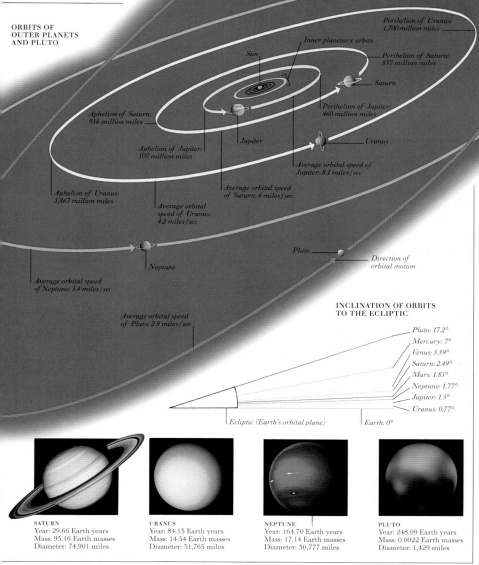

ORBITS OF OUTER PLANETS AND PLUTO

Sun

Inner planetary orbits

Perihelion of Uranus: 1,700 million miles

Perihelion of Saturn: 837 million miles

Saturn

Perihelion of Jupiter: 460 million miles

Aphelion of Saturn: 936 million miles

Aphelion of Jupiter: 507 million miles

Jupiter

Uranus

Average orbital speed of Jupiter: 8.1 miles/sec

Aphelion of Uranus: 1,867 million miles

Average orbital speed of Saturn: 6 miles/sec

Average orbital speed of Uranus: 4.2 miles/sec

Pluto

Direction of orbital motion

Neptune

Average orbital speed of Neptune: 3.4 miles/sec

Average orbital speed of Pluto: 2.9 miles/sec

INCLINATION OF ORBITS TO THE ECLIPTIC

Pluto: 17.2°
Mercury: 7°
Venus: 3.39°
Saturn: 2.49°
Mars: 1.85°
Neptune: 1.77°
Jupiter: 1.3°
Uranus: 0.77°

Ecliptic (Earth's orbital plane)   *Earth: 0°*

SATURN
Year: 29.66 Earth years
Mass: 95.16 Earth masses
Diameter: 74,901 miles

URANUS
Year: 84.13 Earth years
Mass: 14.54 Earth masses
Diameter: 31,765 miles

NEPTUNE
Year: 164.70 Earth years
Mass: 17.14 Earth masses
Diameter: 30,777 miles

PLUTO
Year: 248.09 Earth years
Mass: 0.0022 Earth masses
Diameter: 1,429 miles

The Sun

SOLAR PHOTOSPHERE

THE SUN IS THE STAR AT THE CENTER of the solar system. It is about five billion years old and will continue to shine as it does now for about another five billion years. The Sun is a yellow main sequence star (see pp. 22-23) about 870,000 miles (1.4 million km) in diameter. It consists almost entirely of hydrogen and helium. In the Sun's core, hydrogen is converted to helium by nuclear fusion, releasing energy in the process. The energy travels from the core, through the radiative and convective zones, to the photosphere (visible surface), where it leaves the Sun in the form of heat and light. On the photosphere there are often dark, relatively cool areas called sunspots, which usually appear in pairs or groups and are caused by the cooling effect of the magnetic field. Other types of solar activity are flares, which are usually associated with sunspots, and prominences. Flares are sudden discharges of high-energy radiation and atomic particles. Prominences are huge loops or filaments of gas extending into the solar atmosphere; some last for hours, others for months. Beyond the photosphere is the chromosphere (inner atmosphere) and the extremely rarified corona (outer atmosphere), which extends millions of miles into space. Tiny particles that escape from the corona give rise to the solar wind, which streams through space at hundreds of miles per second. The chromosphere and corona can be seen from Earth when the Sun is totally eclipsed by the Moon.

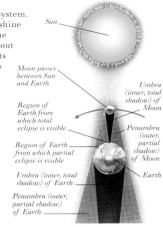

Sun

Moon passes between Sun and Earth

Region of Earth from which total eclipse is visible

Region of Earth from which partial eclipse is visible

Umbra (inner, total shadow) of Moon

Penumbra (outer, partial shadow) of Moon

Umbra (inner, total shadow) of Earth

Penumbra (outer, partial shadow) of Earth

Earth

SURFACE FEATURES

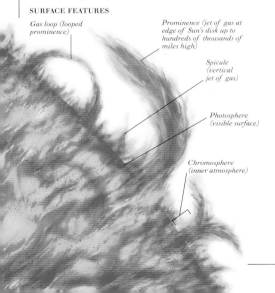

Gas loop (looped prominence)

Prominence (jet of gas at edge of Sun's disk up to hundreds of thousands of miles high)

Spicule (vertical jet of gas)

Photosphere (visible surface)

Chromosphere (inner atmosphere)

TOTAL SOLAR ECLIPSE

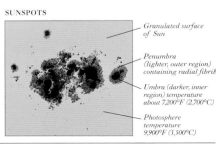

Corona (outer atmosphere of extremely hot, diffuse gas)

Moon covers Sun's disk

SUNSPOTS

Granulated surface of Sun

Penumbra (lighter, outer region) containing radial fibrils

Umbra (darker, inner region) temperature about 7,200°F (2,700°C)

Photosphere temperature 9,900°F (5,500°C)

**EXTERNAL FEATURES AND
INTERNAL STRUCTURE OF THE SUN**

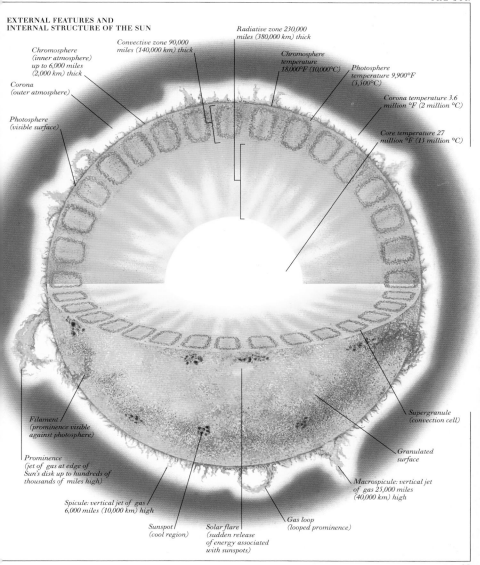

*Radiative zone 230,000
miles (380,000 km) thick*

*Convective zone 90,000
miles (140,000 km) thick*

*Chromosphere
(inner atmosphere)
up to 6,000 miles
(2,000 km) thick*

*Chromosphere
temperature
18,000°F (10,000°C)*

*Photosphere
temperature 9,900°F
(5,500°C)*

*Corona
(outer atmosphere)*

*Corona temperature 3.6
million °F (2 million °C)*

*Photosphere
(visible surface)*

*Core temperature 27
million °F (15 million °C)*

*Filament
(prominence visible
against photosphere)*

*Supergranule
(convection cell)*

*Prominence
(jet of gas at edge of
Sun's disk up to hundreds of
thousands of miles high)*

*Granulated
surface*

*Spicule: vertical jet of gas
6,000 miles (10,000 km) high*

*Macrospicule: vertical jet
of gas 25,000 miles
(40,000 km) high*

*Sunspot
(cool region)*

*Solar flare
(sudden release
of energy associated
with sunspots)*

*Gas loop
(looped prominence)*

Mercury

MERCURY

MERCURY IS THE NEAREST PLANET to the Sun, orbiting at an average distance of about 36 million miles (58 million km). Because Mercury is the closest planet to the Sun, it moves faster than any other planet, travelling at an average speed of nearly 30 miles (48 km) per second and completing an orbit in just under 88 days. Mercury is very small (only 40 percent bigger than the Moon) and rocky. Most of the surface has been heavily cratered by the impact of meteorites, although there are also smooth, sparsely cratered lava-covered plains. The Caloris Basin is the largest crater, measuring about 800 miles (1,300 km) across. It is thought to have been formed when a 38-mile- (60-km-) diameter asteroid hit the planet, and is surrounded by concentric rings of mountains thrown up by the impact. The surface also has many clifflike ridges (called rupes) that are thought to have been formed when the hot core of the young planet cooled and shrank about four billion years ago, buckling the planet's surface in the process. The planet rotates about its axis very slowly, taking nearly 59 Earth days to complete one rotation. As a result, a solar day (sunrise to sunrise) on Mercury is about 176 Earth days—twice as long as the 88-day Mercurian year. Mercury has extreme surface temperatures, ranging from a maximum of 800°F (430°C) on the sunlit side to -270°F (-170°C) on the dark side. At nightfall, the temperature drops very quickly because the planet's atmosphere is almost nonexistent. It consists only of minute amounts of helium and hydrogen captured from the solar wind, plus traces of other gases.

TILT AND ROTATION OF MERCURY

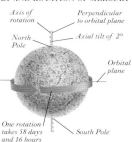

Axis of rotation

Perpendicular to orbital plane

North Pole

Axial tilt of 2°

Orbital plane

One rotation takes 58 days and 16 hours

South Pole

DEGAS AND BRONTË (RAY CRATERS)

Bright ray of ejecta (ejected material)

Brontë

Unmapped region

Degas with central peak

FORMATION OF A RAY CRATER

Debris thrown out by impact

Path of meteorite colliding with planet

Wall of rock thrown up around crater

Impact forms saucer-shaped crater

Fractured rock

METEORITE IMPACT

Path of rocky ejecta (ejected material)

Ejecta forms secondary craters

Loose debris on crater floor

SECONDARY CRATERING

Wall of rock forms ring of mountains

Ray of ejecta (ejected material)

Small secondary crater

Loose ejected rock

Central mountain rings form if floor of large crater recoils from meteorite impact

Falling debris forms ridges on side of wall

RAY CRATER

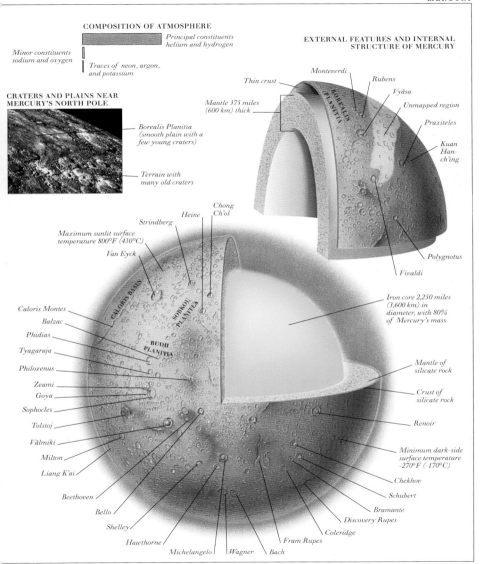

COMPOSITION OF ATMOSPHERE

Principal constituents helium and hydrogen

Minor constituents sodium and oxygen

Traces of neon, argon, and potassium

EXTERNAL FEATURES AND INTERNAL STRUCTURE OF MERCURY

Monteverdi

Rubens

Thin crust

Vyāsa

Mantle 375 miles (600 km) thick

BOREALIS PLANITIA

Unmapped region

Praxiteles

Kuan Han-ch'ing

CRATERS AND PLAINS NEAR MERCURY'S NORTH POLE

Borealis Planitia (smooth plain with a few young craters)

Terrain with many old craters

Polygnotus

Vivaldi

Chong Ch'ol

Heine

Strindberg

Maximum sunlit surface temperature 800°F (430°C)

Van Eyck

CALORIS BASIS

SOBKOU PLANITIA

Caloris Montes

Balzac

Phidias

Tyagaraja

Philoxenus

Zeami

Goya

BUDH PLANITIA

Sophocles

Tolstoj

Vālmiki

Milton

Liang K'ai

Beethoven

Bello

Shelley

Hawthorne

Michelangelo

Wagner

Bach

Fram Rupes

Coleridge

Discovery Rupes

Bramante

Schubert

Chekhov

Minimum dark-side surface temperature -270°F (-170°C)

Renoir

Crust of silicate rock

Mantle of silicate rock

Iron core 2,250 miles (3,600 km) in diameter, with 80% of Mercury's mass

Venus

RADAR IMAGE OF VENUS

VENUS IS A ROCKY PLANET and the second planet from the Sun. Venus spins slowly backwards as it orbits the Sun, causing its rotational period to be the longest in the solar system, at about 243 Earth days. It is slightly smaller than Earth and probably has a similar internal structure, consisting of a semisolid metal core, surrounded by a rocky mantle and crust. Venus is the brightest object in the sky after the Sun and Moon because its clouds reflect sunlight strongly. The main component of the atmosphere is carbon dioxide, which traps heat in a greenhouse effect far stronger than that on Earth. As a result, Venus is the hottest planet, with a maximum surface temperature of about 900°F (480°C). The thick cloud layers contain droplets of sulfuric acid and are driven around the planet by winds at speeds of up to 220 miles (360 km) per hour. Although the planet takes 243 Earth days to rotate once, the high-speed winds cause the clouds to circle the planet in only four Earth days. The high temperature, acidic clouds, and enormous atmospheric pressure (about 90 times greater at the surface than that on Earth) make the environment extremely hostile. However, space probes have managed to land on Venus and photograph its dry, dusty surface. The Venusian surface has also been mapped by probes with radar equipment that can "see" through the cloud layers. Such radar maps reveal a terrain with craters, mountains, volcanoes, and areas where craters have been covered by plains of solidified volcanic lava. There are two large highland regions called Aphrodite Terra and Ishtar Terra.

TILT AND ROTATION OF VENUS

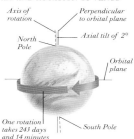

Axis of rotation

Perpendicular to orbital plane

Axial tilt of 2°

North Pole

Orbital plane

One rotation takes 243 days and 14 minutes

South Pole

CLOUD FEATURES

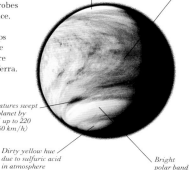

Polar hood

Dark, mid-latitude band

Cloud features swept around planet by winds of up to 220 miles (360 km/h)

Dirty yellow hue due to sulfuric acid in atmosphere

Bright polar band

VENUSIAN CRATERS

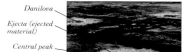

Danilova

Ejecta (ejected material)

Central peak

Howe

FALSE-COLOR RADAR MAP OF THE SURFACE OF VENUS

Metis Regio

Maxwell Montes

Bell Regio

Tethus Regio

Atalanta Planitia

Sedna Planitia

ISHTAR TERRA

Leda Planitia

Eisila Regio

Tellus Regio

Guinevere Planitia

Niobe Planitia

Phoebe Regio

Alpha Regio

Ovda Regio

Themis Regio

Thetis Regio

APHRODITE TERRA

Lavinia Planitia

Aino Planitia

Helen Planitia

Lada Terra

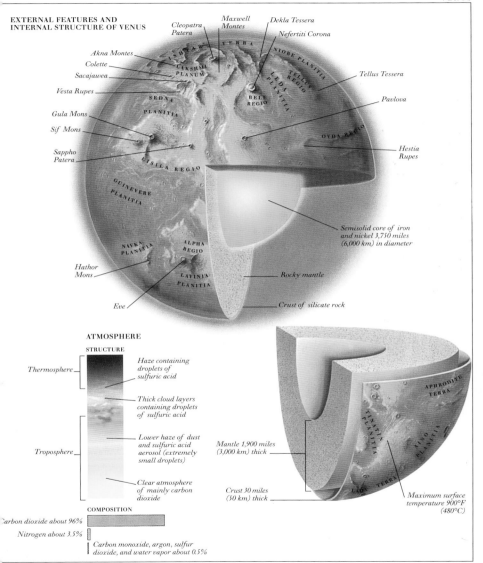

EXTERNAL FEATURES AND INTERNAL STRUCTURE OF VENUS

Cleopatra Patera
Maxwell Montes
Dekla Tessera
Nefertiti Corona
Akna Montes
Colette
Sacajawea
Vesta Rupes
Gula Mons
Sif Mons
Sappho Patera
Hathor Mons
Eve
ISHTAR TERRA
NIOBE PLANITIA
LAKSHMI PLANUM
SEDNA PLANITIA
LEDA PLANITIA
BELL REGIO
TELLUS REGIO
Tellus Tessera
Pavlova
OVDA REGIO
Hestia Rupes
EISILA REGIO
GUINEVERE PLANITIA
NAVKA PLANITIA
ALPHA REGIO
LAVINIA PLANITIA

Semisolid core of iron and nickel 3,750 miles (6,000 km) in diameter

Rocky mantle

Crust of silicate rock

ATMOSPHERE

STRUCTURE

Thermosphere
Troposphere

Haze containing droplets of sulfuric acid

Thick cloud layers containing droplets of sulfuric acid

Lower haze of dust and sulfuric acid aerosol (extremely small droplets)

Clear atmosphere of mainly carbon dioxide

Mantle 1,900 miles (3,000 km) thick

Crust 30 miles (50 km) thick

APHRODITE TERRA
TINATIN PLANITIA
AINO PLANITIA
LADA TERRA

Maximum surface temperature 900°F (480°C)

COMPOSITION

Carbon dioxide about 96%

Nitrogen about 3.5%

Carbon monoxide, argon, sulfur dioxide, and water vapor about 0.5%

The Earth

Axis of rotation

Axial tilt of 23.4°

North Pole

Orbital plane

South Pole

One rotation takes 23 hours and 56 minutes

Perpendicular to orbital plane

THE EARTH

THE EARTH IS THE THIRD of the eight planets that orbit the Sun. It is the largest and densest rocky planet, and the only one known to support life. About 70 percent of the Earth's surface is covered by water, which is not found in liquid form on the surface of any other planet. There are four main layers: the inner core, the outer core, the mantle, and the crust. At the heart of the planet the solid inner core has a temperature of about 11,900°F (6,600°C). The heat from this inner core causes material in the molten outer core and mantle to circulate in convection currents. It is thought that these convection currents generate the Earth's magnetic field, which extends into space as the magnetosphere. The Earth's atmosphere helps screen out some of the harmful radiation from the Sun, stops most meteoroids from reaching the planet's surface, and traps enough heat to prevent extremes of cold. The Earth has one natural satellite, the Moon, which is thought to have formed when a huge asteroid impacted Earth in the distant past.

THE FORMATION OF THE EARTH

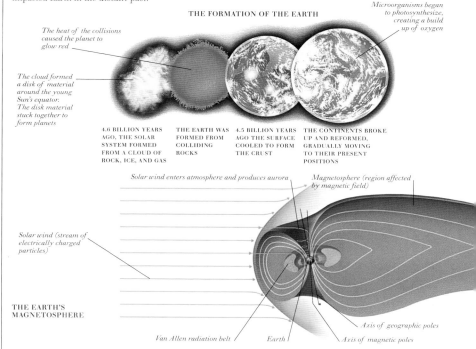

Microorganisms began to photosynthesize, creating a build up of oxygen

The heat of the collisions caused the planet to glow red

The cloud formed a disk of material around the young Sun's equator. The disk material stuck together to form planets

4.6 BILLION YEARS AGO, THE SOLAR SYSTEM FORMED FROM A CLOUD OF ROCK, ICE, AND GAS

THE EARTH WAS FORMED FROM COLLIDING ROCKS

4.5 BILLION YEARS AGO THE SURFACE COOLED TO FORM THE CRUST

THE CONTINENTS BROKE UP AND REFORMED, GRADUALLY MOVING TO THEIR PRESENT POSITIONS

Solar wind enters atmosphere and produces aurora

Magnetosphere (region affected by magnetic field)

Solar wind (stream of electrically charged particles)

THE EARTH'S MAGNETOSPHERE

Van Allen radiation belt

Earth

Axis of geographic poles

Axis of magnetic poles

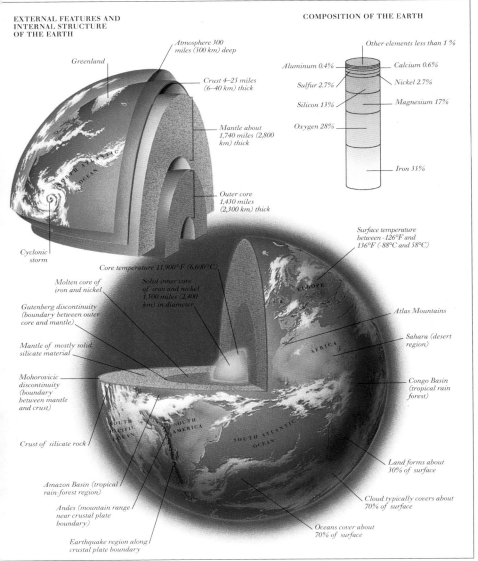

EXTERNAL FEATURES AND INTERNAL STRUCTURE OF THE EARTH

COMPOSITION OF THE EARTH

Greenland

Atmosphere 300 miles (500 km) deep

Crust 4–25 miles (6–40 km) thick

Mantle about 1,740 miles (2,800 km) thick

Outer core 1,430 miles (2,300 km) thick

Cyclonic storm

Other elements less than 1 %

Aluminum 0.4%

Calcium 0.6%

Sulfur 2.7%

Nickel 2.7%

Silicon 13%

Magnesium 17%

Oxygen 28%

Iron 35%

Core temperature 11,900° F (6,600°C)

Surface temperature between -126°F and 136°F (-88°C and 58°C)

Molten core of iron and nickel

Solid inner core of iron and nickel 1,500 miles (2,400 km) in diameter

Gutenberg discontinuity (boundary between outer core and mantle)

Atlas Mountains

Sahara (desert region)

Mantle of mostly solid silicate material

Congo Basin (tropical rain forest)

Mohorovicic discontinuity (boundary between mantle and crust)

Crust of silicate rock

Land forms about 30% of surface

Amazon Basin (tropical rain-forest region)

Cloud typically covers about 70% of surface

Andes (mountain range near crustal plate boundary)

Oceans cover about 70% of surface

Earthquake region along crustal plate boundary

39

The Moon

THE MOON FROM EARTH

THE MOON IS THE EARTH'S only natural satellite. It is relatively large for a moon, with a diameter of about 2,155 miles (3,470 km)—just over a quarter that of the Earth. The Moon takes the same time to rotate on its axis as it takes to orbit the Earth (27.3 days), and so the same side (the near side) always faces us. However, the amount of the surface we can see—the phase of the Moon—depends on how much of the near side is in sunlight. The Moon is dry and barren, with negligible atmosphere and water. It consists mainly of solid rock, although its core may contain molten rock or iron. The surface is dusty, with highlands covered in craters caused by meteorite impacts, and lowlands in which large craters have been filled by solidified lava to form dark areas called maria or "seas." Maria occur mainly on the near side, which has a thinner crust than the far side. Many of the craters are rimmed by mountain ranges that form the crater walls and can be thousands of feet high.

TILT AND ROTATION OF THE MOON

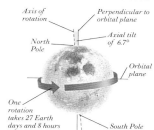

Axis of rotation
Perpendicular to orbital plane
North Pole
Axial tilt of 6.7°
Orbital plane
One rotation takes 27 Earth days and 8 hours
South Pole

CRATERS ON OCEANUS PROCELLARUM

Aristarchus
Cobra Head (head of Schröter's Valley)
Herodotus

NEAR SIDE OF THE MOON

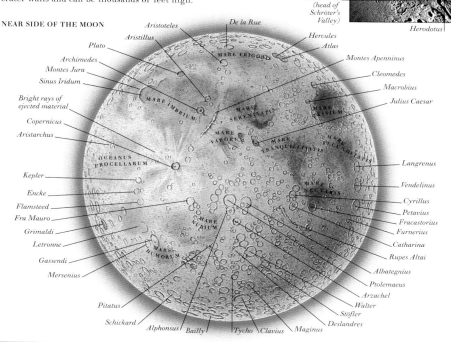

De la Rue
Aristoteles
Aristillus
Plato
Archimedes
Montes Jura
Sinus Iridum
Bright rays of ejected material
Copernicus
Aristarchus
Kepler
Encke
Flamsteed
Fra Mauro
Grimaldi
Letronne
Gassendi
Mersenius
Pitatus
Schickard
Alphonsus
Bailly
Tycho
Clavius
Maginus

Hercules
Atlas
Montes Apenninus
Cleomedes
Macrobius
Julius Caesar
Langrenus
Vendelinus
Cyrillus
Petavius
Fracastorius
Furnerius
Catharina
Rupes Altai
Albategnius
Ptolemaeus
Arzachel
Walter
Stöfler
Deslandres

MARE FRIGORIS
MARE IMBRIUM
MARE SERENITATIS
MARE CRISIUM
MARE VAPORUM
MARE TRANQUILLITATIS
MARE FECUNDITATIS
OCEANUS PROCELLARUM
MARE NECTARIS
MARE NUBIUM
MARE HUMORUM

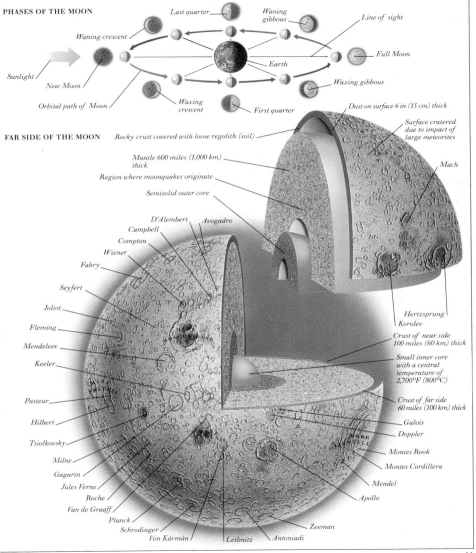

PHASES OF THE MOON

Last quarter

Waning gibbous

Waning crescent

Line of sight

Sunlight

New Moon

Full Moon

Earth

Orbital path of Moon

Waxing crescent

First quarter

Waxing gibbous

FAR SIDE OF THE MOON

Rocky crust covered with loose regolith (soil)

Dust on surface 6 in (15 cm) thick

Surface cratered due to impact of large meteorites

Mantle 600 miles (1,000 km) thick

Mach

Region where moonquakes originate

Semisolid outer core

D'Alembert

Avogadro

Campbell

Compton

Wiener

Fabry

Seyfert

Joliot

Fleming

Mendeleev

Keeler

Pasteur

Hilbert

Tsiolkovsky

Milne

Gagarin

Jules Verne

Roche

Van de Graaff

Planck

Schrodinger

Von Kármàn

Leibnitz

Antoniadi

Zeeman

Apollo

Mendel

Montes Cordillera

Montes Rook

Doppler

Galois

Crust of far side 60 miles (100 km) thick

Small inner core with a central temperature of 2,700°F (800°C)

Crust of near side 100 miles (60 km) thick

Hertzsprung

Korolev

Mars

MARS

MARS, KNOWN AS THE RED PLANET, is the fourth planet from the Sun and the outermost rocky planet. In the 19th century, astronomers first observed what were thought to be signs of life on Mars. These signs included apparent canal-like lines on the surface, and dark patches that were thought to be vegetation. It is now known that the "canals" are an optical illusion, and the dark patches are areas where the red dust that covers most of the planet has been blown away. The fine dust particles are often whipped up by winds into dust storms that occasionally obscure almost all the surface. Residual fine dust in the atmosphere gives the Martian sky a pinkish hue. The northern hemisphere of Mars has many large plains formed of solidified volcanic lava, whereas the southern hemisphere has many craters and large impact basins. There are also several huge, extinct volcanoes, including Olympus Mons, which, at 370 miles (600 km) across and 15 miles (25 km) high, is the largest known volcano in the solar system. The surface also has many canyons and branching channels. The canyons were formed by movements of the surface crust, but the channels are thought to have been formed by flowing water that has now dried up. The Martian atmosphere is much thinner than Earth's, with only a few clouds and morning mists. Mars has two tiny, irregularly shaped moons called Phobos and Deimos. Their small size indicates that they may be asteroids that have been captured by the gravity of Mars.

TILT AND ROTATION OF MARS

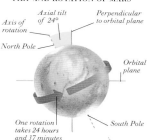

Axis of rotation

Axial tilt of 24°

Perpendicular to orbital plane

North Pole

Orbital plane

One rotation takes 24 hours and 37 minutes

South Pole

SURFACE FEATURES OF MARS

Bright water-ice fog

Fog in canyon 12 miles (20 km) wide at end of Valles Marineris

Syria Planum

NOCTIS LABYRINTHUS (CANYON SYSTEM)

Summit caldera consisting of overlapping collapsed volcanic craters

Gentle slope produced by lava flow

Cloud formation

OLYMPUS MONS (EXTINCT SHIELD VOLCANO)

THE SURFACE OF MARS

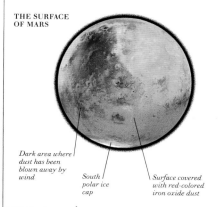

Dark area where dust has been blown away by wind

South polar ice cap

Surface covered with red-colored iron oxide dust

MOONS OF MARS

PHOBOS
Average diameter: 14 miles
Average distance from
planet: 5,800 miles

DEIMOS
Average diameter: 8 miles
Average distance from
planet: 14,600 miles

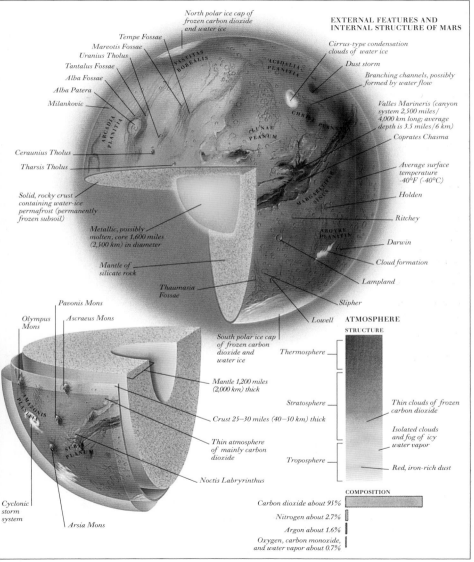

EXTERNAL FEATURES AND
INTERNAL STRUCTURE OF MARS

North polar ice cap of
frozen carbon dioxide
and water ice

Tempe Fossae

Mareotis Fossae

Uranius Tholus

Tantalus Fossae

Alba Fossae

Alba Patera

Milankovic

Ceraunius Tholus

Tharsis Tholus

Solid, rocky crust
containing water-ice
permafrost (permanently
frozen subsoil)

Metallic, possibly
molten, core 1,600 miles
(2,500 km) in diameter

Mantle of
silicate rock

Thaumasia
Fossae

Cirrus-type condensation
clouds of water ice

Dust storm

Branching channels, possibly
formed by water flow

Valles Marineris (canyon
system 2,500 miles /
4,000 km long; average
depth is 3.5 miles/6 km)

Coprates Chasma

Average surface
temperature
-40°F (-40°C)

Holden

Ritchey

Darwin

Cloud formation

Lampland

Slipher

Lowell

South polar ice cap
of frozen carbon
dioxide and
water ice

Pavonis Mons

Olympus
Mons

Ascraeus Mons

Mantle 1,200 miles
(2,000 km) thick

Crust 25–30 miles (40–50 km) thick

Thin atmosphere
of mainly carbon
dioxide

Noctis Labryrinthus

Cyclonic
storm
system

Arsia Mons

ATMOSPHERE

STRUCTURE

Thermosphere

Stratosphere

Troposphere

Thin clouds of frozen
carbon dioxide

Isolated clouds
and fog of icy
water vapor

Red, iron-rich dust

COMPOSITION

Carbon dioxide about 95%

Nitrogen about 2.7%

Argon about 1.6%

Oxygen, carbon monoxide,
and water vapor about 0.7%

Jupiter

JUPITER

JUPITER IS THE FIFTH PLANET from the Sun and the innermost of the four giant planets. It is the largest and the most massive planet, with a diameter about 11 times that of the Earth and a mass about 2.5 times the combined mass of the seven other planets. Jupiter is thought to have a small rocky core surrounded by an inner mantle of metallic hydrogen (liquid hydrogen that acts like a metal). Outside the inner mantle is an outer mantle of liquid hydrogen and helium that merges into the gaseous atmosphere. Jupiter's rapid rate of rotation causes the clouds in its atmosphere to form belts and zones that encircle the planet parallel to the equator. Belts are dark, low-lying, relatively warm cloud layers, and zones are bright, high-altitude, cooler cloud layers. Within the belts and zones, turbulence causes the formation of cloud features such as white ovals and red spots, both of which are huge storm systems. The most prominent cloud feature is a storm called the Great Red Spot, which consists of a spiraling column of clouds three times wider than the Earth that rises about five miles (8 km) above the upper cloud layer. Jupiter has a thin, faint, main ring, inside which is a tenuous halo ring of tiny particles. Beyond the main ring's outer edge is a broad and faint two-part gossamer ring. There are 63 known Jovian moons. The four largest moons (called the Galileans) are Ganymede, Callisto, Io, and Europa. Ganymede and Callisto are cratered and icy. Europa is smooth and icy and is thought to have a subsurface water ocean. Io is covered in bright red, orange, and yellow splotches. This coloring is caused by sulfurous material from active volcanoes that shoot plumes of lava hundreds of miles above the surface.

TILT AND ROTATION OF JUPITER

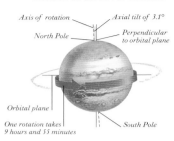

Axis of rotation

Axial tilt of 3.1°

North Pole

Perpendicular to orbital plane

Orbital plane

One rotation takes 9 hours and 55 minutes

South Pole

GREAT RED SPOT AND WHITE OVAL

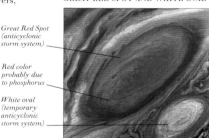

Great Red Spot (anticyclonic storm system)

Red color probably due to phosphorus

White oval (temporary anticyclonic storm system)

INNER RINGS OF JUPITER

Main ring

Halo ring

GALILEAN MOONS OF JUPITER

EUROPA
Diameter: 1,950 miles
Average distance from planet: 416,900 miles

CALLISTO
Diameter: 2,985 miles
Average distance from planet: 1,168,200 miles

GANYMEDE
Diameter: 3,270 miles
Average distance from planet: 664,900 miles

IO
Diameter: 2,263 miles
Average distance from planet: 262,100 miles

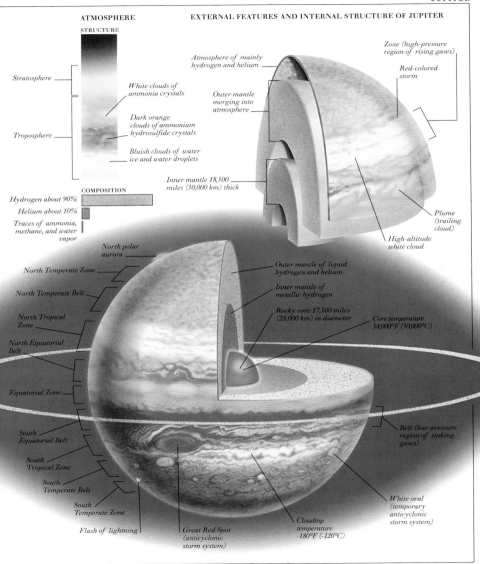

ATMOSPHERE

STRUCTURE

Stratosphere

Troposphere

White clouds of ammonia crystals

Dark orange clouds of ammonium hydrosulfide crystals

Bluish clouds of water ice and water droplets

COMPOSITION

Hydrogen about 90%

Helium about 10%

Traces of ammonia, methane, and water vapor

EXTERNAL FEATURES AND INTERNAL STRUCTURE OF JUPITER

Atmosphere of mainly hydrogen and helium

Outer mantle merging into atmosphere

Inner mantle 18,500 miles (30,000 km) thick

Zone (high-pressure region of rising gases)

Red-colored storm

Plume (trailing cloud)

High-altitude white cloud

North polar aurora

North Temperate Zone

North Temperate Belt

North Tropical Zone

North Equatorial Belt

Equatorial Zone

South Equatorial Belt

South Tropical Zone

South Temperate Belt

South Temperate Zone

Flash of lightning

Outer mantle of liquid hydrogen and helium

Inner mantle of metallic hydrogen

Rocky core 17,500 miles (28,000 km) in diameter

Core temperature 54,000°F (30,000°C)

Belt (low-pressure region of sinking gases)

White oval (temporary anticyclonic storm system)

Great Red Spot (anticyclonic storm system)

Cloudtop temperature -180°F (-120°C)

45

Saturn

FALSE-COLOR IMAGE OF SATURN

S ATURN IS THE SIXTH PLANET from the Sun. It is a gas giant almost as big as Jupiter, with an equatorial diameter of about 75,000 miles (120,500 km). Saturn is thought to consist of a small core of rock and ice surrounded by an inner mantle of metallic hydrogen (liquid hydrogen that acts like a metal). Outside the inner mantle is an outer mantle of liquid hydrogen that merges into a gaseous atmosphere. Saturn's clouds form belts and zones similar to those on Jupiter, but obscured by overlying haze. Storms and eddies, seen as red or white ovals, occur in the clouds. Saturn has an extremely thin but wide system of rings that is about half a mile (1 km) thick but extends outward to about 260,000 miles (420,000 km) from the planet's surface. The main rings comprise thousands of narrow ringlets, each made of icy rock lumps that range in size from tiny particles to chunks several yards across. The D, E, and G rings are very faint, the F ring is brighter, and the A, B, and C rings are bright enough to be seen from Earth with binoculars. In 2009, a huge dust ring was discovered 4 million miles (6 million km) beyond the main system. Saturn has more than 60 known moons, some of which orbit inside the rings and are thought to exert a gravitational influence on the shapes of the rings. Unusually, seven of the moons are co-orbital—they share an orbit with another moon. Astronomers believe that such co-orbital moons may have originated from a single satellite that broke up.

TILT AND ROTATION OF SATURN

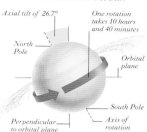

Axial tilt of 26.7°

One rotation takes 10 hours and 40 minutes

North Pole

Orbital plane

South Pole

Perpendicular to orbital plane

Axis of rotation

FALSE-COLOR IMAGE OF SATURN'S CLOUD FEATURES

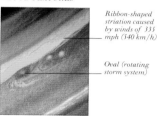

Ribbon-shaped striation caused by winds of 335 mph (540 km/h)

Oval (rotating storm system)

INNER RINGS OF SATURN

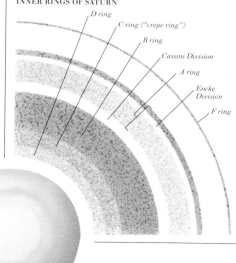

D ring

C ring ("crepe ring")

B ring

Cassini Division

A ring

Encke Division

F ring

MOONS OF SATURN

ENCELADUS
Diameter: 509 miles
Average distance from
planet: 148,000 miles

TETHYS
Diameter: 652 miles
Average distance from
planet: 183,000 miles

DIONE
Diameter: 695 miles
Average distance from
planet: 254,000 miles

MIMAS
Diameter: 247 miles
Average distance from
planet: 115,600 miles

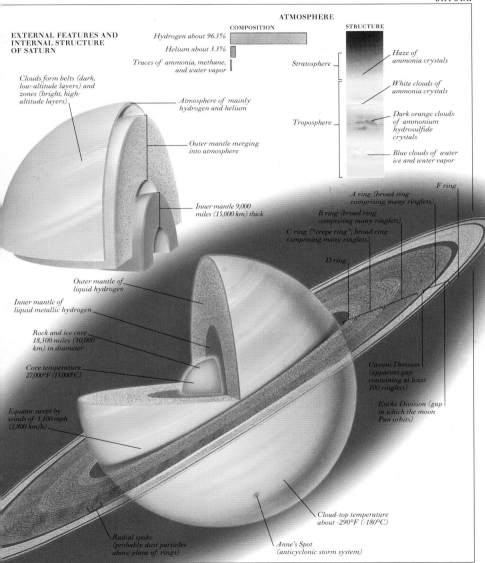

**EXTERNAL FEATURES AND
INTERNAL STRUCTURE
OF SATURN**

ATMOSPHERE

COMPOSITION

Hydrogen about 96.3%

Helium about 3.3%

Traces of ammonia, methane,
and water vapor

STRUCTURE

Stratosphere

Troposphere

Haze of
ammonia crystals

White clouds of
ammonia crystals

Dark orange clouds
of ammonium
hydrosulfide
crystals

Blue clouds of water
ice and water vapor

Clouds form belts (dark,
low-altitude layers) and
zones (bright, high-
altitude layers)

Atmosphere of mainly
hydrogen and helium

Outer mantle merging
into atmosphere

Inner mantle 9,000
miles (15,000 km) thick

Outer mantle of
liquid hydrogen

Inner mantle of
liquid metallic hydrogen

Rock and ice core
18,500 miles (30,000
km) in diameter

Core temperature
27,000°F (15,000°C)

Equator swept by
winds of 1,100 mph
(1,800 km/h)

F ring

A ring (broad ring
comprising many ringlets)

B ring (broad ring
comprising many ringlets)

C ring ("crepe ring"; broad ring
comprising many ringlets)

D ring

Cassini Division
(apparent gap
containing at least
100 ringlets)

Encke Division (gap
in which the moon
Pan orbits)

Cloud-top temperature
about -290°F (-180°C)

Radial spoke
(probably dust particles
above plane of rings)

Anne's Spot
(anticyclonic storm system)

Uranus

FALSE-COLOR IMAGE OF URANUS

URANUS IS THE SEVENTH PLANET from the Sun and the third largest, with a diameter of about 32,000 miles (51,000 km). It is thought to consist of a dense mixture of different types of ice and gas around a solid core. Its atmosphere contains traces of methane, giving the planet a blue-green hue, and the temperature at the cloud tops is about -350°F (-210°C). Uranus is the most featureless planet to have been closely observed: only a few icy clouds of methane have been seen so far. Uranus is unique among the planets in that its axis of rotation lies close to its orbital plane. As a result of its strongly tilted rotational axis, Uranus rolls on its side along its orbital path around the Sun, whereas other planets spin more or less upright. Uranus is encircled by main rings that consist of rocks interspersed with dust lanes and two distant outer rings made of dust. The rings contain some of the darkest matter in the solar system and are extremely narrow, making them difficult to detect: most of them are less than 6 miles (10 km) wide, whereas most of Saturn's rings are thousands of miles in width. There are 27 known Uranian moons, all of which are icy and most of which are farther out than the rings. The 13 inner moons are small and dark, with diameters of less than 100 miles (160 km), and the five major moons are between about 290 and 1,000 miles (470 and 1,600 km) in diameter. The major moons have a wide variety of surface features. Miranda has the most varied surface, with cratered areas broken up by huge ridges and cliffs 12 miles (20 km) high. Beyond these are nine much more distant moons with diameters less than 90 miles (150 km).

TILT AND ROTATION OF URANUS

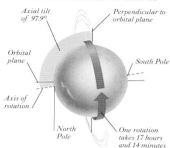

Axial tilt of 97.9°
Perpendicular to orbital plane
Orbital plane
South Pole
Axis of rotation
North Pole
One rotation takes 17 hours and 14 minutes

MAJOR MOONS

MIRANDA
Diameter: 295 miles
Average distance from planet: 80,700 miles

RINGS OF URANUS

Epsilon ring
Lambda ring
Delta ring
Gamma ring
Eta ring
Beta ring
Alpha ring
Rings 4 and 5
Ring 6
Zeta ring

RINGS AND DUST LANES

ARIEL
Diameter: 720 miles
Average distance from planet: 118,800 miles

UMBRIEL
Diameter: 726 miles
Average distance from planet: 165,500 miles

TITANIA
Diameter: 981 miles
Average distance from planet: 270,900 miles

OBERON
Diameter: 946 miles
Average distance from planet: 362,000 miles

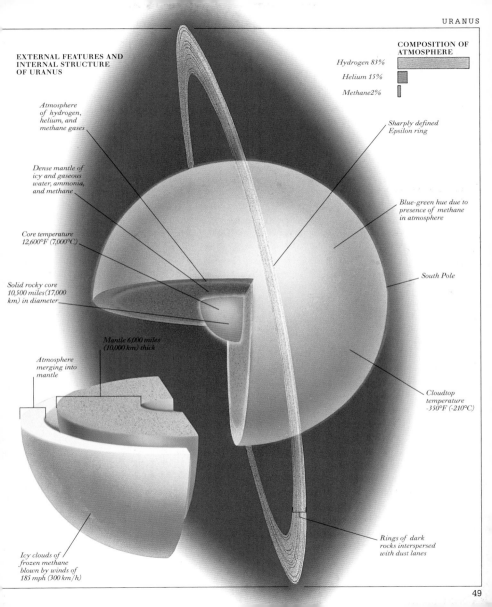

EXTERNAL FEATURES AND INTERNAL STRUCTURE OF URANUS

COMPOSITION OF ATMOSPHERE

Hydrogen 83%

Helium 15%

Methane 2%

Atmosphere of hydrogen, helium, and methane gases

Dense mantle of icy and gaseous water, ammonia, and methane

Core temperature 12,600°F (7,000°C)

Solid rocky core 10,500 miles (17,000 km) in diameter

Mantle 6,000 miles (10,000 km) thick

Atmosphere merging into mantle

Icy clouds of frozen methane blown by winds of 185 mph (300 km/h)

Sharply defined Epsilon ring

Blue-green hue due to presence of methane in atmosphere

South Pole

Cloudtop temperature -350°F (-210°C)

Rings of dark rocks interspersed with dust lanes

Neptune and Pluto

FALSE-COLOR IMAGE OF NEPTUNE

NEPTUNE IS the farthest planet from the Sun, at an average distance of about 2.8 billion miles (4.5 billion km). Neptune is the smallest of the giant planets and is thought to consist of a small rocky core surrounded by a mixture of liquids and gases. Several transient cloud features have been observed in its atmosphere. The largest of these were the Great Dark Spot, which was as wide as the Earth, the Small Dark Spot, and the Scooter. The Great and Small Dark Spots were huge storms that were swept around the planet by winds of about 1,200 miles (2,000 km) per hour. The Scooter was a large area of cirrus cloud. Neptune has six tenuous rings and 13 known moons. Triton is the largest Neptunian moon and the coldest object in the solar system, with a temperature of -390°F (-240°C). Unlike most moons in the solar system, Triton orbits its mother planet in the opposite direction of the planet's rotation. The region extending out from Neptune's orbit is populated by Kuiper Belt objects and dwarf planets. They make a doughnut-shaped belt called the Kuiper Belt. The Kuiper Belt objects are a mix of rock and ice, irregular in shape, and less than 600 miles (1,000 km) across. The larger dwarf planets, which include Pluto, are almost round bodies. Pluto was the first object discovered beyond Neptune and was considered a planet until the dwarf planet category was introduced in 2006. It is made of rock and ice and is 1,365 miles (2,274 km) across. It has three known moons. The largest, Charon, is about half Pluto's size and the two probably had a common origin.

TILT AND ROTATION OF NEPTUNE

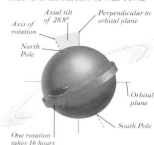

Axis of rotation
Axial tilt of 28.8°
Perpendicular to orbital plane
North Pole
Orbital plane
South Pole
One rotation takes 16 hours and 7 minutes

CLOUD FEATURES OF NEPTUNE

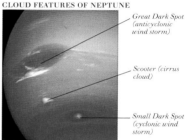

Great Dark Spot (anticyclonic wind storm)
Scooter (cirrus cloud)
Small Dark Spot (cyclonic wind storm)

RINGS OF NEPTUNE

Adams ring and unnamed ring on its inner edge
Arago ring
Lassell ring
Le Verrier ring
Galle ring

HIGH-ALTITUDE CLOUDS

Methane cirrus clouds 25 miles (40 km) above main cloud deck
Cloud shadow
Main cloud deck blown by winds at speeds of about 12,000 miles (2,000 km/h)

MOONS OF NEPTUNE

TRITON
Diameter: 1,681 miles
Average distance from planet: 220,500 miles

PROTEUS
Diameter: 259 miles
Average distance from planet: 75,100 miles

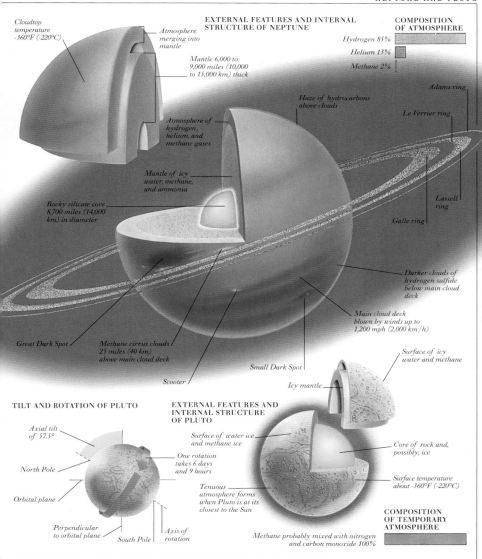

EXTERNAL FEATURES AND INTERNAL STRUCTURE OF NEPTUNE

COMPOSITION OF ATMOSPHERE

Hydrogen 85%

Helium 13%

Methane 2%

Cloudtop temperature -360°F (-220°C)

Atmosphere merging into mantle

Mantle 6,000 to 9,000 miles (10,000 to 15,000 km) thick

Haze of hydrocarbons above clouds

Adams ring

Le Verrier ring

Atmosphere of hydrogen, helium, and methane gases

Mantle of icy water, methane, and ammonia

Rocky silicate core 8,700 miles (14,000 km) in diameter

Lassell ring

Galle ring

Darker clouds of hydrogen sulfide below main cloud deck

Main cloud deck blown by winds up to 1,200 mph (2,000 km/h)

Great Dark Spot

Methane cirrus clouds 25 miles (40 km) above main cloud deck

Scooter

Small Dark Spot

Surface of icy water and methane

Icy mantle

TILT AND ROTATION OF PLUTO

EXTERNAL FEATURES AND INTERNAL STRUCTURE OF PLUTO

Axial tilt of 57.5°

North Pole

Orbital plane

Perpendicular to orbital plane

South Pole

Axis of rotation

One rotation takes 6 days and 9 hours

Surface of water ice and methane ice

Tenuous atmosphere forms when Pluto is at its closest to the Sun

Core of rock and, possibly, ice

Surface temperature about -360°F (-220°C)

COMPOSITION OF TEMPORARY ATMOSPHERE

Methane probably mixed with nitrogen and carbon monoxide 100%

51

Asteroids, comets, and meteoroids

ASTEROID 951 GASPRA

ASTEROIDS, COMETS, AND METEOROIDS are all debris remaining from the nebula from which the solar system formed 4.6 billion years ago. Asteroids are rocky bodies up to about 600 miles (1,000 km) in diameter, although most are much smaller. Most of them orbit the Sun in the asteroid belt, which lies between the orbits of Mars and Jupiter. Cometary nuclei exist in a huge cloud (called the Oort Cloud) that surrounds the planetary part of the solar system. They are made of frozen water and dust and are a few miles in

diameter. Occasionally, a comet is deflected from the Oort Cloud on to a long, elliptical path that brings it much closer to the Sun. As the comet approaches the Sun, the cometary nucleus starts to vaporize in the heat, producing both a brightly shining coma (a huge sphere of gas and dust around the nucleus), and a gas tail, and a dust tail. Meteoroids are small chunks of stone or stone and iron, which are fragments of asteroids or comets. Meteoroids range in size from tiny dust particles to objects tens of meters across. If a meteoroid enters the Earth's atmosphere, it is heated by friction and appears as a glowing streak of light called a meteor (also known as a shooting star). Meteor showers occur when the Earth passes through the trail of dust particles left by a comet. Most meteoroids burn up in the atmosphere. The remnants of the few that are large enough to reach the Earth's surface are termed meteorites.

OPTICAL IMAGE OF HALLEY'S COMET

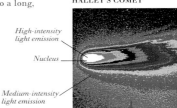

FALSE-COLOR IMAGE OF HALLEY'S COMET

High-intensity light emission

Nucleus

Medium-intensity light emission

Low-intensity light emission

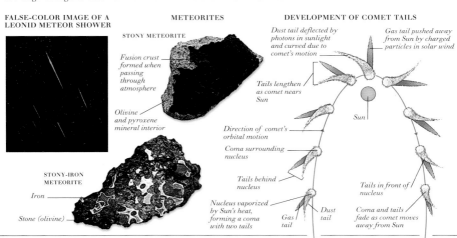

FALSE-COLOR IMAGE OF A LEONID METEOR SHOWER

METEORITES

STONY METEORITE

Fusion crust formed when passing through atmosphere

Olivine and pyroxene mineral interior

STONY-IRON METEORITE

Iron

Stone (olivine)

DEVELOPMENT OF COMET TAILS

Dust tail deflected by photons in sunlight and curved due to comet's motion

Gas tail pushed away from Sun by charged particles in solar wind

Tails lengthen as comet nears Sun

Direction of comet's orbital motion

Coma surrounding nucleus

Sun

Tails behind nucleus

Tails in front of nucleus

Nucleus vaporized by Sun's heat, forming a coma with two tails

Gas tail

Dust tail

Coma and tails fade as comet moves away from Sun

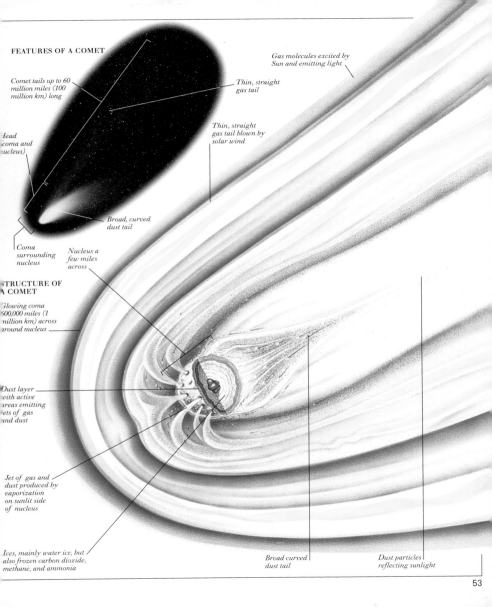

FEATURES OF A COMET

Comet tails up to 60
million miles (100
million km) long

Gas molecules excited by
Sun and emitting light

Thin, straight
gas tail

Thin, straight
gas tail blown by
solar wind

Head
(coma and
nucleus)

Broad, curved
dust tail

Coma
surrounding
nucleus

Nucleus a
few miles
across

STRUCTURE OF
A COMET

Glowing coma
500,000 miles (1
million km) across
around nucleus

Dust layer
with active
areas emitting
jets of gas
and dust

Jet of gas and
dust produced by
vaporization
on sunlit side
of nucleus

Ices, mainly water ice, but
also frozen carbon dioxide,
methane, and ammonia

Broad curved
dust tail

Dust particles
reflecting sunlight

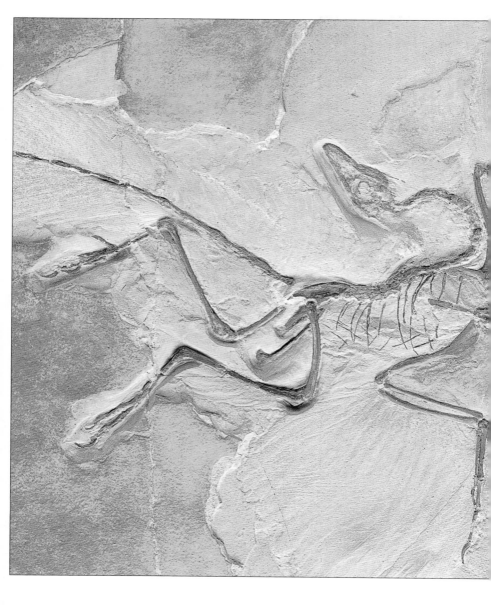

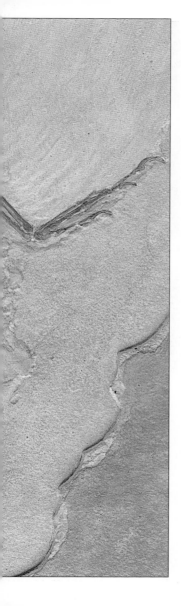

PREHISTORIC EARTH

THE CHANGING EARTH 56
THE EARTH'S CRUST 58
FAULTS AND FOLDS 60
MOUNTAIN BUILDING 62
PRECAMBRIAN TO DEVONIAN PERIOD 64
CARBONIFEROUS TO PERMIAN PERIOD 66
TRIASSIC PERIOD 68
JURASSIC PERIOD 70
CRETACEOUS PERIOD 72
TERTIARY PERIOD 74
QUATERNARY PERIOD 76
EARLY SIGNS OF LIFE 78
AMPHIBIANS AND REPTILES 80
THE DINOSAURS 82
THEROPODS 1 84
THEROPODS 2 86
SAUROPODOMORPHS 1 88
SAUROPODOMORPHS 2 90
THYREOPHORANS 1 92
THYREOPHORANS 2 94
ORNITHOPODS 1 96
ORNITHOPODS 2 98
MARGINOCEPHALIANS 1 100
MARGINOCEPHALIANS 2 102
MAMMALS 1 104
MAMMALS 2 106
THE FIRST HUMANS 108

The changing Earth

THE EARTH FORMED FROM A CLOUD OF DUST and gas drifting through space about 4.6 billion years ago. Dense minerals sank to the center while lighter ones formed a thin rocky crust. However, the first known life-forms—bacteria and blue-green algae—did not appear until about 3.4 billion years ago, and it was only about 700 million years ago that more complex plants and animals began to develop. Since then, thousands of animal and plant species have evolved; some, such as the dinosaurs, survived for many millions of years, while others died out quickly. The Earth itself is continually changing. Although continents neared their present locations about 50 million years ago, they are still drifting slowly over the planet's surface, and mountain ranges such as the Himalayas—which began to form 40 million years ago—are continually being built up and worn away. Climate is also subject to change: the Earth has undergone a series of ice ages interspersed with warmer periods (the most recent glacial period was at its height about 20,000 years ago).

Small mammals appeared (e.g., Crusafontia)

Dinosaurs became extinct

Global mountain building occurred

Multicellular soft-bodied animals appeared (e.g., worms and jellyfish)

Shelled invertebrates appeared (e.g., trilobites)

Marine plants flourished

Land plants appeared (e.g., Cooksonia)

Unicellular organisms appeared (e.g., blue-green algae)

Earth formed

Coral reefs appeared

Vertebrates appeared (e.g., Hemicyclaspis)

More complex types of algae appeared

Amphibians appeared (e.g., Ichthyostega)

CRETACEO

PRECAMBRIAN TIME

CAMBRIAN

ORDOVICIAN

SILURIAN

DEVONIAN

GEOLOGICAL TIMESCALE

MILLIONS OF YEARS AGO (MYA) 4,600	570	510	439	409	363	323	29
						MISSISSIPPIAN (NORTH AMERICA)	PENNSYLVANIAN (NORTH AMERICA)
	CAMBRIAN	ORDOVICIAN	SILURIAN	DEVONIAN		CARBONIFEROUS	
PRECAMBRIAN TIME				PALEOZOIC			

EVOLUTION OF THE EARTH

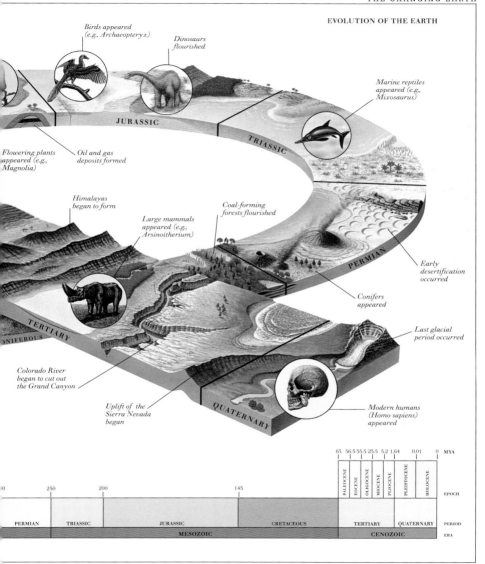

Birds appeared
(e.g., Archaeopteryx)

Dinosaurs
flourished

Marine reptiles
appeared (e.g.,
Mixosaurus)

JURASSIC

TRIASSIC

Flowering plants
appeared (e.g.,
Magnolia)

Oil and gas
deposits formed

Himalayas
began to form

Coal-forming
forests flourished

Large mammals
appeared (e.g.,
Arsinoitherium)

Early
desertification
occurred

PERMIAN

Conifers
appeared

TERTIARY

Last glacial
period occurred

ONIFEROUS

Colorado River
began to cut out
the Grand Canyon

Uplift of the
Sierra Nevada
began

QUATERNARY

Modern humans
(Homo sapiens)
appeared

		65	56.5	35.5	23.5	5.2	1.64		0.01	0	MYA
			PALEOCENE	EOCENE	OLIGOCENE	MIOCENE	PLIOCENE	PLEISTOCENE		HOLOCENE	EPOCH

0	250	200		145					
PERMIAN	TRIASSIC	JURASSIC		CRETACEOUS		TERTIARY		QUATERNARY	PERIOD
		MESOZOIC				CENOZOIC			ERA

57

The Earth's crust

THE EARTH'S CRUST IS THE SOLID outer shell of the Earth. It includes continental crust (about 25 miles/40 km thick) and oceanic crust (about four miles/6 km thick). The crust and the topmost layer of the mantle form the lithosphere. The lithosphere consists of semirigid plates that move relative to each other on the underlying asthenosphere (a partly molten layer of the mantle). This process is known as plate tectonics and helps explain continental drift. Where two plates move apart, there are rifts in the crust. In mid-ocean, this movement results in seafloor spreading and the formation of ocean ridges; on continents, crustal spreading can form rift valleys. When plates move toward each other, one may be subducted beneath (forced under) the other. In mid-ocean, this causes ocean trenches, seismic activity, and arcs of volcanic islands. Where oceanic crust is subducted beneath continental crust or where continents collide, land may be uplifted and mountains formed (see pp. 62–65). Plates may also slide past each other—along the San Andreas fault, for example. Crustal movement on continents may result in earthquakes, while movement under the seabed can lead to tidal waves.

ELEMENTS IN THE EARTH'S CRUST

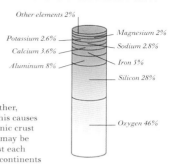

Other elements 2%

Magnesium 2%

Potassium 2.6%

Sodium 2.8%

Calcium 3.6%

Iron 5%

Aluminum 8%

Silicon 28%

Oxygen 46%

FEATURES OF PLATE MOVEMENTS

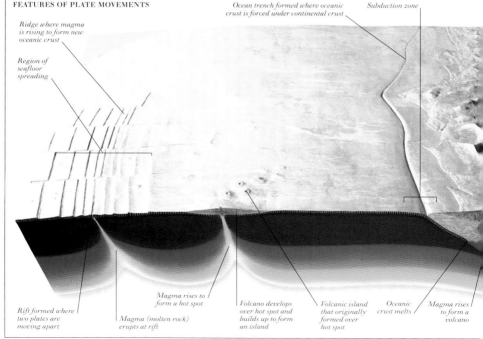

Ocean trench formed where oceanic crust is forced under continental crust

Subduction zone

Ridge where magma is rising to form new oceanic crust

Region of seafloor spreading

Rift formed where two plates are moving apart

Magma (molten rock) erupts at rift

Magma rises to form a hot spot

Volcano develops over hot spot and builds up to form an island

Volcanic island that originally formed over hot spot

Oceanic crust melts

Magma rises to form a volcano

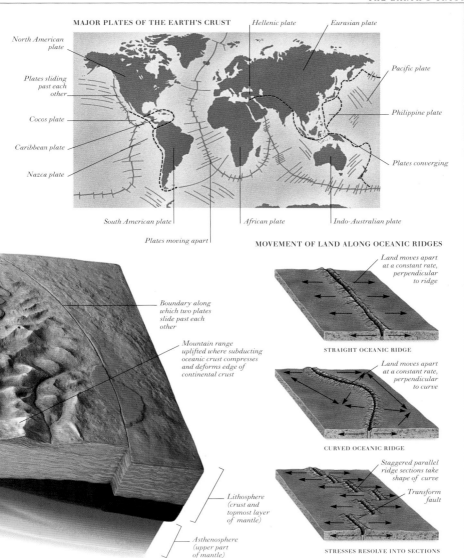

MAJOR PLATES OF THE EARTH'S CRUST

Hellenic plate
Eurasian plate
North American plate
Pacific plate
Plates sliding past each other
Philippine plate
Cocos plate
Caribbean plate
Plates converging
Nazca plate
South American plate
African plate
Indo-Australian plate
Plates moving apart

Boundary along which two plates slide past each other

Mountain range uplifted where subducting oceanic crust compresses and deforms edge of continental crust

Lithosphere (crust and topmost layer of mantle)

Asthenosphere (upper part of mantle)

MOVEMENT OF LAND ALONG OCEANIC RIDGES

Land moves apart at a constant rate, perpendicular to ridge

STRAIGHT OCEANIC RIDGE

Land moves apart at a constant rate, perpendicular to curve

CURVED OCEANIC RIDGE

Staggered parallel ridge sections take shape of curve

Transform fault

STRESSES RESOLVE INTO SECTIONS

Faults and folds

THE CONTINUOUS MOVEMENT of the Earth's crustal plates (see pp. 58–59) can squeeze, stretch, or break rock strata, deforming them and producing faults and folds. A fault is a fracture in a rock along which there is movement of one side relative to the other. The movement can be vertical, horizontal, or oblique (vertical and horizontal). Faults develop when rocks are subjected to compression or tension. They tend to occur in hard, rigid rocks, which are more likely to break than bend. The smallest faults occur in single mineral crystals and are microscopically small, whereas the largest—the Great Rift Valley in Africa, which formed between 5 million and 100,000 years ago—is more than 6,000 miles (9,000 km) long. A fold is a bend in a rock layer caused by compression. Folds occur in elastic rocks, which tend to bend rather than break. The two main types of fold are anticlines (upfolds) and synclines (downfolds). Folds vary in size from a few millimeters long to folded mountain ranges hundreds of miles long, such as the Himalayas (see pp. 62–63) and the Alps, which are repeatedly folding. In addition to faults and folds, other features associated with rock deformations include boudins, mullions, and *en échelon* fractures.

STRUCTURE OF A FOLD

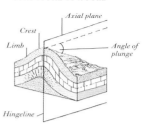

Axial plane
Crest
Limb
Angle of plunge
Hingeline

STRUCTURE OF A FAULT

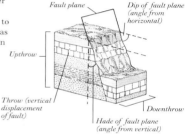

Fault plane
Dip of fault plane (angle from horizontal)
Upthrow
Throw (vertical displacement of fault)
Downthrow
Hade of fault plane (angle from vertical)

STRUCTURE OF A SLOPE

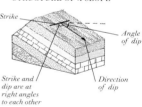

Strike
Angle of dip
Strike and dip are at right angles to each other
Direction of dip

FOLDED ROCK

Steeply dipping limbs
Crest of anticline
Plunge

SECTION THROUGH FOLDED ROCK STRATA THAT HAVE BEEN ERODED

Dipping bed
Anticlinal fold
Monoclinal fold
Mineral-filled fault

Upper Carboniferous Millstone Grit
Lower Carboniferous Limestone

EXAMPLES OF FOLDS

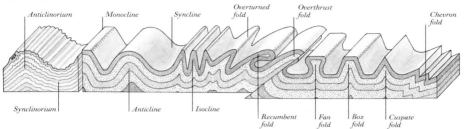

Anticlinorium *Monocline* *Syncline* *Overturned fold* *Overthrust fold* *Chevron fold*

Synclinorium *Anticline* *Isocline* *Recumbent fold* *Fan fold* *Box fold* *Cuspate fold*

EXAMPLES OF FAULTS

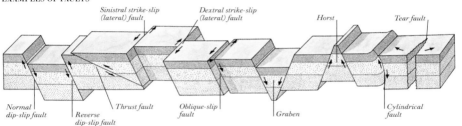

Sinistral strike-slip (lateral) fault *Dextral strike-slip (lateral) fault* *Horst* *Tear fault*

Normal dip-slip fault *Reverse dip-slip fault* *Thrust fault* *Oblique-slip fault* *Graben* *Cylindrical fault*

SMALL-SCALE ROCK DEFORMATIONS

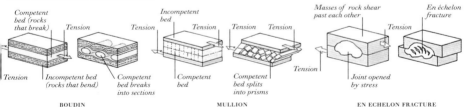

Competent bed (rocks that break) *Tension* *Incompetent bed* *Tension* *Tension* *Masses of rock shear past each other* *Tension* *En échelon fracture*

Tension *Incompetent bed (rocks that bend)* *Competent bed breaks into sections* *Competent bed* *Competent bed splits into prisms* *Joint opened by stress*

BOUDIN **MULLION** **EN ECHELON FRACTURE**

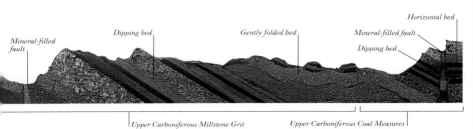

Horizontal bed

Mineral-filled fault *Dipping bed* *Gently folded bed* *Mineral-filled fault* *Dipping bed*

Upper Carboniferous Millstone Grit *Upper Carboniferous Coal Measures*

Mountain building

THE PROCESSES INVOLVED in mountain building—termed orogenesis—occur as a result of the movement of the Earth's crustal plates (see pp. 58–59). There are three main types of mountains: volcanic mountains, fold mountains, and block mountains. Most volcanic mountains have been formed along plate boundaries where plates have come together or moved apart and lava and other debris have been ejected onto the Earth's surface. The lava and debris may have built up to form a dome around the vent of a volcano. Fold mountains are formed

Asia

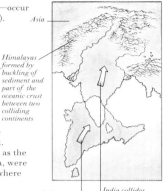

Himalayas formed by buckling of sediment and part of the oceanic crust between two colliding continents

where plates push together and cause the rock to buckle upward. Where oceanic crust meets less dense continental crust, the oceanic crust is forced under the continental crust. The continental crust is buckled by the impact. This is how folded mountain ranges, such as the Appalachian Mountains in North America, were formed. Fold mountains are also formed where two areas of continental crust meet. The Himalayas, for example, began to form when India collided with Asia, buckling the sediments

BHAGIRATHI PARBAT,
HIMALAYAS

India moves north

India collides with Asia about 40 million years ago

and parts of the oceanic crust between them. Block mountains are formed when a block of land is uplifted between two faults as a result of compression or tension in the Earth's crust (see pp. 60–61). Often, the movement along faults has taken place gradually over millions of years. However, two plates may cause an earthquake by suddenly sliding past each other along a faultline.

EXAMPLES OF MOUNTAINS

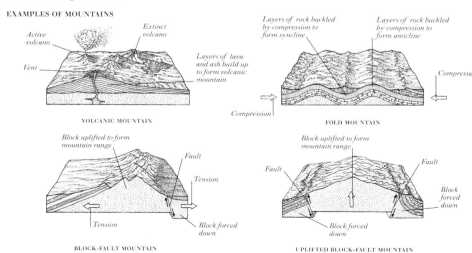

Active volcano

Extinct volcano

Vent

Layers of lava and ash build up to form volcanic mountain

VOLCANIC MOUNTAIN

Layers of rock buckled by compression to form syncline

Layers of rock buckled by compression to form anticline

Compression

Compression

FOLD MOUNTAIN

Block uplifted to form mountain range

Fault

Tension

Tension

Block forced down

BLOCK-FAULT MOUNTAIN

Block uplifted to form mountain range

Fault

Fault

Block forced down

Block forced down

UPLIFTED BLOCK-FAULT MOUNTAIN

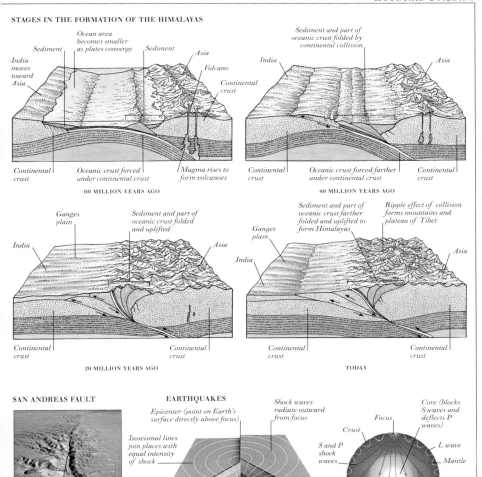

STAGES IN THE FORMATION OF THE HIMALAYAS

60 MILLION YEARS AGO

India moves toward Asia

Sediment

Ocean area becomes smaller as plates converge

Sediment

Asia

Volcano

Continental crust

Continental crust

Oceanic crust forced under continental crust

Magma rises to form volcanoes

40 MILLION YEARS AGO

India

Sediment and part of oceanic crust folded by continental collision

Asia

Continental crust

Oceanic crust forced farther under continental crust

Continental crust

20 MILLION YEARS AGO

Ganges plain

India

Sediment and part of oceanic crust folded and uplifted

Asia

Continental crust

Continental crust

TODAY

Ganges plain

India

Sediment and part of oceanic crust farther folded and uplifted to form Himalayas

Ripple effect of collision forms mountains and plateau of Tibet

Asia

Continental crust

Continental crust

SAN ANDREAS FAULT

Faultline along which two plates may slide past each other, causing an earthquake

EARTHQUAKES

Epicenter (point on Earth's surface directly above focus)

Isoseismal lines join places with equal intensity of shock

Shock waves radiate outward from focus

Focus (point at which earthquake originates)

ANATOMY OF AN EARTHQUAKE

Core (blocks S waves and deflects P waves)

Focus

Crust

S and P shock waves

L wave

Mantle

P wave shadow zone

P wave shadow zone

P wave

PATH OF SHOCK WAVES THROUGH THE EARTH

Precambrian to Devonian periods

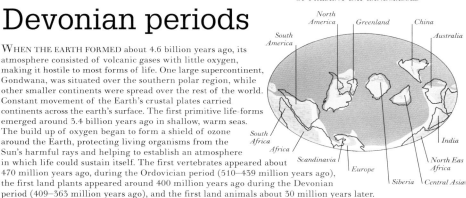

WHEN THE EARTH FORMED about 4.6 billion years ago, its atmosphere consisted of volcanic gases with little oxygen, making it hostile to most forms of life. One large supercontinent, Gondwana, was situated over the southern polar region, while other smaller continents were spread over the rest of the world. Constant movement of the Earth's crustal plates carried continents across the earth's surface. The first primitive life-forms emerged around 3.4 billion years ago in shallow, warm seas. The build up of oxygen began to form a shield of ozone around the Earth, protecting living organisms from the Sun's harmful rays and helping to establish an atmosphere in which life could sustain itself. The first vertebrates appeared about 470 million years ago, during the Ordovician period (510–439 million years ago), the first land plants appeared around 400 million years ago during the Devonian period (409–363 million years ago), and the first land animals about 30 million years later.

EXAMPLES OF PRECAMBRIAN TO DEVONIAN PLANT GROUPS

A PRESENT-DAY CLUBMOSS
(Lycopodium sp.)

A PRESENT-DAY LAND PLANT
(Asparagus setaceous)

FOSSIL OF AN EXTINCT LAND PLANT
(Cooksonia hemisphaerica)

FOSSIL OF AN EXTINCT SWAMP PLANT
(Zosterophyllum llanoveranum)

EXAMPLES OF PRECAMBRIAN TO DEVONIAN TRILOBITES

ACADAGNOSTUS
Group: Agnostidae
Length: ⅓ in (8 mm)

PHACOPS
Group: Phacopidae
Length: 1¾ in (4.5 cm)

OLENELLUS
Group: Olenellidae
Length: 2½ in (6 cm)

ELRATHIA
Group: Ptychopariidae
Length: ¾ in (2 cm)

THE EARTH DURING THE MIDDLE ORDOVICIAN PERIOD

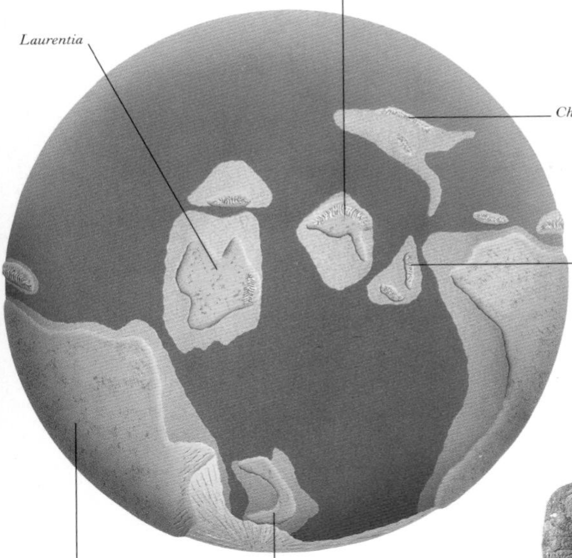
Siberia
Laurentia
China
Kazakstania
Gondwana
Baltica

EXAMPLES OF EARLY MARINE INVERTEBRATES

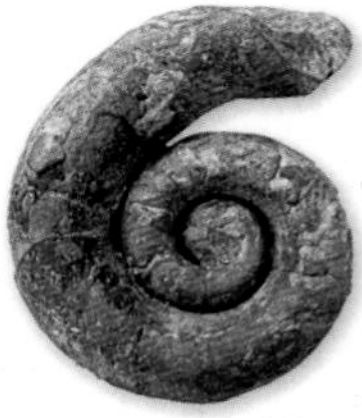

FOSSIL NAUTILOID
(Estonioceras perforatum)

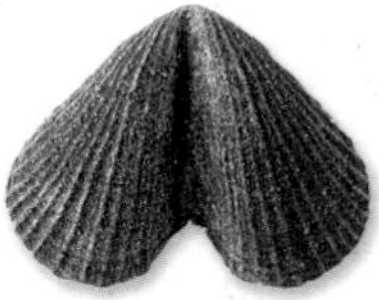

FOSSIL BRACHIOPOD
(Dicoelosia bilobata)

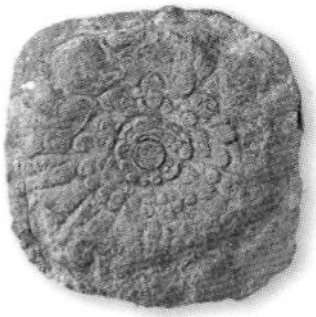

TRACE FOSSIL
(Mawsonites spriggi)

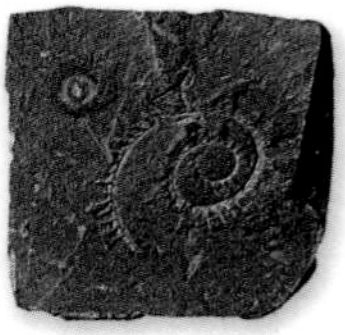

FOSSIL GRAPTOLITE
(Monograptus convolutus)

EXAMPLES OF DEVONIAN FISH

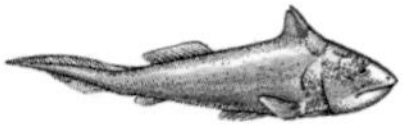

RHAMPHODOPSIS
Group: Ptyctodontidae
Length: 6 in (15 cm)

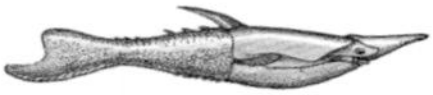

PTERASPIS
Group: Pteraspidae
Length: 10 in (25 cm)

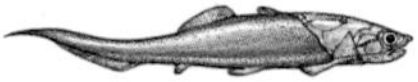

COCCOSTEUS
Group: Coccosteidae
Length: 14 in (35 cm)

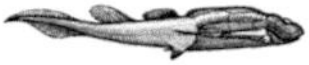

BOTHRIOLEPIS
Group: Bothriolepididae
Length: 16 in (40 cm)

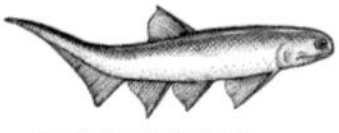

CHEIRACANTHUS
Group: Acanthodidae
Length: 12 in (30 cm)

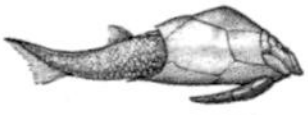

PTERICHTHYODES
Group: Asterolepididae
Length: 6 in (15 cm)

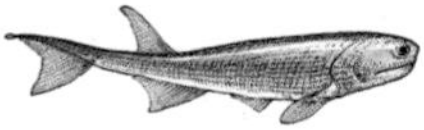

CHEIROLEPIS
Group: Cheirolepidae
Length: 6¾ in (17 cm)

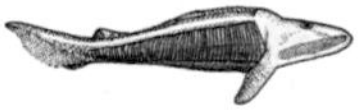

CEPHALASPIS
Group: Cephalaspidae
Length: 8¾ in (22 cm)

Carboniferous to Permian periods

THE CARBONIFEROUS PERIOD (363–290 million years ago) takes its name from the thick, carbon-rich layers—now coal—that were produced during this period as swampy tropical forests were repeatedly drowned by shallow seas. The humid climate across northern and equatorial continents throughout Carboniferous times produced the first dense plant cover on Earth. During the early part of this period, the first reptiles appeared. Their development of a waterproof egg with a protective internal structure ended animal life's dependence on an aquatic environment. Toward the end of Carboniferous times, the earth's continents Laurasia and Gondwana collided, resulting in the huge landmass of Pangaea. Glaciers smothered much of the southern hemisphere during the Permian period (290–245 million years ago), covering Antarctica, parts of Australia, and much of South America, Africa, and India. Ice locked up much of the world's water and large areas of the northern hemisphere experienced a drop in sea level. Away from the poles, deserts and a hot dry climate predominated. As a result of these conditions, the Permian period ended with the greatest mass extinction of life on Earth ever.

LATE CARBONIFEROUS POSITIONS OF PRESENT-DAY LANDMASSES

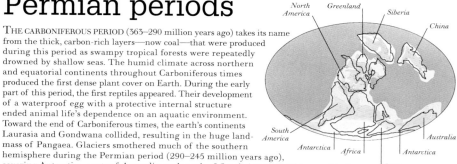

North America
Greenland
Siberia
China
South America
Antarctica
Africa
Australia
Antarctica
India

EXAMPLES OF CARBONIFEROUS AND PERMIAN PLANT GROUPS

A PRESENT-DAY FIR
(Abies concolor)

FOSSIL OF AN EXTINCT FERN
(Zeilleria frenzlii)

FOSSIL OF AN EXTINCT HORSETAIL
(Equisetites sp.)

FOSSIL OF AN EXTINCT CLUBMOSS
(Lepidodendron sp.)

EXAMPLES OF CARBONIFEROUS AND PERMIAN TREES

PECOPTERIS
Group: Marattiaceae
Height: 13 ft (4 m)

PARIPTERIS
Group: Medullosaceae
Height: 16 ft 6 in (5 m)

MARIOPTERIS
Group: Lyginopteridales
Height: 16 ft 6 in (5 m)

MEDULLOSA
Group: Medullosaceae
Height: 16 ft 6 in (5 m)

THE EARTH DURING THE LATE CARBONIFEROUS PERIOD

Siberia

Laurussia

China

Ural Mountains

Caledonian Mountains

Appalachian Mountains

Gondwana

EXAMPLES OF CARBONIFEROUS AND PERMIAN ANIMALS

SKULL OF AN EXTINCT SYNAPSID
(*Dimetrodon loomisi*)

FOSSIL TEETH OF AN EXTINCT SHARK
(*Helicoprion bessonowi*)

MODEL OF AN EXTINCT EARLY REPTILELIKE ANIMAL
(*Westlothiana lizziae*)

LEPIDODENDRON
Group: Lepidodendraceae
Height: 100 ft (30 m)

CORDAITES
Group: Cordaitacea
Height: 33 ft (10 m)

GLOSSOPTERIS
Group: Glossopteridaceae
Height: 26 ft (8 m)

ALETHOPTERIS
Group: Medullosaceae
Height: 16 ft 6 in (5 m)

Triassic period

THE TRIASSIC PERIOD (250–200 million years ago) marked the beginning of what is known as the Age of the Dinosaurs (the Mesozoic era). During this period, the present-day continents were massed together, forming one huge continent known as Pangaea. This landmass experienced extremes of climate, with lush green areas around the coast or by lakes and rivers, and arid deserts in the interior. The only forms of plant life were nonflowering plants, such as conifers, ferns, cycads, and ginkgos; flowering plants had not yet evolved. The principal forms of animal life included diverse, often gigantic, amphibians, rhynchosaurs ("beaked lizards"), and primitive crocodilians. Dinosaurs first appeared about 230 million years ago, at the beginning of the Late Triassic period. Among the earliest dinosaurs were the carnivorous (flesh-eating) herrerasaurids, such as *Herrerasaurus* and *Staurikosaurus*. Early herbivorous (plant-eating) dinosaurs first appeared in Late Triassic times and included *Plateosaurus* and *Technosaurus*. By the end of the Triassic period, dinosaurs dominated Pangaea, possibly contributing to the extinction of many other reptiles.

EXAMPLES OF TRIASSIC PLANT GROUPS

A PRESENT-DAY CYCAD
(Cycas revoluta)

A PRESENT-DAY GINKGO
(Ginkgo biloba)

A PRESENT-DAY CONIFER
(Araucaria araucana)

FOSSIL OF AN EXTINCT FERN
(Pachypteris sp.)

FOSSIL LEAF OF AN EXTINCT CYCAD
(Cycas sp.)

EXAMPLES OF TRIASSIC DINOSAURS

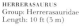

MELANOROSAURUS
Group: Melanorosauridae
Length: 40 ft (12.2 m)

MUSSAURUS
Group: Sauropodomorpha
Length: 6 ft 6 in–10 ft (2–3 m)

HERRERASAURUS
Group: Herrerasauridae
Length: 10 ft (3 m)

PISANOSAURUS
Group: Ornithischia
Length: 3 ft (90 cm)

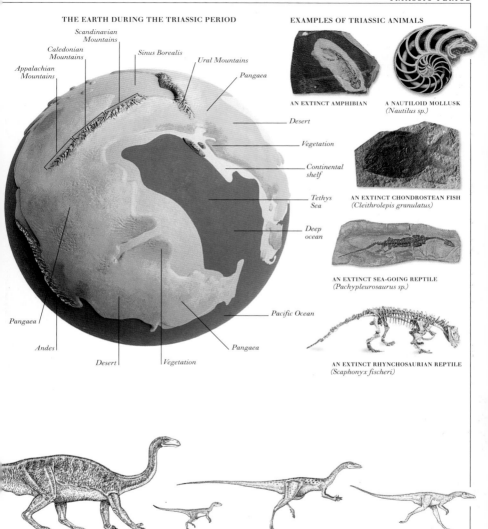

THE EARTH DURING THE TRIASSIC PERIOD

Appalachian Mountains

Caledonian Mountains

Scandinavian Mountains

Sinus Borealis

Ural Mountains

Pangaea

Desert

Vegetation

Continental shelf

Tethys Sea

Deep ocean

Pangaea

Andes

Desert

Vegetation

Pangaea

Pacific Ocean

EXAMPLES OF TRIASSIC ANIMALS

AN EXTINCT AMPHIBIAN

A NAUTILOID MOLLUSK
(Nautilus sp.)

AN EXTINCT CHONDROSTEAN FISH
(Cleithrolepis granulatus)

AN EXTINCT SEA-GOING REPTILE
(Pachypleurosaurus sp.)

AN EXTINCT RHYNCHOSAURIAN REPTILE
(Scaphonyx fischeri)

PLATEOSAURUS
Group: Plateosauridae
Length: 26 ft (7.9 m)

TECHNOSAURUS
Group: Ornithischia
Length: 3 ft 3 in (1 m)

COELOPHYSIS
Group: Coelophysidae
Length: 10 ft (3 m)

STAURIKOSAURUS
Group: Herrerasauridae
Length: 6 ft 6 in (2 m)

Jurassic period

THE JURASSIC PERIOD, the middle part of the Mesozoic era, lasted from 199 to 145 million years ago. During Jurassic times, the landmass of Pangaea broke up into the continents of Gondwana and Laurasia, and sea levels rose, flooding areas of lower land. The Jurassic climate was warm and moist. Plants such as ginkgos, horsetails, and conifers thrived, and giant redwood trees appeared, as did the first flowering plants. The abundance of plant food coincided with the proliferation of herbivorous (plant-eating) dinosaurs, such as the large sauropods (e.g., *Diplodocus*) and stegosaurs (e.g., *Stegosaurus*). Carnivorous (flesheating) dinosaurs, such as *Compsognathus* and *Allosaurus*, also flourished by hunting the many animals that existed—among them other dinosaurs. Further Jurassic animals included shrewlike mammals, and pterosaurs (flying reptiles), as well as plesiosaurs and ichthyosaurs (both marine reptiles).

JURASSIC POSITIONS OF PRESENT-DAY LANDMASSES

North America
Europe
Arabia
Asia
South America
Africa
Antarctica
India
Australia

EXAMPLES OF JURASSIC PLANT GROUPS

A PRESENT-DAY FERN
(*Dicksonia antarctica*)

A PRESENT-DAY HORSETAIL
(*Equisetum arvense*)

A PRESENT-DAY CONIFER
(*Taxus baccata*)

FOSSIL LEAF OF AN EXTINCT CONIFER
(*Taxus sp.*)

FOSSIL LEAF OF AN EXTINCT REDWOOD
(*Sequoiadendron affinis*)

EXAMPLES OF JURASSIC DINOSAURS

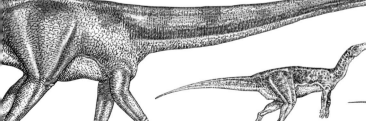

DIPLODOCUS
Group: Diplodocidae
Length: 88 ft (26.8 m)

CAMPTOSAURUS
Group: Iguanodontia
Length: 16–23 ft (4.9–7 m)

DRYOSAURUS
Group: Dryosauridae
Length: 10–15 ft (3–4 m)

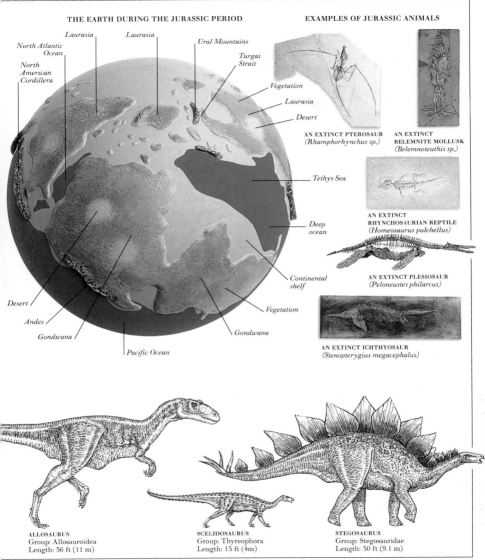

THE EARTH DURING THE JURASSIC PERIOD

EXAMPLES OF JURASSIC ANIMALS

North Atlantic Ocean

North American Cordillera

Laurasia

Laurasia

Ural Mountains

Turgai Strait

Vegetation

Laurasia

Desert

Tethys Sea

Deep ocean

Continental shelf

Vegetation

Desert

Andes

Gondwana

Gondwana

Pacific Ocean

AN EXTINCT PTEROSAUR
(*Rhamphorhynchus sp.*)

**AN EXTINCT
BELEMNITE MOLLUSK**
(*Belemnoteuthis sp.*)

**AN EXTINCT
RHYNCHOSAURIAN REPTILE**
(*Homeosaurus pulchellus*)

AN EXTINCT PLESIOSAUR
(*Peloneustes philarcus*)

AN EXTINCT ICHTHYOSAUR
(*Stenopterygius megacephalus*)

ALLOSAURUS
Group: Allosauroidea
Length: 36 ft (11 m)

SCELIDOSAURUS
Group: Thyreophora
Length: 13 ft (4m)

STEGOSAURUS
Group: Stegosauridae
Length: 30 ft (9.1 m)

Cretaceous period

THE MESOZOIC ERA ENDED WITH the Cretaceous period, which lasted from 146 to 65 million years ago. During this period, Gondwana and Laurasia were breaking up into smaller landmasses that more closely resembled the modern continents. The climate remained mild and moist but the seasons became more marked. Flowering plants, including deciduous trees, replaced many cycads, seed ferns, and conifers. Animal species became more varied, with the evolution of new mammals, insects, fish, crustaceans, and turtles. Dinosaurs evolved into a wide variety of species during Cretaceous times; more than half of all known dinosaurs—including *Iguanodon, Deinonychus, Tyrannosaurus,* and *Hypsilophodon*—lived during this period. At the end of the Cretaceous period, however, most dinosaurs became extinct. The reason for this mass extinction is unknown but it is thought to have been caused by climatic changes due to either a catastrophic meteor impact with the Earth or extensive volcanic eruptions.

CRETACEOUS POSITIONS OF PRESENT-DAY LANDMASSES

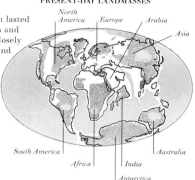

North America   Europe   Arabia
Asia
South America   Australia
Africa   India
Antarctica

EXAMPLES OF CRETACEOUS PLANT GROUPS

A PRESENT-DAY CONIFER
(*Pinus muricata*)

A PRESENT-DAY DECIDUOUS TREE
(*Magnolia sp.*)

FOSSIL OF AN EXTINCT FERN
(*Sphenopteris latiloba*)

FOSSIL OF AN EXTINCT GINKGO
(*Ginkgo pluripartita*)

FOSSIL LEAVES OF AN EXTINCT DECIDUOUS TREE
(*Cercidyphyllum sp.*)

EXAMPLES OF CRETACEOUS DINOSAURS

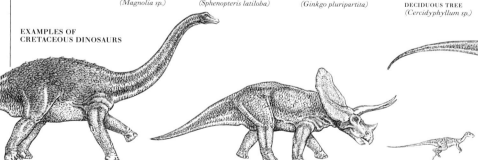

SALTASAURUS
Group: Saltasauridae
Length: 40 ft (12.2 m)

TOROSAURUS
Group: Ceratopsidae
Length: 25 ft (7.6 m)

HYPSILOPHODON
Group: Ornithopoda
Length: 4 ft 6 in—7 ft 6 in (1.4–2.3 m)

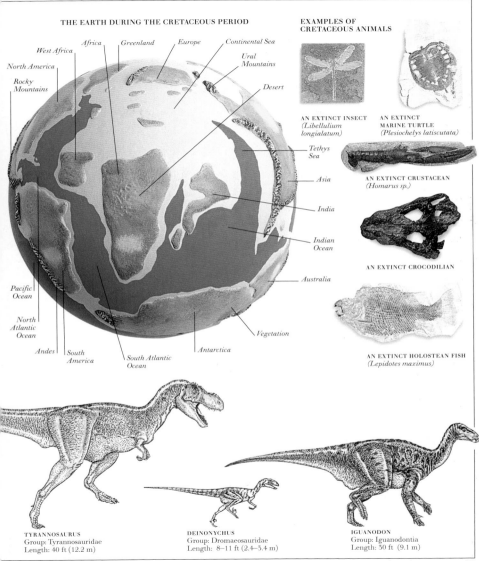

THE EARTH DURING THE CRETACEOUS PERIOD

West Africa
Africa
Greenland
Europe
Continental Sea
North America
Rocky Mountains
Ural Mountains
Desert
Tethys Sea
Asia
India
Indian Ocean
Pacific Ocean
North Atlantic Ocean
Andes
South America
South Atlantic Ocean
Antarctica
Australia
Vegetation

EXAMPLES OF CRETACEOUS ANIMALS

AN EXTINCT INSECT
(*Libellulium longialatum*)

AN EXTINCT MARINE TURTLE
(*Plesiochelys latiscutata*)

AN EXTINCT CRUSTACEAN
(*Homarus* sp.)

AN EXTINCT CROCODILIAN

AN EXTINCT HOLOSTEAN FISH
(*Lepidotes maximus*)

TYRANNOSAURUS
Group: Tyrannosauridae
Length: 40 ft (12.2 m)

DEINONYCHUS
Group: Dromaeosauridae
Length: 8–11 ft (2.4–3.4 m)

IGUANODON
Group: Iguanodontia
Length: 30 ft (9.1 m)

Tertiary period

**TERTIARY POSITIONS OF
PRESENT-DAY LANDMASSES**

North America · Europe · Asia · South America · Africa · Australia · Antarctica

FOLLOWING THE DEMISE OF THE DINOSAURS at the end of the Cretaceous period, the Tertiary period (65–1.6 million years ago), which formed the first part of the Cenozoic era (65 million years ago–present), was characterized by a huge expansion of mammal life. Placental mammals nourish and maintain the young in the mother's uterus; only a few groups of placental mammals existed during Cretaceous times, compared with a few dozen during the Tertiary period. One of these included the first hominid (see pp.108–109), *Ardipithecus*, which appeared in Africa. By the beginning of the Tertiary period, the continents had almost reached their present position. The Tethys Sea, which had separated the northern continents from Africa and India, began to close up, forming the Mediterranean Sea and allowing the migration of terrestrial animals between Africa and western Europe. India's collision with Asia led to the formation of the Himalayas. During the middle part of the Tertiary period, the forest-dwelling and browsing mammals were replaced by mammals such as the horses, better suited to grazing the open savannahs that began to dominate. Repeated cool periods throughout the Tertiary period established the Antarctic as an icy island continent.

EXAMPLES OF TERTIARY PLANT GROUPS

A PRESENT-DAY OAK
(Quercus palustris)

A PRESENT-DAY BIRCH
(Betula grossa)

**FOSSIL LEAF OF AN
EXTINCT BIRCH**
(Betulites sp.)

**FOSSILIZED STEM OF
AN EXTINCT PALM**
(Palmoxylon sp.)

**EXAMPLES OF TERTIARY
ANIMAL GROUPS**

HYAENODON
Group: Hyaenodontidae
Length: 6 ft 6 in (2 m)

TITANOHYRAX
Group: Pliohyracidae
Length: 6 ft 6 in (2 m)

PHORUSRHACOS
Group: Phorusrhacidae
Length: 5 ft (1.5 m)

SAMOTHERIUM
Group: Giraffidae
Length: 10 ft (3 m)

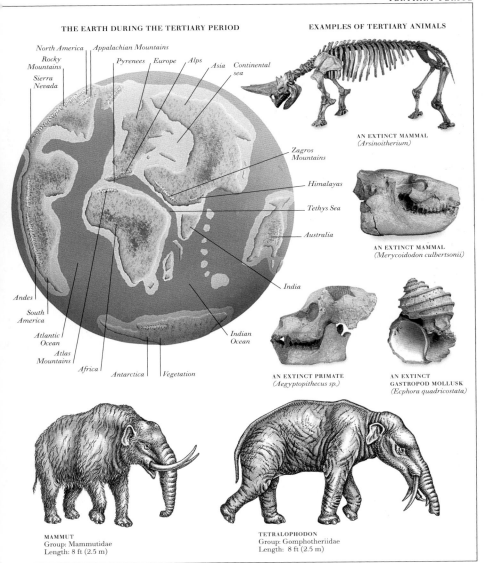

THE EARTH DURING THE TERTIARY PERIOD

EXAMPLES OF TERTIARY ANIMALS

North America
Rocky Mountains
Sierra Nevada
Appalachian Mountains
Pyrenees
Europe
Alps
Asia
Continental sea
Zagros Mountains
Himalayas
Tethys Sea
Australia
India
Andes
South America
Atlantic Ocean
Atlas Mountains
Africa
Antarctica
Vegetation
Indian Ocean

AN EXTINCT MAMMAL
(*Arsinoitherium*)

AN EXTINCT MAMMAL
(*Merycoidodon culbertsonii*)

AN EXTINCT PRIMATE
(*Aegyptopithecus sp.*)

AN EXTINCT GASTROPOD MOLLUSK
(*Ecphora quadricostata*)

MAMMUT
Group: Mammutidae
Length: 8 ft (2.5 m)

TETRALOPHODON
Group: Gomphotheriidae
Length: 8 ft (2.5 m)

Quaternary period

THE QUATERNARY PERIOD (1.6 million years ago–present) forms the second part of the Cenozoic era (65 million years ago–present): it has been characterized by alternating cold (glacial) and warm (interglacial) periods. During cold periods, ice sheets and glaciers have formed repeatedly on northern and southern continents. The cold environments in North America and Eurasia, and to a lesser extent in southern South America and parts of Australia, have caused the migration of many life-forms toward the Equator. Only the specialized ice age mammals such as *Mammuthus* and *Coelodonta*, with their thick wool and fat insulation, were suited to life in very cold climates. Humans developed throughout the Pleistocene period (1.6 million–10,000 years ago) in Africa and migrated northward into Europe and Asia. Modern humans, *Homo sapiens*, lived on the cold European continent 30,000 years ago and hunted other mammals. The end of the last ice age and the climatic changes that occurred about 10,000 years ago brought extinction to many Pleistocene mammals, but enabled humans to flourish.

QUATERNARY POSITIONS OF PRESENT-DAY LANDMASSES

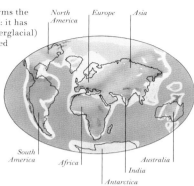

North America
Europe
Asia
South America
Africa
India
Australia
Antarctica

EXAMPLES OF QUATERNARY PLANT GROUPS

A PRESENT-DAY BIRCH
(Betula lenta)

A PRESENT-DAY SWEEETGUM
(Liquidambar styraciflua)

FOSSIL LEAF OF A SWEETGUM
(Liquidambar europeanum)

FOSSIL LEAF OF A BIRCH
(Betula sp.)

EXAMPLES OF QUATERNARY ANIMAL GROUPS

PROCOPTODON
Group: Macropodidae
Length: 10 ft (3 m)

DIPROTODON
Group: Diprotodontidae
Length: 10 ft (3 m)

TOXODON
Group: Toxodontidae
Length: 10 ft (3 m)

MAMMUTHUS
Group: Elephantidae
Length: 10 ft (3 m)

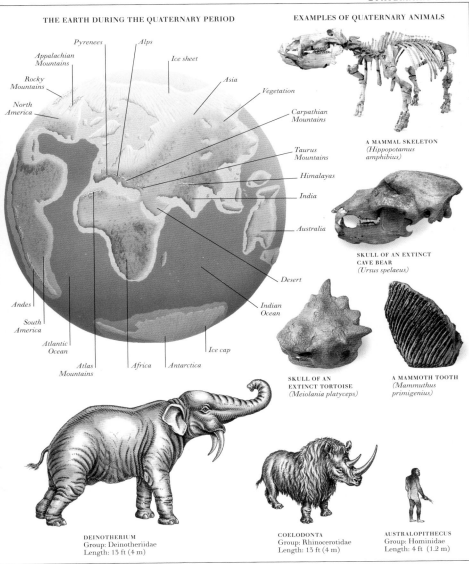

THE EARTH DURING THE QUATERNARY PERIOD

Pyrenees
Alps
Appalachian Mountains
Ice sheet
Rocky Mountains
Asia
North America
Vegetation
Carpathian Mountains
Taurus Mountains
Himalayas
India
Australia
Desert
Andes
Indian Ocean
South America
Atlantic Ocean
Atlas Mountains
Ice cap
Africa
Antarctica

EXAMPLES OF QUATERNARY ANIMALS

A MAMMAL SKELETON
(Hippopotamus amphibius)

SKULL OF AN EXTINCT CAVE BEAR
(Ursus spelaeus)

SKULL OF AN EXTINCT TORTOISE
(Meiolania platyceps)

A MAMMOTH TOOTH
(Mammuthus primigenius)

DEINOTHERIUM
Group: Deinotheriidae
Length: 13 ft (4 m)

COELODONTA
Group: Rhinocerotidae
Length: 13 ft (4 m)

AUSTRALOPITHECUS
Group: Hominidae
Length: 4 ft (1.2 m)

77

Early signs of life

FOR ALMOST A THOUSAND MILLION YEARS after its formation, there
was no known life on Earth. The first simple, sea-dwelling organic
structures appeared about 3.5 billion years ago; they may have
formed when certain chemical molecules joined together.
Prokaryotes, single-celled microorganisms such as blue-green
algae, were able to photosynthesize (see pp. 138–139), and thus
produce oxygen. A thousand million years later, sufficient
oxygen had built up in the Earth's atmosphere to allow
multicellular organisms to proliferate in the Precambrian
seas (before 570 million years ago). Soft-bodied jellyfish,
corals, and seaworms flourished about 700 million years
ago. Trilobites, the first animals with hard body frames,
developed during the Cambrian period (570–510 million
years ago). However, it was not until the beginning of the
Devonian period (409–363 million years ago) that early
land plants, such as *Asteroxylon*, formed a water-
retaining cuticle, which ended their dependence on an
aquatic environment. About 360 million years ago, the
first amphibians (see pp. 80–81) crawled onto the land,
although they probably still returned to the water to lay
their soft eggs. By the time the first reptiles and synapsids
appeared late in the Carboniferous, animals with
backbones had become fully independent of water.

STROMATOLITIC LIMESTONE

*Alternate
layers of
mud and
sand*

*Layers bound
by algae*

*Layered
structure*

Limestone

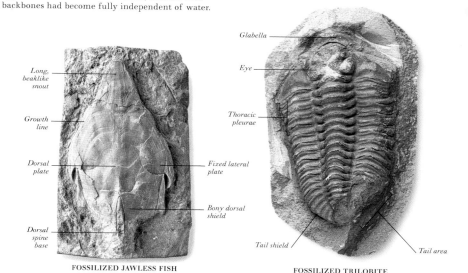

*Long,
beaklike
snout*

*Growth
line*

*Dorsal
plate*

*Dorsal
spine
base*

Glabella

Eye

*Thoracic
pleurae*

*Fixed lateral
plate*

*Bony dorsal
shield*

Tail shield

Tail area

FOSSILIZED JAWLESS FISH

FOSSILIZED TRILOBITE

Ambulacral groove

Small ossicles of upper surface

Central disk

Iron pyrites

FOSSILIZED STARFISH

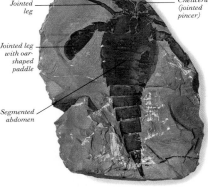

Row of ossicles

Broad disk

Short arm

Row of ossicles

UPPER SURFACE OF FOSSILIZED STARFISH

LOWER SURFACE OF FOSSILIZED STARFISH

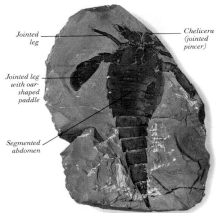

Jointed leg

Chelicera (jointed pincer)

Jointed leg with oar-shaped paddle

Segmented abdomen

UNDERSIDE OF FOSSILIZED EURYPTERID

Telson (tail spine)

Abdominal segments

Shell contains eight somites (thoracic segments)

Hingeless, bivalved shell

FOSSIL OF AN EXTINCT SHRIMP

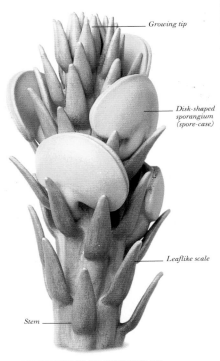

Growing tip

Disk-shaped sporangium (spore-case)

Leaflike scale

Stem

RECONSTRUCTION OF ASTEROXYLON

Amphibians and reptiles

THE EARLIEST KNOWN AMPHIBIANS, such as *Acanthostega* and *Ichthyostega*, lived about 363 million years ago at the end of the Devonian period (409–363 million years ago). Their limbs may have evolved from the muscular fins of lungfishlike creatures. These fish can use their fins to push themselves along the bottom of lakes and some can breathe at the water's surface. While amphibians (see pp. 182–183) can exist on land, they are dependent on a wet environment because their skin does not retain moisture and most species must return to the water to lay their eggs. Evolving from amphibians, reptiles (see pp. 184–187) first appeared during the Carboniferous period (363–290 million years ago): *Westlothiana*, a possible early reptile, lived on land 338 million years ago. The development of the amniotic egg, with an embryo enclosed in its own wet environment (the amnion) and protected by a waterproof shell, freed reptiles from the amphibian's dependence on a wet habitat. A scaly skin protected the reptile from desiccation on land and enabled it to exploit ways of life closed to its amphibian ancestors. Reptiles include the dinosaurs, which came to dominate life on land during the Mesozoic era (245–65 million years ago).

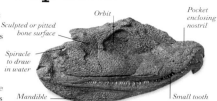

FOSSIL SKULL OF ACANTHOSTEGA

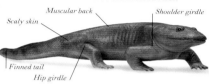

MODEL OF ICHTHYOSTEGA

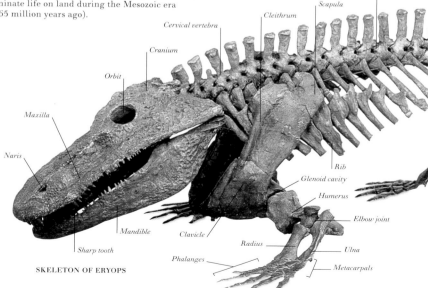

SKELETON OF ERYOPS

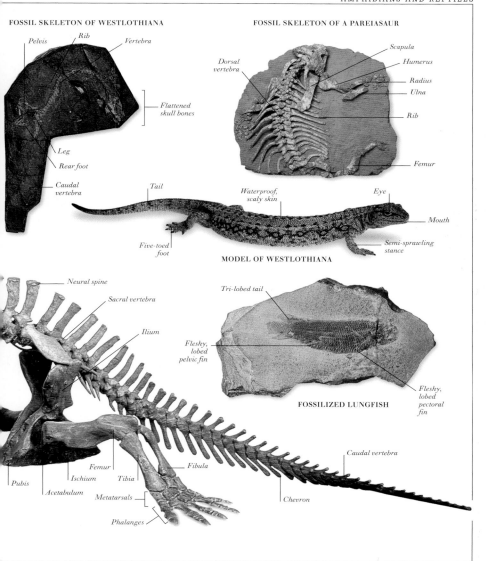

FOSSIL SKELETON OF WESTLOTHIANA

Pelvis
Rib
Vertebra
Flattened skull bones
Leg
Rear foot
Caudal vertebra

FOSSIL SKELETON OF A PAREIASAUR

Dorsal vertebra
Scapula
Humerus
Radius
Ulna
Rib
Femur

Tail
Waterproof, scaly skin
Eye
Mouth
Five-toed foot
Semi-sprawling stance

MODEL OF WESTLOTHIANA

Neural spine
Sacral vertebra
Ilium

Tri-lobed tail
Fleshy, lobed pelvic fin
Fleshy, lobed pectoral fin

FOSSILIZED LUNGFISH

Femur
Fibula
Pubis
Ischium
Tibia
Acetabulum
Metatarsals
Phalanges
Chevron
Caudal vertebra

The dinosaurs

THE DINOSAURS WERE A LARGE GROUP of reptiles that were the dominant land vertebrates (animals with backbones) for most of the Mesozoic era (245–65 million years ago). They appeared some 230 million years ago and were distinguished from other scaly, egg-laying reptiles by an important feature: dinosaurs had an erect limb stance. This enabled them to keep their bodies well above the ground, unlike the sprawling and semisprawling stance of other reptiles. The head of the dinosaur's femur (thighbone) fit into a socket in its pelvis (hip-bone), producing efficient and mobile locomotion. Dinosaurs are categorized into two groups according to the structure of their pelvis: saurischian (lizard-hipped) and ornithischian (bird-hipped) dinosaurs. In the case of most saurischians, the pubis (part of the pelvis) jutted forward, while in ornithischians it slanted back, parallel to the ischium (another part of the pelvis). Dinosaurs ranged in size from smaller than a domestic cat to the biggest land animals ever known. The Dinosauria were the most successful land vertebrates ever, and survived for 165 million years, until most became extinct 65 million years ago.

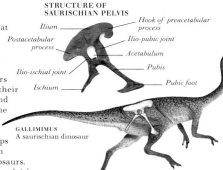

STRUCTURE OF SAURISCHIAN PELVIS

Ilium
Hook of preacetabular process
Postacetabular process
Ilio-pubic joint
Acetabulum
Pubis
Ilio-ischial joint
Ischium
Pubic foot

GALLIMIMUS
A saurischian dinosaur

POSITION OF PELVIS IN A SAURISCHIAN DINOSAUR

STRUCTURE OF ORNITHISCHIAN PELVIS

Ilium
Preacetabular process
Postacetabular process
Ilio-pubic joint
Prepubis
Ilio-ischial joint
Acetabulum
Pubis
Ischium

HYPSILOPHODON
An ornithischian dinosaur

POSITION OF PELVIS IN AN ORNITHISCHIAN DINOSAUR

BAROSAURUS
A saurischian dinosaur

COMPARISON OF ANIMAL STANCES

SPRAWLING STANCE
The thighs and upper arms project straight out from the body so that the knees and elbows are bent at right angles.

COMMON IGUANA
(Iguana iguana)
A present-day reptile

ERECT STANCE
The thighs and upper arms project straight down from the body so that the knees and elbows are straight.

SEMISPRAWLING STANCE
The thighs and upper arms project downwards and outwards so that the knees and elbows are slightly bent.

DWARF CROCODILE
(Osteolaemus tetraspis)
A present-day reptile

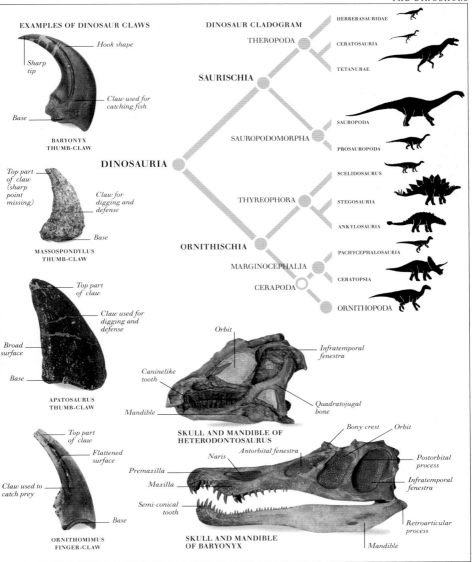

EXAMPLES OF DINOSAUR CLAWS

Hook shape

Sharp tip

Base

Claw used for catching fish

BARYONYX THUMB-CLAW

Top part of claw (sharp point missing)

Claw for digging and defense

Base

MASSOSPONDYLUS THUMB-CLAW

Top part of claw

Claw used for digging and defense

Broad surface

Base

APATOSAURUS THUMB-CLAW

Top part of claw

Flattened surface

Claw used to catch prey

Base

ORNITHOMIMUS FINGER-CLAW

DINOSAUR CLADOGRAM

HERRERASAURIDAE

THEROPODA

CERATOSAURIA

TETANURAE

SAURISCHIA

SAUROPODA

SAUROPODOMORPHA

PROSAUROPODA

DINOSAURIA

SCELIDOSAURUS

THYREOPHORA

STEGOSAURIA

ANKYLOSAURIA

PACHYCEPHALOSAURIA

ORNITHISCHIA

MARGINOCEPHALIA

CERATOPSIA

CERAPODA

ORNITHOPODA

Orbit

Infratemporal fenestra

Caninelike tooth

Quadratojugal bone

Mandible

SKULL AND MANDIBLE OF HETERODONTOSAURUS

Bony crest *Orbit*

Antorbital fenestra

Naris

Premaxilla

Postorbital process

Maxilla

Infratemporal fenestra

Semi-conical tooth

Retroarticular process

SKULL AND MANDIBLE OF BARYONYX

Mandible

Theropods 1

AN ENORMOUSLY SUCCESSFUL SUBGROUP of the Saurischia, the bipedal (two-footed) theropods ("beast feet") emerged 230 million years ago in Late Triassic times; the oldest known example comes from South America. Theropods spanned the age of most dinosaurs (230–65 million years ago) and beyond, and included most of the known predatory dinosaurs. The typical theropod had smallish arms with sharp, clawed fingers; powerful jaws lined with sharp teeth; an S-shaped neck; long, muscular hind limbs; and clawed, usually four-toed feet. Many theropods may have been warm-blooded; most were exclusively carnivorous. Theropods ranged from animals no larger than a chicken to huge creatures, such as *Tyrannosaurus* and *Baryonyx*. The group also included ostrichlike omnivores and herbivores with toothless beaks, such as *Struthiomimus* and *Gallimimus*. Birds are dinosaurs and evolved from within a group of tetanuran theropods called maniraptorans. *Archaeopteryx*, small and feathered, was the first known bird and lived alongside other dinosaurs.

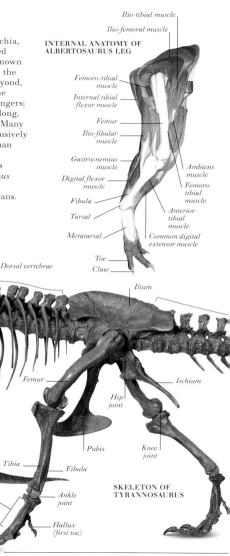

INTERNAL ANATOMY OF ALBERTOSAURUS LEG

Ilio-tibial muscle
Ilio-femoral muscle
Femoro-tibial muscle
Internal tibial flexor muscle
Femur
Ilio-fibular muscle
Gastrocnemius muscle
Digital flexor muscle
Fibula
Tarsal
Metatarsal
Toe
Claw
Ambiens muscle
Femoro-tibial muscle
Anterior tibial muscle
Common digital extensor muscle

SKELETON OF TYRANNOSAURUS

Cranium
Supraoccipital crest
Orbit
Cervical vertebrae
Naris
Dorsal vertebrae
Cervical rib
Scapula
Shoulder joint
Ulna
Mandible
Serrated tooth
Phalanges
Metacarpals
Wrist joint
Elbow joint
Coracoid
Rib
Humerus
Femur
Ilium
Ischium
Hip joint
Knee joint
Pubis

EXTERNAL FEATURES OF TYRANNOSAURUS

Naris
Eye
Thigh
Forelimb
Hand
Knee
Ankle
Toe
Claw
Foot
Scaly skin
Tail
Hind limb
Metatarsals
Phalanges
Tibia
Fibula
Ankle joint
Hallux (first toe)

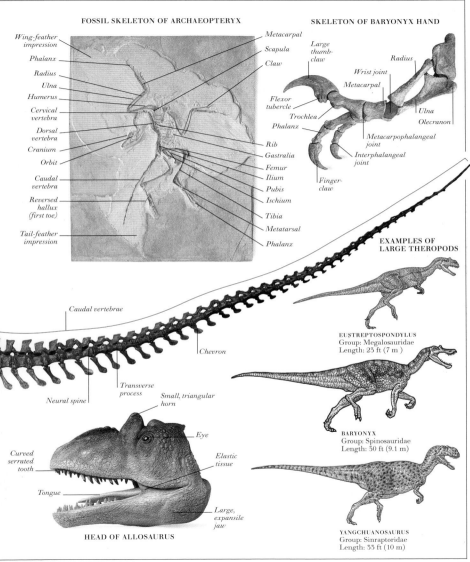

FOSSIL SKELETON OF ARCHAEOPTERYX

Wing-feather impression
Phalanx
Radius
Ulna
Humerus
Cervical vertebra
Dorsal vertebra
Cranium
Orbit
Caudal vertebra
Reversed hallux (first toe)
Tail-feather impression

Metacarpal
Scapula
Claw

Rib
Gastralia
Femur
Ilium
Pubis
Ischium
Tibia
Metatarsal
Phalanx

SKELETON OF BARYONYX HAND

Large thumb-claw
Flexor tubercle
Trochlea
Phalanx
Finger-claw

Radius
Wrist joint
Metacarpal
Ulna
Olecranon
Metacarpophalangeal joint
Interphalangeal joint

Caudal vertebrae
Chevron
Transverse process
Neural spine

EXAMPLES OF LARGE THEROPODS

EUSTREPTOSPONDYLUS
Group: Megalosauridae
Length: 25 ft (7 m)

BARYONYX
Group: Spinosauridae
Length: 30 ft (9.1 m)

YANGCHUANOSAURUS
Group: Sinraptoridae
Length: 33 ft (10 m)

Small, triangular horn
Eye
Curved serrated tooth
Elastic tissue
Tongue
Large, expansile jaw

HEAD OF ALLOSAURUS

Theropods 2

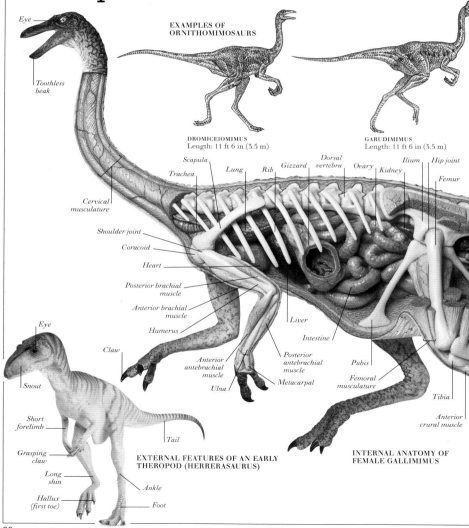

Eye

Toothless beak

Cervical musculature

EXAMPLES OF ORNITHOMIMOSAURS

DROMICEIOMIMUS
Length: 11 ft 6 in (3.5 m)

GARUDIMIMUS
Length: 11 ft 6 in (3.5 m)

Scapula

Trachea

Lung

Rib

Gizzard

Dorsal vertebra

Ovary

Kidney

Ilium

Hip joint

Femur

Shoulder joint

Coracoid

Heart

Posterior brachial muscle

Anterior brachial muscle

Humerus

Liver

Intestine

Anterior antebrachial muscle

Ulna

Metacarpal

Posterior antebrachial muscle

Pubis

Femoral musculature

Tibia

Anterior crural muscle

Eye

Snout

Short forelimb

Grasping claw

Long shin

Hallux (first toe)

Ankle

Foot

Claw

Tail

EXTERNAL FEATURES OF AN EARLY THEROPOD (HERRERASAURUS)

INTERNAL ANATOMY OF FEMALE GALLIMIMUS

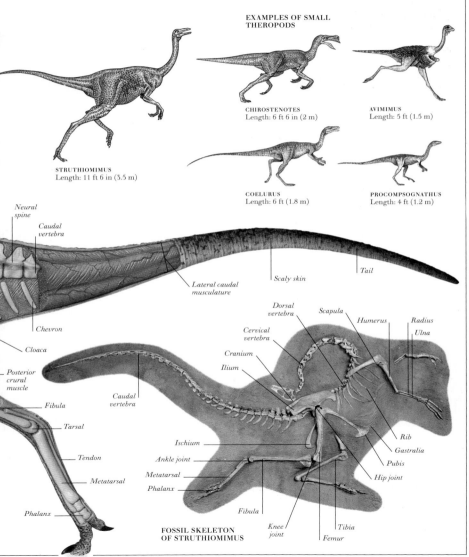

EXAMPLES OF SMALL THEROPODS

CHIROSTENOTES
Length: 6 ft 6 in (2 m)

AVIMIMUS
Length: 5 ft (1.5 m)

STRUTHIOMIMUS
Length: 11 ft 6 in (3.5 m)

COELURUS
Length: 6 ft (1.8 m)

PROCOMPSOGNATHUS
Length: 4 ft (1.2 m)

Neural spine

Caudal vertebra

Chevron

Cloaca

Posterior crural muscle

Fibula

Tarsal

Tendon

Metatarsal

Phalanx

Lateral caudal musculature

Scaly skin

Tail

Caudal vertebra

Dorsal vertebra

Cervical vertebra

Cranium

Ilium

Scapula

Humerus

Radius

Ulna

Rib

Gastralia

Pubis

Hip joint

Ischium

Ankle joint

Metatarsal

Phalanx

Fibula

Knee joint

Femur

Tibia

FOSSIL SKELETON OF STRUTHIOMIMUS

Sauropodomorphs 1

THECODONTOSAURUS

THE SAUROPODOMORPHA ("lizard-feet forms") were herbivorous, usually quadrupedal (four-footed) dinosaurs. A suborder of the Saurischia, they were characterized by small heads, bulky bodies, and long necks and tails. Sauropodomorphs have often been split into two groups: prosauropods and sauropods. Prosauropods lived from Late Triassic to Early Jurassic times (225–180 million years ago) and included beasts such as the small *Anchisaurus* and one of the first very large dinosaurs, *Plateosaurus*. By Middle Jurassic times (about 165 million years ago), sauropods had replaced prosauropods and spread worldwide. They included the heaviest and longest land animals ever, such as *Diplodocus* and *Brachiosaurus*. Sauropods persisted to the end of the Cretaceous period (65 million years ago). Many of these dinosaurs moved in herds, protected from predatory theropods by their huge bulk and powerful tails, which they could use to lash out at attackers. Sauropodomorphs were the most common large herbivores until Late Jurassic times (about 145 million years ago), and appear to have survived in both southern and northern continents until the end of the Cretaceous period.

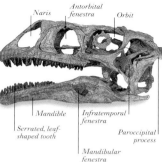

SKULL AND MANDIBLE OF PLATEOSAURUS

Naris
Antorbital fenestra
Orbit
Mandible
Infratemporal fenestra
Serrated, leaf-shaped tooth
Paroccipital process
Mandibular fenestra

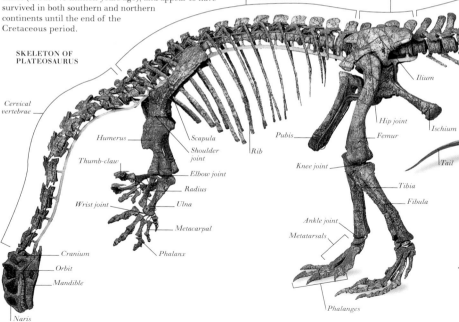

SKELETON OF PLATEOSAURUS

Dorsal vertebrae
Sacral vertebrae
Cervical vertebrae
Ilium
Humerus
Scapula
Shoulder joint
Pubis
Hip joint
Ischium
Thumb-claw
Rib
Femur
Tail
Elbow joint
Radius
Knee joint
Wrist joint
Ulna
Tibia
Fibula
Metacarpal
Ankle joint
Metatarsals
Cranium
Phalanx
Orbit
Mandible
Phalanges
Naris

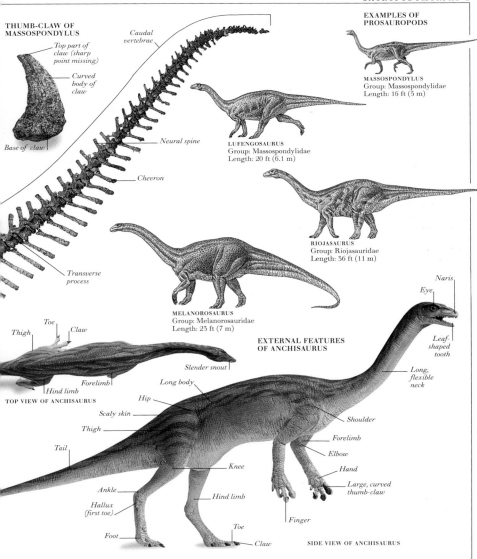

THUMB-CLAW OF MASSOSPONDYLUS

Top part of claw (sharp point missing)

Curved body of claw

Base of claw

Caudal vertebrae

Neural spine

Chevron

Transverse process

EXAMPLES OF PROSAUROPODS

MASSOSPONDYLUS
Group: Massospondylidae
Length: 16 ft (5 m)

LUFENGOSAURUS
Group: Massospondylidae
Length: 20 ft (6.1 m)

RIOJASAURUS
Group: Riojasauridae
Length: 36 ft (11 m)

MELANOROSAURUS
Group: Melanorosauridae
Length: 23 ft (7 m)

Thigh
Toe
Claw
Forelimb
Hind limb

TOP VIEW OF ANCHISAURUS

Slender snout

Long body

Hip

Scaly skin

Thigh

Tail

Knee

Ankle

Hallux (first toe)

Foot

Hind limb

Toe

Claw

EXTERNAL FEATURES OF ANCHISAURUS

Naris

Eye

Leaf-shaped tooth

Long, flexible neck

Shoulder

Forelimb

Elbow

Hand

Large, curved thumb-claw

Finger

SIDE VIEW OF ANCHISAURUS

Sauropodomorphs 2

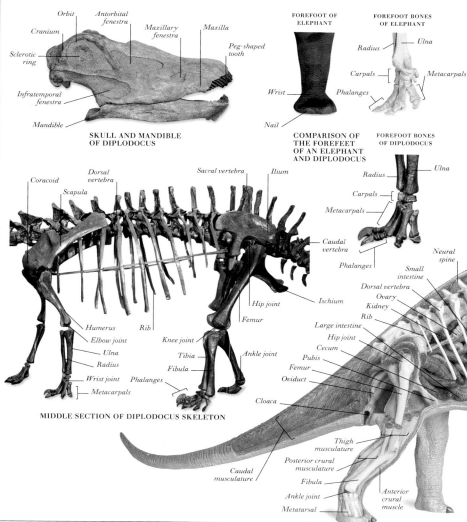

Orbit
Cranium
Antorbital fenestra
Maxillary fenestra
Maxilla
Sclerotic ring
Peg-shaped tooth
Infratemporal fenestra
Mandible

SKULL AND MANDIBLE OF DIPLODOCUS

FOREFOOT OF ELEPHANT
Wrist
Nail

FOREFOOT BONES OF ELEPHANT
Radius
Ulna
Carpals
Metacarpals
Phalanges

COMPARISON OF THE FOREFEET OF AN ELEPHANT AND DIPLODOCUS

FOREFOOT BONES OF DIPLODOCUS
Radius
Ulna
Carpals
Metacarpals
Phalanges

Coracoid
Dorsal vertebra
Scapula
Sacral vertebra
Ilium
Caudal vertebra
Hip joint
Ischium
Femur
Humerus
Rib
Elbow joint
Knee joint
Ulna
Radius
Tibia
Ankle joint
Fibula
Wrist joint
Phalanges
Metacarpals

MIDDLE SECTION OF DIPLODOCUS SKELETON

Neural spine
Small intestine
Dorsal vertebra
Ovary
Kidney
Rib
Large intestine
Hip joint
Cecum
Pubis
Femur
Oviduct
Cloaca
Thigh musculature
Posterior crural musculature
Caudal musculature
Fibula
Ankle joint
Anterior crural muscle
Metatarsal

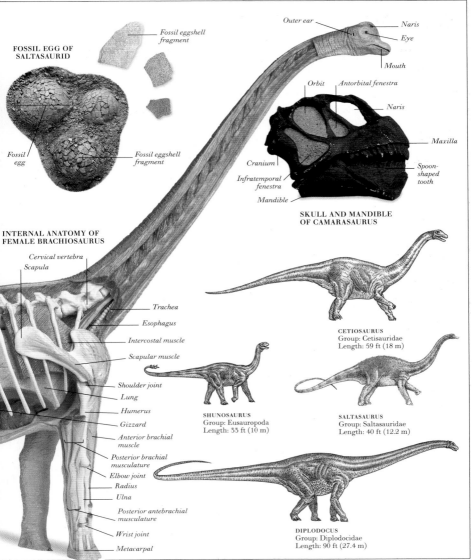

FOSSIL EGG OF SALTASAURID

Fossil eggshell fragment

Fossil egg

Fossil eggshell fragment

Outer ear
Naris
Eye
Mouth

Orbit
Antorbital fenestra
Naris
Maxilla
Cranium
Spoon-shaped tooth
Infratemporal fenestra
Mandible

SKULL AND MANDIBLE OF CAMARASAURUS

INTERNAL ANATOMY OF FEMALE BRACHIOSAURUS

Cervical vertebra
Scapula

Trachea
Esophagus
Intercostal muscle
Scapular muscle
Shoulder joint
Lung
Humerus
Gizzard
Anterior brachial muscle
Posterior brachial musculature
Elbow joint
Radius
Ulna
Posterior antebrachial musculature
Wrist joint
Metacarpal

CETIOSAURUS
Group: Cetisauridae
Length: 59 ft (18 m)

SHUNOSAURUS
Group: Eusauropoda
Length: 33 ft (10 m)

SALTASAURUS
Group: Saltasauridae
Length: 40 ft (12.2 m)

DIPLODOCUS
Group: Diplodocidae
Length: 90 ft (27.4 m)

Thyreophorans 1

THYREOPHORANS ("SHIELD BEARERS") were a group of quadrupedal armored dinosaurs. They were one clade among several within the Ornithischia (bird-hipped dinosaurs), they were characterized by rows of bony studs, plates, or spikes along the back, which protected some from predators and may have helped others regulate body temperature. Up to 30 ft (9 m) long, with a small head and small cheek teeth, thyreophorans had shorter forelimbs than hind limbs and probably browsed on low-level vegetation. The earliest thyreophorans were small and lived in Early Jurassic times (about 200 million years ago) in Europe, North America, and China. Stegosaurs, such as *Stegosaurus* and *Kentrosaurus*, replaced these older forms. The earliest stegosaur remains come mainly from China. Several genera of stegosaurs survived into the Early Cretaceous period (145–100 million years ago). Ankylosaurs, with a combination of beak and teeth in close proximity, and cheek teeth adapted for cropping vegetation, appeared at the same time as stegosaurs. They originated in the Late Jurassic period (155 million years ago) and in North America survived until 65 million years ago.

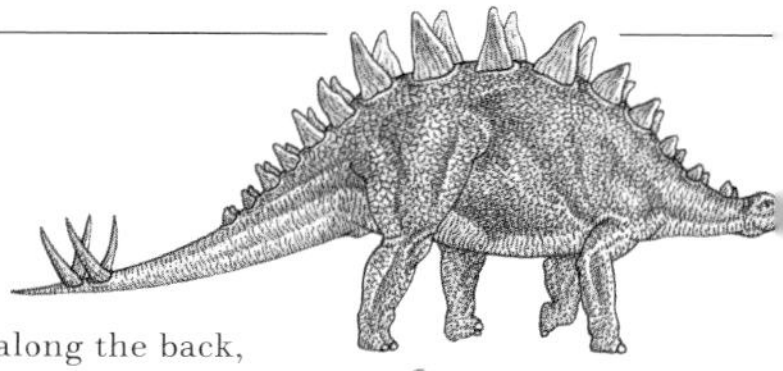

TUOJIANGOSAURUS
Group: Stegosauridae
Length: 23 ft (7 m)

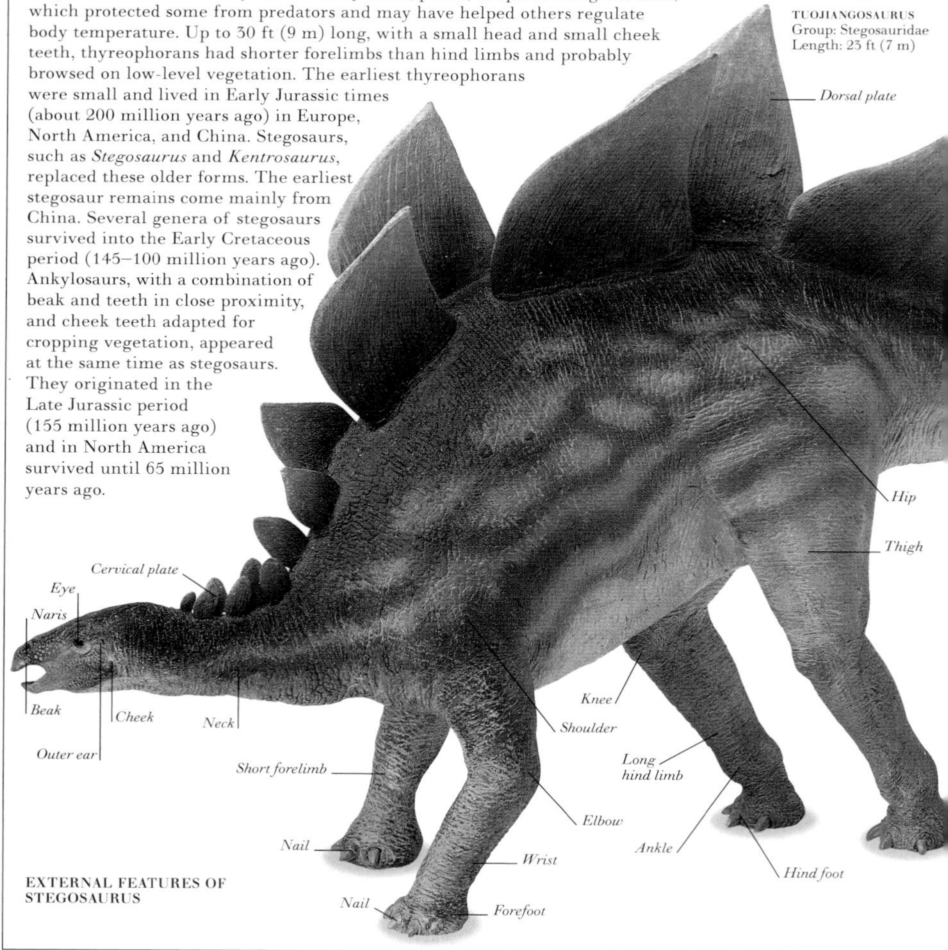

Dorsal plate

Hip

Thigh

Cervical plate

Eye

Naris

Beak

Cheek

Neck

Outer ear

Short forelimb

Knee

Shoulder

Long hind limb

Elbow

Ankle

Nail

Wrist

Hind foot

EXTERNAL FEATURES OF STEGOSAURUS

Nail

Forefoot

EXAMPLES OF STEGOSAURS

HUAYANGOSAURUS
Group: Huayangosauridae
Length: 13 ft (4 m)

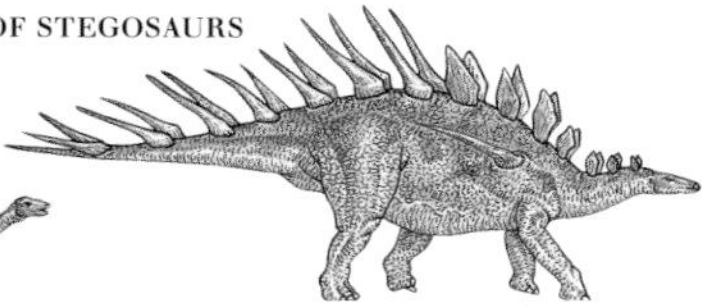

KENTROSAURUS
Group: Stegosauridae
Length: 16 ft (4.9 m)

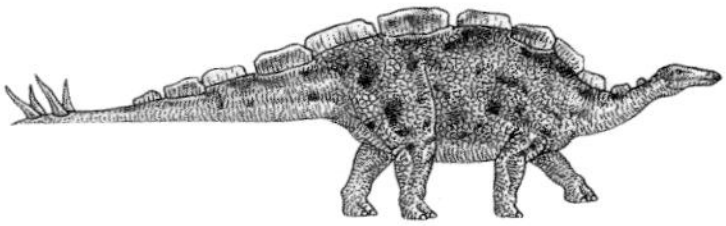

WUERHOSAURUS
Group: Stegosauridae
Length: 20 ft (6.1 m)

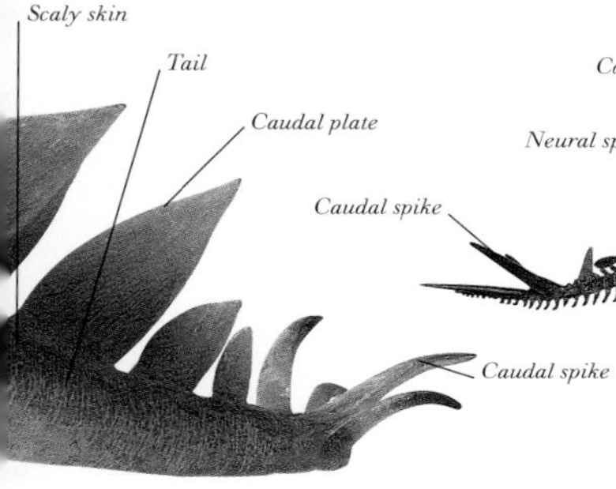

EXAMPLES OF STEGOSAUR SKELETONS

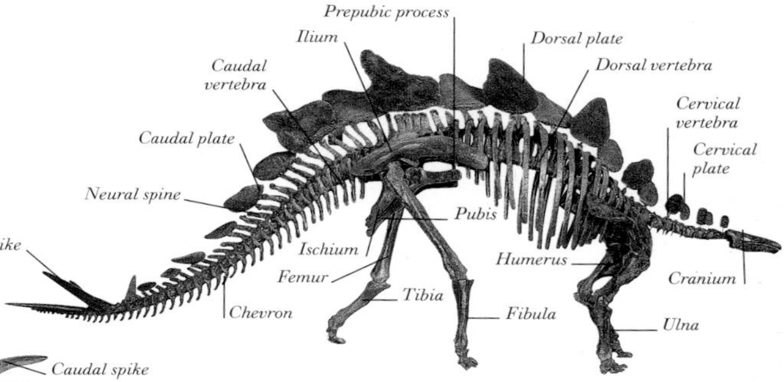

Scaly skin

Tail

Caudal plate

Caudal spike

Caudal spike

Prepubic process

Ilium

Caudal vertebra

Caudal plate

Neural spine

Ischium

Femur

Chevron

Pubis

Tibia

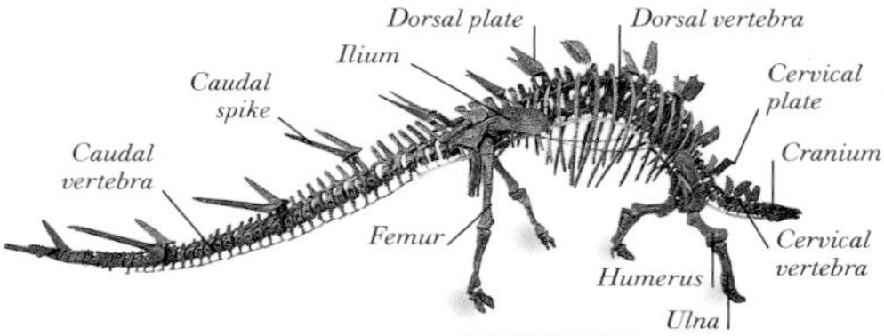

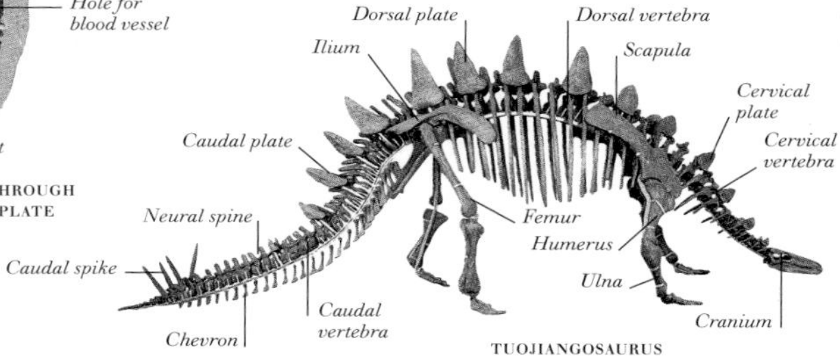

Dorsal plate

Dorsal vertebra

Cervical vertebra

Cervical plate

Humerus

Cranium

Fibula

Ulna

STEGOSAURUS

DORSAL PLATE OF STEGOSAURUS

Front edge

Pointed top

Back edge

Base

Large surface area for radiating and absorbing heat

Hole for blood vessel

SIDE VIEW OF DORSAL PLATE

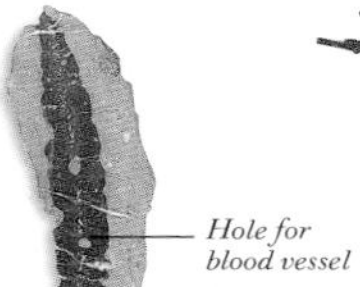

SECTION THROUGH DORSAL PLATE

Dorsal plate

Ilium

Caudal spike

Caudal vertebra

Dorsal vertebra

Cervical plate

Cranium

Femur

Humerus

Cervical vertebra

Ulna

KENTROSAURUS

Dorsal plate

Ilium

Caudal plate

Neural spine

Caudal spike

Chevron

Caudal vertebra

Dorsal vertebra

Scapula

Femur

Humerus

Cervical plate

Cervical vertebra

Ulna

Cranium

TUOJIANGOSAURUS

93

Thyreophorans 2

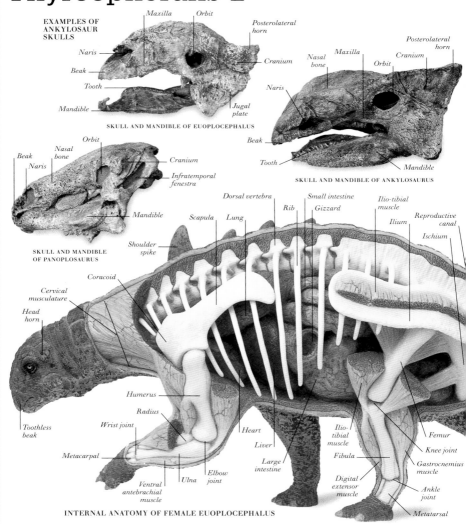

EXAMPLES OF
ANKYLOSAUR
SKULLS

Maxilla
Orbit
Posterolateral horn
Naris
Cranium
Beak
Tooth
Mandible
Jugal plate

SKULL AND MANDIBLE OF EUOPLOCEPHALUS

Nasal bone
Maxilla
Orbit
Posterolateral horn
Cranium
Naris
Beak
Tooth
Mandible

SKULL AND MANDIBLE OF ANKYLOSAURUS

Beak
Nasal bone
Orbit
Naris
Cranium
Infratemporal fenestra
Mandible

SKULL AND MANDIBLE
OF PANOPLOSAURUS

Dorsal vertebra
Small intestine
Rib
Gizzard
Ilio-tibial muscle
Ilium
Scapula
Lung
Reproductive canal
Ischium
Shoulder spike
Coracoid
Cervical musculature
Head horn
Humerus
Radius
Wrist joint
Heart
Femur
Metacarpal
Knee joint
Toothless beak
Ilio-tibial muscle
Fibula
Gastrocnemius muscle
Liver
Ventral antebrachial muscle
Ulna
Elbow joint
Large intestine
Digital extensor muscle
Ankle joint
Metatarsal

INTERNAL ANATOMY OF FEMALE EUOPLOCEPHALUS

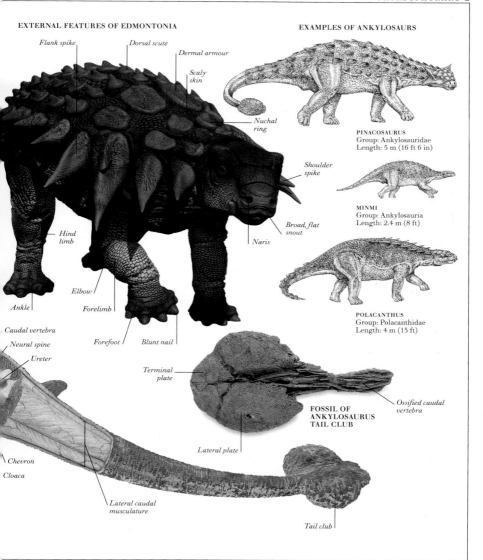

EXTERNAL FEATURES OF EDMONTONIA

Flank spike

Dorsal scute

Dermal armour

Scaly skin

Nuchal ring

Shoulder spike

Broad, flat snout

Naris

Hind limb

Elbow

Forelimb

Ankle

Forefoot

Blunt nail

Caudal vertebra

Neural spine

Ureter

Chevron

Cloaca

Terminal plate

Lateral plate

Lateral caudal musculature

Tail club

EXAMPLES OF ANKYLOSAURS

PINACOSAURUS
Group: Ankylosauridae
Length: 5 m (16 ft 6 in)

MINMI
Group: Ankylosauria
Length: 2.4 m (8 ft)

POLACANTHUS
Group: Polacanthidae
Length: 4 m (13 ft)

Ossified caudal vertebra

FOSSIL OF ANKYLOSAURUS TAIL CLUB

Ornithopods 1

IGUANODON TOOTH

ORNITHOPODS ("BIRD FEET") were a group of ornithischian ("bird-hipped") dinosaurs. These bipedal and quadrupedal herbivores had a horny beak, plant-cutting or grinding cheek teeth, and a pelvic and tail region stiffened by bony tendons. They evolved teeth and jaws adapted to pulping vegetation and flourished from the Middle Jurassic to the Late Cretaceous period (165–65 million years ago) in North America, Europe, Africa, China, Australia, and Antarctica. Some ornithopods were no larger than a dog, while others were immense creatures up to 49 ft (15 m) long. Iguanodonts, an ornithopod group, had a broad, toothless beak at the end of a long snout, large jaws with long rows of ridged, closely packed teeth for grinding vegetation, a bulky body, and a heavy tail. *Iguanodon* and some other iguanodonts had large thumb-spikes that were strong enough to stab attackers. Another group, the hadrosaurs, such as *Gryposaurus* and *Hadrosaurus*, lived in Late Cretaceous times (97–65 million years ago) and with their broad beaks are sometimes known as "duckbills." They were characterized by their deep skulls and closely packed rows of teeth, while some, such as *Corythosaurus* and *Lambeosaurus*, had tall, hollow, bony head crests.

SKELETON OF IGUANODON

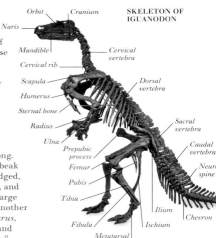

Orbit
Cranium
Naris
Mandible
Cervical vertebra
Cervical rib
Scapula
Dorsal vertebra
Humerus
Sternal bone
Radius
Sacral vertebra
Ulna
Caudal vertebra
Prepubic process
Femur
Neural spine
Pubis
Tibia
Ilium
Chevron
Fibula
Ischium
Metatarsal

EXTERNAL FEATURES OF MANTELLISAURUS

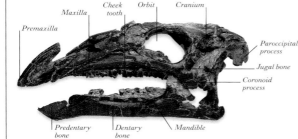

Thigh
Heavy, stiff tail

SKULL AND MANDIBLE OF YOUNG MANTELLISAURUS

Maxilla
Cheek tooth
Orbit
Cranium
Premaxilla
Paroccipital process
Jugal bone
Coronoid process
Predentary bone
Dentary bone
Mandible

Knee

Hind limb

Ankle
Toe
Foot

Hooflike nail

EXAMPLES OF IGUANODONTS

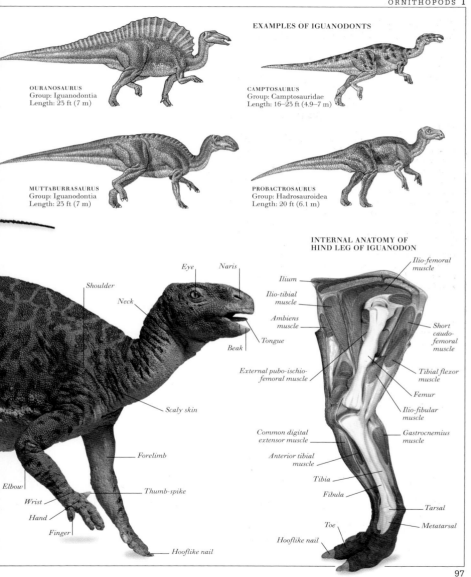

OURANOSAURUS
Group: Iguanodontia
Length: 23 ft (7 m)

CAMPTOSAURUS
Group: Camptosauridae
Length: 16–23 ft (4.9–7 m)

MUTTABURRASAURUS
Group: Iguanodontia
Length: 25 ft (7 m)

PROBACTROSAURUS
Group: Hadrosauroidea
Length: 20 ft (6.1 m)

**INTERNAL ANATOMY OF
HIND LEG OF IGUANODON**

Eye

Naris

Shoulder

Neck

Ilium

Ilio-femoral muscle

Ilio-tibial muscle

Ambiens muscle

Short caudo-femoral muscle

Beak

Tongue

External pubo-ischio-femoral muscle

Tibial flexor muscle

Femur

Ilio-fibular muscle

Scaly skin

Gastrocnemius muscle

Common digital extensor muscle

Anterior tibial muscle

Forelimb

Tibia

Fibula

Elbow

Wrist

Thumb-spike

Hand

Tarsal

Metatarsal

Finger

Toe

Hooflike nail

Hooflike nail

Ornithopods 2

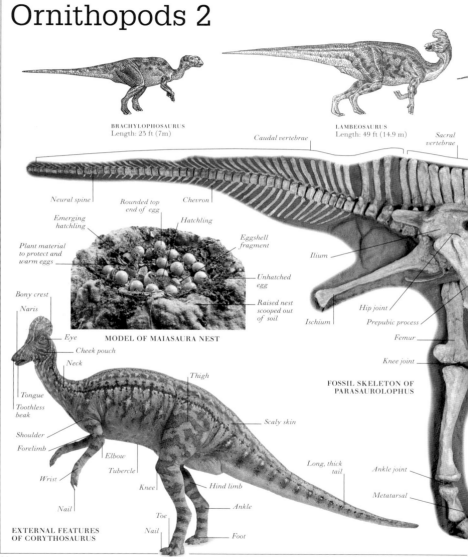

BRACHYLOPHOSAURUS
Length: 23 ft (7m)

LAMBEOSAURUS
Length: 49 ft (14.9 m)

Caudal vertebrae

Sacral vertebrae

Neural spine

Rounded top end of egg

Chevron

Emerging hatchling

Hatchling

Eggshell fragment

Plant material to protect and warm eggs

Ilium

Unhatched egg

Raised nest scooped out of soil

Bony crest

Naris

MODEL OF MAIASAURA NEST

Hip joint

Ischium

Prepubic process

Eye

Cheek pouch

Femur

Neck

Knee joint

Thigh

FOSSIL SKELETON OF PARASAUROLOPHUS

Tongue

Toothless beak

Scaly skin

Shoulder

Forelimb

Elbow

Long, thick tail

Ankle joint

Tubercle

Metatarsal

Wrist

Knee

Hind limb

Nail

Ankle

EXTERNAL FEATURES OF CORYTHOSAURUS

Toe

Nail

Foot

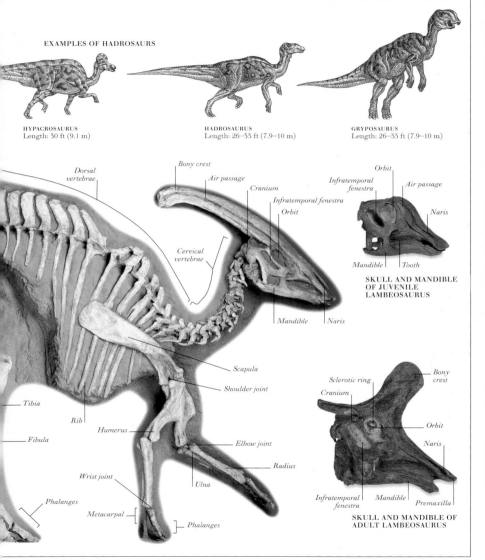

EXAMPLES OF HADROSAURS

HYPACROSAURUS
Length: 30 ft (9.1 m)

HADROSAURUS
Length: 26–35 ft (7.9–10 m)

GRYPOSAURUS
Length: 26–35 ft (7.9–10 m)

Dorsal vertebrae

Bony crest

Air passage

Cranium

Infratemporal fenestra

Orbit

Cervical vertebrae

Mandible

Naris

Orbit

Infratemporal fenestra

Air passage

Naris

Mandible

Tooth

SKULL AND MANDIBLE OF JUVENILE LAMBEOSAURUS

Scapula

Shoulder joint

Tibia

Rib

Humerus

Fibula

Elbow joint

Radius

Wrist joint

Ulna

Phalanges

Metacarpal

Phalanges

Sclerotic ring

Cranium

Bony crest

Orbit

Naris

Infratemporal fenestra

Mandible

Premaxilla

SKULL AND MANDIBLE OF ADULT LAMBEOSAURUS

Marginocephalians 1

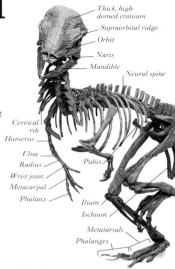

HEAD-BUTTING PRENOCEPHALES

MARGINOCEPHALIA ("margined heads") were a group of bipedal and quadrupedal ornithischian dinosaurs with a narrow shelf or deep, bony frill at the back of the skull. Marginocephalians were probably descended from the same ancestor as the ornithopods and lived in what are now North America, Africa, Asia, and Europe during the Cretaceous period (145–65 million years ago). They were divided into two groups: Pachycephalosauria ("thick-headed lizards"), such as *Pachycephalosaurus* and *Stegoceras*, and Ceratopsia ("horned faces"), such as *Triceratops* and *Psittacosaurus*. The thick skulls of Pachycephalosauria may have protected their brains during possible head-butting contests fought to win territory and mates; their hips and spines may also have been strengthened to withstand the shock. The bony frill of Ceratopsia would have added to their frightening appearance when charging; the neck was strengthened for impact and to support the huge head, with its snipping beak and powerful slicing toothed jaws. A charging ceratopsian would have been a formidable opponent for even the largest predators. Ceratopsians were among the most abundant herbivorous dinosaurs of the Late Cretaceous period (97–65 million years ago).

Thick, high-domed cranium
Supraorbital ridge
Orbit
Naris
Mandible
Neural spine
Cervical rib
Humerus
Ulna
Radius
Wrist joint
Metacarpal
Phalanx
Pubis
Ilium
Ischium
Metatarsals
Phalanges

EXAMPLES OF SKULLS OF PACHYCEPHALOSAURS

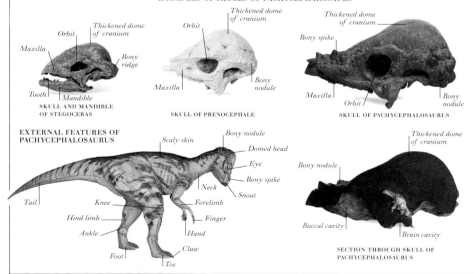

Thickened dome of cranium
Orbit
Maxilla
Bony ridge
Tooth
Mandible
SKULL AND MANDIBLE OF STEGOCERAS

Thickened dome of cranium
Orbit
Maxilla
Bony nodule
SKULL OF PRENOCEPHALE

Thickened dome of cranium
Bony spike
Maxilla
Orbit
Bony nodule
SKULL OF PACHYCEPHALOSAURUS

EXTERNAL FEATURES OF PACHYCEPHALOSAURUS
Scaly skin
Bony nodule
Domed head
Eye
Bony spike
Neck
Snout
Tail
Knee
Hind limb
Ankle
Forelimb
Finger
Hand
Claw
Foot
Toe

Thickened dome of cranium
Bony nodule
Buccal cavity
Brain cavity
SECTION THROUGH SKULL OF PACHYCEPHALOSAURUS

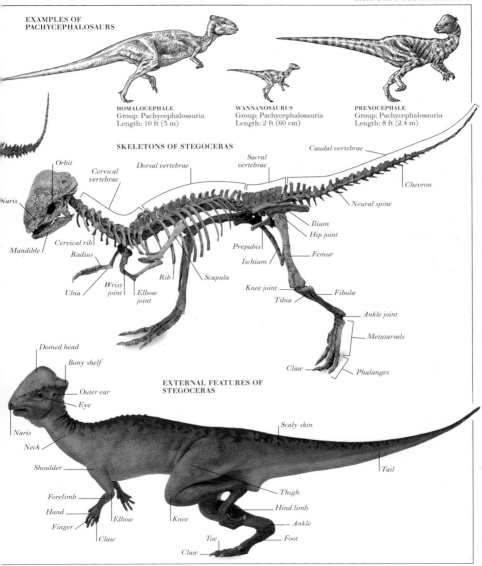

EXAMPLES OF PACHYCEPHALOSAURS

HOMALOCEPHALE
Group: Pachycephalosauria
Length: 10 ft (3 m)

WANNANOSAURUS
Group: Pachycephalosauria
Length: 2 ft (60 cm)

PRENOCEPHALE
Group: Pachycephalosauria
Length: 8 ft (2.4 m)

SKELETONS OF STEGOCERAS

Caudal vertebrae

Sacral vertebrae

Dorsal vertebrae

Cervical vertebrae

Orbit

Chevron

Naris

Neural spine

Ilium

Hip joint

Mandible

Cervical rib

Prepubis

Femur

Radius

Ischium

Ulna

Wrist joint

Rib

Scapula

Knee joint

Fibula

Elbow joint

Tibia

Ankle joint

Metatarsals

Claw

Phalanges

EXTERNAL FEATURES OF STEGOCERAS

Domed head

Bony shelf

Outer ear

Eye

Scaly skin

Naris

Neck

Tail

Shoulder

Thigh

Forelimb

Hind limb

Hand

Elbow

Knee

Ankle

Finger

Claw

Toe

Foot

Claw

Marginocephalians 2

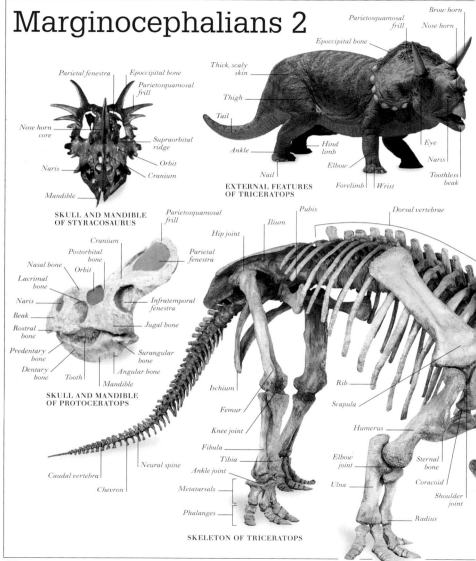

SKULL AND MANDIBLE OF STYRACOSAURUS

Parietal fenestra
Epoccipital bone
Parietosquamosal frill
Nose horn core
Supraorbital ridge
Naris
Orbit
Cranium
Mandible

EXTERNAL FEATURES OF TRICERATOPS

Parietosquamosal frill
Epoccipital bone
Brow horn
Nose horn
Thick, scaly skin
Thigh
Tail
Ankle
Nail
Hind limb
Elbow
Forelimb
Wrist
Eye
Naris
Toothless beak

SKULL AND MANDIBLE OF PROTOCERATOPS

Cranium
Postorbital bone
Nasal bone
Orbit
Lacrimal bone
Naris
Beak
Rostral bone
Predentary bone
Dentary bone
Tooth
Mandible
Surangular bone
Angular bone
Jugal bone
Infratemporal fenestra
Parietal fenestra
Parietosquamosal frill

SKELETON OF TRICERATOPS

Parietosquamosal frill
Hip joint
Ilium
Pubis
Dorsal vertebrae
Ischium
Femur
Knee joint
Fibula
Tibia
Ankle joint
Metatarsals
Phalanges
Caudal vertebra
Neural spine
Chevron
Rib
Scapula
Humerus
Elbow joint
Ulna
Sternal bone
Coracoid
Shoulder joint
Radius

EXTERNAL FEATURES OF PSITTACOSAURUS

Eye

Cheek horn

Beak

Claw

Finger

Forelimb

Elbow

Scaly skin

Thigh

Knee

Claw

Toe

Ankle

Hind limb

Parietosquamosal frill

Tail

Cranium

Orbit

Brow horn core

Nose horn core

Naris

Cervical rib

Infratemporal fenestra

Jugal bone

Tooth

Metacarpals

Phalanges

Mandible

Predentary bone

Rostral bone

EXAMPLES OF CERATOPSIA

PROTOCERATOPS
Group: Protoceratopsidae
Length: 9 ft (2.7 m)

STYRACOSAURUS
Group: Centrosaurinae
Length: 18 ft (5.5 m)

TRICERATOPS
Group: Chasmosaurinae
Length: 30 ft (9.1 m)

PACHYRHINOSAURUS
Group: Centrosaurinae
Length: 18 ft (5.5 m)

LEPTOCERATOPS
Group: Leptoceratopsidae
Length: 7 ft (2.1 m)

Mammals 1

**TETRALOPHODON
CHEEK TEETH**

SINCE THE EXTINCTION of most of the dinosaurs 65 million years ago, mammals (along with birds) have been the dominant vertebrates on land. This class includes terrestrial, aerial, and aquatic forms. Having developed from the therapsids, the first true mammals—small, nocturnal, shrewlike creatures, such as *Megazostrodon*—appeared over 200 million years ago during the Triassic period (250–200 million years ago). Mammals had several features that differed from those of their ancestors: an efficient four-chambered heart allowed these warm-blooded animals to sustain high levels of activity; a covering of hair helped them maintain a constant body temperature; an improved limb structure gave them more efficient locomotion; and the birth of live young and the immediate supply of food from the mother's milk aided their rapid growth. Since the end of the Mesozoic era (65 million years ago), the number of major mammal groups and the abundance of species in each have varied dramatically. For example, the Perissodactyla (the group that includes *Coelodonta* and modern horses) was a common group during the Early Tertiary period (about 54 million years ago). Today, the mammalian groups with the most species include the Rodentia (rats and mice), the Chiroptera (bats), the Primates (monkeys and apes), the Carnivora (bears, cats, and dogs), and the Artiodactyla (cattle, deer, and pigs), while the Proboscidea group, which formerly included many genera, such as *Phiomia*, *Moeritherium*, *Tetralophodon*, and *Mammuthus*, now has only three species of elephant. In Australia and South America, millions of years of continental isolation led to increased diversity of the marsupials, a group of mammals distinct from the placentals (see p. 74) that existed elsewhere.

Long tail aids balance

Insulating hair

Neural spine

Scapula

Cervical vertebra

Humerus

Nasal horn

Naris

Orbit

Mandible

Radius

Premaxilla bone

Ulna

Chisel-edged molar

Metacarpal

Phalanx

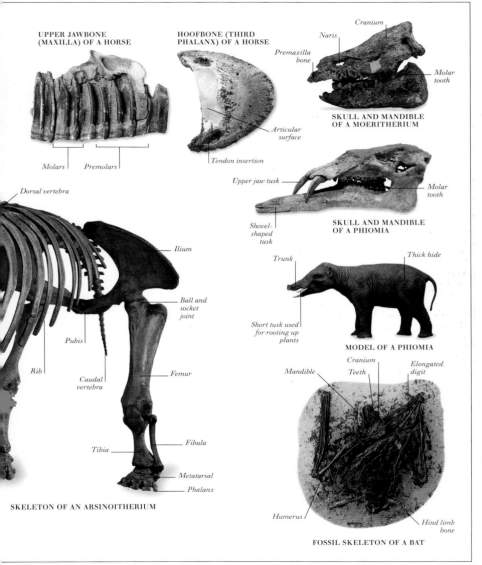

UPPER JAWBONE (MAXILLA) OF A HORSE

Molars

Premolars

HOOFBONE (THIRD PHALANX) OF A HORSE

Articular surface

Tendon insertion

Cranium

Naris

Premaxilla bone

Molar tooth

SKULL AND MANDIBLE OF A MOERITHERIUM

Upper jaw tusk

Molar tooth

Shovel-shaped tusk

SKULL AND MANDIBLE OF A PHIOMIA

Trunk

Thick hide

Short tusk used for rooting up plants

MODEL OF A PHIOMIA

Dorsal vertebra

Ilium

Ball and socket joint

Pubis

Rib

Caudal vertebra

Femur

Tibia

Fibula

Metatarsal

Phalanx

SKELETON OF AN ARSINOITHERIUM

Mandible

Cranium

Teeth

Elongated digit

Humerus

Hind limb bone

FOSSIL SKELETON OF A BAT

Mammals 2

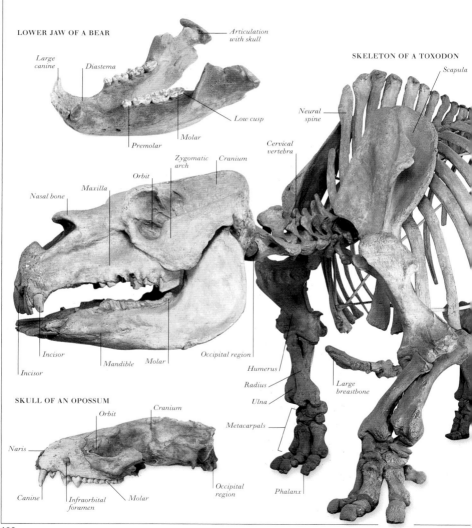

LOWER JAW OF A BEAR

Large canine

Diastema

Articulation with skull

Low cusp

Premolar

Molar

SKELETON OF A TOXODON

Scapula

Neural spine

Cervical vertebra

Zygomatic arch

Cranium

Orbit

Maxilla

Nasal bone

Incisor

Mandible

Molar

Occipital region

Humerus

Radius

Ulna

Metacarpals

Large breastbone

Incisor

SKULL OF AN OPOSSUM

Orbit

Cranium

Naris

Occipital region

Canine

Infraorbital foramen

Molar

Phalanx

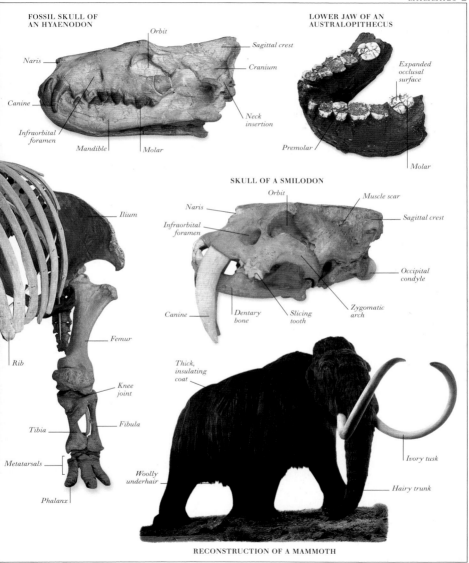

FOSSIL SKULL OF AN HYAENODON

Orbit
Naris
Sagittal crest
Cranium
Canine
Neck insertion
Infraorbital foramen
Mandible
Molar

LOWER JAW OF AN AUSTRALOPITHECUS

Expanded occlusal surface
Premolar
Molar

SKULL OF A SMILODON

Orbit
Muscle scar
Naris
Sagittal crest
Infraorbital foramen
Occipital condyle
Canine
Dentary bone
Slicing tooth
Zygomatic arch

Ilium
Rib
Femur
Knee joint
Tibia
Fibula
Metatarsals
Phalanx

RECONSTRUCTION OF A MAMMOTH

Thick, insulating coat
Woolly underhair
Ivory tusk
Hairy trunk

The first humans

MODERN HUMANS BELONG TO THE MAMMALIAN order of primates (see pp. 202–203), which originated about 55 million years ago; primates included the only extant hominid species. The earliest hominid was *Ardipithecus* ("ground ape") and *Australopithecus* ("southern ape"), both small-brained intermediates between apes and humans that were capable of standing and walking upright. *Homo habilis*, the earliest member of the genus Homo, appeared at least 2 million years ago. This larger-brained "handy man" began making tools for hunting. *Homo ergaster* first appeared in Africa about 1.8 million years ago and spread into Asia about 800,000 years later. Smaller-toothed than *Homo habilis*, H. ergaster—followed by Homo erectus—developed fire as a tool, which enabled it to cook food. Neanderthals, a near relative of modern humans, originated about 200,000 years ago, and *Homo sapiens* (modern humans) appeared in Africa about 100,000 years later. The two coexisted for thousands of years, but by 30,000 years ago, *Homo sapiens* had become dominant and the Neanderthals had died out. Classification of *Homo sapiens* in relation to its ancestors is enormously problematic: modern humans must be classified not only by bone structure, but also by specific behavior—the ability to plan future action; to follow traditions; and to use symbolic communication, including complex language and the ability to use and recognize symbols.

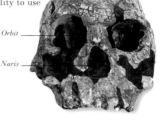

JAWBONE OF AUSTRALOPITHECUS
(SOUTHERN APE)

Larger jawbone than modern human

Large back tooth

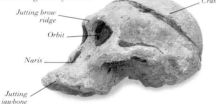

Cranium

Jutting brow ridge

Orbit

Naris

Jutting jawbone

SKULL OF AUSTRALOPITHECUS
(SOUTHERN APE)

Orbit

Naris

SKULL OF HOMO HABILIS
(FIRST MEMBER OF HOMO GENUS)

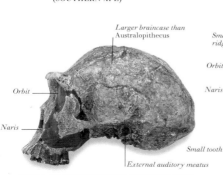

Larger braincase than Australopithecus

Orbit

Naris

External auditory meatus

SKULL OF HOMO ERECTUS (UPRIGHT MAN)

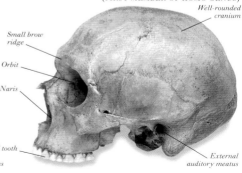

Well-rounded cranium

Small brow ridge

Orbit

Naris

Small tooth

External auditory meatus

SKULL OF HOMO SAPIENS (MODERN HUMAN)

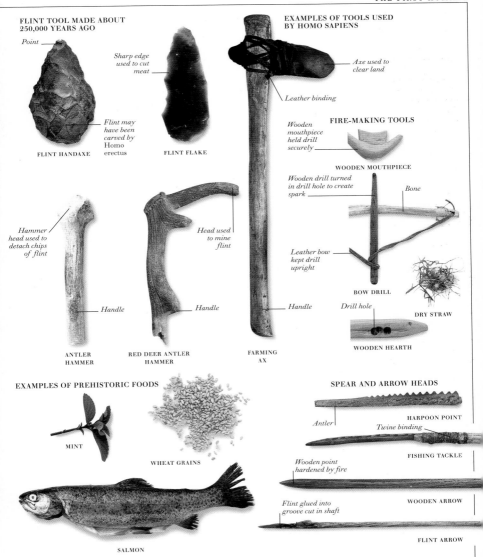

FLINT TOOL MADE ABOUT 250,000 YEARS AGO

Point

Sharp edge used to cut meat

Flint may have been carved by Homo erectus

FLINT HANDAXE

FLINT FLAKE

Hammer head used to detach chips of flint

Handle

ANTLER HAMMER

Head used to mine flint

Handle

RED DEER ANTLER HAMMER

Handle

FARMING AX

EXAMPLES OF TOOLS USED BY HOMO SAPIENS

Axe used to clear land

Leather binding

FIRE-MAKING TOOLS

Wooden mouthpiece held drill securely

WOODEN MOUTHPIECE

Wooden drill turned in drill hole to create spark

Bone

Leather bow kept drill upright

BOW DRILL

DRY STRAW

Drill hole

WOODEN HEARTH

EXAMPLES OF PREHISTORIC FOODS

MINT

WHEAT GRAINS

SALMON

SPEAR AND ARROW HEADS

HARPOON POINT

Antler

Twine binding

FISHING TACKLE

Wooden point hardened by fire

WOODEN ARROW

Flint glued into groove cut in shaft

FLINT ARROW

PLANTS

PLANT VARIETIES · 112
FUNGI AND LICHENS · · · · · · · · · · · · · · · · · · 114
ALGAE AND SEAWEEDS · · · · · · · · · · · · · · · · 116
LIVERWORTS AND MOSSES · · · · · · · · · · · · · 118
HORSETAILS, CLUBMOSSES, AND FERNS · · · · · 120
GYMNOSPERMS 1 · 122
GYMNOSPERMS 2 · 124
MONOCOTYLEDONS AND DICOTYLEDONS · · · · · 126
HERBACEOUS FLOWERING PLANTS · · · · · · · · · 128
WOODY FLOWERING PLANTS · · · · · · · · · · · · 130
ROOTS · 132
STEMS · 134
LEAVES · 136
PHOTOSYNTHESIS · 138
FLOWERS 1 · 140
FLOWERS 2 · 142
POLLINATION · 144
FERTILIZATION · 146
SUCCULENT FRUITS · · · · · · · · · · · · · · · · · · · 148
DRY FRUITS · 150
GERMINATION · 152
VEGETATIVE REPRODUCTION · · · · · · · · · · · · · 154
DRYLAND PLANTS · 156
WETLAND PLANTS · 158
CARNIVOROUS PLANTS · · · · · · · · · · · · · · · · · 160
EPIPHYTIC AND PARASITIC PLANTS · · · · · · · · 162

Plant varieties

THERE ARE MORE THAN 300,000 SPECIES of plant.
They show a wide diversity of forms and life-styles, ranging, for example,
from delicate liverworts, adapted for life in a damp habitat, to cacti, capable of surviving
in the desert, and from herbaceous plants, such as corn, which completes its life-cycle in one year,
to the giant redwood tree, which can live for thousands of years. This diversity reflects the adaptations
of plants to survive in a wide range of habitats. This is seen most clearly in the flowering plants (phylum
Angiospermophyta), which are the most numerous, with over 250,000 species, and the most widespread,
being found from the tropics to the poles. Despite their diversity, plants share certain characteristics: typically,
plants are green, and make their food by photosynthesis; and most plants live in or on a substrate, such as
soil, and do not actively move. Algae (kingdom Protista) and fungi (kingdom Fungi) have
some plantlike characteristics and are often studied alongside plants, although they
are not true plants.

FLOWERING PLANT
Bromeliad
(*Acanthostachys strobilacea*)

Leaf

GREEN ALGA
Micrograph of desmid
(*Micrasterias sp.*)

Pyrenoid
(small protein
body)

Chloroplast

Sinus
(division between
two halves of cell)

Cell wall

FERN
Tree fern
(*Dicksonia antarctica*)

Rachis
(main axis
of pinnate leaf)

Petiole
(leaf stalk)

Ramentum
(brown scale)

Base of dead
frond (leaf)

Trunk

Adventitious
root

Epiphytic
fern growing
at base

BRYOPHYTE
Moss
(*Bryum sp.*)

Seta
(stalk)

Immature capsule

Sporophyte
(spore-
producing
plant)

Capsule
(site of spore
production)

"Leaf"

Gametophyte
(gamete-producing
plant)

FLOWERING PLANT
Succulent
(*Kedrostis africana*)

*Petiole
(leaf stalk)*

Leaf

FLOWERING PLANT
Micrograph of cross-section
through leaf of marram grass
(*Ammophila arenaria*)

*Sclerenchyma
(strengthening
tissue)*

*Cuticle
(waterproof
covering)*

Stem

Xylem } *Vascular
Phloem* } *tissue*

*Stiff trichome
(hair)*

*Caudex
(swollen
stem
base)*

*Interlocked
trichomes (hairs)*

*Epidermis
(outer layer
of cells)*

*Hinge cells
(cause curling of leaf to
reduce water loss)*

*Mesophyll
(photosynthetic
tissue)*

Root

Spine *Flower*

*Bract
(leaflike structure)*

Inflorescence

Stem

*Pinna
(leaflet)*

FLOWERING PLANT
Couch grass
(*Agropyron repens*)

FLOWERING PLANT
Pitcher plant
(*Sarracenia purpurea*)

Sepal

*Fruit
surrounded
by floral parts*

*Caryopsis
(type of
dry fruit)*

*Rachis
(main axis of
grass inflorescence)*

*Umbrella
of style*

Frond (leaf)

*Pitcher (leaf
modified to trap
insects)*

*Pedicel
(flower
stalk)*

Hood

Node

*Downward-pointing
hair (encourages
insect prey into
pitcher)*

*Midrib of
pinna (leaflet)*

Wing

*Lamina
(blade)*

*Round, hollow
stem*

*Sheathing
leaf base*

*Adventitious
root*

*Immature
pitcher*

Fungi and lichens

FUNGI WERE ONCE THOUGHT OF AS PLANTS but are now classified as a separate kingdom. This kingdom includes not only the familiar mushrooms, puffballs, stinkhorns, and molds, but also yeasts, smuts, rusts, and lichens. Most fungi are multicellular, consisting of a mass of threadlike hyphae that together form a mycelium. However, the simpler fungi (e.g., yeasts) are microscopic, single-celled organisms. Typically, fungi reproduce by means of spores. Most fungi feed on dead or decaying matter, or on living organisms. A few fungi obtain their food from plants or algae, with which they have a symbiotic (mutually advantageous) relationship. Lichens are a symbiotic partnership between algae and fungi. Of the six types of lichens, the three most common are crustose (flat and crusty), foliose (leafy), and fruticose (shrublike). Some lichens (e.g., *Cladonia floerkeana*) are a combination of types. Lichens reproduce by means of spores or soredia (powdery vegetative fragments).

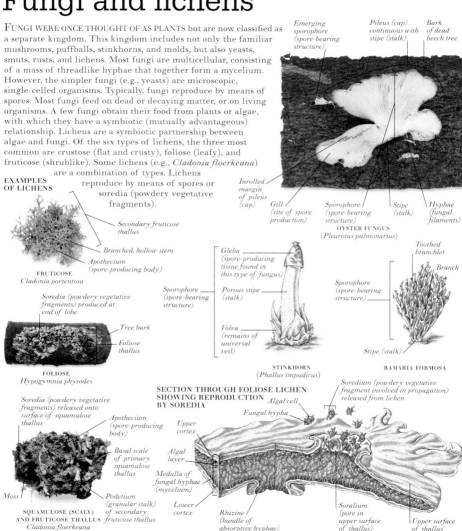

EXAMPLES OF LICHENS

Secondary fruticose thallus

Branched, hollow stem

Apothecium (spore-producing body)

FRUTICOSE
Cladonia portentosa

Soredia (powdery vegetative fragments) produced at end of lobe

Tree bark

Foliose thallus

FOLIOSE
Hypogymnia physodes

Soredia (powdery vegetative fragments) released onto surface of squamulose thallus

Apothecium (spore-producing body)

Basal scale of primary squamulose thallus

Moss

Podetium (granular stalk) of secondary fruticose thallus

SQUAMULOSE (SCALY) AND FRUTICOSE THALLUS
Cladonia floerkeana

Emerging sporophore (spore-bearing structure)

Pileus (cap) continuous with stipe (stalk)

Bark of dead beech tree

Inrolled margin of pileus (cap)

Gill (site of spore production)

Sporophore (spore-bearing structure)

Stipe (stalk)

Hyphae (fungal filaments)

OYSTER FUNGUS
(*Pleurotus pulmonarius*)

Gleba (spore-producing tissue found in this type of fungus)

Sporophore (spore-bearing structure)

Porous stipe (stalk)

Volva (remains of universal veil)

STINKHORN
(*Phallus impudicus*)

Toothed branchlet

Branch

Sporophore (spore-bearing structure)

Stipe (stalk)

RAMARIA FORMOSA

SECTION THROUGH FOLIOSE LICHEN SHOWING REPRODUCTION BY SOREDIA

Algal cell

Fungal hypha

Soredium (powdery vegetative fragment involved in propagation) released from lichen

Upper cortex

Algal layer

Medulla of fungal hyphae (mycelium)

Lower cortex

Rhizine (bundle of absorptive hyphae)

Soralium (pore in upper surface of thallus)

Upper surface of thallus

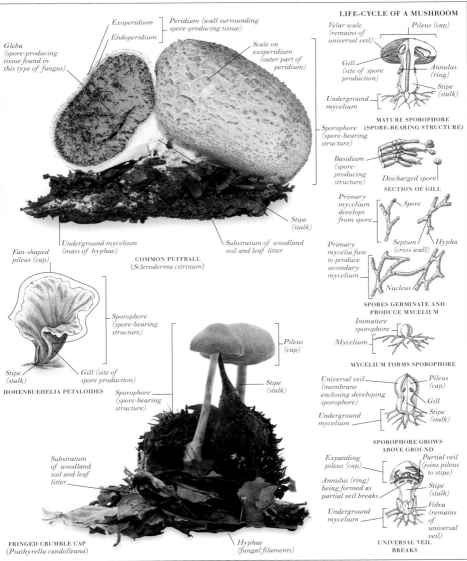

Gleba (spore-producing tissue found in this type of fungus)

Exoperidium

Endoperidium

Peridium (wall surrounding spore-producing tissue)

Scale on exoperidium (outer part of peridium)

Sporophore (spore-bearing structure)

Stipe (stalk)

Underground mycelium (mass of hyphae)

Substratum of woodland soil and leaf litter

COMMON PUFFBALL
(*Scleroderma citrinum*)

Fan-shaped pileus (cap)

Sporophore (spore-bearing structure)

Stipe (stalk)

Gill (site of spore production)

HOHENBUEHELIA PETALOIDES

Sporophore (spore-bearing structure)

Pileus (cap)

Stipe (stalk)

Substratum of woodland soil and leaf litter

FRINGED CRUMBLE CAP
(*Psathyrella candolleana*)

Hyphae (fungal filaments)

LIFE-CYCLE OF A MUSHROOM

Velar scale (remains of universal veil)

Pileus (cap)

Gill (site of spore production)

Annulus (ring)

Stipe (stalk)

Underground mycelium

MATURE SPOROPHORE
(SPORE-BEARING STRUCTURE)

Basidium (spore-producing structure)

Discharged spore

SECTION OF GILL

Primary mycelium develops from spore

Spore

Septum (cross wall)

Hypha

Primary mycelia fuse to produce secondary mycelium

Nucleus

SPORES GERMINATE AND PRODUCE MYCELIUM

Immature sporophore

Mycelium

MYCELIUM FORMS SPOROPHORE

Universal veil (membrane enclosing developing sporophore)

Pileus (cap)

Gill

Underground mycelium

Stipe (stalk)

SPOROPHORE GROWS ABOVE GROUND

Expanding pileus (cap)

Partial veil (joins pileus to stipe)

Annulus (ring) being formed as partial veil breaks

Stipe (stalk)

Underground mycelium

Volva (remains of universal veil)

UNIVERSAL VEIL BREAKS

Algae and seaweeds

ALGAE ARE NOT TRUE PLANTS. They form a diverse group of plantlike organisms that belong to the kingdom Protista. Like plants, algae possess the green pigment chlorophyll and make their own food by photosynthesis (see pp. 138-139). Many algae also possess other pigments by which they can be classified; for example, the brown pigment fucoxanthin is found in the brown algae. Some of the 10 phyla of algae are exclusively unicellular (single-celled); others also contain aggregates of cells in filaments or colonies. Three phyla—the Chlorophyta (green algae), Rhodophyta (red algae), and Phaeophyta (brown algae)—contain larger, multicellular, thalloid (flat), marine organisms commonly known as seaweeds. Most algae can reproduce sexually. For example, in the brown seaweed *Fucus vesiculosus*, gametes (sex cells) are produced in conceptacles (chambers) in the receptacles (fertile tips of fronds); after their release into the sea, antherozoids (male gametes) and oospheres (female gametes) fuse; the resulting zygote settles on a rock and develops into a new seaweed.

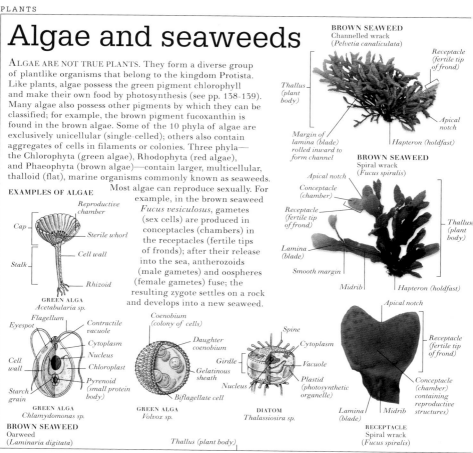

EXAMPLES OF ALGAE

GREEN ALGA
Acetabularia sp.
- Reproductive chamber
- Cap
- Sterile whorl
- Cell wall
- Stalk
- Rhizoid

GREEN ALGA
Chlamydomonas sp.
- Flagellum
- Eyespot
- Cell wall
- Starch grain
- Contractile vacuole
- Cytoplasm
- Nucleus
- Chloroplast
- Pyrenoid (small protein body)

GREEN ALGA
Volvox sp.
- Coenobium (colony of cells)
- Daughter coenobium
- Girdle
- Gelatinous sheath
- Biflagellate cell

DIATOM
Thalassiosira sp.
- Spine
- Cytoplasm
- Vacuole
- Plastid (photosynthetic organelle)
- Nucleus

BROWN SEAWEED
Oarweed
(*Laminaria digitata*)
- Thallus (plant body)

BROWN SEAWEED
Channelled wrack
(*Pelvetia canaliculata*)
- Thallus (plant body)
- Receptacle (fertile tip of frond)
- Apical notch
- Margin of lamina (blade) rolled inward to form channel
- Hapteron (holdfast)

BROWN SEAWEED
Spiral wrack
(*Fucus spiralis*)
- Apical notch
- Conceptacle (chamber)
- Receptacle (fertile tip of frond)
- Lamina (blade)
- Smooth margin
- Midrib
- Thallus (plant body)
- Hapteron (holdfast)

RECEPTACLE
Spiral wrack
(*Fucus spiralis*)
- Apical notch
- Receptacle (fertile tip of frond)
- Conceptacle (chamber) containing reproductive structures
- Lamina (blade)
- Midrib

- Lamina (blade) palmately divided

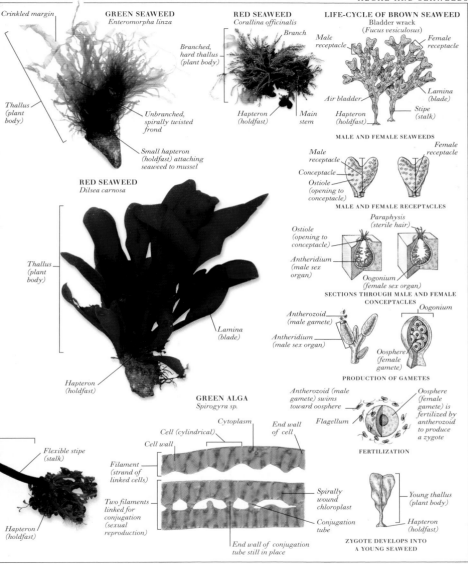

GREEN SEAWEED
Enteromorpha linza

Crinkled margin

Thallus (plant body)

Unbranched, spirally twisted frond

Small hapteron (holdfast) attaching seaweed to mussel

RED SEAWEED
Corallina officinalis

Branch

Branched, hard thallus (plant body)

Hapteron (holdfast)

Main stem

RED SEAWEED
Dilsea carnosa

Thallus (plant body)

Lamina (blade)

Hapteron (holdfast)

LIFE-CYCLE OF BROWN SEAWEED
Bladder wrack
(*Fucus vesiculosus*)

Male receptacle

Female receptacle

Air bladder

Lamina (blade)

Hapteron (holdfast)

Stipe (stalk)

MALE AND FEMALE SEAWEEDS

Male receptacle

Female receptacle

Conceptacle

Ostiole (opening to conceptacle)

MALE AND FEMALE RECEPTACLES

Paraphysis (sterile hair)

Ostiole (opening to conceptacle)

Antheridium (male sex organ)

Oogonium (female sex organ)

SECTIONS THROUGH MALE AND FEMALE CONCEPTACLES

Antherozoid (male gamete)

Antheridium (male sex organ)

Oogonium

Oosphere (female gamete)

PRODUCTION OF GAMETES

GREEN ALGA
Spirogyra sp.

Antherozoid (male gamete) swims toward oosphere

Flagellum

Oosphere (female gamete) is fertilized by antherozoid to produce a zygote

FERTILIZATION

Cytoplasm

Cell (cylindrical)

Cell wall

End wall of cell

Filament (strand of linked cells)

Two filaments linked for conjugation (sexual reproduction)

Spirally wound chloroplast

Conjugation tube

End wall of conjugation tube still in place

Young thallus (plant body)

Hapteron (holdfast)

ZYGOTE DEVELOPS INTO A YOUNG SEAWEED

Flexible stipe (stalk)

Hapteron (holdfast)

Liverworts and mosses

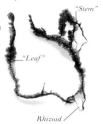

"Stem"

"Leaf"

Rhizoid

LIVERWORTS AND MOSSES ARE SMALL, LOW-GROWING PLANTS that belong to the phylum Bryophyta. Bryophytes do not have true stems, leaves, or roots (they are anchored to the ground by rhizoids), nor do they have the vascular tissues (xylem and phloem) that transport water and nutrients in higher plants. With no outer, waterproof cuticle, bryophytes are susceptible to drying out, and most grow in moist habitats. The bryophyte life-cycle has two stages. In stage one, the green plant (gametophyte) produces male and female gametes (sex cells), which fuse to form a zygote. In stage two, the zygote develops into a sporophyte that remains attached to the gametophyte. The sporophyte produces spores, which are released and germinate into new green plants. Liverworts (class Hepaticae) grow horizontally and may be thalloid (flat and ribbonlike) or "leafy." Mosses (class Musci) typically have an upright "stem" with spirally arranged "leaves."

A THALLOID LIVERWORT
Marchantia polymorpha

Archegoniophore (stalked structure carrying archegonia)

Disk

Lobe

Stalk

Gemma cup

Thallus (plant body)

Gemma (detachable tissue that produces new plants)

Thallus (plant body)

Apical notch

Toothed margin of cup

DETAIL OF GEMMA CUP

Disk

Lobe

Stalk

Rhizoid

SIDE VIEW OF ARCHEGONIOPHORE

Lobe

Disk

Ray (radial groove)

Stalk

ARCHEGONIOPHORE FROM BELOW

Pore

Ray (radial groove)

MICROGRAPH OF LOBE

Gemma cup

Thallus (plant body)

Midrib

Archegoniophore (stalked structure carrying archegonia)

FEMALE GAMETOPHYTE

MICROGRAPH OF THALLUS
Conocephalum conicum

Position of air chamber

Pore for exchange of gases

Upper surface

Rhizoid

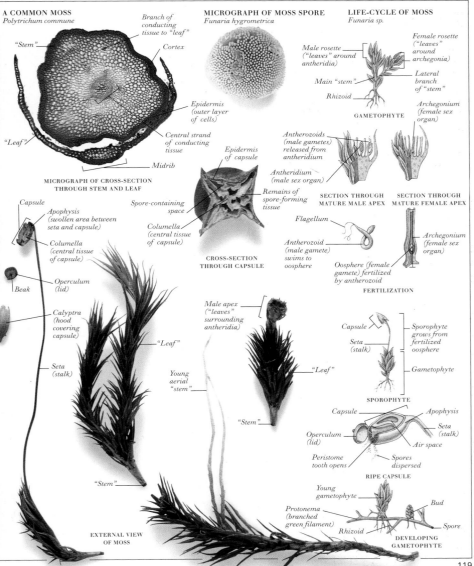

A COMMON MOSS
Polytrichum commune

"Stem"

Branch of
conducting
tissue to "leaf"

Cortex

Epidermis
(outer layer
of cells)

Central strand
of conducting
tissue

"Leaf"

Midrib

**MICROGRAPH OF CROSS-SECTION
THROUGH STEM AND LEAF**

Capsule

Apophysis
(swollen area between
seta and capsule)

Columella
(central tissue
of capsule)

Operculum
(lid)

Beak

Calyptra
(hood
covering
capsule)

Seta
(stalk)

"Leaf"

"Stem"

**EXTERNAL VIEW
OF MOSS**

MICROGRAPH OF MOSS SPORE
Funaria hygrometrica

Epidermis
of capsule

Spore-containing
space

Remains of
spore-forming
tissue

Columella
(central tissue
of capsule)

**CROSS-SECTION
THROUGH CAPSULE**

Male apex
("leaves"
surrounding
antheridia)

"Leaf"

Young
aerial
"stem"

"Stem"

LIFE-CYCLE OF MOSS
Funaria sp.

Male rosette
("leaves" around
antheridia)

Female rosette
("leaves"
around
archegonia)

Main "stem"

Lateral
branch
of "stem"

Rhizoid

Archegonium
(female sex
organ)

GAMETOPHYTE

Antherozoids
(male gametes)
released from
antheridium

Antheridium
(male sex organ)

**SECTION THROUGH
MATURE MALE APEX**

Archegonium
(female sex
organ)

**SECTION THROUGH
MATURE FEMALE APEX**

Flagellum

Antherozoid
(male gamete)
swims to
oosphere

Oosphere (female
gamete) fertilized
by antherozoid

FERTILIZATION

Capsule

Seta
(stalk)

Sporophyte
grows from
fertilized
oosphere

Gametophyte

SPOROPHYTE

Capsule

Apophysis

Operculum
(lid)

Seta
(stalk)

Air space

Peristome
tooth opens

Spores
dispersed

RIPE CAPSULE

Young
gametophyte

Bud

Protonema
(branched
green filament)

Spore

Rhizoid

**DEVELOPING
GAMETOPHYTE**

119

Horsetails, clubmosses, and ferns

HORSETAILS, CLUBMOSSES, AND FERNS are primitive land plants, which, like higher plants, have stems, roots, and leaves, and vascular systems that transport water, minerals, and food. However, unlike higher plants, they do not produce seeds when reproducing. Their life-cycles involve two stages. In stage one, the sporophyte (green plant) produces spores in sporangia. In stage two, the spores germinate, developing into small, short-lived gametophyte plants that produce male and female gametes (sex cells); the gametes fuse to form a zygote from which a new sporophyte plant develops. Horsetails (phylum Sphenophyta) have erect, green stems with branches arranged in whorls; some stems are fertile and have a single spore-producing strobilus (group of sporangia) at the tip. Clubmosses (phylum Lycopodophyta) typically have small leaves arranged spirally around the stem, with spore-producing strobili at the tip of some stems. Ferns (phylum Filicinophyta) typically have large, pinnate fronds (leaves); sporangia, grouped together in sori, develop on the underside of fertile fronds.

FROND
Male fern
(*Dryopteris filix-mas*)

CLUBMOSS
Lycopodium sp.

Stem with spirally arranged leaves

Branch

Strobilus (group of sporangia)

CLUBMOSS
Selaginella sp.

Epidermis (outer layer of cells)

Cortex (layer between epidermis and vascular tissue)

Vascular tissue — Phloem, Xylem

Lacuna (air space)

Rhizophore (leafless branch)

Shoot apex

Branch

Creeping stem with spirally arranged leaves

MICROGRAPH OF CROSS-SECTION THROUGH CLUBMOSS STEM

HORSETAIL
Common horsetail
(*Equisetum arvense*)

Apex of sterile shoot

Sporangiophore (structure carrying sporangia)

Strobilus (group of sporangia)

Non-photosynthetic fertile stem

Collar of small brown leaves

Young shoot

Lateral branch

Photosynthetic sterile stem

Node

Internode

Node

Tuber

Rhizome

Adventitious root

Endodermis (inner layer of cortex)

Vascular tissue

Sclerenchyma (strengthening tissue)

Epidermis (outer layer of cells)

Chlorenchyma (photosynthetic tissue)

Parenchyma (packing tissue)

Cortex (layer between epidermis and vascular tissue)

Hollow pith cavity

Vallecular canal (longitudinal channel)

Carinal canal (longitudinal channel)

MICROGRAPH OF CROSS-SECTION THROUGH HORSETAIL STEM

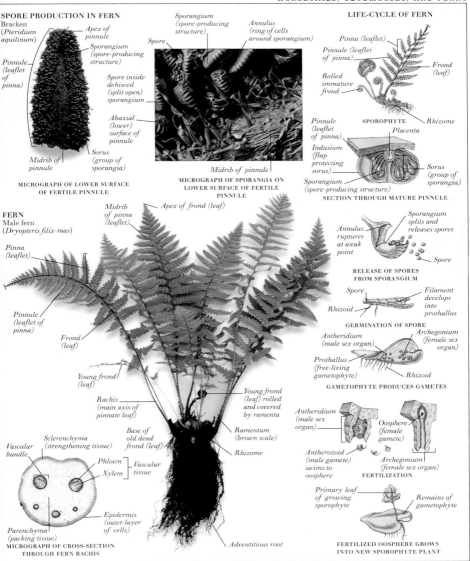

SPORE PRODUCTION IN FERN

Bracken
(*Pteridium
aquilinum*)

Apex of
pinnule

Sporangium
(spore-producing
structure)

Pinnule
(leaflet
of
pinna)

Midrib of
pinnule

Sorus
(group of
sporangia)

MICROGRAPH OF LOWER SURFACE
OF FERTILE PINNULE

Sporangium (spore-producing
structure)

Spore

Annulus
(ring of cells
around sporangium)

Spore inside
dehisced
(split open)
sporangium

Abaxial
(lower)
surface of
pinnule

Midrib of pinnule

MICROGRAPH OF SPORANGIA ON
LOWER SURFACE OF FERTILE
PINNULE

LIFE-CYCLE OF FERN

Pinna (leaflet)

Pinnule (leaflet
of pinna)

Rolled
immature
frond

Frond
(leaf)

Rhizome

SPOROPHYTE

Pinnule
(leaflet
of pinna)

Indusium
(flap
protecting
sorus)

Sporangium
(spore-producing structure)

Placenta

Sorus
(group of
sporangia)

SECTION THROUGH MATURE PINNULE

FERN
Male fern
(*Dryopteris filix-mas*)

Pinna
(leaflet)

Pinnule
(leaflet of
pinna)

Frond
(leaf)

Young frond
(leaf)

Midrib
of pinna
(leaflet)

Apex of frond (leaf)

Rachis
(main axis of
pinnate leaf)

Base of
old dead
frond (leaf)

Young frond
(leaf) rolled
and covered
by ramenta

Ramentum
(brown scale)

Rhizome

Sporangium
splits and
releases spores

Annulus
ruptures
at weak
point

Spore

RELEASE OF SPORES
FROM SPORANGIUM

Spore

Rhizoid

Filament
develops
into
prothallus

GERMINATION OF SPORE

Antheridium
(male sex organ)

Prothallus
(free-living
gametophyte)

Archegonium
(female sex
organ)

Rhizoid

GAMETOPHYTE PRODUCES GAMETES

Antheridium
(male sex
organ)

Antherozoid
(male gamete)
swims to
oosphere

Oosphere
(female
gamete)

Archegonium
(female sex organ)

FERTILIZATION

FERN (cross-section)

Vascular
bundle

Sclerenchyma
(strengthening tissue)

Phloem
Xylem

Vascular
tissue

Epidermis
(outer layer
of cells)

Parenchyma
(packing tissue)

MICROGRAPH OF CROSS-SECTION
THROUGH FERN RACHIS

Adventitious root

Primary leaf
of growing
sporophyte

Remains of
gametophyte

FERTILIZED OOSPHERE GROWS
INTO NEW SPOROPHYTE PLANT

Gymnosperms 1

THE GYMNOSPERMS ARE FOUR RELATED PHYLA of seed-producing plants; their seeds, however, lack the protective, outer covering that surrounds the seeds of flowering plants. Typically, gymnosperms are woody, perennial shrubs or trees, with stems, leaves, and roots, and a well-developed vascular (transportat) system. The reproductive structures in most gymnosperms are cones: male cones produce microspores in which male gametes (sex cells) develop; female cones produce megaspores in which female gametes develop. Microspores are blown by the wind to female cones, male and female gametes fuse during fertilization, and a seed develops. The four gymnosperm phyla are the conifers (phylum Coniferophyta), mostly tall trees; cycads (phylum Cycadophyta), small palmlike trees; the ginkgo or maidenhair tree (phylum Ginkgophyta), a tall tree with bilobed leaves; and gnetophytes (phylum Gnetophyta), a diverse group of plants, mainly shrubs, but also including the horizontally growing welwitschia.

LIFE-CYCLE OF SCOTS PINE
(*Pinus sylvestris*)

Needle (foliage leaf)

Cone

Ovuliferous scale (ovule- then seed-bearing structure)

MALE CONES YOUNG FEMALE CONE

Pollen grain in micropyle (entrance to ovule)

Ovuliferous scale

Pollen grain

Nucleus

Air sac

Ovule (contains female gamete)

POLLINATION

Integument (outer part of ovule)

Pollen tube (carries male gamete from pollen grain to ovum)

Archegonium (containing female gamete)

FERTILIZATION

Seed

Seed

Wing

MATURE FEMALE CONE AND WINGED SEED

SCALE AND SEEDS
Pine (*Pinus sp.*)

Ovuliferous scale (ovule- then seed-bearing structure)

Wing of seed derived from ovuliferous scale

Seed

Wing scar

Seed

Seed scar

Point of attachment to axis of cone

OVULIFEROUS SCALE FROM THIRD-YEAR FEMALE CONE

Plumule (embryonic shoot)

Cotyledon (seed leaf)

Root

GERMINATION OF PINE SEEDLING

Microsporangium (structure in which pollen grains are formed)

Microsporophyll (modified leaf carrying microsporangia)

Ovule (contains female gametes)

Bract scale

Axis of cone

Scale leaf

Ovuliferous scale (ovule- then seed-bearing structure)

Axis of cone

MICROGRAPH OF LONGITUDINAL SECTION THROUGH YOUNG MALE CONE

MICROGRAPH OF LONGITUDINAL SECTION THROUGH SECOND-YEAR FEMALE CONE

WELWITSCHIA
(*Welwitschia mirabilis*)

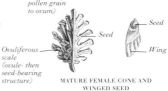
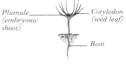

Frayed end of leaf

SMOOTH CYPRESS
(*Cupressus glabra*)

Immature female cone

Ovuliferous scale (ovule- then seed-bearing structure)

Mature female cone

Immature male cone

Scalelike leaf

Stem

Ovuliferous scale

Ovule (contains female gamete)

CROSS-SECTION THROUGH IMMATURE CONE

Ovuliferous scale (ovule- then seed-bearing structure)

Seed

CROSS-SECTION THROUGH MATURE CONE

Woody scale

Opening between woody scales through which seeds are released

DISCARDED CONE

YEW
(*Taxus baccata*)

Single ovule (contains female gamete)

Scale

Female "cone"

Developing seed

Scale

Scale

FEMALE "CONES" AT VARIOUS STAGES OF DEVELOPMENT

Seed

Aril (fleshy outgrowth from seed)

Stem

Needle (foliage leaf)

CYCAD
Sago palm
(*Cycas revoluta*)

Pinnate leaf

Scale leaf

Continuously growing leaf

Pinna (leaflet)

Old leaf base

Stem covered by scale leaves

MAIDENHAIR TREE
(*Ginkgo biloba*)

Stem

Petiole (leaf stalk)

Girdle scar

Bilobed leaf

Immature cone

Stalk scar

Woody stem

Site of cone growth

Adaxial (upper) surface of leaf

Abaxial (lower) surface of leaf

Frayed end of leaf

Gymnosperms 2

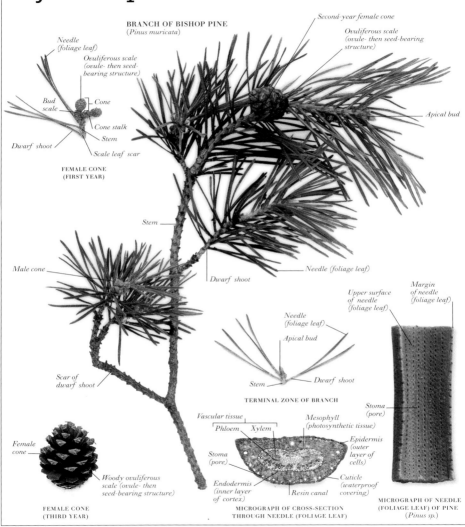

BRANCH OF BISHOP PINE
(*Pinus muricata*)

Second-year female cone

*Ovuliferous scale
(ovule- then seed-bearing
structure)*

*Needle
(foliage leaf)*

*Ovuliferous scale
(ovule- then seed-
bearing structure)*

*Bud
scale*

Cone

Cone stalk

Stem

Dwarf shoot

Scale leaf scar

Apical bud

**FEMALE CONE
(FIRST YEAR)**

Stem

Male cone

Stem

Needle (foliage leaf)

Dwarf shoot

*Margin
of needle
(foliage leaf)*

*Upper surface
of needle
(foliage leaf)*

*Needle
(foliage leaf)*

Apical bud

Stem   *Dwarf shoot*

TERMINAL ZONE OF BRANCH

*Scar of
dwarf shoot*

*Stoma
(pore)*

*Female
cone*

Vascular tissue

Phloem   *Xylem*

*Mesophyll
(photosynthetic tissue)*

*Stoma
(pore)*

*Epidermis
(outer
layer of
cells)*

*Woody ovuliferous
scale (ovule- then
seed-bearing structure)*

*Endodermis
(inner layer
of cortex)*

*Cuticle
(waterproof
covering)*

Resin canal

**FEMALE CONE
(THIRD YEAR)**

**MICROGRAPH OF CROSS-SECTION
THROUGH NEEDLE (FOLIAGE LEAF)**

**MICROGRAPH OF NEEDLE
(FOLIAGE LEAF) OF PINE**
(*Pinus sp.*)

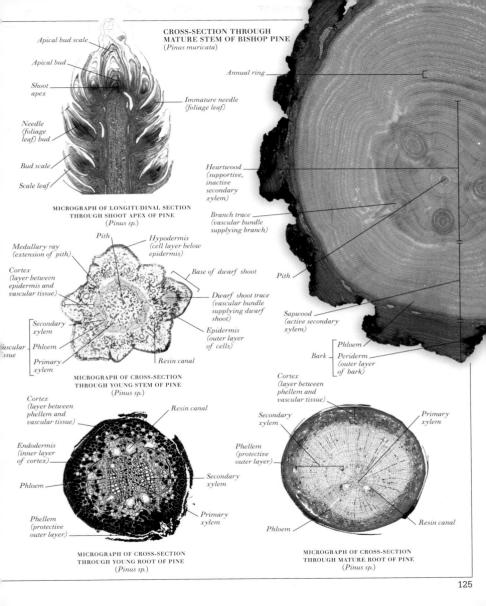

CROSS-SECTION THROUGH MATURE STEM OF BISHOP PINE
(*Pinus muricata*)

Apical bud scale

Apical bud

Shoot apex

Immature needle (foliage leaf)

Needle (foliage leaf) bud

Bud scale

Scale leaf

MICROGRAPH OF LONGITUDINAL SECTION THROUGH SHOOT APEX OF PINE
(*Pinus sp.*)

Annual ring

Heartwood (supportive, inactive secondary xylem)

Branch trace (vascular bundle supplying branch)

Pith

Sapwood (active secondary xylem)

Phloem

Bark — *Periderm (outer layer of bark)*

Pith

Hypodermis (cell layer below epidermis)

Medullary ray (extension of pith)

Cortex (layer between epidermis and vascular tissue)

Base of dwarf shoot

Dwarf shoot trace (vascular bundle supplying dwarf shoot)

Epidermis (outer layer of cells)

Secondary xylem

Phloem

Primary xylem

Vascular tissue

Resin canal

MICROGRAPH OF CROSS-SECTION THROUGH YOUNG STEM OF PINE
(*Pinus sp.*)

Cortex (layer between phellem and vascular tissue)

Resin canal

Cortex (layer between phellem and vascular tissue)

Secondary xylem

Primary xylem

Endodermis (inner layer of cortex)

Phellem (protective outer layer)

Phloem

Secondary xylem

Phloem

Primary xylem

Resin canal

Phellem (protective outer layer)

MICROGRAPH OF CROSS-SECTION THROUGH YOUNG ROOT OF PINE
(*Pinus sp.*)

MICROGRAPH OF CROSS-SECTION THROUGH MATURE ROOT OF PINE
(*Pinus sp.*)

Monocotyledons and dicotyledons

FLOWERING PLANTS (PHYLUM ANGIOSPERMOPHYTA) are divided into two classes: monocotyledons (class Monocotyledoneae) and dicotyledons (class Dicotyledoneae). Typically, monocotyledons have seeds with one cotyledon (seed leaf); their foliage leaves are narrow with parallel veins; the flower components occur in multiples of three; sepals and petals are indistinguishable and are known as tepals; vascular (transport) tissues are scattered in random bundles throughout the stem; and, since they lack stem cambium (actively dividing cells that produce wood), most monocotyledons are herbaceous (see pp. 128-129).

CROSS-SECTION THROUGH MONOCOTYLEDONOUS LEAF BASES

Dicotyledons have seeds with two cotyledons; leaves are broad with a central midrib and branched veins; flower parts occur in multiples of four or five; sepals are generally small and green; petals are large and colorful; vascular bundles are arranged in a ring around the edge of the stem; and, because many dicotyledons possess wood-producing stem cambium, there are woody forms (see pp. 130-131) as well as herbaceous ones.

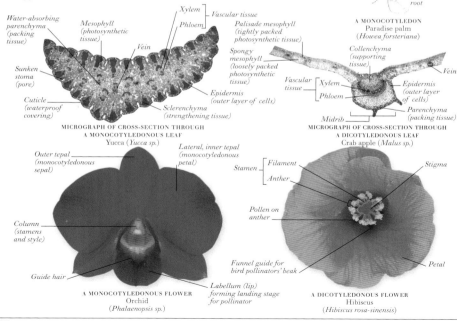

Vein (parallel venation)

Leaflet

Petiole (leaf stalk)

Emerging leaf

Leaf base

Adventitious root

A MONOCOTYLEDON
Paradise palm
(*Howea forsteriana*)

Water-absorbing parenchyma (packing tissue)

Mesophyll (photosynthetic tissue)

Vein

Sunken stoma (pore)

Cuticle (waterproof covering)

Xylem ⎤ Vascular tissue
Phloem ⎦

Sclerenchyma (strengthening tissue)

Epidermis (outer layer of cells)

MICROGRAPH OF CROSS-SECTION THROUGH A MONOCOTYLEDONOUS LEAF
Yucca (*Yucca sp.*)

Palisade mesophyll (tightly packed photosynthetic tissue)

Spongy mesophyll (loosely packed photosynthetic tissue)

Vascular tissue
Xylem
Phloem

Midrib

Collenchyma (supporting tissue)

Vein

Epidermis (outer layer of cells)

Parenchyma (packing tissue)

MICROGRAPH OF CROSS-SECTION THROUGH A DICOTYLEDONOUS LEAF
Crab apple (*Malus sp.*)

Outer tepal (monocotyledonous sepal)

Lateral, inner tepal (monocotyledonous petal)

Stamen ⎡ Filament
⎣ Anther

Pollen on anther

Column (stamens and style)

Guide hair

Labellum (lip) forming landing stage for pollinator

A MONOCOTYLEDONOUS FLOWER
Orchid
(*Phalaenopsis sp.*)

Stigma

Funnel guide for bird pollinators' beak

Petal

A DICOTYLEDONOUS FLOWER
Hibiscus
(*Hibiscus rosa-sinensis*)

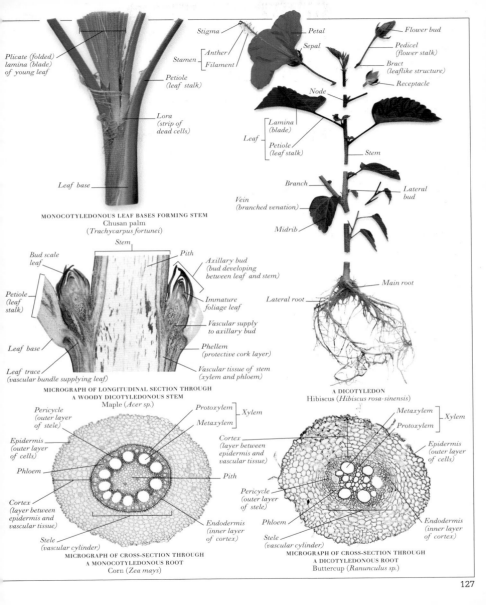

Plicate (folded) lamina (blade) of young leaf

Petiole (leaf stalk)

Stamen { Anther, Filament

Stigma

Petal

Sepal

Flower bud

Pedicel (flower stalk)

Bract (leaflike structure)

Receptacle

Node

Lora (strip of dead cells)

Leaf { Lamina (blade), Petiole (leaf stalk)

Stem

Leaf base

Branch

Lateral bud

Vein (branched venation)

Midrib

MONOCOTYLEDONOUS LEAF BASES FORMING STEM
Chusan palm
(*Trachycarpus fortunei*)

Stem

Bud scale leaf

Pith

Axillary bud (bud developing between leaf and stem)

Petiole (leaf stalk)

Immature foliage leaf

Vascular supply to axillary bud

Leaf base

Phellem (protective cork layer)

Leaf trace (vascular bundle supplying leaf)

Vascular tissue of stem (xylem and phloem)

Lateral root

Main root

Lateral root

MICROGRAPH OF LONGITUDINAL SECTION THROUGH A WOODY DICOTYLEDONOUS STEM
Maple (*Acer sp.*)

A DICOTYLEDON
Hibiscus (*Hibiscus rosa-sinensis*)

Pericycle (outer layer of stele)

Epidermis (outer layer of cells)

Phloem

Cortex (layer between epidermis and vascular tissue)

Stele (vascular cylinder)

Protoxylem } Xylem
Metaxylem

Pith

Endodermis (inner layer of cortex)

Metaxylem } Xylem
Protoxylem

Cortex (layer between epidermis and vascular tissue)

Epidermis (outer layer of cells)

Pericycle (outer layer of stele)

Phloem

Stele (vascular cylinder)

Endodermis (inner layer of cortex)

MICROGRAPH OF CROSS-SECTION THROUGH A MONOCOTYLEDONOUS ROOT
Corn (*Zea mays*)

MICROGRAPH OF CROSS-SECTION THROUGH A DICOTYLEDONOUS ROOT
Buttercup (*Ranunculus sp.*)

Herbaceous flowering plants

HERBACEOUS FLOWERING PLANTS TYPICALLY HAVE GREEN, NON-WOODY STEMS, and tend to be relatively short-lived. Many herbaceous plants live for only one or two years. Annuals (e.g., sweet peas) grow from seed, produce flowers and then seeds, and die within a single year. Biennials (e.g., carrots) have a two-year life cycle. In the first year, seeds grow into plants, which produce leaves and store food in underground storage organs; the stems and foliage then die back in winter. In the second year, new stems grow from the storage organs, produce leaves, flowers, and seeds, and then die. Some herbaceous plants (e.g., potatoes) are perennial. They grow back year after year, producing shoots and flowers in spring, storing food in underground tubers or rhizomes during summer, dying back in the fall, and surviving underground during winter.

Young plant forming

Petiole (stalk) of young leaf

Lateral root

Stipule (structure at base of leaf)

Trifoliate leaf

Node

Simple ovate leaflet

Root nodule

Main root

SWEET PEA
(*Lathyrus odoratus*)

STRAWBERRY
(*Fragaria* x *ananassa*)

Runner (creeping stem)

Lateral root scar

Remains of leaves

Stem

Leaf scar

Rib

Lateral root

Tap root

CARROT
(*Daucus carota*)

Leaf base

Spine (modified leaf)

Slender rhizome

Leaf scar

Petiole (leaf stalk)

Stem tuber

Adventitious root

Stem

Narrow, succulent leaf

Simple deltoid leaf

ROCK STONECROP
(*Sedum rupestre*)

POTATO
(*Solanum tuberosum*)

Adventitious root

PARTS OF HERBACEOUS FLOWERING PLANTS

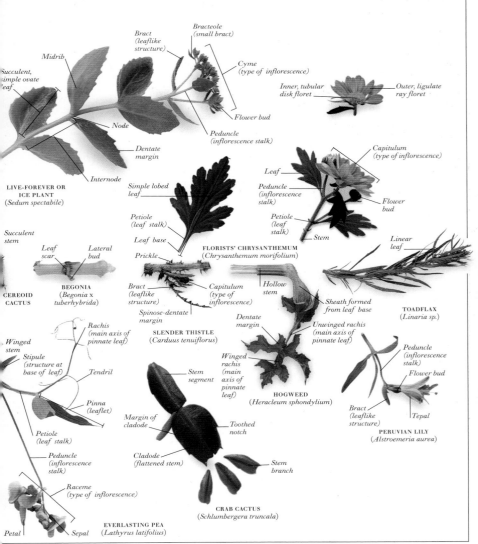

Bract
(leaflike
structure)

Bracteole
(small bract)

Cyme
(type of inflorescence)

Midrib

Succulent,
simple ovate
leaf

Node

Dentate
margin

Flower bud

Peduncle
(inflorescence stalk)

Inner, tubular
disk floret

Outer, ligulate
ray floret

**LIVE-FOREVER OR
ICE PLANT**
(*Sedum spectabile*)

Internode

Simple lobed
leaf

Petiole
(leaf stalk)

Leaf base

Capitulum
(type of inflorescence)

Leaf

Peduncle
(inflorescence
stalk)

Flower
bud

Petiole
(leaf
stalk)

Stem

Linear
leaf

Succulent
stem

Leaf
scar

Lateral
bud

Prickle

Bract
(leaflike
structure)

Capitulum
(type of
inflorescence)

Hollow
stem

Sheath formed
from leaf base

TOADFLAX
(*Linaria sp.*)

FLORISTS' CHRYSANTHEMUM
(*Chrysanthemum morifolium*)

**CEREOID
CACTUS**

BEGONIA
(*Begonia* x
tuberhybrida)

Spinose-dentate
margin

Dentate
margin

Unwinged rachis
(main axis of
pinnate leaf)

Peduncle
(inflorescence
stalk)

Flower bud

Rachis
(main axis of
pinnate leaf)

SLENDER THISTLE
(*Carduus tenuiflorus*)

Winged
stem

Stipule
(structure at
base of leaf)

Tendril

Stem
segment

Winged
rachis
(main
axis of
pinnate
leaf)

HOGWEED
(*Heracleum sphondylium*)

Bract
(leaflike
structure)

Tepal

PERUVIAN LILY
(*Alstroemeria aurea*)

Pinna
(leaflet)

Petiole
(leaf stalk)

Margin of
cladode

Toothed
notch

Peduncle
(inflorescence
stalk)

Cladode
(flattened stem)

Stem
branch

Raceme
(type of inflorescence)

Petal

Sepal

EVERLASTING PEA
(*Lathyrus latifolius*)

CRAB CACTUS
(*Schlumbergera truncata*)

Woody flowering plants

WOODY FLOWERING PLANTS ARE PERENNIAL, that is, they continue to grow and reproduce for many years. They have one or more permanent stems above ground, and numerous smaller branches. The stems and branches have a strong woody core that supports the plant and contains vascular tissue for transporting water and nutrients. Outside the woody core is a layer of tough, protective bark, which has lenticels (tiny pores) in it to enable gases to pass through. Woody flowering plants may be shrubs, which have several stems arising from the soil; bushes, which are shrubs with dense branching and foliage; or trees, which typically have a single upright stem (the trunk) that bears branches. Deciduous woody plants (e.g., roses) shed all their leaves once a year and remain leafless during winter. Evergreen woody plants (e.g., ivy) shed their leaves gradually, so retaining full leaf cover throughout the year.

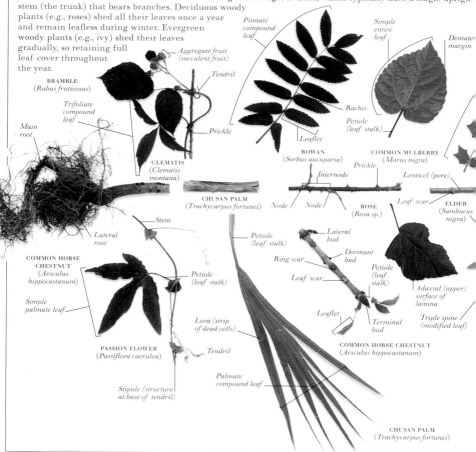

Aggregate fruit (succulent fruit)

Tendril

BRAMBLE
(*Rubus fruticosus*)

Trifoliate compound leaf

Main root

Prickle

Pinnate compound leaf

CLEMATIS
(*Clematis montana*)

Simple entire leaf

Dentate margin

Rachis

Petiole (leaf stalk)

Leaflet

ROWAN
(*Sorbus aucuparia*)

COMMON MULBERRY
(*Morus nigra*)

Prickle

Internode

CHUSAN PALM
(*Trachycarpus fortunei*)

Node   Node

Lenticel (pore)

Leaf scar

ROSE
(*Rosa sp.*)

ELDER
(*Sambucus nigra*)

Stem

Lateral root

COMMON HORSE CHESTNUT
(*Aesculus hippocastanum*)

Simple palmate leaf

PASSION FLOWER
(*Passiflora caerulea*)

Petiole (leaf stalk)

Petiole (leaf stalk)

Lora (strip of dead cells)

Tendril

Stipule (structure at base of tendril)

Palmate compound leaf

Lateral bud

Dormant bud

Ring scar

Leaf scar

Petiole (leaf stalk)

Leaflet

Terminal bud

Adaxial (upper) surface of lamina

Triple spine (modified leaf)

COMMON HORSE CHESTNUT
(*Aesculus hippocastanum*)

CHUSAN PALM
(*Trachycarpus fortunei*)

PARTS OF WOODY FLOWERING PLANTS

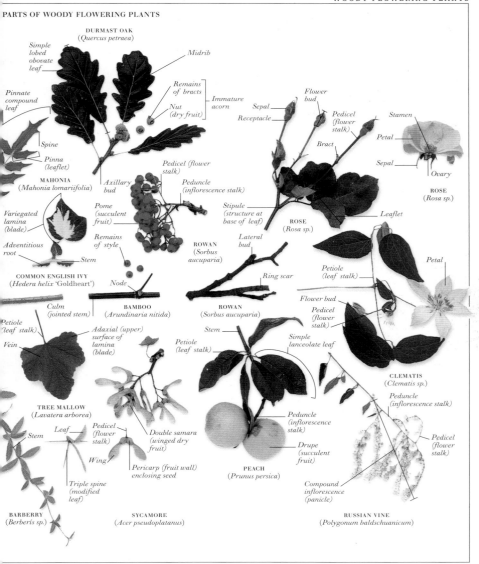

DURMAST OAK
(*Quercus petraea*)

Simple lobed obovate leaf

Midrib

Remains of bracts

Immature acorn

Nut (dry fruit)

Pinnate compound leaf

Spine

Pinna (leaflet)

MAHONIA
(*Mahonia lomariifolia*)

Axillary bud

Pedicel (flower stalk)

Peduncle (inflorescence stalk)

Pome (succulent fruit)

Remains of style

ROWAN
(*Sorbus aucuparia*)

COMMON ENGLISH IVY
(*Hedera helix* 'Goldheart')

Variegated lamina (blade)

Adventitious root

Stem

Node

Culm (jointed stem)

BAMBOO
(*Arundinaria nitida*)

Petiole (leaf stalk)

Vein

TREE MALLOW
(*Lavatera arborea*)

Adaxial (upper) surface of lamina (blade)

Flower bud

Sepal

Receptacle

Pedicel (flower stalk)

Bract

Stamen

Petal

Sepal

Ovary

ROSE
(*Rosa sp.*)

Stipule (structure at base of leaf)

ROSE
(*Rosa sp.*)

Leaflet

Lateral bud

Ring scar

ROWAN
(*Sorbus aucuparia*)

Petiole (leaf stalk)

Flower bud

Pedicel (flower stalk)

Petal

CLEMATIS
(*Clematis sp.*)

Stem

Petiole (leaf stalk)

Simple lanceolate leaf

Peduncle (inflorescence stalk)

Leaf

Pedicel (flower stalk)

Stem

Wing

Double samara (winged dry fruit)

Pericarp (fruit wall) enclosing seed

Triple spine (modified leaf)

BARBERRY
(*Berberis sp.*)

SYCAMORE
(*Acer pseudoplatanus*)

Peduncle (inflorescence stalk)

Drupe (succulent fruit)

PEACH
(*Prunus persica*)

Pedicel (flower stalk)

Compound inflorescence (panicle)

RUSSIAN VINE
(*Polygonum baldschuanicum*)

Roots

ROOTS ARE THE UNDERGROUND PARTS OF PLANTS. They have
three main functions. First, they anchor the plant in the soil.
Second, they absorb water and minerals from the spaces
between soil particles; the roots' absorptive properties are
increased by root hairs, which grow behind the root tip,
allowing maximum uptake of vital substances. Third, the
root is part of the plant's transport system: xylem carries
water and minerals from the roots to the stem and leaves,
and phloem carries nutrients from the leaves to all parts of
the root system. In addition, some roots (e.g., carrots) are food
stores. Roots have an outer epidermis covering a cortex of parenchyma
(packing tissue), and a central cylinder of vascular tissue. This arrangement
helps the roots resist the forces of compression as they grow through the soil.

Split in testa as seed germinates

Cotyledon (seed leaf)

Primary root

Testa (seed coat)

Root hair

CARROT
(*Daucus carota*)

FEATURES OF A TYPICAL ROOT
Buttercup
(*Ranunculus sp.*)

Stele (vascular cylinder)

Phloem sieve tube (through which nutrients are transported)

Root tip (region of cell division)

Pericycle (outer layer of stele)

Companion cell (cell associated with phloem sieve tube)

Root hair

Cortex (layer between epidermis and vascular tissue)

Air space (allowing gas diffusion in the root)

Root hair

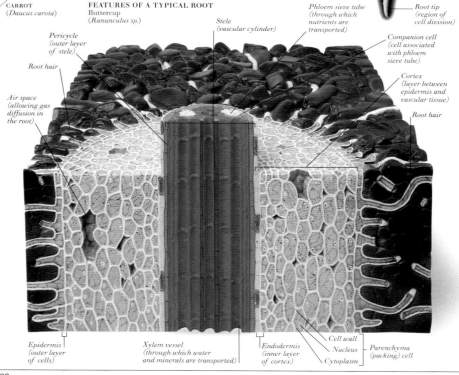

Epidermis (outer layer of cells)

Xylem vessel (through which water and minerals are transported)

Endodermis (inner layer of cortex)

Cell wall

Nucleus

Cytoplasm

Parenchyma (packing) cell

PRIMARY ROOT AND MICROGRAPHS OF SECTIONS THROUGH ROOTS

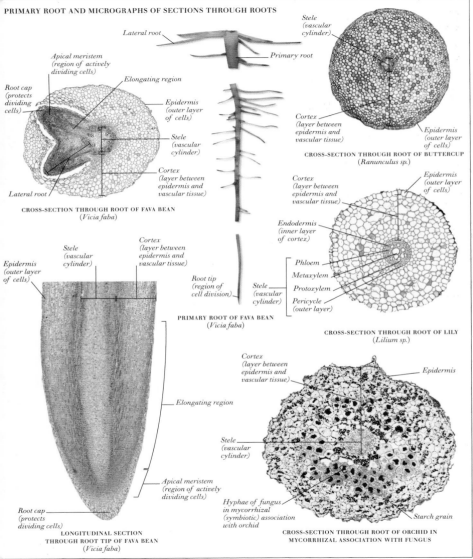

Lateral root

Primary root

Apical meristem (region of actively dividing cells)

Elongating region

Root cap (protects dividing cells)

Epidermis (outer layer of cells)

Stele (vascular cylinder)

Cortex (layer between epidermis and vascular tissue)

Lateral root

CROSS-SECTION THROUGH ROOT OF FAVA BEAN
(*Vicia faba*)

Stele (vascular cylinder)

Cortex (layer between epidermis and vascular tissue)

Epidermis (outer layer of cells)

Root tip (region of cell division)

Elongating region

Apical meristem (region of actively dividing cells)

Root cap (protects dividing cells)

LONGITUDINAL SECTION THROUGH ROOT TIP OF FAVA BEAN
(*Vicia faba*)

PRIMARY ROOT OF FAVA BEAN
(*Vicia faba*)

Stele (vascular cylinder)

Cortex (layer between epidermis and vascular tissue)

Epidermis (outer layer of cells)

CROSS-SECTION THROUGH ROOT OF BUTTERCUP
(*Ranunculus sp.*)

Cortex (layer between epidermis and vascular tissue)

Endodermis (inner layer of cortex)

Phloem
Metaxylem
Protoxylem
Pericycle (outer layer)

Stele (vascular cylinder)

Epidermis (outer layer of cells)

CROSS-SECTION THROUGH ROOT OF LILY
(*Lilium sp.*)

Cortex (layer between epidermis and vascular tissue)

Epidermis

Stele (vascular cylinder)

Hyphae of fungus in mycorrhizal (symbiotic) association with orchid

Starch grain

CROSS-SECTION THROUGH ROOT OF ORCHID IN MYCORRHIZAL ASSOCIATION WITH FUNGUS

Stems

THE STEM IS THE MAIN SUPPORTIVE PART OF A PLANT that grows above ground. Stems bear leaves (organs of photosynthesis), which grow at nodes; buds (shoots covered by protective scales), which grow at the stem tip (apical or terminal buds) and in the angle between a leaf and the stem (axillary or lateral buds); and flowers (reproductive structures). The stem forms part of the plant's transport system: xylem tissue in the stem transports water and minerals from the roots to the aerial parts of the plant, and phloem tissue transports nutrients manufactured in the leaves to other parts of the plant. Stem tissues are also used for storing water and food. Herbaceous (non-woody) stems have an outer protective epidermis covering a cortex that consists mainly of parenchyma (packing tissue) but also has some collenchyma (supporting tissue). The vascular tissue of such stems is arranged in bundles, each of which consists of xylem, phloem, and sclerenchyma (strengthening tissue). Woody stems have an outer protective layer of tough bark, which is perforated with lenticels (pores) to allow gas exchange. Inside the bark is a ring of secondary phloem, which surrounds an inner core of secondary xylem.

MICROGRAPH OF LONGITUDINAL SECTION THROUGH APEX OF STEM
Coleus sp.

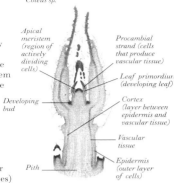

Apical meristem (region of actively dividing cells)

Procambial strand (cells that produce vascular tissue)

Leaf primordium (developing leaf)

Developing bud

Cortex (layer between epidermis and vascular tissue)

Vascular tissue

Pith

Epidermis (outer layer of cells)

YOUNG WOODY STEM
Lime
(Tilia sp.)

EMERGENT BUDS
London plane
(Platanus x acerifolia)

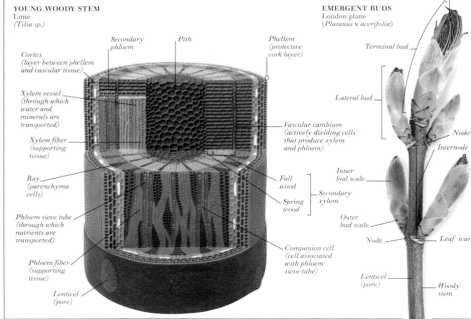

Secondary phloem

Pith

Phellem (protective cork layer)

Cortex (layer between phellem and vascular tissue)

Xylem vessel (through which water and minerals are transported)

Xylem fiber (supporting tissue)

Ray (parenchyma cells)

Phloem sieve tube (through which nutrients are transported)

Phloem fiber (supporting tissue)

Lenticel (pore)

Vascular cambium (actively dividing cells that produce xylem and phloem)

Fall wood

Spring wood

Companion cell (cell associated with phloem sieve tube)

Young leaves emerge

Terminal bud

Lateral bud

Node

Internode

Inner bud scale

Secondary xylem

Outer bud scale

Node

Leaf scar

Lenticel (pore)

Woody stem

MICROGRAPHS OF CROSS-SECTIONS THROUGH VARIOUS STEMS

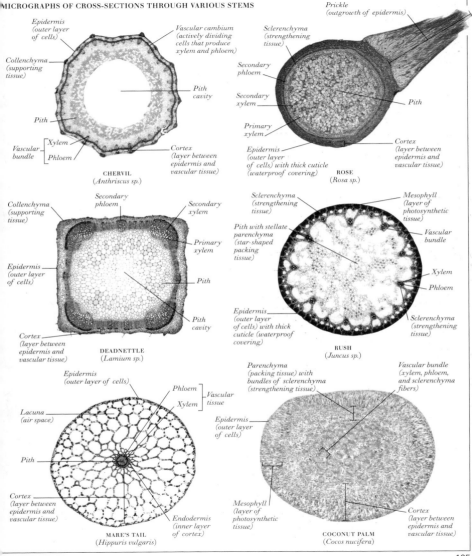

Prickle
(outgrowth of epidermis)

Epidermis
(outer layer
of cells)

Vascular cambium
(actively dividing
cells that produce
xylem and phloem)

Sclerenchyma
(strengthening
tissue)

Collenchyma
(supporting
tissue)

Secondary
phloem

Pith
cavity

Pith

Pith

Secondary
xylem

Vascular
bundle { Xylem
Phloem }

Primary
xylem

Cortex
(layer between
epidermis and
vascular tissue)

Epidermis
(outer layer
of cells) with thick cuticle
(waterproof covering)

Cortex
(layer between
epidermis and
vascular tissue)

CHERVIL
(*Anthriscus sp.*)

ROSE
(*Rosa sp.*)

Collenchyma
(supporting
tissue)

Secondary
phloem

Secondary
xylem

Sclerenchyma
(strengthening
tissue)

Mesophyll
(layer of
photosynthetic
tissue)

Primary
xylem

Pith with stellate
parenchyma
(star-shaped
packing
tissue)

Vascular
bundle

Epidermis
(outer layer
of cells)

Pith

Xylem

Phloem

Cortex
(layer between
epidermis and
vascular tissue)

Pith
cavity

Epidermis
(outer layer
of cells) with thick
cuticle (waterproof
covering)

Sclerenchyma
(strengthening
tissue)

DEADNETTLE
(*Lamium sp.*)

RUSH
(*Juncus sp.*)

Epidermis
(outer layer of cells)

Phloem
Xylem } Vascular
tissue

Parenchyma
(packing tissue) with
bundles of sclerenchyma
(strengthening tissue)

Vascular bundle
(xylem, phloem,
and sclerenchyma
fibers)

Lacuna
(air space)

Epidermis
(outer layer
of cells)

Pith

Cortex
(layer between
epidermis and
vascular tissue)

Endodermis
(inner layer
of cortex)

Mesophyll
(layer of
photosynthetic
tissue)

Cortex
(layer between
epidermis and
vascular tissue)

MARE'S TAIL
(*Hippuris vulgaris*)

COCONUT PALM
(*Cocos nucifera*)

Leaves

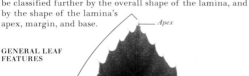

CHECKERBLOOM
(*Sidalcea malviflora*)

LEAVES ARE THE MAIN SITES OF PHOTOSYNTHESIS (see pp. 138-139) and transpiration (water loss by evaporation) in plants. A typical leaf consists of a thin, flat lamina (blade) supported by a network of veins; a petiole (leaf stalk); and a leaf base, where the petiole joins the stem. Leaves can be classified as simple, in which the lamina is a single unit, or compound, in which the lamina is divided into separate leaflets. Compound leaves may be pinnate, with pinnae (leaflets) on both sides of a rachis (main axis), or palmate, with leaflets arising from a single point at the tip of the petiole. Leaves can be classified further by the overall shape of the lamina, and by the shape of the lamina's apex, margin, and base.

SIMPLE LEAF SHAPES

Subacute apex

Acuminate apex

Entire margin

Entire margin

Cuneate base

Cordate base

PANDURIFORM
Croton
(*Codiaeum variegatum*)

LANCEOLATE
Sea buckthorn
(*Hippophae rhamnoides*)

GENERAL LEAF FEATURES

Apex

Lamina (blade)

Midrib

Margin

Lateral vein

Lamina base

Petiole (leaf stalk)

Leaf base

Sweet chestnut
(*Castanea sativa*)

COMPOUND LEAF SHAPES

Terminal pinna (leaflet)

Emarginate apex

Rachis (main axis of pinnate leaf)

Pinna (leaflet)

Petiolule (leaflet stalk)

Petiole (leaf stalk)

ODD PINNATE
False acacia
(*Robinia pseudoacacia*)

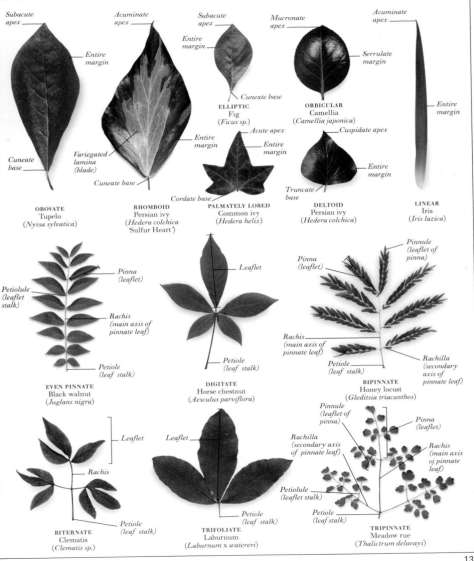

Subacute apex

Entire margin

Cuneate base

OBOVATE
Tupelo
(*Nyssa sylvatica*)

Acuminate apex

Variegated lamina (blade)

Entire margin

Cuneate base

RHOMBOID
Persian ivy
(*Hedera colchica* 'Sulfur Heart')

Subacute apex

Entire margin

Cuneate base

ELLIPTIC
Fig
(*Ficus sp.*)

Acute apex

Entire margin

Entire margin

Cordate base

PALMATELY LOBED
Common ivy
(*Hedera helix*)

Mucronate apex

Serrulate margin

ORBICULAR
Camellia
(*Camellia japonica*)

Cuspidate apex

Entire margin

Truncate base

DELTOID
Persian ivy
(*Hedera colchica*)

Acuminate apex

Entire margin

LINEAR
Iris
(*Iris lazica*)

Pinna (leaflet)

Petiolule (leaflet stalk)

Rachis (main axis of pinnate leaf)

Petiole (leaf stalk)

EVEN PINNATE
Black walnut
(*Juglans nigra*)

Leaflet

Petiole (leaf stalk)

DIGITATE
Horse chestnut
(*Aesculus parviflora*)

Pinna (leaflet)

Pinnule (leaflet of pinna)

Rachis (main axis of pinnate leaf)

Petiole (leaf stalk)

Rachilla (secondary axis of pinnate leaf)

BIPINNATE
Honey locust
(*Gleditsia triacanthos*)

Leaflet

Rachis

Petiole (leaf stalk)

BITERNATE
Clematis
(*Clematis sp.*)

Leaflet

Petiole (leaf stalk)

TRIFOLIATE
Laburnum
(*Laburnum* x *watereri*)

Pinnule (leaflet of pinna)

Rachilla (secondary axis of pinnate leaf)

Petiolule (leaflet stalk)

Pinna (leaflet)

Rachis (main axis of pinnate leaf)

Petiole (leaf stalk)

TRIPINNATE
Meadow rue
(*Thalictrum delavayi*)

Photosynthesis

PHOTOSYNTHESIS IS THE PROCESS by which plants make their food using sunlight, water, and carbon dioxide. It takes place inside special structures in leaf cells called chloroplasts. The chloroplasts contain chlorophyll, a green pigment that absorbs energy from sunlight. During photosynthesis, the absorbed energy is used to join together carbon dioxide and water to form the sugar glucose, which is the energy source for the whole plant; oxygen, a waste product, is released into the air. Leaves are the main sites of photosynthesis, and have various adaptations for that purpose: flat laminae (blades) provide a large surface for absorbing sunlight; stomata (pores) in the lower surface of the laminae allow gases (carbon dioxide and oxygen) to pass into and out of the leaves; and an extensive network of veins brings water into the leaves and transports the glucose produced by photosynthesis to the rest of the plant.

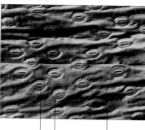

MICROGRAPH OF LEAF
Lily (*Lilium sp.*)

Stoma (pore) | Guard cell (controls opening and closing of stoma) | Lower surface of lamina (blade)

THE PROCESS OF PHOTOSYNTHESIS

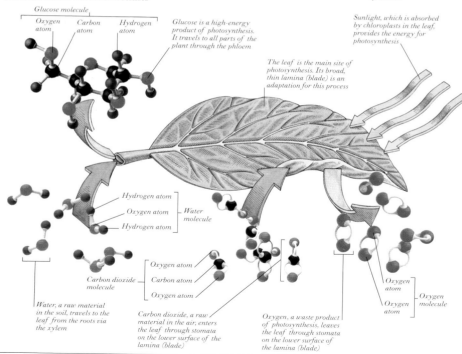

Glucose molecule
Oxygen atom
Carbon atom
Hydrogen atom

Glucose is a high-energy product of photosynthesis. It travels to all parts of the plant through the phloem

Sunlight, which is absorbed by chloroplasts in the leaf, provides the energy for photosynthesis

The leaf is the main site of photosynthesis. Its broad, thin lamina (blade) is an adaptation for this process

Hydrogen atom
Oxygen atom
Hydrogen atom
Water molecule

Carbon dioxide molecule
Oxygen atom
Carbon atom
Oxygen atom

Oxygen atom
Oxygen atom
Oxygen molecule

Water, a raw material in the soil, travels to the leaf from the roots via the xylem

Carbon dioxide, a raw material in the air, enters the leaf through stomata on the lower surface of the lamina (blade)

Oxygen, a waste product of photosynthesis, leaves the leaf through stomata on the lower surface of the lamina (blade)

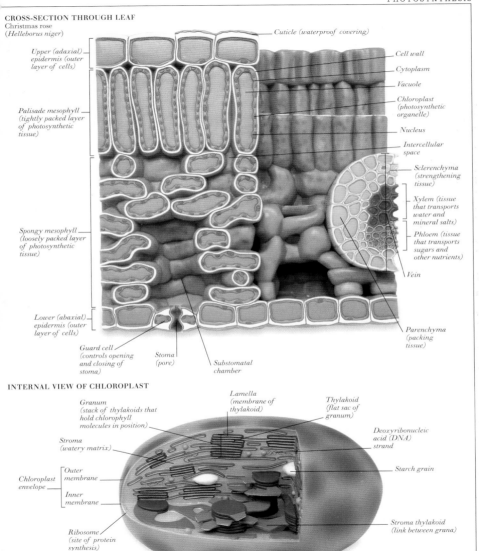

CROSS-SECTION THROUGH LEAF
Christmas rose
(*Helleborus niger*)

Cuticle (waterproof covering)

*Upper (adaxial)
epidermis (outer
layer of cells)*

Cell wall

Cytoplasm

Vacuole

*Chloroplast
(photosynthetic
organelle)*

*Palisade mesophyll
(tightly packed layer
of photosynthetic
tissue)*

Nucleus

*Intercellular
space*

*Sclerenchyma
(strengthening
tissue)*

*Xylem (tissue
that transports
water and
mineral salts)*

*Phloem (tissue
that transports
sugars and
other nutrients)*

*Spongy mesophyll
(loosely packed layer
of photosynthetic
tissue)*

Vein

*Lower (abaxial)
epidermis (outer
layer of cells)*

*Parenchyma
(packing
tissue)*

*Guard cell
(controls opening
and closing of
stoma)*

*Stoma
(pore)*

*Substomatal
chamber*

INTERNAL VIEW OF CHLOROPLAST

*Lamella
(membrane of
thylakoid)*

*Granum
(stack of thylakoids that
hold chlorophyll
molecules in position)*

*Thylakoid
(flat sac of
granum)*

*Deoxyribonucleic
acid (DNA)
strand*

*Stroma
(watery matrix)*

Starch grain

*Chloroplast
envelope*

*Outer
membrane*

*Inner
membrane*

*Stroma thylakoid
(link between grana)*

*Ribosome
(site of protein
synthesis)*

Flowers 1

FLOWERS ARE THE SITES OF SEXUAL REPRODUCTION in flowering plants. Their component parts are arranged in whorls around the receptacle (tip of the flower stalk). The sepals (collectively called the calyx) are outermost; typically small and green, they protect the developing flower. The petals (collectively called the corolla) are typically large and brightly colored; they are found inside the sepals. In monocotyledonous flowers (see pp. 126-127), sepals and petals are indistinguishable; individually they are called tepals (collectively called the perianth). The petals surround the male and female reproductive structures (androecium and gynoecium). The androecium consists of stamens (male organs); each stamen is made up of a filament (stalk) and anther. The gynoecium has one or more carpels (female organs); each carpel consists of an ovary, style, and stigma. Some flowers (e.g., lily) occur singly on a pedicel (flower stalk); others (e.g., elder, sunflower) are arranged in a group (inflorescence) on a peduncle (inflorescence stalk).

A MONOCOTYLEDONOUS FLOWER
Lily
(*Lilium* sp.)

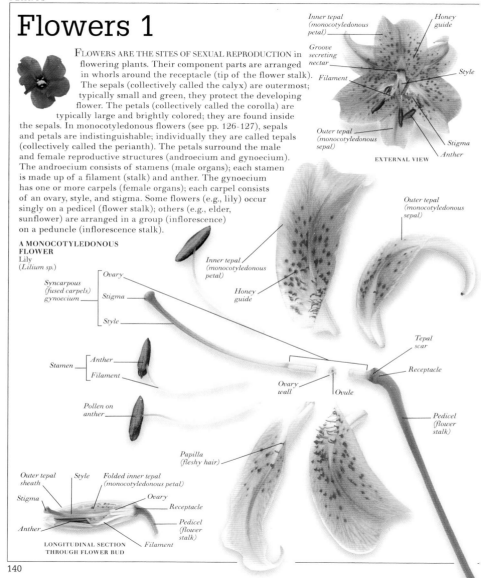

Inner tepal (monocotyledonous petal)

Honey guide

Groove secreting nectar

Filament

Style

Outer tepal (monocotyledonous sepal)

Stigma

Anther

EXTERNAL VIEW

Inner tepal (monocotyledonous petal)

Honey guide

Outer tepal (monocotyledonous sepal)

Syncarpous (fused carpels) gynoecium

Ovary

Stigma

Style

Tepal scar

Receptacle

Stamen

Anther

Filament

Pollen on anther

Ovary wall

Ovule

Pedicel (flower stalk)

Papilla (fleshy hair)

Outer tepal sheath

Style

Folded inner tepal (monocotyledonous petal)

Stigma

Ovary

Receptacle

Anther

Pedicel (flower stalk)

LONGITUDINAL SECTION THROUGH FLOWER BUD

Filament

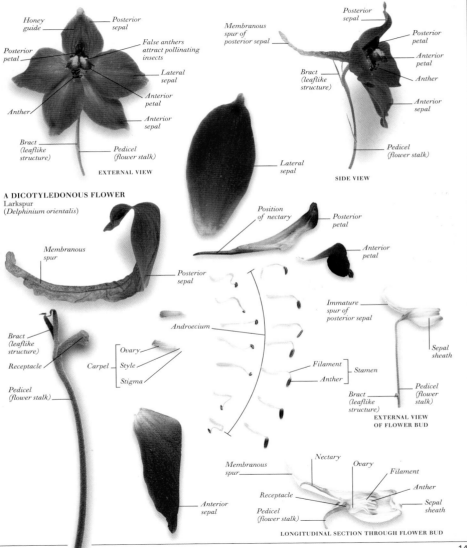

Honey guide

Posterior sepal

False anthers attract pollinating insects

Posterior petal

Lateral sepal

Anterior petal

Anther

Anterior sepal

Bract (leaflike structure)

Pedicel (flower stalk)

EXTERNAL VIEW

Posterior sepal

Membranous spur of posterior sepal

Posterior petal

Anterior petal

Anther

Bract (leaflike structure)

Anterior sepal

Pedicel (flower stalk)

SIDE VIEW

A DICOTYLEDONOUS FLOWER
Larkspur
(*Delphinium orientalis*)

Membranous spur

Lateral sepal

Position of nectary

Posterior petal

Anterior petal

Posterior sepal

Androecium

Immature spur of posterior sepal

Bract (leaflike structure)

Receptacle

Ovary

Style

Stigma

Carpel

Filament

Anther

Stamen

Sepal sheath

Bract (leaflike structure)

Pedicel (flower stalk)

EXTERNAL VIEW OF FLOWER BUD

Pedicel (flower stalk)

Anterior sepal

Membranous spur

Nectary

Ovary

Filament

Anther

Receptacle

Sepal sheath

Pedicel (flower stalk)

LONGITUDINAL SECTION THROUGH FLOWER BUD

141

Flowers 2

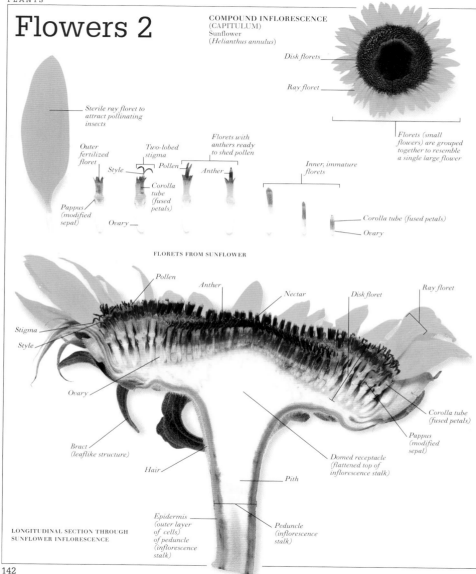

COMPOUND INFLORESCENCE
(CAPITULUM)
Sunflower
(*Helianthus annulus*)

Disk florets

Ray floret

Florets (small flowers) are grouped together to resemble a single large flower

Sterile ray floret to attract pollinating insects

Outer fertilized floret

Two-lobed stigma

Style

Pollen

Anther

Florets with anthers ready to shed pollen

Inner, immature florets

Corolla tube (fused petals)

Ovary

Pappus (modified sepal)

Corolla tube (fused petals)

Ovary

FLORETS FROM SUNFLOWER

Pollen

Anther

Nectar

Disk floret

Ray floret

Stigma

Style

Ovary

Corolla tube (fused petals)

Pappus (modified sepal)

Bract (leaflike structure)

Hair

Domed receptacle (flattened top of inflorescence stalk)

Pith

LONGITUDINAL SECTION THROUGH SUNFLOWER INFLORESCENCE

Epidermis (outer layer of cells) of peduncle (inflorescence stalk)

Peduncle (inflorescence stalk)

ARRANGEMENT OF FLOWERS ON STEM

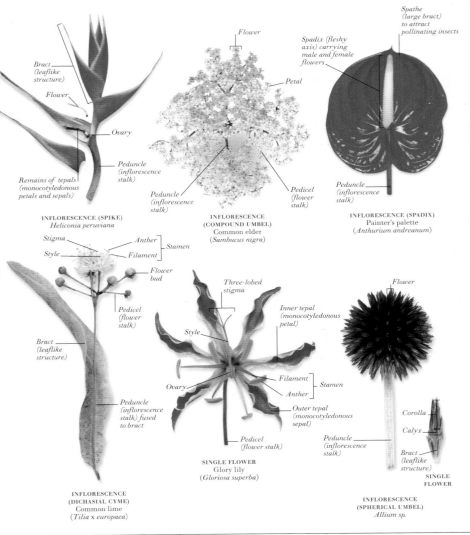

Bract
(leaflike
structure)

Flower

Ovary

Peduncle
(inflorescence
stalk)

Remains of tepals
(monocotyledonous
petals and sepals)

INFLORESCENCE (SPIKE)
Heliconia peruviana

Flower

Petal

Peduncle
(inflorescence
stalk)

Pedicel
(flower
stalk)

**INFLORESCENCE
(COMPOUND UMBEL)**
Common elder
(*Sambucus nigra*)

Spathe
(large bract)
to attract
pollinating insects

Spadix (fleshy
axis) carrying
male and female
flowers

Peduncle
(inflorescence
stalk)

INFLORESCENCE (SPADIX)
Painter's palette
(*Anthurium andreanum*)

Stigma

Anther

Style

Filament

Stamen

Flower
bud

Pedicel
(flower
stalk)

Bract
(leaflike
structure)

Peduncle
(inflorescence
stalk) fused
to bract

**INFLORESCENCE
(DICHASIAL CYME)**
Common lime
(*Tilia x europaea*)

Three-lobed
stigma

Inner tepal
(monocotyledonous
petal)

Style

Ovary

Filament

Anther

Stamen

Outer tepal
(monocotyledonous
sepal)

Pedicel
(flower stalk)

SINGLE FLOWER
Glory lily
(*Gloriosa superba*)

Flower

Corolla

Calyx

Peduncle
(inflorescence
stalk)

Bract
(leaflike
structure)

**SINGLE
FLOWER**

**INFLORESCENCE
(SPHERICAL UMBEL)**
Allium sp.

Pollination

POLLINATION IS THE TRANSFER OF POLLEN (which contains the male sex cells) from an anther (part of the male reproductive organ) to a stigma (part of the female reproductive organ). This process precedes fertilization (see pp. 146-147). Pollination may occur within the same flower (self-pollination), or between flowers on separate plants of the same species (cross-pollination). In most plants, pollination is carried out either by insects (entomophilous pollination) or by the wind (anemophilous pollination). Less commonly, birds, bats, or water are the agents of pollination. Insect-pollinated flowers are typically brightly colored, scented, and produce nectar, on which insects feed. Such flowers also tend to have patterns that are visible only in ultraviolet light, which many insects can see but which humans cannot. These features attract insects, which become covered with the sticky or hooked pollen grains when they visit one flower, and then transfer the pollen to the next flower they visit. Wind-pollinated flowers are generally small, relatively inconspicuous, and unscented. They produce large quantities of light pollen grains that are easily blown by the wind to other flowers.

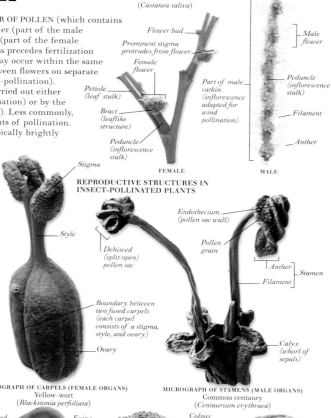

REPRODUCTIVE STRUCTURES IN WIND-POLLINATED PLANT
Sweet chestnut
(*Castanea saliva*)

Flower bud

Prominent stigma protrudes from flower

Female flower

Petiole (leaf stalk)

Bract (leaflike structure)

Peduncle (inflorescence stalk)

Part of male catkin (inflorescence adapted for wind pollination)

Male flower

Peduncle (inflorescence stalk)

Filament

Anther

FEMALE

MALE

REPRODUCTIVE STRUCTURES IN INSECT-POLLINATED PLANTS

Stigma

Style

Dehisced (split open) pollen sac

Boundary between two fused carpels (each carpel consists of a stigma, style, and ovary)

Ovary

Endothecium (pollen sac wall)

Pollen grain

Anther

Filament

Stamen

Calyx (whorl of sepals)

MICROGRAPHS OF POLLEN GRAINS

Exine (outer coat of pollen grain)

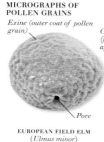

Pore

EUROPEAN FIELD ELM
(*Ulmus minor*)

Colpus (furrow-shaped aperture)

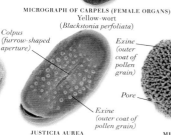

Exine (outer coat of pollen grain)

MICROGRAPH OF CARPELS (FEMALE ORGANS)
Yellow-wort
(*Blackstonia perfoliata*)

JUSTICIA AUREA

Exine (outer coat of pollen grain)

Pore

Baculum (rod-shaped structure)

MEADOW CRANESBILL
(*Geranium pratense*)

MICROGRAPH OF STAMENS (MALE ORGANS)
Common centaury
(*Centaurium erythraea*)

Colpus (furrow-shaped aperture)

Exine (outer coat of pollen grain)

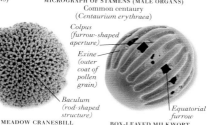

Equatorial furrow

BOX-LEAVED MILKWORT
(*Polygala chamaebuxus*)

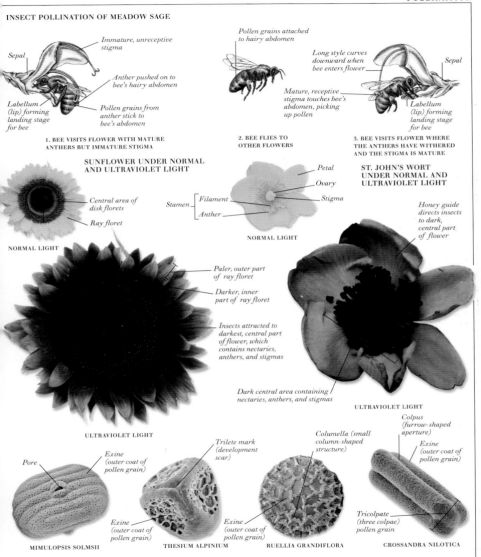

INSECT POLLINATION OF MEADOW SAGE

Sepal

Immature, unreceptive stigma

Anther pushed on to bee's hairy abdomen

Labellum (lip) forming landing stage for bee

Pollen grains from anther stick to bee's abdomen

1. BEE VISITS FLOWER WITH MATURE ANTHERS BUT IMMATURE STIGMA

Pollen grains attached to hairy abdomen

2. BEE FLIES TO OTHER FLOWERS

Long style curves downward when bee enters flower

Mature, receptive stigma touches bee's abdomen, picking up pollen

Sepal

Labellum (lip) forming landing stage for bee

3. BEE VISITS FLOWER WHERE THE ANTHERS HAVE WITHERED AND THE STIGMA IS MATURE

SUNFLOWER UNDER NORMAL AND ULTRAVIOLET LIGHT

Central area of disk florets

Ray floret

NORMAL LIGHT

Petal

Ovary

Stamen { Filament / Anther }

Stigma

NORMAL LIGHT

ST. JOHN'S WORT UNDER NORMAL AND ULTRAVIOLET LIGHT

Honey guide directs insects to dark, central part of flower

Paler, outer part of ray floret

Darker, inner part of ray floret

Insects attracted to darkest, central part of flower, which contains nectaries, anthers, and stigmas

Dark central area containing nectaries, anthers, and stigmas

ULTRAVIOLET LIGHT

ULTRAVIOLET LIGHT

Pore

Exine (outer coat of pollen grain)

MIMULOPSIS SOLMSH

Trilete mark (development scar)

Exine (outer coat of pollen grain)

THESIUM ALPINIUM

Columella (small column-shaped structure)

Exine (outer coat of pollen grain)

RUELLIA GRANDIFLORA

Colpus (furrow-shaped aperture)

Exine (outer coat of pollen grain)

Tricolpate (three colpae) pollen grain

CROSSANDRA NILOTICA

Fertilization

FERTILIZATION IS THE FUSION of male and female gametes (sex cells) to produce a zygote (embryo). Following pollination (see pp. 144-145), the pollen grains that contain the male gametes are on the stigma, some distance from the female gamete (ovum) inside the ovule. To enable the gametes to meet, the pollen grain germinates and produces a pollen tube, which grows down and enters the embryo sac (the inner part of the ovule that contains the ovum). Two male gametes, traveling at the tip of the pollen tube, enter the embryo sac. One gamete fuses with the ovum to produce a zygote that will develop into an embryo plant. The other male gamete fuses with two polar nuclei to produce the endosperm, which acts as a food supply for the developing embryo. Fertilization also initiates other changes: the integument (outer part of ovule) forms a testa (seed coat) around the embryo and endosperm; the petals fall off; the stigma and style wither; and the ovary wall forms a layer (called the pericarp) around the seed. Together, the pericarp and seed form the fruit, which may be succulent (see pp. 148-149) or dry (see pp. 150-151).

In some species (e.g., blackberry), apomixis can occur: the seed develops without fertilization of the ovum by a male gamete but endosperm formation and fruit development take place as in other species.

BANANA
(*Musa 'lacatan'*)

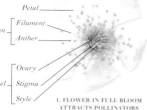

Stamen
- Petal
- Filament
- Anther

Carpel
- Ovary
- Stigma
- Style

1. FLOWER IN FULL BLOOM
ATTRACTS POLLINATORS

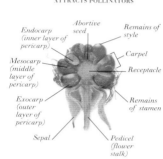

Endocarp (inner layer of pericarp)

Abortive seed

Remains of style

Carpel

Mesocarp (middle layer of pericarp)

Receptacle

Exocarp (outer layer of pericarp)

Remains of stamen

Sepal

Pedicel (flower stalk)

4. PERICARP FORMS
FLESH, SKIN, AND A HARD INNER
LAYER (SHOWN IN CROSS-SECTION)

Exocarp (outer layer of pericarp)

Carpel

Remains of style

Remains of stamen

Remains of sepal

Pedicel (flower stalk)

7. MESOCARP (FLESHY PART OF PERICARP)
OF EACH CARPEL STARTS TO
CHANGE COLOR

Exocarp (outer layer of pericarp)

Drupelet

Remains of style

Remains of stamen

Remains of sepal

Pedicel (flower stalk)

8. CARPELS MATURE INTO DRUPELETS
(SMALL FLESHY FRUITS WITH SINGLE SEEDS
SURROUNDED BY HARD ENDOCARP)

Exocarp (outer layer of pericarp)

Drupelet

Remains of style

Remains of sepal

Remains of stamen

Pedicel (flower stalk)

9. MESOCARP OF DRUPELET BECOMES
DARKER AND SWEETER

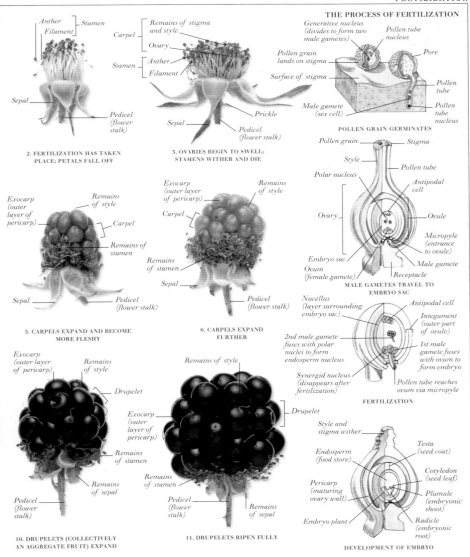

THE PROCESS OF FERTILIZATION

Generative nucleus (divides to form two male gametes)

Pollen tube nucleus

Pollen grain lands on stigma

Pore

Surface of stigma

Male gamete (sex cell)

Pollen tube

Pollen tube nucleus

POLLEN GRAIN GERMINATES

Anther
Filament — Stamen

Carpel

Remains of stigma and style

Ovary

Anther
Filament — Stamen

Sepal

Stamen

Sepal

Prickle

Pedicel (flower stalk)

Pedicel (flower stalk)

2. FERTILIZATION HAS TAKEN PLACE; PETALS FALL OFF

3. OVARIES BEGIN TO SWELL; STAMENS WITHER AND DIE

Pollen grain — Stigma

Style

Pollen tube

Polar nucleus

Antipodal cell

Ovary

Ovule

Embryo sac

Ovum (female gamete)

Micropyle (entrance to ovule)

Male gamete

Receptacle

MALE GAMETES TRAVEL TO EMBRYO SAC

Exocarp (outer layer of pericarp)

Remains of style

Carpel

Remains of stamen

Sepal

Pedicel (flower stalk)

5. CARPELS EXPAND AND BECOME MORE FLESHY

Exocarp (outer layer of pericarp)

Remains of style

Carpel

Remains of stamen

Sepal

Pedicel (flower stalk)

6. CARPELS EXPAND FURTHER

Nucellus (layer surrounding embryo sac)

Antipodal cell

Integument (outer part of ovule)

2nd male gamete fuses with polar nuclei to form endosperm nucleus

Synergid nucleus (disappears after fertilization)

1st male gamete fuses with ovum to form embryo

Pollen tube reaches ovum via micropyle

FERTILIZATION

Exocarp (outer layer of pericarp)

Remains of style

Drupelet

Remains of stamen

Remains of sepal

Pedicel (flower stalk)

10. DRUPELETS (COLLECTIVELY AN AGGREGATE FRUIT) EXPAND

Remains of style

Exocarp (outer layer of pericarp)

Drupelet

Remains of stamen

Pedicel (flower stalk)

Remains of sepal

11. DRUPELETS RIPEN FULLY

Style and stigma wither

Endosperm (food store)

Pericarp (maturing ovary wall)

Embryo plant

Testa (seed coat)

Cotyledon (seed leaf)

Plumule (embryonic shoot)

Radicle (embryonic root)

DEVELOPMENT OF EMBRYO

Succulent fruits

A FRUIT IS A FULLY DEVELOPED and ripened ovary (seed-producing part of a plant's female reproductive organs). Fruits may be succulent or dry (see pp. 150-151). Succulent fruits are fleshy and brightly colored, making them attractive to animals, which eat them and so disperse the seeds away from the parent plant. The wall (pericarp) of a succulent fruit has three layers: an outer exocarp, a middle mesocarp, and an inner endocarp. These three layers vary in thickness and texture in different types of fruits and may blend into each other. Succulent fruits can be classed as simple (derived from one ovary) or compound (derived from several ovaries). Simple succulent fruits include berries, which typically have many seeds, and drupes, which typically have a single stone or pit (e.g., cherry and peach). Compound succulent fruits include aggregate fruits, which are formed from many ovaries in one flower, and multiple fruits, which develop from the ovaries of many flowers. Some fruits, known as false fruits or pseudocarps, develop from parts of the flower in addition to the ovaries. For example, the flesh of the apple is formed from the receptacle (the upper end of the flower stalk).

BERRY
Cocoa
(*Theobroma cacao*)

HESPERIDIUM (A TYPE OF BERRY)
Lemon
(*Citrus limon*)

Pedicel (flower stalk)

Endocarp

Pedicel (flower stalk)

Mesocarp

Exocarp

Leathery exocarp

Seed

Vesicle (juice sac)

Oil gland

Remains of style

Remains of style

Placenta

EXTERNAL VIEW OF FRUIT

LONGITUDINAL SECTION THROUGH FRUIT

Hilum (point of attachment to ovary)

Embryo

Seed

Carpel wall

Carpel

Testa (seed coat)

Cotyledon (seed leaf)

Placenta

EXTERNAL VIEW AND SECTION THROUGH SEED

CROSS-SECTION THROUGH FRUIT

SYCONIUM (A TYPE OF FALSE FRUIT)
Fig
(*Ficus carica*)

Remains of female flowers

Fleshy infolded receptacle

Peduncle (inflorescence stalk)

Pip (seed surrounded by endocarp)

Rema of ma flower

Skin

Pore closed by scales

EXTERNAL VIEW OF FRUIT

LONGITUDINAL SECTION THROUGH FRUIT

FRUIT WITH FLESHY ARIL
Lychee
(*Litchi chinensis*)

Pedicel (flower stalk)

Pedicel (flower stalk)

Seed

Remains of style

Endocarp

EXTERNAL VIEW AND SECTION THROUGH PIT

Aril (fleshy outgrowth from seed stalk)

Drupelet

Pit

Pericarp (fruit wall)

Pericarp (fruit wall)

Pedicel (flower stalk)

Endocarp

Cotyledon (seed leaf)

Embryo

Testa (seed coat)

EXTERNAL VIEW OF FRUIT

LONGITUDINAL SECTION THROUGH FRUIT

REMAINS OF A SINGLE FEMALE FLOWER

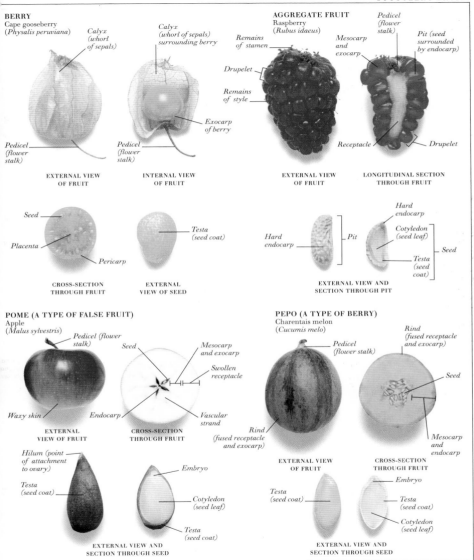

BERRY
Cape gooseberry
(*Physalis peruviana*)

Calyx (whorl of sepals)

Calyx (whorl of sepals) surrounding berry

Pedicel (flower stalk)

Exocarp of berry

Pedicel (flower stalk)

EXTERNAL VIEW OF FRUIT

INTERNAL VIEW OF FRUIT

Seed

Placenta

Pericarp

Testa (seed coat)

CROSS-SECTION THROUGH FRUIT

EXTERNAL VIEW OF SEED

AGGREGATE FRUIT
Raspberry
(*Rubus idaeus*)

Pedicel (flower stalk)

Pit (seed surrounded by endocarp)

Remains of stamen

Mesocarp and exocarp

Drupelet

Remains of style

Receptacle

Drupelet

EXTERNAL VIEW OF FRUIT

LONGITUDINAL SECTION THROUGH FRUIT

Hard endocarp

Hard endocarp

Pit

Cotyledon (seed leaf)

Seed

Testa (seed coat)

EXTERNAL VIEW AND SECTION THROUGH PIT

POME (A TYPE OF FALSE FRUIT)
Apple
(*Malus sylvestris*)

Pedicel (flower stalk)

Seed

Mesocarp and exocarp

Swollen receptacle

Waxy skin

Endocarp

Vascular strand

EXTERNAL VIEW OF FRUIT

CROSS-SECTION THROUGH FRUIT

Hilum (point of attachment to ovary)

Testa (seed coat)

Embryo

Cotyledon (seed leaf)

Testa (seed coat)

EXTERNAL VIEW AND SECTION THROUGH SEED

PEPO (A TYPE OF BERRY)
Charentais melon
(*Cucumis melo*)

Rind (fused receptacle and exocarp)

Pedicel (flower stalk)

Seed

Mesocarp and endocarp

Rind (fused receptacle and exocarp)

EXTERNAL VIEW OF FRUIT

CROSS-SECTION THROUGH FRUIT

Testa (seed coat)

Embryo

Testa (seed coat)

Cotyledon (seed leaf)

EXTERNAL VIEW AND SECTION THROUGH SEED

Dry fruits

DRY FRUITS HAVE A HARD, DRY PERICARP (fruit wall) around their seeds unlike succulent fruits, which have fleshy pericarps (see pp. 148-149). Dry fruits are divided into three types: dehiscent, in which the pericarp splits open to release the seeds; indehiscent, which do not split open; and schizocarpic, in which the fruit splits but the seeds are not exposed. Dehiscent dry fruits include capsules (e.g., love-in-a-mist), follicles (e.g., delphinium), legumes (e.g., pea), and siliquas (e.g., honesty). Typically, the seeds of dehiscent fruits are dispersed by the wind. Indehiscent dry fruits include nuts (e.g., sweet chestnut), nutlets (e.g., goosegrass), achenes (e.g., strawberry), caryopses (e.g., wheat), samaras (e.g., elm), and cypselas (e.g., dandelion). Some indehiscent dry fruits are dispersed by the wind, assisted by "wings" (e.g., elm) or "parachutes" (e.g., dandelion); others (e.g., goosegrass) have hooked pericarps to aid dispersal on animals' fur. Schizocarpic dry fruits include cremocarps (e.g., hogweed), and double samaras (e.g., sycamore maple); these are dispersed by the wind.

NUTLET
Goosegrass
(*Galium aparine*)

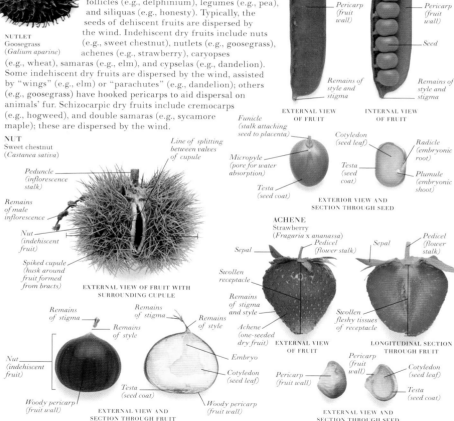

LEGUME
Pea
(*Pisum sativum*)

Pedicel (flower stalk)

Receptacle

Remains of sepal

Remains of stamen

Placenta

Pericarp (fruit wall)

Remains of style and stigma

EXTERNAL VIEW OF FRUIT

Pedicel (flower stalk)

Receptacle

Remains of sepal

Funicle (stalk attaching seed to placenta)

Pericarp (fruit wall)

Seed

Remains of style and stigma

INTERNAL VIEW OF FRUIT

Funicle (stalk attaching seed to placenta)

Micropyle (pore for water absorption)

Testa (seed coat)

Cotyledon (seed leaf)

Radicle (embryonic root)

Testa (seed coat)

Plumule (embryonic shoot)

EXTERIOR VIEW AND SECTION THROUGH SEED

NUT
Sweet chestnut
(*Castanea sativa*)

Line of splitting between valves of cupule

Peduncle (inflorescence stalk)

Remains of male inflorescence

Nut (indehiscent fruit)

Spiked cupule (husk around fruit formed from bracts)

EXTERNAL VIEW OF FRUIT WITH SURROUNDING CUPULE

Remains of stigma

Remains of style

Remains of stigma

Remains of style

Nut (indehiscent fruit)

Embryo

Cotyledon (seed leaf)

Testa (seed coat)

Woody pericarp (fruit wall)

Woody pericarp (fruit wall)

EXTERNAL VIEW AND SECTION THROUGH FRUIT

ACHENE
Strawberry
(*Fragaria* x *ananassa*)

Sepal

Pedicel (flower stalk)

Swollen receptacle

Remains of stigma and style

Achene (one-seeded dry fruit)

EXTERNAL VIEW OF FRUIT

Sepal

Pedicel (flower stalk)

Swollen fleshy tissues of receptacle

LONGITUDINAL SECTION THROUGH FRUIT

Pericarp (fruit wall)

Pericarp (fruit wall)

Cotyledon (seed leaf)

Testa (seed coat)

EXTERNAL VIEW AND SECTION THROUGH SEED

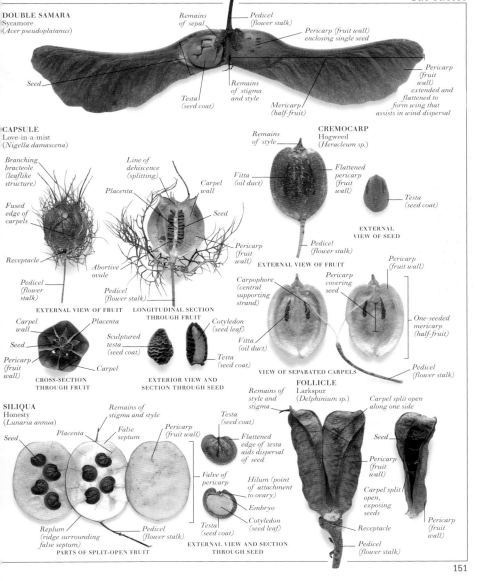

DOUBLE SAMARA
Sycamore
(*Acer pseudoplatanus*)

Remains
of sepal

Pedicel
(flower stalk)

Pericarp (fruit wall)
enclosing single seed

Pericarp
(fruit
wall)
extended and
flattened to
form wing that
assists in wind dispersal

Seed

Remains
of stigma
and style

Testa
(seed coat)

Mericarp
(half-fruit)

CAPSULE
Love-in-a-mist
(*Nigella damascena*)

Branching
bracteole
(leaflike
structure)

Line of
dehiscence
(splitting)

Carpel
wall

Placenta

Fused
edge of
carpels

Seed

Receptacle

Abortive
ovule

Pericarp
(fruit
wall)

Pedicel
(flower
stalk)

Pedicel
(flower stalk)

EXTERNAL VIEW OF FRUIT

**LONGITUDINAL SECTION
THROUGH FRUIT**

Carpel
wall

Placenta

Sculptured
testa
(seed coat)

Cotyledon
(seed leaf)

Seed

Pericarp
(fruit
wall)

Carpel

Testa
(seed coat)

**CROSS-SECTION
THROUGH FRUIT**

**EXTERIOR VIEW AND
SECTION THROUGH SEED**

CREMOCARP
Hogweed
(*Heracleum sp.*)

Remains
of style

Flattened
pericarp
(fruit
wall)

Vitta
(oil duct)

Testa
(seed coat)

Pedicel
(flower stalk)

**EXTERNAL
VIEW OF SEED**

EXTERNAL VIEW OF FRUIT

Carpophore
(central
supporting
strand)

Pericarp
covering
seed

Pericarp
(fruit wall)

One-seeded
mericarp
(half-fruit)

Vitta
(oil duct)

Pedicel
(flower stalk)

VIEW OF SEPARATED CARPELS

SILIQUA
Honesty
(*Lunaria annua*)

Remains of
stigma and style

False
septum

Pericarp
(fruit wall)

Seed

Placenta

FOLLICLE
Larkspur
(*Delphinium sp.*)

Remains of
style and
stigma

Testa
(seed coat)

Flattened
edge of testa
aids dispersal
of seed

Valve of
pericarp

Hilum (point
of attachment
to ovary)

Embryo

Cotyledon
(seed leaf)

Testa
(seed coat)

Carpel split open
along one side

Seed

Pericarp
(fruit
wall)

Carpel split
open,
exposing
seeds

Receptacle

Pericarp
(fruit
wall)

Pedicel
(flower stalk)

Replum
(ridge surrounding
false septum)

Pedicel
(flower stalk)

PARTS OF SPLIT-OPEN FRUIT

**EXTERNAL VIEW AND SECTION
THROUGH SEED**

Germination

GERMINATION IS THE GROWTH OF SEEDS INTO SEEDLINGS. It starts when seeds become active below ground, and ends when the first foliage leaves appear above ground. A seed consists of an embryo and its food supply, surrounded by a testa (seed coat). The embryo is made up of one or two cotyledons (seed leaves) attached to a central axis. The upper part of the axis consists of an epicotyl, which has a plumule (embryonic shoot) at its tip. The lower part of the axis consists of a hypocotyl and a radicle (embryonic root). After dispersal from the parent plant, the seeds dehydrate and enter a period of dormancy. Following this dormant period, germination begins, provided that the seeds have enough water, oxygen, warmth, and, in some cases, light. In the first stages of germination, the seed takes in water; the embryo starts to use its food supply; and the radicle swells, breaks through the testa, and grows downward. Germination then proceeds in one of two ways, depending on the type of seed. In epigeal germination, the hypocotyl lengthens, pulling the plumule and its protective cotyledons out of the soil. In hypogeal germination, the cotyledons remain below ground and the epicotyl lengthens, pushing the plumule upward.

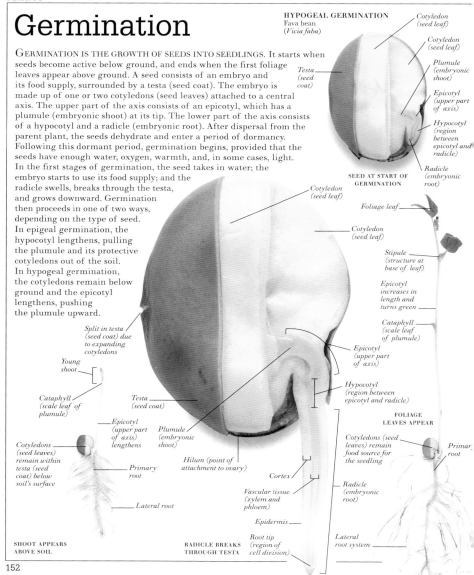

HYPOGEAL GERMINATION
Fava bean (*Vicia faba*)

Cotyledon (seed leaf)

Cotyledon (seed leaf)

Plumule (embryonic shoot)

Epicotyl (upper part of axis)

Hypocotyl (region between epicotyl and radicle)

Testa (seed coat)

Radicle (embryonic root)

SEED AT START OF GERMINATION

Foliage leaf

Cotyledon (seed leaf)

Stipule (structure at base of leaf)

Epicotyl increases in length and turns green

Cataphyll (scale leaf of plumule)

Epicotyl (upper part of axis)

Hypocotyl (region between epicotyl and radicle)

FOLIAGE LEAVES APPEAR

Cotyledons (seed leaves) remain food source for the seedling

Primary root

Radicle (embryonic root)

Lateral root system

Cotyledon (seed leaf)

Cotyledon (seed leaf)

Split in testa (seed coat) due to expanding cotyledons

Young shoot

Cataphyll (scale leaf of plumule)

Testa (seed coat)

Epicotyl (upper part of axis) lengthens

Plumule (embryonic shoot)

Hilum (point of attachment to ovary)

Cortex

Vascular tissue (xylem and phloem)

Epidermis

Cotyledons (seed leaves) remain within testa (seed coat) below soil's surface

Primary root

Lateral root

SHOOT APPEARS ABOVE SOIL

RADICLE BREAKS THROUGH TESTA

Root tip (region of cell division)

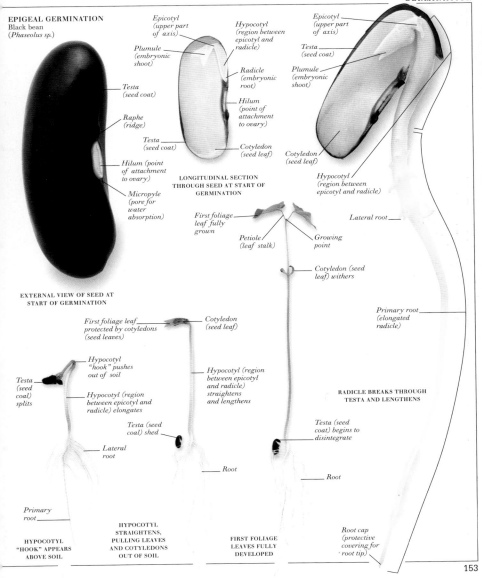

EPIGEAL GERMINATION
Black bean
(*Phaseolus sp.*)

Testa
(seed coat)

Raphe
(ridge)

Hilum (point
of attachment
to ovary)

Micropyle
(pore for
water
absorption)

**EXTERNAL VIEW OF SEED AT
START OF GERMINATION**

Epicotyl
(upper part
of axis)

Plumule
(embryonic
shoot)

Hypocotyl
(region between
epicotyl and
radicle)

Radicle
(embryonic
root)

Hilum
(point of
attachment
to ovary)

Testa
(seed coat)

Cotyledon
(seed leaf)

**LONGITUDINAL SECTION
THROUGH SEED AT START OF
GERMINATION**

Epicotyl
(upper part
of axis)

Testa
(seed coat)

Plumule
(embryonic
shoot)

Cotyledon
(seed leaf)

Hypocotyl
(region between
epicotyl and radicle)

Lateral root

Primary root
(elongated
radicle)

**RADICLE BREAKS THROUGH
TESTA AND LENGTHENS**

Root cap
(protective
covering for
root tip)

First foliage
leaf fully
grown

Petiole
(leaf stalk)

Growing
point

Cotyledon (seed
leaf) withers

First foliage leaf
protected by cotyledons
(seed leaves)

Cotyledon
(seed leaf)

Hypocotyl
"hook" pushes
out of soil

Testa
(seed
coat)
splits

Hypocotyl (region
between epicotyl and
radicle) elongates

Testa (seed
coat) shed

Lateral
root

Primary
root

**HYPOCOTYL
"HOOK" APPEARS
ABOVE SOIL**

Hypocotyl (region
between epicotyl
and radicle)
straightens
and lengthens

Root

**HYPOCOTYL
STRAIGHTENS,
PULLING LEAVES
AND COTYLEDONS
OUT OF SOIL**

Testa (seed
coat) begins to
disintegrate

Root

**FIRST FOLIAGE
LEAVES FULLY
DEVELOPED**

Vegetative reproduction

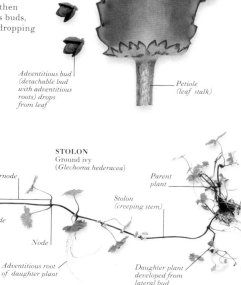

Apex of leaf

Lamina (blade) of leaf

Leaf margin

Notch in leaf margin containing meristematic (actively dividing) cells

Adventitious bud (detachable bud with adventitious roots) drops from leaf

Petiole (leaf stalk)

CORM
Gladiolus
(*Gladiolus sp.*)

MANY PLANTS CAN PROPAGATE THEMSELVES by vegetative reproduction. In this process, part of a plant separates off, takes root, and grows into a new plant. Vegetative reproduction is a type of asexual reproduction; that is, it involves only one parent, and there is no fusion of gametes (sex cells). Plants use various structures to reproduce vegetatively. Some plants use underground storage organs. Such organs include rhizomes (horizontal, underground stems), the branches of which produce new plants; bulbs (swollen leaf bases) and corms (swollen stems), which produce daughter bulbs or corms that separate off from the parent; and stem tubers (thickened underground stems) and root tubers (swollen adventitious roots), which also separate off from the parent. Other propagative structures include runners and stolons, creeping horizontal stems that take root and produce new plants; bulbils, small bulbs that develop on the stem or in the place of flowers, and then drop off and grow into new plants; and adventitious buds, miniature plants that form on leaf margins before dropping to the ground and growing into mature plants.

BULBIL IN PLACE OF FLOWER
Orange lily
(*Lilium bulbiferum*)

Scar left by flower

Leaf

Pedicel (flower stalk)

Terminal bud

Internode

Node

Detachable bulbil formed in place of flower

Node

Peduncle (inflorescence stalk)

Adventitious root of daughter plant

STOLON
Ground ivy
(*Glechoma hederacea*)

Parent plant

Stolon (creeping stem)

Daughter plant developed from lateral bud

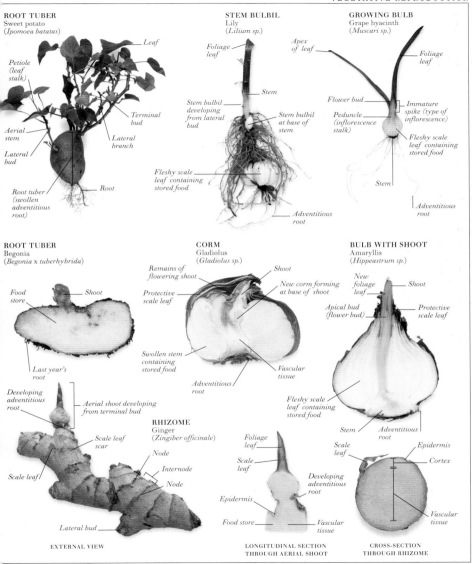

ROOT TUBER
Sweet potato
(*Ipomoea batatas*)

Leaf

Petiole
(leaf
stalk)

Terminal
bud

Aerial
stem

Lateral
branch

Lateral
bud

Root tuber
(swollen
adventitious
root)

Root

STEM BULBIL
Lily
(*Lilium sp.*)

Foliage
leaf

Stem

Stem bulbil
developing
from lateral
bud

Stem bulbil
at base of
stem

Fleshy scale
leaf containing
stored food

Adventitious
root

GROWING BULB
Grape hyacinth
(*Muscari sp.*)

Apex
of leaf

Foliage
leaf

Flower bud

Immature
spike (type of
inflorescence)

Peduncle
(inflorescence
stalk)

Fleshy scale
leaf containing
stored food

Stem

Adventitious
root

ROOT TUBER
Begonia
(*Begonia x tuberhybrida*)

Food
store

Shoot

Last year's
root

Developing
adventitious
root

Aerial shoot developing
from terminal bud

Scale leaf
scar

Node

Internode

Node

Scale leaf

Lateral bud

EXTERNAL VIEW

CORM
Gladiolus
(*Gladiolus sp.*)

Remains of
flowering shoot

Protective
scale leaf

Shoot

New corm forming
at base of shoot

Swollen stem
containing
stored food

Adventitious
root

Vascular
tissue

RHIZOME
Ginger
(*Zingiber officinale*)

Foliage
leaf

Scale
leaf

Developing
adventitious
root

Epidermis

Food store

Vascular
tissue

LONGITUDINAL SECTION
THROUGH AERIAL SHOOT

BULB WITH SHOOT
Amaryllis
(*Hippeastrum sp.*)

New
foliage
leaf

Shoot

Apical bud
(flower bud)

Protective
scale leaf

Fleshy scale
leaf containing
stored food

Stem

Adventitious
root

Scale
leaf

Epidermis

Cortex

Vascular
tissue

CROSS-SECTION
THROUGH RHIZOME

Dryland plants

LEAF SUCCULENT
Lithops sp.

DRYLAND PLANTS (XEROPHYTES) are able to survive in unfavorable habitats. All are found in places where little water is available; some live in high temperatures that cause excessive loss of water from the leaves. Xerophytes show a number of adaptations to dry conditions; these include reduced leaf area, rolled leaves, sunken stomata, hairs, spines, and thick cuticles. One group, succulent plants, stores water in specially enlarged spongy tissues found in leaves, roots, or stems. Leaf succulents have enlarged, fleshy, water-storing leaves. Root succulents have a large, underground water-storage organ with short-lived stems and leaves above ground. Stem succulents are represented by the cacti (family Cactaceae). Cacti stems are fleshy, green, and photosynthetic; they are typically ribbed or covered by tubercles in rows, with leaves being reduced to spines or entirely absent.

STEM SUCCULENT
Golden barrel cactus
(*Echinocactus grusonii*)

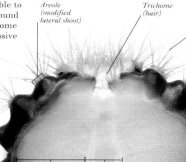

Areole (modified lateral shoot)
Trichome (hair)
Spine (modified leaf)
Waxy cuticle (waterproof covering)
Water-storing parenchyma (packing tissue)
Tubercle (projection from stem surface)
Vascular cylinder (transport tissue)

Spine (modified leaf)
Tubercle (projection from stem surface)
Root

EXTERNAL VIEW

Sinuous (wavy) cell wall
Stoma (pore) controlling exchange of gases

MICROGRAPH OF STEM SURFACE

Spine (modified leaf)
Areole (modified lateral shoot)
Tubercle (projection from stem surface)
Waxy cuticle (waterproof covering)

DETAIL OF STEM SURFACE

Root

LONGITUDINAL SECTION THROUGH STEM

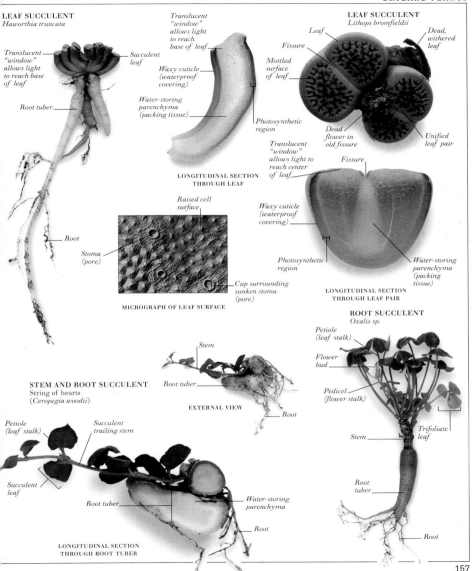

LEAF SUCCULENT
Haworthia truncata

Translucent "window" allows light to reach base of leaf

Succulent leaf

Root tuber

Root

Translucent "window" allows light to reach base of leaf

Waxy cuticle (waterproof covering)

Water-storing parenchyma (packing tissue)

Photosynthetic region

LONGITUDINAL SECTION THROUGH LEAF

LEAF SUCCULENT
Lithops bromfieldii

Leaf

Fissure

Dead, withered leaf

Mottled surface of leaf

Dead flower in old fissure

Unified leaf pair

Translucent "window" allows light to reach center of leaf

Fissure

Waxy cuticle (waterproof covering)

Photosynthetic region

Water-storing parenchyma (packing tissue)

LONGITUDINAL SECTION THROUGH LEAF PAIR

Raised cell surface

Stoma (pore)

Cup surrounding sunken stoma (pore)

MICROGRAPH OF LEAF SURFACE

Stem

Root tuber

Root

EXTERNAL VIEW

STEM AND ROOT SUCCULENT
String of hearts
(*Ceropegia woodii*)

Petiole (leaf stalk)

Succulent trailing stem

Succulent leaf

Root tuber

Water-storing parenchyma

Root

LONGITUDINAL SECTION THROUGH ROOT TUBER

ROOT SUCCULENT
Oxalis sp.

Petiole (leaf stalk)

Flower bud

Pedicel (flower stalk)

Trifoliate leaf

Stem

Root tuber

Root

Wetland plants

WETLAND PLANTS GROW SUBMERGED IN WATER, either partially (e.g., water hyacinth) or completely (e.g., pond weeds), and show various adaptations to this habitat. Typically, there are numerous air spaces inside the stems, leaves, and roots; these aid gas exchange and buoyancy. Submerged parts generally have no cuticle (waterproof covering), enabling the plants to absorb minerals and gases directly from the water; in addition, being supported by the water, they need little of the supportive tissue found in land plants. Stomata, the gas exchange pores, are absent from plants that are completely submerged; in partially submerged plants with floating leaves (e.g., water lilies), stomata are found on the upper leaf surfaces, where they cannot be flooded.

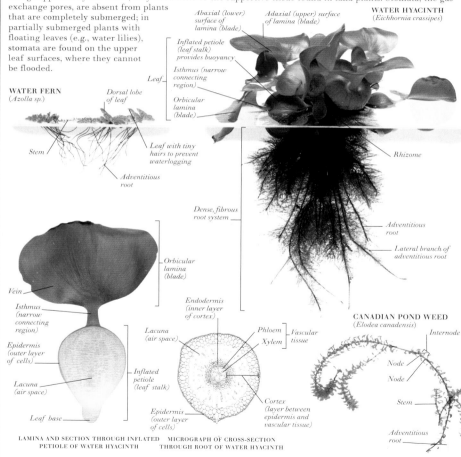

WATER HYACINTH
(*Eichhornia crassipes*)

Abaxial (lower) surface of lamina (blade)

Adaxial (upper) surface of lamina (blade)

Inflated petiole (leaf stalk) provides buoyancy

Isthmus (narrow connecting region)

Leaf

Orbicular lamina (blade)

WATER FERN
(*Azolla sp.*)

Dorsal lobe of leaf

Stem

Leaf with tiny hairs to prevent waterlogging

Adventitious root

Rhizome

Dense, fibrous root system

Orbicular lamina (blade)

Adventitious root

Lateral branch of adventitious root

Vein

Isthmus (narrow connecting region)

Epidermis (outer layer of cells)

Lacuna (air space)

Leaf base

Endodermis (inner layer of cortex)

Lacuna (air space)

Inflated petiole (leaf stalk)

Epidermis (outer layer of cells)

Phloem / Xylem — Vascular tissue

Cortex (layer between epidermis and vascular tissue)

CANADIAN POND WEED
(*Elodea canadensis*)

Internode

Node

Node

Stem

Adventitious root

LAMINA AND SECTION THROUGH INFLATED PETIOLE OF WATER HYACINTH

MICROGRAPH OF CROSS-SECTION THROUGH ROOT OF WATER HYACINTH

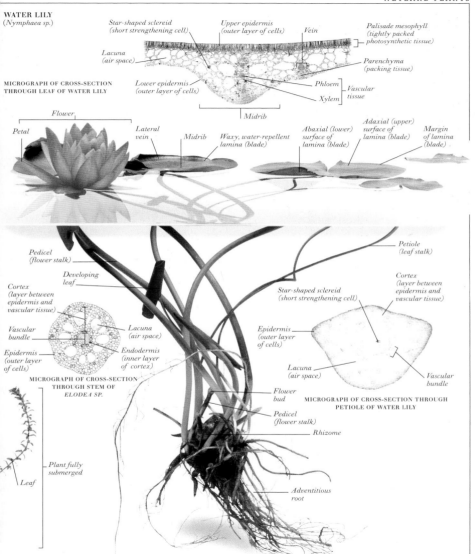

WATER LILY
(*Nymphaea* sp.)

Star-shaped sclereid
(short strengthening cell)

Upper epidermis
(outer layer of cells)

Vein

Palisade mesophyll
(tightly packed
photosynthetic tissue)

Lacuna
(air space)

Parenchyma
(packing tissue)

MICROGRAPH OF CROSS-SECTION
THROUGH LEAF OF WATER LILY

Lower epidermis
(outer layer of cells)

Phloem
Xylem
} Vascular
tissue

Midrib

Flower

Petal

Lateral
vein

Midrib

Waxy, water-repellent
lamina (blade)

Abaxial (lower)
surface of
lamina (blade)

Adaxial (upper)
surface of
lamina (blade)

Margin
of lamina
(blade)

Pedicel
(flower stalk)

Developing
leaf

Petiole
(leaf stalk)

Cortex
(layer between
epidermis and
vascular tissue)

Star-shaped sclereid
(short strengthening cell)

Cortex
(layer between
epidermis and
vascular tissue)

Vascular
bundle

Lacuna
(air space)

Epidermis
(outer layer
of cells)

Epidermis
(outer layer
of cells)

Endodermis
(inner layer
of cortex)

Lacuna
(air space)

Vascular
bundle

MICROGRAPH OF CROSS-SECTION
THROUGH STEM OF
ELODEA SP.

Flower
bud

Pedicel
(flower stalk)

MICROGRAPH OF CROSS-SECTION THROUGH
PETIOLE OF WATER LILY

Rhizome

Plant fully
submerged

Leaf

Adventitious
root

Carnivorous plants

Areola ("window" of transparent tissue)

Fishtail nectary

Wing

Hood

Pitcher

Tubular petiole (leaf stalk)

Areola ("window" of transparent tissue)

CARNIVOROUS (INSECTIVOROUS) PLANTS FEED ON INSECTS and other small animals, in addition to producing food in their leaves by photosynthesis. The nutrients absorbed from trapped insects enable carnivorous plants to thrive in acid, boggy soils that lack essential minerals, especially nitrates, where most other plants could not survive. All carnivorous plants have some leaves modified as traps; many use bright colors and scented nectar to attract prey; and most use enzymes to digest the prey. There are three types of traps. Pitcher plants, such as the monkey cup and cobra lily, have leaves modified as pitcher-shaped pitfall traps, half-filled with water; once lured inside the mouth of the trap, insects lose their footing on the slippery surface, fall into the liquid, and either decompose or are digested. Venus fly traps use a spring-trap mechanism; when an insect touches trigger hairs on the inner surfaces of the leaves, the two lobes of the trap snap shut. Butterworts and sundews entangle prey by sticky droplets on the leaf surface, while the edges of the leaves slowly curl over to envelop and digest the prey.

Dome-shaped hood develops

Fishtail nectary appears

Immature pitcher

Smooth surface

Nectar roll

Mouth

Wing

Downward pointing hair

DEVELOPMENT OF MODIFIED LEAF IN COBRA LILY

Immature trap

Interlocked teeth

Closed trap

VENUS FLY TRAP
(*Dionaea muscipula*)

Red color of trap attracts insects

Phyllode (flattened petiole)

Summer petiole (leaf stalk)

Nectary zone (glands secrete nectar)

Digestive zone (glands secrete digestive enzymes)

Tooth

Lobe of trap

Midrib (hinge of trap)

Trigger hair

Trap (twin-lobed leaf blade)

Spring petiole (leaf stalk)

Digestive gland

Sensory hinge

Trigger hair

Inner surface of trap

MICROGRAPH OF LOBE OF VENUS FLY TRAP

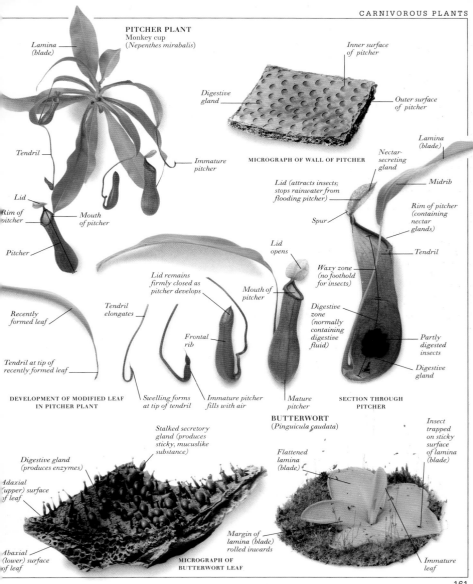

PITCHER PLANT
Monkey cup
(*Nepenthes mirabilis*)

Lamina (blade)

Tendril

Lid

Rim of pitcher

Mouth of pitcher

Pitcher

Immature pitcher

Inner surface of pitcher

Digestive gland

Outer surface of pitcher

MICROGRAPH OF WALL OF PITCHER

Lid (attracts insects; stops rainwater from flooding pitcher)

Spur

Nectar-secreting gland

Lamina (blade)

Midrib

Rim of pitcher (containing nectar glands)

Tendril

Waxy zone (no foothold for insects)

Digestive zone (normally containing digestive fluid)

Partly digested insects

Digestive gland

Recently formed leaf

Tendril at tip of recently formed leaf

Tendril elongates

Lid remains firmly closed as pitcher develops

Frontal rib

Swelling forms at tip of tendril

Immature pitcher fills with air

Lid opens

Mouth of pitcher

Mature pitcher

DEVELOPMENT OF MODIFIED LEAF IN PITCHER PLANT

SECTION THROUGH PITCHER

BUTTERWORT
(*Pinguicula caudata*)

Stalked secretory gland (produces sticky, mucuslike substance)

Digestive gland (produces enzymes)

Adaxial (upper) surface of leaf

Abaxial (lower) surface of leaf

MICROGRAPH OF BUTTERWORT LEAF

Flattened lamina (blade)

Margin of lamina (blade) rolled inwards

Insect trapped on sticky surface of lamina (blade)

Immature leaf

Epiphytic and parasitic plants

EPIPHYTIC AND PARASITIC PLANTS GROW ON OTHER LIVING PLANTS. Typically, epiphytic plants are not rooted in the soil; instead, they live above ground level on the stems and branches of other plants. Epiphytes obtain water from trapped rainwater and from moisture in the air, and minerals from organic matter that has accumulated on the surface of the plant on which they are growing. Like other green plants, epiphytes produce their food by photosynthesis. Epiphytes include tropical orchids and bromeliads (air plants), and some mosses that live in temperate regions. Parasitic plants obtain all their nutrient requirements from the host plants on which they grow. The parasites produce haustoria, rootlike organs that penetrate the stem or roots of the host and grow inward to merge with the host's vascular tissue, from which the parasite extracts water, minerals, and manufactured nutrients. As they have no need to produce their own food, parasitic plants lack chlorophyll, the green photosynthetic pigment, and they have no foliage leaves. Partial parasitic plants (e.g., mistletoe) obtain water and minerals from the host plant but have green leaves and stems and are therefore able to produce their own food by photosynthesis.

EPIPHYTIC ORCHID
Brassavola nodosa

Peduncle (inflorescence stalk)

Pedicel (flower stalk)

Flower

Scale leaf

Aerial root

Leaf

Node

Stem

Bark of tree to which epiphyte is attached

Inflorescence (spike)

Peduncle (inflorescence stalk)

Flower bud

Strap-shaped arching leaf (part of rosette of leaves)

Leaf margin with spines

Overlapping leaf bases in which rainwater is trapped

EPIPHYTIC BROMELIAD
Aechmea miniata

Mass of adventitious roots

Stem

Bark of tree to which epiphyte is attached

Velamen (multi-layered epidermis capable of absorbing water from rain or condensation)

Cortex (layer between epidermis and vascular tissue)

Cortex cell containing chloroplasts

Vascular tissue { *Xylem* / *Phloem* }

Exodermis (outer layer of cortex)

Pith

Endoderm (inner layer of cortex)

MICROGRAPH OF CROSS-SECTION THROUGH AERIAL ROOT OF EPIPHYTIC ORCHID

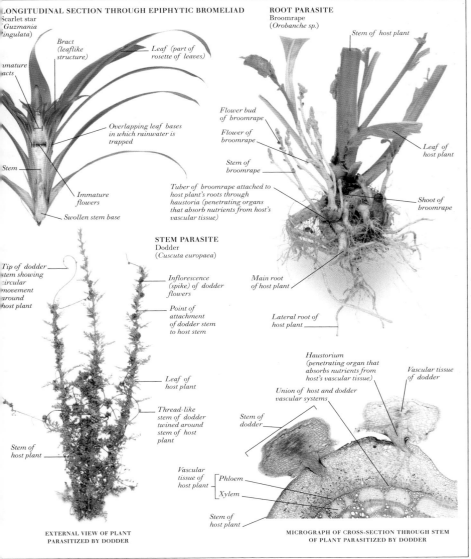

LONGITUDINAL SECTION THROUGH EPIPHYTIC BROMELIAD
Scarlet star
(*Guzmania
lingulata*)

Bract
(leaflike
structure)

Leaf (part of
rosette of leaves)

Immature
bracts

Overlapping leaf bases
in which rainwater is
trapped

Stem

Immature
flowers

Swollen stem base

ROOT PARASITE
Broomrape
(*Orobanche sp.*)

Stem of host plant

Flower bud
of broomrape

Flower of
broomrape

Stem of
broomrape

Leaf of
host plant

Tuber of broomrape attached to
host plant's roots through
haustoria (penetrating organs
that absorb nutrients from host's
vascular tissue)

Shoot of
broomrape

Main root
of host plant

Lateral root of
host plant

STEM PARASITE
Dodder
(*Cuscuta europaea*)

Tip of dodder
stem showing
circular
movement
around
host plant

Inflorescence
(spike) of dodder
flowers

Point of
attachment
of dodder stem
to host stem

Leaf of
host plant

Thread-like
stem of dodder
twined around
stem of host
plant

Stem of
host plant

Vascular
tissue of
host plant

Phloem

Xylem

Stem of
host plant

Haustorium
(penetrating organ that
absorbs nutrients from
host's vascular tissue)

Vascular tissue
of dodder

Union of host and dodder
vascular systems

Stem of
dodder

**EXTERNAL VIEW OF PLANT
PARASITIZED BY DODDER**

**MICROGRAPH OF CROSS-SECTION THROUGH STEM
OF PLANT PARASITIZED BY DODDER**

ANIMALS

Sponges, Jellyfish, and Sea Anemones ········· 166
Insects ········· 168
Arachnids ········· 170
Crustaceans ········· 172
Starfish and Sea Urchins ········· 174
Mollusks ········· 176
Sharks and Jawless Fish ········· 178
Bony Fish ········· 180
Amphibians ········· 182
Lizards and Snakes ········· 184
Crocodilians and Turtles ········· 186
Birds 1 ········· 188
Birds 2 ········· 190
Eggs ········· 192
Carnivores ········· 194
Rabbits and Rodents ········· 196
Ungulates ········· 198
Elephants ········· 200
Primates ········· 202
Dophins, Whales, and Seals ········· 204
Marsupials and Monotremes ········· 206

Sponges, jellyfish, and sea anemones

SPONGES ARE MAINLY MARINE animals that make up the phylum Porifera. They are among the simplest of all animals, having no tissues or organs. Their bodies consist of two layers of cells separated by a jellylike layer (mesohyal) that is strengthened by mineral spicules or protein fibers. The body is perforated by a system of pores and water channels called the aquiferous system. Special cells (choanocytes) with whiplike structures (flagella) draw water through the aquiferous system, thereby bringing tiny food particles to the sponge's cells. Jellyfish (class Scyphozoa), sea anemones (class Anthozoa), and corals (also class Anthozoa) belong to the phylum Cnidaria, also known as Coelenterata. More complex than sponges, coelenterates have simple tissues, such as nervous tissue; a radially symmetrical body; and a mouth surrounded by tentacles with unique stinging cells (cnidocytes).

INTERNAL ANATOMY OF A SPONGE

Amoebocyte
Osculum (excurrent pore)
Choanocyte (collar cell)
Ostium (incurrent pore)
Porocyte (pore cell)
Mesohyal
Spongocoel (atrium; paragaster)
Spicule
Pinacocyte (epidermal cell)
Ostium (incurrent pore)

SKELETON OF A SPONGE

Protein matrix

Pore

EXTERNAL FEATURES OF A SEA ANEMONE

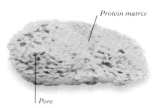

Tentacle

EXAMPLES OF SEA ANEMONES

PARASITIC ANEMONE
(Calliactis parasitica)

JEWEL ANEMONE
(Corynactis viridis)

PLUMOSE ANEMONE
(Metridium senile)

MEDITERRANEAN SEA ANEMONE
(Condylactis sp.)

GREEN SNAKELOCK ANEMONE
(Anemonia viridis)

BEADLET ANEMONE
(Actinia equina)

GHOST ANEMONE
(Actinothoe sphyrodeta)

Sagartia elegans

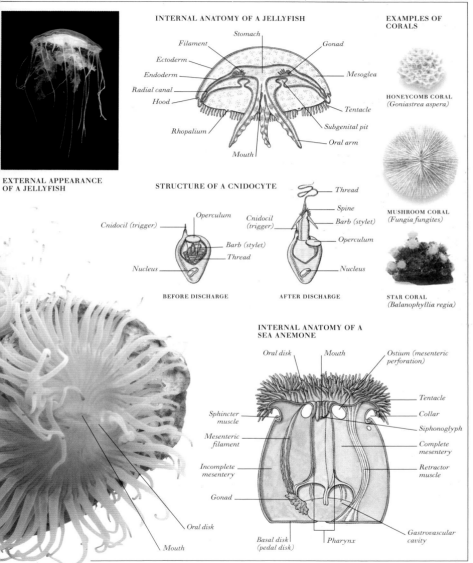

INTERNAL ANATOMY OF A JELLYFISH

Filament
Stomach
Ectoderm
Gonad
Endoderm
Mesoglea
Radial canal
Hood
Tentacle
Rhopalium
Subgenital pit
Oral arm
Mouth

EXTERNAL APPEARANCE OF A JELLYFISH

EXAMPLES OF CORALS

HONEYCOMB CORAL
(Goniastrea aspera)

MUSHROOM CORAL
(Fungia fungites)

STAR CORAL
(Balanophyllia regia)

STRUCTURE OF A CNIDOCYTE

Operculum
Cnidocil (trigger)
Barb (stylet)
Nucleus
Thread

Thread
Spine
Cnidocil (trigger)
Barb (stylet)
Operculum
Nucleus

BEFORE DISCHARGE

AFTER DISCHARGE

INTERNAL ANATOMY OF A SEA ANEMONE

Oral disk
Mouth
Ostium (mesenteric perforation)
Sphincter muscle
Tentacle
Collar
Siphonoglyph
Mesenteric filament
Complete mesentery
Incomplete mesentery
Retractor muscle
Gonad
Basal disk (pedal disk)
Pharynx
Gastrovascular cavity

Oral disk
Mouth

Insects

PUPA (CHRYSALIS)

THE WORD INSECT REFERS to small invertebrate creatures, especially those with bodies divided into sections. Insects, including beetles, ants, bees, butterflies, and moths, belong to various orders in the class Insecta, which is a division of the phylum Arthropoda. Features common to all insects are an exoskeleton (external skeleton); three pairs of jointed legs; three body sections (head, thorax, and abdomen); and one pair of sensory antennae. Beetles (order Coleoptera) are the biggest group of insect, with about 300,000 species (about 30 percent of all known insects). They have a pair of hard elytra (wing cases), which are modified front wings. The principal function of the elytra is to protect the hind wings, which are used for flying. Ants, together with bees and wasps, form the order Hymenoptera, which contains about 200,000 species. This group is characterized by a marked narrowing between the thorax and abdomen. Butterflies and moths form the order Lepidoptera, which has about 150,000 species. They have wings covered with tiny scales, hence the name of their order (Lepidoptera means "scale wings"). The separation of lepidopterans into butterflies and moths is largely artificial, since there are no features that categorically distinguish one group from the other. In general, however, most butterflies fly by day, whereas most moths are night-flyers. Some insects, including butterflies and moths, undergo complete metamorphosis (transformation) during their life-cycle. A butterfly metamorphoses from an egg to a larva (caterpillar), then to a pupa (chrysalis), and finally to an imago (adult).

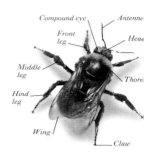

Compound eye — *Antenna* — *Front leg* — *Head* — *Middle leg* — *Thorax* — *Hind leg* — *Wing* — *Claw*

BUMBLEBEE

Compound eye — *Stigma (spot)* — *Vein* — *Abdomen*

DAMSELFLY

EXTERNAL FEATURES OF A BEETLE

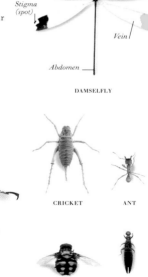

Elytron — *Tarsus* — *Claw* — *Tibia* — *Costal margin* — *Pedicel* — *Apex* — *Femur* — *Vein* — *Flagellum* — *Trochanter* — *Wing* — *Mandible* — *Scape* — *Coxa* — *Labrum* — *Labial palp* — *Abdomen* — *Compound eye* — *Head* — *Prothorax* — *Mesothorax* — *Front leg* — *Scutellum* — *Hind leg* — *Metathorax* — *Middle leg*

CRICKET

ANT

FLY

EARWIG

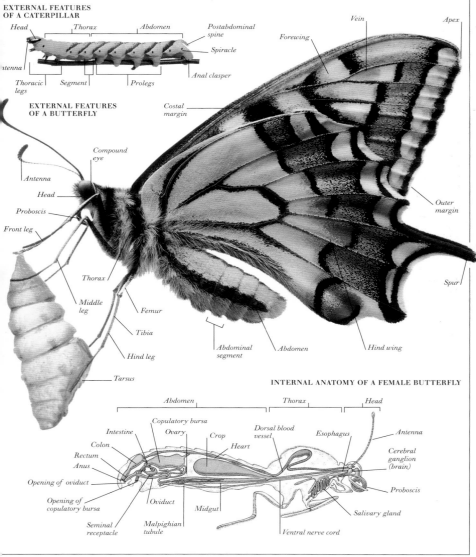

EXTERNAL FEATURES OF A CATERPILLAR

Head
Thorax
Abdomen
Postabdominal spine
Antenna
Spiracle
Thoracic legs
Segment
Prolegs
Anal clasper

EXTERNAL FEATURES OF A BUTTERFLY

Vein
Apex
Forewing
Costal margin
Compound eye
Antenna
Head
Proboscis
Outer margin
Front leg
Thorax
Middle leg
Femur
Tibia
Hind leg
Tarsus
Spur
Abdominal segment
Abdomen
Hind wing

INTERNAL ANATOMY OF A FEMALE BUTTERFLY

Abdomen
Thorax
Head
Copulatory bursa
Intestine
Ovary
Crop
Dorsal blood vessel
Esophagus
Antenna
Colon
Heart
Cerebral ganglion (brain)
Rectum
Anus
Opening of oviduct
Proboscis
Opening of copulatory bursa
Oviduct
Midgut
Salivary gland
Seminal receptacle
Malpighian tubule
Ventral nerve cord

Arachnids

THE CLASS ARACHNIDA INCLUDES SPIDERS (order Araneae) and scorpions (order Scorpiones). The class is part of the phylum Arthropoda, which also includes insects and crustaceans.

Spiders and scorpions are characterized by having four pairs of walking legs; a pair of pincerlike mouthparts called chelicerae; another pair of frontal appendages called pedipalps, which are sensory in spiders but used for grasping in scorpions; and a body divided into two sections (a combined head and thorax called a cephalothorax or prosoma, and an abdomen or opisthosoma). Unlike other arthropods, spiders and scorpions lack antennae. Spiders and scorpions are carnivorous. Spiders poison prey by biting with the fanged chelicerae, scorpions by stinging with the end of the metasoma (tail).

MEXICAN TRUE RED-LEGGED TARANTULA
(Euathlus emilia)

INTERNAL ANATOMY OF A FEMALE SPIDER

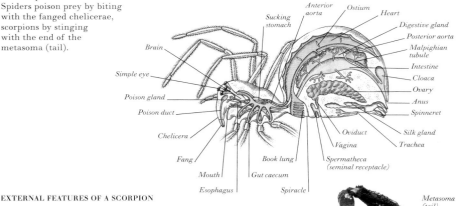

Anterior aorta
Ostium
Sucking stomach
Heart
Digestive gland
Posterior aorta
Malpighian tubule
Intestine
Cloaca
Ovary
Anus
Spinneret
Silk gland
Trachea
Oviduct
Vagina
Spermatheca (seminal receptacle)
Book lung
Gut caecum
Spiracle
Mouth
Esophagus
Fang
Chelicera
Poison duct
Poison gland
Simple eye
Brain

EXTERNAL FEATURES OF A SCORPION

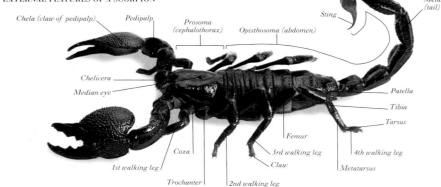

Chela (claw of pedipalp)
Pedipalp
Prosoma (cephalothorax)
Opisthosoma (abdomen)
Sting
Metasoma (tail)
Chelicera
Median eye
Patella
Tibia
Tarsus
Femur
Metatarsus
4th walking leg
3rd walking leg
Claw
2nd walking leg
Coxa
Trochanter
1st walking leg

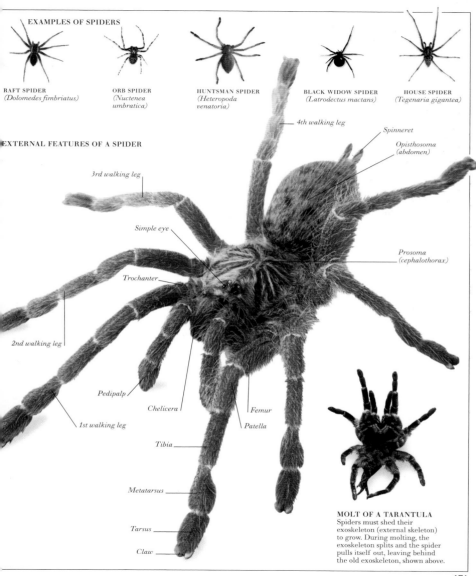

EXAMPLES OF SPIDERS

RAFT SPIDER
(Dolomedes fimbriatus)

ORB SPIDER
(Nuctenea umbratica)

HUNTSMAN SPIDER
(Heteropoda venatoria)

BLACK WIDOW SPIDER
(Latrodectus mactans)

HOUSE SPIDER
(Tegenaria gigantea)

EXTERNAL FEATURES OF A SPIDER

4th walking leg

Spinneret

Opisthosoma
(abdomen)

3rd walking leg

Simple eye

Prosoma
(cephalothorax)

Trochanter

2nd walking leg

Pedipalp

Chelicera

Femur

Patella

1st walking leg

Tibia

Metatarsus

Tarsus

Claw

MOLT OF A TARANTULA
Spiders must shed their exoskeleton (external skeleton) to grow. During molting, the exoskeleton splits and the spider pulls itself out, leaving behind the old exoskeleton, shown above.

Crustaceans

THE SUBPHYLUM CRUSTACEA is one of the largest groups in the phylum Arthropoda. The subphylum is divided into several classes, the most important of which are Malacostraca and Cirripedia. The class Malacostraca includes crayfish, crabs, lobsters, and shrimps. Typical features of malacostracans include a body divided into two sections (a combined head and thorax called a cephalothorax, and an abdomen); an exoskeleton (external skeleton) with a large plate (carapace) covering the cephalothorax; stalked, compound eyes; and two pairs of antennae. The class Cirripedia includes barnacles, which, unlike other crustaceans, spend their adult lives attached to a surface, such as a rock. Other characteristics of cirripedes include an exoskeleton of overlapping calcareous plates; a body consisting almost entirely of thorax (the abdomen and head are minute); and six pairs of thoracic appendages (cirri) used for filter feeding.

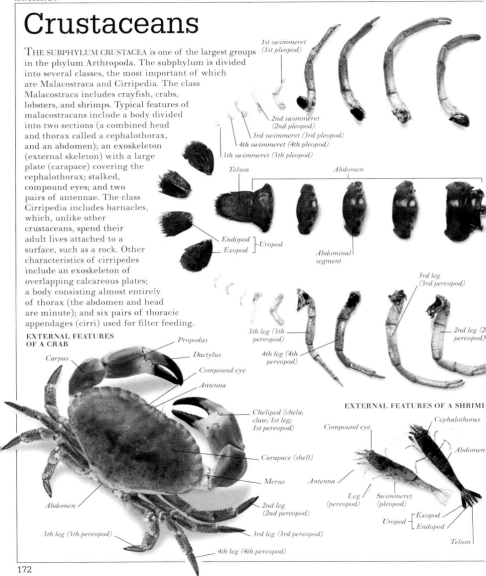

1st swimmeret (1st pleopod)

2nd swimmeret (2nd pleopod)

3rd swimmeret (3rd pleopod)

4th swimmeret (4th pleopod)

5th swimmeret (5th pleopod)

Telson

Abdomen

Endopod
Exopod — Uropod

Abdominal segment

3rd leg (3rd pereopod)

2nd leg (2nd pereopod)

5th leg (5th pereopod)

4th leg (4th pereopod)

EXTERNAL FEATURES OF A CRAB

Carpus

Propodus

Dactylus

Compound eye

Antenna

Cheliped (chela; claw; 1st leg; 1st pereopod)

Carapace (shell)

Merus

2nd leg (2nd pereopod)

Abdomen

3rd leg (3rd pereopod)

5th leg (5th pereopod)

4th leg (4th pereopod)

EXTERNAL FEATURES OF A SHRIMP

Compound eye

Cephalothorax

Abdomen

Antenna

Leg (pereopod)

Swimmeret (pleopod)

Uropod — Exopod
Endopod

Telson

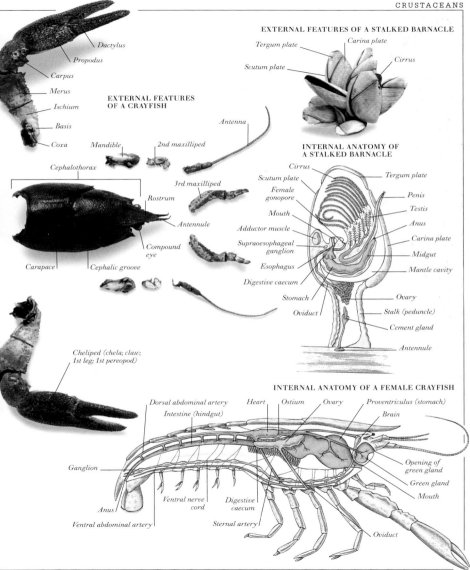

EXTERNAL FEATURES OF A STALKED BARNACLE

Tergum plate
Carina plate
Cirrus
Scutum plate

Dactylus
Propodus
Carpus
Merus
Ischium
Basis
Coxa

EXTERNAL FEATURES OF A CRAYFISH

Mandible
2nd maxilliped
Antenna

Cephalothorax
Rostrum
3rd maxilliped

Antennule
Compound eye

Carapace
Cephalic groove

INTERNAL ANATOMY OF A STALKED BARNACLE

Cirrus
Scutum plate
Tergum plate
Female gonopore
Penis
Mouth
Testis
Adductor muscle
Anus
Supraoesophageal ganglion
Carina plate
Esophagus
Midgut
Digestive caecum
Mantle cavity
Stomach
Ovary
Oviduct
Stalk (peduncle)
Cement gland
Antennule

Cheliped (chela; claw; 1st leg; 1st pereopod)

INTERNAL ANATOMY OF A FEMALE CRAYFISH

Dorsal abdominal artery
Heart
Ostium
Ovary
Proventriculus (stomach)
Intestine (hindgut)
Brain

Ganglion
Opening of green gland
Green gland
Mouth

Anus
Ventral nerve cord
Digestive caecum
Ventral abdominal artery
Sternal artery
Oviduct

Starfish and sea urchins

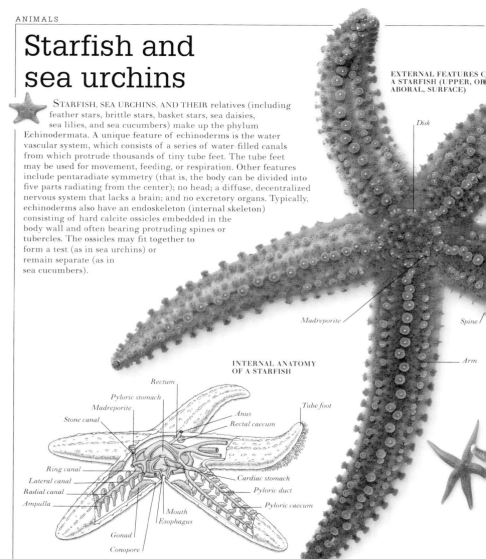

STARFISH, SEA URCHINS, AND THEIR relatives (including feather stars, brittle stars, basket stars, sea daisies, sea lilies, and sea cucumbers) make up the phylum Echinodermata. A unique feature of echinoderms is the water vascular system, which consists of a series of water-filled canals from which protrude thousands of tiny tube feet. The tube feet may be used for movement, feeding, or respiration. Other features include pentaradiate symmetry (that is, the body can be divided into five parts radiating from the center); no head; a diffuse, decentralized nervous system that lacks a brain; and no excretory organs. Typically, echinoderms also have an endoskeleton (internal skeleton) consisting of hard calcite ossicles embedded in the body wall and often bearing protruding spines or tubercles. The ossicles may fit together to form a test (as in sea urchins) or remain separate (as in sea cucumbers).

EXTERNAL FEATURES O[F] A STARFISH (UPPER, OR ABORAL, SURFACE)

Disk

Madreporite

Spine

Arm

INTERNAL ANATOMY OF A STARFISH

Rectum

Pyloric stomach

Madreporite

Stone canal

Anus

Rectal caecum

Tube foot

Ring canal

Lateral canal

Radial canal

Ampulla

Cardiac stomach

Pyloric duct

Pyloric caecum

Mouth

Esophagus

Gonad

Conopore

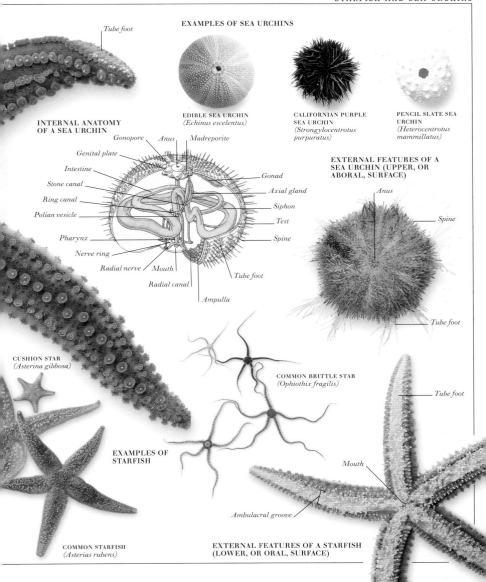

Tube foot

EXAMPLES OF SEA URCHINS

EDIBLE SEA URCHIN
(Echinus escelentus)

CALIFORNIAN PURPLE
SEA URCHIN
*(Strongylocentrotus
purpuratus)*

PENCIL SLATE SEA
URCHIN
*(Heterocentrotus
mammillatus)*

**INTERNAL ANATOMY
OF A SEA URCHIN**

Gonopore
Anus
Madreporite
Genital plate
Intestine
Stone canal
Ring canal
Polian vesicle
Pharynx
Nerve ring
Radial nerve
Mouth
Radial canal
Ampulla
Gonad
Axial gland
Siphon
Test
Spine
Tube foot

**EXTERNAL FEATURES OF A
SEA URCHIN (UPPER, OR
ABORAL, SURFACE)**

Anus
Spine
Tube foot

CUSHION STAR
(Asterina gibbosa)

COMMON BRITTLE STAR
(Ophiothix fragilis)

Tube foot

Mouth

**EXAMPLES OF
STARFISH**

Ambulacral groove

COMMON STARFISH
(Asterias rubens)

**EXTERNAL FEATURES OF A STARFISH
(LOWER, OR ORAL, SURFACE)**

Mollusks

THE PHYLUM MOLLUSCA (MOLLUSKS) is a large group of animals that includes octopuses, snails, and scallops. Octopuses and their relatives—including squid and cuttlefish—form the class Cephalopoda. Cephalopods typically have a head with a radula (a filelike feeding organ) and beak; a well-developed nervous system; sucker-bearing tentacles; a muscular mantle (part of the body wall) that can expel water through the siphon, enabling movement by jet propulsion; and a small shell or no shell. Snails and their relatives—including slugs, limpets, and abalones—make up the class Gastropoda. Gastropods typically have a coiled external shell, although some, such as slugs, have a small internal shell or no shell; a flat foot; and a head with tentacles and a radula. Scallops and their relatives—including clams, mussels, and oysters—make up the class Bivalvia (also called Pelecypoda). Features of bivalves include a shell with two halves (valves); large gills that are used for breathing and filter feeding; and no radula.

EXTERNAL FEATURES OF A SCALLOP

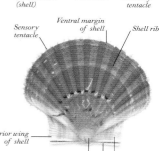

Upper valve (shell) Mantle Ocellus (eye)

Lower valve (shell) Shell rib Sensory tentacle

Sensory tentacle Ventral margin of shell Shell rib

Anterior wing of shell

Umbo Posterior wing of shell

Dorsal margin of shell

INTERNAL ANATOMY OF AN OCTOPUS

Cephalic vein

Skull

Brain

Poison gland

Crop

Digestive caecum

Dorsal mantle cavity

Siphon (funnel)

Buccal mass

Beak

Mantle muscles

Shell rudiment

Stomach

Caecum

Gonad

Systemic heart

Kidney

Branchial heart

Anus

Ctenidium

Ink sac

Muscular septum

Tentacle

Sucker

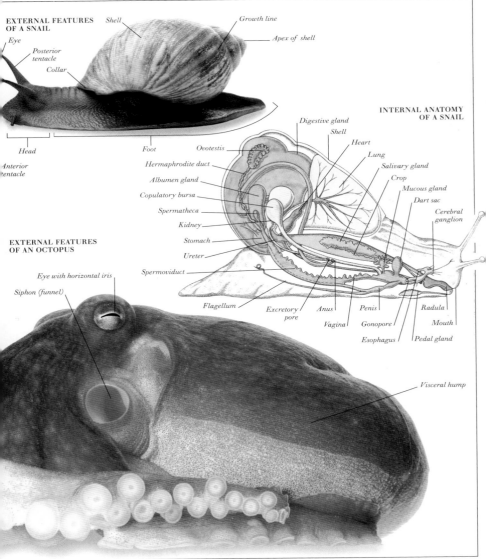

EXTERNAL FEATURES OF A SNAIL

Eye

Posterior tentacle

Collar

Shell

Growth line

Apex of shell

Head

Foot

Anterior tentacle

INTERNAL ANATOMY OF A SNAIL

Digestive gland

Shell

Heart

Lung

Salivary gland

Crop

Mucous gland

Dart sac

Cerebral ganglion

Ovotestis

Hermaphrodite duct

Albumen gland

Copulatory bursa

Spermatheca

Kidney

Stomach

Ureter

Spermoviduct

Flagellum

Excretory pore

Anus

Penis

Radula

Mouth

Vagina

Gonopore

Pedal gland

Esophagus

EXTERNAL FEATURES OF AN OCTOPUS

Eye with horizontal iris

Siphon (funnel)

Visceral hump

Sharks and jawless fish

SHARKS, DOGFISH (WHICH ARE actually small sharks), skates, and rays belong to a class of fishes called Chondrichthyes, which is a division of the superclass Gnathostomata (meaning "jawed mouths"). Also sometimes known as elasmobranchs, sharks and their relatives have a skeleton made of cartilage (hence their common name, cartilaginous fish), a characteristic that distinguishes them from bony fish (see pp. 180-181). Other important features of cartilaginous fish are extremely tough, toothlike scales, and lack of a swim bladder. Jawless fish—lampreys and hagfish—are primitive, eellike fish that make up the order Cyclostomata (meaning "round mouths"), a division of the superclass Agnatha (meaning "without jaws"). In addition to their characteristic round, suckerlike mouths and lack of jaws, cyclostomes also have smooth, slimy skin without scales, and unpaired fins.

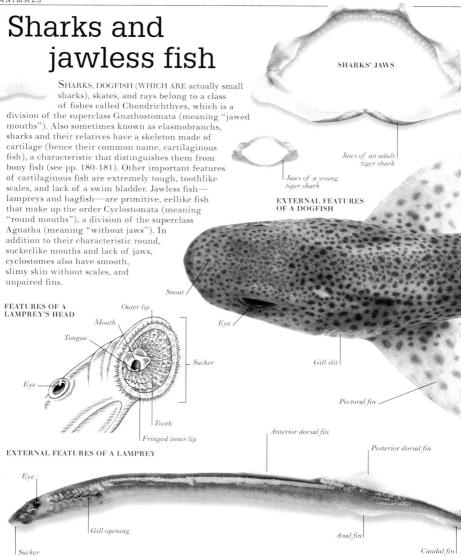

SHARKS' JAWS

Jaws of an adult tiger shark

Jaws of a young tiger shark

EXTERNAL FEATURES OF A DOGFISH

Snout

Eye

Gill slit

Pectoral fin

FEATURES OF A LAMPREY'S HEAD

Outer lip

Mouth

Tongue

Eye

Sucker

Tooth

Fringed inner lip

EXTERNAL FEATURES OF A LAMPREY

Eye

Gill opening

Sucker

Anterior dorsal fin

Posterior dorsal fin

Anal fin

Caudal fin

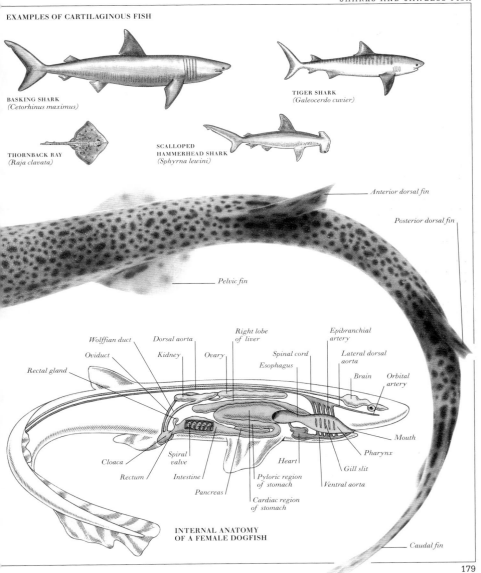

EXAMPLES OF CARTILAGINOUS FISH

BASKING SHARK
(*Cetorhinus maximus*)

TIGER SHARK
(*Galeocerdo cuvier*)

THORNBACK RAY
(*Raja clavata*)

SCALLOPED
HAMMERHEAD SHARK
(*Sphyrna lewini*)

Anterior dorsal fin

Posterior dorsal fin

Pelvic fin

Wolffian duct

Oviduct

Rectal gland

Dorsal aorta

Kidney

Ovary

Right lobe
of liver

Spinal cord

Esophagus

Epibranchial
artery

Lateral dorsal
aorta

Brain

Orbital
artery

Mouth

Cloaca

Spiral
valve

Rectum

Intestine

Pancreas

Heart

Pharynx

Gill slit

Ventral aorta

Pyloric region
of stomach

Cardiac region
of stomach

Caudal fin

INTERNAL ANATOMY
OF A FEMALE DOGFISH

Bony fish

BONY FISH, SUCH AS CARP, TROUT, SALMON, perch, and cod, are by far the best known and largest group of fish, with more than 20,000 species (over 95 percent of all known fish). As their name suggests, bony fish have skeletons made of bone, in contrast to the cartilaginous skeletons of sharks, jawless fish, and their relatives (see pp. 178-179). Other typical features of bony fish include a swim bladder, which functions as a variable-buoyancy organ, enabling a fish to remain effortlessly at whatever depth it is swimming; relatively thin, bonelike scales; a flap (called an operculum) covering the gills; and paired pelvic and pectoral fins. Scientifically, bony fish belong to the class Osteichthyes, which is a division of the superclass Gnathostomata (meaning "jawed mouths").

HOW FISH BREATHE

Fish "breathe" by extracting oxygen from water through their gills. Water is sucked in through the mouth; simultaneously, the opercula close to prevent the water from escaping. The mouth is then closed, and muscles in the walls of the mouth, pharynx, and opercular cavity contract to pump the water inside over the gills and out through the opercula. Some fish rely on swimming with their mouths open to keep water flowing over the gills.

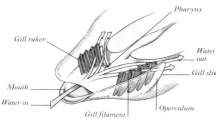

Pharynx
Gill raker
Water out
Gill slit
Mouth
Gill filament
Water in
Operculum

EXAMPLES OF BONY FISH

MANDARINFISH
(Synchiropus splendidus)

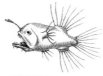

ANGLERFISH
(Caulophryne jordani)

LIONFISH
(Pterois volitans)

OCEANIC SEAHORSE
(Hippocampus kuda)

STURGEON
(Acipenser sturio)

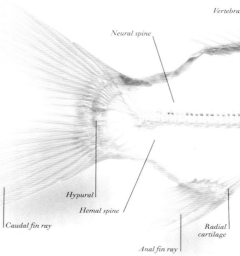

Vertebra
Neural spine
Hypural
Hemal spine
Caudal fin ray
Anal fin ray
Radial cartilage

SNOWFLAKE MORAY EEL
(Echidna nebulosa)

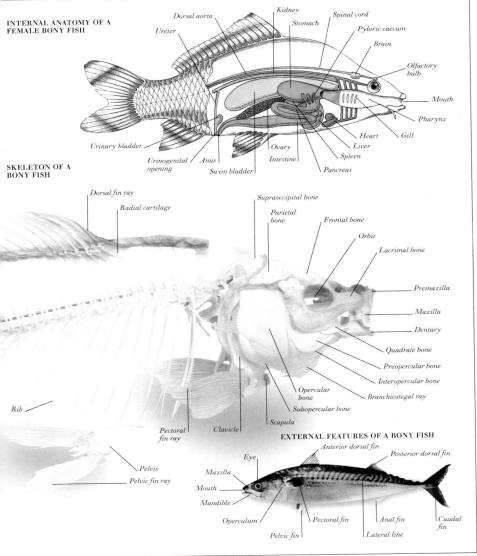

INTERNAL ANATOMY OF A FEMALE BONY FISH

Dorsal aorta

Ureter

Kidney

Stomach

Spinal cord

Pyloric caecum

Brain

Olfactory bulb

Mouth

Pharynx

Gill

Liver

Heart

Spleen

Pancreas

Intestine

Ovary

Swim bladder

Anus

Urinogenital opening

Urinary bladder

SKELETON OF A BONY FISH

Dorsal fin ray

Radial cartilage

Supraoccipital bone

Parietal bone

Frontal bone

Orbit

Lacrimal bone

Premaxilla

Maxilla

Dentary

Quadrate bone

Preopercular bone

Interopercular bone

Branchiostegal ray

Opercular bone

Subopercular bone

Scapula

Clavicle

Pectoral fin ray

Rib

Pelvis

Pelvic fin ray

EXTERNAL FEATURES OF A BONY FISH

Anterior dorsal fin

Posterior dorsal fin

Eye

Maxilla

Mouth

Mandible

Operculum

Pectoral fin

Anal fin

Caudal fin

Pelvic fin

Lateral line

Amphibians

THE CLASS AMPHIBIA INCLUDES FROGS and toads (which make
up the order Anura), and newts and salamanders (which make
up the order Urodela). Amphibians typically have moist,
scaleless, hairless skin; lungs; and are cold-blooded.
They also undergo complete metamorphosis, from
eggs laid in water through various water-living
larval stages (such as tadpoles) to land-living
adults. Typical features of adult frogs and
toads include a squat body with no tail; long,
powerful hind legs; and large, often bulging,
eyes. Adult newts and salamanders typically
have a long body with a well-developed
tail; and relatively short, equal-sized legs.
However, newts and salamanders show
considerable variation; for example, in
some species the adults have minute
legs, external gills rather than lungs,
and spend their entire lives in water.

**INTERNAL ANATOMY
OF A FEMALE FROG**

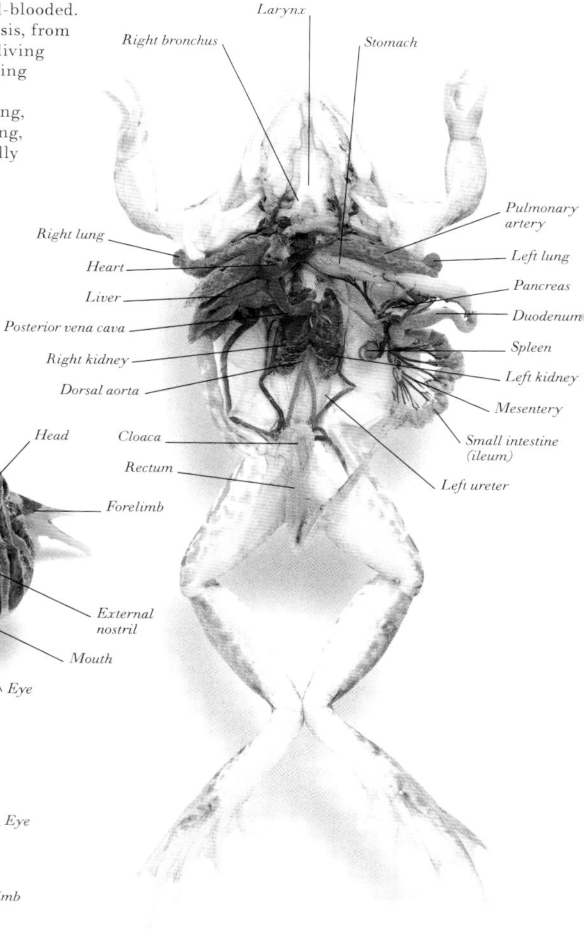

Larynx
Right bronchus
Stomach
Pulmonary artery
Right lung
Left lung
Heart
Pancreas
Liver
Duodenum
Posterior vena cava
Spleen
Right kidney
Left kidney
Dorsal aorta
Mesentery
Cloaca
Small intestine (ileum)
Rectum
Left ureter

**EXTERNAL FEATURES
OF A FROG**

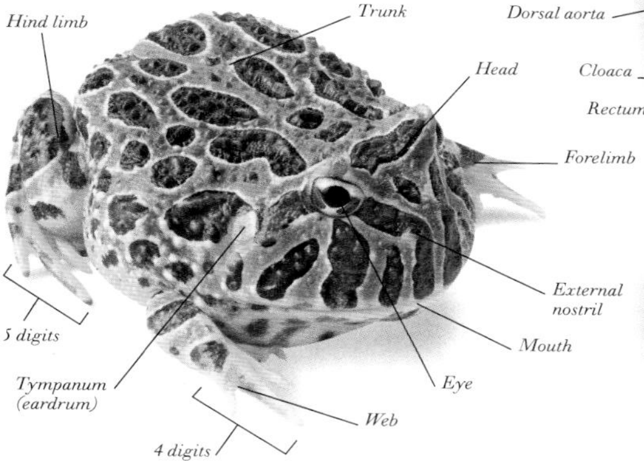

Hind limb
Trunk
Head
Forelimb
5 digits
External nostril
Tympanum (eardrum)
Mouth
Eye
4 digits
Web

**EXTERNAL FEATURES OF A
SALAMANDER**

Eye
Tail
Forelimb
Hind limb
Digit

EGGS (SPAWN)

YOUNG TADPOLES

MATURE TADPOLE

YOUNG FROG

METAMORPHOSIS OF FROGS

Frogs undergo complete metamorphosis. Eggs (spawn) are laid in water and hatch into young tadpoles, which have a tail and external gills but no legs. As the tadpoles grow, the gills disappear, back legs develop, then front legs, and the tail shrinks. Eventually the tail disappears, resulting in a young adult frog.

SKELETON OF A FROG

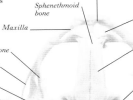

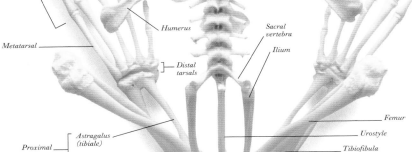

Premaxilla

Sphenethmoid bone

Nasal bone

Maxilla

Frontoparietal bone

Prootic bone

Pterygoid bone

Quadratojugal bone

Squamosal bone

Exoccipital bone

Suprascapula

Vertebra

Radio-ulna

Phalanges

Carpals

Metacarpals

Phalanges

Metatarsal

Humerus

Distal tarsals

Sacral vertebra

Ilium

Femur

Urostyle

Proximal tarsals

Astragalus (tibiale)

Calcaneum (fibulare)

Tibiofibula

Ischium

Lizards and snakes

LIZARDS AND SNAKES BELONG to the order Squamata, a division of the class Reptilia. Characteristic reptilian features include scaly skin, lungs, and cold-bloodedness. Most reptiles lay leathery-shelled eggs, although some hatch the eggs inside their bodies and give birth to live young. Lizards belong to the suborder Lacertilia. Typically, they have long tails, and shed their skin in several pieces. Many lizards can regenerate a tail if it is lost; some can change color; and some are limbless. Snakes make up the suborder Ophidia (also called Serpentes). All snakes have long, limbless bodies; can dislocate their lower jaw to swallow large prey; and have eyelids that are joined together to form a single transparent covering over the front of the eye. Most snakes shed their skin in a single piece. Constrictor snakes kill their prey by squeezing; venomous snakes poison their prey.

EXAMPLES OF SNAKES

MEXICAN MOUNTAIN KING SNAKE
(*Lampropeltis triangulum annulata*)

BANDED M
SN
(*Lamprope
ruthve*

EXTERNAL FEATURES OF A LIZARD

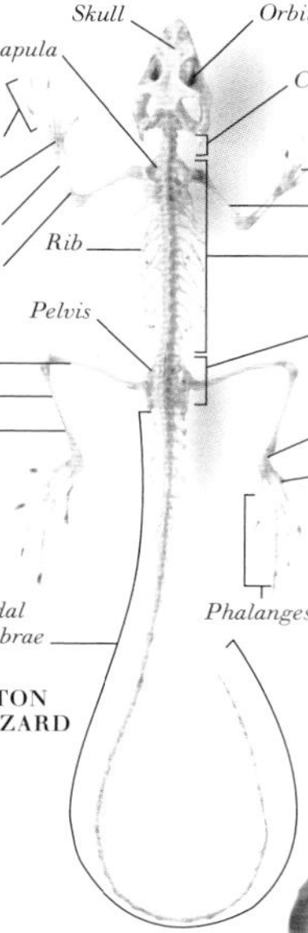

Eye

Mouth

External nostril

Crest

Eardrum

Masseteric scale

Dorsal scale

SKELETON OF A LIZARD

Skull

Orbit

Scapula

Cervical vertebrae

Phalanges

Carpals

Metacarpal

Ulna

Humerus

Radius

Rib

Thoracolumbar vertebrae

Pelvis

Sacrum

Femur

Tibia

Fibula

Tarsals

Metatarsal

Dewlap

Caudal vertebrae

Phalanges

Foreleg

Toe

Belly

Ventral scale

Claw

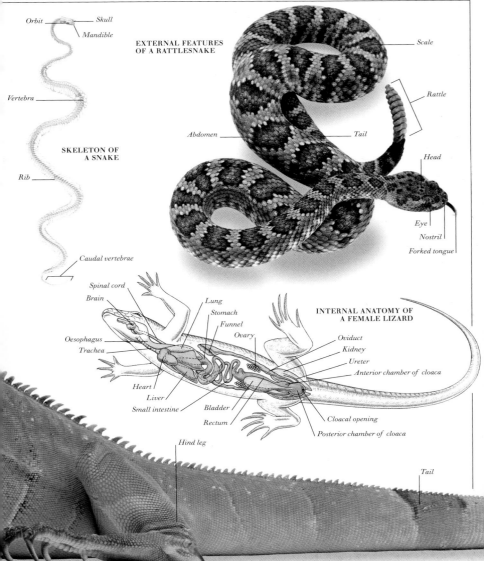

Orbit

Skull

Mandible

Vertebra

**SKELETON OF
A SNAKE**

Rib

Caudal vertebrae

**EXTERNAL FEATURES
OF A RATTLESNAKE**

Scale

Rattle

Abdomen

Tail

Head

Eye

Nostril

Forked tongue

Spinal cord

Brain

Lung

Stomach

Funnel

Ovary

Oesophagus

Trachea

**INTERNAL ANATOMY OF
A FEMALE LIZARD**

Oviduct

Kidney

Ureter

Anterior chamber of cloaca

Heart

Liver

Small intestine

Bladder

Rectum

Cloacal opening

Posterior chamber of cloaca

Hind leg

Tail

Crocodilians and turtles

CROCODILIANS AND TURTLES BELONG to different orders in the class Reptilia. The order Crocodilia includes crocodiles, alligators, caimans, and gharials. Typically, crocodilians are carnivores (flesh-eaters), and have a long snout, sharp teeth for gripping prey, and hard, square scales. All crocodilians are adapted to living on land and in water: they have four strong legs for moving on land; a powerful tail for swimming; and their eyes and nostrils are high on the head so that they stay above water while the rest of the body is submerged. The order Chelonia includes marine turtles, terrapins (freshwater turtles), and tortoises (land turtles). Characteristically, chelonians have a short, broad body encased in a bony shell with an outer horny covering, into which the head and limbs can be withdrawn; and a horny beak instead of teeth.

SKULLS OF CROCODILIANS

GHARIAL
(Gavialis gangeticus)

NILE CROCODILE
(Crocodylus niloticus)

AMERICAN ALLIGATOR
(Alligator mississippiensis)

SKELETON OF A CROCODILE

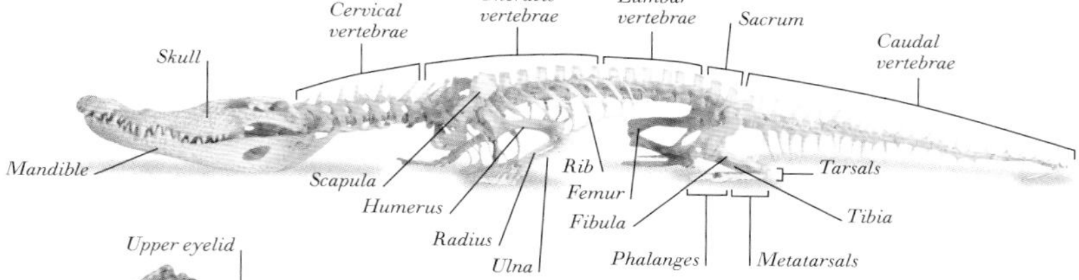

Cervical vertebrae
Thoracic vertebrae
Lumbar vertebrae
Sacrum
Caudal vertebrae
Skull
Mandible
Scapula
Humerus
Radius
Ulna
Rib
Femur
Fibula
Phalanges
Metatarsals
Tarsals
Tibia

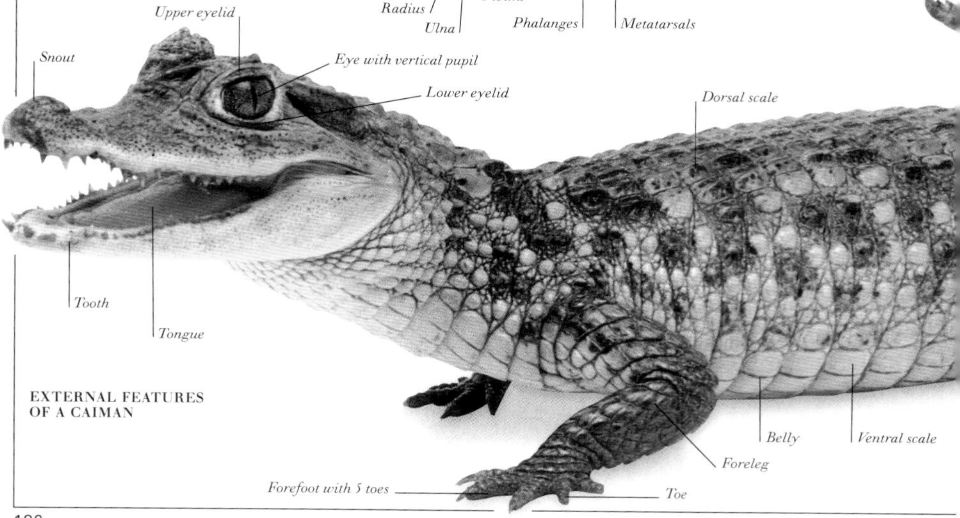

Snout
Upper eyelid
Eye with vertical pupil
Lower eyelid
Dorsal scale
Tooth
Tongue

EXTERNAL FEATURES OF A CAIMAN

Belly
Ventral scale
Foreleg
Forefoot with 5 toes
Toe

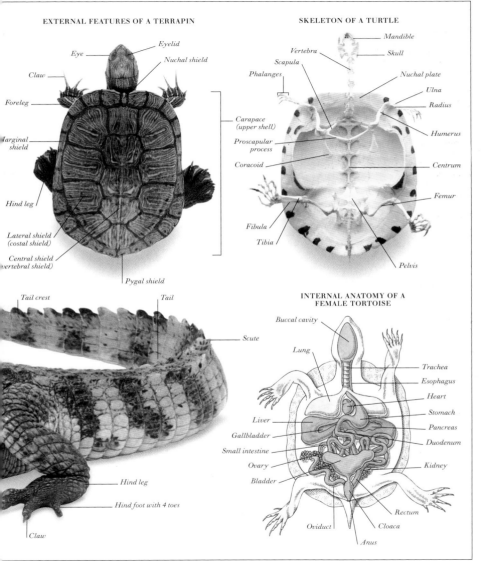

EXTERNAL FEATURES OF A TERRAPIN

Eyelid
Eye
Nuchal shield
Claw
Foreleg
Marginal shield
Hind leg
Lateral shield (costal shield)
Central shield (vertebral shield)
Pygal shield
Carapace (upper shell)
Proscapular process
Coracoid

SKELETON OF A TURTLE

Mandible
Skull
Vertebra
Scapula
Phalanges
Nuchal plate
Ulna
Radius
Humerus
Centrum
Femur
Fibula
Tibia
Pelvis

Tail crest
Tail
Scute
Hind leg
Hind foot with 4 toes
Claw

INTERNAL ANATOMY OF A FEMALE TORTOISE

Buccal cavity
Lung
Trachea
Esophagus
Heart
Stomach
Pancreas
Duodenum
Liver
Gallbladder
Small intestine
Ovary
Bladder
Kidney
Oviduct
Cloaca
Rectum
Anus

Birds 1

BIRDS MAKE UP THE CLASS AVES. There are more than 9,000 species, almost all of which can fly (the only flightless birds are penguins, ostriches, rheas, cassowaries, and kiwis). The ability to fly is reflected in the typical bird features: forelimbs modified as wings; a streamlined body; and hollow bones to reduce weight. All birds lay hard-shelled eggs, which the parents incubate. Birds' beaks and feet vary according to diet and way of life. Beaks range from general-purpose types suitable for a mixed diet (those of thrushes, for example), to types specialized for particular foods (such as the large, curved, sieving beaks of flamingos). Feet range from the webbed "paddles" of ducks, to the talons of birds of prey. Plumage also varies widely, and in many species the male is brightly colored for courtship display whereas the female is drab.

EXTERNAL FEATURES OF A BIRD

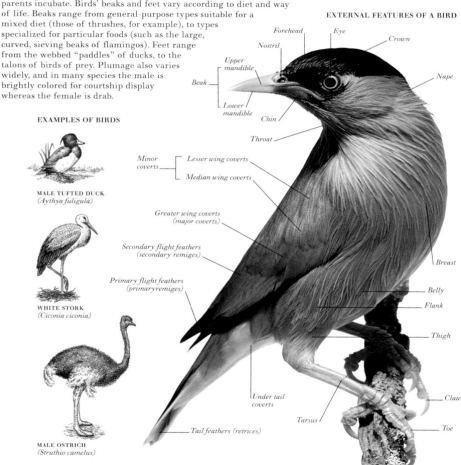

Forehead
Eye
Crown
Nostril
Nape
Upper mandible
Beak
Lower mandible
Chin
Throat

EXAMPLES OF BIRDS

MALE TUFTED DUCK
(*Aythya fuligula*)

WHITE STORK
(*Ciconia ciconia*)

MALE OSTRICH
(*Struthio camelus*)

Minor coverts
Lesser wing coverts
Median wing coverts
Greater wing coverts (major coverts)
Secondary flight feathers (secondary remiges)
Primary flight feathers (primaryremiges)
Under tail coverts
Tail feathers (retrices)
Tarsus
Breast
Belly
Flank
Thigh
Claw
Toe

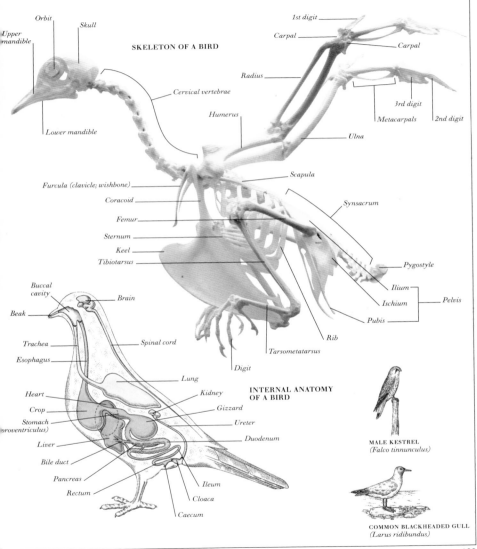

SKELETON OF A BIRD

Orbit
Skull
Upper mandible
Lower mandible
1st digit
Carpal
Carpal
Radius
3rd digit
Metacarpals
2nd digit
Humerus
Ulna
Cervical vertebrae
Furcula (clavicle; wishbone)
Coracoid
Scapula
Synsacrum
Femur
Sternum
Keel
Tibiotarsus
Pygostyle
Ilium
Ischium
Pelvis
Pubis
Rib
Tarsometatarsus
Digit

INTERNAL ANATOMY OF A BIRD

Buccal cavity
Brain
Beak
Trachea
Spinal cord
Esophagus
Lung
Heart
Kidney
Crop
Gizzard
Stomach (proventriculus)
Ureter
Liver
Duodenum
Bile duct
Pancreas
Ileum
Rectum
Cloaca
Caecum

MALE KESTREL
(Falco tinnunculus)

COMMON BLACKHEADED GULL
(Larus ridibundus)

189

Birds 2

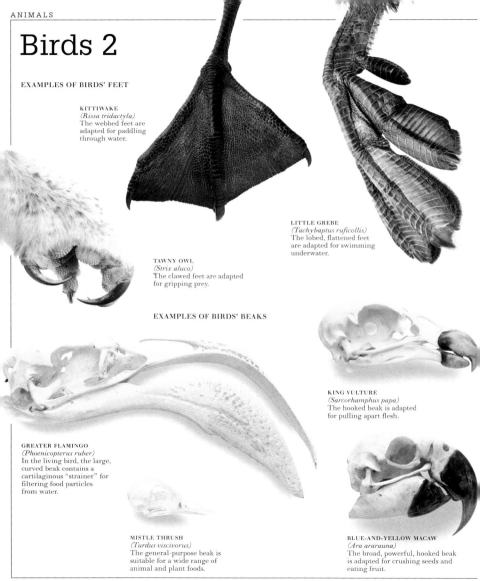

EXAMPLES OF BIRDS' FEET

KITTIWAKE
(Rissa tridactyla)
The webbed feet are
adapted for paddling
through water.

LITTLE GREBE
(Tachybaptus ruficollis)
The lobed, flattened feet
are adapted for swimming
underwater.

TAWNY OWL
(Strix aluco)
The clawed feet are adapted
for gripping prey.

EXAMPLES OF BIRDS' BEAKS

KING VULTURE
(Sarcorhamphus papa)
The hooked beak is adapted
for pulling apart flesh.

GREATER FLAMINGO
(Phoenicopterus ruber)
In the living bird, the large,
curved beak contains a
cartilaginous "strainer" for
filtering food particles
from water.

MISTLE THRUSH
(Turdus viscivorus)
The general-purpose beak is
suitable for a wide range of
animal and plant foods.

BLUE-AND-YELLOW MACAW
(Ara ararauna)
The broad, powerful, hooked beak
is adapted for crushing seeds and
eating fruit.

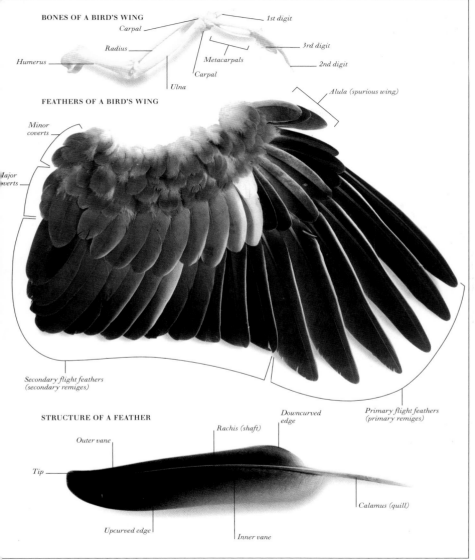

BONES OF A BIRD'S WING

1st digit
Carpal
Radius
3rd digit
Metacarpals
Humerus
2nd digit
Carpal
Ulna
Alula (spurious wing)

FEATHERS OF A BIRD'S WING

Minor
coverts

Major
coverts

Secondary flight feathers
(secondary remiges)

Primary flight feathers
(primary remiges)

STRUCTURE OF A FEATHER

Rachis (shaft)
Downcurved
edge
Outer vane
Tip
Calamus (quill)
Upcurved edge
Inner vane

191

Eggs

AN EGG IS A SINGLE CELL, produced by the female, with the capacity to develop into a new individual. Development may take place inside the mother's body (as in most mammals) or outside, in which case the egg has a protective covering such as a shell. Egg yolk nourishes the growing young. Eggs developing inside the mother generally have little yolk, because the young are nourished from her body. Eggs developing outside may also have little yolk if they are produced by animals whose young go through a larval stage (such as a caterpillar) that feeds itself while developing into the adult form. The shelled eggs of birds and reptiles contain enough yolk to sustain the young until it hatches into a juvenile version of the adult.

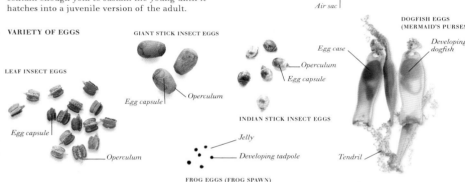

SECTION THROUGH A CHICKEN'S EGG

Yolk
Albumen (egg white)
Yolk sac
Shell
Amnion
Amniotic fluid
Allantoic fluid
Developing chick
Developing wing
Allantois
Shell membrane
Chorioallantoic membrane
Air sac

VARIETY OF EGGS

GIANT STICK INSECT EGGS

LEAF INSECT EGGS

Egg capsule
Operculum

Egg capsule
Operculum

Egg case
Operculum
Egg capsule

INDIAN STICK INSECT EGGS

Jelly
Developing tadpole

FROG EGGS (FROG SPAWN)

DOGFISH EGGS (MERMAID'S PURSE)

Developing dogfish
Tendril

HATCHING OF A QUAIL'S EGG

EGG AT THE POINT OF HATCHING

Rounded end of egg
Shell
Pointed end of egg
Shell membrane
Camouflage coloration
Crack caused by chick pecking through the shell

CUTTING THROUGH THE EGG

Chick
Shell
Shell membrane
Crack extended by more pecking by the chick

BREAKING OUT OF THE EGG

Chick pushes off the top of the shell
Shell membrane
Shell
Eye
Beak
Egg-tooth
Crack runs completely around the shell

EXAMPLES OF BIRDS' EGGS

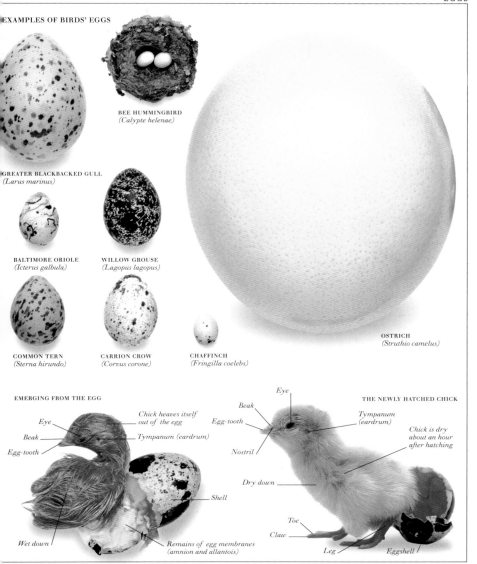

BEE HUMMINGBIRD
(Calypte helenae)

GREATER BLACKBACKED GULL
(Larus marinus)

BALTIMORE ORIOLE
(Icterus galbula)

WILLOW GROUSE
(Lagopus lagopus)

COMMON TERN
(Sterna hirundo)

CARRION CROW
(Corvus corone)

CHAFFINCH
(Fringilla coelebs)

OSTRICH
(Struthio camelus)

EMERGING FROM THE EGG

Eye

Beak

Egg-tooth

Chick heaves itself out of the egg

Tympanum (eardrum)

Shell

Wet down

Remains of egg membranes (amnion and allantois)

THE NEWLY HATCHED CHICK

Eye

Beak

Egg-tooth

Nostril

Tympanum (eardrum)

Chick is dry about an hour after hatching

Dry down

Toe

Claw

Leg

Eggshell

Carnivores

THE MAMMALIAN ORDER CARNIVORA includes cats, dogs, bears, raccoons, pandas, weasels, badgers, skunks, otters, civets, mongooses, and hyenas. The order's name is derived from the fact that most of its members are carnivores (flesh-eaters). Typical carnivore features therefore reflect a hunting life-style: speed and agility; sharp claws and well-developed canine teeth for holding and killing prey; carnassial teeth (cheek teeth) for cutting flesh; and forward-facing eyes for good distance judgment. However, some members of the order—bears, badgers, and foxes, for example— have a more mixed diet, and a few are entirely herbivorous (plant-eating), notably pandas. Such animals have no carnassial teeth and tend to be slower moving than pure flesh-eaters.

EXTERNAL FEATURES OF A MALE LION

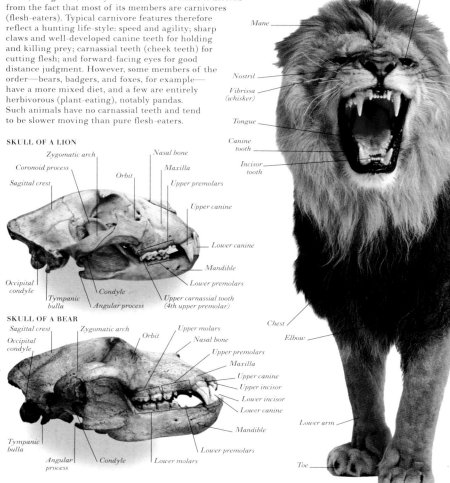

Nose
Eye
Mane
Nostril
Vibrissa (whisker)
Tongue
Canine tooth
Incisor tooth
Chest
Elbow
Lower arm
Toe

SKULL OF A LION

Zygomatic arch
Coronoid process
Sagittal crest
Orbit
Nasal bone
Maxilla
Upper premolars
Upper canine
Lower canine
Mandible
Lower premolars
Occipital condyle
Tympanic bulla
Condyle
Angular process
Upper carnassial tooth (4th upper premolar)

SKULL OF A BEAR

Sagittal crest
Occipital condyle
Zygomatic arch
Orbit
Upper molars
Nasal bone
Upper premolars
Maxilla
Upper canine
Upper incisor
Lower incisor
Lower canine
Mandible
Lower premolars
Lower molars
Tympanic bulla
Angular process
Condyle

EXAMPLES OF CARNIVORES

ALSATIAN DOG
(Canis familiaris)

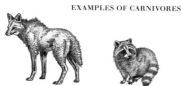

MANED WOLF
(Chrysocyon brachyurus)

RACCOON
(Procyon lotor)

AMERICAN BLACK BEAR
(Ursus americanus)

SKELETON OF A DOMESTIC CAT

Back
Rump
Hip
Rib cage
Caudal vertebrae
Sacrum
Lumbar vertebrae
Thoracic vertebrae
Cervical vertebrae
Skull
Pelvis
Femur
Scapula
Sternum
Humerus
Patella
Rib
Fibula
Ulna
Tibia
Radius
Carpals
Tarsals
Metatarsals
Metacarpals
Belly
Thigh
Knee
Phalanges

INTERNAL ANATOMY OF A MALE DOMESTIC CAT

Brain
Spinal cord
Stomach
Kidney
Diaphragm
Liver
Ureter
Large intestine
Nasal cavity
Small intestine
Buccal cavity
Anus
Nostril
Testis
Tongue
Trachea
Oesophagus
Lung
Hock
Tail
Paw
Heart
Gallbladder
Pancreas
Spleen
Urethra
Bladder
Vas deferens (sperm duct)

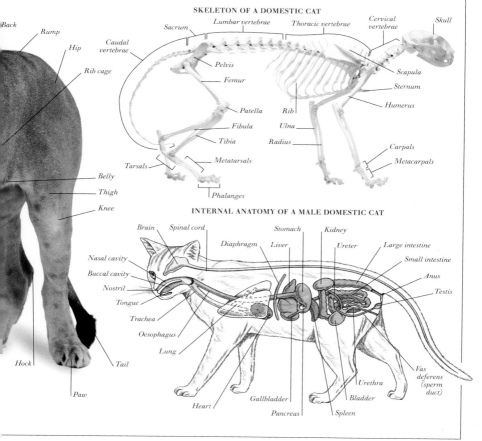

Rabbits and rodents

ALTHOUGH RABBITS AND RODENTS belong to different orders of mammals, they have some features in common. These features include chisel-shaped incisor teeth that grow continually, and eating their feces to extract more nutrients from their plant diet. Rabbits and hares belong to the order Lagomorpha. Characteristically, they have four incisors in the upper jaw and two in the lower jaw; powerful hind legs for jumping; forelimbs adapted for burrowing; long ears; and a small tail. Rodents make up the order Rodentia. This is the largest order of mammals, with more than 1,700 species, including squirrels, beavers, chipmunks, gophers, rats, mice, lemmings, gerbils, porcupines, cavies, and the capybara. Typical rodent features include two incisors in each jaw; short forelimbs for manipulating food; and cheek pouches for storing food.

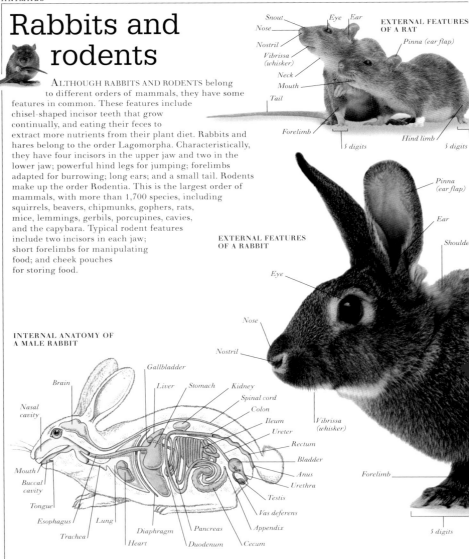

EXTERNAL FEATURES OF A RAT

Snout
Eye
Ear
Nose
Pinna (ear flap)
Nostril
Vibrissa (whisker)
Neck
Mouth
Tail
Forelimb
Hind limb
5 digits
5 digits

Pinna (ear flap)
Ear
Shoulde

EXTERNAL FEATURES OF A RABBIT

Eye
Nose
Nostril
Vibrissa (whisker)
Forelimb
5 digits

INTERNAL ANATOMY OF A MALE RABBIT

Gallbladder
Brain
Liver
Stomach
Kidney
Spinal cord
Nasal cavity
Colon
Ileum
Ureter
Rectum
Bladder
Mouth
Anus
Buccal cavity
Urethra
Tongue
Testis
Esophagus
Vas deferens
Lung
Appendix
Trachea
Diaphragm
Pancreas
Heart
Duodenum
Cecum

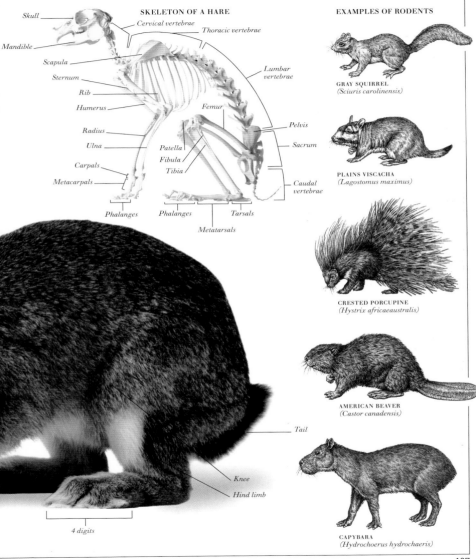

SKELETON OF A HARE

- Skull
- Cervical vertebrae
- Thoracic vertebrae
- Mandible
- Scapula
- Sternum
- Rib
- Humerus
- Radius
- Ulna
- Carpals
- Metacarpals
- Phalanges
- Femur
- Patella
- Fibula
- Tibia
- Phalanges
- Metatarsals
- Tarsals
- Lumbar vertebrae
- Pelvis
- Sacrum
- Caudal vertebrae

Tail

Knee

Hind limb

4 digits

EXAMPLES OF RODENTS

GRAY SQUIRREL
(*Sciuris carolinensis*)

PLAINS VISCACHA
(*Lagostomus maximus*)

CRESTED PORCUPINE
(*Hystrix africaeaustralis*)

AMERICAN BEAVER
(*Castor canadensis*)

CAPYBARA
(*Hydrochoerus hydrochaeris*)

Ungulates

Ungulates is a general term for a large, varied group of mammals that includes horses, cattle, and their relatives. The ungulates are divided into two orders on the basis of the number of toes. Members of the order Perissodactyla (odd-toed ungulates) have one or three toes. Perissodactyls include horses, onagers, and zebras (all of which are one-toed), and rhinoceroses and tapirs (which are three-toed). Members of the order Artiodactyla (even-toed ungulates) have two or four toes. Most artiodactyls have two toes, which are typically encased in hooves to give the so-called cloven hoof. Two-toed, cloven-hoofed artiodactyls include cows and other cattle, sheep, goats, antelopes, deer, and giraffes. The other main two-toed artiodactyls are camels and llamas. Most two-toed artiodactyls are ruminants; that is, they have a four-chambered stomach and chew the cud. The principal four-toed artiodactyls are pigs, peccaries, and hippopotamuses.

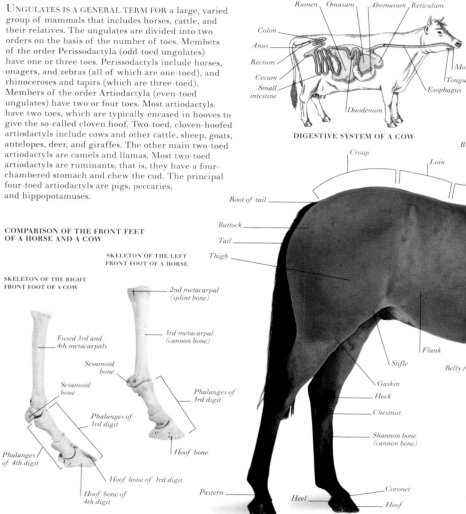

Chambers of stomach

Rumen   Omasum   Abomasum   Reticulum

Colon

Anus

Rectum

Cecum

Small intestine

Duodenum

Mo

Tongu

Esophagus

DIGESTIVE SYSTEM OF A COW

Croup

Loin

B

Root of tail

Buttock

Tail

Thigh

Stifle

Flank

Gaskin   Belly

Hock

Chestnut

Shannon bone (cannon bone)

Coronet

Heel   Hoof

COMPARISON OF THE FRONT FEET OF A HORSE AND A COW

SKELETON OF THE LEFT FRONT FOOT OF A HORSE

SKELETON OF THE RIGHT FRONT FOOT OF A COW

2nd metacarpal (splint bone)

3rd metacarpal (cannon bone)

Fused 3rd and 4th metacarpals

Sesamoid bone

Sesamoid bone

Phalanges of 3rd digit

Phalanges of 3rd digit

Phalanges of 4th digit

Hoof bone of 3rd digit

Hoof bone

Hoof bone of 4th digit

Pastern

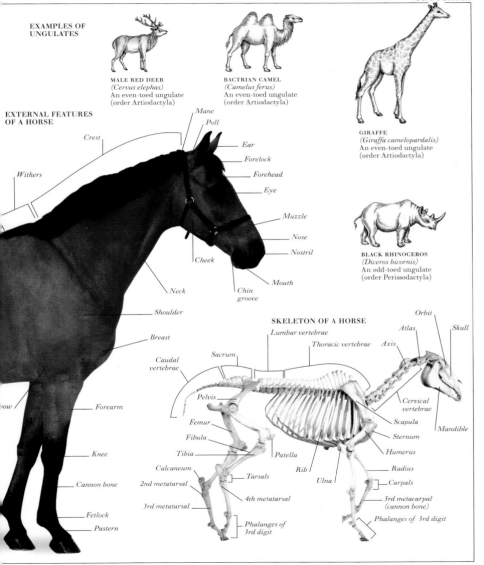

EXAMPLES OF UNGULATES

MALE RED DEER
(Cervus elephas)
An even-toed ungulate
(order Artiodactyla)

BACTRIAN CAMEL
(Camelus ferus)
An even-toed ungulate
(order Artiodactyla)

GIRAFFE
(Giraffa camelopardalis)
An even-toed ungulate
(order Artiodactyla)

BLACK RHINOCEROS
(Diceros bicornis)
An odd-toed ungulate
(order Perissodactyla)

EXTERNAL FEATURES OF A HORSE

Mane
Poll
Crest
Ear
Forelock
Withers
Forehead
Eye
Muzzle
Nose
Nostril
Cheek
Chin groove
Mouth
Neck
Shoulder
Breast
ow
Forearm
Knee
Cannon bone
Fetlock
Pastern

SKELETON OF A HORSE

Orbit
Atlas
Skull
Axis
Lumbar vertebrae
Thoracic vertebrae
Sacrum
Caudal vertebrae
Cervical vertebrae
Pelvis
Scapula
Femur
Sternum
Fibula
Humerus
Tibia
Patella
Calcaneum
Rib
Radius
Tarsals
Ulna
Carpals
2nd metatarsal
4th metatarsal
3rd metacarpal (cannon bone)
3rd metatarsal
Phalanges of 3rd digit
Phalanges of 3rd digit
Mandible

Elephants

THE TWO SPECIES OF elephant—African and Asian—are the only members of the mammalian order Proboscidea. The bigger African elephant is the largest land animal: a fully grown male may be up to 13 ft (4 m) tall and weigh nearly 8 tons (7 metric tons). A fully grown male Asian elephant may be 11 ft (3.3 m) tall and weigh 6 tons (5.4 metric tons). The trunk—an extension of the nose and upper lip—is the elephant's other most obvious feature. It is used for manipulating and lifting, feeding, drinking and spraying water, smelling, touching, and producing trumpeting sounds. Other characteristic features include a pair of tusks, used for defense and for crushing vegetation; thick, pillarlike legs and broad feet to support the massive body; and large ear flaps that act as radiators to keep the elephant cool.

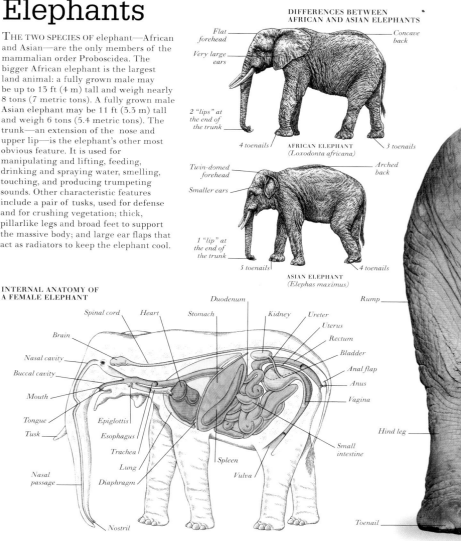

DIFFERENCES BETWEEN AFRICAN AND ASIAN ELEPHANTS

Flat forehead
Very large ears
Concave back
2 "lips" at the end of the trunk
4 toenails
AFRICAN ELEPHANT
(Loxodonta africana)
3 toenails

Twin-domed forehead
Smaller ears
Arched back
1 "lip" at the end of the trunk
5 toenails
ASIAN ELEPHANT
(Elephas maximus)
4 toenails

INTERNAL ANATOMY OF A FEMALE ELEPHANT

Spinal cord   Heart   Stomach   Duodenum   Kidney   Ureter   Rump
Brain   Uterus
Nasal cavity   Rectum
Buccal cavity   Bladder
Mouth   Anal flap
Tongue   Anus
Tusk   Epiglottis   Vagina
Esophagus   Hind leg
Trachea
Lung   Small intestine
Nasal passage   Diaphragm   Spleen   Vulva
Nostril   Toenail

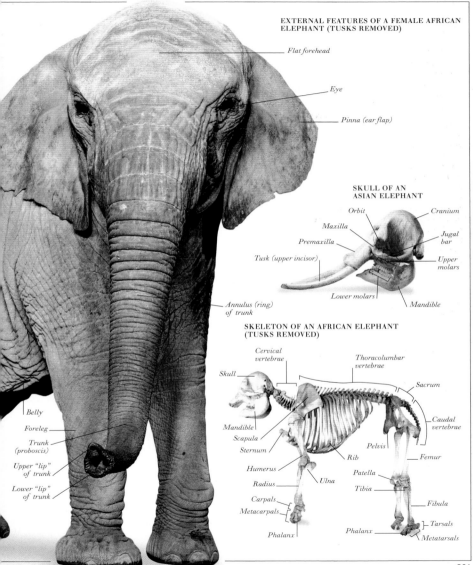

EXTERNAL FEATURES OF A FEMALE AFRICAN ELEPHANT (TUSKS REMOVED)

Flat forehead

Eye

Pinna (ear flap)

Annulus (ring) of trunk

Belly

Foreleg

Trunk (proboscis)

Upper "lip" of trunk

Lower "lip" of trunk

SKULL OF AN ASIAN ELEPHANT

Orbit

Cranium

Maxilla

Jugal bar

Premaxilla

Upper molars

Tusk (upper incisor)

Lower molars

Mandible

SKELETON OF AN AFRICAN ELEPHANT (TUSKS REMOVED)

Cervical vertebrae

Thoracolumbar vertebrae

Skull

Sacrum

Mandible

Caudal vertebrae

Scapula

Pelvis

Sternum

Femur

Rib

Humerus

Patella

Radius

Tibia

Ulna

Carpals

Fibula

Metacarpals

Tarsals

Phalanx

Phalanx

Metatarsals

Primates

THE MAMMALIAN ORDER PRIMATES consists of monkeys, apes, and their relatives (including humans). There are two suborders of primates: Prosimii, the primitive primates, which include lemurs, tarsiers, and lorises; and Anthropoidea, the advanced primates, which include monkeys, apes, and humans. The anthropoids are divided into New World monkeys, Old World monkeys, and hominids. New World monkeys typically have wide-apart nostrils that open to the side; and long tails, which are prehensile (grasping) in some species. This group of monkeys lives in South America, and includes marmosets, tamarins, and howler monkeys. Old World monkeys typically have close-set nostrils that open forward or downward; and non-prehensile tails. This group of monkeys lives in Africa and Asia, and includes langurs, mandrills, macaques, and baboons. Hominids typically have large brains, and no tail. This group includes the apes—chimpanzees, gibbons, gorillas, and orangutans—and humans.

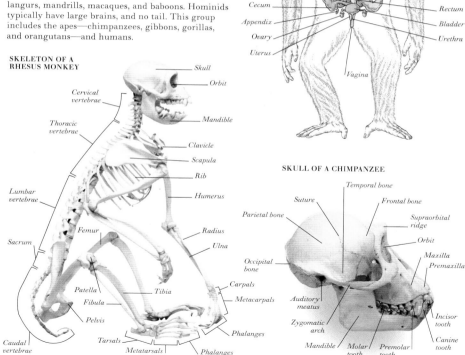

INTERNAL ANATOMY OF A FEMALE CHIMPANZEE

Buccal cavity · Tongue · Trachea · Lung · Liver · Pancreas · Small intestine · Cecum · Appendix · Ovary · Uterus · Brain · Nasal cavity · Spinal cord · Esophagus · Heart · Diaphragm · Stomach · Spleen · Large intestine · Rectum · Bladder · Urethra · Vagina

SKELETON OF A RHESUS MONKEY

Skull · Orbit · Cervical vertebrae · Mandible · Thoracic vertebrae · Clavicle · Scapula · Rib · Humerus · Lumbar vertebrae · Radius · Ulna · Sacrum · Femur · Patella · Tibia · Fibula · Carpals · Pelvis · Metacarpals · Caudal vertebrae · Tarsals · Metatarsals · Phalanges · Phalanges

SKULL OF A CHIMPANZEE

Temporal bone · Suture · Parietal bone · Frontal bone · Supraorbital ridge · Orbit · Maxilla · Premaxilla · Occipital bone · Auditory meatus · Zygomatic arch · Mandible · Molar tooth · Premolar tooth · Incisor tooth · Canine tooth

EXAMPLES OF PRIMATES

RING-TAILED LEMUR
(Lemur catta)
A prosimian

MALE RED HOWLER MONKEY
(Alouatta seniculus)
A New World monkey

MALE MANDRILL
(Mandrillus sphinx)
An Old World monkey

CHIMPANZEE
(Pan troglodytes)
An ape

**EXTERNAL FEATURES OF
A YOUNG GORILLA**

GOLDEN LION TAMARIN
(Leontopithecus rosalia)
A New World monkey

Pinna *(ear flap)*

Shoulder

Brow ridge

Eye

Nostril

Mouth

Upper arm

Thigh

Forearm

Chest

Knee

Elbow

Lower leg

Hand

Foot

Finger

Toe

Toenail

Dolphins, whales, and seals

DOLPHINS, WHALES, AND SEALS belong
to two orders of mammal adapted to living
in water. Dolphins and whales make up the
order Cetacea. Typical cetacean features include
a streamlined, fishlike shape; forelimbs in the form
of flippers; no visible hind limbs; a horizontally flattened
tail; and thick blubber under the skin. There are two groups
of cetaceans: toothed whales, including sperm whales, white whales,
beaked whales, dolphins, and porpoises; and the larger whalebone (baleen)
whales, including rorquals, gray whales, and right whales. The blue whale—a
rorqual—is the largest living animal: an adult may be up to 100 ft (30 m) long
and weigh 145 tons (130 metric tons). Seals and their relatives—sea lions and
walruses—make up the order Pinnipedia. Characteristically, they have a
streamlined, torpedo-shaped body; forelimbs and hind limbs modified as
flippers; thick blubber; and no external ears.

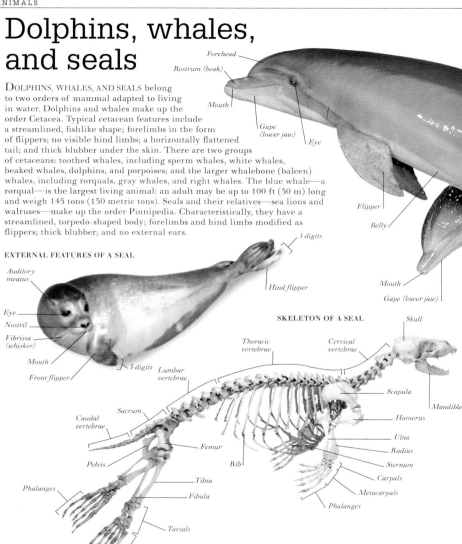

Forehead
Rostrum (beak)
Mouth
Gape (lower jaw)
Eye
Flipper
Belly
Mouth
Gape (lower jaw)

EXTERNAL FEATURES OF A SEAL

Auditory meatus
Eye
Nostril
Vibrissa (whisker)
Mouth
Front flipper
5 digits
Hind flipper
5 digits

SKELETON OF A SEAL

Skull
Thoracic vertebrae
Cervical vertebrae
Lumbar vertebrae
Sacrum
Scapula
Mandible
Caudal vertebrae
Humerus
Ulna
Radius
Femur
Rib
Sternum
Pelvis
Carpals
Tibia
Metacarpals
Phalanges
Fibula
Phalanges
Tarsals
Metatarsals

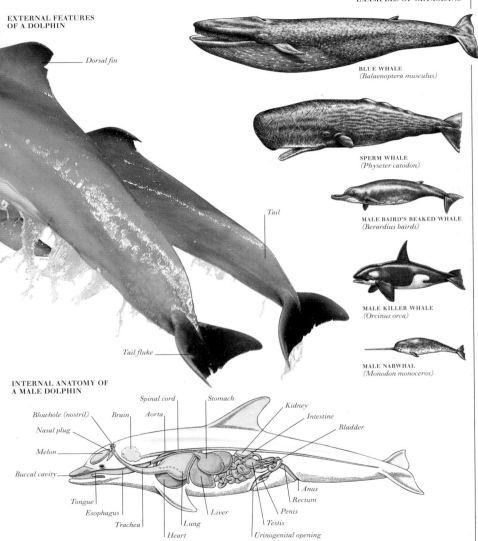

EXAMPLES OF CETACEANS

**EXTERNAL FEATURES
OF A DOLPHIN**

Dorsal fin

Tail

Tail fluke

BLUE WHALE
(Balaenoptera musculus)

SPERM WHALE
(Physeter catodon)

MALE BAIRD'S BEAKED WHALE
(Berardius bairdi)

MALE KILLER WHALE
(Orcinus orca)

MALE NARWHAL
(Monodon monoceros)

**INTERNAL ANATOMY OF
A MALE DOLPHIN**

Spinal cord   _Stomach_   _Kidney_

Blowhole (nostril)   _Brain_   _Aorta_   _Intestine_

Nasal plug   _Bladder_

Melon

Buccal cavity

Anus

Rectum

Tongue   _Penis_

Esophagus   _Testis_

Trachea   _Liver_   _Urinogenital opening_

Heart   _Lung_

205

Marsupials and Monotremes

MARSUPIALS AND MONOTREMES are two orders of mammal that differ from other mammalian groups in the ways that their young develop. The order Marsupalia, the pouched mammals, is made up of kangaroos and their relatives. Typically, marsupials give birth to their young at a very early stage of development. The young then crawls to the mother's pouch (which is on the outside of her abdomen), where it attaches itself to a nipple and remains until fully developed. Most marsupials live in Australia, although the opossums—which are classified as marsupials despite not having a pouch—live in the Americas. The order Monotremata is made up of the platypus and its relatives (the echidnas, or spiny anteaters). The monotremes are primitive mammals that lay eggs, which the mother incubates. The monotremes are found only in Australia and New Guinea.

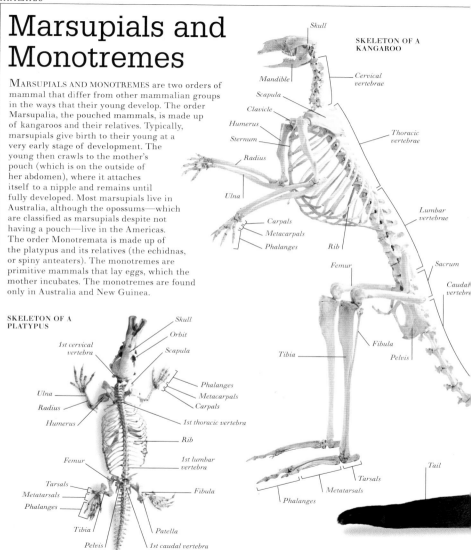

SKELETON OF A KANGAROO

Skull

Mandible

Cervical vertebrae

Scapula

Clavicle

Humerus

Sternum

Radius

Ulna

Thoracic vertebrae

Lumbar vertebrae

Carpals

Metacarpals

Phalanges

Rib

Femur

Sacrum

Caudal vertebrae

Fibula

Tibia

Pelvis

Tarsals

Metatarsals

Phalanges

Tail

SKELETON OF A PLATYPUS

Skull

Orbit

1st cervical vertebra

Scapula

Phalanges

Metacarpals

Carpals

Ulna

Radius

Humerus

1st thoracic vertebra

Rib

Femur

1st lumbar vertebra

Tarsals

Metatarsals

Phalanges

Fibula

Tibia

Patella

Pelvis

1st caudal vertebra

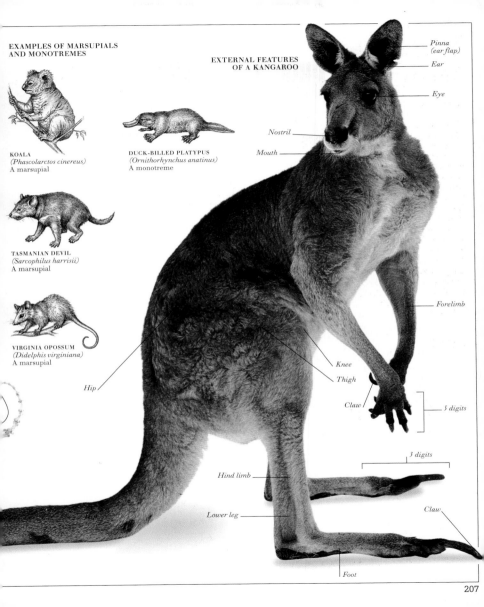

EXAMPLES OF MARSUPIALS AND MONOTREMES

KOALA
(Phascolarctos cinereus)
A marsupial

DUCK-BILLED PLATYPUS
(Ornithorhynchus anatinus)
A monotreme

TASMANIAN DEVIL
(Sarcophilus harrisii)
A marsupial

VIRGINIA OPOSSUM
(Didelphis virginiana)
A marsupial

EXTERNAL FEATURES OF A KANGAROO

Pinna
(ear flap)

Ear

Eye

Nostril

Mouth

Forelimb

Knee

Thigh

Claw

5 digits

3 digits

Hip

Hind limb

Lower leg

Claw

Foot

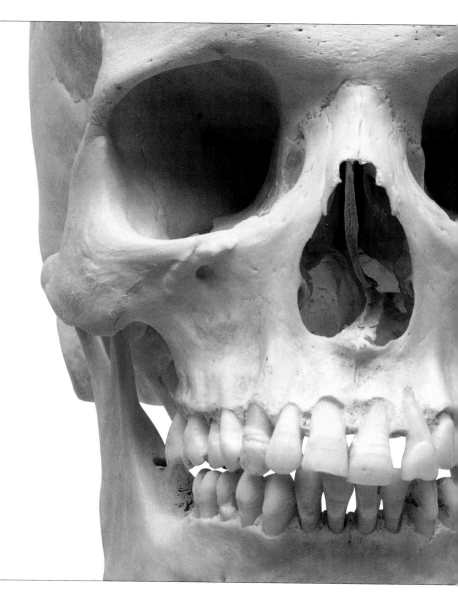

THE HUMAN BODY

BODY FEATURES 210
HEAD 212
BODY ORGANS 214
BODY CELLS 216
SKELETON 218
SKULL 220
SPINE 222
BONES AND JOINTS 224
MUSCLES 1 226
MUSCLES 2 228
HANDS 230
FEET 232
SKIN AND HAIR 234
BRAIN 236
NERVOUS SYSTEM 238
EYE 240
EAR 242
NOSE, MOUTH, AND THROAT 244
TEETH 246
DIGESTIVE SYSTEM 248
HEART 250
CIRCULATORY SYSTEM 252
RESPIRATORY SYSTEM 254
URINARY SYSTEM 256
REPRODUCTIVE SYSTEM 258
DEVELOPMENT OF A BABY 260

Body features

ALTHOUGH THERE IS enormous
variation between the external
appearances of humans, all bodies
contain the same basic features.
The outward form of the
human body depends on the
size of the skeleton, the shape
of the muscles, the thickness
of the fat layer beneath
the skin, the elasticity or
sagginess of the skin, and
the person's age and sex.
Males tend to be taller than
females, with broader
shoulders, more body hair,
and a different pattern of
fat deposits under the skin;
the female body tends to
be less muscular and
has a shallower and
wider pelvis to allow
for childbirth.

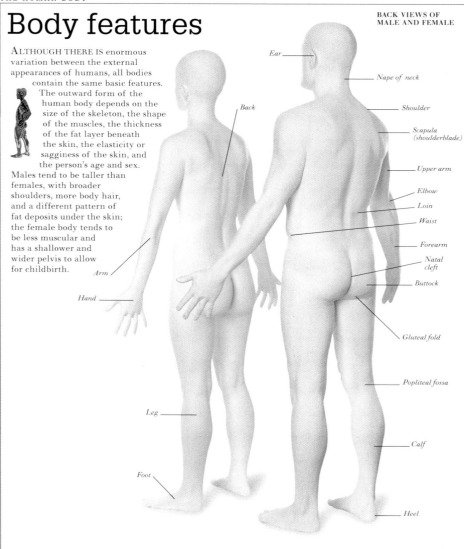

Ear

Nape of neck

Shoulder

Scapula
(shoulderblade)

Back

Upper arm

Elbow

Loin

Waist

Forearm

Natal
cleft

Buttock

Arm

Hand

Gluteal fold

Popliteal fossa

Leg

Calf

Foot

Heel

**FRONT VIEWS OF
MALE AND FEMALE**

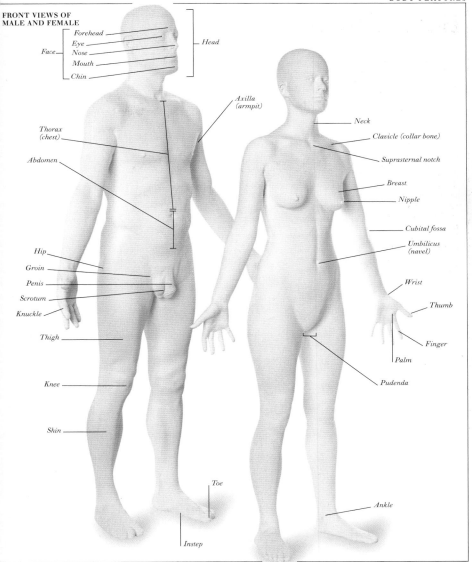

Forehead

Eye

Face — Nose

Mouth

Chin

Head

Axilla
(armpit)

Thorax
(chest)

Abdomen

Hip

Groin

Penis

Scrotum

Knuckle

Thigh

Knee

Shin

Toe

Instep

Neck

Clavicle (collar bone)

Suprasternal notch

Breast

Nipple

Cubital fossa

Umbilicus
(navel)

Wrist

Thumb

Finger

Palm

Pudenda

Ankle

Head

IN A NEWBORN BABY, the head accounts for one-quarter of the total body length; by adulthood, the proportion has reduced to one-eighth. Contained in the head are the body's main sense organs: eyes, ears, olfactory nerves that detect smells, and the taste buds of the tongue. Signals from these organs pass to the body's great coordination center: the brain, housed in the protective, bony dome of the skull. Hair on the head insulates against heat loss, and adult males also grow thick facial hair. The face has three important openings: two nostrils through which air passes, and the mouth, which takes in nourishment and helps form speech. Although all heads are basically similar, differences in the size, shape, and color of features produce an infinite variety of appearances.

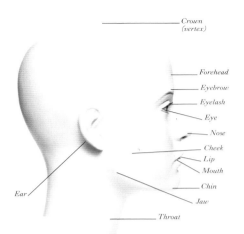

Crown (vertex)
Forehead
Eyebrow
Eyelash
Eye
Nose
Cheek
Lip
Mouth
Chin
Jaw
Ear
Throat

SECTION THROUGH HEAD

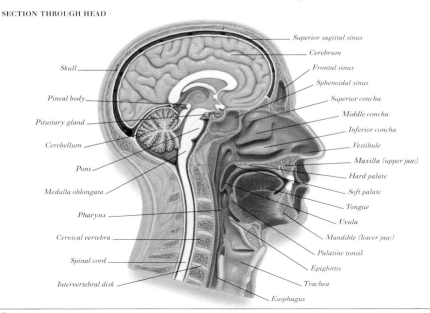

Skull
Pineal body
Pituitary gland
Cerebellum
Pons
Medulla oblongata
Pharynx
Cervical vertebra
Spinal cord
Intervertebral disk

Superior sagittal sinus
Cerebrum
Frontal sinus
Sphenoidal sinus
Superior concha
Middle concha
Inferior concha
Vestibule
Maxilla (upper jaw)
Hard palate
Soft palate
Tongue
Uvula
Mandible (lower jaw)
Palatine tonsil
Epiglottis
Trachea
Esophagus

**FRONT VIEW OF EXTERNAL
FEATURES OF HEAD**

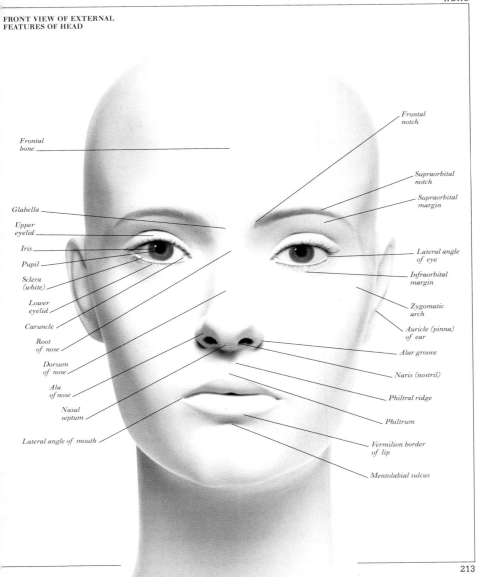

Frontal
notch

Frontal
bone

Supraorbital
notch

Supraorbital
margin

Glabella

Upper
eyelid

Iris

Lateral angle
of eye

Pupil

Infraorbital
margin

Sclera
(white)

Zygomatic
arch

Lower
eyelid

Auricle (pinna)
of ear

Caruncle

Root
of nose

Alar groove

Dorsum
of nose

Naris (nostril)

Ala
of nose

Philtral ridge

Nasal
septum

Philtrum

Lateral angle of mouth

Vermilion border
of lip

Mentolabial sulcus

Body organs

ALL THE VITAL BODY ORGANS except for the brain are enclosed within the trunk or torso (the body apart from the head and limbs). The trunk contains two large cavities separated by a muscular sheet called the diaphragm. The upper cavity, known as the thorax or chest cavity, contains the heart and lungs. The lower cavity, called the abdominal cavity, contains the stomach, intestines, liver, and pancreas, which all play a role in digesting food. Also within the trunk are the kidneys and bladder, which are part of the urinary system, and the reproductive organs, which hold the seeds of new human life. Modern imaging techniques, such as contrast X-rays and different types of scans, make it possible to see and study body organs without the need to cut through their protective coverings of skin, fat, muscle, and bone.

MAJOR INTERNAL STRUCTURES

Thyroid gland
Larynx
Heart
Right lung
Left lung
Liver
Diaphragm
Stomach
Large intestine
Small intestine
Greater omentum

IMAGING THE BODY

SCINTIGRAM OF HEART CHAMBERS

ANGIOGRAM OF RIGHT LUNG

CONTRAST X-RAY OF GALLBLADDER

SCINTIGRAM OF NERVOUS SYSTEM

DOUBLE CONTRAST X-RAY OF COLON

ULTRASOUND SCAN OF TWINS IN UTERUS

ANGIOGRAM OF KIDNEYS

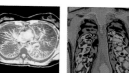

ANGIOGRAM OF ARTERIES OF HEAD

CT SCAN THROUGH FEMALE CHEST

THERMOGRAM OF CHEST REGION

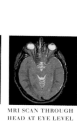

ANGIOGRAM OF ARTERIES OF HEART

MRI SCAN THROUGH HEAD AT EYE LEVEL

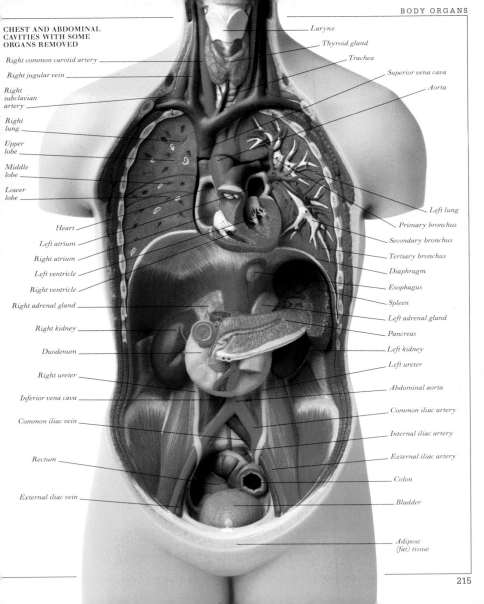

**CHEST AND ABDOMINAL
CAVITIES WITH SOME
ORGANS REMOVED**

Right common carotid artery

Right jugular vein

Right
subclavian
artery

Right
lung

Upper
lobe

Middle
lobe

Lower
lobe

Heart

Left atrium

Right atrium

Left ventricle

Right ventricle

Right adrenal gland

Right kidney

Duodenum

Right ureter

Inferior vena cava

Common iliac vein

Rectum

External iliac vein

Larynx

Thyroid gland

Trachea

Superior vena cava

Aorta

Left lung

Primary bronchus

Secondary bronchus

Tertiary bronchus

Diaphragm

Esophagus

Spleen

Left adrenal gland

Pancreas

Left kidney

Left ureter

Abdominal aorta

Common iliac artery

Internal iliac artery

External iliac artery

Colon

Bladder

Adipose
(fat) tissue

Body cells

EVERYONE IS MADE UP OF BILLIONS OF CELLS, which are the basic structural units of the body. Bones, muscles, nerves, skin, blood, and all other body tissues are formed from different types of cells. Each cell has a specific function but works with other types of cells to perform the enormous number of tasks needed to sustain life. Most body cells have a similar basic structure. Each cell has an outer layer (called the cell membrane) and contains a fluid material (cytoplasm). Within the cytoplasm are many specialized structures (organelles). The most important organelle is the nucleus, which contains vital genetic material and acts as the cell's control center.

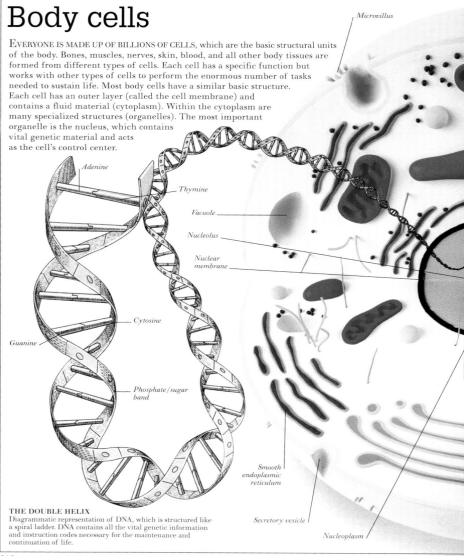

Microvillus

Adenine

Thymine

Vacuole

Nucleolus

Nuclear membrane

Cytosine

Guanine

Phosphate/sugar band

Smooth endoplasmic reticulum

Secretory vesicle

Nucleoplasm

THE DOUBLE HELIX
Diagrammatic representation of DNA, which is structured like a spiral ladder. DNA contains all the vital genetic information and instruction codes necessary for the maintenance and continuation of life.

GENERALIZED HUMAN CELL

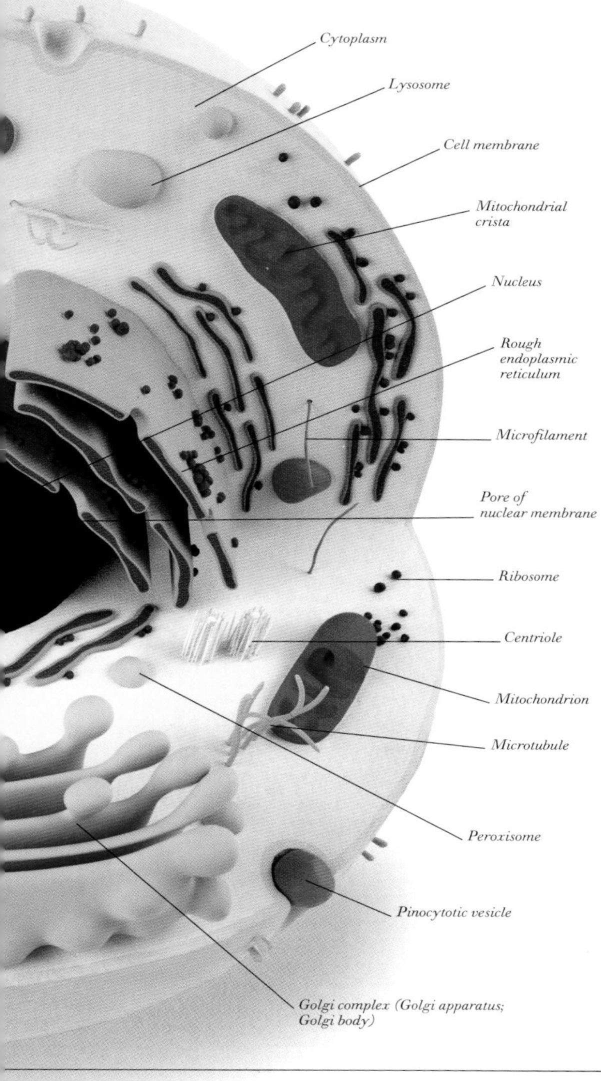

Cytoplasm

Lysosome

Cell membrane

Mitochondrial crista

Nucleus

Rough endoplasmic reticulum

Microfilament

Pore of nuclear membrane

Ribosome

Centriole

Mitochondrion

Microtubule

Peroxisome

Pinocytotic vesicle

Golgi complex (Golgi apparatus; Golgi body)

TYPES OF CELLS

BONE-FORMING CELL

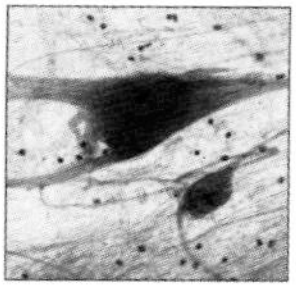

NERVE CELLS IN SPINAL CORD

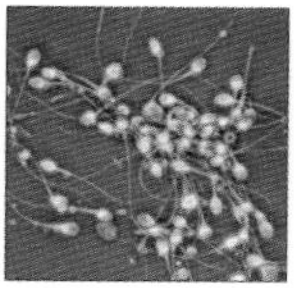

SPERM CELLS IN SEMEN

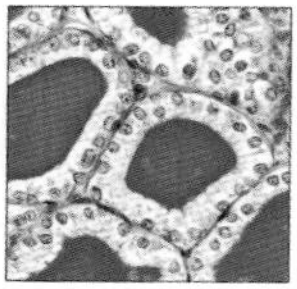

SECRETORY THYROID GLAND CELLS

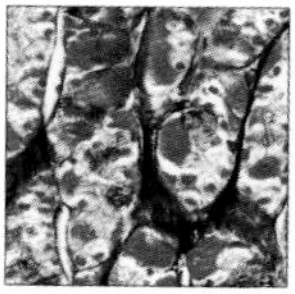

ACID-SECRETING STOMACH CELLS

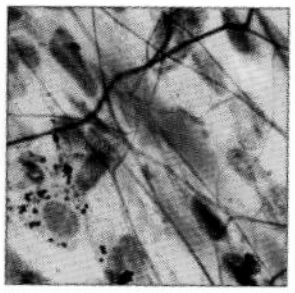

CONNECTIVE TISSUE CELLS

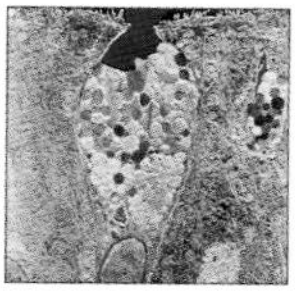

MUCUS-SECRETING DUODENAL CELLS

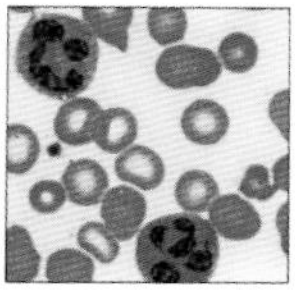

RED AND TWO WHITE BLOOD CELLS

FAT CELLS IN ADIPOSE TISSUE

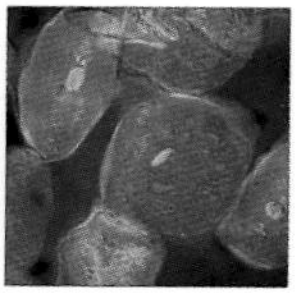

EPITHELIAL CELLS IN CHEEK

Skeleton

THE SKELETON IS A MOBILE FRAMEWORK made up of 206 bones, approximately
half of which are in the hands and feet. Although individual bones are rigid,
the skeleton as a whole is remarkably flexible and allows the human body a
huge range of movement. The skeleton serves as an anchorage for the skeletal
muscles, and as a protective cage for the body's internal organs.
Female bones are usually smaller and lighter
than male bones, and the female pelvis
is shallower and has a wider cavity.

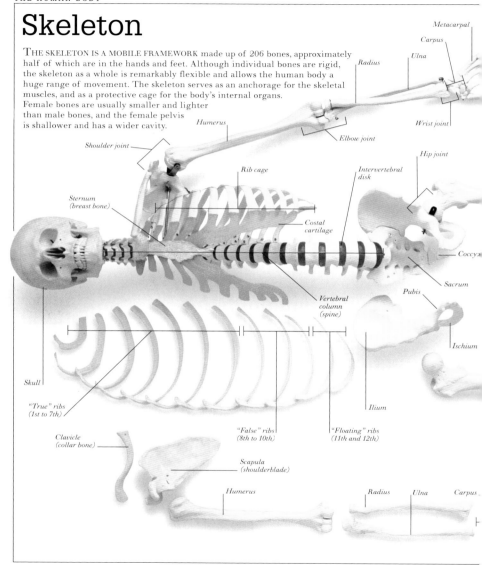

Metacarpal

Carpus

Radius

Ulna

Wrist joint

Humerus

Shoulder joint

Elbow joint

Hip joint

Rib cage

Intervertebral
disk

Sternum
(breast bone)

Costal
cartilage

Coccyx

Sacrum

Pubis

Vertebral
column
(spine)

Ischium

Skull

Ilium

"True" ribs
(1st to 7th)

"False" ribs
(8th to 10th)

"Floating" ribs
(11th and 12th)

Clavicle
(collar bone)

Scapula
(shoulderblade)

Humerus

Radius

Ulna

Carpus

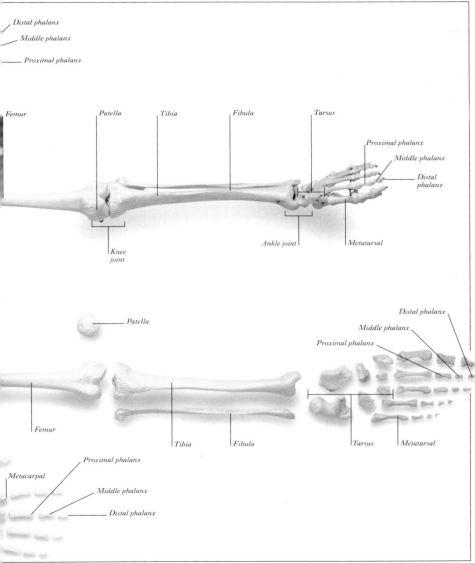

Distal phalanx

Middle phalanx

Proximal phalanx

Femur

Patella

Tibia

Fibula

Tarsus

Proximal phalanx

Middle phalanx

Distal phalanx

Knee joint

Ankle joint

Metatarsal

Patella

Distal phalanx

Middle phalanx

Proximal phalanx

Femur

Tibia

Fibula

Tarsus

Metatarsal

Metacarpal

Proximal phalanx

Middle phalanx

Distal phalanx

Skull

THE SKULL is the most complicated bony structure of the body but every feature serves a purpose. Internally, the main hollow chamber of the skull has three levels that support the brain, with every bump and hollow corresponding to the shape of the brain. Underneath and toward the back of the skull is a large round hole, the foramen magnum, through which the spinal cord passes. To the front of this are many smaller openings through which nerves, arteries, and veins pass to and from the brain. The roof of the skull is formed from four thin, curved bones that are firmly fixed together from the age of about two years. At the front of the skull are the two orbits, which contain the eyeballs, and a central hole for the airway of the nose. The jaw bone hinges on either side at ear level.

RIGHT SIDE VIEW OF A FETAL SKULL

- Anterior fontanelle
- Parietal bone
- Coronal suture
- Frontal bone
- Nasal bone
- Mental symphysis
- Sphenoidal fontanelle
- Mastoid fontanelle
- External auditory meatus
- Lambdoid suture
- Occipital bone

RIGHT SIDE VIEW OF SKULL

- Coronal suture
- Frontal bone
- Greater wing of sphenoid bone
- Frontozygomatic suture
- Parietal bone
- Supraorbital margin
- Squamous suture
- Orbital cavity
- Nasal bone
- Anterior nasal spine
- Maxilla (upper jaw)
- Mandible (lower jaw)
- Lambdoid suture
- Occipital bone
- Temporal bone
- External auditory meatus
- Mastoid process
- Condyle
- Coronoid process
- Zygomatic bone
- Mental foramen

VIEW OF SKULL FROM BELOW

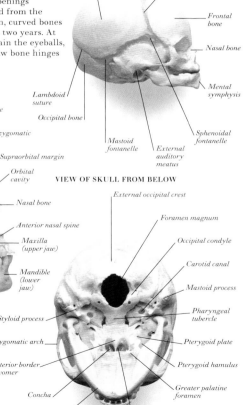

- External occipital crest
- Foramen magnum
- Occipital condyle
- Carotid canal
- Mastoid process
- Pharyngeal tubercle
- Pterygoid plate
- Pterygoid hamulus
- Greater palatine foramen
- Posterior nasal aperture
- Styloid process
- Zygomatic arch
- Posterior border of vomer
- Concha
- Mandible (lower jaw)

FRONT VIEW OF SKULL

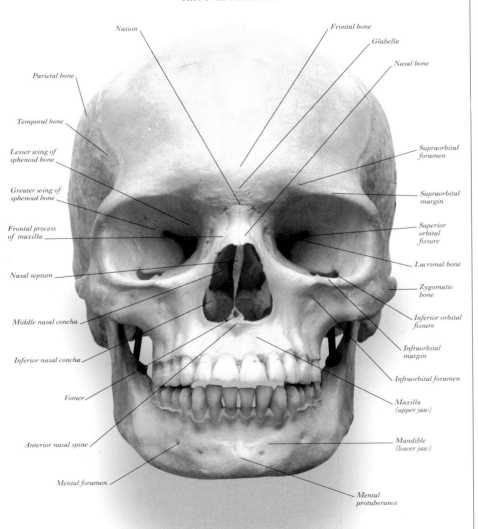

Nasion

Frontal bone

Glabella

Nasal bone

Parietal bone

Temporal bone

Lesser wing of
sphenoid bone

Greater wing of
sphenoid bone

Frontal process
of maxilla

Nasal septum

Middle nasal concha

Inferior nasal concha

Vomer

Anterior nasal spine

Mental foramen

Supraorbital
foramen

Supraorbital
margin

Superior
orbital
fissure

Lacrimal bone

Zygomatic
bone

Inferior orbital
fissure

Infraorbital
margin

Infraorbital foramen

Maxilla
(upper jaw)

Mandible
(lower jaw)

Mental
protuberance

Spine

THE SPINE (OR VERTEBRAL COLUMN) has two main functions:
it serves as a protective surrounding for the delicate spinal
cord and forms the supporting back bone of the skeleton.
The spine consists of 24 separate differently shaped bones
(vertebrae) with a curved, triangular bone (the sacrum) at
the bottom. The sacrum is made up of fused vertebrae; at its
lower end is a small tail-like structure made up of tiny bones
collectively called the coccyx. Between each pair of vertebrae
is a disk of cartilage that cushions the bones during movement.
The top two vertebrae differ in appearance from the others and
work as a pair: the first, called the atlas, rotates around a stout
vertical peg on the second, the axis. This arrangement allows
the skull to move freely up and down, and from side to side.

SPINE DIVIDED INTO VERTEBRAL SECTIONS — FRONT

Cervical vertebrae

Thoracic vertebrae

Lumbar vertebrae

Sacral vertebrae

Coccygeal vertebrae

TYPES OF VERTEBRAE (VIEWED FROM ABOVE)

ATLAS

Lateral mass with superior articular facet

Anterior arch

Posterior arch

Anterior tubercle

Posterior tubercle

Vertebral foramen

Transverse process

Transverse foramen

AXIS

Facet

Dens

Vertebral foramen

Spinous process

Lamina

Transverse process and foramen

CERVICAL VERTEBRA

Body

Superior articular process

Anterior tubercle

Spinous process

Vertebral foramen

Posterior tubercle

Transverse foramen

SKULL AND SPINE

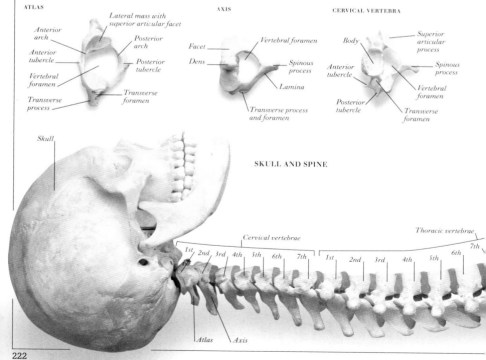

Skull

Cervical vertebrae

1st 2nd 3rd 4th 5th 6th 7th

Atlas Axis

Thoracic vertebrae

1st 2nd 3rd 4th 5th 6th 7th

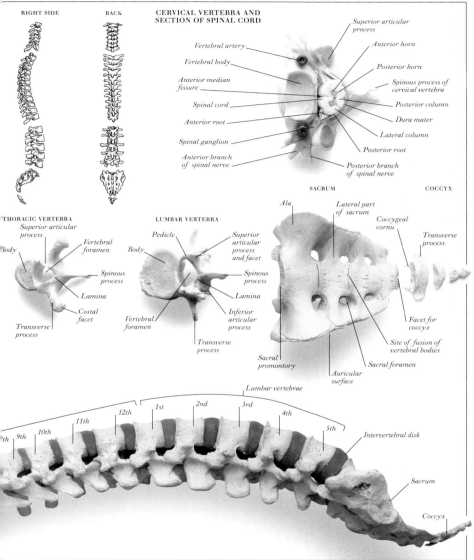

RIGHT SIDE

BACK

CERVICAL VERTEBRA AND SECTION OF SPINAL CORD

Superior articular process

Vertebral artery

Anterior horn

Vertebral body

Posterior horn

Anterior median fissure

Spinous process of cervical vertebra

Spinal cord

Posterior column

Anterior root

Dura mater

Spinal ganglion

Lateral column

Anterior branch of spinal nerve

Posterior root

Posterior branch of spinal nerve

SACRUM

COCCYX

THORACIC VERTEBRA

Superior articular process

Vertebral foramen

Body

Spinous process

Lamina

Costal facet

Transverse process

LUMBAR VERTEBRA

Pedicle

Body

Superior articular process and facet

Spinous process

Lamina

Inferior articular process

Vertebral foramen

Transverse process

Ala

Lateral part of sacrum

Coccygeal cornu

Transverse process

Sacral promontory

Auricular surface

Sacral foramen

Site of fusion of vertebral bodies

Facet for coccyx

Lumbar vertebrae

1st   2nd   3rd   4th   5th

9th   10th   11th   12th

8th

Intervertebral disk

Sacrum

Coccyx

Bones and joints

BONES FORM the body's hard, strong skeletal framework. Each bone has a hard, compact exterior surrounding a spongy, lighter interior. The long bones of the arms and legs, such as the femur (thigh bone), have a central cavity containing bone marrow. Bones are composed chiefly of calcium, phosphorus, and a fibrous substance known as collagen. Bones meet at joints, which are of several different types. For example, the hip is a ball-and-socket joint that allows the femur a wide range of movement, whereas finger joints are simple hinge joints that allow only bending and straightening. Joints are held in place by bands of tissue called ligaments. Movement of joints is facilitated by the smooth hyaline cartilage that covers the bone ends and by the synovial membrane that lines and lubricates the joint.

LIGAMENTS SURROUNDING HIP JOINT

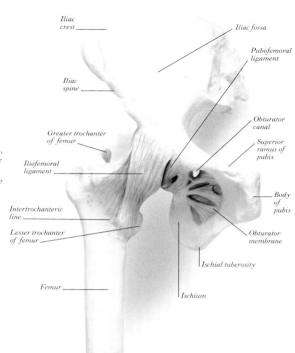

Iliac crest

Iliac fossa

Pubofemoral ligament

Iliac spine

Obturator canal

Greater trochanter of femur

Superior ramus of pubis

Iliofemoral ligament

Body of pubis

Intertrochanteric line

Obturator membrane

Lesser trochanter of femur

Ischial tuberosity

Femur

Ischium

SECTION THROUGH LEFT FEMUR

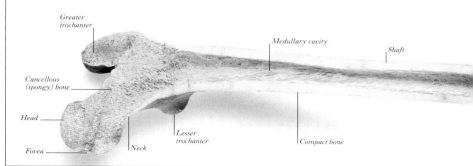

Greater trochanter

Medullary cavity

Shaft

Cancellous (spongy) bone

Head

Lesser trochanter

Neck

Compact bone

Fovea

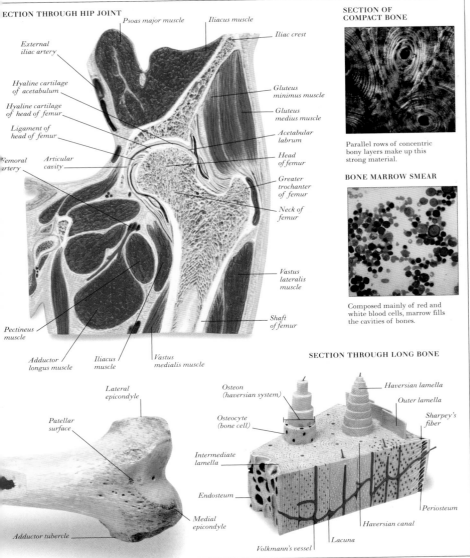

...ECTION THROUGH HIP JOINT

- Psoas major muscle
- Iliacus muscle
- External iliac artery
- Iliac crest
- Hyaline cartilage of acetabulum
- Hyaline cartilage of head of femur
- Gluteus minimus muscle
- Gluteus medius muscle
- Ligament of head of femur
- Acetabular labrum
- Femoral artery
- Articular cavity
- Head of femur
- Greater trochanter of femur
- Neck of femur
- Pectineus muscle
- Vastus lateralis muscle
- Shaft of femur
- Adductor longus muscle
- Iliacus muscle
- Vastus medialis muscle

SECTION OF COMPACT BONE

Parallel rows of concentric bony layers make up this strong material.

BONE MARROW SMEAR

Composed mainly of red and white blood cells, marrow fills the cavities of bones.

- Lateral epicondyle
- Patellar surface
- Medial epicondyle
- Adductor tubercle

SECTION THROUGH LONG BONE

- Osteon (haversian system)
- Haversian lamella
- Outer lamella
- Osteocyte (bone cell)
- Intermediate lamella
- Sharpey's fiber
- Endosteum
- Periosteum
- Volkmann's vessel
- Lacuna
- Haversian canal

Muscles 1

THERE ARE THREE MAIN TYPES OF MUSCLE: skeletal muscle (also called voluntary muscle because it can be consciously controlled); smooth muscle (also called involuntary muscle because it is not under voluntary control); and the specialized muscle tissue of the heart. Humans have more than 600 skeletal muscles, which differ in size and shape according to the jobs they do. Skeletal muscles are attached either directly or indirectly (via tendons) to bones, and work in opposing pairs (one muscle in the pair contracts while the other relaxes) to produce body movements as diverse as walking, threading a needle, and an array of facial expressions. Smooth muscles occur in the walls of internal body organs and perform actions such as forcing food through the intestines, contracting the uterus (womb) in childbirth, and pumping blood through the blood vessels.

SOME OTHER MUSCLES IN THE BODY

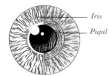

Iris
Pupil

IRIS
The muscle fibers contract and dilate (expand) to alter pupil size.

TONGUE
Interlacing layers of muscle allow great mobility.

ILEUM
Opposing muscle layers transport semidigested food.

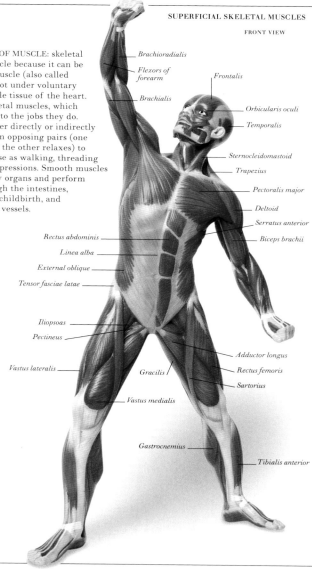

Brachioradialis
Flexors of forearm
Brachialis
Frontalis
Orbicularis oculi
Temporalis
Sternocleidomastoid
Trapezius
Pectoralis major
Deltoid
Serratus anterior
Biceps brachii
Rectus abdominis
Linea alba
External oblique
Tensor fasciae latae
Iliopsoas
Pectineus
Adductor longus
Rectus femoris
Sartorius
Vastus lateralis
Gracilis
Vastus medialis
Gastrocnemius
Tibialis anterior

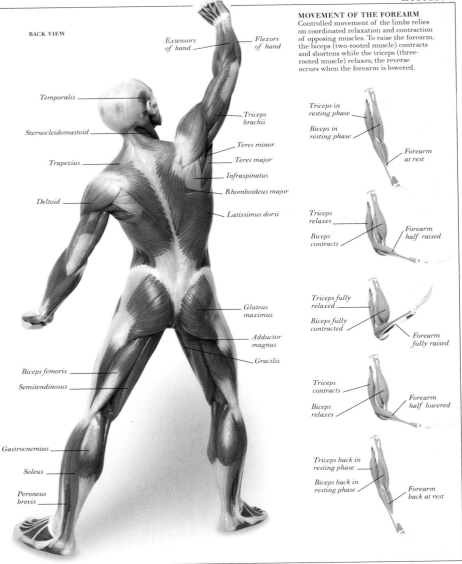

BACK VIEW

Extensors of hand

Flexors of hand

Temporalis

Sternocleidomastoid

Trapezius

Deltoid

Triceps brachii

Teres minor

Teres major

Infraspinatus

Rhomboideus major

Latissimus dorsi

Gluteus maximus

Adductor magnus

Gracilis

Biceps femoris

Semitendinosus

Gastrocnemius

Soleus

Peroneus brevis

MOVEMENT OF THE FOREARM

Controlled movement of the limbs relies on coordinated relaxation and contraction of opposing muscles. To raise the forearm, the biceps (two-rooted muscle) contracts and shortens while the triceps (three-rooted muscle) relaxes; the reverse occurs when the forearm is lowered.

Triceps in resting phase

Biceps in resting phase

Forearm at rest

Triceps relaxes

Biceps contracts

Forearm half raised

Triceps fully relaxed

Biceps fully contracted

Forearm fully raised

Triceps contracts

Biceps relaxes

Forearm half lowered

Triceps back in resting phase

Biceps back in resting phase

Forearm back at rest

Muscles 2

SKELETAL MUSCLE FIBER

MUSCLES OF FACIAL EXPRESSION
A single expression is the result of movement of many muscles; the main muscles of expression are shown in action below.

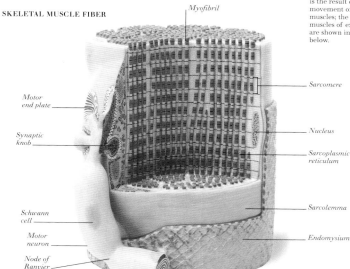

Myofibril

Sarcomere

Nucleus

Sarcoplasmic reticulum

Sarcolemma

Endomysium

Motor
end plate

Synaptic
knob

Schwann
cell

Motor
neuron

Node of
Ranvier

FRONTALIS

CORRUGATOR
SUPERCILII

ORBICULARIS ORIS

TYPES OF MUSCLE

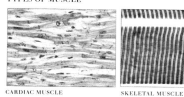

CARDIAC MUSCLE   SKELETAL MUSCLE   SMOOTH MUSCLE

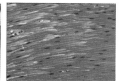

ZYGOMATICUS MAJOR

CONTRACTION OF SKELETAL MUSCLE

RELAXED STATE

CONTRACTED STATE

DEPRESSOR ANGULI
ORIS

**MUSCLES OF
HEAD AND NECK**

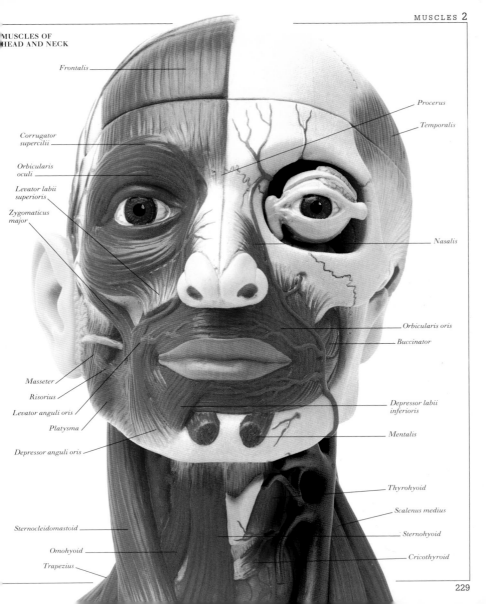

Frontalis

*Corrugator
supercilii*

*Orbicularis
oculi*

*Levator labii
superioris*

*Zygomaticus
major*

Masseter

Risorius

Levator anguli oris

Platysma

Depressor anguli oris

Sternocleidomastoid

Omohyoid

Trapezius

Procerus

Temporalis

Nasalis

Orbicularis oris

Buccinator

*Depressor labii
inferioris*

Mentalis

Thyrohyoid

Scalenus medius

Sternohyoid

Cricothyroid

Hands

THE HUMAN HAND is an extremely versatile tool, capable of delicate manipulation as well as powerful gripping actions. The arrangement of its 27 small bones, moved by 37 skeletal muscles that are connected to the bones by tendons, allows a wide range of movements. Our ability to bring the tips of our thumbs and fingers together, combined with the extraordinary sensitivity of our fingertips due to their rich supply of nerve endings, makes our hands uniquely dextrous.

X-RAY OF LEFT HAND OF A YOUNG CHILD

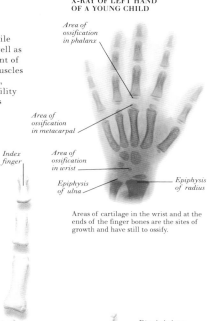

Area of ossification in phalanx

Area of ossification in metacarpal

Area of ossification in wrist

Epiphysis of ulna

Epiphysis of radius

Areas of cartilage in the wrist and at the ends of the finger bones are the sites of growth and have still to ossify.

BONES OF HAND

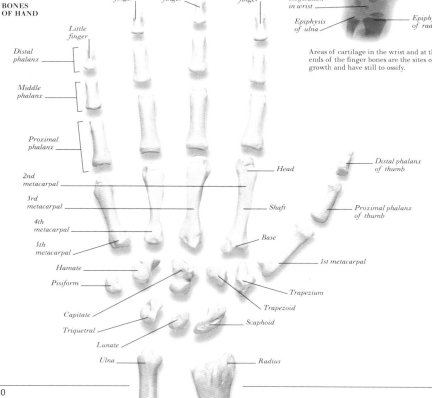

Ring finger

Middle finger

Index finger

Little finger

Distal phalanx

Middle phalanx

Proximal phalanx

2nd metacarpal

3rd metacarpal

4th metacarpal

5th metacarpal

Hamate

Pisiform

Capitate

Triquetral

Lunate

Ulna

Head

Shaft

Base

Distal phalanx of thumb

Proximal phalanx of thumb

1st metacarpal

Trapezium

Trapezoid

Scaphoid

Radius

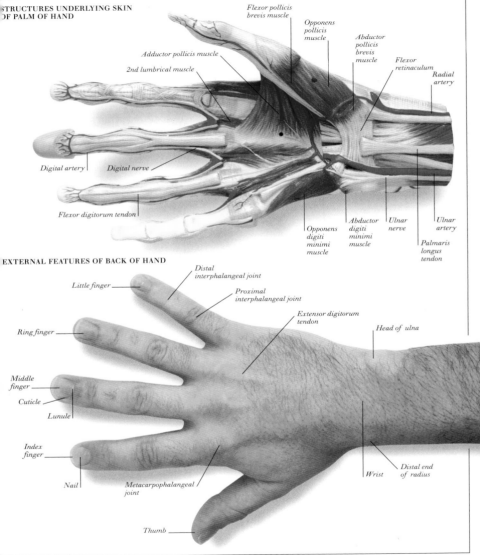

STRUCTURES UNDERLYING SKIN OF PALM OF HAND

Flexor pollicis brevis muscle

Opponens pollicis muscle

Abductor pollicis brevis muscle

Adductor pollicis muscle

2nd lumbrical muscle

Flexor retinaculum

Radial artery

Digital artery

Digital nerve

Flexor digitorum tendon

Opponens digiti minimi muscle

Abductor digiti minimi muscle

Ulnar nerve

Ulnar artery

Palmaris longus tendon

EXTERNAL FEATURES OF BACK OF HAND

Little finger

Distal interphalangeal joint

Proximal interphalangeal joint

Extensor digitorum tendon

Head of ulna

Ring finger

Middle finger

Cuticle

Lunule

Index finger

Nail

Metacarpophalangeal joint

Wrist

Distal end of radius

Thumb

Feet

THE FEET AND TOES are essential elements in body movement. They bear and propel the weight of the body during walking and running, and also help to maintain balance during changes of body position. Each foot has 26 bones, more than 100 ligaments, and 33 muscles, some of which are attached to the lower leg. The heel pad and the arch of the foot act as shock absorbers, providing a cushion against the jolts that occur with every step.

LIGAMENTS OF FOOT

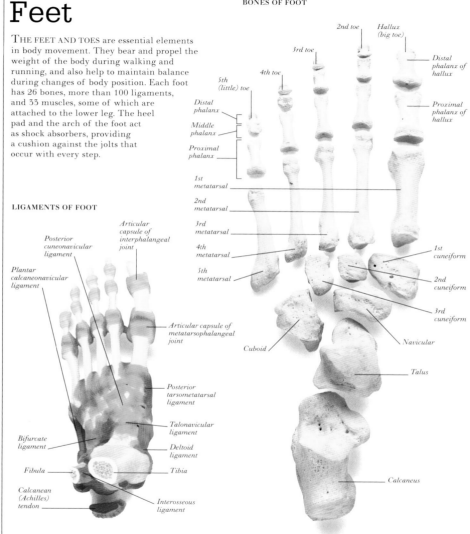

2nd toe

Hallux (big toe)

3rd toe

Distal phalanx of hallux

4th toe

Proximal phalanx of hallux

5th (little) toe

Distal phalanx

Middle phalanx

Proximal phalanx

1st metatarsal

2nd metatarsal

3rd metatarsal

4th metatarsal

5th metatarsal

1st cuneiform

2nd cuneiform

3rd cuneiform

Cuboid

Navicular

Talus

Calcaneus

Posterior cuneonavicular ligament

Articular capsule of interphalangeal joint

Plantar calcaneonavicular ligament

Articular capsule of metatarsophalangeal joint

Posterior tarsometatarsal ligament

Talonavicular ligament

Bifurcate ligament

Deltoid ligament

Fibula

Tibia

Calcanean (Achilles) tendon

Interosseous ligament

STRUCTURES UNDERLYING SKIN OF FOOT

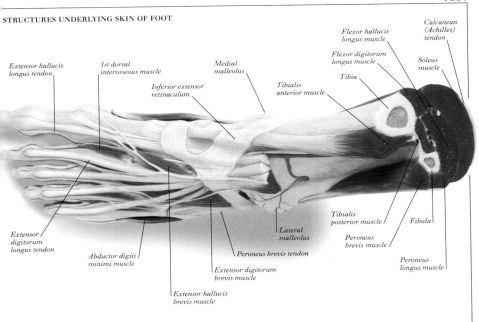

Extensor hallucis longus tendon

1st dorsal interosseous muscle

Inferior extensor retinaculum

Medial malleolus

Tibialis anterior muscle

Flexor hallucis longus muscle

Flexor digitorum longus muscle

Tibia

Calcanean (Achilles) tendon

Soleus muscle

Extensor digitorum longus tendon

Abductor digiti minimi muscle

Extensor hallucis brevis muscle

Extensor digitorum brevis muscle

Peroneus brevis tendon

Lateral malleolus

Tibialis posterior muscle

Peroneus brevis muscle

Fibula

Peroneus longus muscle

EXTERNAL FEATURES OF FOOT

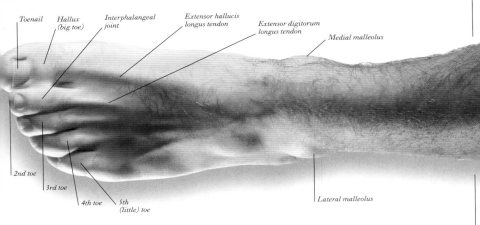

Toenail

Hallux (big toe)

Interphalangeal joint

Extensor hallucis longus tendon

Extensor digitorum longus tendon

Medial malleolus

2nd toe

3rd toe

4th toe

5th (little) toe

Lateral malleolus

Skin and hair

SKIN IS THE BODY'S LARGEST ORGAN, a waterproof barrier that protects the internal organs against infection, injury, and harmful sun rays. The skin is also an important sensory organ and helps to control body temperature. The outer layer of the skin, known as the epidermis, is coated with keratin, a tough, horny protein that is also the chief constituent of hair and nails. Dead cells are shed from the skin's surface and are replaced by new cells from the base of the epidermis, the region that also produces the skin pigment, melanin. The dermis contains most of the skin's living structures, and includes nerve endings, blood vessels, elastic fibers, sweat glands that cool the skin, and sebaceous glands that produce oil to keep the skin supple. Beneath the dermis lies the subcutaneous tissue (hypodermis), which is rich in fat and blood vessels. Hair shafts grow from hair follicles situated in the dermis and subcutaneous tissue. Hair grows on every part of the skin apart from the palms of the hands and soles of the feet.

SECTION OF HAIR

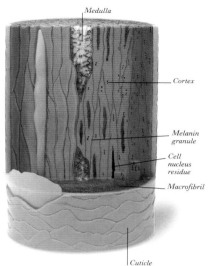

Medulla

Cortex

Melanin granule

Cell nucleus residue

Macrofibril

Cuticle

SECTIONS OF DIFFERENT TYPES OF SKIN

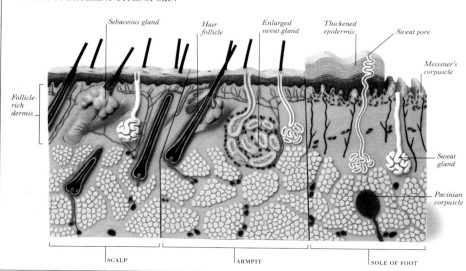

Sebaceous gland

Hair follicle

Enlarged sweat gland

Thickened epidermis

Sweat pore

Meissner's corpuscle

Follicle-rich dermis

Sweat gland

Pacinian corpuscle

SCALP

ARMPIT

SOLE OF FOOT

234

SECTION OF SKIN

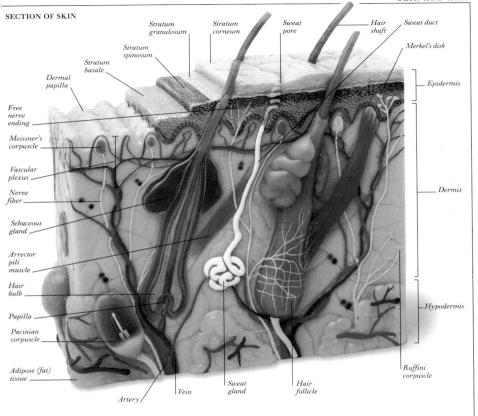

Stratum granulosum

Stratum corneum

Sweat pore

Hair shaft

Sweat duct

Stratum spinosum

Merkel's disk

Stratum basale

Dermal papilla

Stratum spinosum

Epidermis

Free nerve ending

Meissner's corpuscle

Vascular plexus

Nerve fiber

Dermis

Sebaceous gland

Arrector pili muscle

Hair bulb

Papilla

Pacinian corpuscle

Hypodermis

Adipose (fat) tissue

Ruffini corpuscle

Artery

Vein

Sweat gland

Hair follicle

PHOTOMICROGRAPHS OF SKIN AND HAIR

SECTION OF SKIN
The flaky cells at the skin's surface are shed continuously.

SWEAT PORE
This allows loss of fluid as part of temperature control.

SKIN HAIR
Two hairs pushing through the outer layer of skin.

HEAD HAIR
The root and part of the shaft of a hair from the scalp.

Brain

THE BRAIN IS THE MAJOR ORGAN of the central nervous system and the control center for all the body's voluntary and involuntary activities. It is also responsible for the complexities of thought, memory, emotion, and language. In adults, this complex organ is a mere 3 lb (1.4 kg) in weight, containing over 10 billion nerve cells. Three distinct regions can easily be seen—the brainstem, the cerebellum, and the large cerebrum. The brainstem controls vital body functions, such as breathing and digestion. The cerebellum's main functions are the maintenance of posture and the coordination of body movements. The cerebrum, which consists of the right and left cerebral hemispheres joined by the corpus callosum, is the site of most conscious and intelligent activities.

MRI SCAN OF TRANSVERSE SECTION THROUGH BRAIN

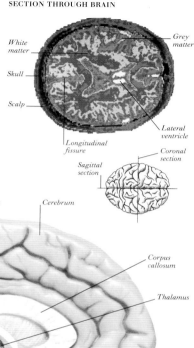

White matter

Grey matter

Skull

Scalp

Lateral ventricle

Longitudinal fissure

Coronal section

Sagittal section

SAGITTAL SECTION THROUGH BRAIN

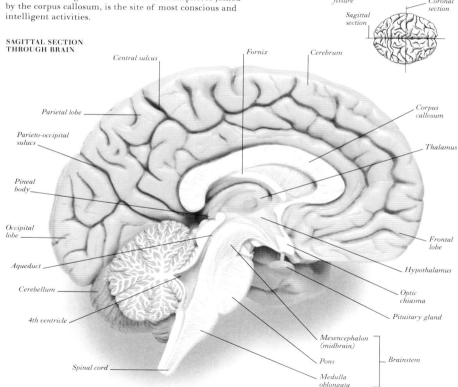

Central sulcus

Fornix

Cerebrum

Parietal lobe

Parieto-occipital sulucs

Pineal body

Occipital lobe

Aqueduct

Cerebellum

4th ventricle

Spinal cord

Corpus callosum

Thalamus

Frontal lobe

Hypothalamus

Optic chiasma

Pituitary gland

Mesencephalon (midbrain)

Pons

Medulla oblongata

Brainstem

SECTION THROUGH SKULL AND BRAIN

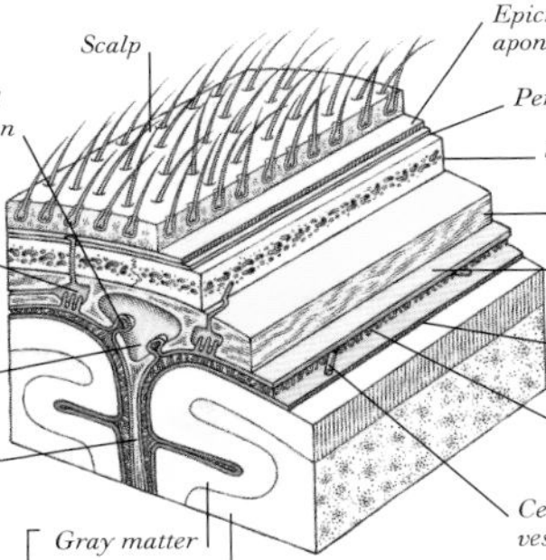

Scalp
Epicranial aponeurosis
Arachnoid granulation
Pericranium
Skull
Dura mater
Lateral lacuna
Arachnoid mater
Superior sagittal sinus
Pia mater
Falx cerebri
Subarachnoid space
Cerebral vessel
Cerebrum { Gray matter / White matter

EXTERNAL ANATOMY OF BRAIN

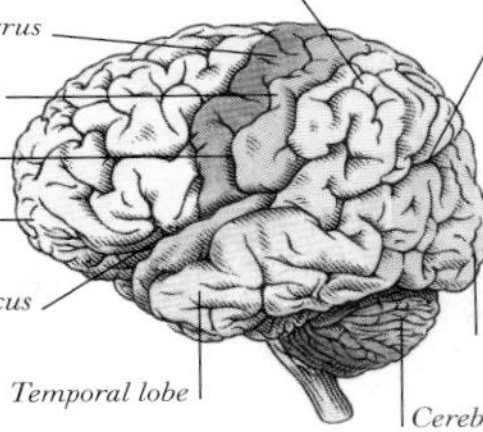

Parietal lobe
Parieto-occipital sulcus
Precentral gyrus
Postcentral gyrus
Central sulcus
Frontal lobe
Lateral sulcus
Temporal lobe
Occipital lobe
Cerebellum

SPECIFIC ROLES OF AREAS OF CEREBRUM

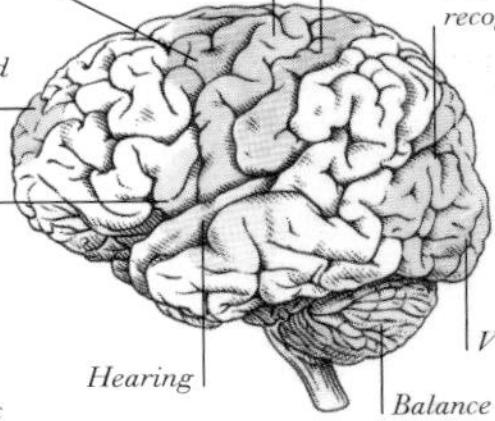

Skilled movements
Basic movements
Sensation
Visual recognition
Behavior and emotion
Speech
Vision
Hearing
Balance and muscle coordination

CORONAL SECTION THROUGH BRAIN

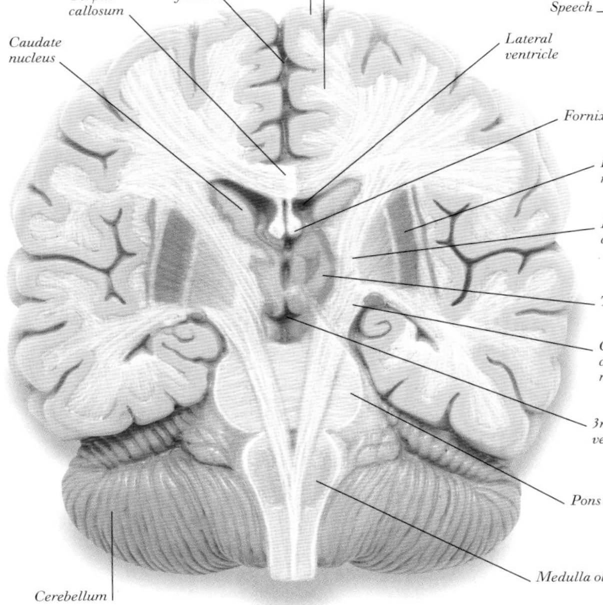

Corpus callosum
Longitudinal fissure
Grey matter / White matter } Cerebrum
Caudate nucleus
Lateral ventricle
Fornix
Lentiform nucleus
Internal capsule
Thalamus
Crus cerebri of midbrain
3rd ventricle
Pons
Medulla oblongata
Cerebellum

NERVE CELLS IN BRAIN

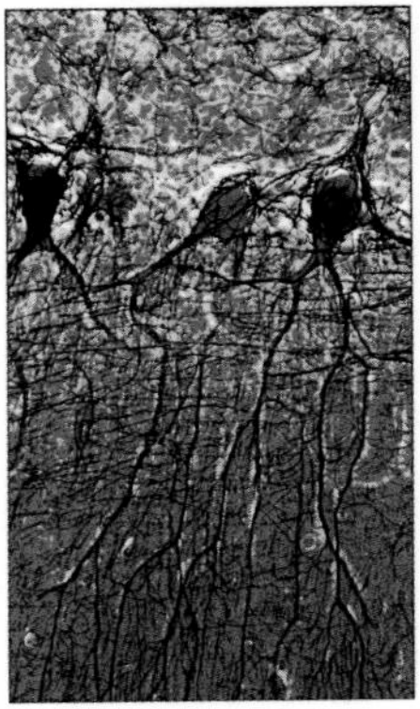

The dark cells are Purkinje's cells, which are among the largest nerve cells in the body.

237

Nervous system

THE NERVOUS SYSTEM IS THE BODY'S internal, electrochemical, communications network. Its main parts are the brain, spinal cord, and nerves. The brain and spinal cord form the central nervous system (CNS), the body's chief controlling and coordinating centers. Billions of long neurons, many grouped as nerves, make up the peripheral nervous system, transmitting nerve impulses between the CNS and other regions of the body. Each neuron has three parts: a cell body, branching dendrites that receive chemical signals from other neurons, and a tubelike axon that conveys these signals as electrical impulses.

CENTRAL AND PERIPHERAL NERVOUS SYSTEMS

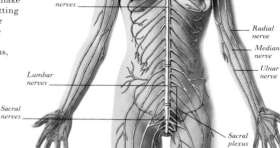

- Cranial nerves
- Cerebrum
- Cerebellum
- Cervical nerves
- Brachial plexus
- Thoracic nerves
- Spinal cord
- Radial nerve
- Median nerve
- Ulnar nerve
- Lumbar nerves
- Sacral nerves
- Sacral plexus
- Femoral nerve
- Pudendal nerve
- Sciatic nerve
- Cutaneous nerve
- Common peroneal nerve
- Posterior tibial nerve
- Superficial peroneal nerve
- Deep peroneal nerve

SECTION THROUGH SPINAL CORD

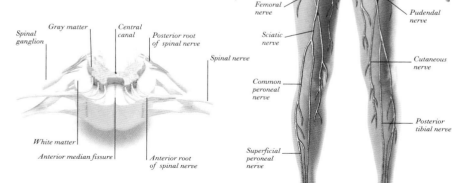

- Spinal ganglion
- Gray matter
- Central canal
- Posterior root of spinal nerve
- Spinal nerve
- White matter
- Anterior median fissure
- Anterior root of spinal nerve

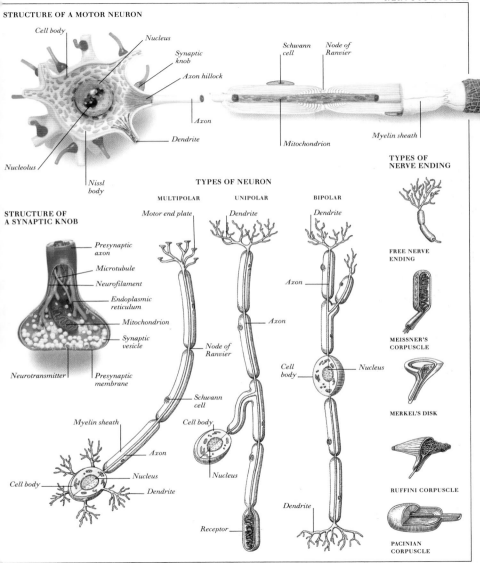

STRUCTURE OF A MOTOR NEURON

Cell body
Nucleus
Synaptic knob
Axon hillock
Schwann cell
Node of Ranvier
Axon
Dendrite
Nucleolus
Nissl body
Mitochondrion
Myelin sheath

TYPES OF NERVE ENDING

STRUCTURE OF A SYNAPTIC KNOB

Presynaptic axon
Microtubule
Neurofilament
Endoplasmic reticulum
Mitochondrion
Synaptic vesicle
Neurotransmitter
Presynaptic membrane

TYPES OF NEURON

MULTIPOLAR
UNIPOLAR
BIPOLAR

Motor end plate
Dendrite
Dendrite

Axon

Axon

Node of Ranvier

Axon

Schwann cell

Cell body

Nucleus

Myelin sheath

Cell body

Axon

Nucleus

Cell body
Nucleus
Dendrite

Nucleus

Dendrite

Receptor

FREE NERVE ENDING

MEISSNER'S CORPUSCLE

MERKEL'S DISK

RUFFINI CORPUSCLE

PACINIAN CORPUSCLE

Eye

THE EYE IS THE ORGAN OF SIGHT. The two eyeballs, protected within bony sockets called orbits and on the outside by the eyelids, eyebrows, and tear film, are directly connected to the brain by the optic nerves. Each eye is moved by six muscles, which are attached around the eyeball. Light rays entering the eye through the pupil are focused by the cornea and lens to form an image on the retina. The retina contains millions of light-sensitive cells, called rods and cones, which convert the image into a pattern of nerve impulses. These impulses are transmitted along the optic nerve to the brain. Information from the two optic nerves is processed in the brain to produce a single coordinated image.

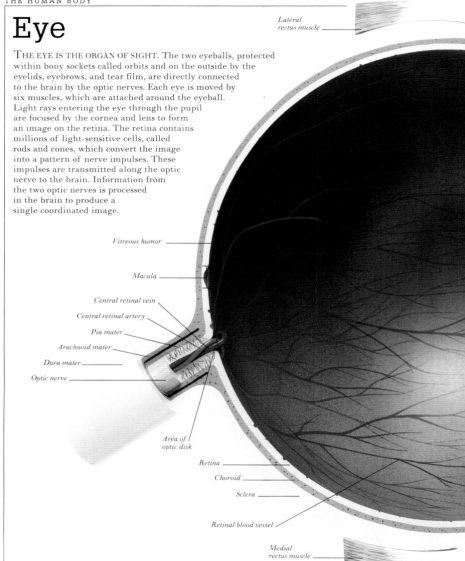

Lateral
rectus muscle

Vitreous humor

Macula

Central retinal vein

Central retinal artery

Pia mater

Arachnoid mater

Dura mater

Optic nerve

Area of
optic disk

Retina

Choroid

Sclera

Retinal blood vessel

Medial
rectus muscle

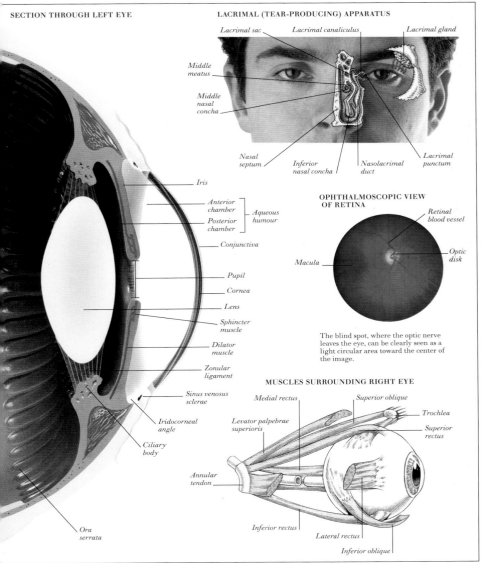

SECTION THROUGH LEFT EYE

LACRIMAL (TEAR-PRODUCING) APPARATUS

Lacrimal sac
Lacrimal canaliculus
Lacrimal gland
Middle meatus
Middle nasal concha
Nasal septum
Inferior nasal concha
Nasolacrimal duct
Lacrimal punctum

Iris
Anterior chamber
Posterior chamber
} Aqueous humour
Conjunctiva
Pupil
Cornea
Lens
Sphincter muscle
Dilator muscle
Zonular ligament
Sinus venosus sclerae
Iridocorneal angle
Ciliary body
Ora serrata

OPHTHALMOSCOPIC VIEW OF RETINA

Retinal blood vessel
Optic disk
Macula

The blind spot, where the optic nerve leaves the eye, can be clearly seen as a light circular area toward the center of the image.

MUSCLES SURROUNDING RIGHT EYE

Medial rectus
Superior oblique
Trochlea
Levator palpebrae superioris
Superior rectus
Annular tendon
Inferior rectus
Lateral rectus
Inferior oblique

Ear

THE EAR IS THE ORGAN OF HEARING AND BALANCE. The outer ear consists of a flap called the auricle or pinna and the auditory canal. The main functional parts-the middle and inner ears-are enclosed within the skull. The middle ear consists of three tiny bones, known as auditory ossicles, and the eustachian tube, which links the ear to the back of the nose. The inner ear consists of the spiral-shaped cochlea, and also the semicircular canals and the vestibule, which are the organs of balance. Sound waves entering the ear travel through the auditory canal to the tympanic membrane (eardrum), where they are converted to vibrations that are transmitted via the ossicles to the cochlea. Here, the vibrations are converted by millions of microscopic hairs into electrical nerve signals to be interpreted by the brain.

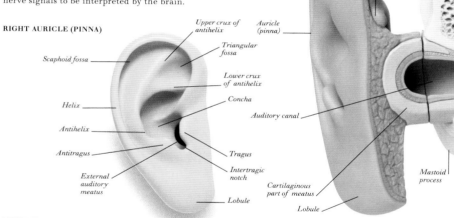

RIGHT AURICLE (PINNA)

- Upper crux of antihelix
- Auricle (pinna)
- Triangular fossa
- Scaphoid fossa
- Lower crux of antihelix
- Concha
- Helix
- Auditory canal
- Antihelix
- Antitragus
- Tragus
- Intertragic notch
- External auditory meatus
- Cartilaginous part of meatus
- Lobule
- Lobule
- Temporal bone
- Cartilage of auricle
- Mastoid process

OSSICLES OF MIDDLE EAR

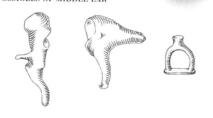

MALLEUS (HAMMER)   INCUS (ANVIL)   STAPES (STIRRUP)

These three tiny bones connect to form a bridge between the tympanic membrane and the oval window. With a system of membranes they convey sound vibrations to the inner ear.

INTERNAL STRUCTURE OF AMPULLA

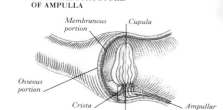

- Membranous portion
- Cupula
- Osseous portion
- Crista
- Ampullar nerve
- Hair cell of crista

LABYRINTH

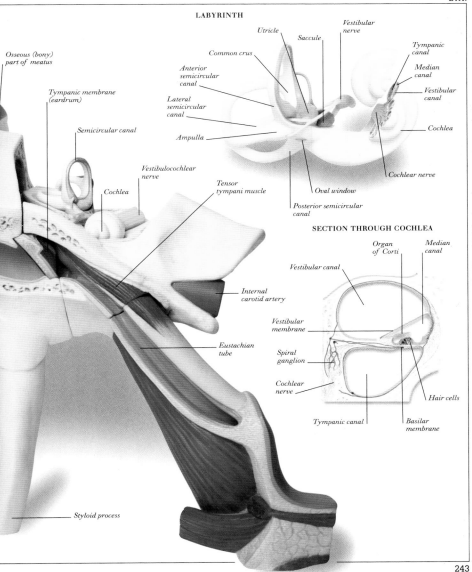

Osseous (bony) part of meatus

Tympanic membrane (eardrum)

Semicircular canal

Vestibulocochlear nerve

Cochlea

Tensor tympani muscle

Internal carotid artery

Eustachian tube

Styloid process

Utricle

Saccule

Vestibular nerve

Common crus

Anterior semicircular canal

Lateral semicircular canal

Ampulla

Oval window

Posterior semicircular canal

Tympanic canal

Median canal

Vestibular canal

Cochlea

Cochlear nerve

SECTION THROUGH COCHLEA

Organ of Corti

Median canal

Vestibular canal

Vestibular membrane

Spiral ganglion

Cochlear nerve

Tympanic canal

Hair cells

Basilar membrane

243

Nose, mouth, and throat

WITH EVERY BREATH, air passes through the nasal cavity down the pharynx (throat), larynx ("voice box"), and trachea (windpipe) to the lungs. The nasal cavity warms and moistens air, and the tiny layers in its lining protect the airway against damage by foreign bodies. During swallowing, the tongue moves up and back, the larynx rises, the epiglottis closes off the entrance to the trachea, and the soft palate separates the nasal cavity from the pharynx. Saliva, secreted from three pairs of salivary glands, lubricates food to make swallowing easier; it also begins the chemical breakdown of food, and helps to produce taste. The senses of taste and smell are closely linked. Both depend on the detection of dissolved molecules by sensory receptors in the olfactory nerve endings of the nose and in the taste buds of the tongue.

STRUCTURE OF TONGUE

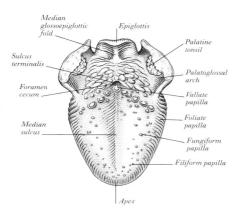

Median glossoepiglottic fold
Epiglottis
Palatine tonsil
Sulcus terminalis
Palatoglossal arch
Foramen cecum
Vallate papilla
Median sulcus
Foliate papilla
Fungiform papilla
Filiform papilla
Apex

TASTE AREAS ON TONGUE

Bitter
Sour
Salt
Sweet

STRUCTURES SURROUNDING PHARYNX

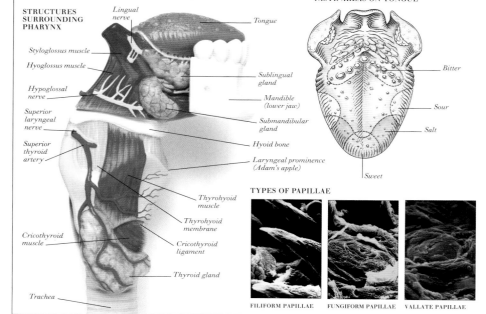

Lingual nerve
Tongue
Styloglossus muscle
Hyoglossus muscle
Hypoglossal nerve
Sublingual gland
Mandible (lower jaw)
Submandibular gland
Superior laryngeal nerve
Superior thyroid artery
Hyoid bone
Laryngeal prominence (Adam's apple)
Thyrohyoid muscle
Thyrohyoid membrane
Cricothyroid muscle
Cricothyroid ligament
Thyroid gland
Trachea

TYPES OF PAPILLAE

FILIFORM PAPILLAE   FUNGIFORM PAPILLAE   VALLATE PAPILLAE

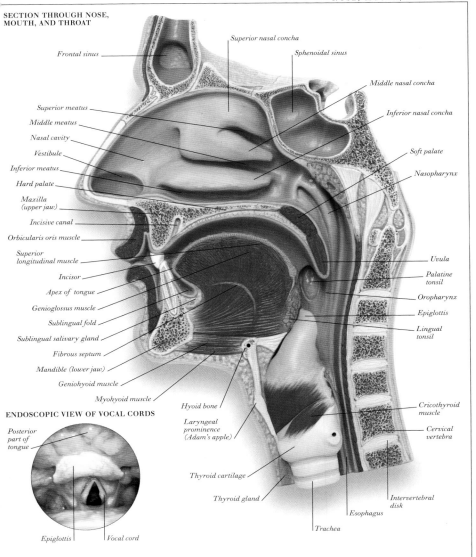

SECTION THROUGH NOSE, MOUTH, AND THROAT

Frontal sinus

Superior nasal concha

Sphenoidal sinus

Middle nasal concha

Inferior nasal concha

Superior meatus

Middle meatus

Nasal cavity

Vestibule

Inferior meatus

Hard palate

Maxilla (upper jaw)

Incisive canal

Orbicularis oris muscle

Superior longitudinal muscle

Incisor

Apex of tongue

Genioglossus muscle

Sublingual fold

Sublingual salivary gland

Fibrous septum

Mandible (lower jaw)

Geniohyoid muscle

Myohyoid muscle

Soft palate

Nasopharynx

Uvula

Palatine tonsil

Oropharynx

Epiglottis

Lingual tonsil

Cricothyroid muscle

Cervical vertebra

Hyoid bone

Laryngeal prominence (Adam's apple)

Thyroid cartilage

Thyroid gland

Intervertebral disk

Esophagus

Trachea

ENDOSCOPIC VIEW OF VOCAL CORDS

Posterior part of tongue

Epiglottis

Vocal cord

245

Teeth

THE 20 PRIMARY TEETH (also called deciduous or baby teeth) usually begin to erupt when a baby is about six months old. They start to be replaced by the permanent teeth when the child is about six years old. By the age of 20, most adults have a full set of 32 teeth although the third molars (commonly called wisdom teeth) may never erupt. While teeth help people to speak clearly and give shape to the face, their main function is the chewing of food. Incisors and canines shear and tear the food into pieces; premolars and molars crush and grind it further. Although tooth enamel is the hardest substance in the body, it tends to be eroded and destroyed by acid produced in the mouth during the breakdown of food.

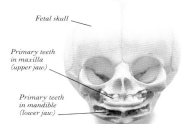

Fetal skull

Primary teeth in maxilla (upper jaw)

Primary teeth in mandible (lower jaw)

FETAL JAWS
By the sixth week of embryonic development areas of thickening occur in each jaw; these areas give rise to tooth buds. By the time the fetus is six months old, enamel has formed on the tooth buds.

DEVELOPMENT OF JAW AND TEETH

Maxilla (upper jaw)

Mandible (lower jaw)

A NEWBORN BABY'S JAWS
The primary teeth can be seen developing in the jaw bones; they begin to erupt around the age of six months.

A FIVE-YEAR-OLD CHILD'S TEETH
There is a full set of 20 erupted primary teeth; the permanent teeth can be seen developing in the upper and lower jaws.

A NINE-YEAR-OLD CHILD'S TEETH
Most of the teeth are primary teeth but the permanent incisors and first molars have now emerged.

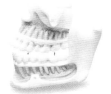

AN ADULT'S TEETH
By the age of 20, the full set of 32 permanent teeth (including the wisdom teeth) should be in position.

THE PERMANENT TEETH

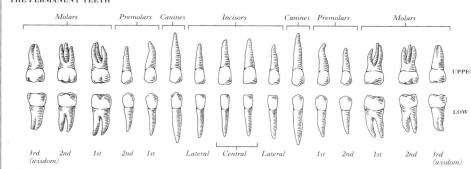

Molars   *Premolars*   *Canines*   *Incisors*   *Canines*   *Premolars*   *Molars*

UPPE

LOW

3rd (wisdom)   2nd   1st   2nd   1st   Lateral   Central   Lateral   1st   2nd   1st   2nd   3rd (wisdom)

STRUCTURE OF A TOOTH

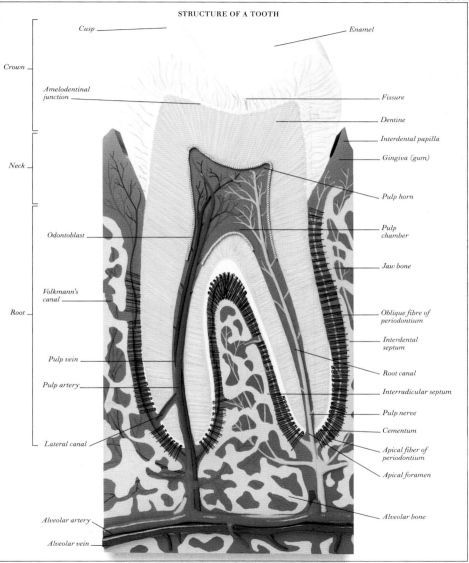

Cusp

Enamel

Crown

Amelodentinal
junction

Fissure

Dentine

Interdental papilla

Neck

Gingiva (gum)

Pulp horn

Odontoblast

Pulp
chamber

Jaw bone

Root

Volkmann's
canal

Oblique fibre of
periodontium

Interdental
septum

Pulp vein

Root canal

Pulp artery

Interradicular septum

Pulp nerve

Cementum

Lateral canal

Apical fiber of
periodontium

Apical foramen

Alveolar bone

Alveolar artery

Alveolar vein

Digestive system

THE DIGESTIVE SYSTEM BREAKS DOWN FOOD into particles so tiny that blood can take nourishment to all parts of the body. The system's main part is a 30 ft (9 m) tube from mouth to rectum; muscles in this alimentary canal force food along. Chewed food first travels through the esophagus to the stomach, which churns and liquidizes food before it passes through the duodenum, jejunum, and ileum—the three parts of the long, convoluted small intestine. Here, digestive juices from the gallbladder and pancreas break down food particles; many filter out into the blood through tiny fingerlike villi that line the small intestine's inner wall. Undigested food in the colon forms feces that leave the body through the anus.

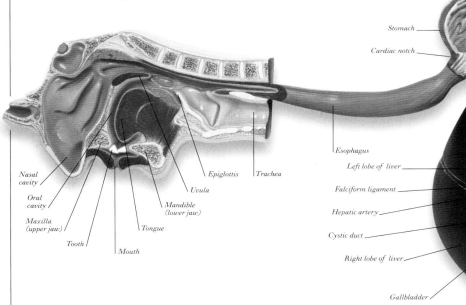

Stomach

Cardiac notch

Esophagus

Left lobe of liver

Falciform ligament

Hepatic artery

Cystic duct

Right lobe of liver

Gallbladder

Nasal cavity

Oral cavity

Maxilla (upper jaw)

Tooth

Mouth

Tongue

Mandible (lower jaw)

Uvula

Epiglottis

Trachea

ENDOSCOPIC VIEWS INSIDE ALIMENTARY CANAL

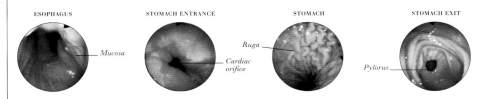

ESOPHAGUS

Mucosa

STOMACH ENTRANCE

Cardiac orifice

STOMACH

Ruga

STOMACH EXIT

Pylorus

ALIMENTARY CANAL

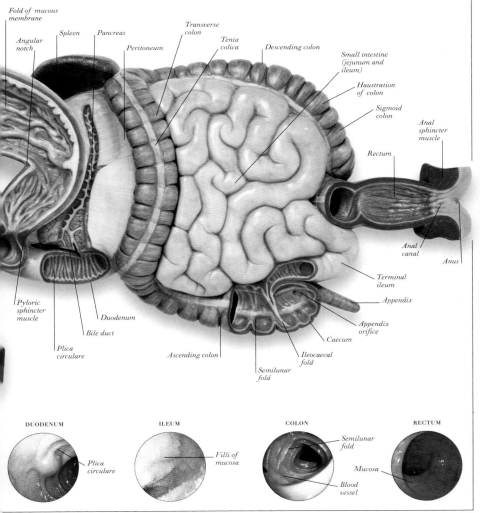

Fold of mucous membrane

Angular notch

Spleen

Pancreas

Peritoneum

Transverse colon

Tenia colica

Descending colon

Small intestine (jejunum and ileum)

Haustration of colon

Sigmoid colon

Anal sphincter muscle

Rectum

Anal canal

Anus

Terminal ileum

Appendix

Appendix orifice

Caecum

Ileocaecal fold

Ascending colon

Semilunar fold

Pyloric sphincter muscle

Duodenum

Bile duct

Plica circulare

DUODENUM

Plica circulare

ILEUM

Villi of mucosa

COLON

Semilunar fold

Blood vessel

RECTUM

Mucosa

Heart

THE HEART IS A HOLLOW MUSCLE in the middle of the chest that pumps blood around the body, supplying cells with oxygen and nutrients. A muscular wall, called the septum, divides the heart lengthwise into left and right sides. A valve divides each side into two chambers: an upper atrium and a lower ventricle. When the heart muscle contracts, it squeezes blood through the atria and then through the ventricles. Oxygenated blood from the lungs flows from the pulmonary veins into the left atrium, through the left ventricle, and then out via the aorta to all parts of the body. Deoxygenated blood returning from the body flows from the vena cava into the right atrium, through the right ventricle, and then out via the pulmonary artery to the lungs for reoxygenation. At rest the heart beats between 60 and 80 times a minute; during exercise or at times of stress or excitement the rate may increase to 200 beats a minute.

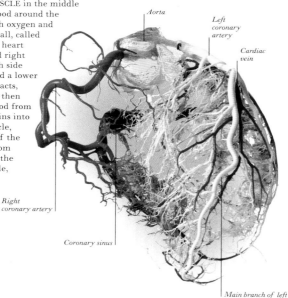

Aorta

Left coronary artery

Cardiac vein

Right coronary artery

Coronary sinus

Main branch of left coronary artery

SECTION THROUGH HEART WALL

Pericardial cavity

Trabecula

Endocardium

Myocardium

Epicardium (visceral pericardium)

Serous pericardium

Fibrous pericardium

HEARTBEAT SEQUENCE

ATRIAL DIASTOLE

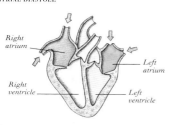

Right atrium

Left atrium

Right ventricle

Left ventricle

Deoxygenated blood enters the right atrium while the left atrium receives oxygenated blood.

STRUCTURE OF HEART

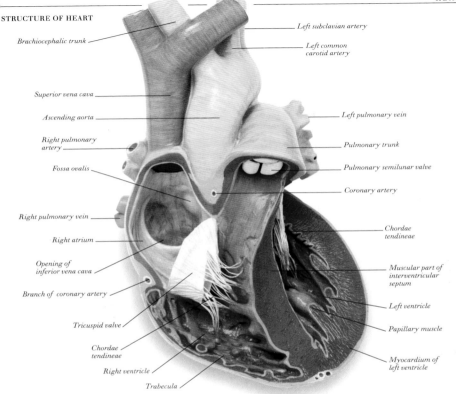

Brachiocephalic trunk

Superior vena cava

Ascending aorta

Right pulmonary artery

Fossa ovalis

Right pulmonary vein

Right atrium

Opening of inferior vena cava

Branch of coronary artery

Tricuspid valve

Chordae tendineae

Right ventricle

Trabecula

Left subclavian artery

Left common carotid artery

Left pulmonary vein

Pulmonary trunk

Pulmonary semilunar valve

Coronary artery

Chordae tendineae

Muscular part of interventricular septum

Left ventricle

Papillary muscle

Myocardium of left ventricle

ATRIAL SYSTOLE (VENTRICULAR DIASTOLE)

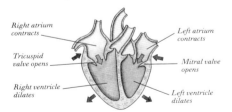

Right atrium contracts

Tricuspid valve opens

Right ventricle dilates

Left atrium contracts

Mitral valve opens

Left ventricle dilates

Left and right atria contract, forcing blood into the relaxed ventricles.

VENTRICULAR SYSTOLE

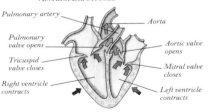

Pulmonary artery

Pulmonary valve opens

Tricuspid valve closes

Right ventricle contracts

Aorta

Aortic valve opens

Mitral valve closes

Left ventricle contracts

Ventricles contract and force blood to the lungs for oxygenation and via the aorta to the rest of the body.

Circulatory system

THE CIRCULATORY SYSTEM consists of the heart and blood vessels, which together maintain a continuous flow of blood around the body. The heart pumps oxygen-rich blood from the lungs to all parts of the body through a network of tubes called arteries, and smaller branches called arterioles. Blood returns to the heart via small vessels called venules, which lead in turn into larger tubes called veins. Arterioles and venules are linked by a network of tiny vessels called capillaries, where the exchange of oxygen and carbon dioxide between blood and body cells takes place. Blood has four main components: red blood cells, white blood cells, platelets, and liquid plasma.

ARTERIAL SYSTEM OF BRAIN

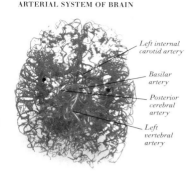

Left internal carotid artery

Basilar artery

Posterior cerebral artery

Left vertebral artery

CIRCULATORY SYSTEM OF HEART AND LUNGS

Superior vena cava

Aorta

Right ventricle

Left ventricle

CIRCULATORY SYSTEM OF LIVER

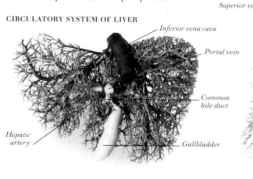

Inferior vena cava

Portal vein

Common bile duct

Hepatic artery

Gallbladder

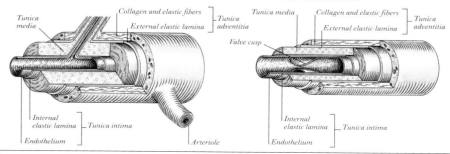

SECTION OF MAIN ARTERY

Tunica media

Collagen and elastic fibers

External elastic lamina

Tunica adventitia

Internal elastic lamina

Tunica intima

Endothelium

Arteriole

SECTION OF MAIN VEIN

Tunica media

Collagen and elastic fibers

External elastic lamina

Tunica adventitia

Valve cusp

Internal elastic lamina

Tunica intima

Endothelium

PRINCIPAL ARTERIES AND VEINS OF CIRCULATORY SYSTEM

Common carotid artery
Subclavian artery
Arch of aorta
Axillary artery
Pulmonary artery
Coronary artery
Brachial artery
Gastric artery
Hepatic artery
Splenic artery
Superior mesenteric artery
Radial artery
Ulnar artery
Palmar arch
Digital artery
Common iliac artery
External iliac artery
Internal iliac artery
Femoral artery
Popliteal artery
Peroneal artery
Anterior tibial artery
Posterior tibial artery
Lateral plantar artery
Dorsal metatarsal artery

Internal jugular vein
Brachiocephalic vein
Subclavian vein
Axillary vein
Cephalic vein
Superior vena cava
Pulmonary vein
Basilic vein
Hepatic portal vein
Median cubital vein
Inferior vena cava
Anterior median vein
Gastroepiploic vein
Palmar vein
Digital vein
Inferior mesenteric vein
Superior mesenteric vein
Common iliac vein
External iliac vein
Internal iliac vein
Femoral vein
Great saphenous vein
Short saphenous vein
Dorsal venous arch
Digital vein

TYPES OF BLOOD CELLS

RED BLOOD CELLS
These cells are biconcave in shape to maximize their oxygen-carrying capacity.

WHITE BLOOD CELLS
Lymphocytes are the smallest white blood cells; they form antibodies against disease.

PLATELETS
Tiny cells that are activated whenever blood clotting or repair to vessels is necessary.

BLOOD CLOTTING

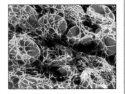

Filaments of fibrin enmesh red blood cells as part of the process of blood clotting.

Respiratory system

THE RESPIRATORY SYSTEM supplies the oxygen needed by body cells and carries off their carbon dioxide waste. Inhaled air passes via the trachea (windpipe) through two narrower tubes, the bronchi, to the lungs. Each lung comprises many fine, branching tubes called bronchioles that end in tiny clustered chambers called alveoli. Gases cross the thin alveolar walls to and from a network of tiny blood vessels. Intercostal (rib) muscles and the muscular diaphragm below the lungs operate the lungs like bellows, drawing air in and forcing it out at regular intervals.

BRONCHIOLE AND ALVEOLI

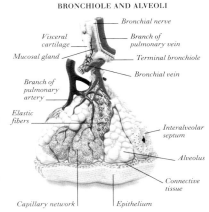

Bronchial nerve
Visceral cartilage
Branch of pulmonary vein
Mucosal gland
Terminal bronchiole
Branch of pulmonary artery
Bronchial vein
Elastic fibers
Interalveolar septum
Alveolus
Capillary network
Connective tissue
Epithelium

SEGMENTS OF BRONCHIAL TREE

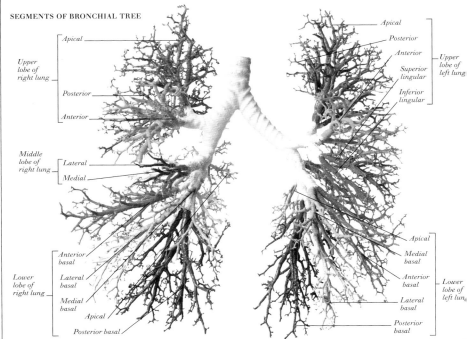

Apical
Upper lobe of right lung
Posterior
Anterior

Middle lobe of right lung
Lateral
Medial

Lower lobe of right lung
Anterior basal
Lateral basal
Medial basal
Apical
Posterior basal

Apical
Posterior
Anterior
Superior lingular
Inferior lingular
Upper lobe of left lung

Apical
Medial basal
Anterior basal
Lateral basal
Posterior basal
Lower lobe of left lung

STRUCTURES OF THORACIC CAVITY

GASEOUS EXCHANGE IN ALVEOLUS

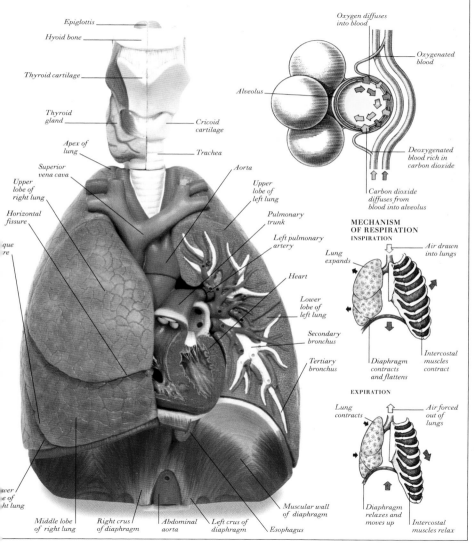

Epiglottis

Hyoid bone

Thyroid cartilage

Thyroid gland

Cricoid cartilage

Apex of lung

Trachea

Superior vena cava

Aorta

Upper lobe of right lung

Upper lobe of left lung

Horizontal fissure

Pulmonary trunk

que re

Left pulmonary artery

Heart

Lower lobe of left lung

Secondary bronchus

Tertiary bronchus

wer e of ht lung

Middle lobe of right lung

Right crus of diaphragm

Abdominal aorta

Left crus of diaphragm

Esophagus

Muscular wall of diaphragm

Oxygen diffuses into blood

Oxygenated blood

Alveolus

Deoxygenated blood rich in carbon dioxide

Carbon dioxide diffuses from blood into alveolus

MECHANISM OF RESPIRATION
INSPIRATION

Lung expands

Air drawn into lungs

Diaphragm contracts and flattens

Intercostal muscles contract

EXPIRATION

Lung contracts

Air forced out of lungs

Diaphragm relaxes and moves up

Intercostal muscles relax

Urinary system

THE URINARY SYSTEM FILTERS WASTE PRODUCTS from the blood and removes them from the body via a system of tubes. Blood is filtered in the two kidneys, which are fist-sized, bean-shaped organs. The renal arteries carry blood to the kidneys; the renal veins remove blood after filtering. Each kidney contains about one million tiny units called nephrons. Each nephron is made up of a tubule and a filtering unit called a glomerulus, which consists of a collection of tiny blood vessels surrounded by the hollow Bowman's capsule. The filtering process produces a watery fluid that leaves the kidney as urine. The urine is carried via two tubes called ureters to the bladder, where it is stored until its release from the body through another tube called the urethra.

ARTERIAL SYSTEM OF KIDNEYS

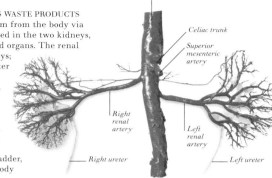

Aorta

Celiac trunk

Superior mesenteric artery

Right renal artery

Left renal artery

Right ureter

Left ureter

SECTION THROUGH LEFT KIDNEY

SECTION OF KIDNEY

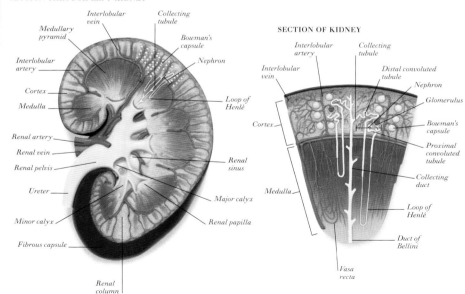

Interlobular vein

Collecting tubule

Medullary pyramid

Bowman's capsule

Interlobular artery

Nephron

Cortex

Medulla

Loop of Henlé

Renal artery

Renal vein

Renal pelvis

Ureter

Renal sinus

Minor calyx

Major calyx

Fibrous capsule

Renal papilla

Renal column

Interlobular artery

Collecting tubule

Interlobular vein

Distal convoluted tubule

Nephron

Glomerulus

Cortex

Bowman's capsule

Proximal convoluted tubule

Collecting duct

Medulla

Loop of Henlé

Duct of Bellini

Vasa recta

MALE URINARY TRACT

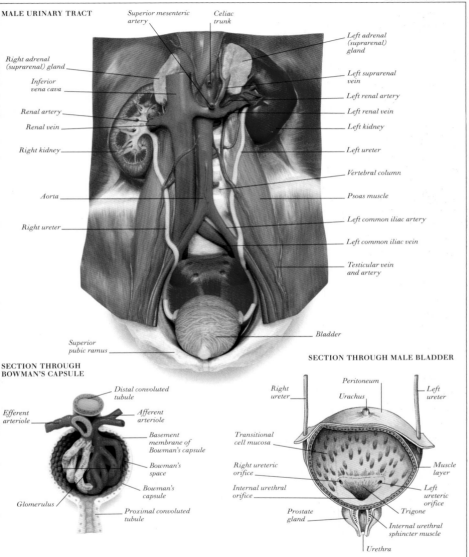

Superior mesenteric artery

Celiac trunk

Left adrenal (suprarenal) gland

Right adrenal (suprarenal) gland

Inferior vena cava

Left suprarenal vein

Left renal artery

Renal artery

Left renal vein

Renal vein

Left kidney

Right kidney

Left ureter

Vertebral column

Aorta

Psoas muscle

Right ureter

Left common iliac artery

Left common iliac vein

Testicular vein and artery

Bladder

Superior pubic ramus

SECTION THROUGH BOWMAN'S CAPSULE

Distal convoluted tubule

Efferent arteriole

Afferent arteriole

Basement membrane of Bowman's capsule

Bowman's space

Bowman's capsule

Glomerulus

Proximal convoluted tubule

SECTION THROUGH MALE BLADDER

Peritoneum

Right ureter

Urachus

Left ureter

Transitional cell mucosa

Right ureteric orifice

Muscle layer

Internal urethral orifice

Left ureteric orifice

Prostate gland

Trigone

Internal urethral sphincter muscle

Urethra

257

Reproductive system

SEX ORGANS LOCATED IN THE PELVIS create new human lives. Each month a ripe egg is released from one of the female's ovaries into a fallopian tube leading to the uterus (womb), a muscular pear-sized organ. A male produces minute tadpolelike sperm in two oval glands called testes. When the male is ready to release sperm into the female's vagina, many millions pass into his urethra and leave his body through the fleshy penis. The sperm travel up through the vagina into the uterus and fallopian tubes, and one sperm may enter and fertilize an egg. The fertilized egg becomes embedded in the uterus wall and starts to grow into a new human being.

SECTION THROUGH OVARY

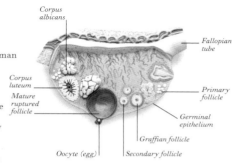

Corpus albicans

Corpus luteum

Mature ruptured follicle

Oocyte (egg)

Fallopian tube

Primary follicle

Germinal epithelium

Graffian follicle

Secondary follicle

SECTION THROUGH FEMALE PELVIC REGION

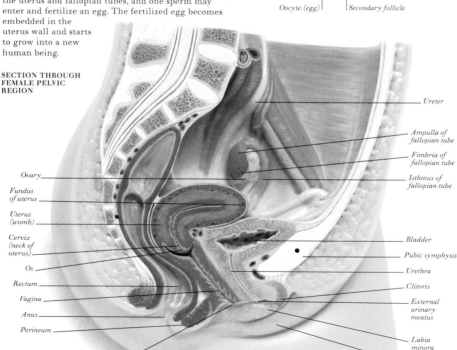

Ovary

Fundus of uterus

Uterus (womb)

Cervix (neck of uterus)

Os

Rectum

Vagina

Anus

Perineum

Introitus (vaginal opening)

Ureter

Ampulla of fallopian tube

Fimbria of fallopian tube

Isthmus of fallopian tube

Bladder

Pubic symphysis

Urethra

Clitoris

External urinary meatus

Labia minora

Labia majora

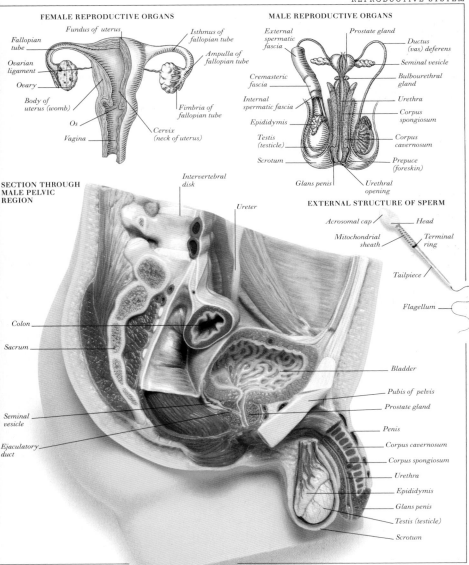

FEMALE REPRODUCTIVE ORGANS

Fundus of uterus
Fallopian tube
Isthmus of fallopian tube
Ampulla of fallopian tube
Ovarian ligament
Ovary
Body of uterus (womb)
Os
Vagina
Cervix (neck of uterus)
Fimbria of fallopian tube

MALE REPRODUCTIVE ORGANS

External spermatic fascia
Prostate gland
Ductus (vas) deferens
Seminal vesicle
Cremasteric fascia
Bulbourethral gland
Internal spermatic fascia
Urethra
Epididymis
Corpus spongiosum
Testis (testicle)
Corpus cavernosum
Scrotum
Prepuce (foreskin)
Glans penis
Urethral opening

SECTION THROUGH MALE PELVIC REGION

Intervertebral disk
Ureter

EXTERNAL STRUCTURE OF SPERM

Acrosomal cap
Head
Mitochondrial sheath
Terminal ring
Tailpiece
Flagellum

Colon
Sacrum
Seminal vesicle
Ejaculatory duct

Bladder
Pubis of pelvis
Prostate gland
Penis
Corpus cavernosum
Corpus spongiosum
Urethra
Epididymis
Glans penis
Testis (testicle)
Scrotum

259

Development of a baby

A FERTILIZED EGG IS NOURISHED AND PROTECTED as it
develops into an embryo and then a fetus during the 40
weeks of pregnancy. The placenta, a mass of blood vessels
implanted in the uterus lining, delivers nourishment and
oxygen, and removes waste through the umbilical cord.
Meanwhile, the fetus lies snugly in its amniotic sac, a bag
of fluid that protects it against any sudden jolts. In the last
weeks of the pregnancy, the rapidly growing fetus turns
head-down: a baby ready to be born.

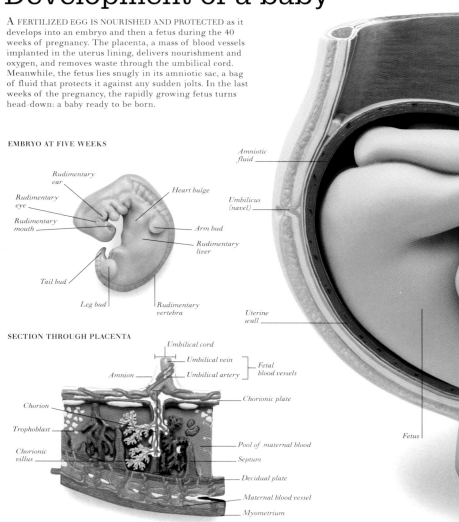

EMBRYO AT FIVE WEEKS

Rudimentary
ear

Rudimentary
eye

Rudimentary
mouth

Tail bud

Leg bud

Rudimentary
vertebra

Heart bulge

Arm bud

Rudimentary
liver

Amniotic
fluid

Umbilicus
(navel)

Uterine
wall

Fetus

SECTION THROUGH PLACENTA

Umbilical cord

Umbilical vein

Umbilical artery

Fetal
blood vessels

Amnion

Chorion

Trophoblast

Chorionic
villus

Chorionic plate

Pool of maternal blood

Septum

Decidual plate

Maternal blood vessel

Myometrium

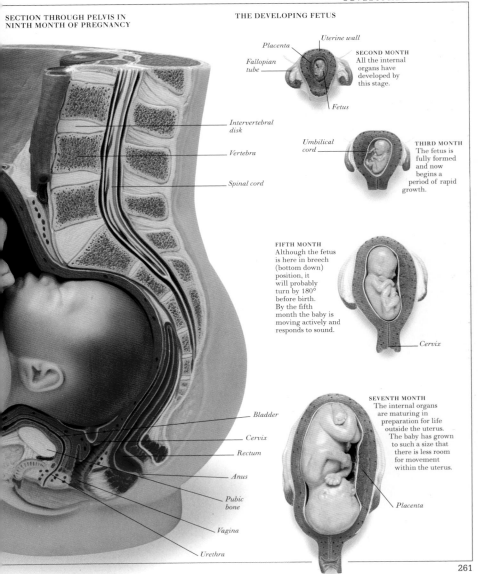

SECTION THROUGH PELVIS IN NINTH MONTH OF PREGNANCY

THE DEVELOPING FETUS

Placenta

Uterine wall

Fallopian tube

SECOND MONTH
All the internal organs have developed by this stage.

Fetus

Intervertebral disk

Vertebra

Spinal cord

Umbilical cord

THIRD MONTH
The fetus is fully formed and now begins a period of rapid growth.

FIFTH MONTH
Although the fetus is here in breech (bottom down) position, it will probably turn by 180° before birth. By the fifth month the baby is moving actively and responds to sound.

Cervix

Bladder

Cervix

Rectum

Anus

Pubic bone

Vagina

Urethra

SEVENTH MONTH
The internal organs are maturing in preparation for life outside the uterus. The baby has grown to such a size that there is less room for movement within the uterus.

Placenta

GEOLOGY, GEOGRAPHY, AND METEOROLOGY

MAPPING THE EARTH ·································· 264
THE ROCK CYCLE ·································· 266
MINERALS ·································· 268
MINERAL FEATURES ·································· 270
VOLCANOES ·································· 272
IGNEOUS AND METAMORPHIC ROCKS ·································· 274
SEDIMENTARY ROCKS ·································· 276
FOSSILS ·································· 278
MINERAL RESOURCES ·································· 280
WEATHERING AND EROSION ·································· 282
CAVES ·································· 284
GLACIERS ·································· 286
RIVERS ·································· 288
RIVER FEATURES ·································· 290
LAKES AND GROUNDWATER ·································· 292
COASTLINES ·································· 294
OCEANS AND SEAS ·································· 296
THE OCEAN FLOOR ·································· 298
THE ATMOSPHERE ·································· 300
WEATHER ·································· 302

Mapping the Earth

THE EARTH'S SURFACE FEATURES can be represented in various ways, such as on maps and globes. The earliest know map of the whole world dates back to between 750–500 BCE. The first globe was constructed in the mid-2nd century BCE, about 100 years after ancient Greek astronomers established that the Earth was spherical. Advances in mathematics, science, and geography—combined with an increasing number of people exploring the world—have meant that Earth's surface features have been mapped with increasing accuracy throughout history. In modern times, advances in technology have revolutionized the mapping process. In 1972, NASA launched the first civilian remote-sensing vehicle into Earth's orbit, which allowed the Earth to be mapped by satellite for the first time. Today, the surface of the Earth is surveyed every day by thousands of satellites, which send mappable data back to Earth to be analyzed and used by a range of people, from cartographers to scientists. The ability to use satellites has substantially sped up data collection—areas that would have once taken months or even years to survey can now be mapped within minutes. However, even with these advances in map-making, globes remain a more accurate way to represent the Earth's surface features. This is because only a globe can correctly represent areas, shapes, sizes, and directions, as there is always distortion when a spherical surface like the Earth's is projected on to the flat surface of a map. A map projection is therefore always a compromise: it shows some features accurately but distorts others. Even satellite mapping does not produce completely accurate maps, although they can show physical features with great clarity.

EXAMPLES OF MAP PROJECTIONS

CYLINDRICAL
PROJECTION

CYLINDRICAL-
PROJECTION MAP

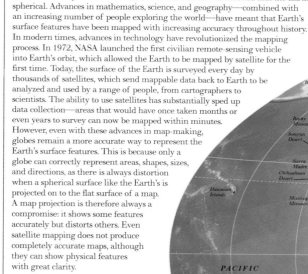

SATELLITE MAPPING OF THE EARTH

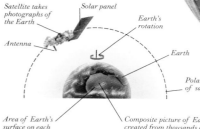

Satellite takes photographs of the Earth

Solar panel

Earth's rotation

Antenna

Earth

Polar orbit of satellite

Area of Earth's surface on each photograph

Composite picture of Earth created from thousands of separate images

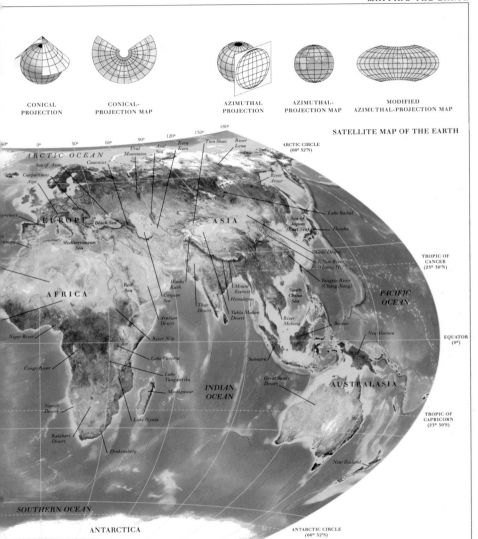

CONICAL
PROJECTION

CONICAL-
PROJECTION MAP

AZIMUTHAL
PROJECTION

AZIMUTHAL-
PROJECTION MAP

MODIFIED
AZIMUTHAL-PROJECTION MAP

SATELLITE MAP OF THE EARTH

180°

150°

120°

90°

60°

30°

0°

30°

ARCTIC CIRCLE
(66° 32'N)

ARCTIC OCEAN

Ural
Mountains

Aral
Sea

Kara
Kum

Tien Shan

River
Lena

Sea of Azov

Caucasus

River
Amur

Carpathians
Alps

renees

EUROPE

Black Sea

ASIA

Sea of
Japan
(East Sea)

Lake Baikal

Honshu

ntains

Mediterranean
Sea

Gobi Desert

Yellow River
(Huang He)

TROPIC OF
CANCER
(23° 30'N)

AFRICA

Red
Sea

Hindu
Kush

Caspian
Sea

Mount
Everest

Himalayas

Takla Makan
Desert

Yangtze River
(Chang Jiang)

South
China
Sea

PACIFIC
OCEAN

Thar
Desert

Arabian
Desert

River
Mekong

Borneo

New Guinea

Niger River

River Nile

EQUATOR
(0°)

Congo River

Lake Victoria

Sumatra

AUSTRALASIA

Lake
Tanganyika

INDIAN
OCEAN

Great Sandy
Desert

Namib
Desert

Madagascar

TROPIC OF
CAPRICORN
(23° 30'S)

Lake Nyasa

Kalahari
Desert

Drakensberg

New Zealand

SOUTHERN OCEAN

ANTARCTICA

ANTARCTIC CIRCLE
(66° 32'S)

30°

0°

30°

60°

90°

120°

150°

180°

GREENWICH
MERIDIAN

EAST OF GREENWICH
MERIDIAN

The rock cycle

HEXAGONAL BASALT
COLUMNS, ICELAND

THE ROCK CYCLE IS A CONTINUOUS PROCESS through which old rocks are transformed into new ones. Rocks can be divided into three main groups: igneous, sedimentary, and metamorphic. Igneous rocks are formed when magma (molten rock) from the Earth's interior cools and solidifies (see pp. 274-275). Sedimentary rocks are formed when sediment (rock particles, for example) becomes compressed and cemented together in a process known as lithification (see pp. 276-277). Metamorphic rocks are formed when igneous, sedimentary, or other metamorphic rocks are changed by heat or pressure (see pp. 274-275). Rocks are added to the Earth's surface by crustal movements and volcanic activity. Once exposed on the surface, the rocks are broken down into rock particles by weathering (see pp. 282-283). The particles are then transported by glaciers, rivers, and wind, and deposited as sediment in lakes, deltas, deserts, and on the ocean floor. Some of this sediment undergoes lithification and forms sedimentary rock. This rock may be thrust back to the surface by crustal movements or forced deeper into the Earth's interior, where heat and pressure transform it into metamorphic rock. The metamorphic rock in turn may be pushed up to the surface or may be melted to form magma. Eventually, the magma cools and solidifies— below or on the surface—forming igneous rock. When the sedimentary, igneous, and metamorphic rocks are exposed once more on the Earth's surface, the cycle begins again.

THE ROCK CYCLE

STAGES IN THE ROCK CYCLE

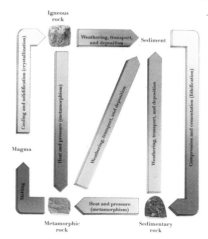

Igneous rock

Weathering, transport, and deposition

Sediment

Cooling and solidification (crystallization)

Heat and pressure (metamorphism)

Weathering, transport, and deposition

Weathering, transport, and deposition

Compression and cementation (lithification)

Magma

Melting

Heat and pressure (metamorphism)

Metamorphic rock

Sedimentary rock

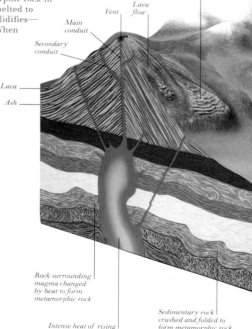

Magma extruded as lava, which solidifies to form igneous rock

Lava flow

Vent

Main conduit

Secondary conduit

Lava

Ash

Rock surrounding magma changed by heat to form metamorphic rock

Intense heat of rising magma melts some of the surrounding rock

Sedimentary rock crushed and folded to form metamorphic rock

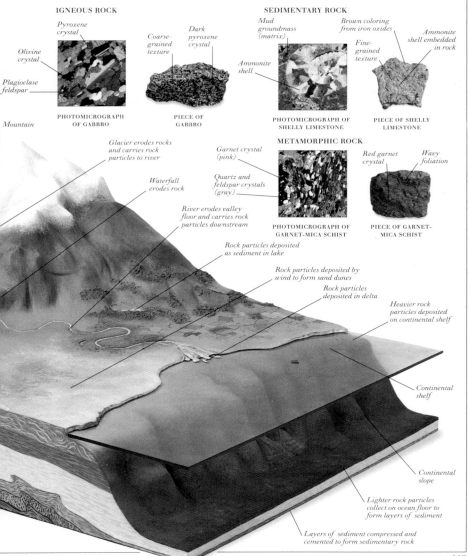

IGNEOUS ROCK

Pyroxene crystal

Olivine crystal

Plagioclase feldspar

Coarse-grained texture

Dark pyroxene crystal

PHOTOMICROGRAPH OF GABBRO

PIECE OF GABBRO

SEDIMENTARY ROCK

Mud groundmass (matrix)

Ammonite shell

Brown coloring from iron oxides

Fine-grained texture

Ammonite shell embedded in rock

PHOTOMICROGRAPH OF SHELLY LIMESTONE

PIECE OF SHELLY LIMESTONE

METAMORPHIC ROCK

Garnet crystal (pink)

Quartz and feldspar crystals (gray)

Red garnet crystal

Wavy foliation

PHOTOMICROGRAPH OF GARNET-MICA SCHIST

PIECE OF GARNET-MICA SCHIST

Mountain

Glacier erodes rocks and carries rock particles to river

Waterfall erodes rock

River erodes valley floor and carries rock particles downstream

Rock particles deposited as sediment in lake

Rock particles deposited by wind to form sand dunes

Rock particles deposited in delta

Heavier rock particles deposited on continental shelf

Continental shelf

Continental slope

Lighter rock particles collect on ocean floor to form layers of sediment

Layers of sediment compressed and cemented to form sedimentary rock

Minerals

A MINERAL IS A NATURALLY OCCURRING SUBSTANCE that has a characteristic chemical composition and specific physical properties, such as habit and streak (see pp. 270-271). A rock, by comparison, is an aggregate of minerals and need not have a specific chemical composition. Minerals are made up of elements (substances that cannot be broken down chemically into simpler substances), each of which can be represented by a chemical symbol. Minerals can be divided into two main groups: native elements and compounds. Native elements are made up of a pure element. Examples include gold (chemical symbol Au), silver (Ag), copper (Cu), and carbon (C); carbon occurs as a native element in two forms, diamond and graphite. Compounds are combinations of two or more elements. For example, sulfides are compounds of sulfur (S) and one or more other elements, such as lead (Pb) in the mineral galena, or antimony (Sb) in the mineral stibnite.

Dendritic (branching) copper

Limonite groundmass (matrix)

COPPER
(Cu)

SULFIDES

Cubic galena crystal

GALENA
(PbS)

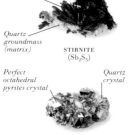

Prismatic stibnite crystal

Quartz groundmass (matrix)

STIBNITE
(Sb_2S_3)

Perfect octahedral pyrites crystal

Quartz crystal

PYRITES
(FeS_2)

Dendritic (branching) gold

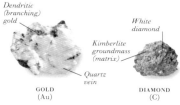

White diamond

Kimberlite groundmass (matrix)

Quartz vein

GOLD
(Au)

DIAMOND
(C)

Hexagonal graphite crystal

GRAPHITE
(C)

OXIDES/HYDROXIDES

Milky quartz groundmass (matrix)

Smoky quartz crystal

SMOKY QUARTZ
(SiO_2)

Rounded bauxite grains in groundmass (matrix)

Mass of specular hematite crystals

SPECULAR HEMATITE
(Fe_2O_3)

BAUXITE
(FeO(OH) and $Al_2O_3.2H_2O$)

Parallel bands of onyx

ONYX
(SiO_2)

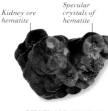

Kidney ore hematite

Specular crystals of hematite

KIDNEY ORE HEMATITE
(Fe_2O_3)

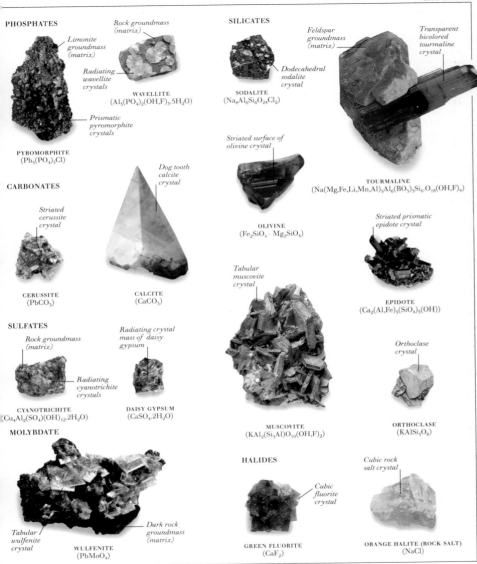

PHOSPHATES

Limonite groundmass (matrix)

Rock groundmass (matrix)

Radiating wavellite crystals

WAVELLITE
($Al_5(PO_4)_2(OH,F)_5.5H_2O$)

Prismatic pyromorphite crystals

PYROMORPHITE
($Pb_5(PO_4)_3Cl$)

CARBONATES

Striated cerussite crystal

CERUSSITE
($PbCO_3$)

Dog tooth calcite crystal

CALCITE
($CaCO_3$)

SULFATES

Rock groundmass (matrix)

Radiating cyanotrichite crystals

CYANOTRICHITE
($Cu_4Al_2(SO_4)(OH)_{12}.2H_2O$)

Radiating crystal mass of daisy gypsum

DAISY GYPSUM
($CaSO_4.2H_2O$)

MOLYBDATE

Tabular wulfenite crystal

Dark rock groundmass (matrix)

WULFENITE
($PbMoO_4$)

SILICATES

Feldspar groundmass (matrix)

Transparent bicolored tourmaline crystal

Dodecahedral sodalite crystal

SODALITE
($Na_8Al_6Si_6O_{24}Cl_2$)

TOURMALINE
($Na(Mg,Fe,Li,Mn,Al)_3Al_6(BO_3)_3Si_6.O_{18}(OH,F)_4$)

Striated surface of olivine crystal

OLIVINE
($Fe_2SiO_4 - Mg_2SiO_4$)

Striated prismatic epidote crystal

EPIDOTE
($Ca_2(Al,Fe)_3(SiO_4)_3(OH)$)

Tabular muscovite crystal

Orthoclase crystal

MUSCOVITE
($KAl_2(Si_3Al)O_{10}(OH,F)_2$)

ORTHOCLASE
($KAlSi_3O_8$)

HALIDES

Cubic fluorite crystal

Cubic rock salt crystal

GREEN FLUORITE
(CaF_2)

ORANGE HALITE (ROCK SALT)
($NaCl$)

Mineral features

MINERALS CAN BE IDENTIFIED BY STUDYING features such as fracture, cleavage, crystal system, habit, hardness, color, and streak. Minerals can break in different ways. If a mineral breaks in an irregular way, leaving rough surfaces, it possesses fracture. If a mineral breaks along well-defined planes of weakness, it possesses cleavage. Specific minerals have distinctive patterns of cleavage; for example, mica cleaves along one plane. Most minerals form crystals, which can be categorized into crystal systems according to their symmetry and number of faces. Within each system, several different but related forms of crystal are possible; for example, a cubic crystal can have six, eight, or 12 sides. A mineral's habit is the typical form taken by an aggregate of its crystals. Examples of habit include botryoidal (like a bunch of grapes) and massive (no definite form). The relative hardness of a mineral may be assessed by testing its resistance to scratching. This property is usually measured using Mohs scale, which increases in hardness from 1 (talc) to 10 (diamond). The color of a mineral is not a dependable guide to its identity as some minerals have a range of colors. Streak (the color the powdered mineral makes when rubbed across an unglazed tile) is a more reliable indicator.

CLEAVAGE

Cleavage in one direction

CLEAVAGE ALONG ONE PLANE

Cleavage in three directions, forming a block cube

CLEAVAGE ALONG THREE PLANES

Horizontal cleavage

Vertical cleavage

CLEAVAGE ALONG TWO PLANES

Cleavage in four directions, forming a double-pyramid crystal

CLEAVAGE ALONG FOUR PLANES

CRYSTAL SYSTEMS

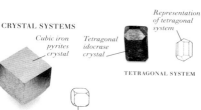

Cubic iron pyrites crystal

Tetragonal idocrase crystal

Representation of tetragonal system

TETRAGONAL SYSTEM

Representation of cubic system

CUBIC SYSTEM

Hexagonal beryl crystal

Representation of hexagonal/trigonal system

HEXAGONAL/TRIGONAL SYSTEM

Orthorhombic barytes crystal

Representation of orthorhombic system

ORTHORHOMBIC SYSTEM

Monoclinic selenite crystal

Representation of monoclinic system

MONOCLINIC SYSTEM

Triclinic axinite crystal

Representation of triclinic system

TRICLINIC SYSTEM

FRACTURE

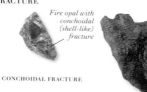

Fire opal with conchoidal (shell-like) fracture

CONCHOIDAL FRACTURE

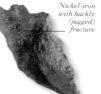

Nickel-iron with hackly (jagged) fracture

HACKLY FRACTURE

Orpiment with uneven fracture

UNEVEN FRACTURE

Garnierite with splintery fracture

SPLINTERY FRACTURE

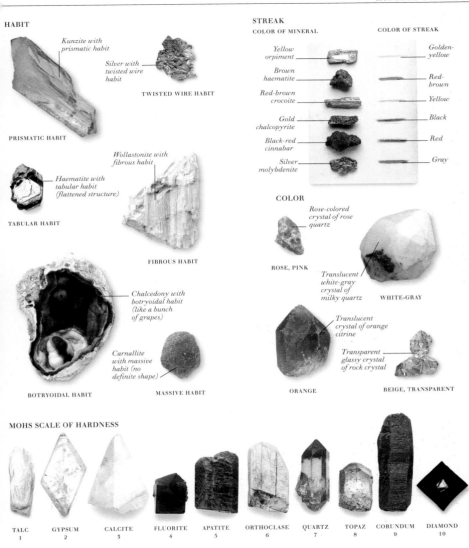

HABIT

Kunzite with prismatic habit

Silver with twisted wire habit

TWISTED WIRE HABIT

PRISMATIC HABIT

Wollastonite with fibrous habit

Haematite with tabular habit (flattened structure)

TABULAR HABIT

FIBROUS HABIT

Chalcedony with botryoidal habit (like a bunch of grapes)

Carnallite with massive habit (no definite shape)

BOTRYOIDAL HABIT

MASSIVE HABIT

STREAK

COLOR OF MINERAL

COLOR OF STREAK

Yellow orpiment

Brown haematite

Red-brown crocoite

Gold chalcopyrite

Black-red cinnabar

Silver molybdenite

Golden-yellow

Red-brown

Yellow

Black

Red

Gray

COLOR

Rose-colored crystal of rose quartz

ROSE, PINK

Translucent white-gray crystal of milky quartz

WHITE-GRAY

Translucent crystal of orange citrine

ORANGE

Transparent glassy crystal of rock crystal

BEIGE, TRANSPARENT

MOHS SCALE OF HARDNESS

TALC
1

GYPSUM
2

CALCITE
3

FLUORITE
4

APATITE
5

ORTHOCLASE
6

QUARTZ
7

TOPAZ
8

CORUNDUM
9

DIAMOND
10

Volcanoes

Folded, rope-like surface

VOLCANOES ARE VENTS OR FISSURES in the Earth's crust through which magma (molten rock that originates from deep beneath the crust) is forced on to the surface as lava. They occur most commonly along the boundaries of crustal plates; most volcanoes lie in a belt called the "Ring of Fire," which runs along the edge of the Pacific Ocean. Volcanoes can be classified according to the violence and frequency of their eruptions.

Nonexplosive volcanic eruptions generally occur where crustal plates pull apart. These eruptions produce runny basaltic lava that spreads quickly over a wide area to form relatively flat cones. The most violent eruptions take place where plates collide. Such eruptions produce thick rhyolitic lava and may also blast out clouds of dust and pyroclasts (lava fragments). The lava does not flow far before cooling and therefore builds up steep-sided, conical volcanoes. Some volcanoes produce lava and ash eruptions, which build up composite volcanic cones. Volcanoes that erupt frequently are described as active; those that erupt rarely are termed dormant; and those that have stopped erupting altogether are termed extinct. As well as the volcanoes themselves, other features associated with volcanic regions include geysers, hot mineral springs, solfataras, fumaroles, and bubbling mud pools.

PAHOEHOE
(ROPY LAVA)

HORU GEYSER,
NEW ZEALAND

VOLCANO TYPES

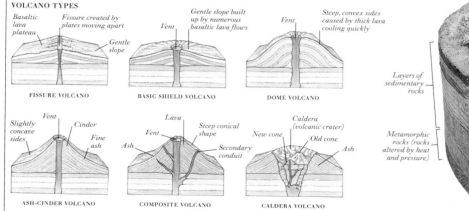

Basaltic lava plateau — *Fissure created by plates moving apart* — *Gentle slope*

FISSURE VOLCANO

Vent — *Gentle slope built up by numerous basaltic lava flows*

BASIC SHIELD VOLCANO

Vent — *Steep, convex sides caused by thick lava cooling quickly*

DOME VOLCANO

Slightly concave sides — *Vent* — *Cinder* — *Fine ash*

ASH-CINDER VOLCANO

Lava — *Vent* — *Ash* — *Steep conical shape* — *Secondary conduit*

COMPOSITE VOLCANO

Caldera (volcanic crater) — *New cone* — *Old cone* — *Ash*

CALDERA VOLCANO

Layers of sedimentary rocks

Metamorphic rocks (rocks altered by heat and pressure)

HOW VOLCANIC PLUGS BECOME EXPOSED

Extinct volcano — *Solidified lava forms plug*

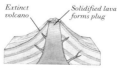

PLUG FORMATION

Plug exposed — *Volcanic cone slowly eroded away*

INITIAL EROSION AROUND PLUG

Resistant lava plug remains — *Volcanic cone completely eroded away*

COMPLETE DENUDATION OF PLUG

LAPILLI
(LAVA FRAGMENTS)

Small piece of solidified lava

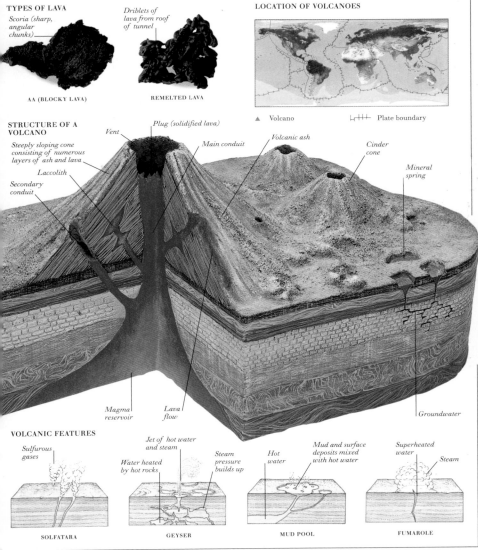

TYPES OF LAVA

Scoria (sharp, angular chunks)

AA (BLOCKY LAVA)

Driblets of lava from roof of tunnel

REMELTED LAVA

LOCATION OF VOLCANOES

▲ Volcano   ⊢┼┼┼ Plate boundary

STRUCTURE OF A VOLCANO

Steeply sloping cone consisting of numerous layers of ash and lava

Laccolith

Secondary conduit

Vent

Plug (solidified lava)

Main conduit

Volcanic ash

Cinder cone

Mineral spring

Magma reservoir

Lava flow

Groundwater

VOLCANIC FEATURES

Sulfurous gases

SOLFATARA

Jet of hot water and steam

Water heated by hot rocks

Steam pressure builds up

GEYSER

Hot water

Mud and surface deposits mixed with hot water

MUD POOL

Superheated water

Steam

FUMAROLE

Igneous and metamorphic rocks

IGNEOUS ROCKS ARE FORMED WHEN MAGMA (molten rock that originates from deep beneath the Earth's crust) cools and solidifies. There are two main types of igneous rock: intrusive and extrusive. Intrusive rocks are formed deep underground where magma is forced into cracks or between rock layers to form structures such as sills, dikes, and batholiths. The magma cools slowly to form coarse-grained rocks such as gabbro and pegmatite. Extrusive rocks are formed above the Earth's surface from lava (magma that has been ejected in a volcanic eruption). The molten lava cools quickly, producing fine-grained rocks such as rhyolite and basalt. Metamorphic rocks are those that have been altered by intense heat (contact metamorphism) or extreme pressure (regional metamorphism). Contact metamorphism occurs when rocks are changed by heat from, for example, an igneous intrusion or lava flow. Regional metamorphism occurs when rock is crushed in the middle of a folding mountain range. Metamorphic rocks can be formed from igneous rocks, sedimentary rocks, or even from other metamorphic rocks.

Cinder cone

Large eroded lava flow

Cedar-tree laccolith

Butte

Plug

CONTACT METAMORPHISM

Metamorphic aureole (region where contact metamorphism occurs)

Hot igneous intrusion

Limestone

Shale

Marble (metamorphosed limestone)

Slate (metamorphosed shale)

Cone sheet

Ring dike

Batholith

Dike

Sill

Dike swarm

Lopolith

IGNEOUS ROCK STRUCTURES

REGIONAL METAMORPHISM

Mountain range

Slate, formed under low pressure and temperature

Compression

Compression

Crust

Mantle

Magma

Schist, formed under medium pressure and temperature

Gneiss, formed under high pressure and temperature

EXAMPLES OF METAMORPHIC ROCKS

Pale feldspar

Dark mica

Dark mineral band

Pale calcite

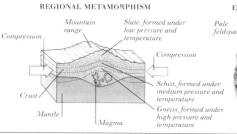

GNEISS

FOLDED SCHIST

SKARN

274

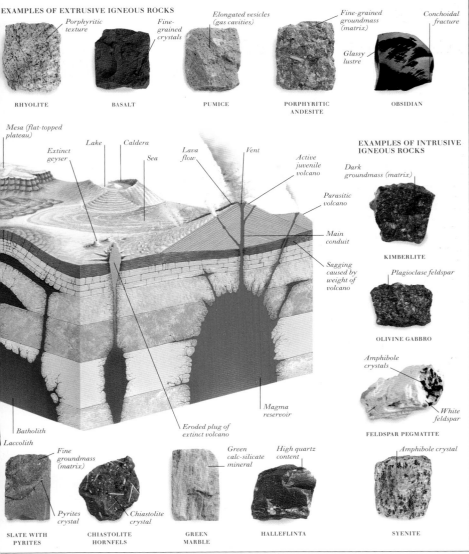

EXAMPLES OF EXTRUSIVE IGNEOUS ROCKS

Porphyritic texture

Fine-grained crystals

Elongated vesicles (gas cavities)

Fine-grained groundmass (matrix)

Conchoidal fracture

Glassy lustre

RHYOLITE

BASALT

PUMICE

PORPHYRITIC ANDESITE

OBSIDIAN

Mesa (flat-topped plateau)

Extinct geyser

Lake

Caldera

Sea

Lava flow

Vent

Active juvenile volcano

Parasitic volcano

Main conduit

Sagging caused by weight of volcano

Batholith

Laccolith

Eroded plug of extinct volcano

Magma reservoir

EXAMPLES OF INTRUSIVE IGNEOUS ROCKS

Dark groundmass (matrix)

KIMBERLITE

Plagioclase feldspar

OLIVINE GABBRO

Amphibole crystals

White feldspar

FELDSPAR PEGMATITE

Amphibole crystal

SYENITE

Fine groundmass (matrix)

Pyrites crystal

Chiastolite crystal

SLATE WITH PYRITES

CHIASTOLITE HORNFELS

Green calc-silicate mineral

GREEN MARBLE

High quartz content

HALLEFLINTA

Sedimentary rocks

SEDIMENTARY ROCKS ARE FORMED BY THE ACCUMULATION and consolidation of sediments (see pp. 266-267). There are three main types of sedimentary rock. Clastic sedimentary rocks, such as breccia or sandstone, are formed from other rocks that have been broken down into fragments by weathering (see pp. 282-283), which have then been transported and deposited elsewhere. Organic sedimentary rocks—for example, coal (see pp. 280-281)—are derived from plant and animal remains. Chemical sedimentary rocks are formed by chemical processes. For example, rock salt is formed when salt dissolved in water is deposited as the water evaporates. Sedimentary rocks are laid down in layers, called beds or strata. Each new layer is laid down horizontally over older ones. There are usually some gaps in the sequence, called unconformities. These represent periods in which no new sediments were being laid down, or when earlier sedimentary layers were raised above sea level and eroded away.

THE GRAND CANYON, USA

EXAMPLES OF UNCONFORMITIES

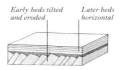

Early beds tilted and eroded   *Later beds horizontal*

ANGULAR UNCONFORMITY

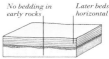

No bedding in early rocks   *Later beds horizontal*

NONCONFORMITY

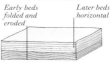

Early beds folded and eroded   *Later beds horizontal*

DISCONFORMITY

SEDIMENTARY LAYERS OF THE GRAND CANYON REGION

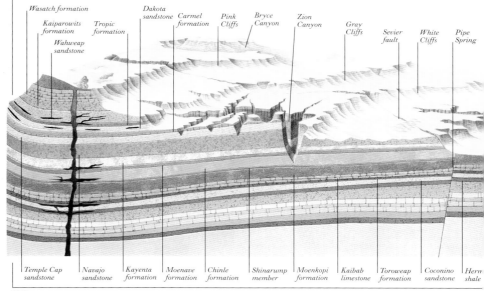

Wasatch formation
Kaiparowits formation
Tropic formation
Wahweap sandstone
Dakota sandstone
Carmel formation
Pink Cliffs
Bryce Canyon
Zion Canyon
Gray Cliffs
Sevier fault
White Cliffs
Pipe Spring

Temple Cap sandstone
Navajo sandstone
Kayenta formation
Moenave formation
Chinle formation
Shinarump member
Moenkopi formation
Kaibab limestone
Toroweap formation
Coconino sandstone
Herm shale

EXAMPLES OF SEDIMENTARY ROCKS

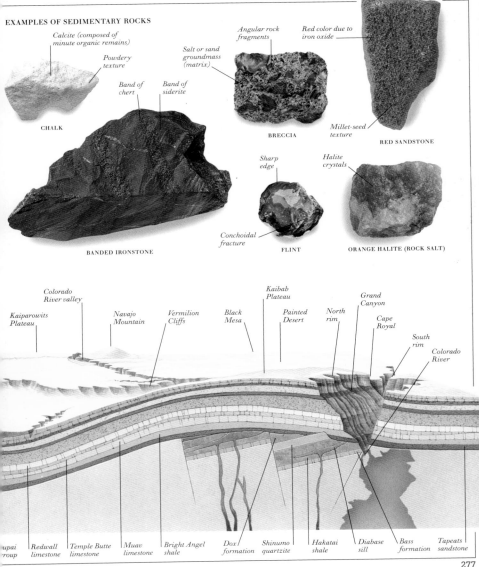

Calcite (composed of minute organic remains)

Powdery texture

CHALK

Band of chert

Band of siderite

BANDED IRONSTONE

Angular rock fragments

Salt or sand groundmass (matrix)

BRECCIA

Red color due to iron oxide

Millet-seed texture

RED SANDSTONE

Sharp edge

Conchoidal fracture

FLINT

Halite crystals

ORANGE HALITE (ROCK SALT)

Kaiparowits Plateau

Colorado River valley

Navajo Mountain

Vermilion Cliffs

Black Mesa

Kaibab Plateau

Painted Desert

North rim

Grand Canyon

Cape Royal

South rim

Colorado River

...upai ...roup

Redwall limestone

Temple Butte limestone

Muav limestone

Bright Angel shale

Dox formation

Shinumo quartzite

Hakatai shale

Diabase sill

Bass formation

Tapeats sandstone

277

Fossils

FOSSILS ARE THE REMAINS of plants and animals that have been preserved in rock. A fossil may be the preserved remains of an organism itself, an impression of it in rock, or preserved traces (known as trace fossils) left by an organism while it was alive, such as organic carbon outlines, fossilized footprints, or droppings. Most dead organisms soon rot away or are eaten by scavengers. For fossilization to occur, rapid burial by sediment is necessary. The organism decays, but the harder parts—bones, teeth, and shells, for example—may be preserved and hardened by minerals from the surrounding sediment. Fossilization may also occur even when the hard parts of an organism are dissolved away to leave an impression called a mold. The mold is filled by minerals, thereby creating a cast of the organism. The study of fossils (paleontology) can not only show how living things have evolved, but can also help to reveal the Earth's geological history—for example, by aiding in the dating of rock strata.

PROCESS OF FOSSILIZATION

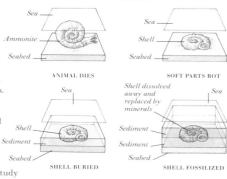

Sea
Ammonite
Seabed

ANIMAL DIES

Sea
Shell
Seabed

SOFT PARTS ROT

Sea
Shell
Sediment
Seabed

SHELL BURIED

Shell dissolved away and replaced by minerals
Sea
Sediment
Sediment
Seabed

SHELL FOSSILIZED

EXAMPLES OF FOSSILS

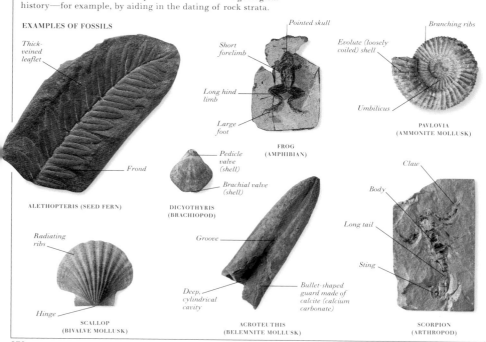

Thick-veined leaflet

Frond

ALETHOPTERIS (SEED FERN)

Radiating ribs

Hinge

SCALLOP (BIVALVE MOLLUSK)

Pointed skull

Short forelimb

Long hind limb

Large foot

FROG (AMPHIBIAN)

Pedicle valve (shell)

Brachial valve (shell)

DICYOTHYRIS (BRACHIOPOD)

Groove

Deep, cylindrical cavity

Bullet-shaped guard made of calcite (calcium carbonate)

ACROTEUTHIS (BELEMNITE MOLLUSK)

Evolute (loosely coiled) shell

Branching ribs

Umbilicus

PAVLOVIA (AMMONITE MOLLUSK)

Claw

Body

Long tail

Sting

SCORPION (ARTHROPOD)

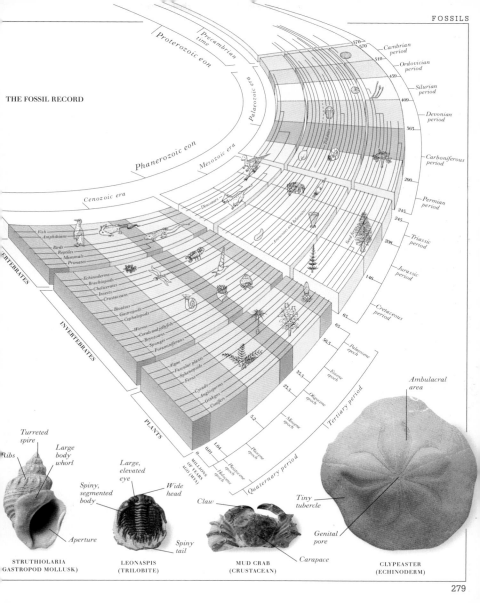

THE FOSSIL RECORD

Precambrian time

Proterozoic eon

Palaeozoic era

Phanerozoic eon

Mesozoic era

Cenozoic era

570 — Cambrian period

510 — Ordovician period

439 — Silurian period

409 — Devonian period

363 — Carboniferous period

290 — Permian period

245 — Permian period

245 — Triassic period

208 — Jurassic period

146 — Cretaceous period

65 — Cretaceous period

65

56.5 — Palaeocene epoch

53.5 — Eocene epoch

23.5 — Oligocene epoch

5.2 — Miocene epoch

1.64 — Pliocene epoch

0.01 — Pleistocene epoch

0.01 — Holocene epoch

Tertiary period

Quaternary period

MILLIONS (OF YEARS AGO (MYA))

VERTEBRATES

Fish
Amphibians
Birds
Reptiles
Mammals
Primates

INVERTEBRATES

Echinoderms
Brachiopods
Chelicerates
Insects
Crustaceans
Bivalves
Gastropods
Cephalopods
Worms
Corals and jellyfish
Bryozoans
Sponges
Foraminiferans

PLANTS

Algae
Vascular plants
Sphenopsids
Ferns
Cycads
Angiosperms
Ginkgos
Conifers

Trilobite

Dinosaur

Ammonites with Belemnites

Seed fern

Ambulacral area

Genital pore

Tiny tubercle

Turreted spire

Large body whorl

Ribs

Aperture

STRUTHIOLARIA
(GASTROPOD MOLLUSK)

Large, elevated eye

Wide head

Spiny, segmented body

Spiny tail

LEONASPIS
(TRILOBITE)

Claw

Carapace

MUD CRAB
(CRUSTACEAN)

CLYPEASTER
(ECHINODERM)

279

Mineral resources

Stalk   *Leaf*

PLANT MATTER

MINERAL RESOURCES CAN BE DEFINED AS naturally occurring substances that can be extracted from the Earth and are useful as fuels and raw materials. Coal, oil, and gas—collectively called fossil fuels—are commonly included in this group, but are not strictly minerals, because they are of organic origin. Coal formation begins when vegetation is buried and partly decomposed to form peat. Overlying sediments compress the peat and transform it into lignite (soft brown coal). As the overlying sediments

OIL RIG, NORTH SEA

accumulate, increasing pressure and temperature eventually transform the lignite into bituminous and hard anthracite coals. Oil and gas are usually formed from organic matter that was deposited in marine sediments. Under the effects of heat and pressure, the compressed organic matter undergoes complex chemical changes to form oil and gas. The oil and gas percolate upwards through water-saturated, permeable rocks and they may rise to the Earth's surface or accumulate below an impermeable layer of rock that has been folded or faulted to form a trap—an anticline (upfold) trap, for example. Minerals are inorganic substances that may consist of a single chemical element, such as gold, silver, or copper, or combinations of elements (see pp. 268-269). Some minerals are concentrated in mineralization zones in rock associated with crustal movements or volcanic activity. Others may be found in sediments as placer deposits—accumulations of high-density minerals that have been weathered out of rocks, transported, and deposited (on riverbeds, for example).

Decayed plant matter

About 60% carbon   PEAT   *About 70% carbon*

Crumbly texture   LIGNITE (BROWN COAL)   *Powdery texture*

About 80% carbon

Shiny surface   BITUMINOUS COAL   *About 95% carbon*

HOW COAL IS FORMED

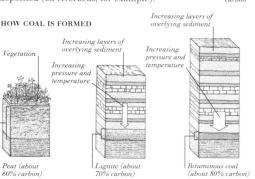

Vegetation

Increasing pressure and temperature

Increasing layers of overlying sediment

Increasing pressure and temperature

Increasing layers of overlying sediment

Increasing pressure and temperature

Peat (about 60% carbon)
PEAT

Lignite (about 70% carbon)
LIGNITE (BROWN COAL)

Bituminous coal (about 80% carbon)
BITUMINOUS COAL

ANTHRACITE COAL

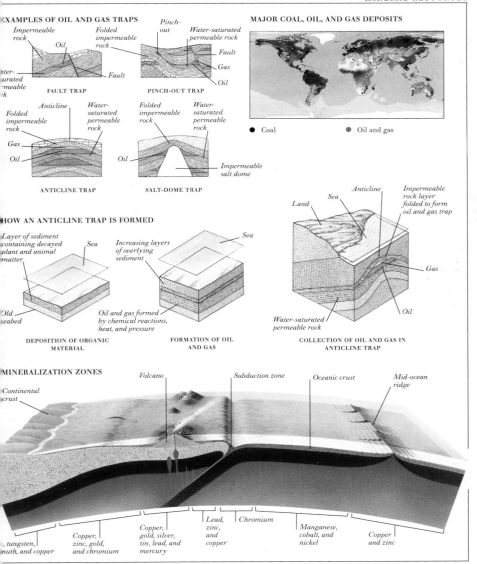

EXAMPLES OF OIL AND GAS TRAPS

Impermeable rock
Oil
Folded impermeable rock
Fault
ter-urated meable k

FAULT TRAP

Pinch-out
Water-saturated permeable rock
Fault
Gas
Oil

PINCH-OUT TRAP

Anticline
Folded impermeable rock
Water-saturated permeable rock
Gas
Oil

ANTICLINE TRAP

Folded impermeable rock
Water-saturated permeable rock
Oil
Impermeable salt dome

SALT-DOME TRAP

MAJOR COAL, OIL, AND GAS DEPOSITS

● Coal   ● Oil and gas

HOW AN ANTICLINE TRAP IS FORMED

Layer of sediment containing decayed plant and animal matter
Sea
Old seabed

DEPOSITION OF ORGANIC MATERIAL

Increasing layers of overlying sediment
Sea
Oil and gas formed by chemical reactions, heat, and pressure

FORMATION OF OIL AND GAS

Land
Sea
Anticline
Impermeable rock layer folded to form oil and gas trap
Gas
Oil
Water-saturated permeable rock

COLLECTION OF OIL AND GAS IN ANTICLINE TRAP

MINERALIZATION ZONES

Continental crust
Volcano
Subduction zone
Oceanic crust
Mid-ocean ridge

, tungsten, muth, and copper
Copper, zinc, gold, and chromium
Copper, gold, silver, tin, lead, and mercury
Lead, zinc, and copper
Chromium
Manganese, cobalt, and nickel
Copper and zinc

Weathering and erosion

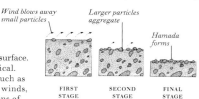

Wind blows away small particles

Larger particles aggregate

Hamada forms

FIRST STAGE   **SECOND STAGE**   **FINAL STAGE**

Weathering is the breaking down of rocks on the Earth's surface. There are two main types: physical (or mechanical) and chemical. Physical weathering may be caused by temperature changes, such as freezing and thawing, or by abrasion from material carried by winds, rivers, or glaciers. Rocks may also be broken down by the actions of animals and plants, such as the burrowing of animals and the growth of roots. Chemical weathering causes rocks to decompose by changing their chemical composition—for example, rainwater may dissolve certain minerals in a rock. Erosion is the wearing away and removal of land surfaces by water, wind, or ice. It is greatest in areas of little or no surface vegetation, such as deserts, where sand dunes may form.

FEATURES OF WEATHERING AND EROSION

FEATURES PRODUCED BY WIND ACTION

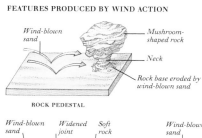

Wind-blown sand

Mushroom-shaped rock

Neck

Rock base eroded by wind-blown sand

ROCK PEDESTAL

Wind-blown sand *Widened joint* *Soft rock*

Hard rock

ZEUGEN

Wind-blown sand

Furrow

Hard rock

Soft rock eroded by wind-blown sand

YARDANG

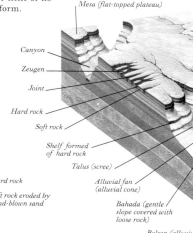

Mesa (flat-topped plateau)

Canyon

Zeugen

Joint

Hard rock

Soft rock

Shelf formed of hard rock

Talus (scree)

Alluvial fan (alluvial cone)

Bahada (gentle slope covered with loose rock)

Bolson (alluvium-filled basin)

EXAMPLES OF PHYSICAL WEATHERING PROCESSES

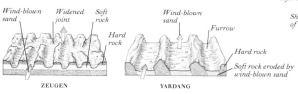

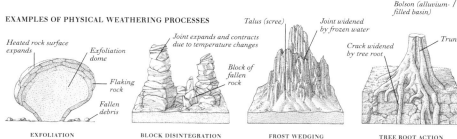

Heated rock surface expands

Exfoliation dome

Flaking rock

Fallen debris

EXFOLIATION (ONION-SKIN WEATHERING)

Joint expands and contracts due to temperature changes

Block of fallen rock

BLOCK DISINTEGRATION

Talus (scree)

Joint widened by frozen water

FROST WEDGING

Crack widened by tree root

Trunk

TREE ROOT ACTION

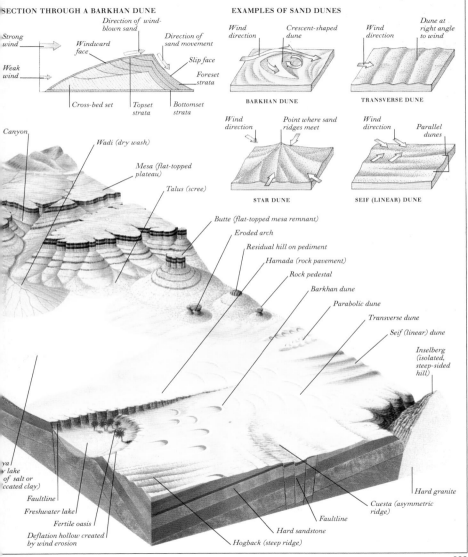

SECTION THROUGH A BARKHAN DUNE

Direction of wind-blown sand
Direction of sand movement
Strong wind
Weak wind
Windward face
Slip face
Foreset strata
Cross-bed set
Topset strata
Bottomset strata

EXAMPLES OF SAND DUNES

Wind direction
Crescent-shaped dune
BARKHAN DUNE

Wind direction
Dune at right angle to wind
TRANSVERSE DUNE

Wind direction
Point where sand ridges meet
STAR DUNE

Wind direction
Parallel dunes
SEIF (LINEAR) DUNE

Canyon
Wadi (dry wash)
Mesa (flat-topped plateau)
Talus (scree)
Butte (flat-topped mesa remnant)
Eroded arch
Residual hill on pediment
Hamada (rock pavement)
Rock pedestal
Barkhan dune
Parabolic dune
Transverse dune
Seif (linear) dune
Inselberg (isolated, steep-sided hill)

...ya ... lake ... of salt or ...ccated clay)
Faultline
Freshwater lake
Fertile oasis
Deflation hollow created by wind erosion
Hogback (steep ridge)
Hard sandstone
Faultline
Cuesta (asymmetric ridge)
Hard granite

Caves

CAVES COMMONLY FORM in areas of limestone, although on coastlines they also occur in other rocks. Limestone is made of calcite (calcium carbonate), which dissolves in the carbonic acid naturally present in rainwater, and in humic acids from the decay of vegetation. The acidic water trickles down through cracks and joints in the limestone and between rock layers, breaking up the surface terrain into clints (blocks of rock), separated by grikes (deep cracks), and punctuated by sink-holes (also called swallow-holes or potholes) into which surface streams may disappear. Underground, the acidic water dissolves the rock around crevices, opening up a network of passages and caves, which can become large caverns if the roofs collapse. Various features are formed when the dissolved calcite is redeposited; for example, it may be redeposited along an underground stream to form a gour (series of calcite ridges), or in caves and passages to form stalactites and stalagmites. Stalactites develop where calcite is left behind as water drips from the roof; where the drops land, stalagmites build up.

STALACTITE WITH RING MARKS

MERGED STALACTITES

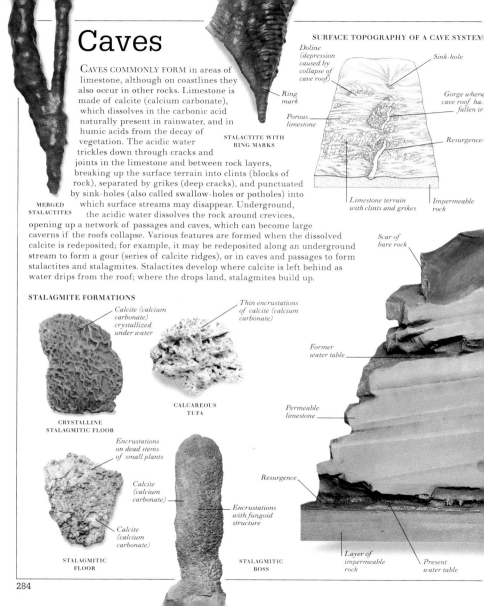

SURFACE TOPOGRAPHY OF A CAVE SYSTEM

Doline (depression caused by collapse of cave roof)

Ring mark

Porous limestone

Sink-hole

Gorge where cave roof has fallen in

Resurgence

Limestone terrain with clints and grikes

Impermeable rock

STALAGMITE FORMATIONS

Calcite (calcium carbonate) crystallized under water

CRYSTALLINE STALAGMITIC FLOOR

Thin encrustations of calcite (calcium carbonate)

CALCAREOUS TUFA

Scar of bare rock

Former water table

Permeable limestone

Encrustations on dead stems of small plants

Calcite (calcium carbonate)

Calcite (calcium carbonate)

STALAGMITIC FLOOR

Resurgence

Encrustations with fungoid structure

STALAGMITIC BOSS

Layer of impermeable rock

Present water table

DEVELOPMENT OF A CAVE SYSTEM

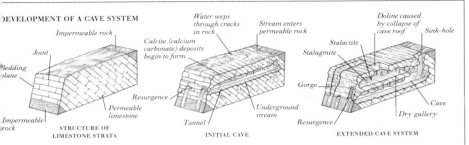

STRUCTURE OF LIMESTONE STRATA

Impermeable rock
Joint
Bedding plane
Impermeable rock
Permeable limestone

INITIAL CAVE

Water seeps through cracks in rock
Stream enters permeable rock
Calcite (calcium carbonate) deposits begin to form
Resurgence
Tunnel
Underground stream

EXTENDED CAVE SYSTEM

Doline caused by collapse of cave roof
Sink-hole
Stalactite
Stalagmite
Gorge
Cave
Dry gallery
Resurgence

INTERCONNECTED CAVE SYSTEM

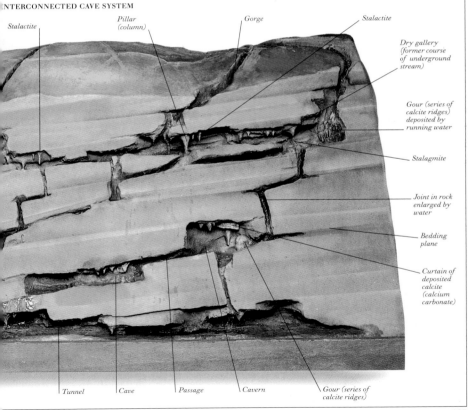

Stalactite
Pillar (column)
Gorge
Stalactite

Dry gallery (former course of underground stream)

Gour (series of calcite ridges) deposited by running water

Stalagmite

Joint in rock enlarged by water

Bedding plane

Curtain of deposited calcite (calcium carbonate)

Tunnel
Cave
Passage
Cavern
Gour (series of calcite ridges)

Glaciers

GLACIER BAY, ALASKA

A VALLEY GLACIER IS A LARGE MASS OF ICE that forms on land and moves slowly downhill under its own weight. It is formed from snow that collects in cirques (mountain hollows also known as corries) and compresses into ice as more and more snow accumulates. The cirque is deepened by frost wedging and abrasion (see pp. 282-283), and arêtes (sharp ridges) develop between adjacent cirques. Eventually, so much ice builds up that the glacier begins to move downhill. As the glacier moves it collects moraine (debris), which may range in size from particles of dust to large boulders. The rocks at the base of the glacier erode the glacial valley, giving it a U-shaped cross-section. Under the glacier, *roches moutonnées* (eroded outcrops of hard rock) and drumlins (rounded mounds of rock and clay) are left behind on the valley floor. The glacier ends at a terminus (the snout), where the ice melts as fast as it arrives. If the temperature increases, the ice melts faster than it arrives, and the glacier retreats. The retreating glacier leaves behind its moraine and also erratics (isolated single boulders). Glacial streams from the melting glacier deposit eskers and kames (ridges and mounds of sand and gravel), but carry away the finer sediment to form a stratified outwash plain. Lumps of ice carried on to this plain melt, creating holes called kettles.

VALLEY GLACIER

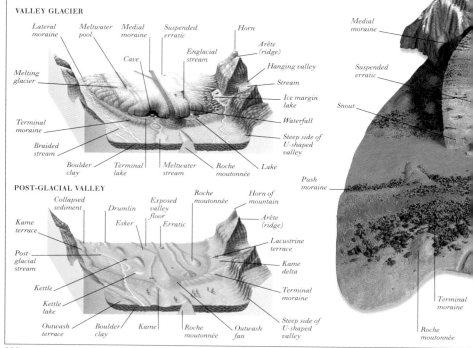

Lateral moraine
Meltwater pool
Medial moraine
Suspended erratic
Horn
Cave
Englacial stream
Arête (ridge)
Hanging valley
Stream
Melting glacier
Ice margin lake
Terminal moraine
Waterfall
Braided stream
Steep side of U-shaped valley
Boulder clay
Terminal lake
Meltwater stream
Roche moutonnée
Lake

Medial moraine
Suspended erratic
Snout
Push moraine
Terminal moraine
Roche moutonnée

POST-GLACIAL VALLEY

Collapsed sediment
Drumlin
Esker
Exposed valley floor
Erratic
Roche moutonnée
Horn of mountain
Arête (ridge)
Kame terrace
Lacustrine terrace
Post-glacial stream
Kame delta
Kettle
Terminal moraine
Kettle lake
Steep side of U-shaped valley
Outwash terrace
Boulder clay
Kame
Roche moutonnée
Outwash fan

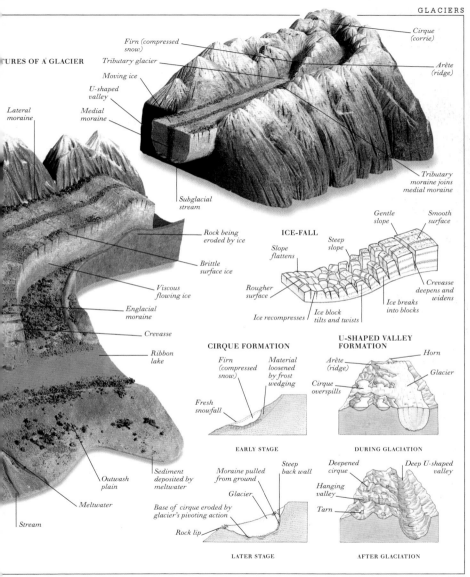

FEATURES OF A GLACIER

Cirque (corrie)

Firn (compressed snow)

Tributary glacier

Moving ice

U-shaped valley

Medial moraine

Lateral moraine

Arête (ridge)

Subglacial stream

Tributary moraine joins medial moraine

Rock being eroded by ice

Brittle surface ice

Viscous flowing ice

Englacial moraine

Crevasse

Ribbon lake

Outwash plain

Meltwater

Stream

Sediment deposited by meltwater

ICE-FALL

Gentle slope

Smooth surface

Steep slope

Slope flattens

Rougher surface

Ice recompresses

Ice block tilts and twists

Ice breaks into blocks

Crevasse deepens and widens

CIRQUE FORMATION

Firn (compressed snow)

Material loosened by frost wedging

Fresh snowfall

EARLY STAGE

Moraine pulled from ground

Steep back wall

Glacier

Base of cirque eroded by glacier's pivoting action

Rock lip

LATER STAGE

U-SHAPED VALLEY FORMATION

Arête (ridge)

Horn

Glacier

Cirque overspills

DURING GLACIATION

Deepened cirque

Deep U-shaped valley

Hanging valley

Tarn

AFTER GLACIATION

Rivers

RIVERS FORM PART of the water cycle—the continuous circulation of water between the land, sea, and atmosphere. The source of a river may be a mountain spring or lake, or a melting glacier. The course that the river subsequently takes depends on the slope of the terrain and on the rock types and formations over which it flows. In its early, upland stages, a river tumbles steeply over rocks and boulders and cuts a steep-sided V-shaped valley. Farther downstream, it flows smoothly over sediments and forms winding meanders, eroding sideways to create broad valleys and plains. On reaching the coast, the river may deposit sediment to form an estuary or delta (see pp. 290-291).

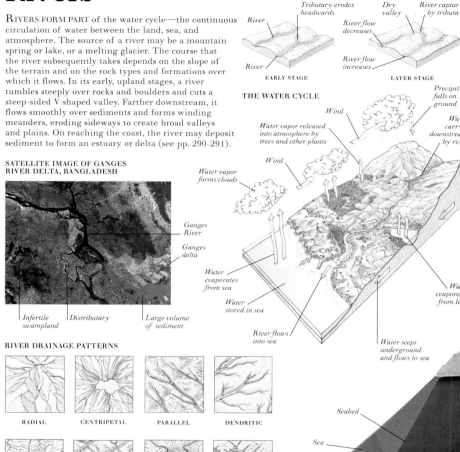

RIVER CAPTURE

Tributary erodes headwards

River

River flow decreases

River

EARLY STAGE

Dry valley

River captur by tributa

River flow increases

LATER STAGE

THE WATER CYCLE

Precipit falls on ground

Wind

Wa carr downstre by ri

Water vapor released into atmosphere by trees and other plants

Wind

Water vapor forms clouds

Water evaporates from sea

Water stored in sea

River flows into sea

Wa evapora from le

Water seeps underground and flows to sea

Seabed

Sea

Sediment layers

SATELLITE IMAGE OF GANGES RIVER DELTA, BANGLADESH

Ganges River

Ganges delta

Infertile swampland   *Distributary*   *Large volume of sediment*

RIVER DRAINAGE PATTERNS

RADIAL   CENTRIPETAL   PARALLEL   DENDRITIC

DERANGED   TRELLISED   ANNULAR   RECTANGULAR

STAGES IN A RIVER'S DEVELOPMENT

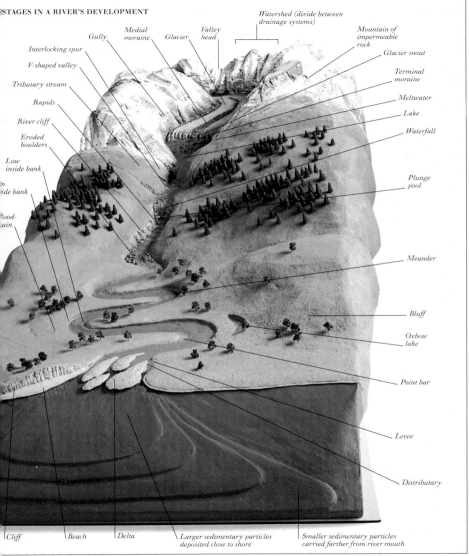

Gully

Medial moraine

Glacier

Valley head

Watershed (divide between drainage systems)

Mountain of impermeable rock

Glacier snout

Interlocking spur

V-shaped valley

Tributary stream

Rapids

River cliff

Eroded boulders

Low inside bank

...side bank

...ood-...ain

Terminal moraine

Meltwater

Lake

Waterfall

Plunge pool

Meander

Bluff

Oxbow lake

Point bar

Levee

Distributary

Cliff

Beach

Delta

Larger sedimentary particles deposited close to shore

Smaller sedimentary particles carried farther from river mouth

River features

RIVERS ARE ONE OF THE MAJOR FORCES that shape the landscape. Near its source, a river is steep (see pp. 288-289). It erodes downward, carving out V-shaped valleys and deep gorges. Waterfalls and rapids are formed where the river flows from hard rock to softer, more easily eroded rock. Farther downstream, meanders may form and there is greater sideways erosion, resulting in a broad river valley. The river sometimes erodes through the neck of a meander to form an oxbow lake. Sediment deposited on the valley floor by meandering rivers and during floods helps to create a floodplain. Floods may also deposit sediment on the banks of the river to form levees. As a river spills into the sea or a lake, it deposits large amounts of sediment, and may form a delta. A delta is an area of sand bars, swamps, and lagoons through which the river flows in several channels called distributaries—the Mississippi delta, for example. Often, a rise in sea level may have flooded the river mouth to form a broad estuary, a tidal section where seawater mixes with fresh water.

HOW WATERFALLS AND RAPIDS ARE FORMED

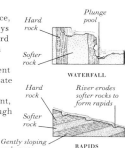

WATERFALL

RAPIDS

A RIVER VALLEY DRAINAGE SYSTEM

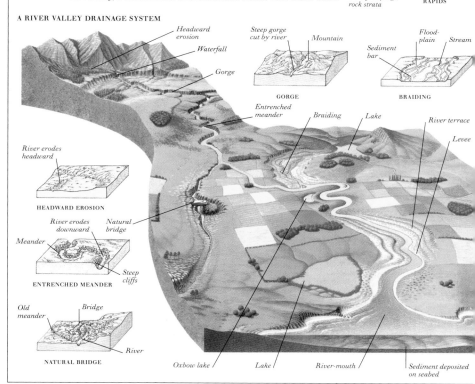

GORGE

BRAIDING

HEADWARD EROSION

ENTRENCHED MEANDER

NATURAL BRIDGE

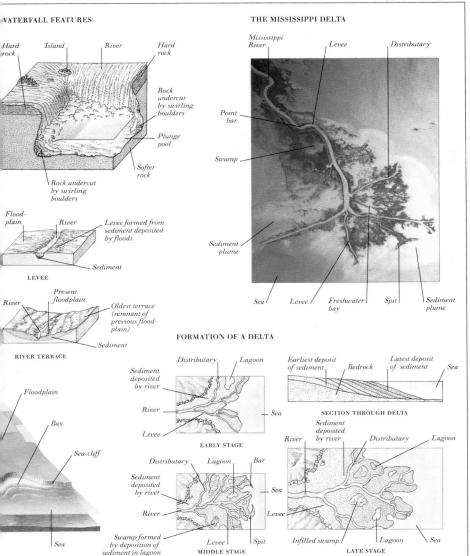

WATERFALL FEATURES

Hard rock

Island

River

Hard rock

Rock undercut by swirling boulders

Plunge pool

Softer rock

Rock undercut by swirling boulders

Flood-plain

River

Levee formed from sediment deposited by floods

Sediment

LEVEE

River

Present floodplain

Oldest terrace (remnant of previous flood-plain)

Sediment

RIVER TERRACE

Floodplain

Bay

Sea-cliff

Sea

THE MISSISSIPPI DELTA

Mississippi River

Levee

Distributary

Point bar

Swamp

Sediment plume

Sea

Levee

Freshwater bay

Spit

Sediment plume

FORMATION OF A DELTA

Distributary

Lagoon

Sediment deposited by river

River

Levee

Sea

EARLY STAGE

Earliest deposit of sediment

Bedrock

Latest deposit of sediment

Sea

SECTION THROUGH DELTA

Distributary

Lagoon

Bar

Sediment deposited by river

River

Sea

Swamp formed by deposition of sediment in lagoon

Levee

Spit

MIDDLE STAGE

River

Sediment deposited by river

Distributary

Lagoon

Levee

Sea

Infilled swamp

Lagoon

Sea

LATE STAGE

Lakes and groundwater

NATURAL LAKE OCCUR WHERE a large quantity of water collects in a hollow in impermeable rock, or is prevented from draining away by a barrier, such as moraine (glacial deposits) or solidified lava. Lakes are often relatively short-lived landscape features, as they tend to become silted up by sediment from the streams and rivers that feed them. Some of the more long-lasting lakes are found in deep rift valleys formed by vertical movements of the Earth's crust (see pp. 58-59)—for example, Lake Baikal in Russia, the world's largest freshwater lake, and the Dead Sea in the Middle East, one of the world's saltiest lakes. Where water is able to drain away, it sinks into the ground until it reaches a layer of impermeable rock, then accumulates in the permeable rock above it; this water-saturated permeable rock is called an aquifer. The saturated zone varies in depth according to seasonal and climatic changes. In wet conditions, the water stored underground builds up, while in dry periods it becomes depleted. Where the upper edge of the saturated zone—the water table—meets the ground surface, water emerges as springs. In an artesian basin, where the aquifer is below an aquiclude (layer of impermeable rock), the water table throughout the basin is determined by its height at the rim. In the center of such a basin, the water table is above ground level. The water in the basin is thus trapped below the water table and can rise under its own pressure along faultlines or well shafts.

LAKE BAIKAL, RUSSIA

EXAMPLES OF SPRINGS

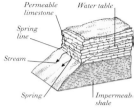

Permeable limestone · *Water table* · *Spring line* · *Stream* · *Spring* · *Impermeable shale*

LIMESTONE SPRING

Permeable gravel · *Water table* · *Spring line* · *Stream* · *Spring* · *Impermeable clay*

COASTAL (VALLEY) SPRING

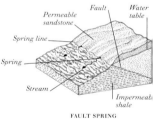

Fault · *Water table* · *Permeable sandstone* · *Spring line* · *Spring* · *Stream* · *Impermeable shale*

FAULT SPRING

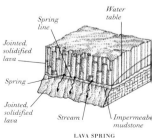

Water table · *Spring line* · *Jointed, solidified lava* · *Spring* · *Jointed, solidified lava* · *Stream* · *Impermeable mudstone*

LAVA SPRING

STRUCTURE OF AN ARTESIAN BASIN

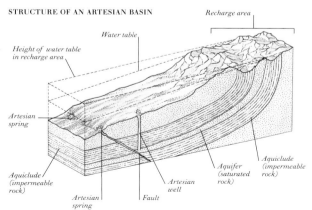

Recharge area

Water table

Height of water table in recharge area

Artesian spring

Aquiclude (impermeable rock)

Artesian spring

Fault

Artesian well

Aquifer (saturated rock)

Aquiclude (impermeable rock)

FEATURES OF A GROUNDWATER SYSTEM

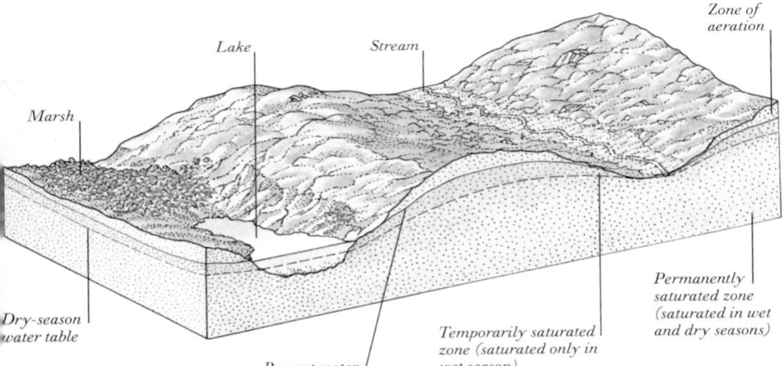

Marsh
Lake
Stream
Zone of aeration

Layer of soil moisture
Zone of aeration
Capillary fringe
Water table
Saturated zone

CLOSE-UP OF SURFACE LAYER

Dry-season water table

Present water table (wet season)

Temporarily saturated zone (saturated only in wet season)

Permanently saturated zone (saturated in wet and dry seasons)

EXAMPLES OF LAKES

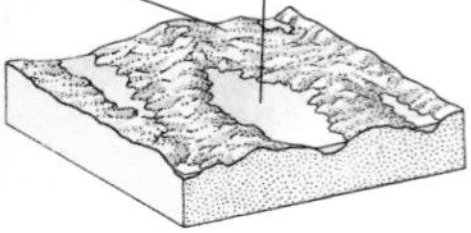

Glacial deposits
Lake in kettle (former site of ice block)

KETTLE LAKE

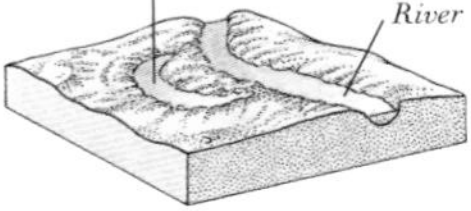

Oxbow lake (cut-off river meander)
River

OXBOW LAKE

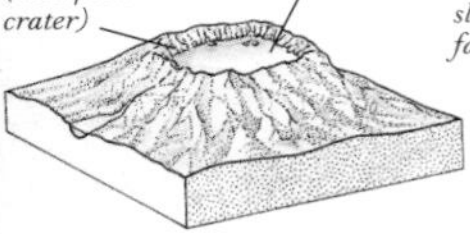

Caldera (collapsed crater)
Volcanic lake

VOLCANIC LAKE

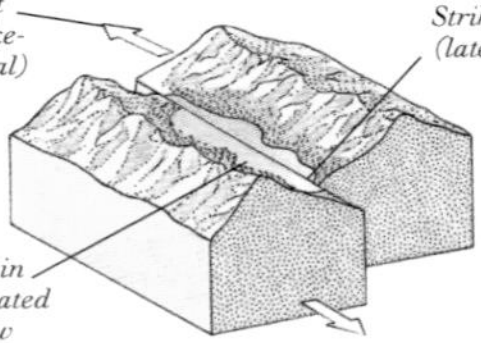

Movement along strike-slip (lateral) fault
Strike-slip (lateral) fault

Lake in elongated hollow

STRIKE-SLIP (LATERAL) FAULT LAKE

Rift valley

High valley walls
Sinking graben (block fault)

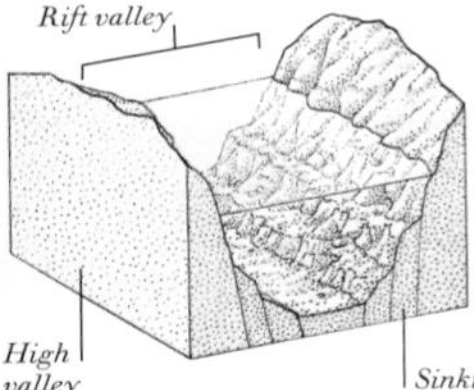

GRABEN (BLOCK-FAULT) LAKE

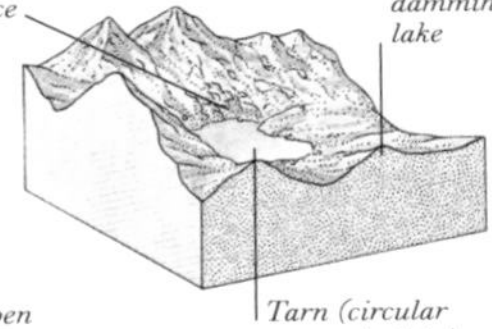

Steep back wall eroded by frost and ice
Moraine or rock lip damming lake

Tarn (circular mountain lake)

TARN

THE DEAD SEA, ISRAEL/JORDAN

River Jordan
Dead Sea
Steep rift-valley walls
Salt left by evaporation
Israel
Shallow flats
Jordan

Coastlines

COASTLINES ARE AMONG THE MOST RAPIDLY changing landscape features. Some are eroded by waves, wind, and rain, causing cliffs to be undercut and caves to be hollowed out of solid rock. Others are built up by waves transporting sand and small rocks in a process known as longshore drift, and by rivers depositing sediment in deltas. Additional influences include the activities of living organisms such as coral, crustal movements, and sea-level variations due to climatic changes. Rising land or a drop in sea level creates an emergent coastline, with cliffs and beaches stranded above the new shoreline. Sinking land or a rise in sea level produces a drowned coastline, typified by fjords (submerged glacial valleys) or submerged river valleys.

FEATURES OF A SEA CLIFF

Cliff-face · Cliff-top · High tide level · Low tide level · Offshore deposits · Wave-cut platform · Undercut area of cliff

FEATURES OF WAVES

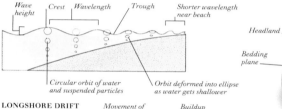

Wave height · Crest · Wavelength · Trough · Shorter wavelength near beach · Circular orbit of water and suspended particles · Orbit deformed into ellipse as water gets shallower

LONGSHORE DRIFT

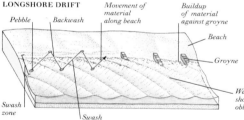

Pebble · Backwash · Movement of material along beach · Buildup of material against groyne · Beach · Groyne · Waves approaching shore at an oblique angle · Swash zone · Swash

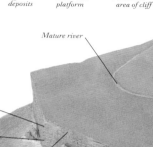

Mature river · Headland · Bedding plane · Sea cliff · Remnants of former headland · Estuary

DEPOSITIONAL FEATURES OF COASTLINES

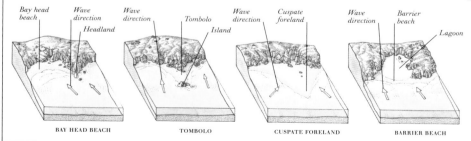

Bay head beach · Wave direction · Headland

Wave direction · Tombolo · Island

Wave direction · Cuspate foreland

Wave direction · Barrier beach · Lagoon

BAY HEAD BEACH · TOMBOLO · CUSPATE FORELAND · BARRIER BEACH

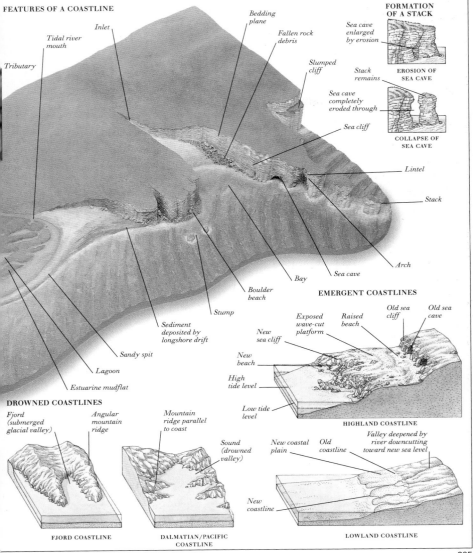

FEATURES OF A COASTLINE

Tidal river mouth

Inlet

Bedding plane

Fallen rock debris

Slumped cliff

Tributary

FORMATION OF A STACK

Sea cave enlarged by erosion

EROSION OF SEA CAVE

Stack remains

Sea cave completely eroded through

COLLAPSE OF SEA CAVE

Sea cliff

Lintel

Stack

Arch

Sea cave

Boulder beach

Bay

Stump

Sediment deposited by longshore drift

Sandy spit

Lagoon

Estuarine mudflat

EMERGENT COASTLINES

Exposed wave-cut platform

Raised beach

Old sea cliff

Old sea cave

New sea cliff

New beach

High tide level

Low tide level

HIGHLAND COASTLINE

DROWNED COASTLINES

Fjord (submerged glacial valley)

Angular mountain ridge

Mountain ridge parallel to coast

Sound (drowned valley)

FJORD COASTLINE

DALMATIAN/PACIFIC COASTLINE

New coastal plain

Old coastline

Valley deepened by river downcutting toward new sea level

New coastline

LOWLAND COASTLINE

Oceans and seas

OCEANS AND SEAS COVER ABOUT 70 PERCENT of the Earth's surface and account for about 97 percent of its total water. These oceans and seas play a crucial role in regulating temperature variations and determining climate. Their waters absorb heat from the Sun, especially in tropical regions, and the surface currents distribute it around the Earth, warming overlying air masses and neighboring land in winter and cooling them in summer. The oceans are never still. Differences in temperature and salinity drive deep current systems, while surface currents are generated by winds blowing over the oceans. All currents are deflected—to the right in the Northern Hemisphere, to the left in the Southern Hemisphere—as a result of the Earth's rotation. This deflective factor is known as the Coriolis force. A current that begins on the surface is immediately deflected. This current in turn generates a current in the layer of water beneath, which is also deflected. As the movement is transmitted downward, the deflections form an Ekman spiral. The waters of the oceans and seas are also moved by the constant ebb and flow of tides. These are caused by the gravitational pull of the Moon and Sun. The highest tides (Spring tides) occur at full and new Moon; the lowest tides (neap tides) occur at first and last quarter.

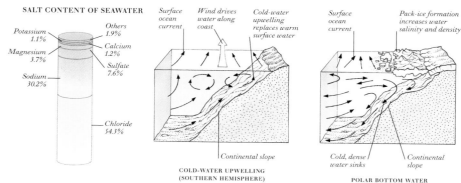

OFFSHORE CURRENTS

SALT CONTENT OF SEAWATER

Potassium 1.1%
Magnesium 3.7%
Sodium 30.2%
Others 1.9%
Calcium 1.2%
Sulfate 7.6%
Chloride 54.3%

Surface ocean current
Wind drives water along coast
Cold-water upwelling replaces warm surface water

Continental slope

COLD-WATER UPWELLING (SOUTHERN HEMISPHERE)

Surface ocean current
Pack-ice formation increases water salinity and density

Cold, dense water sinks
Continental slope

POLAR BOTTOM WATER

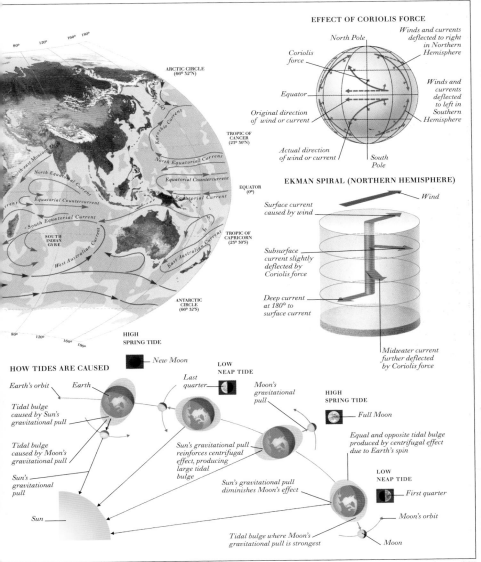

EFFECT OF CORIOLIS FORCE

North Pole

Coriolis force

Winds and currents deflected to right in Northern Hemisphere

Equator

Winds and currents deflected to left in Southern Hemisphere

Original direction of wind or current

Actual direction of wind or current

South Pole

EKMAN SPIRAL (NORTHERN HEMISPHERE)

Surface current caused by wind

Wind

Subsurface current slightly deflected by Coriolis force

Deep current at 180° to surface current

Midwater current further deflected by Coriolis force

ARCTIC CIRCLE (66° 32'N)

Oyashio Current

Kuroshio Current

TROPIC OF CANCER (23° 30'N)

North Equatorial Current

Northeast Monsoon Drift

North Equatorial Current

Equatorial Countercurrent

EQUATOR (0°)

Equatorial Countercurrent

Equatorial Current

Equatorial Current

South Equatorial Current

TROPIC OF CAPRICORN (23° 30'S)

SOUTH INDIAN GYRE

West Australian Current

East Australian Current

ANTARCTIC CIRCLE (66° 32'S)

HIGH SPRING TIDE

New Moon

LOW NEAP TIDE

Last quarter

HOW TIDES ARE CAUSED

Earth's orbit

Earth

Tidal bulge caused by Sun's gravitational pull

Tidal bulge caused by Moon's gravitational pull

Sun's gravitational pull

Sun

Moon's gravitational pull

Sun's gravitational pull reinforces centrifugal effect, producing large tidal bulge

HIGH SPRING TIDE

Full Moon

Equal and opposite tidal bulge produced by centrifugal effect due to Earth's spin

LOW NEAP TIDE

First quarter

Sun's gravitational pull diminishes Moon's effect

Moon's orbit

Tidal bulge where Moon's gravitational pull is strongest

Moon

297

The ocean floor

THE OCEAN FLOOR COMPRISES TWO SECTIONS: the continental
shelf and slope, and the deep-ocean floor. The continental
shelf and slope are part of the continental crust, but may extend far into the ocean.
Sloping quite gently to a depth of about 460 feet (140 m), the continental
shelf is covered in sandy deposits shaped by waves and tidal currents. At
the edge of the continental shelf, the seabed slopes down to the abyssal
plain, which lies at an average depth of about 12,500 feet (3,800 m). On
this deep-ocean floor is a layer of sediment made up of clays, fine oozes
formed from the remains of tiny sea creatures, and occasional mineral-
rich deposits. Echo-sounding and remote sensing from satellites has
revealed that the abyssal plain is divided by a system of mountain ranges,
far bigger than any on land—the mid-ocean ridge. Here, magma
(molten rock) wells up from the Earth's interior and solidifies,
widening the ocean floor (see pp. 58-59). As the ocean floor spreads,
volcanoes that have formed over hot spots in the crust move away
from their magma source; they become extinct and are increasingly
submerged and eroded. Volcanoes eroded below sea level remain as
seamounts (underwater mountains). In warm waters, a volcano that
projects above the ocean surface often acquires a fringing coral reef,
which may develop into an atoll as the volcano becomes submerged.

CONTINENTAL-SHELF FLOOR

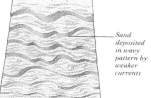

Bedrock
exposed by
tidal scour

Shoreline

Parallel strips
of coarse
material left
by strong
tidal currents

Sand
deposited
in wavy
pattern by
weaker
currents

Irregular patches of
fine sand deposited
by weakest currents

FEATURES OF THE OCEAN FLOOR

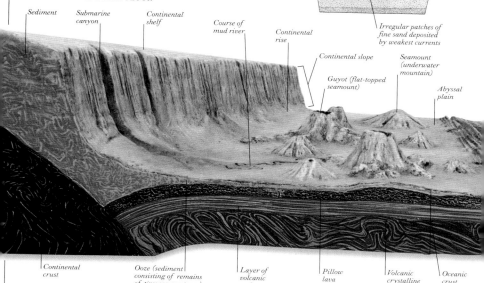

Sediment

Submarine
canyon

Continental
shelf

Course of
mud river

Continental
rise

Continental
slope

Guyot (flat-topped
seamount)

Seamount
(underwater
mountain)

Abyssal
plain

Continental
crust

Ooze (sediment
consisting of remains
of tiny sea creatures)

Layer of
volcanic
rock

Pillow
lava

Volcanic
crystalline
rock

Oceanic
crust

KEY

▢ Calcareous ooze

▢ Pelagic clay

▢ Glacial sediments

▢ Siliceous ooze

▢ Terrigenous sediments

▢ Continental margin sediments

▨ Metalliferous muds

▢ Major nodule fields

DEEP-OCEAN FLOOR SEDIMENTS

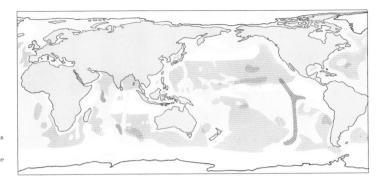

ECHO-SOUND PROFILE OF OCEAN FLOOR

Event mark indicates synchronization of survey equipment

Sand wave

Sand wave

Seabed profile

Minor oscillations caused by ship's movement

Velocity of sound in water (4,898 ft/sec; 1,493 m/sec)

Reference code

Mid-ocean ridge

Ocean trench

Magma (molten rock)

Sediment

DEVELOPMENT OF AN ATOLL

Volcanic island

Coral grows on shoreline

Sea level

FRINGING REEF

Lagoon

Eroded volcanic island subsides

Coral continues to grow, forming barrier reef

BARRIER REEF

Coral continues to grow where waves bring food

Lagoon

Dead coral

Volcanic island becomes submerged

ATOLL

Volcanic island is submerged farther

Coral submerged too deeply to grow

SUBMERGED ATOLL

The atmosphere

Exosphere
(altitude above
300 miles/500 km)

JET STREAM

THE EARTH IS SURROUNDED BY ITS ATMOSPHERE, a blanket of gases that enables life to exist on the planet. This layer has no definite outer edge, gradually becoming thinner until it merges into space, but over 80 percent of atmospheric gases are held by gravity within about 12 miles (20 km) of the Earth's surface. The atmosphere blocks out much harmful ultraviolet solar radiation, and insulates the Earth against extremes of temperature by limiting both incoming solar radiation and the escape of reradiated heat into space. This natural balance may be distorted by the greenhouse effect, as gases such as carbon dioxide have built up in the atmosphere, trapping more heat. Close to the Earth's surface, differences in air temperature and pressure cause air to circulate between the equator and poles. This circulation, together with the Coriolis force, gives rise to the prevailing surface winds and the high-level jet streams.

Corona

ATMOSPHERIC CIRCULATION AND WINDS

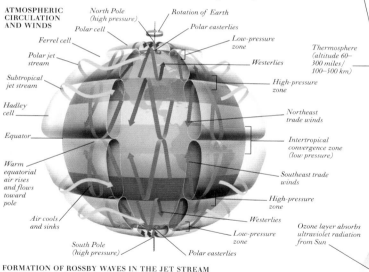

North Pole
(high pressure)

Rotation of Earth

Polar easterlies

Polar cell

Ferrel cell

Low-pressure
zone

Polar jet
stream

Westerlies

Subtropical
jet stream

High-pressure
zone

Hadley
cell

Northeast
trade winds

Equator

Intertropical
convergence zone
(low pressure)

Warm
equatorial
air rises
and flows
toward
pole

Southeast trade
winds

Air cools
and sinks

High-pressure
zone

Westerlies

Low-pressure
zone

South Pole
(high pressure)

Polar easterlies

Thermosphere
(altitude 60–
300 miles/
100–500 km)

Ozone layer absorbs
ultraviolet radiation
from Sun

FORMATION OF ROSSBY WAVES IN THE JET STREAM

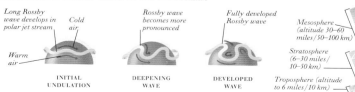

Long Rossby
wave develops in
polar jet stream

Cold
air

Warm
air

**INITIAL
UNDULATION**

Rossby wave
becomes more
pronounced

**DEEPENING
WAVE**

Fully developed
Rossby wave

**DEVELOPED
WAVE**

Mesosphere
(altitude 30–60
miles/50–100 km)

Stratosphere
(6–30 miles/
10–50 km)

Troposphere (altitude
to 6 miles/10 km)

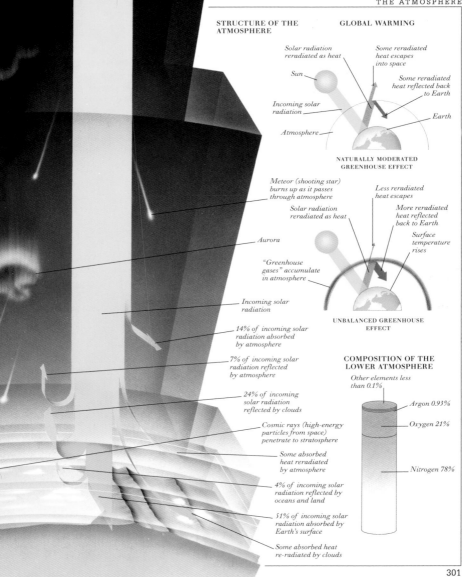

STRUCTURE OF THE ATMOSPHERE

GLOBAL WARMING

Solar radiation reradiated as heat

Sun

Some reradiated heat escapes into space

Some reradiated heat reflected back to Earth

Incoming solar radiation

Earth

Atmosphere

NATURALLY MODERATED GREENHOUSE EFFECT

Meteor (shooting star) burns up as it passes through atmosphere

Aurora

Less reradiated heat escapes

More reradiated heat reflected back to Earth

Solar radiation reradiated as heat

Surface temperature rises

"Greenhouse gases" accumulate in atmosphere

Incoming solar radiation

UNBALANCED GREENHOUSE EFFECT

14% of incoming solar radiation absorbed by atmosphere

7% of incoming solar radiation reflected by atmosphere

COMPOSITION OF THE LOWER ATMOSPHERE

Other elements less than 0.1%

24% of incoming solar radiation reflected by clouds

Argon 0.93%

Cosmic rays (high-energy particles from space) penetrate to stratosphere

Oxygen 21%

Some absorbed heat reradiated by atmosphere

4% of incoming solar radiation reflected by oceans and land

Nitrogen 78%

51% of incoming solar radiation absorbed by Earth's surface

Some absorbed heat re-radiated by clouds

Weather

WEATHER IS DEFINED AS THE ATMOSPHERIC CONDITIONS at a particular time and place; climate is the average weather conditions for a given region over time. Weather is assessed in terms of temperature, wind, cloud cover, and precipitation, such as rain or snow. Good weather is associated with high-pressure areas, where air is sinking. Cloudy, wet, changeable weather is common in low-pressure zones with rising, unstable air. Such conditions occur at temperate latitudes, where warm air meets cool air along the polar fronts. Here, spiraling low-pressure cells known as depressions (mid-latitude cyclones) often form. A depression usually contains a sector of warmer air, beginning at a warm front and ending at a cold front. If the two fronts merge, forming an occluded front, the warm air is pushed upward. An extreme form of low-pressure cell is a hurricane (also called a typhoon or tropical cyclone), which brings torrential rain and exceptionally strong winds.

TYPES OF OCCLUDED FRONT

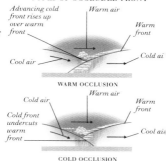

Advancing cold front rises up over warm front

Warm air

Warm front

Cool air

Cold air

WARM OCCLUSION

Cold air

Warm air

Warm front

Cold front undercuts warm front

Cool air

COLD OCCLUSION

FORMS OF PRECIPITATION

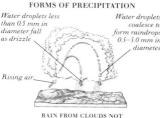

Water droplets less than 0.5 mm in diameter fall as drizzle

Water droplets coalesce to form raindrops 0.5–5.0 mm in diameter

Rising air

RAIN FROM CLOUDS NOT REACHING FREEZING LEVEL

Coalesced water droplets fall as rain

Ice crystal

Snowflakes grown from ice crystals fall as snow

Rising air

Snowflakes melt to fall as rain

RAIN AND SNOW FROM CLOUDS REACHING FREEZING LEVEL

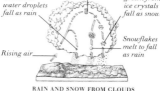

Vertical air currents toss frozen water droplets up and down

Alternate freezing and melting builds up layers of ice

Rising air

Ice falls as hailstones

HAIL

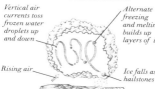

TYPES OF CLOUD

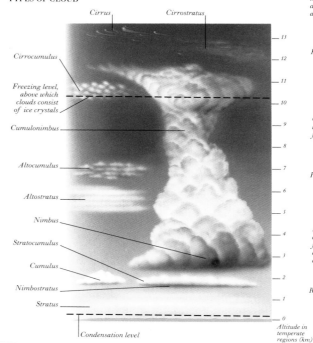

Cirrus

Cirrostratus

Cirrocumulus

Freezing level, above which clouds consist of ice crystals

Cumulonimbus

Altocumulus

Altostratus

Nimbus

Stratocumulus

Cumulus

Nimbostratus

Stratus

Condensation level

— 13
— 12
— 11
— 10
— 9
— 8
— 7
— 6
— 5
— 4
— 3
— 2
— 1
— 0

Altitude in temperate regions (km)

STRUCTURE OF A HURRICANE

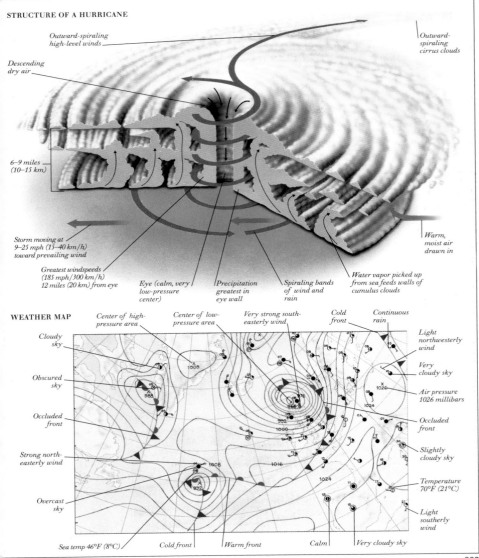

Outward-spiraling high-level winds

Outward-spiraling cirrus clouds

Descending dry air

6–9 miles (10–15 km)

Storm moving at 9–25 mph (15–40 km/h) toward prevailing wind

Warm, moist air drawn in

Greatest windspeeds (185 mph/300 km/h) 12 miles (20 km) from eye

Eye (calm, very low-pressure center)

Precipitation greatest in eye wall

Spiraling bands of wind and rain

Water vapor picked up from sea feeds walls of cumulus clouds

WEATHER MAP

Center of high-pressure area

Center of low-pressure area

Very strong southeasterly wind

Cold front

Continuous rain

Cloudy sky

Light northwesterly wind

Obscured sky

Very cloudy sky

Air pressure 1026 millibars

Occluded front

Occluded front

Strong northeasterly wind

Slightly cloudy sky

Temperature 70°F (21°C)

Overcast sky

Light southerly wind

Sea temp 46°F (8°C)

Cold front

Warm front

Calm

Very cloudy sky

PHYSICS AND CHEMISTRY

THE VARIETY OF MATTER 306
ATOMS AND MOLECULES 308
THE PERIODIC TABLE 310
CHEMICAL REACTIONS 312
ENERGY 314
ELECTRICITY AND MAGNETISM 316
LIGHT 318
FORCE AND MOTION 320

The variety of matter

PLANT AND INSECT (LIVING MATTER)

MATTER IS ANYTHING THAT HAS A MASS. It includes everything from natural substances, such as minerals or living organisms, to synthetic materials. Matter can exist in three distinct states—solid, liquid, and gas. A solid is rigid and retains its shape. A liquid is fluid, has a definite volume, and will take the shape of its container. A gas (also fluid) fills a space, so its volume will be the same as the volume of its container. Most substances can exist as a solid, a liquid, or a gas: the state is determined by temperature. At very high temperatures, matter becomes plasma, often considered to be a fourth state of matter. All matter is composed of microscopic particles, such as atoms and molecules (see pp. 308–309). The arrangement and interactions of these particles give a substance its physical and chemical properties, by which matter can be identified. There is a huge variety of matter because particles can arrange themselves in countless ways, in one substance or by mixing with others. Natural glass, for example, seems to be a solid but is, in fact, a supercool liquid: the atoms are not locked into a pattern and can flow. Pure substances known as elements (see p. 310) combine to form compounds or mixtures. Mixtures called colloids are made up of larger particles of matter suspended in a solid, liquid, or gas, while a solution is one substance dissolved in another.

TYPES OF COLLOID

HAIR GEL (SOLID IN LIQUID)

SHAVING CREAM (AIR IN LIQUID)

MIST (LIQUID IN GAS)

EXAMPLES OF MATTER

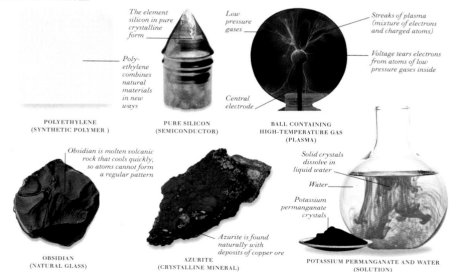

The element silicon in pure crystalline form

Poly-ethylene combines natural materials in new ways

Low pressure gases

Streaks of plasma (mixture of electrons and charged atoms)

Voltage tears electrons from atoms of low pressure gases inside

Central electrode

POLYETHYLENE (SYNTHETIC POLYMER)

PURE SILICON (SEMICONDUCTOR)

BALL CONTAINING HIGH-TEMPERATURE GAS (PLASMA)

Obsidian is molten volcanic rock that cools quickly, so atoms cannot form a regular pattern

Solid crystals dissolve in liquid water

Water

Potassium permanganate crystals

Azurite is found naturally with deposits of copper ore

OBSIDIAN (NATURAL GLASS)

AZURITE (CRYSTALLINE MINERAL)

POTASSIUM PERMANGANATE AND WATER (SOLUTION)

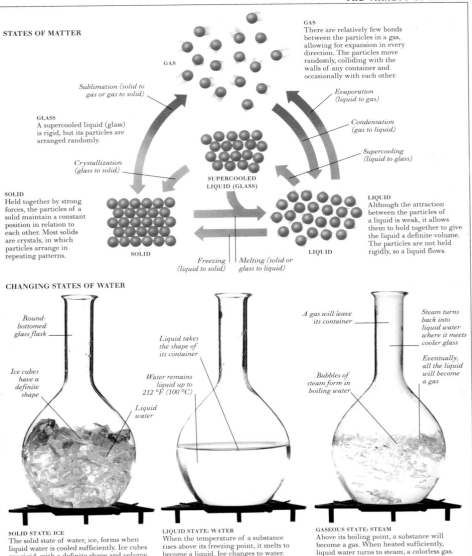

STATES OF MATTER

GAS
There are relatively few bonds between the particles in a gas, allowing for expansion in every direction. The particles move randomly, colliding with the walls of any container and occasionally with each other.

GAS

Sublimation (solid to gas or gas to solid)

Evaporation (liquid to gas)

GLASS
A supercooled liquid (glass) is rigid, but its particles are arranged randomly.

Condensation (gas to liquid)

Crystallization (glass to solid)

Supercooling (liquid to glass)

SUPERCOOLED LIQUID (GLASS)

SOLID
Held together by strong forces, the particles of a solid maintain a constant position in relation to each other. Most solids are crystals, in which particles arrange in repeating patterns.

LIQUID
Although the attraction between the particles of a liquid is weak, it allows them to hold together to give the liquid a definite volume. The particles are not held rigidly, so a liquid flows.

SOLID

LIQUID

Freezing (liquid to solid)   *Melting (solid or glass to liquid)*

CHANGING STATES OF WATER

Round-bottomed glass flask

Ice cubes have a definite shape

Liquid water

Liquid takes the shape of its container

Water remains liquid up to 212 °F (100 °C)

Liquid water

A gas will leave its container

Steam turns back into liquid water where it meets cooler glass

Bubbles of steam form in boiling water

Eventually, all the liquid will become a gas

SOLID STATE: ICE
The solid state of water, ice, forms when liquid water is cooled sufficiently. Ice cubes are rigid, with a definite shape and volume.

LIQUID STATE: WATER
When the temperature of a substance rises above its freezing point, it melts to become a liquid. Ice changes to water.

GASEOUS STATE: STEAM
Above its boiling point, a substance will become a gas. When heated sufficiently, liquid water turns to steam, a colorless gas.

Atoms and molecules

FALSE-COLOR IMAGE OF ACTUAL GOLD ATOMS

ATOMS ARE THE smallest individual parts of an element (see pp. 310-311). They are tiny, with diameters in the order of one ten-thousand-millionth of a meter (10^{-10} m). Two or more atoms join together (bond) to form a molecule of a substance known as a compound. For example, when atoms of the elements hydrogen and fluorine join together, they form a molecule of the compound hydrogen fluoride. So molecules are the smallest individual parts of a compound. Atoms themselves are not indivisible—they possess an internal structure. At their center is a dense nucleus, consisting of protons, which have a positive electric charge (see p. 316), and neutrons, which are uncharged. Around the nucleus are the negatively charged electrons. It is the electrons that give a substance most of its physical and chemical properties. They do not follow definite paths around the nucleus. Instead, electrons are said to be found within certain regions, called orbitals. These are arranged around the nucleus in "shells," each containing electrons of a particular energy. For example, the first shell (1) can hold up to two electrons, in a so-called s-orbital (1s). The second shell (2) can hold up to eight electrons, in s-orbitals (2s) and p-orbitals (2p). If an atom loses an electron, it becomes a positive ion (cation). If an electron is gained, an atom becomes a negative ion (anion). Ions of opposite charges will attract and join together, in a type of bonding known as ionic bonding. In covalent bonding, the atoms bond by sharing their electrons in what become molecular orbitals.

ATOMIC ORBITALS

S-ORBITAL

P-ORBITAL

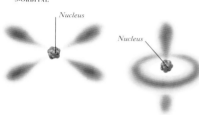

D-ORBITALS

MOLECULAR ORBITALS

Σ- (PI) ORBITAL

Σ- (SIGMA) ORBITAL

SP³-HYBRID ORBITAL

EXAMPLE OF IONIC BONDING

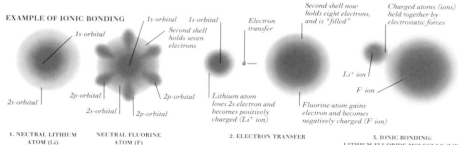

1. NEUTRAL LITHIUM ATOM (Li)

NEUTRAL FLUORINE ATOM (F)

2. ELECTRON TRANSFER

3. IONIC BONDING: LITHIUM FLUORIDE MOLECULE (LiF)

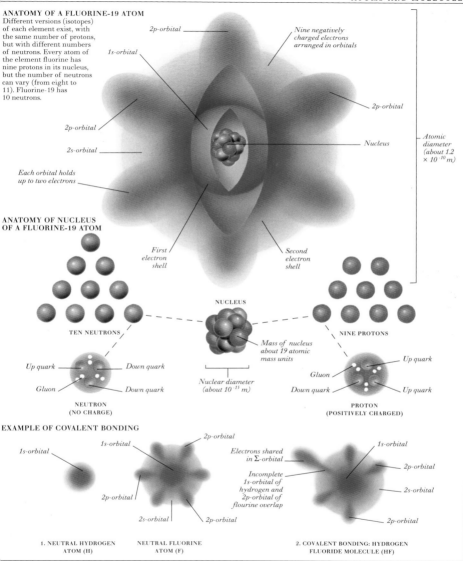

ANATOMY OF A FLUORINE-19 ATOM
Different versions (isotopes) of each element exist, with the same number of protons, but with different numbers of neutrons. Every atom of the element fluorine has nine protons in its nucleus, but the number of neutrons can vary (from eight to 11). Fluorine-19 has 10 neutrons.

2p-orbital

Nine negatively charged electrons arranged in orbitals

1s-orbital

2p-orbital

2p-orbital

2s-orbital

Nucleus

Atomic diameter (about 1.2 × 10⁻¹⁰ m)

Each orbital holds up to two electrons

First electron shell

Second electron shell

ANATOMY OF NUCLEUS OF A FLUORINE-19 ATOM

TEN NEUTRONS

NUCLEUS

Mass of nucleus about 19 atomic mass units

NINE PROTONS

Nuclear diameter (about 10⁻¹⁵ m)

Up quark

Down quark

Gluon

Down quark

NEUTRON (NO CHARGE)

Gluon

Up quark

Down quark

Up quark

PROTON (POSITIVELY CHARGED)

EXAMPLE OF COVALENT BONDING

1s-orbital

1s-orbital

2p-orbital

Electrons shared in Σ-orbital

Incomplete 1s-orbital of hydrogen and 2p-orbital of flourine overlap

1s-orbital

2p-orbital

2p-orbital

2s-orbital

2s-orbital

2p-orbital

2p-orbital

1. NEUTRAL HYDROGEN ATOM (H)

NEUTRAL FLUORINE ATOM (F)

2. COVALENT BONDING: HYDROGEN FLUORIDE MOLECULE (HF)

The periodic table

AN ELEMENT is a substance that consists of atoms of one type only. The 92 elements that occur naturally, and the 17 elements created artificially, are often arranged into a chart called the periodic table. Each element is defined by its atomic number—the number of protons in the nucleus of each of its atoms (it is also the number of electrons present). Atomic number increases along each row (period) and down each column (group). The shape of the table is determined by the way in which electrons arrange themselves around the nucleus: the positioning of elements in order of increasing atomic number brings together atoms with a similar pattern of orbiting electrons (orbitals). These appear in blocks. Electrons occupy shells of a certain energy (see pp. 308-309). Periods are ordered according to the filling of successive shells with electrons, while groups reflect the number of electrons in the outer shell (valency electrons). These outer electrons are important—they decide the chemical properties of the atom. Elements that appear in the same group have similar properties because they have the same number of electrons in their outer shell. Elements in Group 0 have "filled shells," where the outer shell holds its maximum number of electrons, and are stable. Atoms of Group I elements have just one electron in their outer shell. This makes them unstable—and ready to react with other substances.

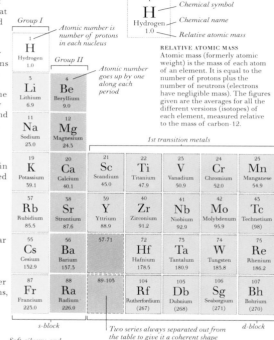

Atomic number

1

H

Hydrogen

Chemical symbol

Chemical name

1.0

Relative atomic mass

RELATIVE ATOMIC MASS
Atomic mass (formerly atomic weight) is the mass of each atom of an element. It is equal to the number of protons plus the number of neutrons (electrons have negligible mass). The figures given are the averages for all the different versions (isotopes) of each element, measured relative to the mass of carbon-12.

Group I

Atomic number is number of protons in each nucleus

Group II

Atomic number goes up by one along each period

1st transition metals

s-block

d-block

Two series always separated out from the table to give it a coherent shape

Soft, silvery, and highly reactive metal

SODIUM: GROUP 1 METAL

Silvery, reactive metal

MAGNESIUM: GROUP 2 METAL

Hard, silvery metal

CHROMIUM: 1ST TRANSITION METAL

METALS AND NON-METALS
Elements at the left-hand side of each period are metals. Metals easily lose electrons and form positive ions. Non-metals, on the right of a period, tend to become negative ions. Semimetals, which have properties of both metals and non-metals, are between the two.

TYPES OF ELEMENT KEY:

- Alkali metals
- Alkaline earth metals
- Transition metals
- Lanthanides
- Actinides
- Poor metals
- Semi-metals
- Non-metals
- Noble gases
- Unknown chemical properties

Radioactive metal

PLUTONIUM: ACTINIDE SERIES METAL

Group I	Group II			1st transition metals				
1 **H** Hydrogen 1.0								
3 **Li** Lithium 6.9	4 **Be** Beryllium 9.0							
11 **Na** Sodium 23.0	12 **Mg** Magnesium 24.3							
19 **K** Potassium 39.1	20 **Ca** Calcium 40.1	21 **Sc** Scandium 45.0	22 **Ti** Titanium 47.9	23 **V** Vanadium 50.9	24 **Cr** Chromium 52.0	25 **Mn** Manganese 54.9
37 **Rb** Rubidium 85.5	38 **Sr** Strontium 87.6	39 **Y** Yttrium 88.9	40 **Zr** Zirconium 91.2	41 **Nb** Niobium 92.9	42 **Mo** Molybdenum 95.9	43 **Tc** Technetium (98)
55 **Cs** Cesium 132.9	56 **Ba** Barium 137.3	57-71	72 **Hf** Hafnium 178.5	73 **Ta** Tantalum 180.9	74 **W** Tungsten 183.8	75 **Re** Rhenium 186.2
87 **Fr** Francium 223.0	88 **Ra** Radium 226.0	89-105	104 **Rf** Rutherfordium (267)	105 **Db** Dubnium (268)	106 **Sg** Seaborgium (271)	107 **Bh** Bohrium (270)

57 **La** Lanthanum 138.9	58 **Ce** Cerium 140.1	59 **Pr** Praseodymium 140.9	60 **Nd** Neodymium 144.2
89 **Ac** Actinium (227)	90 **Th** Thorium 252.0	91 **Pa** Protactinium 251.0	92 **U** Uranium 238.0

DIAMOND

ALLOTROPES OF CARBON
Some elements exist in more than one form—these are known as allotropes. Carbon powder, graphite, and diamond are allotropes of carbon. They all consist of carbon atoms, but have very different physical properties.

Bright yellow crystal

SULFUR:
GROUP 6 SOLID NON-METAL

IODINE:
GROUP 7
SOLID NON-METAL

Purple-black solid turns to gas easily

GRAPHITE   **CARBON POWDER**

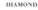

2nd transition metals   *3rd transition metals*

Boron and carbon groups   *Nitrogen and oxygen groups*   *Halogens*   Group 0

					Group III	Group IV	Group V	Group VI	Group VII	2 He Helium 4.0	Period
					5 B Boron 10.8	6 C Carbon 12.0	7 N Nitrogen 14.0	8 O Oxygen 16.0	9 F Fluorine 19.0	10 Ne Neon 20.2	Short period
					13 Al Aluminum 27.0	14 Si Silicon 28.1	15 P Phosphorus 31.0	16 S Sulfur 32.1	17 Cl Chlorine 55.5	18 Ar Argon 40.0	
26 Fe Iron 55.8	27 Co Cobalt 58.9	28 Ni Nickel 58.7	29 Cu Copper 63.5	30 Zn Zinc 65.4	31 Ga Gallium 69.7	52 Ge Germanium 72.6	53 As Arsenic 74.9	54 Se Selenium 79.0	55 Br Bromine 79.9	56 Kr Krypton 83.8	Long period
44 Ru Ruthenium 101.1	45 Rh Rhodium 102.9	46 Pd Palladium 106.4	47 Ag Silver 107.9	48 Cd Cadmium 112.4	49 In Indium 114.8	50 Sn Tin 118.7	51 Sb Antimony 121.8	52 Te Tellurium 127.6	53 I Iodine 126.9	54 Xe Xenon 131.3	
76 Os Osmium 190.2	77 Ir Iridium 192.2	78 Pt Platinum 195.1	79 Au Gold 197.0	80 Hg Mercury 200.6	81 Tl Thallium 204.4	82 Pb Lead 207.2	83 Bi Bismuth 209.0	84 Po Polonium (209)	85 At Astatine (210)	86 Rn Radon (222)	
108 Hs Hassium (269)	109 Mt Meitnerium (278)	110 Ds Darmstadtium (281)	111 Rg Roentgenium (281)	112 Cn Copernicium (285)	113 Uut Ununtrium (286)	114 Uuq Ununquadium (289)	115 Uup Ununpentium (289)	116 Uuh Ununhexium (293)	117 Uus Ununseptium (294)	118 Uuo Ununoctium (294)	

d-block   *p-block*

Unreactive, colorless gas glows red in discharge tube

Yellow, unreactive precious metal

Soft, shiny, reactive metal

Shiny semi-metal

GOLD:
3RD TRANSITION METAL

TIN:
GROUP 4 POOR METAL

ANTIMONY:
GROUP 5 SEMI-METAL

NOBLE GASES
Group 0 contains elements that have a filled (complete) outer shell of electrons, which means the atoms do not need to lose or gain electrons by bonding with other atoms. This makes them stable and they do not easily form ions or react with other elements. Noble gases are also called rare or inert gases.

NEON:
GROUP 0
COLORLESS GAS

61 Pm Promethium (145)	62 Sm Samarium 150.4	63 Eu Europium 152.0	64 Gd Gadolinium 157.5	65 Tb Terbium 158.9	66 Dy Dysprosium 162.5	67 Ho Holmium 164.9	68 Er Erbium 167.3	69 Tm Thulium 168.9	70 Yb Ytterbium 175.0	71 Lu Lutetium 175.0
93 Np Neptunium (257)	94 Pu Plutonium (244)	95 Am Americium (243)	96 Cm Curium (247)	97 Bk Berkelium (247)	98 Cf Californium (251)	99 Es Einsteinium (252)	100 Fm Fermium (257)	101 Md Mendelevium (258)	102 No Nobelium (259)	105 Lr Lawrencium (262)

f-block

Chemical reactions

A CHEMICAL REACTION TAKES PLACE whenever bonds between atoms are broken or made. In each case, atoms or groups of atoms rearrange, making new substances (products) from the original ones (reactants). Reactions happen naturally, or can be made to happen; they may take years, or only an instant. Some of the main types are shown here. A reaction usually involves a change in energy (see pp. 314-315). In a burning reaction, for example, the making of new bonds between atoms releases energy as heat and light. This type of reaction, in which heat is given off, is an exothermic reaction. Many reactions, like burning, are irreversible, but some can take place in either direction, and are said to be reversible. Reactions can be used to form solids from solutions: in a double decomposition reaction, two compounds in solution break down and re-form into two new substances, often creating a precipitate (insoluble solid); in displacement, an element (e.g., copper) displaces another element (e.g., silver) from a solution. The rate (speed) of a reaction is determined by many different factors, such as temperature, and the size and shape of the reactants. To describe and keep track of reactions, internationally recognized chemical symbols and equations are used. Reactions are also used in the laboratory to identify matter. An experiment with candle wax, for example, demonstrates that it contains carbon and hydrogen.

SALT FORMATION (ACID ON METAL)

Glass beaker

Hydrogen gas (H_2) given off

Zinc (Zn) replaces hydrogen in acid (HCl) to form zinc chloride solution ($ZnCl_2$)

Hydrogen in acid driven off when acid meets a reactive metal

Hydrochloric acid (HCl)

Effervescence

Zinc metal chippings (Zn)

Zinc metal chippings (Zn)

THE REACTION
Hydrochloric acid added to zinc produces zinc chloride and hydrogen.
$Zn + 2HCl \rightarrow ZnCl_2 + H_2$

DISPLACEMENT

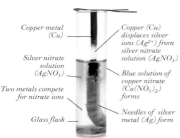

Copper metal (Cu)

Copper (Cu) displaces silver ions (Ag^{2+}) from silver nitrate solution ($AgNO_3$)

Silver nitrate solution ($AgNO_3$)

Blue solution of copper nitrate ($Cu(NO_3)_2$) forms

Two metals compete for nitrate ions

Needles of silver metal (Ag) form

Glass flask

THE REACTION
Copper metal added to silver nitrate solution produces copper nitrate and silver metal.
$Cu + 2AgNO_3 \rightarrow Cu(NO_3)_2 + 2Ag$

BURNING MATTER

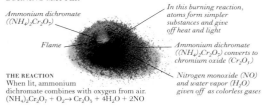

Ammonium dichromate (($NH_4)_2Cr_2O_7$)

In this burning reaction, atoms form simpler substances and give off heat and light

Flame

Ammonium dichromate (($NH_4)_2Cr_2O_7$) converts to chromium oxide (Cr_2O_3)

Nitrogen monoxide (NO) and water vapor (H_2O) given off as colorless gases

THE REACTION
When lit, ammonium dichromate combines with oxygen from air.
$(NH_4)_2Cr_2O_7 + O_2 \rightarrow Cr_2O_3 + 4H_2O + 2NO$

A REVERSIBLE REACTION

Flat-bottomed glass flask

Potassium Chromate solution (K_2CrO_4)

Bright yellow solution contains potassium and chromate ions

1. THE REACTANT
Potassium chromate dissolves in water to form potassium ions and chromate ions.
$K_2CrO_4 \rightarrow 2K^+ + CrO_4^{2-}$

Pipette

Hydrochloric acid (HCl) added in drops

Acid causes reaction to take place

Chromate ions converted to orange dichromate ions

Potassium dichromate (KCr_2O_7) forms

2. THE REACTION
Addition of hydrochloric acid changes chromate ions into dichromate ions.
$2CrO_4^{2-} \rightarrow Cr_2O_7^{2-}$

Pipette

Sodium hydroxide (NaOH) added in drops

Sodium hydroxide (NaOH) neutralizes the acid

Solution turns to bright orange of potassium dichromate

Solution returns to original bright yellow color

Potassium dichromate (KCr_2O_7) re-forms to potassium chromate (K_2CrO_4)

3. REVERSING
Addition of sodium hydroxide changes dichromate ions back into chromate ions.
$Cr_2O_7^{2-} \rightarrow 2CrO_4^{2-}$

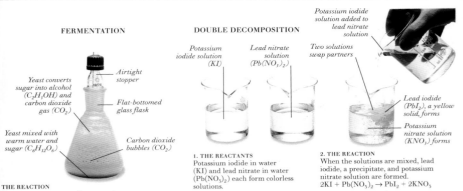

FERMENTATION

Yeast converts sugar into alcohol (C_2H_5OH) and carbon dioxide gas (CO_2)

Airtight stopper

Flat-bottomed glass flask

Yeast mixed with warm water and sugar ($C_6H_{12}O_6$)

Carbon dioxide bubbles (CO_2)

THE REACTION
Yeast converts sugar and warm water into alcohol and carbon dioxide.
$$C_6H_{12}O_6 \rightarrow 2C_2H_5OH + 2CO_2$$

DOUBLE DECOMPOSITION

Potassium iodide solution (KI)

Lead nitrate solution ($Pb(NO_3)_2$)

Two solutions swap partners

Potassium iodide solution added to lead nitrate solution

Lead iodide (PbI_2), a yellow solid, forms

Potassium nitrate solution (KNO_3) forms

1. THE REACTANTS
Potassium iodide in water (KI) and lead nitrate in water ($Pb(NO_3)_2$) each form colorless solutions.

2. THE REACTION
When the solutions are mixed, lead iodide, a precipitate, and potassium nitrate solution are formed.
$$2KI + Pb(NO_3)_2 \rightarrow PbI_2 + 2KNO_3$$

TESTING CANDLE WAX, AN ORGANIC COMPOUND

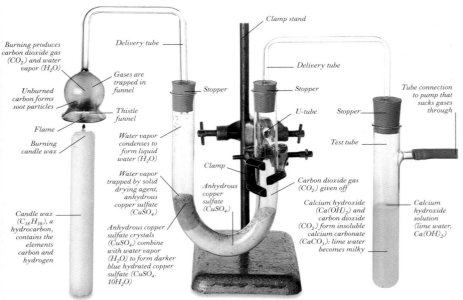

Burning produces carbon dioxide gas (CO_2) and water vapor (H_2O)

Unburned carbon forms soot particles

Flame

Burning candle wax

Candle wax ($C_{18}H_{18}$), a hydrocarbon, contains the elements carbon and hydrogen

Delivery tube

Gases are trapped in funnel

Thistle funnel

Water vapor condenses to form liquid water (H_2O)

Water vapor trapped by solid drying agent, anhydrous copper sulfate ($CuSO_4$)

Anhydrous copper sulfate ($CuSO_4$) crystals combine with water vapor (H_2O) to form darker blue hydrated copper sulfate ($CuSO_4$. $10H_2O$)

Clamp stand

Delivery tube

Stopper

Stopper

U-tube

Anhydrous copper sulfate ($CuSO_4$)

Clamp

Carbon dioxide gas (CO_2) given off

Calcium hydroxide ($Ca(OH)_2$) and carbon dioxide (CO_2) form insoluble calcium carbonate ($CaCO_3$): lime water becomes milky

Tube connection to pump that sucks gases through

Stopper

Test tube

Calcium hydroxide solution (lime water, $Ca(OH)_2$)

1. THE BURNING REACTION
Burning wax produces carbon dioxide gas and water vapor.
$$2C_{18}H_{58} + 55O_2 \rightarrow 36CO_2 + 38H_2O$$

2. TESTING FOR WATER VAPOR
A solid drying agent traps water vapor, proving the presence of hydrogen in the candle wax.
$$CuSO_4 + 10H_2O \rightarrow CuSO_4 . 10H_2O$$

3. TESTING FOR CARBON DIOXIDE
Calcium hydroxide in solution reacts with carbon dioxide, forming a carbonate and turning milky.
$$Ca(OH)_2 + CO_2 \rightarrow CaCO_3 + H_2O$$

313

Energy

ANYTHING THAT HAPPENS—from a pin-drop to an explosion—requires energy. Energy is the capacity for "doing work" (making something happen). Various forms of energy exist, including light, heat, sound, electrical, chemical, nuclear, kinetic, and potential energies. The Law of Conservation of Energy states that the total amount of energy in the universe is fixed—energy cannot be created or destroyed. It means that energy can only change from one form to another (energy transfer). For example, potential energy is energy that is "stored," and can be used in the future. An object gains potential energy when it is lifted; as the object is released, potential energy changes into the energy of motion (kinetic energy). During transference, some of the energy converts into heat. A combined heat and power station can put some of the otherwise "waste" heat to useful effect in local schools and housing. Most of the Earth's energy is provided by the Sun, in the form of electromagnetic radiation (see pp. 316-317). Some of this energy transfers to plant and animal life, and ultimately to fossil fuels, where it is stored in chemical form. Our bodies obtain energy from the food we eat, while energy needed for other tasks, such as heating and transport, can be obtained by burning fossil fuels—or by harnessing natural forces like wind or moving water—to generate electricity. Another source is nuclear power, where energy is released by reactions in the nucleus of an atom. All energy is measured by the international unit, the joule (J). As a guide, one joule is about equal to the amount of energy needed to lift an apple one meter.

SANKEY DIAGRAM SHOWING ENERGY FLOW IN A COAL-FIRED COMBINED HEAT AND POWER STATION

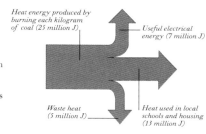

Heat energy produced by burning each kilogram of coal (25 million J)

Useful electrical energy (7 million J)

Waste heat (5 million J)

Heat used in local schools and housing (13 million J)

CROSS-SECTION OF HYDROELECTRIC POWER STATION WITH FRANCIS TURBINE

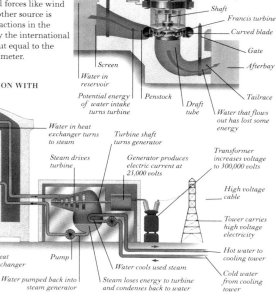

Transformer

Switch gear including circuit braker

Insulator

Bushing

High voltage cable

Rotor house

Gate

Generator unit

Generator rotor turned by turbine

Shaft

Francis turbine

Curved blade

Gate

Afterbay

Screen

Water in reservoir

Potential energy of water intake turns turbine

Penstock

Draft tube

Tailrace

Water that flows out has lost some energy

CROSS-SECTION OF NUCLEAR POWER STATION WITH PRESSURIZED WATER REACTOR

Steam generator

Concrete shielding

Water pressurizer

Steel girder framework

Control rod

Reactor core

Pump

Moderator (water)

Enriched uranium fuel

Coolant (water) takes heat from reactor core to heat exchanger

Heat exchanger

Water in heat exchanger turns to steam

Steam drives turbine

Turbine shaft turns generator

Generator produces electric current at 25,000 volts

Transformer increases voltage to 300,000 volts

High voltage cable

Tower carries high voltage electricity

Hot water to cooling tower

Cold water from cooling tower

Pump

Water pumped back into steam generator

Water cools used steam

Steam loses energy to turbine and condenses back to water

ENERGY SYSTEMS

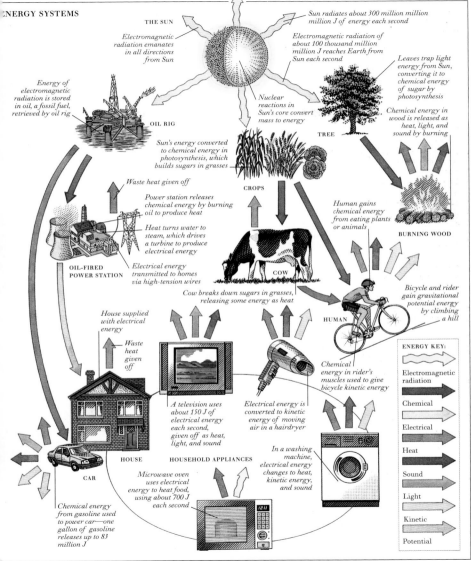

THE SUN

Sun radiates about 300 million million million J of energy each second

Electromagnetic radiation emanates in all directions from Sun

Electromagnetic radiation of about 100 thousand million million J reaches Earth from Sun each second

Leaves trap light energy from Sun, converting it to chemical energy of sugar by photosynthesis

Energy of electromagnetic radiation is stored in oil, a fossil fuel, retrieved by oil rig

OIL RIG

Nuclear reactions in Sun's core convert mass to energy

TREE

Chemical energy in wood is released as heat, light, and sound by burning

Sun's energy converted to chemical energy in photosynthesis, which builds sugars in grasses

CROPS

Human gains chemical energy from eating plants or animals

Waste heat given off

Power station releases chemical energy by burning oil to produce heat

Heat turns water to steam, which drives a turbine to produce electrical energy

OIL-FIRED POWER STATION

Electrical energy transmitted to homes via high-tension wires

COW

BURNING WOOD

Cow breaks down sugars in grasses, releasing some energy as heat

Bicycle and rider gain gravitational potential energy by climbing a hill

HUMAN

House supplied with electrical energy

Waste heat given off

Chemical energy in rider's muscles used to give bicycle kinetic energy

ENERGY KEY:

Electromagnetic radiation

A television uses about 150 J of electrical energy each second, given off as heat, light, and sound

Electrical energy is converted to kinetic energy of moving air in a hairdryer

Chemical

Electrical

HOUSE

HOUSEHOLD APPLIANCES

In a washing machine, electrical energy changes to heat, kinetic energy, and sound

Heat

Sound

CAR

Microwave oven uses electrical energy to heat food, using about 700 J each second

Light

Kinetic

Potential

Chemical energy from gasoline used to power car—one gallon of gasoline releases up to 83 million J

Electricity and magnetism

ELECTRICAL EFFECTS result from an imbalance of electric charge. There are two types of electric charge, named positive (carried by protons) and negative (carried by electrons). If charges are opposite (unlike), they attract one another, while like charges repel. Forces of attraction and repulsion (electrostatic forces) exist between any two charged particles. Matter is normally uncharged, but if

electrons are gained, an object will gain an overall negative charge; if they are removed, it becomes positive. Objects with an overall negative or positive charge are said to have an imbalance of charge, and exert the same forces as individual negative and positive charges. On this larger scale, the forces will always act to regain the balance of charge. This causes static electricity. Lightning, for example, is produced by clouds discharging a huge excess of negative electrons. If charges

LIGHTNING

are "free"—in a wire or material that allows electrons to pass through it—the forces cause a flow of charge called an electric current. Some substances exhibit the strange phenomenon of magnetism—which also produces attractive and repulsive forces. Magnetic substances consist of small regions called domains. Normally unmagnetized, they can be magnetized by being placed in a magnetic field. Magnetism and electricity are inextricably linked, a fact put to use in motors and generators.

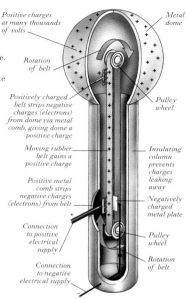

Positive charges at many thousands of volts

Metal dome

Rotation of belt

Positively charged belt strips negative charges (electrons) from dome via metal comb, giving dome a positive charge

Pulley wheel

Moving rubber belt gains a positive charge

Insulating column prevents charges leaking away

Positive metal comb strips negative charges (electrons) from belt

Negatively charged metal plate

Connection to positive electrical supply

Pulley wheel

Connection to negative electrical supply

Rotation of belt

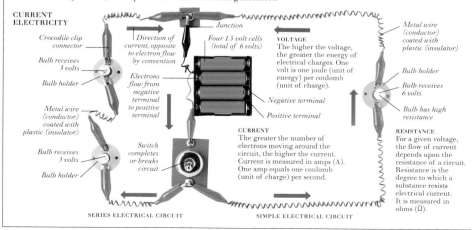

CURRENT ELECTRICITY

Crocodile clip connector

Bulb receives 3 volts

Bulb holder

Metal wire (conductor) coated with plastic (insulator)

Bulb receives 3 volts

Bulb holder

Direction of current, opposite to electron flow by convention

Junction

Four 1.5 volt cells (total of 6 volts)

Electrons flow from negative terminal to positive terminal

Negative terminal

Positive terminal

Switch completes or breaks circuit

VOLTAGE
The higher the voltage, the greater the energy of electrical charges. One volt is one joule (unit of energy) per coulomb (unit of charge).

CURRENT
The greater the number of electrons moving around the circuit, the higher the current. Current is measured in amps (A). One amp equals one coulomb (unit of charge) per second.

Metal wire (conductor) coated with plastic (insulator)

Bulb holder

Bulb receives 6 volts

Bulb has high resistance

RESISTANCE
For a given voltage, the flow of current depends upon the resistance of a circuit. Resistance is the degree to which a substance resists electrical current. It is measured in ohms (Ω).

SERIES ELECTRICAL CIRCUIT

SIMPLE ELECTRICAL CIRCUIT

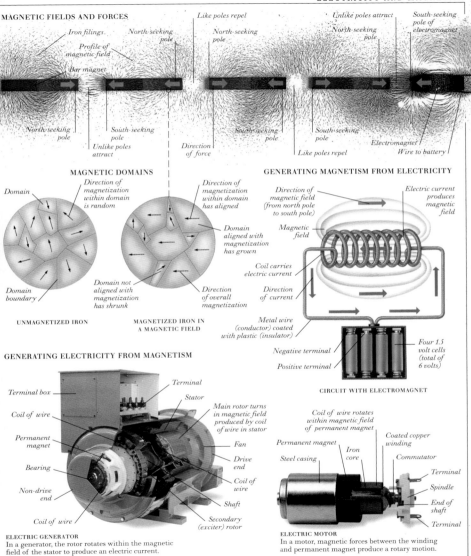

MAGNETIC FIELDS AND FORCES

Iron filings

Profile of magnetic field

Bar magnet

North-seeking pole

Like poles repel

North-seeking pole

North-seeking pole

Unlike poles attract

South-seeking pole of electromagnet

North-seeking pole

South-seeking pole

Unlike poles attract

Direction of force

South-seeking pole

South-seeking pole

Like poles repel

Electromagnet

Wire to battery

MAGNETIC DOMAINS

Domain

Direction of magnetization within domain is random

Domain boundary

Direction of magnetization within domain has aligned

Domain aligned with magnetization has grown

Domain not aligned with magnetization has shrunk

Direction of overall magnetization

UNMAGNETIZED IRON

MAGNETIZED IRON IN A MAGNETIC FIELD

GENERATING MAGNETISM FROM ELECTRICITY

Direction of magnetic field (from north pole to south pole)

Electric current produces magnetic field

Magnetic field

Coil carries electric current

Direction of current

Metal wire (conductor) coated with plastic (insulator)

Negative terminal

Positive terminal

Four 1.5 volt cells (total of 6 volts)

CIRCUIT WITH ELECTROMAGNET

GENERATING ELECTRICITY FROM MAGNETISM

Terminal box

Coil of wire

Permanent magnet

Bearing

Non-drive end

Coil of wire

Terminal

Stator

Main rotor turns in magnetic field produced by coil of wire in stator

Fan

Drive end

Coil of wire

Shaft

Secondary (exciter) rotor

ELECTRIC GENERATOR

In a generator, the rotor rotates within the magnetic field of the stator to produce an electric current.

Coil of wire rotates within magnetic field of permanent magnet

Permanent magnet

Steel casing

Iron core

Coated copper winding

Commutator

Terminal

Spindle

End of shaft

Terminal

ELECTRIC MOTOR

In a motor, magnetic forces between the winding and permanent magnet produce a rotary motion.

Light

INFRARED IMAGE
OF A HOUSE

LIGHT IS A FORM OF ENERGY. It is a
type of electromagnetic radiation, like X-
rays or radio waves. All electromagnetic
radiation is produced by electric charges
(see pp. 316-317): it is caused by the effects
of oscillating electric and magnetic fields as they travel
through space. Electromagnetic radiation is considered to
have both wave and particle properties. It can be thought
of as a wave of electricity and magnetism. In that case,
the difference between the various forms of
radiation is their wavelength. Radiation can
also be said to consist of particles, or packets
of energy, called photons. The difference
between light and X-rays, for instance, is
the amount of energy that each photon
carries. The complete range of radiation is
referred to as the electromagnetic spectrum,
extending from low energy, long wavelength
radio waves to high energy, short wavelength
gamma rays. Light is the only part of the
electromagnetic spectrum that is visible.
White light from the Sun is made up of all
the visible wavelengths of radiation, which
can be seen when it is separated by using a
prism. Light, like all forms of electromagnetic
radiation, can be reflected (bounced back)
and refracted (bent). Different parts of the
electromagnetic spectrum are produced in
different ways. Sometimes visible light—
and infrared radiation—is generated by the
vibrating particles of warm or hot objects.
The emission of light in this way is called
incandescence. Light can also be produced
by fluorescence, a phenomenon in which
electrons gain and lose energy within atoms.

MAXWELLIAN DIAGRAM OF ELECTROMAGNETIC RADIATION AS WAVES

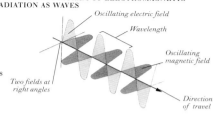

Oscillating electric field

Wavelength

Oscillating
magnetic field

Two fields at
right angles

Direction
of travel

ELECTROMAGNETIC RADIATION AS PARTICLES

Photon thought
of as wave packet
of energy

Red light has
long wavelength

Blue light has about
twice the energy of
red light

Blue light has shorter
wavelength: waves are
more tightly packed

PHOTON OF RED LIGHT

PHOTON OF BLUE LIGHT

SPLITTING WHITE LIGHT INTO THE SPECTRUM

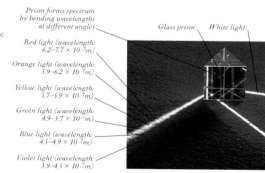

Prism forms spectrum
by bending wavelengths
at different angles

Glass prism   White light

Red light (wavelength:
6.2–7.7×10^{-7}m)

Orange light (wavelength:
5.9–6.2×10^{-7}m)

Yellow light (wavelength:
5.7–5.9×10^{-7}m)

Green light (wavelength:
4.9–5.7×10^{-7}m)

Blue light (wavelength:
4.5–4.9×10^{-7}m)

Violet light (wavelength:
3.9–4.5×10^{-7}m)

THE ELECTROMAGNETIC SPECTRUM

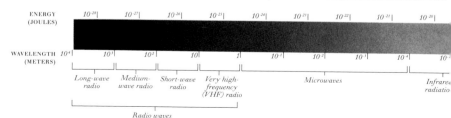

ENERGY (JOULES)	10^{-28}	10^{-27}	10^{-26}	10^{-25}	10^{-24}	10^{-23}	10^{-22}	10^{-21}	10^{-20}

WAVELENGTH (METERS)	10^{4}	10^{3}	10^{2}	10	1	10^{-1}	10^{-2}	10^{-3}	10^{-4}	10^{-}

Long-wave
radio

Medium-
wave radio

Short-wave
radio

Very high-
frequency
(VHF) radio

Microwaves

Infrared
radiatio

Radio waves

ARTIFICIAL LIGHT SOURCES

FLUORESCENT TUBE

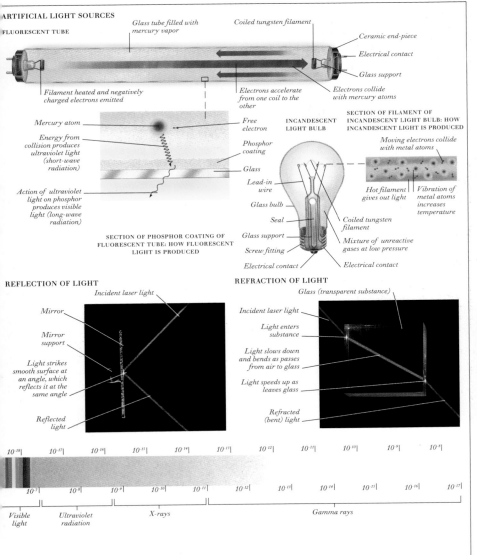

Glass tube filled with mercury vapor

Coiled tungsten filament

Ceramic end-piece

Electrical contact

Glass support

Filament heated and negatively charged electrons emitted

Electrons accelerate from one coil to the other

Electrons collide with mercury atoms

Mercury atom

Free electron

INCANDESCENT LIGHT BULB

SECTION OF FILAMENT OF INCANDESCENT LIGHT BULB: HOW INCANDESCENT LIGHT IS PRODUCED

Energy from collision produces ultraviolet light (short-wave radiation)

Moving electrons collide with metal atoms

Phosphor coating

Glass

Action of ultraviolet light on phosphor produces visible light (long-wave radiation)

Lead-in wire

Glass bulb

Seal

Hot filament gives out light

Vibration of metal atoms increases temperature

Glass support

Screw fitting

Coiled tungsten filament

Mixture of unreactive gases at low pressure

Electrical contact

Electrical contact

SECTION OF PHOSPHOR COATING OF FLUORESCENT TUBE: HOW FLUORESCENT LIGHT IS PRODUCED

REFLECTION OF LIGHT

Incident laser light

Mirror

Mirror support

Light strikes smooth surface at an angle, which reflects it at the same angle

Reflected light

REFRACTION OF LIGHT

Glass (transparent substance)

Incident laser light

Light enters substance

Light slows down and bends as passes from air to glass

Light speeds up as leaves glass

Refracted (bent) light

10^{-18} 10^{-17} 10^{-16} 10^{-15} 10^{-14} 10^{-11} 10^{-12} 10^{-11} 10^{-10} 10^{-9} 10^{-8}

10^{-7} 10^{-8} 10^{-9} 10^{-10} 10^{-11} 10^{-12} 10^{-11} 10^{-14} 10^{-11} 10^{-16} 10^{-17}

Visible light

Ultraviolet radiation

X-rays

Gamma rays

Force and motion

FORCES ARE PUSHES OR PULLS that change the motion of objects. To make a stationary object move, or a moving object stop, a force is needed. A force is also required to change the speed or direction of an object. This change in speed or direction is known as acceleration. Acceleration depends on the size (magnitude) of the force, and on the mass of the object. The effects of forces were first summarized by Isaac Newton in his three laws of motion. The international unit of force, named after him, is the newton (N), which is approximately equal to the weight of one apple. Gravity—the force of attraction between any two masses—can be measured using a newton meter (spring balance). Forces are put to useful effect in machines. A simple machine, such as a wheel and axle, is a device that changes the size or direction of an applied force. It allows an applied force (the effort) to produce another force (the load). A lever uses a bar that turns on a fulcrum to exert force. In all simple machines, there is a relationship between force and distance. A small force (in a compound pulley, for instance) moves through a large distance to lift a heavy object a small distance. This is called the Law of Simple Machines.

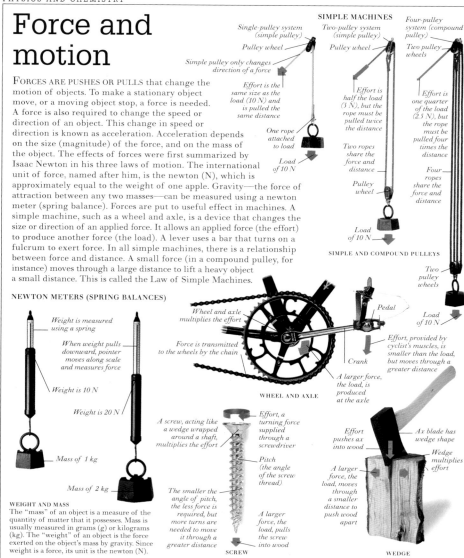

SIMPLE MACHINES

Single-pulley system (simple pulley)

Pulley wheel

Simple pulley only changes direction of a force

Effort is the same size as the load (10 N) and is pulled the same distance

One rope attached to load

Load of 10 N

Two-pulley system (simple pulley)

Pulley wheel

Effort is half the load (5 N), but the rope must be pulled twice the distance

Two ropes share the force and distance

Pulley wheel

Load of 10 N

Four-pulley system (compound pulley)

Two pulley wheels

Effort is one quarter of the load (2.5 N), but the rope must be pulled four times the distance

Four ropes share the force and distance

SIMPLE AND COMPOUND PULLEYS

Two pulley wheels

Load of 10 N

NEWTON METERS (SPRING BALANCES)

Weight is measured using a spring

When weight pulls downward, pointer moves along scale and measures force

Weight is 10 N

Weight is 20 N

Mass of 1 kg

Mass of 2 kg

WEIGHT AND MASS
The "mass" of an object is a measure of the quantity of matter that it possesses. Mass is usually measured in grams (g) or kilograms (kg). The "weight" of an object is the force exerted on the object's mass by gravity. Since weight is a force, its unit is the newton (N).

Wheel and axle multiplies the effort

Force is transmitted to the wheels by the chain

Pedal

Crank

Effort, provided by cyclist's muscles, is smaller than the load, but moves through a greater distance

A larger force, the load, is produced at the axle

WHEEL AND AXLE

A screw, acting like a wedge wrapped around a shaft, multiplies the effort

Effort, a turning force supplied through a screwdriver

Pitch (the angle of the screw thread)

The smaller the angle of pitch, the less force is required, but more turns are needed to move it through a greater distance

A larger force, the load, pulls the screw into wood

SCREW

Effort pushes ax into wood

Ax blade has wedge shape

Wedge multiplies effort

A larger force, the load, moves through a smaller distance to push wood apart

WEDGE

NEWTON'S THREE LAWS OF MOTION

NEWTON'S FIRST LAW
When no force acts on a body, it will
continue in a state of rest or uniform motion.

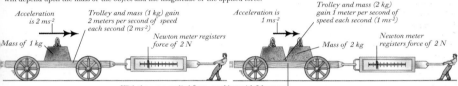

Constant speed

Newton meter shows no applied force

Mass of 1 kg

Mass of trolley is negligible

Trolley is not in motion, and will remain at rest until a force acts

NO FORCE, NO ACCELERATION: STATE OF REST

Newton meter shows no applied force

Mass of 1 kg

Trolley is in motion, and will continue at a constant speed in a straight line until a force acts

NO FORCE, NO ACCELERATION: UNIFORM MOTION

NEWTON'S SECOND LAW
When a force acts on a body, the motion of the body will change. The size of the change
will depend upon the mass of the object and the magnitude of the applied force.

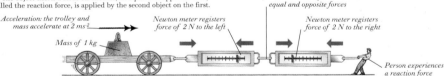

Acceleration is 2 ms^{-2}

Trolley and mass (1 kg) gain 2 meters per second of speed each second (2 ms^{-2})

Newton meter registers force of 2 N

Mass of 1 kg

Acceleration is 1 ms^{-2}

Trolley and mass (2 kg) gain 1 meter per second of speed each second (1 ms^{-2})

Newton meter registers force of 2 N

Mass of 2 kg

With the same applied force, an object with 2 kg mass accelerates at half the rate of object with 1 kg mass

FORCE AND ACCELERATION: SMALL MASS, LARGE ACCELERATION　　　**FORCE AND ACCELERATION: LARGE MASS, SMALL ACCELERATION**

NEWTON'S THIRD LAW
If one object exerts a force on another, an equal and opposite force,
called the reaction force, is applied by the second object on the first.

Newton meters pull on each other with equal and opposite forces

Acceleration: the trolley and mass accelerate at 2 ms^{-2}

Newton meter registers force of 2 N to the left

Newton meter registers force of 2 N to the right

Mass of 1 kg

Person experiences a reaction force

ACTION AND REACTION

THREE CLASSES OF LEVER

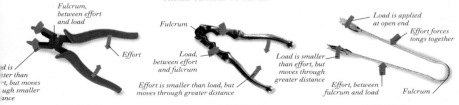

Fulcrum, between effort and load

Effort

d is ...ter than ...t, but moves ...ugh smaller ...ance

CLASS 1 LEVER
Pliers consist of two class 1 levers.

Fulcrum

Load, between effort and fulcrum

Effort is smaller than load, but moves through greater distance

CLASS 2 LEVER
Nutcrackers consist of two class 2 levers.

Load is applied at open end

Effort forces tongs together

Load is smaller than effort, but moves through greater distance

Effort, between fulcrum and load

Fulcrum

CLASS 3 LEVER
Tongs consist of two class 3 levers.

321

RAIL AND ROAD

STEAM LOCOMOTIVES 324

DIESEL TRAINS 326

ELECTRIC AND HIGH-SPEED TRAINS 328

TRAIN EQUIPMENT 330

TROLLEYS AND BUSES 332

THE FIRST CARS 334

ELEGANCE AND UTILITY 336

MASS-PRODUCTION 338

THE "PEOPLE'S CAR" 340

EARLY ENGINES 342

MODERN ENGINES 344

ALTERNATIVE ENGINES 346

BODYWORK 348

MECHANICAL COMPONENTS 350

CAR TRIM 352

HYBRID CAR 354

RACE CARS 356

BICYCLE ANATOMY 358

BICYCLES 360

THE MOTORCYCLE 362

THE MOTORCYCLE CHASSIS 364

MOTORCYCLE ENGINES 366

COMPETITION MOTORCYCLES 368

Steam locomotives

Wagons that are pulled along tracks have been used to transport material since the 16th century, but these trains were drawn by men or horses until the invention of the steam locomotive. Steam locomotives enabled the basic railroad system to realize its true potential. In 1804, Richard Trevithick built the world's first working steam locomotive in South Wales. It was not entirely successful, but it encouraged others to develop new designs. By 1829, the British engineer Robert Stephenson had built the Rocket, considered to be the forerunner of the modern locomotive. The Rocket was a self-sufficient unit, carrying coal to heat the boiler and a water supply for generating steam. Steam passed from the boiler to force the pistons back and forth, and this movement turned the driving wheels, propelling the train forward. Used steam was then expelled in characteristic puffs. Later steam locomotives, like Ellerman Lines and the Mallard, worked in a similar way, but on a much larger scale. The simple design and reliability of steam locomotives ensured that they changed very little in 120 years of use, before being replaced from the 1950s by more efficient diesel and electric power (see pp. 326-329).

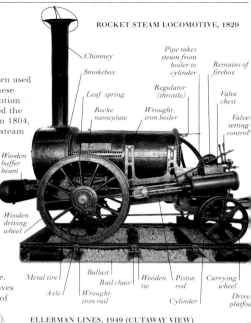

ROCKET STEAM LOCOMOTIVE, 1829

Chimney

Smokebox

Leaf spring

Rocket nameplate

Pipe takes steam from boiler to cylinder

Remains of firebox

Regulator (throttle)

Valve chest

Wrought-iron boiler

Valve setting control

Wooden buffer beam

Wooden driving wheel

Metal tire

Axle

Ballast

Rail chair

Wrought-iron rail

Wooden tie

Piston rod

Cylinder

Carrying wheel

Drive platform

ELLERMAN LINES, 1949 (CUTAWAY VIEW)

Vacuum reservoir

Panel brace

Panel sheeting

Water tank

Coal space

Tender hand brake

Cab

Firebox

Brick arch

Water filler

Hand rail

Buffer

Brake vacuum pipe

Wheel guard

Axle

Axle box

Tender wheel

Brake rigging

Water float to indicate water level

Water float lever

Step

Axle box cover

Footplate

Coupling

Coil spring

Trailing wheel

Grate

Fire drawn into fire tubes

TENDER

CAB INTERIOR OF MALLARD EXPRESS STEAM LOCOMOTIVE, 1938

Steam sanding control

Blower isolator valve

Pressure gauge isolator valve

Vacuum brake isolator valve

Steam chest pressure gauge

Vacuum brake pressure gauge

Blower control

Regulator controls flow of steam to cylinders

Cab side window

Vacuum brake lever

Live steam water injector control

Manual sanding lever

Reverser handle

Driver's seat

Steam-operated reversing shaft lock control

Steam heating isolator valve

Sliding roof vent

Boiler pressure gauge

Gauge glass to show level of water in boiler

Exhaust steam water injector control

Steam heating pressure gauge

Glass deflector

Whistle lever

Cylinder drain cock lever

Control valve for hot water hose

Fireman's seat

Steam heat safety valve

Oil can warming tray

Firebox

Firehole

Firebox door

Fire tube

Steam dome

Mechanical lubricator

Pipe takes steam from boiler to cylinder

Chimney

Thermal siphon

Regulator valve

Superheater tube inside flue tube

Boiler

Blast pipe

Smokebox

Smokebox door

Lubricating pipe

Piston valve

Buffer

Brake shoe

Brake rigging

Coupling rod

Driving wheel

Crank

Expansion lever

Connecting rod

Combination lever

Slide bar

Piston, linked to connecting rod

Bogie frame

Cylinder

Leading wheel

Screw coupling

STEAM LOCOMOTIVE

Diesel trains

Rudolf Diesel first demonstrated the diesel engine in Germany in 1898, but it was not until the 1940s that diesel locomotives were successfully established on both passenger and freight services in the US. Early diesel locomotives like the Union Pacific were more expensive to build than steam locomotives, but were more efficient and cheaper to operate, especially where oil was plentiful. One feature of diesel engines is that the power output cannot be coupled directly to the wheels. To convert the mechanical energy produced by diesel engines, a transmission system is needed. Almost all diesel locomotives have electric transmissions, and are known as diesel-electric locomotives. The diesel engine works by drawing air into the cylinders and compressing it to increase its temperature; a small quantity of diesel fuel is then injected into it. The resulting combustion drives the generator (more recently an alternator) to produce electricity, which is fed to electric motors connected to the wheels. Diesel-electric locomotives are essentially electric locomotives that carry their own power plants, and are used worldwide today. The Deltic diesel-electric locomotive, similar to the one shown here, replaced classic express steam locomotives, and ran at speeds up to 100 mph (160 kph).

FRONT VIEW OF UNION PACIFIC
DIESEL-ELECTRIC LOCOMOTIVE, 1950s

Exhaust vent · Windshield wiper · Horn · Cab front window · Headlight · Cab door · Name of operating railroad · Illuminated locomotive unit number · Railroad crest · Cab step · Step · Motor-driven bogie axle · Air-brake coupling hose · Center buck-eye coupler

PROTOTYPE DELTIC DIESEL-ELECTRIC LOCOMOTIVE, 1956

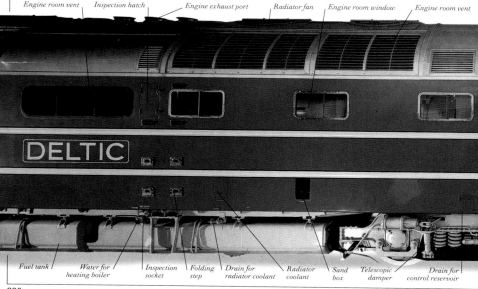

Engine room vent · Inspection hatch · Engine exhaust port · Radiator fan · Engine room window · Engine room vent

DELTIC

Fuel tank · Water for heating boiler · Inspection socket · Folding step · Drain for radiator coolant · Radiator coolant · Sand box · Telescopic damper · Drain for control reservoir

DIESEL ENGINE OF BRITISH RAIL CLASS 20 DIESEL-ELECTRIC LOCOMOTIVE

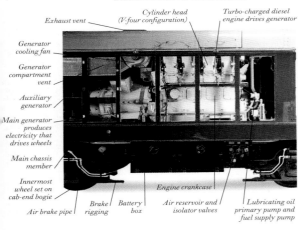

Exhaust vent

Cylinder head
(V-four configuration)

Turbo-charged diesel
engine drives generator

Generator
cooling fan

Generator
compartment
vent

Auxiliary
generator

Main generator
produces
electricity that
drives wheels

Main chassis
member

Innermost
wheel set on
cab-end bogie

Engine crankcase

Brake
rigging

Battery
box

Air reservoir and
isolator valves

Lubricating oil
primary pump and
fuel supply pump

Air brake pipe

EXAMPLES OF FREIGHT CARS

BOX CAR

HOPPER CAR

REFRIGERATOR CAR

LIVESTOCK CAR

FLAT CAR WITH BULKHEADS

AUTOMOBILE CAR

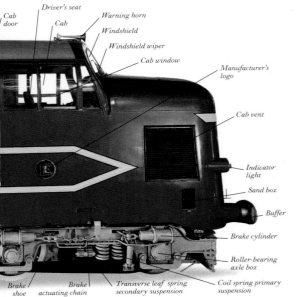

Cab
door

Driver's seat

Cab

Warning horn

Windshield

Windshield wiper

Cab window

Manufacturer's
logo

Cab vent

Indicator
light

Sand box

Buffer

Brake cylinder

Roller-bearing
axle box

Brake
shoe

Brake
actuating chain

Transverse leaf spring
secondary suspension

Coil spring primary
suspension

Electric and high-speed trains

THE FIRST ELECTRIC LOCOMOTIVE ran in 1879 in Berlin, Germany. In Europe, electric trains developed as a more efficient alternative to the steam locomotive and diesel-electric power. Like diesels, electric trains employ electric motors to drive the wheels but, unlike diesels, the electricity is generated externally at a power station. Electric current is picked up either from a catenary (overhead cable) via a pantograph, or from a third rail. Since it does not carry its own power-generating equipment, an electric locomotive has a better power-to-weight ratio and greater acceleration than its diesel-electric equivalent. This makes electric trains suitable for urban routes with many stops. They are also faster, quieter, and cause less pollution. The latest electric French TGV (Train à Grande Vitesse) reaches 185 mph (300 kph); other trains, like the London to Paris and Brussels Eurostar, can run at several voltages and operate between different countries. Simpler electric trains perform special duties—the "People Mover" at Gatwick Airport in London runs between terminals.

HOW ALTERNATING CURRENT (AC) ELECTRIC TRAINS WORK

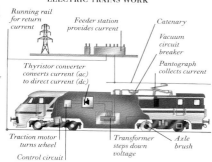

Running rail for return current

Feeder station provides current

Catenary

Vacuum circuit breaker

Pantograph collects current

Thyristor converter converts current (ac) to direct current (dc)

Traction motor turns wheel

Control circuit

Transformer steps down voltage

Axle brush

FRONT VIEW OF PARIS METRO

Route number

Windshield wiper

Unit number

Operator's initials (Régie Autonome des Transports Parisien)

Rubber running wheel

Guard for rubber wheel

Door open/shut indicator light

Driver's seat

Handle

Front light (white)

Rear light (red)

Buffing pad

Rubber guide wheel

FRONT VIEW OF ITALIAN STATE RAILROADS CLASS 402 ELECTRIC LOCOMOTIVE

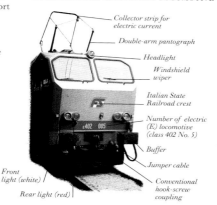

Collector strip for electric current

Double-arm pantograph

Headlight

Windshield wiper

Italian State Railroad crest

Number of electric (E) locomotive (class 402 No. 5)

Buffer

Jumper cable

Conventional hook-screw coupling

Front light (white)

Rear light (red)

SIDE VIEW OF SHANGHAI MAGLEV TRAIN

Automatic door

Onboard levitation magnet

Driver compartment

Guideway

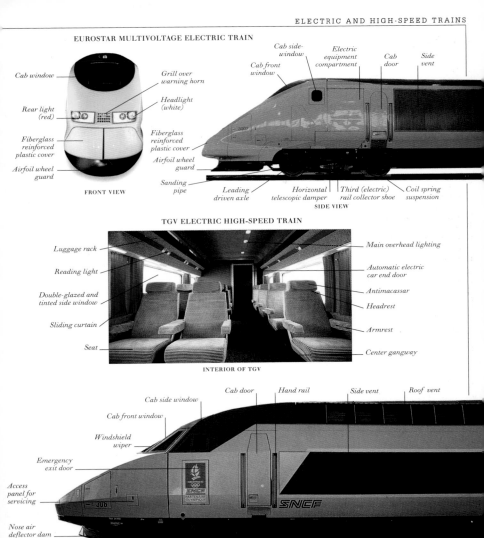

EUROSTAR MULTIVOLTAGE ELECTRIC TRAIN

Cab window

Grill over warning horn

Headlight (white)

Rear light (red)

Fiberglass reinforced plastic cover

Airfoil wheel guard

FRONT VIEW

Cab side-window

Cab front window

Electric equipment compartment

Cab door

Side vent

Fiberglass reinforced plastic cover

Airfoil wheel guard

Sanding pipe

Leading driven axle

Horizontal telescopic damper

Third (electric) rail collector shoe

Coil spring suspension

SIDE VIEW

TGV ELECTRIC HIGH-SPEED TRAIN

Luggage rack

Reading light

Double-glazed and tinted side window

Sliding curtain

Seat

Main overhead lighting

Automatic electric car end door

Antimacassar

Headrest

Armrest

Center gangway

INTERIOR OF TGV

Cab side window

Cab front window

Windshield wiper

Emergency exit door

Access panel for servicing

Nose air deflector dam

Cab door

Hand rail

Side vent

Roof vent

SNCF

Vertical damper

Horizontal damper

SIDE VIEW OF TGV

329

Train equipment

MODERN RAILROAD TRACK consists of two parallel steel rails clipped on to a support called a railroad tie. Railroad ties are usually made of reinforced concrete, although wood and steel are still used. The distance between the inside edges of the rails is the track gauge. It evolved in Britain, which uses a gauge of 4 ft 8½ in (1,435 mm), known as the standard gauge. As engineering grew more sophisticated, narrower gauges were adopted because they cost less to build. The loading gauge, which is equally important, determines the size of the largest loaded vehicle that may pass through tunnels and under bridges with adequate clearance. Safe train operation relies on following a signaling system. At first, signaling was based on a simple time interval between trains, but it now depends on maintaining a safe distance between successive trains traveling in the same direction. Most modern signals are color lights, but older mechanical semaphore signals are still used. On the latest high-speed lines, train drivers receive control instructions by electronic means. Signaling depends on reliable control of the train by effective braking. For fast, modern trains, which have considerable momentum, it is essential that each vehicle in the train can be braked by the driver or by a train control system, such as Automatic Train Protection (ATP). Braking is achieved by the brake shoe acting on the wheel rim (rim brakes), by disc brakes, or, increasingly, by electrical braking.

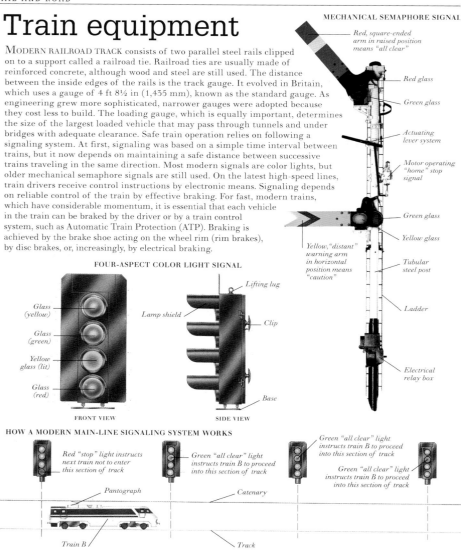

MECHANICAL SEMAPHORE SIGNAL

Red, square-ended arm in raised position means "all clear"

Red glass

Green glass

Actuating lever system

Motor operating "home" stop signal

Green glass

Yellow glass

Yellow, "distant" warning arm in horizontal position means "caution"

Tubular steel post

Ladder

Electrical relay box

FOUR-ASPECT COLOR LIGHT SIGNAL

Lifting lug

Lamp shield

Clip

Glass (yellow)

Glass (green)

Yellow glass (lit)

Glass (red)

Base

FRONT VIEW

SIDE VIEW

HOW A MODERN MAIN-LINE SIGNALING SYSTEM WORKS

Red "stop" light instructs next train not to enter this section of track

Green "all clear" light instructs train B to proceed into this section of track

Green "all clear" light instructs train B to proceed into this section of track

Green "all clear" light instructs train B to proceed into this section of track

Pantograph

Catenary

Train B

Track

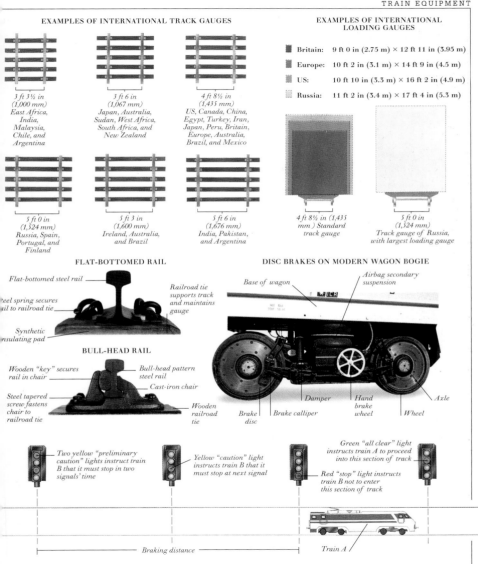

EXAMPLES OF INTERNATIONAL TRACK GAUGES

3 ft 3½ in (1,000 mm)
East Africa, India, Malaysia, Chile, and Argentina

3 ft 6 in (1,067 mm)
Japan, Australia, Sudan, West Africa, South Africa, and New Zealand

4 ft 8½ in (1,435 mm)
US, Canada, China, Egypt, Turkey, Iran, Japan, Peru, Britain, Europe, Australia, Brazil, and Mexico

5 ft 0 in (1,524 mm)
Russia, Spain, Portugal, and Finland

5 ft 3 in (1,600 mm)
Ireland, Australia, and Brazil

5 ft 6 in (1,676 mm)
India, Pakistan, and Argentina

EXAMPLES OF INTERNATIONAL LOADING GAUGES

Britain: 9 ft 0 in (2.75 m) × 12 ft 11 in (3.95 m)
Europe: 10 ft 2 in (3.1 m) × 14 ft 9 in (4.5 m)
US: 10 ft 10 in (3.3 m) × 16 ft 2 in (4.9 m)
Russia: 11 ft 2 in (3.4 m) × 17 ft 4 in (5.3 m)

4 ft 8½ in (1,435 mm) Standard track gauge

5 ft 0 in (1,524 mm) Track gauge of Russia, with largest loading gauge

FLAT-BOTTOMED RAIL

Flat-bottomed steel rail

Steel spring secures rail to railroad tie

Synthetic insulating pad

Railroad tie supports track and maintains gauge

BULL-HEAD RAIL

Wooden "key" secures rail in chair

Steel tapered screw fastens chair to railroad tie

Bull-head pattern steel rail

Cast-iron chair

Wooden railroad tie

DISC BRAKES ON MODERN WAGON BOGIE

Base of wagon

Airbag secondary suspension

Damper

Hand brake wheel

Axle

Brake disc

Brake calliper

Wheel

Two yellow "preliminary caution" lights instruct train B that it must stop in two signals' time

Yellow "caution" light instructs train B that it must stop at next signal

Green "all clear" light instructs train A to proceed into this section of track

Red "stop" light instructs train B not to enter this section of track

Braking distance

Train A

Trolleys and buses

METROLINK TROLLEY, MANCHESTER, UK

AS CITY POPULATIONS exploded in the 1800s, there was an urgent need for mass transportation. Trolleys were an early solution. The first trolleys, like buses, were horse-drawn, but in 1881, electric streetcars appeared in Berlin, Germany. Electric streetcars soon became widespread throughout Europe and North America. Trolleys run on rails along a fixed route, using electric motors that receive power from overhead cables. As road networks developed, motorized buses offered a flexible alternative to trolleys. By the 1930s, they had replaced trolley systems in many cities. City buses typically have doors at both front and rear to make loading and unloading easier. Double-decker designs are popular, occupying the same amount of street space as single-decker buses but able to transport twice the number of people. Buses are also commonly used for inter-city travel and touring. Tour buses have reclining seats, large windows, luggage space, and toilets. Recently, as city traffic has become increasingly congested, many city planners have designed new electric streetcar routes to run alongside bus routes as part of an integrated transportation system.

TROLLEY, c.1900

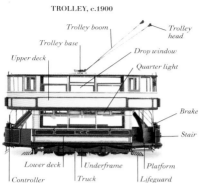

MCW METROBUS, LONDON, UK

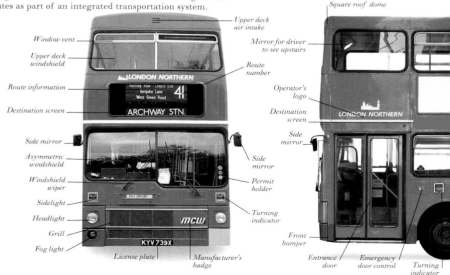

FRONT VIEW

SINGLE-DECKER BUS, NEW YORK CITY

Wheelchair access

Sliding window

Sloped roof dome

Marker light

Repeater indicator

Entrance door

Side mirror

Tinted glass

Route number

Headlight

Air intake

Turning indicator

Tire

Axle

Exit door

Access panel

Sidelight

Entrance door

License plate

Bumper

Bumper

SIDE VIEW

FRONT VIEW

DOUBLE-DECKER TOUR BUS, PARIS, FRANCE

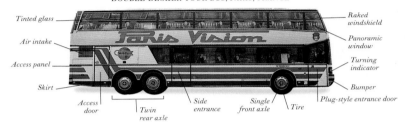

Tinted glass

Raked windshield

Air intake

Panoramic window

Access panel

Turning indicator

Skirt

Bumper

Access door

Twin rear axle

Side entrance

Single front axle

Tire

Plug-style entrance door

Paris Vision

Sliding window vent

Upper saloon window

Advertising panel

Air intake

Lower saloon window

Fleet number

Engine access panel

Rear bumper

Emergency door control

Two-leaf style exit door

Legal lettering

London Buses logo

Tire

Skirt

Axle

LONDON BUSES

M1041

SIDE VIEW

The first cars

THE EARLIEST ROAD VEHICLE powered by an engine, the Cugnot steam traction engine, was built in 1770. More practical steam carriages, such as the Bordino, were available in the early 19th century, but they were heavy and cumbersome. Restrictive laws and the introduction of railroads, faster and able to carry more passengers, saw the decline of "cars" powered by steam. It was not until 1860 that the first practical power unit for road vehicles was developed, with the invention of the internal combustion engine by the Belgian Etienne Lenoir. By around 1890, Karl Benz and Gottlieb Daimler in Germany, and Albert de Dion and Armand Peugeot in France were building cars for sale to the public. These early cars, despite being primitive, expensive, and produced in limited numbers, heralded the age of the automobile.

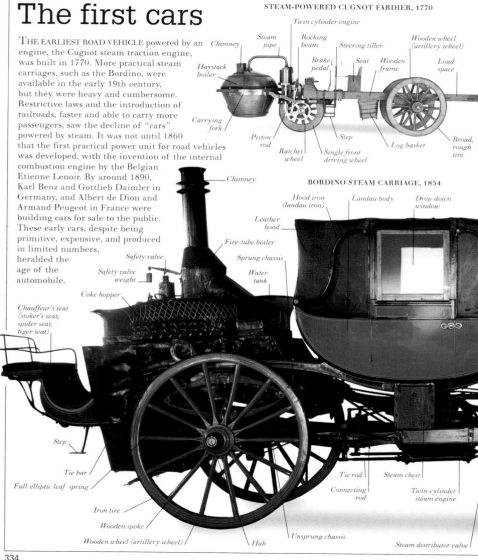

STEAM-POWERED CUGNOT FARDIER, 1770

Twin cylinder engine
Chimney
Steam pipe
Rocking beam
Steering tiller
Wooden wheel (artillery wheel)
Haystack boiler
Brake pedal
Seat
Wooden frame
Load space
Carrying fork
Piston rod
Ratchet wheel
Step
Single front driving wheel
Log basket
Broad, rough tire

BORDINO STEAM CARRIAGE, 1854

Chimney
Hood iron (landau iron)
Landau body
Drop-down window
Leather hood
Fire-tube boiler
Sprung chassis
Safety valve
Safety valve weight
Water tank
Coke hopper
Chauffeur's seat (stoker's seat; spider seat; tiger seat)
Step
Tie bar
Full-elliptic leaf spring
Iron tire
Wooden spoke
Wooden wheel (artillery wheel)
Hub
Unsprung chassis
Tie rod
Connecting rod
Steam chest
Twin-cylinder steam engine
Steam distributor valve

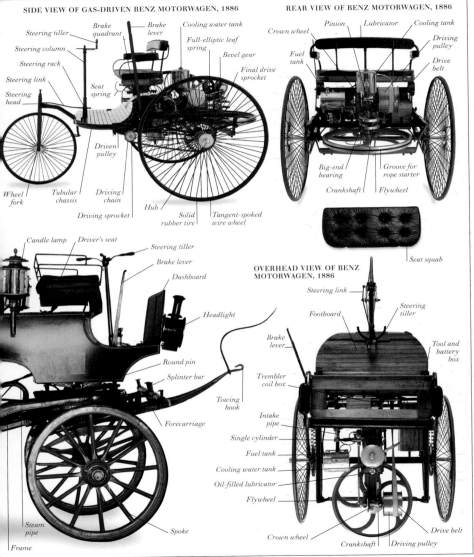

SIDE VIEW OF GAS-DRIVEN BENZ MOTORWAGEN, 1886

Steering tiller
Brake quadrant
Brake lever
Cooling water tank
Full-elliptic leaf spring
Steering column
Bevel gear
Steering rack
Final drive sprocket
Steering link
Steering head
Seat spring
Driven pulley
Wheel fork
Tubular chassis
Driving chain
Driving sprocket
Hub
Solid rubber tire
Tangent-spoked wire wheel

REAR VIEW OF BENZ MOTORWAGEN, 1886

Pinion
Lubricator
Cooling tank
Crown wheel
Driving pulley
Fuel tank
Drive belt
Big-end bearing
Groove for rope starter
Crankshaft
Flywheel
Seat squab

Candle lamp
Driver's seat
Steering tiller
Brake lever
Dashboard
Headlight
Round pin
Splinter bar
Towing hook
Forecarriage
Steam pipe
Spoke
Frame

OVERHEAD VIEW OF BENZ MOTORWAGEN, 1886

Steering link
Footboard
Steering tiller
Brake lever
Tool and battery box
Trembler coil box
Intake pipe
Single cylinder
Fuel tank
Cooling water tank
Oil-filled lubricator
Flywheel
Crown wheel
Crankshaft
Driving pulley
Drive belt

335

Elegance and utility

DURING THE FIRST DECADE OF THE 20TH CENTURY, the motorist who could afford it had a choice of some of the finest cars ever made. These handbuilt cars were powerful and luxurious, using the finest woods, leathers, and cloths, and bodywork made to the customer's individual requirements; some had six-cylinder engines as big as 15 liters. The price of such cars was several times that of an average house, and their yearly running costs were also very high. As a result, basic, utilitarian cars became popular. Costing perhaps one-tenth of the price of a luxury car, these cars had very little trim and often had only single-cylinder engines.

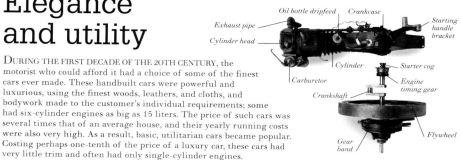

Oil bottle dripfeed • Crankcase • Starting handle bracket • Exhaust pipe • Cylinder head • Cylinder • Starter cog • Carburetor • Engine timing gear • Crankshaft • Gear band • Flywheel

FRONT VIEW OF 1906 RENAULT

SIDE VIEW OF 1906 RENAULT

Canopy • Mahogany framed Windshield • Cast aluminum wheel spider • Rear window • British Automobile Association badge • Bedford cord upholstery • Window blind • British Royal Automobile Club badge • Blind pull • Rearview mirror • Window lift strap • Lamp bracket • Broad lace trim • Oil side lamp • Windshield support • Dashboard radiator • Fender (wing) • Brass bevel • Hood catch • Access panel • Bail handle • Lifting handle • Mirror reflector • Acetylene headlight • Steering spindle • Elliott steering knuckle • Chevron-tread tire • Front axle • Dumb iron • Screwdown greaser • Starting handle • Track rod

Luggage grid • Button-quilted upholstery • Mahogany-framed plate glass window • Round-corner single limousine coachwork • Rear oil lamp • Shock absorber • Hub • Hub cap • Beaded edge tire • Tire security bolt

X 825

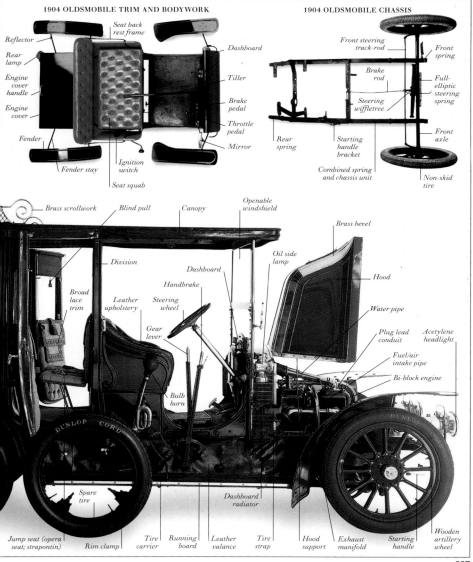

1904 OLDSMOBILE TRIM AND BODYWORK

Reflector
Rear lamp
Engine cover handle
Engine cover
Fender
Fender stay
Seat squab
Ignition switch
Seat back rest frame
Dashboard
Tiller
Brake pedal
Throttle pedal
Mirror

1904 OLDSMOBILE CHASSIS

Front steering track-rod
Front spring
Brake rod
Full-elliptic steering spring
Steering wiffletree
Front axle
Rear spring
Starting handle bracket
Combined spring and chassis unit
Non-skid tire

Brass scrollwork
Blind pull
Canopy
Openable windshield
Brass bevel
Division
Broad lace trim
Leather upholstery
Dashboard
Handbrake
Steering wheel
Gear lever
Bulb horn
Oil side lamp
Hood
Water pipe
Plug lead conduit
Acetylene headlight
Fuel/air intake pipe
Bi-block engine
Spare tire
Dashboard radiator
Jump seat (opera seat; strapontin)
Rim clamp
Tire carrier
Running board
Leather valance
Tire strap
Hood support
Exhaust manifold
Starting handle
Wooden artillery wheel

Mass-production

THE FIRST CARS WERE HAND-ASSEMBLED from individually built parts, a time-consuming procedure that required skilled mechanics and made cars very expensive. This problem was solved, in America, by a Detroit car manufacturer named Henry Ford; he introduced mass-production by using standardized parts, and later combined these with a moving production line. The work was brought to the workers, each of whom performed one simple task in the construction process as the chassis moved along the line. The first mass-produced car, the Ford Model T, was launched in 1908 and was available in a limited range of body styles and colors. However, when the production line was introduced in 1914, the color range was cut back; the Model T became available, as Henry Ford said, in "any color you like, so long as it's black." Ford cut the production time for a car from several days to about 12 hours, and eventually to minutes, making cars much cheaper than before. As a result, by 1920 half the cars in the world were Model T Fords.

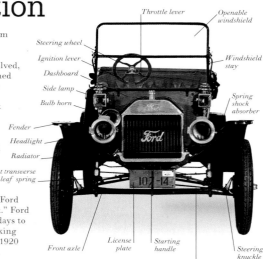

FRONT VIEW OF 1913 FORD MODEL T

Throttle lever

Openable windshield

Steering wheel

Windshield stay

Ignition lever

Dashboard

Side lamp

Bulb horn

Spring shock absorber

Fender

Headlight

Radiator

Front transverse leaf spring

Front axle

License plate

Starting handle

Steering knuckle

Steering spindle connecting-rod

STAGES OF FORD MODEL T PRODUCTION

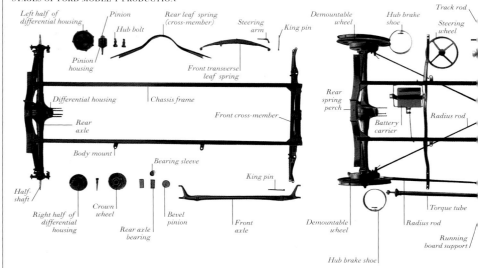

Left half of differential housing

Pinion

Rear leaf spring (cross-member)

Steering arm

King pin

Demountable wheel

Hub brake shoe

Track rod

Steering wheel

Hub bolt

Pinion housing

Front transverse leaf spring

Differential housing

Chassis frame

Front cross-member

Rear spring perch

Radius rod

Rear axle

Battery carrier

Body mount

Bearing sleeve

King pin

Half-shaft

Crown wheel

Rear axle bearing

Bevel pinion

Front axle

Demountable wheel

Radius rod

Torque tube

Running board support

Right half of differential housing

Hub brake shoe

SIDE VIEW OF 1913 FORD MODEL T

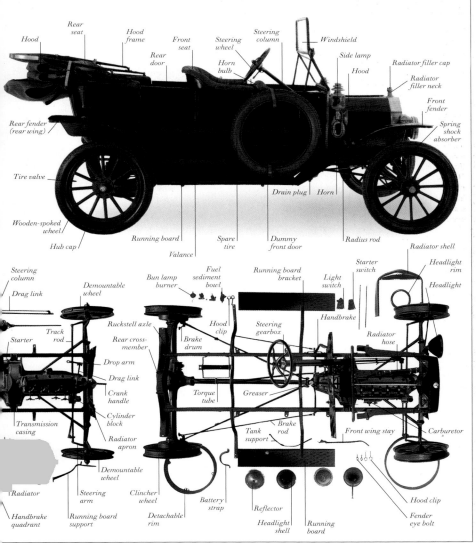

Hood

Rear seat

Hood frame

Rear door

Front seat

Steering wheel

Steering column

Windshield

Horn bulb

Side lamp

Hood

Radiator filler cap

Radiator filler neck

Front fender

Rear fender (rear wing)

Spring shock absorber

Tire valve

Drain plug

Horn

Wooden-spoked wheel

Hub cap

Running board

Valance

Spare tire

Dummy front door

Radius rod

Radiator shell

Steering column

Drag link

Demountable wheel

Bun lamp burner

Fuel sediment bowl

Running board bracket

Light switch

Starter switch

Headlight rim

Headlight

Starter

Track rod

Ruckstell axle

Rear cross-member

Hood clip

Brake drum

Steering gearbox

Handbrake

Radiator hose

Drop arm

Drag link

Crank handle

Cylinder block

Transmission casing

Radiator apron

Torque tube

Greaser

Brake rod

Tank support

Front wing stay

Carburetor

Demountable wheel

Radiator

Steering arm

Running board support

Clincher wheel

Detachable rim

Battery strap

Reflector

Headlight shell

Running board

Hood clip

Fender eye bolt

Handbrake quadrant

The "people's car"

THE MOST POPULAR CAR in the history of car manufacture is the Volkswagen Beetle, originally called the KdF Wagen. The car was developed in Germany in the 1930s by Dr. Ferdinand Porsche. At that time, Germany had only half the number of cars of Britain or France, and Adolf Hitler took a personal interest in the development of the Volkswagen ("people's car"). The intention was to provide a new industry, new jobs, and a car so cheap that anyone with a job could afford it. Dr. Porsche designed a car that was cheap to build and run; its rear-mounted, air-cooled engine cut down the number of parts needed and also reduced weight. However, few civilians managed to obtain the Beetle before the outbreak of World War II in 1939. After the war, the Beetle proved so popular that eventually more than 20 million were sold.

Fuel tank

Steering tie-rod

Fuel tank sender unit

Fuel filler neck

Windshield-wiper motor assembly

Steering box assembly

Steering idler

Frame head

Anti-roll bar

Suspension strut

Brake back plate

Track control arm

Pedal cluster

Dust shroud

Strut insert (shock absorber)

CUSTOMIZED VOLKSWAGEN BEETLE

Front suspension top mount

Gear lever knob

Front road spring

Seat mount

Front suspension top mount

Rear lamp

Air scoop

Quarter light

Hood

Handbrake

Floor pan (platform chassis)

Torsion bar cover

Indicator

Rear brake drum

Trailing arm

Tail pipe

Pressed steel wheel

Fuel filler cap

FLAT-FOUR CYLINDER ARRANGEMENT

Tire

Sports wheel

Counterweight

Piston

Rear shock absorber

Drive shaft

Transaxle (gearbox and final drive)

Heat exchanger

Crankshaft

Clutch and flywheel

Starter motor

Flat-four engine

Big end

Connecting rod (con-rod)

Air filter

Tail pipe

BODY SHELL OF VOLKSWAGEN BEETLE

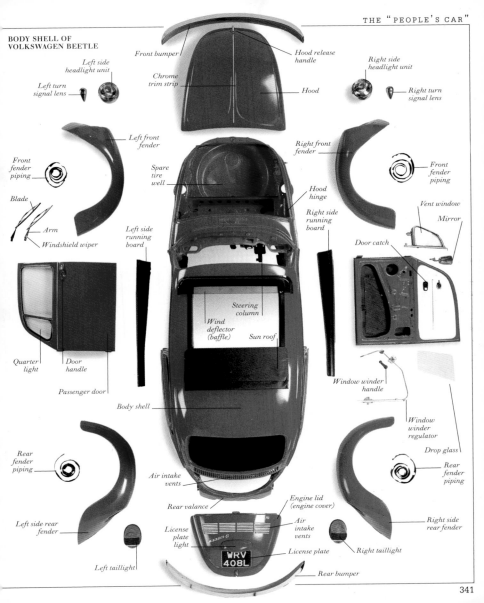

Front bumper

Hood release handle

Left side headlight unit

Left turn signal lens

Chrome trim strip

Hood

Right side headlight unit

Right turn signal lens

Left front fender

Front fender piping

Spare tire well

Right front fender

Front fender piping

Hood hinge

Blade

Arm

Windshield wiper

Left side running board

Right side running board

Vent window

Mirror

Door catch

Wind deflector (baffle)

Steering column

Sun roof

Quarter light

Door handle

Passenger door

Window winder handle

Body shell

Window winder regulator

Drop glass

Rear fender piping

Air intake vents

Rear valance

Engine lid (engine cover)

Air intake vents

Rear fender piping

Left side rear fender

License plate light

License plate

Right side rear fender

Left taillight

WRV 408L

Right taillight

Rear bumper

Early engines

STEAM AND ELECTRICITY were used to power cars until early this century, but neither power source was ideal. Electric cars had to stop frequently to recharge their heavy batteries, and steam cars gave smooth power delivery but were too complicated for the average driver to use. A rival power source, the internal combustion engine, was invented in 1860 by Etienne Lenoir (see pp. 334-335). This engine converted the force of a controlled explosion into rotary motion, to turn the wheels of a vehicle. Early variations on this basic model included sleeve valves, separately cast cylinders, and the two-stroke combustion cycle. Today, many internal combustion engines, including the Wankel rotary and diesels (see pp. 346-347), use the four-stroke cycle, first demonstrated by Nikolaus Otto in 1876. The Otto cycle, often described as "suck, squeeze, bang, blow," has proved the best method of ensuring that the engine turns over smoothly and that exhaust emissions are controllable.

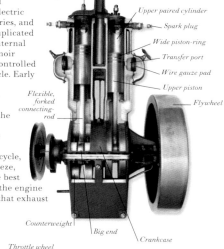

Port linking combustion chambers of upper and lower cylinders

Water connection

Upper paired cylinder

Spark plug

Wide piston-ring

Transfer port

Wire gauze pad

Upper piston

Flywheel

Flexible, forked connecting-rod

Counterweight

Big end

Crankcase

BERSEY ELECTRIC CAB, 1896

Mounting for tray of 40 batteries

Housing for electric motors

SECTIONED WHITE STEAM CAR, 1903

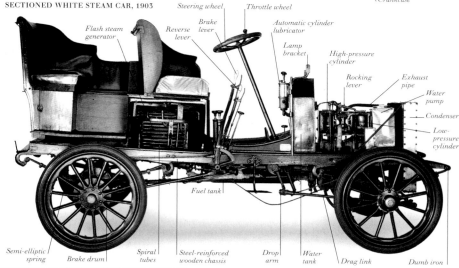

Steering wheel

Brake lever

Throttle wheel

Reverse lever

Automatic cylinder lubricator

Flash steam generator

Lamp bracket

High-pressure cylinder

Rocking lever

Exhaust pipe

Water pump

Condenser

Low-pressure cylinder

Fuel tank

Semi-elliptic spring

Brake drum

Spiral tubes

Steel-reinforced wooden chassis

Drop arm

Water tank

Drag link

Dumb iron

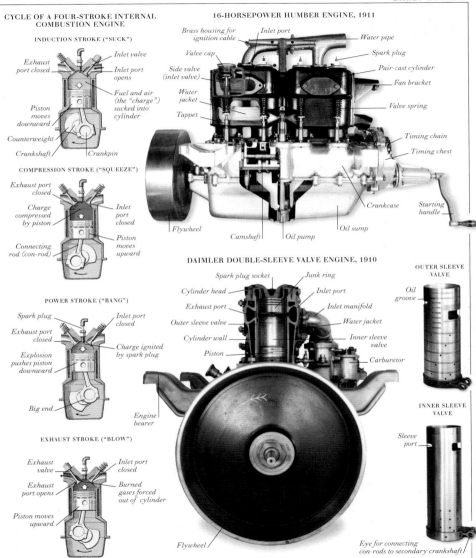

CYCLE OF A FOUR-STROKE INTERNAL COMBUSTION ENGINE

INDUCTION STROKE ("SUCK")

Exhaust port closed
Inlet valve
Inlet port opens
Fuel and air (the "charge") sucked into cylinder
Piston moves downward
Counterweight
Crankshaft
Crankpin

COMPRESSION STROKE ("SQUEEZE")

Exhaust port closed
Charge compressed by piston
Inlet port closed
Connecting rod (con-rod)
Piston moves upward

POWER STROKE ("BANG")

Spark plug
Inlet port closed
Exhaust port closed
Explosion pushes piston downward
Charge ignited by spark plug
Big end

EXHAUST STROKE ("BLOW")

Exhaust valve
Inlet port closed
Exhaust port opens
Burned gases forced out of cylinder
Piston moves upward

16-HORSEPOWER HUMBER ENGINE, 1911

Brass housing for ignition cable
Inlet port
Water pipe
Valve cap
Spark plug
Side valve (inlet valve)
Pair-cast cylinder
Fan bracket
Water jacket
Valve spring
Tappet
Timing chain
Timing chest
Crankcase
Starting handle
Flywheel
Camshaft
Oil pump
Oil sump

DAIMLER DOUBLE-SLEEVE VALVE ENGINE, 1910

Spark plug socket
Junk ring
Cylinder head
Inlet port
Exhaust port
Inlet manifold
Outer sleeve valve
Water jacket
Cylinder wall
Inner sleeve valve
Piston
Carburetor
Engine bearer
Flywheel

OUTER SLEEVE VALVE

Oil groove

INNER SLEEVE VALVE

Sleeve port
Eye for connecting con-rods to secondary crankshaft

Modern engines

TODAY'S GASOLINE ENGINE WORKS on the same basic principles as the first car engines of a century ago, although it has been greatly refined. Modern engines, often made from special metal alloys, are much lighter than earlier engines. Computerized ignition systems, fuel injectors, and multivalve cylinder heads achieve a more efficient combustion of the fuel/air mixture (the charge) so that less fuel is wasted. As a result of this greater efficiency, the power and performance of a modern engine are increased, and the level of pollution in the exhaust gases is reduced. Exhaust pollution levels today are also lowered by the increasing use of special filters called catalytic converters, which absorb many exhaust pollutants. The need to produce ever more efficient engines means that it can take up to seven years to develop a new engine for a family car, at a cost of many millions of dollars.

FRONT VIEW OF A FORD COSWORTH V6 12-VALVE

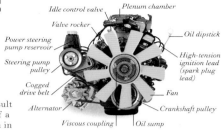

Idle control valve — Plenum chamber
Valve rocker
Oil dipstick
Power steering pump reservoir
High-tension ignition lead (spark plug lead)
Steering pump pulley
Cogged drive belt
Fan
Alternator
Crankshaft pulley
Viscous coupling — Oil sump

FRONT VIEW OF A FORD COSWORTH V6 24-VALVE

Idle control valve — Plenum chamber
Exhaust gas recirculation valve
Camshaft timing gear
Camshaft chain
Steering pump drive pulley
Belt tensioner
Air-conditioning pump
Alternator cooling fan
Oil sump — Drive belt
Crankshaft pulley

SECTIONED VIEW OF A JAGUAR STRAIGHT 6

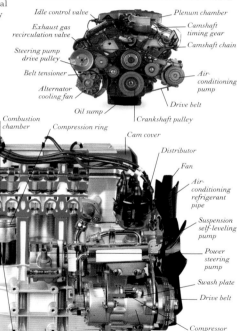

Cam follower (bucket tappet)
Valve spring
Cam lobe
Cam
Combustion chamber
Compression ring
Cam cover
Camshaft
Distributor
Cylinder head
Fan
Valve stem
Air-conditioning refrigerant pipe
Exhaust valve
Suspension self-leveling pump
Cylinder liner
Power steering pump
Water jacket
Piston
Swash plate
Connecting rod (con-rod)
Drive belt
Main bearing housing
Big end
Compressor piston
Transmission adaptor plate
Air-conditioning compressor
Crankshaft counterweight
Oil sump
Oil pick-up pipe
Anti-surge baffle
Crankcase
Oil-control ring (scraper ring)

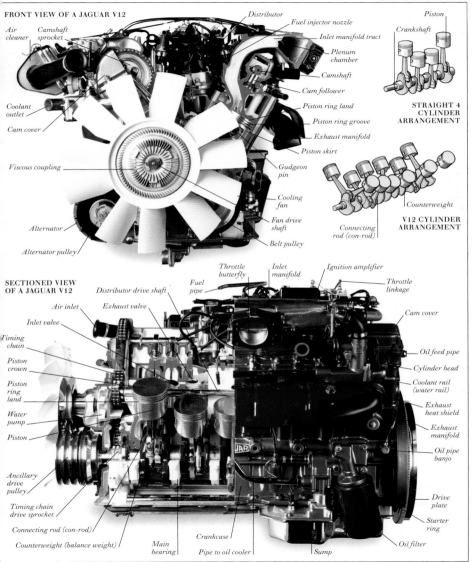

FRONT VIEW OF A JAGUAR V12

Air cleaner
Camshaft sprocket
Distributor
Fuel injector nozzle
Piston
Crankshaft
Inlet manifold tract
Plenum chamber
Camshaft
Cam follower
Piston ring land
Piston ring groove
Exhaust manifold
Piston skirt
Gudgeon pin
Cooling fan
Fan drive shaft
Belt pulley
Coolant outlet
Cam cover
Viscous coupling
Alternator
Alternator pulley

STRAIGHT 4 CYLINDER ARRANGEMENT

Counterweight
Connecting rod (con-rod)

V12 CYLINDER ARRANGEMENT

SECTIONED VIEW OF A JAGUAR V12

Distributor drive shaft
Throttle butterfly
Inlet manifold
Fuel pipe
Ignition amplifier
Throttle linkage
Air inlet
Exhaust valve
Inlet valve
Cam cover
Timing chain
Piston crown
Piston ring land
Water pump
Piston
Oil feed pipe
Cylinder head
Coolant rail (water rail)
Exhaust heat shield
Exhaust manifold
Oil pipe banjo
Ancillary drive pulley
Timing chain drive sprocket
Connecting rod (con-rod)
Counterweight (balance weight)
Main bearing
Pipe to oil cooler
Crankcase
Sump
Drive plate
Starter ring
Oil filter

Alternative engines

ROTARY-ENGINED MAZDA RX-7

THE MOST COMMON TYPE OF ALTERNATIVE ENGINE is the diesel engine, which, instead of igniting the compressed fuel/air mixture with a spark, uses compression alone, heating the mixture to the point where it explodes. A diesel engine's fuel consumption is low in comparison with similarly sized piston engines, despite its heavier, reinforced moving parts and cylinder block. Another type of engine is the rotary-combustion, first successfully developed by Felix Wankel in the 1950s. Its two trilobate (three-sided) rotors revolve in housings shaped in a fat figure-eight. The four sequences of the four-stroke cycle, which occur consecutively in a piston engine, occur simultaneously in a rotary engine, producing power in a continuous stream.

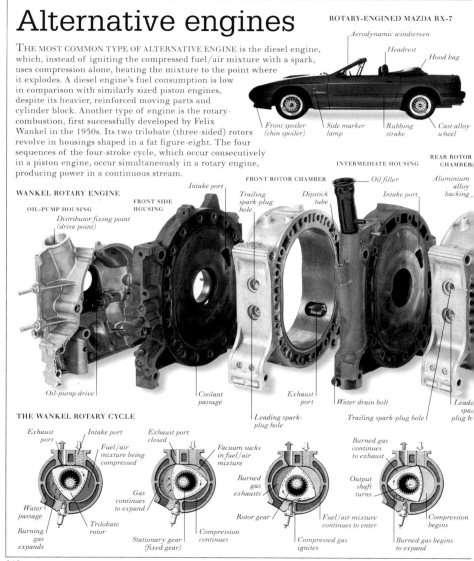

Aerodynamic windscreen

Headrest

Hood bag

Front spoiler (chin spoiler)

Side marker lamp

Rubbing strake

Cast alloy wheel

REAR ROTOR CHAMBER

INTERMEDIATE HOUSING

Oil filler

Aluminium alloy backing

FRONT ROTOR CHAMBER

Intake port

WANKEL ROTARY ENGINE

Intake port

Trailing spark-plug hole

Dipstick tube

Intake port

FRONT SIDE HOUSING

OIL-PUMP HOUSING

Distributor fixing point (drive point)

Oil-pump drive

Coolant passage

Exhaust port

Water drain bolt

Leading spark-plug hole

Trailing spark-plug hole

Lead... spa... plug h...

THE WANKEL ROTARY CYCLE

Exhaust port

Intake port

Fuel/air mixture being compressed

Exhaust port closed

Vacuum sucks in fuel/air mixture

Burned gas continues to exhaust

Gas continues to expand

Burned gas exhausts

Output shaft turns

Water passage

Burning gas expands

Trilobate rotor

Stationary gear (fixed gear)

Compression continues

Rotor gear

Compressed gas ignites

Fuel/air mixture continues to enter

Compressed gas... to expand

Compression begins

Burned gas begins to expand

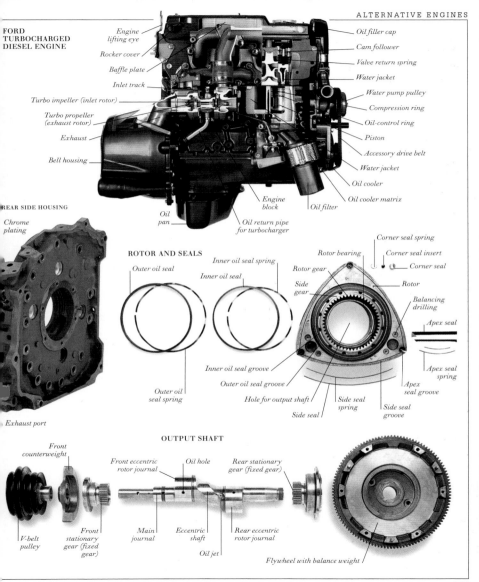

FORD TURBOCHARGED DIESEL ENGINE

Engine lifting eye

Oil filler cap

Rocker cover

Cam follower

Baffle plate

Valve return spring

Inlet track

Water jacket

Turbo impeller (inlet rotor)

Water pump pulley

Turbo propeller (exhaust rotor)

Compression ring

Exhaust

Oil-control ring

Bell housing

Piston

Accessory drive belt

Water jacket

Oil cooler

Oil cooler matrix

Engine block

Oil filter

REAR SIDE HOUSING

Chrome plating

Oil pan

Oil return pipe for turbocharger

Exhaust port

ROTOR AND SEALS

Outer oil seal

Inner oil seal spring

Inner oil seal

Corner seal spring

Corner seal insert

Corner seal

Rotor bearing

Rotor gear

Side gear

Rotor

Balancing drilling

Apex seal

Inner oil seal groove

Outer oil seal groove

Hole for output shaft

Outer oil seal spring

Apex seal groove

Apex seal spring

Side seal spring

Side seal groove

Side seal

OUTPUT SHAFT

Front counterweight

Front eccentric rotor journal

Oil hole

Rear stationary gear (fixed gear)

V-belt pulley

Front stationary gear (fixed gear)

Main journal

Eccentric shaft

Rear eccentric rotor journal

Oil jet

Flywheel with balance weight

Bodywork

RENAULT LOGO

THE BODY OF A MODERN mass-produced car is built on the monocoque (single-shell) principle, in which the roof, side panels, and floor are welded into a single integral unit. This bodyshell protects and supports the car's internal parts. Steel and glass are used to construct the bodyshell, creating a unit that is both light and strong. Its lightness helps to conserve energy, while its strength protects the occupants. Modern bodywork is designed with the aid of computers, which are used to predict factors such as aerodynamic efficiency and impact-resistance. High-technology is also employed on the production line, where robots are used to assemble, weld, and paint the body.

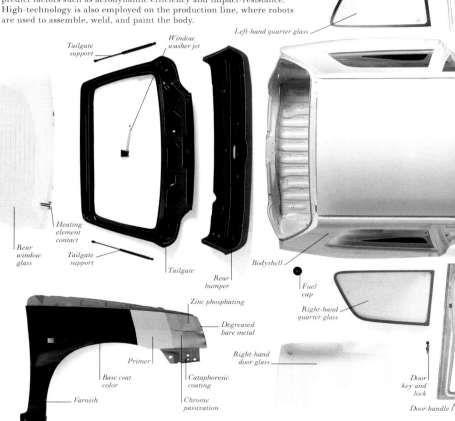

Door handle

Door lock

Left-hand door glass

Left-hand quarter glass

Tailgate support

Window washer jet

Rear window glass

Heating element contact

Tailgate support

Tailgate

Rear bumper

Bodyshell

Fuel cap

Right-hand quarter glass

Zinc phosphating

Degreased bare metal

Primer

Base coat color

Cataphoresic coating

Right-hand door glass

Varnish

Chrome passivation

Door key and lock

Door handle

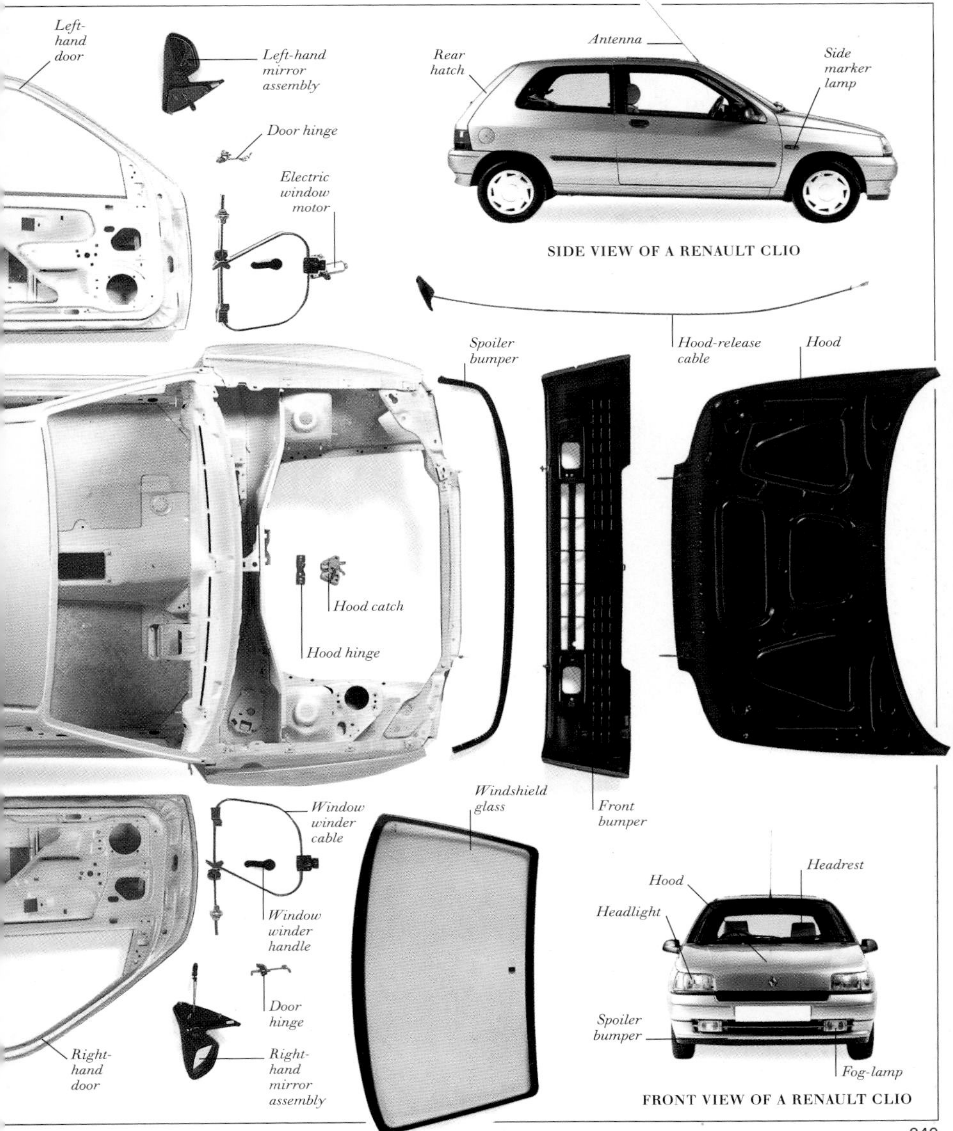

Left-hand door

Left-hand mirror assembly

Door hinge

Electric window motor

Antenna

Rear hatch

Side marker lamp

SIDE VIEW OF A RENAULT CLIO

Spoiler bumper

Hood-release cable

Hood

Hood catch

Hood hinge

Front bumper

Windshield glass

Window winder cable

Window winder handle

Door hinge

Right-hand door

Right-hand mirror assembly

Hood

Headrest

Headlight

Spoiler bumper

Fog-lamp

FRONT VIEW OF A RENAULT CLIO

Mechanical components

A TYPICAL MODERN CAR has several thousand individual mechanical components. These are assembled to form the car's various mechanical systems: engine and exhaust, transmission, steering, suspension, and brakes. To ensure that each system functions properly, components are manufactured to extremely fine tolerances—to within about one ten-thousandth of an inch (one five-hundredth of a millimeter) in some cases.

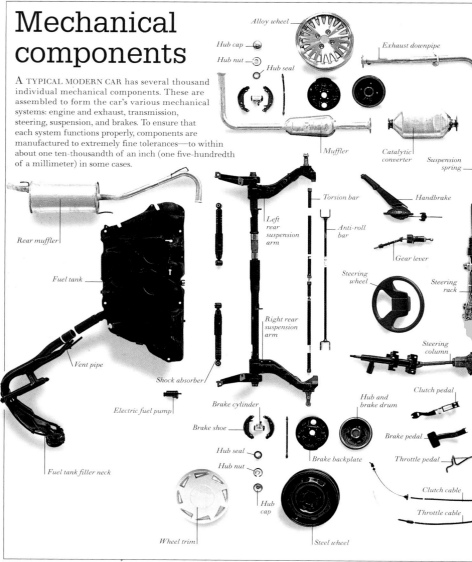

Alloy wheel

Hub cap

Hub nut

Hub seal

Exhaust downpipe

Muffler

Catalytic converter

Suspension spring

Rear muffler

Fuel tank

Torsion bar

Handbrake

Left rear suspension arm

Anti-roll bar

Gear lever

Steering wheel

Steering rack

Right rear suspension arm

Steering column

Vent pipe

Shock absorber

Electric fuel pump

Brake cylinder

Brake shoe

Hub and brake drum

Clutch pedal

Brake pedal

Throttle pedal

Hub seal

Hub nut

Brake backplate

Hub cap

Clutch cable

Throttle cable

Fuel tank filler neck

Wheel trim

Steel wheel

**MECHANICAL COMPONENTS
OF A RENAULT CLIO, 1991**

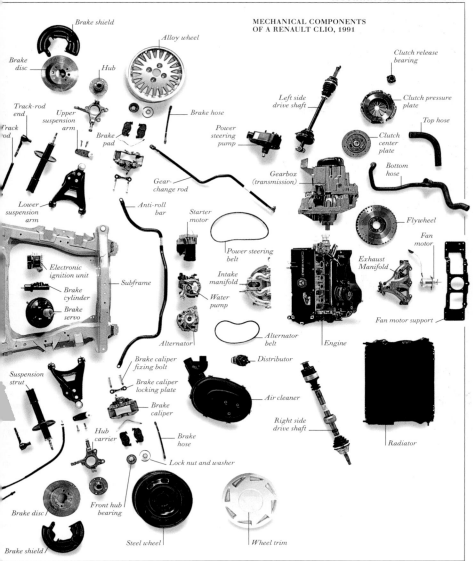

Brake shield

Alloy wheel

Clutch release bearing

Brake disc

Hub

Track-rod end

Upper suspension arm

Brake pad

Brake hose

Power steering pump

Left side drive shaft

Clutch pressure plate

Top hose

Clutch center plate

Track rod

Lower suspension arm

Gear-change rod

Anti-roll bar

Gearbox (transmission)

Bottom hose

Flywheel

Fan motor

Starter motor

Power steering belt

Exhaust Manifold

Electronic ignition unit

Subframe

Intake manifold

Fan motor support

Brake cylinder

Water pump

Brake servo

Alternator

Alternator belt

Engine

Radiator

Suspension strut

Brake caliper fixing bolt

Distributor

Brake caliper locking plate

Brake caliper

Air cleaner

Hub carrier

Brake hose

Right side drive shaft

Lock nut and washer

Brake disc

Front hub bearing

Brake shield

Steel wheel

Wheel trim

Car trim

A MODERN CAR HAS TWO TYPES OF TRIM, according to the materials used: hard (chrome and plastics) and soft (upholstery materials). Safety and comfort are priorities in the trim's design: seats help the occupants to maintain a comfortable posture, rubber seals keep out dirt and moisture, and headlights light the way. Older cars had interior or leather paneling cut and fitted by craftsmen; modern cars use precisely molded plastics and seat fabrics cut by robot-controlled lasers to reduce costs and production time. Doors are now trimmed off the production line so that complex wiring can be built in.

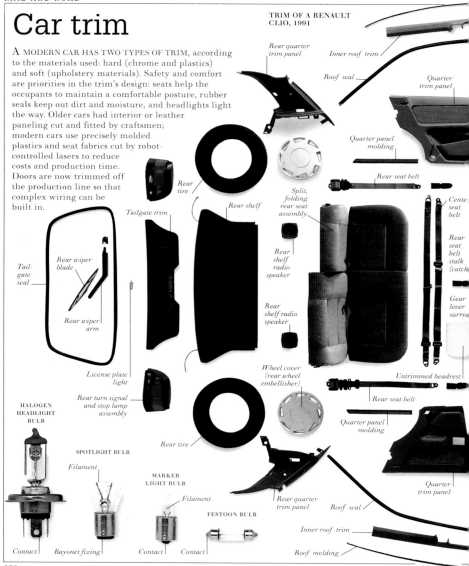

Rear quarter trim panel

Inner roof trim

Roof seal

Quarter trim panel

Quarter panel molding

Rear seat belt

Cente[r] seat belt

Rear seat belt stalk (catch[)]

Gear lever surrou[nd]

Rear tire

Rear shelf

Split, folding rear seat assembly

Tailgate trim

Tail-gate seal

Rear wiper blade

Rear wiper arm

Rear shelf radio speaker

Rear shelf radio speaker

License plate light

Wheel cover (rear wheel embellisher)

Untrimmed headrest

Rear turn signal and stop lamp assembly

Rear seat belt

Quarter panel molding

Rear tire

HALOGEN HEADLIGHT BULB

SPOTLIGHT BULB

Filament

MARKER LIGHT BULB

Filament

FESTOON BULB

Rear quarter trim panel

Roof seal

Quarter trim panel

Inner roof trim

Roof molding

Contact

Bayonet fixing

Contact

Contact

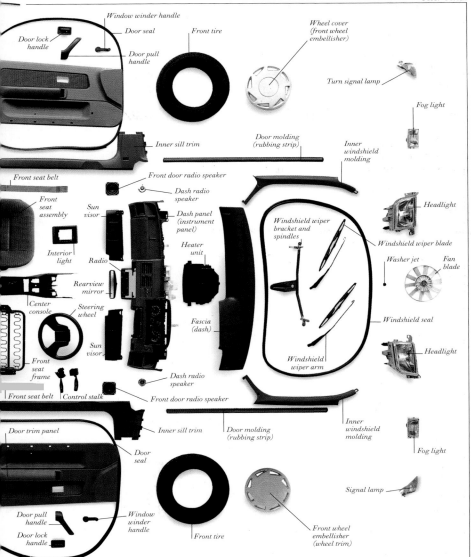

Window winder handle

Door lock handle

Door seal

Door pull handle

Front tire

Wheel cover (front wheel embellisher)

Turn signal lamp

Fog light

Inner sill trim

Door molding (rubbing strip)

Inner windshield molding

Front seat belt

Front door radio speaker

Dash radio speaker

Headlight

Front seat assembly

Sun visor

Dash panel (instrument panel)

Windshield wiper bracket and spindles

Interior light

Heater unit

Windshield wiper blade

Radio

Washer jet

Fan blade

Rearview mirror

Center console

Steering wheel

Windshield seal

Front seat frame

Sun visor

Fascia (dash)

Headlight

Windshield wiper arm

Dash radio speaker

Front seat belt

Control stalk

Front door radio speaker

Inner windshield molding

Door trim panel

Inner sill trim

Door molding (rubbing strip)

Fog light

Door seal

Door pull handle

Window winder handle

Signal lamp

Door lock handle

Front tire

Front wheel embellisher (wheel trim)

353

Hybrid car

THERE HAVE BEEN SEVERAL proposed alternatives to conventional gas- or diesel-powered cars, including cars that use solar or battery power. The object is to lower harmful emissions and conserve natural resources. One of the alternatives already in production is the hybrid car. A hybrid vehicle uses two or more fuels. Examples include diesel-electric trains and mopeds. The latter combine the power of a gasoline engine with pedal power. In a hybrid car, gas consumption is reduced by the provision of additional power by an electric motor during acceleration. The motor is driven by power from on-board batteries that are recharged by an engine-driven generator when the car is decelerating or cruising. Some hybrid cars transfer energy from the wheels to a flywheel during braking. The flywheel drives the generator, which recharges the batteries.

HONDA INSIGHT

Antenna · Aerodynamic roof · Windshield · Side mirror · Plastic front wings · Front air dam · Plastic bumper · Aerodynamic underside components · Cooling intake · Aluminum hood

SIDE VIEW OF 1-LITER VTEC ENGINE

FRONT VIEW OF 1-LITER VTEC ENGINE

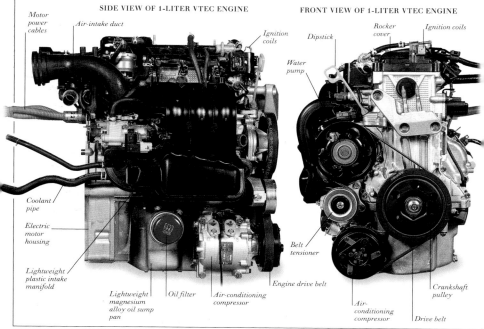

Motor power cables · Air-intake duct · Ignition coils · Dipstick · Rocker cover · Ignition coils · Water pump · Coolant pipe · Electric motor housing · Lightweight plastic intake manifold · Belt tensioner · Lightweight magnesium alloy oil sump pan · Oil filter · Air-conditioning compressor · Engine drive belt · Air-conditioning compressor · Crankshaft pulley · Drive belt

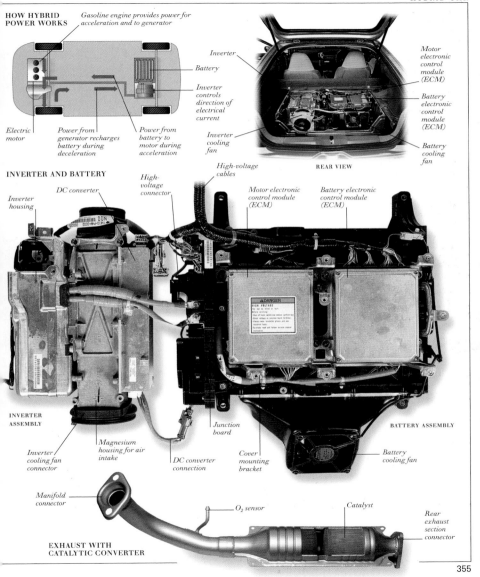

HOW HYBRID POWER WORKS

Gasoline engine provides power for acceleration and to generator

Inverter

Battery

Inverter controls direction of electrical current

Electric motor

Power from generator recharges battery during deceleration

Power from battery to motor during acceleration

Inverter cooling fan

Motor electronic control module (ECM)

Battery electronic control module (ECM)

Battery cooling fan

REAR VIEW

INVERTER AND BATTERY

Inverter housing

DC converter

High-voltage connector

High-voltage cables

Motor electronic control module (ECM)

Battery electronic control module (ECM)

⚠ DANGER
HIGH VOLTAGE

INVERTER ASSEMBLY

Inverter cooling fan connector

Magnesium housing for air intake

DC converter connection

Junction board

Cover mounting bracket

BATTERY ASSEMBLY

Battery cooling fan

Manifold connector

O_2 sensor

Catalyst

Rear exhaust section connector

EXHAUST WITH CATALYTIC CONVERTER

355

Race cars

SINCE THE ADVENT OF DRIVING, race cars have been a major focus of innovation in car design. Features that are now commonplace, such as disc brakes, turbochargers, and even safety belts, were used first on competition cars. Research into race cars has contributed to a new understanding of engine performance, aerodynamics, and tire adhesion, and has led to the development of ultralight materials such as carbon fiber for car bodies. A modern McLaren Formula One car has a low, streamlined body and an open cockpit but, unlike its forerunner, it also has front and rear wings that push the wheels firmly on to the track, huge tires for extra grip, and electronic sensors that continually relay information to the pits about the car's performance.

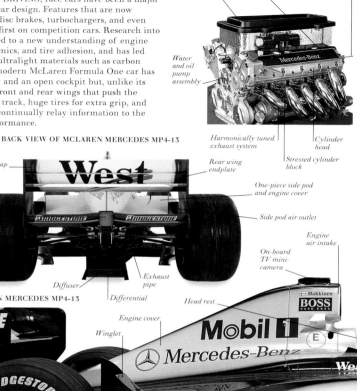

Fuel injection trumpet guard

Cam cover

Gearbox fixing stud

Water and oil pump assembly

Harmonically tuned exhaust system

Cylinder head

Stressed cylinder block

BACK VIEW OF MCLAREN MERCEDES MP4-13

Upper flap

Grooved racing tire

Warning light

Half-shaft

Rear wing endplate

One-piece side pod and engine cover

Side pod air outlet

Engine air intake

On-board TV mini-camera

Diffuser

Exhaust pipe

Differential

SIDE VIEW OF MCLAREN MERCEDES MP4-13

Head rest

Engine cover

Winglet

Rear wing endplate

Alloy wheel

Wheel nut

Side pod

OVERHEAD VIEW OF MCLAREN MERCEDES MP4-13

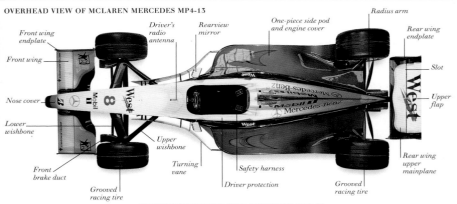

Radius arm

Front wing endplate

Driver's radio antenna

Rearview mirror

One-piece side pod and engine cover

Rear wing endplate

Front wing

Slot

Upper flap

Nose cover

Lower wishbone

Upper wishbone

Front brake duct

Turning vane

Safety harness

Driver protection

Rear wing upper mainplane

Grooved racing tire

Grooved racing tire

FRONT VIEW OF MCLAREN MERCEDES MP4-13

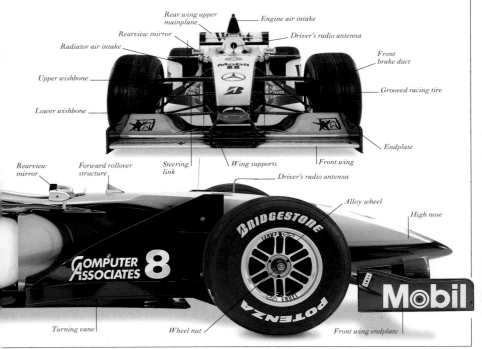

Rear wing upper mainplane

Engine air intake

Rearview mirror

Driver's radio antenna

Radiator air intake

Front brake duct

Upper wishbone

Grooved racing tire

Lower wishbone

Endplate

Steering link

Wing supports

Front wing

Rearview mirror

Forward rollover structure

Driver's radio antenna

Alloy wheel

High nose

COMPUTER ASSOCIATES 8

BRIDGESTONE

POTENZA

Mobil

Turning vane

Wheel nut

Front wing endplate

Bicycle anatomy

THE BICYCLE IS A TWO-WHEELED, light-weight machine, which is propelled by human power. It is efficient, cheap, easily manufactured, and one of the world's most popular forms of transportation. The first pedal-driven bicycle was built in Scotland in 1839. Since then the basic design—of a frame, wheels, brakes, handlebars, and saddle—has been gradually improved, with the addition of a chain, gear system, and pneumatic tires (tires inflated with air). The recent invention of the mountain bike (all-terrain bike) has been an important development. With its strong, rugged frame, wide tires, and 21 gears, a mountain bike enables riders to reach rough and hilly areas that were previously inaccessible to cyclists.

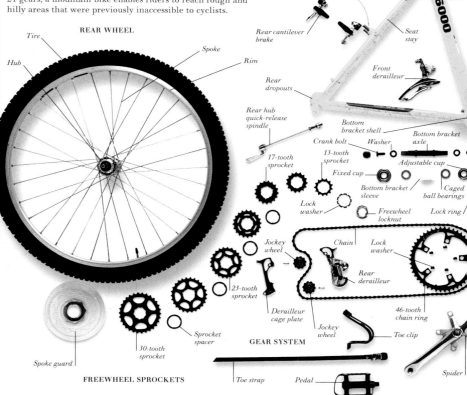

Saddle

Seat post

Seat post quick-release bolt

Cable guide

Straddle wire

Seat tube

6000

USA

Rear cantilever brake

Seat stay

Front derailleur

REAR WHEEL

Tire

Spoke

Hub

Rim

Rear dropouts

Rear hub quick-release spindle

Bottom bracket shell

Bottom bracket axle

Crank bolt

Washer

17-tooth sprocket

13-tooth sprocket

Fixed cup

Adjustable cup

Lock washer

Bottom bracket sleeve

Caged ball bearings

Freewheel locknut

Lock ring

Jockey wheel

Chain

Lock washer

Rear derailleur

23-tooth sprocket

Derailleur cage plate

Jockey wheel

46-tooth chain ring

Toe clip

Sprocket spacer

GEAR SYSTEM

Spoke guard

30-tooth sprocket

Toe strap

Pedal

Spider

FREEWHEEL SPROCKETS

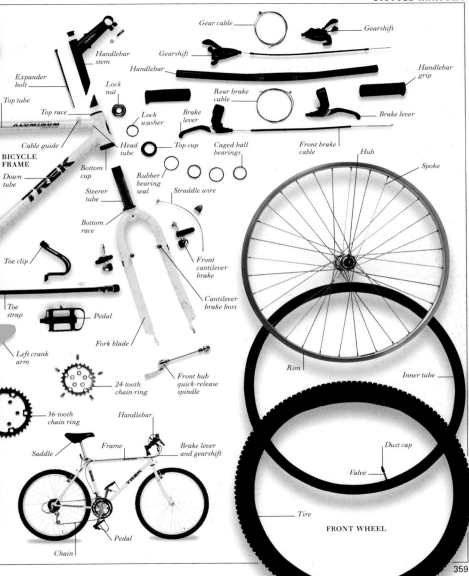

Gear cable

Gearshift

Handlebar
stem

Gearshift

Handlebar

Handlebar
grip

Expander
bolt

Lock
nut

Top tube

Rear brake
cable

Lock
washer

Brake
lever

Top race

Brake lever

ALUMINUM

Cable guide

Head
tube

Top cup

Caged ball
bearings

Front brake
cable

BICYCLE
FRAME

Hub

Spoke

Down
tube

Bottom
cup

Rubber
bearing
seal

Steerer
tube

Straddle wire

Bottom
race

Toe clip

Front
cantilever
brake

Cantilever
brake boss

Toe
strap

Pedal

Fork blade

Rim

Inner tube

Left crank
arm

24-tooth
chain ring

Front hub
quick-release
spindle

36-tooth
chain ring

Handlebar

Saddle

Frame

Brake lever
and gearshift

Dust cap

Valve

Pedal

Tire

FRONT WHEEL

Chain

Bicycles

ALTHOUGH ALL BICYCLES are made up of the same basic components, they can vary greatly in design. A racing bike, such as the Eddy Merckx model, with its light frame and steep head- and seat-angles, is built for speed. Its design forces the rider to adopt the "aerotuck," a crouched, aerodynamic position. While a touring bike resembles the racing bike in many respects, it is designed for comfort and stability on long-distance journeys. Touring bikes are characterized by more relaxed frame angles, heavy chain stays that support the rear panniers, and a long wheelbase (the distance between the wheel axles) for reliable handling. All-round bicycles, known as "hybrids," combine the light weight and speed of sports bikes with the rugged durability of mountain bikes (see pp. 358-359). Bicycles that are not designed for conventional road use include time-trial bikes, which have a short head tube, sloping top tube, "aero" handlebars, and aerodynamic tubing. Most Human Powered Vehicles (HPVs) are recumbents—the rider has a recumbent position—which maximize power output and minimize drag (resistance). Essential to the safety of all riders are helmets, and both front and rear lights; locks protect against theft.

FRONT AND REAR LIGHTS

HELMET

White front light

Red rear light

Hard outer shell

Air vent

Polystyrene padding

Quick-release strap

EDDY MERCKX RACING BICYCLE

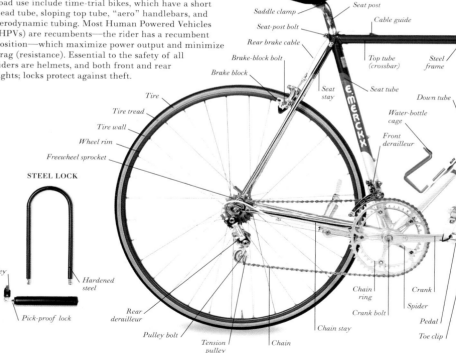

Saddle

Seat post

Saddle clamp

Cable guide

Seat-post bolt

Rear brake cable

Top tube (crossbar)

Steel frame

Brake-block bolt

Seat stay

Seat tube

Brake block

Seat tube

Down tube

Water-bottle cage

Front derailleur

Tire

Tire tread

Tire wall

Wheel rim

Freewheel sprocket

STEEL LOCK

Key

Hardened steel

Pick-proof lock

Rear derailleur

Pulley bolt

Tension pulley

Chain

Chain stay

Chain ring

Crank bolt

Crank

Spider

Pedal

Toe clip

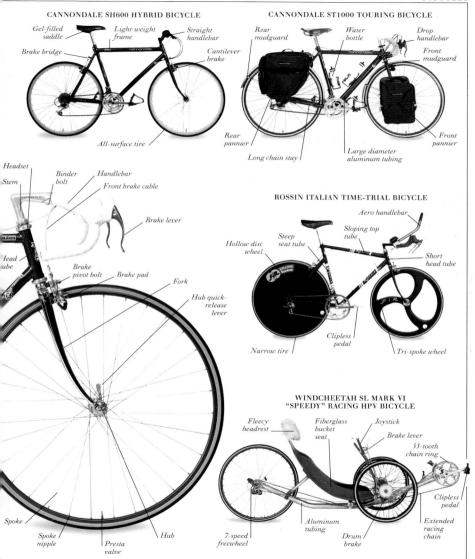

CANNONDALE SH600 HYBRID BICYCLE

Gel-filled saddle

Light-weight frame

Straight handlebar

Brake bridge

Cantilever brake

All-surface tire

CANNONDALE ST1000 TOURING BICYCLE

Rear mudguard

Water bottle

Drop handlebar

Front mudguard

Rear pannier

Long chain stay

Large diameter aluminum tubing

Front pannier

Headset

Stem

Binder bolt

Handlebar

Front brake cable

Brake lever

Head tube

Brake pivot bolt

Brake pad

Fork

Hub quick-release lever

Spoke

Spoke nipple

Presta valve

Hub

ROSSIN ITALIAN TIME-TRIAL BICYCLE

Aero handlebar

Sloping top tube

Steep seat tube

Hollow disc wheel

Short head tube

Narrow tire

Clipless pedal

Tri-spoke wheel

WINDCHEETAH SL MARK VI "SPEEDY" RACING HPV BICYCLE

Fleecy headrest

Fiberglass bucket seat

Joystick

Brake lever

53-tooth chain ring

Clipless pedal

7-speed freewheel

Aluminum tubing

Drum brake

Extended racing chain

The motorcycle

THE MOTORCYCLE HAS EVOLVED from a motorized cycle—a basic bicycle with an engine—into a sophisticated, high-performance machine. In 1901, the Werner brothers established the most viable location for the engine by positioning it low in the center of the chassis (see pp. 364-365): the new Werner became the basis for the modern motorcycle. Motorcycles are used for many purposes—for commuting, delivering messages, touring, and racing—and different machines have been developed according to the demands of different types of rider. The Vespa scooter, for instance, which is small-wheeled, economical, and easy-to-ride, was designed to meet the needs of the commuter. Sidecars provided transportation for the family until the arrival of cheap cars caused their popularity to decline. Enthusiast riders generally favor larger capacity machines that are capable of greater performance and offer more comfort. Four-cylinder machines have been common since the Honda CB750 appeared in 1969. Despite advances in motorcycle technology, many riders are attracted to the traditional looks of motorcycles like the twin-cylinder Harley-Davidson. The Harley-Davidson Glides exploit the style of the classic American V-twin engine, where the cylinders are placed in a V-formation.

1901 WERNER MOTORCYCLE

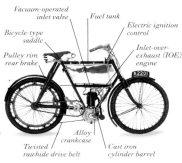

Vacuum-operated inlet valve
Fuel tank
Electric ignition control
Bicycle-type saddle
Inlet-over-exhaust (IOE) engine
Pulley rim rear brake
A220
Alloy crankcase
Twisted rawhide drive belt
Cast iron cylinder barrel

1988 HARLEY-DAVIDSON FLHS ELECTRA GLIDE

1965 BMW R/60 WITH 1952 STEIB CHAIR

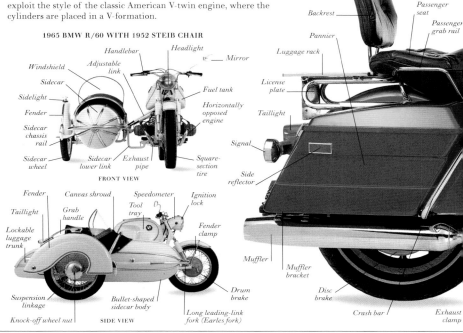

Handlebar
Headlight
Mirror
Windshield
Adjustable link
Sidecar
Fuel tank
Sidelight
Horizontally opposed engine
Fender
Sidecar chassis rail
Sidecar wheel
Sidecar lower link
Exhaust pipe
Square-section tire
Side reflector
Signal

FRONT VIEW

Passenger seat
Passenger grab rail
Backrest
Pannier
Luggage rack
License plate
Taillight

Fender
Canvas shroud
Speedometer
Ignition lock
Taillight
Grab handle
Tool tray
Lockable luggage trunk
Fender clamp
Muffler
Muffler bracket
Disc brake
Suspension linkage
Bullet-shaped sidecar body
Drum brake
Crash bar
Exhaust clamp
Knock-off wheel nut
SIDE VIEW
Long leading-link fork (Earles fork)

1969 HONDA CB750

1963 VESPA GRAND SPORT 160 MARK 1

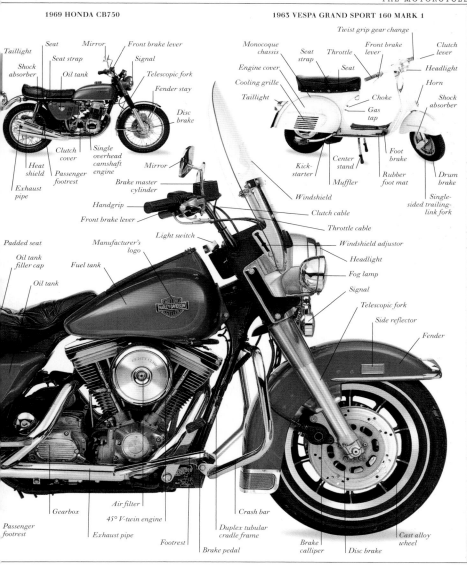

Taillight
Seat
Mirror
Front brake lever
Seat strap
Signal
Shock absorber
Oil tank
Telescopic fork
Fender stay
Disc brake
Clutch cover
Single overhead camshaft engine
Mirror
Heat shield
Passenger footrest
Exhaust pipe
Brake master cylinder
Handgrip
Front brake lever
Light switch

Twist grip gear change
Monocoque chassis
Seat strap
Throttle
Front brake lever
Clutch lever
Engine cover
Seat
Headlight
Cooling grille
Horn
Taillight
Choke
Gas tap
Shock absorber
Kick-starter
Center stand
Muffler
Foot brake
Rubber foot mat
Drum brake
Single-sided trailing-link fork
Windshield
Clutch cable
Throttle cable
Windshield adjustor

Padded seat
Oil tank filler cap
Fuel tank
Manufacturer's logo
Headlight
Fog lamp
Oil tank
Signal
Telescopic fork
Side reflector
Fender
Gearbox
Air filter
45° V-twin engine
Crash bar
Passenger footrest
Exhaust pipe
Footrest
Duplex tubular cradle frame
Brake pedal
Brake calliper
Disc brake
Cast alloy wheel

The motorcycle chassis

THE MOTORCYCLE CHASSIS is the main "body" of the motorcycle, to which the engine is attached. Consisting of the frame, wheels, suspension, and brakes, the chassis performs various functions. The frame, which is built from steel or alloy, keeps the wheels in line to maintain the handling of the motorcycle, and serves as a structure for mounting other components. The engine and gearbox unit is bolted into place, while items such as the seat, the fenders, and the fairing are more easily removable. Suspension cushions the rider from irregularities in the road surface. In most suspension systems, coil springs controlled by an oil damper separate the main mass of the motorcycle from the wheels. At the front, the spring and damper are usually incorporated in a telescopic fork; the rear employs a pivoted swingarm. The suspension also helps to retain maximum contact between the tires and the road, necessary for effective braking and steering. Drum brakes were common until the 1970s, but modern motorcycles use disc brakes, which are more powerful.

1985 HONDA VF750 WITH BODYWORK

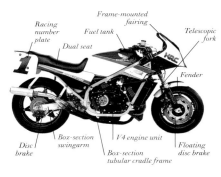

Racing number plate · Fuel tank · Frame-mounted fairing · Telescopic fork · Dual seat · Fender · Disc brake · Box-section swingarm · V4 engine unit · Box-section tubular cradle frame · Floating disc brake

1985 HONDA VF750 WITH BODYWORK REMOVED

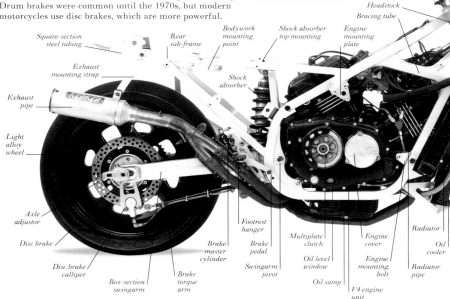

Brake master cylinder · Headstock · Bracing tube · Square-section steel tubing · Rear sub-frame · Bodywork mounting point · Shock absorber top mounting · Engine mounting plate · Exhaust mounting strap · Shock absorber · Exhaust pipe · Light alloy wheel · Axle adjustor · Disc brake · Disc brake calliper · Box-section swingarm · Brake torque arm · Brake master cylinder · Brake pedal · Footrest hanger · Multiplate clutch · Oil level window · Swingarm pivot · Oil sump · V4 engine unit · Engine cover · Engine mounting bolt · Radiator · Oil cooler · Radiator pipe

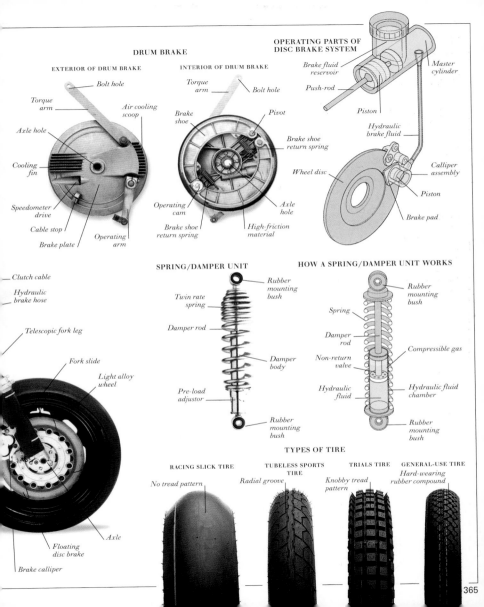

DRUM BRAKE

OPERATING PARTS OF DISC BRAKE SYSTEM

Brake fluid reservoir
Master cylinder
Push-rod
Piston
Hydraulic brake fluid
Wheel disc
Calliper assembly
Piston
Brake pad

EXTERIOR OF DRUM BRAKE

Bolt hole
Torque arm
Air cooling scoop
Axle hole
Cooling fin
Speedometer drive
Cable stop
Brake plate
Operating arm

INTERIOR OF DRUM BRAKE

Torque arm
Bolt hole
Brake shoe
Pivot
Brake shoe return spring
Operating cam
Brake shoe return spring
Axle hole
High-friction material

Clutch cable
Hydraulic brake hose
Telescopic fork leg
Fork slide
Light alloy wheel
Axle
Floating disc brake
Brake calliper

SPRING/DAMPER UNIT

Twin rate spring
Rubber mounting bush
Damper rod
Damper body
Pre-load adjustor
Rubber mounting bush

HOW A SPRING/DAMPER UNIT WORKS

Rubber mounting bush
Spring
Damper rod
Non-return valve
Compressible gas
Hydraulic fluid
Hydraulic fluid chamber
Rubber mounting bush

TYPES OF TIRE

RACING SLICK TIRE
No tread pattern

TUBELESS SPORTS TIRE
Radial groove

TRIALS TIRE
Knobby tread pattern

GENERAL-USE TIRE
Hard-wearing rubber compound

Motorcycle engines

MOTORCYCLE ENGINES must be lightweight and compact and have a good power output. They have between one and six cylinders, can be cooled by air or water, and the capacity of the combustion chamber varies from 49cc (cubic centimeters) to 1500cc. Two types of internal combustion engine are common: the four-stroke, which is used in cars (see pp. 342-343), and the two-stroke. A basic two-stroke engine has only three moving parts—the crankshaft, the connecting rod, and the piston—but the power output is high. The engine fires every two strokes (rather than every four), giving a "power stroke" every revolution (see p. 343). Power is conveyed from the engine to the rear wheel by the transmission system. This usually consists of a clutch, a gearbox, and a final drive system. Clutches are multiplate devices, which run in oil. Gearboxes have five or six speeds and are operated by foot pedal. Shaft and belt drive systems are used in some cases, but chain drive to the rear wheel is most common.

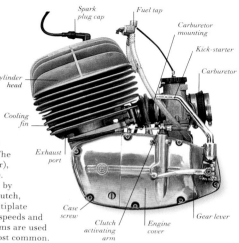

Spark plug cap

Fuel tap

Carburetor mounting

Kick-starter

Carburetor

Cylinder head

Cooling fin

Exhaust port

Case screw

Clutch activating arm

Engine cover

Gear lever

TRANSMISSION SYSTEM

GEARBOX

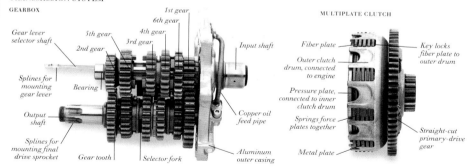

Gear lever selector shaft

5th gear

2nd gear

1st gear

6th gear

4th gear

3rd gear

Input shaft

Splines for mounting gear lever

Bearing

Output shaft

Splines for mounting final drive sprocket

Gear tooth

Selector fork

Copper oil feed pipe

Aluminum outer casing

MULTIPLATE CLUTCH

Fiber plate

Outer clutch drum, connected to engine

Pressure plate, connected to inner clutch drum

Springs force plates together

Metal plate

Key locks fiber plate to outer drum

Straight-cut primary-drive gear

MODERN "O RING" DRIVE CHAIN

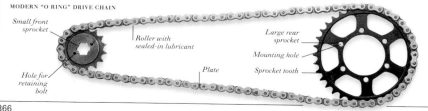

Small front sprocket

Roller with sealed-in lubricant

Large rear sprocket

Mounting hole

Plate

Sprocket tooth

Hole for retaining bolt

**VELOCETTE OVERHEAD
VALVE (OHV) ENGINE**

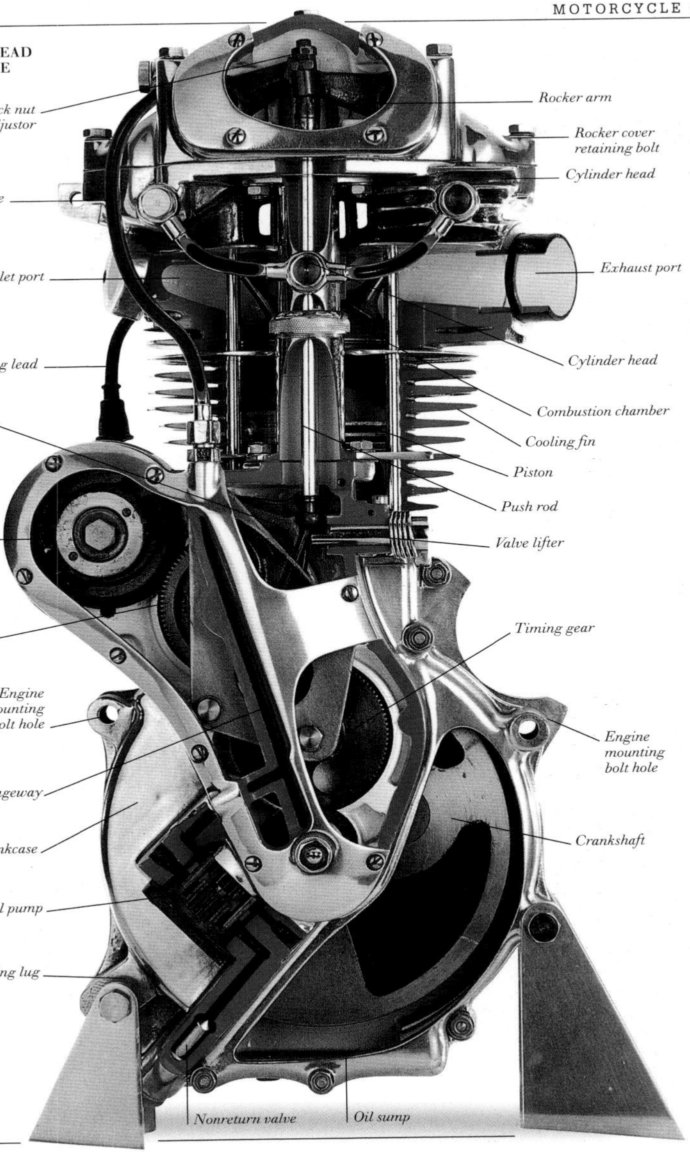

Screw and lock nut
tappet adjustor

Rocker arm

Rocker cover
retaining bolt

Oil feed pipe

Cylinder head

Inlet port

Exhaust port

Spark plug lead

Cylinder head

Combustion chamber

Cam follower

Cooling fin

Piston

Magneto drive

Push rod

Valve lifter

Camshaft gear

Timing gear

Engine
mounting
bolt hole

Engine
mounting
bolt hole

Oil passageway

Crankcase

Crankshaft

Oil pump

Mounting lug

Nonreturn valve

Oil sump

Competition motorcycles

THERE ARE MANY TYPES of motorcycle sport and in each, a specialized machine has evolved to perform to specific requirements. Races take place on roads or tracks or "off-road," in fields, dirt tracks, and even the desert. "Grand Prix" world championships in road-racing are contested by three classes: 125cc; 250cc two-strokes; the top class of 500cc two-strokes; and 900cc four-stroke machines. The latest racing sidecars have more in common with racing cars than motorcycles. The rider and passenger operate within an all-enclosing, aerodynamic fairing. The Suzuki RGV500 shown here, like other Grand Prix machines, carries advertising, which helps to cover the cost of developing motorcycle technology. In Speedway, which originated in the US in 1902, motorcycles operate without brakes or a gearbox. Off-road competition motorcycles have less emphasis on high power output. In Motocross, for example, which is held on rough terrain, they must have high ground clearance, flexible long-travel suspension, and tires with a chunky tread pattern.

1992 HUSQVARNA MOTOCROSS TC610

Throttle cable
Hand protector
Handlebar brace
Radiator air vent
Long seat
Racing number
Flexible plastic fender
Telescopic fork
Light-weight exhaust system
Plastic guard
Axle
Overhead camshaft engine
Gear lever
Knobby tire
Disc brake
Brake calliper
Shock absorber
Alloy swingarm
Shock absorber linkage
Disc brake

1992 SUZUKI RGV500
SIDE VIEW

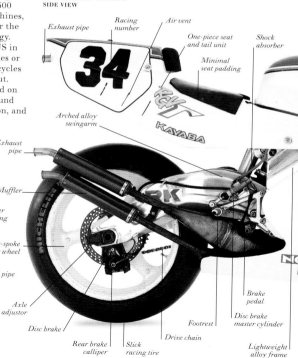

Exhaust pipe
Racing number
Air vent
One-piece seat and tail unit
Shock absorber
Minimal seat padding
Arched alloy swingarm

Exhaust pipe
Vent
Handlebar
Footrest
Rear brake pedal
Drive chain
Wide, slick tire
Exhaust pipe
Muffler
Shock absorber mounting
Three-spoke alloy wheel
Exhaust pipe
Axle adjustor
Disc brake
Rear brake calliper
Slick racing tire
Drive chain
Footrest
Brake pedal
Disc brake master cylinder
Lightweight alloy frame

REAR VIEW

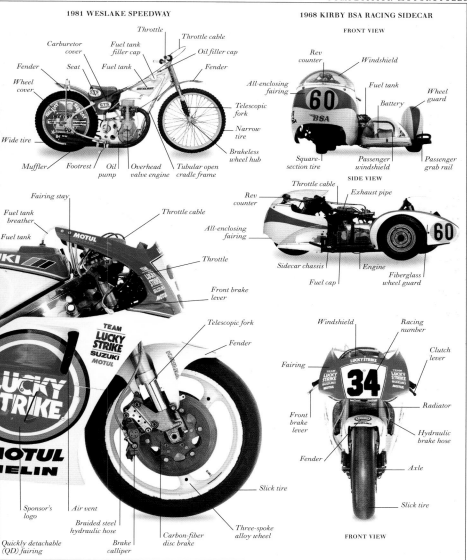

1981 WESLAKE SPEEDWAY

Throttle

Throttle cable

Carburetor cover

Fuel tank filler cap

Oil filler cap

Fender

Seat

Fuel tank

Fender

Wheel cover

Telescopic fork

Wide tire

Narrow tire

Brakeless wheel hub

Muffler

Footrest

Oil pump

Overhead valve engine

Tubular open cradle frame

Fairing stay

Fuel tank breather

Fuel tank

Throttle cable

Throttle

Front brake lever

Telescopic fork

Fender

Sponsor's logo

Air vent

Braided steel hydraulic hose

Brake calliper

Carbon-fiber disc brake

Three-spoke alloy wheel

Slick tire

Quickly detachable (QD) fairing

1968 KIRBY BSA RACING SIDECAR

FRONT VIEW

Rev counter

Windshield

All-enclosing fairing

Fuel tank

Battery

Wheel guard

60

BSA

Square-section tire

Passenger windshield

Passenger grab rail

SIDE VIEW

Throttle cable

Exhaust pipe

Rev counter

All-enclosing fairing

60

Sidecar chassis

Engine

Fiberglass wheel guard

Fuel cap

Windshield

Racing number

Clutch lever

Fairing

34

Radiator

Front brake lever

Hydraulic brake hose

Fender

Axle

Slick tire

FRONT VIEW

369

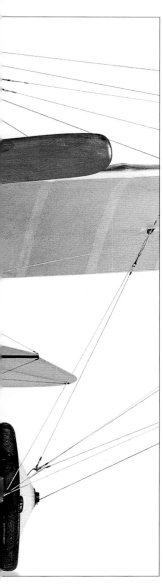

SEA AND AIR

ANCIENT GREEK AND ROMAN SHIPS············372

VIKING SHIPS············374

MEDIEVAL WARSHIPS AND TRADERS············376

THE EXPANSION OF SAIL············378

A SHIP OF THE LINE············380

RIGGING············382

SAILS············384

MOORING AND ANCHORING············386

ROPES AND KNOTS············388

PADDLE WHEELS AND PROPELLERS············390

ANATOMY OF AN IRON SHIP············392

THE BATTLESHIP············394

FRIGATES AND SUBMARINES············396

PIONEERS OF FLIGHT············398

EARLY MONOPLANES············400

BIPLANES AND TRIPLANES············402

WORLD WAR I AIRCRAFT············404

EARLY PASSENGER AIRCRAFT············406

WORLD WAR II AIRCRAFT············408

MODERN PISTON AERO-ENGINES············410

MODERN JETLINERS 1············412

MODERN JETLINERS 2············414

SUPERSONIC JETLINERS············416

JET ENGINES············418

MODERN MILITARY AIRCRAFT············420

HELICOPTERS············422

LIGHT AIRCRAFT············424

GLIDERS, HANG-GLIDERS, AND ULTRALIGHTS···426

Ancient Greek and Roman ships

ROMAN ANCHOR

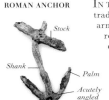

- Stock
- Shank
- Palm
- Acutely angled arm
- Ring
- Crown

IN THE EXPANSIVE EMPIRES OF GREECE AND ROME, powerful fleets were needed for battle, trade, and communication. Greek galleys were powered by a sail and many oars. A new armament, the embolos (ram), was fitted on to the galley bow. Since ramming duels required fast and maneuverable boats, extra rows of oarsmen were added, culminating in the trireme. During the fifth and fourth centuries BC, the trireme dominated the Mediterranean. It was powered by 170 oarsmen, rowing with one oar each. The oarsmen were ranged on three levels, as the model opposite shows. The trireme also carried archers and soldiers for boarding. Galleys were pulled out of the water when not in use, and were kept in dockyard ship-sheds. The merchant ships of the Greeks and Romans were mighty vessels, too. The full-bodied Roman corbita, for example, could hold up to 400 tons (440 metric tons) and carried a cargo of spices, gems, silk, and animals. The construction of these boats was based on a stout hull with planking secured by mortice and tenon. Some of these ships embarked on long voyages, sailing even as far as India. To make them easier to steer, corbitas set a fore sail called an "artemon." It flew from a forward-leaning mast that was a forerunner of the long bowsprits carried by the great clipper ships of the 19th century.

ATTIC VASE SHOWING A GALLEY

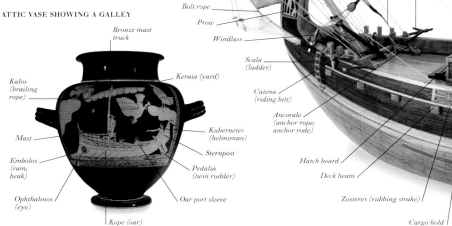

- Double halyard
- Bullseye
- **ROMAN CORBITA**
- Roband (rope band)
- Fore mast
- Ceruchi (lift)
- Heraldic device
- Antenna (yard)
- Buntline
- Ring
- Brace
- Ruden (brail line)
- Artemon (fore sail)
- Fore stay
- Oculus (eye)
- Anchor
- Tabling
- Sheet
- Bolt rope
- Prow
- Windlass
- Scala (ladder)
- Bronze mast truck
- Keraia (yard)
- Catena (riding bitt)
- Kalos (brailing rope)
- Ancorale (anchor rope; anchor rode)
- Kubernetes (helmsman)
- Mast
- Sternpost
- Embolos (ram; beak)
- Pedalia (twin rudder)
- Hatch board
- Deck beam
- Ophthalmos (eye)
- Oar port sleeve
- Zosteres (rubbing strake)
- Kope (oar)
- Cargo hold

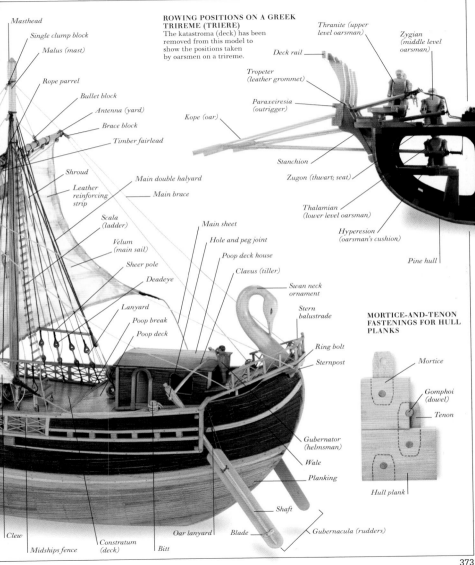

Masthead

Single clump block

Malus (mast)

Rope parrel

Bullet block

Antenna (yard)

Brace block

Timber fairlead

Shroud

Leather reinforcing strip

Main double halyard

Main brace

Scala (ladder)

Velum (main sail)

Sheer pole

Deadeye

Lanyard

Poop break

Poop deck

Clew

Midships fence

Constratum (deck)

Bitt

Oar lanyard

Main sheet

Hole and peg joint

Poop deck house

Clavus (tiller)

Swan neck ornament

Stern balustrade

Ring bolt

Sternpost

Gubernator (helmsman)

Wale

Planking

Shaft

Blade

Gubernacula (rudders)

ROWING POSITIONS ON A GREEK TRIREME (TRIERE)
The katastroma (deck) has been removed from this model to show the positions taken by oarsmen on a trireme.

Thranite (upper level oarsman)

Zygian (middle level oarsman)

Deck rail

Tropeter (leather grommet)

Paraxeiresia (outrigger)

Kope (oar)

Stanchion

Zugon (thwart; seat)

Thalamian (lower level oarsman)

Hyperesion (oarsman's cushion)

Pine hull

MORTICE-AND-TENON FASTENINGS FOR HULL PLANKS

Mortice

Gomphoi (dowel)

Tenon

Hull plank

Viking ships

IN THE DARK AGES and early medieval times, the longships of Scandinavia were one of the most feared sights for people of northern Europe. The Vikings launched raids from Scandinavia every summer in longships equipped with a single steering oar on the right, or "steerboard," side (hence "starboard"). A longship had one row of oars on each side and a single sail. The hull had clinker (overlapping) planks. Prowheads adorned fighting ships during campaigns of war. The sailing longship was also used for local coastal travel. The karv below was probably built as transport for an important family, while the smaller faering (top right) was a rowing boat only. The fleet of William of Normandy that invaded England in 1066 owed much to the Viking boatbuilding tradition, and has been depicted in the Bayeux Tapestry (above). Seals used by port towns and royal courts through the ages provide an excellent record of contemporary ship design. The seal opposite shows how ships changed from the Viking period to the end of the Middle Ages. The introduction of the fighting platform—the castle— and the addition of extra masts and sails changed the character of the medieval ship. Note also that the steering oar has been replaced by a centered rudder.

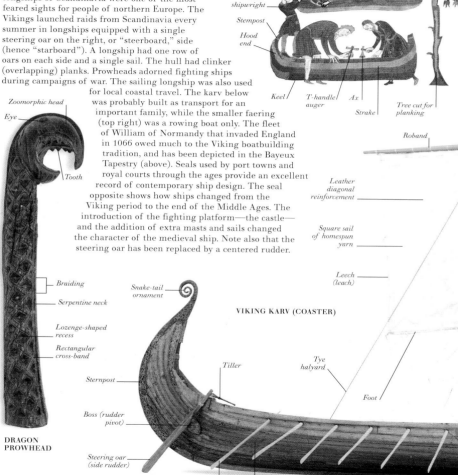

BOATBUILDERS' TOOLS

Shave
Broad ax
Breast auger
Sheer
Master shipwright
Stempost
Hood end
Keel
T-handle auger
Ax
Strake
Tree cut for planking

Roband

Leather diagonal reinforcement

Square sail of homespun yarn

Leech (leach)

VIKING KARV (COASTER)

Snake-tail ornament

Tye halyard

Foot

Tiller

Sternpost

Boss (rudder pivot)

Steering oar (side rudder)

Oar
Starboard (steerboard) side
Keel

Zoomorphic head
Eye
Tooth

Braiding
Serpentine neck
Lozenge-shaped recess
Rectangular cross-band

DRAGON PROWHEAD

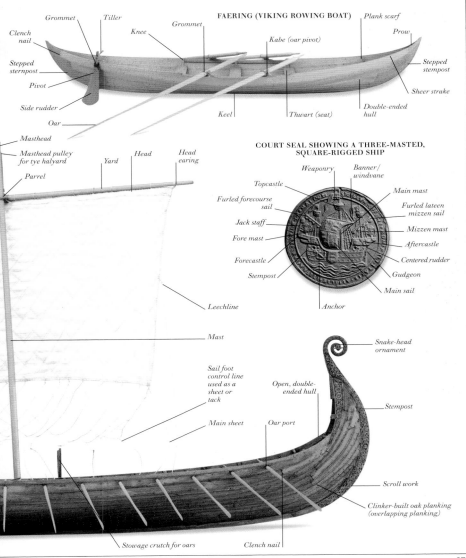

FAERING (VIKING ROWING BOAT)

Grommet

Tiller

Clench nail

Knee

Grommet

Plank scarf

Prow

Stepped sternpost

Kabe (oar pivot)

Stepped stempost

Pivot

Side rudder

Sheer strake

Oar

Keel

Thwart (seat)

Double-ended hull

COURT SEAL SHOWING A THREE-MASTED, SQUARE-RIGGED SHIP

Masthead

Masthead pulley for tye halyard

Parrel

Yard

Head

Head earing

Weaponry

Banner / windvane

Topcastle

Main mast

Furled forecourse sail

Furled lateen mizzen sail

Jack staff

Mizzen mast

Fore mast

Aftercastle

Forecastle

Centered rudder

Stempost

Gudgeon

Main sail

Leechline

Anchor

Mast

Snake-head ornament

Sail foot control line used as a sheet or tack

Open, double-ended hull

Stempost

Main sheet

Oar port

Scroll work

Clinker-built oak planking (overlapping planking)

Stowage crutch for oars

Clench nail

Medieval warships and traders

FROM THE 16TH CENTURY, SHIPS WERE BUILT WITH A NEW FORM OF HULL, constructed from carvel (edge-to-edge) planking. Warships of the time, like King Henry VIII of England's Mary Rose, boasted awesome fire power. This ship carried both long-range cannon in bronze, and short-range, anti personnel guns in iron. Elsewhere, ships took on a multiformity of shapes. Dhows transported slaves from East Africa to Arabia, their fore-and-aft rigged lateen sails allowing them to sail close to the wind around the lands of the Indian Ocean. The Chinese sailed to East Africa and Arabia in junks, trading goods that were carried in watertight compartments. New astronomical tools helped medieval sailors to find their way. Cross-staves and astrolabes were used to measure the altitude of the Sun or stars. One of a choice of four cross-pieces was slid up or down the staff of the cross-stave—which was graduated in degrees of altitude—until its top aligned with the celestial body and its base with the horizon. The sighting rule of the astrolabe was simply lined up with a known body, and its altitude read from marks on the metal disk. With sundials, the sailor could use the shadow of the Sun to show the time of day.

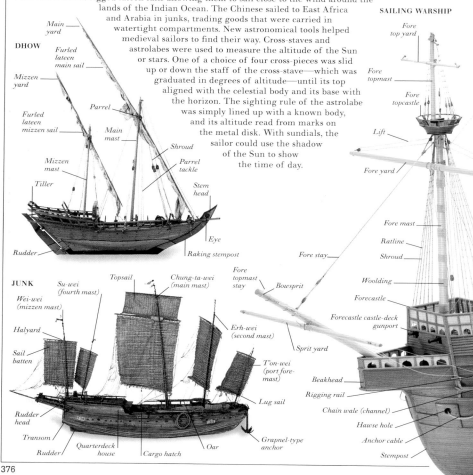

DHOW

Main yard
Furled lateen main sail
Mizzen yard
Furled lateen mizzen sail
Parrel
Main mast
Mizzen mast
Shroud
Parrel tackle
Tiller
Stem head
Rudder
Eye
Raking stempost

JUNK

Su-wei (fourth mast)
Wei-wei (mizzen mast)
Halyard
Sail batten
Topsail
Chung-ta-wei (main mast)
Fore topmast stay
Bowsprit
Erh-wei (second mast)
Sprit yard
T'on-wei (port fore-mast)
Lug sail
Rudder head
Transom
Rudder
Quarterdeck house
Cargo hatch
Oar
Grapnel-type anchor

SAILING WARSHIP

Fore top yard
Fore topmast
Fore topcastle
Lift
Fore yard
Fore mast
Ratline
Shroud
Woolding
Forecastle
Forecastle castle-deck gunport
Beakhead
Rigging rail
Chain wale (channel)
Hawse hole
Anchor cable
Stempost
Fore stay
Fore topmast stay

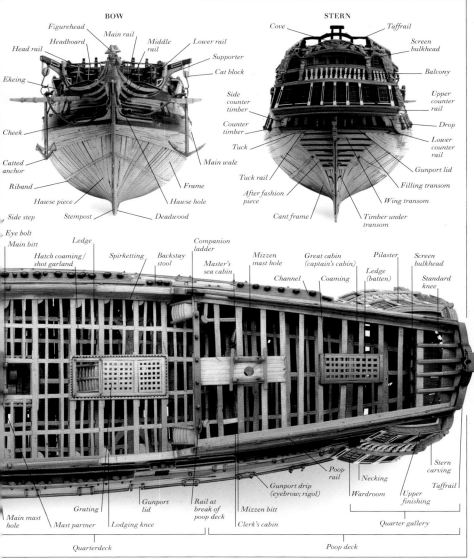

BOW

Figurehead
Main rail
Headboard
Middle rail
Head rail
Lower rail
Supporter
Ekeing
Cat block
Cheek
Catted anchor
Riband
Main wale
Hawse piece
Frame
Side step
Stempost
Hawse hole
Deadwood

STERN

Cove
Taffrail
Screen bulkhead
Balcony
Upper counter rail
Side counter timber
Drop
Counter timber
Lower counter rail
Tuck
Gunport lid
Tuck rail
Filling transom
After fashion piece
Wing transom
Cant frame
Timber under transom

Eye bolt
Main bitt
Ledge
Companion ladder
Pilaster
Hatch coaming / shot garland
Spirketting
Backstay stool
Master's sea cabin
Mizzen mast hole
Great cabin (captain's cabin)
Ledge (batten)
Screen bulkhead
Channel
Coaming
Standard knee

Stern carving
Poop rail
Necking
Taffrail
Main mast hole
Grating
Gunport lid
Rail at break of poop deck
Mizzen bitt
Wardroom
Upper finishing
Mast partner
Lodging knee
Gunport drip (eyebrow; rigol)
Clerk's cabin

Quarterdeck
Poop deck
Quarter gallery

Rigging

MOST SAILING SHIPS HAVE TWO TYPES OF RIGGING. Standing rigging—kept taut by rigging screws or old-fashioned lanyards and deadeyes—refers to the ropes, wires, and chains that support the masts and yards (horizontal spars). Running rigging, which includes types of block and tackle, halyards, and sheets, is used to hoist, lower, or trim sails.

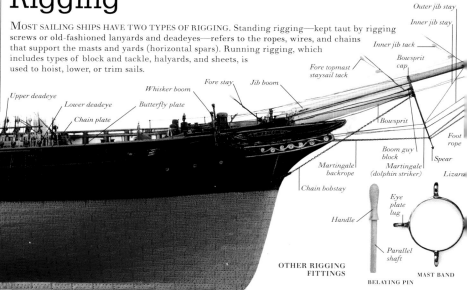

Outer jib stay
Inner jib stay
Inner jib tack
Bowsprit cap
Fore topmast staysail tack
Upper deadeye
Lower deadeye
Butterfly plate
Chain plate
Whisker boom
Fore stay
Jib boom
Fore stay
Jib boom
Bowsprit
Foot rope
Boom guy block
Spear
Martingale backrope
Martingale (dolphin striker)
Lizard
Chain bobstay

OTHER RIGGING FITTINGS

Handle
Eye plate lug
Parallel shaft

BELAYING PIN
MAST BAND

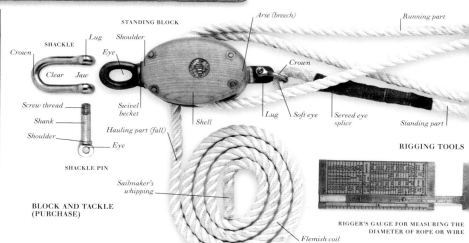

STANDING BLOCK
Arse (breech)
Running part
Lug
Shoulder
Crown
SHACKLE
Eye
Crown
Clear   Jaw
Shoulder
Swivel becket
Lug   Soft eye   Served eye splice
Shell
Standing part
Screw thread
Shank
Shoulder
Eye
Hauling part (fall)
SHACKLE PIN
Sailmaker's whipping

RIGGING TOOLS

BLOCK AND TACKLE
(PURCHASE)

Flemish coil

RIGGER'S GAUGE FOR MEASURING THE
DIAMETER OF ROPE OR WIRE

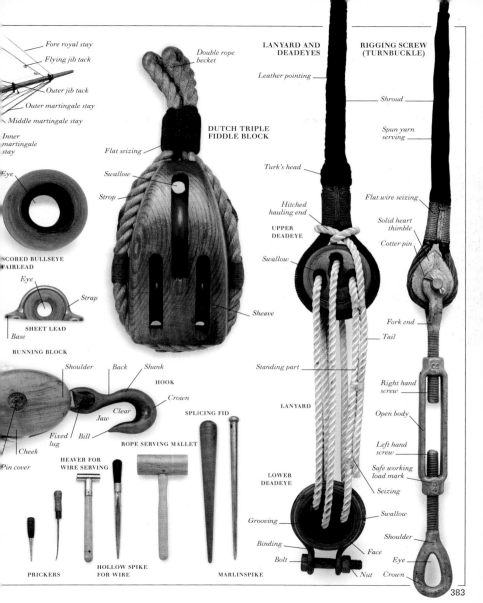

Fore royal stay

Flying jib tack

Outer jib tack

Outer martingale stay

Middle martingale stay

Inner martingale stay

Eye

SCORED BULLSEYE FAIRLEAD

Eye

Strap

SHEET LEAD

Base

RUNNING BLOCK

Cheek

Pin cover

Shoulder   Back   Shank

HOOK

Crown

Clear

Jaw

Fixed   Bill
lug

ROPE SERVING MALLET

HEAVER FOR WIRE SERVING

PRICKERS

HOLLOW SPIKE FOR WIRE

Double rope becket

DUTCH TRIPLE FIDDLE BLOCK

Flat seizing

Swallow

Strop

Sheave

SPLICING FID

MARLINSPIKE

LANYARD AND DEADEYES

Leather pointing

Turk's head

Hitched hauling end

UPPER DEADEYE

Swallow

Standing part

LANYARD

LOWER DEADEYE

Grooving

Binding

Bolt

Sheave

Swallow

Face

Nut

RIGGING SCREW (TURNBUCKLE)

Shroud

Spun yarn serving

Flat wire seizing

Solid heart thimble

Cotter pin

Fork end

Tail

Right hand screw

Open body

Left hand screw

Safe working load mark

Seizing

Swallow

Shoulder

Eye

Crown

Sails

THERE ARE TWO MAIN TYPES OF SAIL, often used in combination. Square sails are driving sails. They are usually attached by parrels to yards, square to the mast to catch the following wind. On fore-and-aft sails, such as lateen and lug sails, the luff (leading edge) usually abuts a mast or a stay. The head of the sail may abut a gaff, and the foot a boom. Around the world, a great range of rigs (sail patterns), such as the ketch, lugger, and schooner, have evolved to suit local needs. Sails are made from strips of cloth, cut to give the sail a belly and strong enough to resist the most violent of winds. Cotton and flax are the traditional sail materials, but synthetic fabrics are now commonly used.

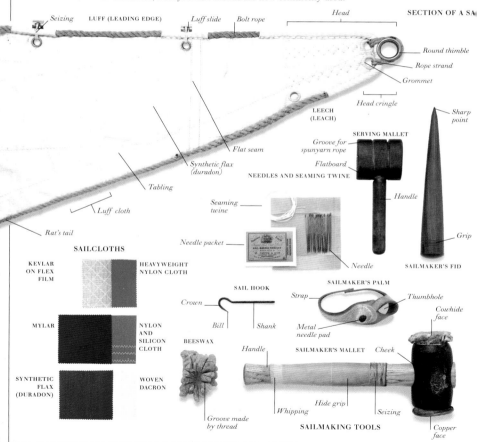

SECTION OF A SAIL

Seizing LUFF (LEADING EDGE) *Luff slide* *Bolt rope* *Head*

Round thimble

Rope strand

Grommet

Head cringle

LEECH (LEACH)

Sharp point

SERVING MALLET

Groove for spunyarn rope

Flatboard

NEEDLES AND SEAMING TWINE

Flat seam

Handle

Synthetic flax (duradon)

Tabling

Seaming twine

Grip

Luff cloth

Needle packet

SAILMAKER'S FID

Rat's tail

Needle

SAILCLOTHS

KEVLAR ON FLEX FILM

HEAVYWEIGHT NYLON CLOTH

SAIL HOOK

SAILMAKER'S PALM

Crown

Strap

Thumbhole

MYLAR

NYLON AND SILICON CLOTH

Bill *Shank*

Metal needle pad

Cowhide face

BEESWAX

Handle

SAILMAKER'S MALLET *Cheek*

SYNTHETIC FLAX (DURADON)

WOVEN DACRON

Groove made by thread

Whipping *Hide grip* *Seizing*

Copper face

SAILMAKING TOOLS

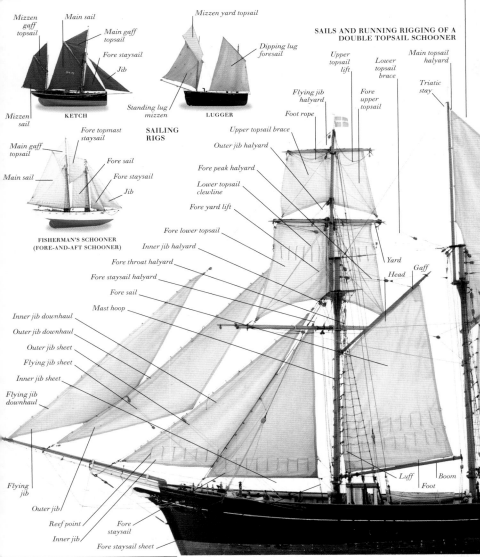

Mizzen gaff topsail

Main sail

Main gaff topsail

Fore staysail

Jib

Mizzen sail

KETCH

Mizzen yard topsail

Dipping lug foresail

Standing lug mizzen

LUGGER

SAILS AND RUNNING RIGGING OF A DOUBLE TOPSAIL SCHOONER

Upper topsail lift

Lower topsail brace

Main topsail halyard

Triatic stay

Flying jib halyard

Fore upper topsail

Foot rope

Upper topsail brace

Outer jib halyard

Fore peak halyard

Lower topsail clewline

Fore yard lift

Fore lower topsail

Inner jib halyard

Yard

Head

Gaff

Fore throat halyard

Fore staysail halyard

Fore sail

Mast hoop

Inner jib downhaul

Outer jib downhaul

Outer jib sheet

Flying jib sheet

Inner jib sheet

Flying jib downhaul

Luff

Boom

Foot

Flying jib

Outer jib

Reef point

Fore staysail

Inner jib

Fore staysail sheet

Main gaff topsail

Fore topmast staysail

Fore sail

Fore staysail

Jib

Main sail

FISHERMAN'S SCHOONER (FORE-AND-AFT SCHOONER)

SAILING RIGS

Mooring and anchoring

For large vessels in open water, anchorage is essential. By holding a ship securely to the seabed, an anchor prevents the vessel from being at the mercy of wave, tide, and current. The earliest anchors were nothing more than stones. In later years, many anchors had a standard design, much like the Admiralty pattern anchor shown on this page. The Danforth anchor is somewhat different. It has particularly deep flukes to give it great holding power. On large sailing ships, anchors were worked by teams of sailors. They turned the drum of a capstan by pushing on bars slotted into the revolving cylinder. This, in turn, lifted or lowered the anchor chain. In calm harbors and estuaries, ships can moor (make fast) without using anchors. Berthing ropes can be attached to bollards both inboard and on the quayside. Berthing ropes are joined to each other by bends, like those opposite.

STONE ANCHOR (KILLICK)

Rope hole

TYPES OF ANCHOR

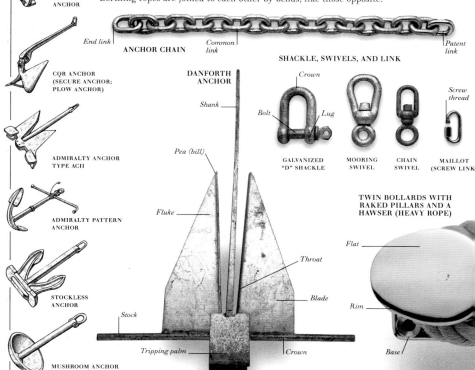

CLOSE-STOWING ANCHOR

CQR ANCHOR (SECURE ANCHOR; PLOW ANCHOR)

ADMIRALTY ANCHOR TYPE ACII

ADMIRALTY PATTERN ANCHOR

STOCKLESS ANCHOR

MUSHROOM ANCHOR (PERMANENT MOORING ANCHOR)

ANCHOR CHAIN

End link

Common link

Patent link

SHACKLE, SWIVELS, AND LINK

DANFORTH ANCHOR

Shank

Pea (bill)

Fluke

Stock

Tripping palm

Crown

Bolt

Lug

GALVANIZED "D" SHACKLE

MOORING SWIVEL

CHAIN SWIVEL

Screw thread

MAILLOT (SCREW LINK)

Throat

Blade

Crown

TWIN BOLLARDS WITH RAKED PILLARS AND A HAWSER (HEAVY ROPE)

Flat

Rim

Base

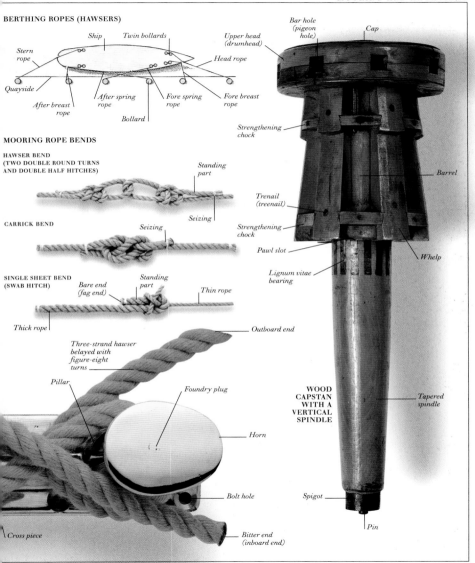

BERTHING ROPES (HAWSERS)

Stern rope

Ship

Twin bollards

Upper head (drumhead)

Head rope

Quayside

After breast rope

After spring rope

Bollard

Fore spring rope

Fore breast rope

MOORING ROPE BENDS

**HAWSER BEND
(TWO DOUBLE ROUND TURNS
AND DOUBLE HALF HITCHES)**

Standing part

Seizing

CARRICK BEND

Seizing

**SINGLE SHEET BEND
(SWAB HITCH)**

Bare end (fag end)

Standing part

Thin rope

Thick rope

Three-strand hawser belayed with figure-eight turns

Pillar

Outboard end

Foundry plug

Horn

Bolt hole

Cross piece

Bitter end (inboard end)

Bar hole (pigeon hole)

Cap

Strengthening chock

Barrel

Trenail (treenail)

Strengthening chock

Pawl slot

Whelp

Lignum vitae bearing

**WOOD
CAPSTAN
WITH A
VERTICAL
SPINDLE**

Tapered spindle

Spigot

Pin

387

Ropes and knots

ALL KINDS OF ROPES ARE USED AT SEA, from thin twines and yarns to thick hawsers. Synthetic fibers have been developed specifically for use at sea. Nylon ropes stretch, and so are ideal for anchoring; polyester (frequently called by the trade name Dacron) has little stretch, so is ideal for halyards and sheets. Different knots have different uses. Knots that join two ropes are called bends; hitches join a rope to another object; and bowlines produce an eye (loop) in the end of a rope. Ropes can be joined by splicing (unraveling the ends and weaving them together) or seizing (lashing the ropes together side by side).

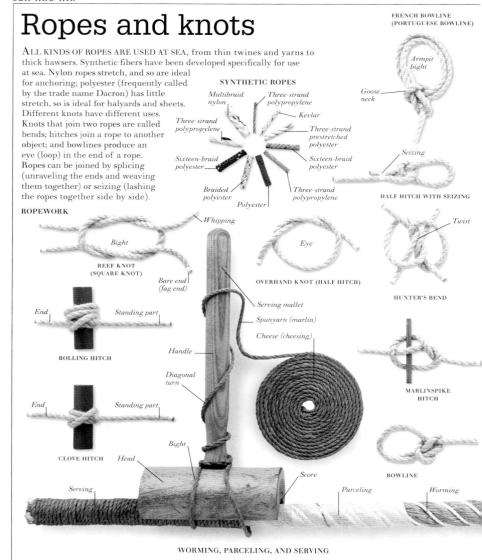

FRENCH BOWLINE (PORTUGUESE BOWLINE)

Armpit bight

Goose neck

Seizing

HALF HITCH WITH SEIZING

SYNTHETIC ROPES

Multibraid nylon

Three-strand polypropylene

Three-strand polypropylene

Kevlar

Three-strand prestretched polyester

Sixteen-braid polyester

Sixteen-braid polyester

Braided polyester

Three-strand polypropylene

Polyester

ROPEWORK

Whipping

Bight

REEF KNOT (SQUARE KNOT)

Bare end (fag end)

Eye

OVERHAND KNOT (HALF HITCH)

Twist

HUNTER'S BEND

End   *Standing part*

ROLLING HITCH

Serving mallet

Spunyarn (marlin)

Cheese (cheesing)

Handle

Diagonal turn

MARLINSPIKE HITCH

End   *Standing part*

CLOVE HITCH   *Head*

Bight

Score

BOWLINE

Serving   *Parceling*   *Worming*

WORMING, PARCELING, AND SERVING

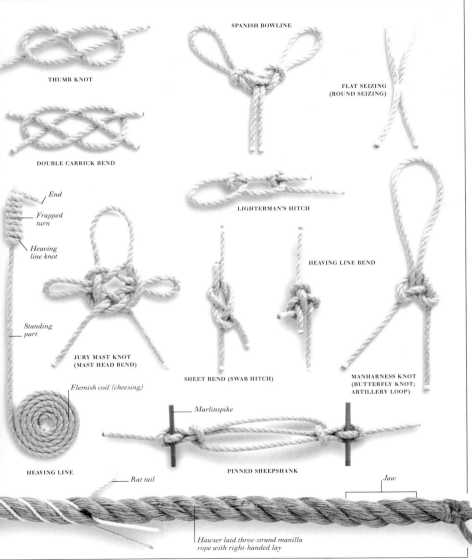

THUMB KNOT

SPANISH BOWLINE

FLAT SEIZING (ROUND SEIZING)

DOUBLE CARRICK BEND

LIGHTERMAN'S HITCH

End

Frapped turn

Heaving line knot

HEAVING LINE BEND

Standing part

JURY MAST KNOT (MAST HEAD BEND)

SHEET BEND (SWAB HITCH)

MANHARNESS KNOT (BUTTERFLY KNOT; ARTILLERY LOOP)

Flemish coil (cheesing)

Marlinspike

Jaw

HEAVING LINE

PINNED SHEEPSHANK

Rat tail

Hawser laid three-strand manilla rope with right-handed lay

Paddle wheels and propellers

THE INVENTION OF THE STEAM ENGINE IN THE 18TH CENTURY made mechanically driven ships fitted with paddle wheels or propellers a viable alternative to sails. Paddle wheels have fixed or feathered floats, and the model shown below features both types. Feathered floats give more propulsive power than fixed floats because they are almost upright at all times in the water. Paddle wheels were superseded by the propeller on oceangoing vessels in the mid-19th century. Propellers are more efficient, work better in rough water, and are less vulnerable in collisions. The first propellers were two-bladed but later three- and four-bladed versions are more powerful; the shape and pitch of blades have also been refined over the years. At the beginning of the 18th century, tillers were superseded on many larger ships by the ship's wheel as a means of steering.

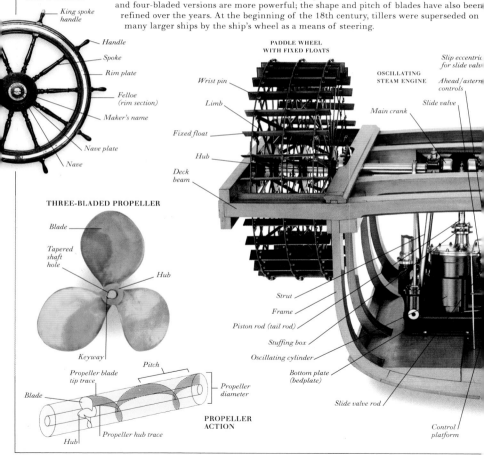

SHIP'S WHEEL

King spoke handle

Handle

Spoke

Rim plate

Felloe (rim section)

Maker's name

Nave plate

Nave

THREE-BLADED PROPELLER

Blade

Tapered shaft hole

Hub

Keyway

Pitch

Propeller blade tip trace

Blade

Hub

Propeller hub trace

Propeller diameter

PROPELLER ACTION

PADDLE WHEEL WITH FIXED FLOATS

Wrist pin

Limb

Fixed float

Hub

Deck beam

OSCILLATING STEAM ENGINE

Slip eccentric for slide valve

Ahead/astern controls

Slide valve

Main crank

Strut

Frame

Piston rod (tail rod)

Stuffing box

Oscillating cylinder

Bottom plate (bedplate)

Slide valve rod

Control platform

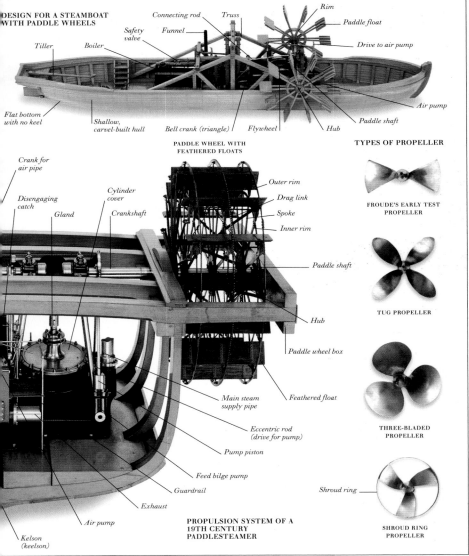

DESIGN FOR A STEAMBOAT WITH PADDLE WHEELS

Connecting rod
Truss
Rim
Paddle float
Safety valve
Funnel
Drive to air pump
Tiller
Boiler
Flat bottom with no keel
Shallow, carvel-built hull
Bell crank (triangle)
Flywheel
Hub
Paddle shaft
Air pump

PADDLE WHEEL WITH FEATHERED FLOATS

Crank for air pipe
Outer rim
Disengaging catch
Drag link
Cylinder cover
Gland
Spoke
Crankshaft
Inner rim
Paddle shaft
Hub
Paddle wheel box
Main steam supply pipe
Feathered float
Eccentric rod (drive for pump)
Pump piston
Feed bilge pump
Guardrail
Exhaust
Air pump
Kelson (keelson)

PROPULSION SYSTEM OF A 19TH CENTURY PADDLESTEAMER

TYPES OF PROPELLER

FROUDE'S EARLY TEST PROPELLER

TUG PROPELLER

THREE-BLADED PROPELLER

Shroud ring

SHROUD RING PROPELLER

Anatomy of an iron ship

IRON PARTS WERE USED IN THE HULLS OF WOODEN SHIPS AS EARLY AS 1675, often in the same form as the wooden parts that they replaced. Eventually, as on the tea clipper Cutty Sark (below), iron rigging was found to be stronger than the traditional rope. The first "ironclads" were warships whose wooden hulls were protected by iron armor plates. Later ironclads actually had iron hulls. The model opposite is based on the British warship HMS Warrior, launched in 1860, the first battleship built entirely of iron. The plan of the iron paddlesteamer (bottom), built somewhat later, shows that this vessel was a sailing ship; but it also boasted a steam propulsion plant amidships that turned two side paddlewheels. Early iron hulls were made from plates that were painstakingly riveted together (as below), but by the 20th century vessels began to be welded together, **TEA** whole sections at a time. The Second World War **CLIPPER** "liberty ship" was one of the first of these "production-line vessels."

Steel yard
Iron wire stay
Steel lower mast
Steel bowsprit
Wooden planking with copper sheathing
Forged iron anchor

RIVETTED PLATES

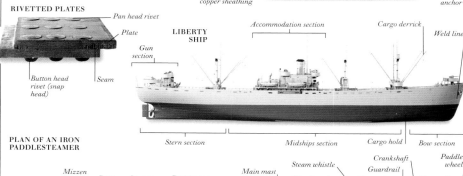

Pan head rivet
Plate
Button head rivet (snap head)
Seam

Gun section
LIBERTY SHIP
Accommodation section
Cargo derrick
Weld line

PLAN OF AN IRON PADDLESTEAMER

Stern section
Midships section
Cargo hold
Bow section

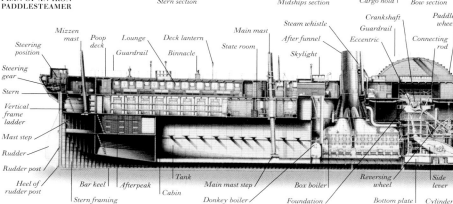

Steering position
Steering gear
Stern
Vertical frame ladder
Mast step
Rudder
Rudder post
Heel of rudder post
Bar keel
Afterpeak
Cabin
Stern framing
Mizzen mast
Poop deck
Guardrail
Lounge
Deck lantern
Binnacle
Tank
Main mast step
Donkey boiler
Main mast
State room
Steam whistle
After funnel
Skylight
Box boiler
Foundation
Crankshaft
Guardrail
Eccentric
Reversing wheel
Bottom plate
Paddle wheel
Connecting rod
Side lever
Cylinder

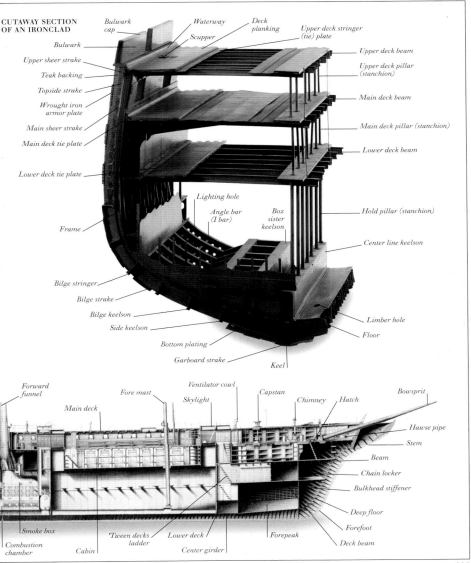

CUTAWAY SECTION OF AN IRONCLAD

Bulwark cap
Waterway
Scupper
Deck planking
Upper deck stringer (tie) plate
Bulwark
Upper deck beam
Upper sheer strake
Upper deck pillar (stanchion)
Teak backing
Topside strake
Main deck beam
Wrought iron armor plate
Main sheer strake
Main deck pillar (stanchion)
Main deck tie plate
Lower deck beam
Lower deck tie plate
Lighting hole
Angle bar (I bar)
Box sister keelson
Hold pillar (stanchion)
Frame
Center line keelson
Bilge stringer
Bilge strake
Bilge keelson
Side keelson
Limber hole
Bottom plating
Floor
Garboard strake
Keel

Forward funnel
Ventilator cowl
Main deck
Fore mast
Skylight
Capstan
Chimney
Hatch
Bowsprit
Hawse pipe
Stem
Beam
Chain locker
Bulkhead stiffener
Deep floor
Forefoot
Smoke box
'Tween decks ladder
Lower deck
Forepeak
Deck beam
Combustion chamber
Cabin
Center girder

The battleship

IN THE EARLY YEARS OF THE 20TH CENTURY, sea warfare—
attacking enemy vessels or defending a ship—was
revolutionized by the introduction of Dreadnought-type
battleships like the Brazilian vessel below. These new
ships combined the latest advances in steam
propulsion, gunnery, and armor plating. The gun
turret was designed to fire shells over huge distances.
It was protected by armor 12 in (30 cm) thick. The
measurements given for the guns of this ship refer
to the bore diameter. Where "weight" is quoted, this
is the weight of the shell that the gun fires. Torpedoes—
as portrayed on the upper cigarette card (right)—were
self-propelled underwater missiles, often steered by gyro-
control. Depth charges were designed in the First World
War for use against submerged U-boats. They are
canisters filled with explosives that are detonated
by depth-sensitive pistols. The lower cigarette
card shows depth charges being fired by
a "thrower," fired from a torpedo tube,
and rolled from the stern. Ship's shields
were fitted to warships from the late
19th century onward. The shield
shown opposite depicts a
traditional ship's cannon.

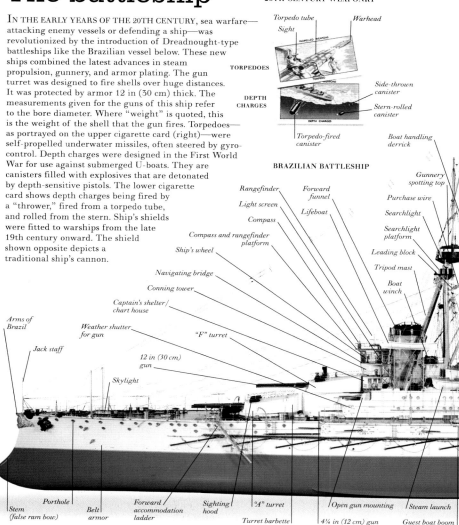

20TH CENTURY WEAPONRY

Torpedo tube   Warhead
Sight

TORPEDOES

DEPTH
CHARGES

Side-thrown
canister

Stern-rolled
canister

Torpedo-fired
canister

Boat handling
derrick

BRAZILIAN BATTLESHIP

Rangefinder   Forward
funnel

Gunnery
spotting top

Light screen   Lifeboat

Purchase wire

Compass

Searchlight

Compass and rangefinder
platform

Searchlight
platform

Ship's wheel

Leading block

Navigating bridge

Tripod mast

Conning tower

Boat
winch

Captain's shelter /
chart house

Arms of
Brazil

Weather shutter
for gun

"F" turret

Jack staff

12 in (30 cm)
gun

Skylight

Stem
(false ram bow)

Porthole

Belt
armor

Forward
accommodation
ladder

Sighting
hood

"A" turret

Open gun mounting

Steam launch

Turret barbette

4¼ in (12 cm) gun

Guest boat boom

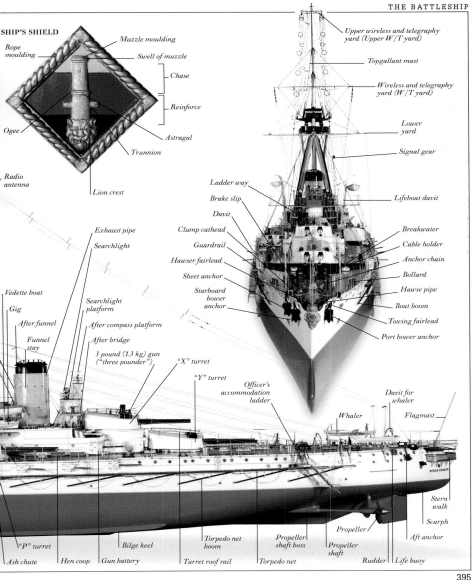

SHIP'S SHIELD

Rope moulding

Muzzle moulding

Swell of muzzle

Chase

Reinforce

Ogee

Astragal

Trunnion

Lion crest

Radio antenna

Upper wireless and telegraphy yard (Upper W/T yard)

Topgallant mast

Wireless and telegraphy yard (W/T yard)

Lower yard

Signal gear

Ladder way

Brake slip

Davit

Clump cathead

Guardrail

Hawser fairlead

Sheet anchor

Starboard bower anchor

Lifeboat davit

Breakwater

Cable holder

Anchor chain

Bollard

Hawse pipe

Boat boom

Towing fairlead

Port bower anchor

Exhaust pipe

Searchlight

Vedette boat

Gig

After funnel

Funnel stay

Searchlight platform

After compass platform

After bridge

3 pound (1.3 kg) gun ("three pounder")

"X" turret

"Y" turret

Officer's accommodation ladder

Davit for whaler

Whaler

Flagmast

Stern walk

Scarph

Aft anchor

"P" turret

Ash chute

Hen coop

Gun battery

Bilge keel

Torpedo net boom

Turret roof rail

Propeller shaft boss

Torpedo net

Propeller shaft

Propeller

Rudder

Life buoy

395

Frigates and submarines

Fʀᴏᴍ ᴛʜᴇ ᴍɪᴅ-19ᴛʜ ᴄᴇɴᴛᴜʀʏ, ᴀʀᴍᴏʀᴇᴅ ꜱʜɪᴘꜱ provided a new challenge to enemy craft. In response, huge revolving gun turrets were developed. These could fire in any direction, could be loaded from the breech very rapidly, and, instead of cannonballs, they discharged exploding shells. Modern fighting ships, like the frigate, combine heavy ship-borne armament with light helicopter weaponry. Submarines function below the surface of the sea. Their speed and ability to fire missiles from under water are their major assets. The nuclear submarine can stay under water for several years without refueling.

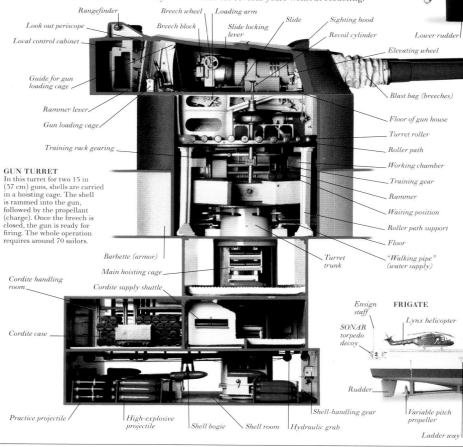

Stabilizer fin
Aft hydroplane
Propeller
Lower rudder

Rangefinder
Look out periscope
Local control cabinet
Breech wheel
Breech block
Loading arm
Slide locking lever
Slide
Sighting hood
Recoil cylinder
Elevating wheel
Guide for gun loading cage
Blast bag (breeches)
Rammer lever
Gun loading cage
Floor of gun house
Training rack gearing
Turret roller
Roller path
Working chamber
Training gear
Rammer
Waiting position
Roller path support
Floor
"Walking pipe" (water supply)

GUN TURRET
In this turret for two 15 in (37 cm) guns, shells are carried in a hoisting cage. The shell is rammed into the gun, followed by the propellant (charge). Once the breech is closed, the gun is ready for firing. The whole operation requires around 70 sailors.

Barbette (armor)
Main hoisting cage
Cordite handling room
Cordite supply shuttle
Turret trunk

Cordite case

Ensign staff
FRIGATE
Lynx helicopter
SONAR torpedo decoy

Rudder
Variable pitch propeller
Ladder way

Practice projectile
High-explosive projectile
Shell bogie
Shell room
Hydraulic grab
Shell-handling gear

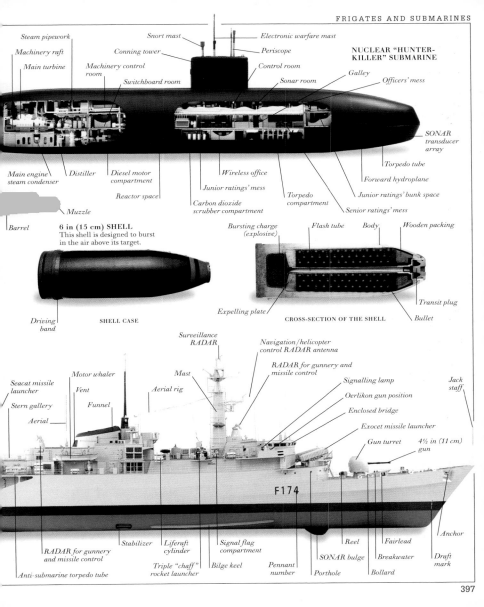

NUCLEAR "HUNTER-KILLER" SUBMARINE

Steam pipework
Machinery raft
Main turbine
Conning tower
Machinery control room
Switchboard room
Snort mast
Electronic warfare mast
Periscope
Control room
Sonar room
Galley
Officers' mess
SONAR transducer array
Torpedo tube
Forward hydroplane
Junior ratings' bunk space
Senior ratings' mess
Main engine steam condenser
Distiller
Diesel motor compartment
Reactor space
Wireless office
Junior ratings' mess
Torpedo compartment
Carbon dioxide scrubber compartment
Muzzle
Barrel

6 in (15 cm) SHELL
This shell is designed to burst in the air above its target.

Driving band
SHELL CASE

Bursting charge (explosive)
Flash tube
Body
Wooden packing
Expelling plate
Transit plug
Bullet
CROSS-SECTION OF THE SHELL

Seacat missile launcher
Stern gallery
Aerial
Motor whaler
Vent
Funnel
Surveillance RADAR
Mast
Aerial rig
Navigation/helicopter control RADAR antenna
RADAR for gunnery and missile control
Signalling lamp
Oerlikon gun position
Enclosed bridge
Exocet missile launcher
Gun turret
4½ in (11 cm) gun
Jack staff

F174

RADAR for gunnery and missile control
Anti-submarine torpedo tube
Stabilizer
Liferaft cylinder
Triple "chaff" rocket launcher
Signal flag compartment
Bilge keel
Pennant number
Porthole
SONAR bulge
Reel
Bollard
Breakwater
Fairlead
Anchor
Draft mark

Pioneers of flight

FLIGHT HAS FASCINATED MANKIND for centuries, and countless unsuccessful flying machines have been designed. The first successful flight was made by the French Montgolfier brothers in 1783, when they flew a balloon over Paris. The next major advance was the development of gliders, notably by the Englishman Sir George Cayley, who in 1845 designed the first glider to make a sustained flight, and by the German Otto Lilienthal, who became known as the world's first pilot because he managed to achieve controlled flights. However, powered flight did not become a practical possibility until the invention of lightweight, gas-driven internal combustion engines at the end of the 19th century. Then, in 1903, the American brothers Orville and Wilbur Wright made the first powered flight in their Wright Flyer biplane, which used a four-cylinder, gas-driven engine. Aircraft design advanced rapidly, and in 1909 the Frenchman Louis Blériot made his pioneering flight across the English Channel (see pp. 400-401). The American Glenn Curtiss also achieved several "firsts" in his Model-D Pusher and its variants, most notably winning the world's first competition for airspeed at Reims in 1909.

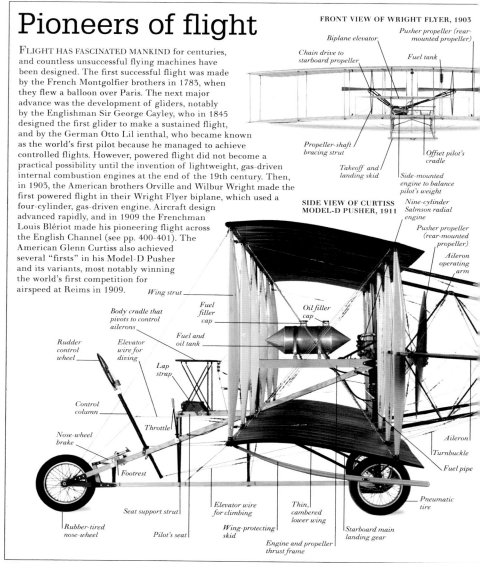

FRONT VIEW OF WRIGHT FLYER, 1903

Pusher propeller (rear-mounted propeller)

Biplane elevator

Chain drive to starboard propeller

Fuel tank

Propeller-shaft bracing strut

Offset pilot's cradle

Takeoff and landing skid

Side-mounted engine to balance pilot's weight

SIDE VIEW OF CURTISS MODEL-D PUSHER, 1911

Nine-cylinder Salmson radial engine

Pusher propeller (rear-mounted propeller)

Aileron operating arm

Wing strut

Body cradle that pivots to control ailerons

Fuel filler cap

Oil filler cap

Fuel and oil tank

Rudder control wheel

Elevator wire for diving

Lap strap

Control column

Throttle

Nose-wheel brake

Footrest

Aileron

Turnbuckle

Fuel pipe

Pneumatic tire

Rubber-tired nose-wheel

Seat support strut

Pilot's seat

Elevator wire for climbing

Wing-protecting skid

Thin, cambered lower wing

Engine and propeller thrust frame

Starboard main landing gear

SIDE VIEW OF WRIGHT FLYER, 1903

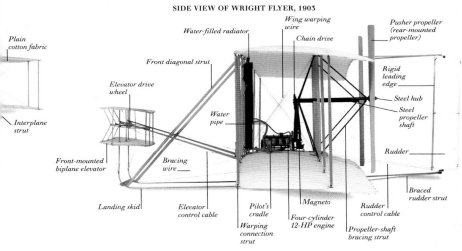

Plain cotton fabric

Interplane strut

Wing warping wire

Water-filled radiator

Chain drive

Pusher propeller (rear-mounted propeller)

Front diagonal strut

Rigid leading edge

Elevator drive wheel

Steel hub

Steel propeller shaft

Water pipe

Front-mounted biplane elevator

Rudder

Bracing wire

Landing skid

Elevator control cable

Warping connection strut

Pilot's cradle

Magneto

Four-cylinder 12-HP engine

Rudder control cable

Braced rudder strut

Propeller-shaft bracing strut

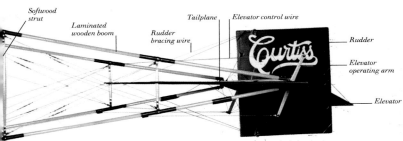

Softwood strut

Laminated wooden boom

Tailplane

Elevator control wire

Rudder bracing wire

Curtiss

Rudder

Elevator operating arm

Elevator

FRONT VIEW OF CURTISS MODEL-D PUSHER, 1911

Rudder control wheel

Anti-lift wire

Fuel and oil tank

Nine-cylinder Salmson radial engine

Elevator operating arm

Aileron operating arm

Starboard aileron

Carved interplane strut

Port aileron

Wing-protecting skid

Wing-protecting skid

Lift wire

Control column

Seat beam

Footrest

Axle

Main landing gear lateral brace

Tubular steel leg

Interplane strut pin-jointed to front spar

Early monoplanes

RUMPLER MONOPLANE, 1908

MONOPLANES HAVE ONE WING on each side of the fuselage. The principal disadvantage of this arrangement in early, wooden-framed aircraft was that single wings were weak and required strong wires to brace them to king posts above and below the fuselage. However, single wings also had advantages: they experienced less drag than multiple wings, allowing greater speed; they also made aircraft more manoeuvrable because single wings were easier to warp (twist) than double wings, and warping the wings was how pilots controlled the roll of early aircraft. By 1912, the French pilot Louis Blériot had used a monoplane to make the first flight across the English Channel, and the Briton Robert Blackburn and the Frenchman Armand Deperdussin had proved the greater speed of monoplanes. However, a spate of crashes caused by broken wings discouraged monoplane production, except in Germany, where all-metal monoplanes were developed in 1917. The wings of all-metal monoplanes did not need strengthening by struts or bracing wires, but despite this, such planes were not widely adopted until the 1930s.

FRONT VIEW OF BLACKBURN MONOPLANE, 1912

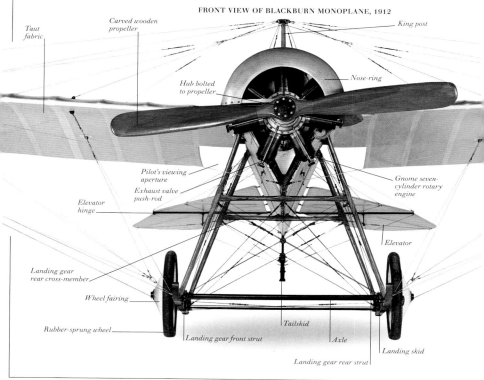

Taut fabric

Carved wooden propeller

King post

Hub bolted to propeller

Nose-ring

Pilot's viewing aperture

Gnome seven-cylinder rotary engine

Exhaust valve push-rod

Elevator hinge

Elevator

Landing gear rear cross-member

Wheel fairing

Rubber-sprung wheel

Tailskid

Landing gear front strut

Axle

Landing skid

Landing gear rear strut

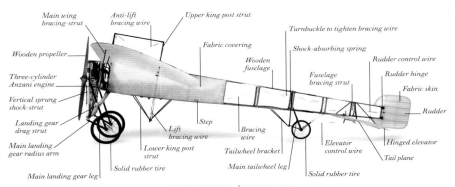

Main wing bracing-strut

Anti-lift bracing wire

Upper king post strut

Wooden propeller

Fabric covering

Turnbuckle to tighten bracing wire

Shock-absorbing spring

Wooden fuselage

Three-cylinder Anzani engine

Rudder control wire

Rudder hinge

Fuselage bracing strut

Fabric skin

Vertical sprung shock-strut

Landing gear drag strut

Rudder

Main landing gear radius arm

Step

Lift bracing wire

Lower king post strut

Bracing wire

Tailwheel bracket

Elevator control wire

Hinged elevator

Main landing gear leg

Solid rubber tire

Main tailwheel leg

Tail plane

Solid rubber tire

SIDE VIEW OF BLÉRIOT XI, 1909

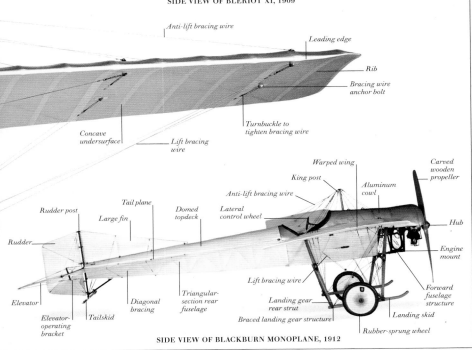

Anti-lift bracing wire

Leading edge

Rib

Bracing wire anchor bolt

Concave undersurface

Lift bracing wire

Turnbuckle to tighten bracing wire

Warped wing

Carved wooden propeller

King post

Aluminum cowl

Rudder post

Anti-lift bracing wire

Lateral control wheel

Tail plane

Large fin

Domed topdeck

Hub

Rudder

Engine mount

Lift bracing wire

Elevator

Diagonal bracing

Triangular-section rear fuselage

Landing gear rear strut

Forward fuselage structure

Elevator-operating bracket

Tailskid

Braced landing gear structure

Landing skid

Rubber-sprung wheel

SIDE VIEW OF BLACKBURN MONOPLANE, 1912

Biplanes and triplanes

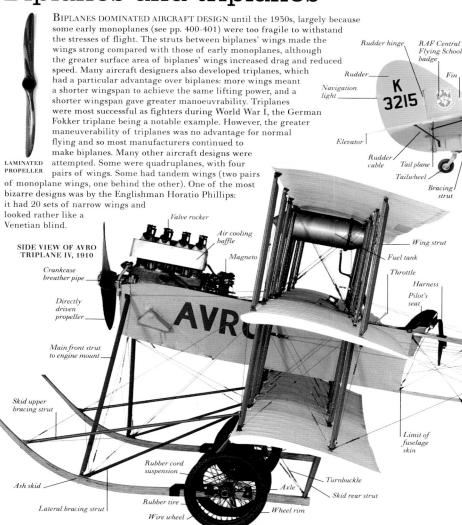

BIPLANES DOMINATED AIRCRAFT DESIGN until the 1930s, largely because some early monoplanes (see pp. 400-401) were too fragile to withstand the stresses of flight. The struts between biplanes' wings made the wings strong compared with those of early monoplanes, although the greater surface area of biplanes' wings increased drag and reduced speed. Many aircraft designers also developed triplanes, which had a particular advantage over biplanes: more wings meant a shorter wingspan to achieve the same lifting power, and a shorter wingspan gave greater manoeuvrability. Triplanes were most successful as fighters during World War I, the German Fokker triplane being a notable example. However, the greater maneuverability of triplanes was no advantage for normal flying and so most manufacturers continued to make biplanes. Many other aircraft designs were attempted. Some were quadruplanes, with four pairs of wings. Some had tandem wings (two pairs of monoplane wings, one behind the other). One of the most bizarre designs was by the Englishman Horatio Phillips: it had 20 sets of narrow wings and looked rather like a Venetian blind.

LAMINATED PROPELLER

Rudder hinge

RAF Central Flying School badge

Rudder

Fin

Navigation light

K 3215

Elevator

Rudder cable

Tail plane

Tailwheel

Bracing strut

SIDE VIEW OF AVRO TRIPLANE IV, 1910

Valve rocker

Air cooling baffle

Magneto

Wing strut

Fuel tank

Throttle

Harness

Pilot's seat

Crankcase breather pipe

Directly driven propeller

AVRO

Main front strut to engine mount

Skid upper bracing strut

Limit of fuselage skin

Ash skid

Rubber cord suspension

Axle

Turnbuckle

Skid rear strut

Lateral bracing strut

Rubber tire

Wheel rim

Wire wheel

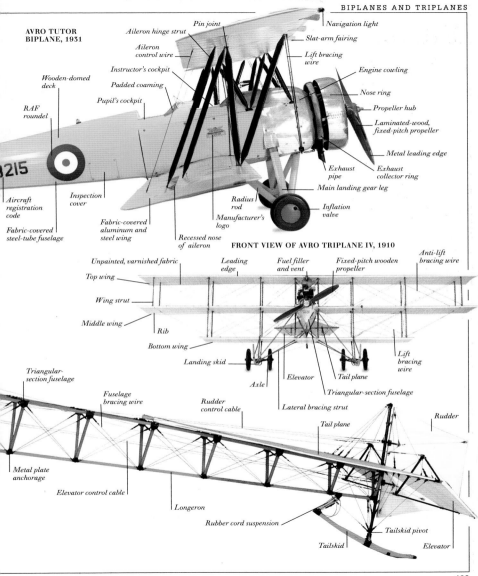

AVRO TUTOR BIPLANE, 1931

Aileron hinge strut

Pin joint

Navigation light

Slat-arm fairing

Aileron control wire

Lift bracing wire

Instructor's cockpit

Engine cowling

Wooden-domed deck

Padded coaming

Nose ring

RAF roundel

Pupil's cockpit

Propeller hub

Laminated-wood, fixed-pitch propeller

Metal leading edge

3215

Exhaust pipe

Exhaust collector ring

Main landing gear leg

Aircraft registration code

Inspection cover

Radius rod

Inflation valve

Fabric-covered steel-tube fuselage

Fabric-covered aluminum and steel wing

Manufacturer's logo

Recessed nose of aileron

FRONT VIEW OF AVRO TRIPLANE IV, 1910

Unpainted, varnished fabric

Leading edge

Fuel filler and vent

Fixed-pitch wooden propeller

Anti-lift bracing wire

Top wing

Wing strut

Middle wing

Rib

Bottom wing

Landing skid

Lift bracing wire

Axle

Elevator

Tail plane

Triangular-section fuselage

Fuselage bracing wire

Rudder control cable

Triangular-section fuselage

Tail plane

Rudder

Metal plate anchorage

Lateral bracing strut

Elevator control cable

Longeron

Rubber cord suspension

Tailskid pivot

Elevator

Tailskid

403

World War I aircraft

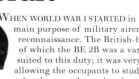

FLYING HELMET

WHEN WORLD WAR I STARTED in 1914, the main purpose of military aircraft was reconnaissance. The British-built BE 2, of which the BE 2B was a variant, was well-suited to this duty; it was very stable in flight, allowing the occupants to study the terrain, take photographs, and make notes. The BE 2 was also one of the first aircraft to drop bombs. One of the biggest problems for aircraft designers during the war was mounting machine-guns. On aircraft that had front-mounted propellers, the field of fire was restricted by the propeller and other parts of the aircraft. The problem was solved in 1915 by the Dutchman Anthony Fokker, who designed an interrupter gear that prevented a machine-gun from firing when a propeller blade passed in front of the barrel. The German LVG CVI had a forward-firing gun to the right of the engine, as well as a rear-cockpit gun, and a bombing capability. It was one of the most versatile aircraft of the war.

PORT WINGS FROM A BE 2B

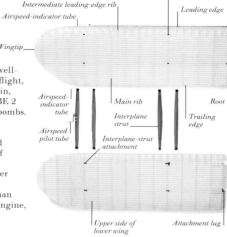

Interplane-strut attachment
Intermediate leading-edge rib
Airspeed-indicator tube
Leading edge
Wingtip
Airspeed-indicator tube
Main rib
Root
Interplane strut
Trailing edge
Airspeed pilot tube
Interplane-strut attachment
Upper side of lower wing
Attachment lug

BE 2B, 1914

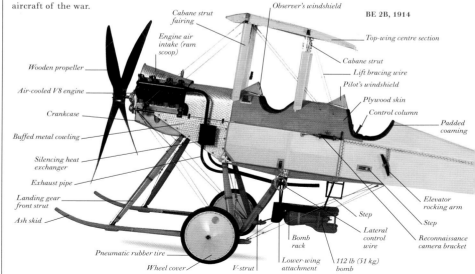

Cabane strut fairing
Observer's windshield
Engine air intake (ram scoop)
Top-wing centre section
Cabane strut
Wooden propeller
Lift bracing wire
Air-cooled V8 engine
Pilot's windshield
Plywood skin
Crankcase
Control column
Buffed metal cowling
Padded coaming
Silencing heat exchanger
Exhaust pipe
Landing gear front strut
Elevator rocking arm
Ash skid
Step
Step
Lateral control wire
Reconnaissance camera bracket
Pneumatic rubber tire
Bomb rack
Wheel cover
V-strut
Lower-wing attachment
112 lb (51 kg) bomb

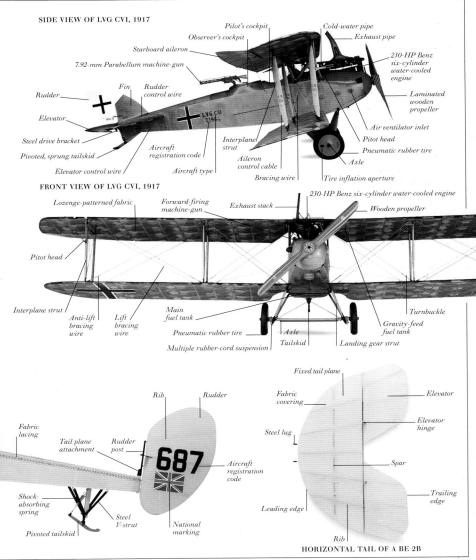

SIDE VIEW OF LVG CVI, 1917

Pilot's cockpit

Observer's cockpit

Starboard aileron

Cold-water pipe

Exhaust pipe

7.92-mm Parabellum machine-gun

230-HP Benz six-cylinder water-cooled engine

Rudder

Fin

Rudder control wire

Elevator

Laminated wooden propeller

Steel drive bracket

Air ventilator inlet

Pivoted, sprung tailskid

Aircraft registration code

Interplane strut

Pitot head

Pneumatic rubber tire

Elevator control wire

Aircraft type

Aileron control cable

Axle

Bracing wire

Tire inflation aperture

FRONT VIEW OF LVG CVI, 1917

Lozenge-patterned fabric

Forward-firing machine-gun

Exhaust stack

230-HP Benz six-cylinder water-cooled engine

Wooden propeller

Pitot head

Interplane strut

Anti-lift bracing wire

Lift bracing wire

Main fuel tank

Turnbuckle

Gravity-feed fuel tank

Pneumatic rubber tire

Axle

Tailskid

Landing gear strut

Multiple rubber-cord suspension

Fabric lacing

Rib

Rudder

Fixed tail plane

Fabric covering

Elevator

Tail plane attachment

Rudder post

Elevator hinge

Steel lug

687

Aircraft registration code

Spar

Shock-absorbing spring

Steel V-strut

Trailing edge

Pivoted tailskid

National marking

Leading edge

Rib

HORIZONTAL TAIL OF A BE 2B

Early passenger aircraft

UNTIL THE 1930s, most passenger aircraft were biplanes, with two pairs of wings and a wooden or metal framework covered with fabric or, sometimes, plywood. Such aircraft were restricted to low speeds and low altitudes because of the drag on their wings. Many had an open cockpit, situated behind or in front of an enclosed—but unpressurized—cabin that carried a maximum of 10 people. The passengers usually sat in wicker chairs that were not bolted to the floor, and the journey could be bumpy when flying through turbulence. Warm clothing, and ear plugs to reduce the effects of prolonged noise, were often required. During the 1930s, powerful, streamlined, all-metal monoplanes, such as the Lockheed Electra shown here, became widespread. By 1939, the advent of pressurized cabins allowed fast flights at high altitudes, where there is less turbulence.

Flying boats were still necessary on many routes until 1945 because of inadequate runways and the frequency of emergency sea landings. World War II, however, resulted in enough good runways being built for land-planes to become standard on all major airline routes.

Green starboard navigation light

Flush-riveted metal-skinned wing

Leading edge

Fuel-jettison valve

Static discharge wick

Split flap in landing position

Roof trim panel

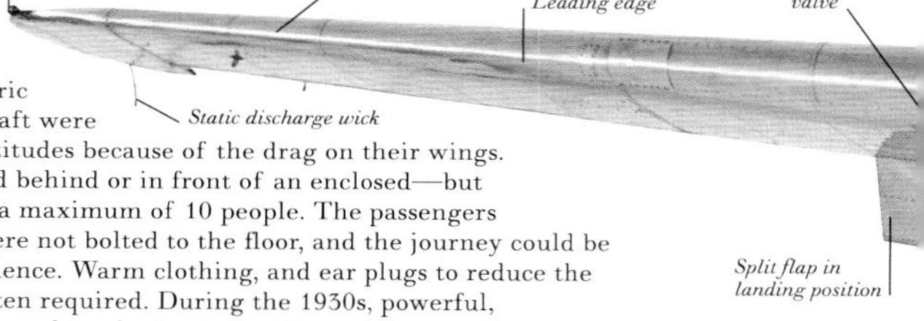

PASSENGER CABIN TRIM PANELS

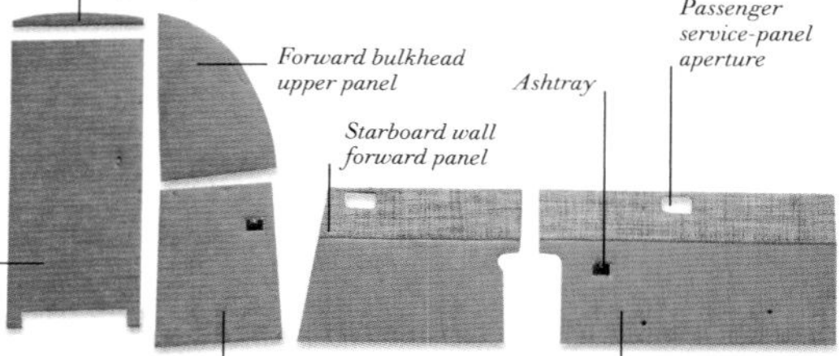

Passenger service-panel aperture

Forward bulkhead upper panel

Ashtray

Starboard wall forward panel

Cockpit door panel

Forward bulkhead lower panel

Starboard wall mid-forward panel

SIDE VIEW OF LOCKHEED ELECTRA, 1934

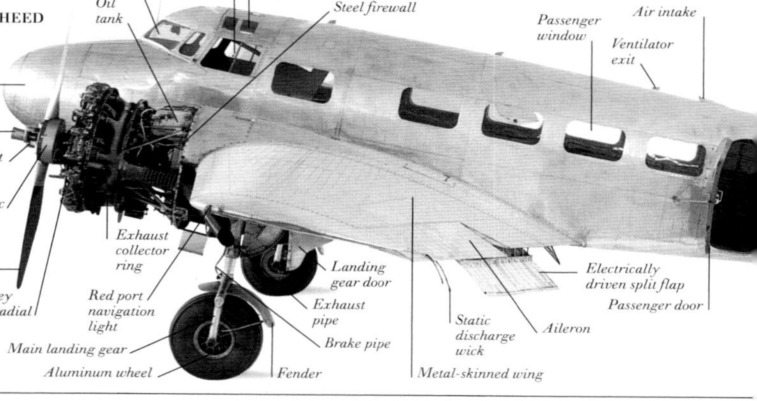

Cockpit windshield

Sliding window

Emergency escape hatch

Steel firewall

Air intake

Passenger window

Ventilator exit

Oil tank

Nose

Propeller pitch-change cylinder

Blade counterweight

Spinner mounting disc

Variable-pitch propeller

Exhaust collector ring

Landing gear door

Electrically driven split flap

Pratt & Whitney nine-cylinder radial engine

Red port navigation light

Exhaust pipe

Passenger door

Main landing gear

Brake pipe

Static discharge wick

Aileron

Aluminum wheel

Fender

Metal-skinned wing

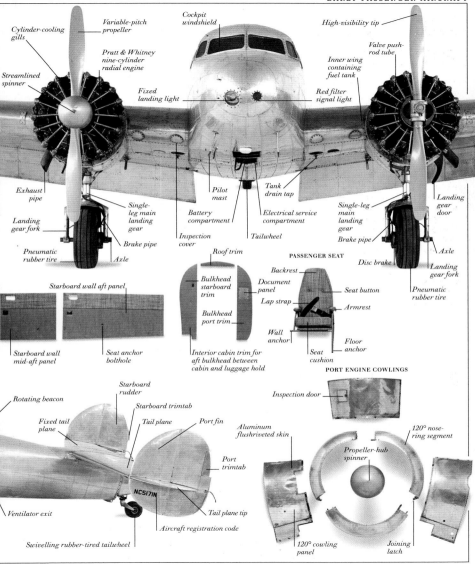

Cylinder-cooling gills

Variable-pitch propeller

Cockpit windshield

High-visibility tip

Streamlined spinner

Pratt & Whitney nine-cylinder radial engine

Valve push-rod tube

Fixed landing light

Inner wing containing fuel tank

Red filter signal light

Exhaust pipe

Single-leg main landing gear

Pilot mast

Tank drain tap

Single-leg main landing gear

Landing gear door

Landing gear fork

Battery compartment

Electrical service compartment

Brake pipe

Axle

Pneumatic rubber tire

Brake pipe

Axle

Inspection cover

Tailwheel

Disc brake

Landing gear fork

Pneumatic rubber tire

Roof trim

PASSENGER SEAT

Starboard wall aft panel

Bulkhead starboard trim

Backrest

Document panel

Seat button

Lap strap

Armrest

Bulkhead port trim

Wall anchor

Floor anchor

Starboard wall mid-aft panel

Seat anchor bolthole

Interior cabin trim for aft bulkhead between cabin and luggage hold

Seat cushion

PORT ENGINE COWLINGS

Rotating beacon

Starboard rudder

Inspection door

Fixed tail plane

Starboard trimtab

Tail plane

Port fin

Aluminum flushriveted skin

120° nose-ring segment

Port trimtab

Propeller-hub spinner

NC517IN

Ventilator exit

Tail plane tip

Aircraft registration code

Swivelling rubber-tired tailwheel

120° cowling panel

Joining latch

World War II aircraft

WHEN WORLD WAR II began in 1939, air forces had already replaced most of their fabric-skinned biplanes with all-metal, stressed-skin monoplanes. Aircraft played a far greater role in military operations during World War II than ever before. The wide range of aircraft duties, and the introduction of radar tracking and guidance systems, put pressure on designers to improve aircraft performance. The main areas of improvement were speed, range, and engine power. Bombers became larger and more powerful—converting from two to four engines—in order to carry a heavier bomb load; the US B-17 Flying Fortress could carry up to 6.8 tons (6.2 metric tons) of bombs over a distance of about 2,000 miles (3,200 km). Some aircraft increased their range by using drop tanks (fuel tanks that were jettisoned when empty to reduce drag). Fighters needed speed and manoeuvrability: the Hawker Tempest shown here had a maximum speed of 435 mph (700 km/h), and was one of the few Allied aircraft capable of catching the German jet-powered V1 "flying bomb." By 1944, Britain had introduced its first turbojet-powered aircraft, the Gloster Meteor fighter, and Germany had introduced the fastest fighter in the world, the turbojet-powered Me 262, which had a maximum speed of 540 mph (868 km/h).

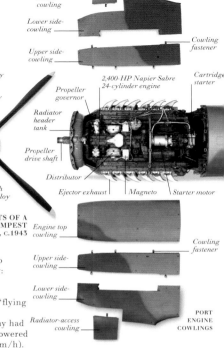

PROPELLER

High-visibility yellow tip

Light-alloy propeller spinner

Variable-pitch aluminum-alloy blade

COMPONENTS OF A HAWKER TEMPEST MARK V, c.1943

STARBOARD ENGINE COWLINGS

Radiator-access cowling

Lower side-cowling

Upper side-cowling

Cowling fastener

2,400-HP Napier Sabre 24-cylinder engine

Cartridge starter

Propeller governor

Radiator header tank

Propeller drive shaft

Distributor

Ejector exhaust

Magneto

Starter motor

Engine top cowling

Upper side-cowling

Lower side-cowling

Radiator-access cowling

Cowling fastener

PORT ENGINE COWLINGS

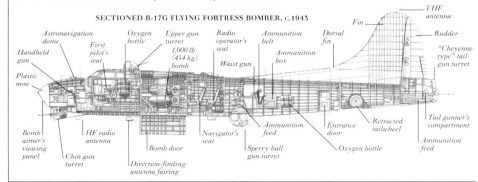

SECTIONED B-17G FLYING FORTRESS BOMBER, c.1943

Astronavigation dome

First pilot's seat

Handheld gun

Plastic nose

Oxygen bottle

Upper gun turret

1,000 lb (454 kg) bomb

Radio operator's seat

Waist gun

Ammunition belt

Ammunition box

Dorsal fin

Fin

VHF antenna

Rudder

"Cheyenne-type" tail-gun turret

Bomb aimer's viewing panel

HF radio antenna

Chin gun turret

Bomb door

Direction-finding-antenna fairing

Navigator's seat

Ammunition feed

Sperry ball gun turret

Entrance door

Oxygen bottle

Retracted tailwheel

Tail gunner's compartment

Ammunition feed

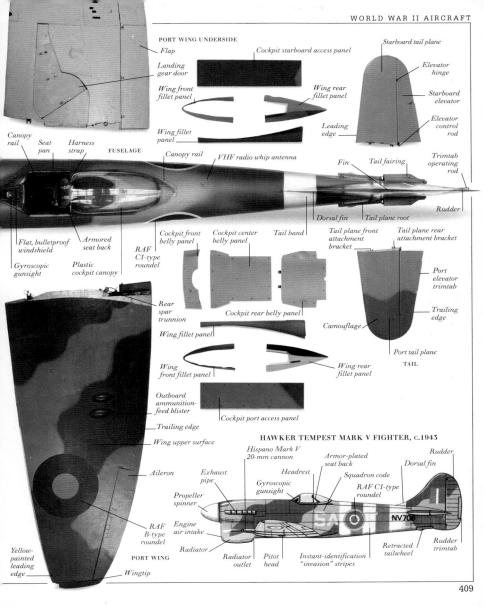

PORT WING UNDERSIDE

Flap

Landing gear door

Wing front fillet panel

Cockpit starboard access panel

Wing rear fillet panel

Wing fillet panel

Starboard tail plane

Elevator hinge

Starboard elevator

Elevator control rod

Leading edge

Canopy rail

Seat pan

Harness strap

FUSELAGE

Canopy rail

VHF radio whip antenna

Fin

Tail fairing

Trimtab operating rod

Dorsal fin

Tail plane root

Rudder

Flat, bulletproof windshield

Armored seat back

RAF C1-type roundel

Cockpit front belly panel

Cockpit center belly panel

Tail band

Tail plane front attachment bracket

Tail plane rear attachment bracket

Gyroscopic gunsight

Plastic cockpit canopy

Port elevator trimtab

Trailing edge

Rear spar trunnion

Cockpit rear belly panel

Wing fillet panel

Camouflage

Port elevator trimtab

Wing front fillet panel

Wing rear fillet panel

Port tail plane

TAIL

Outboard ammunition-feed blister

Cockpit port access panel

Trailing edge

Wing upper surface

HAWKER TEMPEST MARK V FIGHTER, C.1943

Hispano Mark V 20-mm cannon

Armor-plated seat back

Headrest

Squadron code

Rudder

Dorsal fin

Aileron

Exhaust pipe

Gyroscopic gunsight

RAF C1-type roundel

Propeller spinner

RAF B-type roundel

Engine air intake

Radiator

Radiator outlet

Pitot head

Instant-identification "invasion" stripes

Retracted tailwheel

Rudder trimtab

Yellow-painted leading edge

PORT WING

Wingtip

NV708

409

Modern piston aero-engines

MID WEST TWO-STROKE, THREE-CYLINDER ENGINE

PISTON ENGINES today are used mainly to power the vast numbers of light aircraft and microlights, as well as crop-sprayers and crop-dusters, small helicopters, and fire-bombers (which dump water on large fires). Virtually all heavier aircraft are now powered by jet engines. Modern piston aero-engines work on the same basic principles as the engine used by the Wright brothers in the first powered flight in 1903. However, today's engines are more sophisticated than earlier engines. For example, modern aero-engines may use a two-stroke or a four-stroke combustion cycle; they may have from one to nine air- or water-cooled cylinders, which may be arranged horizontally, in-line, in V formation, or radially; and they may drive the aircraft's propeller either directly or through a reduction gearbox. One of the more unconventional types of modern aero-engine is the rotary engine shown here, which has a trilobate (three-sided) rotor spinning in a chamber shaped like a fat figure-eight.

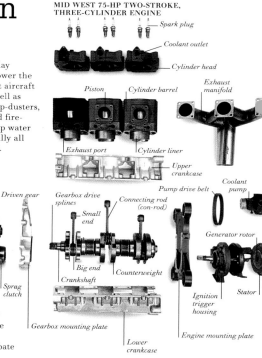

MID WEST 75-HP TWO-STROKE, THREE-CYLINDER ENGINE

Spark plug

Coolant outlet

Cylinder head

Piston

Cylinder barrel

Exhaust manifold

Exhaust port

Cylinder liner

Upper crankcase

Gearbox drive splines

Connecting rod (con-rod)

Small end

Pump drive belt

Coolant pump

Big end

Counterweight

Crankshaft

Generator rotor

Ignition trigger housing

Stator

Gearbox mounting plate

Lower crankcase

Engine mounting plate

Reduction gearbox

Driven gear

Propeller drive flange

Torsional vibration damper

Sprag clutch

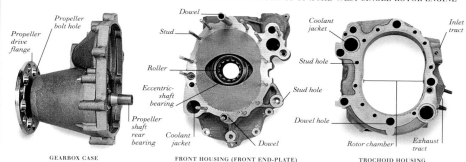

ROTOR AND HOUSINGS OF A MID WEST SINGLE-ROTOR ENGINE

Propeller bolt hole

Propeller drive flange

Dowel

Stud

Roller

Eccentric-shaft bearing

Propeller shaft rear bearing

Coolant jacket

Dowel

Coolant jacket

Stud hole

Stud hole

Dowel hole

Rotor chamber

Inlet tract

Exhaust tract

GEARBOX CASE

FRONT HOUSING (FRONT END-PLATE)

TROCHOID HOUSING

MID WEST 90-HP TWIN-ROTOR ENGINE

Propeller-bolt collar

Propeller drive flange

Reduction gearbox

Lubricating oil feed

Engine front mounting plate

Blanking plate over air inlet

Carburettor

Upper rubber anti-vibration engine mount

Rotor-cooling air duct

Pipe clamp joint

Rotor-cooling air pump

Upper rotor-cooling air duct

Generator housing

Electric cable

Front bearing mount

Oil pump drive shaft cover

Torsional vibration damper

Fuel pipe inlet connection

Fuel drip tray

Blanking plate over exhaust port

Exhaust pipe flange

Lower rubber anti-vibration engine mount

Engine rear mounting plate

Starter motor

Flywheel

OUTPUT SHAFT OF A MID WEST ROTARY ENGINE

Balance weight

Drive gear

Front bearing

Flywheel retaining thread

Eccentric shaft

Drive gear spline

Rear bearing

Rotor bearing

Flywheel

Starter ring teeth

Oil seal spacer ring

Corner bolt

Rotor tip seal

Tip seal groove

Rotor gear teeth

Rotor bearing

Cooling fins

Rotor tip spring

Balancing drilling

Rotor side seal

Side seal spring

Side seal groove

ROTOR AND SEALS

Fixed gear (stationary gear)

Engine mounting

Stud hole

Dowel hole

Coolant jacket

REAR HOUSING (REAR END-PLATE)

Outlet manifold

Pump drive shaft

Fixing stud

Bolt hole

Inlet manifold

Water pump cover and oil pump housing

Thermostat

Oil pump

WATER PUMP HOUSING

Modern jetliners 1

BAE-146 JETLINER

MODERN JETLINERS HAVE ENABLED ordinary people to travel to places where once only the wealthy could afford to go. Compared with the first jetliners (which were introduced in the 1940s), modern ones are much quieter, burn fuel more efficiently, and produce less air pollution. These advances are largely due to the replacement of turbojet engines with turbofan engines (see pp. 418-419). The greater power of turbofan engines at low speeds enables modern jetliners to carry more fuel and passengers than turbojet aircraft; a modern Boeing 747-400 (popularly known as a "jumbo jet") can fly 400 people for 8,500 miles (13,700 km) without needing to refuel. Jetliners fly at high altitudes, typically cruising at 26,000-36,000 ft (8000-11,000 m), where they can use fuel efficiently and usually avoid bad weather. The pilot always controls the aircraft during takeoff and landing, but at other times the aircraft is usually controlled by an autopilot. Autopilots are complex on-board mechanisms that detect deviations from an aircraft's route and make appropriate adjustments to the flight controls. Flight decks are also equipped with radars that warn pilots of approaching hazards, such as mountain ranges, bad weather, and other aircraft.

Shoulder cowling

Engine pylon

Hinged cowling panel

Nose cowling

Fire-extinguisher discharge indicator

Fan duct nozzle

Core-engine jet pipe

Oil-filler door

Push-in door for hand-held fire-extinguisher

Drain mast

TURBOFAN ENGINE COWLING

STRUCTURAL COMPONENTS OF A BAE-146 JETLINER

Oil-filler door for integrated-drive generator

FUSELAGE NOSE-SECTION

FUSELAGE MID-SECTION

Electrically heated, birdproof windshield

Side window

Anchor for open door

Rain gutter

Hinge

Peephole

Finger recess

Static air-pressure plate

Forward main door aperture

VHF omni-range and instrument-landing-system antennas

Light-alloy door frame

Passenger window aperture

Main external operating handle

Multiple-pinned lock

Floor level

Radome

Toilet service connector

FORWARD MAIN DOOR

Anchor for open door

Air temperature probe

Stall warning vane

Pitot head for dynamic air pressure

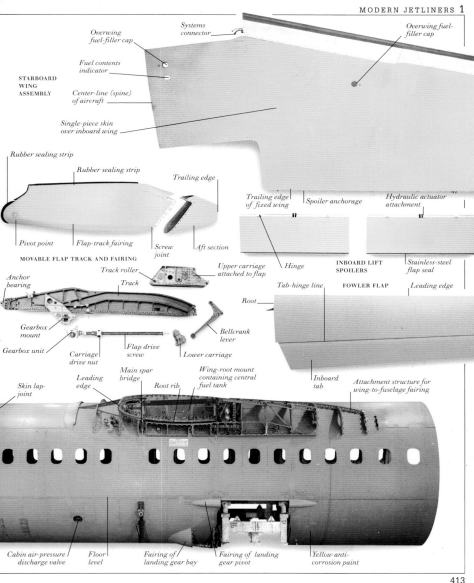

Overwing fuel-filler cap

Systems connector

Overwing fuel-filler cap

Overwing fuel-filler cap

Fuel contents indicator

STARBOARD WING ASSEMBLY

Center-line (spine) of aircraft

Single-piece skin over inboard wing

Rubber sealing strip

Rubber sealing strip

Trailing edge

Trailing edge of fixed wing

Spoiler anchorage

Hydraulic actuator attachment

Pivot point

Flap-track fairing

Screw joint

Aft section

Hinge

INBOARD LIFT SPOILERS

Stainless-steel flap seal

MOVABLE FLAP TRACK AND FAIRING

Upper carriage attached to flap

Tab-hinge line

FOWLER FLAP

Leading edge

Track roller

Anchor bearing

Track

Root

Gearbox mount

Gearbox unit

Carriage drive nut

Flap drive screw

Lower carriage

Bellcrank lever

Main spar bridge

Wing-root mount containing central fuel tank

Inboard tab

Attachment structure for wing-to-fuselage fairing

Skin lap-joint

Leading edge

Root rib

Cabin air-pressure discharge valve

Floor level

Fairing of landing gear bay

Fairing of landing gear pivot

Yellow anti-corrosion paint

413

Modern jetliners 2

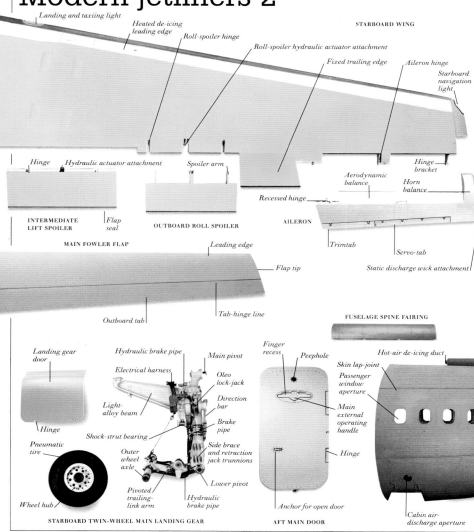

Landing and taxiing light

Heated de-icing leading edge

Roll-spoiler hinge

Roll-spoiler hydraulic actuator attachment

STARBOARD WING

Fixed trailing edge

Aileron hinge

Starboard navigation light

Hinge

Hydraulic actuator attachment

Spoiler arm

Hinge bracket

Aerodynamic balance

Horn balance

Recessed hinge

INTERMEDIATE LIFT SPOILER

Flap seal

MAIN FOWLER FLAP

OUTBOARD ROLL SPOILER

AILERON

Trimtab

Servo-tab

Leading edge

Flap tip

Static discharge wick attachment

Outboard tab

Tab-hinge line

FUSELAGE SPINE FAIRING

Landing gear door

Hydraulic brake pipe

Electrical harness

Main pivot

Oleo lock-jack

Direction bar

Light-alloy beam

Brake pipe

Hinge

Shock-strut bearing

Pneumatic tire

Outer wheel axle

Side brace and retraction jack trunnions

Lower pivot

Pivoted trailing-link arm

Hydraulic brake pipe

Wheel hub

STARBOARD TWIN-WHEEL MAIN LANDING GEAR

Finger recess

Peephole

Hot-air de-icing duct

Skin lap-joint

Passenger window aperture

Main external operating handle

Hinge

Anchor for open door

AFT MAIN DOOR

Cabin air-discharge aperture

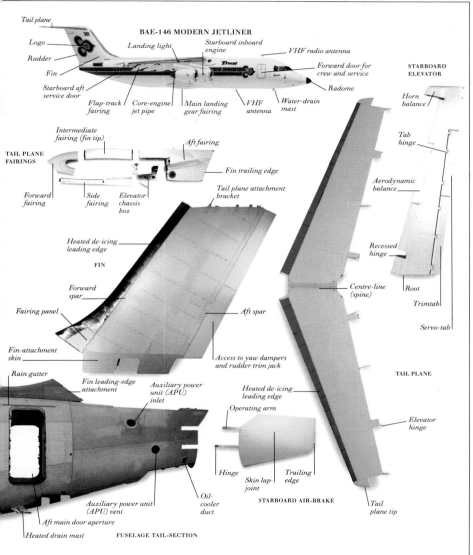

BAE-146 MODERN JETLINER

Tail plane

Logo

Rudder

Fin

Starboard aft service door

Landing light

Starboard inboard engine

VHF radio antenna

Flap-track fairing

Core-engine jet pipe

Main landing gear fairing

VHF antenna

Water-drain mast

Forward door for crew and service

Radome

STARBOARD ELEVATOR

Horn balance

Tab hinge

TAIL PLANE FAIRINGS

Intermediate fairing (fin tip)

Aft fairing

Fin trailing edge

Forward fairing

Side fairing

Elevator chassis box

Tail plane attachment bracket

Aerodynamic balance

FIN

Heated de-icing leading edge

Recessed hinge

Root

Centre-line (spine)

Trimtab

Forward spar

Servo-tab

Fairing panel

Aft spar

Fin-attachment skin

Access to yaw dampers and rudder trim jack

TAIL PLANE

Rain gutter

Fin leading-edge attachment

Auxiliary power unit (APU) inlet

Heated de-icing leading edge

Operating arm

Elevator hinge

Auxiliary power unit (APU) vent

Oil-cooler duct

Hinge

Skin lap-joint

Trailing edge

STARBOARD AIR-BRAKE

Tail plane tip

Aft main door aperture

Heated drain mast

FUSELAGE TAIL-SECTION

415

Supersonic jetliners

COMPUTER-DESIGNED SST

SUPERSONIC AIRCRAFT FLY FASTER than the speed of sound (Mach 1). There are many supersonic military aircraft, but only two supersonic passenger-carrying aircraft (also called SSTs, or supersonic transports) have been produced: the Russian Tu-144, and the Concorde, produced jointly by Britain and France. The Tu-144 was withdrawn in 1978, after only seven months in service. The Concorde remained in service from 1976 until 2003, with a break for modifications from July 2000 until October 2001. Its features included a droop nose, which lowered during takeoff and landing to aid visibility from the cockpit; the pumping of fuel between forward and aft trim tanks helped stabilize the aircraft. The Concorde had a narrow fuselage and shortspan wings to reduce drag during supersonic flight. Its noisy turbojet engines with afterburners enabled it to carry 100 passengers at a cruising speed of Mach 2 at 50,000-60,000 ft (15,000-18,000 m). Once an aircraft is flying faster than Mach 1, it produces a continuous air-pressure wave, which is heard as a "sonic boom."

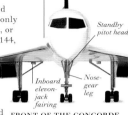

FRONT OF THE CONCORDE

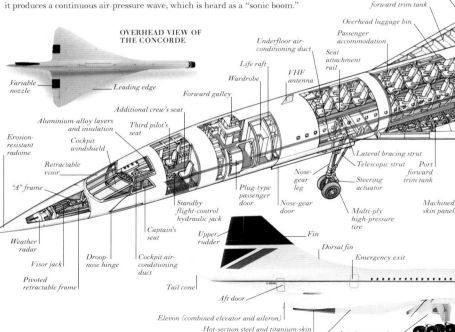

OVERHEAD VIEW OF THE CONCORDE

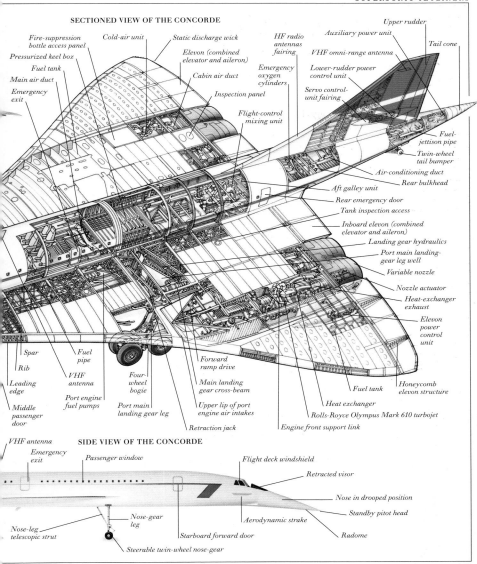

SECTIONED VIEW OF THE CONCORDE

Fire-suppression bottle access panel
Cold-air unit
Static discharge wick
HF radio antennas fairing
Upper rudder
Auxiliary power unit
VHF omni-range antenna
Tail cone
Pressurized keel box
Elevon (combined elevator and aileron)
Fuel tank
Cabin air duct
Emergency oxygen cylinders
Lower-rudder power control unit
Main air duct
Inspection panel
Servo control-unit fairing
Emergency exit
Flight-control mixing unit
Fuel-jettison pipe
Twin-wheel tail bumper
Air-conditioning duct
Rear bulkhead
Aft galley unit
Rear emergency door
Tank inspection access
Inboard elevon (combined elevator and aileron)
Landing gear hydraulics
Port main landing-gear leg well
Variable nozzle
Nozzle actuator
Heat-exchanger exhaust
Elevon power control unit

Spar
Fuel pipe
Rib
VHF antenna
Leading edge
Four-wheel bogie
Forward ramp drive
Main landing gear cross-beam
Fuel tank
Honeycomb elevon structure
Middle passenger door
Port engine fuel pumps
Port main landing gear leg
Upper lip of port engine air intakes
Heat exchanger
Rolls-Royce Olympus Mark 610 turbojet
Retraction jack
Engine front support link

SIDE VIEW OF THE CONCORDE

VHF antenna
Emergency exit
Passenger window
Flight deck windshield
Retracted visor
Nose in drooped position
Standby pitot head
Nose-leg telescopic strut
Nose-gear leg
Starboard forward door
Aerodynamic strake
Radome
Steerable twin-wheel nose-gear

417

Jet engines

JET ENGINES ARE USED BY MOST MILITARY and heavy aircraft, and by many helicopters. The simplest type of jet engine, or gas turbine, is the turbojet. It works by continuously burning a mixture of fuel and air in a combustion chamber to produce a jet of hot exhaust gas that is expelled through a nozzle to produce thrust. The hot gas also spins turbine blades, which, in turn, spin the blades of an air compressor; the compressor forces air into the combustion chamber. Many of the fastest aircraft use turbojets, with additional booster units called afterburners, but their use is restricted by their high noise emission. Most jetliners use turbofan jet engines, which are quieter. An enormous fan, driven by a low-pressure turbine, feeds some air into the compressor but feeds most of it through bypass ducts to join the exhaust jetstream in the tail cone. The bypass stream produces most of the thrust. Many smaller, propeller-driven aircraft use turboprop jet engines, in which the engine powers a propeller.

Fuel sprayer
Turbine rotor
Reverse-flow combustion chamber
Radial diffuser
Exhaust diffuser
Centrifugal compressor
Inducer
Tail cone
Air intake
Jet pipe
Exhaust nozzle
Nose cone
Igniter
Alternator
Nozzle guide vane
Air impingement starter
Combustion chamber casing

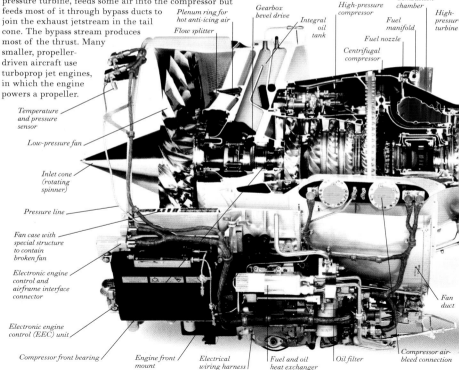

Plenum ring for hot anti-icing air
Flow splitter
Gearbox bevel drive
Integral oil tank
High-pressure compressor
Combustion chamber
High-pressure turbine
Fuel manifold
Fuel nozzle
Centrifugal compressor
Temperature and pressure sensor
Low-pressure fan
Inlet cone (rotating spinner)
Pressure line
Fan case with special structure to contain broken fan
Electronic engine control and airframe interface connector
Electronic engine control (EEC) unit
Compressor front bearing
Engine front mount
Electrical wiring harness
Fuel and oil heat exchanger
Oil filter
Compressor air-bleed connection
Fan duct

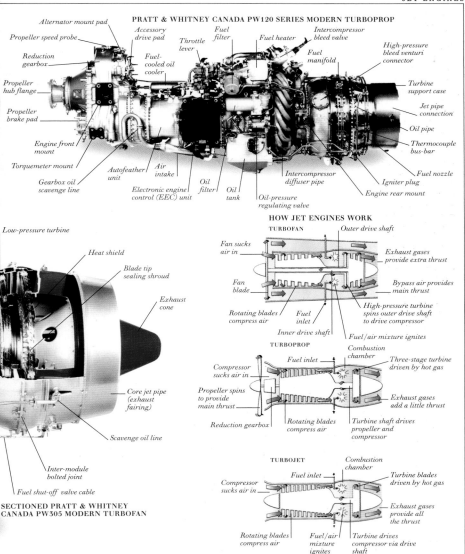

PRATT & WHITNEY CANADA PW120 SERIES MODERN TURBOPROP

Alternator mount pad
Accessory drive pad
Fuel filter
Fuel heater
Intercompressor bleed valve
High-pressure bleed venturi connector
Propeller speed probe
Throttle lever
Fuel manifold
Reduction gearbox
Fuel-cooled oil cooler
Turbine support case
Propeller hub flange
Jet pipe connection
Propeller brake pad
Oil pipe
Thermocouple bus-bar
Engine front mount
Torquemeter mount
Autofeather unit
Air intake
Oil filter
Oil tank
Intercompressor diffuser pipe
Fuel nozzle
Igniter plug
Engine rear mount
Gearbox oil scavenge line
Electronic engine control (EEC) unit
Oil-pressure regulating valve

HOW JET ENGINES WORK

TURBOFAN

Low-pressure turbine
Heat shield
Blade tip sealing shroud
Exhaust cone
Core jet pipe (exhaust fairing)
Scavenge oil line
Inter-module bolted joint
Fuel shut-off valve cable

Fan sucks air in
Outer drive shaft
Exhaust gases provide extra thrust
Bypass air provides main thrust
Fan blade
High-pressure turbine spins outer drive shaft to drive compressor
Rotating blades compress air
Fuel inlet
Inner drive shaft
Fuel/air mixture ignites

TURBOPROP

Compressor sucks air in
Fuel inlet
Combustion chamber
Three-stage turbine driven by hot gas
Propeller spins to provide main thrust
Exhaust gases add a little thrust
Reduction gearbox
Rotating blades compress air
Turbine shaft drives propeller and compressor

TURBOJET

Compressor sucks air in
Fuel inlet
Combustion chamber
Turbine blades driven by hot gas
Exhaust gases provide all the thrust
Rotating blades compress air
Fuel/air mixture ignites
Turbine drives compressor via drive shaft

SECTIONED PRATT & WHITNEY CANADA PW305 MODERN TURBOFAN

Modern military aircraft

MODERN MILITARY AIRCRAFT ARE AMONG THE MOST SOPHISTICATED and expensive products of the 21st century. Fighters need computer-operated controls for maneuverability, powerful engines, and effective air-to-air weapons. Most modern fighters also have guided missiles, radar, and passive, infrared sensors. These developments enable today's fighters to engage in combat with adversaries that are outside visual range. Bombers carry a large weapon load and enough fuel for long-range flights. A few military aircraft, such as the Tornado and the F-14 Tomcat, have variable-sweep ("swing") wings. During takeoff and landing their wings are fully extended, but for high-speed flight and low-level attacks the wings are pivoted fully back. A recent development is the "stealth" bomber, which is designed to absorb or deflect enemy radar in order to remain undetected. Earlier bombers, such as the Tornado, use terrain-following radars to fly so close to the ground that they avoid enemy radar detection.

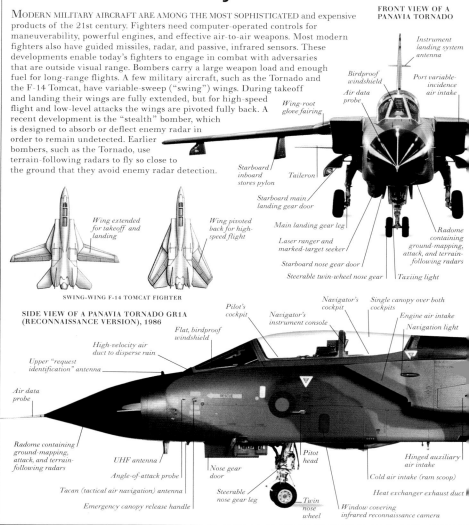

FRONT VIEW OF A PANAVIA TORNADO

Instrument landing system antenna

Birdproof windshield

Port variable-incidence air intake

Air data probe

Wing-root glove fairing

Starboard inboard stores pylon

Taileron

Starboard main landing gear door

Main landing gear leg

Laser ranger and marked-target seeker

Starboard nose gear door

Steerable twin-wheel nose gear

Radome containing ground-mapping, attack, and terrain-following radars

Taxiing light

Wing extended for takeoff and landing

Wing pivoted back for high-speed flight

SWING-WING F-14 TOMCAT FIGHTER

SIDE VIEW OF A PANAVIA TORNADO GR1A (RECONNAISSANCE VERSION), 1986

Pilot's cockpit

Navigator's cockpit

Navigator's instrument console

Single canopy over both cockpits

Engine air intake

Navigation light

Flat, birdproof windshield

High-velocity air duct to disperse rain

Upper "request identification" antenna

Air data probe

Radome containing ground-mapping, attack, and terrain-following radars

UHF antenna

Angle-of-attack probe

Tacan (tactical air navigation) antenna

Emergency canopy release handle

Nose gear door

Steerable nose gear leg

Twin nose wheel

Pitot head

Window covering infrared reconnaissance camera

Hinged auxiliary air intake

Cold air intake (ram scoop)

Heat exchanger exhaust duct

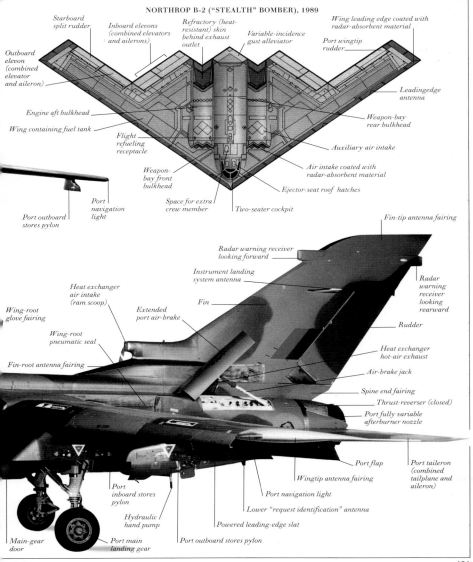

NORTHROP B-2 ("STEALTH" BOMBER), 1989

Starboard split rudder

Inboard elevons (combined elevators and ailerons)

Refractory (heat-resistant) skin behind exhaust outlet

Variable-incidence gust alleviator

Wing leading edge coated with radar-absorbent material

Port wingtip rudder

Outboard elevon (combined elevator and aileron)

Leadingedge antenna

Engine aft bulkhead

Weapon-bay rear bulkhead

Wing containing fuel tank

Flight refueling receptacle

Auxiliary air intake

Weapon-bay front bulkhead

Air intake coated with radar-absorbent material

Space for extra crew member

Ejector-seat roof hatches

Port outboard stores pylon

Port navigation light

Two-seater cockpit

Fin-tip antenna fairing

Radar warning receiver looking forward

Instrument landing system antenna

Heat exchanger air intake (ram scoop)

Fin

Radar warning receiver looking rearward

Wing-root glove fairing

Extended port air-brake

Rudder

Wing-root pneumatic seal

Heat exchanger hot-air exhaust

Fin-root antenna fairing

Air-brake jack

Spine end fairing

Thrust-reverser (closed)

Port fully variable afterburner nozzle

Port flap

Port taileron (combined tailplane and aileron)

Wingtip antenna fairing

Port inboard stores pylon

Port navigation light

Hydraulic hand pump

Lower "request identification" antenna

Main-gear door

Port main landing gear

Powered leading-edge slat

Port outboard stores pylon

421

Helicopters

HELICOPTERS USE ROTATING BLADES for lift, propulsion, and steering. The first machine to achieve sustained, controlled flight using rotating blades was the autogiro built in the 1920s by the Spaniard Juan de la Cierva. His machine had unpowered blades above the fuselage that relied on the flow of air to rotate them and provide lift as the autogiro was driven forward by a conventional propeller. Then, in 1939, the Russian-born American Igor Sikorsky produced his VS-300, the forerunner of modern helicopters. Its engine-driven blades provided lift, propulsion, and steering. It could take off vertically, hover, and fly in any direction, and had a tail rotor to prevent the helicopter body from spinning. The introduction of gas turbine jet engines to helicopters in 1955 produced quieter, safer, and more powerful machines. Because of their versatility in flight, helicopters are today used for many purposes, including crop spraying, traffic surveillance, and transporting crews to deep-sea oil rigs, as well as acting as gunships, air ambulances, and air taxis.

BELL 47G-3B1

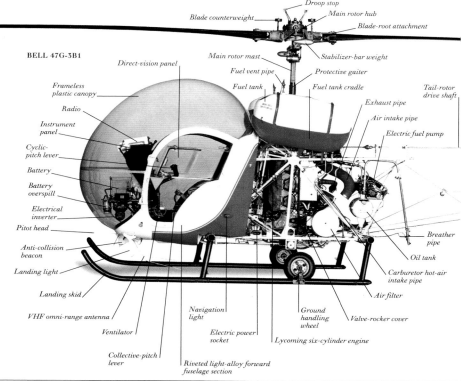

BELL 47G-3B1

Droop stop
Blade counterweight
Main rotor hub
Blade-root attachment
Main rotor mast
Stabilizer-bar weight
Direct-vision panel
Fuel vent pipe
Protective gaiter
Frameless plastic canopy
Fuel tank
Fuel tank cradle
Tail-rotor drive shaft
Radio
Exhaust pipe
Air intake pipe
Instrument panel
Electric fuel pump
Cyclic-pitch lever
Battery
Battery overspill
Electrical inverter
Pitot head
Breather pipe
Anti-collision beacon
Oil tank
Landing light
Carburetor hot-air intake pipe
Landing skid
Air filter
VHF omni-range antenna
Navigation light
Ground handling wheel
Valve-rocker cover
Ventilator
Electric power socket
Lycoming six-cylinder engine
Collective-pitch lever
Riveted light-alloy forward fuselage section

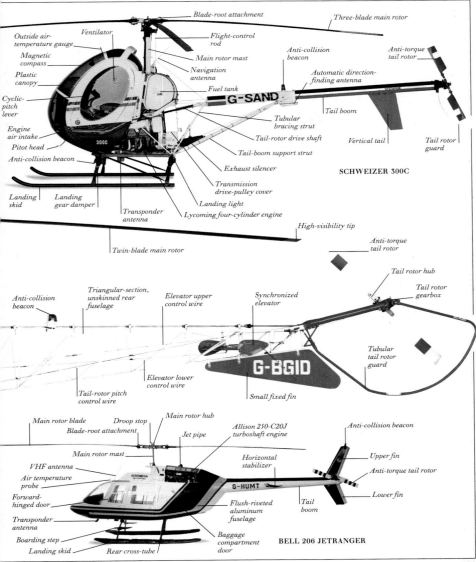

Blade-root attachment

Three-blade main rotor

Outside air-temperature gauge

Ventilator

Flight-control rod

Magnetic compass

Main rotor mast

Anti-collision beacon

Anti-torque tail rotor

Plastic canopy

Navigation antenna

Automatic direction-finding antenna

Cyclic-pitch lever

Fuel tank

G-SAND

Tail boom

Tail rotor guard

Engine air intake

Tubular bracing strut

Pitot head

Tail-rotor drive shaft

Vertical tail

Anti-collision beacon

Tail-boom support strut

Exhaust silencer

SCHWEIZER 300C

Transmission drive-pulley cover

Landing skid

Landing gear damper

Landing light

Transponder antenna

Lycoming four-cylinder engine

High-visibility tip

Twin-blade main rotor

Anti-torque tail rotor

Anti-collision beacon

Triangular-section, unskinned rear fuselage

Elevator upper control wire

Synchronized elevator

Tail rotor hub

Tail rotor gearbox

G-BGID

Tubular tail rotor guard

Tail-rotor pitch control wire

Elevator lower control wire

Small fixed fin

Main rotor blade

Droop stop

Main rotor hub

Allison 250-C20J turboshaft engine

Anti-collision beacon

Blade-root attachment

Jet pipe

Main rotor mast

Horizontal stabilizer

Upper fin

VHF antenna

AEROMEGA HELICOPTERS

Anti-torque tail rotor

Air temperature probe

G-HUMT

Lower fin

Forward-hinged door

Flush-riveted aluminum fuselage

Tail boom

Transponder antenna

Boarding step

Baggage compartment door

BELL 206 JETRANGER

Landing skid

Rear cross-tube

Light aircraft

LIGHT AIRCRAFT, SUCH AS THE ARV SUPER 2 shown here, are small, lightweight, and of simple construction. More than a million have been built since World War I, mainly for recreational use by private owners. Virtually all light aircraft have piston engines, most of which are air-cooled, although some are liquid-cooled. Open cockpits, almost universal in the 1920s, have today been replaced by enclosed cabins. The cabins of high-wing aircraft have one or two doors, whereas those of low-wing aircraft usually have a sliding or hinged canopy. Most modern light aircraft are made of aluminum alloy, although some are made of wood or of fiber-reinforced materials. Light aircraft today also usually have navigational instruments, an electrical system, cabin heating, wheel brakes, and a two-way radio.

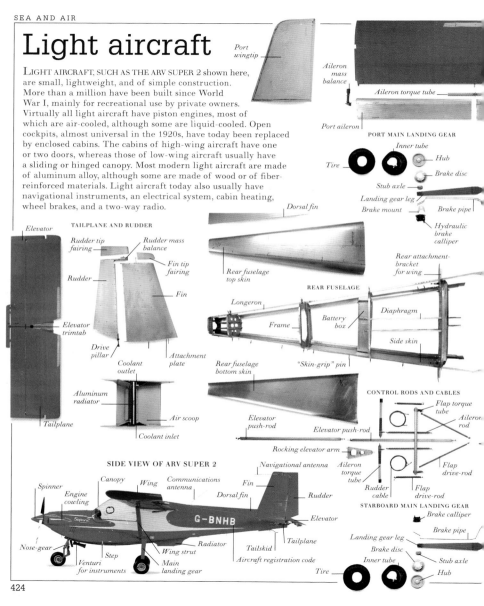

Port wingtip

Aileron mass balance

Aileron torque tube

Port aileron

PORT MAIN LANDING GEAR

Inner tube

Tire

Hub

Brake disc

Stub axle

Landing gear leg

Brake mount

Brake pipe

Hydraulic brake calliper

Dorsal fin

Elevator

TAILPLANE AND RUDDER

Rudder tip fairing

Rudder mass balance

Fin tip fairing

Rudder

Fin

Rear fuselage top skin

Longeron

Rear attachment-bracket for wing

REAR FUSELAGE

Elevator trimtab

Drive pillar

Attachment plate

Coolant outlet

Frame

Battery box

Diaphragm

Side skin

Rear fuselage bottom skin

"Skin-grip" pin

Aluminum radiator

Air scoop

Coolant inlet

Elevator push-rod

CONTROL RODS AND CABLES

Flap torque tube

Aileron rod

Tailplane

Elevator push-rod

Rocking elevator arm

Aileron torque tube

Flap drive-rod

SIDE VIEW OF ARV SUPER 2

Navigational antenna

Rudder cable

Flap drive-rod

Spinner

Canopy

Wing

Communications antenna

Fin

Dorsal fin

Rudder

STARBOARD MAIN LANDING GEAR

Brake calliper

Engine cowling

Elevator

Brake pipe

G-BNHB

Landing gear leg

Nose-gear

Radiator

Venturi for instruments

Step

Wing strut

Main landing gear

Tailskid

Aircraft registration code

Tailplane

Brake disc

Inner tube

Stub axle

Hub

Tire

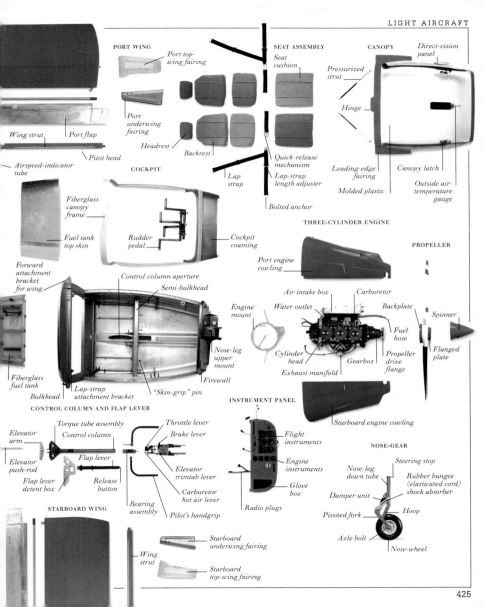

PORT WING

Port top-wing fairing

Port underwing fairing

Wing strut

Port flap

Headrest

Pitot head

Airspeed-indicator tube

SEAT ASSEMBLY

Seat cushion

Backrest

Lap strap

Quick-release mechanism

Lap-strap length adjuster

Lap-strap attachment bracket

Bolted anchor

CANOPY

Direct-vision panel

Pressurized strut

Hinge

Leading-edge fairing

Molded plastic

Canopy latch

Outside air-temperature gauge

COCKPIT

Fiberglass canopy frame

Fuel tank top skin

Rudder pedal

Cockpit coaming

Forward attachment bracket for wing

Control-column aperture

Semi-bulkhead

Engine mount

Nose-leg upper mount

Fiberglass fuel tank

Bulkhead

Lap-strap attachment bracket

"Skin-grip" pin

Firewall

THREE-CYLINDER ENGINE

Port engine cowling

Air intake box

Water outlet

Carburetor

Cylinder head

Exhaust manifold

Gearbox

Backplate

Fuel hose

Propeller drive flange

PROPELLER

Spinner

Flanged plate

Starboard engine cowling

CONTROL COLUMN AND FLAP LEVER

Elevator arm

Torque tube assembly

Control column

Throttle lever

Brake lever

Elevator push-rod

Flap lever

Elevator trimtab lever

Flap lever detent box

Release button

Carburetor hot air lever

Bearing assembly

Pilot's handgrip

INSTRUMENT PANEL

Flight instruments

Engine instruments

Glove box

Radio plugs

NOSE-GEAR

Steering stop

Nose-leg down tube

Rubber bungee (elasticated cord) shock absorber

Damper unit

Pivoted fork

Hoop

Axle bolt

Nose-wheel

STARBOARD WING

Wing strut

Starboard underwing fairing

Starboard top-wing fairing

Gliders, hang-gliders, and ultralights

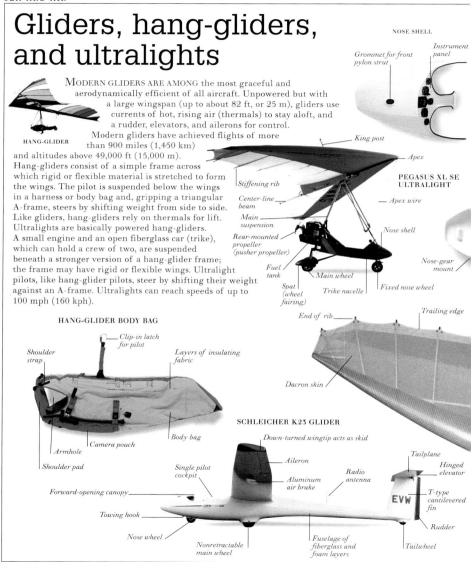

MODERN GLIDERS ARE AMONG the most graceful and aerodynamically efficient of all aircraft. Unpowered but with a large wingspan (up to about 82 ft, or 25 m), gliders use currents of hot, rising air (thermals) to stay aloft, and a rudder, elevators, and ailerons for control. Modern gliders have achieved flights of more than 900 miles (1,450 km) and altitudes above 49,000 ft (15,000 m). Hang-gliders consist of a simple frame across which rigid or flexible material is stretched to form the wings. The pilot is suspended below the wings in a harness or body bag and, gripping a triangular A-frame, steers by shifting weight from side to side. Like gliders, hang-gliders rely on thermals for lift. Ultralights are basically powered hang-gliders. A small engine and an open fiberglass car (trike), which can hold a crew of two, are suspended beneath a stronger version of a hang-glider frame; the frame may have rigid or flexible wings. Ultralight pilots, like hang-glider pilots, steer by shifting their weight against an A-frame. Ultralights can reach speeds of up to 100 mph (160 kph).

HANG-GLIDER

NOSE SHELL

Grommet for front pylon strut

Instrument panel

King post

Apex

PEGASUS XL SE ULTRALIGHT

Stiffening rib

Center-line beam

Main suspension

Rear-mounted propeller (pusher propeller)

Fuel tank

Spat (wheel fairing)

Main wheel

Trike nacelle

Apex wire

Nose shell

Nose-gear mount

Fixed nose wheel

Trailing edge

End of rib

HANG-GLIDER BODY BAG

Clip-in latch for pilot

Shoulder strap

Layers of insulating fabric

Dacron skin

Armhole

Camera pouch

Body bag

Shoulder pad

SCHLEICHER K23 GLIDER

Down-turned wingtip acts as skid

Single pilot cockpit

Aileron

Aluminum air brake

Radio antenna

Tailplane

Hinged elevator

Forward-opening canopy

Towing hook

EVW

T-type cantilevered fin

Rudder

Nose wheel

Nonretractable main wheel

Fuselage of fiberglass and foam layers

Tailwheel

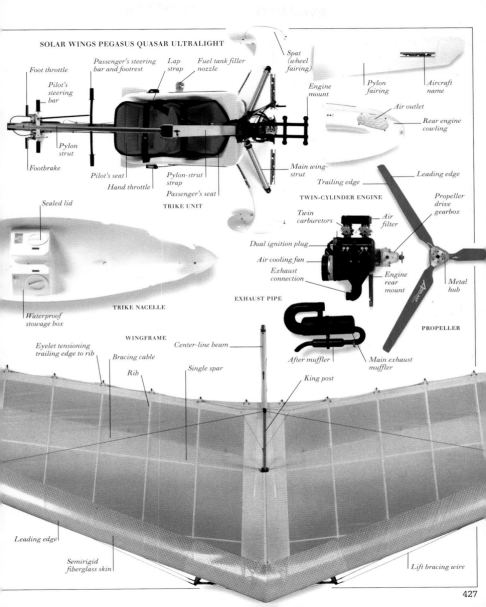

SOLAR WINGS PEGASUS QUASAR ULTRALIGHT

Foot throttle

Pilot's steering bar

Passenger's steering bar and footrest

Lap strap

Fuel tank filler nozzle

Spat (wheel fairing)

Engine mount

Pylon fairing

Aircraft name

Air outlet

Rear engine cowling

Pylon strut

Footbrake

Pilot's seat

Hand throttle

Pylon-strut strap

Passenger's seat

Main wing strut

Trailing edge

Leading edge

TRIKE UNIT

TWIN-CYLINDER ENGINE

Propeller drive gearbox

Sealed lid

Twin carburetors

Air filter

Dual ignition plug

Air cooling fan

Exhaust connection

Engine rear mount

Metal hub

Waterproof stowage box

TRIKE NACELLE

EXHAUST PIPE

PROPELLER

WINGFRAME

Center-line beam

Eyelet tensioning trailing edge to rib

Bracing cable

Rib

Single spar

King post

After muffler

Main exhaust muffler

Leading edge

Semirigid fiberglass skin

Lift bracing wire

427

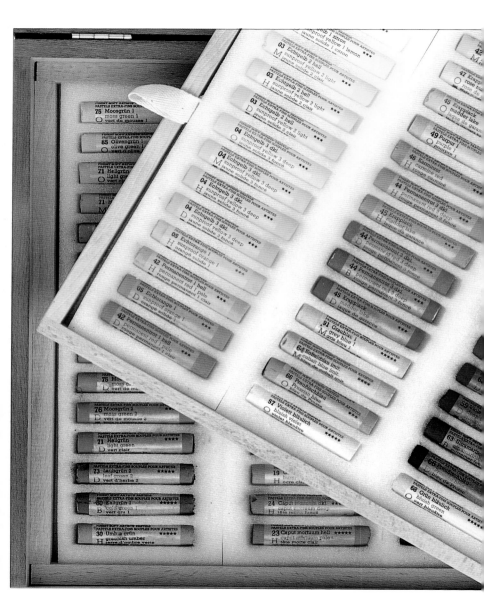

The
Visual Arts

Drawing····································430
Tempera····································432
Fresco····································434
Oils····································436
Watercolor····································438
Pastels····································440
Acrylics····································442
Calligraphy····································444
Printmaking 1····································446
Printmaking 2····································448
Mosaic····································450
Sculpture 1····································452
Sculpture 2····································454

Drawing

DRAWINGS CAN BE FINISHED WORKS OF ART, or preparatory studies for paintings and other visual arts. They can be made using a wide variety of drawing instruments such as pencils, graphite sticks, chalks, charcoal, pens and inks, and silver wires. The most common drawing instrument is the graphite pencil. A graphite pencil consists of a thin rod of graphite mixed with clay, encased in wood. Charcoal is one of the oldest drawing instruments. It is produced by firing twigs of willow, vine, or other woods at high temperatures in airtight containers. Erasers can be used to rub out marks made by drawing materials such as graphite pencils or charcoal, or to achieve a particular effect—such as smudging. Fixative is often applied—using a mouth diffuser or aerosol spray fixative—to prevent smudging once a drawing is finished. Silver lines can be produced by drawing silver wire across specially prepared paper—a technique known as silverpoint. The lines are permanent and cannot be erased. In time, the silver lines oxidize and turn brown.

Hinge

Liquid fixative consisting of dissolved resin

Fixative is sucked into tube and sprayed on to drawing

CHALK, CRAYON, AND CHARCOAL

Calcite (calcium carbonate) mixed with pigment

BLUE CHALK

Iron oxide mixed with chalk

SANGUINE CRAYON

Carbonized wood

WILLOW CHARCOAL

ERASERS

Hard texture

Medium-soft, light line

PLASTIC ERASER

Soft texture

PUTTY ERASER

DRAWING INSTRUMENTS

2B GRAPHITE PENCIL

Very soft, dark line

8B GRAPHITE PENCIL

SILVER WIRE IN A METAL HOLDER

DRAWING BOARD

DRAWING MATERIALS

Graphite stick

Bulldog clip

Colored pencil

Drawing board

Paper

Dip pen

Drawing clip

Pencil sharpener

Sketch book

Ink bottle

Silver lines oxidize to a light brown color

Figures drawn in ink on top of lines

Line drawn in silverpoint using a rule

Complex perspective drawing done as a preparatory study for a painting

Vanishing point located on head of man riding rearing horse

Lines of squared pavement slabs recede toward a single vanishing point

Paper prepared with size (glue) and pigment

EXAMPLE OF A SILVERPOINT DRAWING
The Adoration of the Magi, Leonardo da Vinci, 1481
Pen and ink over silverpoint on paper
6½ × 11½ in (16.5 × 29.2 cm)

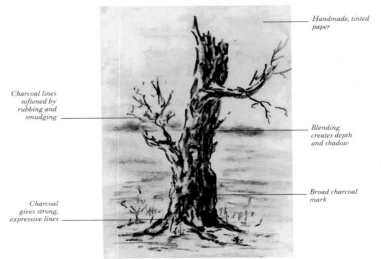

Handmade, tinted paper

Charcoal lines softened by rubbing and smudging

Blending creates depth and shadow

Broad charcoal mark

Charcoal gives strong, expressive lines

EXAMPLE OF A CHARCOAL DRAWING
Charcoal on paper

Tempera

ILLUMINATED MANUSCRIPT

THE TERM TEMPERA is applied to any paint in which pigment is tempered (mixed) with a water-based binding medium—usually egg yolk. Egg tempera is applied to a smooth surface such as vellum (for illuminated manuscripts) or more commonly to hardwood panels prepared with gesso—a mixture of chalk and size (glue). Hog hair brushes are used to apply the gesso. A layer of gesso grosso (coarse gesso) is followed by successive layers of gesso sotile (fine gesso) that are sanded between coats to provide a smooth, yet absorbent ground. The paint is applied with fine sable brushes in thin layers, using light brushstrokes. Tempera dries quickly to form a tough skin with a satin sheen. The luminous white surface of the gesso combined with the overlaid paint produces the brilliant crispness and rich colors particular to this medium. Egg tempera paintings are frequently gilded with gold. Leaves of finely beaten gold are applied to a bole (reddish-brown clay) base and polished by burnishing.

MATERIALS FOR GILDING

Parchment for protecting gold leaf from drafts

Brush

Bowl containing diluted bole

Gold leaf

Gilder's knife

Gilder's tip for picking up gold leaf

Gilder's cushion

Surface prepared with gesso

Gold leaf smoothed and polished with a burnisher

Gold leaf applied in overlapping layers

Bole brushed on to gesso

Burnisher

Agate tip

MATERIALS FOR TEMPERA PANEL PAINTING

Yolk

EGG

White

SIZE (GLUE)

GESSO

MORTAR AND PESTLE

Mortar

Lip

Pestle for crushing and grinding pigments

EGG YOLK BINDING MEDIUM

EXAMPLES OF BRUSHES

FLAT HOG HAIR BRUSH

SABLE BRUSH SIZE 6

SABLE BRUSH SIZE 1

EXAMPLE OF A TEMPERA PAINTING

Presentation in the Temple, Ambrogio Lorenzetti, 1342
Tempera on wood, 8 ft 5⅛ in × 5 ft 6 ⅛in (257 × 168 cm)

Altarpiece commissioned for Siena Cathedral, Italy
Textured gold ornament made by punching motifs into the gilded surface
The red tinge of the bole is just visible beneath the gold
Edge of a sheet of gold leaf
Crisp edge characteristic of tempera painting
Vine black used to create the dim cathedral interior
Highlights on the beard made by applying thin layers of white over dried paint
Red drapery painted in vermilion
Raised right hand and pointing finger is the gesture of prophecy
Receding floor tiles create the impression of depth
Patch of discolored varnish, left from last cleaning

PIGMENTS FOR FLESH-COLOR PAINTING

VERDACCIO

VERMILION AND LEAD WHITE

VERMILION

RED EARTH (IRON OXIDE)

EXAMPLES OF PIGMENTS

MALACHITE

ULTRAMARINE LAPIS LAZULI

VINE BLACK

LEAD TIN YELLOW

Warm flesh tones achieved by layering vermilion and white over an undercoat of verdaccio
Patterned gold halo glitters in candlelight
Ultramarine lapis lazuli, as costly as gold, was reserved for significant figures such as the Virgin Mary
Craquelure (pattern of cracks in the paint)

DETAIL FROM "PRESENTATION IN THE TEMPLE"

Fresco

FRESCO IS A METHOD OF WALL PAINTING. In buon fresco (true fresco), pigments are mixed with water and applied to an intonaco (layer of fresh, damp lime-plaster). The intonaco absorbs and binds the pigments as it dries making the picture a permanent part of the wall surface. The intonaco is applied in sections called giornate (daily sections). The size of each giornata depends on the artist's estimate of how much can be painted before the plaster sets. The junctions between giornate are sometimes visible on a finished fresco. The range of colors used in buon fresco are limited to lime-resistant pigments such as earth colors (below). Slaked lime (burnt lime mixed with water), bianco di San Giovanni (slaked lime that has been partly exposed to air), and chalk can be used to produce fresco whites. In fresco secco (dry fresco), pigments are mixed with a binding medium and applied to dry plaster. The pigments are not completely absorbed into the plaster and may flake off over time.

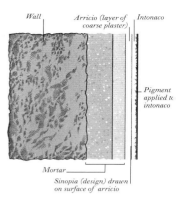

Wall

Arricio (layer of coarse plaster)

Intonaco

Pigment applied to intonaco

Mortar

Sinopia (design) drawn on surface of arricio

EXAMPLES OF EARTH COLOR PIGMENTS

EXAMPLES OF FRESCO BRUSHES

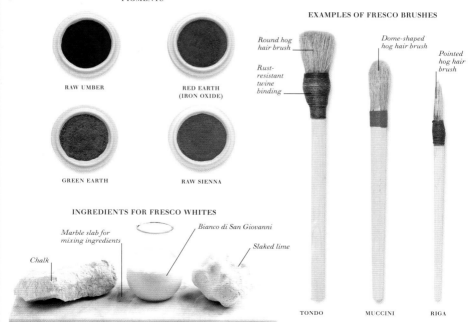

RAW UMBER

RED EARTH (IRON OXIDE)

GREEN EARTH

RAW SIENNA

Round hog hair brush

Rust-resistant twine binding

Dome-shaped hog hair brush

Pointed hog hair brush

INGREDIENTS FOR FRESCO WHITES

Marble slab for mixing ingredients

Bianco di San Giovanni

Slaked lime

Chalk

TONDO

MUCCINI

RIGA

EXAMPLE OF A FRESCO
The Expulsion of the Merchants from the Temple, Giotto, c.1306
Fresco, 78 × 72 in (200 × 185 cm)

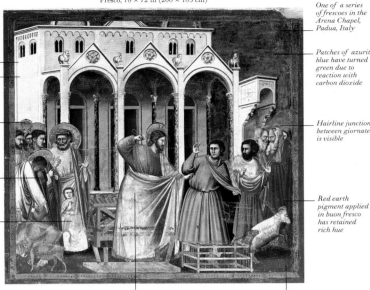

One of a series
of frescoes in the
Arena Chapel,
Padua, Italy

Temple acts as
a backdrop for
the action

Bianco di San
Giovanni often
used for fresco
whites

Gold leaf applied
to apostle's halo

Green earth
pigment applied
to robe

Child painted
on top of
apostle's robe

Patches of azurite
blue have turned
green due to
reaction with
carbon dioxide

Hairline junction
between giornate
is visible

Red earth
pigment applied
in buon fresco
has retained
rich hue

Azurite blue applied in fresco secco has
flaked off to reveal the plaster beneath

Dry, matte surface characteristic
of buon fresco

Paint applied
in buon fresco
to child's face

White dove
represents
the Holy Ghost

Paint applied
in fresco secco
to child's body
has flaked off

**DETAIL FROM "THE
EXPULSION"**

Artist has to finish giornata
before plaster dries

Junction between giornate

A fresco was
generally
worked in
zones from
the top down

Sinopia (design)
sketched in
red earth

Area with little
detail can be
painted quickly,
allowing a
larger giornata
to be completed

Highly detailed
area takes a
longer time to
paint, restricting
the size of the
giornata

GIORNATE (DAILY SECTIONS) IN "THE EXPULSION"

Oils

OIL PAINTS ARE MADE BY MIXING and grinding pigment with a drying vegetable oil such as linseed oil. The paint can be applied to many different surfaces and textures—the most common being canvas. Before painting, the canvas is stretched on a wooden frame and its surface is prepared with layers of size (glue) and primer. The two main types of brushes used in oil painting are stiff hog hair bristle brushes—generally used for covering large areas; and soft hair brushes made from sable or synthetic material—generally used for fine detail. Other tools, including painting knives, can also be used to achieve different effects. Oil paint can be applied thickly (a technique known as impasto), or can be thinned down using a solvent—such as turpentine. Varnishes are sometimes applied to finished paintings to protect their surface and to give them a matte or gloss finish.

KIDNEY-SHAPED PALETTE

DAMMAR RESIN VARNISH

Crystals are dissolved and applied to painting to protect its surface

COMMERCIAL OIL PAINTS

CADMIUM RED

Lightfast opaque color

ULTRAMARINE

Transparent color

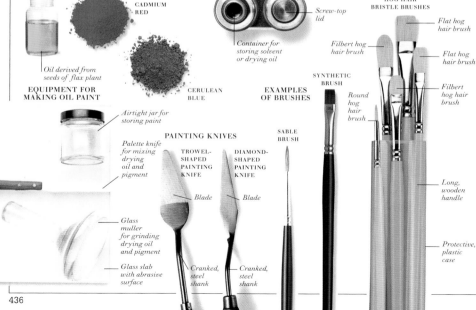

LINSEED OIL

Oil derived from seeds of flax plant

EQUIPMENT FOR MAKING OIL PAINT

EXAMPLES OF PIGMENTS

CADMIUM RED

CERULEAN BLUE

DOUBLE DIPPER (PALETTE ATTACHMENT)

Screw-top lid

Container for storing solvent or drying oil

HOG HAIR BRISTLE BRUSHES

Flat hog hair brush

Filbert hog hair brush

Flat hog hair brush

Filbert hog hair brush

SYNTHETIC BRUSH

Round hog hair brush

EXAMPLES OF BRUSHES

SABLE BRUSH

Long, wooden handle

Protective, plastic case

Airtight jar for storing paint

PAINTING KNIVES

Palette knife for mixing drying oil and pigment

TROWEL-SHAPED PAINTING KNIFE

DIAMOND-SHAPED PAINTING KNIFE

Blade

Blade

Glass muller for grinding drying oil and pigment

Glass slab with abrasive surface

Cranked, steel shank

Cranked, steel shank

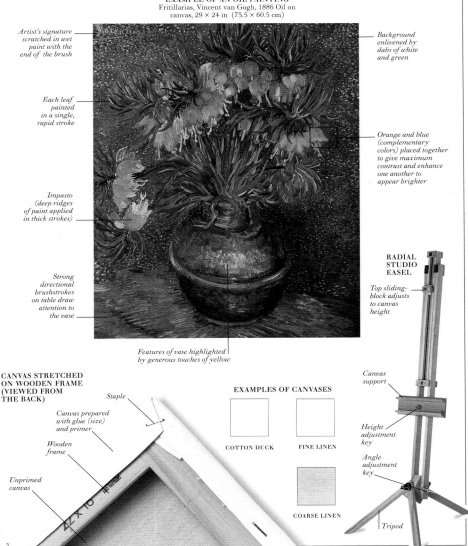

EXAMPLE OF AN OIL PAINTING
Fritillarias, Vincent van Gogh, 1886 Oil on canvas, 29 × 24 in (73.5 × 60.5 cm)

Artist's signature scratched in wet paint with the end of the brush

Background enlivened by dabs of white and green

Each leaf painted in a single, rapid stroke

Orange and blue (complementary colors) placed together to give maximum contrast and enhance one another to appear brighter

Impasto (deep ridges of paint applied in thick strokes)

Strong directional brushstrokes on table draw attention to the vase

Features of vase highlighted by generous touches of yellow

RADIAL STUDIO EASEL

Top sliding-block adjusts to canvas height

Canvas support

Height adjustment key

Angle adjustment key

Tripod

CANVAS STRETCHED ON WOODEN FRAME (VIEWED FROM THE BACK)

Staple

Canvas prepared with glue (size) and primer

Wooden frame

Unprimed canvas

EXAMPLES OF CANVASES

COTTON DUCK

FINE LINEN

COARSE LINEN

Watercolor

GUM ARABIC

Watercolor paint is made of ground pigment mixed with a watersoluble binding medium, usually gum arabic. It is usually applied to paper using soft hair brushes such as sable, goat hair, squirrel, and synthetic brushes. Watercolors are often diluted and applied as overlaying washes (thin, transparent layers) to build up depth of color. Washes can be laid in a variety of ways to create a range of different effects. For example, a wet-in-wet wash can be achieved by laying a wash on top of another wet wash. The two washes blend together to give a fused effect. Sponges are used to modify washes by soaking up paint so that areas of pigment are lightened or removed from the paper. Watercolors can also be applied undiluted—a technique known as dry brush—to create a broken-color effect. Watercolors are generally transparent and allow light to reflect from the surface of the paper through the layers of paint to give a luminous effect. They can be thickened and made opaque by adding body color (Chinese white).

Natural sap from acacia tree

NATURAL SPONGE

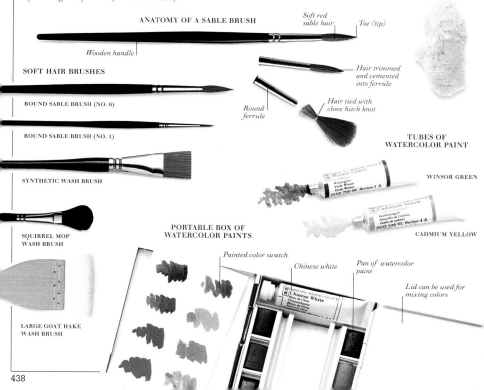

ANATOMY OF A SABLE BRUSH

Soft red sable hair   *Toe (tip)*

Wooden handle

SOFT HAIR BRUSHES

Hair trimmed and cemented into ferrule

ROUND SABLE BRUSH (NO. 6)

Round ferrule   *Hair tied with clove hitch knot*

ROUND SABLE BRUSH (NO. 1)

SYNTHETIC WASH BRUSH

TUBES OF WATERCOLOR PAINT

WINSOR GREEN

Winsergren Verde Winsor Verde Winsor 0102 720 SL Series 1 A

SQUIRREL MOP WASH BRUSH

Kadmiumgelb Amarillo de cadmio Giallo di cadmio 0102 108 SL Series 4 A

CADMIUM YELLOW

PORTABLE BOX OF WATERCOLOR PAINTS

Painted color swatch   *Chinese white*   *Pan of watercolor paint*

Lid can be used for mixing colors

Chinese White

LARGE GOAT HAKE WASH BRUSH

EXAMPLE OF A WATERCOLOR
Burning of the Houses of Parliament, Turner, 1834
Watercolor on paper, 11½ × 17½ in (29.2 × 44.5 cm)

Transparent washes laid on top of each other to create tonal depth

Highlight scratched out with a scalpel

Crowd painted with thin strokes laid over a pale wash

Transparent washes allow light to reflect off the surface of the paper to give a luminous effect

Paper shows through thin wash to give flames added highlight

Undiluted paint applied, then partly washed out, to create the impression of water

EXAMPLES OF WASHES

WASH OVER DRY BRUSH
Wash laid over paint applied with dry brush gives two-tone effect

WET-IN-WET
Two diluted washes left to run together to give fused effect

GRADED WASH
Strong wash applied to tilted paper gives graded effect

DRY BRUSH
Undiluted paint dragged across surface of paper gives broken effect

EXAMPLES OF WATERCOLOR PAPERS

SMOOTH-TEXTURED PAPER

MEDIUM-TEXTURED PAPER

ROUGH-TEXTURED PAPER

COLOR WHEEL OF WATERCOLOR PAINTS

Yellow (primary color)

Secondary colours made by mixing yellow and blue

Secondary colors made by mixing red and yellow

Blue (primary color)

Red (primary color)

Secondary colors made by mixing blue and red

Pastels

PASTELS ARE STICKS OF PIGMENT made by mixing ground pigment with chalk and a binding medium, such as gum arabic. They vary in hardness depending on the proportion of the binding medium to the chalk. Soft pastel—the most common form of pastel—contains just enough binding medium to hold the pigment in stick form. Pastels can be applied directly to any support (surface) with sufficient tooth (texture). When a pastel is drawn over a textured surface, the pigment crumbles and lodges in the fibers of the support. Pastel marks have a particular soft, matte quality and are suitable for techniques such as blending, scumbling, and feathering. Blending is a technique of rubbing and fusing two or more colors on the support using fingers or various tools such as tortillons (paper stumps), soft hair brushes, putty erasers, and soft bread. Scumbling is a technique of building up layers of pastel colors. The side or blunted tip of a soft pastel is lightly drawn over an underpainted area so that patches of the color beneath show through. Feathering is a technique of applying parallel strokes of color with the point of a pastel, usually over an existing layer of pastel color. A thin spray of fixative can be applied— using a mouth diffuser (see pp. 430-431) or aerosol spray fixative—to a finished pastel painting, or in between layers of color, to prevent smudging.

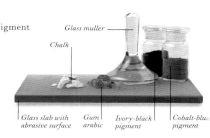

Glass muller

Chalk

Glass slab with abrasive surface | Gum arabic | Ivory-black pigment | Cobalt-blue pigment

EXAMPLES OF SOFT PASTELS

COBALT-BLUE HALF PASTEL

VERMILION HALF PASTEL

OLIVE-GREEN FULL PASTEL

MAUVE FULL PASTEL

BOXED PASTEL SET

EQUIPMENT USED WITH PASTELS

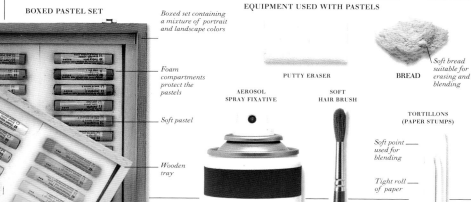

Boxed set containing a mixture of portrait and landscape colors

Foam compartments protect the pastels

Soft pastel

Wooden tray

PUTTY ERASER

AEROSOL SPRAY FIXATIVE

SOFT HAIR BRUSH

BREAD

Soft bread suitable for erasing and blending

TORTILLONS (PAPER STUMPS)

Soft point used for blending

Tight roll of paper

EXAMPLE OF A PASTEL PAINTING
Woman Drying her Neck, Edgar Degas, c.1898
Pastel on cardboard, 24½ x 25½ in (62.5 x 65.5 cm)

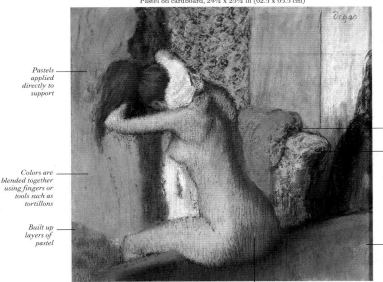

Pastels applied directly to support

Colors are blended together using fingers or tools such as tortillons

Built up layers of pastel

Rich color of fabric created by overlaying yellows and oranges

Broken colors, characteristic of scumbling technique

Toned color of paper visible beneath thinly applied pastels

Pure bright colors laid side by side produce strong contrasts

DETAIL FROM "WOMAN DRYING HER NECK"

Feathering technique used to produce skin tones

EXAMPLES OF TEXTURED PAPERS AND PASTEL BOARDS

WATERCOLOR PAPER (ROUGH TEXTURE)

GLASS PAPER

WATERCOLOR PAPER (MEDIUM TEXTURE)

INGRES PAPER

FLOCKED PASTEL BOARD

CANSON PAPER

EXAMPLES OF COLORED AND TINTED PAPERS

Acrylics

ACRYLIC PAINT IS MADE BY MIXING PIGMENT with a synthetic resin. It can be thinned with water but dries to become water insoluble. Acrylics are applied to many surfaces, such as paper and acrylic-primed board and canvas. A variety of brushes, painting knives, rollers, air-brushes, plastic scrapers, and other tools are used in acrylic painting. The versatility of acrylics makes them suitable for a wide range of techniques. They can be used opaquely or—by adding water—in a transparent, watercolor style. Acrylic mediums can be added to the paint to adjust its consistency for special effects such as glazing and impasto (ridges of paint applied in thick strokes) or to make it more matt or glossy. Acrylics are quick-drying, which allows layers of paint to be applied on top of each other almost immediately.

Sable brush

Hog hair sash brush

Synthetic hog hair brush

Synthetic sable brush

Hog hair brush

Goat hair brush

Synthetic wash brush

Ox hair brush

EXAMPLES OF PAINTS USED IN ACRYLICS

Azo yellow

Phthalo green

Cerulean blue

Phthalo blue

Quinacridone red

Titanium white

Pad of disposable paper palettes

Yellow ocher

Burnt umber

Burnt sienna

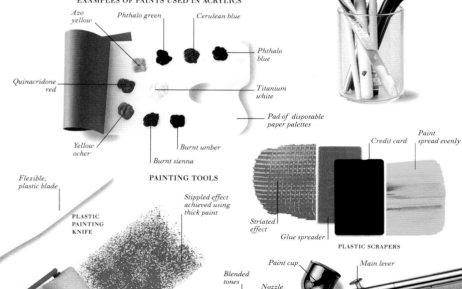

PAINTING TOOLS

Flexible, plastic blade

PLASTIC PAINTING KNIFE

Stippled effect achieved using thick paint

Striated effect

Glue spreader

Credit card

Paint spread evenly

PLASTIC SCRAPERS

Plastic handle

SPONGE ROLLER

Blended tones

Paint cup

Nozzle

Main lever

AIR-BRUSH

Uniform tone

Air hose

EXAMPLE OF AN ACRYLIC PAINTING
Acrylic on canvas, 8 x 10½ in (20.5 x 26.6 cm)

Paint applied evenly using a roller

Cotton duck canvas support (surface)

Masking tape stuck on to canvas to define main shapes, and paint applied within these areas using a roller

Flatness of rollered areas enhanced by adding gel medium to the paint

Imprecise edge around shadow where paint has seeped under masking tape

EXAMPLES OF ACRYLIC PAINTS AND TECHNIQUES

Opaque effect

Extruded (squeezed) effect

Paint applied using painting knife

PURPLE ACRYLIC PAINT

YELLOW ACRYLIC PAINT

ORANGE ACRYLIC PAINT

Transparent, watercolor effect

Translucent, impasto glaze

Thick impasto with coarse texture

BLUE ACRYLIC PAINT DILUTED WITH WATER

GREEN ACRYLIC PAINT MIXED WITH GEL MEDIUM

RED ACRYLIC PAINT MIXED WITH TEXTURE PASTE

Calligraphy

CALLIGRAPHY IS BEAUTIFULLY FORMED LETTERING. The term applies to written text and illumination (the decoration of manuscripts using gold leaf and color). The essential materials needed to practice calligraphy are a writing tool, ink, and a writing surface. Quills are among the oldest writing tools. They are usually made from goose or turkey feathers, and are noted for their flexibility and ability to produce fine lines. A quill point, however, is not very durable and constant recutting and trimming is required. The most commonly used writing instrument in Western calligraphy is a detachable, metal nib held in a penholder. The metal nib is very durable, and there are a wide range of different types. Particular types of nibs—such as copperplate, speedball, and round-hand nibs—are used for specific styles of lettering. Some nibs have integral ink reservoirs and others have reservoirs that are detachable. Brushes are also used for writing, and for filling in outlined letters and painting decoration. Other writing tools used in calligraphy are fountain pens, felt-tip pens, rotring pens, and reed pens. Calligraphy inks may come in liquid form, or as a solid ink stick. Ink sticks are ground down in distilled water to form a liquid ink. The most common writing surfaces for calligraphy are good quality, smooth -surfaced papers. To achieve the best writing position, the calligrapher places the paper on a drawing board set at an angle.

EQUIPMENT USED IN BRUSH LETTERING

Brush rest

Wolf hair brush

Goat hair brush

BRUSHES AND BRUSH REST

Liquid ink made by grinding down ink stick in distilled water

Solid carbon ink stick

Ink stone

INK STICK AND STONE

— Feather

PENS, NIBS, AND BRUSHES USED IN CALLIGRAPHY

PENHOLDER

COPPERPLATE NIB

SPEEDBALL NIB

GOAT HAIR BRUSH

FELT-TIP PEN

ROUND-HAND NIB AND DETACHABLE INK RESERVOIR

WOLF HAIR BRUSH

AUTOMATIC PEN

Feather stripped for better handling

FOUNTAIN PEN AND INK

REED PEN

Barrel —

Barrel

SQUARE SABLE BRUSH

Bottle of permanent black ink

Clip

POINTED SABLE BRUSH

Nib

Hand-cut point

GOOSE-FEATHER QUILL

Nib

Outer cap

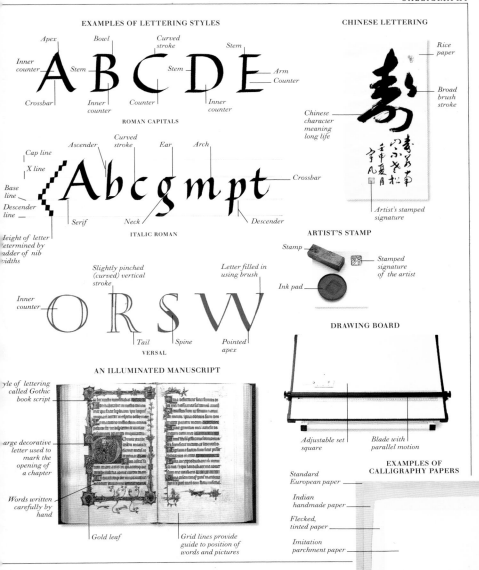

EXAMPLES OF LETTERING STYLES

Apex
Bowl
Curved stroke
Stem
Inner counter
Stem
Stem
Arm
Counter

A B C D E

Crossbar
Inner counter
Counter
Inner counter

ROMAN CAPITALS

Cap line
X line
Ascender
Curved stroke
Ear
Arch
Base line
Descender line
Crossbar

Abcgmpt

Serif
Neck
Descender

ITALIC ROMAN

Height of letter determined by ladder of nib widths

Slightly pinched (curved) vertical stroke
Letter filled in using brush
Inner counter

O R S W

Tail
Spine
Pointed apex

VERSAL

AN ILLUMINATED MANUSCRIPT

style of lettering called Gothic book script

large decorative letter used to mark the opening of a chapter

Words written carefully by hand

Gold leaf

Grid lines provide guide to position of words and pictures

CHINESE LETTERING

Rice paper

Broad brush stroke

Chinese character meaning long life

Artist's stamped signature

ARTIST'S STAMP

Stamp

Stamped signature of the artist

Ink pad

DRAWING BOARD

Adjustable set square

Blade with parallel motion

EXAMPLES OF CALLIGRAPHY PAPERS

Standard European paper

Indian handmade paper

Flecked, tinted paper

Imitation parchment paper

Printmaking 1

PRINTS ARE MADE BY FOUR BASIC printing processes—intaglio, lithographic, relief, and screen. In intaglio printing, lines are engraved or etched into the surface of a metal plate. Lines are engraved by hand using sharp metal tools. They are etched by corroding the metal plate with acid, using acid-resistant ground to protect the areas not to be etched. The plate is then inked and wiped, leaving the grooves filled with ink and the surface clean. Dampened paper is laid over the plate, and both paper and plate are passed through the rollers of an etching press. The pressure of the rollers forces the paper into the grooves, so that it takes up the ink, leaving an impression on the paper. Lithographic printing is based on the antipathy between grease and water. An image is drawn on a surface—usually a stone or metal plate—with a greasy medium, such as tusche (lihographic ink). The greasy drawing is fixed on to the plate by applying an acidic solution, such as gum arabic. The surface is then dampened and rolled with ink. The ink adheres only to the greasy areas and is repelled by the water. Paper is laid on the plate and pressure is applied by means of a press. In relief printing, the nonprinting areas of a wood or linoleum block are cut away using gouges, knives, and other tools. The printing areas are left raised in relief and are rolled with ink. Paper is laid on the inked block and pressure is applied by means of a press or by burnishing (rubbing) the back of the paper. The most common forms of relief printing are woodcut, wood engraving, and linocut. In screen printing, the printing surface is a mesh stretched across a wooden frame. A stencil is applied to the mesh to seal the nonprinting areas and ink is scraped through the mesh to produce an image.

THE FOUR MAIN PRINTING PROCESSES

Paper — — Printed image

— Engraved or etched image

Metal plate — — Inked area

INTAGLIO

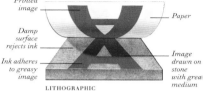

Printed image

Damp surface rejects ink — — Paper

Ink adheres to greasy image — — Image drawn on stone with greasy medium

LITHOGRAPHIC

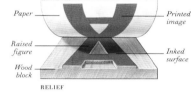

Paper — — Printed image

Raised figure — — Inked surface

Wood block

RELIEF

— Wooden frame

Ink forced through mesh — — Stencil

— Printed image

Paper

SCREEN

LEATHER INK DABBER

EQUIPMENT USED IN INTAGLIO PRINTING

ROCKER   SCRIBER   ROULETTE   SCRAPER   BURNISHER   CLAMP

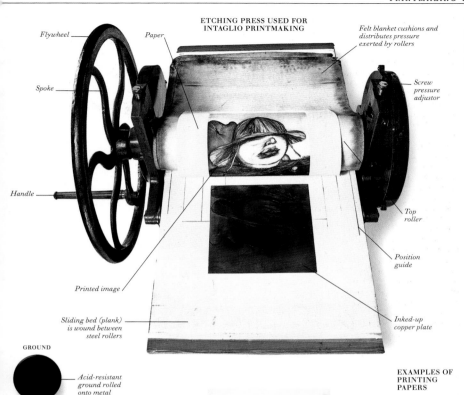

ETCHING PRESS USED FOR INTAGLIO PRINTMAKING

Flywheel

Paper

Felt blanket cushions and distributes pressure exerted by rollers

Spoke

Screw pressure adjustor

Handle

Top roller

Position guide

Printed image

Sliding bed (plank) is wound between steel rollers

Inked-up copper plate

GROUND

Acid-resistant ground rolled onto metal plate before etching

GROUND ROLLER

Gelatine roller

Wooden handle

EXAMPLES OF PRINTING PAPERS

EXAMPLE OF AN INTAGLIO PRINT
Annie with a Sun Hat, Jock McFadyen, 1993
Etched copper plate, 16 × 15¾ in (41 × 40 cm)

Printmaking 2

EXAMPLE OF A LITHOGRAPHIC STONE AND PRINT
Untitled, Frederic M. Pannebaker, 1972

IMAGE DRAWN ON STONE

LITHOGRAPIC PRINT

EXAMPLE OF A SCREEN PRINT
Patrons In An Art Deco Club, Unknown, 1931

SCREEN AND SQUEEGEE

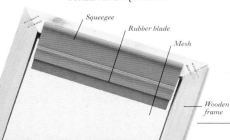

Squeegee

Rubber blade

Mesh

Wooden frame

EQUIPMENT USED IN LITHOGRAPHIC PRINTING

CRAYON AND HOLDER

LITHOGRAPHIC PENCIL

TUSCHE (LITHOGRAPHIC INK) PEN

ERASING STICK

EXPANDABLE SPONGE

TUSCHE (LITHOGRAPHIC INK) STICK

RUBBING INK

INK ROLLER

MILD ACIDIC SOLUTION

GUM ARABIC SOLUTION

WATER-BASED SCREEN PRINTING INKS

BLUE ACRYLIC INK

RED ACRYLIC INK

BROWN TEXTILE INK

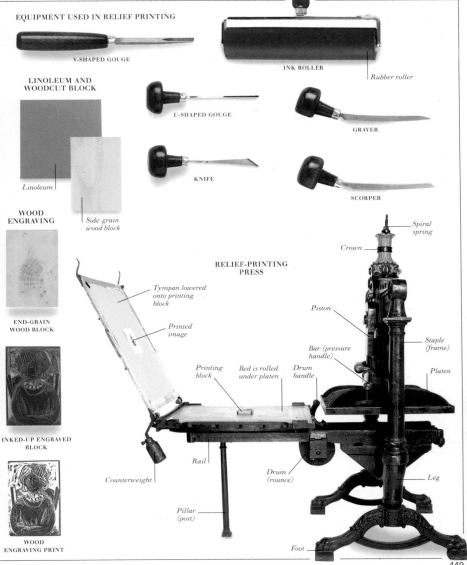

EQUIPMENT USED IN RELIEF PRINTING

V-SHAPED GOUGE

INK ROLLER

Rubber roller

LINOLEUM AND WOODCUT BLOCK

Linoleum

U-SHAPED GOUGE

GRAVER

Side-grain wood block

KNIFE

SCORPER

WOOD ENGRAVING

END-GRAIN WOOD BLOCK

INKED-UP ENGRAVED BLOCK

WOOD ENGRAVING PRINT

RELIEF-PRINTING PRESS

Spiral spring

Crown

Tympan lowered onto printing block

Piston

Printed image

Bar (pressure handle)

Staple (frame)

Printing block

Bed is rolled under platen

Drum handle

Platen

Counterweight

Rail

Drum (rounce)

Leg

Pillar (post)

Foot

449

Mosaic

MOSAIC IS THE ART OF MAKING patterns and pictures from tesserae (small, colored pieces of glass, marble, and other materials). Different materials are cut into tesserae using different tools. Smalti (glass enamel) and marble are cut into pieces using a hammer and a hardy (a pointed blade) embedded in a log. Vitreous glass is cut into pieces using a pair of pliers. Mosaics can be made using a direct or indirect method. In the direct method, the tesserae are laid directly into a bed of cement-based adhesive. In the indirect method, the design is drawn in reverse on paper or cloth. The tesserae are then stuck face-down on the paper or cloth using water-soluble glue. Adhesive is spread with a trowel on to a solid surface—such as a wall—and the back of the mosaic is laid into the adhesive. Finally, the paper or cloth is soaked off to reveal the mosaic. Gaps between tesserae can be filled with grout. Grout is forced into gaps by dragging a grouting squeegee across the face of the mosaic. Mosaics are usually used to decorate walls and floors, but they can also be applied to smaller objects.

EQUIPMENT FOR BREAKING MARBLE

Sawn strip of marble, ready for breaking into cubes

Mosaic hammer

Alicante (red marble) pieces

Hardy (pointed blade) embedded in a log

PLIERS

Hardwearing, tungsten carbide tip

Handle with rubber grip

MOSAIC TOOLS

CEMENT-BASED ADHESIVE

GROUT

SMALTI (GLASS ENAMEL)

RED SMALTI

EXAMPLE OF A MOSAIC (DIRECT METHOD)
Seascape, Tessa Hunkin, 1993
Smalti mosaic on board
31½ in (80 cm) diameter

YELLOW SMALTI

BLUE SMALTI

Gold-leaf smalti

TROWEL

Notch

Steel blade

Wooden handle

GROUTING SQUEEGEE

Wooden handle

Rubber blade

Nicobond

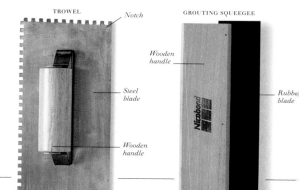

STAGES IN THE CREATION OF A MOSAIC (INDIRECT METHOD)

COLOR SKETCH
A color sketch is drawn
in oil pastel to give a clear
impression of how the finished
mosaic will look.

REVERSE IMAGE
Tesserae are glued face-down
on reverse image on paper.
Mosaic is then attached to solid
surface and paper is removed.

*Geometric
design*

Grout

MOSAIC MOSQUE DESIGN

*Floral
design*

Geometric border

*Andamenti
(line along
which tesserae
are laid)*

*Gold tessera
with ripple
finish*

*Gold tessera
placed upside
down*

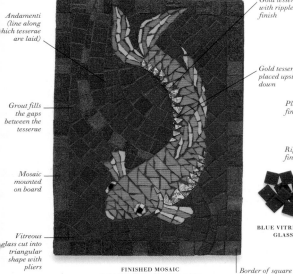

*Grout fills
the gaps
between the
tesserae*

*Mosaic
mounted
on board*

*Vitreous
glass cut into
triangular
shape with
pliers*

FINISHED MOSAIC
Goldfish, Tessa Hunkin, 1993
Vitreous glass mosaic on board
14 × 10 in (35.5 × 25.5 cm)

*Border of square
vitreous glass*

VITREOUS GLASS

**GREEN VITREOUS
GLASS WITH GOLD LEAF**

*Plain
finish*

*Ripple
finish*

**RED VITREOUS
GLASS**

SHEETS OF VITREOUS GLASS

**BLUE VITREOUS
GLASS**

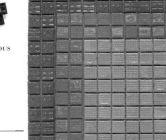

Sculpture 1

THE TWO TRADITIONAL METHODS OF MAKING SCULPTURE are carving and modeling. A carved sculpture is made by cutting away the surplus from a block of hard material such as stone, marble, or wood. The tools used for carving vary according to the material being carved. Heavy steel points, claws, and chisels that are struck with a lump hammer are generally used for stone and marble. Sharp gouges and chisels that are struck with a wooden mallet are used for wood. Sculptures formed from hard materials are generally finished by filing with rasps, rifflers, and other abrasive implements. Modeling is a process by which shapes are built up, using malleable materials such as clay, plaster, and wax. The material is cut with wire-ended tools and modeled with the fingers or a variety of hardwood and metal implements. For large or intricate modeled sculptures an armature (frame), made from metal or wood, is used to provide internal support. Sculptures formed in soft materials may harden naturally or can be made more durable by firing in a kiln. Modeled sculptures are often first designed in wax or another material to be cast later in a metal (see pp. 454-455) such as bronze. The development of many new materials in the 20th century has enabled sculptors to experiment with new techniques such as construction (joining preformed pieces of material such as machine components, mirrors, and furniture) and kinetic (mobile) sculpture.

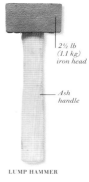

2½ lb
(1.1 kg)
iron head

Ash
handle

LUMP HAMMER

CALLIPERS

Curved leg

Gap measures
distance between
two points on a
sculpture

EXAMPLES OF WOOD-CARVING TOOLS

CABINET RASP

STRAIGHT GOUGE

SALMON BEND GOUGE

CHISEL

Stone for
sharpening
wood-carving
tools

Wing nut

**WIDE
MARBLE
CLAW**

**NARROW
MARBLE
CLAW**

POINT

FLAT CHISEL

BULLNOSE CHISEL

**ARKANSAS
HONE-STONE**

Cedar
box

**EXAMPLES OF RIFFLERS
(FOR STONE, MARBLE, AND WOOD)**

12 IN (30 CM) RIFFLER

Surface for
sharpening
stone-carving
tools

6 IN (15 CM) RIFFLER

DIAMOND WHETSTONE

**CARVING
MALLET**

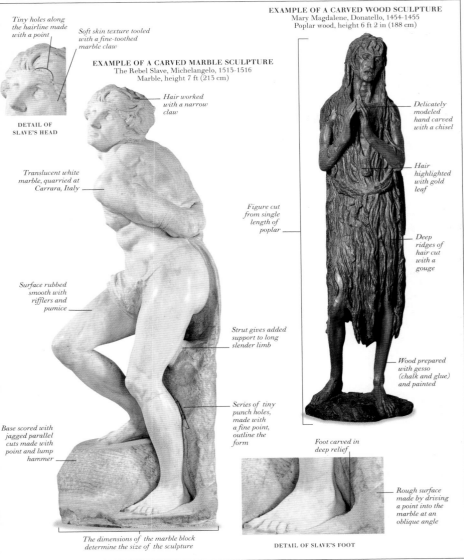

Tiny holes along the hairline made with a point

Soft skin texture tooled with a fine-toothed marble claw

EXAMPLE OF A CARVED WOOD SCULPTURE
Mary Magdalene, Donatello, 1454-1455
Poplar wood, height 6 ft 2 in (188 cm)

EXAMPLE OF A CARVED MARBLE SCULPTURE
The Rebel Slave, Michelangelo, 1513-1516
Marble, height 7 ft (213 cm)

Hair worked with a narrow claw

DETAIL OF SLAVE'S HEAD

Delicately modeled hand carved with a chisel

Translucent white marble, quarried at Carrara, Italy

Hair highlighted with gold leaf

Figure cut from single length of poplar

Deep ridges of hair cut with a gouge

Surface rubbed smooth with rifflers and pumice

Strut gives added support to long slender limb

Wood prepared with gesso (chalk and glue) and painted

Series of tiny punch holes, made with a fine point, outline the form

Base scored with jagged parallel cuts made with point and lump hammer

Foot carved in deep relief

Rough surface made by driving a point into the marble at an oblique angle

The dimensions of the marble block determine the size of the sculpture

DETAIL OF SLAVE'S FOOT

Sculpture 2

EXAMPLES OF MODELING TOOLS

WIRE-ENDED CUTTING TOOL

CURVED MOLDING TOOL

SPATULA-ENDED WAX MODELING TOOL

ROUNDED WAX MODELING TOOL

EXAMPLES OF BRONZE FINISHING TOOLS

HOOKED RIFFLER

POINTED RIFFLER

SPIRIT LAMP (FOR HEATING WAX MODELING TOOLS)

Wick

Brass holder

Glass bowl

Methylated spirit

STAGES IN THE LOST-WAX METHOD OF CASTING
Based on Mars, Giambologna, c.1546

Wax-covered wire armature

ORIGINAL MODEL
An original, solid wax model is made and preserved so that numerous replicas can be cast.

Wax riser (vertical, hollow rod)

Chaplet (iron nail)

Wax runner (horizontal, hollow rod)

HOLLOW WAX FIGURE IS CAST
A new, hollow wax model is cast from the original model. It is filled with a plaster core that is held in place with nails. Wax runners and risers are attached.

Fire-resistant clay

FIGURE IS BAKED IN CASTING MOLD
The model is encased in clay and baked. The wax melts away (through the channels made by the wax rods) and is replaced by molten bronze.

MODELING STAND AND ARMATURE

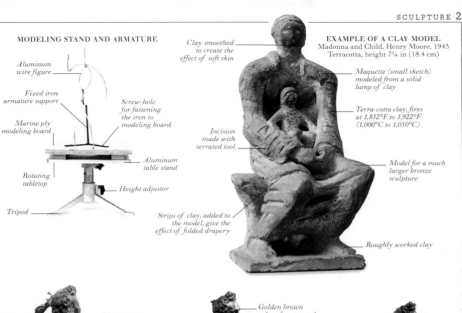

Aluminum wire figure

Fixed iron armature support

Marine ply modeling board

Rotating tabletop

Tripod

Screw-hole for fastening the iron to modeling board

Aluminum table stand

Height adjustor

EXAMPLE OF A CLAY MODEL
Madonna and Child, Henry Moore, 1943
Terracotta, height 7¼ in (18.4 cm)

Clay smoothed to create the effect of soft skin

Maquette (small sketch) modeled from a solid lump of clay

Terra-cotta clay, fires at 1,832°F to 1,922°F (1,000°C to 1,050°C)

Incision made with serrated tool

Model for a much larger bronze sculpture

Strips of clay, added to the model, give the effect of folded drapery

Roughly worked clay

Metal riser

Metal runner

Golden brown color of untreated bronze

Stump left by rod will be filed down

Dark brown patina

Hole left by nail will be plugged with bronze

STATUE IS STRIPPED OF CLAY
When the bronze has cooled, the clay mold is broken open to reveal the bronze statue with solid metal runners and risers.

STATUE IS FINISHED
The nails are pulled out and a large hole is made to remove the plaster core. When the metal rods have been sawn off, the sculpture is filed to refine the surface.

STATUE IS CLEANED
Finally, the work is cleaned and polished. An artificial patina (coloring) is achieved by treating the surface with chemicals.

ARCHITECTURE

ANCIENT EGYPT····································458
ANCIENT GREECE··································460
ANCIENT ROME 1··································462
ANCIENT ROME 2··································464
MEDIEVAL CASTLES AND HOUSES··········466
MEDIEVAL CHURCHES·························468
GOTHIC 1··470
GOTHIC 2··472
RENAISSANCE 1···································474
RENAISSANCE 2···································476
BAROQUE AND NEOCLASSICAL 1···········478
BAROQUE AND NEOCLASSICAL 2···········480
BAROQUE AND NEOCLASSICAL 3···········482
ARCHES AND VAULTS····························484
DOMES···486
ISLAMIC BUILDINGS·····························488
SOUTH AND EAST ASIA··························490
THE 19TH CENTURY·····························492
THE EARLY 20TH CENTURY···················494
MODERN BUILDINGS 1··························496
MODERN BUILDINGS 2··························498

Ancient Egypt

THE CIVILIZATION OF THE ANCIENT EGYPTIANS (which lasted from about 3100 BC until it was finally absorbed into the Roman Empire in 30 BC) is famous for its temples and tombs. Egyptian temples were often huge and geometric, like the Temple of Amon-Re (below and right). They were usually decorated with hieroglyphs (sacred characters used for picture-writing) and painted reliefs depicting gods, Pharaohs (kings), and queens. Tombs were particularly important to the Egyptians, who believed that the dead were resurrected in the afterlife. The tombs were often decorated—as, for example, the surround of the false door opposite—in order to give comfort to the dead. The best-known ancient Egyptian tombs are the pyramids, which were designed to symbolize the rays of the Sun. Many of the architectural forms used by the ancient Egyptians were later adopted by other civilizations; for example, columns and capitals were later used by the ancient Greeks (see pp. 460-461) and ancient Romans (see pp. 462-465).

SIDE VIEW OF HYPOSTYLE HALL, TEMPLE
OF AMON-RE, KARNAK, EGYPT, c. 1290 BC

Cornice decorated with cavetto molding

Campaniform (open papyrus) capital

Architrave

Papyrus-bud capital

Socle

Side aisle   Central nave   Side aisle

Horus, the Sun-god   Architrave   Stone slab forming flat roof of side aisle

Kepresh crown with disk

Chons, the Moon-god | Amon-Re, king of the gods | Hathor, the sky-goddess | Papyrus motif | Cartouche (oval border) containing the titles of the Pharaoh (king) | Socle | Aisle running north-south

LIMESTONE FALSE DOOR WITH HIEROGLYPHS, TOMB OF KING TJETJI, GIZA, EGYPT, c.2400 BC

Lintel

Hieroglyph representing a house

Disk representing sun or light

Eroded image of Tjetji

Limestone stela (slab)

Hoe-shaped hieroglyph representing "mr" sound

Head of false door

Image of Tjetji's wife

Image of Tjetji's daughter

PLANT CAPITAL OF THE PTOLEMAIC-ROMAN PERIOD, EGYPT, 332-30 BC

Palm leaf

Papyrus flower

Papyrus leaf

Papyrus stem

Lotus bud

Lotus stem

Cornice decorated with cavetto molding

Bead molding

Trellis window

Rectangular pier decorated with hieroglyphs

Elevated roof of central nave

Clerestory

Disk representing Sun or light

Architrave

Square abacus

Papyrus-bud capital

Papyriform column

Shaft

Scene depicting a Pharaoh (king) paying homage to the god Amon-Re

Central nave

ANCIENT EGYPTIAN BUILDING DECORATION

DECORATED WINDOW, MEDINET HABU, EGYPT, c.1198 BC

ROPE AND PATERAE DECORATION

CAPITAL WITH THE HEAD OF THE SKY-GODDESS HATHOR, TEMPLE OF ISIS, PHILAE, EGYPT, 283-47 BC

LOTUS AND PAPYRUS FRIEZE DECORATION

Ancient Greece

THE CLASSICAL TEMPLES OF ANCIENT GREECE were built according to the belief that certain forms and proportions were pleasing to the gods. There were three main ancient Greek architectural orders (styles), which can be distinguished by the decoration and proportions of their columns, capitals (column tops), and entablatures (structures resting on the capitals). The oldest is the Doric order, which dates from the seventh century BC and was used mainly on the Greek mainland and in the western colonies, such as Sicily and southern Italy. The Temple of Neptune, shown here, is a classic example of this order. It is hypaethral (roofless) and peripteral (surrounded by a single row of columns). About a century later, the more decorative Ionic order developed on the Aegean Islands. Features of this order include volutes (spiral scrolls) on capitals and acroteria (pediment ornaments). The Corinthian order was invented in Athens in the fifth century BC and is typically identified by an acanthus leaf on the capitals. This order was later widely used in ancient Roman architecture.

CAPITALS OF THE THREE ORDERS OF ANCIENT GREEK ARCHITECTURE

Abacus
Echinus
Annulet
Trachelion (neck)

DORIC CAPITAL, THE PROPYLAEUM (GATEWAY), THE ACROPOLIS, ATHENS, GREECE, 449 BC

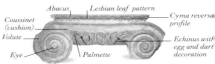

Abacus
Lesbian leaf pattern
Coussinet (cushion)
Volute
Eye
Palmette
Cyma reversa profile
Echinus with egg and dart decoration

IONIC CAPITAL, THE PROPYLAEUM (GATEWAY), TEMPLE OF ATHENA POLIAS, PRIENE, GREECE, c.334 BC

Mask
Abacus
Volute
Cauliculus
Bell-shaped core
Acanthus leaf

CORINTHIAN CAPITAL FROM A STOA (PORTICO), PROBABLY FROM ASIA MINOR

TEMPLE OF NEPTUNE, PAESTUM, ITALY, c.460 BC

Raking cornice
Pediment
Trachelion (neck)
Taenia
Triglyph
Metope
Glyph (channel)
Doric entablature
Pteron (external colonnade)
Euthynteria
Drum
Stylobate
Column of the Doric order

PLAN OF THE TEMPLE OF NEPTUNE, PAESTUM

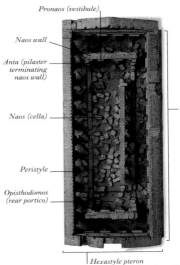

Pronaos (vestibule)

Naos wall

Anta (pilaster terminating naos wall)

Naos (cella)

Peristyle

Opisthodomos (rear portico)

Pteron (external colonnade)

Hexastyle pteron (colonnade of six columns)

ANCIENT GREEK BUILDING DECORATION

Volute

FACADE, TREASURY OF ATREUS, MYCENAE, GREECE, 1350-1250 BC

Meander

FRETWORK, PARTHENON, ATHENS, GREECE, 447-436 BC

ACROTERION, TEMPLE OF APHAIA, AEGINA, GREECE, 490 BC

Griffon (gryphon)

Raking cornice

ANTEFIXA, TEMPLE OF APHAIA, AEGINA, GREECE, 490 BC

Palmette

Volute

Regula (short fillet beneath taenia)

Eaves

Cornice

Frieze

Architrave

Capital

Shaft

Crepidoma (stepped base)

Entasis (slight curve of a column)

Intercolumniation

Fluting

461

Ancient Rome 1

IN THE EARLY PERIOD OF THE ROMAN EMPIRE extensive use
was made of ancient Greek architectural ideas, particularly
those of the Corinthian order (see pp. 460-461). As a result,
many early Roman buildings—such as the Temple of Vesta
(opposite)—closely resemble ancient Greek buildings. A
distinctive Roman style began to evolve in the first century
AD. This style developed the interiors of buildings (the Greeks
had concentrated on the exterior) by using arches, vaults, and
domes inside the buildings, and by ornamenting internal walls.
Many of these features can be seen in the Pantheon. Exterior
columns were often used for decorative, rather than structural,
purposes, as in the Colosseum and the Porta Nigra (see
pp. 464-465). Smaller buildings had timber frames with
wattle-and-daub walls, as in the mill (see pp. 464-465).
Roman architecture remained influential for many centuries,
with some of its principles being used in the 11th century in
Romanesque buildings (see pp. 468-469) and also in the 15th
and 16th centuries in Renaissance buildings (see pp. 474-477).

ANCIENT ROMAN BUILDING DECORATION

FESTOON, TEMPLE OF VESTA,
TIVOLI, ITALY, C.80 BC

RICHLY DECORATED
ROMAN OVUM

INTERIOR OF THE PANTHEON, ROME, ITALY, 118-c.128

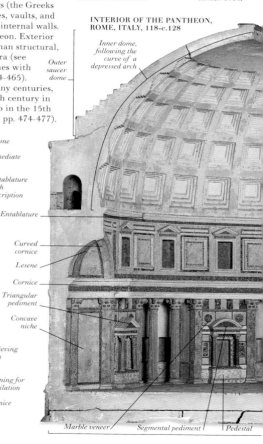

Outer
saucer
dome

Inner dome,
following the
curve of a
depressed arch

Entablature
with
inscription

Entablature

Curved
cornice

Lesene

Cornice

Triangular
pediment

Concave
niche

Relieving
arch

Opening for
ventilation

Cornice

Marble veneer   Segmental pediment   Pedestal

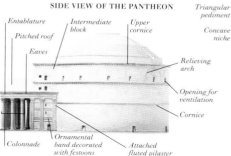

Oculus

Series of concentric,
steplike rings

Outer saucer dome

Intermediate
block

Dentil ornament

Engaged
pediment

Entablature
with
inscription

Raking
cornice

Pediment

Rotunda

Octastyle portico
(eight-column portico)

FRONT VIEW OF THE PANTHEON

SIDE VIEW OF THE PANTHEON

Entablature

Intermediate
block

Upper
cornice

Pitched roof

Eaves

Colonnade

Ornamental
band decorated
with festoons

Attached
fluted pilaster

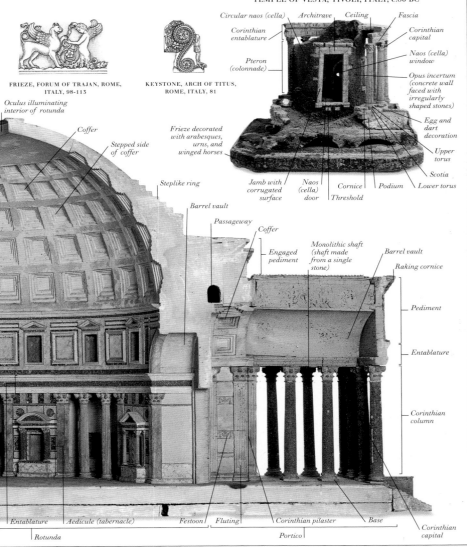

FRIEZE, FORUM OF TRAJAN, ROME,
ITALY, 98-113

KEYSTONE, ARCH OF TITUS,
ROME, ITALY, 81

TEMPLE OF VESTA, TIVOLI, ITALY, c.80 BC

Circular naos (cella)

Corinthian
entablature

Architrave

Ceiling

Fascia

Corinthian
capital

Pteron
(colonnade)

Naos (cella)
window

Opus incertum
(concrete wall
faced with
irregularly
shaped stones)

Egg and
dart
decoration

Upper
torus

Scotia

Lower torus

Jamb with
corrugated
surface

Naos
(cella)
door

Cornice

Threshold

Podium

Oculus illuminating
interior of rotunda

Coffer

Stepped side
of coffer

Frieze decorated
with arabesques,
urns, and
winged horses

Steplike ring

Barrel vault

Passageway

Coffer

Engaged
pediment

Monolithic shaft
(shaft made
from a single
stone)

Barrel vault

Raking cornice

Pediment

Entablature

Corinthian
column

Entablature

Aedicule (tabernacle)

Festoon

Fluting

Corinthian pilaster

Base

Corinthian
capital

Rotunda

Portico

Ancient Rome 2

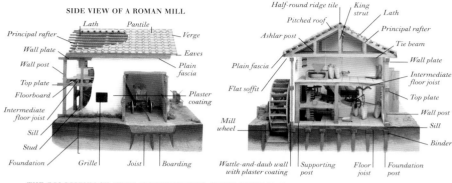

SIDE VIEW OF A ROMAN MILL

- Principal rafter
- Lath
- Pantile
- Verge
- Wall plate
- Eaves
- Wall post
- Plain fascia
- Top plate
- Floorboard
- Plaster coating
- Intermediate floor joist
- Sill
- Stud
- Foundation
- Grille
- Joist
- Boarding

FRONT VIEW OF A ROMAN MILL, 1ST CENTURY BC

- Half-round ridge tile
- King strut
- Lath
- Pitched roof
- Principal rafter
- Ashlar post
- Tie beam
- Plain fascia
- Wall plate
- Flat soffit
- Intermediate floor joist
- Top plate
- Wall post
- Mill wheel
- Sill
- Binder
- Wattle-and-daub wall with plaster coating
- Supporting post
- Floor joist
- Foundation post

THE COLOSSEUM (FLAVIAN AMPHITHEATRE), ROME, ITALY, 70-82

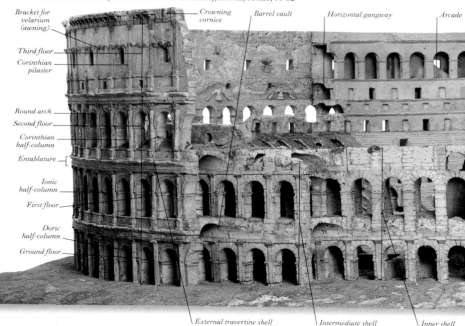

- Bracket for velarium (awning)
- Crowning cornice
- Barrel vault
- Horizontal gangway
- Arcade
- Third floor
- Corinthian pilaster
- Round arch
- Second floor
- Corinthian half-column
- Entablature
- Ionic half-column
- First floor
- Doric half-column
- Ground floor
- External travertine shell
- Intermediate shell
- Inner shell

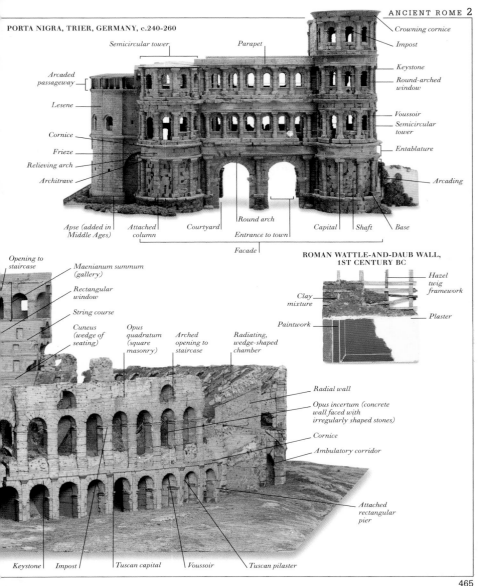

PORTA NIGRA, TRIER, GERMANY, c.240-260

Crowning cornice

Impost

Semicircular tower

Parapet

Keystone

Round-arched window

Arcaded passageway

Lesene

Voussoir

Semicircular tower

Cornice

Entablature

Frieze

Relieving arch

Arcading

Architrave

Apse (added in Middle Ages)

Attached column

Courtyard

Round arch

Entrance to town

Capital

Shaft

Base

Facade

ROMAN WATTLE-AND-DAUB WALL, 1ST CENTURY BC

Opening to staircase

Maenianum summum (gallery)

Rectangular window

String course

Cuneus (wedge of seating)

Opus quadratum (square masonry)

Arched opening to staircase

Radiating, wedge-shaped chamber

Hazel twig framework

Clay mixture

Plaster

Paintwork

Radial wall

Opus incertum (concrete wall faced with irregularly shaped stones)

Cornice

Ambulatory corridor

Attached rectangular pier

Keystone

Impost

Tuscan capital

Voussoir

Tuscan pilaster

Medieval castles and houses

WARFARE WAS COMMON IN EUROPE in the Middle Ages, and many monarchs and nobles built castles as a form of defense. Typical medieval castles have outer walls surrounding a moat. Inside the moat is a bailey (courtyard), protected by a chemise (jacket wall). The innermost and strongest part of a medieval castle is the keep. There are two main types of keep: towers called donjons, such as the Tour de César and Coucy-le-Château, and rectangular keeps ("hall-keeps"), such as the Tower of London. Castles were often guarded by salients (projecting fortifications), like those of the Bastille. Medieval houses typically had timber cruck (tentlike) frames, wattle-and-daub walls, and pitched roofs, like those on medieval London Bridge (opposite).

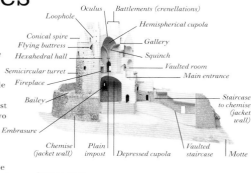

DONJON, TOUR DE CESAR, PROVINS, FRANCE, 12TH CENTURY

Oculus
Loophole
Battlements (crenellations)
Hemispherical cupola
Conical spire
Flying buttress
Gallery
Hexahedral hall
Squinch
Semicircular turret
Vaulted room
Fireplace
Main entrance
Bailey
Staircase to chemise (jacket wall)
Embrasure
Chemise (jacket wall)
Plain impost
Depressed cupola
Vaulted staircase
Motte

Loophole

SALIENT, CAERNARVON CASTLE, BRITAIN, 1283-1323

Timber cruck frame

CRUCK-FRAMED HOUSE, BRITAIN, c.1200

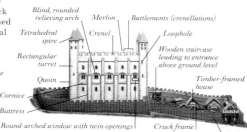

Blind, rounded relieving arch
Merlon
Battlements (crenellations)
Tetrahedral spire
Crenel
Loophole
Rectangular turret
Wooden staircase leading to entrance above ground level
Quoin
Timber-framed house
Cornice
Buttress
Round-arched window with twin openings
Cruck frame
Paling

TOWER OF LONDON, BRITAIN, FROM 1070

Curtain wall
Pointed relieving arch
Semicircular relieving arch
Plain string course
Bracket decorated with scroll molding

Rectangular window
Sunken rectangular panel
Round-arched window
Semicircular salient
Loophole
Lateral circular salient

THE BASTILLE, PARIS, FRANCE, 14TH CENTURY

MEDIEVAL LONDON BRIDGE, BRITAIN, 1176 (WITH 14TH-CENTURY BATTLEMENTED BUILDING, NONESUCH HOUSE, AND TWO-TOWERED GATE)

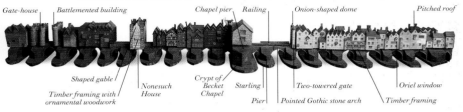

Gate-house

Battlemented building

Chapel pier

Railing

Onion-shaped dome

Pitched roof

Shaped gable

Nonesuch House

Crypt of Becket Chapel

Starling

Two-towered gate

Oriel window

Timber framing with ornamental woodwork

Pier

Pointed Gothic stone arch

Timber framing

DONJON, COUCY-LE-CHATEAU, AISNE, FRANCE, 1225-1245

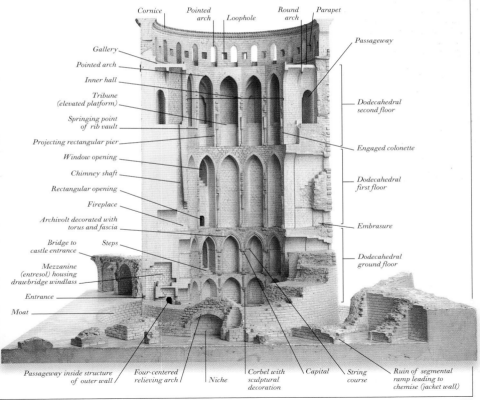

Cornice

Pointed arch

Loophole

Round arch

Parapet

Gallery

Pointed arch

Inner hall

Tribune (elevated platform)

Springing point of rib vault

Projecting rectangular pier

Window opening

Chimney shaft

Rectangular opening

Fireplace

Archivolt decorated with torus and fascia

Bridge to castle entrance

Steps

Mezzanine (entresol) housing drawbridge windlass

Entrance

Moat

Passageway

Dodecahedral second floor

Engaged colonette

Dodecahedral first floor

Embrasure

Dodecahedral ground floor

Passageway inside structure of outer wall

Four-centered relieving arch

Niche

Corbel with sculptural decoration

Capital

String course

Ruin of segmental ramp leading to chemise (jacket wall)

Medieval churches

ABBEY OF ST. FOI, CONQUES, FRANCE, c.1050–c.1130

DURING THE MIDDLE AGES, large numbers of churches were built in Europe. European churches of this period typically have high vaults supported by massive piers and columns. In the 10th century, the Romanesque style developed. Romanesque architects adopted many Roman or early Christian architectural ideas, such as cross-shaped ground-plans—like that of Angoulême Cathedral (opposite)—and the basilican system of a nave with a central vessel and side aisles. In the mid-12th century, flying buttresses and pointed vaults appeared. These features later became widely used in Gothic architecture (see pp. 470–471). Bagneux Church (opposite) has both styles: a Romanesque tower, and a Gothic nave and choir.

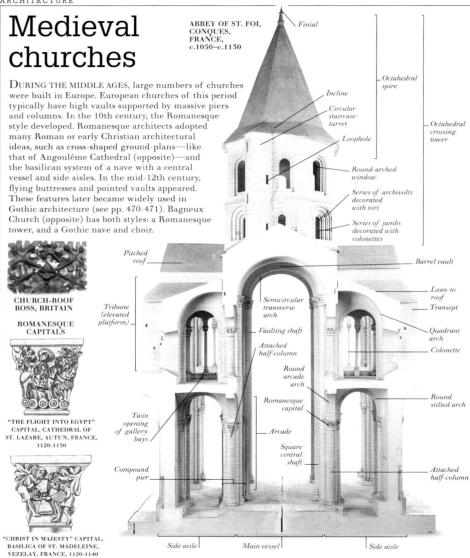

CHURCH-ROOF BOSS, BRITAIN

ROMANESQUE CAPITALS

"THE FLIGHT INTO EGYPT" CAPITAL, CATHEDRAL OF ST. LAZARE, AUTUN, FRANCE, 1120–1130

"CHRIST IN MAJESTY" CAPITAL, BASILICA OF ST. MADELEINE, VEZELAY, FRANCE, 1120–1140

Finial

Octahedral spire

Incline

Circular staircase-turret

Loophole

Octahedral crossing tower

Round-arched window

Series of archivolts decorated with tori

Series of jambs decorated with colonettes

Pitched roof

Barrel vault

Tribune (elevated platform)

Lean-to roof

Semicircular transverse arch

Transept

Vaulting shaft

Quadrant arch

Attached half-column

Colonette

Round arcade arch

Romanesque capital

Round stilted arch

Twin opening of gallery bays

Arcade

Square central shaft

Compound pier

Attached half-column

Side aisle

Main vessel

Side aisle

GROUND-PLAN OF ANGOULEME CATHEDRAL, FRANCE, FROM c.1105

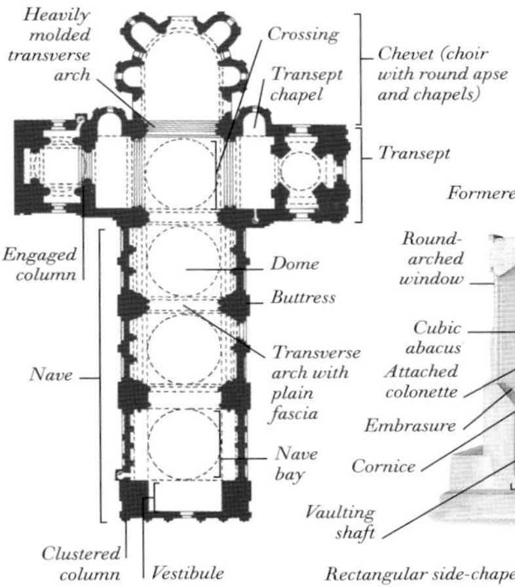

Heavily molded transverse arch
Crossing
Transept chapel
Chevet (choir with round apse and chapels)
Transept
Formeret
Domed rib-vault
Lierne
Round-arched window
Engaged column
Dome
Buttress
Transverse arch with plain fascia
Nave
Cubic abacus
Attached colonette
Embrasure
Cornice
Vaulting shaft
Clustered column
Vestibule
Nave bay
Rectangular side-chapel
Impost with foliated frieze

CHOIR, CHURCH OF ST. SERGE, ANGERS, FRANCE, c.1215-1220

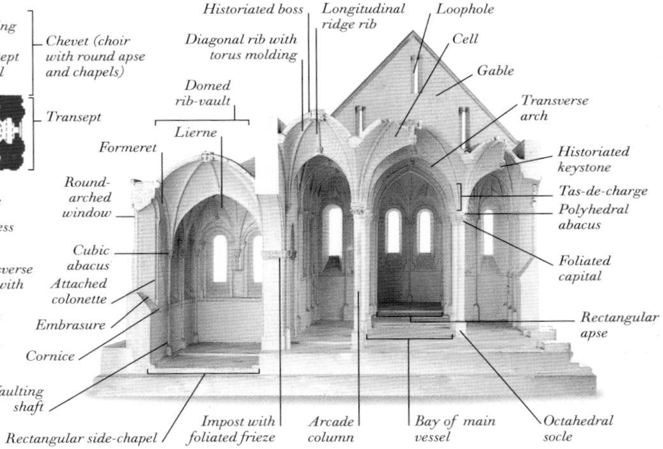

Historiated boss
Longitudinal ridge rib
Loophole
Diagonal rib with torus molding
Cell
Gable
Transverse arch
Historiated keystone
Tas-de-charge
Polyhedral abacus
Foliated capital
Rectangular apse
Arcade column
Bay of main vessel
Octahedral socle

BAGNEUX CHURCH, FRANCE, 1170-1190

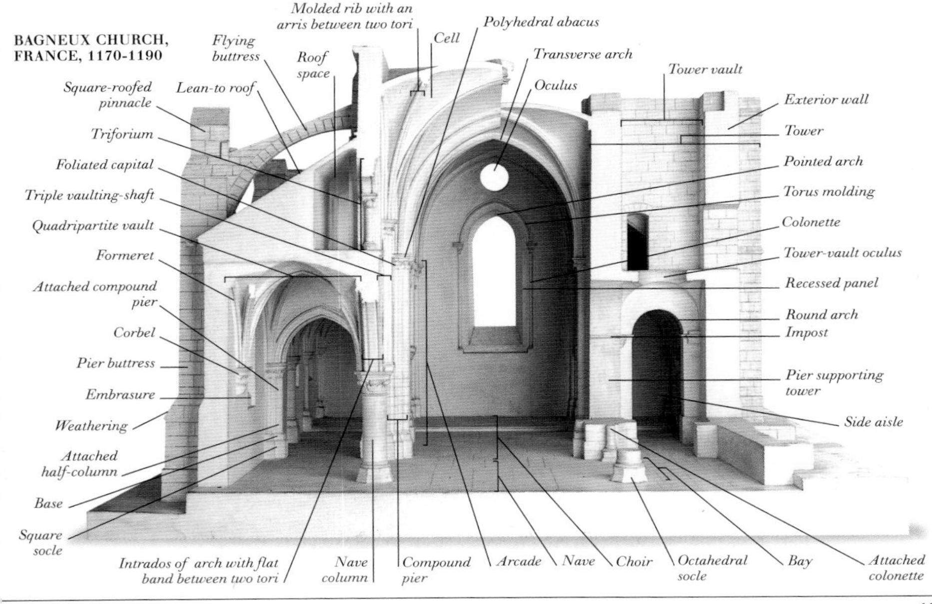

Molded rib with an arris between two tori
Cell
Polyhedral abacus
Flying buttress
Roof space
Transverse arch
Tower vault
Oculus
Square-roofed pinnacle
Lean-to roof
Exterior wall
Tower
Triforium
Pointed arch
Foliated capital
Torus molding
Triple vaulting-shaft
Colonette
Quadripartite vault
Tower-vault oculus
Formeret
Recessed panel
Attached compound pier
Round arch
Corbel
Impost
Pier buttress
Pier supporting tower
Embrasure
Side aisle
Weathering
Attached half-column
Base
Square socle
Intrados of arch with flat band between two tori
Nave column
Compound pier
Arcade
Nave
Choir
Octahedral socle
Bay
Attached colonette

Gothic 1

GOTHIC STAINED GLASS WITH FOLIATED SCROLL MOTIF, ON WOODEN FORM

GOTHIC BUILDINGS are characterized by rib vaults, pointed or lancet arches, flying buttresses, decorative tracery and gables, and stained-glass windows. Typical Gothic buildings include the Cathedrals of Salisbury and old St. Paul's in England, and Notre Dame de Paris in France (see pp. 472-473). The Gothic style developed out of Romanesque architecture in France (see pp. 468-469) in the mid-12th century, and then spread throughout Europe. The decorative elements of Gothic architecture became highly developed in buildings of the English Decorated style (late 13th-14th century) and the French Flamboyant style (15th-16th century). These styles are exemplified by the tower of Salisbury Cathedral and the staircase in the Church of St. Maclou (see pp. 472-473), respectively. In both of these styles, embellishments such as ballflowers and curvilinear (flowing) tracery were used liberally. The English Perpendicular style (late 14th-15th century), which followed the Decorated style, emphasized the vertical and horizontal elements of a building. A notable feature of this style is the hammer-beam roof.

GROUND-PLAN OF SALISBURY CATHEDRAL

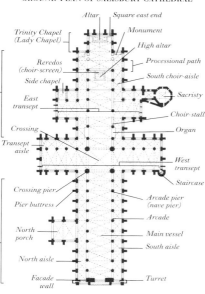

Altar
Square east end
Trinity Chapel (Lady Chapel)
Monument
High altar
Reredos (choir-screen)
Processional path
Side chapel
South choir-aisle
Choir
East transept
Sacristy
Crossing
Choir-stall
Organ
Transept aisle
West transept
Staircase
Crossing pier
Arcade pier (nave pier)
Pier buttress
Arcade
North porch
Main vessel
Nave
South aisle
North aisle
Facade wall
Turret

GOTHIC TORUS WITH BALLFLOWERS

Limestone block
Block members carved into rolls
Block members cut polygonally
Pencil guideline
Early stage of ballflower carving

BLOCK AFTER INITIAL CUTTING

BLOCK WITH MEMBERS CUT INTO ROLLS

Torus
Ballflower
Fillet
Mason's mark

FINISHED BLOCK

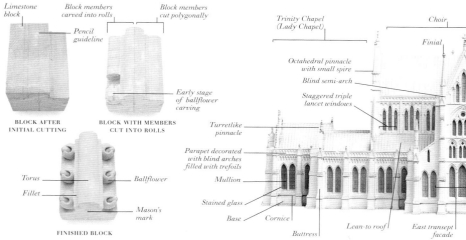

Trinity Chapel (Lady Chapel)
Choir
Finial
Octahedral pinnacle with small spire
Blind semi-arch
Staggered triple lancet windows
Turretlike pinnacle
Parapet decorated with blind arches filled with trefoils
Mullion
Stained glass
Base
Cornice
Buttress
Lean-to roof
East transept facade

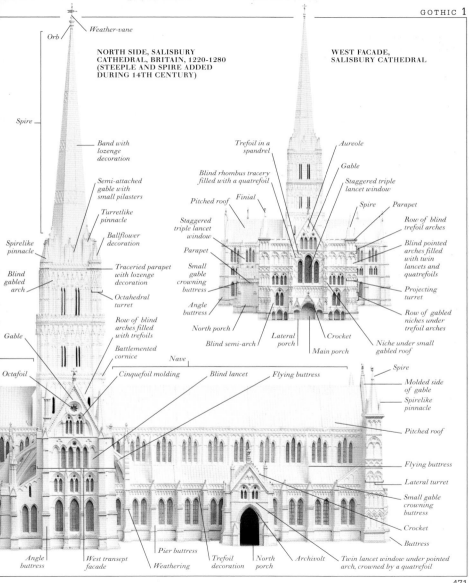

Weather-vane

Orb

**NORTH SIDE, SALISBURY
CATHEDRAL, BRITAIN, 1220-1280
(STEEPLE AND SPIRE ADDED
DURING 14TH CENTURY)**

**WEST FACADE,
SALISBURY CATHEDRAL**

Spire

Band with
lozenge
decoration

Trefoil in a
spandrel

Aureole

Gable

Blind rhombus tracery
filled with a quatrefoil

Staggered triple
lancet window

Semi-attached
gable with
small pilasters

Pitched roof

Finial

Spire

Parapet

Turretlike
pinnacle

Staggered
triple lancet
window

Row of blind
trefoil arches

Ballflower
decoration

Spirelike
pinnacle

Parapet

Blind pointed
arches filled
with twin
lancets and
quatrefoils

Tracericed parapet
with lozenge
decoration

Small
gable
crowning
buttress

Blind
gabled
arch

Projecting
turret

Octahedral
turret

Angle
buttress

Row of gabled
niches under
trefoil arches

Row of blind
arches filled
with trefoils

North porch

Niche under small
gabled roof

Gable

Blind semi-arch

Lateral
porch

Crocket

Battlemented
cornice

Main porch

Nave

Octafoil

Spire

Cinquefoil molding

Blind lancet

Flying buttress

Molded side
of gable

Spirelike
pinnacle

Pitched roof

Flying buttress

Lateral turret

Small gable
crowning
buttress

Crocket

Buttress

Angle
buttress

West transept
facade

Pier buttress

Weathering

Trefoil
decoration

North
porch

Archivolt

Twin lancet window under pointed
arch, crowned by a quatrefoil

Gothic 2

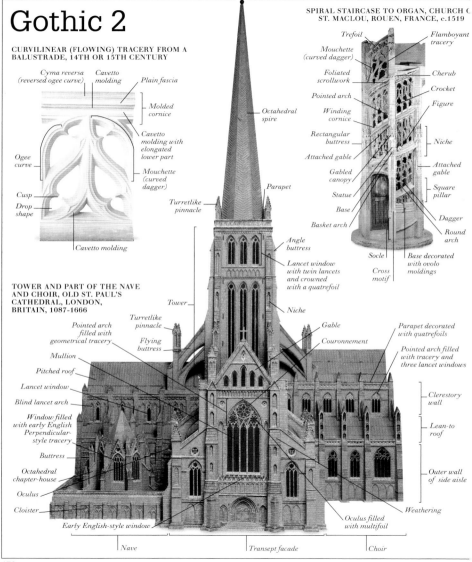

CURVILINEAR (FLOWING) TRACERY FROM A BALUSTRADE, 14TH OR 15TH CENTURY

- Cyma reversa (reversed ogee curve)
- Cavetto molding
- Plain fascia
- Molded cornice
- Cavetto molding with elongated lower part
- Ogee curve
- Mouchette (curved dagger)
- Cusp
- Drop shape
- Cavetto molding

SPIRAL STAIRCASE TO ORGAN, CHURCH OF ST. MACLOU, ROUEN, FRANCE, c.1519

- Trefoil
- Flamboyant tracery
- Mouchette (curved dagger)
- Cherub
- Foliated scrollwork
- Crocket
- Pointed arch
- Figure
- Winding cornice
- Rectangular buttress
- Niche
- Attached gable
- Attached gable
- Gabled canopy
- Square pillar
- Statue
- Dagger
- Base
- Round arch
- Basket arch
- Socle
- Base decorated with ovolo moldings
- Cross motif

- Octahedral spire
- Parapet
- Turretlike pinnacle
- Angle buttress
- Lancet window with twin lancets and crowned with a quatrefoil

TOWER AND PART OF THE NAVE AND CHOIR, OLD ST. PAUL'S CATHEDRAL, LONDON, BRITAIN, 1087-1666

- Tower
- Turretlike pinnacle
- Niche
- Pointed arch filled with geometrical tracery
- Flying buttress
- Gable
- Couronnement
- Parapet decorated with quatrefoils
- Mullion
- Pointed arch filled with tracery and three lancet windows
- Pitched roof
- Lancet window
- Blind lancet arch
- Clerestory wall
- Window filled with early English Perpendicular-style tracery
- Lean-to roof
- Buttress
- Octahedral chapter-house
- Outer wall of side aisle
- Oculus
- Cloister
- Weathering
- Early English-style window
- Oculus filled with multifoil
- Nave
- Transept facade
- Choir

472

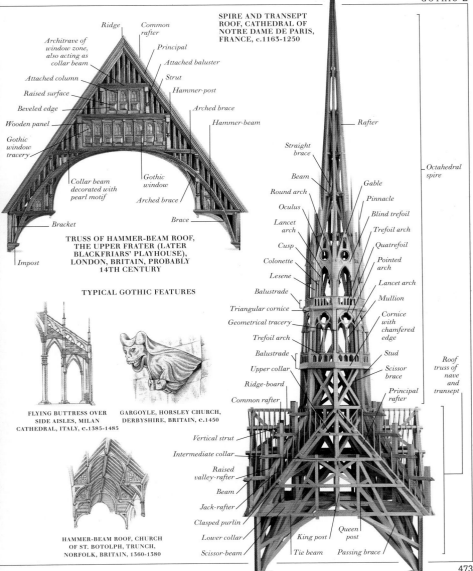

Ridge

Common rafter

Architrave of window zone, also acting as collar beam

Principal

Attached baluster

Attached column

Strut

Raised surface

Hammer-post

Beveled edge

Arched brace

Wooden panel

Hammer-beam

Gothic window tracery

Collar beam decorated with pearl motif

Gothic window

Arched brace

Bracket

Brace

Impost

SPIRE AND TRANSEPT ROOF, CATHEDRAL OF NOTRE DAME DE PARIS, FRANCE, c.1163-1250

TRUSS OF HAMMER-BEAM ROOF, THE UPPER FRATER (LATER BLACKFRIARS' PLAYHOUSE), LONDON, BRITAIN, PROBABLY 14TH CENTURY

TYPICAL GOTHIC FEATURES

FLYING BUTTRESS OVER SIDE AISLES, MILAN CATHEDRAL, ITALY, c.1385-1485

GARGOYLE, HORSLEY CHURCH, DERBYSHIRE, BRITAIN, c.1450

HAMMER-BEAM ROOF, CHURCH OF ST. BOTOLPH, TRUNCH, NORFOLK, BRITAIN, 1360-1380

Rafter

Straight brace

Beam

Round arch

Oculus

Lancet arch

Cusp

Colonette

Lesene

Balustrade

Triangular cornice

Geometrical tracery

Trefoil arch

Balustrade

Upper collar

Ridge-board

Common rafter

Vertical strut

Intermediate collar

Raised valley-rafter

Beam

Jack-rafter

Clasped purlin

Lower collar

Scissor-beam

Gable

Pinnacle

Blind trefoil

Trefoil arch

Quatrefoil

Pointed arch

Lancet arch

Mullion

Cornice with chamfered edge

Stud

Scissor brace

Principal rafter

King post

Queen post

Tie beam

Passing brace

Octahedral spire

Roof truss of nave and transept

473

Renaissance 1

THE RENAISSANCE was a European movement—lasting roughly from the 14th century to the mid-17th century—in which the arts and sciences underwent great changes. In architecture, these changes were marked by a return to the classical forms and proportions of ancient Roman buildings. The Renaissance originated in Italy, and the buildings most characteristic of its style can be found there, such as the Palazzo Strozzi shown here. Mannerism is a branch of the Renaissance style that distorts the classical forms; an example is the Laurentian Library staircase. As the Renaissance style spread to other European countries, many of its features were incorporated into the local architecture; for example, the Château de Montal in France (see pp. 476-477) incorporates aedicules (tabernacles).

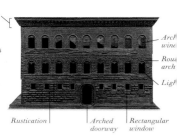

Crowning cornice

Arch wind

Rou arch

Ligh

Rustication

Arched doorway

Rectangular window

SIDE VIEW OF PALAZZO STROZZI, FLORENCE, ITALY, 1489 (BY G. DA SANGALLO, B. DA MAIANO, AND CRONACA)

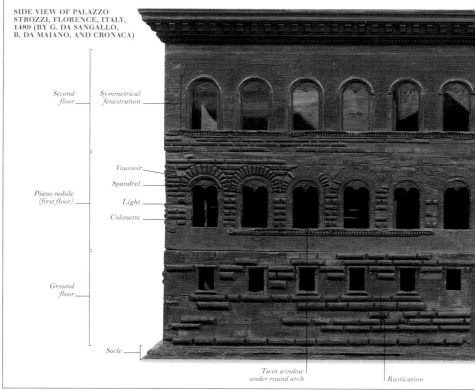

Second floor

Symmetrical fenestration

Voussoir

Spandrel

Piano nobile (first floor)

Light

Colonette

Ground floor

Socle

Twin window under round arch

Rustication

DETAILS FROM ITALIAN RENAISSANCE BUILDINGS

**PANEL FROM DRUM OF DOME,
FLORENCE CATHEDRAL, 1420-1436**

**COFFERING IN DOME,
PAZZI CHAPEL,
FLORENCE, 1429-1461**

**STAIRCASE,
LAURENTIAN LIBRARY,
FLORENCE, 1559**

**PORTICO, VILLA ROTUNDA,
VICENZA, 1567-1569**

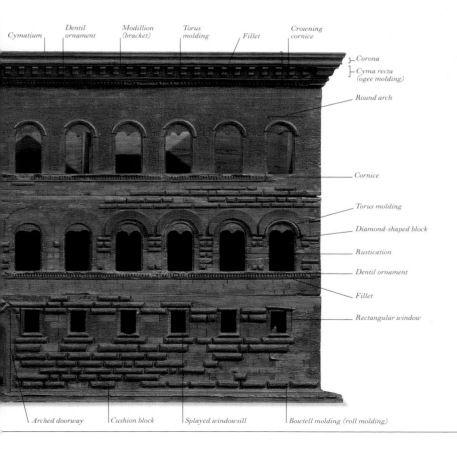

Cymatium

Dentil ornament

Modillion (bracket)

Torus molding

Fillet

Crowning cornice

Corona

Cyma recta (ogee molding)

Round arch

Cornice

Torus molding

Diamond-shaped block

Rustication

Dentil ornament

Fillet

Rectangular window

Arched doorway

Cushion block

Splayed windowsill

Bowtell molding (roll molding)

Renaissance 2

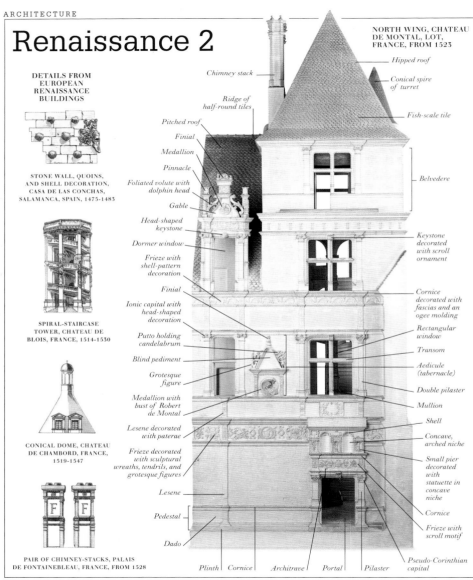

DETAILS FROM EUROPEAN RENAISSANCE BUILDINGS

STONE WALL, QUOINS, AND SHELL DECORATION, CASA DE LAS CONCHAS, SALAMANCA, SPAIN, 1475-1483

SPIRAL-STAIRCASE TOWER, CHATEAU DE BLOIS, FRANCE, 1514-1530

CONICAL DOME, CHATEAU DE CHAMBORD, FRANCE, 1519-1547

PAIR OF CHIMNEY-STACKS, PALAIS DE FONTAINEBLEAU, FRANCE, FROM 1528

Hipped roof

Conical spire of turret

Chimney stack

Fish-scale tile

Ridge of half-round tiles

Pitched roof

Finial

Medallion

Belvedere

Pinnacle

Foliated volute with dolphin head

Gable

Head-shaped keystone

Keystone decorated with scroll ornament

Dormer window

Frieze with shell-pattern decoration

Finial

Cornice decorated with fascias and an ogee molding

Ionic capital with head-shaped decoration

Rectangular window

Putto holding candelabrum

Transom

Blind pediment

Aedicule (tabernacle)

Grotesque figure

Double pilaster

Medallion with bust of Robert de Montal

Mullion

Shell

Lesene decorated with paterae

Concave, arched niche

Frieze decorated with sculptural wreaths, tendrils, and grotesque figures

Small pier decorated with statuette in concave niche

Lesene

Cornice

Pedestal

Frieze with scroll motif

Dado

Plinth   Cornice   Architrave   Portal   Pilaster

Pseudo-Corinthian capital

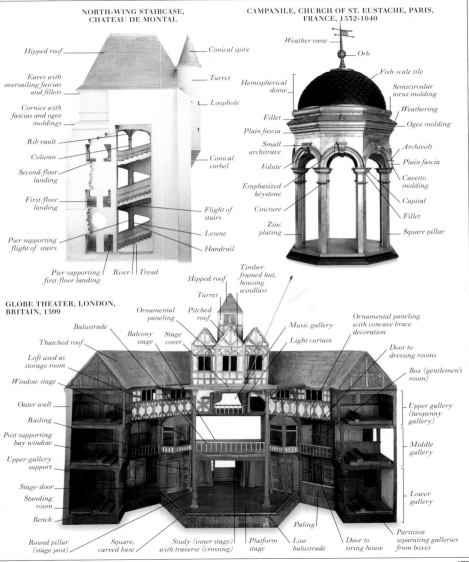

NORTH-WING STAIRCASE, CHATEAU DE MONTAL

Hipped roof

Eaves with oversailing fascias and fillets

Cornice with fascias and ogee moldings

Rib vault

Column

Second-floor landing

First-floor landing

Pier supporting flight of stairs

Pier supporting first-floor landing

Riser

Tread

Conical spire

Turret

Loophole

Conical corbel

Flight of stairs

Lesene

Handrail

CAMPANILE, CHURCH OF ST. EUSTACHE, PARIS, FRANCE, 1532-1640

Weather vane

Orb

Fish-scale tile

Hemispherical dome

Semicircular torus molding

Weathering

Fillet

Ogee molding

Plain fascia

Small architrave

Archivolt

Plain fascia

Volute

Cavetto molding

Emphasized keystone

Capital

Cincture

Fillet

Zinc plating

Square pillar

GLOBE THEATER, LONDON, BRITAIN, 1599

Balustrade

Thatched roof

Loft used as storage room

Window stage

Outer wall

Railing

Post supporting bay window

Upper-gallery support

Stage-door

Standing room

Bench

Round pillar (stage post)

Square, carved base

Study (inner stage) with traverse (crossing)

Platform stage

Low balustrade

Paling

Door to tiring house

Partition separating galleries from boxes

Balcony stage

Stage cover

Ornamental paneling

Pitched roof

Turret

Hipped roof

Timber-framed hut, housing windlass

Music gallery

Light curtain

Ornamental paneling with concave brace decoration

Door to dressing rooms

Box (gentlemen's room)

Upper gallery (twopenny gallery)

Middle gallery

Lower gallery

477

Baroque and neoclassical 1

THE BAROQUE STYLE EVOLVED IN THE EARLY 17TH CENTURY in Rome. It is characterized by curved outlines and ostentatious decoration, as can be seen in the Italian church details (right). The baroque style was particularly widely favored in Italy, Spain, and Germany. It was also adopted in Britain and France, but with adaptations. The British architects Sir Christopher Wren and Nicholas Hawksmoor, for example, used baroque features—such as the concave walls of St. Paul's Cathedral and the curved buttresses of the Church of St. George in the East (see pp. 480-481)—but they did so with restraint. Similarly, the curved buttresses and volutes of the Parisian Church of St. Paul-St. Louis are relatively plain. In the second half of the 17th century, a distinct classical style (known as neoclassicism) developed in northern Europe as a reaction to the excesses of baroque. Typical of this new style were churches such as the Madeleine (a proposed facade is shown below), as well as secular buildings such as the Cirque Napoleon (opposite) and the buildings of the British architect Sir John Soane (see pp. 482-483). In early 18th-century France, an extremely lavish form of baroque developed, known as rococo. The balcony from Nantes (see pp. 482-483) with its twisted ironwork and head-shaped corbels is typical of this style.

DETAILS FROM ITALIAN BAROQUE CHURCHES

SCROLLED BUTTRESS, CHURCH OF ST. MARIA DELLA SALUTE, VENICE, 1631-1682

STATUE OF THE ECSTASY OF ST. THERESA, CHURCH OF ST. MARIA DELLA VITTORIA, ROME, 1645-1652

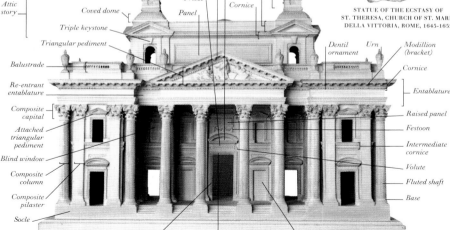

Attached segmental pediment
Round-arched window
Raking cornice
Lantern
Finial
Twin pilaster
Parapet
Attic story
Frieze
Coved dome
Cornice
Panel
Triple keystone
Triangular pediment
Dentil ornament
Urn
Modillion (bracket)
Balustrade
Cornice
Re-entrant entablature
Entablature
Composite capital
Raised panel
Attached triangular pediment
Festoon
Blind window
Intermediate cornice
Composite column
Volute
Composite pilaster
Fluted shaft
Socle
Base
Door jamb
Architrave
Blind door

PROPOSED FACADE, THE MADELEINE (NEOCLASSICAL), PARIS, FRANCE, 1764 (BY P. CONTANT D'IVRY)

CIRQUE NAPOLEON (NEOCLASSICAL), PARIS, FRANCE, 1852 (BY J. I. HITTORFF)

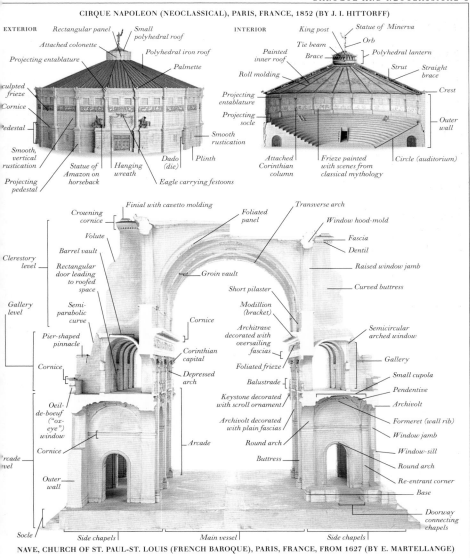

EXTERIOR

- Rectangular panel
- Small polyhedral roof
- Attached colonette
- Polyhedral iron roof
- Projecting entablature
- Palmette
- Sculpted frieze
- Cornice
- Pedestal
- Smooth, vertical rustication
- Projecting pedestal
- Statue of Amazon on horseback
- Hanging wreath
- Dado (die)
- Plinth
- Smooth rustication
- Eagle carrying festoons

INTERIOR

- King post
- Statue of Minerva
- Tie beam
- Orb
- Painted inner roof
- Brace
- Polyhedral lantern
- Roll molding
- Strut
- Straight brace
- Projecting entablature
- Crest
- Projecting socle
- Outer wall
- Attached Corinthian column
- Frieze painted with scenes from classical mythology
- Circle (auditorium)

NAVE, CHURCH OF ST. PAUL-ST. LOUIS (FRENCH BAROQUE), PARIS, FRANCE, FROM 1627 (BY E. MARTELLANGE)

- Finial with cavetto molding
- Foliated panel
- Transverse arch
- Crowning cornice
- Window hood-mold
- Volute
- Fascia
- Clerestory level
- Barrel vault
- Dentil
- Rectangular door leading to roofed space
- Groin vault
- Raised window jamb
- Gallery level
- Semi-parabolic curve
- Short pilaster
- Curved buttress
- Pier-shaped pinnacle
- Cornice
- Modillion (bracket)
- Semicircular arched window
- Corinthian capital
- Architrave decorated with oversailing fascias
- Gallery
- Cornice
- Depressed arch
- Foliated frieze
- Small cupola
- Oeil-de-boeuf ("ox-eye") window
- Balustrade
- Pendentive
- Keystone decorated with scroll ornament
- Archivolt
- Cornice
- Archivolt decorated with plain fascias
- Formeret (wall rib)
- Arcade
- Round arch
- Window jamb
- Arcade level
- Buttress
- Window-sill
- Outer wall
- Round arch
- Re-entrant corner
- Base
- Socle
- Doorway connecting chapels
- Side chapels
- Main vessel
- Side chapels

Baroque and neoclassical 2

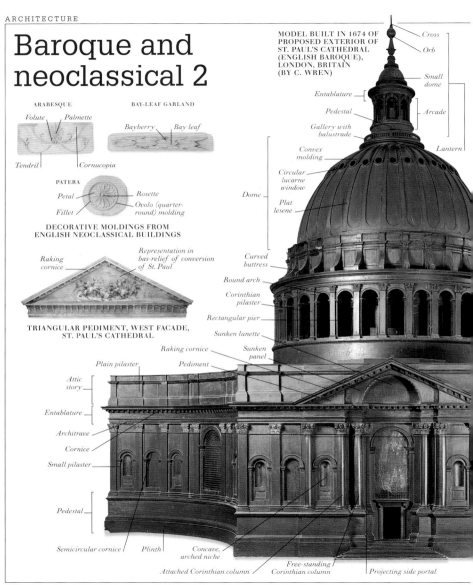

ARABESQUE

Volute
Palmette
Tendril
Cornucopia

BAY-LEAF GARLAND

Bayberry
Bay leaf

PATERA

Petal
Fillet
Rosette
Ovolo (quarter-round) molding

DECORATIVE MOLDINGS FROM
ENGLISH NEOCLASSICAL BUILDINGS

Raking cornice
Representation in bas-relief of conversion of St. Paul

TRIANGULAR PEDIMENT, WEST FACADE,
ST. PAUL'S CATHEDRAL

MODEL BUILT IN 1674 OF
PROPOSED EXTERIOR OF
ST. PAUL'S CATHEDRAL
(ENGLISH BAROQUE),
LONDON, BRITAIN
(BY C. WREN)

Cross
Orb
Small dome
Entablature
Pedestal
Arcade
Gallery with balustrade
Lantern
Convex molding
Circular lucarne window
Dome
Plat lesene
Curved buttress
Round arch
Corinthian pilaster
Rectangular pier
Sunken lunette
Sunken panel
Raking cornice
Pediment
Plain pilaster
Attic story
Entablature
Architrave
Cornice
Small pilaster
Pedestal
Semicircular cornice
Plinth
Concave, arched niche
Attached Corinthian column
Free-standing Corinthian column
Projecting side portal

CHURCH OF ST. GEORGE IN THE EAST (ENGLISH BAROQUE), LONDON, BRITAIN, 1714-1734 (BY N. HAWKSMOOR)

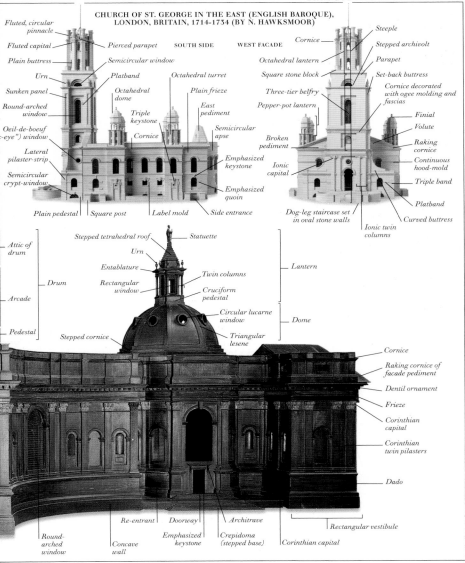

SOUTH SIDE

Fluted, circular pinnacle

Fluted capital

Pierced parapet

Plain buttress

Semicircular window

Urn

Platband

Sunken panel

Octahedral dome

Round-arched window

Oeil-de-boeuf ("ox-eye") window

Triple keystone

Lateral pilaster-strip

Cornice

Semicircular crypt-window

Plain pedestal

Square post

Label mold

Octahedral turret

Plain frieze

East pediment

Semicircular apse

Emphasized keystone

Emphasized quoin

Side entrance

WEST FACADE

Steeple

Cornice

Stepped archivolt

Octahedral lantern

Parapet

Square stone block

Set-back buttress

Three-tier belfry

Cornice decorated with ogee molding and fascias

Pepper-pot lantern

Finial

Volute

Broken pediment

Raking cornice

Ionic capital

Continuous hood-mold

Triple band

Platband

Dog-leg staircase set in oval stone walls

Curved buttress

Ionic twin columns

Attic of drum

Stepped tetrahedral roof

Statuette

Urn

Entablature

Twin columns

Drum

Rectangular window

Cruciform pedestal

Lantern

Arcade

Circular lucarne window

Dome

Pedestal

Stepped cornice

Triangular lesene

Cornice

Raking cornice of facade pediment

Dentil ornament

Frieze

Corinthian capital

Corinthian twin pilasters

Dado

Round-arched window

Re-entrant

Doorway

Architrave

Concave wall

Emphasized keystone

Crepidoma (stepped base)

Corinthian capital

Rectangular vestibule

Baroque and neoclassical 3

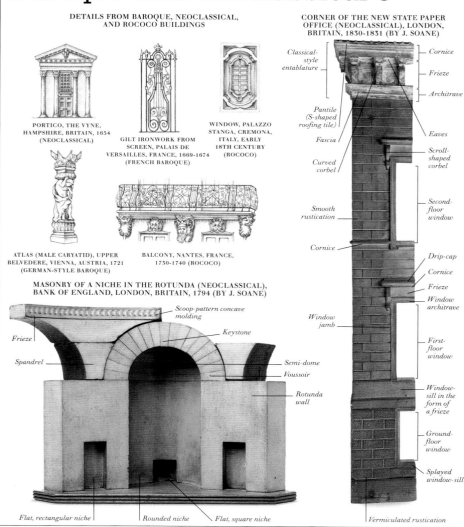

DETAILS FROM BAROQUE, NEOCLASSICAL, AND ROCOCO BUILDINGS

PORTICO, THE VYNE, HAMPSHIRE, BRITAIN, 1654 (NEOCLASSICAL)

GILT IRONWORK FROM SCREEN, PALAIS DE VERSAILLES, FRANCE, 1669-1674 (FRENCH BAROQUE)

WINDOW, PALAZZO STANGA, CREMONA, ITALY, EARLY 18TH CENTURY (ROCOCO)

ATLAS (MALE CARYATID), UPPER BELVEDERE, VIENNA, AUSTRIA, 1721 (GERMAN-STYLE BAROQUE)

BALCONY, NANTES, FRANCE, 1730-1740 (ROCOCO)

MASONRY OF A NICHE IN THE ROTUNDA (NEOCLASSICAL), BANK OF ENGLAND, LONDON, BRITAIN, 1794 (BY J. SOANE)

Scoop-pattern concave molding

Frieze

Keystone

Spandrel

Semi-dome

Voussoir

Rotunda wall

Flat, rectangular niche

Rounded niche

Flat, square niche

CORNER OF THE NEW STATE PAPER OFFICE (NEOCLASSICAL), LONDON, BRITAIN, 1830-1831 (BY J. SOANE)

Classical-style entablature

Cornice

Frieze

Architrave

Pantile (S-shaped roofing tile)

Eaves

Fascia

Scroll-shaped corbel

Curved corbel

Second-floor window

Smooth rustication

Cornice

Drip-cap

Cornice

Frieze

Window architrave

Window jamb

First-floor window

Window-sill in the form of a frieze

Ground-floor window

Splayed window-sill

Vermiculated rustication

TYRINGHAM HOUSE (NEOCLASSICAL), BUCKINGHAMSHIRE, BRITAIN, 1793-1797 (BY J. SOANE)

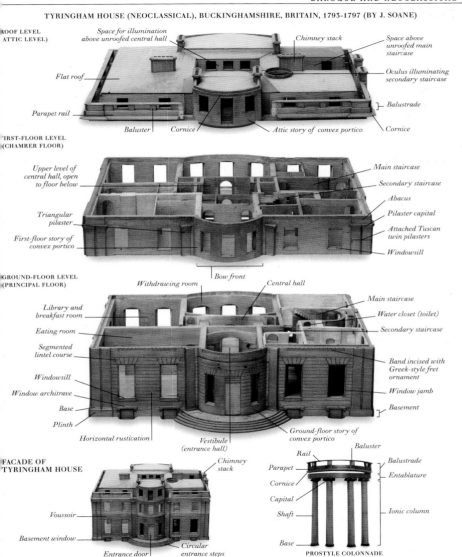

ROOF LEVEL
(ATTIC LEVEL)

Space for illumination above unroofed central hall

Chimney stack

Space above unroofed main staircase

Flat roof

Oculus illuminating secondary staircase

Parapet rail

Balustrade

Baluster

Cornice

Attic story of convex portico

Cornice

FIRST-FLOOR LEVEL
(CHAMBER FLOOR)

Upper level of central hall, open to floor below

Main staircase

Secondary staircase

Abacus

Triangular pilaster

Pilaster capital

Attached Tuscan twin pilasters

First-floor story of convex portico

Windowsill

GROUND-FLOOR LEVEL
(PRINCIPAL FLOOR)

Withdrawing room

Central hall

Library and breakfast room

Main staircase

Water closet (toilet)

Eating room

Secondary staircase

Segmented lintel course

Band incised with Greek-style fret ornament

Windowsill

Window architrave

Window jamb

Base

Basement

Plinth

Horizontal rustication

Vestibule (entrance hall)

Ground-floor story of convex portico

Bow front

FACADE OF
TYRINGHAM HOUSE

Chimney stack

Rail

Baluster

Parapet

Balustrade

Cornice

Entablature

Voussoir

Capital

Basement window

Shaft

Ionic column

Entrance door

Circular entrance steps

Base

PROSTYLE COLONNADE

483

Arches and vaults

ARCHES ARE CURVED STRUCTURES used to bridge spans and to support the weight of upper parts of buildings, such as domes, as in St. Paul's Cathedral (below) and the antique temple (opposite). The voussoirs (wedge-shaped blocks) that form an arch (right) support each other and convert the downward force of the weight of the building into an outward force. This outward force is in turn transferred to buttresses, piers, or abutments. A vault is an arched roof or ceiling. There are four main types of vault (opposite). A barrel vault is a single vault, semicircular in cross-section; a groin vault consists of two barrel vaults intersecting at right-angles; a rib vault is a groin vault reinforced by ribs; and a fan vault is a rib vault in which the ribs radiate from the springing point (where the arch begins) like a fan.

PARTS OF AN ARCH

FRONT

SIDE

ARCHES AND BASE OF DOME, ST. PAUL'S CATHEDRAL, LONDON, BRITAIN, 1675-1710 (BY C. WREN)

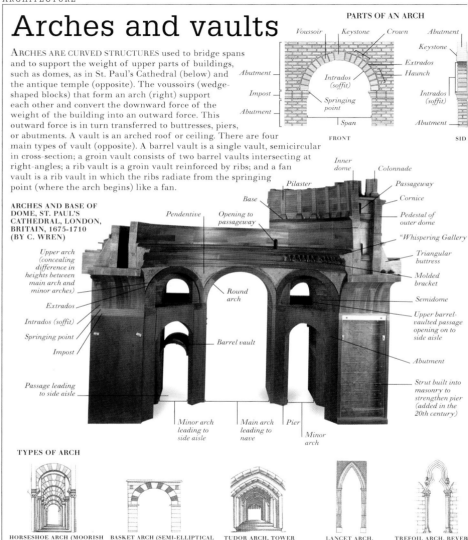

TYPES OF ARCH

HORSESHOE ARCH (MOORISH ARCH), GREAT MOSQUE, CORDORA, SPAIN, 785

BASKET ARCH (SEMI-ELLIPTICAL ARCH), PALATINE CHAPEL, AIX-LA-CHAPELLE, FRANCE, 790-798

TUDOR ARCH, TOWER OF LONDON, BRITAIN, c.1086-1097

LANCET ARCH, WESTMINSTER ABBEY, LONDON, BRITAIN, 1503-1519

TREFOIL ARCH, BEVERMINSTER, YORKSHIRE BRITAIN, c.1300

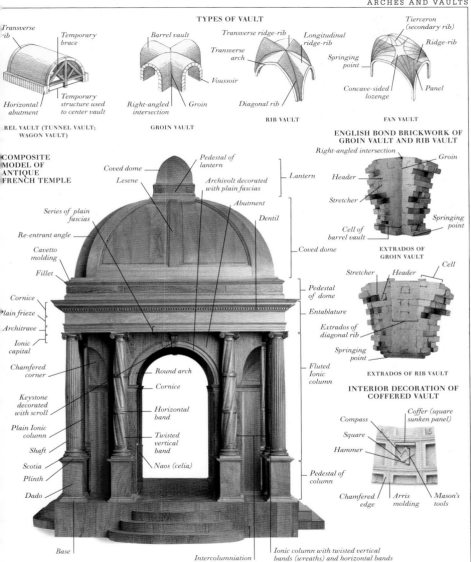

TYPES OF VAULT

BARREL VAULT (TUNNEL VAULT; WAGON VAULT)
- Transverse rib
- Temporary brace
- Horizontal abutment
- Temporary structure used to center vault

GROIN VAULT
- Barrel vault
- Voussoir
- Right-angled intersection
- Groin

RIB VAULT
- Transverse ridge-rib
- Longitudinal ridge-rib
- Transverse arch
- Diagonal rib

FAN VAULT
- Tierceron (secondary rib)
- Ridge-rib
- Springing point
- Concave-sided lozenge
- Panel

ENGLISH BOND BRICKWORK OF GROIN VAULT AND RIB VAULT

EXTRADOS OF GROIN VAULT
- Right-angled intersection
- Groin
- Header
- Stretcher
- Cell of barrel vault
- Springing point

EXTRADOS OF RIB VAULT
- Stretcher
- Header
- Cell
- Extrados of diagonal rib
- Springing point

COMPOSITE MODEL OF ANTIQUE FRENCH TEMPLE

- Coved dome
- Lesene
- Series of plain fascias
- Re-entrant angle
- Cavetto molding
- Fillet
- Cornice
- Plain frieze
- Architrave
- Ionic capital
- Chamfered corner
- Keystone decorated with scroll
- Plain Ionic column
- Shaft
- Scotia
- Plinth
- Dado
- Base
- Pedestal of lantern
- Archivolt decorated with plain fascias
- Abutment
- Dentil
- Lantern
- Coved dome
- Pedestal of dome
- Entablature
- Fluted Ionic column
- Round arch
- Cornice
- Horizontal band
- Twisted vertical band
- Naos (celia)
- Pedestal of column
- Intercolumniation
- Ionic column with twisted vertical bands (wreaths) and horizontal bands

INTERIOR DECORATION OF COFFERED VAULT

- Compass
- Square
- Hammer
- Coffer (square sunken panel)
- Chamfered edge
- Arris molding
- Mason's tools

Domes

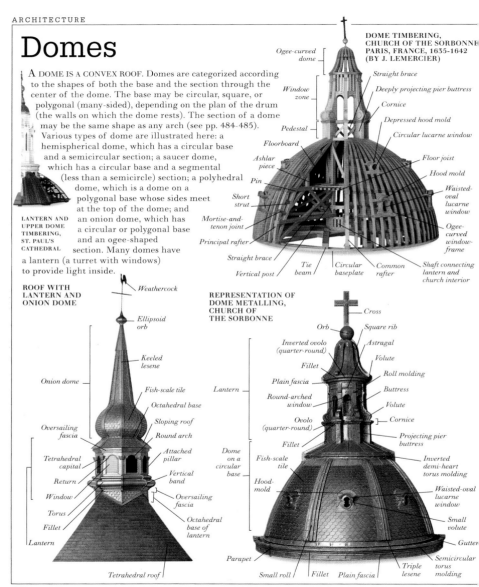

A DOME IS A CONVEX ROOF. Domes are categorized according to the shapes of both the base and the section through the center of the dome. The base may be circular, square, or polygonal (many-sided), depending on the plan of the drum (the walls on which the dome rests). The section of a dome may be the same shape as any arch (see pp. 484–485). Various types of dome are illustrated here: a hemispherical dome, which has a circular base and a semicircular section; a saucer dome, which has a circular base and a segmental (less than a semicircle) section; a polyhedral dome, which is a dome on a polygonal base whose sides meet at the top of the dome; and an onion dome, which has a circular or polygonal base and an ogee-shaped section. Many domes have a lantern (a turret with windows) to provide light inside.

LANTERN AND UPPER DOME TIMBERING, ST. PAUL'S CATHEDRAL

DOME TIMBERING, CHURCH OF THE SORBONNE, PARIS, FRANCE, 1635–1642 (BY J. LEMERCIER)

Ogee-curved dome
Straight brace
Window zone
Deeply projecting pier buttress
Cornice
Depressed hood mold
Pedestal
Circular lucarne window
Floorboard
Ashlar piece
Floor joist
Hood mold
Pin
Waisted-oval lucarne window
Short strut
Mortise-and-tenon joint
Principal rafter
Ogee-curved window-frame
Straight brace
Vertical post
Tie beam
Circular baseplate
Common rafter
Shaft connecting lantern and church interior

ROOF WITH LANTERN AND ONION DOME

Weathercock
Ellipsoid orb
Keeled lesene
Onion dome
Fish-scale tile
Octahedral base
Oversailing fascia
Sloping roof
Round arch
Tetrahedral capital
Attached pillar
Return
Vertical band
Window
Oversailing fascia
Torus
Octahedral base of lantern
Fillet
Lantern
Tetrahedral roof

REPRESENTATION OF DOME METALLING, CHURCH OF THE SORBONNE

Cross
Orb
Square rib
Inverted ovolo (quarter-round)
Astragal
Fillet
Volute
Plain fascia
Roll molding
Lantern
Round-arched window
Buttress
Ovolo (quarter-round)
Volute
Fillet
Cornice
Dome on a circular base
Projecting pier buttress
Fish-scale tile
Inverted demi-heart torus molding
Hood-mold
Waisted-oval lucarne window
Small volute
Parapet
Gutter
Small roll
Fillet
Plain fascia
Triple lesene
Semicircular torus molding

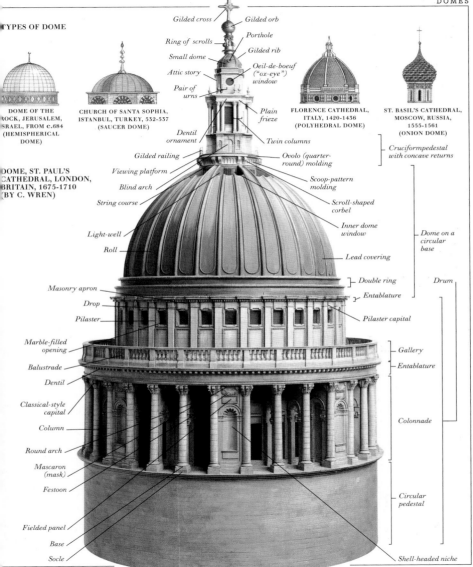

TYPES OF DOME

DOME OF THE
ROCK, JERUSALEM,
ISRAEL, FROM c.684
(HEMISPHERICAL
DOME)

CHURCH OF SANTA SOPHIA,
ISTANBUL, TURKEY, 532-537
(SAUCER DOME)

FLORENCE CATHEDRAL,
ITALY, 1420-1436
(POLYHEDRAL DOME)

ST. BASIL'S CATHEDRAL,
MOSCOW, RUSSIA,
1555-1561
(ONION DOME)

DOME, ST. PAUL'S
CATHEDRAL, LONDON,
BRITAIN, 1675-1710
(BY C. WREN)

Gilded cross
Gilded orb
Porthole
Ring of scrolls
Gilded rib
Small dome
Oeil-de-boeuf
("ox-eye")
window
Attic story
Pair of
urns
Plain
frieze
Dentil
ornament
Twin columns
Gilded railing
Ovolo (quarter-
round) molding
Viewing platform
Scoop-pattern
molding
Blind arch
String course
Scroll-shaped
corbel
Inner dome
window
Light-well
Roll
Lead covering
Masonry apron
Double ring
Drop
Entablature
Pilaster
Pilaster capital
Marble-filled
opening
Gallery
Balustrade
Entablature
Dentil
Classical-style
capital
Column
Colonnade
Round arch
Mascaron
(mask)
Festoon
Fielded panel
Base
Circular
pedestal
Socle
Shell-headed niche

Cruciformpedestal
with concave returns

Dome on a
circular
base

Drum

Islamic buildings

THE ISLAMIC RELIGION was founded by the prophet Muhammad, who was born in Mecca (in present-day Saudi Arabia) about 570 AD. In the following three centuries, Islam spread from Arabia to North Africa and Spain, as well as to India and much of the rest of Asia. The worldwide influence of Islam remains strong today. Common characteristics of Islamic buildings include ogee arches and roofs, onion domes, and walls decorated with carved stone, paintings, inlays, or mosaics. The most important type of Islamic building is the mosque—the place of worship—which generally has a minaret (tower) from which the muezzin (official crier) calls Muslims to prayer. Most mosques have a mihrab (decorative niche) that indicates the direction of Mecca. As figurative art is not allowed in Islam, buildings are ornamented with geometric and arabesque motifs, and inscriptions (frequently Koranic verses).

OPUS SECTILE
MOSAIC DESIGN

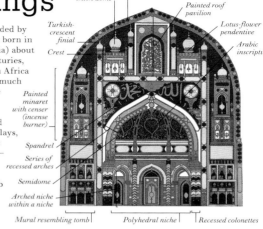

Budlike onion dome
Depressed arch surrounding mihrab
Painted roof pavilion
Turkish-crescent finial
Lotus-flower pendentive
Crest
Arabic inscripti
Painted minaret with censer (incense burner)
Spandrel
Series of recessed arches
Semidome
Arched niche within a niche
Mural resembling tomb
Polyhedral niche
Recessed colonettes

MIHRAB, JAMI MASJID (PRINCIPAL OR CONGREGATIONAL MOSQUE), BIJAPUR, INDIA, c.1636

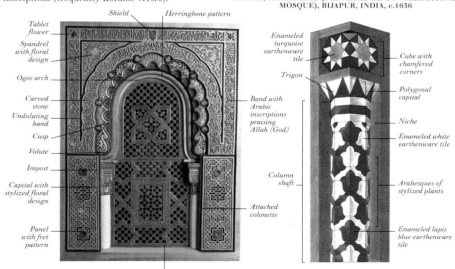

Tablet flower
Shield
Herringbone pattern
Spandrel with floral design
Ogee arch
Carved stone
Undulating band
Cusp
Volute
Impost
Capital with stylized floral design
Panel with fret pattern
Jali (latticed screen) with geometrical patterns

Band with Arabic inscriptions praising Allah (God)
Column shaft
Attached colonette

ARCH, THE ALHAMBRA, GRANADA, SPAIN, 1333-1354

Enameled turquoise earthenware tile
Trigon
Cube with chamfered corners
Polygonal capital
Niche
Enameled white earthenware tile
Arabesques of stylized plants
Enameled lapis blue earthenware tile

MIHRAB WITH COLUMN, EL-AINYI
MOSQUE, CAIRO, EGYPT, 15TH CENTURY

EXAMPLES OF ISLAMIC MOSAICS, EGYPT AND SYRIA

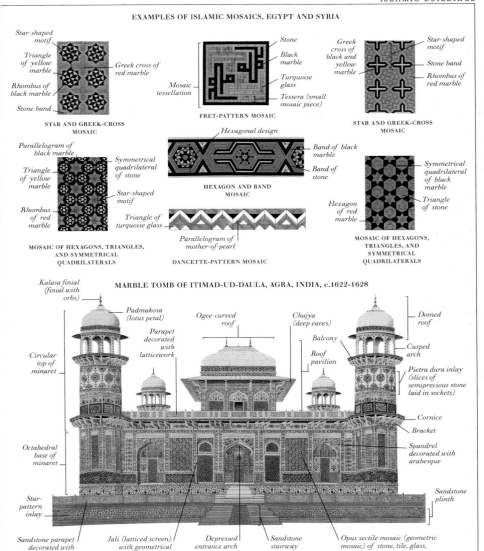

Star-shaped motif
Triangle of yellow marble
Greek cross of red marble
Rhombus of black marble
Stone band

STAR AND GREEK-CROSS MOSAIC

Stone
Black marble
Turquoise glass
Mosaic tessellation
Tessera (small mosaic piece)

FRET-PATTERN MOSAIC

Greek cross of black and yellow marble
Star-shaped motif
Stone band
Rhombus of red marble

STAR AND GREEK-CROSS MOSAIC

Parallelogram of black marble
Triangle of yellow marble
Rhombus of red marble
Symmetrical quadrilateral of stone
Star-shaped motif

MOSAIC OF HEXAGONS, TRIANGLES, AND SYMMETRICAL QUADRILATERALS

Hexagonal design
Band of black marble
Band of stone

HEXAGON AND BAND MOSAIC

Triangle of turquoise glass
Parallelogram of mother-of-pearl

DANCETTE-PATTERN MOSAIC

Symmetrical quadrilateral of black marble
Triangle of stone
Hexagon of red marble

MOSAIC OF HEXAGONS, TRIANGLES, AND SYMMETRICAL QUADRILATERALS

MARBLE TOMB OF ITIMAD-UD-DAULA, AGRA, INDIA, c.1622-1628

Kalasa finial (finial with orbs)
Padmakosa (lotus petal)
Ogee-curved roof
Chajya (deep eaves)
Domed roof
Parapet decorated with latticework
Balcony
Roof pavilion
Cusped arch
Circular top of minaret
Pietra dura inlay (slices of semiprecious stone laid in sockets)
Cornice
Bracket
Spandrel decorated with arabesque
Octahedral base of minaret
Star-pattern inlay
Sandstone plinth
Sandstone parapet decorated with latticework
Jali (latticed screen) with geometrical patterns
Depressed entrance arch
Sandstone stairway
Opus sectile mosaic (geometric mosaic) of stone, tile, glass, and enamel

South and east Asia

THE TRADITIONAL ARCHITECTURE of south and east Asia has been profoundly influenced by the spread from India of Buddhism and Hinduism. This influence is shown both by the abundance and by the architectural styles of temples and shrines in the region. Many early Hindu temples consist of rooms carved from solid rock-faces. However, free-standing structures began to be built in southern India from about the eighth century AD. Many were built in the Dravidian style, like the Temple of Virupaksha (opposite) with its characteristic antarala (terraced tower), perforated windows, and numerous arches, pilasters, and carvings. The earliest Buddhist religious monuments were Indian stupas, which consisted of a single hemispherical dome surmounted by a chattravali (shaft) and surrounded by railings with ornate gates. Later Indian stupas and those built elsewhere were sometimes modified; for example, in Sri Lanka, the dome became bell-shaped, and was called a dagoba. Buddhist pagodas, such as the Burmese example (right), are multistoried temples, each story having a projecting roof. The form of these buildings probably derived from the yasti (pointed spire) of the stupa. Another feature of many traditional Asian buildings is their imaginative roof-forms, such as gambrel (mansard) roofs, and roofs with angle-rafters (below).

DETAILS FROM EAST ASIAN BUILDINGS

KASUGA-STYLE ROOF WITH SUMIGI (ANGLE-RAFTERS), KASUGADO SHRINE OF ENJOJI, NARA, JAPAN, 12TH-14TH CENTURY

TERRACES, TEMPLE OF HEAVEN, BEIJING, CHINA, 15TH CENTURY

GAMBREL (MANSARD) ROOF WITH UPSWEPT EAVES AND UNDULATING GABLES, HIMEJI CASTLE, HIMEJI, JAPAN, 1608-1609

CORNER CAPITAL WITH ROOF BEAMS, POPCHU-SA TEMPLE, POPCHU-SA, SOUTH KOREA, 17TH CENTURY

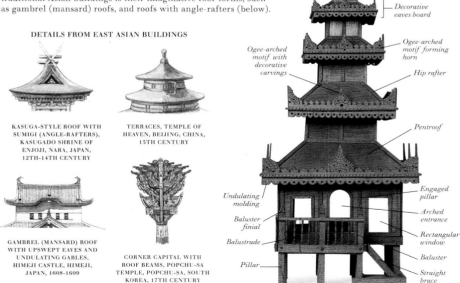

Gilded band

Gilded iron hti (crown)

Dubika (mast)

Arrow motif

Torus molding with spiral carving

Decorative eaves board

Ogee-arched motif with decorative carvings

Ogee-arched motif forming horn

Hip rafter

Pentroof

Undulating molding

Baluster finial

Balustrade

Pillar

Engaged pillar

Arched entrance

Rectangular window

Baluster

Straight brace

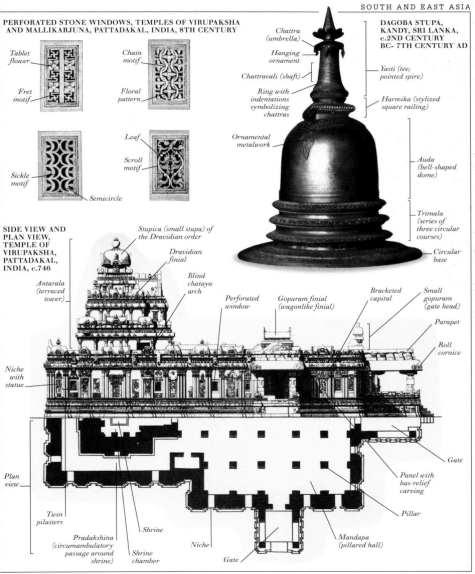

PERFORATED STONE WINDOWS, TEMPLES OF VIRUPAKSHA AND MALLIKARJUNA, PATTADAKAL, INDIA, 8TH CENTURY

Tablet flower

Fret motif

Chain motif

Floral pattern

Sickle motif

Leaf

Scroll motif

Semicircle

DAGOBA STUPA, KANDY, SRI LANKA, c.2ND CENTURY BC- 7TH CENTURY AD

Chattra (umbrella)

Hanging ornament

Chattravali (shaft)

Ring with indentations symbolizing chattras

Ornamental metalwork

Yasti (tee; pointed spire)

Harmika (stylized square railing)

Auda (bell-shaped dome)

Trimala (series of three circular courses)

Circular base

SIDE VIEW AND PLAN VIEW, TEMPLE OF VIRUPAKSHA, PATTADAKAL, INDIA, c.746

Stupica (small stupa) of the Dravidian order

Dravidian finial

Antarala (terraced tower)

Blind chataya arch

Perforated window

Gopuram finial (wagonlike finial)

Bracketed capital

Small gopuram (gate head)

Parapet

Roll cornice

Niche with statue

Gate

Plan view

Panel with bas-relief carving

Twin pilasters

Pillar

Pradakshina (circumambulatory passage around shrine)

Shrine

Shrine chamber

Niche

Gate

Mandapa (pillared hall)

The 19th century

BUILDINGS OF THE 19TH CENTURY are characterized by the use of new materials and by a great diversity of architectural styles. From the end of the 18th century, iron and steel became widely used as alternatives to wood for the framework of buildings, as in the flax-spinning mill shown here. Built in Britain in 1796, this mill exemplifies an architectural style that became common throughout the industrialized world for more than a century. The Industrial Revolution also brought mass-production of building parts—a development that enabled the British architect Sir Joseph Paxton to erect London's Crystal Palace (a building made entirely of iron and glass) in only nine months, ready for the Great Exhibition of 1851. The 19th century saw a widespread revival of older architectural styles. For example, in the US and Germany, Neo-Greek architecture was fashionable; in Britain and France, Neo-Baroque, Neo-Byzantine, and Neo-Gothic styles (as seen in the Palace of Westminster and Tower Bridge) were dominant.

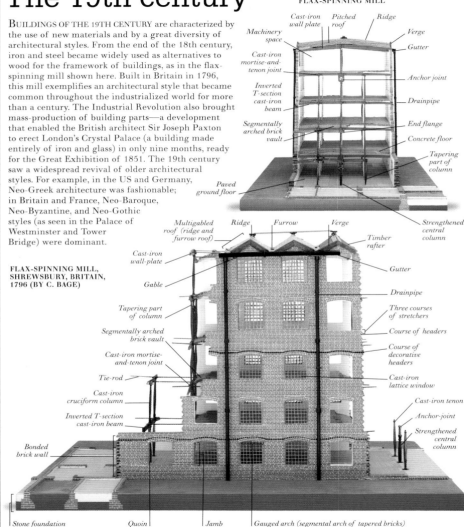

SECTION THROUGH A FLAX-SPINNING MILL

Machinery space
Cast-iron wall plate
Pitched roof
Ridge
Verge
Gutter
Cast-iron mortise-and-tenon joint
Anchor joint
Inverted T-section cast-iron beam
Drainpipe
Segmentally arched brick vault
End flange
Concrete floor
Tapering part of column
Paved ground floor
Strengthened central column

FLAX-SPINNING MILL, SHREWSBURY, BRITAIN, 1796 (BY C. BAGE)

Multigabled roof (ridge and furrow roof)
Ridge
Furrow
Verge
Cast-iron wall-plate
Timber rafter
Gable
Gutter
Tapering part of column
Drainpipe
Three courses of stretchers
Segmentally arched brick vault
Course of headers
Cast-iron mortise-and-tenon joint
Course of decorative headers
Tie-rod
Cast-iron cruciform column
Cast-iron lattice window
Inverted T-section cast-iron beam
Cast-iron tenon
Anchor-joint
Strengthened central column
Bonded brick wall
Stone foundation
Quoin
Jamb
Gauged arch (segmental arch of tapered bricks)

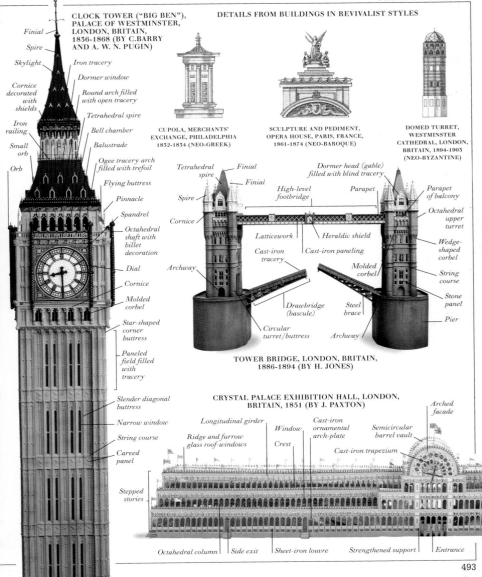

DETAILS FROM BUILDINGS IN REVIVALIST STYLES

CLOCK TOWER ("BIG BEN"),
PALACE OF WESTMINSTER,
LONDON, BRITAIN,
1836-1868 (BY C. BARRY
AND A. W. N. PUGIN)

Finial

Spire

Skylight

Iron tracery

Cornice decorated with shields

Dormer window

Round arch filled with open tracery

Tetrahedral spire

Iron railing

Bell chamber

Small orb

Balustrade

Orb

Ogee tracery arch filled with trefoil

Flying buttress

Pinnacle

Spandrel

Octahedral shaft with billet decoration

Dial

Cornice

Molded corbel

Star-shaped corner buttress

Paneled field filled with tracery

Slender diagonal buttress

Narrow window

String course

Carved panel

Stepped stories

CUPOLA, MERCHANTS'
EXCHANGE, PHILADELPHIA
1832-1834 (NEO-GREEK)

SCULPTURE AND PEDIMENT,
OPERA HOUSE, PARIS, FRANCE,
1861-1874 (NEO-BAROQUE)

DOMED TURRET,
WESTMINSTER
CATHEDRAL, LONDON,
BRITAIN, 1894-1903
(NEO-BYZANTINE)

Tetrahedral spire

Finial

Finial

Dormer head (gable) filled with blind tracery

Parapet

Parapet of balcony

Spire

High-level footbridge

Octahedral upper turret

Cornice

Latticework

Heraldic shield

Wedge-shaped corbel

Cast-iron tracery

Cast-iron paneling

Molded corbel

String course

Archway

Drawbridge (bascule)

Steel brace

Stone panel

Circular turret/buttress

Archway

Pier

TOWER BRIDGE, LONDON, BRITAIN,
1886-1894 (BY H. JONES)

CRYSTAL PALACE EXHIBITION HALL, LONDON,
BRITAIN, 1851 (BY J. PAXTON)

Longitudinal girder

Window

Cast-iron ornamental arch-plate

Arched facade

Ridge and furrow glass roof-windows

Crest

Semicircular barrel vault

Cast-iron trapezium

Octahedral column

Side exit

Sheet-iron louvre

Strengthened support

Entrance

493

The early 20th century

ARCHITECTURE OF THE EARLY 20TH CENTURY is notable for radical new types of steel-and-glass buildings—particularly skyscrapers—and the widespread use of steel-reinforced concrete. The steel-framed skyscraper was pioneered in Chicago in the 1880s, but did not become widespread until the first decades of the 20th century. As construction techniques were refined, skyscrapers became higher and higher; for example, the Empire State Building (right) of 1929-1931 has 102 stories. Many buildings of this period were constructed from lightweight concrete slabs, which could be supported by cantilever beams or by pilotis (stilts). The early 20th century also produced a great variety of architectural styles, some of which are illustrated opposite. Despite their diversity, the styles of this period generally had one thing in common: they were completely new, with few links to past architectural styles. This originality is in marked contrast to 19th century architecture (see pp. 492-493), much of which was revivalist.

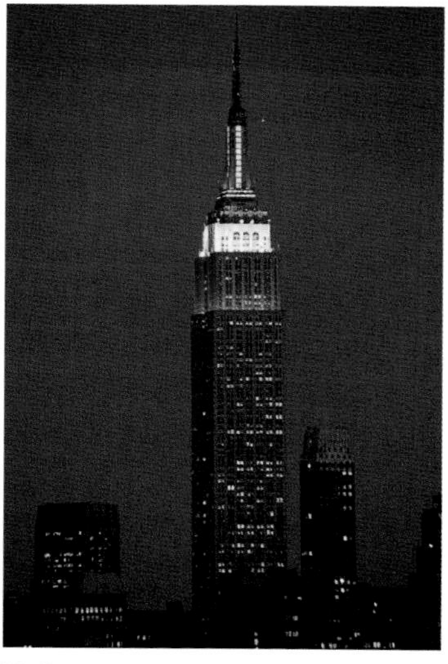

The Empire State Building's top 30 floors were first illuminated in color in 1976 to honor the United States Bicentennial. This marked the beginning of the Lighting Partners Program that today sees the building lit up in specific colors for many occasions. Above, the blue, white, and red lights celebrate Independence Day.

EMPIRE STATE BUILDING, NEW YORK, USA, 1929-19 (BY R. H. SHREVE, T. LAMB, AND A. L. HARMON)

Radio mast
Circular lantern
Art deco splayed seashell form
Stepped plinth
Chamfered corner
Colonnaded story
Ornamentation
Set-back
Ziggurat-style step-back
Steel mullion
Flush window
Vertical pier
Regular fenestration
Windowsill
Solid-panel infill
Curved wall
Fanlike art deco decoration
Decorated stone lintel
Stone structure line
Limestone and granite cladding
Stepped cornice
Flat roof
Parapet
Plinth
Covered driveway
Ground-floor entrance
Base
Square bay

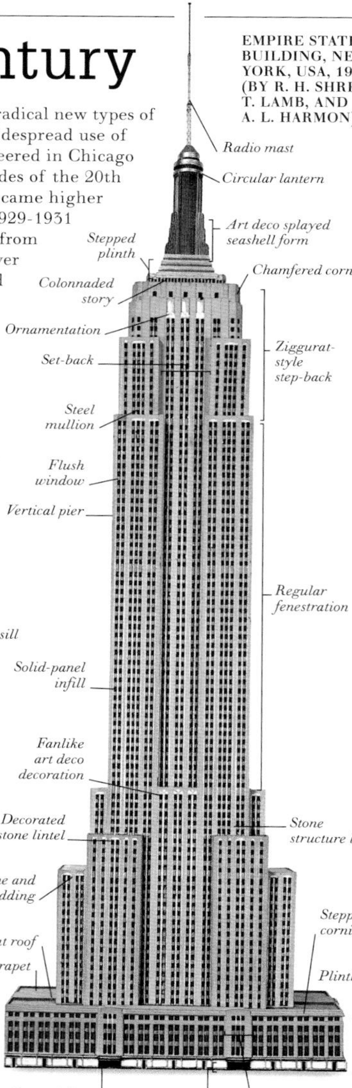

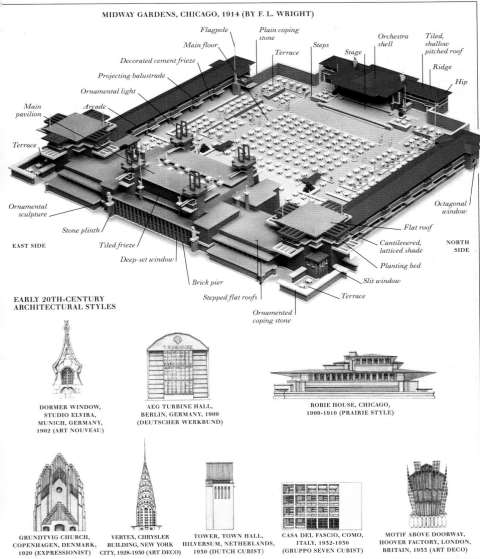

MIDWAY GARDENS, CHICAGO, 1914 (BY F. L. WRIGHT)

Flagpole
Plain coping stone
Main floor
Terrace
Steps
Stage
Orchestra shell
Tiled, shallow pitched roof
Decorated cement frieze
Projecting balustrade
Ornamental light
Ridge
Hip
Arcade
Main pavilion
Terrace
Ornamental sculpture
Stone plinth
Tiled frieze
Deep-set window
Brick pier
Stepped flat roofs
Ornamented coping stone
Terrace
Slit window
Planting bed
Cantilevered, latticed shade
Flat roof
Octagonal window
EAST SIDE
NORTH SIDE

EARLY 20TH-CENTURY ARCHITECTURAL STYLES

DORMER WINDOW, STUDIO ELVIRA, MUNICH, GERMANY, 1902 (ART NOUVEAU)

AEG TURBINE HALL, BERLIN, GERMANY, 1909 (DEUTSCHER WERKBUND)

ROBIE HOUSE, CHICAGO, 1909-1910 (PRAIRIE STYLE)

GRUNDTVIG CHURCH, COPENHAGEN, DENMARK, 1920 (EXPRESSIONIST)

VERTEX, CHRYSLER BUILDING, NEW YORK CITY, 1928-1930 (ART DECO)

TOWER, TOWN HALL, HILVERSUM, NETHERLANDS, 1930 (DUTCH CUBIST)

CASA DEL FASCIO, COMO, ITALY, 1932-1936 (GRUPPO SEVEN CUBIST)

MOTIF ABOVE DOORWAY, HOOVER FACTORY, LONDON, BRITAIN, 1933 (ART DECO)

Modern buildings 1

ARCHITECTURE SINCE ABOUT THE 1950s is generally known as modern architecture. One of its main influences has been functionalism—a belief that a building's function should be apparent in its design. Both the Centre Georges Pompidou (below and opposite) and the Hong Kong and Shanghai Bank (see pp. 498-499) are functionalist buildings: on each, elements of engineering and the building's services are clearly visible on the outside. In the 1980s, some architects rejected functionalism in favor of post-modernism, in which historical styles—particularly neoclassicism—were revived, using modern building materials and techniques. In many modern buildings, walls are made of glass or concrete hung from a frame, as in the Kawana House (right); this type of wall construction is known as curtain walling. Other modern construction techniques include the intricate interlocking of concrete vaults—as in the Sydney Opera House (see pp. 498-499)—and the use of high-tension beams to create complex roof shapes, such as the paraboloid roof of the Church of St. Pierre de Libreville (see pp. 498-499).

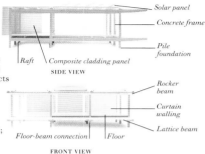

Solar panel

Concrete frame

Pile foundation

Raft   Composite cladding panel

SIDE VIEW

Rocker beam

Curtain walling

Lattice beam

Floor-beam connection   Floor

FRONT VIEW

SERVICES FACADE, CENTRE GEORGES POMPIDOU, PARIS, FRANCE, 1977 (BY R. PIANO AND R. ROGERS)

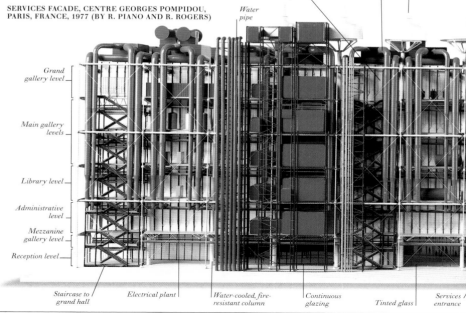

Metal-faced, fire-resistant panel

Air-conditioning duct

Cooling tower

Water pipe

Grand gallery level

Main gallery levels

Library level

Administrative level

Mezzanine gallery level

Reception level

Staircase to grand hall

Electrical plant

Water-cooled, fire-resistant column

Continuous glazing

Tinted glass

Services entrance

PRINCIPAL FACADE, CENTRE GEORGES POMPIDOU

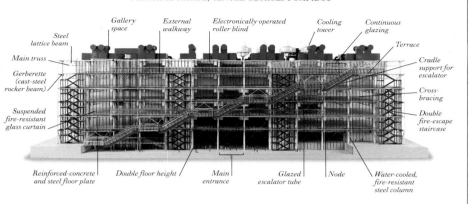

Gallery space
External walkway
Electronically operated roller blind
Cooling tower
Continuous glazing
Terrace
Steel lattice beam
Main truss
Gerberette (cast-steel rocker beam)
Cradle support for escalator
Cross-bracing
Double fire-escape staircase
Suspended fire-resistant glass curtain
Reinforced-concrete and steel floor plate
Double floor height
Main entrance
Glazed escalator tube
Node
Water-cooled, fire-resistant steel column

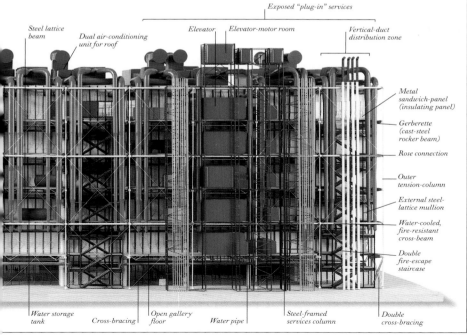

Exposed "plug-in" services
Steel lattice beam
Dual air-conditioning unit for roof
Elevator
Elevator-motor room
Vertical-duct distribution zone
Metal sandwich-panel (insulating panel)
Gerberette (cast-steel rocker beam)
Rose connection
Outer tension-column
External steel-lattice mullion
Water-cooled, fire-resistant cross-beam
Double fire-escape staircase
Water storage tank
Cross-bracing
Open gallery floor
Water pipe
Steel-framed services column
Double cross-bracing

497

Modern buildings 2

HONG KONG AND SHANGHAI BANK, HONG KONG, 1981-1985 (BY N. FOSTER)

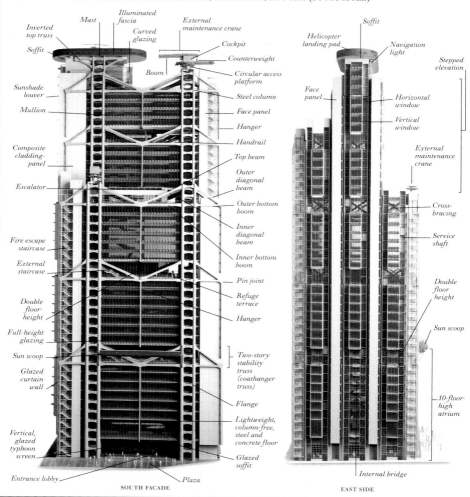

Inverted top truss
Mast
Illuminated fascia
Curved glazing
External maintenance crane
Soffit
Cockpit
Counterweight
Boom
Circular access platform
Soffit
Sunshade louver
Steel column
Face panel
Mullion
Hanger
Handrail
Composite cladding panel
Top beam
Outer diagonal beam
Escalator
Outer bottom boom
Inner diagonal beam
Fire escape staircase
Inner bottom boom
External staircase
Pin joint
Refuge terrace
Double floor height
Hanger
Full-height glazing
Two-story stability truss (coathanger truss)
Sun scoop
Glazed curtain wall
Flange
Lightweight, column-free, steel and concrete floor
Vertical, glazed typhoon screen
Glazed soffit
Entrance lobby
Plaza

SOUTH FACADE

Helicopter landing pad
Soffit
Navigation light
Stepped elevation
Face panel
Horizontal window
Vertical window
External maintenance crane
Cross-bracing
Service shaft
Double floor height
Sun scoop
10-floor-high atrium
Internal bridge

EAST SIDE

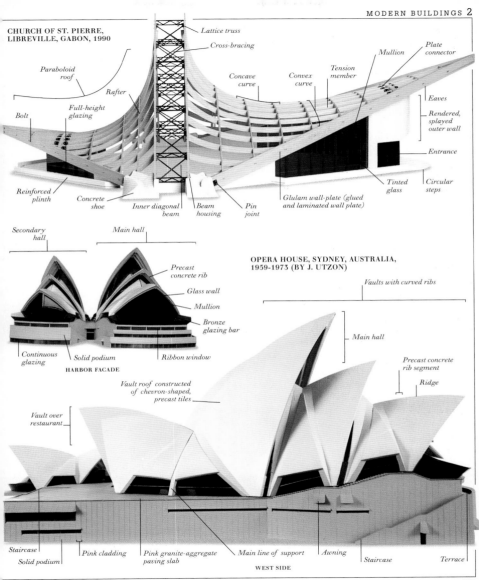

**CHURCH OF ST. PIERRE,
LIBREVILLE, GABON, 1990**

Lattice truss

Cross-bracing

Mullion

Plate connector

Paraboloid roof

Rafter

Concave curve

Convex curve

Tension member

Eaves

Bolt

Full-height glazing

Rendered, splayed outer wall

Entrance

Reinforced plinth

Concrete shoe

Inner diagonal beam

Beam housing

Pin joint

Glulam wall-plate (glued and laminated wall plate)

Tinted glass

Circular steps

Secondary hall

Main hall

**OPERA HOUSE, SYDNEY, AUSTRALIA,
1959-1973 (BY J. UTZON)**

Vaults with curved ribs

Precast concrete rib

Glass wall

Mullion

Main hall

Bronze glazing bar

Precast concrete rib segment

Ridge

Continuous glazing

Solid podium

Ribbon window

HARBOR FACADE

Vault roof constructed of chevron-shaped, precast tiles

Vault over restaurant

Staircase

Solid podium

Pink cladding

Pink granite-aggregate paving slab

Main line of support

Awning

Staircase

Terrace

WEST SIDE

MUSIC

MUSICAL NOTATION ···································· 502

ORCHESTRAS ··· 504

BRASS INSTRUMENTS ································· 506

WOODWIND INSTRUMENTS ······················ 508

STRINGED INSTRUMENTS ·························· 510

GUITARS ·· 512

KEYBOARD INSTRUMENTS ························ 514

PERCUSSION INSTRUMENTS ····················· 516

DRUMS ·· 518

ELECTRONIC INSTRUMENTS ····················· 520

Musical notation

MUSICAL NOTATION IS ANY METHOD by which sounds are written down so that they can be read and performed by others. The present-day conventional system of notation uses a five-line stave (staff)—divided by vertical lines into sections known as bars—on which notes, rests, clefs, key signatures, time signatures, accidentals, and other symbols are written. A note indicates the duration of a sound and, according to its position on the stave, its pitch. Notes can be arranged on the stave in order of pitch to form a scale. A silence in the music is indicated by a rest. The clef, which is placed at the beginning of a stave, fixes the pitch. The key signature, which is placed after the clef, indicates the key. The time signature, placed after the key signature, shows the number of beats in a bar. Accidentals are used to indicate the raising or lowering of the pitch of a note.

ELEMENTS OF MUSICAL NOTATION

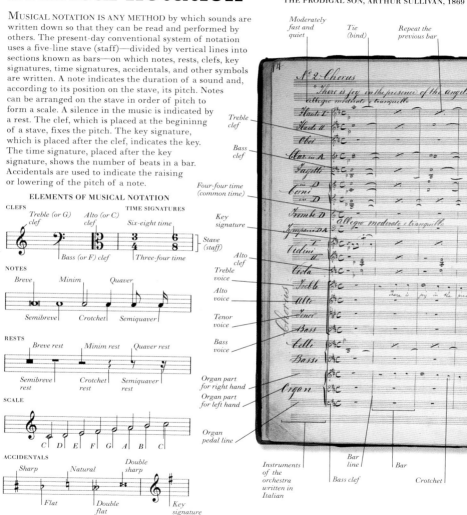

CLEFS
Treble (or G) clef
Alto (or C) clef
Bass (or F) clef

TIME SIGNATURES
Six-eight time
Three-four time

NOTES
Breve
Minim
Quaver
Semibreve
Crotchet
Semiquaver

RESTS
Breve rest
Minim rest
Quaver rest
Semibreve rest
Crotchet rest
Semiquaver rest

SCALE
C D E F G A B C

ACCIDENTALS
Sharp
Natural
Double sharp
Flat
Double flat
Key signature

Moderately fast and quiet
Tie (bind)
Repeat the previous bar
Treble clef
Bass clef
Four-four time (common time)
Key signature
Stave (staff)
Alto clef
Treble voice
Alto voice
Tenor voice
Bass voice
Organ part for right hand
Organ part for left hand
Organ pedal line
Instruments of the orchestra written in Italian
Bar line
Bass clef
Bar
Crotchet

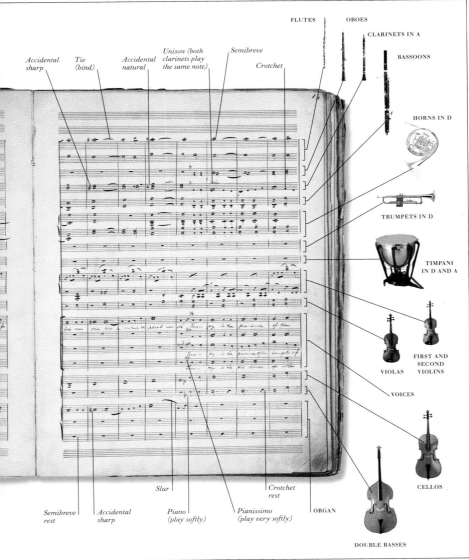

FLUTES

OBOES

CLARINETS IN A

BASSOONS

Accidental sharp

Tie (bind)

Accidental natural

Unison (both clarinets play the same note)

Semibreve

Crotchet

HORNS IN D

TRUMPETS IN D

TIMPANI IN D AND A

FIRST AND SECOND VIOLINS

VIOLAS

VOICES

CELLOS

Slur

Crotchet rest

ORGAN

Semibreve rest

Accidental sharp

Piano (play softly)

Pianissimo (play very softly)

DOUBLE BASSES

503

Orchestras

AN ORCHESTRA IS A GROUP of musicians that plays music written for a specific combination of instruments. The number and type of instruments included in the orchestra depends on the style of music being played. The modern orchestra (also known as a symphony orchestra) is made up of four sections of instruments—stringed, woodwind, brass, and percussion. The stringed section consists of violins, violas, cellos (violoncellos), double basses, and sometimes a harp (see pp. 510-511). The main instruments of the woodwind section are flutes, oboes, clarinets, and bassoons—the piccolo, cor anglais, bass clarinet, saxophone, and double bassoon (contrabassoon) can also be included if the music requires them (see pp. 508-509). The brass section usually consists of horns, trumpets, trombones, and the tuba (see pp. 506-507). The main instruments of the percussion section are the timpani (see pp. 518-519). The side drum, bass drum, cymbals, tambourine, triangle, tubular bells, xylophone, vibraphone, tam-tam (gong), castanets, and maracas can also be included in the percussion section (see pp. 516-517). The musicians are usually arranged in a semi-circle—strings spread along the front, woodwind and brass in the center, and percussion at the back. A conductor stands in front of the musicians and controls the tempo (speed) of the music and the overall balance of the sound, ensuring that no instruments are too loud or too soft in relation to the others.

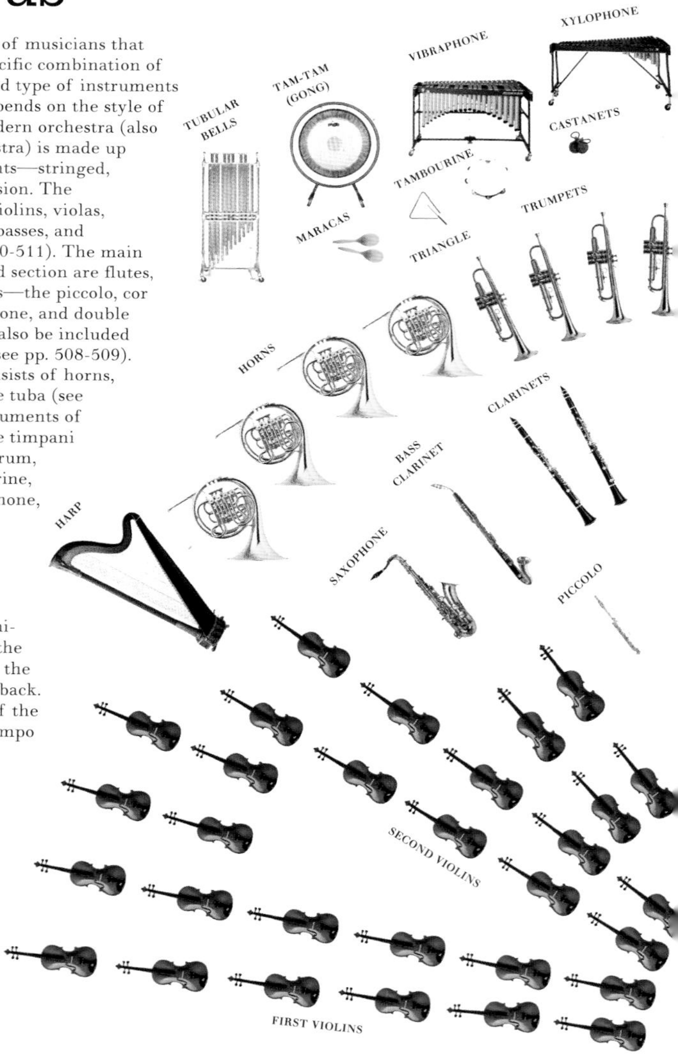

TUBULAR BELLS

TAM-TAM (GONG)

VIBRAPHONE

XYLOPHONE

CASTANETS

TAMBOURINE

TRUMPETS

MARACAS

TRIANGLE

HORNS

CLARINETS

BASS CLARINET

HARP

SAXOPHONE

PICCOLO

SECOND VIOLINS

FIRST VIOLINS

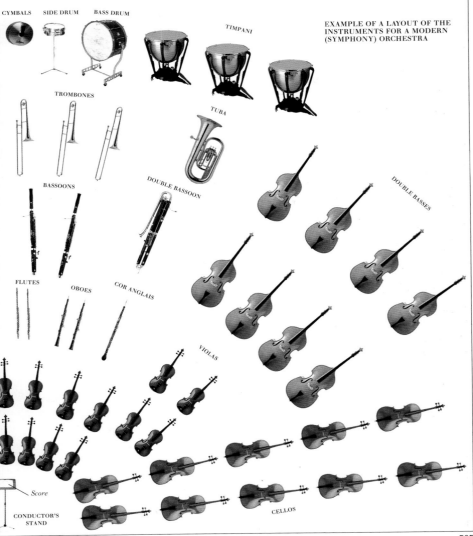

CYMBALS   SIDE DRUM   BASS DRUM

TIMPANI

EXAMPLE OF A LAYOUT OF THE
INSTRUMENTS FOR A MODERN
(SYMPHONY) ORCHESTRA

TROMBONES

TUBA

BASSOONS

DOUBLE BASSOON

DOUBLE BASSES

FLUTES

OBOES   COR ANGLAIS

VIOLAS

Score

CONDUCTOR'S
STAND

CELLOS

Brass instruments

BUGLE

Brass instruments are wind instruments that are made of metal, usually brass. Although they appear in many different shapes and sizes, all brass instruments have a mouthpiece, a length of hollow tube, and a flared bell. The mouthpiece of a brass instrument may be cup-shaped, as in the cornet, or cone-shaped, as in the horn. The tube may be wide or narrow, mainly conical, as in the horn and tuba, or mainly cylindrical, as in the trumpet and trombone. The sound of a brass instrument is made by the player's lips vibrating against the mouthpiece, so that the air vibrates in the tube. By changing lip tension, the player can vary the vibrations and produce notes of different pitches. The range of notes produced by a brass instrument can be extended by means of a valve system. Most brass instruments, such as the trumpet, have piston valves that divert the air in the instrument along an extra piece of tubing (known as a valve slide) when pressed down. The total length of the tube is increased and the pitch of the note produced is lowered. Instead of valves, the trombone has a movable slide that can be pushed away from or drawn toward the player. The sound of a brass instrument can also be changed by inserting a mute into the bell of the instrument.

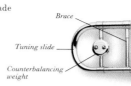

Brace

Tuning slide

Counterbalancing weight

SIMPLIFIED DIAGRAM SHOWING HOW A PISTON VALVE SYSTEM WORKS

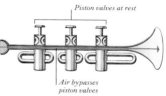

Piston valves at rest

Air bypasses piston valves

PISTON VALVES AT REST

First piston valve pressed down

Second and third piston valves at rest

Air diverted through first valve slide

PISTON VALVE PRESSED DOWN

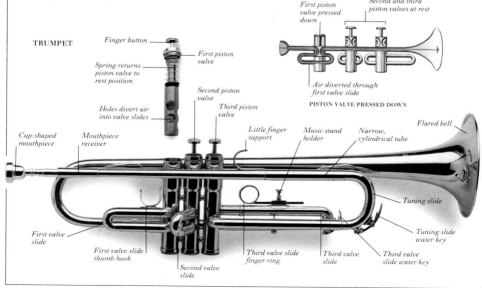

TRUMPET

Finger button

First piston valve

Spring returns piston valve to rest position

Second piston valve

Third piston valve

Holes divert air into valve slides

Little finger support

Music stand holder

Narrow, cylindrical tube

Flared bell

Cup-shaped mouthpiece

Mouthpiece receiver

Tuning slide

First valve slide

First valve slide thumb hook

Second valve slide

Third valve slide finger ring

Third valve slide

Third valve slide water key

Tuning slide water key

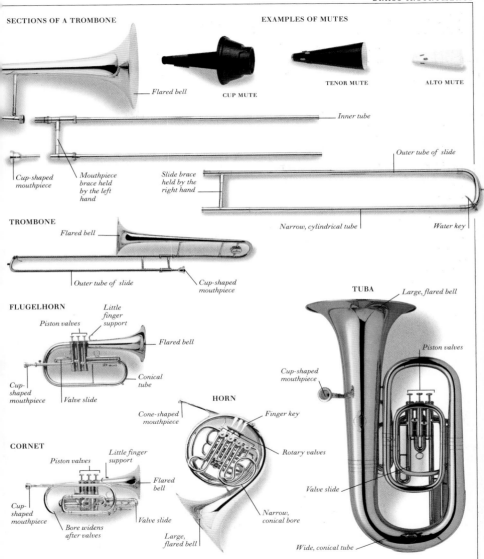

SECTIONS OF A TROMBONE

EXAMPLES OF MUTES

Flared bell

CUP MUTE

TENOR MUTE

ALTO MUTE

Inner tube

Cup-shaped mouthpiece

Mouthpiece brace held by the left hand

Slide brace held by the right hand

Outer tube of slide

Narrow, cylindrical tube

Water key

TROMBONE

Flared bell

Outer tube of slide

Cup-shaped mouthpiece

FLUGELHORN

Little finger support

Piston valves

Flared bell

Cup-shaped mouthpiece

Valve slide

Conical tube

TUBA

Large, flared bell

Piston valves

Cup-shaped mouthpiece

Valve slide

Wide, conical tube

HORN

Cone-shaped mouthpiece

Finger key

Rotary valves

Narrow, conical bore

Large, flared bell

CORNET

Piston valves

Little finger support

Flared bell

Cup-shaped mouthpiece

Bore widens after valves

Valve slide

Woodwind instruments

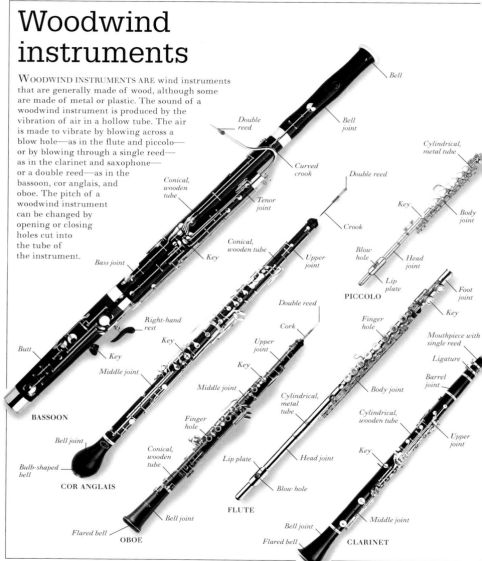

WOODWIND INSTRUMENTS ARE wind instruments that are generally made of wood, although some are made of metal or plastic. The sound of a woodwind instrument is produced by the vibration of air in a hollow tube. The air is made to vibrate by blowing across a blow hole—as in the flute and piccolo—or by blowing through a single reed—as in the clarinet and saxophone—or a double reed—as in the bassoon, cor anglais, and oboe. The pitch of a woodwind instrument can be changed by opening or closing holes cut into the tube of the instrument.

Bell

Double reed

Bell joint

Cylindrical, metal tube

Curved crook

Double reed

Conical, wooden tube

Key

Body joint

Tenor joint

Crook

Conical, wooden tube

Upper joint

Blow hole

Head joint

Bass joint

Key

Lip plate

PICCOLO

Foot joint

Double reed

Key

Finger hole

Cork

Finger hole

Mouthpiece with single reed

Right-hand rest

Key

Upper joint

Ligature

Barrel joint

Butt

Key

Key

Body joint

Middle joint

Cylindrical, metal tube

Cylindrical, wooden tube

Key

BASSOON

Finger hole

Upper joint

Bell joint

Conical, wooden tube

Lip plate

Head joint

Bulb-shaped bell

COR ANGLAIS

Blow hole

FLUTE

Bell joint

Middle joint

Flared bell

OBOE

Bell joint

Flared bell

CLARINET

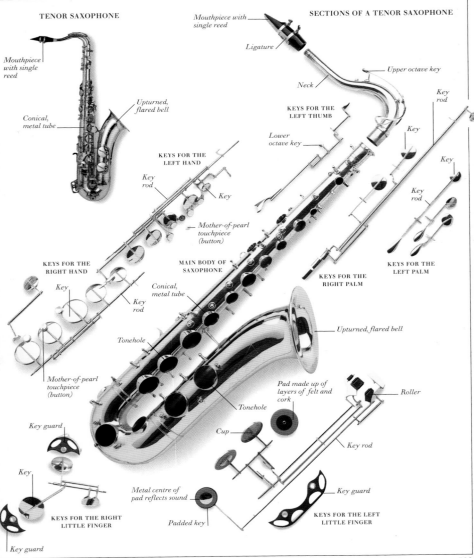

TENOR SAXOPHONE

SECTIONS OF A TENOR SAXOPHONE

Mouthpiece with single reed

Ligature

Upper octave key

Neck

Key rod

Mouthpiece with single reed

Conical, metal tube

Upturned, flared bell

KEYS FOR THE LEFT THUMB

Lower octave key

Key

Key

Key rod

KEYS FOR THE LEFT HAND

Key rod

Key

Mother-of-pearl touchpiece (button)

KEYS FOR THE LEFT PALM

KEYS FOR THE RIGHT HAND

MAIN BODY OF SAXOPHONE

Key

Conical, metal tube

Key rod

KEYS FOR THE RIGHT PALM

Tonehole

Upturned, flared bell

Mother-of-pearl touchpiece (button)

Pad made up of layers of felt and cork

Roller

Key guard

Tonehole

Cup

Key rod

Key

Metal centre of pad reflects sound

Key guard

KEYS FOR THE RIGHT LITTLE FINGER

Padded key

KEYS FOR THE LEFT LITTLE FINGER

Key guard

Stringed instruments

STRINGED INSTRUMENTS PRODUCE SOUND by the vibration of stretched strings. This may be done by drawing a bow across the strings, as in the violin; or by plucking the strings, as in the harp and guitar (see pp. 512-513). The four modern members of the bowed string family are the violin, viola, cello (violoncello), and double bass. Each consists of a hollow, wooden body, a long neck, and four strings. The bow is a wooden stick with horsehair stretched across its length. The vibrations made by drawing the bow across the strings are transmitted to the hollow body, and this itself vibrates, amplifying and enriching the sound produced. The harp consists of a set of strings of different lengths stretched across a wooden frame. The strings are plucked by the player's thumbs and fingers—except the little finger of each hand—which produces vibrations that are amplified by the harp's sound board. The pitch of the note produced by any stringed instrument depends on the length, weight, and tension of the string. A shorter, lighter, or tighter string gives a higher note.

Strings

Scroll eye

Scroll

Peg hole

Ebony tuning pegs

Neck made of maple wood

Fingerboard

Rounded shoulder

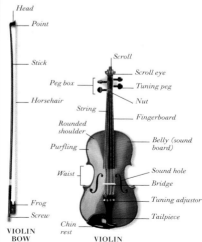

Head

Point

Stick

Horsehair

Scroll

Scroll eye

Peg box

Tuning peg

Nut

String

Fingerboard

Rounded shoulder

Purfling

Belly (sound board)

Waist

Sound hole

Bridge

Tuning adjustor

Tailpiece

Frog

Screw

Chin rest

VIOLIN BOW

VIOLIN

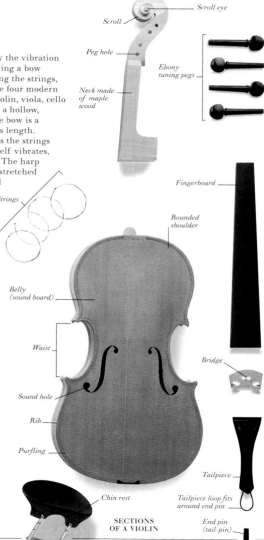

Belly (sound board)

Waist

Sound hole

Rib

Purfling

Bridge

Tailpiece

Chin rest

Tailpiece loop fits around end pin

End pin (tail-pin)

SECTIONS OF A VIOLIN

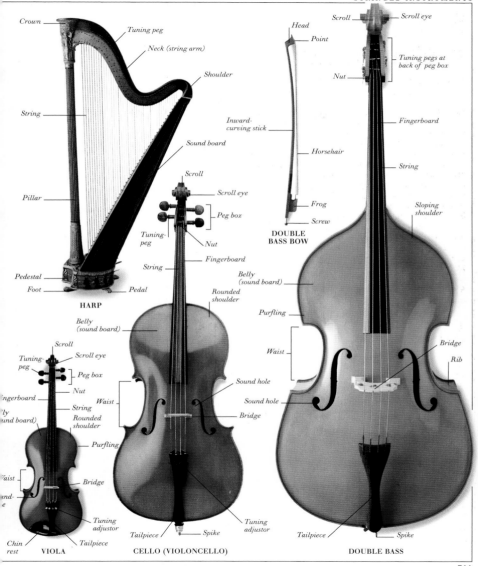

HARP

Crown
Tuning peg
Neck (string arm)
Shoulder
String
Sound board
Pillar
Pedestal
Foot
Pedal

DOUBLE BASS BOW

Head
Point
Inward-curving stick
Horsehair
Frog
Screw

VIOLA

Scroll
Tuning-peg
Scroll eye
Peg box
Nut
Fingerboard
Belly (sound board)
String
Rounded shoulder
Purfling
Waist
Bridge
Tuning adjustor
Chin rest
Tailpiece

CELLO (VIOLONCELLO)

Scroll
Scroll eye
Peg box
Tuning-peg
Nut
Fingerboard
String
Belly (sound board)
Rounded shoulder
Waist
Sound hole
Bridge
Tailpiece
Spike
Tuning adjustor

DOUBLE BASS

Scroll
Scroll eye
Tuning pegs at back of peg box
Nut
Fingerboard
String
Sloping shoulder
Belly (sound board)
Purfling
Waist
Bridge
Rib
Sound hole
Tailpiece
Spike

Guitars

THE GUITAR IS A PLUCKED stringed instrument (see pp. 510-511). There are two types of guitar—acoustic and electric. Acoustic guitars have hollow bodies and six or 12 strings. Plucking the strings produces vibrations that are amplified by their hollow bodies. Electric guitars usually have solid bodies and six strings. Pick-ups placed under the strings convert their vibrations into electronic signals that are magnified by an amplifier, and sent to a loudspeaker where they are converted into sounds (see pp. 520-521). Electric bass guitars are very similar in structure to electric guitars, and produce sound in the same way, but have four strings and play bass notes.

String
Fret
Machine head
Hollow body
Neck
Headstock
Sound hole
B string
G string
Bridge
D string
A string
Low E string
Maker's label

Lining glued along top and bottom edge of rib

Rib

End block

Strap peg

Joint

Transverse (crosswise) strut strengthens back

Back made of two pieces of cherry wood joined together

Saddle

Bridge pin

Bridge

Binding

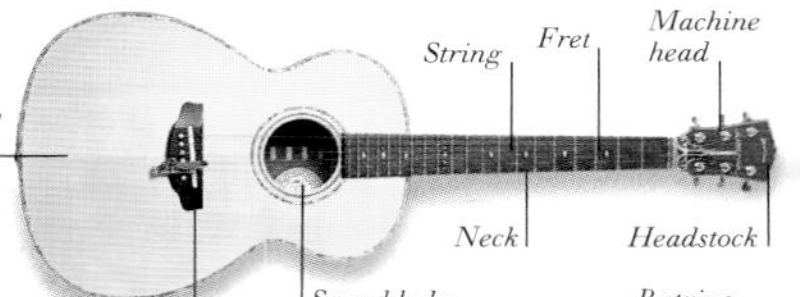

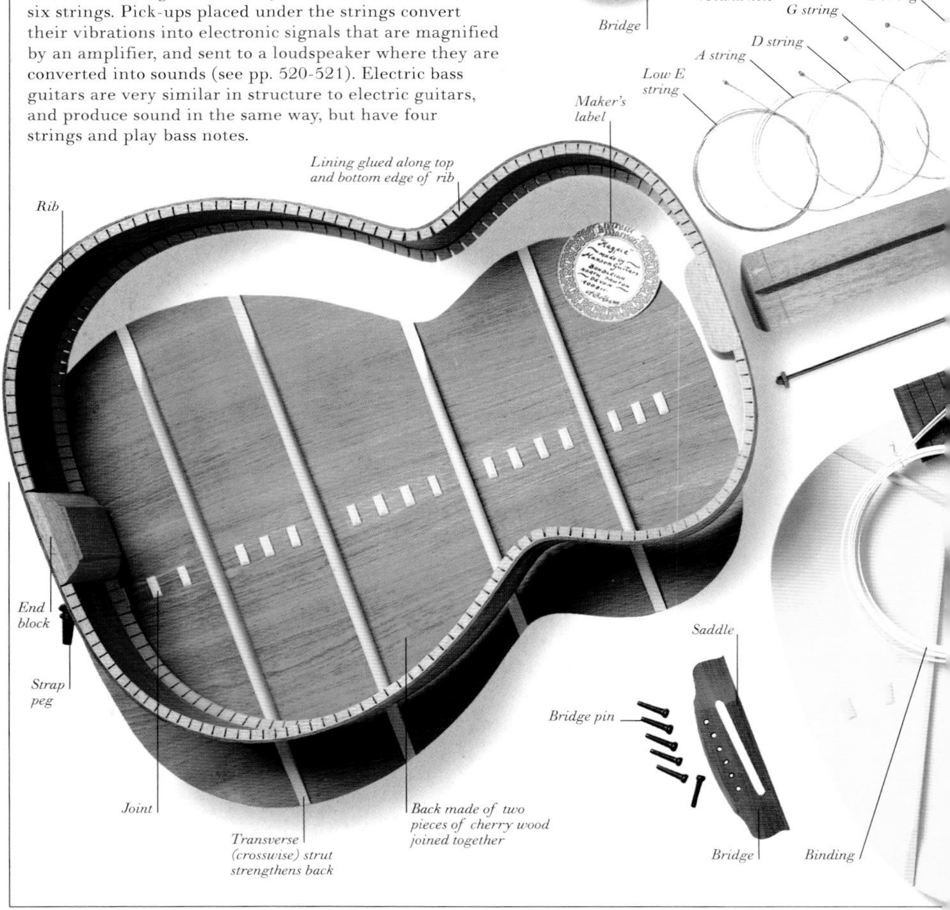

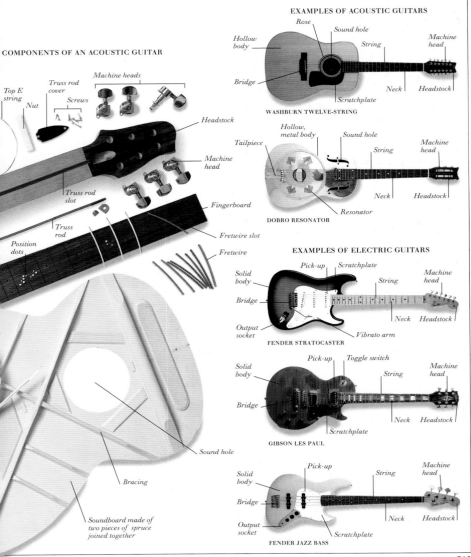

COMPONENTS OF AN ACOUSTIC GUITAR

Top E string

Nut

Truss rod cover

Screws

Machine heads

Headstock

Machine head

Truss rod slot

Truss rod

Position dots

Fingerboard

Fretwire slot

Fretwire

Sound hole

Bracing

Soundboard made of two pieces of spruce joined together

EXAMPLES OF ACOUSTIC GUITARS

Rose

Sound hole

Hollow body

String

Machine head

Bridge

Neck

Headstock

Scratchplate

WASHBURN TWELVE-STRING

Hollow, metal body

Sound hole

Tailpiece

String

Machine head

Neck

Headstock

Resonator

DOBRO RESONATOR

EXAMPLES OF ELECTRIC GUITARS

Pick-up

Scratchplate

Solid body

String

Machine head

Bridge

Output socket

Neck

Headstock

Vibrato arm

FENDER STRATOCASTER

Pick-up

Toggle switch

Solid body

String

Machine head

Bridge

Neck

Headstock

Scratchplate

GIBSON LES PAUL

Pick-up

String

Machine head

Solid body

Bridge

Output socket

Neck

Headstock

Scratchplate

FENDER JAZZ BASS

Keyboard instruments

KEYBOARD INSTRUMENTS are instruments that are sounded by means of a keyboard. The organ and piano are two of the principal members of the keyboard family. The organ consists of pipes that are operated by one or more manuals (keyboards) and a pedal board. The pipes are lined up in rows (known as ranks or registers) on top of a wind chest. The sound of the organ is made when air is admitted into a pipe by pressing a key or pedal. The piano

ORGAN PIPE

consists of wire strings stretched over a metal frame, and a keyboard and pedals that operate hammers and dampers. The piano frame is either vertical—as in the upright piano—or horizontal—as in the grand piano. When a key is at rest, a damper lies against the string to stop it from vibrating. When a key is pressed down, the damper moves away from the string as the hammer strikes it, causing the string to vibrate and sound a note.

UPRIGHT PIANO

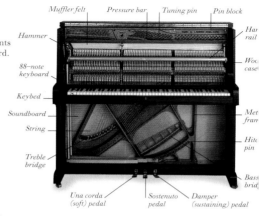

Muffler felt
Pressure bar
Tuning pin
Pin block
Hammer
Har rail
88—note keyboard
Woo case
Keyed
Soundboard
Met fran
String
Treble bridge
Hitc pin
Una corda (soft) pedal
Sostenuto pedal
Damper (sustaining) pedal
Bass brid

ORGAN CONSOLE

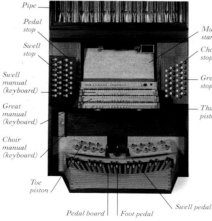

Pipe
Pedal stop
Swell stop
Music stand
Choir stop
Swell manual (keyboard)
Great stop
Great manual (keyboard)
Thumb piston
Choir manual (keyboard)
Toe piston
Pedal board
Foot pedal
Swell pedal

UPRIGHT PIANO ACTION

KEY AT REST

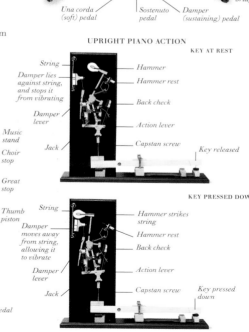

String
Hammer
Damper lies against string, and stops it from vibrating
Hammer rest
Back check
Damper lever
Action lever
Jack
Capstan screw
Key released

KEY PRESSED DOW

String
Hammer strikes string
Damper moves away from string, allowing it to vibrate
Hammer rest
Back check
Damper lever
Action lever
Jack
Capstan screw
Key pressed down

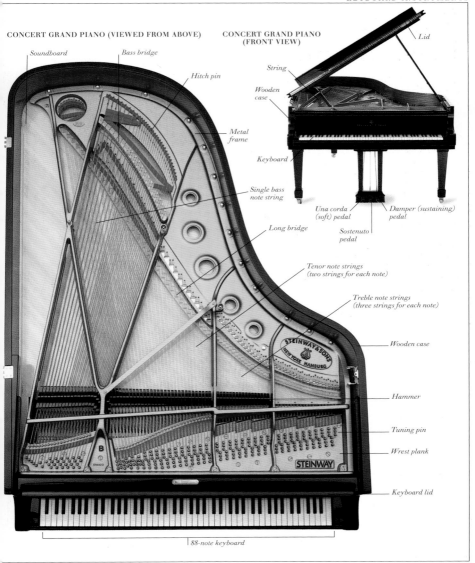

CONCERT GRAND PIANO (VIEWED FROM ABOVE)

CONCERT GRAND PIANO (FRONT VIEW)

Soundboard

Bass bridge

Hitch pin

Metal frame

Single bass note string

Long bridge

Tenor note strings
(two strings for each note)

Treble note strings
(three strings for each note)

Wooden case

Hammer

Tuning pin

Wrest plank

Keyboard lid

88-note keyboard

Lid

String

Wooden case

Keyboard

Una corda
(soft) pedal

Sostenuto
pedal

Damper (sustaining)
pedal

STEINWAY & SONS
NEW YORK HAMBURG

STEINWAY

515

Percussion instruments

PERCUSSION INSTRUMENTS are a large group of instruments that produce sound by being struck, shaken, scraped, or clashed together. Most percussion instruments—such as the tam-tam (gong), cymbals, and maracas—do not have a definite pitch and are used for rhythm and impact, and the distinctive

TEMPLE BLOCKS

timber (color) of their sound. Other percussion instruments—such as the xylophone, vibraphone, and tubular bells—are tuned to a definite pitch and can play melody, harmony, and rhythms. The xylophone and vibraphone each have two rows of bars that are arranged in a similar way to the black and white keys of a piano. Metal tubes are suspended below the bars to amplify the sound. The vibraphone has electrically operated fans that rotate in the tubes and produce a vibrato (wavering pitch) effect.

Tube struck with mallet

Hollow, metal tube

Damper bar

Metal frame

Mechanism linking pedal and damper bar

Row of tubes graduated in length and pitch

Damper pedal

EXAMPLES OF BEATERS

SOFT-HEADED BEATER   *Fell-covered head*

Rosewood head

HARD-HEADED BEATER

Leather-covered head

MALLET

TAM-TAM (GONG)

Tam-tam struck in center with soft-headed beater

Cord

Metal frame

PAISTE

Row of bars graduated in length and pitch

XYLOPHONE

Wooden bar struck with hard-headed beater

onCorde

Hollow, metal tube

Metal stand

Rim

Large, metal disk

CYMBALS

Leather strap fits around player's hand

Pad protects hands from vibrations

Zildjian

Thin, convex disk of copper and tin alloy

SECTIONS OF A MARACA

Wooden handle

Lead shot

Hollow, wooden head

CLAVES

Hardwood sticks clashed together to give a sharp crack

TRIANGLE

Steel rod bent into triangular shape

Steel beater

CASTANETS

Cord

Hollowed wood

VIBRAPHONE

Row of bars graduated in length and pitch

Metal bar struck with soft-headed beater

MUSSER

Metal frame

Damper pedal

Metal tube containing electrically operated fan that produces vibrato (wavering pitch) effect

Electric cable

517

Drums

A DRUM IS A percussion instrument that consists of a drumhead, made of skin or plastic, stretched over one or both ends of a hollow vessel (the body shell). Drums are played in most parts of the world and are made in a number of different shapes and sizes. They can be divided into three groups according to the shape of the body-shell: frame drums (e.g., tambourines), bowl-shaped drums (e.g., timpani), and tubular drums (e.g., congas). Drums are usually sounded by striking the drumhead with the hands or with beaters, such as a hard-headed stick. The drumhead vibrates, and its vibrations are amplified by the hollow body shell. The snare drum has wires—known as snares—stretched across the lower drumhead; the snares vibrate against the lower drumhead when the drum is played. Most drums, such as congas, do not have a definite pitch and can play only rhythms (see pp. 516-517). Other drums, such as timpani, have a definite pitch and can play melody, harmony, and rhythms. They can be tuned by adjusting the tension of the drumhead. Different types of drum can be combined together with other percussion instruments to form a drum set. The basic components of the drum set are bass drum, tom-toms, floor tom (tenor drum), snare drum, and cymbals.

TAMBOURINE

DRUM SET

Crash cymbal

Tension key

Tension rod

Tom-tom

Lug

Hi-hat cymbal

Snare drum

Tripod stand

Chain

Tension screw

Felt-covered beater

Pedal

Pedal

SNARE DRUM (VIEWED FROM BELOW)

Snare mounting

Adjustable damper

Lug

Transparent lower drumhead

Upper drumhead

Snare

Stick

Snare release lever

EXAMPLES OF BEATERS

Acorn

HARD-HEADED STICK

Taper

SOFT-HEADED STICK

Felt-covered head

WIRE BRUSH

Wire bristles

Ride cymbal

Tension key

Tom-tom

Height adjustment key

Tension rod

Lug

Floor tom (tenor drum)

Tension rod

Lug

Wooden body shell

Height adjustment key

Leg

Bass drum

Rubber foot

CONGAS

Metal hoop

Drumhead

Tension rod

Wooden body shell

Tripod stand

Leg

TIMPANUM (KETTLE DRUM)

Drumhead

Tension rod

Metal hoop

Tuning gauge

Copper body shell

Strut

Crown

Tension rod

Tuning pedal

Castor

Electronic instruments

ELECTRONIC DRUMS

ELECTRONIC INSTRUMENTS generate electronic signals that are magnified by an amplifier and sent to a loudspeaker, where they are converted into sounds. Synthesizers, and other electronic instruments, simulate the characteristic sounds of conventional instruments, and also create entirely new sounds. Most electronic instruments are keyboard instruments, but electronic wind and percussion instruments are also popular. A digital sampler records and stores sounds from musical instruments or other sources. When the sound is played back, the pitch of the original sound can be altered. A keyboard can be connected to the sampler so that a tune can be played using the sampled sounds. With a MIDI (Musical Instrument Digital Interface) system, a computer can be linked with other electronic instruments, such as keyboards and electronic drums, to make sounds together or in sequence. It is also possible, using music software, to compose and play music on a home computer.

Drum pad

Height adjustment key

HOME KEYBOARD

Power button
Volume control
Function display
Memory record button
Tone editor control
Demonstration tune button

Pitch modulator
Multiaccompaniment system control
Tone and rhythm pattern selector
Key

Tripod

SYNTHESIZER

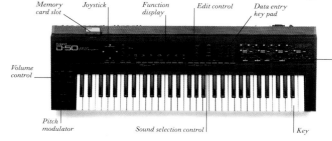

Memory card slot
Joystick
Function display
Edit control
Data entry key pad
Sound structure guide

Volume control

Pitch modulator
Sound selection control
Key

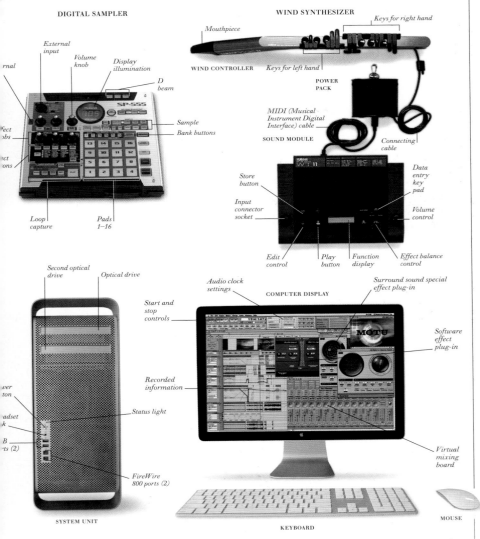

DIGITAL SAMPLER

External input

rnal

Volume knob

Display illumination

D beam

Sample

Bank buttons

ect obs

ct ons

Loop capture

Pads 1–16

WIND SYNTHESIZER

Mouthpiece

Keys for right hand

WIND CONTROLLER

Keys for left hand

POWER PACK

MIDI (Musical Instrument Digital Interface) cable

SOUND MODULE

Connecting cable

Store button

Input connector socket

Data entry key pad

Volume control

Edit control

Play button

Function display

Effect balance control

Second optical drive

Optical drive

Audio clock settings

COMPUTER DISPLAY

Surround sound special effect plug-in

Start and stop controls

Software effect plug-in

Recorded information

ver ton

adset k

B ts (2)

Status light

FireWire 800 ports (2)

Virtual mixing board

SYSTEM UNIT

KEYBOARD

MOUSE

COMPUTER WITH MIDI AND AUDIO SOFTWARE SEQUENCER

521

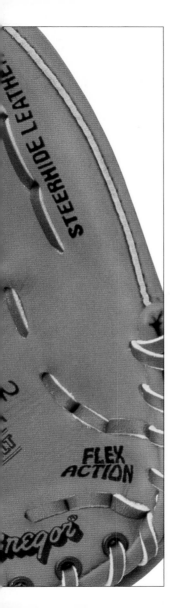

SPORTS

Soccer ··········· 524
Football ··········· 526
Australian Rules and Gaelic Football ······ 528
Rugby ··········· 530
Basketball ··········· 532
Volleyball, Netball, and Handball ······· 534
Baseball ··········· 536
Cricket ··········· 538
Hockey, Lacrosse, and Hurling ······ 540
Track and Field ··········· 542
Racket Sports ··········· 544
Golf ··········· 546
Archery and Shooting ··········· 548
Ice Hockey ··········· 550
Alpine Skiing ··········· 552
Equestrian Sports ··········· 554
Judo and Fencing ··········· 556
Swimming and Diving ··········· 558
Canoeing, Rowing, and Sailing ······· 560
Angling ··········· 562

Soccer

GAMES INVOLVING KICKING A BALL have a long history and were recorded in China as early as 300 BC; in medieval Europe, street football was banned as a menace to the public; only in 1863 were the rules established, specifically banning carrying the ball for all players except the goalkeeper, and separating rugby from soccer. Soccer, officially termed association football, is a team sport in which players attempt to score goals by passing and dribbling the ball down the field past opposing defenders, and kicking or heading the ball into the goal net, outwitting the defending goalkeeper. Each team consists of 10 outfield players (defenders, midfielders, and strikers) and a goalkeeper. Players from the opposing team may challenge the player in possession of the ball, but an illegal or foul tackle results in a penalty if a foul occurs inside the penalty area or a free kick if outside the penalty area. The round ball used in soccer is more easily controlled than the oval balls used in American, Canadian, and Australian rules football and in rugby. The result is a more "open" or flowing game that is played and watched by millions of people worldwide.

ASSISTANT REFEREE'S FLAG

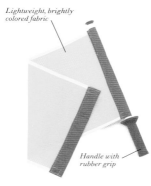

Lightweight, brightly colored fabric

Handle with rubber grip

REFEREE'S EQUIPMENT

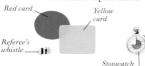

Red card

Yellow card

Referee's whistle

Stopwatch

SOCCER FIELD

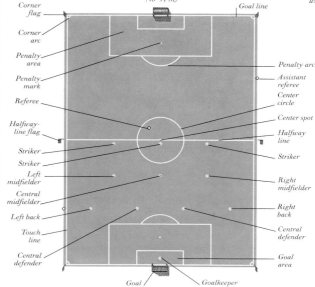

Corner flag

Corner arc

Penalty area

Penalty mark

Referee

Halfway-line flag

Striker

Striker

Left midfielder

Central midfielder

Left back

Touch line

Central defender

130–300 ft (46–91 m)

Goal line

Penalty arc

Assistant referee

Center circle

Center spot

Halfway line

Striker

Right midfielder

Right back

Central defender

Goal area

Goal

Goalkeeper

FIELD MARKINGS

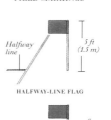

Halfway line

5 ft (1.5 m)

HALFWAY-LINE FLAG

Corner arc

CORNER FLAG

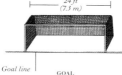

24 ft (7.3 m)

Goal line

GOAL.

GOALKEEPER

Goalkeeper's shirt

Glove

Shin guard

Shorts

Sock

Soccer shoe

SOCCER STRIP

Open-neck collar

Lightweight, man-made fabric team shirt

Team logo

Manufacturer's logo

Ribbed welt

Sponsor's logo

Manufacturer's name

Edge cut to fit perfectly

Motta

lotto

MAKING A SOCCER BALL

Hole punched in panel for stitching

Mitre

MULTIPLEX

Ball size number

5

Mitre

MULTIPLEX

8½–9 in (22–23 cm)

Waxed thread

Needle

Bladder valve

Bladder made from latex rubber

Panels sewn together with ball inside out

Laminated panel

Long cotton sock

Club crest

Team shorts

Synthetic shoelace

Interchangeable nylon cleat

SOCCER SHOE

Football

IN AMERICAN AND CANADIAN FOOTBALL, the object of the game is to get the ball across the opponent's goal line, either by passing or carrying it across (a touchdown), or by kicking it between their goalposts (a field goal). An American football team has 11 players on the field at a time, although up to 40 players can appear for each side in a single game. The agile "offense" tries to score points, and the heavy hitting "defense" holds back the opposition. When in possession of the ball, a team has four chances ("downs"), to move it at least ten yards (nine meters) up the field to make a "first down." The opposition gains possession if they fail, or by tackling and intercepting the ball. Canadian football is played on a larger field, with 12 men on each side. A team has only three chances to achieve a first down. Otherwise, the game is very similar to American football. Helmets, face masks, and layers of body padding are worn by the players for protection.

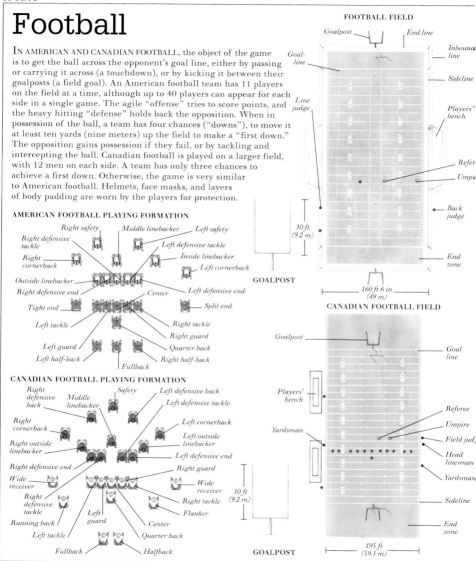

FOOTBALL FIELD

Goalpost — End line — Inbound line — Goal-line — Sideline — Line judge — Players' bench — Refer — Ump — Back judge — End zone

160 ft 6 in (49 m)

AMERICAN FOOTBALL PLAYING FORMATION

Right safety — Middle linebacker — Left safety — Right defensive tackle — Left defensive tackle — Right cornerback — Inside linebacker — Left cornerback — Outside linebacker — Right defensive end — Center — Left defensive end — Tight end — Split end — Left tackle — Right tackle — Right guard — Left guard — Quarter back — Left half-back — Right half-back — Fullback

30 ft (9.2 m)

GOALPOST

CANADIAN FOOTBALL FIELD

Goalpost — Goal line — Players' bench — Referee — Yardsman — Umpire — Field jud — Head linesman — Yardsman — Sideline — End zone

195 ft (59.5 m)

CANADIAN FOOTBALL PLAYING FORMATION

Right defensive back — Middle linebacker — Safety — Left defensive back — Left defensive tackle — Right cornerback — Left cornerback — Right outside linebacker — Left outside linebacker — Right defensive end — Left defensive end — Wide receiver — Right guard — Wide receiver — Right defensive tackle — Right tackle — Running back — Left guard — Flanker — Left tackle — Center — Quarter back — Fullback — Halfback

30 ft (9.2 m)

GOALPOST

PLAYER

- Team logo
- Helmet
- Wrist pad
- Player's number
- Tie to shoulder pads
- Thigh pad
- Pants
- Cleated shoe

PROTECTIVE EQUIPMENT

- Painted white ring
- Lace
- Brown pebbled leather
- 11 in (28 cm)

FOOTBALL

HELMET

- Nonbreakable plastic
- Rubber-coated plastic
- Shock absorber

HELMET

SHOULDER PAD

- Chest protector weight up to 5 lb 8 oz (2.5 kg)

BIKE BIKE
AIR·LITE
BLUE·LASER 40-42

RIB PADS

- Strap ties on to shoulder pad

UPPER ARM PAD

BIKE

- Tail bone pad
- Foam-sponge filling

HIP PAD

ELBOW PAD

FINGERLESS GLOVE

- Screw-in cleat
- Rigid plastic covering

BIKE
44-52

BIKE
44-52

THIGH PAD

SHOE

- Fold-over leather tongue

PANTS

KNEE PAD

REFEREE'S SIGNALS

- **TIME OUT**
- **TOUCHDOWN OR FIELD GOAL**
- **PERSONAL FOUL**
- **OFFSIDE OR ENCROACHMENT**
- **HOLDING**
- **ILLEGAL MOTION**
- **FIRST DOWN**
- **PASS INTERFERENCE**

Australian rules and Gaelic football

VARIETIES OF FOOTBALL have developed all over the world and Australian rules football is considered to be one of the roughest versions, allowing full body tackles even though participants wear no protective padding. The game is played on a large, oval field by two sides, each of 18 players. Players can kick or punch the ball, which is shaped like a rugby ball, but cannot throw it. Running with the ball is permitted, as long as the ball touches the ground at least once every 10 meters. The fullbacks defend two sets of posts. Teams try to score "goals" (six points) between the inner posts or "behinds" (one point) inside the outer posts. Each game has four quarters of 25 minutes, and the team with the most points at the end of the allotted time is the winner. In Gaelic football, an Irish version of soccer (see pp. 524–525), a size 5 soccer ball is used. Each team can have 15 players on the field at a time. Players are allowed to catch, fist, and kick the ball, or dribble it using their hands or feet, but cannot throw it. Teams are awarded three points for getting the ball into the net, and one point for getting it through the posts above the crossbar. Gaelic football is rarely played outside of Ireland.

START OF PLAY

Field umpire

Center circle

AUSTRALIAN RULES FOOTBALL FIELD

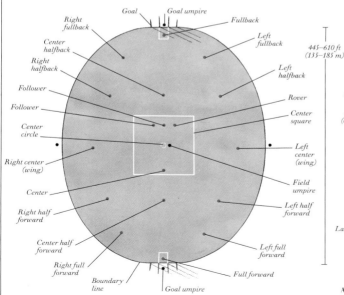

Goal — Goal umpire — Fullback
Right fullback
Center halfback — Left fullback
Right halfback
Left halfback
Follower
Follower — Rover
Center circle — Center square
Right center (wing) — Left center (wing)
Center — Field umpire
Right half forward — Left half forward
Center half forward — Left full forward
Right full forward — Full forward
Boundary line — Goal umpire

445–610 ft (135–185 m)

SCORING

GOAL (6 POINTS)

BEHIND (1 POINT)

21 ft (6.4 m)

Goalpost

21 ft (6.4 m)

Behind post

Behind-line

Goal-line

Goal square

GOALPOSTS

10⅞ in (27.5 cm)

Lace

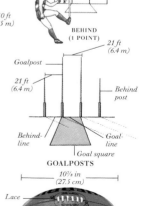

Leather covering

AUSTRALIAN RULES FOOTBALL

AUSTRALIAN RULES FOOTBALL SKILLS

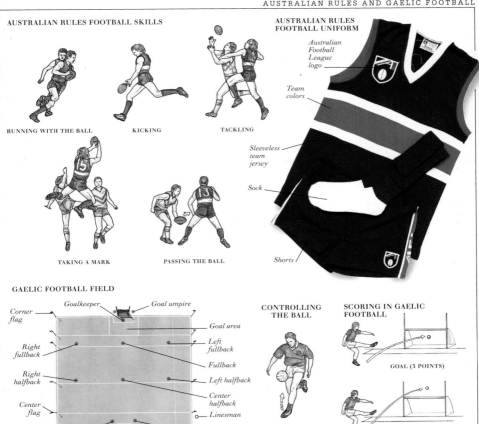

RUNNING WITH THE BALL

KICKING

TACKLING

TAKING A MARK

PASSING THE BALL

AUSTRALIAN RULES FOOTBALL UNIFORM

Australian Football League logo

Team colors

Sleeveless team jersey

Sock

Shorts

GAELIC FOOTBALL FIELD

Corner flag

Goalkeeper

Goal umpire

Goal area

Right fullback

Left fullback

Fullback

Right halfback

Left halfback

Center halfback

Center flag

Linesman

Linesman

Left midfielder

Right midfielder

Midfield line

Referee

Left half-forward

Right half-forward

Right full-forward

Center half-forward

Full forward

Left full-forward

260–295 ft (80–90 m)

CONTROLLING THE BALL

SCORING IN GAELIC FOOTBALL

GOAL (3 POINTS)

POINT (1 POINT)

8½–9 in (22–23 cm)

21ft (6.4 m)

Goalpost

Crossbar

Parallelogram

GOAL

oneills all-ireland

GAELIC FOOTBALL

529

Rugby

RUGBY IS PLAYED WITH AN OVAL BALL, which may be carried, thrown, or kicked. There are two codes of rugby, both played at amateur and professional levels. Rugby Union is played by two teams of 15 players. They can score points in two ways: by placing the ball by hand over the opponents' goal line (a try, scoring four points) or by kicking it over the crossbar of the opponent's goal (a conversion of a try, scoring two points; a penalty kick, scoring three points; or a dropkick, scoring three points). Rugby League developed from the Union game but is played by 13 players. In League games, a try scores four points; a conversion scores two points; a drop goal scores one point, and a penalty kick scores two points. Scrummages occur in both codes when play stops following an infringement.

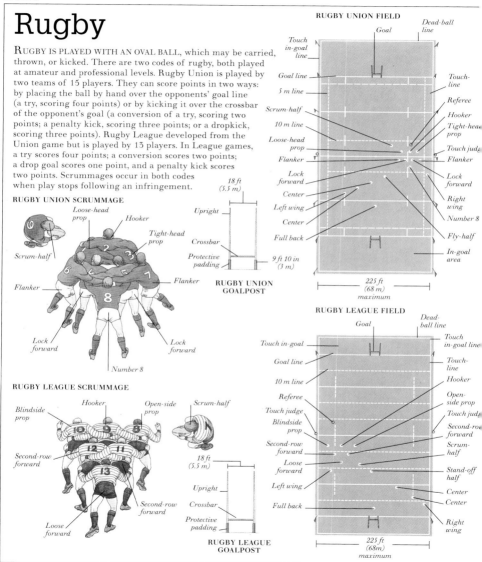

RUGBY UNION FIELD

Touch in-goal line · Goal · Dead-ball line · Goal line · 5 m line · Scrum-half · 10 m line · Loose-head prop · Flanker · Lock forward · Center · Left wing · Center · Full back · Touch-line · Referee · Hooker · Tight-head prop · Touch judge · Flanker · Lock forward · Right wing · Number 8 · Fly-half · In-goal area

225 ft
(68 m)
maximum

RUGBY UNION SCRUMMAGE

Loose-head prop · Hooker · Tight-head prop · Scrum-half · Flanker · Flanker · Lock forward · Lock forward · Number 8

18 ft
(5.5 m)

Upright · Crossbar · Protective padding

9 ft 10 in
(3 m)

RUGBY UNION GOALPOST

RUGBY LEAGUE SCRUMMAGE

Blindside prop · Hooker · Open-side prop · Scrum-half · Second-row forward · Second-row forward · Second-row forward · Loose forward

18 ft
(5.5 m)

Upright · Crossbar · Protective padding

RUGBY LEAGUE GOALPOST

RUGBY LEAGUE FIELD

Touch in-goal · Goal · Dead-ball line · Goal line · 10 m line · Referee · Touch judge · Blindside prop · Second-row forward · Loose forward · Left wing · Full back · Touch in-goal line · Touch-line · Hooker · Open-side prop · Touch judge · Second-row forward · Scrum-half · Stand-off half · Center · Center · Right wing

225 ft
(68m)
maximum

RUGBY SCORING AND SKILLS

GOAL

Goal-line

TRY

PASS

PLACE KICK

FLYING TACKLE

RUGBY UNION PLAYER

Shirt in team color

Team shorts

Knee-high sock

Cleated shoe

RUGBY UNION BALL

Laminated leather panel covered with textured plastic

GILBERT
REPLICA

Four-panel construction

|— 11–12 in (28–30 cm) —|

RUGBY LEAGUE BALL

Eight-panel construction

TETLEY'S
GILBERT

Laminated leather panel covered with textured plastic

|— 11 in (28 cm) —|

Button-up collar

RUGBY LEAGUE SHIRT

Team crest

Short sleeve

RUGBY UNION SHIRT

GILBERT

BEDFORD BLUES

CITY

Ankle support

Circular cleat

RUGBY SHOE

Team color

RUGBY SHIRTS

Team crest

Basketball

BASKETBALL IS A BALL GAME for two teams of five players, originally devised in 1890 by James Naismath for the Y.M.C.A. in Springfield, Massachusetts. The object of the game is to take possession of the ball and score points by throwing the ball into the opposing team's basket. A player moves the ball up and down the court by bouncing it along the ground or "dribbling"; the ball may be passed between players by throwing, bouncing, or rolling. Players may not run with or kick the ball, although pivoting on one foot is allowed. The game begins with the referee throwing the ball into the air and a player from each team jumping up to try and "tip" the ball to a teammate. The length of the game and the number of periods played varies at different levels. There are amateur, professional, and international rules. No game ends in a draw. An extra period of five minutes is played, plus as many extra periods as are necessary to break the tie. In addition to the five players on court, each team has up to seven substitutes, but players may only leave the court with the permission of the referee. Basketball is a noncontact sport and fouls on other players are penalized by a throw-in awarded against the offending team; a free throw at the basket is awarded when a player is fouled in the act of shooting. Basketball is a fast-moving game, requiring both physical and mental coordination. Skillful tactical play matters more than simple physical strength and the agility of the players makes the game an excellent spectator sport.

CHEST PASS

DRIBBLE

OVERHEAD PASS

LAY-UP SHOT

JUMP SHOT

LONG PASS

INTERNATIONAL BASKETBALL COURT

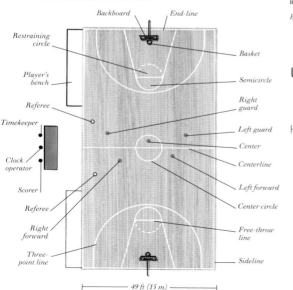

Backboard

End-line

Restraining circle

Basket

Player's bench

Semicircle

Referee

Right guard

Timekeeper

Left guard

Center

Clock operator

Centerline

Scorer

Left forward

Referee

Center circle

Right forward

Free-throw line

Three-point line

Sideline

49 ft (15 m)

BASKET AND BACKBOARD

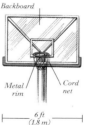

Backboard

Metal rim

Cord net

6 ft (1.8 m)

BASKET AND BACKBOARD STRUCTURE

10 ft (3.05 m)

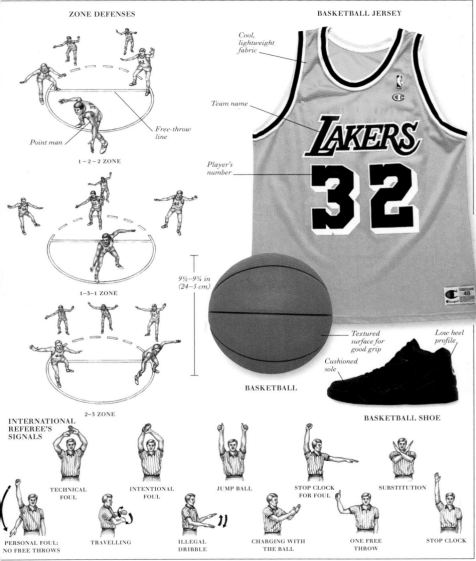

ZONE DEFENSES

BASKETBALL JERSEY

Cool, lightweight fabric

Team name

Player's number

Point man

Free-throw line

1 – 2 – 2 ZONE

1–3–1 ZONE

9½–9¼ in (24–5 cm)

2–3 ZONE

Textured surface for good grip

Cushioned sole

Low heel profile

BASKETBALL

BASKETBALL SHOE

INTERNATIONAL REFEREE'S SIGNALS

TECHNICAL FOUL

INTENTIONAL FOUL

JUMP BALL

STOP CLOCK FOR FOUL

SUBSTITUTION

PERSONAL FOUL: NO FREE THROWS

TRAVELLING

ILLEGAL DRIBBLE

CHARGING WITH THE BALL

ONE FREE THROW

STOP CLOCK

Volleyball, netball, and handball

VOLLEYBALL, NETBALL, AND HANDBALL are fast-moving team sports played with balls on courts with a hard surface. In volleyball, the object of the game is to hit the ball over a net strung across the center of the court so that it touches the ground on the opponent's side. The team of six players can take three hits to direct the ball over the net, although the same player cannot hit the ball twice in a row. Players can hit the ball with their arms, hands, or any other part of their upper body. Teams score points only while serving. The first team to score 15 points, with a two-point margin over their opponent, wins the game. Netball is one of the few sports played exclusively by women. Similar to basketball (see pp. 532–533), it is played on a slightly larger court with seven players instead of five. A team moves the ball toward the goal by throwing, passing, and catching it with the aim of throwing the ball through the opponents' goal net. Players are confined by their playing position to specific areas of the court. Team handball is one of the world's fastest games. Each side has seven players. A team moves the ball by dribbling, passing, or bouncing it as they run. Players may stop, catch, throw, bounce, or strike the ball with any part of the body above the knees. Each team tries to score goals by directing the ball past the opposition's goalkeeper into the net, which is similar to a soccer net.

VOLLEYBALL SHOTS

OVERHAND SERVE

SPIKE (SMASH)

UNDERHAND SERVE

FOREARM PASS (DIG)

UNIFORM

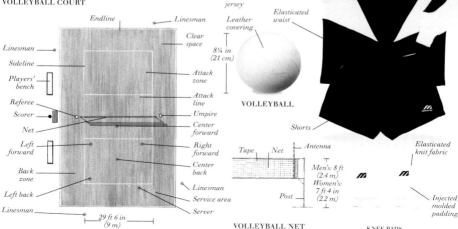

VOLLEYBALL COURT

Endline

Linesman

Linesman

Sideline

Players' bench

Referee

Scorer

Net

Left forward

Back zone

Left back

Linesman

Clear space

Attack zone

Attack line

Umpire

Center forward

Right forward

Center back

Linesman

Service area

Server

29 ft 6 in (9 m)

Ribbed cuff

Cotton-knit jersey

Leather covering

Elasticated waist

Team colors

8¼ in (21 cm)

VOLLEYBALL

Shorts

Elasticated knit fabric

Injected molded padding

Tape

Net

Antenna

Men's: 8 ft (2.4 m)
Women's: 7 ft 4 in (2.2 m)

Post

VOLLEYBALL NET

KNEE PADS

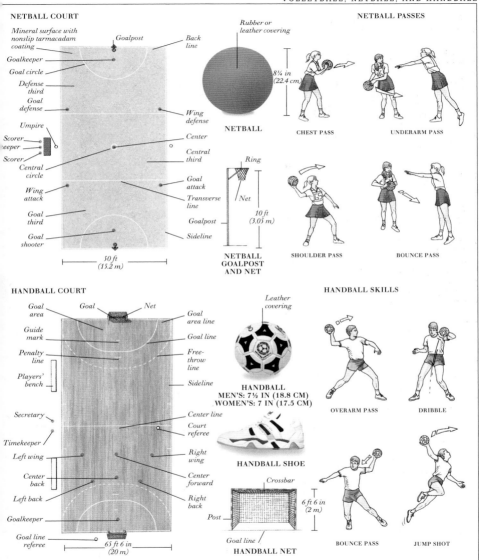

NETBALL COURT

Mineral surface with nonslip tarmacadam coating
Goalpost
Back line
Goalkeeper
Goal circle
Defense third
Goal defense
Wing defense
Umpire
Scorer
keeper
Scorer
Central circle
Wing attack
Center
Central third
Goal attack
Transverse line
Goal third
Goal shooter
Sideline
50 ft (15.2 m)

NETBALL PASSES

Rubber or leather covering
8¼ in (22.4 cm)

NETBALL

CHEST PASS

UNDERARM PASS

SHOULDER PASS

BOUNCE PASS

Ring
Net
10 ft (3.05 m)
Goalpost

NETBALL GOALPOST AND NET

HANDBALL COURT

Goal area
Goal
Net
Goal area line
Guide mark
Goal line
Penalty line
Free-throw line
Players' bench
Sideline
Secretary
Center line
Court referee
Timekeeper
Left wing
Right wing
Center back
Center forward
Left back
Right back
Goalkeeper
Goal line referee
65 ft 6 in (20 m)

Leather covering

HANDBALL
MEN'S: 7½ IN (18.8 CM)
WOMEN'S: 7 IN (17.5 CM)

HANDBALL SHOE

Crossbar
6 ft 6 in (2 m)
Post
Goal line

HANDBALL NET

HANDBALL SKILLS

OVERARM PASS

DRIBBLE

BOUNCE PASS

JUMP SHOT

Baseball

BASEBALL IS A BALL GAME for two teams of nine players. The batter hits the ball thrown by the opposing team's pitcher, into the area between the foul lines. He then runs around all four fixed bases in order to score a run, touching or "tagging" each base in turn. The pitcher must throw the ball at a height between the batter's armpits and knees, a height which is called the "strike zone." A ball pitched in this area that crosses over the "home plate" is called a "strike" and the batter has three strikes in which to try and hit the ball (otherwise he is "struck out"). The fielding team tries to get the batting team out by catching the ball before it bounces, tagging a player of the batting team with the ball who is running between bases, or by tagging a base before the player has reached it. Members of the batting team may stop safely at a base as long as it is not occupied by another member of their team. When the batter runs to first base, his teammate at first base must run on to second—this is called "force play." A game consists of nine innings and each team will bat once during an inning. When three members of the batting team are out, the teams swap roles. The team with the greatest number of runs wins the game.

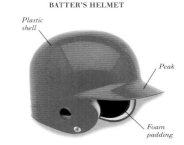

BATTER'S HELMET

Plastic shell

Peak

Foam padding

Wire coated in strong nylon

Plastic-coated foam padding

CATCHER'S MASK

BASEBALL FIELD

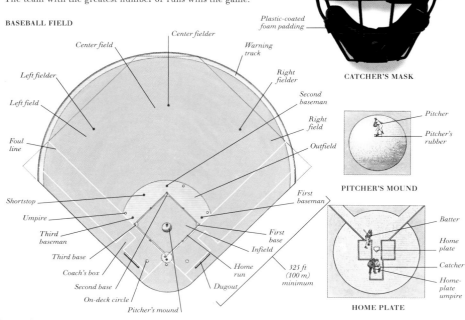

Center fielder

Center field

Warning track

Left fielder

Right fielder

Left field

Second baseman

Foul line

Right field

Outfield

Shortstop

First baseman

Umpire

First base

Third baseman

Infield

Third base

325 ft (100 m) minimum

Home run

Coach's box

Second base

Home plate

On-deck circle

Dugout

Pitcher's mound

Pitcher

Pitcher's rubber

PITCHER'S MOUND

Batter

Home plate

Catcher

Home-plate umpire

HOME PLATE

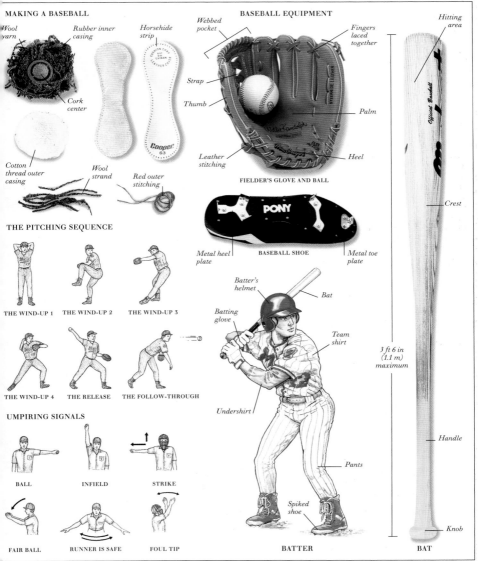

MAKING A BASEBALL

Wool yarn

Rubber inner casing

Horsehide strip

Cork center

Cotton thread outer casing

Wool strand

Red outer stitching

BASEBALL EQUIPMENT

Webbed pocket

Fingers laced together

Strap

Thumb

Palm

Leather stitching

Heel

FIELDER'S GLOVE AND BALL

Metal heel plate

BASEBALL SHOE

Metal toe plate

THE PITCHING SEQUENCE

THE WIND-UP 1

THE WIND-UP 2

THE WIND-UP 3

THE WIND-UP 4

THE RELEASE

THE FOLLOW-THROUGH

UMPIRING SIGNALS

BALL

INFIELD

STRIKE

FAIR BALL

RUNNER IS SAFE

FOUL TIP

Batter's helmet

Bat

Batting glove

Team shirt

Undershirt

Pants

Spiked shoe

BATTER

Hitting area

Crest

3 ft 6 in (1.1 m) maximum

Handle

Knob

BAT

Cricket

CRICKET IS A BALL GAME PLAYED by two teams of eleven players on a pitch with two sets of three stumps (wickets). The bowler bowls the ball down the pitch to the batsman of the opposing team, who must defend the wicket in front of which he stands. The object of the game is to score as many runs as possible. Runs can be scored individually by running the length of the playing strip, or by hitting a ball that lands outside the boundary ("six"), or that lands inside the boundary but bounces or rolls outside ("four"); the opposing team will bowl and field, attempting to dismiss the batsmen. A batsman can be dismissed in one of several ways: by the bowler hitting the wicket with the ball ("bowled"); by a fielder catching the ball hit by the batsman before it touches the ground ("caught"); by the wicket-keeper or another fielder breaking the wicket while the batsman is attempting a run and is therefore out of his ground ("stumped" or "run out"); by the batsman breaking the wicket with his own bat or body ("hit wicket"); by a part of the batsman's body being hit by a ball that would otherwise have hit the wicket ("leg before wicket" ["lbw"]). A match consists of one or two innings and each inning ends when the tenth batsman of the batting team is out, when a certain number of overs (a series of six balls bowled) have been played, or when the captain of the batting team "declares" ending the innings voluntarily.

FORWARD DEFENSIVE STROKE

BACKWARD DEFENSIVE STROKE

ON-DRIVE

OFF-DRIVE

PULL

HOOK

SQUARE CUT

LEG GLANCE

POSSIBLE FIELD POSITIONS FOR AN AWAY SWING BOWLER TO A RIGHT-HANDED BATSMAN (IN RED) AND OTHER FIELD POSITIONS

Long on
Long off
Umpire
Bowler
Boundary line
Nonstriking batsman
Deep mid-wicket
Mid-on
Extra cover
Silly mid-on
Mid-off
Forward short leg
Silly mid-off
Square leg
Cover
Deep square leg
Point
Square-leg umpire
Gulley
Batsman
Third man
Long leg
Second slip
Leg slip
Bowler
Wicket-keeper
Return crease
Fine leg
Sight screen
First slip
Umpire
Nonstriking batsman

CRICKET PITCH

Wicket-keeper

Batsman

Wicket

Bowling crease

66 ft (20 m)

CRICKET BALL AND WICKET

Leather skin

Seam

BALL

Bail

WICKET

Stump

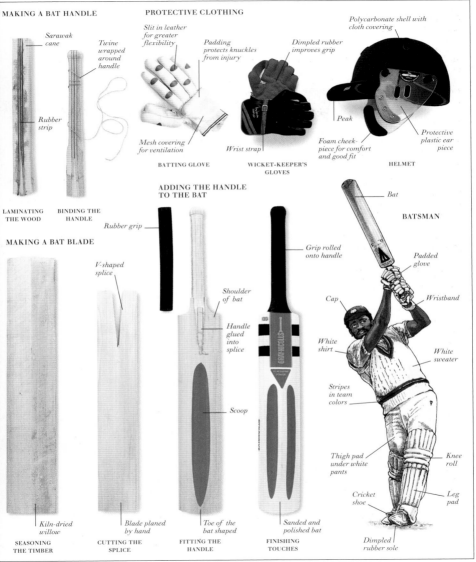

MAKING A BAT HANDLE

Sarawak cane

Twine wrapped around handle

Rubber strip

LAMINATING THE WOOD

BINDING THE HANDLE

MAKING A BAT BLADE

V-shaped splice

Kiln-dried willow

SEASONING THE TIMBER

Blade planed by hand

CUTTING THE SPLICE

PROTECTIVE CLOTHING

Slit in leather for greater flexibility

Padding protects knuckles from injury

Mesh covering for ventilation

BATTING GLOVE

Dimpled rubber improves grip

Wrist strap

WICKET-KEEPER'S GLOVES

Polycarbonate shell with cloth covering

Peak

Foam cheek-piece for comfort and good fit

Protective plastic ear piece

HELMET

ADDING THE HANDLE TO THE BAT

Rubber grip

Grip rolled onto handle

Shoulder of bat

Handle glued into splice

Scoop

Toe of the bat shaped

FITTING THE HANDLE

Sanded and polished bat

FINISHING TOUCHES

Bat

BATSMAN

Padded glove

Cap

Wristband

White shirt

White sweater

Stripes in team colors

Thigh pad under white pants

Knee roll

Cricket shoe

Leg pad

Dimpled rubber sole

Field hockey, lacrosse, and hurling

ALL OVER THE WORLD, TEAM GAMES have evolved that require that a ball be struck or carried, and tossed at the end of a stick. Early forms of these games include hurling, shinty, bandy, and pelota. Field hockey is played by men and women: two teams of 11 players try to gain and keep possession of the ball and score goals by using the hockey stick to propel the ball into their opponents' goal net. Skills such as passing, pushing, or hitting the ball by slapping or lifting it in a flicking movement, and shooting at goal are crucial. Hockey is played indoors and outdoors on grass or synthetic fields. Lacrosse is played internationally as a 12-a-side game for women and as 10-a-side game for men. The women's field has no absolute boundaries but the men's field has clearly defined side-lines and end-lines. The ball is kept in play by being carried, thrown, or batted with the crosse, and rolled or kicked in any direction. In men's and women's lacrosse, play can continue behind the marked goal areas. Similar skills are required in hurling—a Gaelic field game played on the same field as Gaelic football (see pp. 528–529), using the same goalposts and net. In hurling, the ball may be struck with or carried on the hurley and, when off the ground, may be struck with the hand or kicked. Goals (three points) are scored when the ball passes between the posts and under the crossbar; one point is scored when it passes between the posts and over the crossbar.

GOALKEEPER'S EQUIPMENT

Face mask
Hard shell
Air vent

HELMET

Strap

Rigid palm

Padded wrist

GAUNTLET

HOCKEY STICK AND BALL

STICK

Handle | *Tape*

Slazenger FLEX

Steam-bent ash head
Blade

Stitched seam

2¼–3 in
(7–7.5 cm)

|← 3 ft (91 cm) →|

BALL

HOCKEY FIELD

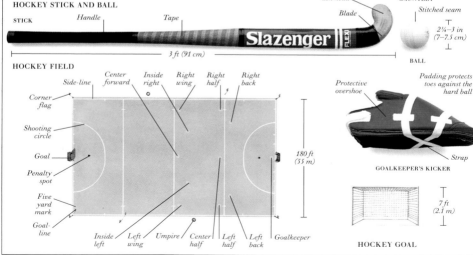

Corner flag
Side-line
Center forward
Inside right
Right wing
Right half
Right back
Shooting circle
Goal
Penalty spot
Five yard mark
Goal-line
Inside left
Left wing
Umpire
Center half
Left half
Left back
Goalkeeper

180 ft
(55 m)

Protective overshoe

Padding protects toes against the hard ball

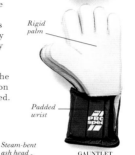

Strap

GOALKEEPER'S KICKER

7 ft
(2.1 m)

HOCKEY GOAL

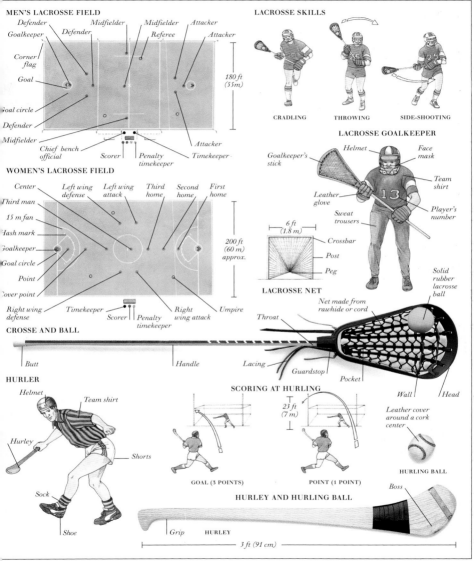

MEN'S LACROSSE FIELD

- *Defender*
- *Goalkeeper*
- *Defender*
- *Midfielder*
- *Midfielder*
- *Referee*
- *Attacker*
- *Attacker*
- *Corner flag*
- *Goal*
- *Goal circle*
- *Defender*
- *Midfielder*
- *Chief bench official*
- *Scorer*
- *Penalty timekeeper*
- *Timekeeper*
- *Attacker*
- *180 ft (55 m)*

WOMEN'S LACROSSE FIELD

- *Center*
- *Left wing defense*
- *Left wing attack*
- *Third home*
- *Second home*
- *First home*
- *Third man*
- *15 m fan*
- *Hash mark*
- *Goalkeeper*
- *Goal circle*
- *Point*
- *Cover point*
- *Right wing defense*
- *Timekeeper*
- *Scorer*
- *Penalty timekeeper*
- *Right wing attack*
- *Umpire*
- *200 ft (60 m) approx.*

CROSSE AND BALL

- *Butt*
- *Handle*

HURLER

- *Helmet*
- *Team shirt*
- *Hurley*
- *Shorts*
- *Sock*
- *Shoe*

LACROSSE SKILLS

CRADLING **THROWING** **SIDE-SHOOTING**

LACROSSE GOALKEEPER

- *Goalkeeper's stick*
- *Helmet*
- *Face mask*
- *Team shirt*
- *Leather glove*
- *Player's number*
- *Sweat trousers*
- *Solid rubber lacrosse ball*

- *6 ft (1.8 m)*
- *Crossbar*
- *Post*
- *Peg*

LACROSSE NET

- *Net made from rawhide or cord*
- *Throat*
- *Lacing*
- *Guardstop*
- *Pocket*
- *Wall*
- *Head*

SCORING AT HURLING

- *23 ft (7 m)*

GOAL (3 POINTS) **POINT (1 POINT)**

- *Leather cover around a cork center*

HURLING BALL

- *Boss*

HURLEY AND HURLING BALL

- *Grip* **HURLEY**
- *3 ft (91 cm)*

Track and field

THE SPORTS that make up track and field are divided into two main groups: track events—which include sprinting, middle- and long-distance running, relay running, hurdling, and walking—and field events that require jumping and throwing skills. Contests designed to test the speed, strength, agility, and stamina of athletes were held by the ancient Greeks over 4,000 years ago. However, the abolition of the Olympic Games in 393 AD meant that track and field events were neglected until the revival of large-scale competitions in the mid-nineteenth century. Modern stadia offer areas reserved for the long jump, triple jump, and pole vault usually situated outside the running track. The javelin, shot, hammer, and discus are thrown within the track area. Most athletes specialize in one or two events but, in the heptathlon, women compete in seven events, held over two days: 200 m and 800 m races, 100 m hurdles, shot put, high jump, and long jump. In the decathlon, men compete in 10 events over two days: 100 m, 400 m, and 1,500 m races, 110 m hurdles, javelin, discus, shot put, pole vault, high jump, and long jump.

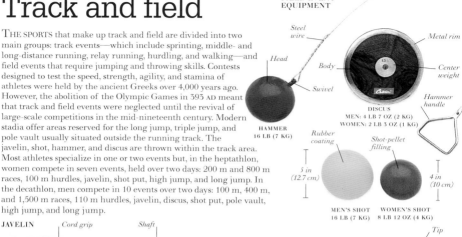

FIELD EVENT EQUIPMENT

Steel wire

Head

Body

Swivel

HAMMER
16 LB (7 KG)

Metal rim

Center weight

Hammer handle

DISCUS
MEN: 4 LB 7 OZ (2 KG)
WOMEN: 2 LB 3 OZ (1 KG)

Rubber coating

Shot-pellet filling

5 in (12.7 cm)

4 in (10 cm)

MEN'S SHOT
16 LB (7 KG)

WOMEN'S SHOT
8 LB 12 OZ (4 KG)

JAVELIN   *Cord grip*   *Shaft*   *Tip*

Men: 8 ft 6 in (2.6 m)
Women: 7 ft 6 in (2.3 m)

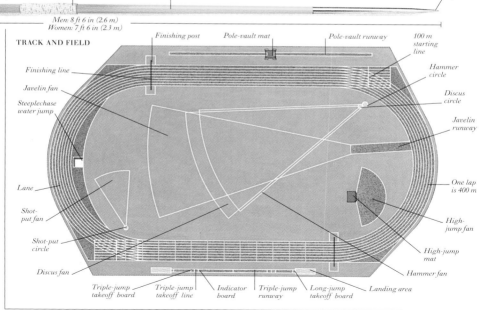

TRACK AND FIELD

Finishing post   *Pole-vault mat*   *Pole-vault runway*   *100 m starting line*

Finishing line

Javelin fan

Steeplechase water jump

Lane

Shot-put fan

Shot-put circle

Discus fan

Triple-jump takeoff board   *Triple-jump takeoff line*   *Indicator board*   *Triple-jump runway*   *Long-jump takeoff board*   *Landing area*

Hammer circle

Discus circle

Javelin runway

One lap is 400 m

High-jump fan

High-jump mat

Hammer fan

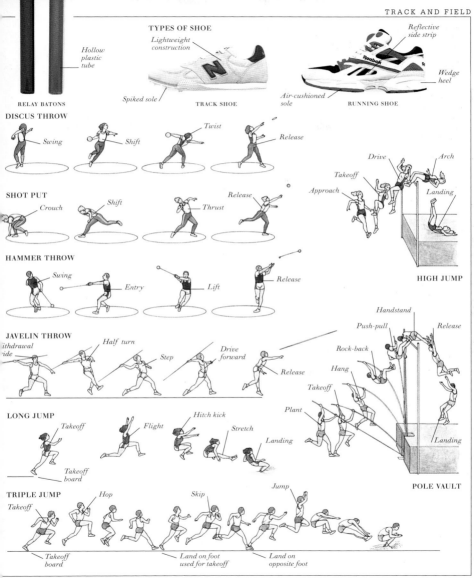

TYPES OF SHOE

Lightweight construction

Spiked sole

TRACK SHOE

Reflective side strip

Reebok

Wedge heel

Air-cushioned sole

RUNNING SHOE

Hollow plastic tube

RELAY BATONS

DISCUS THROW

Swing

Shift

Twist

Release

SHOT PUT

Crouch

Shift

Thrust

Release

HAMMER THROW

Swing

Entry

Lift

Release

JAVELIN THROW

Withdrawal ide

Half turn

Step

Drive forward

Release

LONG JUMP

Takeoff

Flight

Hitch kick

Stretch

Landing

Takeoff board

TRIPLE JUMP

Takeoff

Hop

Skip

Jump

Takeoff board

Land on foot used for takeoff

Land on opposite foot

HIGH JUMP

Approach

Takeoff

Drive

Arch

Landing

POLE VAULT

Handstand

Push-pull

Release

Rock-back

Hang

Takeoff

Plant

Landing

543

Racket sports

PROTECTIVE EYEWEAR

THE OBJECT OF ALL RACKET SPORTS is to make shots the opponent cannot return. Games are played by two players (singles) or four players (doubles). Racket shape and size is tailored to each sport, but all rackets are constructed of wood, plastic, aluminum, or high-performance materials such as fiberglass and carbon graphite. Racket strings are usually synthetic, although natural gut is still used. Tennis is played on a court divided by a low net. Opposing players serve alternate games. At least six games must be won to gain a set, and two or sometimes three sets are needed to win a match. Tennis courts may be concrete, grass, clay, or synthetic, each surface requiring a different style of play. Badminton is an indoor sport that is played with light, flexible rackets and a birdie on a court with a high net. Players can score points only on their serve. The first to reach 15 points (11 points for women's singles) wins the game. Two games are needed to win a match. Squash and racketball are both played in enclosed courts. One player hits the ball against the front wall, and the other tries to return it before it bounces on the floor more than once. Squash rackets have smaller, rounder heads and stiffer frames than badminton rackets. In the United States, the game is played on a narrower court than an international court using a much harder ball. Squash games are played to 15 points (American) or 9 points (international). In racketball, players use a ball that is larger and bouncier than a squash ball. The racket is thick and sturdy, with a large head, short handle, and a thong that loops around the wrist. Points can be won only when serving, and the first player to reach 21 points wins.

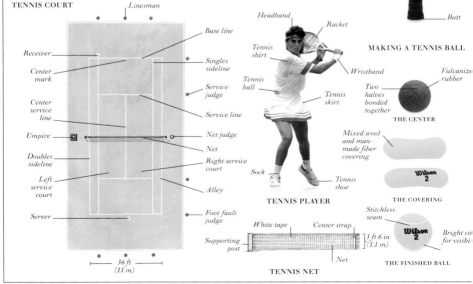

TENNIS RACKET

Synthetic string · Frame · Head · Logo · Throat · Grip · Butt

TENNIS COURT

Linesman · Receiver · Center mark · Center service line · Umpire · Doubles sideline · Left service court · Server · Base line · Singles sideline · Service judge · Service line · Net judge · Net · Right service court · Alley · Foot-fault judge

36 ft (11 m)

TENNIS PLAYER

Headband · Racket · Tennis shirt · Wristband · Tennis ball · Tennis skirt · Sock · Tennis shoe

TENNIS NET

White tape · Center strap · Supporting post · Net · 3 ft 6 in (1.1 m)

MAKING A TENNIS BALL

Vulcanized rubber · Two halves bonded together

THE CENTER

Mixed wool and man-made fiber covering

THE COVERING

Stitchless seam · Bright color for visibility

THE FINISHED BALL

Wilson 2

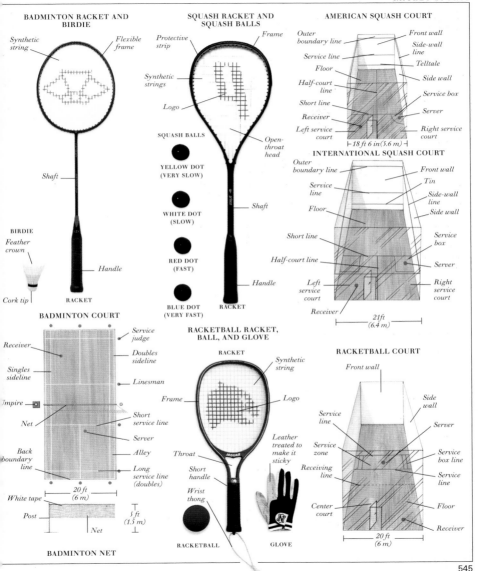

BADMINTON RACKET AND BIRDIE

Synthetic string
Flexible frame
Shaft

BIRDIE
Feather crown
Cork tip
Handle
RACKET

SQUASH RACKET AND SQUASH BALLS

Protective strip
Frame
Synthetic strings
Logo
Shaft
Open-throat head
Handle
RACKET

SQUASH BALLS

YELLOW DOT (VERY SLOW)

WHITE DOT (SLOW)

RED DOT (FAST)

BLUE DOT (VERY FAST)

AMERICAN SQUASH COURT

Outer boundary line
Front wall
Side-wall line
Service line
Telltale
Floor
Side wall
Half-court line
Service box
Short line
Server
Receiver
Left service court
Right service court
├ 18 ft 6 in (5.6 m) ┤

INTERNATIONAL SQUASH COURT

Outer boundary line
Front wall
Service line
Tin
Side-wall line
Floor
Side wall
Short line
Service box
Half-court line
Server
Left service court
Right service court
Receiver
21 ft (6.4 m)

BADMINTON COURT

Service judge
Receiver
Doubles sideline
Singles sideline
Linesman
Umpire
Short service line
Net
Server
Back boundary line
Alley
Long service line (doubles)
20 ft (6 m)

White tape
5 ft (1.5 m)
Post
Net
BADMINTON NET

RACKETBALL RACKET, BALL, AND GLOVE

RACKET
Synthetic string
Frame
Logo
Throat
Leather treated to make it sticky
Short handle
JAGUAR
Wrist thong
RACKETBALL
GLOVE

RACKETBALL COURT

Front wall
Side wall
Service line
Server
Service zone
Service box line
Receiving line
Service line
Center court
Floor
Receiver
20 ft (6 m)

Golf

GOLF BALL AND TEE

THE GAME OF GOLF was first played in Scotland some 400 years ago. Players are required to hit a ball, using a wooden or iron club, from a smooth level point or "teeing ground," down the "fairway," and on to a putting green where the target hole is located. The fairway is a strip of clear land along which there are natural hazards—such as ponds and streams, man-made hazards—such as bunkers (sand pits), and rough (areas of uncut grass). Championship golf courses have 18 holes. The object of the game is to hit the ball into each hole in turn, and to complete the "round" using as few strokes as possible. Players compete individually or in teams, playing the course together in groups of two, three, or four. The two basic forms of competition are match play and stroke play. In match play, the side winning the majority of holes over a certain number of rounds wins the match. In stroke play, the winner is the player who finishes a certain number of rounds having made the fewest strokes.

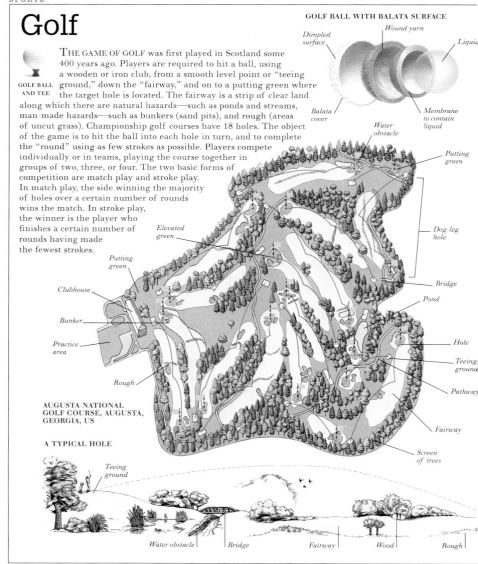

GOLF BALL WITH BALATA SURFACE

Dimpled surface

Wound yarn

Liquid

Balata cover

Membrane to contain liquid

Water obstacle

Putting green

Elevated green

Dog-leg hole

Putting green

Bridge

Clubhouse

Pond

Bunker

Hole

Practice area

Teeing ground

Rough

Pathway

AUGUSTA NATIONAL GOLF COURSE, AUGUSTA, GEORGIA, US

Fairway

Screen of trees

A TYPICAL HOLE

Teeing ground

Water obstacle   *Bridge*   *Fairway*   *Wood*   *Rough*

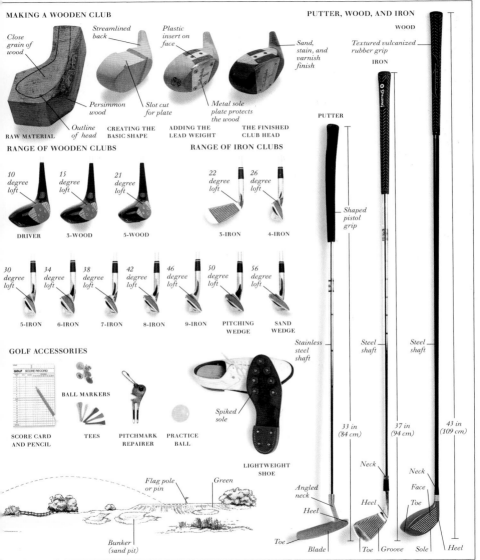

MAKING A WOODEN CLUB

Close grain of wood

Persimmon wood

Outline of head

RAW MATERIAL

Streamlined back

Slot cut for plate

CREATING THE BASIC SHAPE

Plastic insert on face

Metal sole plate protects the wood

ADDING THE LEAD WEIGHT

Sand, stain, and varnish finish

THE FINISHED CLUB HEAD

RANGE OF WOODEN CLUBS

10 degree loft

DRIVER

15 degree loft

3-WOOD

21 degree loft

5-WOOD

30 degree loft

5-IRON

34 degree loft

6-IRON

38 degree loft

7-IRON

42 degree loft

8-IRON

46 degree loft

9-IRON

50 degree loft

PITCHING WEDGE

56 degree loft

SAND WEDGE

RANGE OF IRON CLUBS

22 degree loft

3-IRON

26 degree loft

4-IRON

GOLF ACCESSORIES

BALL MARKERS

SCORE CARD AND PENCIL

TEES

PITCHMARK REPAIRER

PRACTICE BALL

Spiked sole

LIGHTWEIGHT SHOE

Flag pole or pin

Green

Bunker (sand pit)

PUTTER, WOOD, AND IRON

WOOD

Textured vulcanized rubber grip

IRON

PUTTER

Shaped pistol grip

Stainless steel shaft

Steel shaft

Steel shaft

33 in (84 cm)

37 in (94 cm)

43 in (109 cm)

Angled neck

Heel

Toe

Blade

Neck

Heel

Toe

Groove

Neck

Face

Toe

Sole

Heel

Archery and shooting

TARGET SHOOTING AND ARCHERY EVOLVED as practice for hunting and battle skills. Modern bows, although designed according to the principles of early hunting bows, use laminates, fiberglass, dacron, and carbon, and are equipped with sights and stabilizers. Competitors in target archery shoot over distances of 100 ft (30 m), 165 ft (50 m), 230 ft (70 m), and 300 ft (90 m) for men, and 100 ft (30 m), 165 ft (50 m), 200 ft (60 m), and 230 ft (70 m) for women. The closer the shot is to the center of the target, the higher the score. The individual scores are added up, and the archer with the highest total wins the competition. Crossbows are used in match competitions over 33 ft (10 m), and 100 ft (30 m). Rifle shooting is divided into three categories: smallbore, bigbore, and air rifle. Contests take place over a variety of distances and further subdivisions are based on the type of shooting position used: prone, kneeling, or standing. The Olympic biathlon combines cross-country skiing and rifle shooting over a course of approximately 12½ miles (20 km). Additional magazines of ammunition are carried in the butt of the rifles. Bigbore rifles fitted with a telescopic sight can be used for hunting and running game target shooting. Pistol shooting events, using rapid-fire pistols, target pistols, and air pistols, take place over 33 ft (10 m), 82 ft (25 m), and 165 ft (50 m) distances. In rapid-fire pistol shooting, a total of 60 shots are fired from a distance of 83 ft (25 m).

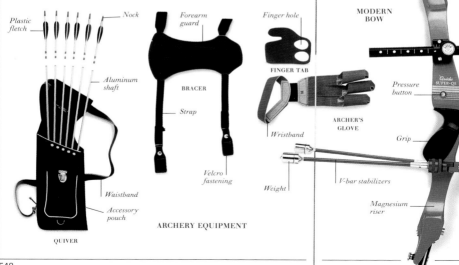

CROSSBOW AND BOLT

Laminated fiberglass bow

Bolt

Bolt rest

1¼ in (45 mm)

CROSSBOW TARGET

Sight

Stirrup held between feet when drawing bow

Hardwood laminate limb

Dacron string

Sight

MODERN BOW

Plastic fletch

Nock

Forearm guard

Finger hole

Aluminum shaft

FINGER TAB

BRACER

Strap

Pressure button

ARCHER'S GLOVE

Wristband

Grip

Velcro fastening

V-bar stabilizers

Weight

Waistband

Accessory pouch

Magnesium riser

ARCHERY EQUIPMENT

QUIVER

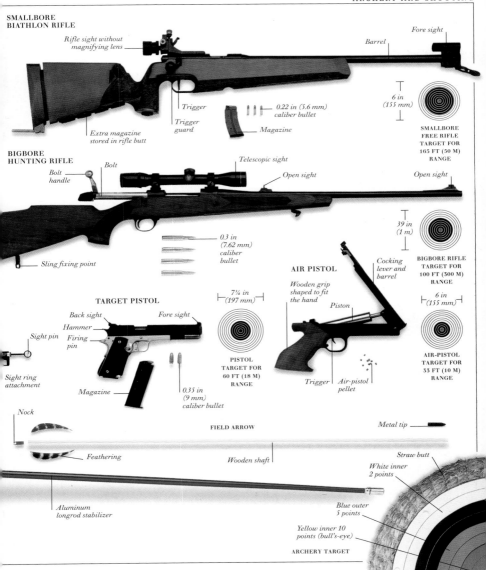

SMALLBORE BIATHLON RIFLE

Rifle sight without magnifying lens

Fore sight

Barrel

Trigger

Trigger guard

0.22 in (5.6 mm) caliber bullet

Magazine

Extra magazine stored in rifle butt

6 in (155 mm)

SMALLBORE FREE RIFLE TARGET FOR 165 FT (50 M) RANGE

BIGBORE HUNTING RIFLE

Bolt handle

Bolt

Telescopic sight

Open sight

Open sight

0.3 in (7.62 mm) caliber bullet

Sling fixing point

39 in (1 m)

BIGBORE RIFLE TARGET FOR 100 FT (300 M) RANGE

AIR PISTOL

Cocking lever and barrel

Wooden grip shaped to fit the hand

Piston

6 in (155 mm)

AIR-PISTOL TARGET FOR 33 FT (10 M) RANGE

TARGET PISTOL

Back sight

Fore sight

Hammer

Firing pin

Sight pin

Sight ring attachment

Magazine

0.35 in (9 mm) caliber bullet

7¼ in (197 mm)

PISTOL TARGET FOR 60 FT (18 M) RANGE

Trigger

Air-pistol pellet

Nock

FIELD ARROW

Metal tip

Feathering

Wooden shaft

Straw butt

White inner 2 points

Aluminum longrod stabilizer

Blue outer 3 points

Yellow inner 10 points (bull's-eye)

ARCHERY TARGET

Ice hockey

ICE HOCKEY IS PLAYED by two teams of six players on an ice rink, with a goal net at each end. The object of this fast, and often dangerous, game is to hit a frozen rubber puck into the opposing team's net with a ice hockey stick. The game begins when the referee drops the puck between the sticks of two players from opposing teams, who "face off." The rink is divided into three areas: defending, neutral, and attacking zones. Players may move with the puck and pass the puck to one another along the ice, but may not pass it more than two zones across the rink markings. A goal is scored when the puck entirely crosses the goal-line between the posts and under the crossbar of the goal. A team may field up to 20 players although only six players are allowed on the ice at one time; substitutions occur frequently. Each game consists of three periods of 20 minutes, divided by breaks of 15 minutes.

GOALKEEPER

ICE HOCKEY RINK

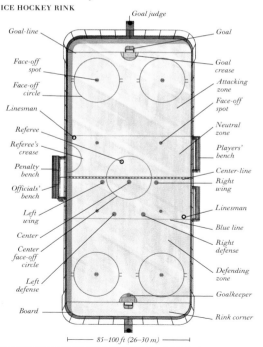

THE FACE OFF

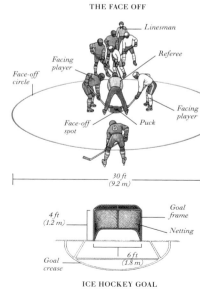

ICE HOCKEY GOAL

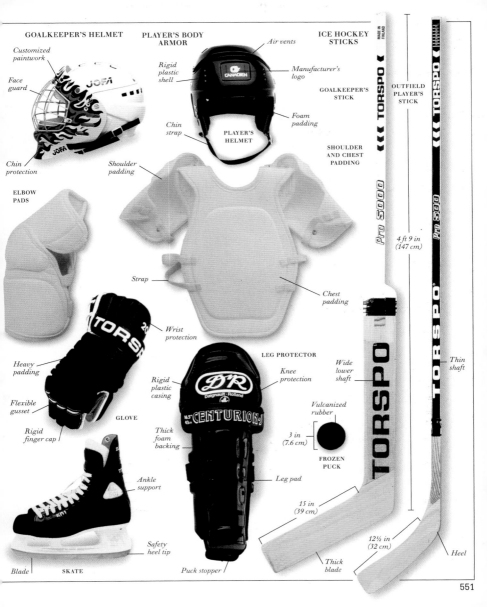

GOALKEEPER'S HELMET

Customized paintwork

Face guard

Chin protection

PLAYER'S BODY ARMOR

Air vents

Rigid plastic shell

Manufacturer's logo

Chin strap

Foam padding

PLAYER'S HELMET

ICE HOCKEY STICKS

GOALKEEPER'S STICK

OUTFIELD PLAYER'S STICK

4 ft 9 in (147 cm)

SHOULDER AND CHEST PADDING

Shoulder padding

ELBOW PADS

Strap

Chest padding

Wrist protection

Heavy padding

Flexible gusset

Rigid finger cap

GLOVE

LEG PROTECTOR

Rigid plastic casing

Knee protection

Thick foam backing

Wide lower shaft

Vulcanized rubber

3 in (7.6 cm)

FROZEN PUCK

Thin shaft

Ankle support

Leg pad

Safety heel tip

15 in (39 cm)

12½ in (32 cm)

Heel

Blade

SKATE

Puck stopper

Thick blade

551

Alpine skiing

COMPETITIVE ALPINE SKIING is divided into four disciplines: downhill, slalom, giant slalom, and super-giant slalom (Super-G). Each one tests different skills. In downhill skiing, competitors race down a slope marked out by control flags, known as "gates," and are timed on a single run only. Competitors wear crash helmets, one-piece Lycra suits, and long skis with flattened tips to minimize air resistance. Slalom and giant slalom skiiers negotiate a twisting course requiring balance, agility, and quick reactions. Courses are defined by pairs of gates. Racers must pass through each pair of gates to complete the course successfully. Competitors are timed on two runs over different courses, and the skier who completes the courses in the shortest time wins. The equipment and protective guards used by slalom skiiers are shown opposite. In Super-G races, competitors ski a single run that combines the technical challenge of slalom with the speed of downhill. The course requires skiers to complete medium-to-long radius turns at high speed, and contain up to two jumps. Clothing is the same as for downhill, but slightly shorter skis are used.

DOWNHILL SKIER

Ski goggles

Helmet

One-piece lycra ski suit

Wrist strap

Ski pole

Basket

Ski boot

Safety binding

Tail

Ski glove

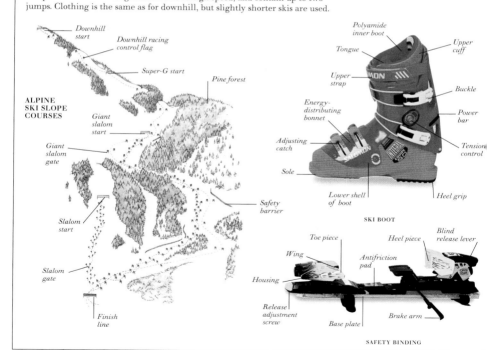

ALPINE SKI SLOPE COURSES

Downhill start

Downhill racing control flag

Super-G start

Pine forest

Giant slalom start

Giant slalom gate

Slalom start

Slalom gate

Finish line

Safety barrier

SKI BOOT

Polyamide inner boot

Tongue

Upper cuff

Upper strap

Buckle

Energy-distributing bonnet

Power bar

Adjusting catch

Tension control

Sole

Lower shell of boot

Heel grip

SAFETY BINDING

Toe piece

Wing

Heel piece

Blind release lever

Antifriction pad

Housing

Release adjustment screw

Base plate

Brake arm

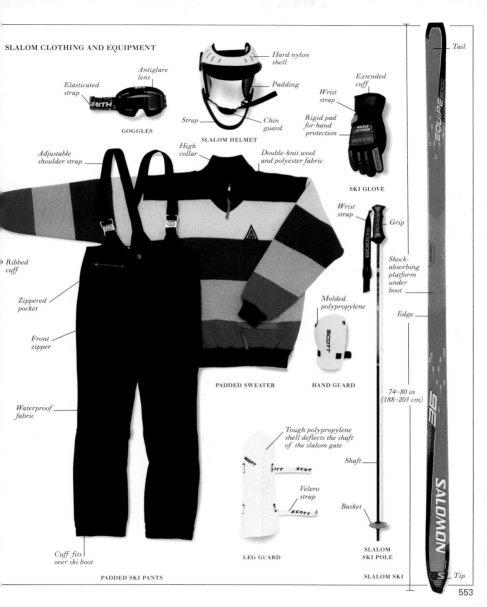

SLALOM CLOTHING AND EQUIPMENT

Elasticated strap

Antiglare lens

GOGGLES

Hard nylon shell

Padding

Strap

Chin guard

SLALOM HELMET

Extended cuff

Wrist strap

Rigid pad for hand protection

SKI GLOVE

Adjustable shoulder strap

High collar

Double-knit wool and polyester fabric

Ribbed cuff

Zippered pocket

Front zipper

Waterproof fabric

Cuff fits over ski boot

PADDED SKI PANTS

PADDED SWEATER

Molded polypropylene

HAND GUARD

Wrist strap

Grip

Shock-absorbing platform under boot

Edge

74–80 in (188–203 cm)

Tough polypropylene shell deflects the shaft of the slalom gate

Velcro strap

LEG GUARD

Shaft

Basket

SLALOM SKI POLE

Tail

Tip

SLALOM SKI

553

Equestrian sports

EQUESTRIAN SPORTS HAVE TAKEN place throughout the world for centuries: events involving mounted horses were recorded in the Olympic Games of 642 BC. Showjumping, however, is a much more recent innovation, and the first competitions were held at the beginning of the 1900s. In this sport, horse and rider must negotiate a course of variable, unfixed obstacles, making as few mistakes as possible. Showjumping fences consist of wooden stands, known as standards or wings, that support planks or poles. Parts of the fence are designed to collapse on impact, preventing injury to the horse and rider. Judges penalize competitors for errors, such as knocking down obstacles, refusing jumps, or deviating from the course. Depending on the type of competition, the rider with the fewest faults, most points, or fastest time wins. There are two basic forms of horse racing—flat races and races with jumps, such as steeplechase or hurdle races. Thoroughbred horses are used in this sport, since they have great strength and stamina and can achieve speeds of up to 40 mph (65 kph). Jockeys wear "silks"— caps and jackets designed in distinctive colors and patterns that help identify the horses. In harness racing, the horse is driven from a light, two-wheeled carriage called a sulky. Horses are trained to trot and to pace, and different races are held for each of these types of gait. In pacing races, the horses wear hobbles to prevent them from breaking into a trot or gallop. Breeds such as the Standardbred and the French Trotter have been developed especially for this sport.

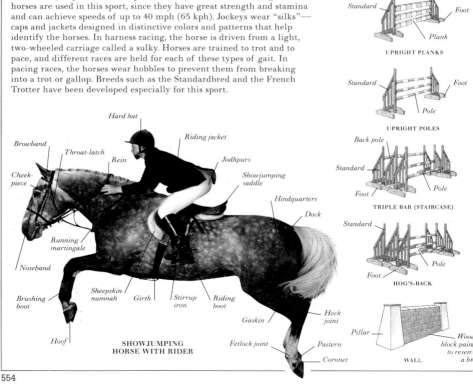

SHOWJUMPING SADDLE

High cantle
Deep seat
Pommel
Forward-cut flap
Knee roll

SHOWJUMPING FENCES

Standard — Foot
Plank

UPRIGHT PLANKS

Standard — Foot
Pole

UPRIGHT POLES

Back pole
Standard
Foot — Pole

TRIPLE BAR (STAIRCASE)

Standard
Foot — Pole

HOG'S-BACK

Pillar
Wood block pair to reser a br

WALL

SHOWJUMPING HORSE WITH RIDER

Hard hat
Riding jacket
Browband
Throat-latch
Rein
Jodhpurs
Cheek-piece
Showjumping saddle
Hindquarters
Dock
Running martingale
Noseband
Brushing boot
Sheepskin numnah
Girth
Stirrup iron
Riding boot
Hoof
Gaskin
Hock joint
Fetlock joint
Pastern
Coronet

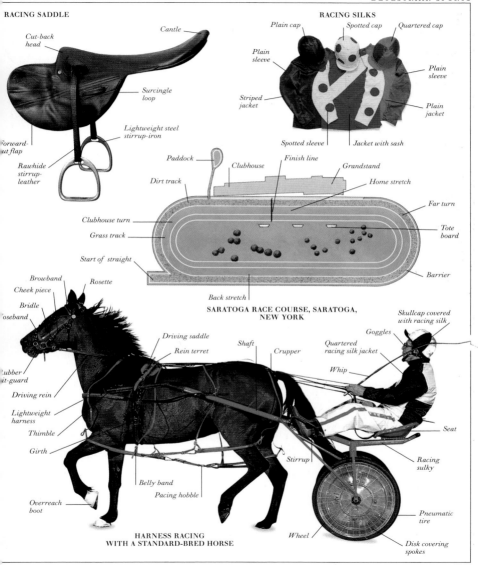

RACING SADDLE

Cut-back head

Cantle

Surcingle loop

Lightweight steel stirrup-iron

Forward-cut flap

Rawhide stirrup-leather

RACING SILKS

Plain cap

Spotted cap

Quartered cap

Plain sleeve

Plain sleeve

Striped jacket

Plain jacket

Spotted sleeve

Jacket with sash

Paddock

Clubhouse

Finish line

Grandstand

Dirt track

Home stretch

Far turn

Clubhouse turn

Grass track

Tote board

Start of straight

Barrier

Back stretch

SARATOGA RACE COURSE, SARATOGA, NEW YORK

Browband

Rosette

Cheek piece

Bridle

Noseband

Rubber bit-guard

Driving rein

Lightweight harness

Thimble

Girth

Overreach boot

Driving saddle

Rein terret

Shaft

Crupper

Skullcap covered with racing silk

Goggles

Quartered racing silk jacket

Whip

Seat

Racing sulky

Belly band

Pacing hobble

Stirrup

Wheel

Pneumatic tire

Disk covering spokes

HARNESS RACING WITH A STANDARD-BRED HORSE

Judo and fencing

COMBAT SPORTS ARE BASED ON THE SKILLS used in fighting. In these sports, the competitors may be unarmed—as in judo and boxing—or armed—as in fencing and kendo. Judo is a system of unarmed combat developed in the East. Translated from the Japanese, the name means "the gentle way." Students learn how to turn an opponent's force to their own advantage. The usual costume is loose white pants and a jacket, fastened with a cloth belt. The color of belt indicates the student's level of expertise, from white-belted novices to the expert "black belts." Competitions take place on a mat or "shiaijo," 30 or 33 ft (9 or 10 m) square in size, bounded by "danger" and "safety" areas to prevent injury. Competitors try to throw, pin, or master their opponent by applying pressure to the arm joints or neck. Judo bouts are strictly monitored, and competitors receive points for superior technique, not for injuring their opponent. Fencing is a combat sport using swords, which takes place on a narrow "piste" 46 ft (14 m) long. Competitors try to touch specific target areas on their opponent with their sword or "foil" while avoiding being touched themselves. The winner is the one who scores the greatest number of hits. Fencers wear clothing made from strong white material that affords maximum protection while allowing freedom of movement, steel mesh masks with padded bibs to protect the fencer's neck, and a long white glove on their sword hand. Fencing foils do not have sharpened blades, and their tips end in a blunt button to prevent injuries. Three types of swords are used—foils, épées, and sabers. Official foil and épée competitions always use an electric scoring system. The sword tips are connected to lights by a long wire that passes underneath each fencer's jacket. A bulb flashes when a hit is made.

JUDO HOLDS AND THROWS

SIDE FOUR QUARTER HOLD

SINGLE WING

BODY DROP

ONE ARM SHOULDER THROW

SHOULDER WHEEL

SWEEPING LOW THROW

STOMACH THROW

KNEE WHEEL

JUDO MAT

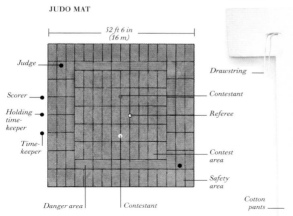

52 ft 6 in (16 m)

Judge

Scorer

Holding timekeeper

Timekeeper

Danger area

Contestant

Danger area

Contestant

UNIFORM

Drawstring

Contestant

Referee

Contest area

Safety area

Cotton pants

Black belt

Heavy-duty cotton jacket

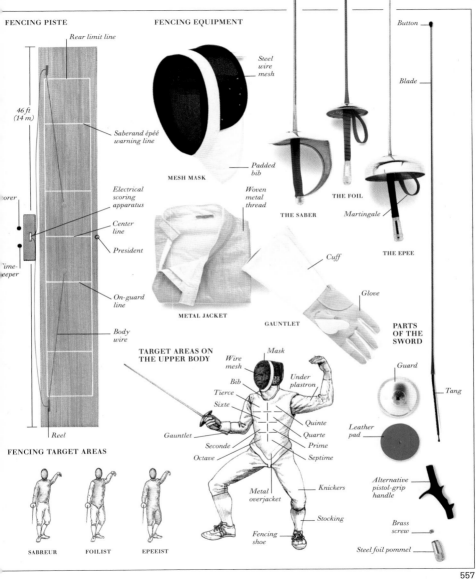

FENCING PISTE

Rear limit line

46 ft
(14 m)

Saberand épéé
warning line

Electrical
scoring
apparatus

Center
line

President

On-guard
line

Body
wire

Reel

Scorer

Timekeeper

FENCING EQUIPMENT

Steel
wire
mesh

Padded
bib

MESH MASK

Woven
metal
thread

METAL JACKET

Cuff

Glove

GAUNTLET

THE FOIL

THE SABER

Martingale

THE EPEE

Button

Blade

**PARTS
OF THE
SWORD**

Guard

Leather
pad

Tang

Alternative
pistol-grip
handle

Brass
screw

Steel foil pommel

**TARGET AREAS ON
THE UPPER BODY**

Mask

Wire
mesh

Bib

Tierce

Sixte

Gauntlet

Seconde

Octave

Metal
overjacket

Under
plastron

Quinte

Quarte

Prime

Septime

Knickers

Stocking

Fencing
shoe

FENCING TARGET AREAS

SABREUR

FOILIST

EPEEIST

Swimming and diving

SWIMMING GOGGLES

SWIMMING WAS INCLUDED in the first
modern Olympic Games in 1896 and diving
events were added in 1904. Swimming is both
an individual and a team sport and races take
place over a predetermined distance in one of the four major
categories of stroke—freestyle (usually front crawl), butterfly,
breaststroke, and backstroke. Competition pools are clearly
marked for racing and antiturbulence lane lines are used to
separate the swimmers and help keep the water calm. The
first team or individual to finish the race is the winner.
Competitive diving is divided into men's and women's
springboard and platform (highboard) events. There are
six official groups of dives: forward dives, backward dives,
armstand dives, twist dives, reverse dives, and inward dives.
Competitors perform a set number of dives and after each
one a panel of judges award marks according to the quality
of execution and the degree of difficulty.

STYLES OF DIVE

Starting position

Hands above head

Legs fully stretched

Flight

Arched back

Toes pointed

Entry

Feet together

Hands close together

FORWARD DIVE

BACKWARD DIVE

SWIMMING POOL

Swimmer
Chief timekeeper
Lane number
Starting block
Lane timekeeper
Placing judge
End wall
Starter
Recorder
Backstroke marker 49 ft (15 m) from end of pool
Side wall
Referee
Anti-turbulence lane line
Backstroke turn indicator 16 ft (5 m) from end of pool
Stroke judge
Bottom line
Turning judge
Turning wall
Lane

75 ft 6 in (23 m)

SWIMWEAR

Latex rubber molds to shape of head

CAPS

Rubber-covered wire

NOSE CLIP

Molded rubber

EARPLUG

High neckline

Man-made stretch fabric

Drawstring

High-cut leg

Strong seam

SWIMSUIT

TRUNKS

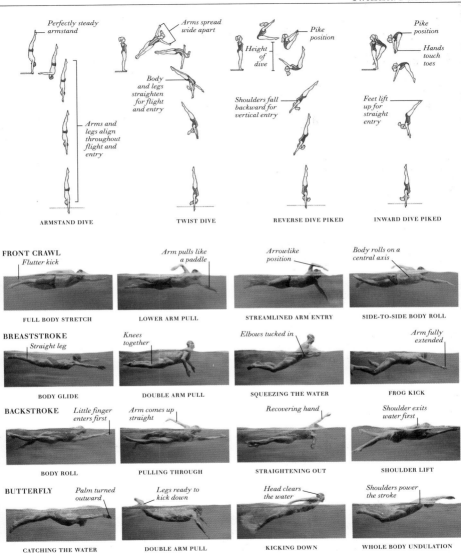

Perfectly steady armstand

Arms and legs align throughout flight and entry

ARMSTAND DIVE

Arms spread wide apart

Body and legs straighten for flight and entry

TWIST DIVE

Pike position

Height of dive

Shoulders fall backward for vertical entry

REVERSE DIVE PIKED

Pike position

Hands touch toes

Feet lift up for straight entry

INWARD DIVE PIKED

FRONT CRAWL
Flutter kick

FULL BODY STRETCH

Arm pulls like a paddle

LOWER ARM PULL

Arrowlike position

STREAMLINED ARM ENTRY

Body rolls on a central axis

SIDE-TO-SIDE BODY ROLL

BREASTSTROKE
Straight leg

BODY GLIDE

Knees together

DOUBLE ARM PULL

Elbows tucked in

SQUEEZING THE WATER

Arm fully extended

FROG KICK

BACKSTROKE
Little finger enters first

BODY ROLL

Arm comes up straight

PULLING THROUGH

Recovering hand

STRAIGHTENING OUT

Shoulder exits water first

SHOULDER LIFT

BUTTERFLY
Palm turned outward

CATCHING THE WATER

Legs ready to kick down

DOUBLE ARM PULL

Head clears the water

KICKING DOWN

Shoulders power the stroke

WHOLE BODY UNDULATION

Canoeing, rowing, and sailing

WATERBORNE SPORTS are as varied as the crafts used. There are two disciplines in rowing; sweep rowing, in which each rower has one oar, and sculling, in which rowers use two oars. There are a number of different Olympic and competitive rowing events for both men and women. The number of rowers and weight classes vary. Some rowing events use a coxswain; a steersman who does not row but directs the crew. Kayaks and canoes are used in straight sprint and slalom races. Slalom races take place over a course consisting of 20 to 25 gates, including at least six upstream gates. In yacht racing, competitors must complete prescribed courses, organized by the race committees, in the shortest possible time, using sail power only. Olympic events include classes for keel boats, dinghies, and catamarans.

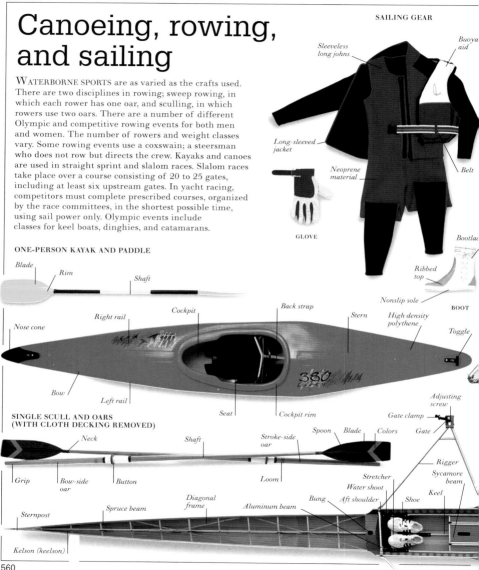

SAILING GEAR

Sleeveless long johns

Buoya aid

Long-sleeved jacket

Neoprene material

Belt

GLOVE

Bootla

Ribbed top

Nonslip sole

BOOT

ONE-PERSON KAYAK AND PADDLE

Blade

Rim

Shaft

Nose cone

Right rail

Cockpit

Back strap

Stern

High density polythene

Toggle

Bow

Left rail

Seat

Cockpit rim

**SINGLE SCULL AND OARS
(WITH CLOTH DECKING REMOVED)**

Neck

Shaft

Stroke-side oar

Spoon

Blade

Colors

Gate

Adjusting screw

Gate clamp

Grip

Bow-side oar

Button

Loom

Stretcher

Water shoot

Aft shoulder

Shoe

Rigger

Sycamore beam

Keel

Sternpost

Spruce beam

Diagonal frame

Aluminum beam

Bung

Kelson (keelson)

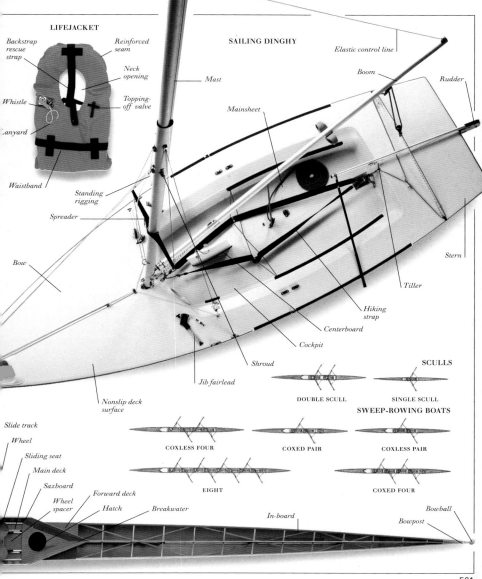

LIFEJACKET

Backstrap rescue strap

Reinforced seam

Neck opening

Whistle

Topping-off valve

Lanyard

Waistband

SAILING DINGHY

Elastic control line

Boom

Mast

Rudder

Mainsheet

Standing rigging

Spreader

Stern

Bow

Tiller

Hiking strap

Centerboard

Cockpit

Shroud

Jib fairlead

Nonslip deck surface

SCULLS

DOUBLE SCULL

SINGLE SCULL

SWEEP-ROWING BOATS

Slide track

Wheel

Sliding seat

Main deck

COXLESS FOUR

COXED PAIR

COXLESS PAIR

Saxboard

Forward deck

Wheel spacer

Hatch

Breakwater

EIGHT

COXED FOUR

In-board

Bowball

Bowpost

Angling

ANGLING MEANS FISHING WITH A ROD, reel, line, and lure.
There are several different types of angling: freshwater
coarse angling, for members of the carp family and pike;
freshwater game angling, for salmon and trout; and sea
angling, for sea fish such as flatfish, bass, and mackerel.
Anglers use a variety of methods for catching fish. These
include bait fishing, in which bait (food to allure the fish)
is placed on a hook and cast into the water; fly fishing, in
which a natural or artificial fly is used to lure the fish;
and spinning, in which a lure that looks like a small fish
revolves as it is pulled through the water. The angler uses
the rod, reel, and line to cast the lure over the water. The
reel controls the line as it spills off the spool and as it is
wound back. Weights may be fixed to
the line so that it will sink. Swivels
are attached to prevent the line
from twisting. When a fish bites,
the hook must become embedded
in its mouth and remain there
while the catch is reeled in.

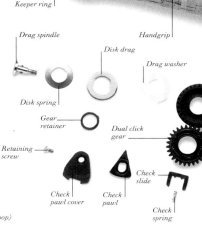

BUTT SECTION

Keeper ring

Handgrip

Drag spindle

Disk drag

Drag washer

Disk spring

Gear retainer

Dual click gear

Retaining screw

Check pawl cover

Check pawl

Check slide

Check spring

REELS

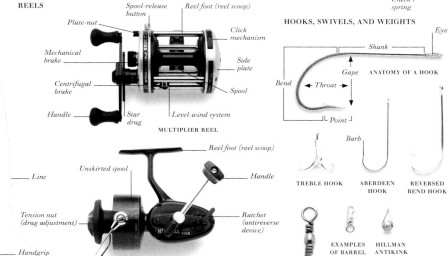

Plate-nut

Spool-release button

Reel foot (reel scoop)

Click mechanism

Mechanical brake

Side plate

Centrifugal brake

Spool

Handle

Star drag

Level-wind system

MULTIPLIER REEL

Line

Handgrip

Reel

Unskirted spool

Reel foot (reel scoop)

Handle

Tension nut (drag adjustment)

Ratchet (antireverse device)

Bail arm

FIXED-SPOOL REEL

HOOKS, SWIVELS, AND WEIGHTS

Eye

Shank

Gape   ANATOMY OF A HOOK

Bend   Throat

Point

TREBLE HOOK

Barb

ABERDEEN HOOK

REVERSED BEND HOOK

EXAMPLES OF BARREL SWIVELS

HILLMAN ANTIKINK WEIGHT

FLY ROD AND REEL

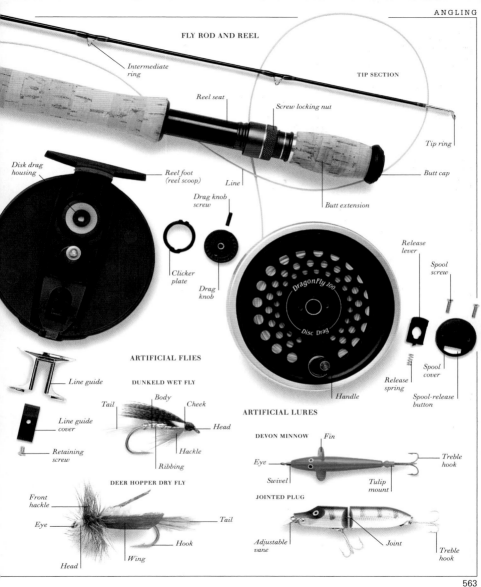

Intermediate ring

TIP SECTION

Reel seat

Screw locking nut

Tip ring

Disk drag housing

Reel foot (reel scoop)

Line

Butt cap

Drag knob screw

Butt extension

Clicker plate

Drag knob

Release lever

Spool screw

DragonFly 100

Disc Drag

Spool cover

Release spring

Handle

Spool-release button

ARTIFICIAL FLIES

Line guide

DUNKELD WET FLY

Tail

Body

Cheek

Line guide cover

Head

Hackle

Retaining screw

Ribbing

ARTIFICIAL LURES

DEVON MINNOW

Fin

Eye

Treble hook

Swivel

Tulip mount

DEER HOPPER DRY FLY

JOINTED PLUG

Front hackle

Eye

Tail

Adjustable vane

Joint

Hook

Treble hook

Head

Wing

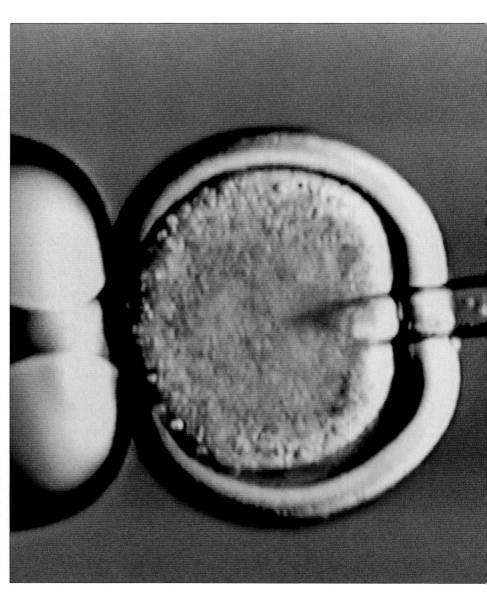

THE MODERN WORLD

PERSONAL COMPUTER ··566
HANDHELD COMPUTER ··568
FLATBED SCANNER ···570
AIRBUS 380 ··572
INKJET PRINTER ···574
THE INTERNET ··576
ELECTRONIC GAMES ··578
DIGITAL CAMERA ···580
DIGITAL VIDEO CAMERA ······································582
HOME CINEMA ··584
PERSONAL MUSIC ··586
CELLPHONES ··588
WEARABLE TECHNOLOGY ····································590
VACUUM CLEANER ··592
IRON AND WASHER-DRYER ···································594
MICROWAVE COMBINATION OVEN ·····················596
TOASTER ···598
DRILL ··600
HOUSE OF THE FUTURE ··602
RENEWABLE ENERGY ···604
CLONING TECHNOLOGY ·······································606
ROBOTS ···608
HIGH-PERFORMANCE MICROSCOPES ····················610
SPACE TELESCOPE ···612
PROBING THE SOLAR SYSTEM 614

Personal computer

PERSONAL COMPUTERS (PCs) fall into two main types: IBM-compatible PCs, known simply as PCs, and Apple Macintosh PCs, known as "Macs." They differ in the way files and programs, and the user's access to them, are organized, and programs must be tailored for each type. However, in most other respects PCs and Macs have much in common. Both contain microchips, or integrated circuits, that store and process data. The "brain" of any PC is a chip known as the central processing unit (CPU), which performs mathematical operations in order to run program instructions and receive, store, and output data. The most powerful personal computer CPUs today can perform more than a billion calculations a second. Data can be input via CDs, USB memory sticks, and other storage media. Highly portable laptop and network PCs are also in widespread use. Most PCs are able to communicate with many other devices, including digital cameras (see pp. 580-81) and smartphones (see pp. 588-89).

LED-backlit glossy wide-screen

Keyboard

Mouse

iMAC

USB ports (4)

Audio in jack

Headphone jack

Firewire 800 port

Ethernet port

Mini display port

Powercord connector

REAR OF iMAC

Webcam

LCD display

Keyboard

Touchpad

Fingerprint reader

Left touchpad button

Right touchpad button

Headphone jacks (2)

Audio in jack

HP PAVILION DV4 LAPTOP

Optical drive

Power connector

USB ports (2)

Expansion port

Remote control

Display

Digital media slot

Security cable slot

RG-45 (network) port

HDMI port

eSATA/ USB port

External monitor port

SIDE VIEW OF HP PAVILION DV4 LAPTOP

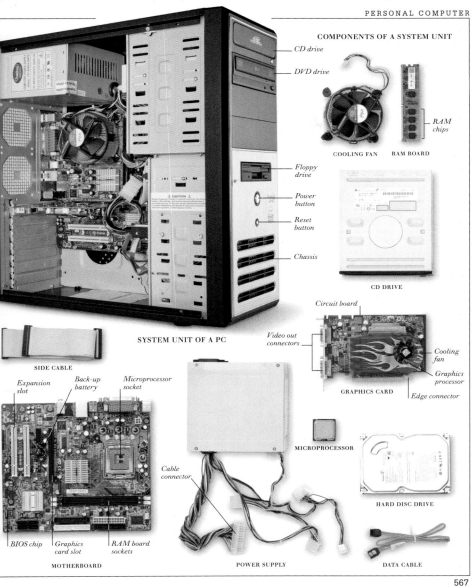

COMPONENTS OF A SYSTEM UNIT

CD drive

DVD drive

RAM chips

COOLING FAN

RAM BOARD

Floppy drive

Power button

Reset button

Chassis

CD DRIVE

SYSTEM UNIT OF A PC

SIDE CABLE

Circuit board

Video out connectors

Cooling fan

Graphics processor

GRAPHICS CARD

Edge connector

Expansion slot

Back-up battery

Microprocessor socket

Cable connector

MICROPROCESSOR

HARD DISC DRIVE

BIOS chip

Graphics card slot

RAM board sockets

MOTHERBOARD

POWER SUPPLY

DATA CABLE

Handheld computer

By THE EARLY 1990s electronic circuitry had been miniaturized to such an extent that it was possible to make small handheld computing devices. The first of these was the Personal Digital Assistant (PDA), which offered features including an address book, calendar, and notepad. In recent years, PDAs have been overtaken by smartphones with internet and email access (see pp. 588–589). A related product is the e-book reader, which stores books in digital form and uses "electronic paper" to mimic the appearance of ink on real paper. An e-book reader no bigger than a thin paperback can store several thousand digital books in its memory. The most recent small computing device is the handheld computer. This looks like a thin flat display, but it is actually a complete computer. Handheld computers are typically controlled by a touch-sensitive screen and have a wireless link to other computers and the internet. They run software applications, or apps, downloaded from the internet. The most popular handheld computer currently is the Apple iPad. It has a multitouch interface that enables its screen to detect the movements of fingertips. In addition to selecting options and apps by touching the screen, images can be enlarged or shrunk by moving fingertips apart or together on the screen.

Sleep/wake button

APPLE IPAD | *Home button* | *App icon*

Touch data is sent as a list of finger positions to the controller where the information is used to zoom in and out of a web page

LCD with buttons displayed

Fingers alter the electric field around nearby sections of the grid

User touches clear protective screen

Touchscreeen electronics interpret the outputs from the grid to work out exactly where the fingers are

Controller

MULTITOUCH INTERFACE

6-in (15-cm) screen

Next page button

Previous page button

Joystick controller

ACER LUMIREAD E-READER

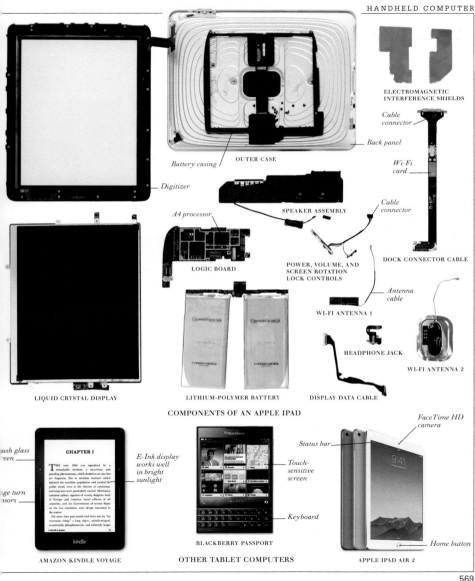

ELECTROMAGNETIC
INTERFERENCE SHIELDS

Cable connector

Back panel

Wi-Fi card

Battery casing OUTER CASE

Digitizer

A4 processor

SPEAKER ASSEMBLY

Cable connector

LOGIC BOARD

POWER, VOLUME, AND
SCREEN ROTATION
LOCK CONTROLS

DOCK CONNECTOR CABLE

Antenna cable

WI-FI ANTENNA 1

LITHIUM-POLYMER BATTERY

HEADPHONE JACK

DISPLAY DATA CABLE

WI-FI ANTENNA 2

LIQUID CRYSTAL DISPLAY

COMPONENTS OF AN APPLE IPAD

ush glass
een

ge turn
sors

CHAPTER I

*E-Ink display
works well
in bright
sunlight*

kindle

AMAZON KINDLE VOYAGE

Status bar

Touch-sensitive screen

Keyboard

BLACKBERRY PASSPORT

OTHER TABLET COMPUTERS

FaceTime HD camera

9:41

Home button

APPLE IPAD AIR 2

Flatbed scanner

SCANNERS CONVERT physical images into electronic form, allowing them to be sent over the internet, displayed on a website, stored on a computer, and manipulated using specialized software. Scanners work by detecting and analyzing light reflected from an opaque image, such as a photographic print. Some can also scan photographic transparencies by analyzing light that has passed through the image. Flatbed scanners contain a unit, called the scan head, that contains a lamp, mirrors, a lens, and an array of CCDs (Charge-Coupled Devices). The carriage passes beneath the image; the lamp shines light on to or through the original; the mirrors reflect the light on to the lens, which focuses it on to the CCD array. Each CCD detects the brightness of light from a particular pixel (picture element) along a· horizontal strip and converts this data into an electric signal. For color images, the light is usually passed through red, green, and blue filters and then directed to the CCD array so that it can be broken down into its component colors. This information is then converted to digital form. The quality of the image depends on its resolution, measured in dpi (Dots Per Inch).

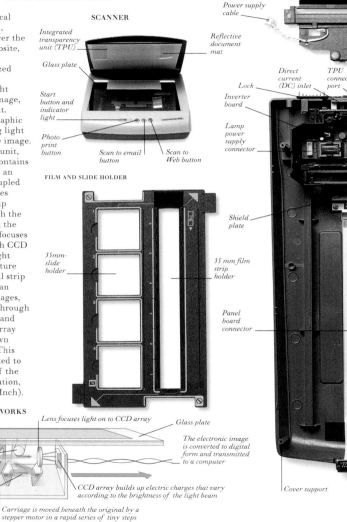

SCANNER

Integrated transparency unit (TPU)

Glass plate

Start button and indicator light

Photo print button

Scan to email button

Scan to Web button

Power supply cable

Reflective document mat

Lock

Direct current (DC) inlet

TPU connec port

Inverter board

Lamp power supply connector

Shield plate

Panel board connector

FILM AND SLIDE HOLDER

35mm-slide holder

35 mm film strip holder

HOW A FLATBED SCANNER WORKS

Original image (photograph or artwork)

Lamp

Lens focuses light on to CCD array

Glass plate

The electronic image is converted to digital form and transmitted to a computer

CCD array builds up electric charges that vary according to the brightness of the light beam

Light beam is reflected from the original to a series of mirrors

Carriage is moved beneath the original by a stepper motor in a rapid series of tiny steps

Cover support

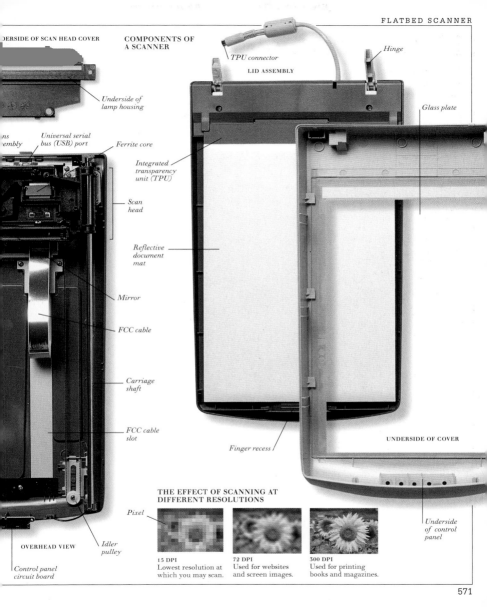

UNDERSIDE OF SCAN HEAD COVER

COMPONENTS OF
A SCANNER

TPU connector

Hinge

LID ASSEMBLY

Underside of
lamp housing

Glass plate

Universal serial
bus (USB) port

Ferrite core

Integrated
transparency
unit (TPU)

Scan
head

Reflective
document
mat

Mirror

FCC cable

Carriage
shaft

FCC cable
slot

UNDERSIDE OF COVER

Finger recess

OVERHEAD VIEW

Idler
pulley

Control panel
circuit board

Underside
of control
panel

THE EFFECT OF SCANNING AT
DIFFERENT RESOLUTIONS

Pixel

15 DPI
Lowest resolution at
which you may scan.

72 DPI
Used for websites
and screen images.

300 DPI
Used for printing
books and magazines.

Airbus 380

CROSS-SECTION
OF FUSELAGE

THE AIRBUS A380 WAS CONCEIVED in the early 1990s to compete with, and if possible replace, the Boeing 747. Work began in earnest on what was then called the A3XX in 1994. Its maiden flight was in April 2005. The A380's shape is subtly molded to minimize drag from its ovoid fuselage. The structure makes extensive use of composite materials, such as thermoplastics and GLARE (aluminum and glass fiber). Its engines are very powerful, but also very efficient. It is claimed that when carrying 550 passengers, the A380 uses only ¾ gallon (2.9 liters) of fuel per passenger per 60 miles (100 km).

Galley area

Personal lighting

Concealed lighting

Storage locker

Window blind

Reclining seat

Seat control panel

Aisle

Folding foot rest

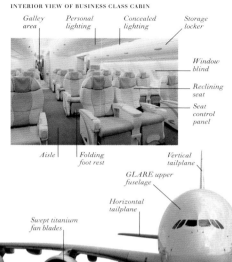

Obstruction light

Swept titanium fan blades

Vertical tailplane

GLARE upper fuselage

Horizontal tailplane

Company logo

Wing landing gear

FRONT VIEW

Split rudder

Jupp-Reese winglet

Upper deck windows

Overwing emergency exit

A380

F-WWOW

Auxiliary Power Unit (APU) exhaust

Horizontal tailplane

Tailcone fairing

Aft door

Belly fairing

Flap track fairings

Body landing gear

SIDE VIEW

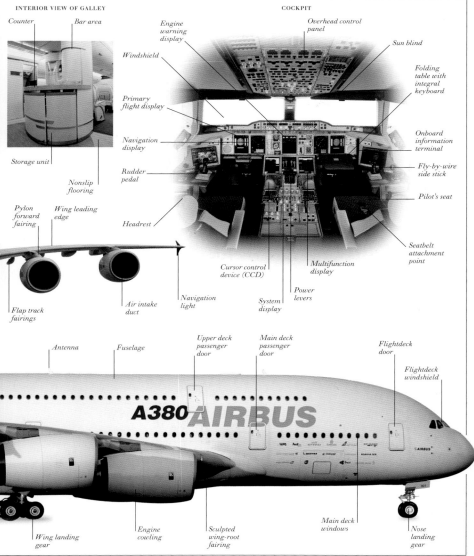

INTERIOR VIEW OF GALLEY

Counter

Bar area

Storage unit

Nonslip flooring

COCKPIT

Engine warning display

Windshield

Primary flight display

Navigation display

Rudder pedal

Headrest

Overhead control panel

Sun blind

Folding table with integral keyboard

Onboard information terminal

Fly-by-wire side stick

Pilot's seat

Seatbelt attachment point

Cursor control device (CCD)

System display

Power levers

Multifunction display

Pylon forward fairing

Wing leading edge

Flap track fairings

Air intake duct

Navigation light

Antenna

Fuselage

Upper deck passenger door

Main deck passenger door

Flightdeck door

Flightdeck windshield

A380 AIRBUS

Wing landing gear

Engine cowling

Sculpted wing-root fairing

Main deck windows

Nose landing gear

573

Inkjet printer

INKJET PRINTERS EXPEL ink droplets from hundreds of tiny jets, or nozzles, on to a medium, such as paper, to print an image. Each droplet corresponds to a single pixel (picture element). Black-and-white printers use only black ink, while color printers overprint combinations of the printing colors (cyan, yellow, magenta, and black) to create a full color range. The printhead containing the nozzles moves sideways across the paper, creating a line of pixels, before the paper moves slightly forward so the next line can be printed. Two basic methods are used to eject ink: thermal, in which ink is heated to form an expanding bubble that expels a droplet from the nozzle, and piezoelectric, in which an electric current expands a crystal causing it to push out the ink droplet. The printer shown here can print digital photographs directly from a memory card.

EPSON STYLUS PHOTO 895 COLOR INKJET PRINTER

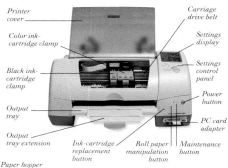

Printer cover

Color ink-cartridge clamp

Black ink-cartridge clamp

Output tray

Output tray extension

Carriage drive belt

Settings display

Settings control panel

Power button

PC card adapter

Ink-cartridge replacement button

Roll paper manipulation button

Maintenance button

Paper hopper

OVERHEAD VIEW WITH OUTER CASING REMOVED

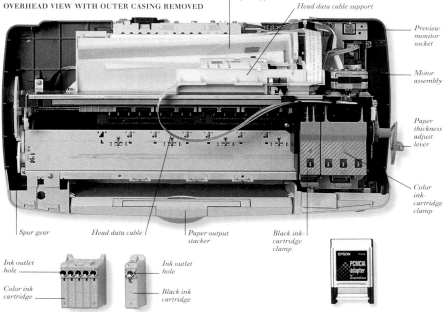

Head data cable support

Preview monitor socket

Motor assembly

Paper thickness adjust lever

Color ink-cartridge clamp

Spur gear

Head data cable

Paper output stacker

Black ink-cartridge clamp

Ink outlet hole

Color ink cartridge

Ink outlet hole

Black ink cartridge

INK CARTRIDGES

PC CARD ADAPTER

PAPER FEED COMPONENTS

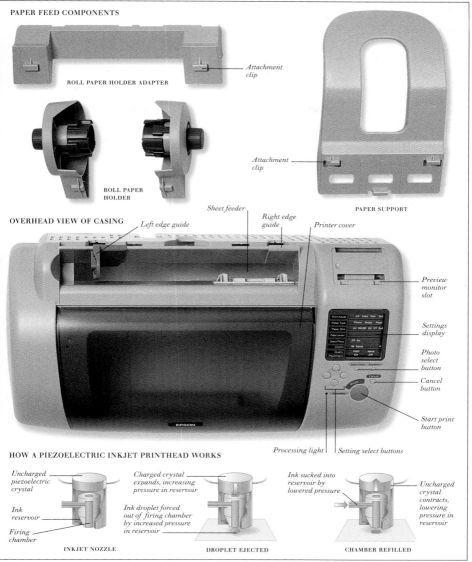

ROLL PAPER HOLDER ADAPTER

Attachment clip

ROLL PAPER HOLDER

Attachment clip

PAPER SUPPORT

OVERHEAD VIEW OF CASING

Left edge guide

Sheet feeder

Right edge guide

Printer cover

Preview monitor slot

Settings display

Photo select button

Cancel button

Start print button

EPSON

Processing light

Setting select buttons

HOW A PIEZOELECTRIC INKJET PRINTHEAD WORKS

Uncharged piezoelectric crystal

Ink reservoir

Firing chamber

INKJET NOZZLE

Charged crystal expands, increasing pressure in reservoir

Ink droplet forced out of firing chamber by increased pressure in reservoir

DROPLET EJECTED

Ink sucked into reservoir by lowered pressure

Uncharged crystal contracts, lowering pressure in reservoir

CHAMBER REFILLED

The internet

THE INTERNET CONSISTS OF TENS of thousands of computer networks linked together to form one huge global network, allowing any computer on one network to communicate with any computer on another. The two main services used on the internet are email and the World Wide Web. Email allows text messages to be sent—along with attached computer files, images, or video clips, for example—to other computers on the internet. The web consists of billions of pages made up of digital files that are stored on computers across the world and can be viewed using a web browser. The web also provides interactive access to various services, for example, banking and shopping.

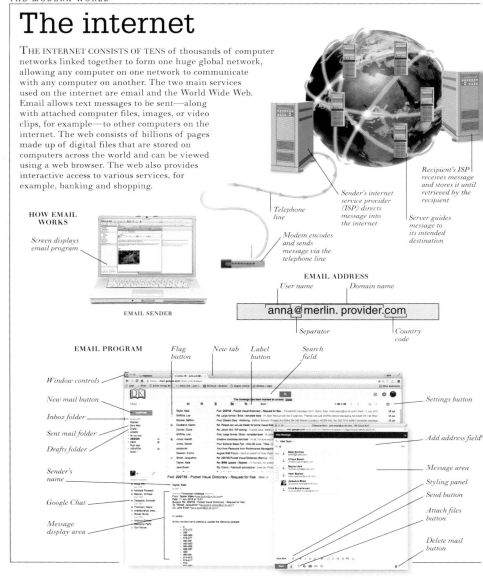

Recipient's ISP receives message and stores it until retrieved by the recipient

Server guides message to its intended destination

Sender's internet service provider (ISP) directs message into the internet

Telephone line

Modem encodes and sends message via the telephone line

HOW EMAIL WORKS

Screen displays email program

EMAIL SENDER

EMAIL ADDRESS

User name   *Domain name*

anna@merlin. provider.com

Separator   *Country code*

EMAIL PROGRAM

Flag button   *New tab*   *Label button*   *Search field*

Window controls

New mail button

Inbox folder

Sent mail folder

Drafts folder

Sender's name

Google Chat

Message display area

Settings button

Add address field

Message area

Styling panel

Send button

Attach files button

Delete mail button

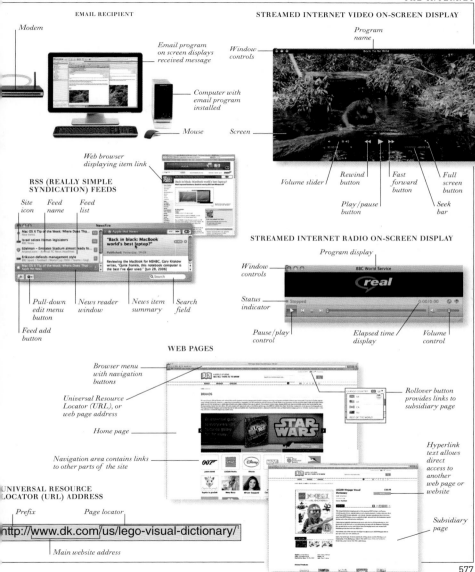

EMAIL RECIPIENT

Modem

Email program on screen displays received message

Computer with email program installed

Mouse

Screen

STREAMED INTERNET VIDEO ON-SCREEN DISPLAY

Program name

Window controls

Born To Be Wild

Volume slider

Rewind button

Fast forward button

Full screen button

Play/pause button

Seek bar

Web browser displaying item link

RSS (REALLY SIMPLE SYNDICATION) FEEDS

Site icon

Feed name

Feed list

NewsFire

Mac OS X Tip of the Week: Where Does Tha...
New Stories

Israel seizes Hamas legislators
BBC News

Edelman – Emirates Stadium almost ready to...
Arsenal.com – Arsenal FC News Headlines

Eriksson defends management style
BBC Sport | Football | World Cup 2006 | News | Engl...

Mac OS X Tip of the Week: Where Does That...
Apple Hot News

Apple Hot News

"Back in black: MacBook world's best laptop?"

Published: Yesterday, 19:09

Reviewing the MacBook for MSNBC, Gary Krakow writes, "Quite frankly, this notebook computer is the best I've ever used." (Jun 28, 2006)

Q Search

Pull-down edit menu button

News reader window

News item summary

Search field

Feed add button

STREAMED INTERNET RADIO ON-SCREEN DISPLAY

Program display

Window controls

BBC World Service

real

Status indicator

Stopped

0:00/0.00

Pause/play control

Elapsed time display

Volume control

WEB PAGES

Browser menu with navigation buttons

Universal Resource Locator (URL), or web page address

Home page

Navigation area contains links to other parts of the site

BRANDS

STAR WARS

007 Disney MARVEL

James Bond LEGO Disney Others

Rollover button provides links to subsidiary page

CHANGE COUNTRY

Hyperlink text allows direct access to another web page or website

LEGO Voyage Visual Dictionary

Subsidiary page

UNIVERSAL RESOURCE LOCATOR (URL) ADDRESS

Prefix   *Page locator*

http://www.dk.com/us/lego-visual-dictionary/

Main website address

Electronic games

MARIO SPORTS MIX WII

VIDEO GAMES HAVE BEEN around since the early 1970s. They are played on PCs, arcade machines, on a TV using a home console, and on portable handheld consoles. Players use devices such as joysticks and control pads with buttons to control movement and action on screen.

The latest generation of consoles uses motion sensor technology to allow players to manipulate objects on screen by simply moving the controller. The most advanced game systems respond to gestures and commands spoken by a player, without any need to use a hand controller. The game itself is stored in the form of digital information on CD, DVD, or microchip—which may be integral or stored in a removable cartridge—or on an internal hard disk. A central processing unit (CPU) (see pp. 566–567) is needed to process commands from the players, while specialized graphics chips are used to process the complex mapping and texturing functions that make modern games appear so realistic.

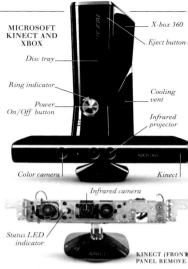

MICROSOFT KINECT AND XBOX

X-box 360
Eject button
Disc tray
Ring indicator
Cooling vent
Power On/Off button
Infrared projector
Color camera
Kinect
Infrared camera
Status LED indicator

KINECT (FRONT PANEL REMOVE

NINTENDO 3DS

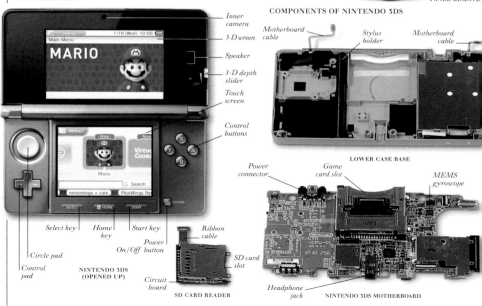

Inner camera
3-D screen
Speaker
3-D depth slider
Touch screen
Control buttons

COMPONENTS OF NINTENDO 3DS

Motherboard cable
Stylus holder
Motherboard cable

LOWER CASE BASE

Power connector
Game card slot
MEMS gyroscope

Select key
Home key
Start key
Ribbon cable
Power On/Off button
SD card slot

Circle pad
Control pad

NINTENDO 3DS (OPENED UP)

Circuit board

SD CARD READER

Headphone jack

NINTENDO 3DS MOTHERBOARD

NINTENDO Wii FIT PLUS

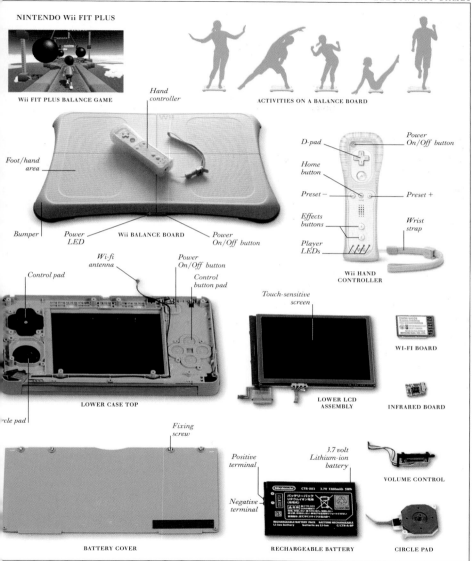

Wii FIT PLUS BALANCE GAME

Hand controller

ACTIVITIES ON A BALANCE BOARD

Foot/hand area

Bumper

Power LED

Wii BALANCE BOARD

Power On/Off button

D-pad

Power On/Off button

Home button

Preset −

Preset +

Effects buttons

Player LEDs

Wrist strap

Wii HAND CONTROLLER

Wi-fi antenna

Control pad

Power On/Off button

Control button pad

Touch-sensitive screen

WI-FI BOARD

LOWER CASE TOP

rcle pad

LOWER LCD ASSEMBLY

INFRARED BOARD

Fixing screw

Positive terminal

Negative terminal

3.7 volt Lithium-ion battery

VOLUME CONTROL

BATTERY COVER

RECHARGEABLE BATTERY

CIRCLE PAD

579

Digital camera

FOR MORE THAN 200 YEARS, CAMERAS recorded pictures as chemical changes in silver-containing substances, on a strip of flexible, celluloid film. The digital camera records pictures in electronic form. At its heart is a specialized integrated circuit known as a charge-coupled device (CCD). This has millions of microunits known as pixels. It works in the opposite way from a miniature computer or TV screen. Instead of electric signals making pixels shine, when light hits a pixel it generates a tiny electrical signal, according to the light's color and brightness. The signals from the CCD's millions of pixels are analogue: they vary continuously in a wavelike fashion. They are converted by a microchip to digital codes of numbers, represented as on-off electronic pulses. The digital signals are processed and fed to the camera's internal memory or a removable memory device such as a data card or memory stick. Photographs can be downloaded from a digital camera to a computer via a cable or in some cases a wireless link. Some digital cameras automatically reduce blurring caused by camera shake or fast movement, some can record video clips as well as still pictures.

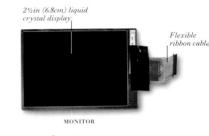

2½in (6.8cm) liquid crystal display

Flexible ribbon cable

MONITOR

Protective steel panel

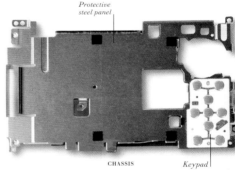

CHASSIS Keypad

Infra receiv (rear)

HOW A DIGITAL CAMERA WORKS

CCD turns light into electronic signals

Lens focuses light

Light from scene

Analogue signals

Analogue to digital converter microchip

Microprocessor

Digital signals

LCD screen

Memory stick

In-camera memory chip

Connector cover

Eyelet for camera strap

CHROMED PLASTIC SIDE COVER

Flash lamp

Nikon

REAR CASE

Menu button

OK (Select) button

Spea

Shoo mode butto

Playt butto

Delete button

Speaker mounting bracket

Speaker

SPEAKER ASSEMBLY

COMPONENTS OF NIKON COOLPIX S1000PJ

Shutter release button

TOP PANEL

Projector button

Focusing lens

Filters

Projector LED

Ribbon cable

PROJECTOR ASSEMBLY

Projector assembly cover

CODEC with speaker driver and video buffet

Display controller chip

SIDE-B

LOGIC BOARD

Projector window

Flash window

Lens

Infrared receiver (front)

Self-timer lamp

Nikon

COOLPIX

NIKKOR 5X WIDE OPTICAL ZOOM VR 5.0–25.0mm1:3.9–5.8

FRONT CASE

Camera module connector

CCD image sensor

CAMERA MODULE

Nikon

LITHIUM ION BATTERY PACK EN-EL12 3.7V 1050mAh 3.9Wh

JFBC

NIKON CORPORATION, JAPAN

Lithium-ion battery

EN-EL12 RECHARGEABLE BATTERY

Lens cover motor

LENS COVER

TYPES OF DIGITAL CAMERA

Mode selector

Shutter button

Nikon

D5000

Lens release button

DIGITAL SLR

18–55mm zoom lens

On/off button

Shutter button

Lens release button

16mm interchangeable lens

DIGITAL CAMERA WITH INTERCHANGEABLE LENS

Water-resistant case

Shutter button

Electronic flash

Strap mount

Lamp

Canon PowerShot D10

Microphone

Lens

UNDERWATER DIGITAL CAMERA

Shutter button

Microphone

Left lens

Right lens

Flash

Lens cover

TWIN CCD

3D HD

FUJIFILM

3-D DIGITAL CAMERA

Digital video camera

A VIDEO CAMERA, OR CAMCORDER, records a scene as a sequence of 25 or 30 still images per second, along with sound. It comprises a video camera to capture light from the scene, a viewfinder through which the scene may be viewed, a screen on which the recorded scene may be viewed, a charge-coupled device (CCD) to convert the visual data into an electric signal, and a means of storing the signal. Digital video cameras convert the signal into digital form—a series of separate measurements of the initial analogue (continuously varying) signal. They record the digital signal, usually on a chip or hard disk. Video cameras often have a slot where a memory card can be inserted to expand the memory and store longer recordings or more still pictures.

COMPONENTS OF A JVC EVERIO VIDEO CAMERA

MONITOR SHELL

MONITOR MOUNT

MONITOR FRAME

Screen connector

2¾-in (6.8-cm) LCD screen

OK button

Grip belt

MONITOR SCREEN

Speaker

Play button

Auto/Manual recording but

Info button

Menu button

AV terminal

LEFT SIDE

Battery

Power/ Charge lamp

Access lamp

Zoom select lever

Power/charge lamp

Access lamp

LEFT OUTER SHELL

Lens cover

Microphone

LCD monitor

TOP VIEW

LENS COVER ASSEMBLY

Speaker

SPEAKER CIRCUIT BOARD

MOTHERBOARD

CHASSIS

Monitor frame

USB terminal

DC terminal

Start/Stop button

LCD monitor

Battery

REAR VIEW

Grip belt

Lens cover switch

RIGHT OUTER SHELL

Grip belt release lever

SDHC CARD

Lens

CCD mounting peg

CCD chip

SENSOR BOARD

Start/Stop button

3.6-volt lithium-ion battery

LENS UNIT

LENS UNIT MOUNT

GRIP BELT FASTENER

Zoom select lever

OK button

RECHARGEABLE BATTERY

GRIP BELT

REAR PANEL

CONTROL UNIT

Home cinema

HOME CINEMA REPLICATES a real "movie theatre" using pictures displayed on a high-quality widescreen television set, such as an LED TV, and surround sound from strategically sited loudspeakers. The source for sound and vision is a DVD (Digital Versatile Disc). Its player uses standard CD (Compact Disc) digital technology, but with a higher density of laser-read microscopic pits—more than 20 billion such pits in multi-level spiral tracks that, stretched out, would extend nearly 25 miles (40km). Blu-ray is a high-quality DVD system that fits much more data on its disc than standard DVDs, allowing High Definition video files to be stored. It is hard for the human ear to discern the direction of low-pitched sounds, so these emanate from a central bass speaker, often built into or below the screen unit. High-pitched sounds, the direction of which is easier to detect, emanate from mid- and high-frequency speakers positioned around the viewer. Light Emitting Diode (LED) TVs shine LEDs through a Liquid Crystal Display (LCD) panel. LCD screens are made up of millions of three-cell pixels, each containing a red, green, and blue sub-pixel. These pixels are controlled by the liquid crystals in the display panel, which regulate the light emitted by the LEDs. This allows all the different combinations of the three colors to be produced, creating the image on-screen. Organic Light Emitting Diode (OLED) TVs have an organic carbon-based layer that produces colored light. While traditional LED screens use several layers to make light and color, OLED screens have just one, and can therefore be thinner and use less energy.

BLU-RAY PLAYER

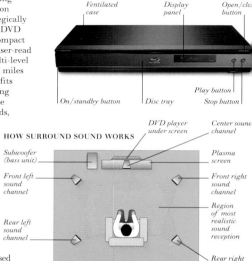

Ventilated case

Display panel

Open/clo button

On/standby button

Disc tray

Play button

Stop button

HOW SURROUND SOUND WORKS

DVD player under screen

Center sound channel

Subwoofer (bass unit)

Plasma screen

Front left sound channel

Front right sound channel

Rear left sound channel

Region of most realistic sound reception

Rear right sound channel

HOW AN OLED SCREEN WORKS

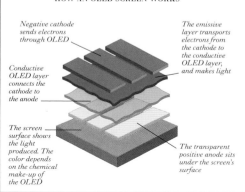

Negative cathode sends electrons through OLED

The emissive layer transports electrons from the cathode to the conductive OLED layer, and makes light

Conductive OLED layer connects the cathode to the anode

The screen surface shows the light produced. The color depends on the chemical make-up of the OLED

The transparent positive anode sits under the screen's surface

WIDE-SCREEN LED TV

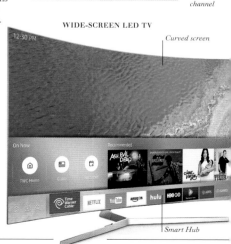

Curved screen

Smart Hub

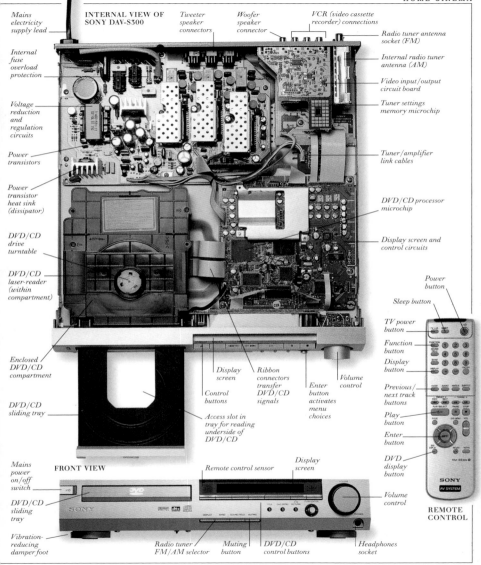

INTERNAL VIEW OF SONY DAV-S300

Mains electricity supply lead

Internal fuse overload protection

Voltage reduction and regulation circuits

Power transistors

Power transistor heat sink (dissipator)

DVD/CD drive turntable

DVD/CD laser-reader (within compartment)

Enclosed DVD/CD compartment

DVD/CD sliding tray

Tweeter speaker connectors

Woofer speaker connector

VCR (video cassette recorder) connections

Radio tuner antenna socket (FM)

Internal radio tuner antenna (AM)

Video input/output circuit board

Tuner settings memory microchip

Tuner/amplifier link cables

DVD/CD processor microchip

Display screen and control circuits

Display screen

Control buttons

Ribbon connectors transfer DVD/CD signals

Access slot in tray for reading underside of DVD/CD

Enter button activates menu choices

Volume control

Power button

Sleep button

TV power button

Function button

Display button

Previous/next track buttons

Play button

Enter button

DVD display button

SONY
AV SYSTEM

REMOTE CONTROL

Mains power on/off switch

DVD/CD sliding tray

Vibration-reducing damper foot

FRONT VIEW

Remote control sensor

Display screen

Radio tuner FM/AM selector

Muting button

DVD/CD control buttons

Headphones socket

Volume control

585

Personal music

THE FIRST BATTERY-DRIVEN PORTABLE source of sound and music was the transistor radio of the 1950s. In the 1970s, the magnetic audio cassette tape allowed recordings to be played on portable tape players. Also, new metal alloys permitted the tiny but high-power magnets needed for lightweight earphones. In the 1980s, compact discs brought music into the digital era. Sony's MD, or minidisc, introduced re-recordable CDs that used magnetic and optical technology. From the mid 1990s, music could be stored in all-electronic digital form in a microchip, usually in the MP3 file format. These files can be transferred between devices and via the Internet. Today, a variety of portable media gadgets can record, play, and store video, photographs, and music in electronic form.

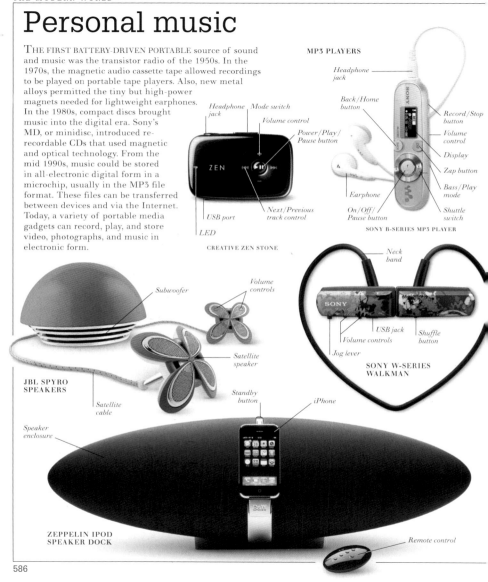

MP3 PLAYERS

Headphone jack

Back/Home button

Record/Stop button

Volume control

Display

Zap button

Bass/Play mode

Earphone

On/Off/ Pause button

Shuttle switch

SONY B-SERIES MP3 PLAYER

Headphone jack

Mode switch

Volume control

Power/Play/ Pause button

ZEN

USB port

Next/Previous track control

LED

CREATIVE ZEN STONE

Neck band

Volume controls

USB jack

Shuffle button

Jog lever

SONY W-SERIES WALKMAN

Subwoofer

Volume controls

Satellite speaker

JBL SPYRO SPEAKERS

Satellite cable

Standby button

iPhone

Speaker enclosure

ZEPPELIN IPOD SPEAKER DOCK

Remote control

Headphone jack

Hold switch

Current song playing

Now Playing
9 of 16
Shake A Leg
AC/DC
Back In Black
0:53   -3:12

Scrubber bar

Select button

menu

Touch-sensitive wheel

Headphones

IPOD CLASSIC

Power button

Volume controls

Water-resistant covering

360° speakers

Audio jack

UE BOOM

Adjustable headband

Foldable hinges

studio

Ear cups

Power button

BEATS BY DRE HEADPHONES

On/Off switch

Clip

Control pad

IPOD SHUFFLE

Cellphones

IN THE EARLY 1990s, THE CELLPHONE (or mobile phone) was a rare luxury, but in recent years it has outsold almost every other electrical gadget—as a professional tool, domestic convenience, and even a fashion accessory. Cellphones have also generally shrunk in size, due to improvements in rechargeable batteries, which now store more electricity for longer in a smaller package, and to smaller, more efficient electronics that use less electricity. A "cellphone" is basically a low-power radio receiver-transmitter, plus a tiny microphone to convert sounds into electrical signals, and a small speaker that does the reverse. When the cellphone is activated, it sends out a radio signal that is answered by nearby mast transmitter-receivers. The phone locks onto the clearest signal and uses this while within range (the range of each transmitter is known as a cell). The phone continuously monitors signal strength and switches to an alternative transmitter when necessary. The phone's liquid crystal display (LCD) shows numbers, letters, symbols, and color pictures. Newer models have a larger screen for more complex color images, and commonly incorporate a camera, radio, and MP3 functionality. Smartphones, which are increasingly widespread, contain additional software and more may be downloaded. Smartphones typically offer internet and email access, PDA-like functions (see pp. 568–569), and may even contain GPS navigation software.

Camera

Rear microphone

Top microphone

App icon

Lightning connector

Headphone jack

Home key

Speaker

I-PHONE 6

HOW A CELLPHONE WORKS

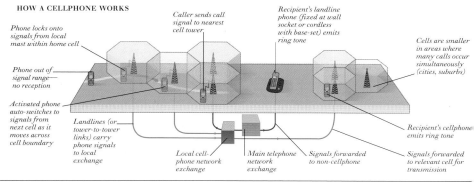

Phone locks onto signals from local mast within home cell

Caller sends call signal to nearest cell tower

Recipient's landline phone (fixed at wall socket or cordless with base-set) emits ring tone

Cells are smaller in areas where many calls occur simultaneously (cities, suburbs)

Phone out of signal range— no reception

Activated phone auto-switches to signals from next cell as it moves across cell boundary

Landlines (or tower-to-tower links) carry phone signals to local exchange

Local cell-phone network exchange

Main telephone network exchange

Signals forwarded to non-cellphone

Recipient's cellphone emits ring tone

Signals forwarded to relevant cell for transmission

COMPONENTS OF BLACKBERRY CURVE 8520

Front housing
ezel
FASCIA

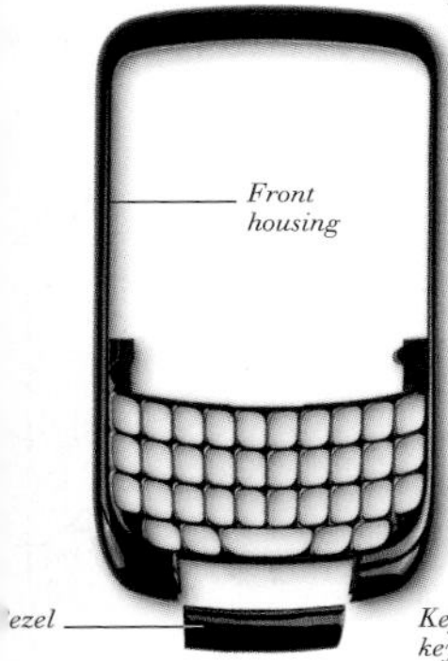

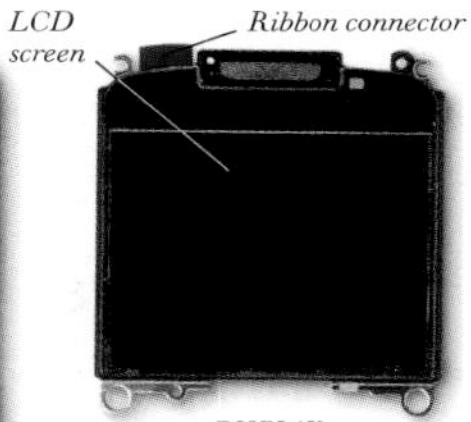

LCD screen
Ribbon connector
DISPLAY

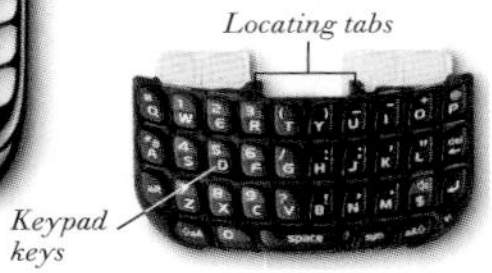

Locating tabs
Keypad keys
KEYPAD

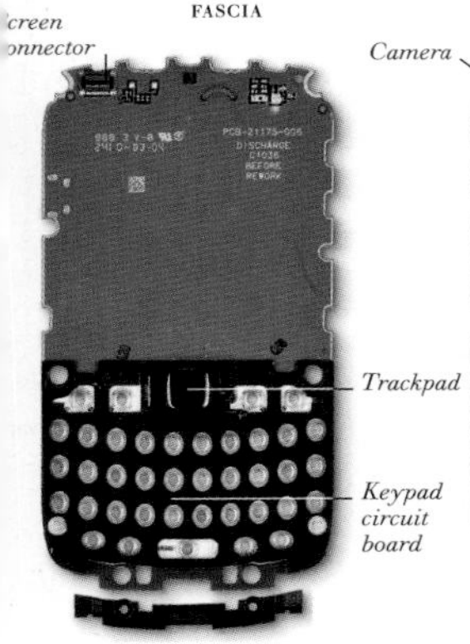

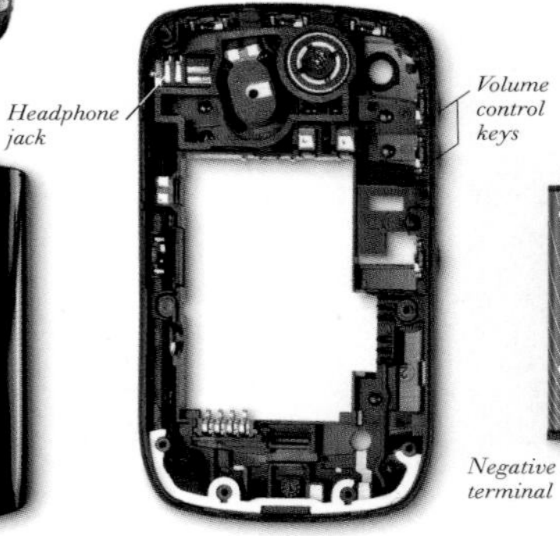

creen
onnector
Trackpad
Keypad circuit board
LOGIC BOARD (FRONT)

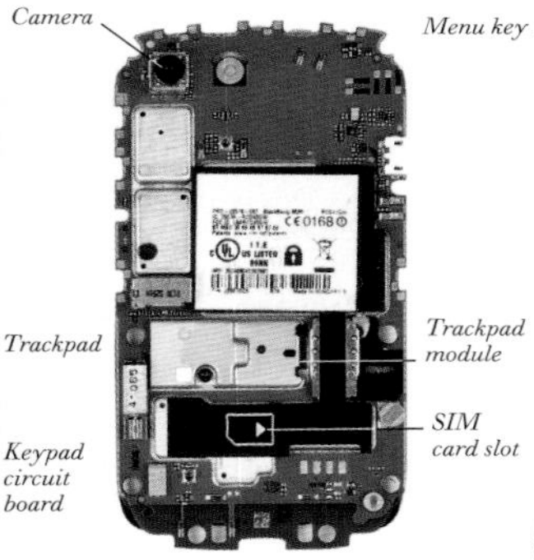

Camera
Trackpad module
SIM card slot
LOGIC BOARD (REAR)

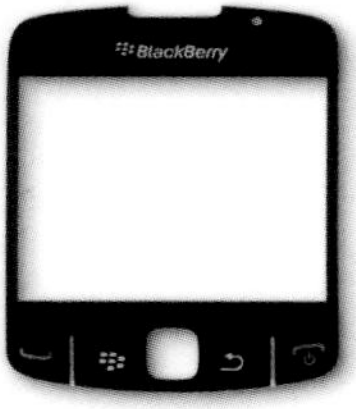

BlackBerry
SCREEN LENS

BATTERY COVER

BLACKBERRY CURVE 8520

Headphone jack
BlackBerry
12:21
Thursday, May 21
(3) Messages
Volume control keys
Screen lens
Micro USB port
Left convenience key
Right convenience key
Trackpad
Send/call key
End/power key
Menu key
Escape/back key
Delete key
Speakerphone key
Left shift key
Right shift key

Headphone jack
Volume control keys
REAR HOUSING

Lithium-ion battery
BlackBerry
Negative terminal
Positive terminal
RECHARGEABLE BATTERY

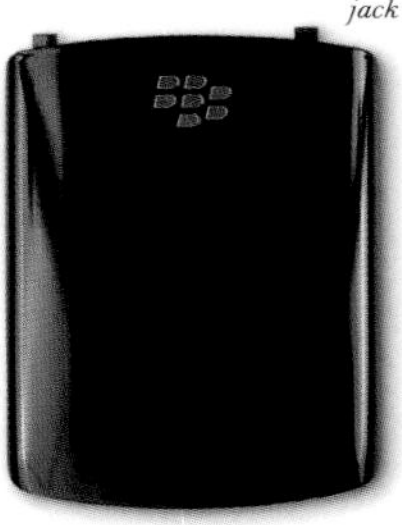

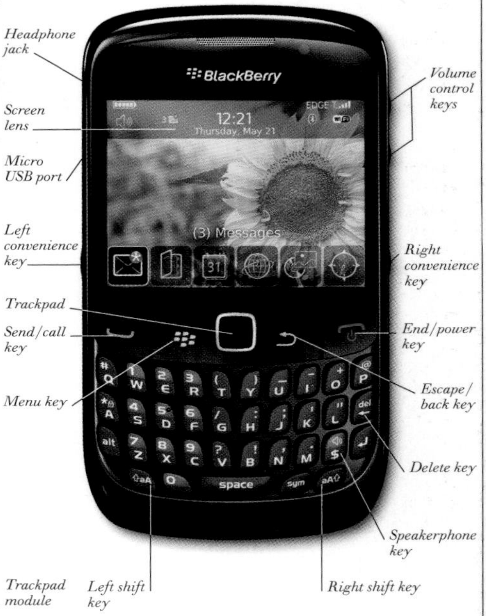

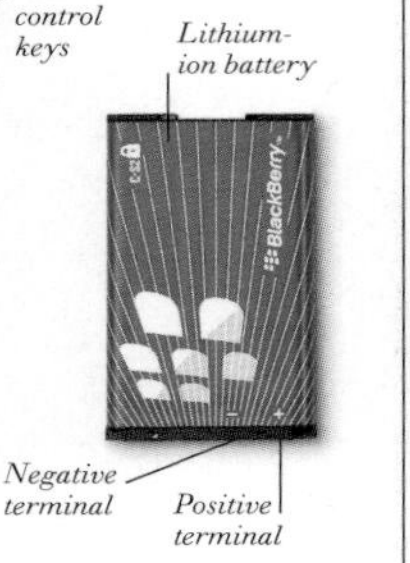

Wearable technology

WEARABLE TECHNOLOGY DEVICES are clothing or accessories, such as jewelery or glasses, that have connected computer devices incorporated in their design. Such devices contain many smart sensors and are connected wirelessly—either via the internet or Bluetooth—to another device, such as a smartphone, that tracks the data the wearable device collects. Wearable technology has been around since the late 1970s, with devices such as the calculator watch and digital hearing aid. However, progress in wearable technology advanced rapidly in the early twenty-first century, when sensors and chip sets became much cheaper and more readily available. Wearable technology can have many different functions. Some devices are used to track medical data, such as measuring heart rate, breathing patterns, and temperature. Others are used to monitor fitness, with many using GPS (below) to track how many steps a user has walked, or how many miles they have run, for example. Some wearable technology is designed to merge the digital world with the physical world—for example, Google Glass, which projects digital information, such as maps and text notifications, onto the glasses' screen without obstructing the view of the real world.

Customizable watch face

On/off button

Interchangeable band

PEBBLE

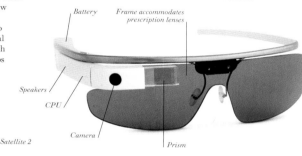

Battery

Frame accommodates prescription lenses

Speakers

CPU

Camera

Prism

GOOGLE GLASS

HOW GPS WORKS

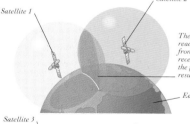

Satellite 1

Satellite 2

The receiver takes a reading of its distance from two satellites. The receiver is located along the plane where the two resultant spheres meet

Earth

Satellite 3

A signal from a third satellite defines two positions on that plane. The position on the Earth's surface is read as the correct location

Optical touchpad

HD camera

RECON JET

Polarized lens

Battery

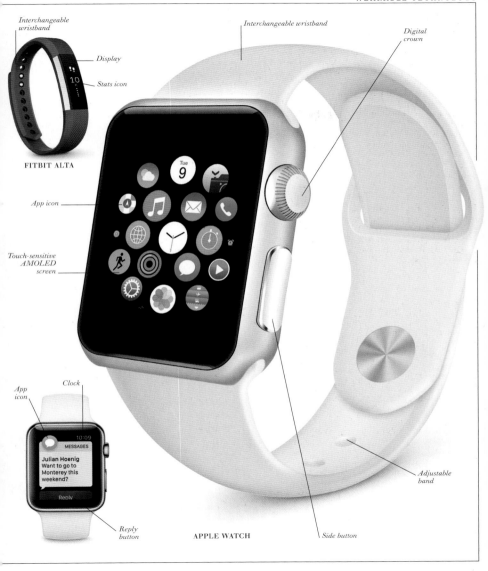

Interchangeable wristband

Display

Stats icon

FITBIT ALTA

Interchangeable wristband

Digital crown

App icon

Touch-sensitive AMOLED screen

App icon

Clock

Tue
9

10:09
MESSAGES
Julian Hoenig
Want to go to Monterey this weekend?

Reply

Reply button

APPLE WATCH

Side button

Adjustable band

Vacuum cleaner

IN A CONVENTIONAL VACUUM CLEANER, an electric motor
spins a fan that sucks in air carrying dust and debris. The air
is forced through tiny pores in a dust bag, trapping most
particles. In the 1990s, James Dyson's dual cyclone "bagless"
design did away with the dust bag—and the reduced airflow
caused by clogging of its pores. An electrically driven fan
creates a partial vacuum within the machine. This sucks air
into the machine past a rotating brush that loosens dirt. The
air flows into a cylinder-shaped bin. As the air whirls around
the bin like a miniature storm, or cyclone, larger particle
are flung outward and fall to the bottom of the bin. The
air then passes through perforations into a cone-shaped
inner bin and then into a series of smaller cones, spinning
faster all the time and flinging smaller and smaller particle
out. The nearly clean air exits the
machine through microfilters that
trap the tiniest particles. Some
Dyson vacuum cleaners run on
a large ball instead of wheels.
The ball makes it easier to
steer the cleaner.

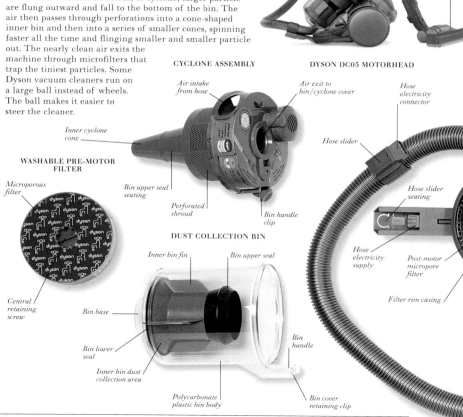

*Wand handle and
brushbar controls*

Upper wand

Lower wand

*Motorized
brushbar
floor tool*

CYCLONE ASSEMBLY

*Air intake
from hose*

*Air exit to
bin/cyclone cover*

*Inner cyclone
cone*

DYSON DC05 MOTORHEAD

*Hose
electricity
connector*

Hose slider

**WASHABLE PRE-MOTOR
FILTER**

*Microporous
filter*

*Bin upper seal
seating*

*Perforated
shroud*

*Bin handle
clip*

*Hose slider
seating*

*Central
retaining
screw*

DUST COLLECTION BIN

*Hose
electricity
supply*

*Post-motor
micropore
filter*

Filter rim casing

Inner bin fin

Bin upper seal

Bin base

*Bin
handle*

*Bin lower
seal*

*Inner bin dust
collection area*

*Polycarbonate
plastic bin body*

*Bin cover
retaining clip*

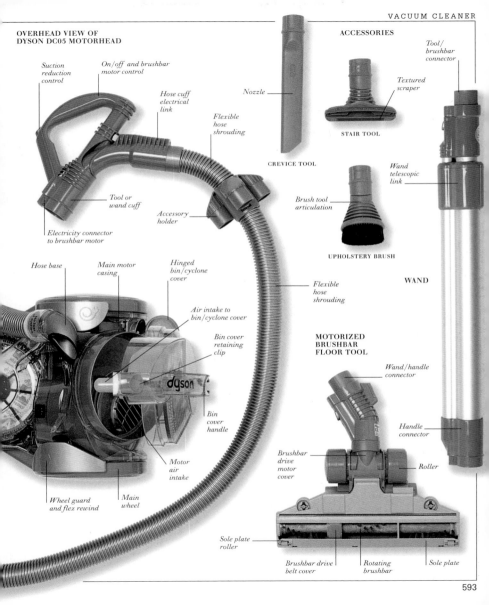

**OVERHEAD VIEW OF
DYSON DC05 MOTORHEAD**

*Suction
reduction
control*

*On/off and brushbar
motor control*

*Hose cuff
electrical
link*

*Flexible
hose
shrouding*

*Tool or
wand cuff*

*Accessory
holder*

*Electricity connector
to brushbar motor*

ACCESSORIES

*Tool/
brushbar
connector*

Nozzle

*Textured
scraper*

STAIR TOOL

CREVICE TOOL

*Wand
telescopic
link*

*Brush tool
articulation*

UPHOLSTERY BRUSH

WAND

Hose base

*Main motor
casing*

*Hinged
bin/cyclone
cover*

*Air intake to
bin/cyclone cover*

*Bin cover
retaining
clip*

*Flexible
hose
shrouding*

dyson

**MOTORIZED
BRUSHBAR
FLOOR TOOL**

*Wand/handle
connector*

*Bin
cover
handle*

*Motor
air
intake*

*Brushbar
drive
motor
cover*

*Handle
connector*

Roller

*Wheel guard
and flex rewind*

*Main
wheel*

*Sole plate
roller*

*Brushbar drive
belt cover*

*Rotating
brushbar*

Sole plate

Iron and washer-dryer

IN THE DAYS BEFORE WASHING MACHINES, laundry was done by hand—washed in a barrel, squeezed in a roller-mangle, hung on a line, and smoothed with an iron heated on the stove. In the 1880s, electrically heated irons were one of the first home electrical appliances. Today's iron still applies heat, sometimes moistened with steam, to dampen and flatten garment fibers. Machines with electric heaters and motors took the strain out of washing from the 1910s. Up to the 1960s, three machines were needed to wash, spin, and dry. Now clothes are swirled in a rotating ribbed tub of hot water, then spun fast to throw off most of the water, before slowly tumbling in electrically heated air to dry—all in one appliance.

FRONT VIEW OF A MIELE WASHER-DRYER

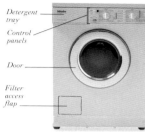

Detergent tray

Control panels

Door

Filter access flap

COMPONENTS OF A STEAM IRON

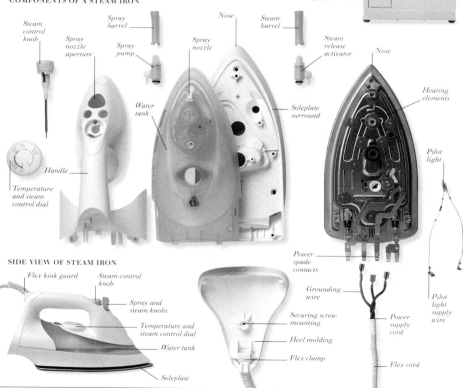

Steam control knob

Spray barrel

Spray nozzle aperture

Spray pump

Nose

Spray nozzle

Steam barrel

Steam release activator

Nose

Water tank

Heating elements

Soleplate surround

Pilot light

Handle

Temperature and steam control dial

Power spade contacts

Grounding wire

Pilot light supply wire

SIDE VIEW OF STEAM IRON

Flex kink guard

Steam control knob

Spray and steam knobs

Temperature and steam control dial

Water tank

Soleplate

Securing screw mounting

Heel molding

Flex clamp

Power supply cord

Flex cord

COMPONENTS OF A MIELE WASHER-DRYER

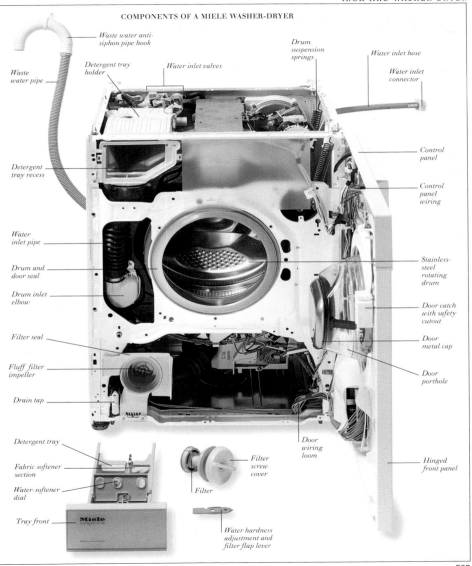

Waste water anti-siphon pipe hook

Detergent tray holder

Water inlet valves

Drum suspension springs

Water inlet hose

Water inlet connector

Waste water pipe

Detergent tray recess

Control panel

Control panel wiring

Water inlet pipe

Drum and door seal

Drum inlet elbow

Stainless-steel rotating drum

Door catch with safety cutout

Door metal cap

Filter seal

Fluff filter impeller

Drain tap

Door porthole

Door wiring loom

Detergent tray

Fabric softener section

Water-softener dial

Filter screw cover

Filter

Hinged front panel

Tray front

Miele

Water hardness adjustment and filter flap lever

595

Microwave combination oven

CONVENTIONAL OVENS use electrically
warmed elements or a flame to heat food.
In a microwave oven heat energy is created
by electromagnetic waves produced by a
magnetron and led by waveguides into the
oven compartment. These microwaves
cannot pass through the compartment's
metal casing, being reflected within and
spread evenly by a fan. But they do pass
through most types of plastic, ceramics, and
glass. Therefore platters or containers made
from these materials are suitable for use in
microwave ovens. A combination oven also
has conventional heating elements, to grill
and "brown" in the traditional fashion, either
alone or in conjunction with microwaves.

MICROWAVE COMBINATION OVEN

Turntable rotator

Door lock

Display screen

Control panel

Metal cook/grill tray (non-microwave)

Glass cooking turntable

Rollers

Metal turntable cover (non-microwave)

Metal grill/griddle (non-microwave)

Under-turntable roller ring (non-microwave)

HOW MICROWAVES HEAT FOOD

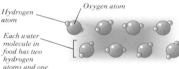

Hydrogen atom

Oxygen atom

Each water molecule in food has two hydrogen atoms and one oxygen atom

Microwaves make water molecules vibrate

Water molecules spin with energy from microwaves

Making the molecules move generates heat

SIDE VIEW OF MICROWAVE COMBINATION OVEN

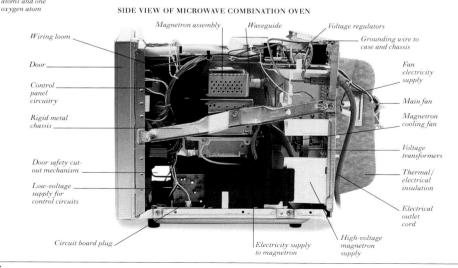

Magnetron assembly

Waveguide

Voltage regulators

Wiring loom

Grounding wire to case and chassis

Door

Fan electricity supply

Control panel circuitry

Main fan

Rigid metal chassis

Magnetron cooling fan

Voltage transformers

Door safety cut-out mechanism

Thermal/ electrical insulation

Low-voltage supply for control circuits

Electrical outlet cord

Circuit board plug

Electricity supply to magnetron

High-voltage magnetron supply

TOP VIEW OF MICROWAVE COMBINATION OVEN

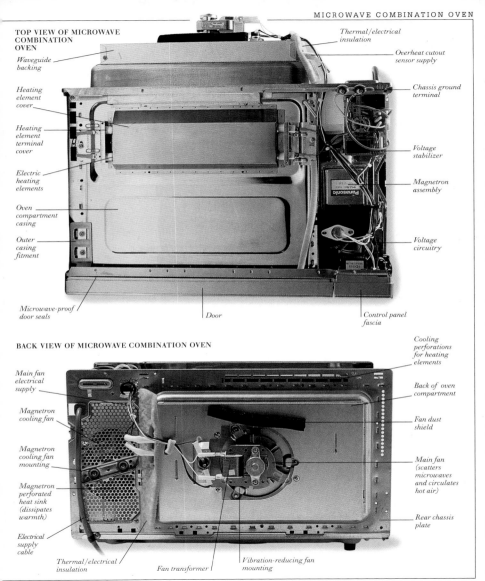

Thermal/electrical insulation

Overheat cutout sensor supply

Waveguide backing

Heating element cover

Heating element terminal cover

Electric heating elements

Oven compartment casing

Outer casing fitment

Chassis ground terminal

Voltage stabilizer

Magnetron assembly

Voltage circuitry

Microwave-proof door seals

Door

Control panel fascia

BACK VIEW OF MICROWAVE COMBINATION OVEN

Cooling perforations for heating elements

Main fan electrical supply

Magnetron cooling fan

Magnetron cooling fan mounting

Magnetron perforated heat sink (dissipates warmth)

Electrical supply cable

Back of oven compartment

Fan dust shield

Main fan (scatters microwaves and circulates hot air)

Rear chassis plate

Thermal/electrical insulation

Fan transformer

Vibration-reducing fan mounting

Toaster

MOST ELECTRIC TOASTERS not only grill slices of bread, but they also pop them up when ready. While the slices rest on a spring-loaded rack, electric heating elements toast the bread. At the same time, a bimetallic strip heats and expands. One of the two metals in this strip expands more quickly than the other, causing the strip to curve. As it bends, it completes an electrical circuit and activates an electromagnet. The magnet attracts a catch, releasing the spring that holds the rack down in the toaster. The elements switch off, and the toasted slices pop up.

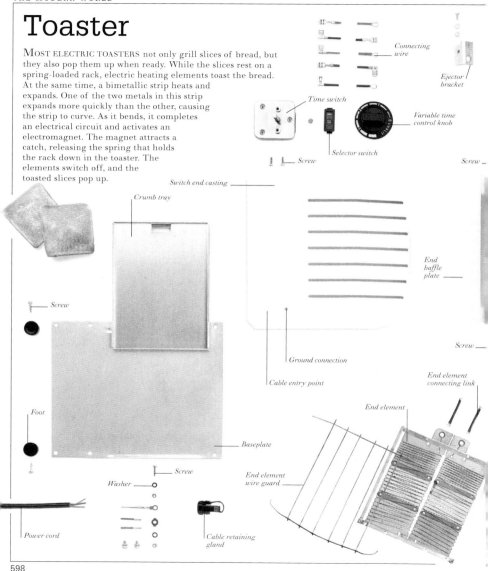

Connecting wire

Ejector bracket

Time switch

Variable time control knob

Selector switch

Screw

Screw

Switch end casting

Crumb tray

End baffle plate

Screw

Screw

Ground connection

Cable entry point

End element connecting link

End element

Foot

Baseplate

End element wire guard

Screw

Washer

Power cord

Cable retaining gland

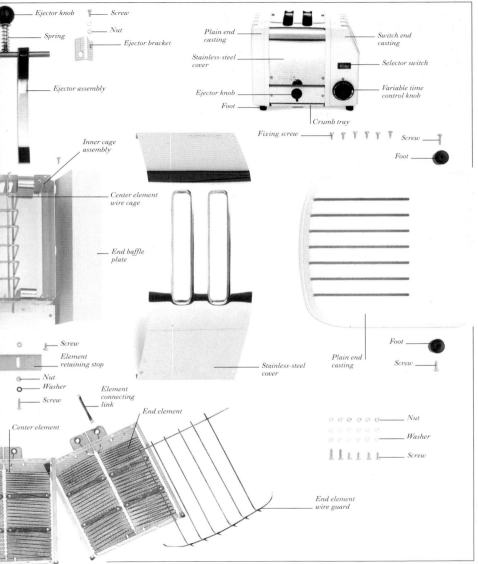

Ejector knob

Screw

Spring

Nut

Ejector bracket

Ejector assembly

Plain end casting

Switch end casting

Stainless-steel cover

Selector switch

Ejector knob

Variable time control knob

Foot

Crumb tray

Fixing screw

Screw

Foot

Inner cage assembly

Center element wire cage

End baffle plate

Plain end casting

Foot

Screw

Screw

Element retaining stop

Stainless-steel cover

Nut

Washer

Screw

Element connecting link

Nut

Washer

Screw

End element

Center element

End element wire guard

Drills

THE ELECTRICALLY POWERED MOTOR OF A POWER DRILL, cooled by a fan, turns a shaft at high speed. The shaft connects, in turn, to a system of gears that rotates a chuck even faster. Clamped by the chuck, a sharp bit cuts out the hole, and at the same time the bit's screw-shaped grooves channel the waste out of the hole. For drilling hard materials, many power drills have a hammer mechanism; when this is operated a ratchet in the gearcase causes the chuck and bit to pound in and out as they drill. A hand drill, although slower and less forceful than a power drill, is easier to control. For cutting wide holes, carpenters often prefer a brace-and-bit. This acts like a lever: the bowed handle of the brace moves a larger distance than the bit, turning the bit with extra force.

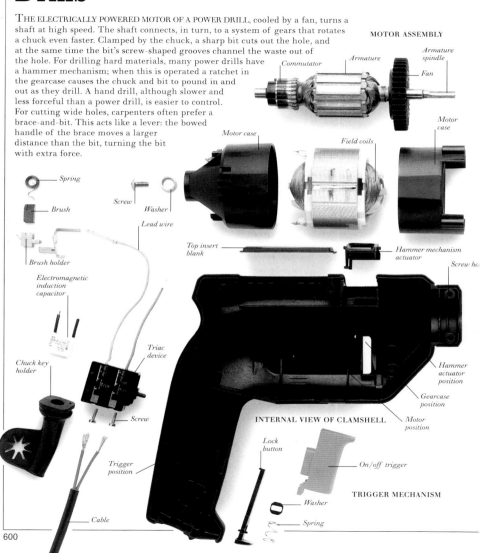

MOTOR ASSEMBLY

Commutator

Armature

Armature spindle

Fan

Motor case

Motor case

Field coils

Spring

Brush

Screw

Washer

Lead wire

Brush holder

Electromagnetic induction capacitor

Top insert blank

Hammer mechanism actuator

Screw ho

Chuck key holder

Triac device

Hammer actuator position

Gearcase position

INTERNAL VIEW OF CLAMSHELL

Motor position

Screw

Trigger position

Lock button

On/off trigger

TRIGGER MECHANISM

Washer

Cable

Spring

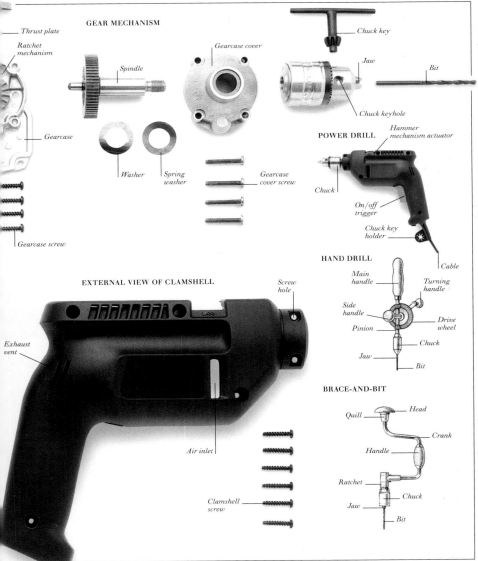

GEAR MECHANISM

Thrust plate

Ratchet mechanism

Spindle

Gearcase cover

Chuck key

Jaw

Bit

Gearcase

Chuck keyhole

Washer

Spring washer

Gearcase cover screw

Gearcase screw

POWER DRILL

Hammer mechanism actuator

Chuck

On/off trigger

Chuck key holder

Cable

HAND DRILL

Main handle

Turning handle

Side handle

Drive wheel

Pinion

Chuck

Jaw

Bit

EXTERNAL VIEW OF CLAMSHELL

Screw hole

Exhaust vent

Air inlet

Clamshell screw

BRACE-AND-BIT

Quill

Head

Crank

Handle

Ratchet

Chuck

Jaw

Bit

House of the future

HOUSES IN THE FUTURE are likely to be more environmentally friendly and energy-efficient than older dwellings, by making better use of materials and intelligent control systems. The Integer house was designed by Cole Thompson Associates, Bree Day Partnership, and Paul Hodgkins Associates, and built in conjunction with the Building Research Establishment in the UK. One of its key features is a large sun room that warms one side of the house. Extensive use is made of recycled, natural, and renewable materials and energy. The walls are made from timber and insulated with fiber from recycled newspaper; waste water from the bathrooms is saved and used to flush the toilets; and a wind turbine and solar panels contribute some of the electricity requirements. Many elements were prefabricated off-site for ease of construction. The Integer house uses only half the energy and a third less water than a traditionally built house.

WALL CONSTRUCTION

Cellulose fiber insulation

Vertical batten

Plasterboard

Vertical batten

Red cedar boarding

Noggin

Skirting board

Breather paper

Floating floor

Cables and ducting

Wooden boarding

SIDE AND REAR VIEW OF THE INTEGER HOUSE

Single-glazed sun room

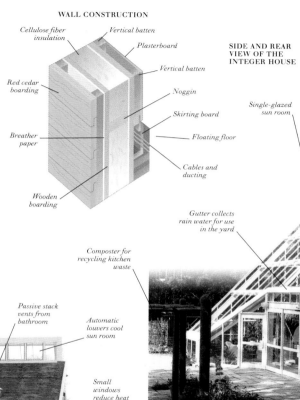

Gutter collects rain water for use in the yard

Composter for recycling kitchen waste

FRONT VIEW OF THE INTEGER HOUSE

Turfed roof helps to regulate temperature

Passive stack vents from bathroom

Automatic louvers cool sun room

Small windows reduce heat loss

Red cedar walls that do not require painting or staining

Intelligent electronic door-lock

Hatch for home deliveries

ROOF CONSTRUCTION

Sedum turf

Mineral wool

Timber trellis

Root-proof membrane

Polyurethane insulation

Vapor barrier

Plywood roof deck

FM and TV antenna feeds into an integrated multimedia network

Solar collector heats water

Automatic louvers to cool sun room

Photovoltaic panel generates electricity

Security light

Window to upper floor home office

Timber bay window to living and dining area

Earth bank insulates lower floor

Blinds that open and close automatically in response to sunshine

SUN ROOM INTERIOR

Renewable energy

RENEWABLE ENERGY COMES from sources that do not become depleted as we use the energy. When a fossil fuel such as coal is burned, it is gone forever, but a renewable source remains available no matter how much is used. The tides, waves, flowing water, sunlight, and the wind are all renewable sources of energy. Wind and water energy are captured by a device called a turbine. The turbine spins and drives an electricity generator. Energy from sunlight, or solar energy, is changed into electricity in two main ways. One uses mirrors to concentrate solar energy and magnify its heating effect which is used to change water into steam to drive turbines. Photovoltaic cells change sunlight directly into electricity. A cell is made from two layers of silicon. One gives out electrons (negative particles) and the other receives them. Sunlight knocks electrons out of atoms where the two layers meet, separating them from the positive particles. The electrons are attracted to one layer of the cell, the positive particles to the other layer. Electrons are naturally attracted to the positive particles, but to come together again, the electrons must flow out of the cell, through an external electric circuit, or load, and back to the other side of the cell, creating a charge. The cell supplies electric current for as long as light keeps falling on it.

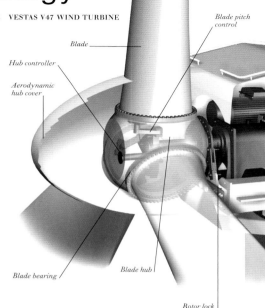

VESTAS V47 WIND TURBINE

Blade pitch control

Blade

Hub controller

Aerodynamic hub cover

Blade bearing

Blade hub

Rotor lock

TIDAL POWER

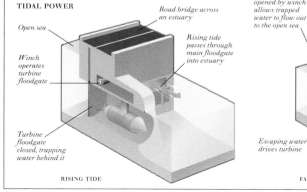

Road bridge across an estuary

Open sea

Winch operates turbine floodgate

Turbine floodgate closed, trapping water behind it

RISING TIDE

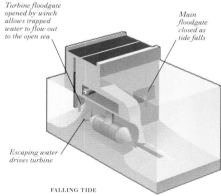

Rising tide passes through main floodgate into estuary

Turbine floodgate opened by winch allows trapped water to flow out to the open sea

Main floodgate closed as tide falls

Escaping water drives turbine

FALLING TIDE

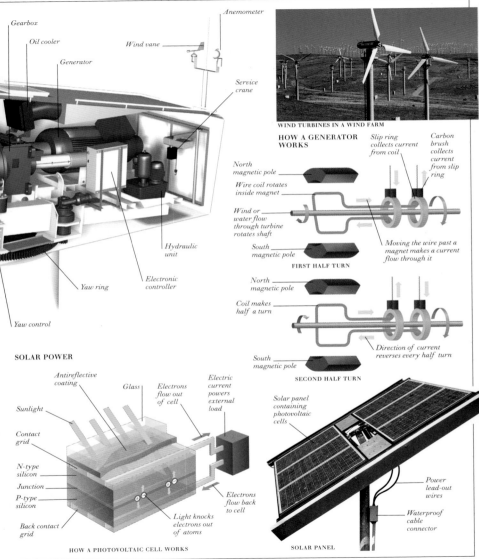

Gearbox

Oil cooler

Generator

Anemometer

Wind vane

Service crane

WIND TURBINES IN A WIND FARM

HOW A GENERATOR WORKS

Slip ring collects current from coil

Carbon brush collects current from slip ring

North magnetic pole

Wire coil rotates inside magnet

Wind or water flow through turbine rotates shaft

South magnetic pole

Moving the wire past a magnet makes a current flow through it

FIRST HALF TURN

North magnetic pole

Coil makes half a turn

South magnetic pole

Direction of current reverses every half turn

SECOND HALF TURN

Hydraulic unit

Electronic controller

Yaw ring

Yaw control

SOLAR POWER

Antireflective coating

Glass

Electrons flow out of cell

Electric current powers external load

Sunlight

Contact grid

N-type silicon

Junction

P-type silicon

Back contact grid

Light knocks electrons out of atoms

Electrons flow back to cell

HOW A PHOTOVOLTAIC CELL WORKS

Solar panel containing photovoltaic cells

Power lead-out wires

Waterproof cable connector

SOLAR PANEL

Cloning technology

IN A LIVING CELL THE GENETIC MATERIAL DNA (deoxyribonucleic acid) contains thousands of units called genes that carry instructions for development, growth, and repair of the living creature. During normal reproduction, half the mother's genetic material contained in an egg cell joins with half the genetic material from the father carried in a sperm cell, to form a unique new genome (set of genes) for a new life. During the early stages of embryo development, the fertilized egg divides into stem cells, which have the potential to become specialized into the hundreds of cell types in a body. Through therapeutic cloning, stem cells can be produced in a laboratory. It is hoped that in the future this technology can be used to grow new tissue that can be transplanted back into the donor to treat illness, without fear of rejection— when the body recognizes a transplanted part as "foreign" because it has different genes, and tries to destroy it. In another form of cloning, performed experimentally using animals, genetic material from a donor animal has been inserted into an egg from another animal that has been emptied of its own genetic material, to produce an animal genetically identical to the donor.

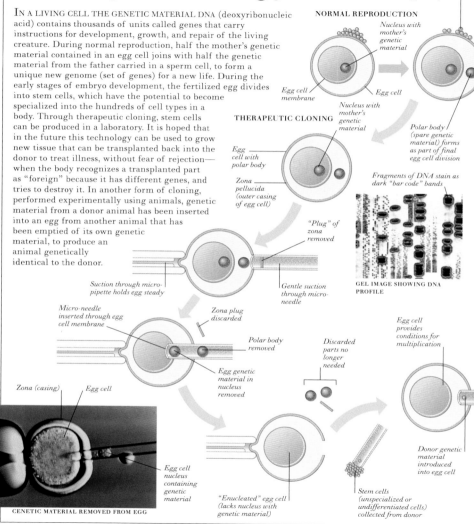

NORMAL REPRODUCTION

Spare cells from egg development

Nucleus with mother's genetic material

Egg cell membrane

Egg cell

Nucleus with mother's genetic material

Polar body (spare genetic material) forms as part of final egg cell division

THERAPEUTIC CLONING

Egg cell with polar body

Zona pellucida (outer casing of egg cell)

Fragments of DNA stain as dark "bar code" bands

"Plug" of zona removed

Suction through micro-pipette holds egg steady

Gentle suction through micro-needle

GEL IMAGE SHOWING DNA PROFILE

Micro-needle inserted through egg cell membrane

Zona plug discarded

Polar body removed

Egg genetic material in nucleus removed

Discarded parts no longer needed

Egg cell provides conditions for multiplication

Zona (casing)   Egg cell

Egg cell nucleus containing genetic material

"Enucleated" egg cell (lacks nucleus with genetic material)

Stem cells (unspecialized or undifferentiated cells) collected from donor

Donor genetic material introduced into egg cell

CENETIC MATERIAL REMOVED FROM EGG

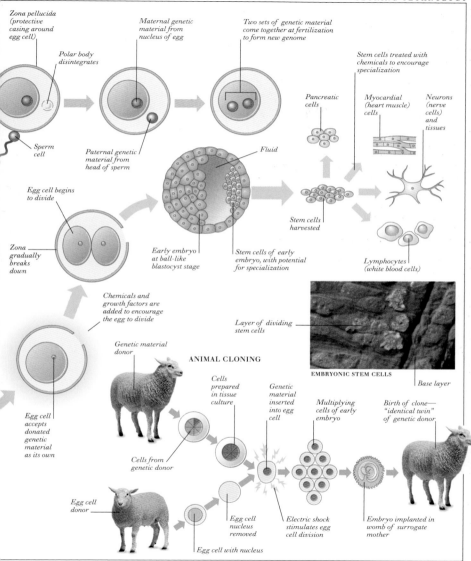

Zona pellucida (protective casing around egg cell)

Polar body disintegrates

Maternal genetic material from nucleus of egg

Two sets of genetic material come together at fertilization to form new genome

Stem cells treated with chemicals to encourage specialization

Pancreatic cells

Myocardial (heart muscle) cells

Neurons (nerve cells) and tissues

Sperm cell

Paternal genetic material from head of sperm

Fluid

Egg cell begins to divide

Zona gradually breaks down

Early embryo at ball-like blastocyst stage

Stem cells of early embryo, with potential for specialization

Stem cells harvested

Lymphocytes (white blood cells)

Chemicals and growth factors are added to encourage the egg to divide

Layer of dividing stem cells

Genetic material donor

ANIMAL CLONING

EMBRYONIC STEM CELLS

Base layer

Egg cell accepts donated genetic material as its own

Cells prepared in tissue culture

Genetic material inserted into egg cell

Multiplying cells of early embryo

Birth of clone— "identical twin" of genetic donor

Cells from genetic donor

Egg cell donor

Egg cell nucleus removed

Electric shock stimulates egg cell division

Embryo implanted in womb of surrogate mother

Egg cell with nucleus

Robots

ROBOTS ARE
MACHINES THAT CAN
carry out a variety of
tasks on their own,
with little or no human
control. Most robots are
mechanical arms used to build
things in factories. The end of the
robot's arm can be equipped with
different tools for gripping, drilling,
cutting, welding, and painting. Robot
toys have become popular, too. They
incorporate sensors that respond to
sounds and sometimes touch. Some of them
can even understand spoken words. Scientists are
also trying to create more advanced, humanlike
robots that can see, hear, learn, and make their own
decisions. ASIMO, a robot developed by the Japanese
car manufacturer Honda, is one of these advanced
humanoid robots. ASIMO stands for Advanced Step
in Innovative MObility. It looks like a small astronaut
wearing a backpack. ASIMO can walk, talk, carry things,
recognize familiar faces, and respond to its name. It was
the first robot that could walk independently and climb
stairs. There are robot toys, too, in the shape of animals
with simple artificial intelligence.

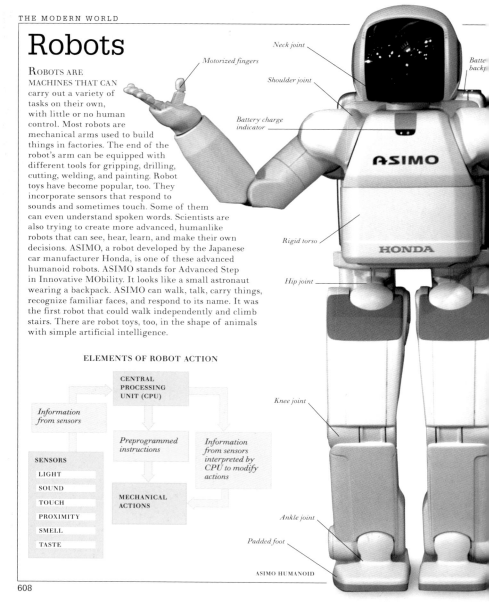

Motorized fingers

Neck joint

Shoulder joint

Battery charge indicator

Battery backpack

Rigid torso

Hip joint

Knee joint

Ankle joint

Padded foot

ASIMO HUMANOID

ELEMENTS OF ROBOT ACTION

CENTRAL PROCESSING UNIT (CPU)

Information from sensors

Preprogrammed instructions

Information from sensors interpreted by CPU to modify actions

SENSORS

LIGHT

SOUND

TOUCH

PROXIMITY

SMELL

TASTE

MECHANICAL ACTIONS

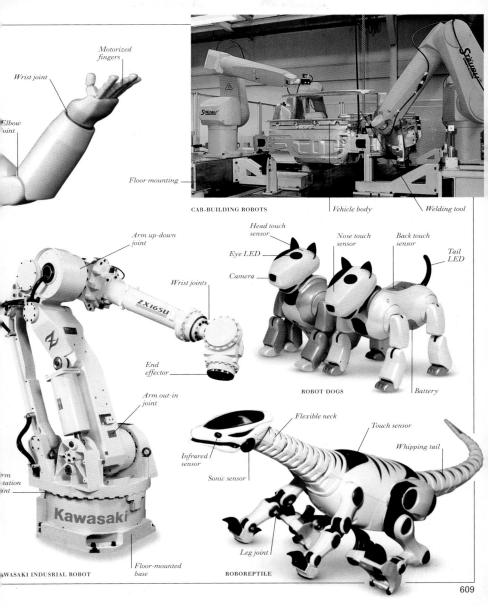

Wrist joint

Motorized fingers

Elbow joint

Floor mounting

CAR-BUILDING ROBOTS

Vehicle body

Welding tool

Arm up-down joint

Wrist joints

End effector

Arm out-in joint

Arm rotation joint

KAWASAKI INDUSRIAL ROBOT

Floor-mounted base

Head touch sensor

Eye LED

Camera

Nose touch sensor

Back touch sensor

Tail LED

ROBOT DOGS

Battery

Flexible neck

Touch sensor

Whipping tail

Infrared sensor

Sonic sensor

Leg joint

ROBOREPTILE

609

High-performance microscopes

OPTICAL MICROSCOPES FORM A MAGNIFIED image by using lenses to bend light. Some special-purpose optical microscopes used in industry and research are designed for observing particular materials, such as living cells. They produce magnifications of up to about 2,000. Electron microscopes produce magnifications of as much as 50 million, although 2 million is more typical. Their images are formed by means of electrons focused by magnetic lenses. There are two main types: scanning electron microscopes (SEMs) scan electrons back and forth across the surface of a specimen; transmission electron microscopes (TEMs) transmit electrons through a thin slice of the specimen.

FEI TECNAI G² TRANSMISSION ELECTRON MICROSCOPE

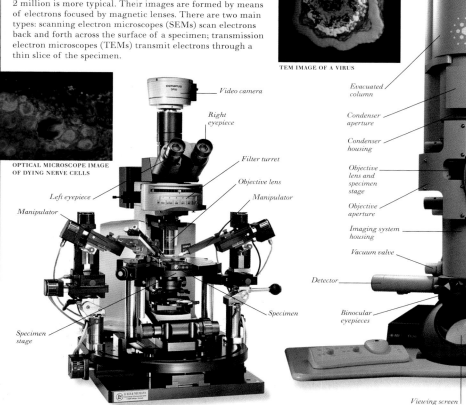

TEM IMAGE OF A VIRUS

Electron gun housing

Evacuated column

Condenser aperture

Condenser housing

Objective lens and specimen stage

Objective aperture

Imaging system housing

Vacuum valve

Detector

Binocular eyepieces

Viewing screen

OPTICAL MICROSCOPE IMAGE OF DYING NERVE CELLS

Video camera

Right eyepiece

Filter turret

Objective lens

Left eyepiece

Manipulator

Manipulator

Specimen

Specimen stage

OLYMPUS BX51W1 OPTICAL MICROSCOPE

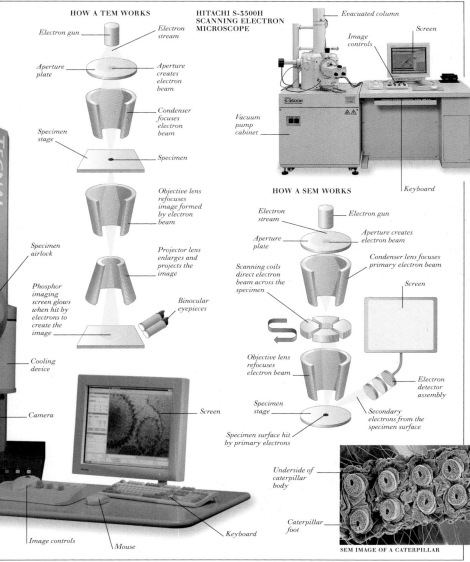

HOW A TEM WORKS

Electron gun
Electron stream
Aperture plate
Aperture creates electron beam
Condenser focuses electron beam
Specimen stage
Specimen
Objective lens refocuses image formed by electron beam
Projector lens enlarges and projects the image
Specimen airlock
Phosphor imaging screen glows when hit by electrons to create the image
Binocular eyepieces
Cooling device
Camera
Screen
Image controls
Mouse
Keyboard

TECNAI

HITACHI S-3500H SCANNING ELECTRON MICROSCOPE

Evacuated column
Image controls
Screen
Vacuum pump cabinet
Keyboard

HOW A SEM WORKS

Electron stream
Electron gun
Aperture plate
Aperture creates electron beam
Condenser lens focuses primary electron beam
Scanning coils direct electron beam across the specimen
Screen
Objective lens refocuses electron beam
Specimen stage
Specimen surface hit by primary electrons
Electron detector assembly
Secondary electrons from the specimen surface

Underside of caterpillar body
Caterpillar foot

SEM IMAGE OF A CATERPILLAR

Space telescope

SPACE TELESCOPES ORBIT THE EARTH hundreds of miles above the ground, their instruments collecting light from stars and galaxies. Telescopes in space have a clearer view than those on Earth, because they are unaffected by the Earth's atmosphere, which absorbs or distorts much of this radiation. There are a variety of types of space telescope designed to observe different types of light. The Hubble Space Telescope observes infrared, ultraviolet, and visible light. It can detect objects that are 100 times fainter than those any telescopes on Earth can see. When this 12-ton (11,000-kilogram), 43-foot (13-meter) long telescope was launched by the Space Shuttle in 1990, it was found that its primary mirror was faulty and its images were blurred. Astronauts fitted extra optics to correct the problem in 1993.

IMAGES TAKEN BY HUBBLE

Pillar of gas

CONE NEBULA

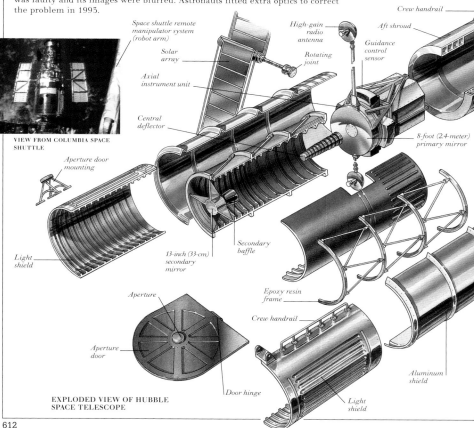

VIEW FROM COLUMBIA SPACE SHUTTLE

Space shuttle remote manipulator system (robot arm)

Solar array

Axial instrument unit

Central deflector

High-gain radio antenna

Rotating joint

Crew handrail

Aft shroud

Guidance control sensor

8-foot (2.4-meter) primary mirror

Aperture door mounting

Light shield

13-inch (33-cm) secondary mirror

Secondary baffle

Epoxy resin frame

Crew handrail

Aperture

Aperture door

Door hinge

Light shield

Aluminum shield

EXPLODED VIEW OF HUBBLE SPACE TELESCOPE

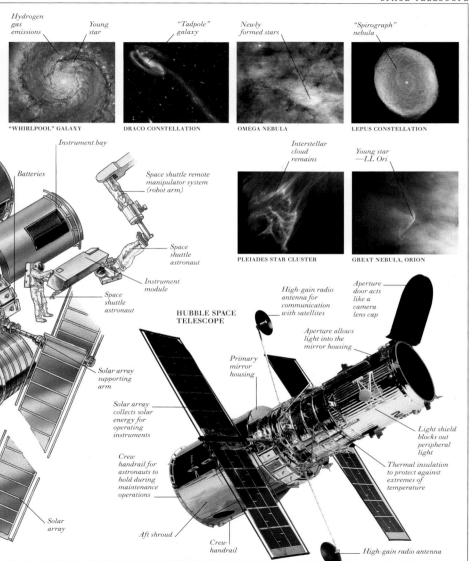

Hydrogen gas emissions

Young star

"WHIRLPOOL" GALAXY

"Tadpole" galaxy

DRACO CONSTELLATION

Newly formed stars

OMEGA NEBULA

"Spirograph" nebula

LEPUS CONSTELLATION

Instrument bay

Batteries

Space shuttle remote manipulator system (robot arm)

Space shuttle astronaut

Instrument module

Space shuttle astronaut

Interstellar cloud remains

PLEIADES STAR CLUSTER

Young star —LL Ori

GREAT NEBULA, ORION

High-gain radio antenna for communication with satellites

HUBBLE SPACE TELESCOPE

Aperture door acts like a camera lens cap

Aperture allows light into the mirror housing

Primary mirror housing

Solar array supporting arm

Solar array collects solar energy for operating instruments

Crew handrail for astronauts to hold during maintenance operations

Light shield blocks out peripheral light

Thermal insulation to protect against extremes of temperature

Solar array

Aft shroud

Crew handrail

High-gain radio antenna

Probing the solar system

SPACE PROBES HAVE VISITED every planet in the solar system. They take photographs and gather data that cannot be collected using Earth-based equipment. Some probes fly past or orbit around planets or moons, while others land. Two Voyager space probes flew past the outer planets in the 1970s and 1980s. Two Viking spacecraft landed on Mars in 1976. The Magellan spacecraft orbited Venus from 1989 and mapped its surface. The Pathfinder spacecraft landed on Mars in 1997 and released a rover vehicle to explore the surface. The Mars Exploration Rover (MER) Mission landed two rovers in 2003. The Cassini space probe reached Saturn in 2004, and in 2005 its mini-probe, Huygens, landed on one of its moons, Titan, and became the first probe to land on a moon of another planet.

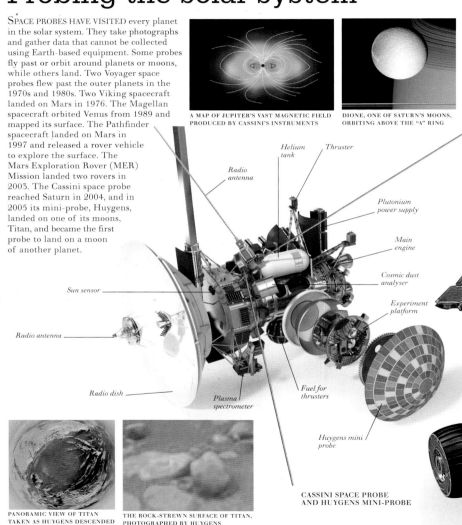

A MAP OF JUPITER'S VAST MAGNETIC FIELD PRODUCED BY CASSINI'S INSTRUMENTS

DIONE, ONE OF SATURN'S MOONS, ORBITING ABOVE THE "A" RING

Helium tank

Thruster

Radio antenna

Plutonium power supply

Main engine

Cosmic dust analyser

Sun sensor

Experiment platform

Radio antenna

Radio dish

Plasma spectrometer

Fuel for thrusters

Huygens mini probe

CASSINI SPACE PROBE AND HUYGENS MINI-PROBE

PANORAMIC VIEW OF TITAN TAKEN AS HUYGENS DESCENDED

THE ROCK-STREWN SURFACE OF TITAN, PHOTOGRAPHED BY HUYGENS

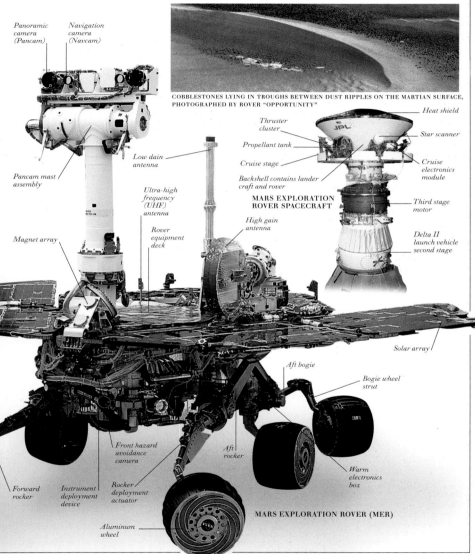

Panoramic camera (Pancam)

Navigation camera (Navcam)

COBBLESTONES LYING IN TROUGHS BETWEEN DUST RIPPLES ON THE MARTIAN SURFACE, PHOTOGRAPHED BY ROVER "OPPORTUNITY"

Pancam mast assembly

Low dain antenna

Ultra-high frequency (UHF) antenna

Rover equipment deck

Magnet array

Thruster cluster

Heat shield

Star scanner

Propellant tank

Cruise stage

Backshell contains lander craft and rover

High gain antenna

Cruise electronics module

MARS EXPLORATION ROVER SPACECRAFT

Third stage motor

Delta II launch vehicle second stage

Solar array

Aft bogie

Bogie wheel strut

Front hazard avoidance camera

Aft rocker

Warm electronics box

Forward rocker

Instrument deployment device

Rocker deployment actuator

MARS EXPLORATION ROVER (MER)

Aluminum wheel

Physical map of the world

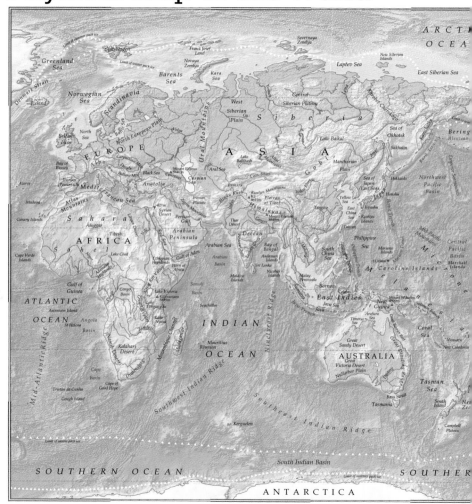

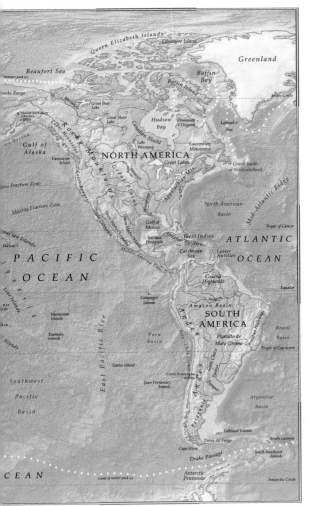

THIS MAP DEPICTS the surface of the Earth today, showing its physical features both above and below sea level. The outer layer of the Earth is called the crust, and it is broken into several pieces called tectonic plates. These plates move slowly on the upper mantle of the Earth. Although tectonic plates move only an inch or so every year, over the course of Earth's history the plates have moved thousands of miles to create new oceans, mountain chains, and continents. Continental drift determines the distribution of the continents, which are propelled by currents rising from the intense heat at the Earth's center. There are seven continents on Earth; these are (from largest to smallest) Asia, Africa, North America, South America, Antarctica, Europe, and Australasia. The physical features of the land are remarkably varied. Among the most notable are mountain ranges, rivers, and deserts. The largest mountain ranges—the Himalayas in Asia and the Andes in South America—extend for thousands of kilometers. The Himalayas include the world's highest mountain, Mount Everest (29,029 ft /8,848 m). The longest rivers are the River Nile in Africa (4,160 ft / 6,695 km) and the Amazon River in South America (4,000 miles /6,437 km). Deserts cover about 20 percent of the total land area. The largest is the Sahara, which covers nearly a third of Africa. Most of Earth is not made up of land, however, but of water—it accounts for about 70 percent of the Earth's surface. The largest single body of water, the Pacific Ocean, alone covers about 30 percent of Earth. The physical features of Earth are not permanent—tectonic forces, weathering and erosion, means that the Earth's surface is constantly changing.

Elevation

						Below sea level	0	250m	500m	1000m	2000m	3000m	4000m	6000m
-6000m	-4000m	-2000m	-1000m	-500m	-250m									
-19,658ft	-13,124ft	-6562ft	-3281ft	-1640ft	-820ft	-328ft/-100m	0	820ft	1640ft	3281ft	6562ft	9843ft	13,124ft	19,685ft

Time zones

The world is divided into 24 time zones, measured in relation to 12 noon Coordinated Universal Time (UTC), on the Greenwich Meridian (0°). Time advances by one hour for every 15° longitude east of Greenwich (and goes back one hour for every 15° west), but the system is adjusted in line with administrative boundaries. Numbers on the map indicate the number of hours that must be added to, or subtracted from UTC to calculate the time in each zone. Thus, the eastern United States (−5) is 5 hours behind UTC.

TYPES OF CALENDAR

GREGORIAN
The 365-day Gregorian calendar was introduced by Pope Gregory XIII in 1582 and is now in use throughout most of the Western world. Every four years (leap year) an extra day is added. Below are the names of the months (and number of days).

January (31)	July (31)
February (28, 29 in leap years)	August (31)
March (31)	September (30)
April (30)	October (31)
May (31)	November (30)
June (30)	December (31)

JEWISH
The Jewish calendar is a lunar calendar adapted to the solar year. It normally has 12 months but in leap years, which occur seven times in every cycle of 19 years, there are 13 months. The years are calculated from the Creation (which is placed at 3761 BC); the months are Nisan, Iyyar, Sivan, Thammuz, Ab, Elul, Tishri, Hesvan, Kislev, Tebet, Sebat, and Adar, with an intercalary month (First Adar) being added in leap years.

ISLAMIC
The Islamic calendar is based on a year of 12 months, each month beginning roughly at the time of the New Moon. The months are Muharram, Safar, Rabi'I, Rabi'II, Jumada I, Jumada II, Rajab, Sha'ban, Ramadan, Shawwal, Dhu l-Qa'dah, and Dhu l-Hijja.

CHINESE
The Chinese calendar is a lunar calendar, with a year consisting of 12 months. Intercalary months are added to keep the calendar in step with the solar year of 365 days. Months are referred to by a number within a year, but also by animal names that, from ancient times, have been attached to years and hours of the day.

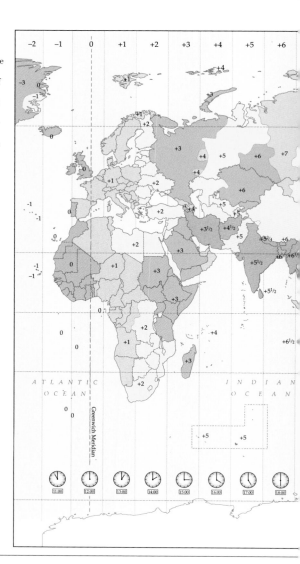

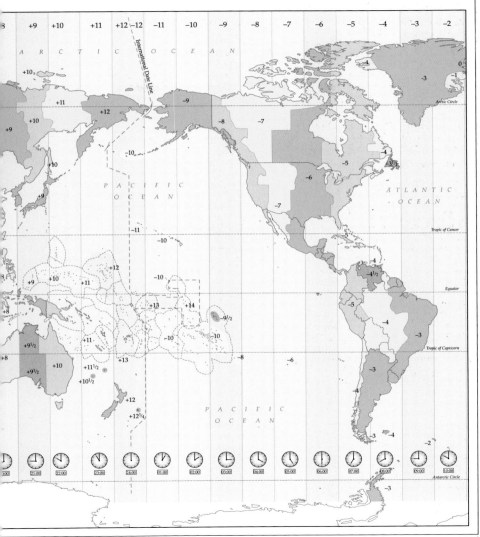

Useful data

UNITS OF MEASUREMENT

METRIC UNIT	EQUIVALENT
Length	
1 centimeter (cm)	10 millimeters (mm)
1 meter (m)	100 centimeters
1 kilometer (km)	1,000 meters
Mass	
1 kilogram (kg)	1,000 grams (g)
1 metric ton (t)	1,000 kilograms
Area	
1 square centimeter (cm²)	100 square millimeters (mm²)
1 square meter (m²)	10,000 square centimeters
1 hectare	10,000 square meters
1 square kilometer (km²)	1,000,000 square meters
Volume	
1 cubic centimeter (cc)	1 milliliter (ml)
1 liter (l)	1,000 milliliters
1 cubic meter (m³)	1,000 liters
Capacity (liquid and dry measures)	
1 centiliter (cl)	10 milliliters (ml)
1 deciliter (dl)	10 centiliters
1 liter (l)	10 deciliters
1 decaliter (dal)	10 liters
1 hectoliter (hi)	10 decaliters
1 kiloliter (kl)	10 hectoliters

IMPERIAL UNIT	EQUIVALENT
Length	
1 foot (ft)	12 inches (in)
1 yard (yd)	3 feet
1 rod (rd)	5½ yards
1 mile (mi)	1,760 yards
Mass	
1 dram (dr)	27.344 grains (gr)
1 ounce (oz)	16 drams
1 pound (lb)	16 ounces
1 hundredweight (cwt) (long)	112 pounds
1 hundredweight (cwt) (short)	100 pounds
1 ton (long)	2,240 pounds
1 ton (short)	2,000 pounds
Area	
1 square foot (ft²)	144 square inches (in²)
9 square feet	1 square yard (yd²)
1 acre	4,840 square yards
1 square mile	640 acres
Volume	
1 cubic foot	1,728 cubic inches
1 cubic yard	27 cubic feet
Capacity (liquid and dry measures)	
1 fluidram (fl dr)	60 minims (min)
1 fluid ounce (fl oz)	8 fluidrams
1 gill (gi)	5 fluid ounces
1 pint (pt)	4 gills
1 quart (qt)	2 pints
1 gallon (gal)	4 quarts
1 peck (pk)	2 gallons
1 bushel (bu)	4 pecks

NUMBER SYSTEMS

ROMAN	ARABIC
I	1
II	2
III	3
IV	4
V	5
VI	6
VII	7
VIII	8
IX	9
X	10
XI	11
XII	12
XIII	13
XIV	14
XV	15
XX	20
XXI	21
XXX	30
XL	40
L	50
LX	60
LXX	70
LXXX	80
XC	90
C	100
CI	101
CC	200
CCC	300
CD	400
D	500
DC	600
DCC	700
DCCC	800
CM	900
M	1,000
MM	2,000

METRIC TO IMPERIAL CONVERSIONS

TO CONVERT	INTO	MULTIPLY BY
Length		
Centimeters	inches	0.3937
Meters	feet	3.2810
Kilometers	miles	0.6214
Meters	yards	1.0940
Mass		
Grams	ounces	0.0352
Kilograms	pounds	2.2050
Metric tons	long tons	0.9843
Metric tons	short tons	1.1025
Area		
Square centimeters	square inches	0.1550
Square meters	square feet	10.7600
Hectares	acres	2.4710
Square kilometers	square miles	0.3861
Square meters	square yards	1.1960
Volume		
Cubic centimeters	cubic inches	0.0610
Cubic meters	cubic feet	35.3100
Capacity		
Liters	pints	1.7600
Liters	gallons	0.2200

IMPERIAL TO METRIC CONVERSIONS

TO CONVERT	INTO	MULTIPLY BY
Length		
Inches	centimeters	2.5400
Feet	meters	0.3048
Miles	kilometers	1.6090
Yards	meters	0.9144
Mass		
Ounces	grams	28.3500
Pounds	kilograms	0.4536
Long tons	metric tons	1.0160
Short tons	metric tons	0.9070
Area		
Square inches	square centimeters	6.4520
Square feet	square meters	0.0929
Acres	hectares	0.4047
Square miles	square kilometers	2.5900
Square yards	square meters	0.8361
Volume		
Cubic inches	cubic centimeters	16.3900
Cubic feet	cubic meters	0.0283
Capacity		
Pints	liters	0.5683
Gallons	liters	4.5460

RULES OF ALGEBRA

EXPRESSION	COMMENTS	EXPRESSION BECOMES
a + a	Simple addition	2a
a + b = c + d	Subtract b from either side	a = c + d - b
ab = cd	Divide both sides by b	a = cd ÷ b
(a + b) (c + d)	Multiplication of bracketed terms	ac + ad + be + bd
a^2 + ab	Use parentheses	a(a + b)
$(a + b)^2$	Expand terms in parentheses	$a^2 + 2ab + b^2$
$a^2 - b^2$	Difference of two squares	(a + b)(a-b)
1/a + 1/b	Find common denominator	(a + b)/ab
a/b ÷ c/d	Dividing by a fraction is the same as multiplying by its reciprocal	a/b × d/c

POWERS OF TEN USED WITH SCIENTIFIC UNITS

FACTOR	NAME	PREFIX	SYMBOL
10^{18}	quintillion	exa-	E
10^{15}	quadrillion	peta-	P
10^{12}	trillion	tera-	T
10^9	billion	giga-	G
10^6	million	mega-	M
10^5	thousand	kilo-	k
10^2	hundred	hecto-	h
10^1	ten	deca-	da
10^{-1}	one-tenth	deci-	d
10^{-2}	one-hundredth	centi-	c
10^{-3}	one-thousandth	milli-	m
10^{-6}	one-millionth	micro-	u
10^{-9}	one-billionth	nano-	n
10^{-12}	one-trillionth	pico-	p
10^{-15}	one-quadrillionth	femto-	f
10^{-18}	one-quintillionth	atto-	a

Note: The American system of numeration for denominations above one million is used in this book. In this system, each of the denominations above one billion (1,000 millions) is 1,000 times the preceding one.

BIOLOGY SYMBOLS

SYMBOL	MEANING
O	female individual (used in inheritance charts)
□	male individual (used in inheritance charts)
♀	female
♂	male
×	crossed with; hybrid
+	wild type
F_1	offspring of the first generation
F_2	offspring of the second generation

TEMPERATURE SCALES

To convert from Fahrenheit (F) to Celsius (C): C = (F—32) × 5 ÷ 9
To convert from Celsius to Fahrenheit: F = (C × 9 ÷ 5) + 32
To convert from Celsius to Kelvin (K): K = C + 273
To convert from Kelvin to Celsius: C = K - 273

Celsius	-20	-10	0	10	20	30	40	50	60	70	80	90	100
Fahrenheit	-4	14	32	50	68	86	104	122	140	158	176	194	212
Kelvin	255	265	273	283	293	303	313	323	333	343	353	363	373

MATHEMATICAL SYMBOLS

SYMBOL	EXPLANATION
+	addition
-	subtraction
×	multiplication
÷	division
=	equals
≠	does not equal
>	greater than
<	less than
≥	greater than or equal to
≤	less than or equal to
∞	infinity
%	percent
π	pi (3.1416)
°	degree
≈	is approximately equal to
∠	angle
∏	parallel to
Σ	summation
u, u	vectors
f(x)	function
!	factorial
√	square root
ξ	universal set
A ∩ B	intersection
A ∪ B	unison
A ⊂ B	subset
Ø	null set

PHYSICS SYMBOLS

SYMBOL	MEANING
α	alpha particle
β	beta ray
γ	gamma ray; photon
ε	electromotive force
η	efficiency; viscosity
λ	wavelength
μ	micro-; permeability
ν	frequency; neutrino
ρ	density; resistivity
σ	conductivity
c	velocity of light
e	electronic charge

CHEMISTRY SYMBOLS

SYMBOL	MEANING
+	plus; together with
−	single bond
•	single bond; single unpaired electron; two separate parts or compounds regarded as loosely joined
=	double bond
≡	triple bond
R	group
X	halogen atom
Z	atomic number

SCIENTIFIC NOTATION

NUMBER	NUMBER BETWEEN 1 AND 10	POWER OF TEN	SCIENTIFIC NOTATION
10	1	10^1	1 3 10^1
150	1.5	$10^2 (= 100)$	1.5 3 10^2
274,000,000	2.74	$10^8 (= 100,000,000)$	2.74 3 10^8
0.0023	2.3	$10^{-3} (= 0.001)$	2.3 3 10^{-3}

TRIGONOMETRY

Angle A (degrees)	sin A	cos A	tan A
0	0	1	0
30	1/2	√3/2	1/√3
45	1/√2	1/√2	1
60	√3/2	1/2	√3
90	1	0	∞

Shapes: Plane

Two-dimensional shapes are termed plane (or flat) shapes. Plane shapes constructed with straight sides, as illustrated here, are called polygons. They are categorized according to the number of sides they have—for example, three-sided polygons are known as triangles. A polygon that has sides of equal length and internal angles of equal size, such as a square, is said to be regular.

AREAS AND PERIMETERS

The formulae for calculating the areas and perimeters of simple plane shapes were devised by Classical Greek mathematicians.

SCALENE TRIANGLE
A triangle (three-sided polygon) with no equal sides or angles.

ISOSCELES TRIANGLE
A triangle with only two sides and two angles equal.

RIGHT-ANGLED TRIANGLE
A triangle with one angle as a right angle (90°).

CIRCLE
r = radius
d = diameter = 2 × r

Circumference = $2 \times \pi \times r$
Area = $\pi \times r^2$
($\pi = 3.1416$)

EQUILATERAL TRIANGLE
A regular triangle.
All angles are 60°.

SQUARE
A regular quadrilateral.
All angles are 90°.

RHOMBUS
A quadrilateral with all sides equal and two pairs of equal angles.

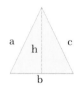

TRIANGLE
Height = h
Sides = a, b, c

Perimeter = $a + b + c$
Area = $\frac{1}{2} \times b \times h$

RECTANGLE
A quadrilateral with four right angles and opposite sides of equal length.

PARALLELOGRAM
A quadrilateral with two pairs of parallel sides.

TRAPEZIUM
A quadrilateral with one pair of parallel sides.

RECTANGLE
Sides = a, b

Perimeter = $2 \times (a + b)$
Area = $a \times b$

PENTAGON
A five-sided polygon. A regular pentagon is shown above.

HEXAGON
A six-sided polygon. A regular hexagon is shown above.

OCTAGON
An eight-sided polygon. A regular octagon is shown above.

Shapes: Solid

Three-dimensional shapes are known as solid shapes and include spheres, cubes, and pyramids. A solid shape with a polygon at each face is called a polyhedron.

SURFACE AREAS AND VOLUMES

Volume refers to the amount of space that a solid object occupies. Its surface area is the sum of the area of each of its faces.

TETRAHEDRON
A four-sided polyhedron. A regular tetrahedron is shown.

CUBE
A regular hexahedron. All sides are equal and all angles are 90°.

OCTAHEDRON
A polyhedron with eight sides.

CYLINDER
Surface area =
$2 \times \pi \times r \times h + 2\pi r^2$
Volume = $\pi \times r^2 \times h$

Height = h
Radius = r

PRISM
A polyhedron of constant cross-sections in planes perpendicular to its longitudinal axis.

PYRAMID
A polygonal base and triangular sides that meet at a point.

TORUS
A doughnutlike, ring shape.

CONE
Surface area =
$\pi \times r \times l + \pi r^2$
Volume = $\frac{1}{3} \times \pi \times r^2 \times l$

Height = h
Radius = r
Side = l

SPHERE
A round shape, as in a ball or an orange.

HEMISPHERE
Formed when a sphere is cut exactly in half.

SPHEROID
An egg-shaped solid object whose cross-section is a circle or an ellipse.

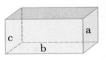

RECTANGULAR BLOCK
Surface area =
$2 (a \times b + b \times c + a \times c)$
Volume = $a \times b \times c$

Sides = a, b, c

CONE
An elliptical or circular base with sides tapering to a single point.

RIGHT CYLINDER
A tube-shaped, solid figure. A right cylinder has parallel faces.

HELIX
A twisted curve. The distance moved in one revolution is its pitch.

Index

A

Aa lava 275
Abacus
  Ancient Egyptian temple 459
  Ancient Greek building 460
  Medieval church 469
  Neoclassical building 485
Abalone 176
Abaxial epidermis 159
Abaxial surface
  Butterwort leaf 161
  Fern pinnule 121
  Mulberry leaf 130
  Water hyacinth leaf 158
  Water lily leaf 159
  Welwitschia leaf 123
Abbey of St. Foi 468
Abdomen
  Crab 172
  Crayfish 172
  Human 211
  Insect 168-169
  Rattlesnake 185
  Scorpion 170
  Shrimp 172
  Spider 171
Abdominal aorta 215, 255
Abdominal artery 173
Abdominal cavity 215
Abdominal segment
  Butterfly 169
  Crayfish 172
  Eurypterid fossil 79
  Extinct shrimp 79
Abductor digiti minimus muscle 231, 233
Abductor pollicis brevis muscle 231
Aberdeen hook 562
Abies Concolor 66
Abomasum 198
Aboral surface
  Sea urchin 175
  Starfish 174
Abortive ovule 151
Abortive seed 146
Abrasion
  Glacier 286
  Weathering and erosion 282
Absolute magnitude
  Hertzsprung-Russell diagram 23
  Stars 22
Absorption lines 22-23
Absorptive hyphae 114
Abutment 484-485
Abyssal plain 298
Acacia tree sap 438
Acadagnostus 64
Acamar 19
Acanthostachys strobilacea 112-113
Acanthostega 80
Acanthus leaf 460
Accelerated electron 319
Acceleration 320-321
  Electric train 328
  Motorcycle 364
Access door 333
Accessory drive pad 419
Accessory pouch 548
Access panel 329, 333
Access slot 585
Accidentals 502-503
Accretion disc 27-29
AC electric train 328
Acer Lumiread e-reader 568

Acer pseudoplatanus 131, 151
Acer sp. 127
Acetabularia sp. 116
Acetabular labrum 225
Acetabulum
  Eryops 81
  Ornithischian 82
  Saurischian 82
Acetylene headlight 556-557
Achenes 150
Achernar 20
Achilles tendon 232-233
Acid
  Intaglio printing 446
  Reversible reaction 312
  Salt formation 312
Acidalia Planitia 43
Acidic solution 446, 448
Acid-resistant ground 446-447
Acid-secreting stomach cell 217
Acipenser sturio 180
Acorn 131
Acoustic guitar 512-513
Acropolis 460
Acrosomal cap 259
Acroterion 460-461
Acroteuthis 278
Acrux
  Centaurus and Crux 21
  Southern stars 21
Acrylic ink 448
Acrylic paint techniques 443
Acrylic-primed board 442
Acrylics 442-443
Actinia equina 166
Actinides 310
Actinium 310
Actinothoe sphyrodeta 166
Action 521
Action lever 514
Active galaxy 12
Active volcano 272
  Igneous and metamorphic rocks 275
  Mountain building 62
Actuating lever system 330
Acuminate leaf apex 136-137
Acute leaf apex 137
Adam's apple 212, 244-245
Adam's ring
  Neptune's rings 50
  Structure of Neptune 51
Adaptation 112
  Dryland plants 156-157
  Wetland plants 158-159
Adaxial epidermis 159
Adaxial surface
  Butterwort leaf 161
  Mulberry leaf 130
  Tree mallow leaf 131
  Water hyacinth leaf 158
  Water lily leaf 159
  Welwitschia leaf 123
Add address field 576
Adductor longus muscle 225, 226
Adductor magnus muscle 227
Adductor muscle 173
Adductor pollicis muscle 231

Adductor tubercle 225
Adenine 216
Adhara 18, 21
Adipose tissue 215, 235
Adjustable damper 518
Adjustable link 362
Adjustable vane 563
Adjusting screw 560
Admiralty anchor Type ACH 586
Admiralty pattern anchor 586
Adrenal gland 215, 257
Adventitious buds 154
Adventitious roots
  Aechmea miniata 162
  Canadian pond weed 158
  Couch grass 113
  Fern 121
  Horsetail 120
  Ivy 131
  Monocotyledon 126
  Potato 128
  Rock stonecrop 128
  Tree fern 112
  Vegetative reproduction 154-155
  Water fern 158
  Water hyacinth 158
  Water lily 159
Advertising 568
Advertising panel 333
Aechmea miniata 162
Aedicule
  Ancient Roman building 463
  Renaissance building 474, 476
AEG Turbine Hall 495
Aegyptopithecus 75
Aeration zone 293
Aerial
  Frigate 397
  Honda Insight 354
  Renault Clio 349
Aerial mammals 104
Aerial rig 397
Aerial root 162
Aerial shoot 155
Aerial stem 119, 155
Aerodynamic balance 414-415
Aerodynamic hub cover 604
Aerodynamic roof 554
Aerodynamic tubing 360
Aerodynamic underside components 554
Aerodynamic windshield 546
Aerofoil guard 529
"Aero" handlebars 360-361
Aerosol spray fixative 430, 440
"Aerotuck" position 360
Aesculus hippocastanum 130
Aesculus parviflora 151
Afferent arteriole 257
A-frame
  Concorde 416
  Gliders, hang-gliders, and ultralights 426
Africa
  Cretaceous period 72-73
  Great Rift Valley 60
  Jurassic period 70
  Late Carboniferous period 66
  Mapping the Earth 264-265
  Middle Ordovician period 64
  Physical map of the world 616-617
  Quaternary period 76-77
  Tertiary period 74-75
  Triassic period 68

African elephant 200-201
African plate 59
African star 595
Aft bogie 615
Aft door 416, 572
Afterbay 314
After breast rope 587
After bridge 595
Afterburner
  Jet engine 418
  Supersonic jetliner 416
Afterburner nozzle 421
Aftercastle
  Sailing warship 377
  Square-rigged ship 375
Aftercastle castle-deck gunport 377
After compass platform 595
After fashion piece 381
After funnel
  Battleship 395
  Iron paddlesteamer 392
Afterpeak 392
After muffler 427
After spring rope 587
Aft fairing 415
Aft galley unit 417
Aft hydroplane 396
Aft main door 414-415
Aft rocker 615
Aft shoulder 560
Aft shroud 612, 613
Aft spar 415
Agate burnisher tip 432
Aggregate fruits 148-149
  Bramble 130
  Development 146-147
Aghulas current 297
Agnatha 178
Agropyron repens 113
Ahead/astern controls 390
Aileron
  ARV light aircraft 424
  BAe-146 components 414
  Curtiss biplane 398-399
  Hawker Tempest components 409
  Lockheed Electra airliner 406
  LVG CVI fighter 405
  Schleicher glider 426
Aileron control wire 403
Aileron hinge strut 403
Aileron mass balance 424
Aileron operating arm 398
Aino Planitia 36-37
Air
  Atmosphere 300
  Oceans and seas 296
  Weather 302-303
Air ambulance 422
Airbag suspension 331
Air bladder 117
Air-brake
  BAe-146 components 415
  Schleicher glider 426
  Tornado 421
Air-brake coupling hose 326
Air-brake jack 421
Air brushes 442
Airbus 380 572-575
Air chamber 118
Air cleaner
  Jaguar V12 engine 345
  Renault Clio 351
Air compression 326
Air-conditioning 496-497
Air-conditioning compressor 344, 354
Air-conditioning duct 417
Air-conditioning pump 344
Air-conditioning refrigerant pipe 344
Air-cooled engine

Motorcycle engine 366
  V8 engine 404
Air cooling baffle 402
Air cooling fan 427
Air cooling scoop 565
Air-cushioned sole 543
Air data probe 420
Air exit 592
Air filter
  Bell-47 helicopter 422
  Harley-Davidson FLHS Electra Glide 363
  Pegasus Quasar 427
  Volkswagen Beetle 340
  ultralight 427
Air hose 442
Air impingement starter 418
Air inlet
  Jaguar V12 engine 345
  Power drill 601
Air intake
  Concorde, the 416
  Double-decker tour bus 333
  Formula One race car 356, 357
  Lockheed Electra airliner 406
  MCW Metrobus 332-333
  Modern military aircraft 420-421
  Single-decker bus 333
  Turbojet engine 418
  Turboprop engine 419
  Vacuum cleaner 592, 593
Air intake box 425
Air-intake duct 354, 573
Air intake vent 541
Air mass 296
Air outlet 556, 427
Air passage
  Lambeosaurus 99
  Parasaurolophus 99
Air pistol 548-549
Air plants 162
Air pressure 303
Air pump
  Oscillating steam engine 391
  Steamboat 391
Air reservoir valve 327
Air resistance 552
Air rifle shooting 548
Air sac
  Chicken's egg 192
  Scots pine 122
Air scoop
  ARV Super 2 424
  Volkswagen Beetle 340
Air spaces
  Clubmoss stem 120
  Mare's tail stem 135
  Moss 119
  Root 132
  Stem 135
  Wetland plants 158-159
Airspeed-indicator tube
  ARV light aircraft 425
  BE 2B wings 404
Airspeed pitot tube 404
Air taxi 422
Air temperature 300
Air temperature probe
  BAe-146 components 412
  Bell Jetranger helicopter 423
Air vent
  Bicycle helmet 360
  Hockey helmet 540
  Suzuki RGV500 368-369
Air ventilator inlet 405
Aisle
  Airbus 380 572
  Ancient Egyptian temple 458
  Cathedral dome 484

Gothic church 470, 472-475
  Medieval church 468-469
Akna Montes 37
Ala 213, 225
Alar groove 213
Alarm vibrator motor 558
Alba Fossae 43
Alba Patera 43
Albaregnus 40
Albertosaurus 84
Albireo 20
Albumen 192
Albumen gland 177
Alcohol fermentation 313
Alcor 19
Alcyone 20
Aldebaran 18, 21
Alderamin 19
Alethopteris 67, 278
Algae 56, 112, 116-117
  Desmid 112
  Earth's evolution 56
  Fossil record 279
  Lichen symbiote 114
Algal cell 114
Algal layer 114
Algebra 621
Algedi 20
Algenib 19, 20
Algieba 18
Algol 19, 20
Alhambra 488
Alhena 18, 21
Alicante 450
Alidade 377
Alimentary canal 248-249
Alioth 18
  The Big Dipper 19
Alkaid 18
  The Big Dipper 19
Alkali metals 310
Allantoic fluid 192
Allantois 192-193
All-around bicycle 360
"All clear" position 330
All-enclosing fairing 369
Alley 544-545
Alligator 186
Allison 250-C20J turboshaft engine 423
Allium sp. 143
Allosaurus 71, 85
Allotropes 311
Alloy disc 517
Alloy frame 368
Alloy wheel
  Formula One race car 356, 357
  Honda VF750 364-365
  Renault Clio 350-351
  Suzuki RGV500 368-369
All-terrain bicycle 358
Alluvial cone 282
Alluvial fan 282
Alluvium-filled basin 282
Almach 19, 20
  Pegasus and Andromeda 19
Al Nair 19, 20
Alnilam 18
Alnitak 18
  Horsehead Nebula 16
  Orion 18
Alouatta seniculus 203
Alpha Centauri 21
Alpha Hydri 20
Alpha Mensae 20
Alphard 18, 21
Alphecca 18, 21
Alpheratz 19, 20
  Pegasus and Andromeda 19
Alphonsus 40
Alpine skiing 552-553
Alps 60, 265, 616

Alrami 21
Alsatian dog 195
Alstroemeria aurea 129
Altair 19, 20
Altar 470
Alternating current 528
Alternative engines 346-347
Alternator
  Diesel train 326
  Ford V6 12-valve engine 344
  Jaguar V12 engine 345
  NPT 501 turbojet 418
  Renault Clio 351
Alternator belt 351
Altitude scale 577
Alto clef 502
Altocumulus cloud 502
Alto mute 507
Altostratus cloud 502
Alto voice 502
Aludra 21
Alula 191
Aluminum 311
  Earth's composition 39
  Earth's crust 58
Aluminum alloy backing 346
Aluminum arrow shaft 548
Aluminum beam 560
Aluminum bonnet 354
Aluminum cowl 401
Aluminum flush-riveted skin 407
Aluminum gearbox casing 366
Aluminum racket 544
Aluminum shield 612
Aluminum wheel 406, 615
Aluminum wire figure 455
Alveolar artery and vein 247
Alveolar bone 247
Alveoli 254-255
Amaryllis 155
Amateur rules 512
Amazon Basin 59
Amazon Kindle Voyage 569
Amazon River 264, 617
Amazonis Planitia 43
Ambiens muscle
  Albertosaurus 84
  Iguanodon 97
Ambulacral groove 79, 175
Ambulatory corridor 465
Amelodental junction 247
American alligator 186
American beaver 197
American black bear 195
American squash court 545
American squash game 544
Americium 311
Ammonia
  Jupiter's atmosphere 45
  Saturn's atmosphere 47
  Structure of Neptune 51
  Structure of Uranus 49
Ammonite 278-279
Ammonite shell 267
Ammonium dichromate 312
Ammonium hydrosulfide
  Jupiter's atmosphere 45
  Saturn's atmosphere 47
Ammophila arenaria 113
Ammunition 548-549
Ammunition box 408
Amnion 192-193, 260
Amniotic egg 80

Amniotic fluid 192, 260
Amniotic sac 260
Amoebocyte 166
AMOLED screen 591
Amphibia 182
Amphibian 80-81, 182-183
  Earth's evolution 56
  Fossil 278-279
  Primitive 68-69, 78
Amphibole 275
Amphitheater 464-465
Amplification
  Drums 518
  Electronic instruments 520
  Guitar 512
  Stringed instruments 510
  Vibraphone 516
  Xylophone 516
Amplifier 520
Amps 516
Ampulla
  Ear 242-243
  Fallopian tube 258-259
  Sea urchin 175
  Starfish 174
Ampullar nerve 242
Anal canal 249
Anal clasper 169
Anal fin
  Bony fish 180-181
  Lamprey 178
Anal fin ray 180
Anal flap 200
Analog signals 580
Anal sphincter muscle 249
Anchisaurus 88-89
Anchor
  74-gun ship 380
  BAe-146 components 412, 414
  Battleship 394-395
  Frigate 397
  Junk 376
  Roman corbita 372
  Square-rigged ship 375
  Tea clipper 592
  Types 586
  Wooden sailing ship 579
Anchor bearing 413
Anchor buoy 379
Anchor cable
  74-gun ship 380
  Sailing warship 376
Anchor chain 586, 595
Anchoring 386-387
Anchor-joint 492
Anchor rode 572
Anchor rope 572-575
Ancient Egyptian building 458-459
Ancient Greek and Roman ships 372-375
Ancient Greek building 460-461, 462
Ancient Greeks 542
Ancient Roman building 462-465, 474
Ancillary drive belt 347
Ancillary drive pulley 345
Anorale 572
Andamenti 451
Andes
  Cretaceous period 75
  Earth's external features 39
  Jurassic period 71
  Quaternary period 77
  Satellite map 264
  Tertiary period 75
  Triassic period 69
Andromeda 19, 20
Andromeda Galaxy 14, 19
Anemometer 605
Anemone viridis 166
Anemophilous pollination 144
Angiogram 214

Angiospermophyta 112, 126
Angiosperms 279
Angle bar 393
Angle buttress 471, 472
Angle-of-attack probe 420
Anglerfish 180
Angling 562-563
Angoulême Cathedral 468-469
Angular branch of animal 295
Angular notch 249
Angular process 194
Angular unconformity 276
Anhydrous copper sulfate 313
Animal cloning 607
Animal life
  Electromagnetic radiation 314
  Primitive 78
Animal remains
  Fossils 279
  Sedimentary rocks 276
Animal stances 82
Animals 56, 67, 78
Anions 308
Ankle
  Anchisaurus 89
  Corythosaurus 98
  Edmontonia 95
  Herrerasaurus 86
  Human 211
  Iguanodon 96
  Pachycephalosaurus 100
  Psittacosaurus 103
  Stegoceras 101
  Stegosaurus 92
  Triceratops 102
  Tyrannosaurus 84
Ankle joint
  Brachiosaurus 90
  Diplodocus 90
  Euoplocephalus 94
  Human 219
  Parasaurolophus 98
  Plateosaurus 88
  Stegoceras 101
  Struthiomimus 87
  Triceratops 102
  Tyrannosaurus 84
Ankylosaurs 83, 92, 94-95
Anne's Spot 47
Annual growth ring 125
Annuals 128
Annular river drainage 288
Annular tendon 241
Annulet 460
Annulus
  Fern 121
  Mushroom 115
Annulus of trunk 201
Ant 168
Anta 461
Antarala 490-491
Antarctica
  Cretaceous period 72-75
  Jurassic period 70
  Late Carboniferous period 66
  Mapping the Earth 264-265
  Physical map of the world 616-617
  Quaternary period 76-77
  Tertiary period 74-75
  Triassic period 68
Antarctic Circle
  Satellite map 265
  Surface currents 297
Antarctic circumpolar current 296
Antares 18, 21
Antefixa 461
Antelope 198
Antenna

Airbus 580 573
Battleship 395
Crab 172
Crayfish 173
Frigate 397
Insects 168-169
Malacostraca 172
Roman corbita 372-373
Shrimp 172
Volleyball net 534
Antennule 173
Anterior antebrachial muscle 86
Anterior aorta 170
Anterior arch 222
Anterior branch of spinal nerve 223
Anterior chamber 241
Anterior chamber of cloaca 185
Anterior crural muscle
  Brachiosaurus 90
  Gallimimus 86
Anterior dorsal fin
  Bony fish 181
  Dogfish 179
  Lamprey 178
Anterior fontanelle 220
Anterior horn 223
Anterior median fissure 223, 258
Anterior median vein 253
Anterior nasal spine 220-221
Anterior petal 141
Anterior root 238
Anterior semicircular canal 243
Anterior sepal 141
Anterior tentacle 177
Anterior tibial artery 253
Anterior tibial muscle
  Albertosaurus 84
  Iguanodon 96
Anterior tubercle 222
Anterior wing of shell 176
Antheridium 117
  Fern 121
  Moss 119
Antherozoids 116-117
  Fern 121
  Moss 119
Anthers 140-143, 145
  Dicotyledons 126-127
  Fertilization 146-147
  Pollination process 144-145
Anthozoa 166
Anthracite coal 280
Anthriscus sp. 155
Anthropoids 202
Anthurium andreanum 143
Antibodies 253
Anticlinal fold 60
Anticline 60-61, 62
Anticline trap 280-281
Anticlinorium 61
Anti-collision beacon 422-423
Anti-corrosion paint 413
Anticyclonic storm system
  Cloud features of Neptune 50
  Jupiter 44-45
  Structure of Saturn 47
Anti-friction pad 552
Anti-glare lens 555
Antihelix 242
Anti-lift bracing wire
  Avro triplane 403
  Blackburn monoplane 401

Blériot XI monoplane 401
LVG CVI fighter 405
Anti-lift wire 399
Antimacassar 329
Antimony 311
Antipodal cell 147
Anti-reflective coating 605
Anti-reverse drive 562
Anti-roll bar
  Renault Clio 550-551
  Volkswagen Beetle 340
Anti-submarine torpedo tube 397
Anti-surge baffle 344
Anti-torque tail rotor 423
Antittygus 242
Anti-vibration engine mount 411
Antler hammer 109
Antler harpoon 109
Antlia 18, 21
Antoniadi 41
Antorbital fenestra
  Baryonyx 83
  Camarasaurus 91
  Diplodocus 90
  Plateosaurus 88
Anura 182
Anus
  Barnacle 175
  Bony fish 181
  Butterfly 169
  Cow 198
  Crayfish 173
  Dolphin 205
  Domestic cat 195
  Elephant 200
  Human 249, 258, 261
  Octopus 176
  Rabbit 196
  Sea urchin 175
  Snail 177
  Spider 170
  Starfish 174
  Tortoise 187
Anvil 242
Aorta
  Anterior 170
  Bony fish 181
  Dogfish 179
  Dolphin 205
  Dorsal 179, 181, 182
  Human 215, 250-251, 252, 255, 256-257
  Posterior 170
  Spider 170
  Ventral 179
Apatite 271
Ape 108, 202-205
Aperture 610, 612, 613
Aperture door 612, 613
Aperture door mounting 612
Aperture plate 611
Apex
  Beetle wing 168
  Butterfly wing 169
  Calligraphy characters 445
  Clubmoss shoot 120
  Fern frond 121
  Fern pinnule 121
  Horsetail shoot 120
  Leaf 136-137, 154-155
  Lung 255
  Moss 119
  Pegasus XL SE
  Pine shoot 125
  Snail shell 177
  Tongue 244-245
  ultralight 426
Apex wire 426
Aphelion 30-31
Aphrodite Terra 36-37
Apical bud
  Bulb 155
  Pine shoot 125
Apical foramen 247

Apical meristem 134
Apical notch
  Seaweed 116
  Thalloid liverwort 118
Apollo 41
Apomixis 146
Apophysis 119
Apotheorium 114
Appalachian mountains
  Late Cretaceous period 67
  Mountain building 62
  Quaternary period 77
  Satellite map 264
  Tertiary period 75
  Triassic period 68
Apparent magnitude 22
Appendix
  Chimpanzee 202
  Human 249
  Rabbit 196
Appendix orifice 249
App icon 590
Apple iMac 567
Apple iPad 568-569
Apple iPhone 6 588
Apple iPod
  Classic 587
  Shuffle 587
Apple Macintosh PCs 566
Approach 545
Apse 465, 469, 481
Aquarius 19, 20
Aquatic mammals 104
Aqueduct 256
Aqueous humor 241
Aquiclude 292
Aquifer 292
Aquiferous system 166
Aquila 19, 20
Ara 20
Ara ararauna 190
Arabesque
  Islamic building 488-489
  Neoclassical molding 80
Arabia
  Cretaceous period 72
  Jurassic period 70
Arabian Desert 265
Arachnids 170-171
Arachnoid granulation 257
Arachnoid mater 237, 240
Aral Sea 265, 616
Araneae 170
Araucaria araucana 68
Arcade
  Ancient Roman building 464-465
  Baroque church 479-481
  Gothic building 470-471
  Medieval church 468-469
  Twentieth-century building 495
Arcadia Planitia 43
Arch 484-485
  Ancient Roman building 462, 464-465
  Asian building 490-491
  Baroque church 479, 480
  Calligraphy characters 445
  Cathedral dome 487
  Features of a coastline 295
  French temple 484-485
  Gothic church 470-473
  High jump 543
  Islamic building 488-489
  Medieval building 466-469
  Nineteenth-century building 492-493
  Renaissance building 474-475
Archaeopteryx 57, 84, 85
Arched brace 473

Arched doorway 474, 475
Arched facade 493
Archegoniophore 118
Archegonium
    Fern 121
    Liverwort 118
    Moss 119
    Scots pine 122
Archery 548-549
Archery screen 577
Archimedes 40
Architrave
    Ancient Egyptian
        temple 458-459
    Ancient Greek temple
        461
    Ancient Roman
        building 465, 465
    Baroque church
        479-481
    French temple 485
    Gothic building 473
    Neoclassical building
        478, 482-485
    Renaissance building
        476-477
Archivolt
    Baroque church 479,
        481
    French temple 485
    Gothic church 471
    Medieval building
        467-468
    Renaissance building
        477
Arch of aorta 255
Arch of Titus 463
Arch-plate 495
Archway 493
    Medieval church 469
    Molding 485
Arctic Circle
    Satellite map 265
    Surface currents 297
Arctic Ocean 265, 617
Arcturus 18, 21
    Hertzsprung-Russell
        diagram 23
Areas 622, 623
Areola 160
Areole 156
Arête 286-287
Argentina 331
Argon
    Atmospheric
        composition 301
    Mars' atmosphere 43
    Mercury's atmosphere 35
    Periodic table 311
    Venus' atmosphere 37
Argyre Planitia 43
Ariel 48
Aries 19, 20
Aril
    Lychee fruit 148
    Yew seed 123
A ring 46-47
Aristarchus 40
Aristillus 40
Aristoteles 40
Arkab Prior 21
Arkansas hone-stone 452
Arm
    74-gun ship 380
    Calligraphy characters
        445
    Gorilla 203
    Human 210
    Lion 194
    Roman anchor 372
    Starfish 174
    Volkswagen Beetle
        341
Armature
    Power drill motor 600
    Sculpture 452, 454-455
Armature spindle 600
Arm bud 260
Armed sports 556-557

Armor
    Battleship 394
    Gun turret 396
    Ironclad 393
Armored dinosaurs 92
Armored seat back 409
Arm out-in joint 608
Armpit 211, 234
Armpit bight 388
Armrest 329, 407
Arm rotation joint 608
Arms of Brazil 594
Armstand dive 558
Arm up-down joint 608
Arrector pili muscle 255
Arrico 454
Arrow head 109
Arse 582
Arsenic 311
Arsia Mons 43
Arsinoitherium 57, 75,
    104-105
Art deco style 495
    Twentieth-century
        building 494, 495
Artemon 372
Arterial system
    Brain 252
    Kidney 256
Arteriole 252
Artery
    Abdominal 173
    Alveolar 247
    Anterior tibial 253
    Axillary 253
    Basilar 252
    Brachial 253
    Central retinal 240
    Common carotid 215,
        251, 253
    Common iliac 215, 253,
        257
    Coronary 250-251, 253
    Digital 231, 253
    Dorsal metatarsal 253
    Epibranchial 179
    External iliac 215, 225,
        253
    Femoral 225, 253
    Gastric 253
    Hepatic 248, 252-253
    Interlobular 256
    Internal carotid 245,
        252
    Internal iliac 215, 253
    Lateral plantar 253
    Orbital 179
    Peroneal 253
    Popliteal 253
    Posterior cerebral 252
    Posterior tibial 253
    Pulmonary 182, 251,
        253, 254-255
    Pulp 247
    Radial 231, 253
    Renal 256-257
    Splenic 253
    Sternal 173
    Subclavian 215, 251,
        253
    Superior mesenteric
        255, 256
    Superior thyroid 244
    Testicular 257
    Ulnar 231, 253
    Umbilical 260
    Vertebral 223, 252
Artesian water 292
Arthropoda 168, 170, 172,
    278
Articular capsule 232
Articular cavity
    Hip joint 225
    Metatarsophalangeal
        joint 232
Artificial elements 310
Artificial fly 562-563
Artificial light 319
Artificial lure 563

Artillery loop 389
Artillery wheel 592
Artiodactyla 104, 198-199
Artist's easel 437
Artist's signature 437, 445
Artist's stamp 445
Art nouveau style 495
Arundinaria nitida 131
ARV Super 2 light aircraft
    424-425
Arzachel 40
Ascender 445
Ascending aorta 251
Ascending colon 249
Asclepias 182
Ascraeus Mons 43
Asexual reproduction 154
Ash
    Mountain building 62
    Rock cycle 266
    Volcano 272-273
Ash chute 595
Ash-cinder volcano 272
Ash eruptions 272
Ash head 540
Ashlar 464, 486
ASIMO humanoid
    608-609
Asia
    Cretaceous period
        72-73
    Himalaya formation
        62-63
    Hominids 108
    Jurassic period 70
    Mapping the Earth
        264-265
    Middle Ordovician
        period 64
    Physical map of
        the world 616-617
    Quaternary period
        76-77
    Tertiary period 74-75
    Triassic period 68
Asian buildings 490-491
Asian elephant 200-201
Asparagus setaceous 64
Ass 198
Association football
    524-525
Astatine 311
Asterias rubens 175
Asterina gibbosa 175
Asteroids 52-53
    Solar system 30
Asteroxylon 78-79
Asthenosphere 58-59
Astragal
    Church of the Sorbonne
        486
    Ship's shield 595
Astragalus 183
Astrolabe 376, 377
Astronavigation dome 408
Asymmetric ridge 283
Atacama Desert 264
Atalanta Planitia 36
Athletics 542-543
Atlantic Ocean 264-265,
    616-617
    Quaternary period 77
    Tertiary period 75
Atlas
    Baroque building 482
    Horse 199
    Human 222
    Moon 40
Atlas mountains 616
    Earth's external
        features 39
    Quaternary period 77
    Satellite map 265
Atmosphere
    Earth 38-39, 64, 300-301
    Jupiter 45
    Mars 45
    Mercury 34-35
    Neptune 51
    Pluto 51

Saturn 47
Uranus 49
Venus 37
Water cycle 288
Atoll 298-299
Atoll development 299
Atomic mass 309, 310
Atomic number 310
Atomic weight 310
Atoms 306, 308-309, 596
    Chemical properties
        310
    Chemical reactions 312
    Periodic table 310
Atrial diastole 250
Atrial systole 251
Atrium
    Hong Kong and
        Shanghai Bank 498
    Human 215, 250-251
    Sponge 166
Attached column
    Ancient Roman
        building 465
    Baroque church 480
    Gothic building 473
    Medieval building 468-
        469
    Neoclassical building
        479
Attach files button 576
Attachment-bracket
    424
Attachment clip 575
Attachment lug 404
Attachment plate 424
Attack line 534
Attack radar 420
Attic
    Baroque church
        480-481
    Cathedral dome 487
    Neoclassical building
        478, 483
Attic vase 372
Attraction 316-317
"A" turret 394
Auda 491
Audio clock settings 521
Audio software sequencer
    521
Auditorium 479
Auditory canal 242
Auditory meatus
    Chimpanzee 202
    Seal 204
Auger 374
Augusta National Golf
    course 546
Aureole 471
Auricle 242
Auricular surface 223
Auriga 18, 21
Aurora 38, 301
Australasia 265, 617
Australia
    Cretaceous period
        72-73
    Jurassic period 70
    Late Carboniferous
        period 66
    Middle Ordovician
        period 64
    Quaternary period
        76-77
    Railroad track gauge
        331
    Satellite map 265
    Tertiary period
        74-75
    Triassic period 68
Australian rules football
    524, 528-529
Australopithecus 77, 108
    Lower jaw 107
    Tertiary period 74
Autofeather unit
    419
Autogiro 422

Automatic cylinder
    lubricator 342
Automatic direction-
    finding aerial 423
Automatic door 328-329
Automatic louvres 602,
    603
Automatic pen 444
Automatic Train
    Protection (ATP) 330
Automobile freight car
    327
Autopilot 412
Autumn wood xylem 134
Auxiliary air intake 420-
    421
Auxiliary generator 327
Auxiliary power unit 417
Auxiliary Power Unit
    (APU) exhaust 572
Auxiliary power unit inlet
    415
Aves 188
Avimimus 87
Avogadro 41
Avro triplane IV 402-403
Avro Tutor biplane
    402-403
Away swing bowler 538
Awning 499
Ax 109, 374
Axial gland 175
Axial instrument unit
    612
Axial tilt
    Earth 38
    Jupiter 44
    Mars 42
    Mercury 34
    Moon 40
    Neptune 50
    Pluto 51
    Saturn 46
    Uranus 48
    Venus 36
Axilla 211
Axillary artery 253
Axillary bud 134
    Dicotyledon stem 127
    Durmast oak 131
    Leaf scars 154
Axillary vein 253
Axinite 270
Axis
    Azolla sp. 158
    Horse 199
    Human 222
    Seed 152-153
    Pine cone 122
Axis of rotation
    Jupiter 44
    Mars 42
    Mercury 34
    Moon 40
    Neptune 50
    Pluto 51
    Pulsar 28
    Saturn 46
    Uranus 48
    Venus 36
Axle
    Avro triplane 402-403
    Blackburn monoplane
        400
    Bus 333
    Curtiss biplane 399
    Honda VF750 565
    Lockheed Electra
        airliner 407
    LVG CVI fighter 405
    Steam locomotive
        324
Axle bolt 425
Axon 239
Aythya fuligula 188
Azimuthal map projection
    265
Azo yellow 442
Azurite 306

B

B-17G Flying Fortress
    bomber 408
Baboon 202
Bach 35
Back
    Block and tackle 383
    Elephant 200
    Horse 198
    Human 210
    Lion 195
Backboard 532
Back bone 222
Back check 514
Back contact grid 605
Background radiation 10
Back/Home button 586
Back judge 526
Back line 535
Back pocket 528
Backrest
    ARV light aircraft 425
    Lockheed Electra
        passenger seat 407
Backs
    Handball 535
    Hockey 540
    Soccer 524
    Volleyball 534
Backshell 615
Back sight 549
Backstay 378, 379, 380
Backstay stool 381
Backstroke 558-559
Backup battery 567
Backward defensive
    stroke 538
Backward dive 558
Backwash 294
Back zones 534
Bacteria 56
Bactrian camel 199
Baculum 144
Badger 194
Badminton 544-545
BAe-146 jetliner
    components 412-415
Baffin Island 264, 617
Baffle 341
Baffle plate 347
Bag[e, C. 492
Baggage compartment
    door 423
Bagneux Church 468-469
Bahada 282
Bail 558
Bail arm 562
Bailey 466
Bail handle 336
Bailly 40
Baird's beaked whale 205
Bait fishing 562
Balaenoptera musculus 205
Balance 252
Balance and muscle
    coordination 237
Balance weight
    Jaguar V12 engine 345
    Mid West rotary engine
        411
Balancing drilling
    Mid West rotary engine
        411
    Wankel rotary engine
        547
Balanophyllia regia 167
Balata surface 546
Balcony 493
    Islamic tomb 489
    Nineteenth-century
        building 493
    Renaissance theater
        477
    Rococo style 478, 482
    Sailing ship 378, 379,
        381
Baleen whale 204

Ball
  Australian rules football 528
  Baseball 557
  Basketball 553
  Cricket 558
  Football 526
  Gaelic football 528-529
  Golf 546
  Handball 555
  Hockey 540
  Hurling 541
  Lacrosse 541
  Netball 555
  Racketball 545
  Rugby 524, 550-551
  Soccer 524
  Squash 545
  Tennis 544
  Volleyball 554
Ballast 524
Ball bearings 358-359
Ballflowers 470-471
Ball marker 547
Ball size number 525
Baltica 65
Baltimore oriole 193
Baluster
  Asian building 490
  Gothic building 473
  Neoclassical building 483
Balustrade
  Asian building 490
  Baroque church 479-480
  Cathedral dome 487
  Gothic church 472-473
  Neoclassical building 478, 483
  Nineteenth-century building 493
  Renaissance theater 477
  Twentieth-century building 495
Balzac 55
Bamboo 131
Banana 146
Banded ironstone 277
Banded milk snake 184
Bandy 540
Bank of England 482
Banner 375
Bar
  Musical notation 502
  Relief-printing press 449
Bar area 573
Barb
  Angling 562
  Cnidocyte 167
Barberry 130-131
Barbette
  Battleship 594
  Gun turret 396
Bar code 606
Bare end
  Reef knot 588
  Single sheet bend 587
Barium 310
Bark
  Bishop pine stem 125
  Epiphyte 162
  Lichen 114
  Perennials 130-131
  Stem 134
  Woody plants 130-131
Bar keel 592
Barkhan dune 285
Bar line 502
Barnacle 172-173
Barnard's Star 23
Baroque style 478-483
Barosaurus 91
Barred spiral galaxy
  Galaxies 12-15
  Milky Way 14-15
  Objects in universe 11

Origin and expansion of universe 10-11
Barrel
  Gun turret 397
  Wood capstan 587
Barrel joint 508
Barrel vault 484-485
  Ancient Roman building 463-464
  Baroque church 479
  Medieval church 468
  Nineteenth-century building 493
Barrier beach 294
Barrier reef 299
Barry, C. 495
Bars 516-517
Bar swivel 562
Baryonyx 83, 84-85
Baryte 270
Basal disk 167
Basal scale 114
Basalt 274-275
Basaltic lava 272
Bascule 493
Base
  Ancient Greek temple 461
  Ancient Roman building 463, 465
  Asian building 491
  Baroque church 479, 481
  Dome 484, 486, 487
  French temple 485
  Gothic church 470, 472
  Medieval church 469
  Neoclassical building 478, 483
  Renaissance theater 477
  Sheet lead 383
  Twentieth-century building 494
  Twin ballasts 386
Baseball 556-557
Base line
  Calligraphy lettering 445
  Tennis 544
Basement 483
Basement membrane of Bowman's capsule 257
Base of phalanx 230
Base plate 552
Bases 536
Basic movements 237
Basic shield volcano 272
Basidium 115
Basilar artery 252
Basilar membrane 243
Basilican system 468
Basilica of St. Madeleine 468
Basilic vein 253
Basket
  Basketball 552
  Ski pole 552-553
Basket arch 472, 484
Basketball 552-553
Basket star 174
Basking shark 179
Bas-relief carving 491
Bass angling 562
Bass bridge
  Concert grand piano 515
  Upright piano 514
Bass clarinet 504
Bass clef 502
Bass drum 504-505, 518-519
Bass formation 277
Bass joint 508
Bass notes 512
Bassoon 503, 504-505, 508
Bass/Play mode 586
Bass voice 502
Bastille 466

Bat
  Baseball 557
  Cricket 559
Bat (animal) 105
Batholiths 274-275
Batsman 558-559
Battery
  74-gun ship 581
  Junk 376
  Wall construction 602
Batter 556-557
Battery
  Bell-47 helicopter 422
  Bersey electric cab 342
  Digital video camera 582
  Hubble Space Telescope 613
  Inverter 355
  Kirby BSA racing sidecar 369
  Battery assembly 555
Battery box 527, 424
Battery carrier 338
Battery compartment 407
Battery cover 579
Battery cooling fan 555
Battery electronic control module (ECM) 515
Battery overspill 422
Battery strap 559
Batting gloves
  Baseball 557
  Cricket 559
Battlemented cornice 471
Battlements 466-467
Battleship 594-595
Bauxite 268
Bay
  Building 468, 469, 494
  Coastline features 295
  River features 291
Bay-head beach 294
Bay-leaf garland 480
Bayonet fixing 352
Bay window 477
BE 2B bomber 404-405
Beach
  Coastline 294-295
  River development 289
Beacon 407, 422-423
Beaded edge tire 336
Beadlet anemone 166
Bead molding 459
Beak
  Ankylosaurus 94
  Attic vase 372
  Bird 188-190
  Ceratopsian 100
  Chelonian 186
  Dolphin 204
  Euoplocephalus 94
  Hatching chick 192-193
  Iguanodon 97
  Moss 119
  Octopus 176
  Ornithopod 96
  Panoplosaurus 94
  Protoceratops 102
  Psittacosaurus 103
  Stegosaurus 92
Beaked whale 204
Beaker 312
Beam
  BAe-146 jetliner 414
  Gothic church 473
  High-tension 496
  Iron paddlesteamer 393
  Modern building 497-499
  Nineteenth-century building 492
  Single skull 560
Bean
  Black 153
  Broad 152
Bear 104, 106, 194-195
Bearing
  Electric generator 317

Jaguar V12 engine 345
Motorcycle gearbox 366
Rotary engine output shaft 411
Bearing assembly 425
Bearing housing 344
Bearing mount 411
Bearing seal 359
Bearing sleeve 358
"Beast feet" 84
Beaten gold 432
Beaters 516, 518-519
Beats 502
Beats by Dre headphones 587
Beaver 196-197
Becket 585
Becket Chapel 467
Bed
  Relief printing press 449
  Sedimentary rocks 276
Bedding plane
  Cave system 284
  Coastline 294-295
Bedford cord upholstery 336
Bedplate 390
Bedrock 298
  Delta formation 291
Bee 168, 379
Bee hummingbird 193
Bee pollination 144-145
Beeswax 384
Beethoven 35
Beetle 168
Begonia 129, 155
Begonia x tuberhybrida 129, 155
Behavior 108, 257
Belaying pin 382
Belemnites 71, 278-279
Belfry
  74-gun ship 380
  Church of St. George in the East 481
Bell 508
Bell 206 Jetranger 423
Bell 47G-3B1 422-423
Bellatrix 18
Bell chamber 493
Bell crank 391
Bell housing 347
Bell joint 508
Bello 55
Bell Regio
  Radar map of Venus 36
  Structure of Venus 37
Belly
  Bird 188
  Caiman 186
  Dolphin 204
  Elephant 201
  Horse 198
  Lion 195
  Lizard 184
  Sail 384
  Viola 511
  Violin 510
Belly-band 555
Belly fairing 572
Belt
  Jupiter 44-45
  Structure of Saturn 47
Belt armor 594
Belt color 556
Belt drive 366
Belt pulley 345
Belt tensioner 344, 564
Belvedere 476
Bench officials
  Ice hockey 550
  Lacrosse 541
Bending 518
Bends 587
Benguela current 297
Benz, Karl 334
Benz Motorwagen 335
Benz six-cylinder engine 405

Berardius bairdi 205
Berberis sp. 130-131
Berkelium 311
Berries 148-149
Bersey electric cab 342
Berthing ropes 587
Beryl 270
Beryllium 310
Beta Hydri 20
Beta Mensae 20
Beta Pictoris 21
Beta ring 48
Betelgeuse 18, 21
  Hertzsprung-Russell diagram 23
  Orion 18
  Universe 10-11
Betula grossa 74
Betula lenta 76
Betulites 74
Bevel gear 335
Bevel pinion 338
Beverley Minster 484
Bhagirathi Parbat 62
Bianco di San Giovanni 434-435
Biathlon rifle 549
Bib 557
Bi-block engine 337
Biceps brachii muscle 226
Biceps femoris muscle 227
Bicycle 360-361
Bicycle anatomy 358-359
Bicycle riding 315
Biennials 128
Biflagellate cell 116
Bifurcate ligament 252
"Big Ben" 493
Bigbore rifle shooting 548-549
Big end
  Flat-four cylinder arrangement 340
  Four-stroke cycle 343
  Jaguar straight six engine 344
  Mid West engine 410
  Trojan engine 342
Big-end bearing 355
Bight 588
Big toe 232-233
Bile duct 189, 249
Bilge keel 395, 597
Bilge keelson 593
Bill
  Danforth anchor 586
  Running block 583
  Sail hook 384
Biloched leaves 123
Bin base 592
Bin cover handle 593
Bin cover retaining clip 592, 593
Binder 464
Binder bolt 361
Binding 583
  Acoustic guitar 512
  Iron paddlesteamer 592
Binding medium 440
Bin handle 592
Bin handle clip 592
Bin lower seal 592
Binnacle box 378
Binocular eyepieces 610, 611
Bin upper seal 592
Bin upper seal seating 592
Biology symbols 621
Bipedal dinosaur 84, 96, 100
Bipinnate leaf 137
Biplane elevator 398-399
Biplanes 402-403, 408
Bipolar neuron 239
Birch 74, 76
Bird 84, 188-191

Beak 190
  Earth's evolution 57
  Feathers 191
  Feet 190
  Fossil record 279
  Wing 191
"Bird feet" 96
Bird-hipped dinosaur 82, 92, 96
Bird of prey 188
Bird pollination 144
Bishop pine 124-125
Bismuth 281, 311
Bit 601
  74-gun ship 580-581
  Roman corbita 373
Bitter end, Hawser 587
Bituminous coal 280
Bivalves 79, 176, 278-279
Blackbacked gull 193
Black bean 155
Black belt 556
Blackberry 130, 146-147
Blackberry Curve 8520 589
Blackberry Passport 589
Blackburn monoplane 400-401
Blackburn, Robert 400
Black dwarf 24-25
Blackheaded gull 189
Black ink cartridge 574
Black ink-cartridge clamp 574
Black holes 28-29
  Galaxies 12
  Massive stars 26-27
Black Mesa 277
Black rhinoceros 199
Black Sea 265, 616
Blackstonia perfoliata 144
Black walnut 137
Black widow spider 171
Bladder
  Bony fish 181
  Chimpanzee 202
  Dolphin 205
  Domestic cat 195
  Elephant 200
  Human 215, 257, 258-259, 261
  Lizard 185
  Rabbit 196
  Soccer ball 525
  Swim 178, 180-181
  Tortoise 187
  Urinary 181
Bladder wrack 117
Blade
  Butterwort 161
  Calligraphy drawing board 445
  Danforth anchor 586
  Dicotyledon leaf 127
  Fencing foil 557
  Golf clubs 547
  Hockey stick 540
  Kayak paddle 560
  Leaf surfaces 136, 138
  Monocotyledon leaf 127
  Propeller 390
  Roman rudder 373
  Sculling oar 560
  Seaweed 116-117
  Vegetative reproduction 154
  Venus fly trap 160
  Volkswagen Beetle 341
  Wetland plants 158-159
  Wind turbine 604
Blade bearing 604
Blade counterweight 406, 422
Blade hub 604
Blade pitch control 604
Blade-root attachment 422-423

Blade tip sealing shroud
419
Blanking plate 411
Blast bag 596
Blaslocyst 525
Blast-pipe 525
Blending 440
Blériot XI monoplane 401
Blériot, Louis
Early monoplane 400
Pioneers of flight 398
Blindage 377
Blind arch
Asian building 491
Cathedral dome 487
Gothic church 470
Blind door 478
Blind pull 536-537
Blind release bar 552
Blinds 603
Blind-side prop 550
Blind spot 241
Blind tracery 493
Blind trefoil 475
Blind window 478
Block and tackle 582-585
Block carving 470
Block cube 270
Block disintegration 282
Block-fault lake 295
Block-fault mountain 62
Blocking pad 550
Blocks 310
Blood cells 253
Blood clotting 253
Blower control 525
Blower isolator valve 525
Blow hole 508
Blowhole 205
Blubber 204
Blue-and-yellow macaw 190
Blue-green alga 56, 78
Blue light 318
Blue line 550
Blue supergiant star
Hertzsprung-Russell
diagram 23
Stellar black hole 29
Bluetooth 590
Blue whale 204-205
Bluff 289
Blunt button 556-557
Blu-ray player 584
BMW R/60 motorcycle 362
Board
Ice hockey rink 550
Modeling 455
Pastels 441
Boarding 464
Board mounting 450-451
Boat boom 595
Boatbuilder's tools 374
Boat handling derrick 595
Boat slide 378
Boat winch 594
Bobstay 379
Body
Anchisaurus 89
Discus 542
Dunkeld wet fly 563
Motorcycle 364-365
Sauropodomorpha 88
Stringed instruments 510
Body bag 426
Body cells 216-217
Body cradle 398
Body drop 556
Body joint
Flute 508
Piccolo 508
Body landing gear 572
Body mount 338
Body organs 214-215
Body padding 526
Body sections
Insect 168
Scorpion 170
Spider 170-171
Body shell 518-519

Bodyshell
Renault Clio 348-349
Volkswagen Beetle 341
Body tackles 528
Body temperature
regulation
Dinosaurs 92
Mammals 104
Body wire 557
Bodywork 348-349
Race cars 356
Volkswagen Beetle 341
Bodywork mounting point
564
Boeing 747-400 412
Bogie axle 326
Bogie frame 325
Bogie main landing gear
416
Bogie wheel strut 615
Boiler
Box boiler 392
Donkey boiler 392
Steamboat with paddle
wheels 391
Steam locomotives
524-525
Boiler pressure gauge 525
Boiler water level 525
Bole base 452-453
Bollard
Battleship 395
Frigate 397
Mooring and anchoring
586-587
Bolson 282
Bolster 378
Bolt
Church of St. Pierre
499
Lower deadeye 383
Shackle 386
Toaster 598
Bolted anchor 425
Bolt hole
Drum brake 365
Mid West rotary engine
411
Twin bollards 587
Bolt rest 548
Bolt rope 372, 384
Bolts 548-549
Bomb 404, 408
Bomb aimer's viewing
panel 408
Bomb door 408
Bomber
Modern military
aircraft 420
World War I aircraft
404-405
World War II aircraft
408-409
Bomb rack 404
Bonaventure mast 377
Bonaventure topcastle 377
Bonaventure topmast 377
Bonaventure top yard 377
Bonaventure yard 377
Bonded brick wall 492
Bonding
Chemical reactions 312
Covalent 309
English bond 485
Gases 307
Ionic 308
Liquids 307
Bone cell 217, 225
Bone marrow smear 225
Bones
Fossil 278
Human 224-225, 230,
252
Bone structure 108
Bone surface 807
Bony crest
Baryonyx 83
Corythosaurus 98
Lambeosaurus 99

Parasaurolophus 99
Bony dorsal shield 78
Bony fish 180-181
Bony frill 100
Bony nodule
Pachycephalosaurus
100
Prenocephale 100
Bony ridge 100
Bony shelf 100, 101
Bony spine 100
Bony strut 85
Bony studs 92
Bony tendons 96
Boom
Battleship 394-395
Curtiss Model-D pusher
599
Double topsail
schooner 385
Guest boat boom 394
Hong Kong and
Shanghai Bank 498
Longboat 380
Rigging 582
Sailing dinghy 561
Boom guy block 382
Boomkin 380
Bootes 18, 21
Bordino Steam Carriage
334-335
Borealis Planitia 35
Borneo 265, 616
Boron 311
Boss
Church roof 468-469
Hurley 541
Viking karv 374
Bothriolepididae 65
Botryoidal habit 270-271
Bottom ballast 377
Bottom bracket 358
Bottom hose 351
Bottom plate 390, 592-593
Bottom race 359
Bottomset strata 283
Boudin 60-61
Boulder beach 295
Boulder clay 286
Bounce pass 535
Boundary
Cricket 538
Mantle crust 59
Outer core-mantle 59
Boundary line
Australian rules football
528
Badminton 545
Cricket 538
Squash 545
Bow
74-gun ship 381
Kayak 560
Sailing dinghy 561
Stringed instruments
510
Wooden sailing ship
578
Bowball 561
Bow drill 109
Bower anchor
Battleship 395
Sailing warship 377
Wooden sailing ship
579
Bow front 485
Bowl 445
Bowler 538
Bowline 388, 389
Bowling crease 538
Bowman's capsule 256
Bowman's space 257
Bow ornament 375
Bowpost 561
Bows 548
Bow section 592
Bow-side oar 560
Bowsprit
Iron paddlesteamer 393

Longboat 380
Rigging 582
Sailing warship 376
Tea clipper 592
Wooden sailing ship
378-379
Bowsprit cap 582
Bowtell molding 475
Box 477
Box boiler 392
Box fold 61
Box freight car 327
Boxing 556
Box-leaved milkwort 144
Box-section tubular
cradle frame 564
Box sister keelson 393
Boxwood staff 577
Brace
Asian building 490
Barrel vault 485
Dome 486
Double topsail
schooner 585
"Ellerman Lines" steam
locomotive 524
Gothic building 473
Neoclassical building
479
Nineteenth-century
building 493
Roman corbita 372
Sailing warship 377
Trombone 506
Wooden sailing ship 378
Brace-and-bit 600-601
Brace block 373
Bracer 548
Brachial artery 253
Brachialis muscle 226
Brachial plexus 238
Brachial valve 278
Brachiocephalic trunk 251
Brachiocephalic vein 253
Brachiopods 278-279
Brachioradialis muscle 226
Brachiosaurus 88, 90-91
Brachylophosaurus 98
Bracing 513
Bracing cable 427
Bracing strut 401-402, 423
Bracing tube 364
Bracing wire
Blériot XI monoplane
401
LVG CVI fighter 405
Wright Flyer 399
Bracken 121
Bracket
Baroque church 479
Cathedral dome 484
Gothic building 473
Islamic tomb 489
Medieval building 466
Neoclassical building
478
Renaissance building
475
Bracket shell 58
Bracteoles
Dehiscent fruit 151
Ice-plant 129
Live-forever 129
Bracts 141-143
Bromeliad 113
Dicotyledon flower 127
Durmast oak 131
Florists'
chrysanthemum 129
Guzmania lingulata 163
Ice-plant 129
Indehiscent fruit 150
Live-forever 129
Peruvian lily 129
Rose 131
Slender thistle 129
Wind-pollinated plant
144
Bract scales 122

Braided polyester 388
Braided stream 286
Braiding
Dragon prowhead 374
River features 290
Brailing rope 372
Brail line 572
Brain
Bird 189
Bony fish 181
Butterfly 169
Chimpanzee 202
Crayfish 173
Dogfish 179
Dolphin 205
Domestic cat 195
Elephant 200
Hominid 108
Human 236-237
Lizard 185
Octopus 176
Rabbit 196
Spider 170
Braincase 108
Brain cavity 100
Brainstem 236
Brake 552, 550
Brake actuating chain 527
Brake arm 552
Brake back plate 340, 550
Brake block 360
Brake bridge 561
Brake cable 365
Brake calliper
ARV light aircraft 424
Disc brake 365
Harley-Davidson FLHS
Electra Glide 363
Honda VF750 364-565
Husqvarna Motocross
TC610 368
Renault Clio 351
Suzuki RGV500 368-369
Wagon bogie 331
Brake cylinder 327,
550-551
Brake disc
ARV light aircraft 424
Renault Clio 351
Wagon bogie 331
Brake drum 339-340, 342
Brake duct 357
Brake fluid 365
Brake hose 351
Brakeless wheel hub 369
Brake lever
ARV light aircraft 425
Benz Motorwagen 335
Bicycle 359
Eddy Merckx racing
bicycle 361
Harley-Davidson FLHS
Electra Glide 363
Kirby BSA 569
Suzuki RGV500 369
White Steam Car 342
"Windcheetah" racing
HPV bicycle 361
Brake master cylinder
Harley-Davidson FLHS
Electra Glide 363
Honda VF750 364
Suzuki RGV500 368
Brake mount 424
Brake pad
Disc brake 365
Eddy Merckx racing
bicycle 361
Renault Clio 351
Wagon bogie 331
Brake pedal
Harley-Davidson FLHS
Electra Glide 363
Honda VF750 364
Oldsmobile bodywork
337
Renault Clio 350
Steam-powered
Cugnot 334

Suzuki RGV500 368
Brake pipe
ARV light aircraft 424
BAe-146 components
414
Lockheed Electra
airliner 406-407
Brake pivot bolt 361
Brake plate 565
Brake quadrant 335
Brake rigging
British Rail Class 20
diesel engine 327
"Ellerman Lines" steam
locomotive 324-325
Brake rod 337, 339
Brake servo 351
Brake shield 551
Brake shoe 550
"Deltic" diesel-electric
locomotive 327
Drum brake 365
"Ellerman Lines" steam
locomotive 325
Renault Clio 350
Brake slip 595
Brake torque arm 364
Brake vacuum pump 324
Braking
Motorcycle 364
Train 330
Braking control system
330
Braking distance 331
Bramante 35
Bramble 130, 146-147
Branched leaf venation 127
Branches
Bishop pine 124
Clubmoss 120
Crab cactus 129
Dicotyledons 127
Horsetail 120
Perennials 130-131
Seaweed 117
Sporophore 114
Woody plants 130-131
Brachial heart 176
Branching bracteole 151
Branchiostegal ray 181
Branchlet 114
Branch trace 125
Brassavola nodosa 162
Brass bevel 336-337
Brass housing for ignition
cable 343
Brassica sp. 132
Brass instruments 504-505,
506-507
Brazil 331
Brazilian battleship
394-395
Brazilian current 296
Brazilian Highlands 264
Bread 598
Breakfast room 483
Breakwater
Battleship 395
Frigate 397
Single scull 561
Breast
Bird 188
Horse 199
Human 211
Breast auger 374
Breast bone 218
Breast stroke 558-559
Breastwork 380
Breather paper 602
Breather pipe 422
Breccia 276-277
Breech 396
Breech block 396
Breeches 557
Breech wheel 396
Breve rest 502
Brick arch 324
Brick pier 495
Brick vault 492

Brick wall 492
Bridge
    Acoustic guitar 512-513
    Battleship 594-595
    Cello 511
    Double bass 511
    Electric guitar 513
    Frigate 397
    Golf course 546
    London Bridge 466-467
    Medieval castle 467
    Modern building 498
    Viola 511
    Violin 510
Bridge pin 512
Bridges 530
Bridle 555
Bright Angel shale 277
B ring 46-47
Britain 331
Brittle stars 174-175
Broad ax 574
Broad disk 79
Broad lace trim 336-337
Broadside 378
Broken pediment 481
Bromeliads 112-113
    Epiphytic 162-163
Bromine 311
Bronchi 254
Bronchial nerve 254
Bronchial tree 254
Bronchial vein 254
Bronchiole and alveoli
    254
Bronchus
    Frog 182
    Human 215, 255
Bronze casting 452
Bronze finishing tools
    454
Bronze mast rock 372
Bronze statue 455
Broomrape 163
Browband 554-555
Brow horn 102
Brow horn core 103
Brown alga 116
Brown scales 121
Brown seaweed 116-117
Brow ridge
    Australopithecus 108
    Gorilla 203
    Homo sapiens 108
Browser menu 577
Brush 452, 444, 600
Brushbar 592, 593
Brushbar drive belt cover
    593
Brushbar motor control
    593
Brush holder 600
Brushing boot 554
Brush lettering equipment
    444
Brush rest 444
Brush tool articulation
    593
Bryce Canyon 276
Bryophyta 118
Bryophytes 112, 118-119
Bryozoans 279
Bryum sp. 112
Buccal cavity
    Bird 189
    Chimpanzee 202
    Dolphin 205
    Domestic cat 195
    Elephant 200
    Pachycephalosaurus
    100
    Rabbit 196
    Tortoise 187
Buccal mass 176
Buccinator muscle 229
Bucket seat 361
Bucket tappet 344
Bud
    Adventitious 154

Aechmea miniata 162
Apical meristem 154
Begonia 129
Bishop pine 124
Broomrape 163
Clematis flower 131
Dicotyledons 127
Durmast oak 131
Florists'
    chrysanthemum 129
Horse chestnut 130
Larkspur 141
Lily 140
Lime 143
London plane 134
Moss 119
*Oxalis sp.*121
Pine needle 125
Rhizome 155
Root tuber 154-155
Rose 131
Rowan twig 131
Stolon 154
Water lily 159
Buddhist style 490
Budh Planitia 35
Bud scale
    Bishop pine 124
    Dicotyledon stem 127
    London plane 134
    Pine shoot apex 125
Buffer
    "Deltic" diesel-electric
    locomotive 527
    "Ellerman Lines" steam
    locomotive 524-525
    Italian State Railroads
    Class 402 528
    "Rocket" steam
    locomotive 524
Buffing pad 528
Bugle 506
Bulb
    Renault Clio 352
    Vegetative reproduction
    154-155
Bulb horn
    1906 Renault 337
    Ford Model T 538
Bulbil 154-155
Bulbourethral gland 259
Bulkhead
    ARV Super 2 425
    Flat freight car 527
Bulkhead stiffener 393
Bulkhead trim 407
Bulldog clip 430
Bullet 397, 549
Bullet block 373
Bullet-shaped guard 278
Bull-head rail 551
Bullnose chisel 452
Bull's-eye 549
Bulwark
    74-gun ship 580
    Ironclad 393
Bumblebee 168
Bumper
    Bus 332-333
    Honda Insight 354
    Renault Clio 348-349
    Volkswagen Beetle 341
Bung 313, 560
Bunkers 546-547
Bunk space 397
Bun lamp burner 559
Buntline 572
Buon fresco 434-435
Buoy 379
Buoyant wetland plants 158
Burmese pagoda 490
Burning reaction 312, 313,
    315
Burnisher 452, 446
Bursting charge 397
Buses 332-333
Business class cabin 572
Bush 605
Bushes 130-131

Bushing 514
Butt
    Bassoon 508
    Lacrosse crosse 541
    Tennis racket 544
Butt cap 563
Butte
    Igneous rock structures
    274
    Weathering and erosion
    285
Buttercup 127, 132-133
Butterfly 168
Butterfly knot 389
Butterfly plate 582
Butterfly swimming
    stroke 558-559
Butterwort 160-161
Butt extension 563
Buttock
    Horse 198
    Human 210
Button head rivet 392
Button-quilted upholstery
    336
Buttress 484
    Baroque church 478-481
    Dome 486
    Gothic church 470-473
    Medieval building 466,
    468-469
    Nineteenth-century
    building 493
Butt section 562

C

3C273 (quasar) 11
Caarduus tenuiflorus 129
Cab 524, 527
Cabane strut 404
Cabbage 132
Cab-end bogie 527
Cabin
    74-gun ship 380-381
    Iron paddlesteamer
    592-593
    Wooden sailing ship 379
Cabin air-discharge
    aperture 414
Cabin air duct 417
Cabin air-pressure
    discharge valve 413
Cabinet rasp 452
Cabin trim 406-407
Cable 600-601
Cable entry point 598
Cable guide 358-359, 360
Cable holder 595
Cable retaining gland 598
Cables and ducting 602
Cable stop 565
Cacti
    Desert survivors 112
    Dryland adaptation 156
    Herbaceous flowering
    plants 129
Cadmium 311
Cadmium red 456
Cadmium yellow 438
Caecum
    Bird 189
    Brachiosaurus 90
    Chimpanzee 202
    Cow 198
    Digestive 176, 175
    Gut 170
    Human 249
    Octopus 176
    Pyloric 181-174
    Rabbit 196
    Rectal 174
Caelum 18
Caernarvon Castle 466
Caiman 186-187
Calamus 191
Calcanean tendon
    232-233

Calcaneum 183, 199
Calcareous ooze 299
Calcareous plates 172
Calcareous tufa 284
Calcite (calcium
    carbonate)
    Blue chalk 450
    Carbonates 269
    Cave 284-285
    Fossils 278
    Mohs scale 271
    Sedimentary rocks 277
    Testing candle wax 313
Calcite curtain 285
Calcite ossicle 174
Calcite ridge 284-285
Calcium 310
    Earth's composition 39
    Earth's crust 58
    Seawater salt content
    296
Calcium line 23
Caldera
    Igneous rock structures
    275
    Lake formation 293
    Volcano 272
Caledonian mountains
    Late Carboniferous
    period 67
    Triassic period 69
Calendars 618
Calf 210
Californian purple sea
    urchin 175
Californium 311
Calliactis parasitica 166
Calligraphy 444-445
Calliper assembly 365
Callipers 452
Callisto 44
Caloris Basin 34-35
Caloris Montes 35
Calypte helenae 193
Calyptra 119
Calyx 140
    Allium sp. 143
    Centaury 144
    Human 256
    Simple succulent berry
    149
Cam 344
Camarasaurus 91
Cambium 126
Cambrian period
    Fossil record 279
    Geological timescale 56
Camcorder 582
Cam cover
    Jaguar straight six
    engine 344
    Jaguar V12 engine 345
    72° VTO engine 356
Camera module 581
Camellia 157
Camels 198-199
Camera 608, 611
    Digital 580-581
    Digital video 582-583
Camera pouch 426
Cam follower
    Ford diesel engine 347
    Jaguar straight six
    engine 344
    Jaguar V12 engine 345
    Velocette OHV engine
    567
Cam lobe 344
Camouflage 409
Camouflage coloration
    192
Campaniform capital 458
Campanile 477
Camptosaurus 70, 97
Camshaft 345-345
Camshaft gear 367
Camshaft sprocket 345
Camshaft timing gear 344
Canada 331

Canadian football 524,
    526-527
Canadian pond weed
    158-159
Canal
    Sea urchin 175
    Starfish 174
Canals 42
Canaries current 296
Cancel button 575
Cancellous bone 224
Cancer 18, 21
Candelabrum 476
Candle lamp 555
Candle wax 312-313
Canes Venatici 18, 21
Canine tooth
    Bear 106, 194
    Chimpanzee 202
    Human 246
    Hyaenodon 107
    Lion 194
    Opossum 106
    Smilodon 107
    Toxodon 106
Canis familiaris 195
Canis Major 18, 21
Canis Minor 18, 21
Canister 594
Cannon 376, 594
Cannon bone 198-199
Cannondale bicycle 361
Canoeing 560-561
Canopus 15
Canopy
    1906 Renault 336-337
    ARV light aircraft
    424-425
    Bell-47 helicopter 422
    Daimler engine 343
    Ford Model T 539
    Hawker Tempest
    components 409
    Oldsmobile engine 336
    Schleicher glider 426
    Schweizer helicopter
    423
Canopy latch 425
Canopy rail 409
Canson paper 441
Cant frame 381
Cantilever beam 494
Cantilever brake 358,
    361
Cantilever brake boss
    359
Cantilevered shade 495
Cantle
    Racing saddle 555
    Showjumping saddle
    554
Canvas
    Acrylic paint 442
    Oil paint 436
    Preparation 437
Canvas shroud 562
Canvas support 457
Canyon
    Sedimentary rocks
    276-277
    Weathering and erosion
    282-283
Cap
    Alga 116
    Fungus 114-115
    Radicle tip 153
    Wood capstan 387
    Wooden sailing ship
    378-379
Cape gooseberry 149
Capella 18, 21
Cape Royal 277
Capillary fringe 293
Capillary network 254
Capital
    Ancient Egyptian
    building 458-459
    Ancient Greek building
    458, 460-461

Ancient Roman
    building 458, 463, 465
Asian building 490, 491
Baroque church 479,
    481
Cathedral dome 487
Domed roof 486
French temple 485
Islamic mosque 488
Medieval building
    467-469
Neoclassical building
    478, 485
Ptolemaic-Roman
    period 459
Renaissance building
    476-477
Romanesque style 468
Capitate bone 250
Capitulum 129, 142
Cap line 445
Capricornus 19, 20
Capstan 587
    74-gun ship 380
    Iron paddlesteamer 593
    Wooden sailing ship
    379
Capstan screw 514
Capsule
    Dry fruit 150-151
    Moss 112, 119
Captain's cabin 379, 581
Captain's seat 416
Captain's shelter 594
Capybara 196-197
Carapace 172-173, 187
Carbon
    Atomic mass 310
    Bows 548
    Candle wax 312-313
    Coal formation 280
    Minerals 268
    Periodic table 311
    Small stars 24-25
    Structure of red
    supergiant 26
Carbonates 269
Carbon atom 138
Carbon bush 605
Carbon dioxide
    Earth's atmosphere
    300
    Gas 312-313
    Mars' atmosphere 43
    Photosynthesis 138
    Respiratory system 255
    Scrubber compartment
    397
    Structure of comet 53
    Venus' atmosphere 37
Carbon graphite racket
    544
Carbonic acid 284
Carboniferous period
    56-57, 66-67
    Reptiles 80
Carbon ink stick 444
Carbonized wood 430
Carbon monoxide
    Mars' atmosphere 43
    Venus' atmosphere 37
Carbon powder 311
Carbon-rich earth layers
    66
Car-building robots 609
Carburetor
    ARV light aircraft 425
    Mid West twin-rotor
    engine 411
    Pegasus Quasar
    ultralight 427
    Two-stroke engine 566
Carburetor cover 569
Carburetor hot-air intake
    pipe 422
Carburetor hot air lever
    425
Cardiac notch 248

Cardiac region of stomach 179
Cardiac stomach 174
Cardiac vein 250
Carduus tenuiflorus 129
Cargo-carrying boat
  Dhow 376
  Junk 376
  Liberty ship 392
  Roman corbita 372-373
  Tea clipper 392
Cargo derrick 392
Cargo hatch 576
Cargo hold 372, 592
Car, hybrid 354
Caribbean plate 59
Caribbean Sea 264, 617
Carina 21
Carinal canal 120
Carina plate 173
Carling 580
Carmel formation 276
Carnallite 271
Carnassial teeth 194
Carnivores 104, 194-195
  Jurassic period 70
  Theropod 84
  Triassic period 68
Carnivorous plants 160-161
  Pitcher plant 113
Carotid canal 220
Carp 180
Carpals 140-141
  Bird 189
  Bird's wing 191
  Domestic cat 195
  Elephant 201
  Frog 183
  Hare 197
  Horse 199
  Kangaroo 206
  Lizard 184
  Platypus 206
  Rhesus monkey 202
  Seal 204
Carp angling 562
Carpathian mountains 77, 265
Carpels 140-141
  Dehiscent fruit 151
  Fertilization 146-147
  Fruit development 148-149
  Insect-pollinated plant 144
  Lemon fruit 148
  Ovary 140
  Stigma 140
  Style 140
Carpel wall 148, 151
Carpophore 151
Carpus
  Crab 172
  Crayfish 173
  Human 218
Carrara white marble 453
Carriage 413, 570
Carriage drivebelt 574
Carriage shaft 571
Carrick bend 587, 589
Carrion crow 193
Carrot 128, 132
Carrying fork 334
Carrying wheel 524
Cartilage
  Auricle 242
  Bony fish 180
  Meatus 242
  Wrist 250
Cartilaginous fish 178-179, 180
Cartouche 458
Cartridge starter 408
Caruncle 213
Carved sculpture 452, 453
Carved stone 488
Carvel-built hull 376, 591
Carvel planking 376, 377

Carving
  Asian building 490-491
  Gothic building 470
  Sculpture 452
Carving mallet 452
Caryopses 113, 150
Cascade 560
Cassette compartment lid 582
Cassini Division 46, 47
Cassini space probe 614
Cassiopeia 19
Cassowaries 188
Cast alloy wheel 346
Cast aluminum wheel spider 336
Castanea sativa 136, 150
Castanets 504, 517
Casting 452, 454
Cast-iron 492-493
Cast-iron chair 331
Cast iron cylinder barrel 363
Castle-deck gunport 576-377
Castles, 374, 466-467
Castor 18, 21
Castor canadensis 197
Cat 104, 194-195
Catalyst 355
Catalytic converter 544, 550, 556
Cataclysm 560
Cataphoresic coating 348
Cataphyll 152
Cat block 381
Catcher's mask 536
Catch glove 550
Catena 372
Catenary 328, 330
Caterpillar 168, 169, 611
  Eggs 192
Catharina 40
Cathead
  74-gun ship 580
  Battleship 595
Cathedral of St. Lazare 468
Cations 308
Catkin 144
Catted anchor 381
Cattle 104, 198
Caucasus 265, 616
Caudal fin 178, 179, 180-181
Caudal musculature 90, 95
Caudal plate 92-93
Caudal spike 92-93
Caudal vertebrae
  Ankylosaurus 95
  Archaeopteryx 85
  Crocodile 186
  Diplodocus 90
  Domestic cat 195
  Elephant 201
  Eryops 81
  Euoplocephalus 95
  Gallimimus 86
  Hare 197
  Horse 199
  Iguanodon 96, 97
  Kangaroo 206
  Kentrosaurus 93
  Lizard 184-185
  Parasaurolophus 98
  Plateosaurus 89
  Platypus 206
  Rhesus monkey 202
  Seal 204
  Stegoceras 101
  Stegosaurus 93
  Struthiomimus 87
  Triceratops 102
  Tuojiangosaurus 93
  Tyrannosaurus 84-85
  Westlothiana 81
Caudate nucleus 257

Gaudex 113
Caudo-femoral muscle 97
Cauliculus 460
Caulophryne jordani 180
Cave bear skull 77
Caves 284-285
  Coastline 294-295
  Glacier 286
Cavetto molding
  Ancient Egyptian building 458-459
  Baroque church 479
  French temple 485
  Gothic building 472
  Renaissance building 477
Cavies 196
Cayley, Sir George 398
CCD (Charge-Coupled Devices) 570
C clef 502
CD/DVD drive 567
Cedar-tree laccolith 274
Ceilings 463, 484
Celestial equator
  Stars of northern skies 18-19
  Stars of southern skies 20-21
Celestial poles 18
Celestial sphere 18
Cell
  Alga 116-117
  Body 217
  Building 469, 485
  Chusan palm leaf 130
  Clubmoss stem 120
  Collar 166
  Dicotyledon 126-127
  Epidermal 166
  Epiphytic orchid 162
  Fern rachis 121
  Horsetail stem 120
  Leaf 126, 159
  Marram grass 113
  Monocotyledon 126-127
  Moss 119
  Mushroom 115
  Photosynthesis 158-159
  Pine 124-125
  Pore 166
  Root 152-153
  Root tip 152
  Sinus 112
  Spirogyra sp. 117
  Stem 134-135
  Wetland plants 158-159
Cell body 239
Cell membrane 217
Cell nuclear membrane 216
Cell nucleus 217
Cell nucleus residue 254
Cello 503-505, 510
Cellophanes 588-589
Cells 607
Cellulose fiber insulation 602
Cell wall
  Alga 112, 116
  Leaf 159
  Palisade mesophyll 139
  Root 132
  Spirogyra sp. 117
  Stem surface 156
Celsius temperature scale 590
Cement-based adhesive 450
Cement gland 173
Cement-rendered wall 494
Cenozoic era 57, 74, 76
  Fossil record 279
Censer 488
Centaurium erythraea 144
Centaurus 18, 21

Centaurus A (radio galaxy) 13
Centaurus and Crux 21
Central Asia 64
Central bulge 12, 14
Central canal 238
Central computer control 528
Central deflector 612
Central electrode 306
Central nervous system 258
Central peak
  Degas and Brönte 34
  Venus' craters 36
Central processing unit (CPU) 590
Central retinal artery 240
Central retinal vein 240
Central shield 187
Central sulcus 236-237
Center
  Australian football 528
  Basketball 532
  Canadian football 526
  Football 526
  Lacrosse 541
  Netball 535
  Rugby 530
Centerboard 561
Center buckeye coupler 326
Center buckeye (Australian rules football 528
  Basketball 532
  Ice hockey 550
  Netball 535
  Soccer 524
Center console 353
Center court 545
Centered rudder 375
Center element 599
Center field 536
Center flag 529
Center forward 540
Center gangway 529
Center Georges Pompidou 496-497
Center girder 393
Center half 540
Center halfback 528, 529
Center half forward 528, 529
Center line 413, 415
  Fencing piste 557
  Ice hockey 550
  Soccer 524
Center-line beam 426-427
Center line keelson 393
Centrifugal brake 562
Centrifugal compressor 418
Centrifugal effect 297
Centriole 217
Centripetal river drainage 288
Centrum 187
Cephalapsis 65
Cephalic groove 173
Cephalic vein
  Human 253
  Octopus 176
Cephalopods 176, 279
Cephalothorax
  Crayfish 173
  Malacostraca 172
  Scorpion 170
  Shrimp 172
  Spider 170-171
Cepheus 19
Ceramic end-piece 319
Ceratopsia 83, 103
Ceratosauria 83
Ceraunius Tholus 43
Cercidyphyllum sp. 72
Cerebellum 212, 236-237, 258
Cerebral areas 237
Cerebral ganglion 169, 177

Cerebral vessel 257
Cerebrum 212, 236-237, 258
Cereoid cactus 129
Cerium 310
Ceropegia woodii 157
Ceruchi 372
Cerussite 269
Cervical musculature
  Euoplocephalus 94
  Gallimimus 86
Cervical nerves 238
Cervical plate 92-93
Cervical rib 84, 96, 100-101, 105
Cervical vertebrae
  Archaeopteryx 85
  Arsinoitherium 104
  Bird 189
  Brachiosaurus 91
  Crocodile 186
  Domestic cat 195
  Elephant 201
  Eryops 80
  Hare 197
  Horse 199
  Human 212, 222, 245
  Iguanodon 96
  Kangaroo 206
  Kentrosaurus 93
  Lizard 184
  Parasaurolophus 99
  Plateosaurus 88
  Platypus 206
  Rhesus monkey 202
  Seal 204
  Stegoceras 101
  Stegosaurus 93
  Struthiomimus 87
  Toxodon 106
  Tuojiangosaurus 93
  Tyrannosaurus 84
Cervix 258-259
Cervus elephus 199
Cesium 310
Cetaceans 204-205
Cetiosaurus 91
Cetorhinus maximus 179
Cetus 19, 20
Chaffinch 193
Chain
  Bicycle 358-359, 360-361
  Drum kit 518
  Wheel and axle 320
  Wooden sailing ship 378
Chain bobstay 582
Chain drive
  Motorcycle clutch 362
  Werner motorcycle 366
  Wright Flyer 398-399
Chain locker 393
Chain motif 491
Chain plate 382
Chain swivel 386
Chain wale 576-577
Chajya 489
Chalcedony 271
Chalk 430
  Tempera 432
  Gesso 434
  Pastel making 440
  Fresco 434
  Sedimentary rocks 277
Chamber
  Building 465, 491
  Gun turret 396
Chambers
  Seaweed 116
  Stomach 198
  Substomatal 139
Chamfered corner 485, 488, 494
Championship golf courses 546
Change 521
Chang Jiang 265
Channel

74-gun ship 381
Sailing warship 376-377
Temple of Neptune 460
Wooden sailing ship 378
Channelled wrack 116
Chapel
  Baroque church 479
  Gothic church 470
  Medieval church 469
Chapel pier 467
Chaplet 454
Chapter-house 472
Charcoal drawing 430-431
Charentais melon 149
Charge
  Four-stroke cycle 343
  Modern engines 344
Charged atom 306, 308
Charged particle 316
Charging with ball 533
Charon 50
Chart house 594
Chase 395
Chassis
  Digital camera 580
  First cars 334-335
  Ford Model T 338
  Kirby BSA sidecar 369
  Microwave combination oven 596
  Monocoque 363
  Motorcycle 362, 364-365
  Oldsmobile chassis 337
  Panhard-system 337
  Volkswagen Beetle 340
  White Steam Car 342
Chassis earth terminal 597
Chassis electrical plug 357
Chassis frame 358
Chassis number 327
Chataya arch 491
Châteaux 474, 476-477
Chatra 491
Chattravali 490-491
Chauffeur's seat 334
Checkerboard 136
Check pawl 562
Cheek
  74-gun ship 381
  Dunkeld wet fly 563
  Horse 199
  Human 212
  Running block 583
  Sailmaker's mallet 384
  Stegosaurus 92
Cheek horn 103
Cheek-piece
  Harness racer 555
  Showjumper 554
Cheek pouch 98, 196
Cheek teeth
  Ankylosaurs 92
  Carnivores 194
  Ornithopods 96
  Tetralophodon 104
  Theropods 84
Cheese 582, 588-589
Cheiracanthus 65
Cheirolepis 65
Chekhov 35
Chela 170, 172, 173
Chelicera 79
Chelicerae 170-171
Chelicerates 279
Cheliped
  Crab 172
  Crayfish 173
Chelonia 186
Chemical bond 307
Chemical change 280-281
Chemical energy 314-315
Chemical equations 312

Chemical properties
  Electrons 308, 310
  Substances 506
Chemical reactions
  312-313
Chemical sedimentary
  rocks 276
Chemical symbols 512
  Periodic table 510-511
Chemical weathering 282
Chemise 466-467
Chemistry symbols 621
Cherry 148
Cherry wood 512
Chert 277
Cherub 472
Chervil 155
Chest
  Gorilla 203
  Human 211, 214
  Lion 194
Chestnut 198
Chest padding 551
Chest pass 532, 535
Chest protector 527
Chevet 469
Chevron 81, 85, 87, 89, 93,
  95-96, 98, 101-102
Chevron fold 61
Chevron-tread tire 336
Chi1 Orionis 18
Chi2 Orionis 18
Chiastolite hornfels 275
Chihuahuan Desert 264
Chile 331
Chimney
  Bordino Steam Carriage
    334
  "Ellerman Lines" steam
    locomotive 525
  Iron paddlesteamer 393
  "Rocket" steam
    locomotive 324
Chimney-shaft 467
Chimney-stack 476, 483
Chimpanzee 202-203
Chin
  Bird 188
  Human 211, 212
China
  Ball games 524
  Late Carboniferous
    period 66-67
  Middle Ordovician
    period 64-65
  Ornithopod 96
  Railroad track gauge
    331 Thyreophorans 92
Chinese calendar 618
Chinese characters 445
Chinese junk 376
Chinese white 438
Chin groove 199
Chin guard 553
Chin gun turret 408
Chinle formation 276
Chin rest 510-511
Chin spoiler 346
Chipmunk 196
Chirostenotes 87
Chisel 452-453
  Chlamydosaurus sp. 116
Chlorenchyma 120
Chloride 296
Chlorine 311
Chlorophyll 138
  Chloroplast 139
  Photosynthesis pigment
    116, 138, 162
Chlorophyta 116
Chloroplast 138-139
  Alga 112
  Chlamydomonas sp.
    116
  Envelope 139
  Epiphytic orchid
    162
  Internal view 139
  Spirogyra sp. 117

Choanocyte 166
Choir 468-469, 470,
  472
Choir manual 514
Choir-screen 470
Choir-stall 470
Choir stop 514
Chondrichthyes 178
Chondrostean fish 69
Chong Ch'ol 55
Chordae tendineae 251
Chorioallantoic
  membrane 192
Chorion 260
Choroid 240
Christian architecture 468
Christmas rose 159
Chromate ion 312
Chrome passivation 348
Chrome plating 347
Chrome trim strip 341
Chromium
  Mineralization zones
    281
  Oxide 312
  Periodic table 510
Chromosphere 32-33
Chrysalis 168
  Chrysanthemum
    morifolium 129
Chryse Planitia 43
Chrysler Building 495
  Chrysocyon brachyurus
    195
Chuck 601
Chuck key 601
Chung-ta-wei 376
Church
  Santa Sophia 487
  Sorbonne 486
  St. Botolph 473
  St. Eustache 477
  St. George in the East
    478, 481
  St. Maclou 470, 472
  St. Maria della Salute
    478
  St. Maria della Vittoria
    478
  St. Paul-St. Louis
    478-479
  St. Pierre de Libreville
    496, 499
  St. Serge 469
Church-roof boss 468
Chusan palm 127, 130
  Ciconia ciconia 188
Ciliary body 241
Cincture 477
Cinder 272
Cinder cone
  Igneous rock structures
    274
  Volcanic structure
    275
Cinema, home 584-585
Cinnabar 271
Cinquefoil molding 471
Circle 479, 622
Circle pad 579
Circuit 516
Circuit board 579, 582,
  585, 589
Circuit board plug 596
Circuit breaker 514
Circular mountain lake
  293
Circulatory system
  252-253
Circumference 622
Cirque 286-287
Cirque formation 287
Cirque Napoleon 478-479
Cirri 172
Cirrocumulus cloud
  302
Cirrostratus cloud
  302
Cirrus 173

Cirrus cloud
  Neptune 50
  Structure of Mars
    43
  Weather 302-303
  Citrus limon 148
City bus 332
Civet 194
Cladding 494, 496,
  498-499
Cladode 129
  Cladonia floerkeana 114
  Cladonia portentosa 114
Clam 176
Clamp
  Cross-stave 377
  Intaglio printing 313
  U-tube 446
Clarinet 503-504, 508
Classical-style
  architecture 474, 478,
    482
Clastic sedimentary rocks
  276
Claves 517
Clavicle
  Bird 189
  Bony fish 181
  Eryops 80
  Human 211, 218
  Kangaroo 206
  Rhesus monkey 202
Clavius 40
Clavus 373
Claw
  Albertosaurus 84
  Anchisaurus 89
  Archaeopteryx 85
  Beetle 168
  Bird 188
  Bumblebee 168
  Caiman 187
  Chick 193
  Crab 172
  Crayfish 173
  Dinosaur 85
  Herrerasaurus 86
  Kangaroo 207
  Lizard 184
  Marble sculpture 452
  Pachycephalosaurus
    100
  Psittacosaurus 103
  Scorpion 170
  Spider 171
  Stegoceras 101
  Terrapin 187
  Tyrannosaurus 84
Clawed feet 190, 206
Clay 298
Clay daub 465
Clay modeling 452,
  455
Clay mounds 286
Clear space 554
Cleavage 270
Clef 502
  Cleithrolepis granulatus
    69
Cleithrum 80
Clematis 130-131, 137
Clench nail 375
Cleomedes 40
Cleopatra Patera 37
Clerestory 459, 472, 479
Clew 375
Clewline 379, 385
Cliffs
  Coastlines 294-295
  River's stages 289
  Sedimentary rocks
    276-277
Climate
  Carboniferous period
    66
  Geological time 56
  Oceans and seas
    296
  Weather 302

Climatic change
  Coastline 294
  Geological time 56
Clincher wheel 359
Clinker-built hull 375
Clinker-built oak planking
  575
Clints 284-285
Clitoris 258
Cloaca
  Bird 189
  Brachiosaurus 90
  Dogfish 179
  Euoplocephalus 94
  Frog 182
  Gallimimus 87
  Lizard 185
  Spider 170
  Tortoise 187
Cloacal opening 185
Clock operator 532
Clock tower 493
Cloister 472
Cloning technology
  606-607
Close-stowing anchor 386
Cloud deck 50-51
Cloud features
  Neptune 50
  Saturn 46
  Venus 36
Clouds
  Earth's atmosphere 301
  Jupiter 44-45
  Mars 42-43
  Neptune 50-51
  Saturn 46-47
  Uranus 48-49
  Venus 36-37
  Water cycle 288
  Weather 302-303
Cloud shadow 50
Clouds of dust and gas
  Life of massive star 24
  Milky Way 14-15
  Nebulae and star
    clusters 16-17
  Origin and expansion of
    universe 11
  Small stars 24
Cloudtop temperature
  Structure of Jupiter 45
  Structure of Neptune 51
  Structure of Saturn 47
  Structure of Uranus 49
Clove hitch 388
Cloven hoof 198
Clubmosses 64, 66,
  120-121
Clump cathead 595
Clustered column 469
Clutch 364, 366
Clutch and flywheel 340
Clutch cable 350, 363, 365
Clutch center plate 351
Clutch cover 363
Clutch lever 363, 369
Clutch pedal 350
Clutch pressure plate 351
Clutch release bearing
  351
  Clypeaster 279
Cnidocytes 166-167
CNS 238
Coal
  Earth's evolution 57
  Mineral resources
    280-281
  Power stations 314
  Sedimentary rocks 276
  Steam locomotive 324
Coal-forming forests 57
Coal measures 61
Coaming 581
Coastal spring 292
Coaster 374-375
Coastlines 294-295
  Cave 284
Cobalt

Mineralization zones
  281
  Periodic table 511
Cobra lily 160-161
  Coccosteus 65
Coccygeal cornu 225
Coccygeal vertebrae 222
Coccyx 218, 222
Cochlea 242-243
Cocking lever 549
Cockpit
  Airbus 380 573
  Avro biplane 403
  Kayak 560
  LVG CVI fighter 405
  Modern military
    aircraft 420-421
  Sailing dinghy 561
  Schleicher glider 426
Cockpit canopy 409
Cockpit coaming 425
Cocoa 148
Coconino sandstone 276
  Cocos nucifera 135
Cocos plate 59
Cod 180
  Codiaeum variegatum 136
Coelenterata 166
Coeliac trunk 256-257
  Coelodonta 76-77, 104
Coeloptysidae 69
  Coelurus 87
Coenobium 116
Coffer 463, 485
Coffered vault 485
Coffering 475
Cogged drive belt 344
Coil spring
  "Ellerman Lines" steam
    locomotive 524
  Motorcycle 364
Coil suspension spring
  "Deltic" diesel-electric
    locomotive 327
  "Eurostar" multi-
    voltage electric train
    329
  Wagon bogie 331
Coke hopper 334
Cold air intake 420
Cold-air unit 417
Cold front 302-303
Cold occlusion 302
Cold-water pipe 405
Cold-water upwelling 296
Coleoptera 168
  Coleus sp. 134
Collagen and elastic fibers
  252
Collapsed crater 293
Collar
  Cathedral of Notre
    Dame de Paris 473
  Sea anemone 167
  Snail 177
Collar-beam 473
Collar bone 211, 218
Collar cell 166
Collar of horsetail 120
Collecting duct 256
Collecting tubule 256
Collective lever 422
Collenchyma 126, 134-135
Colliding plates 272
Colloids 306
Colon
  Butterfly 169
  Cow 198
  Human 215, 249, 259
  Rabbit 196
Colonette
  Gothic church 473
  Islamic building 488
  Medieval building
    467-469
  Neoclassical building
    479
  Renaissance building
    474

Colonnade
  Ancient Greek building
    460-461
  Ancient Roman
    building 462-465
  Cathedral dome 484,
    487
  Neoclassical building
    483
Colonnaded story 494
Color 270
Color changes 512-513
Color ink cartridge 574
Color ink-cartridge
  clamp 574
Color light signals 330
Color wheel 439
Colorado River
  Earth's evolution 57
  Grand Canyon 277
  Valley 277
Colosseum 462, 464-465
Colpus 144
Columba 18, 21
Columella 119, 145
Column
  Ancient Egyptian
    building 458-459
  Ancient Greek building
    458, 460
  Ancient Roman
    building 458, 462-463,
    465
  Baroque church
    480-481
  Cathedral dome 487
  Cave system 285
  French temple 485
  Gothic church 473
  Islamic mosque 488
  Medieval church
    468-469
  Modern building
    496-498
  Monocotyledonous
    flower 126
  Neoclassical building
    478-479, 483
  Nineteenth-century
    building 492-493
  Renaissance building
    477
  Coma 52-53
Coma Berenices 18, 21
Combat sports 556-557
Combination lever 325
Combustion 326
Combustion chamber
  Capacity 366-567
  Iron paddlesteamer
    393
  Jaguar straight six
    engine 344
  Jet engines 418-419
Combustion cycle 410
Comets 30, 52-53
Common bile duct 252
Common blackheaded
  gull 189
Common brittle star 173
Common carotid artery
  215, 251, 253
Common centaury 144
Common crus 243
Common digital extensor
  muscle 84, 97
Common elder 143
Common English ivy 131
Common horse chestnut 130
Common horsetail 120
Common Iguana 82
Common iliac artery 215,
  253, 257
Common iliac vein 215,
  253, 257
Common ivy 137
Common lime 143
Common link 386
Common mulberry 130

Common peroneal nerve
258
Common rafter 475, 486
Common starfish 175
Common tern 195
Common time 502
Communication 108
Communications aerial 424
Commutator 600
Commuters 565
Compact bone 224-225
Compact disc 584, 586
Companion cells 132-134
Companion ladder 581
Companion way 580
Company logo 572
Compass
  Battleship 594
  Vault decoration 485
Compass and rangefinder
  platform 594
Competent bed rock 61
Competition motorcycles
  368-369
Competitions
  Archery 548
  Diving 558
  Judo 556
  Rowing 560
  Skiing 552-555
Complete mesentery 167
Composite capital 478
Composite column 478
Composite pilaster 478
Composite volcano 272
Composter 602
Compound eye
  Beetle 168
  Bumblebee 168
  Butterfly 169
  Crab 172
  Crayfish 173
  Damselfly 168
  Malacostraca 172
  Shrimp 172
Compound inflorescence
  131, 142
Compound leaf 130-131,
  136
Compound pier 468-469
Compound pulleys 320
Compounds 268, 306, 308
Compound succulent fruit
  148-149
Compound umbel 143
Compressible gas 365
Compression
  Faults and folds 60
  Glacier 286
  Igneous and
    metamorphic rocks 274
  Mineral resources 280
  Mountain building 62
  Rock cycle 266
Compression ring
  Ford diesel engine 347
  Jaguar straight six
    engine 344
Compression stroke 343
Compressor 418
Compressor piston 344
Compsognathus 70
Computer
  and Email program
    677
  Electronic instruments
    520
  Laptop 567
  Modern bodywork 348
  Tablet 568-569
Computerized ignition
  system 344
Concave brace 477
Concave molding 482
Concave wall 478, 481
Concealed lighting 572
Conceptacles 116-117
Concert grand piano
  515

Concha
  Ear 242
  Nasal 221, 241
Conchoidal fracture
  Extrusive igneous rocks
    275
  Fracture 270
  Sedimentary rocks
    277
Concorde 416-417
Concrete 492, 494,
  496-499
Concrete shielding 314
Concrete shoe 499
Concrete track 328
Concrete wall 463, 465,
  496
Condensation 307
Condensation
  Nuclear power station
    314
  Testing candle wax
    313
Condensation level 302
Condenser 342
Condenser aperture
  610
Condenser housing
  611
Condenser lens 611
Conducting tissue 119
Conductor
  Electrical circuit 316
  Generating magnetism
    317
  Orchestra 504
Conductor's stand 505
Condylactis sp. 166
Condyle
  Carnivore 194
  Human 220
Cone 625
Cones
  Bishop pine 124
  Gymnosperms 122
  Igneous and
    metamorphic rocks 274
  Pine 122
  Scots pine 122
  Smooth cypress 123
  Welwitschia 123
  Yew 123
Cone sheet 274
Cone stalk 124
Congas 519
Congo Basin 39
Congo River 265
Conical bore 507
Conical dome 476
Conical map projection 265
Conical spire 466, 476
Conical volcano 272
Conifer
  Cretaceous period 72
  Earth's evolution 57
  Fossil record 279
  Gymnosperm 122-125
  Jurassic period 70
  Triassic period 68
Coniferophyta 122
Conjugation 117
Conjunctiva 241
Connecting rod
  Bordino Steam Carriage
    334
  Flat-four cylinder
    arrangement 340
  Four-stroke cycle 343
  Iron paddlesteamer 392
  Jaguar straight six
    engine 344
  Jaguar V12 engine 345
  Mid West two-stroke
    engine 410
  Steamboat with paddle
    wheels 391
Connecting wire
  598
Connectors 569

Conning tower 394, 397
Conocephalum conicum
  118
Con-rod 340, 343-345
Conservation of Energy
  Law 314
Conservatory 602, 603
Console 579
Constellations 18-21, 613
Constratum 373
Constrictor snakes 184
Construction sculpture
  452
Contact 352
Contact grid 605
Contact metamorphism
  274
Contant d'Ivry 478
Contest area 556
Contests
  Head-butting 100
  Shooting 548
Continental crust 58-59
  Mineralization zones
    281
  Mountain building
    62-63
  Ocean floor 298
Continental drift 58, 617
Continental margin
  sediments 299
Continental rise 298
Continental Sea 73, 75
Continental shelf
  Ocean floor 298
  Prehistoric Earth 69, 71
  Rock cycle 267
Continental slope
  Ocean floor 298
  Offshore currents 296
  Rock cycle stages 267
Continents
  Formation of the Earth
    58, 56
  Geological time 56
  Mapping the Earth
    264-265
  Physical map of the
    world 616-617
Contrabassoon 504-505
Contractile vacuole 116
Control cabinet 396
Control circuit 328
Control buttons 585
Control column
  ARV light aircraft 425
  BE 2B bomber 404
  Curtiss biplane 398-399
Control-column aperture
  425
Control flag 552
Controller 332
Control line 561
Control panel 571, 595, 596
Control panel and disc
  tray cover 584
Control panel boards 597
Control panel fascia 597
Control panel microchips
  596
Control panels 594
Control panel wiring 595
Control platform 590
Control reservoir drain 326
Control rod 314, 424
Control room 397
Control stalk 353
Convection cell 33
Convection current 38
Convective zone 24, 33
Converging plates 63
Conversion 550
Convex portico 483
Cook/grill tray 596
Cooking 108
Cooksonia 56
Cooksonia hemispherica
  64
Coolant 314

Coolant inlet 424
Coolant jacket 410-411
Coolant outlet
  ARV light aircraft 424
  Jaguar V12 engine 345
  Mid West two-stroke
    engine 410
Coolant passage 346
Coolant pipe 354
Coolant pump 410
Coolant rail 345
Cooling device 611
Cooling fan 345, 567
Cooling fin
  Drum brake 365
  Mid West rotary engine
    411
  Two-stroke engine 366
  Velocette OHV engine
    367
Cooling intake 534
Cooling perforations 597
Cooling tank 335
Cooling tower
  Center Georges
    Pompidou 496-497
  Nuclear power station
    314
Cooling water tank 335
Co-orbital moons 46
Coping-stone 495
Copper
  Mineral resources
    280-281
  Minerals 268
  Periodic table 311-312
Copper body-shell 519
Copper face 384
Copper nitrate solution
  312
Copper ore 306
Copper plate nib 444
Copper sheathing 392
Copper sulfate 313
Coprates Chasma 43
Copulatory bursa
  Butterfly 169
  Snail 177
Coracoid
  Bird 189
  Diplodocus 90
  Euoplocephalus 94
  Gallimimus 86
  Triceratops 102
  Turtle 187
  Tyrannosaurus 84
Coral 78, 166-167
  Atoll development 299
  Fossil record 279
Corallina officinalis 117
Coral reef
  Earth's evolution 56
  Ocean floor 298
Gor Anglais 504-505, 508
Corbel
  Cathedral dome 487
  Medieval building 467,
    469
  Neoclassical building
    482
  Nineteenth-century
    building 493
  Renaissance building 477
  Rococo style 478
Corbita 372-373
Cor Caroli 18, 21
Cordaites 67
Cordate leaf bases
  136-137
Cordite case 396
Cordite handling room 396
Cordite supply shuttle 396
Core
  Earth 38-39
  Helix Nebula 17
  Massive stars 26-27
  Moon 40
  Neutron stars and black
    holes 28-29

Small stars 24-25
Structure of comet 53
Structure of Earth 63
Structure of Jupiter 45
Structure of Mars 43
Structure of Mercury 35
Structure of Neptune 51
Structure of Pluto 51
Structure of Saturn 47
Structure of Uranus 49
Structure of Venus 37
Core-engine jet pipe 412,
  415
Core jet pipe 419
Core temperature
  Structure of Earth 39
  Structure of Jupiter 45
  Structure of main
    sequence star 24
  Structure of red giant
    25
  Structure of red
    supergiant 26
  Structure of Saturn 47
  Structure of Sun 33
  Structure of Uranus 49
Corinthian capital 460,
  463, 479, 481
Corinthian column
  463-464, 479-480
Corinthian entablature
  463
Corinthian order 460, 462
Corinthian pilaster
  463-464, 480-481
Coriolis force 296-297,
  300
Cork
  Oboe 508
  Stems 134-135
  Woody dicotyledons 127
Corms 154-155
Corn 112
Cornea 241
Corner arc 524
Corner seal 347
Cornet 506
Cornice
  Ancient Egyptian
    temple 458-459
  Ancient Greek building
    460-461
  Ancient Roman
    building 462-465
  Asian building 491
  Baroque church
    479-481
  Dome 484, 486
  French temple 485
  Gothic church 470-473
  Islamic tomb 489
  Medieval building
    466-467, 469
  Neoclassical building
    478-479, 482-483
  Nineteenth-century
    building 493
  Renaissance building
    474-477
  Twentieth-century
    building 494
Cornucopia 480
Corolla 140, 142-143
Corona
  Earth's atmosphere 300
  Palazzo Strozzi 475
  Sun's atmosphere 32-33
Corona Australis 19
Corona Borealis 18, 21
Coronal section through
  brain 236-237
Coronal suture 220
Coronary artery 250-251,
  253
Coronary sinus 250
Corona temperature 33
Coronet 198, 554
Coronoid process 194, 220
Corpus albicans 258

Corpus callosum 236-237
Corpus cavernosum 259
Corpus luteum 258
Corpus spongiosum 259
Corridor 465
Corries 286-287
Corrugator supercilii
  muscle 228-229
Cortex
  Apical meristem 134
  Canadian pond weed
    158-159
  Clubmoss stem 120
  Dicotyledon 127
  Epiphytic orchid 162
  Hair 234
  Horsetail stem 120
  Kidney 256
  Lichen 114
  Monocotyledon 127
  Moss 119
  Pine 125
  Radicle 152
  Rhizome 155
  Root 132-133
  Stems 134-135
  Water hyacinth 158
  Water lily 159
Corundum 271
Corvus 18, 21
Corvus corone 193
Corynactis viridis 166
Corythosaurus 96, 98
Cosmic background
  radiation 10
Cosmic dust analyser 614
Cosmic ray 301
Costal cartilage 218
Costal facet 223
Costal margin 168, 169
Costal shield 187
Cotter pin 383
Cotton duck canvas 437,
  443
Cotyledon 126, 152-153
  Development 132
  Dicotyledon 126
  Dry fruit seed 150-151
  Embryo development
    147
  Epigeal germination
    153
  Hypogeal germination
    152
  Monocotyledon 126
  Pine 122
  Root development 132
  Seed 152-153
  Succulent fruit seed
    148-149
Couch grass 113
Coucy-le-Chateau 466-467
Coulomb 316
Counter
  Calligraphy lettering
    445
Counterbalancing weight
  506
Counter, galley 373
Counter rail 381
Counter timber 381
Counterweight
  Flat-four cylinder
    arrangement 340
  Four-stroke cycle 343
  Hong Kong and
    Shanghai Bank 498
  Jaguar V12 engine 345
  Output shaft 347
  Relief printing press
    449
  Rotary engine output
    shaft 410
  Trojan engine 342
  V12 cylinder
    arrangement 345
Coupling
  Conventional hookscrew
    528

632

"Ellerman Lines" steam
locomotive 324
Coupling rod 325
Corounement 472
Course
Asian building 491
Medieval building
466-467
Neoclassical building
483
Nineteenth-century
building 492-493
Court referee 535
Court
Basketball 532
Handball 535
Netball 535
Volleyball 534
Court seal 375
Courtship display 188
Courtyard 465, 466
Coussinet 460
Covalent bonding 308-309
Cove 581
Coved dome 478, 485
Cover point 541
Cover support 570
Coverts 188, 191
Cow 198
Cowhide face 584
Cowling fastener 408
Cowling panel 407, 412
Coxa
Beetle 168
Crayfish 173
Scorpion 170
Coxswain 560
CQR anchor 586
Crab 172
Crab apple 126
Crab cactus 129
Crab Nebula 28
Cracks 284-285
Cradle frame
Honda VF750 564
Weslake Speedway
motorcycle 569
Cradling 541
Crane 498
Cranial nerves 238
Cranium
Ankylosaurus 94
Archaeopteryx 85
Australopithecus 108
Bat 105
Camarasaurus 91
Diplodocus 90
Elephant 201
Eryops 80
Euoplocephalus 94
Homo sapiens 108
Hyaenodon 107
Iguanodon 96
Kentrosaurus 93
Lambeosaurus 99
Moeritherium 105
Opossum 106
Pachycephalosaurus
100
Panoplosaurus 94
Parasaurolophus 99
Plateosaurus 88
Prenocephale 100
Protoceratops 102
Stegoceras 100
Stegosaurus 93
Struthiomimus 87
Styracosaurus 102
Toxodon 106
Triceratops 103
Tuojiangosaurus 93
Tyrannosaurus 84
Crank 320
Brace-and-bit 601
Eddy Merckx racing
bicycle 360
"Ellerman Lines" steam
locomotive 325
Crank bolt 558, 360

Crankcase
BE 2B bomber 404
British Rail Class 20
diesel engine 327
Humber engine 343
Jaguar straight six
engine 344
Jaguar V12 engine 345
Mid West two-stroke
engine 410
Oldsmobile engine 336
Trojan engine 342
Velocette OHV engine
367
Werner motorcycle 362
Crankcase breather pipe
402
Crank handle 339
Crankpin 543
Crankshaft
Benz Motorwagen 335
Flat-four cylinder
arrangement 340
Four-stroke cycle 343
Iron paddlesteamer 392
Mid West two-stroke
engine 410
Oklsmobile engine 336
Oscillating steam
engine 391
Straight four cylinder
arrangement 345
Two-stroke engine 366
Velocette OHV engine
367
Crankshaft counterweight
344
Crankshaft pulley 344,
355
Crash bar 362-363
Crash cymbal 518
Crash helmet 552
Crater
Mercury's North Pole 35
Northern stars 18
Oceanus Procellarum
40
Southern stars 21
Surface features of
Mars 42
Crayfish 172-173
Crayon 448
Creative Zen Stone 586
Creeping stems 154
Clubmoss 120
Strawberry 128
Cremasteric fascia 259
Cremocarp 150-151
Crenellation 466
Crepidoma 461, 481
Crescent-shaped dune
285
Crest
Building 479, 488, 493
Fold formation 60
Horse 199
Lizard 184
Ship's shield 395
Crested porcupine 197
Cretaceous period 72-73
Fossil record 279
Geological time 56-57
Crevasse 287
Crevice 284
Crevice tool 593
Crew handrail 612, 613
Crew's seat 416
Cricket (animal) 168
Cricket (game) 538-539
Cricoid cartilage 255
Cricothyroid ligament 244
Cricothyroid muscle 229,
244-245
C ring 46-47
Cringle 384
Crista 242
Crocket 471-472
Crocodile clip connector
316

Crocodiles 68, 73, 186-187
Crocodylus niloticus 186
Crocoite 271
Cronaca 474
Crook 508
Crop
Bird 189
Butterfly 169
Octopus 176
Snail 177
Crop-duster 410
Crops 315
Crop-sprayer 410, 422
Cross
Baroque church 480
Dome 486-487
Motif 472
Crossandra nilotica 145
Crossbar
Calligraphy characters
445
Eddy Merckx racing
bicycle 360
Gaelic football 529
Handball 535
Hurling 540
Rugby 530
Cross-bed set 283
Crossbow 548
Cross-bracing 497-499
Cross-country skiing 548
Crosse 540-541
Crossing 469-470, 477
Crossing tower 468
Cross-member 338-339
Cross-piece 376-377, 387
Cross-pollination 144
Cross-staff 377
Cross-stave 376-577
Cross tube 423
Cross wall of hypha 115
Crosswise strut 512
Crotchet rest 502-503
Croton 136
Crouch 543
Croup 198
Crow 193
Crown
Bird 188
Building 484, 490
Danforth anchor 386
Harp 511
Head 212
Relief-printing press
449
Rigging 382-383
Roman anchor 372
Sail hook 384
Shackle 386
Teeth 247
Timpanum 519
Crowning cornice
Ancient Roman
building 464, 465
Baroque church 479
Renaissance building
474-475
Crown wheel
Benz Motorwagen 335
Ford Model T 338
Cruciform column 492
Cruciform pedestal 481,
487
Cruck frame 466
Cruise electronics module
615
Cruise stage 615
Crumb tray 598-599
Crupper 555
Crusafontia 56
Crus cerebri of midbrain
237
Crus of diaphragm 255
Crust
Moon 41
Ocean floor 298
Pulsar 28
Regional
metamorphism 274

Structure of comet 53
Structure of Earth
38-39
Structure of Mars 45
Structure of Mercury 35
Structure of Venus 37
Crustaceans 172-173
Arthropoda 170
Cretaceous period
72-73
Fossil 279
Crustal movement
Coastline 294
Faults and folds 60
Mineralization zones
280
Mountain building 62
Rock cycle 266
Volcano 272
Crustal plate boundary 39
Crustal plates 58-59, 60
Crustose lichen 114
Crutch
Viking karv 375
Crux-Centaurus Arm 14
Crypt 467
Crypt-window 481
Crystalline external crust
28
Crystalline stalagmitic
floor 284
Crystallization 307
Crystal Palace Exhibition
Hall 492-493
Crystals
Faults 60
Intrusive igneous rocks
275
Mineral features
270-271
Minerals 268-269
Solids 307
Crystal systems 270
Ctenidium 176
CT scan 214
Cube 623
Cubic crystal 270
Cubic system 270
Cubital fossa 211
Cuboid bone 252
Cucumis melo 149
Cud 198
Cuesta 283
Culm 131
Cumulonimbus cloud 302
Cumulus cloud 302
Cuneate leaf base 136-137
Cuneus 465
Cup 509
Cup mute 507
Cupola 466, 479, 493
Cupressus glabra 123
Cup-shaped mouthpiece
506-507
Cup surrounding stomata
157
Cupula 242
Cupule 150
Curium 311
Current 296-297
Current electricity 316
Cursor control device
(CCD) 573
Curtain 477, 497
Curtain wall 466, 496, 498
Curtiss, Glenn 598
Curtiss Model-D Pusher
398-399
Curved buttress 478-481
Curved cornice 462
Curvilinear tracery 470,
472
Cuscuta europaea 163
Cushion
Doric capital 460
Rowing positions 573
Cushion star 175
Cusp
Asian building 488

Gothic building 472-473
Structure of a tooth
247
Cuspate fold 61
Cuspate foreland 294
Cusped arch 489
Cuspidate leaf apex 137
Cutaneous nerve 238
Cuticle
Bishop pine needle
124
Dryland plants 156
Golden barrel cactus
156
Hair 234
Haworthia truncata 157
Leaf 139
Lithops brom fieldii 157
Marram grass 113
Monocotyledon leaf 126
Nail 231
Rose stem 135
Rush stem 135
Wetland plants 158
Cuttlefish 176
Cutty Sark 592
Cyanotrichite 269
Cycadophyta 122
Cycads 68, 122-123, 279
Cycas revoluta 68, 123
Cycas sp. 68
Cyclic-pitch lever 422-423
Cyclone assembly 592
Cyclonic storm
Structure of Earth 39
Structure of Mars 43
Structure of Neptune
50
Cyclostomata 178
Cygnus 19, 20
Cylinder
Diesel train 326
Early engines 342-343
"Ellerman Lines" steam
locomotive 325
Iron paddlesteamer 392
Modern piston aero-
engines 410
Motorcycle 362, 366
Oldsmobile engine 336
"Rocket" steam
locomotive 324
Cylinder barrel
Mid West two-stroke
engine 410
Werner motorcycle 362
Cylinder block 339
Cylinder-cooling gills 407
Cylinder drain cock lever
325
Cylinder head
72° V10 engine 356
ARV light aircraft 425
British Rail Class 20
diesel engine 327
Daimler engine 343
Jaguar straight six
engine 344
Jaguar V12 engine 345
Mid West two-stroke
engine 410
Oldsmobile engine 336
Two-stroke engine 366
Velocette OHV engine
367
Cylinder liner
Jaguar Straight six
engine 344
Mid West two-stroke
engine 410
Cylinder shape 623
Cylinder wall 343
Cylindrical fault 61
Cylindrical map
projection 264
Cyma recta 475
Cyma reversa 460,
472
Cymatium 475

Cymbals 504-505,
516-517
Drum kit 518
Cyme 129, 143
Cypress 123
Cypselas 150
Cyrillus 40
Cystic duct 248
Cytoplasm
Chlamydomonas sp.
116
Diatom 116
Human 217
Palisade mesophyll
139
Root cell 132
Thalassiosira sp. 116
Cytosine 216

D

Dacron 548
Dacron sailcloth 584
Dacron skin 426
Dactylus 172-173
Dado
Baroque church
481
French temple 485
Neoclassical building
479
Renaissance building
476
Dagger 472
Dagoba stupa 490-491
Daimler double-sleeve
valve engine 343
Daimler, Gottlieb 334
Daisy gypsum 269
Dakota sandstone 276
D'Alembert 41
Dalmatian coastline 295
Da Maiano, B. 474
Damper
Piano 514
TGV electric high-
speed train 329
Wagon bogie 331
Damper bar 516
Damper body 565
Damper pedal
Concert grand piano
515
Tubular bells 516
Upright piano 514
Vibraphone 517
Damper unit 425
Damp lime-plaster 434
Damselfly 168
Dancette-pattern mosaic
489
Dandelion 150
Danforth anchor 386
Danger area 556
Danilova 36
Dark mica 274
Dark nebulae 16
Darlingtonia californica
160-161
Dart sac 177
Darwin 43
Da Sangallo, G. 474
Dash 557
Dashboard
1906 Renault 337
Bordino Steam Carriage
335
Ford Model T 338
Dashboard radiator
336-337
Dash panel 353
Dash radio speaker
555
Daucus curola 128, 152
Daughter bulbs 154
Daughter plants 154
Davit 395
D-block 310-311

DC converter 555
DC converter connection 355
DC current 528
DC socket 586
Dead-ball line 530
Deadeye
    74-gun ship 380
    Longboat 380
    Rigging 582-583
    Roman corbita 375
    Sailing warship 377
Deadnettle 135
Dead organisms 278
Dead plant encrustations 284
Dead Sea 292-293
Deadwood 381
Debris
    Glacier 286-287
    Mountain building 62
    Ray crater 34
Decathlon 542
Decidual plate 260
Deciduous plants 130-131
Deciduous teeth 246
Deciduous trees 72
Deck
    Greek trireme 373
    Roman corbita 373
Deck beam
    74-gun ship 380
    Ironclad 393
    Paddle steamer 390, 393
    Roman corbita 372
Deck house 373, 376
Deck lantern 392
Deck planking 393
Deck rail 373
Decorative letter 445
Deep cracks 284-285
Deep current systems 296-297
Deepened valley 295
Deep floor 393
Deep mid wicket 538
Deep-ocean floor 298
Deep-ocean floor sediments 299
Deep peroneal nerve 258
Deep relief carving 453
Deep square leg 538
Deer 104, 198-199
Deer hopper dry fly 563
Defenders
    Ice hockey 550
    Lacrosse 541
    Soccer 524
Defending zones 550
Defense 526, 535
Defensive back 526
Defensive end 526
Defensive tackle 526
Deflation hollow 283
Degreased bare metal 348
Dehiscence 150-151
    Fern spore 121
    Pollen sac 144
Dehiscent fruits 150-151
Dehydration 152
De-icing leading edge 414, 415
Deimos 42
Deinonychus 75
Deinotherium 77
Dekla Tessera 37
de la Cierva, Juan 422
Delete mail button 576
Delphinium 150
Delphinium orientalis 141
Delphinium sp. 151
Delphinus 19, 20
Delta
    Coastline 294
    River features 290
    River 288-289
    Rock cycle 266-267

Delta Andromedae 19
Delta Crucis 21
Delta formation 291
Delta Hydri 20
Delta II launch vehicle second stage 615
Delta ring 48
Deltavjalia vjatkensis 81
"Deltic" diesel-electric locomotive 526-527
Deltoid leaf 137
Deltoid ligament 232
Deltoid muscle 226-227
Demountable wheel 358-359
Dendrite 239
Dendritic copper 268
Dendritic gold 268
Dendritic river drainage 288
Deneb 19, 20
    Hertzsprung-Russell diagram 23
Deneb Algedi 19, 20
Deneb Kaitos 19, 20
Denebola 18, 21
Dens 222
Density
    Formation of black hole 29
    Massive stars 26-27
    Small stars 24-25
    Stellar black hole 29
Dentary 181
Dentary bone 96, 102, 107
Dentate leaf margin
    Hogweed 129
    Ice-plant 129
    Live-forever 129
    Mulberry 130
    Rock stonecrop 128
Dentil
    Ancient Roman building 462
    Baroque church 479, 481
    Cathedral dome 487
    French temple 485
    Neoclassical building 478
    Renaissance building 475
Dentine 247
Deoxyribonucleic acid strand 139
Deperdussin, Armand 400
Depressed arch
    Ancient Roman building 462
    Islamic building 488-489
Depressions 302
Depressor anguli oris muscle 228-229
Depressor labii inferioris muscle 229
Depth charge 394
Derailleur cage plate 358
Deranged river drainage 288
Dermal armor 95
Dermal papilla 235
Dermis 234-235
Derrick 392, 395
Descender 445
Descending colon 249
Desert 39, 57
    Carboniferous to Permian period 66
    Mapping the Earth 264-265
    Physical map of the world 616-617
    Rock cycle 266
    Weathering and erosion 282-283
Desertification 57, 76
Desiccated clay 283
Design
    Fresco 454-455
    Modeled sculpture 452

Mosaic 449
Deslandres 40
Desmid 112
Destination screen 332
Detachable bud 154
Detachable ink reservoir 444
Detachable rim 339
Detector 610
Detergent tray 594, 595
Detergent tray holder 595
Detergent tray recess 595
Deuterium nucleus 22
Deutscher Werkbund style 495
Devonian fish 65
Devonian period 64-65, 80
    Fossil record 279
    Geological time 56
    Primitive life 78
Devon minnow 563
Dewlap 184
Dextral strike-slip fault 61
Dhow 376
Diabase sill 277
Diagonal bracing 401
Diagonal reinforcement 574
Diagonal strut 399
Diagonal turn 388
Dial
    Clocktower 493
    Sundial 377
Diameter 622
    Atoms 308
    Earth 30
    Fluorine-19 atom 309
    Fluorine-19 nucleus 309
    Jupiter 26, 44
    Jupiter's moons 44
    Life of massive star 26-27
    Life of small star 21-26
    Mars 30
    Mars' moons 42
    Mercury 30
    Moon 40
    Neptune 31
    Neptune's moons 50
    Planets 30-31
    Pluto 31
    Saturn 27, 46
    Saturn's moons 46
    Stars 22
    Sun 32
    Uranus 27, 48
    Uranus' moons 48
    Venus 30
Diamond 311
    Mineral features 270-271
    Native elements 268
Diamond-shaped painting knife 436
Diamond whetstone 452
Diaphragm
    ARV Super 2 424
    Chimpanzee 202
    Domestic cat 195
    Elephant 200
    Human 215, 254-255
    Rabbit 196
Diastema 106
Diatom 116
Diceros bicornis 199
Dichasial cyme 143
Dicksonia antarctica 70, 112-113
Dicloelosia bilobata 65
Dicotyledon 126-127, 141-143
Dicyothyris 278
Didelphis 106
Didelphis virginiana 207
Diesel-electric train 526
Diesel fuel injection 526

Diesel motor compartment 397
Diesel, Rudolph 526
Diesel train 324, 326-527
Differential 356
Differential housing 338
Diffuser 356
Digestive caecum 173, 176
Digestive enzymes 160
Digestive gland
    Snail 177
    Spider 170
Digestive glands/zones
    Butterwort 161
    Monkey cup 161
    Venus fly trap 160
Digestive system
    Cow 198
    Human 248-249
Digit 105
Digital artery 231, 253
Digital camcorder 582-583
Digital camera
    3-D digital camera 581
    Digital camera with interchangeable lens 581
    Digital SLR 581
    Underwater digital camera 581
Digital extensor muscle 94
Digital flexor muscle 84
Digital media slot 567
Digital nerve 231
Digital sampler 520-521
Digital vein 253
Digital video camera 582-583
Digitate leaf 137
Digits
    Bird 189
    Bird's wing 191
    Frog 182
    Kangaroo 207
    Rabbit 196-197
    Rat 196
    Salamander 182
    Seal 204
Dike 274
Dike swarm 274
Dilator muscle 241
Dilsea carnosa 117
Dimetrodon loomisi 67
Dinghy 560
Dinosaur cladogram 83
Dinosaur 56-57, 80, 82-83
    Fossil record 279
Dionaea muscipula 160
Dione 46, 614
Dip 60
Diplodocus 70, 88, 90-91
Dip pen 430
Dipping bed rock 60-61
Dipping lug foresail 385
Diprotodon 76
Dip-slip fault 61
Dipstick 354
Dipstick tube 346, 356
Dipterus valeciennesi 81
Direct current 528
Direct current (DC) inlet 571
Direction bar 414
Direction-finding aerial fairing 408
Direct method mosaic creation 450
Direct-vision panel
    ARV light aircraft 425
    Bell-47 helicopter 422
Dirt track motorcycle racing 368
Disc brake
    Harley-Davidson FLHS Electra Glide 362-363
    Honda CB750 363
    Honda VF750 564

Husqvarna Motocross TC610 568
Lockheed Electra airliner 407
    Motorcycle 364-365
    Suzuki RGV500 368-369
Disc brake caliper 364, 368-369
Disconformity 276
Discovery Rupes 35
Discus 542-543
Disk
    Basal 167
    Crab 166-167
    Liverwort 118
    Pedal 167
    Sea anemone 166-167
    Starfish 174
    Starfish fossil 79
Disk drag 562-563
Disk florets 129, 142, 145
Displacement reactions 312
Display button 585
Display controller chip 581
Display panel
    Blu-ray recorder 584
Display screen 585, 596
Display screen and control circuits 585
Distal convoluted tubule 256-257
Distal end of radius 231
Distal interphalangeal joint 231
Distal phalanx 219, 230, 232
Distal tarsal 183
Distance lines
    Gaelic football 529
    Rugby 530
Distance running 542
Distance signaling 550
Distilled water 444
Distiller 597
Distributary
    River features 290-291
    Rivers 288-289
Distributor
    Hawker Tempest Mark V 408
    Jaguar straight six engine 344
    Jaguar V12 engine 345
    Renault Clio 351
Distributor drive shaft 345
Distributor fixing point 346
Diving 558-559
DNA 139, 216, 606
Dobro resonator 513
Dock 554
Document panel 407
Document table 571
Dodder 163
Dog 104, 194-195
Dogfish 178-179, 192
Dog-leg hole 546
Dog-leg staircase 481
Doline 284-285
Dolomedes fimbriatus 171
Dolphins 204-205
Dolphin striker 382
Domain name 576
Dome 484, 486-487
    Ancient Roman building 462
    Asian building 490-491
    Baroque church 480-481
    French temple 485
    Islamic building 488
    Medieval building 467, 469
    Neoclassical building 478
    Renaissance building 475-477
Domed receptacle 142

Domed roof 489
Domed topdeck 401
Domed turret 493
Dome metalling 486
Dome of the Rock 487
Dome timbering 486
Dome volcano 62, 272
Donjon 466-467
Donkey boiler 392
Donor genetic material 606, 607
Door
    Ancient Egyptian tomb 458-459
    Ancient Roman building 463
    Baroque church 479
    Bell 206 jetliner 423
    Double-decker touring bus 333
    Gatwick Express "People Mover" 528
    MCW Metrobus 332-333
    Microwave combination oven 596
    Neoclassical building 478
    Renaissance theater 477
    Renault Clio 349
    Single-decker bus 333
    TGV electric high-speed train 329
    Washer-dryer 594
Door catch 341
Door catch with safety cut-out 595
Door frame 412
Door glass 348
Door handle 341, 348
Door hinge 612
Door jamb 478
Door key and lock 348
Door lock 596, 602
Door metal cap 595
Door molding 353
Door porthole 595
Door safety cut-out mechanism 596
Door trim panel 353
Doorway 474-475, 479, 481, 495
Door wiring loom 595
Doppler 41
Dorado 21
Doric capital 460
Doric column 460, 464
Doric half-column 464
Doric order 460
Dormancy
    Horse chestnut bud 130
    Seed 152
Dormant volcano 272
Dormer head 495
Dormer window 476, 493, 495
Dorsal abdominal artery 175
Dorsal aorta
    Bony fish 181
    Dogfish 179
    Frog 182
Dorsal blood vessel 169
Dorsal fin
    ARV light aircraft 424
    Bony fish 181
    Concorde, the 416
    Dogfish 179
    Dolphin 205
    Lamprey 178
    World War II aircraft 408-409
Dorsal fin ray 181
Dorsal interosseous muscle 233
Dorsal lobe 158
Dorsal mantle cavity 176
Dorsal margin of shell 176
Dorsal metatarsal artery 253

Dorsal plate 78, 92-93
Dorsal scale 184, 186
Dorsal scute 95
Dorsal spine base 78
Dorsal venous arch 253
Dorsal vertebrae
  Archaeopteryx 85
  Brachiosaurus 90
  Diplodocus 90
  Eryops 80
  Euoplocephalus 94
  Gallimimus 86
  Iguanodon 96
  kentrosaurus 93
  Parasaurolophus 99
  Pareiasaur 81
  Plateosaurus 88
  Stegoceras 101
  Stegosaurus 93
  Struthiomimus 87
  Tuojiangosaurus 93
  Tyrannosaurus 84
Dorsum 213
Double-arm pantograph 328
Double bass 503-505, 510, 511
Double bassoon 504-505
Double-decker bus 332-333
Double decomposition reaction 312-313
Double-dipper palette attachment 436
Double-ended hull 375
Double flat 502
Double halyard 373
Double helix 216
Double-planet system
  Earth 58
  Pluto 50
Double-pyramid crystal 270
Double reed 508
Double rope becket 383
Doubles 544
Double samaras
  Dry fruit 150-151
  Sycamore 131
Double scull 561
Double sharp 502
Double topsail schooner 385
Dowel
  Mid West single rotor engine 410
  Mortise-and-tenon fastening 373
Dowel hole 410-411
Downfolds 60
Downhaul 385
Downhill skiing 552
"Downs" 526
Downthrow 60
Down tube 360
Dox formation 277
dpi (Dots Per Inch) 570
Draco 19, 20
Draft mark
  Frigate 397
  Wooden sailing ship 379
Drafts folder 576
Draft tube 314
Drag
  Biplanes and triplanes 402
  Cycling 360
  Early monoplane 400
  Early passenger aircraft 406
Drag knob 563
Drag link
  19th century paddlesteamer 391
  Ford Model T 339
  White Steam Car 342
Dragon prowhead 374
Drag spindle 562
Drag washer 562

Drainage systems divide 289
Drain mast 412, 415
Drain pipe 492
Drain plug 339
Drakensberg 265, 616
Dravidian finial 491
Dravidian style 490
Drawbridge 493
Drawbridge windlass 467
Drawing 430-431
Drawing board 430, 444-445
Drawing instruments 430
Drawing materials 430
Dreadnought-type battleship 394
Dressing-room 477
Dribbling
  Basketball 552
  Gaelic football 528
  Handball 534-535
  Soccer 524
Drill 600-601
D ring 46-47
Drip-cap 482
Drive 543
Drive belt 354, 355, 344, 362
Drive bracket 405
Drive chain 366, 368
Drive end 317
Drive gear 411
Driven gear 410
Driven pulley 355
Drive pillar 424
Drive plate 345
Drive point 546
Driver 547
Driver protection 357
Driverless train 328
Driver's platform 324
Driver's radio aerial 357
Driver's seat
  Bordino Steam Carriage 335
  "Deltic" diesel-electric locomotive 327
  "Mallard" express steam locomotive 325
  Paris Metro 328
Drive shaft
  Jet engine 419
  Renault Clio 351
  Volkswagen Beetle 340
Drive sprocket mounting spline 366
Drive-wheel 601
Driving band 397
Driving chain 335
Driving pulley 335
Driving rein 555
Driving saddle 555
Driving sprocket 335
Driving wheel 324-325
Drizzle 302
  Dromiceiomimus 86
Droop nose 416
Droop stop 422-423
Drop 581
Drop arm
  Ford Model T 339
  White Steam Car 342
Drop-down window 334
Drop glass 541
Drop goal 530
Drop handlebar 361
Dropkick 530
Drop tank 408
Drop window 332
Drowned coastline 294-295
Drowned valley 295
Drum 486
  Ancient Greek building 460
  Baroque church 481
  Cathedral dome 487

Relief printing press 449
Washer-dryer 595
Drum and door seal 595
Drum brake
  BMW R/60 362
  Motorcycle 364-365
  Vespa Grand Sport 160 Mark 1 363
  "Windcheetah" racing HPV bicycle 361
Drumhead 387
Drum inlet elbow 595
Drumline 286
Drum pad 520
Drums 518-519, 520
Drum suspension springs 595
Drupelets 146-149
Drupes 131, 148-149
Dry air 303
Dry brush 438-439
Dry fresco 434-435
Dry fruits 150-151
  Couch grass 113
  Durmast oak 131
  Sycamore 131
Dry gallery 284-285
Drying agent 313
Dry lake bed 283
Dryland plants 156-157
  Dryopteris filix-mas 120-121
  Dryosaurus 70
Dry pericarps 150
Dry season 293
Dry wash 283
Dual click gear 562
Dual ignition plug 427
Dual seat 364
Dubhe 18
  The Plough 19
Dubika 490
Duck 188
Duck-billed platypus 206-207
"Duckbills" 96
Duct 496, 497
Duct of Bellini 256
Ductus deferens 259
Duodenum
  Bird 189
  Cow 198
  Elephant 200
  Frog 182
  Human 215, 248-249
  Rabbit 196
  Tortoise 187
Duplex tubular cradle frame 363
Duradon 384
Dura mater 223, 237, 240
Durmast oak 131
Dust
  Asteroids, comets, and meteoroids 52-53
  Mars 42-43
  Moon 41
  Nebulae and star clusters 16-17
  NGC 2997 (spiral galaxy) 12
  Overhead view of our galaxy 14
  Solar system 30
  Venus' atmosphere 37
Dust cap 359
Dust cloud
  Geological time 56
  Large Magellanic Cloud 12
  Mars 42-43
  Milky Way 14-15

Nebulae and star clusters 16-17
Origin and expansion of universe 11
Volcano 272
Dust collection bin 592
Dust lane
  Centaurus A 13
  Horsehead Nebula 16
  NGC 2997 (spiral galaxy) 12
  Optical image of Rings and dust lanes 48
  Trifid Nebula 16
Dust particles 53
Dust shroud 340
Dust storm 43
Dust tail 52-53
Dutch cubist style 495
Dutch shoe 377
Dutch triple field block 585
DVD/CD control buttons 585
DVD/CD drive turntable 585
DVD/CD laser-reader 585
DVD/CD on-screen menu display button 585
DVD/CD processor microchip 585
DVD/CD sliding tray 585
DVD/CD stop button 585
DVD display button 585
DVD player 584-585
Dwarf crocodile 82
Dwarf shoot 124-125
  Dynastes hercules 12
Dyson DC05 vacuum cleaner 592-593
Dysprosium 311

E

Ear
  Calligraphy characters 445
  Elephant 200
  Gorilla 203
  Hare 196
  Horse 198
  Human 210, 212, 242-245
  Kangaroo 207
  Rabbit 196
  Rat 196
Eardrum
  Chick 193
  Frog 182
  Human 243
  Lizard 184
Earles fork 362
Early desertification 57
Early engines 342-343
Early English
  Perpendicular-style tracery 472
Early English-style window 472
Early monoplanes 400-401
Early passenger aircraft 406-407
Early tram 332
Early voyagers 374-375
Earphone 586
Earpiece 588
Earplug 558
Earth 58-59
  Cretaceous period 73
  Energy emission from Sun 22
  Jurassic period 71
  Objects in universe 11
  Phases of the Moon 41
  Primitive life 78-79
  Quaternary period 77
  Solar eclipse 32

Solar system 30
Tertiary period 75
Tides 297
Triassic period 69
Earth-ball fungus 115
Earth bank 603
Earth connection 598
Earth connection 587
Earth formation 56-57
Earth pigments 434
Earthquake anatomy 63
Earthquake region 59
Earthquakes
  Crustal movement 58
  Faults and folds 60
  Mountain building 62-63
Earth's atmosphere 58-59, 78, 300-301
Earth's composition 39
Earth's core 58-59, 63
Earth's crust 58-59, 58-59
  Igneous and metamorphic rocks 274
  Lake formation 292
  Volcano 272
Earth's crustal plates 62, 64
Earth's energy 314
Earth's evolution 56-57
Earth's external features 59
Earth's formation 58, 56, 64
Earth's interior
  Ocean floor 298
  Rock cycle 266
  Structure 39
Earth's layers 58
Earth's magnetic field 38
Earth's mantle 58-39, 58-59
Earth's orbit 297
Earth's rotation 58
  Atmospheric circulation and winds 300
  Oceans and seas 296
  Satellite mapping 264
Earth's satellite 58
Earth's surface
  Atmosphere 300-301
  Formation of the Earth 58-59
  Geological time 56
  Mapping the Earth 264-265
  Mineral resources 280
  Mountain building 62
  Oceans and seas 296
  Physical map of the world 616-617
  Precambrian to Devonian period 64
  Rock cycle 266
Earth's tilt 58
Earth wire 594
Earwig 168
East Africa 331
East Asian buildings 490-491
East Australian current 297
East Greenland current 296
Eaves
  Ancient Greek building 461
  Ancient Roman building 462, 464
  Islamic tomb 489
  Modern building 499
  Neoclassical building 482
  Renaissance building 477
Eaves board 490
Eccentric 392
Eccentric rod 391
Eccentric rotor journal 347
Eccentric shaft 347, 411

Eccentric-shaft bearing 410
  Echidna nebulosa 180
Echidnas 206
  Echinocactus grusonii 156
Echinoderms 174, 279
Echinus 460
  Echinus esculentus 175
Echo-sounding 298
Ecliptic
  Inclination of planetary orbits 31
  Stars of northern skies 18-19
  Stars of southern skies 20-21
  Ecphora 75
Ectoderm 167
Eddy Merckx racing bicycle 360-361
Edible sea urchin 175
  Edmontonia 95
Eel 180
Efferent arteriole 256-257
Effervescence 312
Effort 320-321
Egg cella 606-607
Eggs 192-195
  Amphibian 78, 80
  Baltimore oriole 193
  Bee hummingbird 193
  Bird 188
  Butterfly 168
  Capsule 192
  Carrion crow 193
  Case 192
  Chaffinch 193
  Chicken 192
  Common tern 193
  Dinosaur 82
  Dogfish 192
  Frog 182-183, 192
  Giant stick insect 192
  Greater blackblacked gull 193
  Hatching 192-193
  Human 258, 260
  Indian stick insect 192
  Leaf insect 192
  Maiasaura 98
  Membrane 193
  Ostrich 193
  Quail 192-193
  Reptile 66, 184
  Titanosaurid 91
  Willow grouse 193
Egg tempera 432
Egg-tooth 192-193
Egg white 192
Egg yolk binding medium 432
Egypt 331
Egyptian building 458-459
  Eichhornia crassipes 158
Eighteenth-century building 492
  Baroque 481
  Neoclassical 478, 482-483
Eighth-century building 490-491
Einsteinium 311
Eisila Regio 36-57
Ejaculatory duct 259
Ejecta
  Degas and Bronte 34
  Features of supernova 27
  Ray crater 34
  Venusian craters 52
Ejector assembly 599
Ejector exhaust 408
Ejector-seat roof hatches 421
Ekeing 381
Ekman spiral 296-297
El-Ainyi Mosque 488

Elapsed time display 577
Elasmobranchs 178
Elastic fiber 252, 254
Elastic rocks 60
Elbow
  Anchisaurus 89
  Corythosaurus 98
  Edmontonia 95
  Gorilla 203
  Horse 199
  Human 210
  Iguanodon 97
  Lion 194
  Psittacosaurus 103
  Stegoceras 101
  Stegosaurus 92
  Triceratops 102
Elbow guard 555
Elbow joint
  Brachiosaurus 91
  Diplodocus 90
  Eryops 80
  Euoplocephalus 94
  Human 218
  Parasaurolophus 99
  Plateosaurus 88
  Stegoceras 101
  Triceratops 102
  Tyrannosaurus 84
Elbow pad 527, 551
Elder 130-131, 140 143
Electrical braking 330
Electrical cells 316-317
Electrical charge
  imbalance 316
Electrical circuit 316
  Toaster 598
Electrical contact 519
Electrical effects 316
Electrical energy 314-315
Electrical harness 414
Electrical inverter 422
Electrical plant 496
Electrical relay 596
Electrical relay box 530
Electrical service
  compartment 407
Electrical supply 316
Electrical wiring harness
  418
Electric bass guitars 512
Electric cable 517
Electric car 542
Electric charge 308
Electric coil 517
Electric current 316-317,
  328, 605
Electric equipment
  compartment 329
Electric fuel pump 422
Electric generator 517
Electric guitar 512-513
Electric heating elements
  597
Electric ignition control
  562
Electricity 316-317
Electricity connector to
  brushbar motor 593
Electricity generation
  Diesel train 526
Electric train 526
  Magnetism 317
Electric locomotive 324,
  528-529
Electric motor
  Diesel train 526
  Electric train 528
  Tram 532
Electric motor/generator
  557
Electric motor housing
  554
Electric power line 328,
  402
Electric power socket
  422
Electric scoring system
  556-557

Electric street tramway
  532
Electric toaster 598
Electric train 528-529
Electric transmission 326
Electric trolley 532
Electric window motor
  349
Electrode 306
Electromagnet 317, 598
Electromagnetic
  induction capacitor 600
Electromagnetic radiation
  314-315, 318
Electromagnetic
  spectrum 318-319
Electron 308, 510
  Atomic number 310
  Fluorine-19 509
Electron beam 611
Electron detector
  assembly 611
Electron gun 611
Electron gun housing
  610
Electron microscope 610
Electronic controller 605
Electronic control signals
  550
Electronic control-unit
  connector 556
Electronic drums 520
Electronic engine control
  (EEC) unit 418-419
Electronic games 578-579
Electronic ignition unit
  351
Electronic instruments
  520-521
Electronic signals 512
Electronic warfare mast
  597
Electrons 605
Electron shell 508-509,
  510
Electron stream 611
Electron transfer 508
Electrostatic forces 308,
  316
Electrostatic generator
  516
Electrothermal de-icing
  panel 416
Element retaining stop
  599
Elements 306, 308
  Atomic mass 310
  Minerals 268
  Periodic table 310-311
Elephant 90, 104, 200-201
Elephas maximus 200
Elevated green 546
Elevating wheel 396
Elevation 498
Elevator
  ARV light aircraft 424
  BAe-146 components
    415
  Bell-47 helicopter 423
  Biplanes and triplanes
    402-405
  Curtiss biplane 399
  Early monoplanes
    400-401
  Hawker Tempest
    components 409
  Schleicher glider 426
  World War I aircraft 405
  Wright Flyer 399
Elevator arm 425
Elevator chassis box 415
Elevator control cable
  599, 403
Elevator control rod
  409
Elevator control wire
  Bell-47 helicopter 47
  Bleriot XI monoplane
    401

Curtiss biplane 399
LVG CVI fighter 405
Elevator drive wheel 599
Elevator hinge
  BAe-146 components
    415
  BE 2B tail 405
  Blackburn monoplane
    400
  Hawker Tempest
    components 409
Elevator operating arm
  399
Elevator-operating
  bracket 401
Elevator push-rod
  424-425
Elevator rocking arm 404
Elevator trimtab 424, 409
Elevator wire 398
Eleventh-century building
  466, 468
Elevon 416-417, 421
Elevon-jack fairing 416
Elevon power control unit
  417
"Ellerman Lines" steam
  locomotive 524-525
Elliott steering knuckle
  356
Ellipsoid orb 486
Elliptical galaxy 11-12
Elliptical orbit 30
Elliptic leaf 137
Elm 144, 150
El Nath 18, 21
Elodea canadensis
  158-159
Elodea sp. 159
Elongating root 153, 153
Elrathia 64
Eltanin 19
Elytron 168
Email 576, 577
Email address 576
Email program 576
Email sender 576
Emarginate apex 136
Embellisher 555
Embolus 372
Embrasure 466-467, 469
Embryo 607
  Cotyledon 152-153
  Dry fruit seed 150-151
  Fertilization 146-147
  Germination 152-153
  Human 260
  Reptile 80
  Seed leaf 152
  Succulent fruit seed
    148-149
Embryonic root 150,
  152-153
Embryonic shoot 147
  Epigeal germination
    153
  Hypogeal germination
    152
  Pea seed 150
  Pine 122
  Seed axis 152-153
Embryo sac 146-147
Emergency canopy
  release handle 420
Emergency door control
  552-553
Emergency escape hatch
  406
Emergency exit 416-417
Emergency oxygen
  cylinder 417
Emergent coastlines
  294-295
Emission nebula 11-12,
  14, 16-17
Empire State Building 494
Enamel
  Islamic buildings 488-489
  Teeth 247

Enceladus 46
Encke 40
Encke Division 46-47
Enclosed bridge 397
Enclosed DVD/CD
  compartment 585
Encroachment 527
End 588-589
End baffle plate 598-599
End block 512
End effector 608
EN-EL12 rechargeable
  battery 581
End element 598-599
End-grain wood block
  449
End-line
  Basketball 552
  Football 526
  · Men's Lacrosse 540
  Volleyball 534
End link 586
Endocardium 250
Endocarp 146-147,
  148-149
Endoderm 167
Endodermis
  Bishop pine needle 124
  Canadian pond weed
    stem 158-159
  Dicotyledon 127
  Epiphytic orchid 162
  Fern rachis 121
  Horsetail stem 120
  Mare's tail stem 155
  Monocotyledon 127
  Pine root 125
  Root 152-153
  Water hyacinth root 158
Endonysium 228
Endoperidium 115
Endoplasmic reticulum
  239
Endopod 172
Endoscopic view
  Alimentary canal 248
  Vocal cords 245
Endoskeleton 174
Endosperm 147
Endosteum 225
Endothecium 144
Endothelium 252
End-pin 510
End-plate
  Formula One race car
    556-557
  Modern piston aero-
    engine 410-411
End-plate aerodynamic
  skirt 557
End zone 526
En echelon fractures
  60-61
Energy 314-315
  Chemical reactions 312
  Electron shells 310
  Light 318
  Renewable 604-605
Energy conversion 158
Energy emission from
  Sun 22
Engaged column 469
Engaged pediment
  462-463
Engine 342-347, 410-411,
  418-419
  1906 Renault 337
  1-liter VTEC 554
  72° V10 356
  ARV light aircraft 425
  BAe-146 jetliner 415
  BMW R/60 362
  Bordino Steam Carriage
    334
  Diesel 326
  Early monoplane
    400-401
  Hawker Tempest
    components 408

Helicopter 422-423
Honda CB750 363
Honda VF750 564
Kirby BSA 369
Lockheed Electra
  airliner 406-407
Motorcycles 362, 364,
  366-367
Oldsmobile engine
  336
Pegasus Quasar
  ultralight 427
Pioneers of flight
  398-399
Renault Clio 350-351
Velocette overhead
  valve (OHV) 567
Volkswagen Beetle
  340
Engine aft bulkhead 421
Engine air intake
  BE 2B bomber 404
  Concorde 416
  Formula One race car
    556, 557
  Hawker Tempest
    fighter 409
  Schweizer helicopter
    423
  Tornado 420
Engine and propeller
  thrust frame 398
Engine bearer 343
Engine block 347
Engine cover
  Formula One race car
    556, 557
  Honda VF750 574
  Oldsmobile bodywork
    337
  Two-stroke engine 566
  Vespa Grand Sport 160
  Mark 1 563
  Volkswagen Beetle 341
Engine cowling
  Airbus 380 573
  ARV light aircraft
    424-425
  Avro biplane 403
  Concorde 416
  Hawker Tempest
    components 408
  Lockheed Electra
    airliner 407
  Pegasus Quasar
    ultralight 427
Engine crankcase 327
Engine drive belt 554
Engineering 496
Engine front mount
  418-419
Engine front support link
  417
Engine fuel pump 417
Engine instruments 425
Engine lid 341
Engine lifting eye 547
Engine mounting
  ARV light aircraft 425
  Blackburn monoplane
    401
  Honda VF750 364
  Modern piston aero-
    engine 411
  Pegasus Quasar
    ultralight 427
  Velocette OHV engine
    567
Engine pylon 412
Engine rear mount
  Pegasus Quasar
    ultralight 427
  Turboprop engine 419
Engine room 326
Engine timing gear 336
Engine warning display
  573
Englacial moraine 287
Englacial stream 286

England 92
English baroque style
  480-481
English bond brickwork
  485
English Decorated style
  470
English ivy 131
English Perpendicular
  style 470, 472
Engraving 446
Enif 19, 20
  Pegasus and
    Andromeda 19
Ensign staff 396
Entablature
  Ancient Greek building
    460
  Ancient Roman
    building 462-463
  Baroque church
    480-481
  Cathedral dome 487
  French temple 485
  Neoclassical building
    478-479, 482-483
Entasis 461
Enter button 585
Enteromorpha linza 117
Entomophilous
  pollination 144
Entrance
  Islamic tomb 489
  Medieval building
    466-467
  Modern building
    496-499
  Neoclassical building
    485
  Nineteenth-century
    building 493
  Twentieth-century
    building 494
Entrenched meander 290
Entresol 467
Enucleated egg cell 606
Enzyme 160
Eocene epoch
  Fossil record 279
  Geological timescale 57
Eon
  Fossil record 279
  Geological time 56-57
Épée 556-557
Epibranchial artery 179
Epicardium 250
Epicenter 63
Epicotyl 152-153
Epicranial aponeurosis
  257
Epidermal cell 166
Epidermis
  Apical meristem 134
  Canadian pond weed
    stem 159
  Clubmoss stem 120
  Dicotyledon 126-127
  Epiphytic orchid 162
  Fern rachis 121
  Flower 142
  Horsetail stem 120
  Human 234-235
  Leaf 139
  Marram grass 113
  Monocotyledon 126-127
  Moss 119
  Multilayered 162
  Pine needle 124
  Pine stem 125
  Prickle 135
  Radicle 152
  Rhizome 155
  Root 152-153
  Stem 154-155
  Water hyacinth
    158
  Water lily 159
Epididymis 259
Epidote 269

636

Epigeal germination
    152-153
Epiglottis
Elephant 200
Human 212, 244-245,
    248, 255
Epiphysis 250
Epiphytes 112, 162-163
Epithelial cell 217
Epithelium 254
Epoch
    Fossil record 279
    Geological time 56-57
Epoxy resin frame 612
Epsilon Centauri 21
Epsilon Crucis 21
Epsilon Hydri 20
Epsilon ring 48-49
Epson Stylus Photo 895
    color inkjet printer
    574
Equal-shock intensity
    lines 65
Equator
    Atmosphere 300
    Quaternary period 76
    Saturn 47
    Satellite map 265
    Surface currents 297
Equatorial air 300
Equatorial current
    296-297
Equatorial furrow 144
Equatorial Zone 45
Equestrian sports 554-555
Equisetites sp. 66
Equilateral triangle 622
Equisetum arvense 70, 120
Equuleus 19, 20
Era
    Fossil record 279
    Geological time 56-57
Eraser 450
Erasing stick 448
Erbium 311
Erect limb stance 82
Erh-wei 376
Eridanus 19, 20
E ring 46
Erosion 282-283
    Coastline 294-295
    Lake formation 293
    Ocean floor 298
    River features 290-291
    Rock cycle 267
    Sedimentary rocks 276
Eryops 80-81
Escalator 497-498
Escape/back button 589
Esker 286
Esophagus
    Barnacle 173
    Bird 189
    Brachiosaurus 91
    Butterfly 169
    Chimpanzee 202
    Cow 198
    Dogfish 179
    Dolphin 205
    Domestic cat 195
    Elephant 200
    Human 212, 215, 245,
        248
    Lizard 185
    Rabbit 196
    Snail 177
    Spider 170
    Starfish 174
    Tortoise 187
Estonioceras perforatum
    65
Estuarine mud-flat 295
Estuary 288, 290-294
Eta Centauri 21
Eta Mensae 20
Eta Orionis 18
Eta ring 48
Eta Sagittarii 21

Etching 446
Ethernet port 566
Euathlus emilia 170
Euoplocephalus 94-95
Eurasia 76
Eurasian plate 59
Europa 44
Europe
    Cretaceous period 72-73
    Electric train 528
    Electric tram 552
    Jurassic period 70
    Mapping the Earth
        264-265
    Middle Ordovician
        period 64
    Physical map of the
        world 616-617
    Quaternary period 76
    Railway track gauge 551
    Tertiary period 74-75
    Triassic period 68
European field elm 144
European hard-screw
    coupling 402
Europium 311
"Eurostar" multivoltage
    electric train 528-529
Eurypterid fossil 79
Eustachian tube 243
Eustreptospondylus 85
Euthynteria 460
Evacuated column 610,
    611
Evaporation 307
Event horizon 28-29
Evergreens 130-131
Everlasting pea 129
Evolute shell 278
Evolution
    Earth 56-57
    Living things 278
Excretory pore 177
Excurrent pore 166
Exfoliation 282
Exhaust
    Catalytic converter 355
    Ford diesel engine 347
    Modern mechanics
        350-351
    Paddlesteamer 391
Exhaust clamp 362
Exhaust collector ring
    405, 406
Exhaust cone 419
Exhaust connection 427
Exhaust diffuser 418
Exhaust downpipe 350
Exhaust fairing 419
Exhaust gas recirculation
    valve 344
Exhaust heat shield 345
Exhaust manifold
    1906 Renault 337
    ARV light aircraft 425
    Jaguar V12 engine 345
    Mid West two-stroke
        engine 410
    Renault Clio 351
Exhaust nozzle 418
Exhaust pipe
    Avro biplane 403
    Bell-47 helicopter 422
    BMW R/60 362
    Brazilian battleship 395
    Harley-Davidson FLHS
        Electra Glide 363
    Formula One race car
        356
    Hawker Tempest
        fighter 409
    Honda CB750 363
    Honda VF750 364
    Kirby BSA 369
    Lockheed Electra
        airliner 406-407
    Oldsmobile engine 336
    Pegasus Quasar
        ultralight 427

Suzuki RGV500 368
White Steam Car 342
World War I aircraft
    404-405
Exhaust pipe flange 411
Exhaust port
    "Deltic" diesel-electric
        locomotive 326
    Four-stroke cycle 343
    Mid West 75-HP engine
        410
    Two-stroke engine 367
    Velocette OHV engine
        367
    Wankel engine 347
    Wankel rotary cycle 346
Exhaust silencer 425, 427
Exhaust stack 405
Exhaust steam water
    injector control 325
Exhaust stroke 343
Exhaust system 368
Exhaust tract 410
Exhaust valve 343-345
Exhaust valve push-rod
    400
Exhaust vent
    British Rail Class 20
        diesel engine 327
    Drill 601
    "Union Pacific"
        locomotive 326
Exine 144-145
Exit door 333
Exocarp 146-149
Exocclipital bone 183
Exocet missile launcher
    397
Exodermis 162
Exoperidium 115
Exopod 172
Exoskeleton
    Insect 168
    Malacostraca 172
    Spider 171
Exosphere 300
Exothermic reactions 312
Expander bolt 359
Expandible sponge 448
Expansile jaw 85
Expansion lever 325
Expansion of sail 378-379
Expansion slot 567
Expelling plate 597
Expiration 255
Exploding shell 396, 397
Expressionist style 495
Extended cave system 285
Extended port air-brake
    421
Extensor digitorum brevis
    muscle 233
Extensor digitorum
    longus tendon 233
Extensor digitorum
    tendon 231
Extensor hallucis brevis
    muscle 233
Extensor hallucis longus
    tendon 233
Extensors of hand 227
External anatomy
    Body 210-211
    Brain 257
    Ear 242-243
    Foot 233
    Hand 231
    Sperm 259
External auditory meatus
    Homo erectus 108
    Homo sapiens 108, 220,
        242
External crust 28
External elastic lamina
    252
External iliac artery 215,
    225, 253
External iliac vein 215,
    253

External monitor port 567
External nostril 184
External oblique muscle
    226
External occipital crest
    220
External pubo-ischio-
    femoral muscle 97
External skeleton
    Insect 168
    Malacostraca 172
    Spider 171
External spermatic fascia
    259
External urinary meatus
    258
Extinct geyser 275
Extinction
    Dinosaur 56, 74, 82, 104
    Life 66
    Pleistocene mammals
        76
Extinct volcano 62, 272
    Igneous rock structures
        275
    Mountain building 62
    Ocean floor 298
Extrados 484-485
Extra period 552
Extrusive rocks 274, 275
Eye
    Allosaurus 85
    Amphibian 182
    Anchisaurus 89
    Angling hook 562
    Beetle 168
    Bird 188
    Bony fish 181
    Brachiosaurus 91
    Bumblebee 168
    Butterfly 169
    Caiman 186
    Carnivore 194
    Chick 192-193
    Corythosaurus 98
    Crab 172
    Crayfish 173
    Crocodilian 186
    Deer hopper dry fly 563
    Devon minnow 565
    Dhow 376
    Dogfish 178
    Dolphin 204
    Elephant 201
    Figurehead 374
    Forward-facing 194
    Frog 182
    Gallimimus 86
    Gorilla 203
    Greek and Roman ships
        372
    Herrerasaurus 86
    Horse 198
    Human 211, 212,
        240-241
    Iguanodon 97
    Kangaroo 207
    Knot 388
    Lamprey 178
    Lion 194
    Lizard 184
    Median 170
    Octopus 177
    Pachycephalosaurus
        100
    Psittacosaurus 103
    Rabbit 196
    Rat 196
    Rattlesnake 185
    Rigging 382-383
    Salamander 182
    Scallop 176
    Scorpion 170
    Seal 204
    Shrimp 172
    Simple 170-171
    Snail 177
    Snake 185
    Spider 170

Stegoceras 101
Stegosaurus 92
Terrapin 187
Triceratops 102
Trilobite fossil 78
Tyrannosaurus 84
Westlothiana 87
Eyeball 241
Eye bolt 581
Eyebrow
    74-gun ship 381
    Human 212
Eyelash 212
Eyelid
    Caiman 186
    Human 215
    Snake 184
    Terrapin 187
Eyepieces 610, 611
Eye plate lug 382
Eyespot 116

F

F-14 Tomcat fighter
    420
Fabric 384
Fabric covering
    Aluminum and steel
        wing 403
    BE 2B tail 405
    Blériot XI monoplane
        401
    Steel-tube fuselage
        403
Fabric lacing 405
Fabric skin 401
Fabric softener section
    595
Fabry 41
Facade
    Ancient Greek building
        461
    Ancient Roman
        building 463
    Baroque church
        480-481
    Gothic church 470-472
    Modern building
        496-499
    Neoclassical building
        478, 483
    Nineteenth-century
        building 493
    Renaissance building
        474
Facade pediment 481
Facade wall 470
Face
    Deadeye 383
    Human 211
    Sailmaker's mallet 384
Face mask
    Fencing 557
    Football 526
    Hockey goalkeeper
        540
    Ice hockey goalkeeper
        550
    Lacrosse goalkeeper
        541
    Slalom skiing 553
Facet 222-223
Faering 374-575
Fag end 387, 388
Fairing 364, 369
Fairing of landing gear 413
Fairing panel 415
Fairlead
    Battleship 395
    Frigate 397
    Rigging 383
    Roman corbita 373
Fairway 546
Falciform ligament 248
Falco tinnunculus 189
Falkland current 296
Fall 382

Fallopian tube 258-259, 261
False acacia 136
False anthers 141
False door 458-459
False fruit 148-149
False ram bow 394
"False ribs" 218
False septum 151
Falx cerebri 237
Fan
    Jaguar straight six
        engine 344
    Jet engines 418-419
    Microwave
        combination oven
        596-597
    Power drill 600
Fan blade
    Renault Clio 353
    Turbofan 419
Fancase 418
Fan drive shaft 345
Fan duct nozzle 412
Fan dust shield 597
Fan fold 61
Fang 170
Fan transformer 597
Fan motor 351
Fan vault 484-485
Farming ax 109
Fascia
    Ancient Roman
        building 463-464
    Baroque church 479,
        481
    Cellphones 589
    Dome 486
    French temple 485
    Gothic building 472
    Medieval building 467,
        469
    Modern building 498
    Neoclassical building
        482
    Renaissance building
        476-477
    Renault Clio 353
Fast forward button 577
Fat
    Cells 217
    Tissue 215, 235
Faultline
    Lake formation 292
    Mountain building
        62-63
    Weathering and erosion
        283
Fault plane 60
Faults 60-61, 292
    Mineral resources
        280
    Mountain building 62
    Oil and gas traps 281
    Showjumping
        competitions 554
Fault spring 292
Fault structure 60
Fault trap 281
Fava bean 133, 152
F-block 311
FCC cable 571
F clef 502
Feather 188, 191
Feathered float 391
Feathering 440-441
Feather shuttlecock
    544-545
Feather star 174
Feed add button 577
Feed bilge pump 391
Feeder station 528
Feed list 577
Feed name 577
Feet
    Human 232-233
    Theropods 84
Fei Tecnai G2
    transmission electron
    microscope 610

Feldspar 267, 269, 275
Felloe 590
Felt blanket 447
Felt-covered beater 516
518-519
Felt-tip pen 444
Female
Body 210, 211
Pelvis 218, 258
Reproductive organs
259
Female apex 119
Female cones
Bishop pine 124
Gymnosperm 122
Pine 122, 124
Smooth cypress 123
Yew 123
Female flower organs
140-143
Female flower remains
148
Female flowers 143, 144,
148
Female gametes
Fertilization 146-147
Gymnosperm 122
Seeds pine 122
Seaweed 116-117
Yew 123
Female receptacles 117
Female reproductive
organs
Fern 121
Fruit 148
Moss 119
Plants 144
Femoral artery 225, 253
Femoral musculature 86
Femoral nerve 238
Femoral vein 253
Femoro-tibial muscle 84
Femur
Albertosaurus 84
Archaeopteryx 85
Beetle 168
Bird 189
Brachiosaurus 90
Butterfly 169
Crocodile 186
Dinosaur 82
Domestic cat 195
Elephant 201
Eryops 81
Euoplocephalus 94
Frog 183
Gallimimus 86
Hare 197
Horse 199
Human 218-219,
224-225
Iguanodon 96-97
Kangaroo 206
Kentrosaurus 93
Lizard 184
Parasaurolophus 98
Pareiasaur 81
Plateosaurus 88
Platypus 206
Rhesus monkey 202
Scorpion 170
Seal 204
Spider 171
Stegoceras 101
Stegosaurus 93
Struthiomimus 87
Toxodon 107
Triceratops 102
Tuojiangosaurus 93
Turtle 187
Tyrannosaurus 84
Fencing 556-557
Fender
1906 Renault 336-337
BMW R/60 with Steib
chair 362
Cannondale ST 1000
touring bicycle 361
Ford Model T 338-339

Harley-Davidson FLHS
Electra Glide 363
Honda VF750 564
Husqvarna Motocross
TC610 368
Kirby BSA 369
Lockheed Electra 406
Motorcycle 364
Suzuki RGV500 369
Volkswagen Beetle 341
Weslake Speedway
motorcycle 369
Fender eye bolt 359
Fender jazz bass guitar
513
Fender stay 337, 362,
365
Fender stratocaster guitar
513
Fenestration 474, 494
Fermentation 313
Fermium 311
Fern 120-121
Fossil 66, 279
Life-cycle 121
Prehistoric Earth 68, 70,
72
Tree fern 112-113
Ferrel cell 300
Ferrite core 571
Fertile horsetail stem
120
Fertile oasis 285
Fertilization 146-147
Fern 121
Gymnosperm 122
Scots pine 122
Seaweed 117
Festoon
Ancient Roman
building 462-463
Cathedral dome 487
Neoclassical building
478-479
Fetal skull 220
Fetlock 199, 554
Fetus 260-261
Fiber 154-155
Fiberglass 548
Bow 548
Bucket seat 361
Canopy frame 425
Fuel tank 425
Racket 544
Reinforced plastic cover
329
Wheel guard 369
Fiber insulation 602
Fiber plate 366
Fibrils 32
Fibrin 253
Fibrous capsule 256
Fibrous habit 271
Fibrous pericardium 250
Fibrous septum 245
Fibula
Albertosaurus 84
Brachiosaurus 90
Crocodile 186
Diplodocus 90
Domestic cat 195
Elephant 201
Eryops 81
Euoplocephalus 94
87
Hare 197
Horse 199
Human 219, 232-233
Iguanodon 96-97
Kangaroo 206
Lizard 184
Parasaurolophus 99
Plateosaurus 88
Platypus 206
Seal 204
Stegoceras 101
Stegosaurus 93
Struthiomimus 87

Devon minnow 563
Dorsal 178-179, 181,
205
Helicopter 423
Lockheed Electra
airliner 407
Lungfish 81
LVG CVI fighter 405
Pectoral 178, 180-181
Pelvic 179-181
Schleicher glider 426
Tornado 421
Ventral 179
World War II aircraft
408-409
Final drive and gearbox
340
Final-drive sprocket 335
Fin-attachment skin 415
Fine 558
Fine linen canvas 437
Fine-toothed marble claw
453
Finger
Anchisaurus 89
Gorilla 203
Human 211
Iguanodon 97
Pachycephalosaurus
100
Psittacosaurus 103
Stegoceras 101
Theropod 84
Fingerboard 510-511,
513
Finger-claw 83, 85
Finger hole 508
Finger key 507
Fingerless glove 527
Fingernail 231
Finger recess 571
Finger tab 548
Finial
Asian building 490-491
Baroque church 479,
481
Gothic church 470-471
Islamic building
488-489
Medieval building 468
Neoclassical building
478
Nineteenth-century
building 493
Renaissance building
476
Finish line 542,
554-555
Fin leading-edge
attachment 415
Finned tail 80
Fin-root aerial fairing 421
Fin tip 415
Fin tip fairing 421, 424
Fin trailing edge 415
Fir 66
Fire 108
Fireball 10
Firebox 324-325
Fire-escape 497-498
Fire extinguisher 328
Fire-extinguisher
discharge indicator 412
Fire-hole 325
Fire-making tools 109
Fireman's seat 325
Fire opal 270
Fireplace 466-467
Fire-resistant clay 454
Fire-resistant curtain 497
Fire-resistant panel 496
Fire-tube boiler 334
Fire tubes 324-325
Firewall 406, 425
Firewire ports 560
Firing 452
Firing chamber 575
Firing pin 549
Firn 287

First century 462-464
"First down" 526-527
First pilot's seat 408
First quarter 41
First rate ship 378
First slip 538
First transition metals 310
First violin 503, 504-505
First wheel set 329
Fish
Bony 180-181
Breathing 180
Cartilaginous 178
Fossil 279
Holostean 73
Jawless 178-179
Fish davit 379
Fisherman's schooner 385
Fishing tackle 109
Fish-scale tile 476-477, 486
Fishtail nectaries 160
Fissure 247
Fissures 157
Fissure volcano 272
Fitbit Alta 591
Five-line stave 502
Five yard mark 540
Fixative 430, 440
Fixed float 590
Fixed gear 346-347, 411
Fixed lug 583
Fixed spool reel 562
Fixing screw 599
Fjord 294-295
Flag button 576
Flagella 166
Flagellum
Beetle 168
Chlamydomonas sp. 116
Moss 119
Seaweed gametes 117
Snail 177
Sperm 259
Flag halyard 580
Flagmast 395
Flag pin 547
Flagpole 495
Flaking rock 282
Flamboyant tracery 472
Flame 312-313
Flamingo 188, 190
Flamsteed 40
Flange 492, 498
Flanged plate 425
Flank
Bird 188
Cow 198
Flanker
Canadian football 526
Rugby 530
Flank spike 95
Flap
ARV light aircraft 425
Formula One race car
356, 357
Hawker Tempest
components 409
Lockheed Electra
airliner 406
Tornado 421
Flap drive screw 413
Flap lever 425
Flap seal 413, 414
Flap tip 414
Flap torque tube 424
Flap track 413
Flap-track fairing 413,
415, 572, 573
Flared bell
Brass instruments
506-507
Woodwind instruments
508-509
Flash lamp 580
Flash steam generator 342
Flash tube 597
Flask 312-313
Flat
Musical notation 502

Twin bollards 586
Flatbed scanner 570-571
Flatboard 384
Flat bottom 591
Flat-bottomed rail 331
Flat chisel 452
Flat cone 272
Flatfish angling 562
Flat-four engine 340
Flat freight car 327
Flat horse-races 554
Flat laminae 158
Flat roof
Ancient Egyptian
building 458
Neoclassical building
483
Twentieth-century
building 494-495
Flat seam 584
Flat seizing 383, 389
Flat soffit 464
Flattened pericarp 151
Flattened petiole 160
Flattened stem 129
Flat-topped plateau 275,
282
Flat-topped seamount 298
Flat wire seizing 383
Flavian amphitheater 464
Flax-spinning mill 492
Flesh-eaters 194
Flesh-eating dinosaur 70
Flesh tones 433
Fleshy aril 148
Fleshy axis 143
Fleshy fruit 146-147
Fleshy hair 140
Fleshy infolded receptacle
148
Fleshy scale leaf 155
Fleteh 548
Flexible hose shrouding
593
Flexible ribbon cable 580
Flex kink guard 594
Flexor digitorum longus
muscle 233
Flexor digitorum tendon
231
Flexor hallucis longus
muscle 233
Flexor pollicis brevis
muscle 231
Flexor retinaculum
muscle 231
Flexors of forearm 226
Flexors of hand 227
Flexor tubercle 85
Flex rewind 593
Flight 543
Flight-control hydraulic
jack 416
Flight-control mixing unit
417
Flight-control rod 423
Flight controls 412
Flightdeck door 573
Flightdeck windshield 573
Flight feathers 188, 191
Flight instruments 425
Flight refueling
receptacle 421
Flint 277
Flint tools 108-109
Flipper
Dolphin 204
Seal 204
Flitch-plated wooden
chassis 342
Float 390-591
Floating disc brake
564-565
Floating floor 602
"Floating" rib 218
Flocked pastel board 441
Floodgate 604
Flood-plain 289-291

Floods 290
Floor
　Gun turret 596
　Ironclad 395
　Longboat 380
　Modern building
　　496-498
　Nineteenth-century
　　building 492
　Twentieth-century
　　building 494-495
Floor anchor 407
Floorboard 464, 486
Floor-joist 464
Floor-mounted base 608
　Floor pan 340
Floor torn 518-519
Florence Cathedral 475,
　487
Florets 142
　Florists'
　　chrysanthemum 129
　Ultraviolet light 145
Florida current 296
Florists' chrysanthemum
　129
Flower bud
　Aechmea miniata 162
　Broomrape 163
　Bulb 155
　Clematis 131
　Florists'
　　chrysanthemum 129
　Hibiscus 127
　Ice-plant 129
　Live-forever 129
　Oxalis sp. 157
　Peruvian lily 129
　Rose 131
　Water lily 159
　Wind pollination 144
Flowering plant 57, 70, 72
Flowering shoot 155
Flowers 140-145
　Brassavola nodosa 162
　Bromeliad 113
　Broomrape 163
　Buds 140-141, 145
　Clematis 131
　Color 140, 144-145
　Dicotyledons 126-127,
　　141-145
　Dodder 163
　Epiphytes 162-163
　Everlasting pea 129
　Florists'
　　chrysanthemum 129
　Guzmania lingulata
　　163
　Ice-plant 129
　Involucre 129
　Monocotyledons 126,
　　140-141, 143
　Peruvian lily 129
　Pollination 144-145
　Rose 131
　Russian vine 131
　Scented 144
　Stem arrangements 143
　Ultraviolet light 145
　Vegetative reproduction
　　154
　Water lily 159
　Yew 123
Flower scars 154
Flower spike 143, 155
Flower stalk
　Brassavola nodosa 162
　Bulbil 154
　Clematis 131
　Dry fruit 150-151
　Fertilization 146-147
　Florists'
　　chrysanthemum 129
　Fruit development
　　146-147
　Monocotyledons
　　140-141, 143
　Oxalis sp. 157

Rose 131
Rowan 131
Russian vine 131
Succulent fruit 148-149
Sycamore 131
Water lily 159
Flow splitter 418
Fluff filter impeller 595
Fluid 506
Fluke
　74-gun ship 380
　Danforth anchor 386
Fluorescent light 318-319
Fluorine 308-309, 311
Fluorite 271
　Halides 269
Flush-riveted aluminum
　fuselage 425
Flush-riveted metal-
　skinned wing 406
Flush window 494
Flute 503, 504-505, 508
Fluted pilaster 462
Fluted pinnacle 481
Fluted shaft 478
Flute tube 525
Fluting 461, 463
Flutter kick 559
Fly 168
Fly-by-wire side stick 573
Fly fishing 562
Fly-half 530
Flying boat 406
Flying buttress
　Gothic building 470-473
　Medieval building 466,
　　468-469
　Nineteenth-century
　　building 493
Flying Fortress bomber
　408
Flying helmet 404
Flying jib 385
Flying reptile 70
Flying tackle 531
Fly rod 562-563
Flywheel
　Benz Motorwagen 335
　Early engines 342-343
　Etching press 447
　Mid West rotary engine
　　411
　Oldsmobile engine 336
　Renault Clio 351
　Steamboat 391
Flywheel retaining thread
　411
Flywheel with balance
　weight 347
FM and TV aerial 603
Focker, Anthony 404
Fo'c'sle 380
Focus 65
Focusing lens 581
Fog 42-43
Fog-lamp 349, 355
Fog light 332, 363
Foil 556-557
Foilist 557
Foil pommel 557
Folded rock 60, 266
　Impermeable rock 281
　Mineral resources 280
　Strata 60-61
Folded schist 274
Folding foot rest 572
Folding mountain range
　274
Folding step 526
Folding table with
　integral keyboard 573
Fold mountains 62
Fold of mucous
　membrane 249
Folds 60-61
Foliage leaf
　Bishop pine 124
　Bud 124
　Bulb 155

Germination 152-155
Monocotyledon
　126
Parasitic plant
　162
Pine 124-125
Rhizome 155
Seedling 152-153
Stem bulbil 155
Yew 123
Foliated capital 469
Foliated frieze 469, 479
Foliated panel 479
Foliated scrollwork 472
Foliated volute 476
Foliate papilla 244
Foliose lichen 114
Foliose thallus 114
Follicle
　Dehiscent dry fruit
　　150-151
　Hair 235
　Ovary 258
Fomalhaut 19, 20
Fontanelle 220
Food storage
　Bulb 155
　Corm 155
　Embryo 147
　Rhizome 155
　Root tuber 155
　Scale leaf 155
　Seed 152
　Succulent 156-157
　Swollen stem 113, 155
Foot
　Anchisaurus 89
　Bird 190
　Caiman 186-187
　Corythosaurus 98
　Cow 198
　Diplodocus 90
　Duck 188
　Elephant 90
　Gorilla 203
　Harp 511
　Herrerasaurus 86
　Horse 198
　Human 210
　Iguanodon 96
　Kangaroo 207
　Pachycephalosaurus
　　100
　Relief-printing press
　　449
　Sails 374, 385
　Slug 176
　Snail 177
　Stegoceras 101
　Stegosaurus 92
　Toaster 598-599
　Tyrannosaurus 84
　Tube 174
　Webbed 188
　Westlothiana 81
Football 524, 526-527
Footboard 335
Foot brake 363
Footbridge 493
Foot-fault judge 544
Foot nut 365
Foot pedal 366, 514
Footplate 324
Footrest
　Curtiss biplane 398-399
　Suzuki RGV500 368
　Weslake Speedway
　　motorcycle 369
Footrest hanger 569
Foot rope 378-379, 382,
　385
Foot throttle 427
Foramen cecum 244
Foramen magnum 220
Foraminiferans 279
Force 320-321
　"Force play" 536
Ford Cosworth V6
　12-valve engine 344

Ford Cosworth V6
　24-valve engine 344
Ford, Henry 338
Ford Model T 538-539
Ford turbocharged diesel
　engine 347
Fore-and-aft rigged lateen
　sails 376
Fore-and-aft sails 384
Fore-and-aft schooner 385
Forearm
　Gorilla 203
　Horse 199
　Human 210
　Movement 227
Forearm guard 548
Forearm pass 534
Fore bitt 380
Fore breast rope 387
Forecarriage 335
Forecastle
　74-gun ship 380
　Sailing warship 376
　Square-rigged ship 375
Forecastle-castle-deck
　gunport 376
Forefoot
　Caiman 186
　Diplodocus 90
　Edmontonia 95
　Elephant 90
　Iron paddlesteamer 393
　Stegosaurus 92
Fore hatch tackle 379
Forehead
　Bird 188
　Dolphin 204
　Elephant 200-201
　Horse 199
　Human 211, 212
Foreleg
　Caiman 186
　Elephant 201
　Lizard 184
　Terrapin 187
Forelimb
　Anchisaurus 89
　Bird 188
　Corythosaurus 98
　Edmontonia 95
　Frog 182
　Hare 196
　Herrerasaurus 86
　Iguanodon 97
　Kangaroo 207
　Pachycephalosaurus
　　100
　Psittacosaurus 103
　Rabbit 196
　Rat 196
　Salamander 182
　Stegoceras 101
　Stegosaurus 92
　Thyreophorans 92
　Triceratops 102
　Tyrannosaurus 84
Forelock 199
Fore lower topsail 385
Fore mast
　Iron paddlesteamer 392
　Roman corbita 372
　Sailing warship 376
　Square-rigged ship 375
　Wooden sailing ship
　　379
Fore mast course 379
Foremast hole 380
Fore mast topgallant sail
　379
Fore mast topsail 379
Forepeak 393
Fore royal stay 385
Fore sail 372, 385
Fore sail halyard 380
Foreset strata 283
Fore shroud 379
Foresight
　Rifle 549
　Target pistol 549

Foreskin 259
Fore spring rope 387
Fore stay
　Rigging 382
　Roman corbita 372
　Sailing warship 376
　Wooden sailing ship
　　379
Fore staysail 379, 385
Forest-dwelling mammals
　74
Fore throat halyard 385
Fore top 379
Fore topcastle 376
Fore topgallant mast 379
Fore topmast 376, 379
Fore topmast stay 376, 379
Fore topmast staysail 385
Fore topmast staysail tack
　382
Fore topsail 379
Fore upper topsail 385
Forewing 169
Fore yard 376, 379
Fore yard lift 385
Forged iron anchor 392
Fork
　ARV Super 2 425
　Eddy Merckx racing
　　bicycle 361
　Harley-Davidson FLHS
　　Electra Glide 363
　Honda CB750 363
　Motorcycle 364
　Vespa Grand Sport 160
　　Mark 1 363
Fork blade 359
Forked beam 380
Forked connecting-rod
　342
Fork end 383
Fork slide 365
Formeret 469, 479
Fornax 19, 20
Fornix 236-237
Fortifications 466
Forum of Trajan 463
Forward bulkhead panel
　406
Forward deck 561
Forward defensive stroke
　538
Forward dive 558
Forward door 415, 417
Forward-facing eyes 194
Forward fairing 415
Forward-firing machine-
　gun 405
Forward funnel 393, 395
Forward fuselage
　structure 401
Forward galley 416
Forward hydroplane 397
Forward main door 412
Forward ramp drive 417
Forward rocker 615
Forward rollover
　structure 357
Forwards 532, 534-535
Forward short leg 538
Forward spar 415
Fossa ovalis 251
Fossil fuel 280-281,
　314-315
Fossilization 278
Fossil record 279
Fossils 278-279
　Acanthostega skull 80
　Ankylosaurus tail club
　　95
　Birch leaf 74, 76
　Blue-green algae 78
　Brachiopod 65
　Clubmoss 66
　Eurypterid 79
　Fern 66
　Graptolite 65
　Horsetail 66
　Hyaenodon skull 107

Jawless fish 78
Land plant 64
Lungfish 81
Nautiloid 65
Palm bark 74
Shark teeth 67
Starfish 79
Swamp plant 64
Sweetgum leaf 76
Titanosaurid egg 91
Trilobite 78
Fossil skeleton
　Archaeopteryx 85
　Bat 105
　Parasaurolophus 98
　Pareiasaur 81
　Struthiomimus 87
　Westlothiana 81
Foster, N. 496, 498
Foul lines 536
Fouls 552
Foul tackle 524
Foul tip 557
Foundation
　Ancient Roman
　　building 464
　Iron paddlesteamer 392
　Modern building 496
　Nineteenth-century
　　building 492
Foundry plug 580
Fountain pen 444
Four-aspect color light
　signal 330
Four-chambered heart
　104
Four-cylinder 12-HP
　engine 399
Four-cylinder motorcycle
　365
Four-footed dinosaur 88,
　92, 96, 100
Four-pulley system 320
Four-stroke combustion
　engine 366
Four-stroke cycle 343
Fourteenth century 474
　Arch 488
　Gothic building 471-473
　Medieval building
　　465-467
　Roof 490
　Style 470
Fourth mast 376
Four-wheel bogie 417
Fovea 224
Fowler flap 413, 414
Foxes 194
Fracastorius 40
Fracture 270
Fractured rock 34
Fragaria x ananassa 128,
　150
Fra Mauro 40
Frame
　74-gun ship 381
　ARV light aircraft 424
　Bicycle 558-559
　Cannondale SH600
　　Digital video camera 582
　Hybrid bicycle 361
　Concert grand piano
　　515
　Concorde, the 416
　Harley-Davidson FLHS
　　Electra Glide 363
　Honda VF750 364
　Ironclad 395
　Longboat 380
　Medieval house 466
　Modeled sculpture 452
　Modern building 496
　Motorcycle 364
　Oscillating steam
　　engine 390
　Racing bicycle 360
　Racket 544-545
　Relief-printing press
　　449

Single scull 560
Steam-powered Cugnot 535
Steel 494
Upright piano 514
Weslake Speedway motorcycle 369
Frame angle 560
Frame drum 518
Frame head 540
Frame-mounted fairing 564
Fram Rupes 35
Francis turbine 514
Francium 310
Frapped turn 589
Free nerve ending 235, 239
Freestyle swimming stroke 558
Free-throw line 532-533, 535
Freewheel 361
Freewheel lock nut 358
Freewheel sprocket 360
Freezing 307
Freezing level 302
Freight car 327
Freight service 326
French baroque style 479, 482
French bowline 388
French Flamboyant style 470
French trotter 554
Fresco 434-435
Freshwater bay 291
Freshwater angling 562
Freshwater lake
    Lakes and groundwater 292
    Weathering and erosion 283
Freshwater turtle 186
Fret 512-513
Fret-pattern mosaic 488-489
Fretwork 461, 491
Frieze
    Ancient Egyptian building 459
    Ancient Greek building 461
    Ancient Roman building 463, 465
    Baroque church 479, 481
    Cathedral dome 487
    French temple 485
    Medieval church 469
    Neoclassical building 478-479, 482
    Renaissance building 476
    Twentieth-century building 495
Frigate 396-397
Fring 46-47
Fringed crumble cap 115
Fringilla coelebs 193
Fringing reef 299
Frog 182-183
    Double bass bow 511
    Eggs 183, 192
    Fossil 278
    Violin bow 510
Frog kick 559
Frond
    Fern 120-121
    Seaweed 116-117
    Tree fern 112-113
Front air dam 354
Frontal bone
    Bony fish 181
    Chimpanzee 202
    Human 212-213, 220-221
Frontalis muscle 226, 228-229
Frontal lobe 236-237

Frontal notch 213
Frontal process 221
Frontal rib 161
Frontal sinus 212, 245
Front axle
    1906 Renault 536-537
    Ford Model T 338
    Honda VF750 365
    Husqvarna Motocross TC610 368
    Kirby BSA 369
Front brake cable
    Bicycle 359
    Eddy Merckx racing bicycle 361
Front brake lever 363
Front bumper 332
Front cantilever brake 359
Front crawl 558-559
Front cylinder exhaust pipe 368
Front derailleur 358-360
Front hazard avoidance camera 615
Front leg 168-169
Front light
    Bicycle 360
    Paris Metro 328
    Italian State Railroads Class 402 328
Frontoparietal bone 183
Frontozygomatic suture 220
Front spring 337
Front wheel
    Bicycle 359
Front wing 168
Frost wedging 282, 286-287
Froude's early test propeller 391
Frozen rubber puck 550-551
Fruit
    Bramble 130
    Couch grass 113
    Development 146-147
    Dry 150-151
    Durmast oak 131
    Peach 131
    Pitcher plant 113
    Rowan 131
    Succulent 148-149
    Sycamore 131
Fruit wall 148-149, 150-151
Fruticose lichen 114
Fruticose thallus 114
"F" turret 394
Fucoxanthin 116
Fucus spiralis 116
Fucus vesiculosus 116, 117
Fuel/air intake pipe 337
Fuel and oil heat exchanger 418
Fuel and oil tank 398-399
Fuel cap 348, 369
Fuel contents indicator 413
Fuel-cooled oil cooler 419
Fuel drip tray 411
Fuel filler and vent 403
Fuel filler cap
    Curtiss biplane 398
    Volkswagen Beetle 340
Fuel filler neck 340
Fuel filter 419
Fuel heater 419
Fuel hose 425
Fuel injection 344, 356
Fuel inlet 419
Fuel-jettison pipe 417
Fuel-jettison valve 406
Fuel manifold 418-419
Fuel nozzle 418-419
Fuel pipe
    Concorde 417
    Curtiss biplane 398
    Jaguar V12 345
Fuel reservoir 368

Fuel sediment bowl 559
Fuel shut-off valve cable 419
Fuel sprayer 418
Fuel supply pump 527
Fuel tank
    Avro triplane 402
    Benz Motorwagen 335
    BMW R/60 362
    Concorde, the 417
    "Deltic" diesel-electric locomotive 326
    Harley-Davidson FLHS Electra Glide 363
    Helicopter 422-425
    Honda VF750 364
    Lockheed Electra airliner 407
    LVG CVI fighter 405
    Pegasus XL SE ultralight 426
    Renault Clio 350
    Suzuki RGV500 369
    Volkswagen Beetle 340
    Werner motorcycle 362
    Weslake Speedway motorcycle 369
    White Steam Car 342
    Wright Flyer 398
Fuel tank breather 369
Fuel tank cradle 422
Fuel tank filler cap 369
Fuel tank filler neck 350
Fuel tank filler nozzle 427
Fuel tank sender unit 340
Fuel tank top skin 425
Fuel tap 366
Fuel vent pipe 422
Fulcrum 320-321
Full back
    Australian rules football 527
    Canadian football 526
    Football 526
    Gaelic football 529
    Rugby 530
Full back line 529
Full-elliptic leaf spring 334-335
Full-elliptic steering spring 337
Full forward 528-529
Fumaroles 272-273
Funaria hygrometrica 119
Funaria sp. 119
Functionalism 496
Function button 585
Function display 520-521
Fundus 258
Fungal filament 114-115
Fungi 112, 114-115, 133
Fungia fungites 167
Fungiform papilla 244
Fungoid-structure encrustations 284
Funicle 150
Funnel
    Battleship 395
    Frigate 397
    Iron paddlesteamer 392-395
    Lizard 185
    Octopus 176-177
    Steamboat with paddle wheels 391
Funnel guide 126
Funnel stay 395
Furcula 189
Furled forecourse sail 575
Furled lateen main sail 576
Furled lateen mizzen sail 375, 376
Furnerius 40
Furrow 282
Furud 21
Fused carpels 140, 144, 151
Fused petals 142, 145

Fused receptacles 149
Fuselage 401, 409, 424, 572, 575
Fuselage bottom skin 424
Fuselage bracing wire 403, 426
Fuselage mid-section 412
Fuselage nose-section 412
Fuselage skin 402
Fuselage spine fairing 414
Fuselage tail-section 415
Fuselage top skin 424
Fusion crust 52
Futtock shroud 378

G

Gabbro 267, 274
Gable
    Gothic building 470-473
    Medieval building 467, 469
    Nineteenth-century building 492-493
    Renaissance building 476
Gabled arch 471
Gacrux 21
Gadolium 311
Gaelic football 528-529
Gaff 380, 385
Gagarin 41
Gaia 302
Galactic center 14, 18, 20
Galactic nucleus 12-13
Galactic plane 14-15
Galaxy 10-15, 613
Galena 268
Galeocerdo cuvier 179
Galilean moons 44
Galium aparine 150
Gallbladder
    Domestic cat 195
    Human 248, 252
    Rabbit 196
    Tortoise 187
Galle ring 50-51
Gallery
    74-gun ship 381
    Ancient Roman building 465
    Baroque church 479-480
    Cathedral dome 487
    Frigate 397
    Medieval building 466-468
    Modern building 496-497
    Renaissance theater 477
    Wooden sailing ship 378-379
Galley 372-397
Galley area, business class cabin 572, 573
Galliminus 82, 84, 86-87
Gallium 311
Galois 41
Galvanized "D" shackle 386
Gambrel roof 490
Game target shooting 548
Gamete 154
    Brown seaweed 116-117
    Bryophyte 118-119
    Fern 120-121
    Fertilization 146-147
    Gymnosperm 122
    Moss 112
    Pine 122
    Vegetative reproduction 154
    Yew 125
Gametophyte

Bryophyte 118-119
Fern 120-121
Liverwort 118
Moss 112, 119
Gamma 18, 21
Gamma Centauri 21
Gamma Hydri 20
Gamma Mensae 20
Gamma radiation 10
Gamma ray 22, 318-319
Gamma ring 48
Ganges River 288
Joule 314, 316
Ganges plain 63
Ganges River delta 288
Ganglion 173, 177
Gangway
    74-gun ship 380
    Colosseum 464
    Sailing warship 377
Ganymede 44
Gape
    Angling hook 562
    Dolphin 204
Garboard strake 393
Gargoyle 473
Garnet 267
Garnet-mica schist 267
Garnierite 270
Garudimimus 86
Gas 306-307
    Asteroids, comets, and meteoroids 52-53
    Chemical reactions 313
    Massive stars 26-27
    Mineral resources 280-281
    NGC 2997 (spiral galaxy) 12
    Small stars 24-25
    Stellar black hole 29
Gas blanket 500
Gas cloud
    Earth's formation 56
    Milky Way 14
    Nebulae and star clusters 16-17
    Origin and expansion of universe 10-11
Gas current 29
Gas deposit 57, 281
Gaseous exchange in alveolus 255
Gaseous water 49
Gas exchange 134
    Leaf 138-139
    Photosynthesis process 138
    Root 132
    Sunken stoma 156-157
    Wetland plants 158
Gas formation 280-281
Gas giants
    Jupiter 44-45
    Neptune 50-51
    Saturn 46-47
    Solar system 30-31
    Uranus 48-49
Gaskin 198, 554
Gas loop 32-33
Gas molecule 53
Gassendi 40
Gas shell 16-17, 25
Gas tail 52-53
Gastralia 85, 87
Gas traps 281
Gastric artery 253
Gastrocnemius muscle
    Albertosaurus 84
    Euoplocephalus 94
    Human 226-227
    Iguanodon 97
Gastroepiploic vein 253
Gastropod mollusk 75
Gastropods 176, 279
Gastrovascular cavity 167

Gas turbine 418
Gate
    Building 467, 490-491
    Canoeing 560
    Downhill skiing 552
    Hydroelectric power station 514
Gate clamp 560
Gate-house 467
Gateway 460
Gatwick Express "People Mover" 328
Gauge 330-331
Gauge class 325
Gauged arch 492
Gauntlet 540, 557
Gavialis gangeticus 186
G clef 502
Gear band 336
Gearbox
    ARV light aircraft 425
    Ford Model T 339
    Harley-Davidson FLHS Electra Glide 363
    Motorcycle 364, 366
    Renault Clio 351
    Volkswagen Beetle 340
    Wind turbine 605
Gearbox bevel drive 418
Gearbox case 410
Gearbox drive spline 410
Gearbox fixing stud 356
Gearbox mount 413
Gearbox oil scavenge line 419
Gearbox unit 413
Gear cable 359
Gearcase 601
Gearcase position 600
Gear change 363
Gear-change rod 351
Gear lever
    1906 Renault 337
    Husqvarna Motocross TC610 368
    Renault Clio 350
    Two-stroke engine 366
Gear lever knob 340
Gear lever surround 352
Gear ratios 361
Gear retainer 362
Gear shift 359
Gear system 358, 366
Gears
    Drills 600
    Motorcycle 366
Gelatine roller 447
Gemini 18
Gemma 118
Generative nucleus 147
Generator 517
    British Rail class 20 diesel engine 327
    Diesel train 326
    Electric train 326
    Nuclear power station 314
    Van de Graaff 316
    Wind turbine 605
Generator cooling fan 327
Generator housing 411
Generator rotor
    Hydroelectric power station 514
    Mid West engine 410
Generator unit 314
Genetic material 606, 607
Genioglossus muscle 245
Geniohyoid muscle 245
Genome 607
Genital plate 175
Gentlemen's room 477
Geographic pole 38
Geological time 56-57, 279
Geranium pratense 144
Gerberette 497
Gerbil 196
Germanium 311
German-style baroque 482

Germany 526
Germinal epithelium 258
Germination 152-153
　Cabbage seed 152
　Epigeal 152-153
　Fern spore 121
　Hypogeal 152-153
　Mushroom spore 115
　Pine 122
　Pollen grain 146-147
Gesso 432, 453
Geyser 272-273, 275
Gharial 186
Ghost anemone 166
Giant redwood 112
Giant slalom 552
Giant stars 22-23, 26
Gibbon 202
Gibson Les Paul guitar 513
Gig 595
Gilded band 490
Gilded cross 487
Gilded orb 487
Gilded rib 487
Gilded truck 578-579
Gilding materials 451, 432
Gill
　Bivalves 176
　Bony fish 180-181
　Dogfish 178-179
　Fungi 114-115
　Lamprey 178
　Newt 182
　Salamander 182
　Tadpole 183
Gill filament 180
Gill opening 178
Gill raker 180
Gill slit 178-180
Gilt ironwork 482, 490
Ginger 155
Gingiva 247
Ginkgo 68, 70, 72, 122-123, 279
Ginkgo biloba 68, 123
Ginkgophyta 122
Ginkgo pluripartita 72
Giornate 434-435
Giraffa camelopardalis 199
Giraffe 198-199
Girder 493
Girdle 116
Girdle scar 123
Girth
　Harness racer 555
　Showjumper 554
Gizzard
　Bird 189
　Brachiosaurus 91
　Euoplocephalus 94
　Gallimimus 86
Glabella
　Human skull 213, 221
　Trilobite fossil 78
Glacial deposits 286-287, 292-293
Glacial periods 56-57, 76
Glacial sediments 299
Glacial streams 286
Glacier Bay 286
Glacier features 286-287
Glaciers 286-287
　Prehistoric Earth 66, 76
　River's stages 289
　Rock cycle 266-267
　Weathering and erosion 282
Glacier snout 286, 289
Gladiolus 154-155
Gland
　19th century paddlesteamer 391
　Axial 175
　Butterwort 161
　Cement 175
　Green 173

Monkey cup 161
Mucous 177
Pedal 177
Poison 170, 176
Rectal 179
Salivary 177
Silk 170
Venus fly trap 160
Glans penis 259
GLARE upper fuselage 572
Glass 307
　Buildings 492, 494
　Photovoltaic cell 605
　Tesserae 450
Glass bulb 319
Glass cooking turntable 596
Glass curtain 497
Glass deflector 525
Glass enamel 450
Glass flask 512
Glass mosaic 489
Glass muller 436, 440
Glass pane 494
Glass paper 441
Glass plate 570, 571
Glass prism 518
Glass slab 456, 440
Glass tube 319
Glass wall 496, 499
Glazing
　Acrylic paints 442
　Modern building 496-499
　Twentieth-century building 494
Glazing bar 499
Gleba 114-115
Glechoma hederacea 154
Gleditsia triacanthos 137
Glenoid cavity 80
Gliders 426-427
Global positioning system (GPS) 590
Global warming 301
Globe 264
Globe Theater 477
Globular cluster 12, 16, 21
Globule 24, 26
Glomerulus 256-257
Gloriosa superba 143
Glory lily 143
Gloss finish
　Acrylics 442
　Oil painting 436
Glossopteris 67
Gloster Meteor fighter 408
Glove box 425
Gloves
　Baseball fielder 537
　Cricket batsman 539
　Cricket wicket-keeper 559
　Fencing 556-557
　Football 527
　Ice hockey 551
　Lacrosse goalkeeper 541
　Racketball 545
　Sailing 560
　Skiing 552-553
　Soccer goalkeeper 525
Glucose 158
Glulam wall-plate 499
Gluon 309
Gluteal fold 210
Gluteus maximus muscle 227
Gluteus medius muscle 225
Gluteus minimus muscle 225
Glyph 460
Gnathostomata 178, 180
Gneiss 274
Gnetophytes 122
Gnome seven-cylinder rotary engine 400

Gnomon 377
Goal
　Australian rules football 528
　Gaelic football 529
　Hockey 540
　Hurling 541
　Ice hockey 550
　Lacrosse 541
　Rugby 550-551
　Soccer 524
Goal area
　Gaelic football 529
　Handball 535
　Soccer 524
Goal attack 535
Goal circle 535, 541
Goal crease 541, 550
Goal defense 535
Goal judge 550
Goalkeeper
　Australian rules football 528
　Gaelic football 529
　Handball 534-535
　Hockey 540
　Ice hockey 550
　Lacrosse 541
　Netball 535
　Soccer 524-525
Goalkeeper's equipment 540
Goalkeeper's gloves 525
Goalkeeper's helmet 550-551
Goalkeeper's kicker 540
Goalkeeper's pad 550
Goalkeeper's shirt 525, 550
Goalkeeper's stick 550
Goal line
　Australian rules football 528
　Football 526
　Handball 535
　Hockey 540
　Ice hockey 550
　Rugby 530
　Soccer 524
Goal line referee 555
Goal net 524, 534, 550
Goalposts
　Australian rules football 528
　Football 526
　Gaelic football 529
　Netball 535
　Rugby 530
Goal shooter 535
Goal square 528
Goal third 535
Goal umpire 528-529
Goat 198
Goat hair brush 438, 442
Goat hake wash brush 438
Gobi Desert 265, 617
Goggles
　Harness racing 555
　Skiing 552-553
　Swimming 558
Gold 31, 268, 280-281, 438
Gold chalcopyrite 271
Golden barrel cactus 156
Golden eagle 188
Golden lion tamarin 203
Gold leaf 432
　Fresco 435
　Illumination 444-445
　Smalti 450
　Vitreous glass 451
　Wood sculpture highlighting 455
Golf 546-547
Golgi complex 217
Gomphos 573
Gonad
　Jellyfish 167
　Octopus 176
　Sea anemone 167

Sea urchin 175
Starfish 174
Gondwana
　Cretaceous period 72
　Jurassic period 70-71
　Late Carboniferous period 66-67
　Middle Ordovician period 64-65
Gong 504, 516
Goniastrea aspera 167
Gonopore
　Barnacle 173
　Sea urchin 175
　Snail 177
　Starfish 174
Google Chat 576
Goose-feather quill 444
Goosegrass 150
Goose neck 588
Gopher 196
Gopuram finial 491
Gorge
　Cave 284-285
　River features 290
Gorilla 202-203
Gothic architecture 468, 470-475
Gothic book script lettering 445
Gothic stone arch 467
Gothic torus 470
Gouge
　Relief printing 446, 449
　Woodcarving 454-455
Gour 284-285
Goya 35
GPS 590
Grab handle 362
Graben 61
Graben lake 293
Gracilis muscle 226-227
Graded wash 439
Graffian follicle 258
Graffias 21
Gran Chaco 264, 617
Grand Canyon 57, 226-227
Grand piano 514-515
"Grand Prix" world championships 568
Grandstand 555
Granite-aggregate slab 499
Granite cladding 494
Granular stalk 114
Granum 139
Grape hyacinth 155
Graphics card 567
Graphite 268, 311
Graphite pencil 430
Graphite stick 430
Grapnel-type anchor 376
Grasping tail 202
Grass 113
Grate 324
Grating 380-381
Graver 449
Gravitation (gravity)
　Atmosphere 300
　Force and motion 320
　Neutron stars and black holes 28
　Oceans and seas 296-297
　Universe 10
Gravitational pull 296-297
Gravity-feed fuel tank 405
Gray Cliffs 276
Gray matter 236-237, 238
Gray squirrel 197
Gray whale 204
Grease 446
Greaser 339
Great Bear Lake 264, 617
Great cabin 379, 381
Great Dark Spot 50-51
Greater blackbacked gull 193
Greater flamingo 190

Greater omentum 214
Greater palatine foramen 220
Greater trochanter of femur 224-225
Greater wing coverts 188
Greater wing of sphenoid bone 220-221
Great Lakes 264
Great manual 514
Great Mosque 484
Great Red Spot 44-45
Great Rift Valley 60
Great Sandy Desert 265, 616
Great saphenous vein 253
Great stop 514
Greek ship 372-373
Greek-style fret ornament 485
Green (golf) 547
Green alga 112, 116-117
Green calc-silicate mineral 275
Green chlorophyll pigment 116, 158
Green earth 434-435
Green fluorite 269
Green gland 173
Greenhouse effect 36, 300-301
"Greenhouse gas" 301
Greenland
　Cretaceous period 73
　Late Carboniferous period 66
　Middle Ordovician period 64
　Satellite map 264
Green light 318, 330-331
Green seaweed 117
Green snakelock anemone 166
Green starboard navigation light 406
Greenwich Meridian
　Satellite map 264-265
　Surface currents 296
Gregorian calendar 681
Grid lines 445
Griffon 461
Grikes 284
Grille
　"Eurostar" warning horn 529
　Roman Mill 464
Grill/griddle 596
Grimaldi 40
Grip
　Sailmaker's fid 384
　Sailmaker's mallet 384
Gripe 379
Groin
　Arches and vaults 485
　Human body 211
Groin pad 527
Groin vault 479, 484-485
Grommet 373, 375, 384, 426
Groove
　Rope starter 335
　Serving mallet 384
Grooved racing tire 356, 357
Groove for FCC cable 571
Grooving 383
Grotesque figure 476
Ground handling wheel 422
Ground ivy 154
Ground-mapping radar 420
Groundmass 268-269
Ground roller 447
Groundwater 292-293
　Volcanic structure 273
Grout 450-451
Growing point 153
Growing tip 79

Growth line
　Fossilized jawless fish 78
　Snail 177
Groyne 294
Grundtvig Church 495
Gruppo Seven Cubist 495
Grus 19, 20
Gryphon 461
Gryposaurus 96, 99
Guanine 216
Guard
　Basketball 532
　Fencing foil 557
　Football 526
Guard cell 138-139
Guardrail 591-592, 595
Guardstop 541
Gubernator 373
Gudgeon 375
Gudgeon pin 345
Gudgeon strap 378
Guest boat boom 594
Guiana Highlands 264, 617
Guidance control sensor 612
Guide hair 126
Guide mark 555
Guide wheel 528
Guinevere Planitia 36, 37
Guitars 510, 512-513
Gula Mons 37
Gulf of Mexico 264, 617
Gulf Stream 296
Gull 189, 193
Gulley 538
Gully 289
Gum 247
Gum arabic 438
　Lithographic printing 446, 448
　Pastel making 440
Gun
　1.5 kg gun 395
　5 pound gun 395
　4½ in gun 397
　4¾ in gun 594
　11 cm gun 397
　12 cm gun 594
　12 in gun 594
　30 cm gun 594
　Battleship 594
　Frigate 397
　Measurements 594
　Sailing warship 376
　Wooden sailing ship 378, 379
Gun battery 395
Gun carriage 377
Gun deck 380
Gun loading cage 396
Gunnery control radar dish 397
Gunnery spotting top 394
Gunport 381
　Sailing warship 376-377
　Wooden sailing ship 379
Gun position 397
Gun section 392
Gunship 422
Gun turret 396-397
　Battleship 394
　Frigate 397
　World War II aircraft 408
Gut cecum 170
Gutenberg discontinuity 39
Gutter 486, 492, 602
Guyot 298
Guzmania lingulata 162-163
Gymnosperm 122-125
Gynoecium 140
Gypsum 271
Gyroscopic gunsight 409

H

Habit 270-271
Habitat 112
  Dryland plants 156-157
  Wetland plants 158-159
Hackle 565
Hackly fracture 270
Hadar 21
Hadley cell 300
Hadrosaur 96, 98-99
Hadrosaurus 96, 99
Hafnium 310
Hagfish 178
Hail 302
Hair 234-235
  Cobra lily 160
  Golden barrel cactus 156
  Inflorescence 140, 142
  Insulating 104, 107
  Mammal 104
  Marram grass 113
  Monocotyledon 126
  Pitcher plant 115
  Root 152
  Venus fly trap 160
  Water fern leaf 158
Hair bulb 255
Hair cell 242-243
Hairdryer 315
Hair follicle 234-235
Hair gel 306
Hair-like nasal leaf 277
Hair shaft 235
Hakatai shale 277
Hale-Bopp Comet 53
Halfback 526, 529
Halfback flank 528
Half-column 464, 468-469
Half-court line 545
Half-forward 529
Half-forward flank 528
Half fruit 151
Half hitch 388
Half-shaft
  Ford Model T 338
  Formula One race car 356
  Half turn 543
Halide 269
Halite crystal 277
Hall
  Asian building 491
  Hypostyle 458
  Medieval building 466-467
  Modern building 496, 499
  Neoclassical building 483
Halleflinta 275
Halley's Comet 52
"Hall-keeps" 466
Hallux
  Anchisaurus 89
  Archaeopteryx 85
  Herrerasaurus 86
  Human 232
  Tyrannosaurus 84
Halo 14
Halogen headlight bulb 352
Halogens 311
Halo ring 44
Halyard
  Double topsail schooner 385
  Junk 376
  Longboat 380
  Rigging 382
  Roman corbita 372, 373
  Viking karv 374
Hamada 282-283
Hamal 19, 20
Hamate bone 230
Hammer 242, 285
  Antler 109
  Athletics 542

Concert grand piano 515
Mosaic 450
Target pistol 549
Upright piano 514
Hammer actuator 600-601
Hammer-beam roof 470, 473
Hammerhead shark 179
Hammer throw 543
Hand
  Anchisaurus 89
  Human 210
  Iguanodon 97
  Pachycephalosaurus 100
  Primate 203
  Stegoceras 101
  Tyrannosaurus 84
Handball 534-535
Handbrake 557, 359-340, 350
Handbrake control shaft 338
Handbrake quadrant 359
Hand drill 600-601
Handheld gun 408
Handle
  Belaying pin 382
  Brace-and-bit 601
  Steam iron 594
Handlebars
  Bicycle 358-359
  BMW R/60 362
  Cannondale SH600 hybrid bicycle 561
  Cannondale ST 1000 touring bicycle 361
  Eddy Merckx racing bicycle 361
  Suzuki RGV500 368
Handle connector 593
Handling
  Motorcycle 360
  Touring bicycle 364
Hand protector 368
Hand rail
  "Ellerman Lines" steam locomotive 524
  Modern building 498
  Renaissance building 477
  Sailmaker's mallet 384
  Serving mallet 384, 388
  Ship's wheel 390
  TGV electric high-speed train 529
  Twentieth-century building 494
Hands 230-231
Handstand 543
Hand throttle 427
Handy Billy 382-383
"Handy man" 108
Hanger 498
Hang-gliders 426-427
Hanging valley 286-287
Hapteron 116-117
Hard disk drive 567
Hard endocarp 146-147, 149
Hard granite 283
Hard hat 554
Hard-headed beater 516, 518-519
Hard metals 310
Hardness 270-271
Hard palate 212, 245
Hard rock 60
  Faults and folds 60
  Glacier 286
  River features 290-291
  Weathering and erosion 282
Hard trim 352
Hardwood implements 452

Hardwood laminate limb 548
Hardwood panels 432
Hardwood sticks 517
Hardy 450
Hare 196-197
Harley-Davidson FLHS Electra Glide 362-363
Harmika 491
Harmon, A.L. 494
Harmonically-tuned exhaust system 356
Harmony
  Drums 518
  Percussion instruments 516
Harness
  Avro triplane IV 402
  Equestrian sports 555
Harness racing 554
Harness strap 407
Harp 504, 510-511
Harpoon point 109
Hash mark 541
Hastate leaf 128
Hatch
  Cargo 576
  For home deliveries 602
  Iron paddlesteamer 393
  Single scull 561
Hatch board 372
Hatch coaming 381
Hatching egg 192-193
Hatchling 98
Hathor Mons 37
Haunch 484
Haustoria 163
Haustration of colon 249
Haversian system 225
Hawker Tempest 408-409
Hawksmoor, N. 478, 481
Haworthia truncata 157
Hawse hole
  74-gun ship 381
  Sailing warship 376
  Wooden sailing ship 378
Hawse piece 381
Hawse pipe 393, 395
Hawser 386-387
Hawser fairlead 395
Hawthorne 55
Haystack boiler 334
Haze 37, 47
Head
  74-gun ship 380
  Allosaurus 85
  Beetle 168
  Brace-and-bit 601
  Bumblebee 168
  Butterfly 169
  Caterpillar 169
  Ceratopsian 100
  Deer hopper dry fly 565
  Double bass bow 511
  Double topsail schooner 385
  Dunkeld wet fly 563
  Femur 224-225
  Frog 182
  Hammer 542
  Human 211, 212-213
  Insect 168
  Lacrosse crosse 541
  Lamprey 178
  Pachycephalosaurus 100
  Phalanx 230
  Prosauropod 88
  Racing bicycle 360
  Racing saddle 554
  Rattlesnake 185
  Sail 375, 384
  Sauropodomorph 88
  Serving mallet 388
  Snail 177
  Sperm 259
  Stegoceras 101
  Stegosaurus 92

Tennis racket 544
Thyrophoran 92
Ulna 231
Violin bow 510
Headband 544
Head beam 380
Headboard 381
Head-butting contest 100
Head crest 96
Head cringle 384
Head data cable 574
Head data cable support 574
Head earing 375
Headers
  Brickwork 485
  Nineteenth-century building 492
Head horn 94
Head joint 508
Headlight
  Bordino Steam Carriage 335
  Bulbs 352
  Ford Model T 338-339
  Renault Clio 349, 353
  Volkswagen Beetle 341
Headland 294
Headlight
  BMW R/60 362
  "Eurostar" multi-voltage electric train 529
  Harley-Davidson FLHS Electra Glide 363
  Italian State Railroads Class 402 528
  MCW Metrobus 332
  Single-decker bus 333
  "Union Pacific" locomotive 326
  Vespa Grand Sport 160
  Mark 1 363
Head linesman 526
Headphone jack 578, 586, 587
Head rail 580-381
Headrest
  Airbus 380 273
  ARV light aircraft 425
  Formula One race car 356
  Hawker Tempest fighter 409
  Mazda RX-7 346
  Renault Clio 349, 352
  TGV electric high-speed train 529
  "Windcheetah" racing HPV bicycle 361
Head rope 387
Headset 561
Headstock
  Acoustic guitar 512-513
  Electric guitar 513
  Honda VF750 364
Head tube 359-361
Headward erosion 290
Headwaters 288
Hearing 237, 242
Heart
  Bird 189
  Bony fish 181
  Branchial 176
  Butterfly 169
  Chimpanzee 202
  Crayfish 173
  Dogfish 179
  Dolphin 205
  Domestic cat 195
  Elephant 200
  Euoplocephalus 94
  Frog 182
  Gallimimus 86
  Human 214-215, 250-251
  Lizard 185
  Mammal 104
  Octopus 176

Rabbit 196
Snail 177
Spider 170
Systemic 176
Tortoise 187
Heartbeat sequence 250-251
Heart bulge 260
Heartwood 125
Heat 314-315
  Chemical reactions 312
  Global warming 300-301
  Igneous and metamorphic rocks 274
Heat absorption 92
Heated filament 319
Heater element contacts 548
Heater unit 353
Heat exchanger
  Concorde 417
  Nuclear power station 314
  Volkswagen Beetle 341
Heat exchanger air intake 421
Heat exchanger exhaust duct 420
Heat exchanger hot-air exhaust 421
Heating element cover 597
Heating elements 594
Heating element terminal cover 597
Heat radiation 92
Heat shield
  Jet engine 419
  Motorcycle 363
  Space probes 614
Heat trapping 300
Heaver for wire serving 383
Heaving line 389
Heavy chemical elements 27
Hedera colchica 137
Hedera helix 131, 137
Heel
  Horse 198
  Human 210
  Rudder post 392
Heel molding 594
Heine 55
Heka 18
Helen Planilia 36
Helianthus annulus 142
Heliconia peruviana 143
Helicoprion bessonowi 67
Helicopter landing-pad 498
Helicopters 396, 410, 422-423
Helium
  Jupiter 44-45
  Massive stars 26
  Mercury's atmosphere 35
  Neptune's atmosphere 51
  Pluto's atmosphere 51
  Periodic table 311
  Saturn 46-47
  Small stars 24-25
  Sun 32
  Uranus' atmosphere 49
Helium-3 nucleus 22
Helium-4 nucleus 22
Helium line 23
Helium tank 614
Helix 242, 623
Helix Nebula 17
Helleborus niger 139
Hellenic plate 59
Helmet
  Baseball batter 536
  Bicycle 360

Cricket 539
Football 526-527
Hockey goal keeper 540
Hurling 541
Ice hockey 550-551
Lacrosse goalkeeper 541
Skiing 542
Helmsman 372-375
Hemal spine 180
Hematite 268
Hemicyclaspis 56
Hemisphere 623
Hemispherical dome 477, 486-487, 490-491
Hen coop 395
Hepaticae 118
Hepatic artery 248, 252-253
Hepatic portal vein 253
Heptathlon 542
Heracleum sp. 151
Heracleum sphondylium 129
Heraldic device 372
Herbaceous plants 126, 128-129
  Structure 112-113
  Woody 130-131
Herbaceous stems 154
Herbivores
  Carnivora 194
  Jurassic period 70
  Marginocephalian 100
  Ornithopodian 96
  Prosauropods 88-89
  Sauropodomorphian 88
  Triassic period 68
Hercules 19, 20, 40
Herds 88
Hermaphrodite duct 177
Hermit shale 276
Herodotus 40
Herrerasaurids 68, 86
Herring-bone pattern 488
Hertzsprung 41
Hertzsprung-Russell diagram 22-23
Hesperidium 148
Hestia Rupes 37
Heterocentrotus mammillatus 175
Heterodontosaurus 83
Heteropoda venatoria 171
Hexagon 622
Hexagonal system 270
HF radio aerial 408
HF radio aerials fairing 417
Hibiscus 126-127
Hide 105
Hide grip 584
Hieroglyphs 458-459
High altar 470
High-altitude cloud 45, 50
Highboard diving 558
High-density minerals 280
High-energy particle 301
High-energy radiation 22
High-explosive projectile 596
High-gain antenna 615
High-gain radio antenna 612, 613
High-jump 542
Highland coastline 295
High-level jet streams 300
High nose 557
High-performance microscopes 610-611
High-pressure areas 302-303
High-pressure bleed venturi connector 419
High-pressure compressor 418
High-pressure cylinder 342
High-pressure turbine 418

High-pressure zone 500
High-speed trains 578
High Spring tide 296-297
High temperature gas 506
High-tension beam 496
High-tension ignition lead 544
High tension wire 315
High tide 296-297
High-velocity air duct 420
High voltage cable 314, 555
High-voltage connector 555
High-voltage magnetron lead 544
Hi-hat cymbal 518
Hilbert 41
Hillman anti-kink weight 562
Hilum
  Dehiscent fruit seed 151
  Epigeal germination 153
  Hypogeal germination 152
  Succulent fruit seed 148-149
Himalayas
  Formation 60, 62-63
  Geological time 56-57
  Mapping the Earth 265
  Mountain building 62-63
  Physical map of the world 617
  Quaternary period 77
  Tertiary period 74
Himeji Castle 490
Hind foot
  Caiman 187
  Stegosaurus 92
Hindgut 173
Hind leg
  Amphibian 182
  Beetle 168
  Bumblebee 168
  Butterfly 169
  Caiman 187
  Elephant 200
  Frog 182
  Hare 196
  Iguanodon 97
  Lizard 185
  Rabbit 196
  Terrapin 187
Hind limb
  Anchisaurus 89
  Corythosaurus 98
  Edmontonia 95
  Frog 182
  Iguanodon 96
  Kangaroo 207
  Pachycephalosaurus 100
  Prosauropod 88
  Psittacosaurus 103
  Rabbit 197
  Rat 196
  Salamander 182
  Stegoceras 101
  Stegosaurus 92
  Theropods 84
  Thyreophoran 92
  Triceratops 102
  Tyrannosaurus 84
Hindlimb bone 105
Hind wing 168-169
  ARV light aircraft 425
  BAe-146 components 412-415
Hinge 571
Hinge bracket 414
Hinge cell 113, 160
Hinged bin/cyclone cover 595
Hingeless bivalve shell 79
Hingeline 60
Hip

Anchisaurus 89
Human 211
Kangaroo 207
Lion 195
Midway Gardens 495
Stegosaurus 92
Hip girdle 80
Hip joint 218, 224-225
  Brachiosaurus 90
  Diplodocus 90
  Gallimimus 86
  Parasaurolophus 98
  Plateosaurus 88
  Stegoceras 101
  Struthiomimus 87
Hip pad 527
Hippeastrum sp. 155
Hipped roof 476-477
Hippocampus kuda 180
Hippophae rhamnoides 136
Hippopotamus 198
Hippopotamus amphibius 77
Hippuris vulgaris 135
Hip-rafter 490
Hispano Mark V 20-mm cannon 409
Histoitated boss 469
Historiated keystone 469
Hitachi S-5500H scanning electron microscope 611
Hitched hauling end 383
Hitch-kick 543
Hitch pin
  Concert grand piano 515
  Upright piano 514
Hittorff, J.I. 479
Hobbles 554
Hock 195, 198
Hockey 540-541
Hock joint 554
Hog hair brush 432, 434
Hog's-back 283
Hog's back jump 554
Hogweed 129, 150-151
Hohenbuehelia petaloides 115
Hoisting cage 396
Holden 43
Holdfast 116-117
Holding 527
Holding timekeeper 556
Hold pillar 393
Hole and peg joint 373
Hollow disk wheel 361
Hollow pith cavity 120
Holmium 311
Holocene epoch
  Fossil record 279
  Geological timescale 57
Holostean fish 73
Homarus sp. 73
Home cinema 584-585
Home key 578
Homeosaurus pulchellus 71
Home page 577
Home plate 536
Home run 536
"Home" signal 330
Hominid 74-75, 108-109, 202
Homocephale 101
Homo erectus 108
Homo habilis 108
Homo sapiens 57, 76, 108-109
Honda CB750 362-363
Honda Insight 354
Honda VF750 364-365
Hone-stone 452
Honesty 150-151
Honeycomb coral 167
Honey guides 140-141, 145
Honey locust 157

Hong Kong and Shanghai Bank 496, 498
Honshu 265, 616
Hood
  1906 Renault 357
  Battleship 394
  Ford Model T 339
  Gun turret 396
  Jellyfish 167
  Pitcher plant 160
  Renault Clio 349
  Volkswagen Beetle 340-341
Hood bag 346
Hood catch 336, 349
Hood end 374
Hood frame 339
Hood iron 334
Hood-mold 479, 481, 486
Hood-release cable 349
Hood-release handle 341
Hoof 198, 554
Hoofbone 105, 198
Hooflike nail 36-37
Hook
  Angling 562
  Cricket 538
  Deer hopper dry fly 563
  Devon minnow 563
  Rigging 383
  Sail 384
Hooked beak 190
Hooked pericarps 150
Hooked riffler 454
Hooker 530
Hoop 580, 625
Hoover Factory 495
Hop 543
Hopper freight car 327
Horizontal bed rock 61
Horizontal cleavage 270
Horizontal muffler 529
Horizontal fissure 255
Horizontally opposed engine 362
Horizontal movement 60
Horizontal, stabilizer 425
Horizontal tailplane 572
Horn
  Ford Model T 339
  Glacier 286-287
  Mooring 387
  Musical instrument 505, 504
  "Union Pacific" locomotive 326
  Vespa Grand Sport 160
Horn balance 414, 415
Horn bulb 339
"Horned faces" 100
Horny beak 96
Horse 104-105, 198-199
Horse chestnut 150, 137
Horse-drawn vehicle 552
Horsehair bow 510-511
Horsehead Nebula 16
Horse riding 554-555
Horseshoe arch 484
Horsetail 120-121
Horsley Church 473
Horst 61
Horu Geyser 272
Hose base 595
Hose cuff electrical link 593
Hose electricity supply connector 592
Hose slider 592
Hose slider seating 592
Host plants 162-165
Hot-air de-icing duct 414
Hot mineral springs 272
Hot spot
  Black holes 29
  Earth's crust 58
  Ocean floor 298

Hot water jet 273
Hound 578
Hour line 577
Household appliances 315
House of the future 602-603
Housing
  Alpine skiing 552
  Electric motor 342
House spider 171
Howe 36
Howea forsteriana 126
Howler monkey 202
HP Pavilion DV4 laptop 566
Hti 490
Huang He 265
Huayangosaurus 93
Hub
  1906 Renault 356
  ARV light aircraft 424
  Benz Motorwagen 335
  Bicycle wheels 358-359
  Blackburn monoplane 400-401
  Bordino Steam Carriage 334
  Eddy Merckx racing bicycle 361
  Paddle wheel 390-391
  Pegasus Quasar ultralight 427
  Propellers 390
  Renault Clio 351
  Wright Flyer 399
Hub and brake drum 350
Hub bearing 351
Hubble Space Telescope 612-613
Hub bolt 358
Hub brake shoe 358
Hub cap
  1906 Renault 356
  Ford Model T 339
  Renault Clio 350
Hub carrier 351
Hub controller 604
Hub nut 350
Hub quick release lever 361
Hub seal 350
Hudson Bay 264, 617
Hull
  Carvel-built 376, 391
  Clinker-built 375
  Cross-section 378
  Double-ended 375
  Greek and Roman ships 372-373
  Iron and wood 392
Hull plank 393
Human body 210-211
Human classification 108
Human Powered Vehicles (HPV) 358, 360
Humans 57, 76, 108, 202, 315
Humber engine 343
Humboldt current 296
Humerus
  Archaeopteryx 85
  Arsinoitherium 104
  Bird 189, 191
  Brachiosaurus 91
  Crocodile 186
  Diplodocus 90
  Eryops 80
  Euoplocephalus 94
  Frog 183
  Gallimimus 86
  Hare 197
  Horse 199
  Human 218
  Iguanodon 96
  Kangaroo 206
  Kentrosaurus 93

Pareiasaur 81
Plateosaurus 88
Stegoceras 100
Struthiomimus 87
Toxodon 106
Triceratops 102
Tyrannosaurus 84
Humic acid 284
Hunter-killer submarine 396-397
Hunter's bend 388
Hunting 108, 548
Huntsman spider 171
Hurdle races 554
Hurdling 542
Hurling 540-541
Hurricane 302-303
Husk 150
Husqvarna Motocross TC610 568
Huygens mini-probe 614
Hyaenodon 74, 107
Hyaenodon 107
Hyaline cartilage 225
Hybrid bicycle 360-361
Hybrid car 354
Hybrid power 355
Hydrated copper sulfate 313
Hydraulic actuator attachment 413, 414
Hydraulic brake calliper 424
Hydraulic brake hose 369
Hydraulic brake pipe 414
Hydraulic fluid
  Disc brake 365
  Spring/muffler unit 365
Hydraulic grab 396
Hydraulic hand-pump 421
Hydraulic hose 369
Hydraulic unit 605
Hydrocarbon 313
Hydrochloric acid 312
Hydrochoerus hydrochaeris 197
Hydroelectric power-station 314
Hydrogen 508, 510
  Candle wax 312-313
  Covalent bonding 309
  Jupiter's atmosphere 45
  Massive stars 26
  Mercury's atmosphere 35
  Nebulae and star clusters 16-17
  Neptune's atmosphere 51
  Nuclear fusion in Sun 22
  Salt formation 312
  Saturn's atmosphere 47
  Small stars 24-25
  Sun 22
  Uranus' atmosphere 49
Hydrogen alpha line 23
Hydrogen atom 138, 596
Hydrogen beta line 23
Hydrogen fluoride 308
Hydrogen gamma line 25
Hydrogen gas 312
Hydrogen nucleus 22
Hydrogen requirement 158
Hydrogen sulfide 51
Hydroplane 396-397
Hydroxide 268
Hydrus 20
Hyena 194
Hymenoptera 168
Hyoglossus muscle 244
Hyoid bone 244-245, 255
Hypacrosaurus 99
Hypaethral temple 460-461
Hyperesion 373
Hyperlink 577

Hyphae
  Fungus 114-115
  Mycorrhizal association 133
Hypocotyl 152-153
Hypodermis
  Gynosperm 125
  Human 235
Hypogeal germination 152-153
Hypoglossal nerve 244
Hypogymnia physodes 114
Hypostyle hall 458-459
Hypothalamus 236
Hypsilophodon 72, 82
Hypural 180
Hystrix africaeaustralis 197

I

I bar 393
IBM-compatible PCs 566
Ice 66, 307
  Glacier 286-287
  Weathering and erosion 282
Ice age 56
Ice-age mammals 76
Ice block
  Ice-fall 287
  Lake formation 293
Ice cap 287
Ice crystal 302
Ice cube 307
Ice erosion 287
Ice-fall 287
Ice hockey 550-551
Ice margin lake 286
Ice-plant 128-129
Ice sheet 76
Ichthyosaur 70-71
Ichthyostega 56, 80
Icicle formation 293
Icterus galbula 193
Idle control valve 344
Idocrase 270
Igneous intrusion 274
Igneous rock 266-267, 274-275
Igniter 418
Igniter plug 419
Ignition amplifier 345
Ignition coils 354
Ignition control 362
Ignition lever 338
Ignition lock 362
Ignition switch 337
Ignition trigger housing 410
Iguana iguana 82
Iguanodon 73, 96-97
Ileocaecal fold 249
Ileum
  Bird 189
  Frog 182
  Human 226, 249
  Rabbit 196
Iliac crest 224-225
Iliac fossa 224
Iliac spine 224
Iliacus muscle 225
Ilio-femoral muscle 84, 97
Ilio-fibular muscle 84, 97
Ilio-ischial joint 82
Iliopsoas muscle 226
Ilio-pubic joint 82
Ilio-tibial muscle
  Albertosaurus 84
  Euoplocephalus 94
  Iguanodon 97
Ilium
  Archaeopteryx 85
  Bird 189
  Diplodocus 90
  Eryops 81

Euoplocephalus 94
Frog 185
Gallimimus 86
Human 218
Iguanodon 96-97
Kentrosaurus 93
Ornithischian 82
Parasaurolophus 98
Plateosaurus 88
Saurischian 82
Stegoceras 100-101
Stegosaurus 93
Struthiomimus 87
Toxodon 107
Tuojiangosaurus 93
Tyrannosaurus 84
Illuminated manuscript 432
Illumination 444-445
iMac 566
Image controls 611
Imaging system housing 610
Imaging the body 214
Imago 168
Immature pitcher 161
Immature spur 141
Impasto 436-437, 442
Impeller 347
Imperial-Metric conversions 620
Impermeable clay 292
Impermeable mudstone 292
Impermeable rock
 Cave 284-285
 Lake 292
 Mineral resources 280-281
 River's stages 289
Impermeable salt dome 281
Impermeable shale 292
Impost
 Ancient Roman building 465
 Cathedral dome 484
 Gothic building 475
 Islamic building 488
 Medieval building 466, 469
In-board 561
Inboard elevon 417, 421
Inboard elevon-jack fairing 416
Inboard end 587
Inboard engine 415
Inboard lift spoilers 413
Inboard trimtab 413
Inbound line 526
Inbox folder 576
Incandescent light 518-519
In-camera memory chip 580
Incident laser light 319
Incisive canal 245
Incisor teeth
 Bear 194
 Chimpanzee 202
 Elephant 201
 Human 245, 246
 Lion 194
 Rabbit 196
 Rodent 196
 Toxodon 106
Incline 468
Incompetent bed rock 61
Incomplete mesentery 167
Incurrent pore 166
Incus 242
Indehiscent fruit 150
Index finger 250-251
India
 Cretaceous period 72-73

Jurassic period 70
Himalaya formation 62-63
Late Carboniferous period 66
Middle Ordovician period 64
Mountain building 62-63
Quaternary period 76-77
Railroad track gauge 331
Tertiary period 74-75
Threophorans 92
Triassic period 68
Indian ocean 75, 75, 77, 265, 616
Indian stick insect 192
Indicator
 "Deltic" diesel-electric locomotive 327
 Bus 333
 Harley-Davidson FLHS Electra Glide 363
 Honda CB750 365
 MCW Metrobus 332
 Volkswagen Beetle 340
Indicator assembly 352
Indicator board 542
Indicator lamp 553
Indicator lens 341
Indirect method mosaic creation 450-451
Indium 311
Indo-Australian plate 59
Inducer 418
Induction stroke 343
Indus 20
Indusium 121
Industrial Revolution 492
Inert gas 311
Inferior articular process 225
Inferior concha 212, 241
Inferior extensor retinaculum 233
Inferior meatus 245
Inferior mesenteric vein 253
Inferior nasal concha 221, 241, 245
Inferior oblique muscle 241
Inferior orbital fissure 221
Inferior rectus muscle 241
Inferior vena cava 215, 252-253, 257
Infertile swamp 288
Infield 536-537
Infilled swamp 291
Inflated petiole 158
Inflation valve 405
Inflorescences 140
 Aechmea miniata 162
 Bromeliad 113
 Catkin 144
 Compound 142-143
 Couch grass 113
 Dodder 163
 Stem arrangements 143
Inflorescence stalk 140-143
 Aechmea miniata 162
 Brassavola nodosa 162
 Everlasting pea 129
 Indehiscent fruit 150
 Peach 131
 Peruvian lily 129
 Rowan 131
 Russian vine 131
 Succulent fruit 148
 Vegetative reproduction 154-155
 Wind-pollinated plant 144
Inflorescence types
 Capitulum 129, 142

Compound umbel 143
Dichasial cyme 143
Raceme 129
Single flower 143
Spadix 143
Spherical umbel 143
Spike 143, 155, 162
Infraorbital foramen 221
Infraorbital margin 213, 221
Infrared radiation 518-519
 Energy emission from Sun 22
 Infrared map of our galaxy 15
Infrared board 579
Infrared camera 578
Infrared receiver 580
Infrared sensor 609
Infraspinatus muscle 227
Inframtemporal fenestra
 Baryonyx 85
 Camarasaurus 91
 Diplodocus 90
 Heterodontosaurus 83
 Lambeosaurus 99
 Panoplosaurus 94
 Parasaurolophus 99
 Plateosaurus 88
 Protoceratops 102
 Triceratops 103
Infratemporal foramen 106-107
Ingres paper 441
Initial cave 285
Ink 430, 444
Ink-cartridge replacement button 574
Ink cartridges 574
Ink dabber 446
Inkjet nozzle 575
Inkjet printer 574-575
Ink outlet hole 574
Ink pad 445
Ink reservoir 444, 575
Ink roller 448, 449
Ink sac 176
Ink stick 444
Ink stone 444
Inlay 488-489
Inlet 295
Inlet cone 418
Inlet manifold
 Daimler engine 345
 Jaguar V12 engine 345
 Mid West single-rotor engine 411
Inlet manifold tract 345
Inlet-over-exhaust (IOE) engine 362
Inlet port 345, 367
Inlet rotor 347
Inlet tract 411
Inlet valve 345, 345, 362
Inner bin fin 592
Inner bud scales 134
Inner cage assembly 599
Inner clutch drum 366
Inner core 58-59, 41
Inner counter 445
Inner cyclone cone 592
Inner dome 484
Inner floret 129, 142
Inner jib downhaul 585
Inner jib halyard 585
Inner jib stay 582
Inner jib tack 582
Inner layer of cortex
 Dicotyledon 127
 Epiphytic orchid 162
 Monocotyledon 127
 Wetland plants 158-159
Inner mantle 44-47
Inner martingale stay 583
Inner membrane 139
Inner planetary orbits 31
Inner posts 528

Inner tepal 126, 140, 143
Inner tube 359, 424, 507
Inner vane 191
Innings 536, 538
Inorganic substances 280
Inscription 488
Insectivorous plants 113, 160-161
Insects 168-169, 279
 Cretaceous 72-73
 Plant food 160-161
 Pollinators 144-145
Inselberg 283
Insoluble solids 312
Inspection cover
 Avro biplane 403
 Lockheed Electra airliner 407
Inspection door 407
Inspection panel 417
Inspiration 255
Instep 211
Instrument bay 615
Instructor's cockpit 403
Instrument console 420
Instrument deployment device 615
Instrument landing system aerial 420-421
Instrument module 613
Instrument panel
 ARV light aircraft 425
 Bell-47 helicopter 422
 Renault Clio 353
 Schweizer helicopter 426
Insulating column 316
Insulating hair 104, 107
Insulation 500
Insulator
 Electric circuit 316
 Generating magnetism 317
 Hydroelectric power station 314
Intaglio printing 446-447, 448
Intake manifold 351, 354
Intake pipe 335
Intake port 346
Integral ink reservoir 444
Integrated transparency unit (TPU) 570, 571
Integrated transport system 332
Integument
 Ovule 147
 Scots pine 122
Intelligent electronic door-lock 602
Intentional foul 533
Interalveolar septum 254
Intercellular leaf space 139
Interception 526
Inter-City travel 332
Intercolumniation 461, 485
Intercompressor bleed valve 419
Intercompressor diffuser pipe 419
Intercostal muscle 91, 255
Interdental papilla 247
Interdental septum 247
Interglacial period 76
Integer house 602, 603
Interior light 355
Interlobular artery 256
Interlobular vein 256
Interlocking spur 289
Intermediate housing 346
Intermediate lamella 225
Intermediate ring 563
Internal capsule 237
Internal carotid artery 243, 252

Internal combustion engine
 First cars 334
 Motorcycle engine 366
 Pioneers of flight 398
Internal crust 28
Internal elastic lamina 252
Internal fuse overload protection 585
Internal iliac artery 215, 253
Internal iliac vein 253
Internal jugular vein 253
Internal skeleton 174
Internal spermatic fascia 259
Internal urethral orifice 257
Internal urethral sphincter muscle 257
International referees signals 535
International rules 532
International squash 544-545
International track gauge 331
Internet 576-577
Internet service provider (ISP) 576
Internode
 Canadian pond weed 158-159
 Horsetail 120
 Ice-plant 129
 Live-forever 129
 London plane 134
 Rhizome 155
 Rock stonecrop 128
 Rose stem 130
 Stem 134
 Stolon 154
Interoperatior bone 181
Interosseous ligament 232
Interphalangeal joint
 Baryonyx 85
 Human 251, 233
Interplane strut 599, 404-405
Interradicular septum 247
Interrupter gear 404
Interstellar cloud remains 613
Intertragic notch 242
Intertrochanteric line 225
Intertropical convergence zone 300
Interventricular septum 251
Intervertebral disc 212, 218, 223, 245, 261
Intestinal muscle 226
Intestine
 Bony fish 181
 Butterfly 169
 Chimpanzee 202
 Cow 198
 Crayfish 173
 Dogfish 179
 Dolphin 205
 Elephant 200
 Frog 182
 Gallimimus 86
 Human 214
 Large 195, 202
 Lizard 185
 Sea urchin 175
 Small 182, 185, 187, 195, 198, 200, 202
 Spider 170
 Tortoise 187
Intrados 469, 484
Introitus 258
Intrusive rocks 26, 275
Invasion stripes 409
Invertebrates
 Earth's evolution 56
 Fossil record 279
 Insects 168-169

Marine 65
Inverted ovolo 486
Inverter 555
Inverter board 570
Inverter cooling fan 555
Inverter cooling fan connector 555
Inverter housing 555
Inward dive 558, 559
Io 44
Iodine 311
Ion 308
Ionic bonding 308
Ionic capital 460
 Baroque church 481
 French temple 485
 Renaissance building 476
Ionic column
 Baroque church 481
 French temple 485
 Neoclassical building 483
Ionic half-column 464
Ionic order 460
Iota Centauri 21
Iota Pegasi 19
Iota Sagittarii 21
Ipomoea batatas 154
Iran 331
Ireland 331
Iridium 311
Iridocorneal angle 241
Iris
 Human 213, 226, 241
 Linear leaf 137
 Octopus 177
Iris lazica 157
Iron 311
 Earth's composition 39
 Earth's crust 58
 Golf club 547
 Magnetic domains 317
 Meteorite 52
 Nineteenth-century buildings 492
 Structure of Mercury 35
 Structure of Venus 37
Iron armature support 455
Ironclad 392-393
Iron club 546-547
Iron fillings 317
Iron hull 392-393
Iron oxide
 Earth pigments 434
 Flesh-colored pigments 435
 Sanguine crayon 430
 Sedimentary rocks 267, 277
Iron oxide dust 42
Iron paddlesteamer 392-393
Iron pyrite 79, 270
Iron railing 493
Iron roof 479
Iron ship 392-393
Iron, steam 594
Iron tracery 493
Iron tire 354
Ironwork 478, 482
Irregular galaxy 10-12, 15
Irreversible reactions 312
Ischial tuberosity 224
Ischium
 Archaeopteryx 85
 Bird 189
 Crayfish 173
 Diplodocus 90
 Eryops 81
 Euoplocephalus 94
 Frog 183
 Human 218, 224
 Iguanodon 96
 Ornithischian 82
 Parasaurolophus 98
 Plateosaurus 88

Saurischian 82
Stegoceras 100-101
Stegosaurus 95
Struthiomimus 87
Triceratops 102
Tyrannosaurus 84
Ishtar Terra 36-37
Islamic buildings 488-489
Islamic calendar 618
Islamic mosaic 489
Islands 291, 294
Isocline 61
Isolated single boulders 286
Isolated steep-sided hill 283
Isolator valve 525, 527
Isosceles triangle 622
Isoseismal lines 63
Isotopes 310
ISP 576
Israel 293
Isthmus
 Reproductive system
 258-259
 Water hyacinth 158
Italian State Railroads
 Class 402 528
Italic Roman lettering 445
Item link 577
Itonaco 434
Ivy 130-131, 137

J

Jack 514
Jacket-wall 466
Jack-rafter 473
Jack staff
 Battleship 394
 Frigate 397
 Square-rigged ship 375
 Wooden sailing ship 379
Jacob's ladder 378
Jagged fracture 270
Jaguar straight six engine
 344
Jaguar V12 engine 345
Jali 488-489
Jamb
 Ancient Roman temple
 463
 Baroque church 479
 Medieval church 468
 Neoclassical building
 478, 482-483
 Nineteenth-century
 building 492
Jami Masjid 488
Javelin 542-543
Jaw
 Allosaurus 85
 Australopithecus
 107-108
 Ceratopsian 100
 Dolphin 204
 Horse 105
 Human 220, 247
 Ornithopod 96
 Shark 178
 Snake 184
 Theropods 84
Jawless fish 78, 178-179,
 180
JBL Spyro speakers 586
Jeer 377
Jejunum 249
Jelly 192
Jellyfish 78, 166-167
 Earth's evolution 56
 Fossil record 279
Jet engine 412, 418-419
Jetliners 412-415
Jet pipe 418-419, 423

Jet pipe connection
 419
Jetstream 300, 418
Jewel anemone 166
Jewel Box 11
Jewish calendar 618
Jib boom 379, 382
Jib fairhead 561
Jib halyard 580
Jibsail 378, 379, 385
Jib sheet 585
Jib stay 582
Jib tack 382, 383
Jockey 554-555
Jockey wheel 358
Jodhpurs 554
Joint
 Cave 284-285
 Coastline 295
 Faults and folds 61
 Jointed plug 19
 Weathering and erosion
 282
Jointed leg 79, 168
Jointed pincer 79
Jointed solidified lava 292
Jointed stem 131
Joints 224-225, 608
Joist 464, 486
Jones, H. 493
Jordan 293
Jordan River 293
Journal 347
Joystick 361, 520
Judo 556-557
Jugal 94
Jugal bar 201
Jugal bone 96, 102-103
Jugal plate 94
Juglans nigra 137
Jugular vein 215
Juice sac 148
"Jumbo jet" 412
Jumps 552, 554
Jump seat 357
Jump shot 532, 535
Junction
 Electrical circuit 316
 Giornata 434-435
 Photovoltaic cell 605
Junction board 555
Juncus sp. 15
Junior ratings' mess 397
Junk 376
Junk ring 343
Jupiter 30-31, 44-45,
 614
Jupp-Reese winglet 572
Jurassic period 70-71
 Fossil record 279
 Geological time 57
Jury mast knot 389
Justicia aurea 144
Juvenile volcano 275
JVC Everio camcorder 582

K

Kabe 575
Kaibab limestone 276
Kaibab Plateau 277
Kaiparowits formation
 276
Kaiparowits Plateau 277
Kalahari Desert 265, 616
Kalanchoe
 daigremontiana 154
Kalasa finial 489
Kalos 372
Kame delta 286
Kame terrace 286
Kangaroo 206-207
Kappa Pegasi 19
Kara Kum 265
Karv 374
Kasugado Shrine of Enjoji
 490
Kasuga-style roof 490
Katastroma 373

Kaus Australis 19, 20
 Sagittarius 21
Kaus Borealis 21
Kaus Meridionalis 21
Kawana House 496
Kawasaki industrial robot
 609
Kayak 560
Kayenta formation 276
Kazakstania 65
Kedrostis africana 113
Keel
 Battleship 395
 Bird 189
 Frigate 397
 Ironclad 393
 Iron paddlesteamer
 392
 Longboat 380
 Sailing warship 377
 Viking ship 374-375
 Wooden sailing ship
 378
Keel boat 560
Keeled leeene 486
Keeler 41
Keelson (Kelson) 560
 19th century paddle
 steamer 391
 Ironclad 393
Keep 466
Keeper ring 562
Kendo 556
Kentrosaurus 92-93
Kepler 40
Keraia 372
Keratin 234
Kestrel 189
Ketch 384, 385
Kettle 286
Kettle drum 519
Kettle lake 293
 Post-glacial valley
 286
Kevlar 384, 388
Key
 Concert grand piano
 515
 Home keyboard 520
 Motorcycle clutch 366
 Musical notation 502
 Steel lock 360
 Synthesizer 520
 Upright piano 514
 Woodwind instruments
 508-509
Keyboard 521, 566, 611
Keyboard instruments
 514-515, 520
Key guard 509
Keypad 589
Key rod 509
Key signature 502
Keystone 484
 Ancient Roman
 building 463, 465
 Baroque church 479,
 481
 French temple 485
 Medieval church 469
 Neoclassical building
 478, 482
 Renaissance building
 476-477
Keyway 390
Kick-stand 363
Kick-starter 363, 366
Kidney
 Bird 189
 Bony fish 181
 Brachiosaurus 90
 Dogfish 179
 Dolphin 205
 Domestic cat 195
 Elephant 200
 Frog 182
 Gallimimus 86
 Human 215, 256-257
 Lizard 185

Octopus 176
Rabbit 196
Snail 177
Tortoise 187
Kidney ore hematite 268
Kidney-shaped palette 436
Killer whale 205
Killick 386
Kiln 452
Kimberlite 268, 275
Kinetic energy 314-315
Kinetic sculpture 452
King pin 338
King-post 473, 479
 Early monoplane
 400-401
 Pegasus Quasar
 ultralight 427
 Pegasus XL SE
 ultralight 426
King-post strut 401
King spoke handle 390
Ring strut 464
King vulture 190
Kirby BSA racing sidecar
 369
Kittiwake 190
Kiwis 188
Knee
 Anchisaurus 89
 Corythosaurus 98
 Faering 375
 Gorilla 203
 Horse 199
 Human 211
 Iguanodon 96
 Kangaroo 207
 Lion 195
 Pachycephalosaurus
 100
 Psittacosaurus 103
 Rabbit 197
 Stegoceras 101
 Stegosaurus 92
 Tyrannosaurus 84
 Wooden ships 381
Knee joint
 Brachiosaurus 90
 Diplodocus 90
 Euoplocephalus 94
 Human 219
 Parasaurolophus 98
 Plateosaurus 88
 Stegoceras 101
 Struthiomimus 87
 Toxodon 107
 Triceratops 102
 Tyrannosaurus 84
Knee of the head 378
Knee pad 527, 534
Knee roll 539, 554
Knife
 Palette 436
 Relief printing 446, 449
Knighthead 380
Knots 388-389
Knuckle 210
Koala 207
Kochab 18
Kope 372-373
Korolev 41
Krypton 311
Kuan Han-ch'ing 35
Kubernetes 372
Kuiper belt 30, 50
Kunzite 271
Kuroshio current 297

L

Label button 576
Labellum 126, 145
Label mold 481
Labia 258
Labial palp 168
Labrum 168
Laburnum x watereri 137
Laccolith 273-275

Lacerta 19, 20
Lacertilia 184
Lacrimal apparatus 241
Lacrimal bone
 Bony fish 181
 Human 221
 Protoceratops 102
Lacrimal canaliculus 241
Lacrimal gland 241
Lacrimal punctum 241
Lacrimal sac 241
Lacrosse 540-541
Lacuna
 Bones and joints 225
 Clubmoss 120
 Mare's tail 133
 Wetland plants 158-159
Lacustrine terrace 286
Lada Terra 36, 37
Ladder
 74-gun ship 381
 Battleship 394
 Frigate 396
 Iron paddlesteamer
 392, 393
 Roman corbita 372-373
 Train equipment 330
 Wooden sailing ship
 378
Ladder way 395-396
Lady Chapel, Salisbury
 Cathedral 470
Lagomorpha 196
Lagoon
 Atoll development 299
 Coastline 294-295
 River features 290-291
Lagoon Nebula 21
Lagopus lagopus 193
Lagostomus maximus 197
Lake Baikal 265
Lake Erie 264
Lake Huron 264
Lake Michigan 264
Lake Nyasa 265
Lake Ontario 264
Lakes 292-293
 Glacier 286-287
 Groundwater system 293
 Igneous rock structures
 275
 River features 290
 River's stages 289
 Rock cycle 266-267
 Weathering and erosion
 285
Lake Superior 264
Lake Tanganyika 265, 616
Lake Victoria 265, 616
Lakshmi Planum 37
Lambda Andromedae 19
Lambda Pegasi 19
Lambdoid suture 220
Lambeosaurus 96, 98-99
Lamb, T. 494
Lamella 159
Lamina 136
 Butterwort 161
 Couch grass 113
 Dicotyledon leaf 127
 Human 222-223
 Leaf 138
 Monocotyledon leaf 127
 Seaweed 116-117
 Succulent 113
 Vegetative reproduction
 154
 Water hyacinth leaf 158
 Water lily leaf 159
Laminaria digitata
 116-117
Laminates 548
Lamium sp. 135
Lamp 570, 571
Lamp bracket 336, 342
Lamp cluster 341
Lampland 43
Lamprey 178
Lampropeltis ruthveni 184

*Lampropeltis triangulum
 annulata* 184
Lamp shield 550
Lanceolate leaf 120, 131,
 136
Lancet 471
Lancet arch 473, 484
Lancet window 470-472
Land 59
 Amphibians 80
 Animals 64
 Atmosphere 301
 Plants 56, 64
 Rivers 288
 Vertebrates 82
Landau body 334
Landau iron 334
Landing 477
Landing and taxiing light
 414
Landing gear 406-407,
 424-425, 573
Landing-gear muffler 423
Landing gear door
 BAe-146 components 414
 Concorde 416
 Hawker Tempest
 components 409
 Lockheed Electra
 airliner 406-407
Landing gear drag strut
 401
Landing gear fork 407
Landing gear front strut
 400, 404
Landing gear hydraulics
 417
Landing gear leg 424
Landing gear rear cross-
 member 400
Landing gear rear strut
 400-401
Landing gear strut 405
Landing light
 BAe-146 jetliner
 components 414-415
 Bell-47 helicopter 422
 Lockheed Electra
 airliner 407
 Schweizer helicopter
 423
Landing skid
 Avro triplane 403
 Blackburn monoplane
 400-401
 Helicopter 422-423
 Wright Flyer 399
Land movement 59
Land plants 56, 78
Landscape features
 290-291, 294
Land surface removal 282
Land turtle 186
Lane
 Athletic track 542
 Swimming pool 558
Lane time-keeper 558
Langrenus 40
Language 108
Langur 202
Lantern 486
 Baroque church
 480-481
 French temple 485
 Neoclassical building
 478-479
 Twentieth-century
 building 494
 Wooden sailing ship
 379
Lanthanides 310
Lanthanum 310
Lanyard
 Lifejacket 561
 Oar 373
 Rigging 382-383
 Roman corbita 373
Lap 542
Lapilli 272

Lap strap
  ARV light aircraft 425
  Curtiss biplane 398
  Lockheed Electra
    passenger seat 407
  Pegasus Quasar
    ultralight 427
Laptop computer 566, 567
Laptops 567
Large intestine
  Brachiosaurus 90
  Chimpanzee 202
  Domestic cat 195
  Euoplocephalus 94
Large Magellanic Cloud
  Hydrus and Mensa 20
  Our galaxy and nearby
    galaxies 15
  Stars of southern skies
    20-21
Large mammals 57
Larkspur 141, 151
Larus marinus 193
Larus ridibundus 193
Larva 168
Laryngeal prominence
  212, 244-245
Larynx
  Amphibian 182
  Human 214-215, 244
Laser ranger 420
Lateen sail 376, 378, 384
Lateral angle 213
Lateral bracing strut
  402-403, 416
Lateral branch
  Adventitious roots
    158-159
  Horsetail 120
  Vegetative reproduction
    154
Lateral bud 134
  Begonia 129
  Dicotyledon 127
  Horse chestnut 130
  Leaf scars 154
  London plane tree 134
  Rhizome 155
  Rowan twig 131
  Stem bulbil 155
  Stolon 154
Lateral canal
  Human 247
  Starfish 174
Lateral caudal
  musculature 87
Lateral column 223
Lateral control wheel 401
Lateral control wire 404
Lateral dorsal aorta 179
Lateral epicondyle 225
Lateral fault 61
Lateral fault lake 293
Lateral lacuna 237
Lateral line 181
Lateral malleolus 233
Lateral mass 222
Lateral moraine 286-287
Lateral plantar artery 253
Lateral plate 78
Lateral rectus muscle
  240-241
Lateral root 133
  Broomrape host 163
  Carrot 128
  Dicotyledon 127
  Germination 152-153
  Horse chestnut 130
  Seedling 152-153
  Strawberry 128
  Sweet pea 128
Lateral root scar 128
Lateral sepal 141
Lateral shield 187
Lateral shoot 156
Lateral strike-slip fault 61
Lateral sulcus 237
Lateral tepal 126

Lateral vein 156, 159
Lateral ventricle 237
Lath 464
Lathyrus latifolius 129
Lathyrus odoratus 128
Latissimus dorsi muscle
  227
Latrodectus mactans 171
Lattice-beam 496-497
Latticed screen 488-489
Latticed shade 495
Lattice-truss 499
Lattice window 492
Lattice-work 495
Laurasia
  Cretaceous period 72
  Jurassic period 70-71
  Late Carboniferous
    period 66-67
Laurentia 65
Laurentian Library
  474-475
Lava 62
  Igneous and
    metamorphic rocks
    274-275
  Mountain building
    62
  Rock cycle 266
  Volcano 272-273
Lava eruptions 272
Lava flow 275
  Contact metamorphism
    274-275
  Mars 42
  Rock cycle 266
Lava fragments 272
Lavatera arborea 131
Lava types 275
Lavinia Planitia 36-37
Lawrencium 311
Layering
  Fresco 434-435
  Pastel colors 440
Lay-up shot 552
LCD see Liquid crystal
  display (LCD)
LCD monitor 585
Leach 574, 584
Lead
  Mineralization zones
    281
  Minerals 268
  Periodic table 311
Lead covering 487
Leading block 394
Leading edge
  Avro biplane 405
  Avro triplane 405
  BAe-146 components
    415, 414-415
  BE 2B tail 405
  BE 2B wings 404
  Blackburn monoplane
    401
  Concorde, the 416-417
  Hawker Tempest
    components 409
  Lockheed Electra
    airliner 406
  Northrop B-2 bomber
    421
  Pegasus Quasar
    ultralight 427
  Wright Flyer 399
Leading-edge aerial 421
Leading-edge fairing 425
Lead-in wire 519
Lead iodide 313
Lead nitrate 313
Lead shot 517
Lead wire 600
Leaf axis 137
Leaf bases 128, 136-137
  Aechmea miniata 162
  Couch grass 113
  Dicotyledon 127
  Florists'
    chrysanthemum 129

Guzmania lingulata
  162-163
Hogweed 129
Monocotyledon 126-127
Sago palm 123
Seedling leaf 152
Water hyacinth 158
Leaf blade
  Butterwort 161
  Dicotyledon 127
  Leaf surface 156, 158
  Monocotyledon 127
  Vegetative reproduction
    154
  Venus fly trap 160
  Wetland plants 158-159
Leaf insert 192
Leafless branch 120
Leaflets 136-137
  Everlasting pea 129
  Fern 120-121
  Horse chestnut leaf 130
  Mahonia 130-131
  Monocotyledon 126
  Pinna 121, 136-137
  Rose 131
  Rowan 130
  Sago palm 123
  Tree fern 112-113
Leaflet stalk 137
Leaf-like structures
  141-143
  Dehiscent fruit 151
  Dicotyledon flower 127
  Guzmania lingulata
    163
  Ice plant 129
  Live-forever 129
  Peruvian lily 129
  Slender thistle 129
  Wind pollination 144
Leaf margin 129
  Aechmea miniata 162
  Slender thistle 129
  Vegetative reproduction
    154
Leaf notch 154
Leaf primordium 134
  Begonia 129
  Elder 130
  Horse chestnut 130
  Ice-plant 128-129
  London plane 134
  Rock stonecrop 128
Leaf shape 136-137
Leaf sheath 129
Leaf spring 358
Leaf spring suspension
  327
Leaf stalk 128, 136-137
  Chusan palm 130
  Clematis 131
  Cobra lily 160
  Common horse
    chestnut 130
  Dicotyledon 127
  Everlasting pea 129
  Florists'
    chrysanthemum 129
  Kedrostis africana 113
  Maidenhair tree 123
  Monocotyledon 126-127
  Mulberry 130
  Oxalis sp. 157
  Passion flower 130
  Peach 131
  Seedling 153
  Strawberry 128
  String of hearts 157
  Tree fern 112
  Tree mallow 131
  Vegetative reproduction
    154-155
  Venus fly trap 160
  Water lily 159
  Wind pollination 144
Leaf succulents
  Haworthia truncata 157

Lithops bromfieldii 157
Lithops sp. 156
Leaf trace 127
Leaf venation 129
Leafy liverwort 118
Leafy thallus 114
Lean-to roof 468-470, 472
Leather ball making 525
Leather grommet 575
Leather hood 334
Leather ink dabber 446
Leather pad 557
Leather upholstery 337
Leather valance 337
Leathery exocarps 148
Leaves 136-137
  Abaxial surface 123, 130
  Adaxial surface 123,
    130
  Aechmea miniata 162
  Apex 136-137
  Apical meristem 134
  Barberry 130-131
  Bishop pine 124
  Brassavola nodosa 162
  Bromeliad 112-113
  Broomrape 163
  Butterwort 161
  Canadian pond weed
    158-159
  Carnivorous plants
    160-161
  Cheekerbloom 156
  Chusan palm 130
  Classification 136-137
  Clematis 150-151
  Clubmoss 120
  Cobra lily 160
  Couch grass 113
  Dicotyledon 126-127
  Dryland plants 156-157
  Durmast oak 131
  Epiphyte 162-163
  Fern 120-121
  Florists'
    chrysanthemum 129
  Germination 152-153
  Guzmania lingulata
    162-163
  Haworthia truncata 157
  Hinge cell 113
  Hogweed 129
  Horsetail 120
  Intercellular space 159
  Ivy 131
  Kedrostis africana 113
  Lamina 156
  Lithops bromfieldii 157
  Liverwort 118
  London plane tree 134
  Maidenhair tree 123
  Margin 136
  Marram grass 113
  Midrib 136
  Monkey cup 161
  Monocotyledon 126-127
  Moss 112, 119
  Mulberry 130
  Orange lily 154
  Oxalis sp. 157
  Parasite host 163
  Passion flower 130
  Peach 131
  Photosynthesis 134,
    158-159
  Pine 122, 124-125
  Pitcher development
    161
  Pitcher plant 113,
    160-161
  Primordia 134
  Rock stonecrop 128
  Rose 150-151
  Rosettes 162-163
  Rowan 130
  Sago palm 123
  Scots pine 122
  Seedling 152-153
  Slender thistle 129

Smooth cypress 123
Stomata 159
Strawberry 128
Tendrils 161
Toadflax 129
Tree fern 112-113
Tree mallow 131
Vegetative reproduction
  154-155
Veins 136, 158-159
Venus fly trap 160
Water fern 158
Water hyacinth 158
Water lily 159
Welwitschia 122-123
Xerophyte 156-157
Yew 123
Le Corbusier 494
LEDs 584, 609
Leda Planitia 36, 37
Ledge 381
Leech 574, 584
Leechline 375
Left edge guide 575
Leg
  Amphibian 182
  Caiman 186-187
  Crab 172
  Crayfish 172-173
  Crocodilian 186
  Elephant 200
  Frog 182
  Gorilla 203
  Human 210
  Kangaroo 207
  Lizard 184-185
  Relief-printing press
    449
  Salamander 182
  Scorpion 170
  Shrimp 172
  Spider 170-171
  Tadpole 183
  Terrapin 187
  Tripod congas stand
    519
"Leg before wicket" 538
Leg bud 260
Leg pad 559, 551
Leg protector 551
Leg slip 538
Legumes 150
Leibnitz 41
Lemercier, J. 486
Lemming 196
Lemon 148
Lemur 202-203
Lemur catta 203
Lena River 265
Lenoir, Etienne
  Early engines 342
  First cars 334
Lens
  Flatbed scanner 570
  Human body 241
  Microscope 610, 611
Lens cover 581
Lens cover assembly 582
Lenticels 130-131, 154
Lentiform nucleus 237
Leo 18, 21
Leo Minor 18, 21
Leonaspis 279
Leonid meteor shower 52
Leontopithecus rosalia 203
Lepidodendron 66-67
Lepidoptera 168
Lepidotes maximus 73
Leptoceratops 103
Lepus 21
Lesbian leaf pattern 460
Lesene
  Ancient Roman
    building 462, 465
  Baroque church
    480-481
  Dome 486
  French temple 485
  Gothic church 473

Renaissance building
  476-477
Lesser trochanter of
  femur 225
Lesser wing covert
  188
Lesser wing of sphenoid
  bone 221
Letterine 40
Lettering 444-445
Levator anguli oris
  muscle 229
Levator labii superioris
  muscle 229
Levator palpebrae
  superioris muscle 241
Levee 289-291
Level-wind system
  562
Lever 520-321
Le Verrier ring 50-51
Liang K'ai 35
Libellulium longialatum
  73
Liberty ship 392
Libra 18, 21
Library 483, 496
Licence holder 552
Lichens 114-115
Lid
  Moss 119
  Pitchers 161
  Ships for war and trade
    377
Lid assembly 571
Lierne 469
Lifeboat 394
Lifeboat davit 395
Life buoy 395
Life-cycle
  Brown seaweed 117
  Fern 121
  Insect 168
  Moss 119
  Mushroom 115
  Plants 112
  Scots pine 122
Lifeguard 532
Lifejacket 561
Life of massive star 26-27
Life of small star 24-25
Life-raft 416
Liferaft cylinder 397
Lift
  Athletics 543
  Center Georges
    Pompidou 497
  Double topsail
    schooner 385
  Roman corbita 372
  Sailing warship
    376-377
  Wooden sailing ship
    378
Lift bracing wire
  Biplanes and triplanes
    403
  Early monoplane
    400-401
  Pegasus Quasar
    ultralight 427
  World War I aircraft
    404-405
Lifting handle 336
Lifting lug 330
Lift spoiler 413, 414
Lift wire 399
Ligament
  Bifurcate 252
  Cricothyroid 244
  Deltoid 252
  Falciform 248
  Foot 232
  Hip joint 224
  Iliofemoral 224
  Interosseous 252
  Ovarian 258
  Periodontal 247

Plantar calcaneonavicular 252
Posterior cuneonavicular 252
Posterior tarsometatarsal 252
Pubofemoral 224
Talonavicular 252
Zonular 241
Ligature 508, 509
Light 314-315, 318-319
Chemical reactions 512
Renaissance building 474
Seed germination 152
Translucent "window" 157
Twentieth-century building 495
Ultraviolet 145
Light aircraft 410, 424-425
Light Emitting Diode 585
Lighterman's hitch 389
Light hour 14
Lighting hole 393
Light level sensor 581
Lightning 45, 516
Lights
  Bicycle 360
  MCW Metrobus 332
Light screen 594
Light shield 612, 615
Light switch 339
Lightweight plastic intake manifold 354
Light-well 487
Light year 14
Lignite 280
Lignum vitae bearing 387
Ligulate ray floret 129
Lilienthal, Otto 398
Lilium bulbiferum 154
Lilium sp. 155, 158, 140-141, 155
Lily
  Bulbil 154-155
  Flower 140-141
  Leaf surface 158
Limb
  Mammal 104
  Paddlesteamer 390
  Reptile 80
  Structure of a fold 60
Limber hole 393
Lime 143
Lime-resistant pigment 434
Limestone
  Cave 284
  Contact metamorphism 274
  Faults and folds 60
  Fossilized blue-green alga 78
  Lower Carboniferous 60
Limestone block 470
Limestone cladding 494
Limestone false door 459
Limestone spring 292
Limestone strata 284
Lime water 313
Linaria sp. 129
Line 562
Linea alba 226
Linear dune 283
Linear leaf 129, 137
Linebacker 526
Line guide 563
Line judge 526
Line of sight 41
Linesman
  Badminton 545
  Gaelic football 529
  Ice hockey 550

Soccer 524
Tennis 544
Volleyball 534
Lingual nerve 244
Lingual tonsil 245
Link 386
Linocut 446
Linoleum block 446, 449
Linseed oil 436
Lintel
  Building 459, 494
  Coastline 295
  Lintel course 483
Lion 194-195
Lion crest 395
Lionfish 180
Lip
  Flower 126, 145
  Human 212-215
  Lamprey 178
  Pollination 145
Lip of trunk 200-201
Lip plate 508, 508
Lip tension 506
Liquidambar styraciflua 76
Liquid crystal display (LCD)
  Apple iPad 568
  HP Pavilion DV4 laptop 567
  JVC Everio camcorder 582-583
  Nikon Coolpix S1000PJ 580
  Televisions 584
Liquid helium 45
Liquid hydrogen 44-47
Liquid ink 444
Liquids 506-507
Litchi chinensis 148
Lithification 266
Lithium 308, 310
Lithium fluoride molecule 308
Lithium-ion battery 589
Lithium-ion rechargeable battery 579
Lithium-polymer battery 569
Lithographic printing 446
Lithographic printing equipment 448
Lithops bromfieldii 157
Lithops sp. 156
Lithosphere 58-59
Little finger 230-231
Little grebe 190
Little toe 232-233
Live-forever 128-129
Liver
  Bird 189
  Bony fish 181
  Chimpanzee 202
  Dogfish 179
  Dolphin 205
  Domestic cat 195
  Euoplocephalus 94
  Frog 182
  Gallimimus 86
  Human 214, 248, 252
  Lizard 185
  Rabbit 196
  Tortoise 187
Liverworts 112, 118-119
Livestock freight car 327
Living organisms 306
Lizard 184-185, 582
"Lizard-feet forms" 88
Lizard-hipped dinosaurs 82, 88-89
Llama 198
Load 320-321
Loading arm 596
Loading gauge 330-331
Load space 354

Lobby 498
Lobe
  Liverwort 118
  Venus fly trap 160
Lobed leaf 129, 131
Lobsters 172
Lobule 242
Local Arm 14
Local control cabinet 596
Lock button 600
Lock forward 530
Lockheed Electra airliner 406-407
Lock nut 351, 359
Locks 360
Lock washer 358-359
Locomotion 104
Locomotives 324-329
Lodging knee 381
Loft 477
Log basket 354
Logic board 581
Loin
  Horse 198
  Human 210
London Bridge 466-467
London plane tree 134
Longboat 380
Long bridge 515
Long-distance cycling 360
Long-distance running 542
Longeron 403, 424
Longitudinal channels 120
Longitudinal fissure 236-237
Long jump 542-543
Long leading-link fork 362
Long leg 538
Long off 538
Long on 538
Long pass 532
Long radius turns 552
Longrod stabilizer 549
Longship 374-375
Longshore drift 294-295
Long-travel suspension 368
Long-wave radio 318
Look out periscope 396
Loom 560
Loop 388-389
Looped prominence 32-33
Loophole
  Medieval building 466-469
  Renaissance building 477
Loop of Henlé 256
Loose forward 530
Loose-head prop 530
Lopolith 274
Lora 127, 130
Lorises 202
Lost-wax casting method 454
Lotus flower 488
Lotus petal 489
Loudspeaker 520
Lounge 392
Louvre 493, 498
Love-in-a-mist 150-151
Lowell 45
Lower Carboniferous Limestone 60
Lower crankcase 410
Lower crux of antihelix 242
Lower deadeye 382-383
Lower deck 393
Lower-energy radiation 22
Lower epidermis 139, 159
Lower eyelid 213
Lower fin 423

Lower haze 37
Lower LCD assembly 579
Lower lobe of lung 215, 254-255
Lower seat axis 152-153
Lower topsail 385
Lower-wing attachment 404
Lower yard 395
Low gain antenna 615
Lowland coastline 295
Low Neap tide 297
Low pressure areas 500, 502-503
Low pressure gases 506
Low tides 296-297
Low-voltage supply 596
Loxodonta africana 200
Lozenge 471, 485
Lubricant 566
Lucarne window 480-481, 486
Lufengosaurus 89
Luff 584-585
Lug 582, 586
Lugger 384
Lug sail
  Junk 376
  Sail types 584
Lumbar nerves 238
Lumbar vertebrae
  Crocodile 186
  Domestic cat 195
  Hare 197
  Horse 199
  Human 222-223
  Kangaroo 206
  Platypus 206
  Rhesus monkey 202
  Seal 204
Lumbrical muscle 251
Lump hammer 452-453
Lunae Planum 43
Lunaria annua 151
Lunate bone 230
Lunette 480
Lung
  Amphibian 182
  Bird 189
  Brachiosaurus 91
  Chimpanzee 202
  Dolphin 205
  Domestic cat 195
  Elephant 200
  Euoplocephalus 94
  Frog 182
  Gallimimus 86
  Human 214-215, 252, 254-255
  Lizard 184-185
  Rabbit 196
  Snail 177
  Snake 184
  Spider 170
  Tortoise 187
Lungfish 80, 81
Lunule 231
Lures 562-563
Lutetium 311
LVG CVI fighter 405
Lychee 148
Lycoming four-cylinder engine 425
Lycoming six-cylinder engine 422
Lycopodophyta 64, 120
Lymphocytes 253
Lynx 18, 21
Lynx helicopter 596
Lyra 19, 20
Lysosome 217

M

M22 (globular cluster) 21
Macaques 202
Macaws 190
Mach 41

Machine-gun 404-405
Machine heads 512-513
Mackerel angling 562
Maquette 455
Macrobius 40
Macrofibril 234
Macrospicule 33
Macs 566
Macula 240-241
Madagascar 265, 616
Madreporite 174, 175
Madrillus sphinx 203
Maeniaum summum 465
Magazine 548-549
Magellanic Cloud 15, 20
Maginus 40
Maglev train 528-329
Magma
  Igneous and Metamorphic rocks 26
  Mountain building 63
  Ocean floor 298-299
  Rock cycle 266
  Volcanoes 272
Magma reservoir
  Igneous rock structures 275
  Volcanic structure 273
Magnesium 310
  Earth's composition 39
  Earth's crust 58
  Seawater salt content 296
Magnesium alloy oil sump pan 354
Magnesium housing for air intake 355
Magnesium riser 548
Magnet 598, 605
Magnet array 615
Magnetic axis 28
Magnetic compass 425
Magnetic field 38
Magnetism 316-517
Magneto
  Avro triplane 402
  Hawker Tempest components 408
  Wright Flyer 399
Magneto drive 367
Magnetosphere 38
Magnetron assembly 596, 597
Magnetron cooling fan 596, 597
Magnetron cooling fan mounting 597
Magnetron perforated heat sink 597
Magnitude 22
Magnolia 57, 72
Mahonia 130-131
Maidenhair tree 122-123
Maillot 586
Main deck passenger door 573
Main deck windows 573
Main engines 614
Main fan 596, 597
Main fan electrical supply 597
Main-line signaling system 330-331
Main motor casing 593
Mainrail head 379
Main sail
  Dhow 376
  Roman corbita 373
  Sailing rigs 385
  Square-rigged ship 375
Mains earthing wire 596
Mains electricity supply lead 585

Main sequence star
  Massive stars 26
  Objects in universe 11
  Small stars 24
  Stars 22-23
Mains flex 594
Mains flex clamp 594
Main sheer strake 393
Main sheet
  Longboat 380
  Roman corbita 373
  Sailing dinghy 561
  Viking karv 375
Main shroud 378
Mains lead 597-598
Main spar bridge 413
Mains power on/off switch 585
Mains spade contacts 594
Main stay 377, 379
Mains supply lead 594
Maintenance button 574
Main topcastle 377
Main topgallant mast 577, 578
Main topgallant sail 579
Main topgallant stay 379
Main topmast 377, 379
Main topmast topcastle 377
Main topsail 379
Main topsail halyard 385
Main topsail yard 379
Main top yard 377
Main turbine 397
Main wale 381
Main wheel 426, 595
Main wing bracing-strut 401
Main wing-strut 427
Main yard
  Dhow 376
  Sailing warship 377
  Wooden sailing ship 379
Maize 127
Major calyx 256
Major coverts 188, 191
Malachite 453
Malacostraca 172
Malaysia 331
Male
  Bladder 257
  Body 210, 211
  Pelvis 259
  Reproductive organs 259
  Urinary tract 257
Male apex 119
Male catkin 144
Male cone 122-123, 24
Male fern 120-121
Male flower organs 140-145
Male flowers
  Fertilization 146-147
  Gymnosperms 122
  Painter's palette 143
  Seaweed 116-117
  Succulent fruit 148
  Wind-pollinated plant 144
"Mallard" express steam locomotive 324-325
Mallet
  Marble carving 452
  Ships and sailing 383, 384, 388
  Tubular bells 516
Malleus 242
Malpighian tubule
  Butterfly 169
  Spider 170
Malus 573
Malus sp. 126
Malus sylvestris 149
Mammals 104-107
  Carnivora 194

Cetacea 204
Cretaceous period 72
Earth's evolution 56-57
Fossil record 279
Jurassic period 70
Lagomorpha 196
Large 57
Marsupalia 206
Monotremata 206
Pinnipedia 204
Primates 202
Proboscidea 200
Rodentia 196
Shrewlike 70
Small 56
Tertiary period 74-75
Ungulates 198
Mammoth 107
Mammut 75
Mammuthus 76, 77, 104
Mandapa 491
Mandarinfish 180
Mandible
Acanthostega 80
Ankylosaurus 94
Arsinoitherium 104
Baryonyx 83
Bat 105
Bear 194
Beetle 168
Bird 188-189
Bony fish 181
Camarasaurus 91
Chimpanzee 202
Crayfish 173
Crocodile 186
Diplodocus 90
Elephant 201
Eryops 80
Euoplocephalus 94
Hare 197
Heterodontosaurus 85
Horse 199
Human 220-221,
244-245
Kangaroo 206
Lambeosaurus 99
Lion 194
Moeritherium 105
Panoplosaurus 94
Parasaurolophus 99
Phiomia 105
Platosaurus 88
Protoceratops 102
Rattlesnake 185
Rhesus monkey 202
Seal 204
Stegoceras 100-101
Styracosaurus 102
Toxodon 106
Triceratops 103
Turtle 187
Tyrannosaurus 84
Mandrills 202-203
Mane 194, 199
Manganese 281, 510
Manharness knot 389
Manifold connector 355
Manilla rope 389
Manipulator 610
Man-of-war 378
Mansard roof 490
Mantellisaurus 96-97
Mantle
Earth 38-39, 58-59, 63
Mars 43
Mercury 35
Moon 41
Mollusks 176-177
Neptune 51
Pluto 51
Regional
metamorphism 274
Uranus 49
Venus 37
Maple 127
Map projections 264-265
Mapping the Earth
264-265

Maracas 504,
516-517
Marble 274
Marble block 455
Marble breaking
equipment 450
Marble mosaic 489
Marble sculpture 452
Marble tessera 450
Marble veneer 462
Marchantia polymorpha
118
Mare Crisium 40
Mare Fecunditatis 40
Mare Frigoris 40
Mare Humorum 40
Mare Imbrium 40
Mare Ingenii 41
Mare Moscoviense 41
Mare Nectaris 40
Mare Nubium 40
Mare Orientale 41
Mareotis Fossae 43
Mare Serenitatis 40
Mare Smithii 41
Mare's tail 135
Mare Tranquillitatis 40
Mare Vaporum 40
Margaritifer Sinus 43
Margin
Lamina 116-117, 161
Leaf 129, 136-137
Needle 124
Water lily leaf 159
Marginal shield 187
"Margined heads" 100
Marginocephalians 83,
100-103
Maria 40
Marine invertebrates
65
Marine plants 56
Marine reptiles 57, 70
Marine sediments 280
Markab 19, 20
Markeb 21
Marlin 588
Marlinspike 383, 589
Marmosets 202
Marram grass 113
Mars 30, 42-43, 615
Mars Exploration Rover
(MER) 615
Mars Exploration Rover
spacecraft 615
Marsh 293
Marsupials 104, 206-207
Martellange, E. 479
Martingale 582, 557
Martingale stay 583
Mary Rose 376
Mascaron 487
Mask 460, 487, 536
Ancient Roman
building 465
Cathedral dome 484
Neoclassical building
482
Masonry apron 487
Mason's mark 470
Mason's tools 485
Mass
Atoms and molecules
309, 520
Earth 30
Jupiter 26, 44
Mars 30
Mercury 30
Neptune 31
Planets 30-31
Pluto 31
Saturn 31
Stars 22
Uranus 31
Venus 30
Massive habit 270-271
Massive stars 26-27

Massospondylidae 89
Mass-production 358-359,
492
Mass transportation 552
Mast
Battleship 594
Frigate 594
Greek galley 372
Iron paddlesteamer 392
Junk 576
Longboat 380
Roman corbita 373
Sailing 561
Sailing warship 376-377
Submarine 397
Tea clipper 392
Three-masted square-
rigged ship 375
Viking karv 375
Wooden sailing ship
378-379
Mast band 382
Master cylinder
Disc brake 365
Harley-Davidson FLHS
Electra Glide 363
Honda VF750 564
Master shipwright 374
Master's sea cabin 381-
Masthead
Roman corbita 373
Viking karv 375
Wooden sailing ship
378
Mast head bend 589
Masthead pulley for tye
halyard 575
Mast hoop 385
Mastoid fontanelle 220
Mastoid process 220, 242
Mast partner 381
Mast step 592
Mast truck 372
Matar 21
Match play 546
Maternal blood pool 260
Maternal blood vessel 260
Mathematical symbols
621
Mato Grosso 264, 617
Matter 306-307
Electrical charge 316
Identification 512
Mature ruptured follicle
258
Mawsonites spriggi 65
Maxilla
Ankylosaurus 94
Baryonyx 83
Bear 194
Bony fish 181
Camarasaurus 91
Chimpanzee 202
Diplodocus 90
Elephant 201
Eryops 80
Euoplocephalus 94
Frog 183
Horse 105
Human 212, 220-221,
244-245, 246, 248
Iguanodon 96
Lion 194
Pachycephalosaurus 100
Prenocephale 100
Stegoceras 100
Toxodon 106
Maxillary fenestra 90
Maxilliped 173
Maxwellian diagram 318
Maxwell Montes 36, 37
Mazda RX-7 546
McLaren Mercedes MP4-
13 556-557
MCW Metrobus 552-555
ME 262 fighter 408
Meadow cranesbill 144
Meadow rue 137
Meadow sage 145

Meander 461
Meanders 288-289, 290
Measurement units 620
Meatus 242-245
Mechanical semaphore
signal 550
Mechanical weathering
282
Mechanics 350-351
Mechanism of respiration
255
Medallion 476
Media guide button 577
Medial epicondyle 225
Medial malleolus 253
Medial rectus muscle
240-241
Median canal 243
Median cubital vein 253
Median eye 170
Median glossoepiglottic
fold 244
Median nerve 238
Median sulcus 244
Median wing coverts 188
Medieval castles 466-467
Medieval churches
468-469
Medieval houses 466-467
Medinet Habu, Egypt 459
Mediterranean Sea 74,
265, 616
Mediterranean sea
anemone 166
Medium-wave radio 318
Medulla 114, 254, 256
Medulla oblongata 212,
256-257
Medullary cavity 224
Medullary pyramid 256
Medullary ray 125
Medullosa 66
Megaspores 122
Megazostrodon 104
Megrez 19
Meiolania 77
Meissner's corpuscle
234-235, 239
Mekong River 265
Melanin 234
Melanosaurus 68, 88-89
Melon 149, 205
Meltwater 287, 289
Meltwater pool 286
Membrane
Chloroplasts 139
Chorioallantoic 192
Egg 193
Shell 192
Thylakoid 139
Memory stick 581
Mendel 41
Mendeleev 41
Mendelevium 311
Meninges 257
Menkalinan 21
Menkar 19, 20
Menkent 21
Mensa 20, 21
Mental foramen 213,
220-221
Mentalis muscle 229
Mental protuberance 221
Mental symphysis 220
Mentolabial sulcus 213
Merak 19
Merchants' Exchange 493
Mercury 30, 34-35
Mercury (metal) 281, 311,
519
Mericarp 151
Meristematic cells 154
Merlon 466
Mermaid's purses
192

Mersenius 40
Merus 172, 175
Merycoidodon 75
Mesa 275, 277, 282
Mesentery 167, 182
Mesocarp 146-147, 148,
148-149
Mesoglea 167
Mesohyal 166
Mesophyll 155
Bishop pine needle 124
Dicotyledon leaf 126
Marram grass 113
Monocotyledon leaf
126
Palisade layer 139
Spongy layer 139
Mesosphere 300
Mesothorax 168
Mesozoic era
Cretaceous period 72
Dinosaurs 82
Fossil record 279
Geological timescale 57
Jurassic period 70
Reptiles 80
Triassic period 68
Mess 597
Message area 576
Message display area 576
Metacarpals
Archaeopteryx 85
Arsinoitherium 104
Baryonyx 83
Bird 189, 91
Brachiosaurus 91
Cow 198
Diplodocus 90
Domestic cat 195
Elephant 90, 201
Eryops 80
Euoplocephalus 94
Frog 183
Gallimimus 86
Hare 197
Horse 198-199
Human 218-219, 230
Kangaroo 206
Lizard 184
Parasaurolophus 99
Plateosaurus 88
Platypus 206
Rhesus monkey 202
Seal 204
Stegoceras 100
Toxodon 106
Triceratops 103
Tyrannosaurus 84
Metacarpophalangeal
joint 85
Metal cook/grill tray 596
Metal grill/griddle 596
Metalliferous muds 299
Metalling 486
Metal modeling
implements 452
Metal needle pad 384
Metal nib 444
Metal riser 455
Metal runner 455
Metals 510
Metal tire 324
Metal wire conductor
516-517
Metamorphic aureole 26
Metamorphic rocks 26,
274-275, 266-267
Metamorphosis
Amphibian 182
Frog 183
Insect 168
Metasoma 170
Metatarsals
Albertosaurus 84
Archaeopteryx 85
Brachiosaurus 90
Crocodile 186
Domestic cat 195
Elephant 201

Eiyops 81
Euoplocephalus 94
Frog 183
Hare 197
Horse 199
Human 218-219, 252
Iguanodon 96-97
Kangaroo 206
Lizard 184
Parasaurolophus 98
Plateosaurus 88
Platypus 206
Rhesus monkey 202
Scorpion 170
Seal 204
Spider 171
Stegoceras 100-101
Struthiomimus 87
Toxodon 107
Triceratops 102
Meterhorax 168
Metaxylem 127, 132-133
Meteor 52, 301
Meteorite
Asteroids, comets, and
meteoroids 52
Earth's atmosphere 38
Moon 41
Ray crater 34
Meteorite impact 34, 40
Meteoroids 52-53
Solar system 30
Methane
Jupiter 45
Neptune and Pluto
50-51
Saturn 47
Uranus 48-49
Methane cirrus clouds
50-51
Metis Regio 36
Metope 460
Metric-Imperial
conversions 620
Metridium senile 166
Metrobus 552-553
Metrolink tram 532
Mexican hat plant 154
Mexican mountain king
snake 184
Mexican true red-legged
tarantula 170
Mexico 331
Mezzanine 467,
496
Miaplacidus 21
Mica 26, 270
Mice 104, 196
Michelangelo 35
Micrasternas sp. 112
Microfilament 217
Microneedle 606
Microorganisms 58, 78
Microphone 581
Micropipette 606
Microporous filter 592
Microprocessor
Personal computer
567
Digital camera 580
Microscopes 610-611
Microsoft Kinect 578
Microsporangium 122
Microspores 122
Microsporophyll 122
Microtubule 217, 239
Micro-USB (Universal
Serial Bus) socket 589
Microwave oven 315
Microwave radiation 10
Microwave combination
oven 596-597
Microwaves 318, 596
Midbrain 236
Middle ear ossicles
242
Middle finger 230-231
Middle leg
Beetle 168

Bumblebee 168
Butterfly 169
Middle lobe of lung 215,
254-255
Middle meatus 241,
245
Middle nasal concha 212,
221, 241, 245
Middle phalanx 219, 230,
232
Middle rail 581
Midfielders
Gaelic football 529
Lacrosse 541
Soccer 524
Midgut 173
Mid-latitude band 36
Mid-latitude cyclones 502
Mid-ocean ridge 281,
298-299
Mid-off 538
Mid-on 538
Midrib
Dicotyledon leaf
126-127
Durmast oak leaf 131
Fern fronds 121
Hogweed leaf 129
Ice-plant leaf 129
Live-forever leaf 129
Liverwort 118
Monkey cup 161
Moss leaf 119
Spiral wrack 116
Sweet chestnut leaf 136
Tree fern 115
Venus fly trap 160
Water lily leaf 159
Midships fence 573
Midships section 592
Midwater current 297
Midway Gardens 495
Mid West single-rotor
engine 411
Mid West twin-rotor
engine 411
Mid West two-stroke
engine 410
Miele washer-dryer 594,
595
Mihrab 488
Milan Cathedral 475
Milankovic 43
Milk snake 184
Milk teeth 246
Milky quartz 268, 271
Milky Way 14-15
Northern stars 18
Solar system 30
Stars of southern skies
20
Mill 462, 464, 492
Millstone grit 60-61
Milne 41
Milton 55
Mimas 46
Mimosa 21
Mimulopsis solmsii 145
Minaret 488-489
Mineral-filled fault 60-61
Mineral-rich deposits
298
Minerals 268-269
Carnivorous plants 160
Epiphytes 162
Fossils 278
Mineral features 270-271
Mineral resources
280-281
Photosynthesis 158-159
Wetland plants 158
Xylem vessel 154
Mineral spicules 166
Mineral spring 273
Mineral wool 603
Minim 502
Minmi 95
Minor calyx 256
Minor coverts 188, 191

Mint 109
Mintaka 18
Miocene epoch
Fossil record 279
Geological timescale 57
Mira 19, 20
Mirach 19, 20
Miranda 48
Mirfak 19, 20
Mirzam 18, 21
Missile launcher 397
Mississippian period 56
Mississippi Delta 290-291
Mississippi-Missouri River
264, 617
Mississippi River 291
Mist 306
Mistle thrush 190
Mistletoe 162
Mitochondrial crista 217
Mitochondrial sheath 259
Mitochondrion 217, 259
Mitral valve 251
Mixosaurus 91
Mizar 19
Mizzen backstay 378
Mizzen bitt 381
Mizzen course 379
Mizzen mast
Dhow 376
Iron paddlesteamer 392
Junk 376
Sailing warship 377
Square-rigged ship 575
Wooden sailing ship
378
Mizzen sail 375, 385
Mizzen shroud 378
Mizzen stay 378
Mizzen top 378
Mizzen topcastle 377
Mizzen topgallant sail 379
Mizzen topmast 377, 378
Mizzen topsail 379
Mizzen yard 376-377, 378
Moat 466-467
Mobile sculpture 452
Modeling 452
Modeling tools 454
Modem 576, 577
Moderator 314
Modern buildings 496-499
Modern engines 544-545
Modern humans 57
Modern jetliners 412-415
Modern military aircraft
420-421
Modern piston aero-
engines 410-411
Mode switch 586
Modified cuticle 157
Modified lateral shoots
156
Modified leaflets 129
Modified leaves
Barberry 150-151
Cobra lily 160
Dryland plants 156-157
Everlasting pea 129
Golden barrel cactus
156
Pitcher development 161
Spines 156
Strawberry 128
Modified shoots 156
Modified stipules 128-129
Modillion
Baroque church 479
Neoclassical building
478
Renaissance building
475
Moenave formation 276
Moenkopi formation 276
Moeritherium 104
Mohorovic discontinuity
59
Mohs scale 270-271
Molar tooth

Arsinoitherium 104
Australopithecus 107
Bear 106, 194
Chimpanzee 202
Elephant 201
Horse 105
Human 246
Hyaenodon 107
Moeritherium 105
Opossum 106
Phiomia 105
Toxodon 106
Mold 278
Molded bracket 484
Molded corbel 493
Molding 485
Ancient Egyptian
temple 458-459
Asian building 490
Baroque church
480-481
Dome 486-487
Gothic church 471-472
Medieval building 466,
469
Neoclassical building
479-480, 482
Renaissance building
475-477
Ship's shield 395
Molding tool 454
Molds 114
Molecular orbitals 308
Molecules 306, 308-309
Mollusks 176-177
Belemnite 71
Nautiloid 69
Molten bronze 454
Molten core 39
Molten rock
Igneous and
metamorphic rocks 274
Matter 306
Ocean floor 298
Plate movements 58
Rock cycle 266
Volcanoes 272
Molting 171
Molybdate 269
Molybdenum 310
Mongooses 194
Monkey cup 161
Monkeys 202-203
Monitor
Digital camera 580
Monoceros 18, 21
Monoclinal fold 60
Monocline 61
Monoclinic system 270
Monococque chassis 363
Monococque shell 348
Monocotyledonous petals
140, 145
Monocotyledonous sepals
126, 140, 143
Monocotyledons 126-127,
140-141, 143
Monodon monoceros 205
Monograptus convolutus
65
Monolithic shaft 463
Monoplanes 400-401, 402,
406
Monoterrenes 206-207
Montes Apenninus 40
Montes Cordillera 41
Montes Jura 40
Montes Rook 41
Monteverdi 35
Montgolfier brothers 398
Monument 470
Moon 40-41
Objects in universe 11
Solar eclipse 32
Tides 296-297
Moonquake region 41
Moons
Jupiter 44
Mars 42

Neptune 50
Saturn 46
Solar system 30
Uranus 48
Mooring 386-387
Moorish arch 484
Moraine 286-287, 292-295
Moray eel 180
Mortar 452
Mortice 373
Mortise 486, 492
Morus nigra 130
Mosaic 450-451
Islamic building
488-489
Tools 450
Mosque 484, 488
Mosses 112, 114, 118-119
Epiphytic 162
Life-cycle 119
Structure 119
Moth 168
Motherboard
Digital camcorder 583
Personal computer 567
Motherboard cable 578
Mother's milk 104
Motion 320-321
Motion sensor 579
Motocross motorcycle
racing 368
Motor air intake 593
Motor assembly 574
Motorcar chassis 362,
364-365
Motorcycle engines
366-367
Motorcycle racing 368
Motorcycles 362-363
Motorcycle sidecar 362,
369
Motor-driven bogie axle
326
Motor electronic control
module (ECM) 355
Motor end plate 228, 239
Motorhead 592, 593
Motorized buses 332
Motor neuron 228, 239
Motor operating signal
330
Motor whaler 397
Motte 466
Mouchette 472
Mounds 286
Mountain bikes 358, 360
Mountain building 56, 58,
62-63
Mountain hollows 286
Mountain lake 288
Mountain ranges
Faults and folds 60
Geological time 56
Igneous and
metamorphic rocks 274
Mapping the Earth
264-265
Mountain building 62
Ocean floor 298
Physical map of the
world 616-617
Plate movements 59
Mountain ridge 295
Mountain ring 54
Mountains 62-63, 267
Mountain spring 288
Mounting bush 565
Mounting splines 366
Mouse 521, 566, 611
Mouse and collar 579
Mouth
Barnacle 173
Bony fish 180-181
Cobra lily 160
Cow 198
Crayfish 175
Dogfish 179
Dolphin 204
Elephant 200

Frog 182
Gorilla 203
Horse 199
Human 211, 212,
244-245, 248
Jellyfish 167
Kangaroo 204
Lamprey 178
Lizard 184
Pitcher plant 161
Rabbit 196
Rat 196
Sea anemone 166-167
Seal 204
Sea urchin 175
Snail 177
Spider 170
Starfish 174-175
Mouth diffuser 450, 440
Mouthpiece
Brass instruments 506
Clarinet 508
Tenor saxophone 509
Trumpet 506
Wind synthesizer 521
Movement
Gas particles 307
Objects 320
MP3 players 586
MRI scan
Head 214
Brain 236
Mt. Everest 265, 616
Mu Andromedae 19
Muav limestone 277
Muccini brush 434
Mucosa 248
Mucosal gland 254
Mucous gland 177
Mucronate leaf apex 137
Mucus-secreting
duodenal cells 217
Mud 267, 273
Mud crab 279
Mud flat 295
Mud pools 272-273
Mud river 298
Mulberry 130
Muliphein 21
Mullion
Gothic church 470,
472-473
Modern building
497-499
Renaissance building
476
Small-scale rock
formation 60-61
Twentieth-century
building 494
Multicellular animals 56
Multicellular organisms
78
Multicellular soft-bodied
animals 56
Multifoil 472
Multifunction display 573
Multigabled roof 492
Multiplait nylon 388
Multiplate clutch 364,
366
Multiple fruits 148-149
Multiplier reel 562
Multi-ply tire 416
Multipolar neuron 239
Multitouch interface 568
Mu Orionis 18
Mu Pegasi 19
Musa 'lacatan' 146
Muscari sp. 155
Musci 118
Muscle 226-229
Abductor digiti
minimus 251, 253
Adductor longus 225
Adductor magnus 227
Adductor pollicis 231
Abductor pollicis brevis
231

Anal sphincter 249
Arrector pili 235
Cricothyroid 244-245
Dilator 241
Dorsal interosseous 233
Energy system 315
Extensor digitorum
brevis 233
Extensor hallucis brevis
233
Flexor digitorum
longus 233
Flexor hallucis longus
233
Flexor pollicis brevis
231
Flexor retinaculum
231
Genioglossus 245
Geniohyoid 245
Gluteus medius 225
Gluteus minimus 225
Hyoglossus 244
Iliacus 225
Inferior oblique 241
Inferior rectus 241
Intercostal 255
Internal urethral
sphincter 257
Lateral rectus 240-241
Levator palpebrae
superioris 241
Lumbrical 231
Medial rectus 240-241
Myohyoid 245
Opponens digiti minimi
251
Opponens pollicis
231
Orbicularis oris 245
Papillary 251
Pectineus 225
Peroneus brevis 233
Peroneus longus 233
Psoas major 225, 257
Pyloric sphincter 249
Soleus 233
Sphincter 241
Styloglossus 244
Superior longitudinal
245
Superior oblique 241
Superior rectus 241
Tensor tympani 243
Thyrohyoid 244
Tibialis anterior 233
Tibialis posterior 233
Urethral sphincter 257
Vastus lateralis 225
Vastus medialis 225
Muscovite 269
Muscular septum 176
Mushroom anchor 386
Mushroom coral 167
Mushrooms 114, 115
Music 514, 586
Musical Instrument
Digital Interface (MIDI)
system 520-521
Musical manuscript
502-503
Musical notation 502-503
Musical score 502-503,
505
Music gallery 477
Musicians 504
Music software
520
Mussels 176
Mussosaurus 68
Mutes 506-507
Muttaburrasaurus 97
Muzzle 199, 397
Mycelium 114-115
Mycorrhizal association
133
Myelin sheath 239
Mylar 384
Myocardium 250-251

Myofibril 228
Myohyoid muscle 245
Myometrium 260

N

Nail
  Corythosaurus 98
  Edmontonia 95
  Elephant 90
  Human 251
  Iguanodon 96-97
  Stegosaurus 92
  Triceratops 102
Nair Al Zaurak 19, 20
Naismath, James 552
Namib Desert 265, 616
Naos 461, 463, 485
Nape 188, 210
Napier Saber 24-cylinder
  engine 408
Naris
  Anchisaurus 89
  Ankylosaurus 94
  Arsinoitherium 104
  Australopithecus 108
  Baryonyx 83
  Brachiosaurus 91
  Camarasaurus 91
  Corythosaurus 98
  Edmontonia 95
  Eryops 80
  Euoplocephalus 94
  Homo erectus 108
  Homo habilis 108
  Homo sapiens 108
  Hyaenodon 107
  Iguanodon 96
  Lambeosaurus 99
  Moeritherium 105
  Opossum 106
  Panoplosaurus 94
  Parasaurolophus 99
  Plateosaurus 88
  Protoceratops 102
  Smilodon 107
  Stegoceras 100-101
  Stegosaurus 92
  Styracosaurus 102
  Triceratops 102-103
  Tyrannosaurus 84
Narrow gauge track 331
Narwhal 205
Nasal bone
  Ankylosaurus 94
  Bear 194
  Frog 183
  Human 220-221
  Lion 194
  Panoplosaurus 94
  Protoceratops 102
  Toxodon 106
Nasal cavity
  Chimpanzee 202
  Domestic cat 195
  Elephant 200
  Human 245, 248
  Rabbit 196
Nasal horn 104
Nasalis 229
Nasal passage 200
Nasal plug 205
Nasal septum 213, 221,
  241
Nash 21
Nasion 213
Nasolacrimal duct 241
Nasopharynx 245
Natal cleft 210
Natal cocoon 24, 26
Native elements 268
Natural bridge 290
Natural elements 310
Natural fly 562
Natural forces 314
Natural glass 306
Natural gut strings 544
Natural lakes 292

Natural satellites 40
Natural sponge 438
Nautiloid mollusk 69
  Fossil 65
Navajo Mountain 277
Navajo sandstone 276
Nave
  Ancient Egyptian
    temple 458-459
  Baroque church 479
  Cathedral dome 484
  Gothic church 470-475
  Medieval church
    468-469
  Ship's wheel 390
Navel 211, 260
Nave plate 390
Navicular bone 232
Navigating bridge 394
Navigational aerial
  423-424
Navigation area 577
Navigation buttons 577
Navigation camera
  (Navcam) 615
Navigation display 573
Navigation light 575
Navigator's cockpit 420
Navigator's seat 408
Navka 37
Nazea plate 59
Neanderthals 108
Neap tides 296-297
Nebulae 16-17
  Cone 612
  Galaxies 12-13
  Great, Orion 613
  Life of massive star 26
  Milky Way 14-15
  NGC 1566 (Seyfert
    galaxy) 13
  Omega 613
  Small stars 24
  Structure of nebula 24
Neck
  Acoustic guitar
    512-513
  Anchisaurus 89
  Calligraphy character
    445
  Corythosaurus 98
  Electric guitar 513
  Golf club 547
  Harp 511
  Horse 199
  Human 211, 224-225,
    247, 258-259
  Iguanodon 97
  Pachycephalosaurus
    100
  Rat 196
  Sauropodomorpha 88
  Sculling oar 560
  Stegoceras 101
  Stegosaurus 92
  Stringed instruments
    510
  Tenor saxophone 509
  Theropod 84
  Violin 510
Necking 581
Nectar 142, 160-161
Nectaries 141, 144-145
  160-161
Needles
  Bishop pine 124
  Pine 124-125
  Scots pine 122
  Yew 123
Nefertiti Corona 37
Negative electric charge
  316
Negative ions 308, 310
Neo-Baroque style
  492-493
Neo-Byzantine style
  492-493
Neoclassical style 478-485,
  496

Neodymium 310
Neo-Gothic style 492-493
Neo-Greek style 492-493
Neon 35, 311
Nepenthes mirabilis 161
Nephron 256
Neptune 31, 50-51
Neptunides polychromus
  12
Neptunium 311
Nerve
  Ampullar 242
  Bronchial 254
  Cervical 238
  Cochlear 243
  Common peroneal 258
  Cranial 238
  Cutaneous 258
  Deep peroneal 258
  Femoral 238
  Hypoglossal 244
  Lingual 244
  Lumbar 238
  Median 238
  Optic 240
  Posterior tibial 258
  Pudendal 258
  Pulp 247
  Radial 238
  Sacral 238
  Sciatic 258
  Spinal 223, 238
  Superficial peroneal 258
  Superior laryngeal 244
  Thoracic 238
  Ulnar 231, 238
  Vestibular 243
  Vestibulocochlear 243
Nerve cell 217, 257, 259
Nerve cord 173
Nerve fiber 235
Nerve ring 175
Nervous system 176,
  238-239
Nervous tissue 166
Netball 534-535
Network port 566
Neural spine
  Arsinoitherium 104
  Bony fish 180
  Brachiosaurus 90
  Eryops 81
  Euoplocephalus 95
  87
  Iguanodon 96
  Parasaurolophus 98
  Plateosaurus 89
  Stegoceras 100-101
  Stegosaurus 93
  Toxodon 106
  Triceratops 102
  Tuojiangosaurus 93
  Tyrannosaurus 85
Neurofilament 239
Neuron 239
Neurotransmitter 259
Neutralization 312
Neutrino 22
Neutron 22, 28
Neutrons 308, 309, 310
Neutron stars 28-29,
  26-27
New Guinea 265, 616
New mail button 576
New Moon 41
News item summary 577
News reader window 577
New State Paper Office 482
New tab 576
Newton (N) 320
Newton, Isaac 320
Newton meter 320-321
Newton's laws of motion
  320-321
Newts 182
New World monkeys
  202-203
New Zealand 265, 272

Next key 568
NGC 1566 (Seyfert galaxy)
  13
NGC 2997 (spiral galaxy)
  12
NGC 4406 (elliptical
  galaxy) 11
NGC 4486 (elliptical
  galaxy) 12
NGC 5236 (spiral galaxy) 11
NGC 5754 (colliding
  galaxies) 9
NGC 6656 (globular
  cluster) 21
NGC 6822 (irregular
  galaxy) 11
Nib types 444
Niche
  Ancient Roman
    building 462
  Asian temple 491
  Baroque church 480
  Cathedral dome 487
  Gothic church 471-472
  Islamic building 488
  Medieval building 467
  Neoclassical building 482
  Renaissance building
    476
Nickel 37, 49, 281, 311
Nickel-iron 270
Nigella damascena 151
Nikon Coolpix S1000PJ
  580-581
Nile crocodile 186
Nile River 264-265
Nimbostratus cloud 302
Nimbus cloud 302
Nineteenth-century
  buildings 479, 482,
  492-493, 494
Ninth-century building
  490
Nintendo 3DS 578
Nintendo Wii Fit Plus
  579
Niobe Planitia 36, 37
Niobium 310
Nippers 450
Nipple
  Human 211
  Marsupials 206
Nissl body 239
Nitrate ions 312
Nitrates 160
Nitrogen
  Atmospheric
    composition 301
  Helix Nebula 17
  Mars' atmosphere 43
  Periodic table 311
  Pluto's atmosphere 51
  Venus' atmosphere 37
Nitrogen dioxide gas 312
Nobelium 311
Noble gases 310-311
Nock 548
Noctis Labyrinthus 42, 43
Nocturnal mammals 104
Node
  Bamboo 131
  Brassavola nodosa 1
    62
  Canadian pond weed
    158-159
  Couch grass 113
  Dicotyledons 127
  Horsetail 120
  Ice-plant 129
  Live-forever 129
  Modern buildings 497
  Rhizome 155
  Rock stonecrop 128
  Rose stem 130
  Stems 134
  Stolon 154
  Strawberry 128
Node of Ranvier
  228, 239

Nodule fields 299
Nodules 128
Noggin 602
Nonconformity 276
Non-drive end 317
Nonesuch House 467
Nonexplosive eruptions
  272
Nonflowering plants 68
Nonmetals 310
Nonreturn valve 367
Nonskid tire 357
Nonslip flooring 573
North America
  Appalachian Mountains
    62
  Cretaceous period 72-73
  Jurassic period 70
  Late Carboniferous
    period 66
  Mapping the Earth
    264-265
  Middle Ordivician
    period 64
  Physical map of the
    world 616-617
  Quaternary period 76-77
  Tertiary period 74-75
  Triassic period 68
North American
  Cordillera 71
North American period 56
North American plate 59
North Atlantic current 296
North Atlantic Gyre 296
North Atlantic Ocean 59,
  71, 75
North East Africa 64
Northeasterly wind 303
Northeast monsoon 297
Northeast trade winds
  300
North Equatorial Belt 45
North Equatorial current
  296-297
Northern Hemisphere
  296-297
North Galactic Pole 15
North magnetic polar
  region 28
North Pacific current 296
North Pacific Gyre 296
North polar aurora 45
North polar ice cap 43
North Pole
  Atmospheric circulation
    and winds 300
  Coriolis force 297
  Jupiter 44
  Mars 42
  Mercury 34
  The Moon 40
  Neptune 50
  Pluto 51
  Pulsar 28
  Saturn 46
  Uranus 48
  Venus 36
North rim 277
North Temperate Zone 45
North Tropical Zone 45
Northwesterly wind 303
Nose
  B-17 bomber 408
  Concorde, the 416-417
  Iron 594
  Horse 198
  Human 211-212,
    244-245
  Lion 194
  Lockheed Electra
    airliner 406
  Rabbit 196
  Rat 196
Noseband 554, 555
Nose clip 558
Nose cone 418, 560
Nose cover 357
Nose cowling 412

Nose-end bogie 327
Nose-gear
  ARV light aircraft
    424-425
  Concorde, the 417
  Tornado 420
Nose horn 102, 103
Nose landing gear 573
Nose ring
  Avro biplane 405
  Blackburn monoplane
    400
Nose wheel
  ARV light aircraft 425
  Curtiss biplane 398
  Pegasus XL SE
  Tornado 420
  ultralight 426
Nostril
  Bird 188
  Chick 193
  Crocodilians 186
  Dolphin 205
  Domestic cat 195
  Elephant 200
  Frog 182
  Gorilla 203
  Horse 198
  Human 215
  Kangaroo 207
  Lion 194
  Lizard 184
  Monkey 202
  Rat 196
  Rattlesnake 185
  Seal 204
Nostril pocket 80
Notes 502, 506
Nothosaurian reptile 69
Notre Dame de Paris 470,
  475
Nozzle
  Concorde, the 416-417
  Jet engines 418-419
  Tornado 421
  Vacuum cleaner 593
NPT 301 turbojet 418
N-type silicon 605
Nu Andromedae 19
Nucellus 147
Nuchal plate 187
Nuchal ring 95
Nuchal shield 187
Nuclear energy 314
Nuclear fusion
  Massive stars 26
  Small stars 24
  Stars 22
  Sun 32
Nuclear "hunter-killer"
  submarine 396-397
Nuclear power station
  314
Nuclear reactions 315
Nucleolus 216, 239
Nucleoplasm 216
Nucleus
  Asteroids, comets, and
    meteoroids 52-53
  Atoms and molecules
    308, 509
  Chlamydomonas sp. 116
  Cnidocytes 167
  Egg cell 606, 607
  Endosperm 147
  Fungal cell 115
  Galaxies 12-13
  Generalized human cell
    216
  Muscle cell 228
  Neuron 239
  Overhead view of our
    galaxy 14
  Palisade mesophyll cell
    139
  Pollen 122
  Pollen tube 147
  Roots 132
  Scots pine pollen 122

Side view of our galaxy 14
Synergid 147
  Thalassiosira sp. 116
Nuctenea umbratica 171
Number systems 620
Nunki 19, 20-21
Nu Orionis 18
Nut
  Deadeye 383
  Dry fruit 150
  Durmast oak 131
  Toaster 598
Nutcrackers 521
Nutlets 150
Nutrients
  Carnivorous plants 160
  Epiphyte supply 162
  Phloem sieve tube 154
  Plant transport 139
Nylon and silicon cloth 584
Nymphaea sp. 159
Nyssa sylvatica 137

O

O_2 sensor 355
Oak 74
Oar
  Greek and Roman ships 372-373
  Junk 376
  Longboat 380
  Viking ships 374-375
Oarweed 116-117
Oasis 285
Oberon 48
Ob-Irtysh River 265
Objective aperture 610
Objective lens 610, 611
Object mass 320
Oblique-slip fault 61
Oboe 504-505, 508
Obovate leaves 137
Observer's cockpit 405
Observer's windshield 404
Obsidian 275, 306
Obstruction light 572
Obturator canal 224
Obturator membrane 224
Occipital bone 202, 220
Occipital condyle 107, 194, 220
Occipital lobe 236-237
Occipital region 106
Occluded fronts 302-303
Ocean currents 296-297
Ocean floor 298-299, 266-267
Oceanic crust
  Earth's crust 58-59
  Mineralization zones 281
  Mountain building 62-63
  Ocean floor 298
Oceanic seahorses 180
Ocean ridges 58-59
Oceans 39, 296-297, 301
Ocean trenches
  Ocean floor features 299
  Offshore currents 296
  Plate movements 58
Oceanus Procellarum 40
Ocellus 176
Octafoil 471
Octagon 622
Octahedron 623
Octastyle portico 462
Octave 557
Octopus 176-177
Ocular end 377
Oculus

Ancient Roman building 462-463
Gothic church 472-475
Medieval building 466, 469
Neoclassical building 483
Roman corbita 372
Odd-toed ungulates 198-199
Odontoblast 247
Oeil-de-boeuf window
  Baroque church 479, 481
  Cathedral dome 487
Oerlikon gun position 397
Off-road motorcycle racing 368
Offshore deposits 294
Ogee 595
Ogee arch 488
Ogee-arched motif 499
Ogee curve 472
Ogee-curved dome 486
Ogee-curved roof 489
Ogee molding 475-477, 481
Ogee tracery 503
Ohms 316
Oil
  Clutches 366
  Diesel trains 526
  Energy storage 515
  Mineral resources 280-281
Oil bottle dripfeed 336
Oil cooler 547, 564, 605
Oil-cooler duct 415
Oil cooler matrix 547
Oil deposit formation 57
Oil deposits 281
Oil dipstick 544
Oil duct 151
Oil feed 411
Oil feed pipe 345, 366, 367
Oil filter
  1-liter VTEC engine 354
  Ford diesel engine 547
  Jaguar V12 engine 345
  Turbofan engine 418
  Turboprop engine 419
Oil-fired power station 315
Oil formation 280-281
Oil muffler 364
Oil paints 436-437
Oil pipe banjo 345
Oil-pressure regulating valve 419
Oil pump
  Humber engine 343
  Mid West single-rotor engine 411
  Velocette OHV engine 367
  Weslake speedway bike 369
Oil rig 315
Oil side lamp 336-337
Oil sump
  Honda VF750 364
  Humber engine 343
  Modern engines 344-345
  Velocette OHV engine 367
Oil tank
  Bell-47 helicopter components 422
  Harley-Davidson FLHS Electra Glide 363
  Lockheed Electra airliner 406
  Turbofan engine 418
  Turboprop engine 419
Oil traps 281
Oldsmobile 336-337
Old World monkeys 202-203
Olecranon 85

OLED 584
Olenellus 64
Oleo lock-jack 414
Olfactory bulb 181
Oligocene epoch
  Fossil record 279
  Geological timescale 57
Olivine
  Igneous rock 267
  Meteorites 52
  Silicates 269
Olivine gabbro 275
Olympus BX51W1 optical microscope 610
Olympus Mons 42-43
Omasum 198
Omega Centauri 21
Omicron Andromedae 19
Omicron¹ Canis Majoris 21
Omicron² Canis Majoris 21
Omicron Orionis 18
Omicron Sagittarii 21
Omnivores 84
Omohyoid muscle 229
Onboard information panel 573
One-toed ungulates 198
Onion dome 467, 486-488
Onion-skin weathering 282
On/off/pause button 586
On-screen display 577
Onyx 268
Oocyte 258
Oogonium 117
Oort Cloud 30, 52
Oosphores 116-117
  Fern 121
  Moss 119
Ooze 298
Open cluster 16
Open gun mounting 394
Opera House, Paris 493
Opera House, Sydney 496, 499
Opercula 180
Opercular bone 181
Operculum
  Bony fish 180-181
  Cnidocyte 167
  Giant stick insect eggs 192
  Indian stick insect eggs 192
  Leaf insect eggs 192
  Moss 119
Ophidia 184
Ophiothrix fragilis 175
Ophiuchus 19, 20
Ophthalmos 372
Opisthodomos 461
Opisthosoma 170-171
Opossums 206, 207
Opponens digiti minimi muscle 251
Opponens pollicis muscle 251
Opportunity 615
Optical drive 567
Optical map of our galaxy 14-15
Optical microscope 610
Optic chiasma 256
Optic disk 240-241
Optic nerve 240
Option connector 571
Opus incertum 463, 465
Opus quadratum 465
Opus sectile mosaic 488-489
Oral arm 167
Oral cavity 248
Oral disk 166-167
Oral surface 175
Orange citrine 271
Orange halite 269, 277
Orange light 318

Orangutans 202
Ora serrata 241
Orb 486
  Baroque church 480
  Cathedral dome 487
  Gothic church 471
  Neoclassical building 479
  Nineteenth-century building 493
  Renaissance building 477
Orbicularis oculi muscle 226, 229
Orbicularis oris muscle 228-229, 245
Orbicular lamina 138
Orbicular leaves 137
Orbit
  Acanthostega 80
  Ankylosaurus 94
  Archaeopteryx 85
  Arsinoitherium 104
  Australopithecus 108
  Baryonyx 83
  Bear 194
  Bird 189
  Bony fish 181
  Camarasaurus 91
  Chimpanzee 202
  Diplodocus 90
  Elephant 201
  Eryops 80
  Euoplocephalus 94
  Heterodontosaurus 83
  Homo erectus 108
  Homo habilis 108
  Homo sapiens 108
  Horse 199
  Hyaenodon 107
  Iguanodon 96
  Lambeosaurus 99
  Lion 194
  Lizard 184
  Opossum 106
  Outer planetary 51
  Pachycephalosaurus 100
  Panoplosaurus 94
  Parasaurolophus 99
  Plateosaurus 88
  Platypus 206
  Prenocephale 100
  Protoceratops 102
  Rattlesnake 185
  Rhesus monkey 202
  Smilodon 107
  Stars of northern skies 18
  Stars of southern skies 20
  Stegoceras 100-101
  Styracosaurus 102
  Toxodon 106
  Triceratops 103
  Tyrannosaurus 84
Orbital artery 179
Orbital cavity 220
Orbital motion 31, 52
Orbital plane
  Earth 38
  Jupiter 44
  Mars 42
  Mercury 34
  Neptune 50
  Pluto 51
  Saturn 46
  The Moon 40
  Uranus 48
  Venus 36
Orbitals 308-309, 310
Orbital speed (velocity)
  Mercury 34
  Solar system 30-31
Orb spider 171
Orchestra layout 504-505
Orchestral instruments 504-505

Musical notation 502-505
Orchestras 504-505
Orchestra shell 495
Orchids 126, 133, 162
Orcinus orca 205
Ordovician period 64-65
  Fossil record 279
  Geological time 56
  Primitive life 78
Organ 514, 502-503
Organic compound 313
Organic material deposition 281
Organic remains 276-277, 280
Organ of Corti 243
Oriel window 467
"O Ring" drive chain 366
Orion 18, 21, 24
Orion Arm 14
Orion Nebula 15, 17, 18
Orion's belt 15-16
Ornament
  Asian building 491
  Baroque church 479, 481
  Cathedral dome 487
  Islamic building 488
  Neoclassical building 483
Ornithischia 68-69, 82-83
  Marginocephalians 100
  Ornithopods 96
  Stegosaurs 92-93
  Thyreophorans 92
Ornithomimosaurs 86-87
Ornithopods 83
Ornithopods 96-97, 98-99
Ornithorhynchus anatinus 207
Orobanche sp. 163
Orogenesis 62-63
Orogeny 245
Oropharynx 245
Orpiment 270-271
Orthoclase 269, 271
Orthorhombic system 270
Os 258-259
Oscillating cylinder 390
Oscillating electric field 318
Oscillating magnetic field 318
Oscillating steam engine 390-391
Osculum 166
Osmium 311
Ossicles 79, 174
Ossicles of middle ear 242
Osteichthyes 180
Osteocyte 225
Osteolaemus tetraspis 82
Osteon 225
Ostiole 117
Ostium
  Crayfish 173
  Sea anemone 167
  Spider 170
  Sponge 166
Ostrich 188, 193
Otters 194
Otto cycle 342
Otto, Nikolaus 342
Ouranosaurus 97
Outboard ammunition-feed blister 409
Outboard elevon 421
Outer bud scale 134
Outer casing fitment 597
Outer core 58-59, 41
Outer ear
  Brachiosaurus 91
  Stegoceras 101
  Stegosaurus 92
Outer electrons 310-311
Outer envelope 25-26
Outer fertilized floret 142
Outer jib downhaul 585

Outer jib halyard 585
Outer jib sheet 585
Outer jib stay 582
Outer lamella 225
Outer mantle
  Jupiter 44-45
  Saturn 46-47
Outer tepals
  Glory lily 143
  Lily 140
  Monocotyledons 126
Outfield 556
Outlet manifold 411
Output tray 574
Outrigger 373, 577
Outwash fan 286
Outwash plain 287
Outwash terrace 286
Ovary
  Barnacle 173
  Bony fish 181
  Brachiosaurus 90
  Butterfly 169
  Chimpanzee 202
  Crayfish 173
  Dogfish 179
  Epigeal germination 153
  Fertilization 146-147
  Flower 140-143
  Gallimimus 86
  Human 258-259
  Hypogeal germination 152
  Insect pollination 144
  Lizard 185
  Rose 131
  Spider 170
  Succulent fruit 148-149
  Tortoise 188
Ovate leaf
  Ice-plant 129
  Live-forever 129
  Strawberry 128
Ovda Regio 36, 37
Oven compartment 597
Overarm pass 555
Overhand knot 388
Overhand serve 554
Overhead camshaft engine 368
Overhead control panel 573
Overhead pass 532
Overhead valve engine (OHV) 367, 369
Over-reach fold 555
Overs 558
Oversailing fascia 477, 482, 486
Overthrust fold 61
Overturned fold 61
Overwing emergency exit 572
Oviduct
  Barnacle 173
  Brachiosaurus 90
  Butterfly 169
  Crayfish 173
  Dogfish 179
  Lizard 185
  Spider 170
  Tortoise 187
Ovolo 486
Ovolo molding
  Cathedral dome 487
  Gothic church 472
  Neoclassical building 480
Ovotestis 177
Ovules 140-143
  Bishop pine 124
  Dehiscent fruit 151
  Fertilization 146
  Pine 122
  Scots pine 122
  Smooth cypress 123
  Yew 123

Ovuliferous scales
    Bishop pine 124
    Pine 122
    Scots pine 122
    Smooth cypress 123
    Yew 125
Ovum
    Ancient Roman
        building 462
    Fertilization 146-147
    Scots pine 122
Oxalis sp. 157
Oxbow lake 293
    River features 290
    River's stages 289
"Ox-eye" window
    Baroque church 479,
        481
    Cathedral dome 487
Oxides 268
Oxygen
    Atmospheric
        Atom 596
    Composition 301
    Early microorganisms
        78
    Earth's composition 59
    Earth's crust 58
    Earth's formation 58,
        64
    Helix Nebula 17
    Mars' atmosphere
        43
    Mercury's atmosphere
        35
    Periodic table 311
    Photosynthesis 158
    Seed germination 152
    Structure of red
        supergiant 26
    Respiration 255
Oxygenated blood 255
Oxygen bottle 408
Oxygen group 311
Ovashio current 297
Oyster fungus 114
Oysters 176
Ozone 64
Ozone layer 300

P

Pachycephalosaurus 69,
    85, 100
Pachypteris sp. 68
Pachyrhinosaurus 105
Pacific coastline 295
Pacific Ocean 264-265,
    272, 616-617
Pacific plate 59
Pacing races 554
Pacing sulky 554-555
Pacinian corpuscle
    254-255
Pack-ice 296
Packing tissue
    Dicotyledon leaf 126
    Fern rachis 121
    Golden barrel cactus
        156
    Haworthia truncata 157
    Horsetail stem 120
    Leaf succulents 157
    Lithops bromfieldii
        157
    Monocotyledon leaf
        126
    Roots 132-133
    Stem 134-135
    Stem succulents 156
    String of hearts 157
    Water lily leaf 159
Padded coaming
    Avro biplane 403
    BE 2B bomber 404
Paddle
    Eurypterid fossil 79
    Kayak 560

Paddlesteamer
    19th century 390-391
    Iron 392-393
Paddle wheels 390-391,
    392
Padmakosa 489
Page locator 577
Pagoda 490
Pahoehoe 272
Painted Desert 277
Painting knives 456, 442
Painting tools 442
Pair-cast cylinder 343
Paired cylinder 342
Palace of Westminster
    492-493
Palais de Fontainebleau
    476
Palais de Versailles 482
Palatine Chapel
    Aix-le-Chapelle 484
Palatine tonsil 212,
    244-245
Palatoglossal arch 244
Palazzo Stanga 482
Palazzo Strozzi 474-475
Pale calcite 26
Pale feldspar 26
Paleocene epoch
    Fossil record 279
    Geological timescale
        57
Paleontology 278
Paleozoic era
    Fossil record 279
    Geological time 56
    Palette 143, 436
Palette knife 456
Paling 466, 477
Palisade mesophyll 126,
    159
Palladium 311
Palm
    Danforth anchor 586
    Hand 211
    Roman anchor 372
    Sailmaker's 584
    Tertiary plant 74
Palmar arch 253
Palmaris longus tendon
    231
Palmar vein 253
Palmate leaves 130, 136
Palmate venation 129
Palmette 460-461, 479-480
Pamirs 616
Pampas 264, 617
Panavia Tornado GR1A
    420-421
Pancam mast assembly
    615
Pancreas
    Bird 189
    Bony fish 181
    Chimpanzee 202
    Dogfish 179
    Domestic cat 195
    Frog 182
    Human 215, 249
    Rabbit 196
    Tortoise 187
Pandas 194
Panduriform leaves
    136
Pane 494
Panel 485
    Asian building 491
    Baroque church
        479-481
    Cathedral dome 487
    Gothic building 473
    Islamic building 488
    Medieval building 466,
        469
    Modern building
        496-498
    Neoclassical building
        478-479

Nineteenth-century
    building 495
Renaissance building
    475
Twentieth-century
    building 494
Panel board connector
    570
Pangaea 66, 68-69, 70
Panniers 360, 361, 362
Panoplosaurus 94
Panicle 131
Panoramic camera
    (Pancam) 615
Pantheon 462-463
Pantile 464, 482
Pantograph 528, 530
Pan troglodytes 202
Paper
    Acrylic paint 442
    Calligraphy 444, 445
    Pastels 440
    Printing processes 446,
        447
    Watercolors 438
Paper feed components
    575
Paper hopper 574
Paper output stacker 574
Paper stumps 440
Paper support 575
Papilla
    Flower 140
    Hair 255
    Renal 256
    Tongue 244
Papillary muscle 251
Pappus 142
Papyriform column 459
Parabellum machine-gun
    405
Parabolic dune 283
Paraboloid roof 496, 499
Parachute seed dispersal
    150
Paradise palm 126
Paragaster 166
Parallel dunes 283
Parallelogram 622
Parallel river drainage
    288
Parallel shaft 382
Parallel venation 126
Parana River 264, 617
Parapet
    Ancient Roman
        building 465
    Asian building 491
    Baroque church 481
    Dome 486
    Gothic church 470-472
    Islamic tomb 489
    Medieval building 467
    Neoclassical building
        478, 483
    Nineteenth-century
        building 495
    Twentieth-century
        building 494
Parapet rail 483
Paraphysis 117, 119
Parasaurolophus 98-99
Parasitic anemone 166
Parasitic cone 272-273
Parasitic plants 162-163
Parasitic volcano 275
Paraxeiresia 575
Parceling 388
Parchment
    Gilding 452
    Imitation 445
Pareiasaur 81
Parenchyma
    Dicotyledon leaf 126
    Dryland plants 156-157
    Fern rachis 121
    Golden barrel cactus
        156
    Horsetail stem 120

Monocotyledon leaf 126
Pine stem 125
Roots 132
Stems 134-135
Water lily leaf 159
Parent plant 154
Parietal bone
    Bony fish 181
    Chimpanzee 202
    Human 220-221
Parietal fenestra 102
Parietal lobe 236-237
Parieto-occipital sulcus
    236-237

Parietosquamosal frill
    102-103
Paripteris 66
Paris Metro 528
Paroccipital process
    Iguanodon 96
    Plateosaurus 88
Parrel
    Dhow 376
    Longboat 380
    Sailing warship 377
    Viking karv 375
Parrel beads 384
Parrel tackle 576
Parthenon 461
Partial solar eclipse 32
Partial veil 115
Particle attraction 307
Particle properties 318
Passiflora caerulea 130
Passing brace 473
Passion flower 130
Passive stack vents 602
Pastels 440-441
Pastern 198-199, 554
Pasteur 41
Patagonia 264, 617
Patella
    Domestic cat 195
    Elephant 201
    Hare 197
    Horse 199
    Human 219
    Platypus 206
    Rhesus monkey 202
    Scorpion 170
    Spider 171
Patellar surface 225
Patera
    Neoclassical building 480
    Renaissance building
        476
Pause/play control 577
Paved floor 492
Pavilion 489, 495
Paving slab 499
Pavlova 57
Pavlovia 278
Pavo 20
Pavonis Mons 43
Paw 195
Pawl 580
Pawl slot 587
Paxton, J. 492-493
Pazzi Chapel 475
PCB *see* printed circuit
    board (PCB)
PC card adapter 574
PCs 566
PDAs 568
Pea
    Dry fruit 150
    Danforth anchor 586
Peach 131, 148
Peacock 20
Peak halyard 380
Peat 280
Pebble 590
Peccaries 198
Pecopteris 66
Pectinous muscle 225-226
Pectoral fin
    Bony fish 180-181
    Lamprey 178

Pectoral fin ray 181
Pectoralis major muscle
    226
Pedal board 514
Pedal cluster 540
Pedal disc 167
Pedal-driven bicycle 358
Pedal gland 177
Pedals
    Bass drum 518
    Bicycle 320, 358-359
    Eddy Merckx racing
        bicycle 360
    Harp 511
    Hi-hat cymbal 518
    Piano 514
    Rossin Italian time-trial
        bicycle 361
Pedal-muffler bar
    mechanism 516
Pedal stop 514
Pedestal
    Ancient Roman
        building 462
    Baroque church
        480-481
    Dome 484, 486-487
    French temple 485
    Harp 511
    Neoclassical building
        479
    Renaissance building
        476
Pedice 168
Pedicel
    Brassavola nodosa 162
    Clematis 131
    Dicotyledon flower 127
    Dry fruit 150-151
    Fertilization 146-147
    Florists'
        chrysanthemum 129
    Flowers 140-141, 143
    Fruit development
        146-147
    Oxalis sp. 157
    Pitcher plant 113
    Rose 131
    Rowan 131
    Russian vine 131
    Succulent fruit 148-149
    Sycamore 131
    Vegetative reproduction
        154
    Water lily 159
Pedicle of vertebra 223
Pedicle valve 278
Pediment
    Ancient Greek building
        460
    Ancient Roman
        building 462-463
    Baroque church 480-481
    Neo-Baroque building
        493
    Neoclassical building
        478
    Renaissance building
        476
Pedipalp 170-171
Peduncle 140, 142-143
    Aechmea miniata 162
    Brassavola nodosa 162
    Everlasting pea 129
    Indehiscent fruit 150
    Peach 131
    Peruvian lily 129
    Rowan 131
    Russian vine 131
    Succulent fruit 148-149
    Toadflax 129
    Vegetative reproduction
        154
    Wind-pollinated plant
        144
Peephole 412, 414

Pegasus 19, 20
Pegasus Quasar
    ultralight 426-427
Pegasus XL SE ultralight
    427
Peg-box 510-511
Pegmatite 26
Peg of vertebra 222
Pelagic clay 299
Pelecypoda 176
Peloneustes philarcus 71
Pelota 540
Pelvetia canaliculata 116
Pelvic fin
    Bony fish 180-181
    Dogfish 179
Pelvis
    Bird 189
    Bony fish 181
    Dinosaur 81
    Domestic cat 195
    Elephant 201
    Hare 197
    Horse 199
    Human 256, 258, 259
    Kangaroo 206
    Lizard 184
    Platypus 206
    Rhesus monkey 202
    Seal 204
    Turtle 187
Penalty area 524
Penalty box 524
Penalty kick 530
Penalty spot 529, 540
Pencils 450
Pencil sharpener 430
Pencil slate sea urchin
    175
Pendentive 479, 484, 488
Penguins 188
Penis
    Barnacle 173
    Dolphin 205
    Human 211, 259
    Snail 177
Pennant number 397
Pennsylvanian period 56
Penny washer 383
Pens 430
Penstock 314
Pentagon 622
Pentaradiate symmetry
    174
Pentroof 490
Penumbra 32
Pepo 149
Pepper-pot lantern 481
Perch 180
Percolation 280
Percussion instruments
    516-517
    Drums 518-519
    Electronic 520
    Orchestral
        arrangement 504-505
Perennials 128, 130-131
Pereopod 172-173
Perforated abroad 592
Perianth 140
Pericardial cavity 250
Pericarp 148
    Dry fruit 150-151
    Embryo development
        147
    Fruit development
        146-147
    Succulent fruit 148-149
    Sycamore 131
Pericranium 237
Pericycle 127, 132
Periderm 125
Peridium 115
Perihelion 30-31
Perimeters 622
Perineum 258
Periodic table 310-311
Periodontal ligament 247
Periodontium 247

Periosteum 225
Peripheral nervous system 258
Peripheral temple 460-461
Periscope 396, 397
Perissodactyla 104, 198-199
Peristome tooth 119
Peristyle 461
Peritoneum 249, 257
Permeable limestone
  Caves 284-285
  Lake formation 292
Permeable rock 292
Permeable sandstone 292
Permian period 66-67
  Fossil record 279
  Geological time 57
Peroneal artery 255
Peroneus brevis muscle 227, 233
Peroneus brevis tendon 233
Peroneus longus muscle 233
Peroxisome 217
Perseus 19, 20
Perseus Arm 14-15
Persian ivy 137
Personal computer 566-567
Personal digital assistants (PDAs) 568
Personal lighting 572
Personal music 586-587
Perspective drawing 431
Peru current 296
Peruvian lily 129
Petal molding 480
Petals 140-145
  Clematis 131
  Color 140, 144-145
  Dicotyledons 127
  Everlasting pea 129
  Fertilization 146
  Insect pollination 145
  Monocotyledons 126
  Peruvian lily 129
  Rose 151
  Water lily 159
Petavius 40
Petiole 128, 136-157
  Chusan palm 130
  Clematis 131
  Cobra lily 160
  Dicotyledons 127
  Everlasting pea 129
  Florists' chrysanthemum 129
  Horse chestnut 130
  Kedrostis africana 113
  Maidenhair tree 123
  Monocotyledons 126-127
  Mulberry 130
  Oxalis sp. 157
  Passion flower 130
  Peach 131
  Rock slonecrop 128
  Seedling 153
  Strawberry 128
  String of hearts 157
  Tree fern 112
  Tree mallow 131
  Vegetative reproduction 154
  Venus fly trap 160
  Water Inacinth 158
  Water lily 159
  Wind-pollinated plant 144
Petiolule 157
Petrol 315
Peugeot, Armand 554
Phacops 64
Phaeophyta 16

Phaet 21
Phalaenopsis sp. 126
Phalanges
  Cow 198
  Crocodile 186
  Diplodocus 90
  Domestic cat 195
  Elephant 90
  Eryops 80-81
  Frog 183
  Hare 197
  Horse 198-199
  Kangaroo 206
  Lizard 184
  Parasaurolophus 99
  Plateosaurus 88
  Platypus 206
  Rhesus monkey 202
  Seal 204
  Stegoceras 100-101
  Triceratops 102-103
  Turtle 187
  Tyrannosaurus 84
Phalanx
  African elephant 201
  Archaeopteryx 85
  Arsinoitherium 104
  Baryonyx 85, 87
  Horse 105
  Human 219, 230
  Plateosaurus 88
  Stegoceras 100
  Struthiomimus 87
  Toxodon 107
Phallus impudicus 114
Phanerozoic eon 279
Pharyngeal tubercle 220
Pharynx
  Bony fish 180-181
  Dogfish 179
  Human 212, 244
  Sea anemone 167
  Sea urchin 175
Phascolarctos cinereus 207
Phaseolus sp. 153
Phases of the Moon 41
Phekda 19
Phellem
  Pine root 125
  Stem 154-155
  Woody dicotyledon 127
Phi Andromedae 19
Phidias 35
Philippine plate 59
Phillips, Horatio 402
Philoxenus 35
Philtral ridge 213
Philtrum 213
Phiomia 104
Phloem 138
  Bishop pine 124-125
  Clubmoss stem 120
  Dicotyledons 126-127
  Dodder host 163
  Epiphytic orchid 162
  Fern rachis 121
  Horsetail stem 120
  Marram grass 113
  Monocotyledons 126-127
  Parasite host 163
  Photosynthesis 138
  Pine root/stem 125
  Radicle 152
  Root 152-153
  Sieve tube 134
  Stem 154-155
  Water hyacinth root 158
  Water lily leaf 159
Phloem fibers 134-135
Phloem sieve tube 134
Phobos 42
Phoebe Regio 36
Phoenicopterus ruber 190
Phoenix 19, 20
Phorusrhacos 74
Phosphates 269
Phosphate/sugar band 216

Phosphor imaging screen 611
Phosphorus 311
Photomicrographs of skin and hair 255
Photons 518
Photo print button 570
Photo select button 575
Photosphere 32-35
Photosynthesis 112, 116, 134, 136, 158-159
  Carnivorous plants 160-161
  Organelle 116, 139
Photosynthetic cells 139
  Bishop pine 124
  Coconut palm stem 135
  Water lily leaf 159
Photosynthetic region 157
Photosynthetic tissue
  Cacti 156
  Dicotyledon leaf 126
  Horsetail stem 120
  Marram grass 113
  Monocotyledon leaf 126
  Rush stem 155
Photovoltaic cell 603
Photovoltaic panel 603
Phyla 116
Phyllode 160
Phylum 116
Physalis peruviana 149
Physeter catodon 205
Physical weathering 282
Physics symbols 621
Pi2 Orionis 18
Pi3 Orionis 18
Pi4 Orionis 18
Pi5 Orionis 18
Pi6 Orionis 18
Pia mater 257, 240
Piano 503, 514
Piano nobile 474, 494
Piano, R. 496
Piazza 474
Pi Canis Majoris 21
Piccolo 504, 508
Pictor 21
Pier 484
  Ancient Egyptian temple 459
  Ancient Roman building 465
  Baroque church 480
  Gothic church 470
  Medieval building 467-469
  Renaissance building 476-477
  Twentieth-century building 495
Pier buttress 469-471, 486
Pietra dura inlay 489
Piezoelectric inkjet printhead 575
Pigments 433, 434, 436
Pigs 104, 198
Pilaster
  74-gun ship 581
  Ancient Greek building 461
  Ancient Roman building 465-465
  Asian temple 490-491
  Baroque church 479-481
  Cathedral dome 484, 487
  Gothic church 471
  Neoclassical building 478, 483
  Renaissance building 476
Pileus 114-115
Pillar
  Asian buildings 490-491
  Domed roof 486
  Gothic church 472

Ironclad 393
Renaissance building 477
Twin bollards 587
Pillow lava 298
Pilotis 494
Pilot light 594
Pilot's cockpit
  LVG CVI fighter 405
  Tornado 420
Pilot's cradle 398-399
Pilot's seat
  Airbus 380 575
  Avro biplane 402
  Curtiss biplane 398
  Pegasus Quasar ultralight 427
Pin
  Capstan 587
  Dome timbering 486
Pinacocyte 166
Pineal body 212, 236
Pine hull 575
Pines 122, 124-125
Pinguicula caudata 161
Pinion
  Benz Motorwagen 355
  Ford Model T 538
  Hand drill 601
Pinna
  Elephant 201
  Everlasting pea 129
  Fern 121
  Gorilla 203
  Human 242-243
  Kangaroo 207
  Leaves 136-157
  Rabbit 196
  Rat 196
  Sago palm 123
  Tree fern 112-113
Pinnacle
  Baroque church 479, 481
  Gothic church 470, 472-473
  Medieval church 469
  Nineteenth-century building 493
  Renaissance building 476
Pinnate leaves 136-157
  Mahonia 130-131
  Rowan 150
  Sago palm 123
Pinned sheepshank 389
Pinnipedia 204
Pinnule 121, 137
Pinocytotic vesicle 217
Pintle strap 378
Pinus muricata 72, 124-125
Pinus sp. 122, 124-125
Pinus sylvestris 122
Pi Pegasi 19
Pipette 512
Pips 148-149
Pi Sagittarii 21
Piscis 19, 20
Pisiform bone 230
Piste 556, 557
Pistol shooting 548
Piston
  Disc brake 365
  Early engines 342-543
  "Ellerman Lines" steam locomotive 525
  Ford diesel engine 547
  Mid West two-stroke engine 410
  Modern engines 344-345
  Relief-printing press 449
  Steam locomotive 324
  Two-stroke engine 366

Velocette OHV engine 367
Volkswagen Beetle 340
Piston engines 410-411, 424
Piston rod 324, 334, 590
Piston valves
  Brass instruments 506
  Cornet 507
  "Ellerman Lines" steam locomotive 525
  Flugelhorn 507
  Stringed instruments 510
  Trumpet 506
  Tuba 507
Pisum sativum 150
Pitatus 40
Pitch
  Brass instruments 506
  Drums 518
  Musical notation 502
  Percussion instruments 516
  Propeller action 390
  Screw thread angle 520
  Woodwind instruments 508
Pitched roof
  Ancient Roman building 462, 464
  Gothic church 471-472
  Medieval building 466-468
  Nineteenth-century building 492
  Renaissance building 476-477
  Twentieth-century building 495
Pitcher 556
Pitcher plants 113, 160-161
Pitches
  Australian rules football 528
  Baseball 536
  Cricket 538
  Gaelic football 529
  Lacrosse 540
Pitching wedge
  Baseball 537
  Golf 547
Pitfall traps 160
Pitot head
  ARV light aircraft 425
  BAe-146 jetliner components 412
  Bell-47 helicopter 422
  Concorde 416-417
  Hawker Tempest fighter 409
  LVG CVI fighter 405
  Schweizer helicopter 423
  Tornado 420
Pitot mast 407
Pitot tube
  Astrolabe 377
  BAe-146 jetliner components 414
  Viking ships 574-575
Pixel 570, 571
Place kick 530
Placenta
  Dry fruit 150-151

Fern pinnule 121
Human 260
Succulent fruit 148-149
Placental mammals 74, 104
Placer deposits 280
Plagioclase feldspar 275
Plains viscacha 197
Planck 41
Plane shapes 622
Planetary nebula
  Nebulae and star clusters 17
  Small stars 24-25
Planetary rotation 30
Planets
  Jupiter 44-45
  Mars 42-43
  Mercury 34-35
  Neptune 50-51
  Pluto 50-51
  Saturn 46-47
  Solar system 30-31
  Uranus 48-49
  Venus 36-37
Planking
  Ironclad 393
  Longboat 380
  Roman corbita 373
  Sailing warship 377
  Tea clipper 592
Plantar calcaneonavicular ligament 252
Plant bodies 116
Plant capital 459
Plant-eating dinosaurs 68, 70
Plant matter 280
Plant remains
  Fossils 278-279
  Mineral resources 280
  Sedimentary rocks 276
Plants 56, 66
  Electromagnetic radiation 314
  Flowering 57, 70, 72
  Fossil record 279
  Non-flowering 68
Plant variety 112-113
Plasma 506
Plasma spectrometer 614
Plaster 452, 464-465
Plasterboard 602
Plastic bumper 354
Plastic fletch 548
Plastic front wings 554
Plastic insulator 316, 317
Plastic rackets 544
Plastid 116
Platanus x acerifolia 134
Platband 481
Plate
  Etching press 477
  Motorcycle clutch 366
  "O Ring" drive chain 366
Plateau
  Neptune's rings 50
  Structure of Neptune 51
Plateaus 276-277
Plate boundaries 62, 273
Plate clip 587
Platelets 253
Plate movements 58-59
  Faults and folds 60
  Mountain building 62-65
Platen 449
Plateosaurus 69, 88-89
Plate tectonics 58-59, 617
Platform
  Cathedral dome 487
  Early tram 332
  Medieval building 467-468
  Modern building 498
Platform diving 558

Platlorm stage 477
Platinum 511
Plat Iesene 480
Plato 40
Platypus 206-207
Platysma 229
Playa 283
Play button 585
Player's bench
  Basketball 532
  Football 526
  Handball 535
  Ice hockey 550
  Volleyball 534
Play/pause control 577
Plaza 498
Pleiades 14, 16, 19, 20
Pleistocene epoch
  Fossil record 279
  Geological timescale 57
Pleistocene period 76
Plenum chamber 344-345
Plenum ring 418
Pleopod 172
Plesiochelys latiscutata 73
Plesiosaurs 70-71
Pleurotus pulmonarius
  114
Plica circulare 249
Plicate lamina 127
Pliers 521
Plinth
  Baroque church 480
  French temple 485
  Islamic tomb 489
  Modern building 499
  Neoclassical building
    479, 483
  Renaissance building 476
  Twentieth-century
    building 494-495
Pliocene epoch
  Fossil record 279
  Geological timescale 57
Plough anchor 386
Plug-ins 521
Plug lead conduit 337
Plugs 272-275
  Igneous rock structures
    274
Plumage 188
Plume 45
Plumose anemone 166
Plumule 147, 152-153
Plunge 60
Plunge pool 289, 291
Pluto 31, 50-51
Plutonium 310-311
Plutonium power supply
  614
Plywood roof deck 603
Plywood skin 404
Pneumatic tires 358, 555
Podetium 114
Podium 463, 499
Point
  Angling hook 562
  Cricket 538
  Double bass bow 511
  Sailmaker's fid 384
  Sculpting tool 452-453
  Violin bow 510
Point bar
  Mississippi Delta 291
  River's stages 289
Pointed arch 466, 467,
  469, 472
Pointed hog hair brush 434
Pointed riffler 454
Pointed sable brush 444
Pointing 383
Poison duct 170
Poison gland
  Octopus 176
  Spider 170
Polacanthus 95
Polar band 36
Polar body 606, 607
Polar bottom water 296

Polar easterlies 300
Polar fronts 302
Polar hood 36
Polaris 14, 18-19
Polar jet stream 300
Polar nuclei 146
Poles 297, 500
Pole star 14, 18
Pole vault 542
Polian vesicle 175
Poll 199
Pollen 140, 142, 144-145
  Dicotyledon flower 126
  Fertilization 146-147
Pollen-forming structures
  122
Pollen grains 144-145
  Fertilization 146-147
  Pine 122
  Scots pine 122
Pollen sac wall 144
Pollen tubes
  Fertilization 146-147
  Scots pine 122
Pollination 144-145, 122
Pollux 18, 21
Polonium 311
Polycarbonate plastic bin
  592
Polyester 588
Polygala chamaebuxus
  144
Polygnotus 35
Polygonum
  baldschuanicum 131
Polyhedral dome 486-487
Polypropylene rope 388
Polythene 306
Polytrichum commune 119
Polyurethane insulation
  603
Pome 131, 149
Pommel 554
Pond weeds 158
Pons 212, 256-257
Poop break 373
Poop deck
  74-gun ship 381
  Iron paddlesteamer 392
  Roman corbita 373
Poop rail
  74-gun ship 381
  Wooden sailing ship
    378
Poor metals 310-311
Popchu-Sa Temple 490
Popliteal artery 253
Popliteal fossa 210
Porch 470-471
Porcupines 196-197
Pore
  Bishop pine needle 124
  Blackberry 147
  Dryland plants 156-157
  Elder stem 130
  Epigeal germination
    153
  False fruit 148
  Gas exchange 158, 160
  Golden barrel cactus
    156
  Haworthia truncata 157
  Leaf 138-139
  Liverwort 118
  Monocotyledon leaf 126
  Nuclear membrane 217
  Perennial bark 130-131
  Pollen grain 144-145
  Seed 153
  Sponge 166
  Water absorption 150,
    153
  Wetland plants 158
  Woody plants 130-131
  Woody stems 134
Porifera 166
Porocyte 166
Porous limestone 284
Porous stipe 114

Porphyritic andesite 275
Porpoises 204
Porrima 21
Porsche, Ferdinand 340
Port
  Trojan two-stroke
    engine 342
  Wooden sailing ship
    379
Portal 476, 480
Portal vein 252
Porta Nigra 462, 465
Port bower anchor 377,
  395
Port foremast 376
Porthole
  Battleship 394
  Dome 487
  Frigate 397
Portico
  Ancient Greek building
    460-461
  Ancient Roman
    building 462-463
  Neoclassical building
    482-483
  Renaissance building
    475
Portugal 331
Portuguese bowline 388
Position guide 447
Positive electric charge
  316
Positive ions 308, 310
Positive metal comb 316
Positive terminal 316, 317
Positron 22
Post 481, 486
Postabdominal spine 169
Postacetabular process 82
Postcentral gyrus 237
Post-crural musculature
  90
Posterior antebrachial
  musculature 86, 91
Posterior aorta 170
Posterior arch 222
Posterior border of vomer
  220
Posterior brachial muscle
  86, 91
Posterior branch of spinal
  nerve 223
Posterior cerebral artery
  252
Posterior chamber 241
Posterior chamber of
  cloaca 185
Posterior column 223
Posterior crural muscle 87
Posterior cuneonavicular
  ligament 232
Posterior dorsal fin
  Bony fish 181
  Dogfish 179
  Lamprey 178
Posterior horn 223
Posterior nasal aperture
  220
Posterior nasal spine 220
Posterior part of tongue
  245
Posterior petal 141
Posterior root 223, 238
Posterior semicircular
  canal 243
Posterior sepal 141
Posterior tarsometatarsal
  ligament 232
Posterior tentacle 177
Posterior tibial artery 253
Posterior tibial nerve 238
Posterior tubercle 222
Posterior vena cava 182
Posterior wing of shell 176
Posterolateral horn 94
Post-glacial stream 286
Post-glacial valley 286
Post-modernism 296, 496

Post-motor micropore
  filter 592
Potassium 35, 58, 286,
  310
Potassium chromate
  solution 312
Potassium dichromate
  ions 312
Potassium iodide 312-313
Potassium nitrate 313
Potassium permanganate
  306
Potato 128
Potential energy 314, 315
Potholes 284
Pouch 206
Power bar 552
Power drill 600-601
Power button
  Home cinema 585
  Inkjet printer 574
  Personal computer
    566-567
Power levers 573
Power output 360, 366
Power/play/pause button
  586
Power stations 314, 315
Power steering belt 351
Power steering pump 544,
  351
Power stroke 343
Power-to-weight ratio
  328
Power transistor heat sink
  (dissipator) 585
Power transistors 585
Practice projectile 396
Pradakshina 491
Praesepe 18
Prairie style 495
Praseodymium 310
Pratt & Whitney Canada
  turbofan engine
  418-419
Pratt & Whitney Canada
  turboprop engine 419
Pratt & Whitney radial
  engine 406-407
Praxiteles 35
Preacetabular process 82
Precambrian period 56,
  64-65, 279
Precambrian seas 78
Precentral gyrus 237
Precious metals 311
Precipitate 312
Precipitation 288, 302-303
Predatory dinosaurs 84
Predatory theropods 85
Predentary bone
  Arsinoitherium 104
  Iguanodon 96
  Lambeosaurus 99
  Protoceratops 102
  Triceratops 103
Prefix 577
Prehensile tail 202
Prehistoric foods 109
Pre-load adjustor 365
Premaxilla
  Baryonyx 83
  Arsinoitherium 104-105
  Bony fish 181
  Chimpanzee 202
  Elephant 201
  Frog 183
  Iguanodon 96
  Lambeosaurus 99
Premolars
  Australopithecus 107
  Bear 106, 194
  Chimpanzee 202
  Horse 105
  Human 246
  Lion 194
Prenocephale 100-101
Preopercular bone
  181

Preparatory drawing
  430-431
Prepubic process
  Iguanodon 96
  Parasaurolophus 98
  Stegosaurus 95
Prepubis
  Ornithischian 82
  Stegoceras 100-101
Prepuce 259
Preserved remains 278
Press
  Etching 447
  Lithographic printing
    446
  Relief-printing 449
Pressed steel wheel 340
Pressure
  Formation of black hole
    29
  Igneous and
    metamorphic rocks 274
  Mineral resources 280
  Stellar black hole 29
  Volcanic features 273
Pressure line 418
Pressure plate 366
Pressurized cabin 406
Pressurized keel box 417
Pressurized strut 425
Pressurized water reactor
  314
Presta valve 361
Presynaptic axon 239
Presynaptic membrane
  239
Preview monitor slot 575
Preview monitor socket
  574
Previous file button 577
Previous key 568
Previous/next track
  buttons 585
Previous track control 587
Prickers 383
Prickle
  Blackberry 147
  Bramble stem 130
  Rose stem 130
  Slender thistle 129
Primary bronchus 215
Primary colors 439
Primary-drive gear 366
Primary flight display 573
Primary flight feathers
  188, 191
Primary follicle 258
Primary leaf 121
Primary mirror 612
Primary mirror housing
  613
Primary mycelium 115
Primary remiges 188, 191
Primary root 132-133
  Germination 152-153
  Seedling 152-153
Primary teeth 246
Primary thallus 114
Primary xylem 125, 153
Primates 108, 202-205,
  279
Primer 548, 436
Primitive crocodilians 68
Primitive life-forms 64
Primitive mammals 206
Principal arteries and
  veins 253
Principal rafter
  Ancient Roman mill 464
  Dome 486
  Gothic building 473
Printer 574-575
Printer cover 574, 575
Printing block 449
Printing papers 447
Print making 446-447,
  448-449
Prism 318, 623, 590
Prismatic habit 271

Privy 380
Probactosaurus 97
Probes, space 614-615
Proboscidea 104
Proboscis 169, 201
Procambial strand 134
Procerus muscle 229
Processing cooling fan
  567
Processing light 575
Processional path 470
Procompsognathus 87
Procoptodon 76
Procyon 8, 21
Procyon lotor 195
Production line
  Mass-production 338
  Modern bodywork 348
  Modern trim 352
Programme display 577
Program name 577
Projectile 396
Projector assembly 581
Projector lens 611
Prokaryotes 78
Prolegs 169
Promethium 311
Prominence 32-33
Pronaos 461
Pro-otic bone 183
Propagative structures
  154-155
Propellant 396
Propellant tank 615
Propeller 390-391
  ARV light aircraft 425
  Battleship 395
  Biplanes and triplanes
    402-405
  Early monoplanes
    400-401
  Ford diesel engine 347
  Frigate 397
  Hawker Tempest
    components 408
  Lockheed Electra
    airliner 406-407
  Pegasus Quasar
    ultralight 427
  Pioneers of flight
    598-599
  Submarine 396
  World War I aircraft
    404-405
Propeller-bolt collar 411
Propeller brake pad 419
Propeller drive flange
  ARV light aircraft 425
  Modern piston aero-
    engines 410-411
Propeller drive gearbox
  427
Propeller drive shaft 408
Propeller-hub spinner 407
Propeller shaft
  Brazilian battleship 395
  Wright Flyer 399
Propeller-shaft boss 595
Propeller-shaft bracing
  strut 388-599
Propeller shaft rear
  bearing 410
Propeller speed probe 419
Propeller spinner 408, 409
Propodus 172, 173
Propylaeum 460
Prosauropods 83
Proscapular process 187
Prosimians 203
Prosimii 202
Prosoma 170, 171
Prostate gland 257, 259
Prostyle colonnade 483
Protactinium 310
Protective clothing
  Cricket 559
  Football 528
  Ice hockey 550-551

Protective eyewear 544
Protective gaiter 422
Protective outer layer 125
Protective root covering 155
Protective scale 154
Protective scale leaf 155
Protein body 112
Protein fibers 166
Protein matrix 166
Protein synthesis site 159
Proterozoic eon 279
Proteus 50
Prothallus 121
Prothorax 168
Protista 112, 116
Protoceratops 102-103
Protogalaxies 10-11
Proton 308, 316
  Atomic mass 310
  Atomic number 310
  Fluorine-19 309
  Nuclear fusion 22
Protonema 119
Protostar 24, 26
Protoxylem
  Dicotyledon root 127
  Monocotyledon root 127
  Root 132-133
Proventriculus
  Bird 189
  Crayfish 173
Prow 572, 575
Prowhead 374
Proxima Centauri 18
Proximal convoluted tubule 256-257
Proximal interphalangeal joint 231
Proximal phalanx 230, 232
Prunus persica 131
Psathyrella candolleana 115
Pseudocarps 148-149
Pseudo-Corinthian capital 476
Psi Sagittarii 21
Psittacosaurus 100, 103
Psoas major muscle 225, 257
Pteraspis 65
Pterichthyodes 65
Pteridium aquilinum 121
Pterois volitans 180
Pteron 460-461, 463
Pterosaurs 70-71
Pterygoid bone 185
Pterygoid hamulus 220
Pterygoid plate 220
Ptolemaeus 40
Ptolemaic-Roman period 459
"P" turret 595
P-type silicon 605
Pubic bone 261
Pubic ramus 257
Pubic symphysis 258
Pubis
  Archaeopteryx 85
  Bird 189
  Diplodocus 90
  Eryops 81
  Gallimimus 86
  Human 218, 224, 259
  Iguanodon 96
  Ornithischian 82
  Plateosaurus 88
  Saurischian 82
  Stegosaurus 93
  Struthiomimus 87
  Tyrannosaurus 84
Pubofemoral ligament 224
Pudenda 211
Pudendal nerve 238
Puffballs 114
Pugin, A.W.N. 493
Pull-down edit menu button 577
Pulley bolt 560

Pulley rim rear brake 362
Pulley wheel
  Simple pulleys 520
  Van de Graaff generator 316
Pulmonary artery
  Frog 182
  Human 251, 255, 254-255
Pulmonary semilunar valve 251
Pulmonary trunk 251, 255
Pulmonary vein 251, 255, 254
Pulp artery and vein 247
Pulp chamber 247
Pulp horn 247
Pulp nerve 247
Pulsar 28
Pumice 275
  Marble carving 453
Pump
  Nuclear power station 314
  Testing angle wax 513
Pump drive belt 410
Pump drive shaft 411
Pump piston 391
Pupa 168
Pupil
  Caiman 186
  Human 213, 226, 241
Pupil's cockpit 405
Puppis 18, 21
Purchase 582-583
Purchase wire 594
Pure substances 306
Purfling 510, 511
Purkinje's cells 257
Purlin 473
Pusher propeller
  Pegasus Quasar ultralight 426
  Pioneers of flight 398-399
Push moraine 286
Push-rod 365, 367
Putter 547
Putting green 546
Putto 476
Putty eraser 430, 440
Pygal shield 187
Pygostyle 189
Pylon 314
Pylon fairing 427
Pylon forward fairing 573
Pylon strut 427
Pyloric cecum
  Bony fish 181
  Starfish 174
Pyloric duct 174
Pyloric region of stomach 179
Pyloric sphincter muscle 249
Pyloric stomach 174
Pyramid 458, 625
Pyrenees 77, 265
Pyrenoid 112, 116
Pyrites 268
  Intrusive igneous rocks 275
Pyroclasts 272
Pyromorphite 269
Pyroxene 52, 267
Pyxis 18

Q

Quadrant arch 468
Quadrate bone 181
Quadratojugal bone
  Frog 183
  Heterodontosaurus 83
Quadrilateral 489
Quadripartite vault 469

Quadrupedal dinosaurs 88, 92, 96, 100
Quadruplanes 402
Quark 309
Quarter back 526
Quarterdeck 380-581
Quarterdeck house 376
Quarter gallery 381
Quarter glass 348
Quarter light 340-341
Quarter panel molding 352
Quarter trim panel 352
Quartz
  Color 271
  Metamorphic rock 267
  Oxides/hydroxides 268
Quasar (quasi-stellar object)
  Galaxies 12
  Objects in universe 11
  Origin and expansion of universe 10-11
Quasar nucleus 13
Quaternary period 57, 76-77
  Fossil record 279
Quatrefoil 471-473
Quaver 502
Quayside 387
Queen-post 473
Quercus palustris 74
Quercus petraea 131
Quick-release mechanism 425
Quick-release strap 560
Quill
  Drill 601
  Feather 191
  Writing tool 444
Quinacridone red 442
Quiver 548
Quoin
  Baroque church 481
  Medieval building 466
  Nineteenth-century building 492
  Renaissance building 476

R

Rabbit line 380
Rabbits 196-197
Raccoons 194-195
Race car 356-357
Raceme 129
Rachilla 137
Rachis 136-137
  Bipinnate leaf 137
  Couch grass 113
  Everlasting pea 129
  Feather 191
  Fern 121
  Hogweed 129
  Pinnate leaf 136-137
  Rowan leaf 130
  Tree fern 112
  Tripinnate leaf 137
Racing bicycle 560
Racing chain 361
Racing colors 554-555
Racing saddle 554
Racing sidecar 368-369
Racing "silks" 554-555
Racing tire 365
  Formula One race car 356-357
  Suzuki RGV500 368-369
Racketball 544-545
Racket sports 544-545
Radar
  Modern jetliners 412
  Modern military aircraft 420-421
  World War II aircraft 408

RADAR antenna 397
RADAR for gunnery and missile control 397
Radial canal
  Jellyfish 167
  Sea urchin 175
  Starfish 174
Radial cartilage 180
Radial diffuser 418
Radial engine
  Curtiss biplane 398-399
  Lockheed Electra airliner 406-407
Radial groove 365
Radial nerve
  Human 238
  Sea urchin 175
Radial river drainage 288
Radial spoke 47
Radial studio easel 437
Radial wall 465
Radiation 38
  Electromagnetic 314
  Energy emission from Sun 22
  Galaxies 12-13
  Nebulae and star clusters 16
  Ozone formation 64
  Universe 10
Radiative zone
  Structure of main sequence star 24
  Structure of Sun 33
Radiator
  1906 Renault 356-357
  ARV light aircraft 424
  Ford Model T 538-539
  Hawker Tempest fighter 409
  Honda VF750 564
  Kirby BSA 569
  Renault Clio 351
  Wright Flyer 399
Radiator-access cowling 408
Radiator air vent 368
Radiator apron 339
Radiator fan 326
Radiator filler neck 339
Radiator outlet 409
Radiator pipe 364
Radiator shell 339
Radicle
  Dry fruit 150
  Embryo development 147
  Epigeal germination 153
  Hypogeal germination 152
Radio
  Bell-47 helicopter 422
  Renault Clio 353
  Streamed internet 577
Radio aerial 426
Radio antenna 395
Radio galaxies 12-13
Radio image 13
Radio lobe 13
Radio mast 494
Radio operator's seat 408
Radio plugs 425
Radio speaker 353
Radio tuner aerial socket (FM) 585
Radio tuner FM/AM selector 585
Radio-ulna 183
Radio wave beam 28
Radio-wave emission 15
Radio waves
  Electromagnetic

spectrum 318
Pulsar 28
Radio image of Centaurus A 13
Radium 310
Radius
  Archaeopteryx 85
  Arsinoitherium 104
  Baryonyx 85
  Bird 189, 191
  Circle 622
  Crocodile 186
  Diplodocus 90
  Domestic cat 195
  Elephant 90, 201
  Eryops 80
  Euoplocephalus 94
  Hare 197
  Horse 199
  Human 218, 230-231
  Iguanodon 96
  Kangaroo 206
  Lizard 184
  Parasaurolophus 99
  Pareiasaur 81
  Plateosaurus 88
  Platypus 206
  Rhesus monkey 202
  Seal 204
  Stegoceras 100-101
  Struthiomimus 87
  Toxodon 106
  Triceratops 102
  Turtle 187
Radius arm 357
Radius rod
  Avro Tutor biplane 403
  Ford Model T 538-539
Radome
  BAe-146 jetliner 415
  Concorde, the 416-417
  Tornado 420
Radon 311
Radula 176-177
RAF Central Flying School badge 402
RAF roundels 403, 409
Raft 496
Raft spider 171
Rail
  Electric tram 332
  Kayak 560
  Neoclassical building 483
  Relief-printing press 449
  Train 330-351
  Wooden sailing ship 379
Rail chair 324
Railing
  Asian building 490-491
  Cathedral dome 487
  Medieval building 467
  Nineteenth-century building 493
  Renaissance theater 477
Railroad crest 326
Railroad system 324
Rain 302
  Rain erosion 294
  Rain gutter 412, 415
Rainwater
  Caves 284
  Weathering and erosion 282
Raised beach 295
Raja clavata 179
Raked windshield 333
Raking cornice
  Ancient Greek building 460-461

Ancient Roman building 462-463
Baroque church 480-481
Neoclassical building 478
Raking stempost 376
Ram 572
Ramaria formosa 114
Ramentum 112, 121
Rammer 396
Ramp 467, 494
Ram scoop
  BE 2B bomber 404
  Tornado 420-421
Rangefinder
  Battleship 394
  Gun turret 396
Ranks 514
Ranunculus sp. 127, 132-133
Raphe 153
Rapid-fire pistols 548
Rapids
  River features 290
  River's stages 289
Rare earths 510
Rare gases 311
Ras Algethi 20
Ras Alhague 19, 20
Rasp 452
Raspberry 149
Rat 104, 196
Ratchet
  Brace-and-bit 601
  Fixed-spool reel 562
Ratchet mechanism 601
Ratchet wheel 334
Rating 378
Rating's mess 397
Ratline 576, 379
Rat's tail 384
Rat tail 589
Rattlesnake 185
Raw sienna 434
Raw umber 434
Ray
  Branchiostegal 181
  Caudal fin 180
  Dorsal fin 181
  Jawless fish 178
  Liverwort 118
  Mercury 34
  Near side of the Moon 40
  Parenchyma cells 134
  Pectoral fin 181
Ray crater 34
Ray florets
  Florists' chrysanthemum 129
  Sunflower 142, 145
Reactants 312
Reactive metals 310-311
Reactor core 314
Reactor space 397
Rear axle 358
Rear axle adjustor 364, 568
Rear bearing 411
Rear brake 362
Rear brake cable 359, 360
Rear brake calliper 368
Rear brake pedal 368
Rear bulkhead 417
Rear cantilever brake 358
Rear chassis plate 597
Rear cylinder exhaust pipe 568
Rear derailleur 358, 360
Rear door 339
Rear dropouts 358
Rear hatch 349
Rear hub quick-release spindle 358
Rear indicator 362

Rear lamp
  Oldsmobile trim 337
  Volkswagen Beetle 340
Rear leaf spring 338
Rear light
  Bicycle 360
  Italian State Railroads
    Class 402 528
  Paris Metro 328
Rear limit line 557
Rear-mounted propeller
  Pegasus Quasar
    ultralight 426
  Pioneers of flight
    598-599
Rear oil lamp 356
Rear shelf 352
Rear shock absorber 340
Rear subframe 364
Rear tail light 329
Rearview mirror
  1906 Renault 336
  Formula One race car
    357
  Renault Clio 353
Receiver
  American squash 545
  Badminton 545
  International squash
    545
  Racketball 545
  Tennis 544
Receiving line 545
Receptacles
  Algae 116
  Dicotyledon flower 127
  Dry fruit 150-151
  Fertilization 147
  Flower 140-36
  Rose 131
  Seaweed 116-117
  Succulent fruit 148-149
Recessed arch 488
Recessed hinge 414, 415
Rechargeable battery
  Nintendo Wii Fit
    Plus 579
Recharge area 292
Reclining seat 572
Recoil cylinder 396
Recon Jet 590
Reconnaissance camera 420
Recorded information 521
Recording light 585
Record/Stop button 586
Rectal cecum 174
Rectal gland 179
Rectangle 622
Rectangular block 623
Rectangular cross-band
  574
Rectangular pier 465, 467,
  480
Rectangular river
  drainage 288
Rectangular window
  Ancient Roman
    building 465
  Asian building 490
  Baroque church 481
  Medieval building 466
  Renaissance building
    474, 476
Rectum
  Bird 189
  Butterfly 169
  Chimpanzee 202
  Cow 198
  Dogfish 179
  Dolphin 205
  Elephant 200
  Frog 182
  Human 215, 248-249,
    258-259, 261
  Lizard 185
  Rabbit 196
  Starfish 174
  Tortoise 187

Rectus abdominis muscle
  226
Rectus femoris muscle
  226
Recumbent fold 61
Red algae 116
Red blood cells 217,
  253
Red-brown crocoite 271
Red card 524
Red cedar boarding 602
Red deer 199
Red dwarf 23
Red earth 433, 434-435
Red filter signal light 407
Red giant
  Small stars 24-25
  Stars 22-23
Red howler monkey 203
Red light 318
  Main-line signaling
    system 330, 331
  Red light photon 318
Red marble 450
Red port navigation light
  406
Red sandstone 277
Red seaweeds 117
Red spot 44-45
Red supergiant
  Massive stars 26-27
  Stars 22-23
Reduction gearbox
  Early piston aero-
    engines 410-411
  Jet engines 419
  Turboprop engine 419
Redwall limestone 277
Red warning light
  Italian State Railroads
    Class 402 528
  Paris Metro 328
Redwood trees 70
Reed pen 444
Reef knot 388
Reef point 585
Reel
  Angling equipment
    562-563
  Fencing piste 557
  Frigate 397
Reel foot 562-563
Reel scoop 562-563
Reel seat 563
Reentrant angle 485
Reentrant corner 479
Referee
  Basketball 532
  Football 526
  Gaelic football 529
  Ice hockey 550
  Judo 556
  Lacrosse 541
  Rugby 530
  Soccer 524
  Swimming 558
  Volleyball 534
Referee's crease 550
Refe'ree's equipment 524
Referee's signals
  Basketball 533
  Football 527
Reflection 318
Reflection nebula 16
Reflector
  Ford Model T 339
  Oldsmobile trim 337
Refraction 318-319
Refractory (heat-resistant)
  skin 421
Refrigerator freight car
  527
Régie Autonome des
  Transports Parisien 328
Regional metamorphism
  274
Regional weather 302
Registers 514
Regolith (soil) 41

Regula 461
Regulator
  "Mallard" express
    steam locomotive 325
  "Rocket" steam
    locomotive 324
Regulator valve 525
Regulus 18, 21
Rein 554
Reinforce 395
Reinforced concrete 494,
  497
  Ties 550
Reinforced plinth
  499
Rein terret 555
Relative atomic mass
  310
Relay baton 543
Relay running 542
Release 537, 543
Release adjustment screw
  552
Release button 425
Release lever 563
Release spring 563
Relief 458
Relief printing 446
Relief printing equipment
  449
Relieving arch
  Ancient Roman
    building 462, 465
  Medieval building
    466-467
Remiges 188, 191
Remote control 584, 585
Remote control sensor
  585
Removable archery
  screen 377
Renaissance buildings
  474-477
Renal artery 256-257
Renal column 256
Renal papilla 256
Renal pelvis 256
Renal sinus 256
Renal vein 256-257
Renault (1906) 336-337
Renault Clio 348-353
Renault logo 348
Renewable energy
  604-605
Renoir 35
Repeater indicator
  333
Repeating pattern
  507
Replum 151
Reply button 590
Reproduction
  Algae 116-117
  Cloning 606-607
  Fertilization 146-147
  Flowering plants 140
  Liverwort 118
  Moss 118-119
  Vegetative 154-155
Reproductive canal 94
Reproductive chamber
  116
Reproductive organs
  259
Reproductive structures
  Flower 140-143
  Pollination 144
Reproductive system
  258-259
Reptiles 80-81, 184-187
  Carboniferous period
    66
  Dinosaurs 82-85
  Fossil record 279
  Jurassic period 70
  Present-day 82
  Rhynchosaurian 71
  Synapsid skull 67
  Triassic period 68

Reptilia 184, 186
Repulsion 316-317
"Request identification"
  aerial 421
Rerradiated heat 300-301
Reredos 470
Rescue strap 561
Reservoir 314
Reset button 560
Resin canal
  Bishop pine needle 124
  Pine root-stem 125
Resistance 316
Resonator 513
Respiration 255
Respiratory system 254-255
Rest
  Musical notation 502
  Newton's first motion
    law 321
Resurgence 284-285
Retaining bolt hole 366
Retaining screw 562, 563
Reticulum
  Digestive system of a
    cow 198
  Southern stars 20
Retina 240-241
Retraction jack 417
Retractor muscle 167
Retreating glacier 286
Retrices 188
Retroarticular process 83
Return 486-487
Rev counter 569
Reversed bend hook 562
Reversed dive piked 559
Reverse dip-slip fault 61
Reverse dive 558
Reverse-flow combustion
  chamber 418
Reverse lever 342
Reverser handle 325
Reverse shock wave 27
Reversible reactions 312
Reversing shaft lock
  control 325
Reversing wheel 392
Revivalist style 493-494
Rewind button 577
Rhamphodopsis 65
Rhamphorhynchus sp. 71
Rheas 188
Rhenium 310
Rhesus monkey 202
Rhinoceroses 198-199
Rhizine 114
Rhizoids 118-119
  Alga 116
  Fern 121
  Liverwort 118
  Moss 119
Rhizomes 154-155
  Fern 121
  Herbaceous flowering
    plants 128
  Horsetail 120
  Water hyacinth 158
  Water lily 159
Rhizophore 120
Rho1 Sagittarii 21
Rhodium 311
Rhodophyta 116
Rhomboideus major
  muscle 227
Rhomboid leaves 137
Rhombus 622
Rhopalium 167
Rhynchosaurian reptile 71
Rhynchosaurs 68-69, 71
Rhyolite 274-275
Rhyolitic lava 272
Rhythm
  Drums 518
  Percussion instruments
    516
Rhythm pattern selector
  520
Rib

Acoustic guitar 512
  Archaeopteryx 85
Avro triplane 403
Baroque church 479
BE 2B tail 405
BE 2B wings 404
Bird 189
  Brachiosaurus 90
Concorde, the 417
Crocodile 186
  Diplodocus 90
Dome 486-487
Domestic cat 195
Double bass 511
Elephant 201
  Eryops 80
  Euoplocephalus 94
  Gallimimus 86
Hare 197
Herbaceous (lowering
  plant 128
Horse 199
Kangaroo 206
Lizard 184
Medieval church 469
Modern building 499
Pareiasaur 81
Pegasus Quasar
  ultralight 426-427
Pegasus XL SE
  ultralight 426
  Plateosaurus 88
Platypus 206
Rhesus monkey 202
Seal 204
Snake 185
  Stegoceras 101
  Struthiomimus 87
  Toxodon 107
  Triceratops 102
  Tyrannosaurus 84
Violin 510
  Westlothiana 81
Riband 381
Ribbon connectors 585
Ribbon Lake 287
Ribbon window 499
Rib cage
  Carnivores 195
  Human 218
Ribosome
  Chloroplast 139
  Human cell 217
Rib vault 469, 484-485
  Gothic building 470
  Medieval building 467
  Renaissance building
    477
Rice paper 445
Ride cymbal 519
Ridge
  Epigeal germination 153
  False septum 151
  Gothic building 473
  Modern building 499
  Nineteenth-century
    building 492
  Seed 153
  Twentieth-century
    building 495
Ridge and furrow roof 492
Ridge-board 473
Ridge-rib 469, 485
Ridges 286-287
Ridge tile 464, 476
Riding bit 372
Riding jacket 554
Riffler 452, 453, 454
Rifle 548, 549
Rift valley 58
  Lake formation 292-293
Rig 584-585
Riga brush 434
Rigel
  Northern stars 18
  Orion 18

Southern stars 21
  Star magnitudes 22
Rigger 560
Rigger's gauge 582
Rigging 582-583
  Iron 392
  Sailing dinghy 561
  Wooden sailing ship
    378-379
Rigging rail 376
Rigging tools 582-583
Right-angled triangle 622
Right cylinder 623
Right edge guide 575
Right whales 204
Rigid rock 60
Rigol 381
Rim
  Bicycle wheel 358-359
  Kayak paddle 560
  Paddle wheel 391
  Tam-tam 516
  Twin bollards 386
Rim brake 330
Rim clamp 337
Rim of pitcher 161
Rim plate 390
Rim section 590
Rind 149
Ring
  74-gun ship 380
  Mushroom 115
  Roman corbita 372
Ring 1986 U1R 48
Ring 1986 U2R 48
Rig 6 48
Ring bolt 373
Ring canal
  Sea urchin 175
  Starfish 174
Ring dyke 26
Ring finger 230-231
"Ring of Fire" 272
Ring of trunk 201
Rings
  Jupiter 44-45
  Neptune 50-51
  Saturn 46-47
  Uranus 48-49
Rings 4 and 5 48
Ring scar 130, 131
Ring-tailed lemur 203
Rink corner 550
  Riojasaurus 89
Ripple finish 451
Riser
  Bronze casting 454, 455
  Staircase 477
Rising air
  Atmospheric circulation
    and winds 300
  Precipitation 302
Rising land 294
Risorius muscle 229
  Rissa tridactyla 190
Ritchey 45
River Amur 265, 616
River banks 289, 290
Riverbed 289
River capture 288
River cliff 289, 290
River course 288
River development 289
River drainage patterns
  288
River features 290-291
River flow 290
River mouth 290
Rivers 288-289
  Physical map of the
    world 617
  River features 290-291
  Rock cycle 266-267
  Weathering and erosion
    282
River source
  River features 290
  Rivers 288
River's stages 288-289

River terrace 290-291
River valley 288, 289, 290
Rivetted plates 592
Road spring 540
Roband 572, 574
Robie House 495
Robinia pseudoacacia 136
Roboreptile 609
Robots 608-609
Robot dogs 609
Roche 41
Roches moutonnées 286
Rock compression 60
Rock crystal 271
Rock cycle 266-267
Rock debris 295
Rock deformations 60, 61
Rocker 446
Rocker arm 366
Rocker-beam 496-497
Rocker cover 547, 554
Rocker deployment actuator 615
Rock erosion 282
"Rocket" steam locomotive 524
Rocket launcher 397
Rock ground mass 269
Rocking beam 354
Rocking elevator arm 424
Rocking lever 342
Rock layer
  Caves 284
  Faults and folds 60
Rock lip
  Cirque formation 287
  Tarn lake 295
Rock mounds 286
Rock particles 266-267
Rock pavement 282-283
Rock pedestal 282-283
Rock prisms 61
Rocks
  Faults and folds 60-61
  Fossils 278-279
  Igneous and metamorphic rocks 274-275
  Mineral resources 280
  Minerals 268
  Rock cycle 266-267
  Sedimentary rocks 276
  Weathering and erosion 282
Rock salt
  Halides 269
  Sedimentary rocks 276-277
Rock scar 284
Rock stonecrop 128
Rock strata 60, 61
  Fossils 278
Rock stress 60, 61
Rock tension 60, 61
Rocky Mountains 75, 75, 77, 264, 617
Rocky planets
  Mars 42-43
  Mercury 34-35
  Solar system 30-31
  Venus 36-37
Rococo style 478
Rod 562-563
Rodentia 104, 196
Rodents 196-197
Rod-shaped structure 144
Rogers, R. 496
Roll 400
Roller
  Mid West single-rotor engine 410
  Motorized brushbar floor tool 593
  "O Ring" drive chain 366

Painting tool 442
Printing equipment 447, 449
Tenor saxophone 509
Roller-bearing axle box 527
Roller-blind 497
Roller path 396
Rollers 596
Rolling hitch 588
Rollover button 577
Roll paper holder 575
Roll paper holder adapter 575
Roll paper manipulation button 574
Roll spoiler 414
Roll-spoiler hydraulic actuator attachment 414
Rolls-Royce Olympus Mark 610 turbojet 417
Roman anchor 372
Roman architecture 462-465
  Roman corbita 372-375
Romanesque style 468, 470
Roman mill 464
Roman ships 572-573
Roof boss 468
Roof construction 603
Roof dome 352, 353
Roofed space 479
Roofing tile 482
Roofless temple 460
Roof molding 352
Roofs 484
  Ancient Egyptian temple 458-459
  Ancient Roman building 462
  Asian building 490
  Baroque church 481
  Dome 486
  Gothic building 470-475
  Hammer-beam 470, 475
  Islamic building 488-489
  Medieval building 467, 468
  Modern building 496-499
  Neoclassical building 479, 483
  Nineteenth-century building 492
  Renaissance building 476-477
  Twentieth-century building 494-495
Root
  BAe-146 jetliner components 413, 415
  BE 2B wings 404
  Tooth 247
Root canal 247
Root cap
  Broad bean 133
  Radicle 153
Root growth 282
Root hairs 132
Root nodule 128
Root of tail 198
Root parasite 163
Root-proof membrane 605
Root rib 413
Roots 132-133
  Adventitious 112-113
  Amaryllis 155
  Begonia 155
  Brassavola nodosa 162
  Broomrape host 163
  Carrot 128
  Cell division 135
  Clubmoss 120
  Couch grass 113

Dehiscent fruit 150
Dicotyledons 127
Elongation region 133
Embryo 147
Epigeal germination 153
Epiphytes 162-163
Fern 121
Germination 152-153
Ginger 155
Gladiolus 155
Golden barrel cactus 156
Grape hyacinth 155
Horse chestnut 130
Horsetail 121
Hypogeal germination 152
Ivy 131
Kedrostis africana 113
Lily 155
Monocotyledons 126-127
Mycorrhizal association 133
Oxalis sp. 157
Pine seedling 122
Potato 128
Rock stonecrop 128
Seedling 152-153
String of hearts 157
Sweet pea 128
Sweet potato 155
Vegetative reproduction 154-155
Water hyacinth 158
Water transport 138
Root scar 128
Root succulents 157
Root tip 152-153
  Radicle 152-153
Root tubers 154-155, 157
Rope and paterae decoration 459
Rope band 372
Rope hole 586
Rope molding 395
Rope parrel 373
Rope preventer 578
Rope strand 384
Rope wooldings 579
Rope work 388
Rorquals 204
Rosa sp. 130-131, 135
Rose 130-131
Rose quartz 271
Rosette
  Epiphytic plants 162-163
  Neoclassical building 480
Rosette Nebula 11
Rossby waves 300
Rossin Italian time-trial bicycle 361
Rostellum 16
Rostral bone 102, 103
Rostrum
  Crayfish 173
  Dolphin 204
Rotary engine 346-347
  Blackburn monoplane 400
  Modern piston aero-engines 410-411
Rotary valves 507
Rotating beacon 407
Rotating drum 595
Rotating joint 612
Rotational period 36
Rotor
  Mid West rotary engine 411
  Rotor and seals 347
Rotor blade 423

Rotor chamber
  Mid West single-rotor engine 410
  Wankel rotary engine 346
Rotor gear 346-347
Rotor gear teeth 411
Rotor house 314
Rotor hub
  Bell-47 helicopter 422
  S42 Schweizer helicopter 423
Rotor journal 347
Rotor lock 604
Rotor mast 422-423
Rotunda 462-465, 482
Rough 546
Rough endoplasmic reticulum 217
Rough terrain motorcycle racing 368
Rough-textured paper 439, 441
Roulette 446
Rounce 449
Round arch
  Ancient Roman building 464-465
  Baroque church 479-480
  Dome 484, 486-487
  French temple 485
  Gothic church 475
  Medieval building 467-469
  Nineteenth-century building 495
  Renaissance building 474-475
Round-arched window
  Ancient Roman building 465
  Baroque church 481
  Dome 486
  Medieval building 466, 468-469
  Neoclassical building 478
Round ball 524
Round-corner single limousine coachwork 336
Roundel
  Avro biplane 403
  Hawker Tempest fighter 409
Roundhead nib 444
Roundhouse 580
Round pin 335
Round shot 378
Round thimble 384
Route information 552
Rover 528
Rover equipment deck 615
Rowan 130-131
Rowing 560-561
Rowing boat 575
Rowing positions on a Greek trireme 373
RSS (really simple syndication) feeds 577
Rubber bungee shock absorber 425
Rubber cord suspension 402-403
Rubber guide wheel 328
Rubber mounting bush 565
Rubber puck 550-551
Rubber roller 449
Rubber sealing strip 413
Rubber-sprung wheel 400-401
Rubber tire 402
Rubber-tired running wheel 528
Rubber wheel-guard 328
Rubber wheels

Paris Metro 328
  "People Mover" 528
Rubbing
  Charcoal drawing 431
  Relief printing 446
Rubbing ink 448
Rubbing strake
  Mazda RX-7 546
  Roman corbita 572
Rubbing strip 553
Rubens 35
Rubidium 510
Rubus fruticosus 130, 146-147
Rubus idaeus 149
Ruckman 528
Rucknover 528
Ruckstell axle 339
Rudder
  ARV light aircraft 424
  Avro biplane 402
  Avro triplane 403
  BAe-146 jetliner 415
  Battleship 395
  BE 2B bomber 405
  Blackburn monoplane 401
  Blériot XI 401
  Concorde 416-417
  Curtiss biplane 399
  Dhow 376
  Frigate 396
  Greek and Roman ships 572-375
  Iron paddlesteamer 392
  Junk 376
  Lockheed Electra airliner 407
  Longboat 380
  LVG CVI fighter 405
  Northrop B-2 bomber 421
  Sailing dinghy 561
  Sailing warship 377
  Schleicher glider 426
  Submarine 396
  Tornado 421
  Viking boats 374-375
  Wooden sailing ship 578
  World War II aircraft 408-409
  Wright Flyer 399
Rudder cable
  ARV light aircraft 424
  Avro biplane 402
Rudder chain 378
Rudder head 376
Rudder hinge
  Avro biplane 402
  Blériot XI monoplane 401
Rudder mass balance 424
Rudder pedal 425, 573
Rudder post
  BE 2B bomber 405
  Blackburn monoplane 401
  Iron paddlesteamer 392
Rudder strut 399
Rudder tip fairing 414
Rudder trimtab 409
Ruden 572
Rudimentary ear 260
Rudimentary eye 260
Rudimentary liver 260
Rudimentary mouth 260
Rudimentary vertebra 260
Ruellia grandiflora 145
Ruffini corpuscle 235, 239
Ruga 248
Rugby 524, 530-531
Rugby League 530-531
Rugby Union 530
Rules of algebra 621

Rumen 198
Ruminants 198
Rumpler monoplane 400
Run 536
Runners
  Bronze casting 454-455
  Rock stonecrop 128
  Strawberry 128
  Vegetative reproduction 154
Running 542
Running back 526
Running block 583
Running board
  Ford Model T 339
  1906 Renault 337
  Volkswagen Beetle 341
Running martingale 554
Running part 382
Running rail 328
Running rigging 582-583, 585
Running shoe 543
Running track 542
Running wheel 528
Runs 538
Rupes 34
Rupes Altai 40
Rush 155
Russian vine 131
Rustication
  Neoclassical building 479, 482-483
  Renaissance building 474-475
Rusts 114
Ruthenium 511

S

62 Sagittarii 21
Sabik 20
Sable brush
  Acrylics 442
  Calligraphy 444
  Oil paints 436
  Tempera 432
  Watercolors 438
Sabers 556-557
Saberur 557
Saber warning line 557
Sacajawea 37
Saccule 243
Sacral foramen 223
Sacral nerves 238
Sacral plexus 238
Sacral promontory 223
Sacral vertebra 183
Sacral vertebrae
  Diplodocus 90
  Eryops 81
  Human 223
  Iguanodon 96
  Parasaurolophus 99
  Plateosaurus 88
  Stegoceras 101
Sacristy 470
Sacrum
  Crocodile 186
  Domestic cat 195
  Elephant 201
  Hare 197
  Horse 199
  Human 218, 223, 259
  Kangaroo 206
  Lizard 184
  Rhesus monkey 202
  Seal 204
Saddle
  Acoustic guitar 512
  Bicycle 358-359
  Cannondale SH600 hybrid bicycle 561
  Eddy Merckx racing bicycle 360
  Horse racing 555
  Show jumping 554
  Werner motorcycle 362

Saddle clamp 360
Safety area 556
Safety barrier 552
Safety belt 556
Safety binding 552
Safety harness 357
Safety valve
  Bordino steam carriage 334
  Steamboat 391
Safe working load mark 585
Sagartia elegans 166
Sagitta 20
Sagittal crest 107, 194
Sagittal section through brain 236
Sagittarius 19-21
Sagittarius Arm 14
Sago palm 123
Sahara 39, 265, 615
Sail
  Roman corbita 372-373
  Square-rigged ship 375
  Types 384-385
  Viking karv 374
Sail batten 376
Sailcloths 584
Sail foot control line 375
Sail hook 384
Sailing 560-561
Sailing rigs 384-385
Sailing warship 376-377
Sailmaker's whipping 582
Sailmaking tools 584
Sail patterns 579, 584
Saiph 18
Salamanders 182
Salient 466
Salisbury Cathedral 470-471
Saliva 244
Salivary gland
  Butterfly 169
  Snail 177
Salmon 109, 180
Salmon angling 562
Salmon bend gouge 452
Salmson radial engine 398-399
Salt
  Dead Sea 293
  Seawater sail content 296
Saltasaurus 72, 91
Salt-dome trap 281
Salt formation 312
Salt groundmass 277
Salt lakes 292
Samaras
  Dry fruit 150
  Sycamore 131, 150
Samarium 311
Sambucus nigra 130-131, 143
Samotherium 74
San Andreas fault 58, 62-63
Sand-bars 290
Sand box 526, 527
Sand dunes
  Rock cycle 267
  Weathering and erosion 282-283
Sand groundmass 277
Sanding pipe 529
Sand-pits 546
Sandstone
  Marble tomb of Itimad-Ud-Daula 489
  Sedimentary rocks 276
Sand wave 290
Sand wedge 547
Sandy deposits 298
Sandy spit 295
Sanguine crayon 430
Sankey diagram 514
Sappho Patera 37

Sapwood 125
Saratoga Race Course 555
Sarcolemma 24
Sarcomere 24
Sarcophilus harrisii 207
Sarcoplasmic reticulum 24
Sarcorhamphus papa 190
Sarracenia purpurea 113
Sartorius muscle 226
Satellite 264
Satellite cable 586
Satellite map 264-265
Satellite speaker 586
Saturated zone 292-293
Saturn 46-47, 614
  Solar system 31
Saucer dome 486-487
  Ancient Roman building 462
Saurischia 82-83, 84, 88
Sauropoda 83
Sauropodomorpha 83, 88
Sauropodomorphs 88-91
Sauropods 70, 88
Savannah 74
Save as draft button 576
Saxboard 561
Saxophone 504, 508-509
Scala 572-573
Scale (musical) 502
Scale leaf scar 124, 155
Scale leaves
  Bishop pine 124
  Bulb 155
  Corm 155
  Epiphytic orchid 162
  Hypogeal germination 152
  Pine 122, 125
  Plumule 152
  Rhizome 155
  Sago palm 155
  Stem bulbil 155
Scalene triangle 622
Scalenus medius muscle 229
Scale of degrees 577
Scales
  Asteroxylon 79
  Bishop pine 124
  Bony fish 180
  Bract 122
  Brassavola nodosa 162
  Caiman 186
  Cartilaginous fish 178
  Crocodilians 186
  Dicotyledons 127
  False fruit 148
  Fern fronds 121
  Insects 168
  Lepidoptera wings 168
  Lizard 184
  Mushroom 115
  Ovuliferous 122-124
  Pine cone 122
  Pine shoot apex 125
  Rattlesnake 185
  Sago palm 122
  Tree fern 112
  Yew 123
Scallop 176
  Fossil 278
Scalloped hammerhead shark 179
Scalp 254, 256-257
Scaly lichens 114
Scaly skin
  Anchisaurus 89
  Corythosaurus 98
  Dinosaurs 82
  Edmontonia 95
  Iguanodon 97
  Pachycephalosaurus 100
  Psittacosaurus 103
  Reptile 80
  Snake 184

Stegosaurus 92
Triceratops 102
Tyrannosaurus 84
Westlothiana 81
Scandinavia 64, 69
Scandium 310
Scan head 571
Scanner 570-571
Scanning coils 611
Scanning electron microscope (SEM) 610, 611
Scan to email button 570
Scan to web button 570
Scapania undulata 118
Scape 168
Scaphoid bone 230
Scaphoid fossa 242
Scaphonyx fischeri 69
Scapula
  Archaeopteryx 85
  Arsinoitherium 104
  Bird 189
  Bony fish 181
  Brachiosaurus 91
  Crocodile 186
  Diplodocus 90
  Domestic cat 195
  Elephant 201
  Eiryops 80
  Euoplocephalus 94
  Gallimimus 86
  Hare 197
  Horse 199
  Human 210, 218
  Iguanodon 96
  Kangaroo 206
  Lizard 184
  Parasaurolophus 99
  Pareiasaur 81
  Plateosaurus 88
  Platypus 206
  Rhesus monkey 202
  Seal 204
  Stegoceras 101
  Struthiomimus 87
  Toxodon 106
  Triceratops 102
  Tuojiangosaurus 93
  Turtle 187
  Tyrannosaurus 84
Scapular muscle 91
Scarlet star 162-163
Scarph 395
Scars
  Horse chestnut 130
  Leaf 128-30, 134
  Rowan twig 131
Scavenge oil line 419
Scelidosaurus 71
Scent 144
Scheat 19, 20
Schedar 19
Schickard 40
Schist 26
Schizoearpic dry fruits 150-151
Schleicher K23 glider 426
Schlumbergera truncata 129
Schooner 384-385
Schrödinger 41
Schubert 55
Schwann cell 228, 239
Schweizer 300c 423
Sciatic nerve 238
Scientific notation 621
Scintigram 214
Scissor brace 475
Sciurus carolinensis 197
Sclera 215, 240
Sclereid 159
Sclerenchyma
  Fern rachis 121
  Horsetail stem 120
  Marram grass 113
  Monocotyledon leaf 126
  Stems 134-135
Sclerenchyma fibers 135

Scleroderma citrinum 115
Sclerotic ring 90, 99
Scooter 50-51
Score 588
Scorecard 547
Scorer
  Basketball 532
  Fencing contest 557
  Judo contest 556
  Lacrosse 541
  Netball 535
  Volleyball 534
Scoria 273
Scoring
  Australian rules football 528
  Badminton 544
  Baseball 556
  Basketball 532
  Cricket 538
  Gaelic football 529
  Hockey 540
  Hurling 540-541
  Netball 534
  Rugby 530-531
  Tennis 544
  Volleyball 534
Scorper 449
Scorpion 170, 278
Scorpiones 170
Scorpius 19, 20
Scotia 463, 485
Scots pine 122
Scraper 46
Scraper ring 344
Scratchplate 513
Scree 282-283
Screen
  Computer 576, 577, 611
  French baroque building 482
  Hydroelectric power station 514
  Islamic building 488-489
  Screen printing 448
  Streamed internet video 577
  Twentieth-century building 494
Screen bulkhead 381
Screen lens 589
Screen printing 446, 448
Screw 320
  Acoustic guitar 513
  Double bass bow 511
  Power drill 600
  Toaster 598
  Violin bow 510
Screw coupling 525
Screw down greaser 556
Screw fitting 319
Screw hole 600
Screw joint 413
Screw link 386
Screw locking nut 563
Screw pressure adjustor 447
Scriber 446
Scroll
  Cello 511
  Double bass 511
  Viola 511
  Violin 510
Scrolled buttress 478
Scroll motif 470, 491
Scroll molding 466
Scroll ornament 476, 479, 485
Scroll-shaped corbel 482, 487
Scrollwork 472
Scrotum 211, 259
Scrum-half 550
Scrummages 550
Scull 561
Sculling 560
Scull oar 560

Sculpted wing-root fairing 575
Sculptor 19, 20
Sculptural decoration 467
Sculpture 452-455, 493, 495
Sculptured testa 151
Scumbling 440-441
Scupper 595
Scute 186
Scutellum 168
Scutum 19
Scutum plate 175
Scyphozoa 166
Sea
  Anticline trap 281
  Fossils 278
  Hurricane structure 303
  River features 290-291
Sea anemone 166-167
Sea angling 562
Seabed
  Fossils 278
  Ocean floor 298
  River features 290
  Rivers 288
Seabed profile 299
Sea buckthorn 136
Seacat missile launcher 397
Sea-cave 295
Sea-cliff 294-295
  River features 291
Sea creature remains 298
Sea cucumber 174
Sea daisies 174
Sea-dwelling organic structures 78
Seafloor spread 58
Seahorse 180
Sea level 66
Sea-level variations 294
Sea lilies 174
Sea lion 204
Seals 204-205
Seam
  Rivetted plates 392
Seaming twine 384
Seamounts 298
Sea of Japan 265, 616
Seasons 72
Seat
  1906 Renault 337
  Driver's 525, 528
  Faering 375
  Fireman's 525
  First cars 334-335
  Ford Model T 339
  Greek trireme 373
  Harley-Davidson FLHS Electra Glide 363
  Honda CB750 565
  Honda VF750 564
  Husqvarna Motocross TC610 368
  Kayak 560
  Longboat 380
  Motorcycle 364
  Racing sulky 555
  Renault Clio 352-355
  Showjumping saddle 554
  Suzuki RGV500 568
  TGV electric high-speed train 329
  Vespa Grand Sport 160
  Mark 1 363
  Weslake Speedway motorcycle 369
Seat angle 360
Seat assembly 425, 553

Seat attachment rail 416
Seat back rest frame 337, 352-353
Seat beam 399
Seatbelt attachment point 573
Seat belt catch 552
Seat control panel 572
Seat cushion 407, 425
Sea temperature 303
Seating 465
Seat mount 540
Seat pan 409
Seat post 358, 360
Seat post quick-release boll 358
Seat spring 555
Seat squab 335, 337
Seat stay 358, 360
Seat support strut 398
Seat tube 358, 360, 361
Sea urchins 174-175
Seawater
  River features 290
  Salt content 296
Seaweeds 116-117
Seaworm 78
Sebaceous gland 234-235
Secondary baffle 612
Secondary bronchus 215
Secondary colors 459
Secondary conduit 272-273
  Rock cycle 266
Secondary crater 34
Secondary flight feathers 188, 191
Secondary follicle 258
Secondary mirror 612
Secondary mycelium 115
Secondary phloem 154-155
Secondary remiges 188, 191
Secondary rotor 317
Secondary suspension 327
Secondary thallus 114
Secondary vascular tissue 134
Secondary xylem 125, 134-135
Second-century building 462
Second electron shell 309
Second mast 376
Second-row forward 550
Second slip 538
Second toe 252
Second violins 503, 504-505
Second wheel set 529
Secretory gland 161
Secretory thyroid gland cells 217
Secretory vesicle 216
Secure anchor 586
Security light 605
Sediment
  Coastlines 294-295
  Fossils 278
  Glaciers 286-287
  Lakes 292
  Mineral resources 280
  Mountain building 62-65
  Ocean floor 298-299
  River features 290-291
  Rivers 288
  Rock cycle 266-267
Sedimentary rocks 276-277
  Igneous and metamorphic rocks 274
  Rock cycle 266-267
Sedna Planitia 36-37
Sedum rupestre 128
Sedum spectabile 128-129
Seed

Apomixis 146
Apple 149
Cape gooseberry 149
Dehydration 152
Dispersal 148-151
Dormancy 152
Dry fruit 150-151
Embryo development 147
Fig 148
Germination 152, 152-155
Goosegrass 150
Gymnosperms 122
Hilum 148-149, 151-155
Hogweed 151
Honesty 151
Larkspur 151
Lemon 148
Love-in-a-mist 151
Lychee 148
Melon 149
Parts 152-153
Pea 150
Pine 122
Raspberry 149
Root development 132
Scots pine 122
Smooth cypress 125
Strawberry 150
Succulent fruit 148-149
Sweet chestnut 150
Sycamore 151, 151
Wind dispersal 150
Wings 150-151
Yew 123
Seed axis 152-153
Seed coat 152, 152-153
Dry fruit 150-151
Embryo development 147
Epigeal germination 155
Hypogeal germination 152
Succulent fruit 148-149
Seed fern 278
Seed leaves 126, 152-153
Dry fruit 150-151
Embryo development 147
Epigeal germination 155
Hypogeal germination 152
Pine 122
Succulent fruit 148-149
Seedlings
Epigeal germination 155
Hypogeal germination 152
Pine 122
Seed-producing organs 148-149
Seed scar 122
Seed stalks 150
Seed wings 151
Seek bar 577
Segmental arch 492
Segmental pediment 462, 478
Segnosauria 83
Seif dune 283
Seismic activity 58
Seizing 383, 384, 387, 588-589
Selaginella sp. 120
Select key 578
Selector fork 566
Selector switch 598-599
Selenite 270
Selenium 511
Self-pollination 144
SEM 601, 611
Semaphore signal 550
Semen 217
Semiarch 470-471
Semibreve 502-505

Semibulkhead 425
Semicircle 552
Semicircular canals 243
Semicircular tower 465
Semiconductor 506
Semidome 484, 482, 488
Semielliptical arch 484
Semielliptic leaf spring 342
Semilunar fold 249
Semi-metals 310-311
Seminal receptacle 169
Spider 170
Seminal vesicle 259
Semiquaver 502
Semisolid core 37
Semisolid outer core 41
Semisprawling stance 82
Westlothiana 81
Semitendinosus muscle 227
Send button 576
Sender's name 576
Senior ratings' mess 597
Sensors 590
Sensory antenna 168
Sensory hinge 160
Sensory tentacle 176
Sent mail folder 576
Sepal 140-143
Clematis 151
Dicotyledons 126-127
Dry fruit 150-151
Everlasting pea 129
Fertilization 146-147
Monocotyledons 126
Peruvian lily 129
Pitcher plant 113
Pollination 145
Rose 151
Succulent fruit 149
Sepal remains 146-147
Sepal sheath 141
Separated carpels 151
Separator 576
Septime 557
Septum 115
False 115
Interventricular 251
Nasal 213, 241
Placenta 260
Sequencer 521
Sequoiadendron sp. 70
Series electrical circuit 316
Serif 445
Serous pericardium 250
Serpens Caput 18, 21
Serpens Cauda 19, 20
Serpentes 184
Serpentine neck 574
Serrated tooth 84, 85, 88
Serrate leaf margins 129
Serratus anterior muscle 226
Server 554, 544, 545, 576
Server Service 544
Service area 554
Service box line 545
Service court 544, 545
Service crane 605
Service door 415
Service judge 544, 545
Service line 544, 545
Service shaft 498
Service zone 545
Serving 588
Serving mallet 583, 584, 589
Servo control-unit fairing 417
Servo-tab 414, 415
Sesamoid bone 198
Seta 112, 119
Set-back buttress 481
Set square 445
Settings button 576
Settings control panel 574
Settings display 574, 575
Setting select buttons 575

Seven Sisters 14
Seventeenth century 474
Building 479-481, 488
Capital 490
Dome 486-487
Roof 490
Style 478
Tomb 489
Seventh century
Building 491
Sever fault 276
Sex cells 154
Fertilization 146-147
Gametophyte plants 120
Gymnosperms 122
Liverwort 118
Moss 118-119
Sextans 21
Sexual reproduction
Algae 116-117
Bryophytes 119
Flowering plants 140-147
Mosses 118-119
Seaweed 116-117
Spirogyra sp. 117
Seyfert 41
Seyfert galaxies 12-13
Shackle 382, 586
Shackle pin 582
Shaft
Ancient Egyptian column 459
Ancient Greek temple 461
Ancient Roman building 463, 465
Arrow 548
Asian building 490-491
Badminton racket 545
Electric generator 517
Feather 191
Femur 225
French temple 485
Golf club 547
Harness racer 555
Hydroelectric power station 514
Javelin 542
Kayak paddle 560
Medieval church 468-469
Modern building 498
Neoclassical building 478, 485
Nineteenth-century building 493
Phalanx 250
Power drill 600
Roman Corbita 375
Sculling oar 560
Ski pole 553
Squash racket 545
Shaft drive 366
Shale
Contact metamorphism 274
Grand Canyon 277
Shallow carvel-built hull 391
Shallow Hats 293
Shank
Anatomy of a hook 562
Danforth anchor 586
Hook 583
Roman anchor 372
Sail hook 384
Shackle pin 582
Shannon bone 198
Shape
Chemical reactants 312
Matter 306-307
Periodic table 310
Shapes (plane; solid) 622
Sharks 178-179, 180
Sharp 502
Sharpey's fiber 225
Shaula 19, 20
Shave 374

Shaving foam 306
Shearing 61
Sheave 585
Sheave for cat tackle 380
Sheep 198
Sheepskin numnah 554
Sheer 374
Sheerplank 380
Sheer pole 373
Sheet strake 575, 593
Sheet 572, 575, 582
Sheet anchor 595
Sheet bend 589
Sheet feeder 575
Sheet-iron louvre 493
Sheet lead 383
Shelf formation 282
Shell
579 cm shell 597
6 in shell 397
Building 464, 476
Chelonians 186
Crab 172
Dorsal margin 176
Egg 192-195
Exploding 394, 396-597
Fossil 278
Massive stars 26
Mollusk 176-177
Octopus 176
Rib 176
Rudiment 176
Scallop 176
Small stars 24-25
Snail 177
Standing block 582
Terrapin 187
Ventral margin 176
Shell bogie 596
Shell case 597
Shelled invertebrates 56
Shelley 35
Shell-like fracture 270
Shell room 396
Shelly limestone 267
"Shiaijo" 556
Shield 594-595
"Shield bearers" 92
Shield plate 570
Shield volcano 42
Shin
Herrerasaurus 86
Human 211
Shinarump member 276
Shin guard
Slalom skiing 553
Soccer 525
Shinty 540
Shinumo quartzite 277
Ship 587
74-gun ship 379, 380-381
Ship of the line 380-381
Ship's cannon 376, 379
Ship's shield 594-595
Ship's wheel 578, 390, 594
Shipwright 374
Shiv 383
Shiver 585
Shock absorber
1906 Renault 356
ARV light aircraft 425
Football helmet 527
Honda CB750 365
Honda VF750 564
Renault Clio 350
Suzuki RGV500 368
Vespa Light aircraft 160
Mark 1 363
Volkswagen Beetle 340
Shock-absorbing platform 555
Shock-absorbing spring 401, 405
Shock-strut 401
Shock waves 27

Path 63
Athletics 543
Basketball 533
Golf 547
Handball 535
Rowing 560
Shoes
Baseball 537
Football 527
Hurling 541
Riding 554
Rugby 531
Sailing 560
Ski 552
Soccer 525
Shoot
Broomrape 163
Embryo 147
Horsetail 120
Hypogeal germination 152
Pine 125
Vegetative reproduction 155
Shoot apex 125
Shooting 548-549
Shooting circle 540
Shooting positions 548
Shoreline
Coastlines 294
Continental-shelf floor 298
Short line 545
Shorts
Australian rules football 529
Hurling 541
Soccer 525
Volleyball 554
Short saphenous vein 255
Shortstop 536
Short-wave radio 318
Shot
Field events equipment 542
Gun 378
Shot garland 581
Shot put 543
Shot-put circle 542
Shot-put fan 542
Shoulder
Anchisaurus 89
Cello 511
Corythosaurus 98
Double bass 511
Gorilla 203
Harp 511
Horse 199
Human 210
Iguanodon 97
Rabbit 196
Rigging 582-585
Stegoceras 101
Stegosaurus 92
Viola 511
Violin 510
Shoulderblade 210, 218
Shoulder cowling 412
Shoulder girdle 80
Shoulder joint
Brachiosaurus 91
Gallimimus 86
Human 218
Parasaurolophus 99
Plateosaurus 88
Triceratops 102
Tyrannosaurus 84
Shoulder pad 426
Shoulder padding 551
Shoulder pass 535
Shoulder spikes
Edmontonia 95
Euoplocephalus 94
Shoulder wheel throw 556
Showjumping 554
Shreve, R.H. 494
Shrewlike mammals 70
Shrimp 172
Fossil 79

Shrine 490-491
Shroud
Dhow 376
Longboat 380
Rigging 583
Roman corbita 373
Sailing dinghy 561
Sailing warship 576
Shrubs 130-151
Shuffle button 586
Shutter button 581
Shutter for gun 394
Shuttlecock 544-545
Shuttle switch 586
Sickle motif 491
Sidalcea malviflora 136
Side aisle
Cathedral dome 484
Gothic church 472-473
Medieval church 469
Side bench 380
Side brace and retraction jack trunnions 414
Sidecar
BMW R/60 562
Motorcycle racing 368-369
Side chapel 469-470, 479
Side counter timber 581
Side-cowling 408
Side drum 504-505
Side fairing 415
Side forequarter hold 556
Side gear 347
Side housing 346-347
Side lamp 338-339
Sidelight 352, 353, 562
Sideline
Badminton 545
Basketball 532
Football 526
Handball 535
Hockey 540
Men's lacrosse 540
Netball 535
Tennis 541
Volleyball 534
Side marker lamp 346, 349
Side plate 562
Side pod 356, 357
Side reflector 562, 563
Side rudder 374-575
Side-shooting 541
Side vent 329
Side wall 545, 558
Side-wall line 545
Sideways erosion
River features 290
Rivers 288
Sierra Madre 264, 617
Sierra Nevada 57, 75
Sieve tubes 154
Sieving beak 188
Sif Mons 37
Sight 394
Sight pin 549
Sight screen 538
Sighting hood
Battleship 394
Gun turret 396
Sighting rule 376-377
Sights 548-549
Sigma Canis Majoris 21
Sigmoid colon 249
Signal flag compartment 597
Signal gear 395
Signaling systems 550-551
Sikorsky, Igor 422
Silence 502
Silencer
Harley-Davidson FLHS Electra Glide 362
Renault Clio 350
Suzuki RGV500 368

Vespa Grand Sport 160
Mark 1 563
Weslake Speedway
  motorcycle 569
Silencing heat exchanger
  404
Silicate core 51
Silicate dust 55
Silicate material 39
Silicate rock 59
Silicates 269
Siliceous ooze 299
Silicon 26
  Earth's composition 59
  Earth's crust 58
  Periodic table 311
  Variety of matter 306
Siliquas 150-151
Silk gland 170
Sill 26
  Ancient Roman mill
    464
  Renaissance building
    475
  Twentieth-century
    building 494
Sill trim 553
Silly mid-off 538
Silly mid-on 558
Silurian period
  Fossil record 279
  Geological time 56
Silver
  Mineral resources
    280-281
  Minerals 268
  Periodic table 311-312
  Streak 271
Silver lines 430-431
Silver molybdenite 271
Silver nitrate solution 312
Silverpoint 430, 431
Silver wire 430
Silvery metals 310
SIM (Subscriber Identity
  Module) card slot 589
Simple electrical circuit
  316
Simple eye 170-171
Simple leaves 136-137
  Entire 130
  Hastate 128
  Lanceolate 131
  Lobed 131
Simple machines 320
Simple Machines Law
  320
Simple succulent fruits
  148-149
Single bass note siring
  515
Single-celled micro-
  organisms 78
Single clump block
  575
Single cylinder 335
Single-decker bus 552, 553
Single flowers 140-141,
  143
Single front driving wheel
  334
Single-glazed
  conservatory 602
Single-leg main landing
  gear 407
Single overhead cam
  engine 363
Single-piece skin 413
Single-pulley system 320
Single reed 508, 509
Singles 544
Single scull 560, 561
Single sheet bend 387
Single-sided trailing-link
  fork 363
Single wing hold
  556

Singularity
  Formation of black hole
    29
  Stellar black hole 29
Sinistral strike-slip fault
  61
Sink-holes 284-285
Sinking land 294
Sinopia 434, 435
Sinous venosus sclerae
  241
Sinuous cell wall 156
Sinus
  Frontal, 212, 245
  Green alga 112
  Renal 256
  Superior sagittal 212
Sinus Borealis 69
Sinus Irid um 40
Siphon
  Octopus 176-177
  Sea urchin 175
Siphonoglyph 167
Sirius
  Canis Major 21
  Northern stars 18
  Our galaxy and nearby
    galaxies 15
  Southern stars 21
  Spectral absroplion
    lines 23
  Star magnitudes 22
Sirius A 23
Sirius B 23
Site icon 577
Sixteenth century
  Building 476-477
  Staircase 472
  Style 462, 470
Size (glue) 431, 432, 436
Skarn 26
Skate
  Chondrichthyes 178
  Ice hockey 550, 551
Skeletal muscle 228
Skeletal muscle fiber 228
Skeleton
  Archaeopteryx 85
  Arsinoitherium 104-105
  Baryonyx hand 85
  Bat 105
  Bird 189
  Bony fish 180-181
  Cow's foot 198
  Crocodile 186
  Diplodocus 90
  Domestic cat 195
  Elephant 201
  Eryops 80-81
  Frog 185
  Hare 197
  Horse 199
  Human 218-219
  Iguanodon 96
  Kangaroo 206
  Kentrosaurus 93
  Lizard 184
  Parasurolophus 98-99
  Pareiasaur 81
  Platcosaurus 88-89
  Platypus 206
  Rhesus monkey 202
  Seal 204
  Snake 185
  Spider 171
  Sponge 166
  Stegoceras 100-101
  Stegosaurus 95
  Struthiomimus 87
  Toxodon 106
  Triceralops 102-103
  Tuofiaigosairus 95
  Turile 187
  Tyrannosaurus 84-85
  Westlothiana 81
Sketch book 450
Skid 402, 404
Skid beam 580
Ski goggles 552, 555

Skiing 552, 553
Skilled movements 237
Skin
  Amphibian 80, 182
  Drumhead 518
  Lizard 184
  Reptile 80
  Snake 184
  Succulent fruits 148-149
  Waterproof 81
Skin and hair 234-235
"Skin-grip" pin 424-425
Skin lap-joint 413, 414,
  415
Skin tones 441
Ski pole 552
Skirting board 602
Skis 552
Skull
  Acanthostega 80
  Alligator 186
  Ankylosaurus 94
  Australopithecus 108
  Baryonyx 85
  Bear 194
  Bird 189
  Camarasaurus 91
  Chimpanzee 202
  Crocodilians 186
  Diplodocus 90
  Domestic cat 195
  Elephant 201
  Euoplocephalus 94
  Fetal 220
  Gharial 186
  Hadrosaurs 96
  Hare 197
  Heterodontosaurus 85
  Homo erect us 108
  Homo habilis 108
  Horse 199
  Human 108, 212, 218,
    220-221, 222, 236-237
  Hyaenodon 107
  Iguanodon 96
  Kangaroo 206
  Lambeosaurus 99
  Lion 194
  Lizard 184
  Marginocephalian 100
  Moeritherium 105
  Octopus 176
  Opossum 106
  Pachycephalosaurus 100
  Pachycephdlosaurus
    100
  Phiomia 105
  Plateosaurus 88
  Platypus 206
  Prenocephale 100
  Protoceratops 102
  Rattlesnake 185
  Rhesus monkey 202
  Seal 204
  Smilodon 107
  Stegoceras 100
  Styracosaurus 102
  Synapsid reptile 67
  Tortoise 77
  Turtle 187
Skull bones 81
Skullcap 555
Skunks 194
Skylight
  Battleship 394
  Building 495, 494
  Iron paddlesteamer
    392-393
Skyscraper 494
Slab
  Ancient Egyptian
    building 458-459
  Modern building 499
  Twentieth-century
    building 494
Slaked lime 434
Slalom
  Skiing 552
  Canoeing 560

Slalom clothing 553
Slalom equipment 553
Slalom gate 552
Slat 421
Slate 274, 275
Sleep button 585
Sleeper 524, 331
Sleeve port 343
Sleeve valve 345
Slender thistle 129
Slick racing tire 365
  Kirby BSA 369
  Suzuki RGV500 569
Slide 396
Slide bar 325
Slide brace 507
Slide locking lever 396
Slide track 561
Sliding bed 447
Sliding curtain 529
Sliding seat 561
Sliding window 333
Sling fixing point 349
Slip face 285
Slip faults 61
Slipher 43
Slope structure 60
Sloping roof 486
Slug 176
Slumped cliff 295
Slur 503
Smallbore rifle shooting
  548
Smallbore rifle target 549
Small intestine
  Brachiosaurus 90
  Chimpanzee 202
  Cow 198
  Domestic cat 195
  Elephant 200
  Euoplocephalus 94
  Frog 182
  Human 214, 249
  Lizard 185
  Tortoise 187
Small Magellanic Cloud
  Hydrus and Mensa 20
  Our galaxy and nearby
    galaxies 15
  Stars of southern skies
    20
Small stars 24-25
Small theropods 87
Small-scale rock
  deformities 61
Smalti 450
Smalti mosaic 450
Smart Hub 584
Smartphones 588-589
Smash 534
Smell 244
Smilodon 107
Smokebox 324, 325
Smoky quartz 268
Smooth cypress 125
Smooth endoplasmic
  reticulum 216
Smudging 430, 431
Smuts 114
Snail 176-177
Snake-bead ornament
  375
Snakes 184-185
Snap head 392
Snare 518
Snare drum 518
Snort mast 397
Snout
  Anchisaurus 89
  Caiman 186
  Croeodilians 186
  Dogfish 178
  Edmontonia 95
  Herrerasaurus 86
  Iguanodonts 96
  Jawless fish fossil 78
  Pachycephalosaurus
    100
  Rat 196

Snow
  Glaciers 286-287
  Weather 302
Snowflake moray eel 180
Snowflakes 302
Soane, J. 478, 482-483
Sobkou Planitia 35
Soccer 524-525
Soccer uniform 525
Socle
  Ancient Egyptian
    temple 458
  Baroque church 479
  Cathedral dome 487
  Gothic church 472
  Medieval church 469
  Neoclassical building
    478-479
  Renaissance building
    474
Soda lite 269
Sodium 35, 58
  Periodic table 310
  Seawater salt content
    296
Sodium hydroxide 312
Sodium lines 23
Soffit 464, 484, 498
Soft eye 382
Soft hair brush 436, 338,
  440
Soft-headed beater 516,
  517, 519
Soft metals 310
Soft palate 212, 245
Soft pastels 440
Soft pedal 514, 515
Soft rock
  River features 290
  Weathering and erosion
    282
Software effect plug-in
  521
Solanum tuberosum 128
Solar array 612, 613, 615
Solar array supporting
  arm 613
Solar cell 605
Solar collector 605
Solar day 34
Solar eclipse 32
Solar flare 32-33
Solar panel 496, 605
Solar power 605
Solar radiation 300-301
Solar system 38, 30-31,
  614-615
Solar wind
  Earth's magnetosphere
    38
  Structure of comet 53
  Sun 32
Solarium 494
Solar Wings Pegasus
  Quasar ultralight 427
Sole of foot 234
Soleplate 593
Soleplate roller 593
Soleplate surround 594
Soleus muscle 227, 233
Solfataras 272-273
Solid body 512, 513
Solid crystals 506
Solid heart thimble 385
Solidified lava
  Lake formation 292
  Volcanoes 272-273
Solid ink stick 444
Solid rubber tire 335
Solids 306-307
  Chemical reactions 312
Solid shapes 622
Solutions 306, 312-313
Sonic sensor 609
Sombrero 12
Somites 79
SONAR bulge 397
SONAR torpedo decoy
  396

SONAR transducer array
  397
Sonic boom 416
Sonoran Desert 264
Sony B-series MP3 player
  586
Sony DAV-S300 585
Sony DSC-W series 114
Sony W-series walkman
  586
Soot particles 313
Sophocles 35
Soralium 114
Sorbus aucuparid 130-131
Soredia 114
Sori 120-121
Sostenuto pedal 514, 515
Sound 514-515
  Coastline 295
  Musical notation 502
Soundboard
  Acoustic guitar 513
  Concert grand piano
    515
  Harp 511
  Upright piano 514
  Viola 511
  Violin 510
Sound channels 584
Sound hole
  Acoustic guitar 512-513
  Cello 511
  Double bass 511
  Viola 511
  Violin 510
Sound module 521
South Africa 64
South America 264, 617
  Cretaceous period
    72-75
  Jurassic period 70
  Late Carboniferous
    period 66
  Middle Ordivician
    period 64
  Quaternary period
    76-77
  Tertiary period 74-75
  Triassic period 68
South American plate 59
South Asian buildings
  490-491
South Atlantic Gyre 296
  Satellite map 265
South Atlantic Ocean 59,
  73
Southeast trade winds
  300
Southeasterly wind 303
South Equatorial Belt 45
South equatorial current
  296-297
Southerly wind 303
Southern Hemisphere
  296-297
Southern polar region 64
South Galactic Pole 15
South Indian Gyre 297
South magnetic polar
  region 28
South Pacific Gyre 296
South Pacific Ocean 59
South polar ice cap
  Structure of Mars 43
  Surface of Mars 42
South Pole
  Atmospheric circulation
    and winds 300
  Coriolis force 297
  Earth 58
  Jupiter 44
  Mars 42
  Mercury 34
  The Moon 40
  Neptune 50
  Pluto 51
  Pulsar 28
  Saturn 46
  Uranus 48-49
  Venus 36

South rim 277
South seeking pole 517
South Temperate Belt 45
South Temperate Zone 45
Space 500-501
Space probes 614-615
Space shuttle astronaut 613
Space shuttle remote manipulator system (robot arm) 612, 613
Space telescope 612-613
Spadix 145
Span 484
Spandrel
  Gothic church 471
  Islamic building 488-489
  Neoclassical building 482
  Nineteenth-century building 495
  Renaissance building 474
Spanish bowline 389
Spar
  BAe-146 jetliner components 415
  BE 2B tail 405
  Concorde, the 417
  Pegasus Quasar ultralight 427
Spare tire 357, 359
Spare wheel well 341
Spark plug 342-343, 410
Spark plug cap 566
Spark plug hole 346
Spark plug lead 344
Spar trunnion 409
Spat 426-427
Spathe 145
  Horsetails 120
Spawn 182-185, 192
Speaker
  Digital video 585
  Electronic music system 521
  Headphones 586
  System unit 567
Speaker assembly 580
Spear 582
Spear head 109
Specimen 610, 611
Specimen airlock 611
Specimen stage 610, 611
Spectral absorption lines 22-23
Spectral type 22-23
Specular hematite 268
Speech 237
Speed
  Forces 320
  Gearbox 366
Speedball nib 444
Speedometer 362
Speedometer drive 565
Sperm 258-259
Spermatheca
  Snail 177
  Spider 170
Sperm cell 217, 607
Sperm duct 195
Spermoviduct 177
Sperm whale 204-205
Sperry-ball gun turret 408
Sphenethmoid bone 183
Sphenoidal fontanelle 220
Sphenoidal sinus 212, 245
Sphenoid bone 220
Sphenopsids 279
Sphenopteris latiloba 72
Sphere 623
Spherical umbel 145

Spheroid 623
Sphincter muscle
  Anal 249
  Iris 241
  Pyloric 249
  Sea anemone 167
  Urethral 257
Sphyrna lewini 179
Spica 18, 21
Spicule 52, 55
Spieules 166
Spider
  Arachnid 170-171
  Bicycle 358, 360
Spider seat 354
Spigot 587
Spike
  Aechmea miniata 162
  Dodder 163
  Double bass 511
  Flower 143
  Grape hyacinth 155
  Thyreophorans 92-93
  Volleyball 534
Spiky cupule 150
Spinal column 258
Spinal cord
  Bird 189
  Bony fish 181
  Chimpanzee 202
  Dogfish 179
  Dolphin 205
  Domestic cat 195
  Elephant 200
  Human 212, 217, 225, 256, 258, 261
  Lizard 185
  Rabbit 196
Spinal ganglion 223, 238, 245
Spinal nerve 223, 238
Spindle 601
Spine
  Aechmea miniata 162
  Barberry 130-131
  Bromeliad 113
  Calligraphy character 445
  Cnidocyte 167
  Diatom 116
  Drvland plants 129
  Herbaceous flowering plants 128-129
  Human 218, 222-223
  Mahonia 150-151
  Modern jetliners 413, 415
  Neural 180
  Sea urchin 174
  Starfish 174
Spine end fairing 421
Spinner
  ARV light aircraft 424-425
  Hawker Tempest components 408
  Hawker Tempest fighter 409
  Lockheed Electra airliner 407
  Turbofan engine 418
Spinneret 170-171
Spinner mounting disc 406
Spinning lure 562
Spinose-dentate margin 129
Spinous process 222-223
Spiny anteaters 206
Spiny leaflets 130-131
Spiracle
  Acanthostega 80
  Caterpillar 169
  Spider 170
Spiral arm
  Galaxies 12-15
  Milky Way 14

Spiral ganglion 243
Spiraling clouds 302
Spiraling low-pressure cells 302
Spiraling rain 305
Spiraling winds 302-305
Spiral scroll 460
Spiral spring 449
Spiral staircase 472, 476
Spiral tubes 542
Spiral valve 179
Spiral wrack 116
Spire
  Asian building 490-491
  Gothic church 470-471, 475
  Medieval building 466, 468
  Nineteenth-century building 493
  Renaissance building 476-477
Spirit lamp 454
Spirketting 381
Spirogyra sp. 117
Spit 291
Splayed window-sill 475, 482
Spleen
  Bony fish 181
  Chimpanzee 202
  Domestic cat 195
  Elephant 200
  Frog 182
  Human 215, 249
Splenic artery 255
Splicing bd 383
Splint bone 198
Splinter bar 555
Splintery fracture 270
Split flap 406
Split line 151
Split-open pollen sac 144
Split rudder 421, 572
Spoiler 546, 549
Spoiler anchorage 415
Spoiler arm 414
Spoke
  Bicycle wheel 358-359
  Bordino Steam Carriage 335
  Eddy Merckx racing bicycle 361
  Etching press 447
  Paddle wheel 391
  Ship's wheel 390
Spoked wheel
  Bievcle 358-359
  Pacing sulky 555
Spoke guard 358
Spoke nipple 361
Sponge roller 442
Sponges 166-167
  Fossils 279
Spongocoel 166
Spongy bone 224
Spongy mesophyll 126, 159
Spongy tissues 156
Spool 562
Spoon 560
Spoon-shaped tooth 91
Sporangia 120-121
Sporangiophore 120
Sporangium 79
Spore-case 79
Spore-producing structures
  Fern 121
  Fungi 114-115
  Lichen 114
  Moss 112
Spores
  Clubmoss 120
  Fern 120-121
  Fungi 114-115
  Horsetail 120
  Lichen 114
  Liverworts 118

Mosses 1 18-119
  Mushroom 115
Sporophores 114-115
Sporophytes
  Clubmoss 120
  Fern 120-121
  Horsetail 120
  Liverworts 118
  Moss 112, 118-119
Sports tire 365
Sports wheel 540
Sprag clutch 410
Spray and steam knobs 594
Spray barrel 594
Spray nozzle 594
Spray pump 594
Spreader 561
Spring
  Lakes and Groundwater 292
  Motorcycle 566
  Power drill 600
  Toaster 599
Spring and chassis unit 337
Spring balance 320
Springboard diving 558
Spring/muffler unit 565
Springing point 467, 484-485
Spring line 292
Spring perch 338
Spring petiole 160
Spring shock absorber 358-359
Spring tides 296-297
Spring-trap mechanism 160
Spring washer 601
Spring wood xylem 134
Sprint races 560
Sprinting 542
Sprilsail 378
Sprit yard 376
Sprocket 358, 366
Spruce 513
Spruce beam 560
Sprung chassis 334
Spunyarn 388
Spun yarn serving 385
Spur 169
Spur gear 574
Spurious wing 191
Squadron code 409
Squamala 184
Squamosal bone 183
Squamous suture 220
Squainulose lichens 114
Squamulose thallus 114
Square 622
Square cut 538
Square knot 388
Square leg 538
Square-leg umpire 558
Square masonry 465
Square rib 486
Square-rigged ship 375
Square sail 374, 378, 584
Square-section steel tubing 364
Square-section tire 362, 369
Squash 544, 545
Squeegee 448
Squid 176
Squinch 466
Squirrel 196-197
Squirrel hair brush 458
Squirrel mop wash brush 458
SST 416-417
St. John's wort 145
St. Basil's Cathedral 487
St. Paul's Cathedral
  Baroque style 478, 480-481

Dome 480, 486-487
  Old 470, 472
Stabilizer 597, 548
Stabilizer-bar weight 422
Stabilizer fin 596
Stable elements 310, 311
Stack 295
Staff 577, 596
Staff 477, 495
Stage-door 477
Stained glass 470
Stainless steel cover 599
Staircase
  Ancient Roman building 465
  Baroque church 481
  Gothic church 470, 472
  Medieval building 466
  Modern building 496-497, 499
  Neoclassical building 483
  Renaissance building 474-477
Staircase turret 468
Stairs 477
Stair tool 593
Stairway 489
Stalactites 284-285
Stalagmites 284-285
Stalagmitic boss 284
Stalagmitic floor 284
Stalk
  Algae 116
  Barnacle 173
  Dicotyledons 127
  Flower 140
  Fungi 114-115
  Liverwort 118
  Monocotyledons 128
  Moss 112, 119
  Pitcher plant 113
  Seaweed 117
  Stem succulent 113
  Water lily 159
Stalked barnacle 173
Stalked secretory glands 161
Stalk scar 125
Stall warning vane 412
Stamen remains 146-147, 150
Stamens 140-143
  Anther 140-143
  Dicotyledon flower 126-127
  Fertilization 146-147
  Filament 140-145
  Insect-pollination 144
  Monocotyledon flower 126
  Rose 131
Stamp 445
Stance
  Dinosaurs 82
  Hominids 108
  Westlothiana 81
Stanchion 373, 595
Standard 554
Standardized horse 554, 555
Standard European paper 445
Standard knee 581
Standby pitot head 416-417
Standing block 382
Standing lug mizzen 385
Standing part
  Hawser bend 587
  Rigging 382-583
  Single sheet bend 587
Standing position 548
Standing rigging 382-585
Standoff half 530
Stapes 242
Staple 449
Starbirlh region 16
Starboard side 574

Starch grains 159
  Chlamydomonas sp. 116
Orchid root 133
Star clusters 16-17, 615
  Objects in universe 11
  Our galaxy and nearby galaxies 14
Star coral 167
Star drag 562
Star dune 283
Starfish 174-175
  Fossil 79
Star formation in Orion 24
Starling 467
Star magnitudes 22
Stars 22-25, 613
  Massive stars 26-27
  Milky Way 14-15
  Neutron stars and black holes 28-29
  Small stars 24-25
  Star clusters 16, 615
  Sun 52-55
Star scanner 615
Star-shaped parenchyma 135
Star-shaped sclereids 159
Stars of northern skies 18-19
Stars of southern skies 20-21
Starter 359, 558
Starter cog 356
Starter motor
  Hawker Tempest components 408
  Mid West twin-rotor engine 411
  Renault Clio 351
  Volkswagen Beetle 540
Starter ring 545
Starling block 558
Starting handle 336-337, 338, 345
Starling line (100m) 542
Start print button 575
Stale room 395
Static air-pressure plate 412
Static discharge wick 406
Static electricity 516
Stationary gear' 346-347, 411
Slalor 410
Statue 472, 478
Statue creation 455
Statuette 476, 481
Status indicator 577
Staurikosaurus 69
Stay 525, 592
Staysail 378, 383
"Stealth" bomber 420-421
Steam 275, 507
  Locomotives 324, 325
  Nuclear power station 314
  Oil-fired power station 315
Steam barrel 594
Steamboat with paddle wheels 391
Steam car 334, 342
Steam chest 554
Steam chest pressure gauge 525
Steam condenser 397
Steam control knob 594
Steam dome 525
Steam engine 590-591
Steam generator 314
Steam grating 380
Steam iron 594
Steam launch 594
Steam locomotive 324, 325
Steam pipe 334-335
Steam pipework 397

Steam-powered Cugnol "Fardier" 554
Steam release activator 594
Steam whistle 392
Steel 492
Steel and concrete floor 498
Steel and titanium skin 416
Steel beater 517
Steel brace 493
Steel column 497-498
Steel floor-plate 497
Steel frame 560, 564
Steel girder framework 514
Steel lattice-beam 497
Steel lock 360
Steel mullion 494
Steel point 452
Steel rails 550
Steel-reinforced concrete 494
Steel sleeper 330
Steel wheel 340, 550-551
Steeple 471, 481
Steeplechase 554
Steep ridge 283
Steerboard side 374
Steerer tube 359
Steering 350, 364
Steering actuator 416
Steering arm 338-339
Steering box assembly 340
Steering column
   Benz Motorwagen 335
   Ford Model T 359
   Renault Clio 350
   Volkswagen Beetle 341
Steering gear 392
Steering gearbox 339
Steering head 355
Steering idler 340
Steering knuckle 338
Steering link 355
Steering oar 374
Steering pump pulley 344
Steering rack 355, 350
Steering spindle 356
Steering stop 425
Steering tie-rod 340
Steering tiller 534-335, 557
Steering track-rod 357
Steering wheel
   1906 Renault 357
   Ford Model T 358-359
   Renault Clio 350, 353
   White Steam Car 342
Steering windetree 357
Stegoceras 100-101
Stegosauria 83
Stegosaurus 71, 92
Steib chair 362
Stela 459
Stele
   Dicotyledons 127
   Monocotyledons 127
   Root 132-133
Stellar core 17
Stellar spectral absorption lines 22-23
Stellate parenchyma 135
Stem 154-155
   Aechmea miniata 162
   Asteroxylon 79
   Bamboo 131
   Barberry 130-131
   Battleship 394
   Begonia 129
   Bishop pine 124-125
   Brassavola nodosa 162
   Bromeliad 113
   Broomrape 163
   Calligraphy character 445
   Canadian pond weed 158-159

Chusan palm 130
Clubmoss 120
Corallina officinalis 117
Couch grass 115
Crab cactus 129
Dicotyledons 126-127
Dodder 163
Eddy Merckx racing bicycle 361
Epiphytes 162-163
Everlasting pea 129
Florists' chrysanthemum 129
Flower arrangements 143
Golden barrel cactus 156
Guzmania lingulata 162-163
Hogweed 129
Horsetail 120
Ice-plant 128-129
Iron paddlesteamer 395
Ivy 131
Kedrostis africana 113
Live-forever 128-129
Liverwort 118
Maidenhair tree 123
Maple 127
Monocotyledons 126-127
Moss 119
Parasitic plants 163
Passion flower 130
Peach 131
Perennials 130-131
Sago palm 123
Strawberry 128
String of hearts 157
Vegetative reproduction 154-155
Water fern 158
Welwitschia 123
Woody plants 130-131
Woody stem 134
Yew 123
Stem bases
   Bulbil 155
   Guzmania lingulata 162-163
Stem branch 129
Stem bulbils 155
Stem cambium 126
Stem cells 606, 607
Stem head 376
Stempost
   74-gun ship 381
   Dhow 376
   Longboat 380
   Sailing warship 376
   Viking ships 374-375
Stem projections 156
Stem segments 129
Stem succulents 113, 156-157
Stem tubers 128, 154
Stencil 446
Step
   74-gun ship 381
   ARV light aircraft 424
   BE 2B bomber 404
   Blériot XI monoplane 401
   Medieval building 467
   Modern building 499
   Neoclassical building 485
   Steam-powered Cugnot 534
   Twentieth-century building 495
   Wooden sailing ship 378
Stephenson, Robert 324
Stepped roof 481
Stepped sternpost 375
Stepped sternpost 375
Sterile hairs 117, 119
Sterile ray 119
Sterile ray floret 142

Sterile shoot 120
Sterile whorl 116
Stern
   74-gun ship 381
   Iron paddlesteamer 392
   Kayak 560,
   Sailing dinghy 561
   Wooden sailing ship 378-379
Sterna hirundo 193
Sternal artery 175
Sternal bone 96, 102
Stern balustrade 373
Stern carving 381
Stern framing 392
Stern gallery 397
Stern lantern 379
Sternocleidomastoid muscle 226-227, 229
Sternohyoid muscle 229
Sternpost
   Greek galley 372
   Iron paddlesteamer 395
   Sailing warship 377
   Single scull 560
   Viking ships 374-375
   Wooden sailing ship 378
Stern quarter gallery 379
Stern rope 587
Stern section 592
Sternum
   Bird 189
   Domestic cat 195
   Elephant 201
   Hare 197
   Horse 199
   Human 218
   Kangaroo 206
   Seal 204
Stern walk 395
Stibnite 268
Stick insect 192
Stiff brush 436
Stifle 198
Stigma
   Damselfly 168
   Dicotyledon flower 126-127
   Fertilization 146-147
   Flower 140-143
   Pollination 144-145
Stigma remains 146-147, 150-151
Stilt 494
Stilted arch 468
Sting 170
Stinging cells 166
Stinkhorn 114
Stipe 114-115, 116-117
Stippled effect 442
Stipule
   Begonia 129
   Everlasting pea 129
   Passion flower 130
   Rose 131
   Seedling leaf 152
   St. John's wort 145
   Strawberry 128
Stirrup
   Crossbow 548
   Ossicles of middle ear 242
   Saddle 555
Stoa 461
   Ancient Roman building 463, 465
   Islamic building 488
Stock
   74-gun ship 380
   Danforth anchor 386
   Roman anchor 372
Stockless anchor 386
Stöfler 40
Stoker's seat 534
Stolons 154
Stomach
   Barnacle 173
   Bird 189

Bony fish 181
Chimpanzee 202
Cow 198
Crayfish 173
Dogfish 179
Dolphin 205
Domestic cat 195
Elephant 200
Frog 182
Human 214, 248
Jellyfish 167
Lizard 185
Octopus 176
Rabbit 196
Ruminants 198
Snail 177
Starfish 174
Tortoise 187
Stomach throw 556
Stomata
   Dryland plants 156-157
   Golden barrel cactus 156
   Haworthia truncata 157
   Monocotyledon leaf 126
   Photosynthesis role 138-139
   Pine needle 124
   Wetland plants 158
Stone
   Succulent fruits 148
   Lithographic printing 446, 448
   Sculpture 452
Stone canal 174, 175
Stone plate 446, 448
Stony-iron meteorite 52
Stony meteorite 52
Stop lamp assembly 352
Stop signal 330
Stopwatch 524
Storage locker 572
Storage organs
   Bulb 155
   Corm 155
   Rhizome 155
   Scale leaf 155
   Seed 152
   Succulent tissue 156-157
   Swollen stem 113, 155
   Tubers 128, 155
   Underground 154-155
Storage unit 573
Store button 521
Stores pylon 420-421
Stork 188
Storm 503
Straddle wire 358, 559
Straight 555
Straight four cylinder arrangement 345
Straight gouge 452
Straight handlebar 361
Strake
   Concorde 416-417
   Ironclad 393
   Roman corbita 372
   Viking ships 374-375
Strapontin 337
Strap-shaped leaf 162
Strata 276
   Faults and folds 60-61
   Sedimentary rocks 276
Stratocumulus cloud 302
Stratosphere
   Earth's atmosphere 300-301
   Jupiter's atmosphere 45
   Mars' atmosphere 43
   Saturn's atmosphere 47
Stratum basale 235
Stratum corneum 235
Stratum granulosum 235
Stratum spinosum 235
Stratus cloud 302
Strawberry 128, 150
Straw butt 549
Streak 270-271

Stream
   Glaciers 286-287
   Groundwater system 293
   Spring examples 292
Streamed internet radio on-screen display 577
Streamed internet video on-screen display 577
Streamlined spinner 407
Strengthening tissue
   Fern rachis 121
   Horsetail stem 120
   Marram grass 113
   Monocotyledon leaf 126
   Stems 134-135
   Water lily leaf 159
Stress 61
Stretcher
   Brickwork 485
   Nineteenth-century building 492
   Single scull 560
Stretches 555
Striated effect 442
Striation 46
Strike
   Baseball 536
   Baseball umpire signal 537
   Slope structure 60
Striker 524
Strike-slip fault 61
Strike-slip fault lake 293
Strike zone 536
Strindberg 35
String
   Acoustic guitar 512-513
   Cello 511
   Concert grand piano 515
   Double bass 511
   Electric guitar 513
   Harp 511
   Upright piano 514
   Viola 511
String arm 511
String course
   Ancient Roman building 465
   Cathedral dome 487
   Medieval building 466-467
   Nineteenth-century building 493
Stringed instruments 510, 511
   Guitar 512, 513
   Orchestral arrangement 504, 505
Strings
   Guitar 512-513
   Racket 544
   Violin 510
Strix aluco 190
Strobili 120
Stroke judge 558
Stroke play 546
Strokes 546
Stroke-side oar 560
Stroma 139
Stroma thylakoid 139
Strongylocentrotus purpuratus 175
Strontium 310
Strop 383
Strut
   Dome 484, 486
   Gothic building 473
   Marble sculpture support 455
   Neoclassical building 479
   Paddlesteamer 390
   Timpanum 519
Strut insert 340
Struthio camelus 188
   Egg 193

Struthiolaria 279
Struthiomimus 84, 87
Stub axle 424
Stud
   Ancient Roman mill 464
   Gothic building 473
   Mid West single rotor engine 410
Studding sail boom 378
Studding sail yard 378
Studio Elvira 495
Study 477
Stuffing box 590
Stump
   Coastline 295
   Wicket 558
Stupa 490-491
Stupica 491
Sturgeon 180
Style 140-143
   Fertilization 146-147
   Monocotyledon flower 126
   Pitcher plant 113
   Pollination 144-145
   Rowan fruit 131
Style of the gnomon 377
Style remains
   Dry fruit 150-151
   Fruit development 146-147
   Succulent fruit 148-149
Stylet 167
Styling panel 576
Stylobate 460
Styloglossus muscle 244
Styloid process 220, 243
Styracosaurus 102, 103
Subacute leaf apex 136-137
Subarachnoid space 237
Subclavian artery 215, 251, 253
Subclavian vein 253
Subduction 58
Subduction zone 281
Sublime 351
Subgenital pit 167
Subglacial stream 287
Sublimation 307
Sublingual fold 245
Sublingual gland 244-245
Submandibular gland 244
Submarine 396-397
Submarine canyon 298
Submerged atoll 299
Submerged glacial valleys 294-295
Submerged river valleys 294
Subopercular bone 181
Substitutions 532, 550
Substomatal chamber 139
Substrate 112
Substratum 115
Subsurface current 297
Subtropical jet stream 300
Subwoofer 586
Succulent fruits 148-149, 150
   Bramble 150
   Development 146-147
   Peach 131
   Rowan 131
Succulent leaves 128, 157
Succulent plants 156-157
Succulents 112
   Leaf 157
   Stem 156-157
   Stem and root 157
   Trailing stem 157
Succulent stem 129
Sucker
   Lamprey 178
   Octopus 176
Sucking stomach 170
Suction reduction control 595
Sugar
   Fermentation 312

Formation 158
Photosynthesis 315
Transport 159
Sulcus terminalis 244
Sulfates 269, 296
Sulfides 268
Sulfur 59, 268
  Periodic table 311
Sulfur dioxide 57
Sulfuric acid 36-57
Sulfurous gases 273
Sulky 554-555
Sumatra 265, 616
Sumigi 490
Summer petiole 160
Summit caldera 42
Sump 343, 344-345
Sump pan 554
Sun 32-33, 58
  Atmosphere 301
  Comet tails 48
  Earth's energy 314
  Electromagnetic
    radiation 314-315
  Energy emission from
    Sun 22
  Light 318
  Milky Way 14
  Objects in universe 11
  Oceans and seas
    296-297
  Ozone formation 64
  Solar eclipse 52
  Solar system 30-31
  Stars 22-25
Sun blind 573
Sun roof 341
Sun scoop 498
Sun sensor 614
Sunspots 32-33
Sun visor 350, 353
Supai group 277
Superclusters 10
Supercooling 307
Supercool liquid 506-507
Superficial peroneal
  nerve 238
Superficial skeletal
  muscles 226-227
Superfluid neutrons 28
Super-giant slalom
  (Super-G) skiing 552
Supergiant stars
  Massive stars 26
  Stars 22-25
  Stellar black hole 29
Supergranule 33
Superheater 325
Superior articular facet
  222
Superior articular process
  222-223
Superior concha 212
Superior laryngeal nerve
  244
Superior longitudinal
  muscle 245
Superior meatus 212
Superior mesenteric
  artery 253, 256
Superior mesenteric trunk
  257
Superior mesenteric vein
  255
Superior nasal concha
  245
Superior oblique muscle
  241
Superior orbital fissure
  221
Superior ramus of pubis
  224, 257

Superior rectus muscle
  241
Superior sagittal sinus
  212, 237
Superior thyroid artery
  244
Superior vena cava 215,
  251, 252-253, 255
Supernova
  Massive stars 26-27
  Nebulae and star
    clusters 16
  Neutron stars and black
    holes 29
Supernova remnant
  Nebulae and star
    clusters 16-17
  X-ray image of Crab
    Nebula 28
Supersonic flight 416
Supersonic jetliners
  416-417
Supersonic transport
  416-417
Supporter 381
Supporting tissue
  Bishop pine stem 125
  Dicotyledon leaf 126
  Stems 154-155
Supraesophageal
  ganglion 173
Supraoccipital bone 181
Supraoccipital crest 84
Supraorbital fissure 221
Supraorbital foramen 221
Supraorbital margin 213,
  220, 221
Supraorbital notch 213
Supraorbital ridge
  Chimpanzee 202
  Stegoceras 100
  Styracosaurus 102
Suprarenal gland 257
Suprarenal vein 257
Suprascapula 183
Suprasternal notch 211
Surangular bone 102
Surcingle loop 555
Surface areas 623
Surface currents 296-297
Surface deposits 273
Surface layer 295
Surface ocean current 296
Surface streams 284
Surface temperature 39
  Stars 22
Structure of main
  sequence star 24
Structure of Mars 43
Structure of Mercury 35
Structure of Neptune 51
Structure of red giant
  25
Structure of red
  supergiant 26
Structure of Venus 37
  Sun 33
Surface terrain 284
Surface vegetation 282
Surface winds 300
Surrogate mother 607
Surround sound 584
Surround sound special
  effect plug-in 521
Surveillance RADAR 397
Suspended erratic 286
Suspension
  "Deltic" diesel-electric
    locomotive 327
  Motocross racing 368
  Motorcycle 364
  Ultralight 426
Suspension arm 350-351
Suspension linkage 362
Suspension spring 350
Suspension strut 340, 351
Suspension top mount
  340
Sustaining pedal 514, 515

Suture 202
Su-wei 376
Suzuki RGV500 368,
  369
Swab hitch 387,
  589
Swallow 585
Swallow-hole 284
Swamp 290-291
Swan neck ornament
  375
Swash plate 344
Swash zone 294
S waves 63
Sweat duct 235
Sweat gland 234-235
Sweat pore 234-235
Sweep rowing 560
Sweep-rowing boat 561
Sweeping low throw 556
Sweet chestnut 136, 144,
  150
Sweetgum 76
Sweet pea 128
Sweet potato 154
Swell manual 514
Swell of muzzle 595
Swell pedal 514
Swell stop 514
Swept titanium fan blades
  572
Swifting tackle 377
Swim bladder 178,
  180-181
Swimmeret 172
Swimming 558, 559
Swimming pool 558
Swimwear 558
Swingarm 364, 368
"Swing-wings" 420
Switch 316
Switchboard room 397
Switch end casting
  598-599
Switch gear 314
Switch becket 382
Swivels
  Mooring and anchoring
    386
  Angling 562, 563
Swivel suspension ring
  577
Swollen leaf base 154-155
Swollen stem base
  Guzmania lingulata
    165
  Kedrostis africana
    113
  Oxalis sp. 157
Swollen stem 154-155
Sword 556-557
Sycamore 131, 150-151
Sycamore beam 560
Syconium 148
Syenite 275
Symbiosis
  Lichens 114
  Mycorrhizal association
    133
Symbols
  Communication 108
  Music 502, 503
Symphony orchestra 504,
  505
Synapsid reptile skull 67
Synaptic knob 228, 239
Synaptic vesicle 239
Syncarpous gynoecium
  140
Synchiropus splendidus
  180
Synchronized elevator
  425
Syncline 60, 61, 62
Synclinorium 61
Synergid nucleus 147
Synsacrum 189
Synthesizer 520
Synthetic brush 436, 438

Synthetic flax 384
Synthetic hog hair brush
  442
Synthetic materials 306
Synthetic polymer 306
Synthetic resin 442
Synthetic ropes 388
Synthetic sable brush 442
Synthetic strings 544, 545
Synthetic wash brush 438,
  442
Syria Planum 42, 45
System display 573
Systems connector 413
System unit 567

T

Tabernacle 463, 474, 476
Tab hinge 415
Tablet computer 568-569
Tablet flower 488, 491
Tabling 572, 584
Tabular habit 271
Tacan aerial 420
Tachybaptus ruficollis 190
Tack 375
Tackling
  Australian rules football
    528, 529
  Football 526
  Rugby 551
  Soccer 524
Tactical air navigation
  (Tacan) aerial 420
Tadpoles 182-183, 192
Taenia 460
Taenia colica 249
Taffrail 378, 381
Tail
  Amphibian 182
  Anchisaurus 89
  BE 2B bomber 404
  Caiman 187
  Calligraphy character
    445
  Corythosaurus 98
  Crocodilians 186
  Deer hopper dry fly
    563
  Dolphin 205
  Dunkeld wet fly 563
  Hare 196
  Hawker Tempest
    components 409
  Herrerasaurus 86
  Horse 198
  Ichthyostega 80
  Iguanodon 96
  Iguanodonts 96
  Kangaroo 206
  Lion 195
  Lizard 184-185
  Lungfish 81
  Monkey 202
  Ornithopods 96
  Pachycephalosaurus
    100
  Prehensile 202
  Rabbit 196-197
  Rat 196
  Rattlesnake 185
  Rigging 382-383
  Salamander 182
  Sauropodomorpha 88
  Schweizer helicopter
    423
  Scorpion 170
  Ski 552-553
  Stegoceras 101
  Stegosaurus 93
  Tadpole 185
  Triceratops 102
  Tyrannosaurus 84
  Westlothiana 81
Tail area 78
Tail boom 423

Tail bud 260
Tail bumper 417
Tail club 95
Tail cone 416-417, 418
Tailcone fairing 572
Tail crest 187
Taileron 420-421
Tail fairing 409
Tail feathers 188
Tail fluke 205
Tailgate 348
Tail gunner's
  compartment 408
Tail-gun turret 408
Taillight
  BMW R/60 562
  Harley-Davidson FLHS
    Electra Glide 562
  Honda CB750 563
  Mark 1 563
  Vespa Grand Sport 160
Tailpiece 510, 511
Tail-pin 510
Tail pipe 340
Tailplane
  ARV light aircraft 424
  BAe-146 jetliner 415
  BK 2B tail 405
  Biplanes and triplanes
    402-403
  Blackburn monoplane
    401
  Blériot XI monoplane
    401
  Curtiss biplane 399
  Hawker Tempest 409
  Lockheed Electra
    airliner 407
  Schleicher glider 426
Tailplane fairing 415
Tailplane root 409
Tailplane tip 407, 415
Tailrace 314
Tail rod 390
Tail rotor 422-423
Tail-rotor drive shaft 422,
  423
Tail rotor gearbox 423
Tail shield 78
Tailskid
  ARV light aircraft 424
  Avro triplane 403
  BE 2B bomber 405
  Blackburn monoplane
    400-401
  LVG CVI fighter 405
Tail spike 92
Tail spine 79
Tail unit 368
Tailwheel
  Avro biplane 402
  B-17 bomber 408
  Hawker Tempest
    fighter 409
  Lockheed Electra
    airliner 407
  Schleicher glider 426
Tailwheel leg 401
Takeoff and landing skid
  398
Takla Makan Desert 265
Talc 270-271
Tallow coating 379
Talonavicular ligament
  232
Talons 188
Talus 282-285
Talus bone 232
Tamarins 202, 203
Tambourine 504, 518
Tam-tam 504, 516
Tandem wings 402
Tank 592
Tank drain tap 407
Tank inspection access
  417
Tank support 339
Tantalum 310

Tantalus Fossae 43
Tapeats sandstone 277
Tapir 198
Tappet 343
Tappet adjustor 367
Tap root 128
Tarantula Nebula 26-27
  Large Magellanic Cloud
    12
Tarantulas 170-171
Target areas 556, 557
Target hole 546
Target pistol 548, 549
Target shooting 548, 549
Tarn 295
  U-shaped valley
    formation 287
Tarsal bone
  Albertosaurus 84
    87
  Iguanodon 97
Tarsals
  Crocodile 186
  Domestic cat 195
  Elephant 201
  Frog 183
  Hare 197
  Horse 199
  Kangaroo 206
  Lizard 184
  Platypus 206
  Rhesus monkey 202
  Seal 204
Tarsiers 202
Tarsomere 13
Tarsometatarsus 189
Tarsus
  Beetle 168
  Bird 188
  Human 219
  Scorpion 170
  Spider 171
Tas-de-charge 469
Tasmanian devil 207
Taste 244
Taste bud 244
Tau Orionis 18
Taurus 19, 20
Taurus mountains 77
Tau Sagittarii 21
Tawny owl 190
Taxing light 414, 420
Taxus baccata 70, 123
Tea clipper 392
Team crest 531
Team jersey 529
Team name 553
Tear fault 61
Technetium 310
Technosaurus 69
Tee 546
Teeing ground 546
Tee peg 547
Teeth
  Ankylosaurus 92
  Bear 106
  Caiman 186
  Canine 194, 202
  Carnassial 194
  Carnivores 194
  Ceratopsian 100
  Cheek 194
  Chimpanzee 202
  Crocodilians 186
  Extinct shark 67
  Hadrosaur 96
  Hominid 108
  Horse 105
  Human 246-247
  Iguanodont 96
  Incisor 194, 196, 201,
    202
  Lamprey 178
  Leaf-shaped 88-89
  Molar 194, 201, 202
  Ornithopod 96
  Premolar 194, 202
  Rabbit 196
  Rodents 196

Theropod 84
Thyreophoran 92
Venus fly trap 160
Teeth development 246
Tegenaria gigantea 171
Telephone line 576
Telescope, space 612-613
Telescopic fork
　Harley-Davidson FLHS
　Electra Glide 563
　Honda CB750 563
　Honda VF750 564
　Husqvarna Motocross
　TC610 368
　Motorcycle 364
　Suzuki RGV500 368
　Weslake Speedway
　motorcycle 569
Telescopic muffler 326,
　529
Telescopic sight 548, 549
Telescopic strut 416
Television 315
Telltale 545
Tellurium 311
Tellus Regio 36, 37
Tellus Tessera 37
Telson 172
　Fossil 79
TEM 610, 611
Tempe Fossae 43
Tempera 432, 433
Temperate latitudes 502
Temperature
　Atmosphere 300-301
　Chemical reactions
　312-313
　Formation of black hole
　29
　Germination 152
　Matter 306-307
　Mineral resources 280
　Oceans and seas 296
　Stellar black hole 29
　Weather 302-303
Temperature and
　pressure sensor 418
Temperature and steam
　control dial 594
Temperature changes
　Atmosphere 301
　Oceans and seas 296
　Weathering and erosion
　282
Temperature scales 621
Tempered pigment 432
Temple 484-485
　Ancient Egyptian 458
　Ancient Greek 460-461
　Ancient Roman 462-465
　Asian 490
Temple blocks 516
Temple Butte limestone
　277
Temple Cap sandstone
　276
Temple of Amon-Re
　458-459
Temple of Aphaia 461
Temple of Athena Polias
　460
Temple of Heaven 490
Temple of Isis 459
Temple of Mallikarjuna
　491
Temple of Neptune
　460-461
Temple of Vesta 462-463
Temple of Virupaksha
　490-491
Tempo 504
Temporal bone
　Chimpanzee 202
　Human 220-221, 242
Temporal lobe 257
Temporalis muscle
　226-227, 229
Tendon
　Achilles 232-233

Annular 241
Calcanean 232-233
Extensor digitorum
　longus 233
Extensor digitorum 231
Extensor hallucis
　longus 233
Flexor digitorum 251, 87
Palmaris longus 231
Peroneus brevis 233
Tendril
　Arabesque 480
　Clematis 150
　Dogfish egg 192
　Everlasting pea 129
　Monkey cup 161
　Passion flower 130
Tennis 544
Tennis racket 544
Tenon
　Flax spinning mill 492
　Hull plank fastening
　373
Tenor drum 518-519
Tenor joint 508
Tenor mule 507
Tenor note strings 515
Tenor saxophone 509
Tenor voice 502
Tension
　Drums 518
　Faults and folds 60-61
　Mountain building 62
Tension column 497
Tension control 552
Tension key 518, 519
Tension member 499
Tension pulley 360
Tension rod 518, 519
Tension screw 518
Tensor fasciae latae
　muscle 226
Tensor tympani muscle
　243
Tentacle
　Coelenterates 166
　Jellyfish 167
　Mollusks 176-177
　Scallop 176
　Sea anemone 166-167
　Snail 177
Tenth century
　Building 490
　Style 468
Tepal 468
Tepal scar 140
Tepal
　Flower parts 140, 143
　Monocotyledons 126
　Peruvian lily 129
Terbium 311
Teres major muscle 227
Teres minor muscle 227
Tergum plate 173
　Egg 192
Terminal box 317
Terminal bronchiole 254
Terminal bud
　Bishop pine 124
　Horse chestnut 130
　London plane 134
　Rhizome 155
　Root tuber 154-155
　Stems 154
　Stolon 154
Terminal ileum 249
Terminal lake 286
Terminal moraine
　Glaciers 286
　Rivers 289
Terminal pinna 136
Terminal ring 259
Terminus 286
Terrace
　Asian building 490-491
　Modern building
　497-499
　Twentieth-century
　building 494-495
Terracotta clay 455

Terrain-following radar
　420
Terrapin 186-187
Terrestrial animal 74
Terrestrial mammal 104
Terrigenous sediment 299
Tertiary bronchus 215
Tertiary period 57, 74, 75
　Fossil record 279
Tessellation 489
Tessera 450, 489
Test 174-175
Testa 152
　Dry fruit 150-151
　Embryo development
　147
　Epigeal germination
　153
　Hypogeal germination
　152
　Succulent fruit seed
　148-149
Testicle 259
Testicular artery 257
Testicular vein 257
Test is
　Barnacle 173
　Dolphin 205
　Domestic cat 195
　Human 259
　Rabbit 196
Test tube 313
Tetanurae 83
Tethus Regio 36
Tethys 46
Tethys Sea
　Cretaceous period 73
　Jurassic period 71
Tertiary period 74, 75
　Triassic period 69
Tetragonal system 270
Tetrahedron 623
Tetralophodon 75, 104
Text 444
Textured papers 441
Textured scraper 593
TGV electric high-speed
　train 529
Thalamian 373
Thalamus 236-237
Thalassiosira sp. 116
Thalictrum delavayi 137
Thallium 311
Thalloid liverwort 118
Thallus
　Algae 116-117
　Lichen 114
　Liverwort 118
　Seaweed 116-117
T-handle auger 374
Thar Desert 265, 616
Tharsis Tholus 43
Thatched roof 477
Thaumasia Fossae 43
The Big Dipper 19
Themis Regio 36
Therapeutic cloning 606
Theobroma cacao 148
Therapsids 104
Thermal/electrical
　insulation 596, 597
Thermal insulation 613
Thermals 426
Thermocouple bus-bar
　419
Thermogram 214
Thermosphere
　Earth's atmosphere
　300
　Mars' atmosphere 43
　Venus' atmosphere 37
Thermostat 411
Theropoda 83
Theropods 84-87
Thesium alpinium 145
Theta1 Sagittarii 21
Theta Andromedae 19
Theta Pegasi 19
Thetis Regio 36

Thick skull 46
Thigh
　Anchisaurus 89
　Bird 188
　Corythosaurus 98
　Gorilla 203
　Horse 198
　Human 211
　Iguanodon 96
　Kangaroo 207
　Lion 195
　Psittacosaurus 103
　Stegoceras 101
　Stegosaurus 92
　Triceratops 102
　Tyrannosaurus 84
Thigh musculature 90
Thigh pad 527
Thimble
　Harness racing 555
　Rigging 383, 384
Third-century building
　465
Third horse 541
Third man 538, 541
Third rail 328
Third stage motor 615
Thirteenth century
　Building 467, 469-471
　Style 470
Thirty-five mm file strip
　holder 570
Thistle funnel 313
Thole pin 580
Thoracic cavity 255
Thoracic leg 169
Thoracic nerve 238
Thoracic pleurae 78
Thoracic segment 79
Thoracic vertebrae
　Crocodile 186
　Domestic cat 195
　Hare 197
　Horse 199
　Human 222
　Kangaroo 206
　Platypus 206
　Rhesus monkey 202
　Seal 204
Thoracolumbar vertebrae
　Elephant 201
　Lizard 184
Thorax
　Cirripedia 172
　Human 211
　Insects 168-169
Thorium 310
Thornback ray 179
Thoroughbred horse 554
Thranite 373
Thread 167
Three-blade main rotor
　423
Three-cylinder Anzani
　engine 401
Three-cylinder engine
　425
Three-lobed stigma 143
Three-masted square-
　rigged ship 375
Three-point line 532
Three pounder 395
Three-toed ungulates 198
Threshold 463
Throat
　Angling hook 562
　Bird 188
　Danforth anchor 386
　Human 212, 244-245
　Lacrosse crosse 541
　Racketball racket 545
　Squash racket 545
　Tennis racket 544
Throatlatch 199
Throttle
　Avro triplane 402
　Curtiss biplane 398
　"Rocket" steam
　locomotive 324

Suzuki RGV500 363
Vespa Grand Sport 160
Mark 1 563
Weslake Speedway
　motorcycle 569
Throttle butterfly 545
Throttle cable 550
　Harley-Davidson FLHS
　Electra Glide 563
　Husqvarna Motocross
　TC610 368
　Kirby BSA racing
　sidecar 369
　Suzuki RGV500 569
　Weslake Speedway
　motorcycle 569
Throttle lever 419, 425
Throttle linkage
　Ford Model T 338
　Jaguar V12 engine 345
　Oldsmobile trim 337
　Renault Clio 350
Throttle wheel 342
Throw
　Judo 556
　Structure of a fault 60
Thrower 394
Throw-in 532
Thrushes 188
Thrust 545
Thruster 614
Thruster cluster 615
Thrust fault 61
Thrust plate 601
Thrust-reverser 421
Thulium 311
Thumb 211, 230-231
Thumb-claw
　Anchisaurus 89
　Apatosaurus 83
　Baryonyx 83, 85
　Massospondylus 83, 89
　Plateosaurus 88
Thumbhole 384
Thumb knot 389
Thumb piston 514
Thumb-spike 96-97
Thwart 573, 575, 580
Thylakoid 139
Thymine 216
Thyrophora 83
Thyreophorans 92-93,
　94-95
Thyristor converter 328
Thyrohyoid membrane
　244
Thyrohyoid muscle 229,
　244
Thyroid cartilage 245, 255
Thyroid gland 214-215,
　217, 244-245, 255
Tibetan plateau 63
Tibia
　Archaeopteryx 85
　Beetle 168
　Butterfly 169
　Crocodile 186
　Diplodocus 90
　Domestic cat 195
　Elephant 201
　Eryops 81
　Gallimimus 86
　Hare 197
　Horse 199
　Human 219, 232-233
　Iguanodon 96-97
　Kangaroo 206
　Lizard 184
　Parasaurolophus 99
　Plateosaurus 88
　Platypus 206
　Rhesus monkey 202
　Scorpion 170
　Seal 204
　Spider 171
　Stegoceras 101
　Stegosaurus 93
　Struthiomimus 87
　Toxodon 107

Triceratops 102
Turtle 187
Tyrannosaurus 84
Tibiale 183
Tibial flexor muscle 97
Tibialis anterior muscle
　226, 233
Tibialis posterior muscle
　233
Tibiofibula 183
Tibiotarsus 189
Tidal bulge 297
Tidal currents 296-297,
　298
Tidal flow 296
Tidal levels 295
Tidal power 604
Tidal river-mouth 295
Tidal scour 298
Tidal waves 58
Tides 294, 297
Tie
　Basketball match 532

Bordino Steam Carriage
　334
　Musical notation 502,
　505
Tie-beam
　Ancient Roman mill 464
　Dome 486
　Gothic church 473
　Neoclassical building
　479
　Tie plate 393
　Tierceron 485
　Tie rod 354, 340
　Tiger seat 334
　Tiger shark 178-179
　Tight end 526
　Tight-head prop 530
Tile
　Dome 486
　Islamic mosque 488
　Modern building 499
　Neoclassical building
　482
　Renaissance building
　476-477
Tiled roof 495
Tilia sp. 154
Tilia x europaea 143
Tiller
　Dhow 376
　First cars 334-335
　Longboat 380
　Oldsmobile trim 337
　Roman orbita 373
　Sailing dinghy 561
　Steamboat with paddle
　wheels 391
　Viking ships 374-375
Till and rotation
　Jupiter 44
　Mars 42
　Mercury 34
　The Moon 40
　Neptune 50
　Pluto 51
　Saturn 46
　Uranus 48
　Venus 36
Timber 516
Timber frame
　Ancient Roman
　building 462, 464-465
　Dome 486
　Medieval building
　466-467
　Renaissance building
　477
Timber head 580
Timber rafter 492
Timber trellis 603
Time interval signal
　330
Timekeeper
　Basketball 532
　Fencing contest 557

Handball 555
Judo contest 556
Lacrosse 541
Netball 555
Swimming 558
Time signature 502
Time switch 598
Time-trial bicycle 360
Time zones 618-619
Timing chain 343, 345
Timing chest 343
Timing gear 367
Timpani 503, 504, 505, 518
Tympanum 519
Tin 311
Mineralization zones 281
Squash 545
Tinatin Planitia 37
Tinted paper 441
Tip of dodder stem 163
Tip ring 563
Tip section 563
Tire
1906 Renault 356-357
ARV light aircraft 424
Avro triplane 402
BAe-146 jetliner 414
Bicycle 358-359
Blériot XI monoplane 401
BMW R/60 362
Cannondale SH600 hybrid bicycle 361
Curtiss biplane 398
Double-decker tour bus 355
Eddy Merckx racing bicycle 360
First cars 334-335
General use 365
Lockheed Electra airliner 407
MCW Metrobus 333
Metal 324
Motocross racing 368
Motorcycle 365
Pacing sulky 555
Pneumatic 358, 555
Race car 356-357
Renault Clio 352-353
"Rocket" steam locomotive 324
Rossin Italian time-trial bicycle 361
Single-decker bus 333
Slick racing 365
Suzuki RGV500 368-369
Trials 365
Tubeless sports 565
Volkswagen Beetle 340
World War I aircraft 404-405
Tire carrier 337
Tire tread 360, 365, 368
Tire wall 360
Tissue culture 607
Titan 614
Titania 48
Titanium 310
Titanohyrax 74
Toad 182
Toadflax 129
Toaster 598-599
Toe
Albertosaurus 84
Anchisaurus 89
Archaeopteryx 85
Bird 188
Caiman 186-187
Corythosaurus 98
Golf club 547
Gorilla 203
Herrerasaurus 86
Human 211, 232-233
Iguanodon 96-97
Lion 194
Lizard 184

Pachycephalosaurus 100
Psittacosaurus 103
Stegoceras 101
Tyrannosaurus 84
Toe clip 360
Toenail
Elephant 200
Gorilla 203
Human 233
Toe piston 514
Toe strap 358-359
Toggle switch 513
Toilet 416, 485
Tolstoj 35
Tomb 458-459, 489
Tomb of Itimad-ud-daula 489
Tomb of King Tjetji 459
Tombolo 294
Tom-toms 518-519
Tondo brush 434
Tone editor control 520
Tonehole 509
Tone pattern selector 520
Tongs 321
Tongue
Allosaurus 85
Caiman 186
Chimpanzee 202
Corythosaurus 98
Cow 198
Dolphin 205
Domestic cat 195
Elephant 200
Human 212, 226, 244, 248
Iguanodon 97
Lamprey 178
Lion 194
Rabbit 196
Rattlesnake 185
Ski boot 552
T'on-wei 376
Tool and battery box 335
Tool brush-head connector 593
Tool or wand cuff 593
Tools
Rigging 382-383
Sailmaking 384
Viking boatbuilding 374
Tooth
Acanthostega 80
Anchisaurus 89
Ankylosaurus 94
Arsinoitherium 104
Australopithecus 108
Baryonyx 83
Camarasaurus 91
Diplodocus 90
Dragon prowhead 374
Eryops 80
Euoplocephalus 94
Heterodontosaurus 83
Homo habilis 108
Human 108, 246-247, 248
Iguanodon 96
Lambeosaurus 99
Moeritherium 105
Pastels application 440
Phiomia 105
Plateosaurus 88
Protoceratops 102
Smilodon 107
Triceratops 103
Tyrannosaurus 84
Toothless beak
Ankylosaurs 92
Corythosaurus 98
Euoplocephalus 94
Gallimimus 86
Theropods 84
Triceratops 102
Topaz 271
Topcastle 373, 377
Topgallant mast
Battleship 395

Sailing warship 377
Wooden sailing ship 378-379
Top hose 351
Topmast 377, 378
Topping lift 380
Topping-up valve 561
Top-plate 464
Top race 359
Topsail
74-gun ship 379
Double topsail schooner 385
Junk 376
Topset strata 283
Topside strake 393
Top sliding block 437
Tornado GR1A 420-421
Torosaurus 73
Toroweap formation 276
Torpedo 394-397
Torque arm 364, 365
Torque arm mount 419
Torque tube 338-339
Torque tube assembly 425
Torrential rain 302
Torsional vibration muffler 410-411
Torsion bar 350
Tortillon 440, 441
Tortoise 186
Tortoise skull 77
Torus
Ancient Roman building 463
Asian building 490
Dome 486
Gothic building 470
Medieval building 467-469
Renaissance building 475, 477
Shapes: solid 623
Total solar eclipse 32
Tote board 555
Touch-down 526
Touch-in goal line 530
Touch judge 530
Touch line
Rugby 530
Soccer 524
Touchpad 566
Touchpiece 509
Touchscreen 568-569, 578-579, 591
Touch sensor 609
Tour buses 332
Tour de César 466
Touring bicycle 360, 361
Tourmaline 269
Tower
Ancient Roman building 465
Asian building 490-491
Clock 493
Gothic church 472
Islamic building 488
Medieval building 466-467, 468-469
Modern building 496-497
Nineteenth-century building 492-493
Renaissance building 476
Twentieth-century building 495
Tower Bridge 492-493
Tower vault 469
Towing fairlead 395
Towing hook 335, 426
Town Hall 495
Toxodon 76, 106, 107
TPU connector 571
Trabecula 250-251
Trace fossils 278

Tracery
Gothic building 470-473
Nineteenth-century building 493
Trachea
Bird 189
Brachiosaurus 91
Chimpanzee 202
Dolphin 205
Domestic cat 195
Elephant 200
Gallimimus 86
Human 212, 215, 244-245, 248, 255
Lizard 185
Rabbit 196
Spider 170
Tortoise 187
Trachelion 460
Trachycarpus fortunei 127, 130
Track 413
Track control arm 340
Track events 542, 543
Track gauge 330, 331
Track rod
Elegance and utility 336-337
Ford Model T 338-339
Renault Clio 351
Track shoe 543
Traction motor 328
Trade winds 300
Traffic congestion 332
Traffic surveillance 422
Tragus 242
Trailboard 379
Trailing arm 340
Trailing edge
BAe-146 jetliner components 413, 414, 415
BE 2B tail 405
BE 2B wings 404
Hawker Tempest components 409
Pegasus Quasar ultralight 426-427
Trailing-link arm 414
Trailing wheel 524
Train equipment 330-331
Training gear 396
Trains
Diesel 326-327
Electric 328-329
High-speed 328-329
Steam 324-325
Trams 332-333
Transaxle 340
Transept
Gothic church 470, 473
Medieval church 468-469
Transfer port 342
Transformation 168
Transformer 314, 328
Transform fault 59
Transistor 584
Transitional cell mucosa 257
Transition metals 310, 311
Transit plug 397
Translucent crystal 271
Translucent impasto glaze 443
Translucent white marble 453
Translucent "window" 157
Transmission 350-351
Transmission adaptor plate 344
Transmission electron microscope (TEM) 610, 611
Transmission system 326, 366
Transom
74-gun ship 381
Junk 376

Longboat 380
North wing, Chateau de Montal 476
Sailing warship 377
Transparency holder 570
Transparent glassy crystal 271
Transparent lower drumhead 518
Transparent tissue 160
Transparent wash 439
Transpiration 136
Transponder aerial 423
Transportation lock 571
Transportation system 332
Transport tissue
Golden barrel cactus 156
Monocotyledons 126
Photosynthesis 158-159
Transversary 377
Transverse arch 485
Baroque church 479
Medieval church 468-469
Transverse colon 249
Transverse dune 283
Transverse foramen 222
Transverse leaf spring 338
Transverse line 555
Transverse process
Human 222-223
Plateosaurus 89
Tyrannosaurus 85
Transverse rib 485
Transverse strut 512
Trapezium 17, 622
Trapezium bone 230
Trapezius muscle 226-227, 229
Trapezoid bone 230
Traps
Butterwort 161
Cobra lily 160
Monkey cup 161
Pitcher plant 115, 160-161
Sundew 160
Venus fly trap 160
Traveler 580
Traveling 555
Travertine shell 464
Tray fascia 595
Tread 47
Tread pattern 365
Treasury of Atreus 461
Treble bridge 514
Treble clef 502
Treble hook 562-563
Treble note strings 515
Treble voice 502
Tree 66-67, 130-131
Energy storage 315
Epiphytes 162-163
Gymnosperms 122-125
Tree fern 112-113
Tree mallow 131
Tree root action 282
Treenail 387
Trefoil
Gothic church 470-473
Nineteenth-century building 493
Trefoil arch 473, 484
Trellis window 459
Trellised river drainage 288
Trembler coil box 335
Trenail 387
Trestle trees 378
Trevithick, Richard 324
Triac device 600
Trials tire 565
Triangle
Shapes: plane 622
Musical instrument 504, 517

Steamboat with paddle wheels 391
Triangle mosaic 489
Triangular buttress 484
Triangular fossa 242
Triangular horn 85
Triangular lesene 481
Triangular pediment 462
Triangular-section fuselage
Avro triplane 403
Bell-47 helicopter 423
Blackburn monoplane 401
Triangulum 19, 20
Triangulum Australe 21
Triassic period 68-69
Fossil record 279
Geological time 57
Triatic stay 385
Tribune 467-468
Tributary
Coastlines 295
Rivers 288
Tributary moraine 287
Tributary stream 289
Triceps brachii muscle 227
Triceratops 100, 102-103
Trichome 156
Marram grass 113
Triclinic system 270
Tricolpate pollen grain 145
Tricuspid valve 251
Triere 373
Trifid Nebula 16
Trifoliate leaves 128, 130
Laburnum 137
Oxalis sp. 157
Triforium 469
Trigger
Air pistol 549
Biathlon smallbore rifle 549
Cnidocyte structure 167
Trigger hair 160
Trigger mechanism 600
Trigger position 600
Triglyph 460
Trigon 488
Trigonal system 270
Trigone 257
Trigonometry 621
Trike nacelle 426-427
Trilete mark 145
Trilobate rotor 346
Tri-lobed tail 81
Trilobites 64, 78
Earth's evolution 56
Fossil record 279
Trim 352-353
1906 Renault 356-357
Oldsmobile trim 337
Renault Clio 350-351
Volkswagen Beetle 341
Trimala 491
Trimtab 407, 414, 415
Trim tank 416-417
Trinity Chapel, Salisbury Cathedral 470
Tripinnate leaves 157
Triplanes 402-403
Triple bar jump 554
Triple jump 542
Triple spine 130-131
Tripod mast 394
Tripod stand
Congas 519
Drum kit 518
Electronic drums 520
Modeling stand 455
Radial studio easel 4 37
Tripping palm 386
Tripping ring 372
Triquetral bone 230
Trireme 372-373

Tri-spoke wheel 561, 568, 569
Triton 50
Trochanter
  Beetle 168
  Scorpion 170
  Spider 171
Trochlea
  Baryonyx 85
  Human 241
Trochoid housing 410
Trojan two-stroke engine 542
Trolley 332
Trombone 504, 505, 506, 507
Tropeter 573
Trophoblast 260
Tropic formation 276
Tropic of Cancer
  Satellite map 265
  Surface currents 297
Tropic of Capricorn
  Satellite map 265
  Surface currents 297
Tropical cyclone 302
Tropical orchids 162
Tropical rainforest 39, 66
Troposphere
  Earth's atmosphere 300
  Jupiter's atmosphere 45
  Mars' atmosphere 43
  Saturn's atmosphere 47
  Venus' atmosphere 37
Trout 180
Trout angling 562
Truck
  Early tram 332
  Greek galley 372
  Longboat 380
  Wooden sailing ship 378-379
Trumpet 504, 506, 503
Truncate leaf base 137
Trunk
  Elephant 200-201
  Mammoth 107
  Phiomia 105
  Tree fern 112
  Woody flowering plant 130-131
Trunnion 595
Truss
  Gothic church 473
  Modern building 497-499
  Steam boat with paddle wheels 391
Truss rod 513
Try 530, 531
T-section beam 492
Tsiolkovsky 41
T-type cantilevered fin 426
Tu-144 416
Tuba 504, 505
Tube fret 174, 175
Tubeless sports tire 365
Tuber
  Broomrape 145
  Dryland plants 157
  Horsetail 120
  Potato 128
  Vegetative reproduction 155
Tubercle
  Corythosaurus 98
  Golden barrel cactus 156
  Sea urchins 174
  Starfish 174
  Stem projections 156
Tubular bells 504, 516
Tubular chassis 355
Tubular drums 518
Tubular open cradle frame 569
Tubular petioles 160

Tuck 581
Tudor arch 484
Tufted duck 188
Tug propeller 391
Tulip mount 563
Tuner/amplifier link cables 585
Tuner settings memory microchip 585
Tungsten
  Mineralization zones 281
  Periodic table 310
Tungsten carbide lip 450
Tungsten filament 319
Tunica adventitia 252
Tunica intima 252
Tunica media 252
Tuning adjustor 510-511
Tuning pedal 519
Tuning peg 510, 511
Tuning pin 514, 515
Tuning slide 506
Tunnel
  Cave 285
  Trains 330
Tunnel vault 485
Tuojiangosaurus 92
Tupelo 157
Turbine
  Energy 314-315
  Floodgate 604
  Jet engines 418-419
Turbo-charged diesel engine 327
Turbocharger 356
Turbofan engine 418-419
  Landing gear 412
Turbo impeller 347
Turbojet engine 418-419
  Landing gear 412
  Supersonic jetliner 416
Turbo propeller 347
Turboprop engine 418-419
Turdus viscivorus 190
Turfed roof 602, 603
Turgai strait 71
Turkish crescent finial 488
Turk's head 383
Turnbuckle
  Avro triplane 402
  Blackburn monoplane 401
  Curtiss biplane 398
  LVG CVI fighter 405
  Rigging screw 383
Turn indicator 358
Turning force 520
Turning indicator 332, 333
Turning judge 558
Turning vane 357
Turns 555
Turntable 596
Turntable rotator 596
Turpentine 456
Turret 486
  Baroque church 481
  Battleship 394-395
  Gothic church 470-471
  Gun turret 396
  Medieval building 466, 468
  Nineteenth-century building 493
  Renaissance building 476-477
Turtle 72-75, 186-187
Tuscan capital 465
Tuscan pilaster 465, 483
Tusche 446
Tusche pen 448
Tusche stick 448
Tusk
  Elephant 200-201
  Mammoth 107
  Phiomia 105

TV mini-camera 356
TV power button 585
Tweeter loudspeaker connectors 585
Twelfth century
  Building 466-467
  Church 469, 473
  Roof 490
  Style 468, 470
Twentieth-century buildings 494-495
Twin-blade main rotor 423
Twin carbon-fiber disc brake 369
Twin carburetors 427
Twin-cylinder engine
  Harley-Davidson 362
  Pegasus Quasar ultralight 427
  Steam-powered Cugnot 334
Twin-domed forehead 200
Twine 384
Twin-lobed leaf blade 160
Twin nose-wheel 420
Twin rate spring 365
Twin rear axle 333
Twin rudder 372
Twin-wheel main landing gear 414
Twin-wheel nose-gear 417, 420
Twist 388
Twist dive 558, 559
Twisted wire habit 271
Two-lobed stigma 142
Two-pulley system 520
Two-seater cockpit 421
Two-stroke combustion engine 366
Two-toed ungulates 198
Two-towered gate 467
Tyagaraja 35
Tycho 40
Tye 577
Tye halyard 574
Tympan 449
Tympanic bullet 194
Tympanic canal 243
Tympanic membrane 243
Tympanum
  Frog 182
  Quail chick 195
Typhoon 302
Tyrannosaurus 75, 84-85
Tyringham House 483

U

UE Boom speakers 587
UHF aerial 420
UK loading gauges 331
Ulmus minor 144
Ulna
  Archaeopteryx 85
  Arsinoitherium 104
  Baryonyx 85
  Bird 189, 191
  Brachiosaurus 91
  Crocodile 186
  Diplodocus 90
  Domestic cat 195
  Elephant 90, 201
  Eryops 80
  Euoplocephalus 94
  Hare 197
  Horse 199
  Human 218, 230
  Iguanodon 96
  Kangaroo 206
  Kentrosaurus 93
  Lizard 184
  Parasaurolophus 99
  Pareiasaur 81
  Plateosaurus 88
  Platypus 206
  Rhesus monkey 202
  Seal 204

Stegoceras 100, 101
Stegosaurus 93
Struthiomimus 87
Toxodon 106
Triceratops 102
Tuojiangosaurus 93
Turtle 187
Tyrannosaurus 84
Ulnar artery 231, 253
Ulnar nerve 231, 238
Ultra-high frequency (UHF) antenna 615
Ultralights 410, 426-427
Ultramarine lapis lazuli 433
Ultrasound scan 214
Ultraviolet light 145, 319
Ultraviolet radiation 22, 319
Ultraviolet solar radiation 300
Umbels 143
Umbilical artery and vein 260
Umbilical cord 260-261
Umbilicus 211, 260
Umbo 176
Umbra 52
Umbrella 491
Umbriel 48
UMD drive ribbon cable 579
Umpire
  Badminton 545
  Baseball 536
  Cricket 538
  Football 526
  Hockey 540
  Lacrosse 541
  Netball 535
  Tennis 544
  Volleyball 534
Umpire signals 537
Una corda pedal 514, 515
Unarmed combat 556
Underarm pass 535
Underframe 332
Underground mycelium 115
Underground stem 154
Underground storage organs 154-155
Underground stream 284-285
Underground water
  Lake formation 292
  Rivers 288
Underhand serve 534
Under plastron 557
Under-turntable roller ring 596
Underwater digital camera 581
Underwater mountains 298
Underwing flaps 425
Ungulates 198-199
Unicellular organisms 56
Unified leaf pair 157
Uniform motion 321
"Union Pacific" diesel train 326
Unipolar neuron 239
Unison 503
Unit number 328
Units of measurement 620
Universal resource locator (URL) address 577
Universal serial bus (USB) ports 566, 567, 570
Universal veil 114-115
Universe 10-11
Unmapped region
  Degas and Brönte 34
  Structure of Mercury 35
Unnilennium 311
Unnilhexium 310

Unniloctium 311
Unnilpentium 310
Unnilquandium 310
Unnilseptium 310
Unreactive gas mixture 319
Unreactive metals 311
Unstable elements 310
Unukalhai 21
Upcurved edge 191
Upfold 60
Upfold trap 280
Upholstery 336-337
Upholstery brush 593
Uplifted block fault mountain 62
Upper arm 210
Upper Belvedere 482
Upper Carboniferous Coal Measures 61
Upper Carboniferous Millstone Grit 60-61
Upper crankcase 410
Upper crux of antihelix 242
Upper deadeye 382-383
Upper deck 380
Upper deck passenger 573
Upper deck windows 572
Upper epidermis 159
Upper eyelid 213
Upper fin 423
Upper finishing 581
Upper Frater 473
Upper gallery 579
Upper head 587
Upper jaw 212, 220-221, 244-245, 246, 248
Upper jaw tusk 105
Upper joint
  Clarinet 508
  Cor Anglais 508
  Oboe 508
Upper lobe of lung 215, 254-255
Upper octave key 509
Upper rudder 416-417
Upper seed axis 152-153
Upper sheer strake 393
Upper topsail 585
Upper wireless and telegraphy yard 395
Upright man 108
Upright piano 514
Upright planks jump 554
Upright poles jump 554
Upsilon Sagittarii 21
Upstream gates 560
Upthrow 60
Urachus 257
Ural mountains
  Cretaceous period 73
  Jurassic period 71
  Late Carboniferous period 67
  Mapping the Earth 265
  Physical map of the world 616
  Triassic period 69
Uranium 310
Uranium fuel 314
Uranus 18-19, 48-49
  Solar system 31
Ureter
  Bird 189
  Bony fish 181
  Domestic cat 195
  Elephant 200
  Frog 182
  Human 215, 256-259
  Lizard 185
  Rabbit 196
  Snail 177
Ureteric orifice 257
Urethra
  Chimpanzee 202

Domestic cat 195
Human 256-257, 259, 261
Rabbit 196
Urethral opening 259
Urethral sphincter muscle 257
Urinary bladder 181
Urinary system 256-257
Urinogenital opening
  Bony fish 181
  Dolphin 205
URL 577
Uropod 478, 481, 487
Urodela 182
Uropod 172
Urostyle 183
Ursa Major 18, 19
Ursa Minor 18, 21
Ursus americanus 195
Ursus spelaeus 77, 106
U-shaped gouge 449
USB ports 566
USB port 566, 586
USB programmer assembly 591
User name 576
U-shaped valley 286-287
Uterine wall 260-261
Uterus
  Chimpanzee 202
  Elephant 200
  Human 258-259
Utricle 243
U-tube 313
Utzon, J. 499
Uvula 212, 245, 248

V

V1 "flying bomb" 408
V12 cylinder arrangement 345
V4 engine unit
  British Rail Class 20 diesel 327
  Honda VF750 564
Vacuole
  Chlamydomonas sp. 116
  Diatom 116
  Human cell 216
  Palisade mesophyll 159
Vacuum brake lever 325
Vacuum circuit braker 528
Vacuum cleaner 592-593
Vacuum operated inlet valve 362
Vacuum pump cabinet 611
Vacuum reservoir 324
Vacuum valve 610
Vagina
  Chimpanzee 202
  Elephant 200
  Human 258-259, 261
  Snail 177
  Spider 170
Valance
  1906 Renault 337
  Ford Model T 339
  Volkswagen Beetle 341
Valency electrons 310
Vallate papillae 244
Vallecular canal 120
Valles Marineris 43
Valley
  Coastline 294
  Glacier 286-287
  Grand Canyon 277
  Mountain 62
  River features 290
  River 288-289
  Rock cycle stages 267

Valley floor erosion 267
Valley head 289
Valley rafter 475
Valley spring 292
Valmiki 35
Valve 359
Valve chest 524
Valve cusp 252
Valve lifter 367
Valve return spring 347
Valve rocker 544, 402
Valves
  Bivalves 176
  Dehiscent fruit 151
  Indehiscent fruit 150
  Scallop 176
Valve slide 506, 507
Valve spring 545, 544
Valve system 506
Vanadium 510
Van Allen radiation belt 58
Van de Graaff 41
Van de Graaff generator
  316
Vane 191
Van Eyck 35
Vang 378
Vanishing point 431
Vapor barrier 603
Variable incidence air
  intake 420
Variable incidence gust-
  alleviator 421
Variable nozzle 416-417
Variable pitch aluminum-
  alloy blade 408
Variable pitch propeller
  396
Variable time control
  knob 598-599
Variegated lamina 131,
  157
Varnish 548, 456
Vasa recta 256
Vascular cambium
  154-155
Vascular plants 279
Vascular plexus 255
Vascular strand 149
Vascular system 162-163
Vascular tissue 156
  Aerial shoot 155
  Apical meristem 154
  Bishop pine 124
  Canadian pond weed
    159
  Clubmoss stem 120
  Corm 155
  Dicotyledon 127
  Dodder 163
  Epiphytic orchid 162
  Fern rachis 121
  Higher plants 118-119
  Horsetail stem 120
  Marram grass 113
  Monocotyledon 126-127
  Parasite host 163
  Perennials 130-151
  Pine needle 124
  Pine root/stem 125
  Radicle 152
  Rhizome 155
  Root 152-155
  Stem 154-155
  Water hyacinth root 158
  Water lily leaf 159
  Woody plants 130-131
Vas deferens
  Domestic cat 195
  Human 259
  Rabbit 196
Vastitas Borealis 43
Vastus lateralis muscle
  225-226
Vastus medialis muscle
  225-226
Vault 484-485, 496
  Ancient Roman
    building 462-464

Baroque church 479
Gothic building 470
Medieval building
  467-469
Modern building 496,
  499
Nineteenth-century
  building 492-493
Renaissance building
  477
Vaulting shaft 468-469
V-belt pulley 347
VCR connections 585
Vedette boat 395
Vega 19, 20
  Our galaxy and nearby
    galaxies 15
Vegetable oil 436
Vegetative reproduction
  154-155
Veil 114-115
Vein
  Alveolar 247
  Anterior median 253
  Axillary 253
  Basilic 253
  Brachiocephalic 253
  Bronchial 254
  Cardiac 255
  Central retinal 240
  Cephalic 176, 253
  Common iliac 215, 253,
    257
  Dicotyledon leaf
    126-127
  Digital 253
  External iliac 215, 253
  Femoral 253
  Gastroepiploic 253
  Great saphenous 253
  Hepatic portal 253
  Hogweed leaf 129
  Inferior mesenteric 253
  Inferior vena cava 215,
    252-253, 257
  Insect 168, 169
  Interlobular 256
  Internal iliac 253
  Internal jugular 253
  Jugular 215
  Leaf 136, 158-159
  Median cubital 253
  Monocotyledon leaf 126
  Palmar 253
  Portal 252
  Pulmonary 251, 253, 254
  Pulp 247
  Renal 256-257
  Short saphenous 253
  Subclavian 253
  Superior mesenteric
    253
  Superior vena cava 215,
    251, 252-253, 255
  Suprarenal 257
  Testicular 257
  Tree mallow leaf 131
  Umbilical 260
  Water lily root 158
  Water lily leaf 159
Vela 18, 21
Velamen 162
Velarium 464
Velar scale 115
Vela Supernova Remnant
  17
Vellum 432
Velocette overhead valve
  (OHV) engine 367
Velum 573
Vena cava
  Frog 182
  Inferior 215, 252-253,
    257
  Superior 215, 251,
    252-253, 255
Vendelinus 40
Veneer 462
Venomous snake 184

Vent
  Frigate 397
  Igneous rock structures
    275
  Mountain building 62
  Rock cycle 266
  Suzuki RGV500 568
  Volcano 272-273
Ventilation 462
Ventilator 422, 425
Ventilator exit 406-407
Ventral abdominal artery
  173
Ventral antebrachial
  muscle 94
Ventral aorta 179
Ventral fin 179
Ventral margin of shell
  176
Ventral nerve cord 169,
  175
Ventral scale 184, 186
Ventricle
  Brain 256-257
  Heart 215, 250-251,
    252
Ventricular diastole
  251
Ventricular systole 251
Venturi 424
Venus 56-57
  Solar system 30
  Venus fly trap 160
Verdaccio 433
Verge 464, 492
Vermiculated rustication
  482
Vermilion 433
Vermilion border of lip
  215
Vermilion Cliffs 277
Versal lettering 445
Vertebra 261
  Bony fish 180
  Cervical 212, 222
  Frog 183
  Lumbar 222-223
  Rattlesnake 185
  Rudimentary 260
  Thoracic 222-223
  Turtle 187
  Westlothiana 81
Vertebral artery 223, 252
Vertebral body 223
Vertebral column 218,
  222, 257
Vertebral foramen
  222-223
Vertebral shield 187
Vertebrates 56, 64, 104
  Fossil record 279
Vertex
  Building 495
  Human body 212
Vertical air current 302
Vertical batten 602
Vertical cleavage 270
Vertical frame ladder 392
Vertical movement
  Faults and folds 60
  Lake formation 292
Vertical muffler 329
Vertical pupil 186
Vertical ridge 129
Vertical spindle 587
Vertical stroke 445
Vertical tailplane 572
Very high frequency
  (VHF) radio 318
Vesicle 148
Vespa Grand Sport 160
  Mark 1 363
Vespa scooter 362, 363
Vessel
  Baroque church 479
  Gothic church 470
  Medieval church
    468-469
Vesta Rupes 57

Vestas A47 wind turbine
  604
Vestibular canal 243
Vestibular membrane 243
Vestibular nerve 243
Vestibule
  Ancient Greek temple
    461
  Baroque church 481
  Human body 212, 245
  Medieval church 469
  Neoclassical building
    483
Vestibulocochlear nerve
  245
Vestibulocochlear nerve
  245
VHF aerial
  B-17 bomber 408-409
  BAe-146 jetliner 415
  Bell Jetranger
    helicopter 423
  Concorde 416-417
  VHF radio 518
VHF omni-range aerial
  Bell-47 helicopter 422
  Concorde, the 417
VHF omni-range and
  instrument-landing-
  system aerial 412
Vibraphone 504, 516, 517
Vibration-reducing fan
  mounting 597
Vibration-reducing
  muffler foot 58
Vibrations
  Brass instruments 506
  Stringed instruments
    510
Vibrato arm 513
Vibrato effect 516, 517
Vibrissa
  Lion 194
  Rabbit 196
  Rat 196
  Seal 204
Vicia faba 133, 152
Video
  Digital 582-583
  Streamed internet 577
Video camera 610
Video input/output circuit
  board 585
Viewfinder 582
Viewing screen 610
Viewing window 581
Viewing window objective
  lens aperture 580
Viking ships 574-575
Villa Rotunda 475
Villi of mucosa 248
Viola 503, 504, 505, 510,
  511
Violent eruptions 272
Violet light 518
Violin 503, 504, 505, 510
Violoncello 510-511
Virginia opossum 207
Virgo 18, 21
Virtual mixing board
  521
Visceral cartilage 254
Visceral hump 177
Visceral pericardium
  250
Viscous coupling 344-345
Visible light 518-519
Vision 237
Visor 416-417
Visual recognition 237
Vitreous glass mosaic
  451
Vitreous glass tessera 450,
  451
Vitreous humor
  240
Vitta 151
Vivaldi 35
Vocal cords 245
Voices 503
Volans 21

Volcanic activity
  Mineralization zones
    280
  Rock cycle 266
Volcanic eruption 26
Volcanic gases 64
Volcanic island 58, 299
Volcanic lake 293
Volcanic lava
  Jupiter 44
  Mars 42
  The Moon 40
  Venus 36
Volcanic mountain 62
Volcanic rock 298, 506
Volcano 58, 63, 272-275
  Jupiter 44
  Locations 273
  Mars 42
  Mineralization zones
    281
  Mountain building
    62-63
  Ocean floor 298
  Vent 62
  Venus 36
Volkmann's canal 247
Volkmann's vessel 225
Volkswagen Beetle
  540-541
Volleyball 534-535
Voltage 306, 516
Voltage circuitry 597
Voltage reduction and
  regulation circuits 585
Voltage regulators 596
Voltage stabilizer 597
Voltage transformers 596
Volume 306, 507
Volume control
  Electronic instruments
    520, 521
  Home cinema 585
  Nintendo Wii Fit
    Plus 579
  Personal music 586-587
Volumes 623
Volume slider 577
Volute
  Ancient Greek building
    460-461
  Baroque church 479,
    481
  Dome 486
  Islamic building 488
  Neoclassical building
    478, 480
  Renaissance building
    476-477
Volva 114-115
Volvox sp. 116
Vomer 221
Von Kármán 41
Voussoir 484-485
  Ancient Roman
    building 465
  Neoclassical building
    482
  Renaissance building
    474
V-shaped gouge 449
V-shaped valley
  River features 290
  Rivers 288-289
V-strut 404-405
VTEC engine 363
V-twin engine 362, 563
Vulpecula 19
Vulture 190
Vulva 200
Vyāsa 35
Vyne 482

W

Wadi 283
Wagner 35
Wagon 524

Wagon bogie 350
Wagon vault 485
Wahweap sandstone 276
Waist
  74-gun ship 580-581
  Human 210
  Stringed instruments
    510-511
Waistband 548
Waist gun 408
Wale
  74-gun ship 581
  Roman corbita 573
  Sailing warship 576-577
Walkway 497
Wall
  Ancient Greek temple
    461
  Ancient Roman
    building 462, 465
  Baroque building
    478-479, 481
  Carpel 148, 151
  Cell 112, 117, 132, 139
  Concrete 496
  Fruit 148-151
  Fungal tissue 115
  Glass 496
  Gothic church 470
  Islamic building 488
  Medieval building
    466-467, 469
  Modern building
    498-499
  Neoclassical building
    479, 482
  Nineteenth-century mill
    492
  Ovary 140, 150
  Renaissance building
    476-477
  Twentieth-century
    building 494
Wall anchor 407
Wall construction 602
Wall foundation 602
Wall painting 434
Walrus 204
Walter 40
Wand 592, 593
Wand handle and
  brushbar controls 592
Wand/handle connector
  593
Wand telescopic link 593
Wankel, Felix 346
Wankel rotary engine
  346-347
Wannanosaurus 101
Wardrobe 416
Wardroom 381
Warhead 394
Warm air 300, 302-303
Warm blood
  Mammals 104
  Theropods 84
Warm electronics box 615
Warm front 302-303
Warm occlusion 302
Warm periods 56
Warning horn 527, 529
Warning light 528, 556
Warship
  74-gun ship 379,
    580-581
  Battleship 394-395
  Frigate 396-397
  Ironclad 392-393
  Man-of-war 378-379,
  Sailing warship 576-577
  Submarine 396-397
Wasatch formation 276
Washable pre-motor filter
  592
Wash cant 578
Washer-dryer 594-595
Wash over dry brush 439
Washburn 12-string
  guitar 513

667

Washer
  Bicycle 358
  Power drill 600–601
  Toaster 598–599
Washer jet 353
Washes 458, 459
Washing machine 315
Wasp 168
Waste heat 314–315
Waste water anti-siphon
  pipe hook 595
Waste water pipe 595
Water 58, 66
  Absorption 150
  Amphibian 80
  Changing states 307
  "Deltic" diesel-electric
    locomotive 526
  Energy generation
    314–315
  Epiphyte supply 162
  Fermentation 313
  Lithographic printing
    446
  Mars 42
  Molecule 138
  Oceans and seas 296
  Photosynthesis 138
  Pollination 144
  Reversible reactions
    312
  Seed germination
    152–153
  Solutions 306
  Storage organs 156–157
  Transport 134, 139
Water and oil pump
  assembly 356
Waterborne sports
  560–561
Water-closet 483
Watercolor 458–459
Watercolor paint pan 458
Watercolor paper 439,
  441
Watercolor-style acrylic
  painting 442, 443
Water connection 542
Water-cooled engine 366
Water cycle 288
Water density 296
Water droplets 45
Waterfall 291
  Glacier 286
  River 289–290
  Rock cycle 267
Water fern 158
Water float 524
Water hardness
  adjustment and filter
  flap lever 595
Water hyacinth 158
Water ice
  Jupiter's atmosphere
    45
  Mercury's atmosphere
    47
  Structure of comet 53
  Structure of Mars 43
  Structure of Neptune 51
Water-ice fog 42
Water-ice permafrost 43
Water inlet connector 595
Water inlet hose 595
Water inlet pipe 595
Water inlet valves 595
Water jacket
  Daimler engine 343
  Ford diesel engine 347
  Humber engine 343
  Jaguar straight six
    engine 344
Water key 506, 507
Water lily 158–159
Waterline 380
Water obstacle 546
Water outlet 425
Water passage
  346

Water pipe
  1906 Renault 337
  Humber engine 343
  Wright Flyer 399
Water pressurizer 314
Waterproof acrylic paint
  442
Waterproof cable
  connector 605
Waterproof covering
  Bishop pine needles
    124
  Golden barrel cactus
    156
  Haworthia truncata 157
  Lithops bromfieldii 157
  Monocotyledon leaf 126
  Rush stem 135
  Wetland plants 158
Waterproof shell 80
Waterproof ski clothing
  553
Waterproof skin 81
Waterproof stowage box
  427
Water pump
  Hybrid car 354
  Jaguar V12 engine 345
  Renault Clio 351
  White Steam Car 542
Water pump pulley 347
Water rail 545
Water reactor 314
Water-retaining cuticle 78
Water salinity 296
Water-saturated
  permeable rock
  292
  Lakes and groundwater
    292
  Mineral resources
    280–281
Watershed 289
Water shoot 560
Water softener dial 595
Water-soluble glue 450
Water storage tank 497
Water-storing
  parenchyma 156–157
Water supply
  Gun turret 396
  Steam locomotive 324
Water table
  Cave system 284
  Lake formation 292
Water tank
  Bordino Steam Carriage
    334
  "Ellerman Lines" steam
    locomotive 324
  Steam iron 594
  White Steam Car 542
Wezen 18
  Canis Major 21
Water vapor
  Chemical reactions
    312–313
  Hurricane structure 303
  Jupiter's atmosphere 45
  Mars' atmosphere 43
  Saturn's atmosphere 47
  Venus' atmosphere 37
  Water cycle 288
Water vascular system
  174
Waterway 380, 393
Wattle-and-daub
  Ancient Roman
    building 462, 464–465
  Medieval house 466
Wave 294, 298
  Erosion 294
  Features 294
  Properties 318
Wave-cut platform 295
Waveguide 596, 597
Wavelength 318
Wavellite 269
Wavering pitch 516, 517
Wavy foliation 267
Wax modeling 452
Wax riser 454

Wax runner 454
Waxy cuticle 156, 157
Waxy fruit skin 149
Waxy zone 161
Weapon-bay bulkhead 421
Weaponry 375
Wearable technology
  590–591
Weasel 194
Weather 502–503
Weathercock 486
Weathering 282–283
  Gothic church 471–472
  Medieval church 469
  Mineral deposits 280
  Renaissance building 477
  Rock cycle 266
  Sedimentary rocks 276
Weather radar 416
Weather shutter for gun
  394
Weather-vane 471, 477
Web
  Frog 182
  Internet 576
Webbed feet 188, 190
Web browser 577
Web pages 577
Webcam 566
Website address 577
Weight
  Arch 484
  All-round bicycle 360
  Bolts 548
  Measurement 320
  Motorcycle engine 366
  Newton meters 320
Weights 562
Wei-wei 376
Welding tool 608
Weld line 392
Welt 122–123
Welwitschia mirabilis
  122–123
Werner motorcycle 362
Weslake Speedway
  motorcycle 369
West Africa 73
West Australian current
  297
Westerlies 300
Westlothiana 67, 80–81
Westminster Abbey 484
Westminster Cathedral
  495
Wet-in-wet wash 438, 439
Wetland plants 158–159
Wet season 295
Wet wash 438
Wezen 18
  Canis Major 21
Whaler 395
Whales 204–205
Wheat 109, 150
Wheel
  1906 Renault 337
  Alloy 356, 357
  Bicycle 358–359
  Diesel motor output 326
  First cars 354–355
  Force/motion 320
  Ford Model T 338–339
  Harley-Davidson FLHS
  Electra Glide 363
  Mars exploration rover
    (MER) 615
  Mazda RX-7 346
  Motorcycle 364
  Pacing sulky 555
  Paddle 390–391
  Renault Clio 350–351
  Rossin Italian time-trial
    bicycle 361
  Ship 378, 390, 394
  Single scull 561
  Volkswagen Beetle 340
  Weslake Speedway
    motorcycle 369

Wheel axle
  BAe-146 jetliner 414
  Touring bicycle 360
Wheelbase 360
Wheelchair access 333
Wheel fairing
  Blackburn monoplane
    400
  Pegasus Quasar
    ultralight 427
  Pegasus XL-SE
    ultralight 426
Wheel fork 335
Wheel guard 324, 369, 593
Wheel hub 414
Wheel nut 356, 357
Wheel sets 327, 329
Wheel spacer 561
Whelp 387
Whetstone 452
Whip 555
Whipping 384, 388
Whisker
  Lion 194
  Rabbit 196
  Rat 196
  Seal 204
Whisker boom 582
"Whispering Gallery" 484
Whistle
  Iron paddlesteamer 392
  Life jacket 561
  Referee 524
Whistle lever 325
White belt 556
White blood cells 217,
  253
White Cliffs 276
White diamond 268
White dwarfs
  Small stars 24–25
  Stars 22–23
White feldspar 275
White-gray crystal 271
White light 318
White matter
  Cerebrum 236–237
  Spinal cord 238
White of eye 213
White oval
  Jupiter 44–45
  Saturn 46
White spirit 436
White Steam Car 542
White stork 188
White warning light
  528
White whale 204
Whorls
  Flower 140
  Green alga cell 116
  Sepals 144, 149
Wicket 538
Wicket-keeper 538
Widened joint 282
Wide receiver 526
Wiener 41
Wi-fi antenna 569, 579
Wi-fi board 579
Wii balance board 579
Wii hand controller 579
Willow grouse 193
Wind
  Atmosphere 300
  Ekman spiral 297
  Energy generation
    314
  Oceans and seas
    296–297
  Rock cycle 266–267
  Water cycle 288
  Weather 302
  Weathering and erosion
    282–283
Windspeed 303
Windcheetah SL Mark VI
  "Speedy" racing HPV
  bicycle 361
Wind chest 514

Wind controller 521
Wind deflector 341
Wind-dispersed seeds
  150–151
Wind erosion 282–283
  Coastline 294
Winding cornice 472
Wind instruments 508,
  509
  Brass 506, 507
  Electronic 520
  Woodwind 508, 509
Windlass
  Buildings 467, 477
  Roman corbita 372
Windlass bar 380
Window
  Ancient Egyptian
    building 459
  Ancient Roman
    building 463, 465
  Asian building
    490–491
  Baroque church
    479–481
  Dome 486–487
  Dormer 495
  Double-decker tour bus
    333
  "Eurostar" multi-
    voltage electric train 329
  Gothic building 470–475
  MCW Metrobus 333
  Medieval building
    466–469
  Modern building 498,
    499
  Neoclassical building
    478, 482–483
  Nineteenth-century
    building 492–493
  Renaissance building
    474, 476
  Rococo style 482
  Single-decker bus 333
  TGV electric highs-
    peed train 329
  Twentieth-century
    building 494–495
Window blind 336, 572
Window controls 576, 577
Window-frame 486
Window glass 348
Window jamb 479, 482,
  483
Windowsill
  Baroque church 479
  Neoclassical building
    482–485
  Twentieth-century
    building 494
Window stage 477
Wind-pollinated plants
  144
Windshield
  Airbus 380 573
  BAe-146 jetliner
    components 412
  BE 2B bomber 404
  BMW R/60 sidecar 362
  Concorde, the 416–417
  "Deltic" diesel-electric
    locomotive 527
  Double-decker tour bus
    333
  Ford Model T 339
  Harley-Davidson FLHS
  Electra Glide 363
  Honda Insight 354
  Hawker Tempest
    components 409
  Kirby BSA racing
    sidecar 362
  Lockheed Electra
    airliner 406–407
  Tornado 420
Windshield wiper
  "Deltic" diesel-electric
    locomotive 527

"Eurostar" multi-
  voltage electric train 329
Italian State Railroads
  Class 402 528
MCW Metrobus 332
Paris Metro 528
TGV electric high-
  speed train 329
"Union Pacific"
  locomotive 326
Volkswagen Beetle 341
Windsor green 438
Windspeed 303
Wind synthesizer 521
Wind turbine 604, 605
Wind-up 557
Windvane 375, 605
Windward face 283
Wing
  1906 Renault 336
  Alula 191
  ARV light aircraft
    424–425
  Australian rules football
    528
  Avro biplane 403
  BAe-146 jetliner
    components 413, 414
  BE 2B wings 404
  Beetle 168
  Biplanes and triplanes
    402
  Bird 188, 191
  Blackburn monoplane
    401
  Bones 191
  Bumblebee 168
  Butterfly 169
  Cobra lily 160
  Coverts 188
  Curtiss biplane 398
  Deer hopper dry fly
    563
  Developing 192
  Dry fruit 150–151
  Early monoplanes 400
  Feather 188, 191
  Ford Model T 338
  Formula One race car
    357
  Gliders, hang-gliders,
    and ultralights 426
  Handball 535
  Hawker Tempest
    components 409
  Hockey 540
  Ice hockey 550
  Lockheed Electra
    airliner 406
  Pine seed 122
  Pitcher plant 113
  Rugby 530
  Scots pine seed 122
  Showjumping fence
    554
  Ski boot safety binding
    552
  Spurious 191
  Sycamore 131
Wing assembly 413
Wing attack 535, 541
Wing case 168
Wing defense
  Lacrosse 541
  Netball 535
Winged seeds
  Scots pine 122
  Sycamore 131, 151
Winged stem 129
Wing end-plate 357
Wing-feather impression
  85
Wing fillet panel 409
Wingframe 427
Wing landing gear 572,
  573
Wing leading edge 573
Winglet 356
Wing mirror 354

Wing piping 541
Wing-protecting skid
598-599
Wing-root glove fairing
420-421
Wing-root mount 415
Wing stay 559
Wing strut
  ARV light aircraft
  424-425
  Avro triplane 402-403
  Curtiss biplane 398
Wing supports 557
Wingtip
  ARV light aircraft 424
  BE 2B wings 404
  Hawker Tempest
  components 409
  Schleicher glider 426
Wingtip aerial fairing 421
Wing vein 168, 169
Wing warping 400
Wire armature 454, 455
Wire bristle brush 519
Wire coil 605
Wire-ended cutting tool
454
Wire-end tools 452
Wire gauze pad 542
Wireless and telegraphy
yard 595
Wireless office 597
Wires 518
Wire wheel 402
Wiring loom 596
Wishbone
  Bird 189
  Formula One race car
  357
Withdrawal stride 543
Withdrawing-room 483
Withers 199
Wolf 195
Wolffian duct 179
Wolf hair brush 444
Wollastonite 271
Womb 258-259
Women's lacrosse field
540, 541
Women's shot 542

Wood
  Golf club 547
  Sculpture 454
Wood block 446, 449
Wood capstan 587
Woodcarving 452, 453
Woodcut 446
Wooden arrow 109
Wooden artillery wheel
557
Wooden bar 516
Wooden boarding 602
Wooden body 510
Wooden body-shell 519
Wooden buffer 324
Wooden case 514, 515
Wooden-domed deck 403
Wooden driving wheel 524
Wooden frame
  Harp 511
  Printing mesh 446, 448
  Sculpture 452
  Steam-powered Cugnot
  "Fardier" 334
Wooden golf clubs 546, 547
Wood engraving 446, 447
Wood engraving print 449
Wooden grip 549
Wooden hearth 109
Wooden "key" 551
Wooden packing 597
Wooden panel 473
Wooden sailing ship
578-579
Wooden sleeper 324, 331
Wooden spoke 554
Wooden-spoked wheel
539
Wooden stands 554
Wooden wheel 534
Woodwind instruments
504, 505, 508, 509
Woodwork 467
Woody flowering plants
126, 130-131
Woody pericarps 150
Woody plants 126
Woody scales
  Bishop pine cone 124
  Smooth cypress 123
Woody stem 134-135

Woofer loudspeaker
connector 585
Woolding 576
Work 514
Working chamber 396
World War I aircraft
404-405
World War II aircraft
408-409
World Wide Web 576
Worming 388
Worms
  Earth's evolution 56
  Fossil record 279
Woven dacron 384
Wrack 116-117
Wren, C. 478
  Baroque church 480
  Cathedral dome 484, 487
Wrest plank
  Concert grand piano 515
  Upright piano 514
Wright brothers
  Modern piston aero-
  engines 410
  Pioneers of flight
  598-599
Wright, F. L. 495
Wright Flyer 598-599
Wrist
  Corythosaurus 98
  Human 211, 230-231
  Iguanodon 97
  Stegosaurus 92
  Triceratops 102
Wrist joint
  Baryonyx 85
  Brachiosaurus 91
  Diplodocus 90
  Euoplocephalus 94
  Human 218
  Parasaurolophus 99
  Plateosaurus 88
  Robot 608
  Stegoceras 100, 101
  Tyrannosaurus 84
Wrist pin 390
Wrist position 444
Writing tools 444
Wrought iron boiler 524

Wrought iron rail 324
Wuerhosaurus 93
Wulfenite 269

X

Xerophytes 156-157
Xi2 Sagittarii 21
Xi Orionis 18
Xi Pegasi 19
X line 445
X-ray 518-519
  Colon 214
  Gallbladder 214
  Hand 230
X-ray emission 28
X-ray image of Crab
  Nebula 28
"X" turret 395
Xylem
  Bishop pine 124
  Clubmoss stem 120
  Dicotyledons 126-127
  Dodder host 163
  Epiphytic orchid 162
  Fern rachis 121
  Higher plants 118-119
  Horsetail stem 120
  Marram grass 113
  Monocotyledons
  126-127
  Pine needle 124
  Pine root/stem 125
  Radicle 152
  Root 132
  Stem 134-135
  Water hyacinth root
  158
  Water lily leaf 159
Xylem fibers 134-135

Y

Yacht racing 560
Yangchuanosaurus 85
Yangtze River 265, 616
Yard 582
  Battleship 395
  Double topsail

schooner 385
Greek and Roman ships
372, 373
Steel 392
Tea clipper 392
Viking karv 375
Yardang 282
Yardarm 379
Yardsman 526
Yasti 490, 491
Yaw control 605
Yaw ring 605
Year
  Earth 30
  Jupiter 30
  Mars 30
  Mercury 26, 34
  Neptune 31
  Planets 30-31
  Pluto 31
  Saturn 31
  Uranus 31
  Venus 30
Yeast
  Fermentation 313
  Fungi 114
Yellow card 524
Yellow light 318,
351
Yellow ocher 442
Yellow orpiment 271
Yellow River 265, 616
Yellow warning arm
530
Yellow-wort 144
Yew 125
Y.M.C.A. 532
Yolk 192
Yolk sac 192
Ytterbium 311
Yttrium 310
"Y" turret 595
Yucca 126
Yucca sp. 126

Z

Zagros Mountains
75
Zap button 586

Zea mays 127
Zeami 35
Zebra 198
Zeeman 41
Zeilleria frenzlii 66
Zeppelin ipod speaker
dock 586
Zeta Centauri 21
Zeta Sagittarii 21
Zeugen 282
Ziggurat-style step-back
494
Zinc 281, 512
Zinc phosphating 348
Zinc plating 477
Zingiber officinale 155
Zion Canyon 276
Zirconium 310
Zona pellucida 606, 607
Zone
  Jupiter 44-45
  Structure of Saturn 47
Zone defenses 533
Zonular ligament 241
Zoomorphic head 374
Zosteres 572
Zosterophyllum
  llanoveranum 64
Zubenelgenubi 18, 21
Zubeneschamali 18, 21
Zugon 573
Zygian 573
Zygomatic arch
  Bear 194
  Chimpanzee 202
  Human 215,
  220
  Lion 194
  Smilodon 106
  Toxodon 107
Zygomatic bone 220-221
Zygomaticus major
muscle 228-229
Zygote
  Bryophyte 118-119
  Fertilization 146-147
  Plant formation 146
  Primitive land plants
  120
  Seaweed 116-117

Acknowledgments

Dorling Kindersley would like to thank (in order of sections):

The Universe
(consultant editors—Sue Becklake, Gevorkyan Tatyana Alekseyevna):

John Becklake; the Memorial Museum of Cosmonautics, Moscow; The Cosmos Pavilion, Moscow; The United States Space and Rocket Centre, Alabama; Broadhurst, Clarkson and Fuller Ltd.; Susannah Massey

Prehistoric Earth
(consultant editors—William Lindsay, Martyn Bramwell, Dr. Ralph E. Molnar, David Lambert):

Dr. Monty Reid, Andrew Neuman, and the staff of the Royal Tyrrell Museum of Palaeontology, Drumheller, Alberta; Dr. Angela Milner and the staff of the Department of Palaeontology, the Natural History Museum, London; Professor W. Ziegler and the staff, in particular Michael Loderstaedt, of the Naturmuseum Senckenburg, Frankfurt; Dr. Alexander Liebau, Axel Hunghrebüller, Reiner Schoch, and the staff of the Institut und Museum für Geologie und Paläontologie der Universität, Tübingen; Rupert Wild of the Institut für Paläontologie, Staatliches Museum für Naturkunde, Stuttgart; Dr. Scheiber of the Stadtmuseum, Nördlingen; Professor Dr. Dietrich Herm of Staatssammlung für Paläontologie und Historische Geologie, München; Dr. Michael Keith-Lucas of the Department of Botany, University of Reading; Richard Walker; American Museum of Natural History, New York

Plants
(consultant editor—Richard Walker):

Diana Miller; Lawrie Springate; Karen Sidwell; Chris Thody; Michelle End; Susan Barnes and Chris Jones of the EMU Unit of the Natural History Museum, London; Jenny Evans of Kew Gardens, London; Kate Biggs of the Royal Horticultural Society Gardens, Wisley, Surrey; Spike Walker of Microworld Services; Neil Fletcher; John Bryant of Bedgebury Pinetum, Kent; Dean Franklin

Animals
(consultant editor—Richard Walker):

David Manning's Animal Ark; Intellectual Animals; Howletts Zoo, Canterbury; John Dunlop; Alexander O'Donnell; Sue Evans of the Royal Veterinary College, London; Dr. Geoff Potts and Fred Frettsome of the Marine Biological Association of the United Kingdom, Plymouth; Jeremy Adams of the Booth Museum of Natural History, Brighton; Derek Telling of the Department of Anatomy, University of Bristol; the Natural History Museum, London; Andy Highfield of the Tortoise Trust; Brian Harris of the Aquarium, London Zoo; the Invertebrate Department, London Zoo; Dr. Harold McClure of the Yerkes Regional Primate Research Center, Emory University, Atlanta, Georgia; Nielson Lausen of the Harvard Medical School, New England Regional Primates Research

Centre, Southborough, Massachusetts; Dr. Paul Hopwood of the Department of Veterinary Anatomy, University of Sydney; Dean Franklin

The Human Body
(consultant editors—Dr. Frances Williams, Dr. Fiona Payne, Richard Cummins FRCS):
Derek Edwards and Dr. Martin Collins, British School of Osteopathy; Dr. M.C.E. Hutchinson of the Department of Anatomy, United Medical and Dental Schools of Guy's and St. Thomas' Hospitals, London. Models—Barry O'Rorke (Bodyline Agency) and Pauline Swaine (MOT Model Agency)

Geology, Geography, and Meteorology
(consultant editor—Martyn Bramwell):
Dr. John Nudds of the Manchester Museum, Manchester; Dr. Alan Wooley and Dr. Andrew Clark of the Natural History Museum, London; Graham Bartlett of the National Meteorological Library and Archive, Bracknell; Tony Drake of BP Exploration, Uxbridge; Jane Davies of the Royal Society of Chemistry, Cambridge; Dr. Tony Waltham of Nottingham Trent University, Nottingham; staff of the Smithsonian Institute, Washington; staff of the United States Geological Survey, Washington; staff of the National Geographic Society, Washington; staff of Edward Lawrence Associates (Export Ltd.), Midhurst; John Farndon; David Lambert

Rail and Road
***Rail* (consultant editor—John Coiley)**
Michael Ashworth of the London Transport Museum

***Road* (consultant editors—David Burgess-Wise, Hugo Wilson)**
The National Motor Museum, Beaulieu; Alf Newell of Renault UK Ltd.; David Suter of Cheltenham Cutaway Exhibits Ltd.; Francesca Riccini of the Science Museum, London. Signore Amadelli of the Museo dell' Automobile Carlo Biscaretti di Ruffia; Paul Bolton of the Mazda MCL Group; Duncan Bradford of Reg Mills Wire Wheels; John and Leslie Brewster of Autocavan; David Burgess-Wise; Trevor Cass of Garrett Turbo Service; John Corbett of The Patrick Collection; Gary Crumpler of Williams Grand Prix Engineering Ltd.; Mollie Easterbrooke and Duncan Gough of Overland Ltd.; Arthur Fairley of the Vauxhall Motor Company; Paul Foulkes-Halbard of Filching Manor Motor Museum; Frank Gilbert of I. Wilkinson and Son Ltd.; Paolo Gratton of Gratton Museum; Colvin Gunn of Gunn and Son; Judy Hogg of Ecurie Bertelli; Milton Holman of Dream Cars; Ian Matthews of IMAT Electronics; Eric Neal of Jaguar Cars Ltd.; Paul Niblett, Keith Davidson, Mark Reumel, and David Woolf of Michelin Tyre plc; Doug Nye; Kevin O'Keefe of O'Keefe Cars; Seat UK; Ian Whitley, Raj Johal and Andy Faiers of the Honda Institute; Roger Smith; Jim Stirling of Ironbridge Gorge Museum, Staffordshire; Jon Taylor; Doug Thompson; Martyn Watkins of Ford Motor Company Ltd.; John Cattermole, Customer Services Manager at London Northern Buses; F. W. Evans Cycles Ltd.; Trek UK Ltd. (Bicycle); Sam Grimmer; Colin Uttley

Physics and Chemistry
(consultant editor—Jack Challoner)

Sea and Air
***Sea* (consultant editors—Geoff Hales and Harvey B. Loomis):**

David Spence, Gillian Hutchinson, David Topliss, Simon Stephens, Robert Baldwin, Jonathan Betts, all of the National Maritime Museum, London; Ian Friel; Simon Turnage of Captain O.M. Watts of London Ltd.; Davey and Company Ltd., Great Dunmow; Avon Inflatables Ltd., Llanelli; Musto Ltd., Benfleet; Peter Martin of Spencer Rigging Ltd., Southampton; Peter Rowson of Ratseys Sailmakers, Southampton; Swiftech Ltd., Wallingford; Colin Scattergood of the Barrow Boat Company Ltd., Colchester; Professor J.S. Morrison of the Trireme Trust, Cambridge; The Cutty Sark Maritime Trust; Adrian Daniels of Kelvin Hughes Marine Instruments, London; Arthur Credland of Hull City Council Museums and Art Galleries; The Hull Maritime Society; Gerald Clark; Peter Fitzgerald of the Science Museum, London; Alec Michael of HMB Subwork Ltd., Great Yarmouth, and Ray Ward of the OSEL Group, Great Yarmouth; Richard Bird of UWI, Weybridge; Walker Marine Instruments, Birmingham; The International Sailing Craft Association; The Exeter Maritime Museum; Jane Wilson of the Trinity Lighthouse Company, London; The Imperial War Museum Collections; Thorn Security Ltd.; Michael Bach

***Air* (consultant editor—Bill Gunston):**
Aeromega Helicopters, Stapleford; Aero Shopping, London; Avionics Mobile Services Ltd., Watford; Roy Barber and John Chapman of the RAF Museum, Hendon; Mitch Barnes Aviation, London; Mike Beach; British Caledonian Flight Training Ltd.; Fred Coates of Helitech (Luton) Ltd.; Michael Cuttell and CSE Aviation Ltd., Oxford; Dowty Aerospace Landing Gear, Gloucester; Guy Hartcup of the Airship Association; Anthony Hooley, Chris Walsh, and David Cord of British Aerospace Regional Aircraft Ltd.; Ken Huntley of Mid-West Aero Engines Ltd.; Imperial War Museum, Duxford; The London Gliding Club, Dunstable; Musée des Ballons, Calvados; Noel Penny Turbines Ltd.; Andy Pavey of Aviation Scotland Ltd.; Tony Pavey of Thermal Aircraft Developments, London; the Commanding Officer and personnel of RAF St Athan; the Commanding Officer and personnel of RAF Wittering; The Science Museum, London; Ross Sharp of the Science Museum, Wroughton; The Shuttleworth Collection; Skysport Engineering; Mike Smith; Solar Wings Ltd., Marlborough; Julian Temple of Brooklands Museum Trust Ltd.; Kelvin Wilson of Flying Start

Architecture
(consultant editor—Alexandra Kennedy):
Stephen Cutler for advice and text; Gavin Morgan of the Museum of London, London; Chris Zeuner of the Weald and Downland Museum, Singleton, Sussex; Alan Hills and James Putnam of the British Museum, London; Dr. Simon Penn and Michael Thomas of the Avoncroft Museum of Buildings, Bromsgrove,

Worcestershire; Christina Scull of Sir John Soane's Museum, London; Paul Kennedy and John Williamson of the London Door Company, London; Lou Davis of The Original Box Sash Window Company, Windsor; Goddard and Gibbs Studios Ltd., London, for access to stained glass windows; The Royal Courts of Justice, Strand, London; Charles Brooking and Peter Dalton for access to the doors and windows in the Charles Brooking Collection, University of Greenwich, Dartford, Kent; Clare O'Brien of the Shakespeare Globe Trust, Shakespeare's Globe Museum, Bear Gardens, Southwark, London; Ken Teague of the Horniman Museum, London; Canon Haliburton, Mike Payton, Ken Stones, and Anthony Webb of St Paul's Cathedral, London; Roy Spring of Salisbury Cathedral; Reverend Gillean Craig of the Church of St George in the East, London; the Science Museum, London; Dr. Neil Bingham; Lin Kennedy of Historic Royal Palaces; Katy Harris of Sir Norman Foster and Partners; Production Design, Thames Television plc, London; Dominique Reynier of Le Centre Georges Pompidou, Paris; Denis Roche of Le Musée National des Monuments Français, Paris; Franck Gioria and students of Les Compagnons du Devoir, Paris, for access to construction models; Frank Folliot of Le Musée Carnavalet, Paris; Dr. Martina Harms of Hessische Landesmuseums, Darmstadt; Jefferson Chapman of the University of Tennessee, Knoxville, for access to the model of the Hypostyle Hall, Temple of Amon-Re; staff of the Palazzo Strozzi, Florence; staff of the Sydney Opera House, Sydney; staff of the Empire State Building, New York; Nick Jackson; Ann Terrell

The Visual Arts
(consultant editor—Pip Seymour):
Rosemary Simmons; Michael Taylor of Paupers Press, London; Tessa Hunkin and Emma Biggs of Mosaic Workshop, London; John Tiranti, Jonathan Lyons of Alec Tiranti Ltd., London; Chris Hough; Dr. Ashok Roy; Satwinder Sehmi of Alphabet Soup, London; Phillip Poole of Cornelissens, London; George Weil and Sons Ltd., London; The National Gallery, London; Chris Webster of the Tate Gallery, London; China Art Cultural Centre, London; London Graphic Centre, London; A.P. Fitzpatrick, London; Flowers Graphics, London; Intaglio Printmaker, London; Falkiner Papers, London; Edgar Udny and Co., London; John Green

Music
(consultant editor—Susan Sturrock):
Boosey and Hawkes Music Publishers Ltd., London, for permission to reproduce extract from The Prodigal Son by Arthur Sullivan; The Bass and Drum Cellar, London; Empire Drums and Percussion, London; Argents (part of World of Music), London; Bill Lewington Ltd., London; Frobenius organ at Kingston Parish Church, Surrey; Yamaha-Kemble Music (UK) Ltd., Tilbrook, Milton Keynes; Yamaha Atelier, London; Akai (UK) Ltd., Hounslow, Middlesex; Casio Electronics Co. Ltd., London; Roland (UK) Ltd., Fleet, Hampshire; Richard Schulman; Andy Brown of Musictrack

Sports
The Sports Council Information Centre, London; The British Olympic Games Committee; Brian Crennell of Black's Leisure Group (First Sport); Lillywhites of Piccadilly, London; Mitre Sports International Ltd., Huddersfield; David Bloomfield of the Football Association; Denver Athletics Ltd., Norfolk; Greg Everest and Keith Birley of the British League of Australian Rules Football; Peter McNally of the Gaelic Athletic Association; Jeremy Garman of James Gilbert Ltd.; Rex King of the Rugby Football Union, Twickenham; Neil Tunnicliffe and John Huxley of the Rugby Football League, Leeds; Wayne Patterson of the Basketball Hall of Fame, Springfield, Connecticut; Brian Coleman of the English Basketball Association; All American Imports, Northampton; George Bulman of the English Volleyball Association; Julie Longdon of Mizuno Mallory (UK) Ltd.; Juliet Stanford of the All- England Netball Association; Jeff Rowland of the British Handball Association; Cally Melin of Adidas UK Ltd.; Patrick Donnely of the Baseball Hall of Fame, Cooperstown, New York; Ian Lepage and Stephen Barlow of the Hockey Association, Milton Keynes; Alison Taylor and Anita Mason of the All England Women's Lacrosse Association, Birmingham; David Shuttleworth of the English Lacrosse Union; Les Barnett and Jock Bentley of the British Athletic Federation Ltd., Birmingham; Mike Gilks of the Badminton Association of England; Gurinder Purewall for advice on archery; Chris McCartney of the US Archery Association; Geoff Doe of the National Smallbore Rifle Association, Bisley, Surrey, for information and reference material on shooting; Fagan Sports Goods Distributors, Surrey; Konrad Bartelski for advice on skiing; The British Ski Federation, Edinburgh; Mike Barnett of Snow and Rock of London; Sally Spurway of Mast-Co. Ltd., Reading; Sarah Morgan for advice on equestrian sports, Steve Brown and the New York Racing Association Inc, New York; Danrho of London; Alan Skipp and James Chambers of the Amateur Fencing Association, London; Carla Richards of the US Fencing Association; Hamilton Bland and John Dryer of the Amateur Swimming Association, Loughborough; Cotswold Camping Ltd., London; Tim Spalton of Glyn Locke (Racing Shells) Ltd., Chalgrove; Terry Friel of the US Rowing Association; House of Hardy; Leeda Fishing Tackle

The Modern World
John Lewis, Brent Cross, for the loan of products for photography; Apple Computers UK; Palm Inc.; Epson UK; Naynesh Mistry of Brother UK; Nintendo; Sony UK; Nokia Mobile Phones Ltd.; Sony Ericsson; Tony Broad of Garmin Europe; Dualit Ltd.; Black and Decker Ltd.; James Honour of the Buildings Research Establishment; Craig Anders of Cole Thompson Associates; Vestas Wind Systems; Bryan Adams of MIT; Dr. Julian Heath of *Microscopy and Analysis*; Fei UK Ltd.; Steve Parker; Ian Graham

PHOTOGRAPHY:
M. Alexander; Peter Anderson; Colin Bowling; Charles Brooks; Jane Burton; Peter Chadwick; Simon Clay; Gordon Clayton; John Coiley; Andy Crawford; Geoff Dann; Philip Dowell; John Downs; Mike Dunning; Torla Evans; David Exton; Paul Forrester; Robert and Anthony Fretwell of Fretwell Photography Ltd..; Philip Gatward; Steve Gorton; Anna Hodgson; Gary Kevin; J. Heseltine; Cyril Laubscher; John Lepine; Lynton Gardiner (American Museum of Natural History, New York); Steve Gorton; Michelangelo Gratton; Judith Harrington; Peter Hayman; Anna Hodgson; Colin Keates; Gary Kevin; Dave King; Bob Langrish; Brian D.Morgan; Nick Nicholls; Nick Parfitt; Tim Parmenter and Colin Keates (Natural History Museum, London); Tim Ridley; Dave Rudkin; Philippe Sebert; James Stevenson; Clive Streeter; Harry Taylor; Matthew Ward; Jerry Young

PHOTOGRAPHIC ASSISTANCE:
Kevin Zak; Gary Ombler; Govind Mittal

ILLUSTRATORS:
Julian Baum; Rick Blakeley; Kuo Rang Chen; Karen Cochrane; Simone End; Ian Fleming; Roy Flooks; Mark Franklin; David Gardner; Will Giles; Mick Gillah; David Hopkins; Selwyn Hutchinson; Mei Lim; Linden Artists; Nick Loates; Chris Lyon; Kathleen McDougall; Coral Mula; Sandra Pond; Dave Pugh; Colin Rose; Graham Rosewarne; John Temperton; Halli Verrinder; John Woodcock; Chris Woolmer

MODEL MAKERS:
Roby Braun; David Donkin; Morrison Frederick; Gordon Models; John Holmes; Graham High and Jeremy Hunt of Centaur Studios; Richard Kemp; Kelvin Thatcher; Paul Wilkinson

ADDITIONAL DESIGN ASSISTANCE:
Stefan Morris; Ulysses Santos; Suchada Smith; Niyati Gosain; Jomin Johny; Ridhi Khanna; Amit Malhotra; Payal Rosalind Malik; Anamica Roy; Ira Sharma; Balwant Singh

ADDITIONAL EDITORIAL ASSISTANCE:
Helen Castle; Colette Connolly; Camela Decaire; Nick Harris; Andrea Horth; Stewart McEwen; Damien Moore; Kate Taylor; Melanie Tham; Pragati Nagpal; Suparna Sengupta; Anita Kakar; Divya Chandhok

INDEX: Kay Wright; Lynn Bresler

Picture credits:

The publisher would like to thank the following for their kind permission to reproduce their photographs:

2011 Research In Motion Limited 589tr; Action Plus 530tc; Alamy images David Kilpatrick 581tr, 581cra; Nikreates 586ca; NordicImages 591tr; © PG Pictures/Apple Inc. 591r; Oleksiy Maksymenko Photography 568cra; © Stanca Sanda/Apple Inc. 588tr; Arthur Turner 579cla; © Chris Wilson/Apple Inc. 587tl; © Amazon. com, Inc. 569bl; Anglo Australian Telescope Board 11cl, 11cra, 11cbl, 12tr, 12bc, 13tl, 13bl, 14tl, 16b, 17tc, 17bl, 22tl/D.Malin 16tl, 26tr, 27tl; © Apple Inc. 569br, 587br, 591bl; Austin Brown and the Aviation Picture Library 426tl; Baptistery, Florence/Alison Harris 453r; © Beats Electronics 587bl; © Blackberry 569bc; Biophoto Associates 217ca, 217cra, 228cbc, 228cbc 230tr; BRE Imaging 602bl, 602r, 603tr, 603br; Paul Brierley 311bra; Bowers & Wilkins: B&W Group Ltd 586b; British Aerospace/Anthony Hooley 412tl, 415tl; British Aerospace (Commercial Aircraft) Ltd 416tl; By permission of the British Library 432tl, 445bl; British Museum 459tl, 459tr, 460tr, 460tc, 460tb, 489b; BP Exploration 299; Duncan Brown 25tl; Frank Lloyd Wright, American, 1867-1959, Model of Midway Gardens, 1914, executed by Richard Tiekner, mixed media, 1987, 41.9 x 81.3 x 76.2, 1989.48. view 1. Photography courtesy of the Art Intitute of Chicago 495t; J.A. Coiley 351cr; Bruce Coleman Ltd/Andy Price 272tl; Canon Europe 581crb; Corbis Joseph Sohm/Visions of America 494l; Corbis Jon Stokes/Science Photo Library 576cl; Wu Ching-teng/Xinhua Press 568br; Haruyoshi Yamaguchi/Sygma 608r; Courtesy of the Board of Trustees of the Victoria and Albert Museum, London 454-455b; Creative Labs, Inc. 586tc; Dorling Kindersley Owen Peyton Jones 566cr, 582-585, 589; Dreamstime.com Vasimila 431b; Dyson 592tr; European Passenger Services 329tl; ESA /PLV 11bl; European Southern Observatory (ESO) 53tl; Fei Co. 610tc, 610r; © Fitbit 591tl; French Railways 329tr; FUJIFILM UK 581br; Geoscience Features 311cla; Robert Harding Picture Library 62tl; Getty Images Tony Cordoza 584tr; GraphicaArtis 448clb; Bill Johnson/The Denver Post 448tl; © MacFormat Magazine/James Looker 590cr; Photodisc/Ryan McVay 577tl; Harman International Industries, Incorporated JBL 586cl; Hitachi High-Technologies Co. Ltd 61 1tr; Michael Holford/ British Museum 372bl, Michael Holford 374tr;

Honda 354tr, 355b; Hutchison Picture Library 60cl; iFixit Miroslav Djuric 580-581 (Nikon Coolpix S1000PJ); Brett Hartt 578cra; The Image Bank/Edward Bower 306tr; Jet Propulsion Laboratory 11cbr; 30bc; 31bc; 31bcr; 38tl; 42crb; 44cb; 44cbr; 44bc; 46tl; 46cr; 46cb; 46bc; 46br; 50tl; 50cra; 50cl; 50c; 50cr; 50br; Kawasaki (UK) 609bl; KeyMed Ltd 248bl, 249bl, 249bcl; Department of Prints and Drawings, Uffizi, Florence/Philip Gatward 431tc/Uffizi, Florence/Philip Gatward 433tl; Robin Kerrod/ Spacecharts 615br; Dr. D.N. Landon (Institute of Neurology) 228bl,br; Life Science Images/Ron Boardman 244bl, 244br; The Lund Observatory 15bc; Brian Morrison 329tl, 329tr; © The Henry Moore Foundation 455tr; Used with permission from Mierosoft 578tr; Musée d'Orsay, Paris/ Philippe Sebert 437tc, 441tc; Musée du Louvre, Paris/Philippe Sebert 453tl, 453l, 453br; Musictrack/MOTU Digital performer 521bcl; NASA/AUI 15tr; NASA and The Hubble Heritage Team (AURA/STScI) 44tl; NASA Dr. R. Albrecht, ESA/ESO Space Telescope European Coordinating Facility 51fbr; CXC/ ASU/J. Hester et al 28cra; JPL/DLR 44br; JPL JHUAPL 42br; JPL-Caltech/University of Arizona 42fbr; NASA/JPL 11 cbr, 11br, 30tl, 30bl, 30br, 30bc, 31bc, 31bcr, 31bl, 34cr, 38tl, 40tl, 40cr, 42cr, 44cb, 44cbr, 44bc, 44cr, 46crb, 46tl, 46cr, 46cb, 46bc, 46br, 48tl, 48cra, 48bca, 48bc, 48br, 50tl, 50bc, 50bc, 50cbr, 50br, 50cr, 52cr, 612cr, 612tr, 613tl, 613tcl, 613cr, 613tr, 615c, 615cr, 615tr, 615cr, 615c; National Maritime Museum 373br, 392-393b; National Medical Slide Bank 217cr; Nature Photographers/Paul Sterry 286tl; Newage International 317bl; Nintendo 578tl, 578clb, 579tl, 579tr, 579cra; Olympus 610cl, 61 0bi; Oxford Scientific Films/Breck P. Kent 166tl; © Pebble 590tr; Planet Earth 274tr; Press Association Images AP 609cr; Quadrant 526tr; Margaret Robinson 352tl; Giotto The Expulsion of the Merchants from the Temple Scala 435tc, 435bl, 435br; RapidRepair.com Ben Levy 569ca (iPad Components); © Recon Instruments Inc 590br; Rex Features Jonathan Hordle 609br; Roland UK 521tl; © Samsung 584br; © SanDisk/ Western Digital Corporation (WDC) 583crb; Science Photo Library 10bl, 13tr, 214bcr, 214bl, 236tr/Michael Abbey 225tc/Agema Infrared Systems 318tl/AGFA 220tl/Alex Barte 605tr/ David Becker 607cr/ Biophoto Associates: 217crb/Dr. Jeremy Burgess/ Science Photo Library 132tr; Dr. Jeremy Burgess 235bcl/CNRI 214tl, 214cl, 214c, 214cr, 214bl, 214clb, 214crb, 214blc, 214br, 217cb, 235bcr, 238tl, 249bcr, 253tr,

253cra, 256tl; Science Photo library /Earth Satellite Corporation 288cl, 293br/Dr. Brian Eyden 228cbr/Professor C. Ferlaut 300tl/ Vaughan Fleming 311tl/Simon Fraser/U.S. Dept.of Energy 214bcl, 266tl/Eric Grave 217br/ Hale Observatories 32br/Max Planck Institute for Radio Astronomy 15tl/Jan Hinsch 225tc/ Jodrell Bank 11tr, 13c /Manfred Kage 217c, 235br, 237br/Dr. William C. Keel 13br/Keith Kent 564c/James King-Holmes 316tl, 606bl/ Russ Lappa 310bra/John Mead 605br/Astrid & Hans-Freider Michler 217tr/ Dennis Milon 52bl/NASA 11cla, 12tl, 15tr, 30c, 32tl, 35tl, 36tl, 36cl, 36cr, 36bc, 42tr, 52tl, 291tr, 300tl/National Optical Astro Observatory 52tr/NIBSC 253crb/ Omikron 244bc/David Parker 63bl, 304-305, 308br/Alfred Pasieka 606cr/Philippe Plailly 508tl/Quest 611br/Roussel-UCLAF/CNRI 217tc/ Rev Ronald Royer 32cr/Royal Observatory, Edinburgh/D Malin 11tl, 11cr,12c, 16cl, 16c, 17br/David Scharf 235bl/Dr. Kaus Schiller 248bcl, 248bcr, 248br/Secchi-Lecaque/Koussel-UCLAF/CNRI 253br/H. Sochurek 214cb/ Stammers/Thompson 230tl/Sheila Terry 234tl/ US Department of Energy 310bc/US Geological Survey/Science Photo Library 8-9, 30bcr, 42tl, 42bl/Tom Van Sant/Geosphere Project, Santa Monica/Science Photo Library 273tr, 281tr, 296tr, 297tl/Dr. Christopher B. Williams/(Saint Marks Hospital) 249br; Oxford Scientific Films/ Animals/ Breck P. Kent 167tl; Pratt & Whitney Canada 418-419b, 419t; Science Museum 306bl, 306bcl; 306 bcr, 324t, 326-327b), 330tr, 351ct, 331 cb; Sony Corporation 586tr, 586cr; Sporting Pictures 524tl, 544cr; TechRepublic Bill Detwiler 578-579b; Tony Stone Worldwide 280tl; J.M.W. Turner The Burning of the Houses of Parliament Tate Gallery 439tc; © Ultimate Ears/UE Boom 2 587tr; Vision 26tr, 27c; Jerry Young 306tl; Dr. Robert Youngson 241cr; courtesy of Vestas Wind Systems 604t; Zefa 217bc/Janicek 276tl/H. Sochurek 210tl, 250tl, 254tl/G. Steenmans 292tl

(a=above, b=below/bottom, c=center, f=far, l-left, r=right, t=top)

All other images © Dorling Kindersley
For further information see: www.dkimages.com

Every effort has been made to trace the copyright holders. Dorling Kindersley apologizes for any unintentional omissions and would be pleased, in any such cases, to add an acknowledgment in future editions.

Some pages in this book previously appeared in the Visual Dictionary series published by Dorling Kindersley. Contributors to this series include:

Project Art Editors: Duncan Brown, Ross George, Nicola Liddiard, Andrew Nash, Clare Shedden, Bryn Walls

Designers: Lesley Betts, Paul Calver, Simone End, Ellen Woodward

Additional design assistance: Sandra Archer, Christina Betts, Alexandra Brown, Nick Jackson, Susan Knight

Project Editors: Fiona Courtney-Thompson, Paul Docherty, Tim Fraser, Stephanie Jackson, Mary Lindsay

Editorial Assistant: Emily Hill

Additional editorial assistance: Susan Bosanko, Edward Bunting, Candace Burch, Deirdre Clark, Jeanette Cossar, Danièle Guitton, Jacqui Hand, David Harding, Nicholas Jackson, Edwina Johnson, David Lambert, Gail Lawther, David Learmount, Paul Jackson, Christine Murdock, Bob Ogden, Cathy Rubinstein, Louise Tucker, Dr. Robert Youngson

Picture Researchers: Vere Dodds, Danièle Guitton, Anna Lord, Catherine O'Rourke, Christine Rista, Sandra Schneider, Vanessa Smith, Clive Webster

Series Editor: Martyn Page

Series Art Editor: Paul Wilkinson

Managing Art Editors: Philip Gilderdale, Steve Knowlden

Art Director: Chez Picthall

Managing Editor: Ruth Midgley

Production: Jayne Simpson